WHY DO YOU NEED
A THESAURUS?

Thesaurus is Latin for "treasure house." And that's exactly what *Webster's New Roget's A–Z Thesaurus* offers you—a rich compendium that quickly and easily provides every writer or speaker with the perfect word to fit the occasion. Acclaimed scholar and writing expert Charlton Laird has organized this handy word-finder with synonyms, specific examples of general words, and antonyms, all listed under the most commonly used words. Its singular design enables you readily to discover the word you want—a great improvement on the traditional thesaurus, which requires you to read through long, confusing lists or flip from page to page. With its comprehensive word choice and attention to wide areas of meaning, *Webster's New Roget's A–Z Thesaurus* is an indispensable reference work . . . and the last word on finding the *right* word.

Webster's New Roget's A–Z Thesaurus

BY **CHARLTON LAIRD**

CONTENTS

THESAURUS STAFF

FOREWORD

This edition of *Webster's New Roget's A–Z Thesaurus* derives ultimately from Charlton Laird's original thesaurus, which was first published in 1948 under the title *Laird's Promptory.* A pioneering work, the *Promptory* established the pattern of arranging entries in alphabetical order, thus making it unnecessary to consult a separate index. This arrangement has since been widely adopted by other publishers.

The entry arrangement and editorial principles are still much in evidence in the present edition. The work draws heavily on the successful innovations of its predecessors and offers new contributions drawn from the evolving database of *Webster's New College Dictionary.* The typefaces and page layout match those of the companion paperback volume, *Webster's New Compact Office Dictionary.*

GUIDE TO THE USE OF THIS BOOK

I. ARRANGEMENT OF ENTRIES

All headwords, including single words, hyphenated and unhyphenated compounds, and phrases, are listed in strict alphabetical order and are set in large, boldface type.

account *n.* ...
accountant *n.* ...
account for *v.* ...
acquaintance *n.* ...
acquainted (with) *a.* ...
acquaint with *v.* ...
acting *a.* ...

Idiomatic phrases that are listed within an entry have also been alphabetized.

action *n.* ... —**bring action** ... —**see action**... —**take action** ...

II. PART-OF-SPEECH LABELS

Part-of-speech labels are given for all headwords, including single words, hyphenated and open compounds, and phrases. Generally, a word having more than one part of speech is given a separate entry block for each part of speech.

abuse *n.* misuse, debasement, degradation, ...
abuse *v.* insult, injure, hurt, ...

Sometimes, though, its synonyms can be conveniently grouped together in a single entry block.

above *a., prep.* 1 [High in position] over, high, higher, superior, ...

III. THE ENTRY BLOCK

A. *Synonyms*—Every entry block lists synonyms (words or phrases that are similar in meaning).

wholly *a.* totally, entirely, fully; see COMPLETELY.
therefore *a., conj.* accordingly, consequently, hence, wherefore, for, since, inasmuch as, ...

Since we do not have space to list every synonym at every entry block, we have chosen certain entry blocks or numbered senses to be the primary location of synonyms belonging to a particular family of meanings. These primary locations are "main entries." Main entries always contain more than three synonyms.

dwell *v.* live, inhabit, stay, lodge, stop, settle, remain, live in, live at, continue, ...

Entry blocks or numbered senses containing only three synonyms are "brief entries." Brief entries always refer the user to a primary location of synonyms in the Thesaurus and often refer to two or more main entries.

abide *v.* 1 [To lodge] stay, room, reside; see DWELL. ...

locate *v.* ... **2** [To take up residence] settle down, establish oneself, inhabit; see DWELL, SETTLE 5.

When we wish to call the user's attention to another, closely related, family of synonyms, we have placed a cross-reference from one main entry to another.

settle *v.* ... **5** [To establish residence] locate, lodge, become a citizen, reside, ... establish a home, keep house; see also DWELL.

All cross-references appear in small capitals.

B. *Definitions*—Distinct senses located in a single entry block are numbered consecutively in boldface numerals and may be further distinguished by brief definitions or explanatory notes in brackets.

capital *n.* **1** [A seat of government] ... **2** [Money and property] ... **3** [A letter usually used initially] ...
calm *a.* **1** [*Said especially of persons*] ... **2** [*Said often of things*] ...

C. *Lists of Examples*—Often, a writer or speaker is looking not for other words similar to a word at hand, but for a specific thing in a general category. So, in addition to providing synonyms, the Thesaurus also provides lists of concrete examples.

boat *n.* *Types of small boats include the following:* sailboat, rowboat, shell, scull, skull, kayak, dugout, canoe, scow, raft, ...
verb *n.* *Verbs include the following:* finite, active, passive, transitive, intransitive, modal, auxiliary, linking, ...
writer *n.* ... *Major writers include the following—British:* Daniel Defoe, Jonathan Swift, Henry Fielding, Samuel Johnson, ... ; *Spanish:* Miguel de Cervantes, Jorge Luis Borges; *Yiddish:* I. B. Singer.

D. *Antonyms*—Antonyms (words that are opposite or nearly opposite in meaning) are listed after the synonyms.

insulted *a.* slandered, libeled, reviled, disgraced, ... shamed; see also HURT. —*Ant.* PRAISED, admired, extolled.
a *a., indefinite article, prep.* **1** ... . —*Ant.* THE, this, that.

Antonyms in small capitals are Thesaurus entries that the user will find especially useful.

E. *The Asterisk*—A headword, a run-on idiomatic phrase, a definition in brackets, a synonym, or an antonym may be marked with an asterisk. An asterisk is intended to alert the user that the term or definition is slang, informal, dialectal, regional, archaic, etc. The user is thus cautioned to consider whether that term is appropriate for his or her purposes. A dictionary will usually provide information on a word marked with an asterisk.

IV. SUGGESTIONS FOR USING THE THESAURUS

For convenience, here is a summary of things to keep in mind while you use this Thesaurus:

1. Look up any word that you have thought of but are, for some reason, not fully satisfied with.
2. Unless you have thought of a rare word, you should find: (a) a main

entry, with many alternative terms, some antonyms, and possibly a "see also" cross-reference, or (b) a brief entry, with three synonyms and one or more cross-references.
3. If you have turned to a main entry, check to see whether more than one meaning is recognized, and, if so, pick the one you want. The various meanings will be numbered in boldface numerals.
4. Work through the list, looking for a term that meets your needs. Try the cross-reference at the end if you need it.
5. If you find a word or phrase you may want to use but do not know very well, look it up in a dictionary.
6. If you have turned to a brief entry, it will provide a few common synonyms. If you are not satisfied with any of them, turn to the main entry cross-referred there. The entry to which you are referred may have more than one grammatical use—*fast* can be an adjective, adverb, noun, or verb. Choose synonyms having the same part of speech as your original, brief entry.

V. ABBREVIATIONS AND SYMBOLS USED IN THIS BOOK

a.	adjective or adverb (i.e., modifier)
abbrev.	abbreviated, abbreviation
adj.	adjective
Ant.	antonyms
conj.	conjunction
etc.	and the like
interj.	interjection
n.	noun
poss.	possessive
prep.	preposition
pron.	pronoun
v.	verb
*	slang, informal, dialectal, regional, archaic, etc.

A

a *a., **indefinite article**, prep.* **1** [The indefinite article; *before vowels, written "an"*] some, one, any, each, some kind of, some particular, any of, any one of, a certain.—*Ant.* THE, this, that. **2** [An indication of frequency] per, every, at the rate of; see EACH 2.

abandon *n.* unrestraint, spontaneity, freedom, exuberance, spirit, enthusiasm, vigor.

abandon *v.* **1** [To give up] leave, quit, withdraw, discontinue, break off, go off from, cast away, cast aside, let go, cease, cast off, discard, vacate, give away, part with, evacuate, surrender, yield, desist, concede, renounce, abdicate, lose hope of, go back on, secede, waive, forgo, back down from, lay aside, dispose of, have done with, throw in the towel*, break the habit. **2** [To leave someone or something in trouble] desert, forsake, ostracize, back out on, break with, break up with, run away, defect, reject, disown, cast off, maroon, depart from, throw overboard, jettison, leave behind, slip away from, stand up*, leave in the lurch, turn one's back on, run out on*, walk out on*, doublecross*, let down, drop.

abandoned *a.* deserted, desolate, destitute, desperate, empty, unused, vacated, left, neglected, relinquished, lonely, forsaken, solitary, hopeless, cast off, cast aside, cast away, forgotten, shunned, forlorn, avoided, outcast, rejected, helpless, unfortunate, alone, discarded, scorned, lost, doomed, friendless, wretched, thrown overboard*, out on a limb*, waiting at the church*, left in the lurch, in the cold, left holding the bag*.—*Ant.* INHABITED, befriended, in use.

abbreviate *v.* shorten, cut, condense; see DECREASE 2.

abbreviation *n.* contraction, abridgment, sketch, brief, abstract, synopsis, reduction, abstraction, condensation, digest, résumé, outline, summary, short form; see also SUMMARY.

abdicate *v.* relinquish, give up, withdraw; see ABANDON 1.

abdomen *n.* midsection, belly, gut*; see STOMACH.

abduct *v.* capture, seize, carry off; see KIDNAP.

abide *v.* **1** [To lodge] stay, room, reside; see DWELL. **2** [To submit to] put up with, bear, bear with, withstand; see also ENDURE 2. **—abide**

by follow, observe, comply with; see FOLLOW 3.

ability *n.* aptitude, intelligence, innate qualities, powers, potency, worth, talent, gift, genius, capability, competence, proficiency, adeptness, qualifications, knowledge, self-sufficiency, technique, craft, skill, artistry, cunning, skillfulness, dexterity, facility, flair, finesse, mastery, cleverness, deftness, experience, ingenuity, strength, understanding, faculty, comprehension, makings, sense, what it takes*, brains, knack, the hang of something, know-how*.—*Ant.* IGNORANCE, incompetence, inexperience.

able *a.* intelligent, ingenious, worthy, talented, gifted, fitted, capable, effective, efficient, qualified, masterful, adequate, competent, expert, experienced, skilled, learned, clever, suitable, smart, crafty, cunning, bright, knowing, dexterous, endowed, deft, apt, agile, adept, alert, adaptable, smooth, ready, versatile, equal to, suited, suited to, well-rounded, mighty, powerful, strong, robust, sturdy, brawny, vigorous, courageous, fit for, sharp, cut out for*.—*Ant.* STUPID, bungling, unadaptable.

able-bodied *a.* fit, powerful, sturdy; see STRONG 1.

abnormal *a.* strange, irregular, unnatural; see UNUSUAL 2.

abnormality *n.* peculiarity, singularity, malformation; see IRREGULARITY.

aboard *a.* on board, on ship, shipped, loaded, on board ship, freight on board, being shipped, en route, consigned, in transit, being transported, embarked, afloat, at sea, on deck, traveling.

abolish *v.* suppress, eradicate, terminate, exterminate, obliterate, annul, remove, revoke, end, finish, nullify, set aside, annihilate, repeal, subvert, reverse, rescind, prohibit, extinguish, cancel, erase, root out, pull up, uproot, demolish, invalidate, overturn, overthrow, declare null and void, do away with, stamp out, undo, throw out, put an end to, inhibit, dispense with, cut out, raze, squelch*, ravage; see also DESTROY.

abort *v.* miscarry, fall short, terminate; see FAIL 1.

about *a., prep.* **1** [Approximately] roughly, nearly, in general; see APPROXIMATELY. **2** [Concerning] regarding, respecting, touching, of, on, in relation to, relative to, relating to, as regards, in regard to, in which, with respect to, in the matter of, with reference to, referring to, so far as something is concerned, in connection with, concerned with, thereby, wherein, as for, dealing with. **3** [Around] surrounding, round about, on all sides; see AROUND.

above *a., prep.* **1** [High in position] over, high, higher, superior, beyond, raised, above one's head, in a higher place, aloft, overhead, toward the sky; see also HIGHER, OVER 1.—*Ant.* BELOW, low, beneath. **2** [Referring to something earlier] before, foregoing, earlier; see PRECEDING. — **above all** in the first place, chiefly, especially; see PRINCIPALLY.

aboveboard *a.* candidly, honestly, frankly; see OPENLY 1.

abrasive *a.* **1** grinding, sharpening, cutting; see ROUGH 1. **2** irritating, annoying, caustic; see DISTURBING.

abreast *a.* in line, equal, side by side; see BESIDE.

abroad *a.* away, at large, adrift, wandering, elsewhere, overseas, traveling, touring, outside, distant, far away, gone, out of the country, removed.

abrupt *a.* **1** [*Said of things, usually landscape*] uneven, jagged, precipitous; see STEEP. **2** [*Said of people or their actions*] blunt, hasty, gruff; see RUDE.

absence *n.* **1** [The state of being elsewhere] truancy, nonattendance, nonappearance, loss, vacancy, cut*, hooky*. **2** [The state of lacking something] deficiency, need, inadequacy; see LACK 1.

absent *a.* away, missing, elsewhere, vanished, gone, gone out, not at home, not present, out, wanting, lacking, abroad, lost, astray, nowhere to be found, on vacation, AWOL*, playing hooky*.

absent-minded *a.* preoccupied, dreamy, listless, lost, absent, thoughtless, oblivious, inattentive, daydreaming, unaware, unconscious, withdrawn, removed, faraway, distracted, remote, forgetful, in the clouds.—*Ant.* OBSERVANT, attentive, alert.

absolute *a.* **1** [Without limitation] total, complete, entire, infinite, unqualified, supreme, full, unrestricted, unlimited, unconditional, unbounded, independent, wholehearted, sheer, pure, unmitigated, utter, unabridged, thorough, clean, outright, downright, ideal, simple, perfect, full, blanket, all-out, out-and-out.—*Ant.* RESTRICTED, limited, qualified. **2** [Without limit in authority] supreme, authoritarian, domineering, arbitrary, official, autocratic, tyrannical, fascist,

haughty, overbearing, czarist, nazi, totalitarian, oppressive, antidemocratic, imperial, dogmatic, commanding, controlling, compelling, despotic, intimidating, fanatic, dictatorial, arrogant, with an iron hand, high and mighty*.—*Ant.* LENIENT, tolerant, temperate. **3** [Certain] positive, unquestionable, undeniable; see CERTAIN 2.

absolutely *a.* **1** [Completely] utterly, unconditionally, thoroughly; see COMPLETELY. **2** [Positively] unquestionably, certainly, definitely; see SURELY.

absolve *v.* pardon, set free, clear; see EXCUSE.

absorb *v.* digest, take in, ingest, use up, assimilate, blot, imbibe, swallow, consume, incorporate, sop up, soak up, sponge up.

absorbed *a.* assimilated, taken in, swallowed up, consumed, drunk, imbibed, dissolved, incorporated, fused, united, digested.—*Ant.* REMOVED, unassimilated, unconsumed.

absorbent *a.* porous, spongy, permeable, penetrable, receptive, retentive, thirsty.—*Ant.* impermeable, impervious, solid.

absorbing *a.* engaging, exciting, enthralling; see INTERESTING.

absorption *n.* assimilation, digestion, osmosis, saturation, penetration, fusion, intake, union, merging, blending, consumption, ingestion, swallowing up, taking in, reception, retention, incorporation, appropriation, drinking in, suction, sopping up, soaking up, sponging up, inhalation.—*Ant.* REMOVAL, ejection, discharge.

abstain *v.* refrain, refrain from, renounce, desist, withhold, avoid, stop, deny oneself, refuse, decline, hold back, shun, evade, cease, dispense with, do without, fast, starve oneself, have nothing to do with, let alone, do nothing, keep from, keep one's hands off, swear off, lay off*, turn over a new leaf, have no hand in, take the pledge.—*Ant.* JOIN, indulge, gorge.

abstinence *n.* abstaining, temperance, denial, self-denial, self-control, self-restraint, continence, fasting, frugality, renunciation, avoidance, sobriety, austerity, refraining, nonindulgence, chastity, moderation, soberness, asceticism, teetotalism.—*Ant.* INDULGENCE, intemperance, overindulgence.

abstract *a.* conceptual, intellectual, ideal; see OBSCURE 1.

absurd *a.* preposterous, ridiculous, ludicrous; see STUPID.

absurdity *n.* improbability, foolishness, senselessness; see NONSENSE 1, 2.

abundance *n.* bounty, more than enough, profusion; see PLENTY.

abundant *a.* sufficient, ample, copious; see PLENTIFUL 2.

abundantly *a.* plentifully, lavishly, richly, handsomely, in large measure, profusely, amply, sufficiently, generously, affluently, inexhaustibly, many times over, to one's heart's content, off the fat of the land; see also ADEQUATELY.

abuse *n.* misuse, debasement, degradation, desecration, injury, damage, harm, hurt, wrong, injustice, insult, mistreatment, violation, malevolence, mishandling, mismanagement, pollution, defilement, perversion, prostitution.—*Ant.* CARE, respect, veneration.

abuse *v.* insult, injure, hurt, harm, damage, impair, offend, overwork, ill-treat, misuse, maltreat, mistreat, wrong, persecute, molest, victimize, oppress, ruin, mar, spoil, do wrong to, mishandle, pervert, profane, prostitute, desecrate, pollute, harass, manhandle, do an injustice to, violate, defile, impose upon, deprave, taint, debase, corrupt.—*Ant.* DEFEND, protect, befriend.

abused *a.* wronged, injured, harmed; see HURT.

academic *a.* scholastic, erudite, scholarly; see LEARNED.

academy *n.* preparatory school, boarding school, finishing school, secondary school, prep school; see also SCHOOL 1.

accelerate *v.* quicken, speed up, hurry; see HASTEN 2.

acceleration *n.* speeding up, hastening, increase of speed, quickening, hurrying, stepping up, picking up speed; see also SPEED.

accent *n.* stress, beat, stroke, emphasis, pitch, accentuation, inflection, intonation, rhythm, meter, cadence.

accept *v.* receive, get, admit, be resigned, give in to, believe, trust, surrender, suffer, endure, allow, tolerate, take in one's stride, consent, acquiesce; see also AGREE.

acceptable *a.* satisfactory, agreeable, pleasing; see PLEASANT 2.

acceptance *n.* recognition, assent, approval; see AGREEMENT 1.

accepted *a.* taken, received, assumed, approved, adopted, recognized, endorsed, verified, acclaimed, welcomed, engaged, hired, claimed, delivered, used, employed, affirmed, upheld, authorized, preferred, acknowledged, accredited, allowed, settled, established, sanctioned, unopposed, customary, authentic, confirmed, chosen, acceptable, popular, formally admitted, stereotyped, orthodox, standard, conventional, current, taken for granted, credited,

OK'd*; see also POPULAR 1, 3.—*Ant.* REFUSED, denied, nullified.

access *n.* admittance, entree, introduction; see ENTRANCE 1, 2.

accessible *a.* approachable, obtainable, attainable; see AVAILABLE.

accessories *n.* frills, ornaments, adornments, decorations, additions, attachments, gimmicks*, doodads*.

accessory *n.* 1 [An accomplice] helper, aid, assistant; see ASSOCIATE. 2 [Something added] attachment, consequence, attendant, complement, supplement, addition.

accident *n.* luck, fortune, contingency, occurrence, circumstance, event, occasion; see also CHANCE 1.

accidental *a.* adventitious, chance, coincidental; see AIMLESS, UNFORTUNATE.

accidentally *a.* unintentionally, involuntarily, unwittingly, unexpectedly, inadvertently, casually, by chance, haphazardly, incidentally, randomly, not purposely, by a fluke*.—*Ant.* DELIBERATELY, voluntarily, intentionally.

accommodate *v.* 1 [To render a service] help, aid, comfort, make comfortable, oblige, suit, serve, gratify, please, arrange, settle, provide, benefit, tender, supply, furnish, assist, support, sustain, do a favor, indulge, humor, pamper, accept, put oneself out for, do a service for. 2 [To suit one thing to another] fit, adapt, correspond; see ADJUST 1. 3 [To provide lodging] house, lodge, put up; see ENTERTAIN 2.

accommodations *n.* quarters, rooms, lodging, housing, apartment, hotel, room and board, roof over one's head; see also HOME 1.

accompanied *a.* chaperoned, attended, escorted, shown around, shown about, not alone.

accompaniment *n.* harmony, instrumental music, musical background; see MUSIC 1.

accompany *v.* escort, attend, be with, follow, keep company with, guard, guide, usher, show in, show around, show the way, conduct, go along, go along with, chaperon, associate with, consort with, look after, go hand in hand with, go side by side with, hang around with*.

accomplice *n.* confederate, helper, aid; see ASSOCIATE.

accomplish *v.* fulfill, perform, finish; see ACHIEVE, SUCCEED 1.

accomplished *a.* 1 [Done] completed, consummated, concluded; see FINISHED. 2 [Skilled] proficient, expert, skillful; see ABLE.

accomplishment *n.* execution, fulfillment, attainment; see SUCCESS 2.

accordingly *a.* in consequence, consequently, equally, respectively, duly, subsequently, in respect to, thus, hence, therefore, as a result, as a consequence, as the case may be, under the circumstances, as things go, to that end, in that event.

according to *prep.* in accordance with, as, to the degree that, conforming to, in keeping with, in line with, in agreement with, consistent with, commensurate with.

account *n.* statement, record, report; see RECORD 1. —**give a good account of oneself** acquit oneself creditably, do well, do oneself proud*, behave courageously. —**on account** charged, in layaway, on layaway, on call; see also UNPAID 1. —**on account of** because of, by virtue of, since; see BECAUSE. —**on no account** for no reason, no way, under no circumstances; see NEVER. —**on someone's account** because of someone, for someone's sake, in someone's behalf; see BECAUSE. —**take account of** judge, evaluate, investigate; see EXAMINE 1. —**take into account** judge, allow for, weigh; see CONSIDER.

accountant *n.* bookkeeper, auditor, CPA; see CLERK.

account for *v.* clarify, justify, elucidate; see EXPLAIN.

accumulate *v.* hoard, get together, gather, amass, amalgamate, collect, heap, store, assemble, concentrate, compile, pile up, accrue, scrape up, stockpile, store up, acquire, gain, load up, rake up, unite, add to, build up, gain control of, roll in*, bank; see also GET 1.

accuracy *n.* efficiency, exactness, precision, correctness, skillfulness, sharpness, incisiveness, mastery, dependability, strictness, certainty, sureness.—*Ant.* ERROR, inaccuracy, mistake.

accurate *a.* **1** [Free from error] exact, correct, perfect; see RIGHT 1. **2** [Characterized by precision] deft, reliable, trustworthy, true, correct, exact, specific, dependable, skillful, methodical, systematic, distinct, particular, realistic, authentic, genuine, careful, close, critical, detailed, factual, severe, rigorous, rigid, strict, meticulous, sharp, faithful, punctual, scientific, objective, rational, unmistakable, reasonable, right, explicit, definite, defined, on the button*, on the dot*, on the nose*, solid.—*Ant.* INCOMPETENT, faulty, slipshod.

accurately *a.* correctly, precisely, exactly; see CAREFULLY 1.

accusation *n.* indictment, allegation, denunciation, slur, complaint, citation, charge, insinuation, imputation, smear*, frame-up*, rap*.

accuse *v.* denounce, charge, indict; see BLAME.

accused *a.* arraigned, indicted, incriminated, charged with, under suspicion, alleged to be guilty, apprehended, held for questioning, liable, involved, under attack, under fire, implicated.—*Ant.* DISCHARGED, acquitted, cleared.

accuser *n.* prosecutor, plaintiff, adversary; see OPPONENT 1.

accustomed *a.* usual, customary, habitual; see CONVENTIONAL 1. —**accustomed to** in the habit of, used to, inclined to; see ADDICTED (TO).

ace *a.* expert, first-rate, outstanding; see DISTINGUISHED 2, ABLE.

ace *n.* expert, master, champion; see SPECIALIST.

ache *n.* twinge, pang, spasm; see PAIN 2.

ache *v.* pain, throb, be sore; see HURT.

achieve *v.* complete, end, terminate, conclude, finish, finish up, finish off, do, perform, execute, fulfill, carry out, carry through, bring about, settle, effect, bring to a conclusion, close, stop, produce, realize, actualize, discharge, wind up, work out, adjust, resolve, solve, accomplish, make an end of, enact, manage, contrive, negotiate, sign, seal, bring to pass, see it through, get done, close up, carry to completion, follow through, deliver, knock off*, fill the bill*, round out*, come through, polish off*, clean up*, mop up*, put across*, pull off*, make short work of*, put through, go all the way*, go the limit*, call it a day*, put the finishing touch on*, dispose of.—*Ant.* ABANDON, fail, give up.

achievement *n.* fulfillment, feat, exploit, accomplishment, triumph, hit, success, realization, creation, completion, execution, actualization, masterpiece, performance, deed, act, enactment, victory, conquest, attainment, feather in one's cap.—*Ant.* FAILURE, blunder, collapse.

acid *a.* sharp, tart, biting; see SOUR.

acid *n.* **1** [A sour substance] strong acid, weak acid, corrosive, Lewis acid. *Common acids include the following:* vinegar, lemon juice; citric, ascorbic, lactic, nicotinic, boric, acetic, sulfuric, hydrochloric, formic, stearic, phosphoric, carbolic, nitric, benzoic, amino, fatty. **2** [A drug] lysergic acid, LSD, mescaline; see DRUG.

acidity *n.* sourness, bitterness, tartness, sharpness, pungency, harshness, causticity.

acknowledge *v.* **1** [To admit] concede, confess, declare; see ADMIT 2.

2 [To recognize the authority of] endorse, certify, confirm, uphold, support, recognize, ratify, approve, defend, subscribe to, accede to, attest to, take an oath by, defer to.

acknowledged *a.* admitted, confessed, recognized, unquestioned, accepted, authorized, confirmed, received, sanctioned, accredited, approved, out-and-out.

acknowledgment *n.* greeting, reply, answer, response, nod, confession, statement, apology, guarantee, return, support, signature, receipt, letter, card, contract, applause, vote of thanks, IOU.

acquaintance *n.* **1** [A person one knows] colleague, associate, neighbor; see FRIEND. **2** [Acquired knowledge] familiarity, awareness, experience; see AWARENESS, EXPERIENCE.

acquainted (**with**) *a.* introduced, on speaking terms, having some connections; see FAMILIAR WITH.

acquaint with *v.* introduce, make acquainted, present; see INTRODUCE 3.

acquire *v.* take, earn, procure; see GET 1.

acquired *a.* reached, inherited, accrued, derived, granted, endowed, bequeathed, handed down, transmitted, allowed, awarded, passed on, willed to, attained, accomplished, learned, adopted, earned, collected, gathered, harvested, secured, procured, obtained, captured, regained, realized, gotten by the sweat of one's brow, dug out*, raked in*, cornered*, netted, salted away*, grabbed; see also WON.

acquisition *n.* inheritance, gift, donation, grant, wealth, riches, fortune, profit, gain, earnings, wages, salary, income, winnings, return, returns, proceeds, benefit, prize, reward, award, accomplishment, achievement, premium, bonus, fee, commission, pension, annuity, allowance, gain, dividend.

acquit *v.* clear, absolve, vindicate; see EXCUSE.

acquittal *n.* absolution, clearance, exoneration, dismissal, deliverance, amnesty, discharge, pardon, reprieve, exemption, liberation, release, freedom.—*Ant.* PUNISHMENT, sentence, imprisonment.

acre *n.* plot, acreage, bit of land, estate; see also PROPERTY 2.

acrobat *n.* tumbler, clown, trampolinist, aerialist, trapeze artist, trapezist, contortionist, tightrope walker, stuntman, figure skater, circus performer, ballet dancer, gymnast.

across *a.*, *prep.* crosswise, crossed, to the opposite side of, over, opposite, on the other side, from side to side

of, from one side to another, transversely, in front of, opposite to, beyond.

act *n.* **1** [An action] deed, performance, exploit; see ACTION 2. **2** [An official or legal statement] law, proposal, judgment, order, commitment, verdict, amendment, announcement, edict, ordinance, decree, statute, writ, bull, warrant, summons, subpoena, document, bill, code, clause, law of the land*. **3** [A division of a play] scene, prologue, epilogue, introduction; first act, second act, third act, etc. **4** [A pose] falsification, feigning, affectation; see PRETENSE 1.

act *v.* **1** [To perform an action] do, execute, carry out, carry on, operate, transact, accomplish, achieve, consummate, carry into effect, perpetrate, persist, labor, work, officiate, function, preside, serve, go ahead, step into, take steps, play a part, begin, move, enforce, maneuver, create, practice, develop, make progress, be active, commit, fight, combat, respond, keep going, answer, pursue, put forth energy, hustle*, get going*.—*Ant.* WAIT, await, rest. **2** [To conduct oneself] behave, seem, appear, carry oneself, give the appearance of, represent oneself as, take on, play one's part, impress one as, put on airs; see also BEHAVE. **3** [To take part in a play] perform, impersonate, represent, act out, simulate, pretend, mimic, burlesque, parody, feign, portray, rehearse, take a part, dramatize, star, play the part of, debut. —**act up** goof off*, be naughty, create a disturbance; see MISBEHAVE. —**act upon** (or **on**) **1** [To act in accordance with] adjust, regulate, behave; see ACT 1, 2. **2** [To influence] affect, sway, impress; see INFLUENCE.

acting *a.* substituting, alternate, assistant; see TEMPORARY.

acting *n.* pretending, feigning, simulating, gesturing, ranting, dramatizing, performing, behaving, playing, showing off, impersonation, depiction, portrayal, pantomime, rendition, dramatics, theatricals, performance, dramatic action, mime.

action *n.* **1** [Any state opposed to rest and quiet] activity, conflict, business, occupation, work, response, reaction, movement, industry, bustle, turmoil, stir, flurry, animation, vivacity, enterprise, energy, liveliness, alertness, vigor, commotion, rush, motion, mobility, haste, speed, go*, life, doings. **2** [An individual deed] feat, exploit, performance, performing, execution, blow, stroke, maneuver, step, stunt, achievement, act, deed, thing, stratagem, something done, accomplishment, commission, effort, enterprise, move, movement, doing, effect, transaction, exertion, operation, handiwork, dealings, procedure. —**bring action** accuse, start a lawsuit, take to court; see SUE. —**see action** do battle, engage in combat, fight; see FIGHT. —**take action** become active, do, initiate activity; see ACT 1.

actions *n.* deportment, conduct, manners; see BEHAVIOR.

activate *v.* stimulate, initiate, arouse; see BEGIN 1.

active *a.* busy, eventful, lively, dynamic, energetic, alive, mobile, hasty, going, rapid, progressive, speedy, walking, traveling, movable, bustling, humming, efficient, functioning, working, moving, restless, swarming, rustling, flowing, in process, in effect, in force, simmering, overflowing, streaming, stirring, effective, at work, operating, operative, agitated, brisk, industrious, enthusiastic, agile, quick, nimble, rapid, dexterous, spry, fresh, sprightly, frisky, wiry, alert, ready, sharp, keen, wide-awake, animated, enlivened, ardent, purposeful, persevering, resolute, aggressive, forceful, intense, determined, diligent, hardworking, assiduous, enterprising, inventive, vigorous, strenuous, eager, zealous, bold, daring, dashing, high-spirited, hopping*, going full blast, in high gear*, snappy*, on the ball*, peppy*.

activity *n.* motion, movement, liveliness; see ACTION 1.

actor *n.* player, performer, character actor, character actress, star, comedian, impersonator, leading man, leading woman, entertainer, performing artist, television star, villain, motion picture actor, stage player, supporting actor, mimic, mime, clown, ventriloquist, pantomimist, performance artist, understudy, Thespian, protagonist, headliner, bit player*, ham*, extra, matinee idol; see also CAST 2.

actress *n.* comedienne, starlet, leading lady; see ACTOR, CAST 2.

actual *a.* original, real, exact; see GENUINE 1.

actually *a.* truly, in fact, as a matter of fact; see REALLY 1.

acute *a.* **1** [Crucial] decisive, important, vital; see CRITICAL. **2** [Sharp] severe, keen, cutting; see INTENSE. **3** [Shrewd] clever, bright, perceptive; see INTELLIGENT.

acutely *a.* keenly, severely, sharply; see VERY.

ad* *n.* announcement, display, notice; see ADVERTISEMENT.

AD or **A.D.** *abbrev.* of the Christian era, after Christ, post-Christian, year of our Lord.

adage *n.* axiom, saying, maxim; see PROVERB.

adapt *v.* modify, revise, adjust; see ALTER 1.

adaptability *n.* changeability, flexibility, versatility, adjustability, conformability, pliancy, docility, compliancy, pliability, plasticity.

adaptable *a.* adjustable, elastic, pliable; see FLEXIBLE.

add *v.* **1** [To bring together, usually by mathematics] total, sum up, sum, figure, figure up, count up, compute, calculate, add up, tally, reckon, enumerate.—*Ant.* DECREASE, subtract, take away. **2** [To make a further remark] append, say further, continue, write further, annex, supplement, affix, add a postscript, reply, tack on. —**add to** augment, amplify, expand; see INCREASE. —**add up** be plausible, be probable, be reasonable, be logical, stand to reason, hold water; see also MAKE SENSE. —**add up to** indicate, signify, imply; see MEAN 1.

addict *n.* drug abuser, user, crackhead*, cokehead*, head*, dope fiend*, drug fiend*, mainliner*, junkie*, alcoholic, druggie*, freak*.

addicted (**to**) *a.* disposed to, inclined, in the habit of, prone, accustomed, attached, abandoned, wedded, devoted, predisposed, used to, imbued with, fanatic about, obsessed with, hooked on*.

addiction *n.* fixation, inclination, bent; see HABIT 2, OBSESSION.

addition *n.* **1** [That which has been added] additive, gain, profit, dividend, bonus, interest, raise, supplement, reinforcement, appendage, appendix, accessory, attachment, extension, increase, annex.—*Ant.* LOSS, reduction, shrinkage. **2** [A real estate development] annex, annexation, subdivision, shopping center, development, tract, extension, expansion, branch, construction.

additional *a.* supplementary, new, further; see EXTRA.

address *n.* **1** [A formal speech] oration, lecture, sermon; see SPEECH 3. **2** [Place at which one may be reached] residence, legal residence, home, quarters, living quarters, dwelling, headquarters, place of business, box number, Web address, URL, website, home page, Internet address; see also HOME 1.

address *v.* **1** [To provide directions for delivery] label, mark, prepare for mailing; see WRITE 2. **2** [To speak formally to an assemblage] lecture, lecture to, discuss, give a talk, give an address, give a speech, take the floor, harangue, rant, sermonize, spout off*, spiel*.

adept *a.* skillful, proficient, capable; see ABLE.

adequate *a.* sufficient, equal to the need, satisfactory; see ENOUGH 1.

adequately *a.* sufficiently, appropriately, suitably, fittingly, satisfactorily, abundantly, copiously, acceptably, tolerably, decently, modestly, fairly well, well enough, capably, good enough, to an acceptable degree, competently; see also WELL 2, 3.—*Ant.* INADEQUATELY, badly, insufficiently.

adhere (to) *v.* 1 [To serve] follow, be devoted to, practice; see OBEY. 2 [To stick to] attach, cling, hold fast; see STICK 1.

adhesive *a.* gummy, clinging, gluey; see STICKY.

ad infinitum *a.* endlessly, forever, ceaselessly; see REGULARLY.

adjacent *a.* beside, alongside, bordering; see NEAR 1.

adjective *n.* modifier, article, determiner, attribute, attributive, qualifier, descriptive word, limiting word, adjectival construction, identifier, qualifying word.

adjourn *v.* leave, postpone, discontinue; see SUSPEND 2.

adjournment *n.* intermission, pause, break; see RECESS 1.

adjust *v.* 1 [To bring to agreement] settle, arrange, conclude, complete, accord, reconcile, clarify, conform, allocate, regulate, organize, systematize, coordinate, straighten, standardize, clean up. 2 [To place or regulate parts] fix, connect, square, balance, regulate, tighten, fit, repair, focus, fine-tune, readjust, rectify, correct, set, mend, improve, overhaul, grind, sharpen, renovate, polish, bring into line, align, calibrate, put in working order, temper, service.

adjustable *a.* adaptable, stretchable, tractable; see FLEXIBLE.

adjustment *n.* settlement, arrangement, pay, remuneration, reimbursement, compensation, compromise, reconciliation, agreement, making up, improvement, regulation, fixing, adaptation, correction, calibration.

ad-lib* *v.* improvise, make up, devise; see INVENT 1.

administer *v.* 1 [To manage] conduct, direct, control; see MANAGE 1. 2 [To furnish] extend, dispense, give; see OFFER 1.

administration *n.* 1 [The direction of affairs] government, supervision, command; see MANAGEMENT. 2 [Those who direct affairs] directors, administrators, officers, supervisors, superintendents, advisors, command, executives, strategists, officials, committee, board, board of directors, executive, executive

branch, legislature, president, presidency, chief executive, CEO, CFO, cabinet, ministry, commander, chairman, general, admiral, commander in chief, central office, headquarters, management, consulate, embassy, legation, bureau, department, Washington, party in power, brass*, front office*, the powers that be, the man*. 3 [The period in which a political administration is operative] term of office, regime, tenure; see sense 2.

administrative *a.* executive, controlling, ruling; see GOVERNING.

administrator *n.* manager, director, chairman; see EXECUTIVE.

admirable *a.* worthy, attractive, good; see EXCELLENT.

admiration *n.* praise, deference, approval, regard, fondness, esteem, respect, appreciation, favor, adoration, applause, glorification, idolatry, honor, recognition, valuing, liking, love, high regard, high opinion, reverence, veneration, homage.—*Ant.* OBJECTION, disregard, distrust.

admire *v.* esteem, honor, applaud, praise, extol, respect, approve, revere, venerate, laud, boost, glorify, reverence, hold dear, appreciate, credit, commend, value, treasure, prize, look up to, rate highly, pay homage to, idolize, adore, hail, put a high price on, have a high opinion of, think highly of, show deference to, think well of, take stock in, put stock in, put on a pedestal.—*Ant.* BLAME, censure, deride.

admirer *n.* supporter, believer, patron; see FOLLOWER.

admissible *a.* proper, suitable, right; see PERMITTED.

admission *n.* 1 [The act of granting entrance] acceptance, admittance, permission, reception, welcome, recognition, acknowledgment, confirmation, selection, initiation.—*Ant.* REMOVAL, rejection, expulsion. 2 [The entrance fee] cover charge, fee, price, ticket, charges, toll, tax, minimum, donation, cover*, gate. 3 [Something acknowledged] statement, disclosure, confession, acknowledgment, affirmation, concession, divulgence, declaration, confirmation, assertion, testimony, allegation, deposition, affidavit.—*Ant.* DENIAL, disallowance, repudiation.

admit *v.* 1 [To grant entrance] bring in, give access to, allow entrance to; see RECEIVE 4. 2 [To confess] acknowledge, indicate, disclose, unveil, uncover, expose, proclaim, declare, open up, bring to light, go over, go into details, confide to, tell, relate, narrate, enumerate, divulge, reveal, communicate, make known, tell the whole story, plead guilty, own up to, talk, sing*, cough up*, come clean*, spill the beans*.—*Ant.* HIDE, cover up, obscure.

admonish *v.* reprove, chide, rebuke; see SCOLD.

admonition *n.* advice, caution, exhortation; see WARNING.

adolescence *n.* young adulthood, puberty, teens; see YOUTH 1.

adolescent *a.* pubescent, juvenile, youthful; see YOUNG 1.

adolescent *n.* youngster, minor, teenager; see YOUTH 3.

adopt *v.* 1 [To take as a son or daughter] father, mother, take in, raise, make one's heir, take as one's own, naturalize, foster. 2 [To take as one's own] embrace, appropriate, pick, choose, select, transfer, seize, take up, take over, choose, assume, use, utilize, imitate, borrow, mimic.—*Ant.* DENY, repudiate, reject.

adoption *n.* choosing, election, choice; see SELECTION 1.

adorable* *a.* delightful, lovable, cute; see CHARMING.

adoration *n.* devotion, homage, veneration; see WORSHIP 1.

adore *v.* 1 [To worship] venerate, revere, glorify; see WORSHIP. 2 [To love] cherish, treasure, prize; see LOVE 1.

adorn *v.* beautify, embellish, ornament; see DECORATE.

adorned *a.* trimmed, decked, garnished; see ORNATE.

adult *a.* of age, grown, developed; see MATURE.

adult *n.* mature person, grown-up, fully developed member of a species; see MAN 2, WOMAN 1.

adulterate *v.* dilute, lessen, taint; see POLLUTE, WEAKEN.

adultery *n.* promiscuity, infidelity, unfaithfulness; see FORNICATION.

advance *n.* 1 [The act of moving forward] impetus, progression, motion; see PROGRESS 1. 2 [Promotion] enrichment, betterment, increase; see IMPROVEMENT 1. —**in advance** ahead of, earlier, in time; see BEFORE.

advance *v.* 1 [To move forward physically] progress, proceed, move on, forge ahead, press on, push ahead, go on, go forth, gain ground, make headway, step forward, come to the front, conquer territory, march on, move onward, continue ahead, push on, press on.—*Ant.* STOP, halt, stand still. 2 [To propose] set forth, introduce, suggest; see PROPOSE 1. 3 [To promote] further, encourage, urge; see PROMOTE 1. 4 [To lend] loan, provide with, furnish; see LEND. 5 [To improve] develop, make progress, get better; see IMPROVE 2.

advanced *a.* 1 [Superior] precocious, first, exceptional; see EXCELLENT. 2 [Aged] seasoned, venerable, time-honored; see OLD 1, 3. 3 [Progressive] radical, unconventional, ahead of the times; see LIBERAL.

advancement *n.* 1 [Promotion in rank] improvement, elevation, raise; see PROMOTION 1. 2 [Progress] gain, headway, progression; see PROGRESS 1.

advantage *n.* luck, favor, approval, help, aid, sanction, good, patronage, support, preference, odds, protection, start, leg up*, helping hand, upper hand, leverage, hold, opportunity, dominance, superiority, supremacy, lead, influence, power, mastery, authority, prestige, sway, pull*, edge*, ace in the hole*.—*Ant.* WEAKNESS, handicap, disadvantage. —**take advantage of** exploit, profit by, utilize; see DECEIVE, USE 1.

adventure *n.* happening, experience, episode; see EVENT.

adventurer *n.* explorer, pirate, soldier of fortune, daredevil, hero, pioneer, mountain climber, big game hunter, romantic; see also PIONEER 2, TRAVELER.

adventurous *a.* bold, daring, courageous; see BRAVE.

adverse *a.* untimely, improper, unfortunate; see UNFAVORABLE.

adversely *a.* negatively, resentfully, unsympathetically; see UNFAVORABLY.

adversity *n.* misfortune, distress, trouble; see DIFFICULTY 1, 2.

advertise *v.* publicize, proclaim, herald, announce, declare, notify, warn, display, exhibit, show, reveal, expose, disclose, unmask, divulge, uncover, communicate, publish abroad, issue, broadcast, print, circulate, show off, parade, propagate, disseminate, inform, celebrate, spread, call public attention to, promulgate, give out, plug*, play up*; see also DECLARE.

advertised *a.* announced, posted, noted, publicized, billed, printed, published, made public, broadcast, emphasized, pointed out, displayed, exhibited, shown, offered, presented, put on sale, flaunted, plugged*, boosted, built up, pushed*.

advertisement *n.* announcement, notice, publicity, exhibit, exhibition, display, circular, handbill, placard, poster, public notice, broadcast, bill, proclamation, classified advertisement, sample, endorsement, want ad*, buildup*, plug*, ballyhoo, blurb*, spread*, classified.

advice *n.* guidance, instruction, consultation, suggestion, preaching, information, admonition, forewarning, warning, caution, a word to the wise, injunction, lesson, directions, opinion, counsel, advisement, encouragement, persuasion, prescription, recommendation, proposition, proposal, view, help, aid, judgment.

advise *v.* recommend, prescribe, guide, exhort, direct, admonish, warn, point out, instruct, counsel, advocate, suggest, urge, prompt, show, tell, inform, caution, charge, encourage, preach, teach, persuade, offer an opinion to, forewarn, prepare, straighten out.—*Ant.* DECEIVE, misdirect, lead astray.

advisor *n.* counselor, instructor, consultant.—*Ant.* FRIEND, TEACHER.

advisory *a.* consulting, having power to advise, prudential; see HELPING.

advocate *v.* bolster, push, further, advance; see also PROMOTE 1.

aerial *a.* in the air, atmospheric, flying; see HIGH 2.

aesthetic *a.* creative, artistic, tasteful; see BEAUTIFUL.

affair *n.* **1** [Business; *often plural*] concern, responsibility, matter, duty, topic, subject, case, circumstance, thing, question, function, private concern, personal business, calling, employment, occupation, profession, pursuit, avocation, obligation, job, province, realm, interest, mission, assignment, task; see also JOB 1. **2** [An illicit love affair] liaison, rendezvous, intimacy, romance, relationship.

affect *v.* impress, sway, induce; see INFLUENCE.

affected *a.* **1** [Being subject to influence] moved, touched, melted, influenced, awakened, sympathetic, stimulated, stirred, grieved, overwhelmed, moved to tears, hurt, excited, struck, impressed, overwrought, concerned, compassionate, sorry, troubled, distressed.—*Ant.* INDIFFERENT, unmoved, untouched. **2** [Insincere or artificial] pretentious, melodramatic, unnatural, stilted, superficial, theatrical, stiff, strained, overdone, disingenuous, ostentatious, hollow, shallow, showy, fake, stuck-up*.—*Ant.* SIMPLE, natural, genuine.

affection *n.* love, friendship, liking, attachment, goodwill, partiality, passion, ardor, friendliness, amiability, amicability, concern, regard, desire, closeness, kindness, devotion, tenderness, fondness.—*Ant.* HATRED, dislike, enmity.

affectionate *a.* kind, tender, friendly; see LOVING.

affidavit *n.* testimony, sworn statement, affirmation; see OATH 1.

affinity *n.* **1** [Attraction based on affection] fondness, liking, close-

ness; see AFFECTION. **2** [Similarity] likeness, resemblance, kinship; see SIMILARITY.

affirmative *a.* agreeing, consenting, concurring, approving, assenting, supporting.—*Ant.* NEGATIVE, contradictory, noncommittal. —**in the affirmative** favorably, in assent, in agreement, with an affirmative answer; see also YES.

afflict *v.* injure, torment, trouble; see HURT.

affliction *n.* trouble, hardship, plight; see DIFFICULTY 1, 2.

affluent *a.* wealthy, well-off, well-to-do; see RICH 1.

afford *v.* have enough for, bear, manage, be able to, have the means for, be financially able, swing*, be in the market for.

afire *a.* flaming, on fire, blazing; see BURNING.

afloat *a.* adrift, at sea, sailing; see FLOATING.

afoot *a.* on foot, hiking, marching; see WALKING.

afraid *a.* hesitant, anxious, apprehensive, disturbed, frightened, fearful, nervous, uneasy, fidgety, alarmed, intimidated, discouraged, disheartened, perplexed, worried, perturbed, upset, panic-stricken, cowardly, scared, terrified, terrorized, shocked, frozen, aghast, alarmed, startled, aroused, horrified, petrified, stunned, rattled, struck dumb, trembling, distressed, jittery*, jumpy, leery, shaky.—*Ant.* CONFIDENT, self-assured, poised.

African *a.* North African, Saharan, sub-Saharan, East African, West African, Central African, South African.

aft *a.* rearward, behind, astern; see BACK.

after *a., prep.* **1** [Behind in space] back of, in the rear, behind; see BACK. **2** [Following] next, later, subsequent; see FOLLOWING.

afternoon *n.* PM, siesta time, early afternoon, late afternoon, mid-afternoon.

afterward *a.* later, after, subsequently, in a while, a while later, afterwards, by and by, eventually, soon, on the next day, ultimately, another time, then, at a later time.

again *a.* anew, afresh, newly, once more, once again, repeatedly, over, from the beginning, on and on, another time, over again, a second time, recurrently, ditto. —**again and again** repeatedly, once again, continuously; see AGAIN. —**as much again** doubled, twice as much, multiplied; see DOUBLE.

against *prep.* **1** [Counter to] in the face of, into, toward, opposite to, facing. **2** [In contact with] on, upon, in collision with, touching; see also NEXT 2. **3** [Contrary to] in opposition to, opposed to, counter to, adverse to, in violation of, versus, over against. **4** [Opposite] facing, fronting, corresponding; see OPPOSITE 3.

age *n.* **1** [The period of one's existence] span, lifetime, duration; see LIFE 4. **2** [A particular point or time in one's life] infancy, childhood, girlhood, boyhood, adolescence, adulthood, youth, middle age, old age, senility. **3** [A period of time] epoch, era, period, time, century, millennium, decade, generation, interval, term; see also LIFE 4. —**of age** adult, twenty-one, having attained majority; see MATURE.

age *v.* grow feeble, decline, wane, advance in years, wrinkle, waste away, have one foot in the grave, become long in the tooth.

aged *a.* gray, elderly, worn; see OLD.

agency *n.* **1** [Place where business is transacted] firm, bureau, company; see OFFICE 3, BUSINESS 4. **2** [That by which something is done] power, auspices, action; see MEANS 1.

agenda *n.* list, plan, schedule; see PROGRAM 2.

agent *n.* broker, promoter, operator, representative, salesman, saleswoman, salesperson, assistant, emissary, intermediary, appointee, servant, executor, attorney, lawyer, go-between, surrogate, mediary, deputy, minister, envoy, middleman, commissioner, delegate, proxy, substitute, steward, functionary, ambassador, proctor, negotiator, advocate, coagent, press agent, booking agent.

aggravate *v.* exasperate, annoy, provoke; see BOTHER 2.

aggravation *n.* **1** [A cause of aggravation] worry, affliction, distress; see DIFFICULTY 1, 2, TROUBLE 1. **2** [Annoyance] irritation, provocation, exasperation; see ANNOYANCE 1.

aggression *n.* offensive, assault, invasion; see ATTACK 1.

aggressive *a.* warlike, attacking, combative, threatening, advancing, offensive, firm, strong, assertive, disruptive, disturbing, hostile, intrusive, contentious, destructive, intruding, invading, assailing, barbaric, up in arms, on the warpath.—*Ant.* SERENE, peace-loving, peaceful.

agile *a.* nimble, quick, spry, deft, vigorous, athletic, sure-footed, light-footed, frisky, spirited, lithe, sprightly, supple, dexterous, rapid, active, ready, alive, buoyant, energetic, stirring, brisk, lively, swift, alert, bustling.—*Ant.* AWKWARD, slow, clumsy.

agility *n.* nimbleness, dexterity, spryness, quickness, briskness, swiftness, deftness, adroitness, fleetness, friskiness, liveliness, alertness.

agitate *v.* stir, move, arouse; see EXCITE.

agitated *a.* disturbed, upset, aroused; see EXCITED.

ago *a.* gone, since, past; see BEFORE.

agony *n.* suffering, torture, anguish; see PAIN 1, 2.

agree *v.* coincide, get along, side with, harmonize with, match up, concur, stand together, parallel, go along with, fit in, suit, say "yes" to, conform, go hand in hand with, equal, correspond, go together, synchronize, measure up to, square with*, click*, hit it off with, see eye to eye.—*Ant.* DIFFER, disagree, debate. —**agree about** come to terms, see eye to eye, settle; see SETTLE 1. —**agree on** come to terms, make an arrangement, make a bargain; see SETTLE 1. —**agree to** promise, consent, approve; see ACCEPT. —**agree with** coincide, accord, harmonize; see AGREE.

agreeable *a.* pleasing, satisfactory, acceptable; see PLEASANT 1, 2.

agreeably *a.* kindly, politely, pleasantly, well, wonderfully, satisfactorily, genially, cheerfully, peacefully; see also FAVORABLY.—*Ant.* OPPOSITE, disagreeably, negatively.

agreement *n.* **1** [The state of being in accord] conformity, friendship, accordance, accommodation, correspondence, harmony, concord, unison, concert, common view, understanding, brotherhood, affiliation, alliance, fellowship, companionship, goodwill, cooperation, assent, approval, compromise, treaty, pact, contract, bargain, settlement, satisfaction, affinity, closeness, concurrence, reconciliation, uniformity, balance, kinship, peace, love, unity, union, tie.—*Ant.* DISAGREEMENT, enmity, disunity. **2** [An expression of agreement] approval, treaty, contract; see DEAL 1.

agriculture *n.* tillage, cultivation, horticulture; see FARMING.

ahead *a.* before, earlier, in advance, ahead of, advanced, preceding, foremost, leading, in the lead, at the head of, in the foreground, to the fore, in the vanguard, first, in front of, preliminary.—*Ant.* behind, back, toward the end. —**get ahead** advance, prosper, progress; see SUCCEED.

aid *n.* comfort, benefit, favor; see HELP 1.

ailing *a.* ill, feeble, weak; see SICK.

ailment *n.* sickness, infirmity, disease; see ILLNESS 1, 2.

aim *n.* intention, object, plan; see PURPOSE 1. —**take aim** point, direct, train; see AIM, *v.*

aim *v.* train, steer, level, direct, set up, set one's sights, sight, take aim, zero in on, draw a bead on.

aimed *a.* proposed, marked, intended for, earmarked, directed, designed, dedicated, calculated, leveled, trained, steered, set, planned, anticipated.

aimless *a.* purposeless, pointless, erratic, thoughtless, careless, heedless, nonchalant, rambling, wandering, blind, random, unsettled, flighty, capricious, wayward, without aim, chance, haphazard, to no purpose, drifting, stray, accidental, undirected, casual, indecisive, irresolute, fitful, fanciful, fickle, eccentric, unplanned, helpless, unpredictable, shiftless.—*Ant.* CAREFUL, purposeful, planned.

air *n.* 1 [The gaseous envelope of the earth] atmosphere, aerosphere, stratosphere, troposphere, thermosphere, substratosphere, ozonosphere, ozone layer, mesosphere, ionosphere, chemosphere, homosphere, heterosphere, exosphere, mesopause, stratopause, aeropause, tropopause; wind, breeze, draft, the open air, sky, oxygen, the open, ventilation, the out-of-doors. 2 [The apparent quality] look, mien, demeanor; see LOOKS. —**in the air** prevalent, abroad, current; see FASHIONABLE, POPULAR 1. —**off the air** not being broadcast, closed, signed off; see QUIET. —**on the air** broadcasting, going on, televising, telecasting, being telecast, live. —**up in the air** undecided, unsettled, unsure; see UNCERTAIN.

air *v.* ventilate, open, freshen, air out, circulate air, air-condition, expose to air, draw in air, fan, refresh, cool, purify.

aired *a.* 1 [Exposed to the air] ventilated, opened, freshened, purified, hung out, sunned, dried.—*Ant.* CLOSED, stuffy, dark. 2 [Exposed to public attention] exposed, disclosed, discussed, revealed, told, unveiled; see also EXPOSED.—*Ant.* SECRET, undisclosed, concealed.

air force *n.* aviation service, air power, air cover; see ARMY 1.

airline *n.* air carrier, commercial airline, air freight carrier; see BUSINESS 4.

airman *n.* pilot, copilot, navigator; see PILOT.

airplane *n.* aircraft, aeroplane, airliner; see PLANE 3.

airport *n.* airfield, spaceport, flying field, landing field, airstrip, hangar, heliport, terminal, runway.

airtight *a.* impermeable to air, closed, sealed; see TIGHT 2.

airy *a.* windy, breezy, draughty, exposed, ventilated, open, spacious, lofty, atmospheric, well-ventilated, aerial, out-of-doors, outdoors, in the open.

aisle *n.* passageway, opening, way, walk, path, course, clearing, avenue, corridor, passage, gangway, alley, lane.

alarm *n.* drum, siren, horn, tocsin, signal, foghorn, fire siren, call, SOS, red light, hoot, blast, shout, warning sound, danger signal, cry, yell, scream, air-raid siren.

alarmed *a.* frightened, fearful, aroused; see AFRAID.

alarming *a.* frightening, foreboding, distressing; see DISTURBING.

album *n.* collection, register, index, scrapbook, notebook, photograph album, stamp book, portfolio, commonplace book.

alcohol *n.* spirits, liquor, intoxicant; see DRINK 2.

alcoholic *a.* hard, fermented, distilled; see STRONG 4.

alcoholic *n.* addict, heavy drinker, sot; see DRUNKARD.

alcoholism *n.* intoxication, insobriety, dipsomania; see DRUNKENNESS.

alert *a.* wary, on guard, wide-awake; see OBSERVANT. —**on the alert** watchful, vigilant, on guard; see OBSERVANT.

alert *v.* inform, put on guard, signal; see WARN.

alibi *n.* proof of absence, plea, explanation, declaration, defense, statement, case, allegation, avowal, assurance, profession, excuse, assertion, answer, reply, retort, vindication.

alien *a.* exotic, strange, unknown; see FOREIGN.

alien *n.* foreigner, stranger, refugee, displaced person, outsider, migrant, colonist, immigrant, guest, visitor, newcomer, barbarian, settler, stateless person, intruder, squatter, interloper, invader, noncitizen, man without a country, extraterrestrial.—*Ant.* INHABITANT, native, citizen.

alienate *v.* estrange, turn away, set against, withdraw the affections of, make unfriendly, come between, disunite, separate, divide, part, turn off*.—*Ant.* UNITE, reconcile, acclimate.

align *v.* arrange, straighten, regulate; see ADJUST 1, 2.

alike *a.* like, same, equal, identical, matching, selfsame, akin, similar, comparable, parallel, resembling, related, approximate, equivalent, allied, of a kind, twin, one, indistinguishable, facsimile, duplicate, matched, mated, one and the same, all one, in the same boat, on all fours with.

alimony *n.* upkeep, maintenance, support; see PAYMENT 1.

alive *a.* live, animate, living, breathing, existing, existent, vital, not dead, mortal, organic, extant, viable, growing, having life, conscious, alive and kicking*, above ground*, among the living.—*Ant.* DEAD, lifeless, inanimate.

all *a.* **1** [Completely] totally, wholly, entirely; see COMPLETELY. **2** [Each] every, any, each and every, any and every, every member of, without exception, barring no one, bar none, beginning and end, alpha and omega, from A to Z.—*Ant.* no, not any, none. **3** [Exclusively] alone, nothing but, solely; see ONLY 1.

all *n.* everything, everyone, every person, sum, collection, group, ensemble, total, totality, sum total, quantity, unit, entity, whole kit and caboodle*; lock, stock and barrel*; the works*.—*Ant.* NONE, nobody, nothing. —**after all** nevertheless, in spite of everything, despite; see ALTHOUGH. —**at all** anyhow, ever, in any way, in any case, in any respect, under any condition, under any circumstances, anyway, anywise, in the least, in any manner, to any extent, in the least degree, anyways*. —**in all** all told, collectively, on the whole; see ALTOGETHER.

allegedly *a.* assertedly, according to the statement, supposedly; see APPARENTLY.

allegiance *n.* fidelity, homage, fealty; see LOYALTY.

allergic to *a.* sensitive to, affected by, subject to, susceptible to, repelled by, oversensitive to.—*Ant.* IMMUNE, unaffected by, hardened to.

allergy *n.* hypersensitive reaction, hypersensitivity, antipathy to certain substances; see ILLNESS 2.

alley *n.* back street, lane, rear way; see ROAD 1. —**up** (or **down**) **one's alley*** suited to one's abilities, in keeping with one's tastes, enjoyable, useful, what the doctor ordered*.

alliance *n.* **1** [The state of being allied] connection, membership, affinity, participation, cooperation, support, union, agreement, common understanding, marriage, kinship, relation, collaboration, federation, friendship, partnership, coalition, association, affiliation, confederation, implication, bond, tie. **2** [The act of joining] fusion, combination, coupling; see UNION 1. **3** [A union] league, federation, company; see ORGANIZATION 2.

allied *a.* unified, confederated, associated; see UNITED.

allot *v.* earmark, allocate, dole; see ASSIGN, DISTRIBUTE.

allotment *n.* portion, lot, part; see SHARE.

all-out *a.* total, wholehearted, complete; see ABSOLUTE 1.

allow *v.* permit, let, sanction, grant, consent to, tolerate, favor, yield, bear, approve of, give leave, endorse, certify, have no objection to, release, pass, authorize, license, warrant, put up with, give the green light to*, give the go-ahead to.—*Ant.* DENY, forbid, prohibit. —**allow for** take into account, take into consideration, provide for; see CONSIDER.

allowable *a.* permissible, proper, legal; see ADMISSIBLE.

allowance *n.* salary, wage, wages, commission, fee, hire, remittance, stipend, gift, grant, pension, alimony, palimony, annuity, settled rate, endowment, scholarship, fellowship, prize, subsidy, pay, bequest, legacy, inheritance, contribution, aid, handout, pocket money. —**make allowances for** weigh, excuse, rationalize; see CONSIDER.

alloy *n.* compound, mixture, combination; see METAL. *Common metal alloys include the following:* amalgam, pewter, brass, bronze, cast iron, Babbitt metal, britannia metal, gunmetal, pinchbeck, wrought iron, steel, vanadium steel, titanium steel, chrome steel, nichrome, tungsten steel, stainless steel, nonmagnetic steel, chromium steel, high tensile steel, cobalt steel, finishing steel, structural steel, carbon steel, sterling silver, white gold, aluminum metals, ferrous metals, nonferrous metals, nickel-silver.

all right *a.* **1** [Adequately] tolerably, acceptably, fairly well; see ADEQUATELY. **2** [Yes] agreed, very well, OK*; see YES. **3** [Certainly] without a doubt, definitely, positively; see SURELY. **4** [Uninjured] safe, well, unhurt; see WHOLE. **5** [Correct] exact, precise, right; see RIGHT 1.

all-time *a.* unsurpassed, record-breaking, to the greatest extent; see BEST 1.

ally *n.* confederate, partner, collaborator; see ASSOCIATE.

almanac *n.* calendar, yearbook, annual, register, world almanac, chronicle, journal, record, register of the year.

almighty *a.* **1** [Omnipotent] invincible, all-powerful, mighty; see POWERFUL 1. **2** [Divine] infinite, eternal, godlike, all-knowing, all-seeing, deathless, immortal, celestial, godly, pervading.

almost *a.* all but, nearly, approximately, roughly, to all intents, as good as, near to, substantially, essentially, in effect, on the verge of, relatively, for all practical purposes, to that effect, not quite, about to, with some exceptions, in the vicinity of, bordering on, within sight of, with little tolerance, close upon, in the neighborhood of, about, just about*, not quite, most*, around*, within a hair of.

aloft *a.* on high, overhead, up; see ABOVE 1, OVER 1.

alone *a.* lone, lonely, solitary, deserted, abandoned, individual, forsaken, desolate, detached, friendless, unaccompanied, isolated, lonesome, apart, by oneself, single, widowed, unattached, unconnected.—*Ant.* ACCOMPANIED, attended, escorted.—**let alone** **1** [Besides] not to mention, also, in addition to; see BESIDES. **2** [Neglect] ignore, isolate, refrain from disturbing; see NEGLECT 2. —**let well enough alone** forget, ignore, let alone; see NEGLECT 2.

along *a., prep.* **1** [Near] by, at, adjacent; see NEAR 1. **2** [Ahead] on, onward, forward; see AHEAD. **3** [Together with] with, accompanying, in addition to, in company with, along with, side by side, coupled with, at the same time, simultaneously. —**all along** all the time, from the beginning, constantly; see REGULARLY. —**get along** **1** [To succeed] prosper, get by, make ends meet; see SUCCEED 1. **2** [To advance] progress, move on, push ahead; see ADVANCE 1. **3** [To agree] accord, stand together, equal; see AGREE.

alongside *a., prep.* parallel to, close by, close at hand, by the side of, at the side of, along the side, side by side, equal with, on the same plane with, almost touching, neck and neck.—*Ant.* BEYOND, ahead, behind.

aloof *a.* remote, reserved, distant; see INDIFFERENT.

aloud *a.* vociferously, audibly, noisily; see LOUDLY.

alphabet *n.* letters, runes, pictographs, ideographs, characters, symbols, signs, hieroglyphs, cryptograms, phonemes, morphemes, phonetic characters; see also LETTER 1.

alphabetical *a.* alphabetic, systematic, logical, consecutive, progressive, one after another, step by step, graded, planned, ordered, letter by letter, from A to Z, indexed.

alphabetize *v.* arrange alphabetically, index, systematize; see ORDER 3.

alpine *a.* mountainous, high, lofty, snowcapped, rocky, soaring, rangy, snow-clad, elevated, towering; see also HIGH 1, 2.

already *a.* previously, by now, now, even now, by this time, at present, just now, in the past, up to now, by that time, then.

also *a.* too, likewise, besides, as well, in addition, additionally, along with, more than that, over and above, in conjunction with, thereto, together with, ditto, more, moreover, further, furthermore, including, plus, to boot.—*Ant.* WITHOUT, excluding, otherwise.

alter *v.* **1** [To change for a purpose] vary, turn, diminish, replace, mutate, warp, alternate, remodel, renovate, evolve, translate, disguise, restyle, revolutionize, reduce, substitute, reorganize, increase, intensify, shape, shift, modify, transform, remake, convert, reform, re-form, tailor, adjust, adapt, invert, reverse, reconstruct. **2** [To become different] convert, develop, decay; see CHANGE 2.

alteration *n.* conversion, modification, revision; see CHANGE 1.

altered *a.* modified, converted, revised; see CHANGED 2.

alternate *a.* alternative, substitute, makeshift; see TEMPORARY.

alternate *n.* replacement, equivalent, double; see SUBSTITUTE.

alternate *v.* **1** [To take or do by turns] substitute, follow in turn, happen by turns, follow one another, do by turns, do one then the other, relieve, fill in for, exchange. **2** [To fluctuate] vary, rise and fall, shift; see WAVER.

alternative *n.* option, discretion, opportunity; see CHOICE.

although *conj.* though, even though, despite, still, despite the fact that, in spite of, even if, while, however, for all that.

altitude *n.* elevation, loftiness, eminence; see HEIGHT.

altogether *a.* all told, collectively, on the whole, in the aggregate, in sum total, in a mass, in all, all things considered, by and large, all, taking all things together, as a whole, for the most part.

always *a.* **1** [Constantly] periodically, continually, ceaselessly; see REGULARLY. **2** [Forever] perpetually, eternally, evermore; see FOREVER.

AM or **A.M.** *abbrev.* ante meridiem, antemeridian, after midnight, morning, early hours, before noon, forenoon, dawn, sunup.

amass *v.* gather, hoard, store up; see ACCUMULATE.

amateur *n.* beginner, novice, learner, nonprofessional, dabbler, recruit, dilettante, hopeful, neophyte, initiate, apprentice, freshman, tenderfoot, rookie*, greenhorn, cub.—*Ant.* VETERAN, professional, expert.

amaze *v.* astonish, perplex, astound; see SURPRISE.

amazement *n.* astonishment, awe, bewilderment; see WONDER 1.

amazing *a.* astonishing, astounding, marvelous; see UNUSUAL 1.

ambassador *n.* representative, envoy, minister; see DIPLOMAT.

ambiguity *n.* doubtfulness, incertitude, vagueness; see UNCERTAINTY 2.

ambiguous *a.* equivocal, enigmatic, vague; see OBSCURE 1.

ambition *n.* hope, earnestness, aspiration, yearning, eagerness, longing, craving, passion, lust, itch, hunger, thirst, appetite, energy, ardor, zeal, enthusiasm, spirit, vigor, enterprise, get up and go*, what it takes*.—*Ant.* INDIFFERENCE, apathy, laziness.

ambitious *a.* aspiring, longing, hopeful, zealous, hungry, thirsty, inspired, industrious, goal-oriented, enthusiastic, energetic, avid, sharp, climbing, ardent, designing, earnest, enterprising, aggressive, Type A, resourceful, pushy*.

ambush *n.* pitfall, snare, deception; see TRAP 1.

ambush *v.* waylay, ensnare, lay for, bushwhack, set a trap, keep out of sight, decoy, entrap, hook in, lurk, lie in wait for, surround, hem in; see also ATTACK.

amend *v.* correct, mend, revise; see ALTER 1.

amendment *n.* bill, measure, act, clause, motion, revision, codicil, supplement, rider.

American *a.* **1** [Related to the Western Hemisphere] continental, North American, Latin American, South American, Central American, Pan-American. **2** [Related to the United States of America] republican, constitutional, democratic, patriotic, all-American.

American *n.* citizen of the United States, United States national, Yankee, Northerner, Southerner, Native American, Indian, pioneer.

Americanism *n.* patriotism, nationalism, isolationism, provincialism, flag waving, fair play, free enterprise, America first, spirit of '76*.

amiable *a.* pleasant, genial, charming; see FRIENDLY.

ammunition *n. Types of ammunition include the following:* projectile, charge, grenade, buckshot, gunpowder, cartridge, bullet, bomb, missile, hand grenade, fuse, fuze, shrapnel, torpedo, shell, ball, cannonball, shot, ammo*; see also BOMB, BULLET, EXPLOSIVE, GAS 3, SHOT 1.

among *prep.* between, in between, in the midst of, in the middle of, encompassed by, surrounded by, in connection with, amid, amongst, amidst, in the company of, betwixt*.

amount *n.* **1** [The total of several quantities] sum, product, sum total; see WHOLE. **2** [Price] expense, output, outlay; see PRICE. **3** [Quantity] bulk, mass, number; see QUANTITY.

amount to *v.* reach, extend to, come to, effect, be equal to, approximate, check with, total up to, be in all, be in the whole, total, tally with, add up to, be tantamount to.

ample *a.* sufficient, plentiful, adequate; see ENOUGH 1.

amplify *v.* expand, augment, elaborate; see INCREASE.

amply *a.* enough, sufficiently, copiously; see ADEQUATELY.

amputate *v.* cut off, sever, cut away; see REMOVE.

amuse *v.* divert, cheer, enliven; see ENTERTAIN 1.

amusement *n.* recreation, pastime, play; see ENTERTAINMENT.

amusing *a.* engaging, diverting, enchanting; see ENTERTAINING.

analysis *n.* study, investigation, interpretation; see EXAMINATION 1.

analyze *v.* dissect, examine, investigate, separate, break down, disintegrate, take apart, resolve into elements, determine the essential features of.

anarchy *n.* turmoil, chaos, mob rule; see DISORDER.

anatomy *n.* physique, form, figure; see BODY 1.

ancestor *n.* progenitor, forebear, father, mother, forefather, foremother, parent, sire, forerunner, author, predecessor, originator, precursor, grandfather, grandmother, procreator, patriarch, relative, begetter, founder, kinsman.

ancestral *a.* inborn, innate, inherited; see INHERENT.

ancestry *n.* lineage, heritage, parentage; see FAMILY.

anchor *n.* stay, tie, grapnel, mooring, grappling iron, support, mainstay, ballast, safeguard, security, protection, hold, fastener, grip, defense, protection, foothold.

anchor *v.* make port, tie up, moor, berth, bring a ship in, drop anchor, cast anchor.

ancient *a.* antique, antiquated, aged; see OLD 1, 2, 3.

and *conj.* in addition, in addition to, also, plus, together with, as well as, furthermore, moreover.

anecdote *n.* tale, incident, episode; see STORY.

anemic *a.* pallid, weak, sickly; see PALE 1.

anesthetic *n.* sedative, painkiller, opiate; see DRUG.

angel *n.* Angel of Death, good angel, dark angel, archangel, guardian angel, spirit, cherub, celestial spirit, saint.—*Ant.* DEVIL, demon, Satan.

angelic *a.* saintly, good, humble, heavenly, spiritual, kind, radiant, beautiful, divine, holy, pure, lovely, devout, virtuous, above reproach, righteous, cherubic.—*Ant.* WICKED, demonic, evil.

anger *n.* wrath, rage, fury, passion, temper, bad temper, animosity, indignation, hatred, resentment, ire, hot temper, impatience, vexation, annoyance, provocation, violence, turbulence, excitement, frenzy, tantrum, exasperation, huff, irritation, dander*.—*Ant.* PATIENCE, mildness, calm.

anger *v.* infuriate, annoy, irritate; see ENRAGE.

angle *n.* 1 [Shape formed by intersecting lines or intersecting planes] notch, crotch, elbow, fork, cusp, incline, decline, Y, V, point where two lines meet.—*Ant.* CURVE, arc, oval. 2 [Point of view] standpoint, outlook, perspective; see VIEWPOINT.

angle for *v.* plot for, scheme for, maneuver for; see PLAN 1.

angler *n.* fisher, fisherwoman, sportsman; see FISHERMAN.

angrily *a.* heatedly, indignantly, irately, grouchily, crisply, sharply, savagely, hotly, fiercely, tartly, bitterly, furiously, wildly, violently.—*Ant.* CALMLY, softly, quietly.

angry *a.* enraged, fierce, fiery, irate, raging, fuming, infuriated, furious, wrathful, stormy, indignant, outraged, cross, vexed, resentful, irritated, bitter, ferocious, offended, sullen, annoyed, provoked, displeased, riled, affronted, huffy, hostile, rabid, mad, hot under the collar*, boiling, steamed up*, at the boiling point, with one's back up*, fit to be tied*, all worked up, up in arms.—*Ant.* CALM, quiet, restrained. —**get angry** become enraged, become furious, lose one's temper, get mad, blow up*, blow one's cool*, lose one's cool*, get hot under the collar*, get steamed up*, fly off the handle*, blow a fuse*.

anguish *n.* wretchedness, pain, agony; see PAIN 1.

angular *a.* sharp-cornered, intersecting, crossing, oblique, with corners, Y-shaped, V-shaped, forked, bent, crooked, pointed, triangular, rectangular, jagged, staggered, zigzag.—*Ant.* ROUND, parallel, side by side.

animal *a.* bestial, beastly, swinish, brutish, wild, beastlike, untamed,

mammalian, bovine, canine, feline, reptilian.

animal *n.* living thing, creature, critter*, being, human being, beast, worm, mollusk, jellyfish, fish, crustacean, amphibian, reptile, insect, arachnid, bird, mammal, vertebrate, invertebrate, wild animal, domestic animal; see also BIRD, FISH, INSECT, MAN 1.

animate *v.* activate, vitalize, make alive, arouse, give life to, energize, put life into, breathe new life into.

animated *a.* spirited, vivacious, lively; see HAPPY.

animosity *n.* dislike, enmity, ill will; see HATRED.

ankle *n.* anklebone, joint, tarsus; see BONE, FOOT 2.

annex *n.* extension, additional quarters, new wing; see ADDITION 1, 2.

annex *v.* append, attach, affix; see ADD.

annihilate *v.* demolish, exterminate, obliterate; see DESTROY.

anniversary *n.* holiday, saint's day, birth date, birthday, yearly observance of an event, feast day, ceremony, annual meeting, biennial, triennial, quadrennial, quinquennial, silver anniversary, golden anniversary, diamond jubilee, jubilee, festival, centennial, centenary, red-letter day.

announce *v.* proclaim, publish, state; see DECLARE.

announced *a.* reported, given out, broadcast, issued, circulated, proclaimed, declared, published, disclosed, divulged, released, made known, disseminated, revealed, publicized, made public.—*Ant.* HIDDEN, unannounced, unrevealed.

announcement *n.* declaration, notification, prediction, proclamation, communication, publication, report, statement, advertisement, decision, news, tidings, returns, bulletin, edict, white paper, message, notice, interim report, survey, advice, item, communiqué, speech, release, handbill, poster, pamphlet, circular, billboard, brochure, form letter, fax, e-mail, telegram, cablegram, letter, leaflet; see also ADVERTISEMENT.—*Ant.* SECRET, ban, silence.

announcer *n.* broadcaster, telecaster, commentator, sportscaster, newscaster, anchor, moderator, emcee, weatherman, disc jockey.

annoy *v.* pester, irritate, trouble; see BOTHER 2.

annoyance *n.* 1 [A feeling of annoyance] vexation, irritation, pique, uneasiness, disgust, displeasure, provocation, nervousness, exasperation, indignation, touchiness, perturbation, moodiness, mortification, vexation, worry, distress, unhappiness, discontent, heartache, misery, aches and pains, dissatisfaction, impatience, peeve*.—*Ant.* JOY, pleasure, delight. **2** [A source of annoyance] worry, inconvenience, nuisance; see DIFFICULTY 1, 2, TROUBLE 1.

annoying *a.* irritating, bothersome, vexatious; see DISTURBING.

annual *a.* yearly, each year, every year, once a year, lasting a year, anniversary, seasonal.

annually *a.* each year, once a year, periodically; see YEARLY.

annul *v.* invalidate, render void, repeal, revoke; see also CANCEL.

annulment *n.* invalidation, nullification, dissolution; see CANCELLATION.

anonymous *a.* unsigned, nameless, unknown, unnamed, unacknowledged, unclaimed, unidentified, secret, of unknown authorship, without a name, bearing no name, incognito, pseudonymous.—*Ant.* NAMED, signed, acknowledged.

another *a.* **1** [Additional] one more, a further, an added; see EXTRA. **2** [Different] a separate, a distinct, some other; see DIFFERENT.

another *pron.* someone else, a different person, one more, an additional one, something else.

answer *n.* **1** [A reply] response, return, statement, retort, echo, repartee, password, rebuttal, reaction, approval, acknowledgment, sign, rejoinder, comeback.—*Ant.* QUESTION, query, request. **2** [A solution] discovery, find, disclosure, revelation, explanation, interpretation, clue, resolution, key, the why and the wherefore.

answer *v.* **1** [To reply] reply, respond, rejoin, retort, acknowledge, give answer, say, echo, return, refute, react, rebut, argue, plead, claim, remark, talk back, shoot back*.—*Ant.* QUESTION, inquire, ask. **2** [To provide a solution] solve, elucidate, clarify; see EXPLAIN. —**answer for** be responsible for, take the blame for, accept the responsibility for, pay for, atone for, be liable for, take upon oneself, sponsor, do at one's own risk, take the rap for*. —**answer to** be responsible to, be ruled by, respect the authority of; see RESPECT 2.

answerable *a.* responsible, liable, accountable; see RESPONSIBLE 1.

antagonism *n.* enmity, hostility, opposition; see HATRED.

antagonistic *a.* opposing, hostile, inimical; see UNFRIENDLY.

antecedent *a.* preliminary, previous, prior; see PRECEDING.

antenna *n.* aerial, TV antenna, receiving wire; see WIRE.

anthem *n.* hymn, song of devotion, song of praise; see SONG.

antibiotic *n.* antitoxin, wonder drug, bacteriostat; see MEDICINE 2.

antibody *n.* immunizer, neutralizer, immunoglobulin; see PREVENTION.

anticipate *v.* expect, forecast, prophesy, predict, hope for, look forward to, wait for, count on, plan on, have a hunch about, bargain for, hold in view, have in prospect, assume, suppose, divine, conjecture, promise oneself, lean upon, entertain the hope of, await, reckon on, count on, have a funny feeling about*, feel it in one's bones.—*Ant.* FEAR, be surprised by, be caught unawares by.

anticipated *a.* foreseen, predictable, prepared for; see EXPECTED, LIKELY 1.

anticipation *n.* expectancy, outlook, trust, prospect, impatience, preoccupation, hope, prevision, presentiment, intuition, foresight, inkling, premonition, apprehension, foreboding, awareness, forethought, hunch, a feeling in one's bones.—*Ant.* SURPRISE, shock, wonder.

antidote *n.* antitoxin, counteractant, remedy; see MEDICINE 2.

antique *a.* ancient, archaic, prehistoric; see OLD 3.

antique *n.* relic, artifact, heirloom, survival, rarity, monument, vestige, ruin.

antiseptic *a.* clean, germ-free, sterilized; see PURE 2.

antiseptic *n.* disinfectant, detergent, prophylactic, preservative, preventive, preventative, counterirritant, sterilizer, immunizing agent, vaccine, germicide, microbicide, fumigant; see also MEDICINE 2.

antitoxin *n.* vaccine, antibody, serum; see MEDICINE 2.

antlers *n.* horns, prongs, rack; see HORN 2.

anxiety *n.* concern, trouble, misgiving; see FEAR.

anxious *a.* **1** [Disturbed in mind] apprehensive, concerned, dreading; see TROUBLED. **2** [Eager] desirous, eager, fervent; see ZEALOUS.

any *a.* either, whatever, any sort of, any kind of, any one, each, some, several, each and every, all, one and all; see also EACH 1, SOME.

any *pron.* any sort, any kind, some number, some amount, any one thing.

anybody *pron.* anyone, everyone, everybody, all, the whole world, the public, the rabble, the masses, each and every one, any person, any one of.—*Ant.* NOBODY, no one, somebody.

anyhow *a.* in any event, at any rate,

nevertheless, at all, in any case, regardless, anyway, in any way, in whatever way, under any circumstances, in one way or the other, in any respect, in either way, whatever happens, irregardless*, somehow or other.

anyone *pron.* any person, one, anyone at all; see ANYBODY.

anyplace* *a.* everywhere, wherever, in any place; see ANYWHERE.

anything *pron.* everything, all, anything at all, any, any one thing, aught, whatever one wants, you name it*.—*Ant.* NOTHING, something, one thing.

anyway *a.* in any event, nevertheless, in any manner; see ANYHOW.

anywhere *a.* wherever, in any place, all over, everywhere, in whatever place, wherever you go, anyplace*.—*Ant.* NOWHERE, in no place, somewhere. —**get anywhere*** prosper, thrive, advance; see SUCCEED 1.

apart *a.* 1 [Separated] disconnected, distant, disassociated; see SEPARATED. 2 [Separately] freely, exclusively, alone; see INDEPENDENTLY. —**take apart** dismember, dissect, reduce to its parts; see ANALYZE, DIVIDE. —**tell apart** characterize, discriminate, differentiate; see DISTINGUISH 1.

apartment *n.* rooms, quarters, flat, suite, penthouse, residence, home, duplex, pad*, walk-up.

apartment building *n.* tenement, hotel, apartment house, condominium, high-rise apartments.

apathetic *a.* unemotional, unresponsive, unconcerned; see INDIFFERENT.

apathy *n.* dullness, insensitivity, unconcern; see INDIFFERENCE.

ape *n.* great ape, primate, simian, gorilla, orangutan, chimpanzee, baboon, bonobo, gibbon; see also MONKEY.

ape *v.* copy, mimic, impersonate; see IMITATE 1.

apiece *a.* respectively, separately, individually; see EACH.

apologetic *a.* regretful, self-incriminating, atoning, rueful, contrite, remorseful, sorry, penitent, down on one's knees*.—*Ant.* STUBBORN, obstinate, unrepentant.

apologize *v.* beg pardon, excuse oneself, atone, ask forgiveness, make amends, give satisfaction, clear oneself, make up with someone, confess, admit one's guilt, retract something said, eat crow*, eat one's words.—*Ant.* INSULT, offend, hurt.

apology *n.* regrets, plea, justification; see EXPLANATION.

apostle *n.* messenger, witness, disciple; see FOLLOWER.

appall *v.* amaze, horrify, dismay; see SHOCK 2.

appalling *a.* horrifying, shocking, dreadful; see FRIGHTFUL.

apparatus *n.* appliance, machinery, outfit; see EQUIPMENT.

apparel *n.* clothes, attire, garments; see DRESS 1.

apparent *a.* 1 [Open to view] visible, clear, manifest; see OBVIOUS 1. 2 [Seeming, but not actual] seeming, possible, plausible; see LIKELY 1.

apparently *a.* obviously, at first sight, in plain sight, unmistakably, at a glance, indubitably, perceptibly, plainly, patently, evidently, clearly, openly, supposedly, overtly, conspicuously, palpably, tangibly, presumably, possibly, manifestly, most likely, reasonably, seemingly, reputedly, as if, as though, to all appearances, in almost every way, allegedly, as it were, on the face of it, to the eye.—*Ant.* SURELY, certainly, undoubtedly.

appeal *n.* 1 [A plea] request, bid, claim, suit, petition, motion, question, entreaty, prayer, invocation, supplication, address, demand, overture, application, proposition, proposal.—*Ant.* DENIAL, refusal, renunciation. 2 [Attractiveness] charm, glamour, interest, allure, charisma, seductiveness, sex appeal, class*.

appeal *v.* 1 [To ask another seriously] plead, make a request, petition; see BEG. 2 [To be attractive or interesting] be pleasing, draw attention, be tempting; see FASCINATE.

appear *v.* 1 [To become visible] emerge, rise, come into view, come forth, come out, come forward, be in sight, become plain, loom, arrive, come to light, enter the picture, recur, materialize, become visible, loom up, break through, show up, crop up, burst forth, turn up, stand out, spring up, bob up, see the light of day, meet the eye, break cover.—*Ant.* DISAPPEAR, depart, vanish. 2 [To seem] look, be likely to be, be apparently; see SEEM.

appearance *n.* 1 [Looks] bearing, mien, features; see LOOKS. 2 [That which only seems to be real] impression, idea, image, reflection, air, mirage, vision, facade, dream, illusion, semblance, seeming.—*Ant.* FACT, being, substance. —**keep up appearances** be outwardly proper, hide one's faults, keep up with the Joneses; see DECEIVE. —**make (or put in) an appearance** appear publicly, be present, come; see ARRIVE.

appease *v.* comply with, meet the requirements of, assuage; see SATISFY 1, 3.

appeasement *n.* amends, settlement, reparation, conciliation, compromise; see also SATISFACTION 2.

appendix *n.* supplement, attachment, addendum; see ADDITION 1.

appetite *n.* hunger, thirst, craving, longing, urge, need for food, need to drink, starvation, empty stomach, thirstiness, ravenousness, desire; see also HUNGER, THIRST.—*Ant.* INDIFFERENCE, satiety, surfeit.

appetizing *a.* savory, tasty, delectable; see DELICIOUS.

applaud *v.* clap, cheer, acclaim; see PRAISE 1.

applause *n.* ovation, cheers, clapping; see PRAISE 2.

appliance *n.* instrument, machine, apparatus; see DEVICE 1. *Common household appliances include the following:* broiler, deep-fryer, coffee maker, can opener, blender, mixer, food processor, electric frying pan, oven, toaster oven, microwave, stove, dishwasher, disposal, refrigerator, freezer, waffle iron, trash compactor, hair dryer, electric toothbrush, shaver, curling iron, clothes dryer, washing machine, iron, water heater, sewing machine, vacuum cleaner, paper shredder, electric fan, air conditioner, space heater.

applicable *a.* suitable, appropriate, usable; see FIT.

applicant *n.* petitioner, aspirant, appellant; see CANDIDATE.

application *n.* 1 [Putting to use] employment, bringing to bear, utilization; see USE 1. 2 [The ability to apply oneself] devotion, zeal, diligence; see ATTENTION. 3 [A request] petition, entreaty, demand; see APPEAL 1. 4 [The instrument by which a request is made] petition, form, blank, paper, letter, credentials, certificate, statement, requisition, draft, check, bill.

applied *a.* used, related, enforced, practiced, utilized, brought to bear, adapted, devoted, adjusted, activated.

apply *v.* 1 [To make a request] petition, make a demand, appeal; see BEG. 2 [To make use of] utilize, employ, practice, exploit; see also USE 1. 3 [To be relevant (to)] be pertinent, pertain, bear on, bear upon, have a bearing on, relate to, allude to, concern, touch on, touch upon, involve, affect, regard, have reference to, connect, refer, suit, be in relationship, hold true, come into play. —**apply oneself (to)** attend to, dedicate oneself, address oneself, be occupied with, keep one's mind on, direct oneself to, concentrate on, persevere, persist in, be industrious, buckle down.

appoint *v.* select, designate, elect; see DELEGATE 1, 2.

appointed *a.* selected, chosen, delegated; see NAMED 2.

appointment *n.* 1 [The act of appointing] designation, election, selection, nomination, approval, choice, promotion, assignment, authorization, installation, delegation, certification, empowering. 2 [An engagement] interview, meeting, rendezvous, assignation, invitation, errand, something to do, date. —**keep an appointment** show up, be on time, be there; see ARRIVE.

appraisal *n.* examination, evaluation, assessment; see ESTIMATE.

appraise *v.* assess, evaluate, assay; see PRICE.

appreciable *a.* considerable, sizable, measurable; see LARGE 1.

appreciate *v.* 1 [To be grateful for] welcome, enjoy, be obliged for, be indebted for, acknowledge, never forget, give thanks for, overflow with gratitude for; see also THANK.—*Ant.* COMPLAIN, find fault with, minimize, object to. 2 [To recognize the worth of] esteem, honor, praise; see ADMIRE.

appreciation *n.* 1 [Sense of gratitude] thankfulness, recognition, gratefulness; see GRATITUDE. 2 [Favorable opinion] esteem, enjoyment, love, affection, attraction, commendation, high regard; see also ADMIRATION.

appreciative *a.* grateful, obliged, satisfied; see THANKFUL.

apprehend *v.* 1 [To understand] perceive, comprehend, grasp; see UNDERSTAND 1. 2 [To arrest] seize, place under arrest, take into custody; see ARREST.

apprehension *n.* 1 [Foreboding] trepidation, dread, misgiving; see FEAR. 2 [Understanding] comprehension, grasp, perspicacity; see JUDGMENT 1. 3 [Arrest] capture, seizure, detention; see ARREST.

apprehensive *a.* fearful, worried, uncertain; see TROUBLED.

apprentice *n.* beginner, student, learner; see AMATEUR.

approach *n.* 1 [A way] path, entrance, gate; see WAY 1, 2. 2 [Plan of action] method, program, procedure; see PLAN 2.

approach *v.* 1 [To approach personally] appeal to, address, speak to, talk to, propose something to, request of, make advances to, make overtures to, take aside, talk to in private, buttonhole, corner, descend on.—*Ant.* AVOID, shun, turn away. 2 [To come near in space] drift toward, loom up, creep up, drive up, near, go near, draw near, close in, surround, come near to, come up to, bear down on, edge up to, ease up to, head into; see also APPEAR 1.—*Ant.* LEAVE, recede, depart. **3** [To come near in time] be imminent, threaten, near, draw near, impend, stare someone in the face.—*Ant.* EXTEND, stretch out, recede. **4** [To approximate] come near, take after, come close to; see RESEMBLE.

approaching *a.* nearing, advancing, impending, oncoming, touching, approximating, coming, drawing near, next to come, threatening, rising, moving closer, gaining.

appropriate *a.* proper, suitable, suited, fitting; see also FIT.

appropriate *v.* **1** [To seize] secure, usurp, take possession of; see GET 1. **2** [To provide money] set aside, set apart, allocate, assign to a particular use, reserve, apportion, devote, allow for, budget, allot.

appropriately *a.* fittingly, suitably, justly, aptly, rightly, properly, agreeably, happily, fortunately.—*Ant.* BADLY, inappropriately, improperly.

appropriation *n.* stipend, grant, fund, allotment, allowance, allocation, contribution, cash, budget, gift, remuneration, donation, support, pay.

approval *n.* **1** [Favorable opinion] regard, esteem, favor; see ADMIRATION. **2** [Sanction] endorsement, support, consent; see PERMISSION.

approve *v.* ratify, affirm, encourage, support, endorse, seal, confirm, license, favor, consent to, agree to, sanction, empower, charter, validate, legalize, recognize, accredit, recommend, authorize, second, subscribe to, allow, go along with, maintain, vote for, advocate, establish, pass, OK*, give the green light to*, hold with.—*Ant.* OPPOSE, reject, veto.

approved *a.* certified, authorized, validated, passed, affirmed, legalized, ratified, sanctioned, permitted, endorsed, vouched for, praised, recognized, recommended, backed, supported, upheld, made official, agreed to, allowed, proven, ordered, established, OK'd*.—*Ant.* REFUSED, censured, disapproved.

approximate *a.* rough, inexact, uncertain, guessed, imprecise, imperfect, close, surmised, unscientific, by means of trial and error, almost, more or less, not quite, coming close, fair, nearly correct.

approximately *a.* nearly, closely, roughly, close to, near to, almost, around, about, in general, in round numbers, not quite, not far from, more or less, practically, just about, on the edge of, for all practical purposes, bordering on, generally.

apron *n.* cover, smock, bib; see CLOTHES.

apt *a.* **1** [Quick to learn] adept,

clever, bright; see INTELLIGENT. **2** [Inclined] prone, tending, liable; see LIKELY 4.

aptitude *n.* capability, competence, talent; see ABILITY.

Arabian *a.* Arabic, Semitic, from Arabia, Middle Eastern, Near Eastern, Moorish, Levantine.

arbitrary *a.* willful, tyrannical, temporary, unpremeditated, irrational, generalized, deceptive, superficial, unscientific, unreasonable, whimsical, fanciful, determined by no principle, optional, uncertain, inconsistent, discretionary, subject to individual will.

arbitrate *v.* settle, adjust, reconcile; see NEGOTIATE.

arbitrator *n.* arbiter, referee, mediator; see JUDGE.

arc *n.* bend, curve, segment of a circle; see ARCH.

arch *n.* arc, curve, vault, dome, cupola, bend, arching, archway, curvature, cove.

arch *v.* extend, round, stretch, curve, bend, shape, hunch, cover, hump, hook, arch over.—*Ant.* STRAIGHTEN, unbend, flatten.

archaic *a.* antiquated, old, ancient; see OLD-FASHIONED.

architect *n.* planner, designer, draftsman, artist, engineer, builder, master builder, designer of buildings.

architecture *n.* construction, planning, designing, building, structure, architectonics, house-building, shipbuilding, bridge-building.

archives *n.* **1** [Place to store documents] repository, vault, library; see MUSEUM. **2** [Documents] chronicles, annals, public papers; see RECORDS.

arctic *a.* polar, frozen, icy; see COLD 1.

ardent *a.* fervent, impassioned, warm; see ZEALOUS.

arduous *a.* hard, severe, laborious; see DIFFICULT 1.

area *n.* section, lot, neighborhood, plot, zone, belt, sector, space, spot, patch, square, quarter, block, precinct, ward, field, territory, district, ghetto, town, township, region, tract, enclosure, parcel, division, city, county, parish, diocese, principality, dominion, kingdom, empire, state; see also MEASURE 1.

arena *n.* field, pit, ground, park, coliseum, square, stadium, playing field, amphitheater, bowl, stage, platform, course, gymnasium, gym*.

argue *v.* plead, appeal, explain, justify, show, reason with, dispute, contend, wrangle, oppose, battle, demonstrate, establish, have it out, put up an argument, bicker, have a brush with.—*Ant.* AGREE, ignore, get along with.

argument *n.* 1 [An effort to convince] debate, exchange, contention; see DISCUSSION. 2 [Verbal disagreement] controversy, quarrel, row; see DISPUTE.

argumentative *a.* hostile, contentious, factious; see QUARRELSOME.

arid *a.* parched, barren, dried; see DRY 1.

arise *v.* 1 [To get up] rise, stand up, turn out, get out of bed, get out of a chair, get to one's feet, jump up, roll out, hit the deck*.—*Ant.* FALL, SIT, LIE. 2 [To ascend] mount, go up, climb; see RISE 1.

aristocracy *n.* nobility, privileged class, superior group, ruling class, noblemen, the elite, gentry, high society, upper classes, persons of rank, patricians.

aristocrat *n.* nobleman, noblewoman, peer, lord, noble, baron, earl, prince, patrician, ruler, gentleman, thoroughbred, duke, viscount, count, king, emperor, empress, queen, princess, duchess, countess, baroness, knight, lady, marquis; see also KING 1, LADY 2.

aristocratic *a.* patrician, refined, well-bred; see NOBLE 1, 2, 3.

arithmetic *n.* computation, calculation, ciphering*; see MATHEMATICS.

arm *n.* 1 [The upper human limb] member, appendage, forelimb, forearm, fin*, flapper*, soupbone*. 2 [Anything resembling an arm] bend, crook, projection, cylinder, sofa-end, branch, limb, rod, bough, offshoot, wing, prong, stump, hook, handle. —**at arm's length** at a distance, not friendly, not intimate, aloof. —**with open arms** warmly, affectionately, joyously; see EAGERLY.

arm *v.* furnish with weapons, load, give firearms to, issue weapons to, equip with arms, outfit, fit out.—*Ant.* DISARM, demilitarize, deactivate.

armchair *n.* easy chair, rocker, recliner; see CHAIR.

armed *a.* equipped, outfitted, in battle formation, loaded, provided with arms, fortified, protected, fitted out, in arms, well-armed.—*Ant.* UNARMED, vulnerable, unprotected.

armistice *n.* truce, cease-fire, temporary peace; see PEACE.

armor *n.* shield, chain mail, armor plate, helmet, bulletproof vest, tank, armored car.

armory *n.* ordnance headquarters, training center, drilling place, depot, arsenal, drill center, shooting range, National Guard building, reserve corps headquarters.

arms *n.* armament, armor, ammunition, firearms, munitions, guns, small arms, instruments of war, deadly weapons, lethal weapons, pistols, rifles, machine guns, submachine guns, equipment, supplies, ordnance, artillery, materiel, hardware, ammo*; see also WEAPON. —**bear arms** carry weapons, be armed, be militant; see ARM. —**take up arms** go to war, rebel, do battle; see FIGHT. —**up in arms** hostile, indignant, willing to fight; see ANGRY.

army *n.* 1 [Military land forces] armed force, standing army, regulars, soldiery, troops, men, cavalry, infantry, artillery, air corps, reserves. 2 [A unit of an army] division, regiment, armored division, airborne division, infantry division, battalion, company, corps, brigade, flight, wing, amphibious force, task force, detail, detachment, squad, troop, patrol, unit, command, formation, point, column, legion, platoon, outfit.

aroma *n.* fragrance, perfume, odor; see SMELL 1, 2.

around *a.,* **prep.** 1 [Surrounding] about, in this area, on all sides, on every side, in circumference, neighboring, in the vicinity of, all around, round about, encompassing, nearby, in a circle, along a circuit, all about, close to, on various sides, round and round, right and left.—*Ant.* DISTANT, remote, far-off. 2 [Approximately] almost, about, close to; see APPROXIMATELY. —**have been around*** have had wide experience, be worldly, be sophisticated; see EXPERIENCED.

arouse *v.* move, stir up, stimulate; see EXCITE.

arrange *v.* 1 [To put in order] regulate, systematize, put in order; see ORDER 3. 2 [To make ready] determine, plan, devise, contrive, prepare for, get ready, make ready, draft, scheme, design, provide, make preparations for, set the stage for, prepare, put into shape, make plans for, line up, organize, adjust, manage, direct, establish, decide, resolve.—*Ant.* BOTHER, disorganize, disturb.

arrangement *n.* 1 [The result of arranging] method, system, form; see ORDER 3. 2 [An agreement] settlement, adjustment, compromise; see AGREEMENT 1. 3 [A design] pattern, composition, combination; see DESIGN.

arrest *n.* appropriation, imprisonment, apprehension, commitment, confinement, incarceration, capture, captivity, protective custody, taking by force, taking into custody, constraint, duress, seizure, detention, bust*.—*Ant.* FREEDOM, acquittal, release. —**under arrest** arrested, caught, apprehended, taken into custody, seized, taken in, handcuffed, confined, jailed, imprisoned, detained, shut up, penned up, put in irons, sent to prison, sent to jail, busted*, pinched*, booked, collared*, nabbed*, sent up the river*.

arrest *v.* apprehend, hold, place under arrest, take into custody, capture, imprison, jail, incarcerate, detain, secure, seize, get, catch, take prisoner, nab*, pick up, bust*.—*Ant.* FREE, liberate, parole.

arrival *n.* **1** [The act of arriving] entrance, advent, coming, entry, appearance, landing, homecoming, debarkation, approach, return, meeting.—*Ant.* DEPARTURE, leaving, leave-taking. **2** [That which has arrived] passenger, visitor, tourist, guest, newcomer, delegate, traveler, cargo, freight, mail, shipment, package, parcel.

arrive *v.* enter, land, disembark, alight, dismount, halt, roll up*, reach one's destination, get in, visit, make shore, drop anchor, reach home, appear, get to, hit*, blow into*, breeze in*, check in*, pull in, hit town*.—*Ant.* LEAVE, go, depart.

arrogance *n.* insolence, smugness, vanity, audacity, haughtiness; see also PRIDE 2.

arrogant *a.* domineering, autocratic, sneering; see EGOTISTIC.

arrogantly *a.* proudly, haughtily, insolently, loftily, with one's nose in the air*.

arrow *n.* shaft, dart, missile; see WEAPON.

arson *n.* setting fire to property, pyromania, deliberate burning of property; see CRIME.

art *n.* representation, illustration, abstraction, imitation, modeling, description, portrayal, design, composition, performance, drama, poetry, fiction, singing, dancing, playing an instrument, personification, sketching, molding, shaping, painting, characterization, creating, sculpting, carving; see also ARCHITECTURE, DANCE 1, LITERATURE 1, MUSIC 1, PAINTING, SCULPTURE.

artery *n.* **1** [Main channel of communication or travel] highway, thoroughfare, line, supply route, canal; see also ROAD 1, WAY 2. **2** [Blood vessel] aorta, arteriole, arterial passageway; see VEIN 3.

artful *a.* clever, adroit, ingenious; see ABLE.

article *n.* **1** [An individual thing] object, item, commodity; see THING 1. **2** [Nonfiction appearing in a periodical] essay, editorial, report; see WRITING 2.

articulate *v.* **1** [To speak clearly] enunciate, pronounce, verbalize; see SPEAK 1. **2** [To join] fit together, combine, connect, link; see also JOIN 1.

artificial *a.* imitation, synthetic, counterfeit; see FALSE 3.

artillery *n.* gunnery, ordnance, cannon; see ARMS, CANNON.

artist *n.* master, creator, painter, composer, virtuoso, musician, poet, novelist, dramatist, essayist, actress, actor, playwright, writer, performing artist, cartoonist, opera singer, instrumentalist, dancer, ballerina, sculptor, etcher, engraver, designer, architect, photographer.

artistic *a.* inventive, skillful, imaginative, discriminating, creative, graceful, talented, accomplished, well-executed, well-wrought, pleasing, sublime, aesthetic, cultured, tasteful, exquisite, sensitive, fine, elegant, harmonious, grand, stimulating, elevated, noble, beautiful.

artistry *n.* workmanship, skill, proficiency; see ABILITY.

as *a., conj., prep.* **1** [While] in the process of, in the act of, on the point of; see WHILE 1. **2** [Because] since, inasmuch as, for the reason that; see BECAUSE. **3** [To the same degree that] in the same way that, in the same manner that, equally, comparatively, similarly. **4** [For the purpose, use, etc. of] just for, serving as, functioning as, acting as, being. —**as a matter of fact** truly, actually, indeed; see REALLY 1. —**as if** just as if, just as though, in such a way that, as if it were, supposing, as would be if, as might be if, just like*. —**as is*** as it stands, as usual, just the same, the same way. —**as it were** so to speak, figuratively speaking, in a way, as it seems, as it would seem, in some sort, in a manner, so to say, kind of*, in a manner of speaking, sort of*. —**as though** just as, just as if, just as though; see AS IF.

ascend *v.* go upward, climb, soar; see RISE 1.

ascent *n.* upward path, climbing, ascension; see RISE 1.

ashamed *a.* embarrassed, shamed, regretful, meek, repentant, penitent, apologetic, debased, abashed, conscience-stricken, mortified, uncomfortable, hesitant, perplexed, bewildered, shamefaced, bowed down, disconcerted, sputtering, stammering, stuttering, gasping, floundering, rattled, muddled, confused, blushing, flustered, distraught, humbled, feeling like a jackass, off balance, in the hole*, taken down a peg, red in the face*, looking silly, at a loss.

ashes *n.* cinders, dust, powder, slag, embers, charcoal, soot.

Asian *a.* Asiatic, Eastern, Far Eastern, Oriental, Siberian, Middle

Eastern, Mideastern, Near Eastern, South Asian, Southeast Asian.

aside *a.* to the side, to one side, on one side, at rest, out, by oneself, apart, at one side, by itself, alone, alongside, out of the way, aloof, away, in safekeeping, abreast, at a short distance, by. —**aside from** apart from, in addition to, excluding; see BESIDES.

ask *v.* request, query, question, interrogate, examine, cross-examine, demand, raise a question, inquire, frame a question, order, command, put questions to, requisition, bid, charge, petition, call upon, invite, urge to, challenge, pry, investigate, quiz, grill, needle*, sound out, pump*, put through the third degree*.—*Ant.* ANSWER, refute, rejoin.

asleep *a.* sleeping, dreaming, quiet, resting, snoring, in a sound sleep, fast asleep, sound asleep, slumbering, reposing, taking a siesta, hibernating, dozing, wakeless, napping, unconscious, dead to the world*, in the land of Nod, snoozing*, conked out*, out like a light*.—*Ant.* AWAKE, waking, alert. —**fall asleep** go to sleep, doze, drop off*; see SLEEP.

aspect *n.* 1 [Looks] countenance, face, features; see LOOKS. 2 [View] perspective, regard, slant; see VIEWPOINT.

aspiration *n.* yearning, eagerness, inclination; see AMBITION.

aspire *v.* strive, struggle, yearn; see TRY 1.

aspiring *a.* ambitious, hopeful, enthusiastic; see ZEALOUS.

ass *n.* 1 [A stupid person] dolt, dunce, blockhead; see FOOL. 2 [A donkey] burro, jackass, jennet; see ANIMAL.

assailant *n.* antagonist, foe, enemy; see OPPONENT.

assassin *n.* murderer, slayer, butcher; see KILLER.

assassinate *v.* slay, slaughter, put to death; see KILL 1.

assassination *n.* killing, shooting, slaying; see MURDER.

assault *n.* 1 [An attack] harm, advance, onslaught; see ATTACK. 2 [A rape] attack, abduction, violation; see RAPE.

assault *v.* 1 [To attack] assail, advance, strike; see ATTACK. 2 [To rape] attack, violate, ravish; see RAPE.

assemble *v.* 1 [To bring together] rally, call, convoke, muster, round up, group, convene, summon, mobilize, call together, accumulate, amass, invite, gather, collect, hold a meeting, unite, pack them in, throw a party*, herd together, rally round,

gather around, gang around*.—*Ant.* SCATTER, break up, send away. 2 [To put together] piece together, set up, erect, construct, join, unite, solder, mold, weld, glue.—*Ant.* BREAK, disassemble, break down.

assembly *n.* 1 [A gathering of persons] assemblage, meeting, association; see GATHERING. 2 [The process of bringing parts together] construction, collection, piecing together, fitting, joining, assembling, modeling, attachment, adjustment, welding, soldering, molding, fixing.—*Ant.* SEPARATION, dismantling, wrecking.

assent *n.* approval, authorization, consent; see PERMISSION.

assert *v.* state, say, affirm; see DECLARE.

assertion *n.* affirmation, statement, report; see DECLARATION.

assess *v.* 1 [To tax] charge, exact tribute, exact from; see TAX 1. 2 [To estimate] judge, reckon, guess; see ESTIMATE.

assets *n.* holdings, possessions, capital; see PROPERTY.

assign *v.* commit, commission, authorize, hand over, earmark, allocate, detail, appoint, allot, prescribe, nominate, name, select, hold responsible, empower, entrust, allow, cast, deputize, attach, charge, accredit, hire, elect, ordain, enroll, relegate, draft.—*Ant.* MAINTAIN, reserve, keep back.

assignment *n.* 1 [An appointment] designation, authorization, nomination; see APPOINTMENT 1. 2 [Something assigned] job, responsibility, task; see DUTY 2.

assimilate *v.* 1 [To absorb] take up, digest, incorporate; see ABSORB. 2 [To understand] grasp, learn, comprehend; see UNDERSTAND 1.

assist *v.* support, aid, serve; see HELP.

assistance *n.* support, comfort, compensation; see HELP 1.

assistant *n.* aide, deputy, henchman, friend, follower, adherent, auxiliary, lieutenant, associate, companion, colleague, partner, helper, apprentice, fellow-worker, secretary, helping hand, patron, backer, bodyguard, aide-de-camp, ally, accessory, clerk, collaborator, confederate, mate, helpmate, accomplice, copartner, co-worker, flunky, man Friday, girl Friday, right arm*, yes man*, right-hand man, friend in need*.—*Ant.* ENEMY, rival, antagonist.

associate *n.* comrade, brother-in-arms, peer, colleague, partner, copartner, friend, ally, buddy*, accomplice, assistant, aide, attendant, henchman, confederate, auxiliary, co-worker, helper, collaborator, fellow-worker, helping hand, right-hand man, man Friday, girl Friday, teammate; see also ASSISTANT.—*Ant.* ENEMY, foe, antagonist.

associate *v.* 1 [To unite with] work with, join with, get along with, be friendly with; see also GO WITH, JOIN 2. 2 [To relate] correlate, link, connect, join; see also COMPARE.

association *n.* 1 [The act of associating] frequenting, fraternization, friendship, acquaintanceship, cooperation, assistance, relationship, affiliation, agreement, participation, companionship, fellowship, familiarity, friendliness, camaraderie, membership, acquaintance, mingling, union, community.—*Ant.* DISAGREEMENT, severance, rupture. 2 [The process of intellectual comparison] connection, comparison, linking, correlation, relation, mental connection, train of thought, connection of ideas in thought, recollection, impression, remembering, combination. 3 [An organization] union, federation, corporation; see ORGANIZATION 2.

assorted *a.* varied, miscellaneous, mixed; see VARIOUS.

assortment *n.* variety, combination, group; see COLLECTION.

assume *v.* suppose, presume, posit, understand, gather, find, theorize, presuppose, ascertain, draw the inference, divine, get the idea, have an idea that, suspect, postulate, regard, consider, infer, hypothesize, guess, conjecture, suppose as fact, deem, imagine, surmise, opine, judge, estimate, speculate, fancy, take the liberty, be of the opinion, dare say, deduce, conclude, put two and two together, be inclined to think, hold the opinion, think, calculate, hope, feel, be afraid, believe, have faith, take it, expect, allow, reckon*.—*Ant.* DOUBT, be surprised, be unaware that.

assumed *a.* presumed, understood, presupposed, counted on, inferred, given, granted, taken as known, conjectured, accepted, supposed, hypothetical, hypothesized.

assumption *n.* 1 [The act of taking for granted] supposition, presupposition, presumption, conjecture, assuming, suspicion, surmise, theorization, hypothesization.—*Ant.* PROOF, demonstration, establishing. 2 [Something assumed] hypothesis, theory, postulate; see OPINION 1.

assurance *n.* 1 [A guarantee] insurance, support, pledge; see PROMISE 1. 2 [Confidence] conviction, trust, certainty; see FAITH 1.

assure *v.* 1 [To guarantee] vouch for, aver, attest; see GUARANTEE. 2 [To convince] prove, persuade, reassure; see CONVINCE.

assured *a.* 1 [Certain] sure,

undoubted, guaranteed; see CERTAIN. 2 [Confident] self-possessed, bold, unhesitating; see CONFIDENT.

astonish *v.* shock, amaze, astound; see SURPRISE.

astonishing *a.* surprising, startling, extraordinary; see UNUSUAL 1.

astonishment *n.* surprise, amazement, bewilderment; see WONDER 1.

astound *v.* amaze, shock, startle; see SURPRISE.

astray *a.* straying, roaming, adrift; see WANDERING 1.

astronaut *n.* space traveler, cosmonaut, spaceman, spacewoman, space pilot, rocket man, spacewalker.

asunder *a.* apart, in two, in half, to shreds, into bits and pieces, dismantled, dissected, in two parts, divided, into separate parts, separated, disjoined, rent, carved, dismembered, torn apart, split; see also BROKEN 1, TORN.—*Ant.* WHOLE, together, sound.

at *prep.* 1 [Position] on, by, near to, about, occupying the precise position of, in the vicinity of, placed at, situated at, found in, in front of, appearing in; see also IN 1, NEAR 1. 2 [Direction] toward, in the direction of, through; see TO 1.

atheism *n.* heresy, agnosticism, godlessness, ungodliness, impiety, positivism, denial of God, iconoclasm, unbelief, nihilism, irreligion, irreverence, rationalism, infidelity, materialism, skepticism, freethinking, disbelief; see also DOUBT.

athlete *n.* acrobat, gymnast, player, contestant, champion, sportsman, sportswoman, amateur, professional, semiprofessional, contender, challenger, letterman, muscle man*, jock*. *Athletes include the following:* baseball player, football player, basketball player, soccer player, rugby player, boxer, wrestler, swimmer, golfer, tennis player, volleyball player, jockey, trackman, javelin thrower, high-jumper, discus thrower, shot putter, biathlete, decathlete, triathlete, skier, ski jumper, slalom racer, runner, marathon runner, relay runner, long jumper, pole vaulter, hurdler, equestrian, polo player, hockey player, skater, bicyclist, cyclist, fencer, swordsman, cricket player, miler.

athletic *a.* muscular, husky, wiry, springy, slim, fast, solid, strapping, hardy, robust, strong, vigorous, powerful, brawny, sinewy, sturdy, manly, well-proportioned, well-built, Herculean, Amazonian, built like an ox*.—*Ant.* SICK, weak, fat.

athletics *n.* gymnastics, sports, games; see SPORT 3.

atmosphere *n.* 1 [The air] layer of

air, gaseous envelope, air pressure; see AIR 1. **2** [A pervading quality] environment, climate, mood; see CHARACTER 1, CHARACTERISTIC.

atmospheric *a.* climatic, meteorological, aerial; see AIRY.

atom *n.* grain, mite, speck, particle, molecule, iota; see also BIT 1, ELEMENT. *Parts of atoms include the following:* electron, proton, neutron, positron, neutrino, quark, antiquark, meson, baryon, nucleon, boson, fermion, muon, photon, lepton, hadron, hyperon.

atom bomb *n.* atomic bomb, nuclear weapon, nuclear device, thermonuclear device, hydrogen bomb, A-bomb, H-bomb.

atomic *a.* microscopic, tiny, diminutive; see MINUTE 1.

atone for *v.* compensate for, do penance for, make amends for; see PAY FOR.

atrocity *n.* **1** [Brutality] inhumanity, wickedness, barbarity; see CRUELTY. **2** [A cruel deed] abomination, outrage, horror; see CRIME.

attach *v.* **1** [To join] connect, append, add; see JOIN 1. **2** [To attribute] associate, impute, ascribe; see GIVE 1.

attachment *n.* **1** [Affection] fondness, liking, devotion; see AFFECTION. **2** [Something attached] accessory, adjunct, annex; see ADDITION 1.

attack *n.* **1** [Offensive tactical action] assault, raid, onslaught, advance, charge, thrust, offense, drive, aggression, onset, outbreak, skirmish, encounter, volley, shooting, barrage, siege, firing, trespass, blockade, crossfire, invasion, offensive, intrusion, intervention, onrush, inroad, encroachment, incursion.—*Ant.* WITHDRAWAL, retreat, retirement. **2** [Verbal attack] libel, slander, denunciation; see BLAME.

attack *v.* **1** [To fight offensively; *used of an army*] assault, beset, besiege, invade, storm, advance, infiltrate, raid, assail, march against, shell, board, take by surprise, make a push, bombard, bomb, go over the top, lay siege to, open fire, shoot at, snipe at, lay into*, launch an attack, ambush, strafe, waylay, engage, set upon, torpedo, push, combat, attempt violence against, charge, strike the first blow, bayonet, stab, close with, rake, have at, counterattack.—*Ant.* RETREAT, fall back, recoil. **2** [To assault; *used of an individual*] molest, beat, overwhelm; see FIGHT, RAPE. **3** [To assail with words] revile, refute, reprove; see BLAME. **4**

[To proceed vigorously with] take up, deal with, start on; see ACT 1.

attacked *a.* assaulted, bombed, bombarded, assailed, stoned, torpedoed, fired upon, stormed, under attack, strafed, invaded, besieged; see also RUINED 1.

attacker *n.* aggressor, fighter, assailant, antagonist, invader, foe, enemy, criminal, plunderer, intruder, trespasser, violator, ravager, spoiler, felon.—*Ant.* VICTIM, prey, martyr.

attain *v.* win, achieve, accomplish; see SUCCEED.

attempt *n.* trial, struggle, endeavor; see EFFORT.

attempt *v.* endeavor, strive, venture; see TRY 1.

attend *v.* be present at, frequent, sit in on, be a guest, revisit, haunt, be a member, be a habitué, make an appearance.—*Ant.* LEAVE, be missing, absent oneself.

attendance *n.* **1** [The act of attending] presence, participation, appearance, being present, putting in an appearance, turning up, showing up.—*Ant.* ABSENCE, nonappearance, nonattendance. **2** [The persons attending] audience, spectators, assembly; see GATHERING.

attendant *n.* aide, orderly, valet, nurse, usher, bellhop, servant, domestic, secretary, understudy, disciple, pupil, companion, caregiver, escort, flight attendant, steward, stewardess, maid; see also ASSISTANT.

attention *n.* observation, observance, regard, vigilance, mindfulness, inspection, heed, heedfulness, watching, listening, consideration, intentness, study, alertness, thought, application, diligence, caution, preoccupation, thoroughness, recognition, concentration, care.

attitude *n.* mood, opinion, idea, belief, air, demeanor, condition of mind, state of feeling, position, reaction, bias, set, leaning, bent, inclination, propensity, cast, emotion, temper, temperament, sensibility, disposition, mental state, notion, philosophy, view, orientation, nature, makeup, frame of mind, character; see also VIEWPOINT.

attorney *n.* attorney at law, barrister, counsel; see LAWYER.

attract *v.* **1** [To draw] pull, drag, bring; see DRAW 1. **2** [To allure] entice, lure, charm; see FASCINATE.

attraction *n.* **1** [The act of drawing toward] magnetism, drawing power, allure, fascination, temptation, pull, gravitation, affinity, inclination, tendency, enticement; see also APPEAL 2. **2** [An event] spectacle, display, demonstration; see EVENT.

attractive *a.* good-looking, winning, engaging; see BEAUTIFUL, HANDSOME.

attribute *n.* property, quality, trait; see CHARACTERISTIC.

attribute *v.* ascribe, impute, connect with; see GIVE 1.

auction *n.* disposal, bidding, public sale; see SALE.

auction *v.* put on sale, sell at auction, put on the block; see SELL.

audible *a.* perceptible, discernible, distinct, loud enough to be heard, capable of being heard, within ear-shot, within hearing distance, hearable, sounding, resounding, loud, deafening, roaring, aloud, clear, plain, emphatic; see also HEARD.

audience *n.* witnesses, spectators, patrons; see GATHERING.

audit *n.* checking, scrutiny, inspection; see EXAMINATION 1.

audit *v.* examine, check, inspect; see EXAMINE 1.

auditorium *n.* hall, lecture room, theater, playhouse, movie house, reception hall, amphitheater, assembly hall, opera house, music hall, concert hall, chapel, assembly room. *Sections of an auditorium include the following:* stage, proscenium, orchestra, parquet, stalls, boxes, pit, orchestra circle, dress circle, balcony, gallery, top gallery, tiers, box office.

auger *n.* bit, twist drill, screw auger; see DRILL 2.

augment *v.* enlarge, expand, magnify; see INCREASE.

aunt *n.* mother's sister, father's sister, uncle's wife, grandaunt, great-aunt, auntie*; see also RELATIVE.

auspices *n.* protection, aegis, support, sponsorship, backing.

austere *a.* harsh, hard, ascetic; see SEVERE 1, 2.

austerity *n.* sternness, severity, strictness, harshness, hardness, grimness, stiffness, seriousness, rigidity, gravity, rigor, formality; see also DETERMINATION.

authentic *a.* **1** [Reliable] trustworthy, authoritative, factual; see RELIABLE. **2** [Genuine] real, true, actual; see GENUINE 1.

authenticate *v.* verify, confirm, validate; see PROVE.

author *n.* writer, journalist, columnist, dramatist, playwright, tragedian, humorist, biographer, poet, novelist, short-story writer, essayist, paperback writer, mystery writer, science-fiction writer, contributor, scriptwriter, screenwriter, correspondent, reporter, copywriter, ghostwriter, encyclopedist, lexicographer, scholar, publicist, critic, annotator, hack writer, freelance

writer, adman; see also EDITOR, WRITER.

authoritative *a.* **1** [Official] definitive, authentic, well-documented; see RELIABLE. **2** [Authorized] lawful, legal, mandatory; see APPROVED, AUTHORIZED. **3** [Suggestive of authority] dogmatic, autocratic, domineering; see ABSOLUTE 2.

authority *n.* **1** [Power based on right] right, authorization, jurisdiction; see POWER 2. **2** [The appearance of having authority] prestige, political influence, esteem; see INFLUENCE. **3** [One who knows] expert, scholar, professional; see SPECIALIST.

authorization *n.* sanction, signature, support; see PERMISSION.

authorize *v.* **1** [To allow] permit, tolerate, suffer; see ALLOW. **2** [To approve] sanction, ratify, endorse; see APPROVE.

authorized *a.* allowed, official, legal, lawful, mandatory, authoritative, decisive, valid, standard, sanctioned, confirmed; see also APPROVED.

auto *n.* car, vehicle, wheels*; see AUTOMOBILE.

autobiography *n.* memoirs, personal history, self-portrayal, confession, life, experiences, diary, adventures, biography, life story, journal, letters.

autocratic *a.* dictatorial, domineering, aggressive; see ABSOLUTE 2.

autograph *n.* name, signature, John Hancock*; see SIGNATURE.

automated *a.* mechanical, mechanized, motorized, computerized, automatic, electronic, programmed, cybernetic; see also AUTOMATIC.

automatic *a.* self-starting, motorized, self-regulating, automated, mechanized, under its own power, electric, cybernetic, computerized, self-moving, self-propelled, programmed, electronic, self-activating, push-button, involuntary, unthinking, mechanical, instinctive, spontaneous, reflex, reflexive, intuitive, unintentional, unforced, unconscious.

automobile *n.* motor car, car, vehicle, passenger car, machine, auto, wheels*. *Types of automobiles include the following:* subcompact, squad car, hearse, limousine, sedan, hardtop, compact, sports car, convertible, station wagon, taxicab, hatchback, limo*, van, minivan, conversion van, recreational vehicle, RV, sport utility vehicle, SUV, stretch limo*, jeep, crate*, buggy*, clunker*, jalopy*. *Principal parts of an automobile include the following:* wheels, tires, fenders, chassis, motor, radiator, engine, fan, cylinders, carburetor, exhaust, muffler, throttle, gear shift, clutch, steering wheel, transmission, universal joint, generator, distributor, alternator, windshield, windshield wipers, catalytic converter, brakes, starter, speedometer, odometer, spark plugs, axles, emergency brake, accelerator, shock absorbers, pistons, intake and exhaust valves, fuel pump, gas tank, control panel, steering column, instrument gauges, water pump, air conditioner, heater, radio, audiocassette player, CD player, belts, hoses, filters, drive shaft, oil pan, computer module, battery, seats, seat belts, headlights, brake lights, turn signals, sun visors.

autonomous *a.* self-governing, self-ruling, independent; see FREE 1.

autonomy *n.* liberty, independence, sovereignty; see FREEDOM 1.

autopsy *n.* post-mortem examination, dissection, investigation; see EXAMINATION 1.

autumn *n.* harvest time, Indian summer, fall; see FALL 3.

auxiliary *a.* **1** [Subsidiary] secondary, accessory, subservient; see SUBORDINATE. **2** [Supplementary] spare, supplemental, reserve; see EXTRA.

available *a.* accessible, usable, ready, convenient, serviceable, prepared, handy, on call, ready for use, open to, derivable from, obtainable, attainable, practicable, achievable, feasible, possible, procurable, realizable, reachable, within reach, at one's disposal, at one's beck and call, at hand, at one's elbow, on tap*, on deck*.—*Ant.* OCCUPIED, unavailable, unobtainable.

avalanche *n.* **1** [A mass moving down a slope] mudslide, snowslide, landslide, rockslide, icefall. **2** [Any overwhelming mass] flood, deluge, torrent; see PLENTY.

avenue *n.* street, boulevard, drive; see ROAD 1.

average *a.* ordinary, medium, mediocre; see COMMON 1.

average *n.* midpoint, standard, center, median, norm, middle, mean, typical kind, rule, average person.—*Ant.* EXTREME, highest, lowest. **—on the average** usually, commonly, ordinarily; see REGULARLY.

average *v.* **1** [To compute an average] split the difference, find the mean, find the arithmetic average; see BALANCE 2. **2** [To do, etc., on an average] complete, make, receive; see DO 1, EARN 2, PERFORM 1. **—average out** stabilize, balance, make even; see EQUALIZE.

avert *v.* turn aside, sidetrack, shove

aside, shunt, turn away from, look away, look another way.

aviation *n.* flying, flight, aeronautics, theory of flight, aeronautical engineering, piloting, aerodynamics, airmanship.

aviator *n.* flier, airman, copilot; see PILOT 1.

avid *a.* eager, enthusiastic, desirous; see ZEALOUS.

avoid *v.* keep away from, flee from, abstain from, shrink from, escape from, evade, shun, elude, dodge, give someone the slip, draw back from, hold off, turn aside from, recoil from, keep at arm's length, withdraw, back out of, shirk, let alone, keep out of the way of, keep clear of, keep at a respectful distance, let well enough alone, keep in the background, keep one's distance, keep away from, refrain from, steer clear of, lay off*, pass up*, shake off.—*Ant.* FACE, meet, undertake.

avoidance *n.* evasion, delay, elusion, escape, retreat, restraint, abstention, nonparticipation, evasive action, temperance, flight, recoil, recession, escape mechanism, dodge.—*Ant.* MEETING, encounter, participation.

await *v.* wait for, anticipate, expect; see ANTICIPATE.

awake *a.* alert, vigilant, observant; see CONSCIOUS.

awake *v.* open one's eyes, become aware, gain consciousness, see the light, stir, get up, come out of sleep, rub one's eyes, rise up, stretch one's limbs, show signs of life, arise, wake up, rise and shine*.—*Ant.* SLEEP, doze off, slumber.

awaken *v.* awake, call, play reveille, arouse, rouse, wake up, excite, stir up, stimulate.

awakening *n.* rebirth, arousal, renewal; see REVIVAL 1.

award *n.* citation, honor, scholarship; see PRIZE.

award *v.* grant, confer, bestow; see GIVE 1.

aware *a.* knowledgeable, cognizant, informed; see CONSCIOUS.

awareness *n.* sensibility, mindfulness, discernment, cognizance, consciousness, alertness, keenness, attentiveness, recognition, comprehension, perception, apprehension, appreciation, experience.

away *a.* absent, not present, distant, at a distance, not here, far afield, at arm's length, remote, out of, far off, apart, beyond, off.—*Ant.* HERE, present, at hand. **—do away with** **1** [To eliminate] get rid of, cancel, take away; see ELIMINATE, REMOVE 1. **2** [To kill] slay, execute, put to death; see KILL 1.

awe *n.* wonder, fright, admiration; see REVERENCE.

awesome *a.* striking, moving, impressive; see GRAND.

awful *a.* **1** [Frightful] horrible, terrible, dreadful; see FRIGHTFUL. **2** [Shocking] appalling, disgusting, repulsive; see OFFENSIVE 2. **3** [*Very great] gigantic, colossal, stupendous; see BIG 1.

awfully *a.* **1** [Badly] poorly, imperfectly, clumsily; see BADLY 1. **2** [*Very] very much, indeed, truly; see VERY.

awhile *a.* for a moment, briefly, momentarily, for a short time, for some time, not for long, temporarily, for a little while, for a spell*.—*Ant.* FOREVER, permanently, for a long time.

awkward *a.* clumsy, bungling, ungraceful, gawky, floundering, stumbling, ungainly, unwieldy, unable, fumbling, bumbling, lacking dexterity, without skill, unskilled, inept, unfit, inexperienced, shuffling, uncouth, incompetent, rusty, green, amateurish, butterfingered*, all thumbs, with two left feet.—*Ant.* ABLE, dexterous, smooth.

awkwardly *a.* clumsily, unskillfully, lumberingly, ineptly, ponderously, uncouthly, gracelessly, inelegantly, incompetently, artlessly, amateurishly, ungracefully, stiffly, woodenly, rigidly, with difficulty, with embarrassment.—*Ant.* GRACEFULLY, skillfully, adroitly.

awkwardness *n.* ineptitude, inability, incompetence, ineptness, artlessness, crudeness, heavy-handedness, ungainliness, oafishness, ungracefulness, gracelessness.—*Ant.* ABILITY, grace, competence.

awning *n.* canvas covering, canopy, sunshade; see COVER 1.

ax *n.* hatchet, adz, tomahawk, battleax, poleax, pickax, mattock, cleaver, broadax, hand ax. —**have an ax to grind*** want something, have a purpose, complain about something; see WANT 1.

axis *n.* shaft, pivot, axle, pole, stem, support, dividing line, spindle, arbor, line of symmetry, line of rotation, line of revolution.

axle *n.* shaft, spindle, pin; see AXIS.

B

babble *n.* jabber, chatter, twaddle; see NONSENSE 1.

babble *v.* talk incoherently, talk foolishly, rant, rave, gush, run on, go on*, gossip, murmur, chat, chatter, prattle, tattle, jabber, blurt, run off at the mouth*, talk off the top of one's head*, rattle on, gab*, cackle, blab, sputter, gibber, blabber*, clatter; see also TALK 1.

baby *a.* infantile, babyish, juvenile; see CHILDISH.

baby *n.* suckling, babe, child, toddler, tot, brat, young one, little one, papoose*, bambino, chick, kid*, cherub, little shaver*, bundle of joy*, another mouth to feed*.—*Ant.* MAN, adolescent, grown-up.

baby *v.* pamper, coddle, pet, spoil, fondle, caress, nurse, cherish, foster, cuddle, make much of, humor, indulge; see also PAMPER.

baby-sit *v.* watch, care for, sit; see GUARD.

bachelor *n.* unmarried man, single man, stag, free man*, single, lone wolf*.—*Ant.* HUSBAND, married man, benedict.

back *a.* rear, after, backward, hindmost, behind, astern, hind, rearward, aft, to the rear, in the rear, dorsal, caudal, following, posterior, terminal, in the wake, in the background, final.—*Ant.* FRONT, forward, head.

back *n.* **1** [The rear part or side] hind part, posterior, stern, poop, aft, tailpiece, tail, back end.—*Ant.* FRONT, fore part, fore. **2** [The rear of the torso] posterior, backside, spinal area; see SPINE. **3** [One who plays behind the line, especially in football] linebacker, fullback, halfback, quarterback, cornerback, safety, running back, tailback, wingback, slot back, blocking back. —**behind someone's back** in secret, slyly, hidden; see SECRETIVE. —**(flat) on one's back** ill, bedridden, helpless; see SICK. —**get off someone's back*** let alone, ignore, stop nagging; see NEGLECT 1. —**get one's back up*** become angry, be stubborn, lose one's temper; see RAGE 1. —**go back on** betray, reject, turn against; see DECEIVE. —**in back of** at the rear, behind, coming after; see FOLLOWING. —**turn one's back on** reject, desert, fail; see ABANDON 1. —**with one's back to the wall** desperate, cornered, stopped; see HOPELESS.

back *v.* **1** [To push backward] drive back, repel, repulse; see PUSH 2. **2** [To further] uphold, stand behind, encourage; see SUPPORT 2. **3** [To equip with a back] stiffen, reinforce, line; see LINE 1, STRENGTHEN. —

back down withdraw, recoil, back out; see RETREAT. —**back off** fall back, withdraw, retire; see RETREAT. —**back out of** withdraw, shrink from, escape; see RETREAT. —**back up** 1 [To move backward] fall back, withdraw, reverse; see RETREAT. 2 [To support] aid, assist, help; see SUPPORT 2.

back and forth *a.* zigzag, in and out, from side to side; see TO AND FRO.

backbone *n.* 1 [Line of bones in the back supporting the body] spinal column, vertebrae, chine; see SPINE 2. 2 [Determination] firmness, fortitude, resolution; see DETERMINATION.

backed *a.* 1 [Propelled backward] driven back, shoved, repelled, repulsed, pushed, retracted.—*Ant.* AHEAD, moved forward, impelled. 2 [Supported] upheld, encouraged, approved, heartened, aided, assisted, advanced, promoted, sustained, fostered, favored, championed, advocated, supplied, maintained, asserted, established, helped, bolstered, propped, furthered, seconded, prompted, served, pushed, boosted, primed.—*Ant.* OPPOSED, discouraged, obstructed. 3 [Supplied with a back, or backing] stiffened, built up, strengthened; see REINFORCED.

backer *n.* benefactor, supporter, follower; see PATRON.

backfire *v.* 1 [To explode] burst, erupt, detonate; see EXPLODE. 2 [To go awry] boomerang, ricochet, have an unwanted result; see FAIL 1.

background *n.* 1 [Setting] backdrop, framework, environment; see SETTING. 2 [The total of one's experiences] education, qualifications, preparation, grounding, rearing, credentials, capacities, accomplishments, achievements, attainments, deeds, actions; see also EXPERIENCE, KNOWLEDGE 1. —**in the background** retiring, unseen, out of sight; see OBSCURE 3, UNNOTICED, WITHDRAWN.

backhanded *a.* obscure, sarcastic, equivocal; see INDIRECT.

backing *n.* 1 [Assistance] subsidy, encouragement, aid; see HELP 1. 2 [Support] reinforcement, buttress, lining; see SUPPORT 2.

backlash *n.* response, repercussion, resentment; see REACTION.

backlog *n.* reserve, supply, stock; see RESERVE 1.

backslide *v.* revert, break faith, fall from grace; see RELAPSE.

backstop *n.* screen, net, barrier; see FENCE.

backward *a.* 1 [To the rear] rearward, astern, behind, retrograde, regressive.—*Ant.* FORWARD, progressive, onward. 2 [Reversed] turned around, counterclockwise, inverted; see REVERSED. 3 [Behind in development] underdeveloped, slow, slow to develop, retarded, delayed, arrested, checked, late, undeveloped, underprivileged; see also DULL 3. —**bend over backward** try hard to please, conciliate, be fair; see TRY 1.

bacon *n.* flitch, Canadian bacon, salt pork; see MEAT. —**bring home the bacon*** provide for, be the breadwinner, achieve; see EARN 2, PROVIDE 1, SUCCEED 1, SUPPORT 3.

bacteria *n.* bacilli, microbes, microscopic organisms; see GERM.

bad *a.* 1 [Wicked] evil, sinful, immoral, wrong, corrupt, base, foul, gross, profane, naughty, degenerate, decadent, depraved, heartless, degraded, debauched, indecent, mean, scandalous, nasty, vicious, fiendish, devilish, criminal, murderous, sinister, monstrous, dangerous, vile, rotten*, dirty, crooked.—*Ant.* GOOD, honest, pure. 2 [Spoiled] rancid, decayed, putrid; see ROTTEN 1, 2. 3 [Below standard] defective, inferior, imperfect; see POOR 2. 4 [In poor health] ill, diseased, ailing; see SICK. 5 [Injurious] hurtful, damaging, detrimental; see HARMFUL. 6 [*Very good] stylish, effective, sharp*; see FASHIONABLE, EXCELLENT. —**go bad** degenerate, deteriorate, rot; see SPOIL. —**not bad*** all right, pretty good, passable; see FAIR 2.

badge *n.* 1 [Outward evidence] marker, symbol, identification; see EMBLEM. 2 [A device worn as evidence] pin, emblem, seal, medal, insignia, shield, epaulet, ribbon, medallion, marker, feather, rosette, clasp, button, signet, crest, star, chevron, stripe.

badger *v.* harass, annoy, pester; see BOTHER 2.

badly *a.* 1 [In an ineffectual or incompetent manner] wrongly, imperfectly, ineffectively, inefficiently, poorly, unsatisfactorily, crudely, boorishly, unskillfully, defectively, weakly, haphazardly, clumsily, carelessly, negligently, incompetently, stupidly, blunderingly, mistakenly, awkwardly, faultily, shiftlessly, abominably, awfully, terribly*.—*Ant.* CAREFULLY, competently, adequately. 2 [*To a marked degree] severely, seriously, greatly; see VERY. —**go badly** miscarry, fall short, dissatisfy; see DISAPPOINT, FAIL 1.

baffle *v.* perplex, puzzle, bewilder; see CONFUSE.

bag *n.* purse, sack, pouch, grip, handbag, tote bag, knapsack, backpack, carpetbag, kit, satchel, saddlebag, gunny sack, suitcase, briefcase, attaché case, duffel bag, pack, container, feedbag, quiver, packet, pocketbook, holster, vanity bag, valise, case, wallet, haversack, holdall, carryall. —**in the bag*** absolute, sure, definite; see CERTAIN 2. —**left holding the bag*** framed*, tricked, deserted; see ABANDONED.

bag *v.* trap, seize, get; see CATCH 1.

baggage *n.* luggage, gear, bags, trunks, valises, suitcases, overnight cases, parcels, paraphernalia, effects, equipage, equipment, packs, things.

baggy *a.* slack, unshapely, bulging; see LOOSE 1.

bail *n.* bond, surety, recognizance, pledge, warrant, guaranty, collateral.

bail *v.* 1 [To dip] scoop, spoon out, dredge; see DIP 2. 2 [To empty] clear, drain, deplete; see EMPTY.

bail out *v.* 1 [Secure the release of] give security for, post bail for, assure, underwrite, guarantee, warrant, insure, deliver, go bail for, spring*. 2 [Run away] desert, blow*, retreat; see ESCAPE.

bait *n.* lure, inducement, bribe; see ATTRACTION.

bait *v.* 1 [To torment] anger, nag, tease; see BOTHER 2. 2 [To lure] entice, attract, draw; see FASCINATE.

bake *v.* roast, toast, warm; see COOK.

baked *a.* parched, scorched, dried, toasted, warmed, heated, cooked, grilled, burned, charred, roasted, incinerated.

baker *n.* pastry chef, chef, *pâtissier* (French); see COOK.

bakery *n.* bake shop, pastry shop, confectionery, bread store, patisserie, cake shop.

balance *n.* 1 [Whatever remains] excess, surplus, residue; see REMAINDER. 2 [An equilibrium] poise, counterpoise, symmetry, offset, equivalence, counterbalance, tension, equalization, equality of weight, parity.—*Ant.* INCONSISTENCY, top-heaviness, imbalance. 3 [An excess of credits over debits] surplus, dividend, credit balance; see PROFIT 2. —**in the balance** undetermined, undecided, critical; see UNCERTAIN.

balance *v.* 1 [To offset] counterbalance, compensate for, allow for; see sense 2. 2 [To place in balance] place in equilibrium, steady, stabilize, neutralize, set, level, equalize, support, poise, oppose, even, weigh, counteract, make equal, compensate, tie, adjust, square, parallel, coordinate, readjust, pair off, equate, match, level off, attune, harmonize, tune, accord, correspond.—*Ant.* UPSET, turn over, topple. 3 [To demonstrate that debits and credits

are in balance] estimate, compare, audit; see CHECK 2.

balanced *a.* 1 [Made even] equalized, poised, offset, in equilibrium, evened, counterweighted, equivalent, stabilized, symmetrical, counterpoised, counterbalanced, on an even keel.—*Ant.* UNSTABLE, unbalanced, unequal. 2 [Audited] validated, confirmed, certified; see APPROVED.

balance of power *n.* equilibrium, distribution, apportionment; see BALANCE 2.

balcony *n.* gallery, mezzanine, terrace; see UPSTAIRS.

bald *a.* hairless, shaven, shaved, bare, featherless, glabrous, shiny, smooth, like a billiard ball; see also SMOOTH 3.—*Ant.* HAIRY, covered, hirsute.

balderdash *n.* senseless talk, gibberish, bombast; see NONSENSE 1.

bale *n.* bundle, bunch, parcel; see PACKAGE.

baik *v.* turn down, demur, desist; see REFUSE.

balky *a.* contrary, obstinate, perverse; see STUBBORN.

ball *n.* 1 [A spherical body] marble, globe, spheroid, sphere, balloon, rounded object, orb, globule, globular object, pellet, pill, drop, knot. 2 [A game played with a ball] baseball, football, catch; see SPORT 3. 3 [A dance] grand ball, promenade, reception; see PARTY 1. —**carry the ball*** assume responsibility, take control, bear the burden; see LEAD 1. —**get the ball rolling*** initiate action, commence, start; see BEGIN 1. —**have something on the ball*** be skilled, have ability, be efficient; see ABLE.

ballad *n.* carol, chant, folk song; see SONG.

ballast *n.* sandbags, counterbalance, counterweight; see WEIGHT 2.

ballet *n.* toe dancing, choreography, dance on *pointe* (French); see DANCE 1.

ballet dancer *n.* ballerina, danseuse, danseur; see DANCER.

balloon *n.* dirigible, aircraft, airship, weather balloon, hot-air balloon, radiosonde, barrage balloon, lighter-than-air craft, toy balloon, zeppelin, observation balloon, blimp*, gasbag.

ballot *n.* tally, ticket, poll; see VOTE 1.

balm *n.* 1 [Anything healing and soothing] solace, consolation, comfort, relief, refreshment, remedy, cure. 2 [A healing ointment] salve, lotion, dressing; see MEDICINE 2.

bamboozle *v.* swindle, trick, dupe; see DECEIVE.

ban *n.* taboo, prohibition, limitation; see REFUSAL.

ban *v.* outlaw, prevent, declare illegal; see FORBID, PREVENT.

banal *a.* dull, trite, hackneyed; see COMMON 1.

band *n.* **1** [A beltlike strip] circuit, meridian, latitude, circle, ring, orbit, zodiac, circumference, zone, ribbon, belt, line, strip, stripe, tape, sash, twine, scarf, bandage, girdle, thong, wristband, bond, tie, binding, stay, truss, belt, cord, harness, brace, strap, binding, waistband, collar, hatband, cable, rope, link, chain, line, string, guy wire. **2** [A company of people] group, collection, association; see GATHERING. **3** [A group of musicians] orchestra, company, troupe, ensemble, group, combo. *Kinds of bands include the following:* military, brass, marching, concert, parade, jazz, stage, dance, Dixieland, jug, string, rock, swing.

bandage *n.* compress, cast, gauze; see DRESSING 3.

bandage *v.* tie, fix, bind up; see BIND 1, FASTEN.

bandit *n.* burglar, thief, raider; see ROBBER.

bang *n.* **1** [A loud report] blast, roar, detonation; see NOISE 1. **2** [A blow] hit, cuff, whack; see BLOW. **3** [*A thrill] enjoyment, pleasant feeling, kick*; see EXCITEMENT.

bang *v.* **1** [To beat] strike, slam, whack; see HIT 1. **2** [To make a noise] crash, clatter, rattle; see SOUND.

banish *v.* exile, deport, cast out, expel, expatriate, ostracize, sequester, excommunicate, transport, outlaw, extradite, isolate, dismiss.—*Ant.* RECEIVE, welcome, accept.

banishment *n.* expatriation, deportation, expulsion; see EXILE 1.

banister *n.* railing, handrail, guardrail; see RAIL 1.

bank *n.* **1** [Ground rising above adjacent water] ledge, embankment, edge; see SHORE. **2** [A financial establishment] national bank, state bank, commercial bank, savings bank, savings and loan association, thrift, lender, mortgage company, Federal Reserve Bank, private bank, countinghouse, banking house, exchequer, credit union, trust company, treasury.

bank *v.* **1** [To deposit money] save, put in the bank, enter in an account; see DEPOSIT 2. **2** [To tilt on a curve] lean, bend, slope; see LEAN 1. — **bank on*** depend on, believe in, be sure about; see TRUST 1.

banker *n.* treasurer, teller, officer of the bank, broker, financier, capital-

ist, investment banker, moneylender.

banking *n.* investment, funding, moneylending; see BUSINESS 1.

bankrupt *a.* failed, out of business, broke*; see RUINED 3.

bankruptcy *n.* insolvency, destitution, distress; see FAILURE 1.

banner *n.* colors, pennant, flag; see EMBLEM.

banquet *n.* repast, fete, feast; see DINNER.

baptism *n.* dedication, christening, initiation; see CEREMONY 2.

baptize *v.* immerse, purify, regenerate, sprinkle, dip, christen, name.

bar *n.* **1** [A relatively long, narrow object] strip, stake, stick, crossbar, boom, rib, crosspiece, pole, spar, rail, yard, yardarm, lever, rod, crowbar, shaft, slab. **2** [A counter serving refreshments, especially drinks] barroom, tavern, cocktail lounge, saloon, public house, counter, hotel, inn, canteen, beer parlor, cabaret, restaurant, cafeteria, roadhouse, brass rail, snack bar, beer garden, watering hole*, dive*, pub*, grill. **3** [The legal profession] lawyers, counselors, barristers, solicitors, jurists, attorneys, bar association, advocates, judiciary. **4** [An obstruction] hindrance, obstacle, hurdle; see BARRIER. **5** [A relatively long, narrow area] strip, stripe, ribbon; see BAND 1.

bar *v.* **1** [To raise a physical obstruction] barricade, dam, dike, fence, wall, erect a barrier, brick up, blockade, clog, exclude, shut out, lock out, keep out, bolt, cork, plug, seal, stop, impede, roadblock.—*Ant.* OPEN, free, clear. **2** [To obstruct by refusal] ban, forbid, deny, refuse, prevent, stop, boycott, ostracize, preclude, shut out, keep out, exclude, exile, reject, outlaw, condemn, discourage, interfere with, restrain, frustrate, circumvent, override, segregate, interdict, veto, blackball, freeze out*.—*Ant.* ALLOW, admit, welcome. **3** [To close] shut, lock, seal; see CLOSE 4.

barbarian *n.* savage, brute, cannibal, rascal, ruffian, monster, yahoo, Philistine, Hun, Vandal, troglodyte, clod; see also BEAST 2.

barbaric *a.* inhuman, brutal, fierce; see CRUEL.

barbarity *n.* savageness, cruelty, brutality; see CRUELTY.

barbecue *n.* **1** [A grill] roaster, grill, broiler; see APPLIANCE. **2** [A picnic] cookout, wiener roast, picnic; see MEAL 2.

barbecue *v.* grill, sear, broil; see COOK.

bare *a.* **1** [Without covering] uncovered, bald, stripped; see NAKED 1, OPEN 4. **2** [Plain] unadorned, sim-

ple, unornamented; see MODEST 2.
3 [Without content] barren, void, unfurnished; see EMPTY.

barefaced *a.* **1** [Open] unconcealed, clear, apparent; see OBVIOUS 1, 2. **2** [Impudent] shameless, audacious, bold; see RUDE 2.

barefoot *a.* shoeless, barefooted, unshod; see NAKED 1.

barely *a.* almost, scarcely, just; see HARDLY.

bargain *n.* **1** [An agreement] pact, compact, contract; see DEAL 1. **2** [An advantageous purchase] good value, good deal, discount, reduction, sale price, marked-down price, buy*, steal*, giveaway*, deal. —**into the bargain** in addition, too, additionally; see ALSO.

bargain *v.* **1** [To trade] barter, do business, merchandise; see BUY, SELL. **2** [To negotiate] make terms, arrange, confer; see NEGOTIATE 1. —**bargain for** expect, plan on, foresee; see ANTICIPATE.

bargaining *n.* trade, transaction, haggling; see BUSINESS 1.

bark *n.* **1** [An outer covering, especially of trees] peel, cork, husk; see COVER 1, SHELL 1. **2** [A short, explosive sound] yelp, yap, grunt; see NOISE 1.

bark *v.* yelp, yap, bay, howl, cry, growl, snarl, yip*, woof, arf. —**bark up the wrong tree** miscalculate, misdirect one's effort, make a mistake; see MISJUDGE 2.

barn *n.* outbuilding, shed, outhouse, shelter, lean-to, coop, hutch, sty, pen, kennel, stable.

barnyard *n.* feedyard, pen, corral, stableyard, lot, feedlot, run.

barred *a.* **1** [Equipped or marked with bars] striped, banded, streaked, pleated, pied, motley, calico, mottled, dappled, cross-hatched, veined, ribbed, ridged, marked, piped, lined. **2** [Prohibited] banned, outlawed, unlawful; see ILLEGAL.

barrel *n.* cask, keg, vat, tub, receptacle, container, vessel.

barren *a.* **1** [Incapable of producing young] impotent, infertile, childless; see STERILE 1. **2** [Incapable of producing vegetation] fallow, unproductive, fruitless; see STERILE 2.

barricade *n.* obstacle, bar, obstruction; see BARRIER.

barricade *v.* obstruct, block, fortify; see BAR 1.

barrier *n.* bar, obstruction, difficulty, hindrance, obstacle, hurdle, stumbling block, fence, sound barrier, restriction, restraint, impediment, drawback, check, stop, stay, bulwark, barricade, rampart, wall, earthwork, embankment, blockade, barbed wire, bamboo curtain, iron curtain.—*Ant.* WAY, path, trail.

barroom *n.* tavern, saloon, pub*; see BAR 2.

barter *n.* trade, exchange, traffic; see BUSINESS 1.

barter *v.* trade, bargain, swap*; see BUY, SELL.

base *a.* low, foul, sordid; see VULGAR.

base *n.* **1** [A point from which action is initiated] camp, field, landing field, airport, airfield, airstrip, port, headquarters, terminal, base camp, home base, firebase, base of operations, center, depot, supply base, dock, harbor, station. **2** [The bottom, thought of as a support] root, foot, footing; see FOUNDATION 2. **3** [Foundation of a belief or statement] principle, authority, evidence; see BASIS. **4** [A goal, especially in baseball] mark, bound, station, plate, post, goal; first base, second base, third base, home plate. —**off base*** erring, mistaken, incorrect; see WRONG 2.

baseball *n.* ball, little league, the national pastime; see SPORT 3.

baseball player *n.* pitcher, catcher, infielder, batter, shortstop, left fielder, right fielder, center fielder, first baseman, second baseman, third baseman, designated hitter, ballplayer, slugger*.

based *a.* confirmed, planted, founded; see ESTABLISHED 2.

basement *n.* cellar, excavation, storage room, wine cellar, furnace room, vault, crypt.

bashful *a.* retiring, reserved, timid; see HUMBLE 1, MODEST 2, SHY.

basic *a.* essential, central, primary; see FUNDAMENTAL, NECESSARY.

basically *a.* fundamentally, primarily, radically; see ESSENTIALLY.

basin *n.* pan, tub, bowl; see CONTAINER.

basis *n.* support, foundation, justification, reason, explanation, background, source, authority, principle, groundwork, assumption, premise, backing, sanction, proof, evidence, nucleus, center.

bask *v.* relax, enjoy, indulge oneself; see WALLOW.

basket *n.* bushel, crate, bin; see CONTAINER.

basketball *n.* hoops*, cage meet, roundball*; see SPORT 3.

bastard *a.* illegitimate, natural, false, mongrel, baseborn, misbegotten.—*Ant.* TRUE, legitimate, wellborn.

bastard *n.* **1** [An illegitimate child] out-of-wedlock birth, whoreson*, love child, woods colt*, Sunday's child*. **2** [*A rascal] scoundrel, cheat, SOB*; see RASCAL.

baste *v.* **1** [To sew temporarily]

stitch, catch, tack; see SEW. **2** [To dress cooking meat with fat or sauce] moisten, grease, season; see COOK.

bat *n.* club, racket, stick; see STICK. **—blind as a bat** sightless, unseeing, blinded; see BLIND 1. **—go to bat for*** intervene for, support, back up; see DEFEND 2. **—have bats in one's belfry*** be mad, be eccentric, be peculiar; see INSANE. **—not bat an eye*** not be surprised, not be shocked, not be amazed, ignore, remain unruffled; see also NEGLECT 1. **—(right) off the bat*** at once, without delay, instantly; see IMMEDIATELY.

bat *v.* strike, whack, sock*; see HIT 1.

batch *n.* stack, group, shipment; see BUNCH.

bath *n.* **1** [The act of cleansing the body] washing, sponge bath, shower, tub, bath, steam bath, sauna, soak*, dip, soaking*. **2** [An enclosure prepared for bathing] bathroom, toilet, shower, washroom, powder room, lavatory, steam room, sauna, Turkish bath, sitz bath, hot tub, whirlpool, spa, Jacuzzi (trademark), mikvah (Jewish), public baths, shower room.

bathe *v.* soap, cleanse, scrub; see WASH 1.

bathrobe *n.* robe, dressing gown, kimono; see CLOTHES.

bathroom *n.* shower, toilet, lavatory; see BATH 2, TOILET.

battalion *n.* unit, force, corps; see ARMY 2.

batter *n.* **1** [One who bats] hitter, pinch hitter, switch-hitter; see BASEBALL PLAYER. **2** [Baking mixture] dough, mix, paste, recipe, concoction, mush; see also MIXTURE 1.

battery *n.* **1** [Cells which generate or store electricity] dry cell, storage cells, storage battery, energy unit, flashlight battery, solar battery, atomic battery, electric cell. **2** [The act of beating] assault, attack, thumping, beating, physical violence, mugging.

battle *n.* strife, contention, struggle, combat, bombing, fighting, bloodshed, clash, onslaught, onset, barrage, conflict, warfare, fray, assault, crusade, military campaign, hostilities, havoc, carnage; see also FIGHT. **—give** (or **do**) **battle** fight back, struggle, engage in battle; see ATTACK, FIGHT.

battlefield *n.* field of battle, battleground, front, theater of war, disputed territory, no man's land.

battleship *n.* man of war, floating fortress, battlewagon*; see SHIP.

bawl *v.* weep, shed tears, sob; see

CRY 1. **—bawl out*** chide, berate, admonish; see SCOLD.

bay *n.* inlet, gulf, bayou, loch, bight, sound, fiord, firth, estuary, strait, narrows, road, arm of the sea, mouth, lagoon, cove, harbor.

bayonet *n.* spike, lance, pike; see KNIFE.

BC or **B.C.** *abbrev.* before Christ, pre-Christian, Old-Testament; see OLD 3.

be *v.* **1** [To have being] live, stay, be alive, exist, remain, continue, endure, go on, stand, subsist, breathe, last, prevail, abide, survive, move, act, do, hold, have place.—*Ant.* DIE, disappear, stop. **2** [To mean] signify, denote, imply; see MEAN 1.

beach *n.* seaside, sand, the coast; see SHORE.

beached *a.* stranded, marooned, aground; see ABANDONED.

beacon *n.* flare, lantern, guide, signal fire, lighthouse, lamp, beam, radar, sonar, airline beacon, radio beacon, air control beacon.

bead *n.* drop, droplet, pellet, grain, particle, speck, dot, dab, pea, shot, pill, driblet.

beads *n.* necklace, pendant, string of jewels; see NECKLACE.

beak *n.* nose, prow, bill, mandible, projection, proboscis, snout, nozzle.

beam *n.* **1** [A relatively long, stout bar] timber, brace, scantling, rafter, stringer, stud, two-by-four, strut, joist, bolster, axle, girder, sleeper, stay, crosspiece, prop, support, trestle, spar, pole, crossbar, T-beam, I-beam, steel beam, boom, post, column, pillar, sill, jamb, cantilever, shaft, scaffolding; see also BAR 1. **2** [Radio waves intended as a guide] direction finder, unidirectional radio signal, radar; see BEACON. **—off the beam*** faulty, incorrect, inaccurate; see WRONG 2. **—on the beam*** alert, on target, efficient; see ABLE.

beam *v.* **1** [To emit] transmit, broadcast, give out; see SEND 1. **2** [To shine] radiate, glitter, glare; see SHINE 1. **3** [To smile] grin, laugh, smirk; see SMILE.

beaming *a.* **1** [Giving forth beams] radiant, glowing, gleaming; see BRIGHT 1. **2** [In very genial humor] grinning, animated, sunny; see HAPPY.

bean *n.* *Varieties include the following:* kidney, navy, lima, soy, castor, black, pinto, string, black-eyed, black-eye, garbanzo, green, wax; see also VEGETABLE. **—full of beans*** **1** lively, vital, energetic; see ACTIVE. **2** mistaken, erring, incorrect; see WRONG 2. **—spill the beans*** divulge information, tell secrets, talk; see TELL 1.

bear *n.* grizzly, polar bear, brown

bear, black bear, cinnamon bear, kodiak bear, sloth bear, koala, Bruin, *ursus* (Latin); see also ANIMAL.

bear *v.* **1** [To suffer] tolerate, support, undergo; see ENDURE 2. **2** [To support weight] sustain, hold up, shoulder; see SUPPORT 1. **3** [To give birth to] deliver, bring to birth, bring forth; see PRODUCE 1. —**bear down on** (or **upon**) **1** [To press] squeeze, compress, push; see PRESS 1. **2** [To try] endeavor, strive, attempt; see TRY 1. —**bear out** confirm, substantiate, support; see PROVE. —**bear up** persist, persevere, carry on; see ENDURE 2. —**bear upon** pertain to, refer to, relate to, regard; see also CONCERN 1. —**bear with** tolerate, be patient with, suffer, put up with; see also ENDURE 2.

bearable *a.* endurable, tolerable, passable, admissible, supportable, sufferable.

beard *n.* whiskers, brush, Van Dyke, chin whiskers, imperial, muttonchops, goatee, spade beard, forked beard, side whiskers.

bearded *a.* bewhiskered, bushy, unshaven; see HAIRY.

bearing *n.* **1** [A point of support] frame, ball bearing, roller bearing; see SUPPORT 2. **2** [Manner of carriage] mien, deportment, manner; see BEHAVIOR, POSTURE 1.

beast *n.* **1** [A large animal] brute, creature, lower animal; see ANIMAL. **2** [A person of brutish nature] monster, brute, degenerate, animal, fiend, swine, pervert, lout, savage, barbarian, monstrosity, Bluebeard; see also PERVERT.

beastly *a.* brutal, savage, coarse, repulsive, gluttonous, obscene, unclean, piggish, hoggish, irrational, boorish, brutish, depraved, abominable, loathsome, vile, low, degraded, sensual, foul, base, disgusting, inhuman, gross, vulgar.—*Ant.* REFINED, sweet, nice.

beat* *a.* weary, fatigued, worn-out; see TIRED.

beat *n.* **1** [A throb] thump, pound, quake, flutter, pulse, pulsation, cadence, flow, vibration, turn, ripple, pressure, impulse, quiver, shake, surge, swell, palpitation, undulation, rhythm. **2** [A unit of music] accent, vibration, division, stress, measure, rhythm.

beat *v.* **1** [To thrash] hit, punish, whip, pistol-whip, flog, trounce, spank, scourge, switch, lash, slap, cuff, box, strap, birch, cane, horsewhip, buffet, pommel, tap, rap, strike, bump, pat, knock, pound, club, punch, bat, flail, batter, maul, whack, hammer, clout, smack, bang, swat, slug*, beat black and blue*, whale*, belt*, whack, beat the tar out of*, beat the daylights out of*,

beat the hell out of*, knock the stuffing out of*, wallop*, lick*, paste*, bash*, work over*, thwack. **2** [To pulsate] pound, thump, pulse; see THROB. **3** [To worst] overcome, surpass, conquer; see DEFEAT 2, 3. **4** [To mix] stir, whip, knead; see MIX 1.

beaten *a.* **1** [Defeated] worsted, humbled, thwarted, bested, disappointed, frustrated, baffled, conquered, overthrown, subjugated, ruined, mastered, trounced, undone, vanquished, crushed, overwhelmed, overpowered, licked*, done in*, done for*, kayoed*, mugged, skinned*, trimmed*, had it*, washed up*, sunk*.—*Ant.* SUCCESSFUL, victorious, triumphant. **2** [Made firm and hard] hammered, tramped, stamped, rolled, milled, forged, trod, pounded, tramped down, tamped.—*Ant.* SOFT, spongy, loose. **3** [Made light by beating] whipped, frothy, foamy, mixed, churned, creamy, bubbly, meringued.

beater *n.* whipper, mixer, eggbeater; see APPLIANCE.

beating *n.* thrashing, whipping, drubbing; see DEFEAT.

beatnik *n.* bohemian, hippie, nonconformist; see RADICAL.

beautiful *a.* lovely, attractive, appealing, comely, pleasing, pretty, fair, fine, nice, dainty, good-looking, delightful, charming, enticing, fascinating, admirable, rich, graceful, ideal, delicate, refined, elegant, symmetrical, well-formed, shapely, well-made, splendid, gorgeous, brilliant, radiant, exquisite, dazzling, resplendent, magnificent, superb, marvelous, wonderful, grand, awe-inspiring, imposing, majestic, excellent, impressive, handsome, divine, blooming, rosy, beauteous, statuesque, well-favored, bewitching, personable, taking, alluring, slender, svelte, lissome, lithe, bright-eyed, easy on the eyes*.—*Ant.* UGLY, deformed, hideous.

beautifully *a.* gracefully, exquisitely, charmingly, attractively, prettily, delightfully, appealingly, seductively, alluringly, elegantly, gorgeously, splendidly, magnificently, ideally, tastefully, sublimely, handsomely, superbly, divinely.

beauty *n.* **1** [A pleasing physical quality] grace, comeliness, fairness, pulchritude, charm, delicacy, elegance, attraction, fascination, allurement, shapeliness, majesty, attractiveness, good looks, glamour, loveliness, bloom.—*Ant.* UGLINESS, homeliness, deformity. **2** [A beautiful woman] goddess, belle, siren, enchantress, seductress, Venus, *femme fatale* (French), vision, knockout*, looker*, charmer*.—*Ant.* WITCH, blemish, fright.

because *conj.* on account of, in consequence of, in view of, by reason of, for the reason that, for the sake of, in behalf of, on the grounds that, in the interest of, as a result of, as things go, by virtue of, in that, since, by the agency of, due to*, being as how*, owing to.

beckon *v.* signal, motion, sign; see SUMMON.

become *v.* develop into, change into, turn into, grow into, eventually be, emerge as, turn out to be, come to be, shift, assume the form of, be reformed, be converted to, convert, mature, shift toward, incline to, melt into; see also GROW 2.

becoming *a.* attractive, beautiful, neat, agreeable, handsome, seemly, comely, tasteful, well-chosen, fair, trim, graceful, flattering, effective, excellent, acceptable, welcome, nice.

bed *n.* 1 [A place of rest] mattress, cot, couch, bedstead, berth, bunk, hay*, sack*. *Beds include the following:* single bed, double bed, davenport, cot, four-poster, trundle bed, twin bed, fold-away bed, Murphy bed, hammock, futon, feather bed, stretcher, folding bed, bunk bed, litter, cradle, crib, bassinet, king-size bed, queen-size bed, water bed, hospital bed, sofa bed, day bed. 2 [A foundation] base, bottom, groundwork; see FOUNDATION 2. 3 [A seed plot] patch, row, planting; see GARDEN.

bedding *n.* bedclothes, bed linen, thermal blankets, covers, bedcovers, pillows, coverlets, sheets, quilts, spreads, comforters.

bed down *v.* turn in, retire, hit the hay*; see SLEEP.

bedlam *n.* confusion, pandemonium, clamor; see CONFUSION, NOISE 2.

bedridden *a.* incapacitated, confined to bed, laid up; see DISABLED.

bedroom *n.* sleeping room, guest room, master bedroom; see ROOM 2.

bedspread *n.* spread, quilt, comforter; see BEDDING.

bedtime *n.* slumbertime, time to retire, sack time*; see NIGHT.

beef *n.* 1 [Bovine flesh used as food] cow's flesh, beefsteak, red meat; see MEAT. 2 [A grown animal of the genus *Bos*] bovine, bull, steer; see COW. 3 [*A complaint] dispute, protestation, gripe*; see OBJECTION.

beef up* *v.* intensify, augment, increase; see STRENGTHEN.

beer *n.* malt beverage, malt liquor, brew, suds*. *Varieties include the following:* lager, bock beer, ale, stout, porter, pale ale, pilsener, bitter, light beer, dark beer.

before *a.* previously, earlier, in the past, since, gone by, in old days, heretofore, former, formerly, back, sooner, up to now, ahead, in front, in the forefront, in advance, facing.—*Ant.* AFTERWARD, in the future, to come.

before *prep.* prior to, previous to, in front of, ahead of, under jurisdiction of, antecedent to.—*Ant.* BEHIND, following, at the rear.

beforehand *a.* previously, already, in anticipation; see BEFORE.

befriend *v.* encourage, advise, stand by; see HELP.

beg *v.* entreat, implore, beseech, supplicate, crave, solicit, pray for, urge, plead, sue, importune, petition, apply to, request, press, appeal to, requisition, conjure, adjure, apostrophize, dun, canvass; see also ASK.—*Ant.* ADMIT, concede, accede.

beggar *n.* pauper, poor person, hobo, tramp, indigent, vagrant, poverty-stricken person, destitute person, dependent, bankrupt, panhandler*, moocher*, bum*.

begging *a.* anxious, in need, imploring, supplicating; see also WANTING 1.

begin *v.* 1 [To initiate] start, cause, inaugurate, make, occasion, impel, produce, effect, set in motion, launch, mount, start in, start on, start up, start off, induce, do, create, bring about, get going, set about, institute, lead up to, undertake, enter upon, open, animate, motivate, go ahead, lead the way, bring on, bring to pass, act on, generate, drive, actualize, introduce, originate, found, establish, set up, trigger, give birth to, take the lead, plunge into, lay the foundation for, break ground.—*Ant.* END, finish, terminate. 2 [To come into being, or start functioning] commence, get under way, set out, start in, start out, come out, arise, rise, dawn, sprout, originate, crop up, come to birth, come into the world, be born, emanate, come into existence, occur, burst forth, issue forth, come forth, bud, grow, flower, blossom, break out, set to work, kick off, jump off*, go to it*, dig in*, take off*, see the light of day.—*Ant.* STOP, cease, subside.

beginner *n.* novice, apprentice, rookie*; see AMATEUR.

beginning *n.* 1 [The origin in point of time or place] source, outset, root; see ORIGIN 2. 2 [The origin, thought of as the cause] germ, heart, antecedent; see ORIGIN 3.

begun *a.* started, initiated, instituted, under way, in motion, in progress, on foot, inaugurated, happening, proceeding, going, active, underway, existing, operative, working, in force.

behalf *n.* interest, benefit, sake; see WELFARE.

behave v. act with decorum, follow the golden rule, do unto others as you would have others do unto you, be nice, be good, be civil, mind one's p's and q's, be orderly, play one's part, live up to, observe the law, reform, mind one's manners, comport oneself, deport oneself, behave oneself, be on one's best behavior, act one's age, avoid offense, toe the line, play fair.

behavior n. bearing, deportment, comportment, demeanor, air, presence, carriage, conduct, manners, actions, attitudes, way of life, speech, talk, tone, morals, habits, tact, social graces, correctness, decorum, form, convention, propriety, taste, management, routine, practice, what's done, style, expression, performance, code, role, observance, course, guise, act, deed, ethics, way, front.

behind a., prep. **1** [To the rear in space] back of, following, after; see BACK. **2** [Late in time] tardy, dilatory, behind time; see LATE 1, SLOW 2. **3** [Slow in progress] sluggish, slow-moving, delayed, backward, underdeveloped, retarded, behind schedule, belated; see also SLOW 2.—Ant. FAST, rapid, on time.

being n. **1** [Existence] presence, actuality, animation; see LIFE 1. **2** [The essential part] nature, core, marrow; see ESSENCE 1. **3** [A living thing] creature, conscious agent, beast; see ANIMAL. —**for the time being** temporarily, tentatively, for now, for the present; see also BRIEFLY, NOW.

belated a. remiss, tardy, overdue; see LATE 1, SLOW 3.

belief n. idea, opinion, faith, creed, tenet, doctrine, principle, feeling, hope, intuition, view, expectation, acceptance, trust, notion, persuasion, position, understanding, conviction, confidence, suspicion, knowledge, conclusion, presumption, surmise, hypothesis, thinking, judgment, certainty, impression, assumption, conjecture, fancy, theory, guess, conception, inference.

believable a. trustworthy, credible, acceptable; see CONVINCING.

believe v. accept, hold, think, understand, consider, swear by, conceive, affirm, conclude, be of the opinion, have faith, have no doubt, take at one's word, take someone's word for, be convinced, be certain of, give credence to, rest assured.—Ant. DENY, doubt, suspect. —**believe in** swear by, look to, have faith in; see TRUST 1.

believer n. convert, devotee, adherent, apostle, disciple, prophet, confirmed believer; see also FOLLOWER.

believing a. maintaining, trusting,

presuming, assuming, holding, accepting, under the impression.

belittle v. lower, disparage, decry; see ABUSE.

bell n. chimes, siren, signal, gong, buzzer; see also ALARM.

belligerent a. warlike, pugnacious, hostile; see AGGRESSIVE.

bellow n. howl, cry, roar; see CRY 1.

bellow v. howl, call, shout; see CRY 2, YELL.

belly n. paunch, abdomen, gut*; see STOMACH.

bellyache* v. whine, grumble, protest; see COMPLAIN.

belong v. **1** [To be properly placed] fit in, have a place, relate; see FIT 1. **2** [To be acceptable in a group; said of persons] fit in, have a place, have its place, be born so, be a member, take one's place with, be one of, be counted among, be included in, owe allegiance to, be a part of, be one of the family.—Ant. DIFFER, fight, not fit in. —**belong to** pertain to, relate to, be occupied by, be enjoyed by, be owned by, be in the possession of, be at the disposal of, be the property of, concern, come with, go with, fall under.—Ant. ESCAPE, be free, have no owner.

belongings n. possessions, goods, things*; see PROPERTY 1.

beloved a. loved, adored, worshiped, cherished, dear, favorite, idolized, precious, prized, dearest, yearned for, revered, treasured, favored, doted on, nearest to someone's heart, dearly beloved, after someone's own heart, darling, admired, popular, well-liked, cared for, respected, pleasing.—Ant. HATED, abhorred, disliked.

beloved n. fiancé, sweetheart, object of someone's affection; see LOVER 1.

below a., prep. **1** [Lower in position] beneath, underneath, down from; see UNDER 1. **2** [Lower in rank or importance] inferior, subject, under; see SUBORDINATE. **3** [Farther along in written material] later, on a following page, in a statement to be made, hereafter, subsequently.—Ant. ABOVE, earlier, on a former page. **4** [On earth] existing, in this world, here below, under the sun, on the face of the earth, in this our life, here. **5** [In hell] in the underworld, damned, condemned; see DAMNED 1.

belt n. girdle, ribbon, string; see BAND 1. —**below the belt** unjust, foul, unsporting; see UNFAIR. —**tighten one's belt** endure hunger, suffer, bear misfortune; see ENDURE 2. —**under one's belt** past, finished, completed; see DONE 1.

bench n. **1** [A long seat] pew, seat, stall; see CHAIR 1. **2** [A long table] workbench, desk, counter; see TABLE 1.

bend *n.* crook, bow, arch; see CURVE.

bend *v.* twist, contort, deform, round, crimp, flex, spiral, coil, crinkle, detour, curl, buckle, crook, bow, incline, deflect, double, loop, twine, curve, arch, wind, stoop, lean, waver, zigzag, reel, crumple, meander, circle, swerve, diverge, droop.—*Ant.* STRAIGHTEN, extend, stretch.

bending *a.* twisting, veering, curving, buckling, twining, spiraling, looping, doubling, drooping, leaning, inclining, bowing, arching, curling, winding, stooping, crumpling, waving, wavering.

beneath *a., prep.* 1 [Under] below, underneath, in a lower place; see UNDER 1. 2 [Lower in rank or importance] subject to, inferior to, under; see SUBORDINATE.

benefactor *n.* helper, protector, angel*; see PATRON.

beneficiary *n.* recipient, receiver, inheritor; see HEIR.

benefit *n.* gain, profit, good; see ADVANTAGE.

benefit *v.* serve, profit, avail; see HELP.

bent *a.* curved, warped, hooked, beaked, looped, sinuous, twined, crooked, bowed, contorted, stooped, doubled over, limp, wilted, drooping, humped, slumped, hunched, humpbacked, bowlegged, inclined; see also TWISTED 1.—*Ant.* STRAIGHT, rigid, erect.

bent *n.* leaning, tendency, propensity; see INCLINATION 1.

bequeath *v.* grant, hand down, pass on; see GIVE 1.

berry *n. Common berries include the following:* raspberry, blackberry, blueberry, loganberry, boysenberry, cranberry, huckleberry, gooseberry, currant, strawberry, mulberry.

berth *n.* place, situation, employment; see JOB 1, PROFESSION 1. —**give a wide berth** keep clear of, evade, stay away from; see AVOID.

beside *prep.* at the side of, at the edge of, adjacent to, next to, adjoining, alongside, near, close at hand, by, with, abreast, side by side, bordering on, neighboring, overlooking, next door to, to one side, nearby, connected with.

besides *a.* in addition to, additionally, moreover, over and above, added to, likewise, further, furthermore, beyond, exceeding, secondly, more than, apart from, extra, in excess of, plus, also, in other respects, exclusive of, with the exception of, as well as, not count-

ing, other than, too, to boot, on top of that, aside from, else.

best *a.* 1 [Generally excellent] first, greatest, finest, highest, transcendent, prime, premium, supreme, incomparable, crowning, paramount, matchless, unrivaled, unparalleled, second to none, unequaled, inimitable, beyond compare, superlative, foremost, peerless, first-rate; see also EXCELLENT.—*Ant.* WORST, poorest, lowest. 2 [Applied especially to actions and persons] noblest, sincerest, most praiseworthy; see NOBLE.

best *n.* first, favorite, choice, finest, top, pick, prime, flower, cream, cream of the crop. —**all for the best** favorable, fortunate, advantageous; see HELPFUL 1, HOPEFUL 2. —**as best one can** skillfully, ably, capably; see ABLE. —**at best** good, highest, most favorable; see BEST. —**at one's best** well, in one's prime, capable; see ABLE, STRONG 1. —**get** (or **have**) **the best of** outdo, surpass, defeat; see EXCEED. —**make the best of** suffer, tolerate, get by; see ENDURE 2. —**with the best** excellently, well, ably; see ABLE.

best *v.* worst, get the better of, overcome; see DEFEAT 3.

bestow *v.* bequeath, present, offer; see GIVE 1.

bet *n.* gamble, wager, venture, pot, hazard, tossup, stake, speculation, betting, raffle, uncertainty, chance, lottery, game of chance, sweepstakes, risk, ante, long shot*, shot in the dark*.

bet *v.* wager, gamble, stake, bet on, bet against, venture, hazard, trust, play against, speculate, play for, put money down, put money on, risk, chance, make a bet, take a chance, lay down, buy in on*, lay odds, lay even money*. —**you bet*** certainly, by all means, yes indeed; see SURELY, YES.

betray *v.* 1 [To deliver into the hands of an enemy] delude, trick, double-cross*; see DECEIVE. 2 [To reveal] divulge, disclose, make known; see REVEAL.

betrayal *n.* treason, treachery, disloyalty; see DECEPTION, DISHONESTY.

betrayer *n.* renegade, deceiver, conspirator; see TRAITOR.

better *a.* 1 [Superior] greater, finer, preferred, bigger, stronger, higher; see also BEST. 2 [Recovering health] convalescent, improved in health, improving, on the road to recovery, on the mend.—*Ant.* SICK, failing, wasting away. —**for the better** favorable, fortunate, helpful; see HOPEFUL 2. —**get** (or **have**) **the better of** outdo, overcome, defeat; see EXCEED.

better *v.* ameliorate, revamp, refine; see IMPROVE 1.

between *prep.* separating, within, bounded by, amidst, amid, among, in, in between, mid, intervening, in the midst of, in the middle, centrally located, surrounded by, midway, halfway, in the thick; see also AMONG. —**between you and me** confidentially, privately, personally; see SECRETLY.

beverage *n.* liquor, refreshment, draft; see DRINK 2.

bewilder *v.* confound, disconcert, puzzle; see CONFUSE.

bewildered *a.* confused, amazed, misguided, lost, astonished, thunderstruck, shocked, muddled, upset, dazed, giddy, dizzy, reeling, puzzled, misled, uncertain, surprised, baffled, disconcerted, appalled, aghast, adrift, at sea, off the track, awed, stupefied, astounded, struck speechless, breathless, befuddled, startled, struck dumb, dumbfounded, dazzled, stunned, electrified, confounded, staggered, petrified, awestruck, flabbergasted, flustered, rattled, up in the air*, stumped*.

beyond *a., prep.* on the other side, on the far side, over there, in advance of, away, out of range, a long way off, yonder, past, free of, clear of, farther off, ahead, behind, more remote.—*Ant.* HERE, on this side, nearer.

bias *n.* bent, preference, leaning; see INCLINATION 1.

bias *v.* influence, prejudice, sway; see INFLUENCE.

Bible *n.* the Good Book, God's word, the Word, Scripture, the Scriptures, the Canon, the Testaments, Sacred History, Holy Writ, the Holy Bible, the Word of God, Testament, the Old Testament, the New Testament.

bibliography *n.* catalog, compilation, list of books; see LIST.

bicker *v.* wrangle, squabble, dispute; see QUARREL.

bicycle *n.* cycle, bike*, two-wheeler; see VEHICLE.

bid *n.* proposal, proposition, declaration; see SUGGESTION 1.

bid *v.* **1** [To propose a price for purchase] venture, bid for, submit a bid; see OFFER 1. **2** [To order] tell, charge, direct; see COMMAND 1.

big *a.* **1** [Of great size] huge, great, swollen, fat, obese, bloated, overgrown, gross, mammoth, wide, grand, vast, immense, considerable, substantial, massive, extensive, spacious, colossal, gigantic, titanic, monstrous, towering, mighty, magnificent, enormous, giant, tremendous, whopping*.—*Ant.* LITTLE, tiny, small. **2** [Grown, or partially grown] grown-up, full-grown, adult;

see MATURE. **3** [Important] prominent, significant, influential; see IMPORTANT 1, 2. **4** [Pompous] presumptuous, pretentious, imperious; see EGOTISTIC. **5** [Generous] magnanimous, liberal, unselfish; see GENEROUS, KIND.

bigot *n.* narrow-minded person, opinionated person, racist, chauvinist, xenophobe, jingoist, hatemonger, dogmatist, redneck*; see also RADICAL.

bigoted *a.* biased, dogmatic, opinionated; see PREJUDICED.

bigotry *n.* intolerance, narrowmindedness, injustice; see FANATICISM, PREJUDICE.

big shot* *n.* big wheel*, bigwig*, VIP*; see EXECUTIVE.

bill *n.* **1** [A statement of account] invoice, statement of indebtedness, request for payment; see STATEMENT 2. **2** [A piece of paper money] Federal Reserve note, bank note, greenback; see MONEY 1. **3** [A statement prepared for enactment into law] measure, proposal, piece of legislation; see LAW 3. **4** [A beak] nib, mandible, projection; see BEAK. —**fill the bill*** meet requirements, be satisfactory, serve the purpose; see SATISFY 3.

bill *v.* dun, solicit, render account of indebtedness, draw upon.

billboard *n.* outdoor advertisement, display panel, poster board; see ADVERTISEMENT, ANNOUNCEMENT.

billfold *n.* card case, pocketbook, purse; see WALLET.

bin *n.* storeroom, granary, silo; see CONTAINER.

binary *a.* double, twofold, digital; see DOUBLE.

bind* *n.* dilemma, tight situation, quandary; see PREDICAMENT.

bind *v.* **1** [To constrain with bonds] truss up, tie up, shackle, fetter, cinch, clamp, chain, leash, constrict, manacle, enchain, lace, pin, restrict, hamper, handcuff, muzzle, hitch, secure, yoke, pin down, fix, strap, tether, bind up, lash down, clamp down on, hogtie. **2** [To hold together or in place] secure, attach, adhere; see FASTEN. **3** [To obligate] oblige, necessitate, compel; see FORCE. **4** [To dress] treat, dress, bandage; see HEAL. **5** [To join] unite, put together, connect; see JOIN 1.

binding *a.* obligatory, requisite, required; see NECESSARY.

binding *n.* **1** [The act of joining] merging, coupling, junction; see UNION 1. **2** [Anything used to bind] tie, adhesive, binder; see FASTENER. **3** [A cover] wrapper, jacket, book cover; see COVER 1.

biography *n.* life story, saga, memoir, journal, experiences, autobiography, life, adventures, life history, confessions, profile, sketch, biographical account; see also RECORD 1, STORY.

biological *a.* organic, life, living, zoological, botanical, concerning life.

biology *n.* science of organisms, ecology, natural science, natural history, nature study, life science; see also SCIENCE 1.

bird *n. Types of birds include the following:* sparrow, starling, robin, blue jay, hawk, meadowlark, owl, vulture, buzzard, woodpecker, cardinal, kingfisher, chickadee, swallow, skylark, nightingale, nuthatch, whippoorwill, thrush, finch, warbler, bluebird, cuckoo, bobolink, wren, gull, eagle, osprey, blackbird, dove, duck, goose, pheasant, chicken, parakeet, parrot, canary, penguin, dodo, crane, heron, egret, mockingbird, ostrich. **—eat like a bird** fast, starve, nibble; see DIET. **—for the birds*** ridiculous, absurd, useless; see STUPID, WORTHLESS.

birth *n.* delivery, parturition, nativity, beginning, blessed event, visit from the stork.—*Ant.* DEATH, decease, demise. **—give birth** bring forth, have a child, reproduce; see PRODUCE 1.

birthday *n.* natal day, name day, celebration; see ANNIVERSARY.

biscuit *n.* cracker, wafer, roll; see BREAD.

bishop *n.* father, archbishop, primate; see MINISTER 1, PRIEST.

bit *n.* 1 [A small quantity] piece, fragment, crumb, dot, particle, jot, trifle, mite, iota, whit, splinter, parcel, portion, droplet, trickle, driblet, morsel, pinch, snip, shred, atom, speck, molecule, shard, chip, fraction, sliver, segment, section, lump, slice, shaving, sample, specimen, scale, flake, excerpt, scrap, part, division, share, trace, item, chunk, paring, taste, mouthful, stub, butt, stump, a drop in the bucket*, peanuts*, chicken feed*, gob, hunk*. 2 [A small degree] jot, minimum, inch, hairbreadth, trifle, iota, mite, fraction, tolerance, margin, whisker, hair, skin of one's teeth. **—do one's bit** participate, share, do one's share; see JOIN 2. **—every bit** wholly, altogether, entirely; see COMPLETELY.

bite *n.* 1 [What one takes in the mouth at one time] mouthful, chew, taste, spoonful, forkful, morsel, nibble. 2 [The result of being bitten] wound, sting, laceration; see INJURY. 3 [A quick meal] snack, nibble, brunch; see FOOD.

bite *v.* 1 [To seize or sever with the teeth] snap, gnaw, sink one's teeth into, nip, nibble, chew, mouth, gulp, worry, taste, masticate, clamp, champ, munch, bite into, crunch, mangle, chaw*; see also EAT 1, TASTE 1. 2 [To be given to biting] snap, be vicious, attack; see HURT. 3 [To cut or corrode] rot, decay, decompose; see RUST.

biting *a.* 1 [Acidulous] sharp, keen, tangy; see SOUR. 2 [Sarcastic] caustic, acrimonious, bitter; see SARCASTIC.

bitten *a.* chewed, torn, lacerated, slashed, gulped, gnawed, nibbled, tasted, devoured, eaten, stung, pierced, mangled, punctured, cut, ripped.

bitter *a.* 1 [Acrid] astringent, acid, tart; see SOUR. 2 [Intense] sharp, harsh, severe; see INTENSE. 3 [Sarcastic] acrimonious, caustic, biting; see SARCASTIC.

bitterness *n.* tartness, piquancy, pungency, acidity, sourness, acridity, brackishness, brininess.

bizarre *a.* odd, fantastic, grotesque; see UNUSUAL 2.

blab *v.* disclose, tell, divulge; see REVEAL.

black *a.* 1 [Opposite to white] dark, blackish, raven, coal-black, dusky, dingy, murky, inklike, somber, swarthy, swart, jet, inky, ebony, pitch-black, black as coal, sooty, gunmetal, flat black, jet black, black as night*.—*Ant.* WHITE, colored, colorful. 2 [Without light] gloomy, shadowy, clouded; see DARK 1.

black *n.* 1 [A chromatic color least resembling white] carbon, darkest gray, jet, sable, ebony, blackness.—*Ant.* WHITE, blond, brightness. 2 [A Negro] colored person*, Negro, African, Afro-American, African-American. **—in the black** successful, lucrative, gainful; see PROFITABLY.

blacken *v.* darken, deepen, make black; see SHADE 2.

black magic *n.* sorcery, witchcraft, necromancy; see MAGIC 1, 2.

blackmail *n.* hush money, tribute, protection*; see BRIBE.

blackmail *v.* extort, coerce, shake down*; see BRIBE, FORCE.

blackness *n.* gloom, duskiness, murkiness; see DARKNESS 1.

black out *v.* 1 [To delete] rub out, eradicate, blot out; see CANCEL, ERASE. 2 [To faint] pass out, lose consciousness, swoon; see FAINT. 3 [To darken] put out the lights, make dark, cause a blackout in; see SHADE 2.

blade *n.* 1 [A cutting instrument] edge, sword, saber; see KNIFE. 2 [A relatively long leaf] frond, spear, shoot; see LEAF.

blame *n.* disapproval, condemnation, denunciation, abuse, disparagement, depreciation, opposition, disfavor, objection, reproach, criticism, repudiation, reprimand, invective, slur, accusation, reproof, attack, chiding, rebuke, impeachment, complaint, diatribe, tirade, charge, indictment, recrimination, arraignment, implication, calumny, frowning upon.—*Ant.* PRAISE, commendation, appreciation.

blame *v.* charge, condemn, criticize, arraign, challenge, involve, attack, brand, implicate, arrest, sue, prosecute, slander, impeach, bring to trial, connect with, indict, impute, put the finger on*, smear, point the finger at*, bring home to, dis*. —**be to blame** guilty, at fault, culpable; see WRONG 2.

blameless *a.* faultless, not guilty, inculpable; see INNOCENT 1.

bland *a.* flat, dull, insipid; see TASTELESS 1.

blank *a.* white, clear, virgin, fresh, plain, empty, untouched, pale, new, spotless, vacant, hollow, meaningless.

blank *n.* **1** [An empty space] void, hollow, hole, cavity, vacancy, womb, gulf, nothingness, hollowness, abyss, opening, vacuum, gap, interval; see also EMPTINESS. **2** [A form] questionnaire, data sheet, information blank; see FORM 5. —**draw a blank** be unable to remember, lose one's memory, disremember*; see FORGET.

blanket *n.* quilt, comforter, throw, electric blanket, thermal blanket, afghan, stadium blanket.

blanket *v.* envelop, conceal, bury; see COVER 1.

blank out *v.* delete, black out, cross out; see CANCEL, ERASE.

blast *n.* **1** [An explosion] burst, eruption, detonation; see EXPLOSION. **2** [A loud sound] roar, din, bang; see NOISE 1. **3** [An explosive charge] gunpowder, TNT, dynamite; see EXPLOSIVE. —**(at) full blast** at full speed, rapidly, quickly; see FAST 1.

blast *v.* blow up, dynamite, detonate; see EXPLODE. —**blast off** rocket, climb, soar up; see RISE 1.

blaze *n.* conflagration, combustion, burning; see FIRE.

blaze *v.* flame, flash, flare up; see BURN.

bleach *v.* blanch, wash out, whiten; see FADE.

bleak *a.* dreary, desolate, bare, cheerless, wild, exposed, barren, windswept, blank, disheartening, weary, melancholy, lonely, flat, somber, distressing, depressing, comfortless, joyless, uninviting, dull, sad, mournful, monotonous, waste, gloomy, dismal, unsheltered, unpopulated, desert, deserted, scorched, stony, burned over, bull-

dozed, cleared, frozen.—*Ant.* GREEN, verdant, fruitful.

bleed *v.* lose blood, shed blood, be bleeding, hemorrhage, gush, spurt, be bled, open a vein, draw blood; see also FLOW.

blemish *n.* flaw, defect, stain, spot, smudge, imperfection, disfigurement, defacement, blot, blur, chip, taint, tarnish, smirch, stigma, brand, deformity, dent, discoloration, mole, pock, blister, birthmark, wart, scar, impurity, speckle, bruise, freckle, pimple, patch, lump, zit*.—*Ant.* PERFECTION, flawlessness, consummation.

blend *n.* combination, compound, amalgam; see MIXTURE 1.

blend *v.* combine, mingle, compound; see MIX 1.

bless *v.* baptize, canonize, glorify, honor, dedicate, make holy, pronounce holy, exalt, give benediction to, absolve, anoint, ordain, hallow, consecrate, beatify, sanctify, enshrine, offer, render acceptable to, sacrifice, commend.

blessed *a.* **1** [Marked by God's favor, especially in heaven] saved, redeemed, glorified, translated, exalted, rewarded, resurrected, sanctified, glorious, beatified, holy, spiritual, religious.—*Ant.* DOOMED, lost, accursed. **2** [Consecrated] sacred, dedicated, sanctified; see DIVINE.

blessing *n.* **1** [Benediction] commendation, sanctification, laying on of hands, absolution, baptism, unction, consecration, Eucharist.—*Ant.* CURSE, damnation, anathema. **2** [Anything that is very welcome] boon, benefit, good, advantage, help, asset, good fortune, stroke of luck, godsend, windfall, miracle, manna from heaven, lucky break.—*Ant.* NUISANCE, obstacle, disadvantage.

blight *n.* disease, withering, mildew; see DECAY.

blight *v.* decay, spoil, ruin; see SPOIL.

blind *a.* **1** [Without sight] sightless, unseeing, eyeless, blinded, visionless, in darkness, dim-sighted, groping, deprived of sight, sun-blind, undiscerning, stone-blind, moon-blind, blind as a bat.—*Ant.* OBSERVANT, perceptive, discerning. **2** [Without looking] obtuse, unseeing, by guesswork, by calculation, with instruments; see also BLINDLY, UNAWARE. **3** [Without passage] obstructed, blocked, without egress; see TIGHT 2, 3. **4** [Random] chance, accidental, unplanned; see AIMLESS.

blind *v.* darken, shadow, dim; see SHADE 2.

blindly *a.* at random, wildly, in all directions, frantically, heedlessly, carelessly, recklessly, passionately, thoughtlessly, impulsively, inconsiderately, unreasonably, without rhyme or reason, senselessly, instinctively, madly, pell-mell, purposelessly, aimlessly, indiscriminately.—*Ant.* CAREFULLY, deliberately, considerately.

blindness *n.* sightlessness, purblindness, myopia, astigmatism, night blindness, snow blindness, color blindness.—*Ant.* SIGHT, vision, seeing.

blink *v.* 1 [To wink rapidly] flicker, bat one's eyes, flutter one's eyelids; see WINK. 2 [To twinkle] glimmer, flash on and off, shimmer; see SHINE 1.

bliss *n.* joy, rapture, ecstasy; see HAPPINESS.

blister *n.* vesicle, sac, weal, welt, blood blister, water blister, second-degree burn; see also SORE.

blister *v.* scald, irritate, mark; see HURT.

blizzard *n.* snowstorm, williwaw, snow squall; see STORM.

bloc *n.* cabal, group, ring; see FACTION.

block *n.* 1 [A mass, usually with flat surfaces] slab, chunk, piece, square, cake, cube, slice, segment, loaf, clod, bar, hunk. 2 [The area between streets] vicinity, square, lots; see NEIGHBORHOOD. 3 [The distance of the side of a city block] street, city block, intersection; see DISTANCE 3. 4 [An obstruction] hindrance, bar, obstacle; see BARRIER. —**knock someone's block off*** thrash, hit, beat up*; see BEAT 1.

block *v.* 1 [To impede] interfere with, prevent, close off; see HINDER. 2 [In sports, to impede a play] throw a block, tackle, check; see STOP 1. —**block out** 1 [To obscure] conceal, screen, cover; see HIDE 1. 2 [To plan] outline, sketch, chart; see PLAN 2.

blockade *n.* barricade, encirclement, strategic barrier; see BARRIER.

blockhead *n.* nitwit, fool, imbecile; see FOOL.

blond *a.* fair, fair-skinned, pale, light, light-skinned, lily-white, white-skinned, creamy, whitish, milky, albino, pearly, platinum, gray-white, towheaded, snowy, light-haired, golden-haired, fair-haired, yellow-haired, sandy-haired, ash-blond, bleached, strawberry-blond, bleached-blond.

blood *n.* lifeblood, plasma, serum, vital fluid, vital juices, gore, sanguine fluid. —**bad blood** malice, rancor, feud; see ANGER, HATRED. —**in cold blood** 1 heartlessly, ruthlessly, unmercifully; see BRUTALLY. 2 cruelly, intentionally, indifferently; see DELIBERATELY. —**make**

someone's blood boil disturb, infuriate, agitate; see ENRAGE. —**make someone's blood run cold** terrify, horrify, scare; see FRIGHTEN.

bloodless *a.* pallid, wan, anemic; see PALE 1.

bloodshed *n.* slaughter, butchery, gore; see BATTLE, MURDER.

bloodshot *a.* inflamed, streaked, red; see BLOODY 1.

bloody *a.* 1 [Showing blood] bleeding, bloodstained, blood-spattered, gaping, unstaunched, grisly, crimson, open, wounded, dripping blood, raw, blood-soaked.—*Ant.* WHOLE, unhurt, uninjured. 2 [Fiercely fought] savage, heavy, murderous; see CRUEL.

bloom *n.* blossom, floweret, efflorescence; see FLOWER.

bloom *v.* flower, burst into bloom, open, bud, prosper, grow, wax, bear fruit, thrive, germinate, flourish, mature, be in peak condition, blossom, come out in flower, be in flower.

blooming *a.* flowering, blossoming, in flower; see BUDDING, GROWING.

blossom *n.* bloom, floweret, bud; see FLOWER.

blossom *v.* flower, blow*, burst into blossom; see BLOOM.

blossoming *n.* blooming, flowering, budding; see BUDDING, GROWING.

blot *n.* spot, stain, smudge; see BLEMISH.

blot *v.* smudge, blotch, soil; see DIRTY. —**blot out** 1 [To mark out] deface, cross out, scratch out, delete; see also CANCEL. 2 [To obscure] darken, blur, shroud; see SHADE 2.

blouse *n.* pullover, overblouse, jersey; see CLOTHES, SHIRT.

blow *n.* hit, strike, swing, bump, wallop, rap, bang, whack, thwack, cuff, smack, uppercut, knock, clout, slam, bruise, swipe*, kick, stroke, punch, jab, gouge, lunge, thrust, swat, poke, prod, slap, the old one-two*, belt*, lick*, crack, kayo*, K.O.*.

blow *v.* 1 [To send forth air rapidly] puff, blast, pant, fan, whiff, whisk, whisper, puff away, exhale, waft, breathe, whistle. 2 [To carry on the wind] waft, flutter, bear, whisk, drive, fling, whirl, flap, flip, wave, buffet, sweep. 3 [To play a wind instrument] pipe, toot, mouth; see PLAY 3. 4 [To sound when blown] trumpet, vibrate, blare; see SOUND. 5 [To give form by inflation] inflate, swell, puff up, pump up; see also FILL 1. 6 [*To fail] miss, flounder, miscarry; see FAIL 1. 7 [*To spend] lay out, pay out, waste, squander; see also SPEND. —**blow up** 1 [To fill] pump up, puff up, swell, inflate; see also FILL 1. 2 [To explode]

erupt, rupture, go off; see EXPLODE.
3 [To destroy with explosives] bomb,
dynamite, detonate; see ATTACK,
DESTROY. **4** [*To lose one's temper]
become enraged, rave, lose self-control; see RAGE 1.

blowing *a.* blasting, puffing, fanning, panting, whisking, breathing,
gasping, fluttering, flapping, waving, streaming, whipping, drifting,
tumbling, gliding, straining; see
also FLYING.—*Ant.* MOTIONLESS,
standing still, hovering.

blown *a.* buffeted, fluttered, fanned;
see BLOWING.

blowout *n.* eruption, blast, detonation, tear, break, puncture, rupture,
leak, flat tire, flat.

blue *a., n.* **1** [One of the primary colors] *Tints and shades of blue include
the following:* indigo, sapphire, turquoise, lapis lazuli, aquamarine,
blue-black, azure, sky-blue, bluegreen; royal, Prussian, navy, powder, baby, cobalt, peacock, robin's
egg, pale, light, dark, deep, electric,
etc., blue; see also COLOR. **2**
[Despondent] depressed, moody,
melancholy; see SAD 1. —**once in a
blue moon** rarely, infrequently,
once in a while; see SELDOM. —**out
of the blue** without warning,
unpredicted, unforeseen; see UNEXPECTED.

blues *n.* **1** [A state of despondency;
often with "the"] depressed spirits,
melancholy, dejection; see GLOOM.
2 [Rhythmic lamentation in a minor
key] dirge, lament, torch song; see
MUSIC 1.

bluff *n.* **1** [A bank] cliff, precipice,
promontory; see HILL, MOUNTAIN 1.
2 [A trick] ruse, deception, delusion;
see TRICK 1.

bluff *v.* fool, mislead, trick; see
DECEIVE.

blunder *n.* mistake, lapse, oversight;
see ERROR.

blunt *a.* **1** [Dull] unsharpened,
unpointed, round; see DULL 1. **2**
[Abrupt] brusque, curt, bluff; see
RUDE 2.

blur *v.* obscure, cloud, smear; see
SHADE 2.

blurt out *v.* speak unthinkingly, jabber, utter; see TALK 1.

blush *v.* change color, flush, redden,
turn red, glow, have rosy cheeks,
turn scarlet.

blushing *a.* coloring, dyeing, staining, reddening, turning red, flushing, glowing, changing color, burning, red as a rose, rosy-red, with
burning cheeks*.

bluster *v.* brag, swagger, strut; see
BOAST.

board *n.* **1** [A piece of thin lumber]
plank, lath, strip; see LUMBER. **2**
[Meals] food, fare, provisions; see
FOOD, MEAL 2. **3** [A body of persons

having specific responsibilities]
jury, council, cabinet; see COMMITTEE. —**across the board** general,
universal, common; see UNIVERSAL
2. —**go by the board** be lost, be
ruined, vanish; see FAIL 1. —**on
board** present, in transit, en route;
see ABOARD.

board *v.* **1** [Cover] cover up, close
up, batten down; see COVER 1. **2** [Go
aboard] embark, cast off, go on
board ship; see LEAVE 1. **3** [Take
care of] lodge, room, house; see
FEED.

boast *n.* brag, vaunt, source of pride,
pretension, self-satisfaction, bravado.

boast *v.* gloat, triumph, swagger,
bully, exult, show off, vaunt, swell,
brag, strut, bluff, flaunt, bluster,
flourish, blow*, sound off*, crow, pat
oneself on the back, blow one's own
horn*, attract attention.—*Ant.*
APOLOGIZE, humble oneself, admit
defeat.

boastful *a.* bragging, pretentious,
bombastic; see EGOTISTIC.

boat *n. Types of small boats include
the following:* sailboat, rowboat,
shell, scull, kayak, dugout, canoe,
scow, raft, launch, motorboat, dory,
catboat, tartan, hydrofoil, speedboat, yawl, sloop, cutter, ketch,
schooner, lifeboat, barge, punt, outrigger, dinghy, racer, hydroplane,
catamaran, skiff, gondola, longboat,
war canoe, flatboat, riverboat, canal
boat. —**in the same boat** in the
same situation, in a similar situation, in the same condition, concurrently; see also TOGETHER 2. —**miss
the boat*** miss, fall short, neglect;
see FAIL 1. —**rock the boat*** upset,
disturb, distort; see CONFUSE.

bobsled *n.* sleigh, toboggan, coaster;
see SLED.

bodily *a.* carnal, fleshly, gross,
somatic, solid, physical, corporeal,
unspiritual, tangible, material, substantial, human, natural, normal,
organic; see also BIOLOGICAL, PHYSICAL 1.

body *n.* **1** [The human organism]
frame, physique, form, figure,
shape, make, carcass*, build,
makeup. **2** [A corpse] cadaver, corpus delecti (Latin), dust, clay, carcass*, dead body, relics, the dead,
the deceased, mummy, skeleton,
ashes, carrion, bones, remains,
stiff*, goner. **3** [The central portion
of an object] chassis, basis, groundwork, frame, fuselage, assembly,
trunk, hull, bed, box, skeleton, scaffold, anatomy, bones, guts*. **4**
[Individuals having an organization] society, group, party; see
ORGANIZATION 2. **5** [A unified or
organized mass] reservoir, supply,

variety; see COLLECTION. **—keep body and soul together** stay alive, endure, earn a living; see SURVIVE 1.

boil *v.* steep, seethe, stew, bubble, simmer, steam, parboil, boil over, evaporate, sterilize; see also COOK. **—boil down** condense, summarize, sum up; see DECREASE 2.

boiling *a.* stewing, steeping, percolating, steaming, bubbling, seething, simmering, evaporating, boiling over; see also COOKING.

boisterous *a.* tumultuous, uproarious, noisy; see LOUD 2, RUDE 2.

bold *a.* **1** [Courageous] intrepid, fearless, daring; see BRAVE. **2** [Impertinent] presumptuous, impudent, brazen; see RUDE 2. **3** [Prominent] strong, clear, plain; see DEFINITE 2.

boldly *a.* **1** [Said of animate beings] impetuously, headlong, intrepidly, fearlessly, recklessly, courageously, dauntlessly, daringly, valiantly, stoutly, resolutely, brazenly, firmly.—*Ant.* COWARDLY, fearfully, cravenly. **2** [Said of inanimate objects] prominently, conspicuously, saliently, sharply, clearly, plainly, openly, abruptly, steeply, eminently, vividly, strongly, palpably, commandingly, showily, compellingly.—*Ant.* VAGUELY, inconspicuously, unobtrusively.

boldness *n.* audacity, impudence, daring; see COURAGE.

bolster *v.* prop, hold up, reinforce, sustain; see also SUPPORT 1, 2.

bolt *n.* staple, brad, nut, skewer, peg, rivet, pin, spike, stud, coupling, key; see also NAIL, SCREW.

bomb *n.* weapon, high explosive, charge; see EXPLOSIVE. *Types of bombs include the following:* incendiary, multiple warhead, high explosive, demolition glider, time, smoke, delayed action, antipersonnel, smart, etc. bomb; atom bomb, atomic bomb, A-bomb, cobalt bomb, hydrogen bomb, H-bomb; torpedo, depth charge, cherry bomb, hand grenade, Molotov cocktail*, stink bomb.

bomb *v.* shell, bombard, torpedo, napalm, blow up, wipe out, blast, attack from the air, zero in on, raid, dive-bomb.

bombing *n.* bombardment, shelling, attack; see ATTACK.

bond *n.* **1** [A link] attachment, union, obligation, connection, relation, affinity, affiliation, bond of union, restraint; see also FRIENDSHIP, MARRIAGE, RELATIONSHIP. **2** [A secured debenture] security, warranty, debenture, certificate, registered bond, government bond, municipal bond, long-term bond, short-term bond, junk bond*. **3**

[Bail] surety, guaranty, warrant; see BAIL.

bondage *n.* servitude, serfdom, subjugation; see SLAVERY 1.

bone *n.* *Bones of the human body include the following:* cranium, skull, frontal bone, temporal bone, parietal bone, occipital bone, cheekbone, mandible, jawbone, spinal column, vertebrae, backbone, rib cage, clavicle, collarbone, shoulder blade, humerus, radius, ulna, carpal, metacarpal, phalanges, pelvis, illium, hipbone, femur, thighbone, patella, kneecap, tibia, shinbone, fibula, tarsal, metatarsal. **—feel in one's bones** be convinced, expect, be sure; see TRUST 1. **—have a bone to pick*** have a complaint, be angry, express an objection; see COMPLAIN. **—make no bones about*** confess, reveal, expose; see ADMIT 2.

bonus *n.* gratuity, reward, additional compensation; see GIFT 1, TIP 2.

bony *a.* emaciated, skinny, scrawny; see THIN 2.

book *n.* publication, work, volume, booklet, pamphlet, reprint, preprint, offprint, hardcover, softcover, text, edition, brochure, folio, copy, monograph, writing, scroll, periodical, magazine, paperback. *Kinds of books include the following:* manual, handbook, reference book, cookbook, children's book, atlas, guidebook, story book, song book, trade book, textbook, workbook, hymnbook, Bible, treatise, tract. **—by the book** strictly, according to rule, rigidly; see LEGALLY, OFFICIALLY 1. **—in one's book** in one's opinion, for oneself, to one's mind; see PERSONALLY 2. **—in the book** practiced, done, established, prevalent; see also KNOWN 2. **—know like a book** understand, comprehend, be aware of; see KNOW 1. **—one for the books*** source of amazement, shock, novelty; see SURPRISE 2. **—on the books** listed, noted, set down; see RECORDED. **—throw the book at*** accuse, charge with every possible offense, be overzealous with; see BLAME.

bookkeeper *n.* controller, comptroller, accountant, auditor; see also CLERK.

boom *n.* **1** [A loud noise] roar, blast, blare; see NOISE 1. **2** [Sudden increase, especially sudden prosperity] rush, growth, inflation; see INCREASE.

boom *v.* **1** [To make a loud sound] roar, reverberate, thunder; see SOUND. **2** [To increase rapidly] prosper, expand, swell; see GROW 1. **—lower the boom on*** take action against, move against, beat, overcome; see also ATTACK.

boon *n.* benefit, good fortune, help; see BLESSING 2.

boor *n.* peasant, yokel, rustic, lout, clown, bumpkin, churl, oaf, lubber, bear, plowman, lumpkin, gaffer, yahoo, hick*, rube*, hayseed*, clod, clodhopper.

boorish *a.* awkward, clumsy, churlish; see RUDE 1, 2.

boost *n.* 1 [Aid] assistance, aid, helping hand; see HELP 1. 2 [An increase] addition, advance, hike*; see INCREASE.

boost *v.* 1 [To raise] shove, hoist, advance; see RAISE 1. 2 [To promote] encourage, support, advertise; see PROMOTE 1, 2. 3 [To increase] raise, heighten, expand; see INCREASE.

boot *n.* hip boot, bootee, wader, galosh, jackboot, chukka boot, combat boot, hiking boot, ski boot, cowboy boot, riding boot. —**bet your boots*** be certain, rely on it, trust in it; see DEPEND ON.

booth *n.* stall, counter, nook, kiosk, pew, berth, compartment, shed, manger, cubbyhole, coop, pen, hut, enclosure, stand, cubicle, box.

bootleg *a.* illegal, unlawful, contraband; see ILLEGAL.

booty *n.* plunder, spoils, winnings, stolen goods, ill-gotten gains, seizure, prize, haul*, pickings, loot, take*.

booze* *n.* liquor, alcohol, whiskey; see DRINK 2.

border *n.* 1 [Edge] hem, end, trim; see DECORATION 2, FRINGE. 2 [Boundary] frontier, outpost, perimeter; see BOUNDARY, EDGE 1.

border *v.* be adjacent to, adjoin, abut on; see JOIN 3. —**border on** lie next to, abut, touch; see JOIN 3.

bordering *a.* rimming, bounding, neighboring, fringing, edging, lining, verging, connecting, on the edge of, flanking; see also NEAR 1.

bore *n.* nuisance, pest, tiresome person; see TROUBLE.

bore *v.* 1 [To pierce by rotary motion] drill, ream, perforate; see PENETRATE. 2 [To weary] fatigue, tire, put to sleep; see TIRE 2.

bored *a.* wearied, fatigued, jaded, dull, irked, annoyed, bored to death*, in a rut, sick and tired, bored stiff*, bored silly*, fed up*; see also TIRED.—*Ant.* EXCITED, thrilled, exhilarated.

boredom *n.* lack of interest, tiresomeness, apathy, doldrums, listlessness, monotony, indifference, tedium, the blahs*.

boring *a.* tedious, stupid, monotonous; see DULL 3, 4.

born *a.* intrinsic, innate, inherent; see NATURAL 1.

borrow *v.* accept the loan of, obtain the use of, take a loan, go into debt, get temporary use of, use, rent, hire,

obtain, give a note for, sponge*, hit up for*, bum*, beg, chisel*, mooch*.—*Ant.* LEND, loan, give back.

borrowed *a.* appropriated, taken, acquired, assumed, adopted, hired, plagiarized, imported, cultivated, imitated.—*Ant.* owned, possessed, purchased.

boss *n.* supervisor, manager, administrator; see EXECUTIVE.

botanical *a.* concerning plants, vegetable, floral, arboreal, herbaceous, horticultural, agricultural; see also BIOLOGICAL.

botany *n.* phytology, natural history, horticulture; see BIOLOGY, SCIENCE.

botch *v.* bungle, spoil, mar, ruin, wreck, mutilate, fumble, distort, blunder, mishandle, do clumsily, muddle, make a mess of, trip, flounder, err, fall down, be mistaken, misjudge, mismanage, miscalculate, misconstrue, misestimate, execute clumsily, do unskillfully, stumble, put one's foot in it*, goof up*, butcher, screw up*, mess up, put out of whack*; see also FAIL 1.—*Ant.* SUCCEED, fix, do well.

both *a.* the two, both together, the one and the other, the pair, the couple, one as well as the other.

bother *n.* 1 [Worry] vexation, distress, anxiety; see CARE 2. 2 [A cause of worry] problem, concern, care; see DIFFICULTY 1, 2, TROUBLE.

bother *v.* 1 [To take trouble] put oneself out, fret, go out of one's way, make a fuss about, fuss over, take pains, make an effort, exert oneself, concern oneself, be concerned about, worry about. 2 [To give trouble] plague, vex, annoy, perplex, pester, molest, irritate, irk, provoke, insult, harass, heckle, aggravate, badger, discommode, disturb, discompose, mortify, goad, intrude upon, disquiet, pursue, hinder, impede, carp at, scare, exasperate, bore, afflict, taunt, torment, torture, bedevil, browbeat, tease, tantalize, ride, rub the wrong way, pick on, nag, needle*, bug*, get under someone's skin*.—*Ant.* HELP, please, delight.

bothered *a.* annoyed, agitated, disturbed; see TROUBLED.

bothersome *a.* annoying, irksome, troublesome; see DISTURBING.

bottle *n.* flask, flagon, decanter, cruet, jug, urn, canteen, cruse, jar, gourd, carafe, hip flask, vial, vacuum bottle, container. —**hit the bottle*** get drunk, imbibe, booze*; see DRINK 2.

bottom *n.* underside, base, nadir, foot, depths, bed, floor, underpart, deepest part, sole, ground.—*Ant.* TOP, peak, pinnacle. —**at bottom** fundamentally, basically, actually;

see REALLY 1. —**be at the bottom of** originate, be the reason for, activate; see CAUSE. —**bet one's bottom dollar*** bet, risk, wager; see GAMBLE.

bottomless a. deep, unfathomable, boundless; see INFINITE.

bottom line* n. 1 [Profits or losses] net income, net loss, net profits; see INCOME, PROFIT 2, LOSS 3. 2 [Final decision] conclusion, determination, last word; see END 2.

bottoms n. low land, marsh, bottomland; see SWAMP.

bough n. limb, arm, fork; see BRANCH 2.

bought a. purchased, procured, budgeted for, requisitioned, paid for, on order, to be delivered, contracted for, acquired; see also ORDERED 1.—*Ant.* STOLEN, sold, given away.

boulder n. stone, slab, crag; see ROCK 1.

boulevard n. street, avenue, highway; see ROAD 1.

bounce v. ricochet, recoil, carom, rebound, glance off, spring back, leap, hop, bolt, vault, skip, bob, buck, jump, bound, jerk up and down, snap back, boomerang, backlash.

bound a. 1 [Literally confined in bonds] fettered, shackled, trussed up, manacled, chained, enchained, handcuffed, hobbled, captive, pinioned, muzzled, in leash, tied up, harnessed, bound hand and foot, pinned down, tethered, picketed, secured, roped, gagged.—*Ant.* FREE, unrestrained, loose. 2 [Figuratively constrained] impelled, compelled, obliged, obligated, restrained, under compulsion, constrained, forced, coerced, driven, pressed, urged, necessitated, under necessity, made, having no alternative, required, duty-bound. —**bound to** certain to, sure to, destined to; see INEVITABLE.

bound v. 1 [To move in leaps] leap, spring, vault; see JUMP 1. 2 [To rebound] bounce, ricochet, recoil; see BOUNCE. 3 [To set limits] restrict, confine, circumscribe; see DEFINE 1. —**out of bounds** off limits, not permitted, restricted; see ILLEGAL.

boundary n. outline, border, verge, rim, beginning, end, confine, bounds, radius, terminus, landmark, march, extremity, compass, side, hem, frame, skirt, termination, margin, line, barrier, frontier, outpost, perimeter, parameter, extent, circumference, horizon, periphery, fringe, mark, confines, limit, borderland.

bounded a. limited, enclosed, bordered; see SURROUNDED.

bounty n. prize, premium, bonus; see PAY 1, 2.

bouquet n. nosegay, garland, corsage, boutonniere, flower arrangement, wreath, spray.

bow n. longbow, crossbow, single-piece bow; see WEAPON.

bow n. 1 [Front of a boat] forepart, bowsprit, prow, head, nose, stem, fore; see also FRONT 1. 2 [A bend from the waist] nod, curtsey, bowing and scraping; see ACKNOWLEDGMENT. —**take a bow** accept praise, be congratulated, feel honored; see BEND.

bow v. 1 [To bend] curtsey, stoop, dip; see BEND. 2 [To submit] surrender, acquiesce, capitulate; see YIELD 1.

bowels n. viscera, entrails, guts; see INSIDES.

bowl n. vessel, tureen, pot, saucer, crock, jar, urn, pitcher, basin, casserole, boat; see also CONTAINER, DISH.

bowling n. lawn bowling, tenpins, boccie; see SPORT 3.

box n. receptacle, crate, carton; see CONTAINER.

box v. 1 [To enclose in a box] confine, package, crate; see PACK 2. 2 [To fight for sport] spar, punch, slug; see FIGHT.

boxer n. pugilist, fighter, prize-fighter; see FIGHTER 1.

boxing n. pugilism, prizefighting, fisticuffs*; see SPORT 3.

boy n. lad, youth, stripling, fellow, schoolboy, youngster, whippersnapper, kid*, junior, little gentleman; see also CHILD.

boycott v. withhold patronage, hold aloof from, ostracize; see AVOID, STRIKE 2.

boyfriend n. young man, beau*, companion, steady*, lover, sweetheart, flame, suitor, paramour, main man*, old man*.

boyhood n. school days, formative period, adolescence; see CHILDHOOD, YOUTH 1.

boyish a. juvenile, youthful, adolescent; see CHILDISH, YOUNG 1.

Boy Scout n. Cub Scout, Explorer, Eagle Scout; see SCOUT 2.

brace n. prop, bolster, stay, support, lever, beam, girder, block, rib, buttress, reinforcement, bearing, truss, bracket, strengthener, band, bracer, stirrup, arm, splint, boom, bar, staff, rafter, jack, crutch.

brace v. prop, bolster, hold up; see SUPPORT 1.

bracelet n. charm bracelet, wristlet, bangle; see JEWELRY.

brag v. swagger, exult, gloat; see BOAST.

braggart n. boaster, blowhard*, windbag*, showoff, swaggerer, strutter, hot dog*, blusterer, bragger, know-it-all*, big talker.

brain n. 1 [The organ of intelligence] cerebrum, gray matter, brain cells; see HEAD 1. 2 [The intelligence] intellect, genius, mentality; see MIND 1. 3 [*A very intelligent person] academician, scholar, egghead*; see INTELLECTUAL. —**have on the brain** be obsessed with, be involved with, fuss over, stew about; see also BOTHER 2.

brainwash* v. indoctrinate, instill, mold; see CONVINCE, INFLUENCE, TEACH.

brake n. check, hamper, curb, deterrent, obstacle, damper, hindrance, restraint, governor.

bramble n. brier, thorn, burr, stinging nettle, prickly shrub, thistle, bramble bush, hedge.

branch n. 1 [A part, usually of secondary importance] subsidiary, outpost, subdivision; see DIVISION 2. 2 [A secondary shoot] bough, limb, offshoot, sprig, twig, bud, arm, fork, growth.

branch off v. diverge, separate, part; see DIVIDE.

branch out v. expand, extend, add to; see GROW 1, INCREASE.

brand n. 1 [A trademark] brand name, make, kind, label, seal, name. 2 [A mark on the body] stigma, scar, sear, welt, range brand, earmark.

brand v. blaze, stamp, imprint; see MARK 1.

brandish v. flourish, gesture, warn; see THREATEN.

brass n. 1 [An alloy of copper and zinc] copper alloy, pinchbeck, brassware, yellow metal. 2 [*High-ranking officials] officers, front office, brass hats*; see OFFICER 3. 3 [*Impudence] effrontery, impertinence, audacity; see RUDENESS.

brat n. impudent child, unruly child, youngster, kid*; see also CHILD.

brave a. fearless, daring, dauntless, valiant, intrepid, undaunted, undismayed, confident, unabashed, chivalrous, valorous, heroic, bold, imprudent, adventurous, reckless, foolhardy, dashing, forward, audacious, gallant, resolute, militant, defiant, hardy, unafraid, stout, stouthearted, lionhearted, manly, firm, plucky, high-spirited, unshrinking, strong, stalwart, unflinching, unyielding, indomitable, game, unconquerable, spunky*, nervy*, gutsy*.—Ant. COWARDLY, timid, craven.

bravely a. courageously, fearlessly, valiantly, boldly, daringly, dauntlessly, intrepidly, heroically, gallantly, hardily, stoutly, manfully, staunchly, with courage, with fortitude, resolutely, valorously, spiritedly, audaciously, chivalrously,

firmly, indomitably, with guts*, like a man*.—Ant. COWARDLY, fearfully, timidly.

bravery n. valor, guts*, fearlessness; see COURAGE, STRENGTH.

brawl n. fracas, squabble, riot; see FIGHT 1.

breach n. violation, infringement, transgression; see CRIME, VIOLATION.

bread n. loaf, baked goods, the staff of life. Types of bread include the following: whole wheat, rye, salt-rising, leavened, unleavened, yeast, quick, corn, sourdough, raisin, French, Italian, white, black, Boston brown, potato, hardtack, flatbread, pita, matzo, pumpernickel, bun, roll, bagel, biscuit, muffin. Breadlike foods include the following: spoon bread, cake, dumpling, turnover, cookie, English muffin, scone, shortbread, Indian bread. —**break bread** partake, have a meal, indulge; see EAT 1. —**know which side one's bread is buttered on** be prudent, save, look out for number one*; see UNDERSTAND 1.

breadth n. largeness, extent, vastness, compass, magnitude, greatness, extensiveness, scope, broadness, width, comprehensiveness, amplitude; see also SIZE 2.

break n. 1 [The act of breaking] fracture, rift, split, schism, cleavage, breach, rupture, eruption, bursting, failure, division, parting, collapse.—Ant. REPAIR, mending, restoration. 2 [A pause] intermission, interim, lapse; see PAUSE. 3 [Fortunate change or event] good luck, advantage, favorable circumstances; see LUCK 1.

break v. 1 [To start a rupture] burst, split, crack, rend, sunder, sever, fracture, tear, cleave, break into, break through, force open, puncture, split, snap, slash, gash, dissect, slice, disjoin, separate; see also CUT. 2 [To shatter] smash, shiver, crash, break up, crush, splinter, pull to pieces, burst, break into pieces, break into smithereens*, fall apart, fall to pieces, collapse, break down, come apart, come unglued, go to wrack and ruin, get wrecked, bust*, split up; see also DISINTEGRATE and sense 1. 3 [To bring to ruin or to an end] demolish, annihilate, eradicate; see DESTROY. 4 [To happen] come to pass, occur, develop; see HAPPEN 2. —**break down** 1 [To analyze] examine, investigate, dissect; see ANALYZE. 2 [To malfunction] fail, stop, falter, misfire, give out, go down, crack up*, cease, backfire, conk out*, peter out*, fizzle out*, collapse, go kaput*, come unglued*, run out of gas*. —**break in** 1 [Train] educate, instruct, prepare; see TEACH. **2** [Intrude] rob, burglarize, trespass; see MEDDLE 2, STEAL. —**break off** end, cease, discontinue; see STOP 2. —**break out 1** [To start] begin, commence, occur; see BEGIN 2. **2** [To escape] burst out, flee, depart; see LEAVE 1. **3** [To erupt] get blemishes, have acne, get a rash, get hives, get pimples. —**break through** penetrate, force a way, intrude; see PENETRATE. —**break up 1** [To scatter] disperse, disband, separate; see DISINTEGRATE, DIVIDE. **2** [To stop] put an end to, halt, terminate; see STOP 2. **3** [To distress] hurt, sadden, wound; see HURT. **4** [*To end relations] discontinue, break off, stop; see END 1.

breakable *a.* fragile, delicate, frail; see WEAK 2.

breakage *n.* harm, wreckage, ruined goods; see DAMAGE 2.

breakdown *n.* collapse, stoppage, disruption; see FAILURE 1.

breakfast *n.* morning meal, first meal of the day, early meal, brunch, continental breakfast; see also MEAL 2.

breaking *a.* bursting, splitting, cracking, rending, sundering, parting, severing, exploding, erupting, shattering, splintering, fracturing, tearing, cleaving, snapping, breaking up, dispersing, separating, smashing, shivering, crashing, splintering, disintegrating, collapsing, caving in, falling, busting*, going to pot.—*Ant.* STRONG, stable, enduring.

breakthrough *n.* discovery, finding, invention; see DISCOVERY.

breakwater *n.* pier, wharf, jetty; see DOCK.

breast *n.* **1** [The forepart of the body above the abdomen] thorax, heart, bosom; see CHEST 2. **2** [An enlarged mammary gland or glands] bosom, chest, teat, tit*, nipple, bust, udder, boob*, jug*, knocker*. —**beat one's breast** repent, humble oneself, be sorry; see APOLOGIZE, REGRET 1. —**make a clean breast of** confess, reveal, expose; see ADMIT 2.

breath *n.* inspiration, expiration, inhalation, exhalation, breathing, gasp, sigh, pant, wheeze. —**catch one's breath** rest, stop, slow down; see PAUSE. —**in the same breath** simultaneously, concurrently, at the same time; see TOGETHER 2. —**out of breath** gasping, choking, out of wind; see BREATHLESS. —**save one's breath*** be quiet, stop talking, never mind; see SHUT UP 1. —**take someone's breath away** thrill, stimulate, invigorate; see EXCITE. —**under one's breath** quietly, in a

whisper, murmuring; see WHISPERING.

breathe *v.* respire, inhale, exhale, draw in, breathe in, breathe out, gasp, pant, wheeze, snort, sigh, huff, puff, scent, sniff.

breathless *a.* out of breath, winded, spent, exhausted, tired, used up, gasping, choking, wheezing, short-winded, puffing, panting, asthmatic, short of breath, out of wind.

breed *n.* strain, variety, kind; see RACE 1.

breed *v.* **1** [To produce] give birth to, deliver, bring forth; see PRODUCE 1. **2** [To cause] bring about, effect, produce; see BEGIN 1.

breeze *n.* draft, gust, blast; see WIND. —**in a breeze*** effortlessly, readily, simply; see EASILY. —**shoot the breeze*** converse, chat, chatter; see TALK 1.

brew *n.* concoction, preparation, distillation, compound, broth, liquor, blend, beer, ale; see also DRINK 1, 2.

brew *v.* concoct, ferment, plot; see COOK.

bribe *n.* fee, reward, hush money, lure, gift, graft, compensation, remuneration, protection, bait, tip, blackmail, price, present, gratuity.

bribe *v.* corrupt, get to, reward, tip, coax, hire, entice, tempt, pervert, lure, buy, influence, buy off, fix*.

brick *n.* cube, chunk, section, block, slab, cinder block, glass block, adobe brick, building brick, paving stone, floor tile; see also STONE.

bridal *a.* nuptial, marriage, wedding, matrimonial, marital, conjugal, wedded.

bride *n.* spouse, mate, partner; see WIFE.

bridegroom *n.* groom, mate, spouse; see HUSBAND.

bridge *n.* **1** [An elevated structure] viaduct, platform, catwalk, gangplank, drawbridge, trestle, aqueduct, scaffold. *Types of bridges include the following:* arch, pier, girder, concrete arch, suspension, cantilever, bascule, pontoon, swing, floating, covered, cable-stayed, steel arch, lift, truss. **2** [A game at cards] contract bridge, auction bridge, duplicate bridge; see GAME 1. **3** [A link] connection, bond, tie; see JOINT 1, LINK.

bridge *v.* connect, span, link; see JOIN 1.

brief *a.* **1** [Abrupt] hasty, curt, blunt; see RUDE 2. **2** [Short in time] short-term, fleeting, concise; see SHORT 2. —**in brief** concisely, to the point, cut short, abbreviated; see also BRIEFLY.

briefing *n.* instruction, training session, orientation; see INTRODUCTION 4, PREPARATION 1.

briefly *a.* shortly, curtly, abruptly, tersely, quickly, hastily, hurriedly, momentarily, fleetingly, suddenly, temporarily, in passing, casually, lightly, briskly, in brief, in outline, in a few words, in a capsule, in a nutshell.

bright *a.* **1** [Shining or vivid] gleaming, shiny, glittering, luminous, lustrous, burnished, polished, sparkling, mirrorlike, glowing, flashing, scintillating, shimmering, incandescent, twinkling, illumined, light, golden, silvery, illuminated, shining, irradiated, glistening, radiant, burning, glaring, beaming, glimmering, splendid, resplendent, brilliant, dazzling, alight; aglow, lighted up, full of light, ablaze, flamelike, moonlit, sunlit, on fire, phosphorescent, blazing, glossy, colored, colorful, tinted, intense, deep, sharp, rich, tinged, hued, touched with color, fresh, clear, ruddy, psychedelic.—*Ant.* DULL, clouded, dark. **2** [Intelligent] clever, quick, alert; see INTELLIGENT. **3** [Not rainy] clear, sunny, mild; see FAIR 3. **4** [Cheerful] lively, vivacious, joyful; see HAPPY.

brighten *v.* **1** [To become brighter] clear up, lighten, grow calm, improve, grow sunny, glow. **2** [To make brighter] polish, intensify, lighten; see SHINE 3.

brightly *a.* lustrously, radiantly, splendidly, brilliantly, dazzlingly, sparklingly, glowingly, gleamingly, shinily, gaily, freshly, vividly, colorfully, cleverly, sunnily.—*Ant.* dully, dingily, darkly.

brightness *n.* shine, luster, illumination; see LIGHT 1.

brilliant *a.* **1** [Shining] dazzling, gleaming, sparkling; see BRIGHT 1. **2** [Showing remarkable ability] ingenious, profound, smart; see INTELLIGENT.

brilliantly *a.* **1** [Very brightly] shiningly, radiantly, blazingly; see BRIGHTLY. **2** [With superior intelligence] cleverly, shrewdly, knowledgeably; see INTELLIGENTLY.

brim *n.* margin, rim, border; see EDGE 1.

bring *v.* **1** [To transport] convey, take along, bear; see CARRY 1, PICK UP 6. **2** [To be worth in sale] sell for, earn, bring in; see PAY 2. **3** [To cause] produce, effect, make; see BEGIN 1. **—bring about 1** [To achieve] do, accomplish, realize; see ACHIEVE, SUCCEED 1. **2** [To cause] produce, effect, do; see BEGIN 1, MANAGE 1. **—bring forth** deliver, bear, yield; see PRODUCE 1, 2. **—bring off** accomplish, realize, execute; see ACHIEVE, SUCCEED 1. **—bring out 1** [To excite] elicit, arouse, evoke; see EXCITE. **2** [To publish] print, issue, put out; see

PUBLISH 1. **3** [To produce a play] present, put on the stage, exhibit; see PERFORM 2. **4** [To intensify] heighten, sharpen, magnify; see EMPHASIZE, INCREASE. **—bring up 1** [To rear] educate, teach, train; see RAISE 2, SUPPORT 3. **2** [To discuss] tender, submit, advance; see DISCUSS, PROPOSE 1.

bringing *n.* fetching, carrying, transporting, accompanying, introducing, shipping, bearing, hauling, bringing in, getting, providing, procuring.

brink *n.* limit, brim, rim; see EDGE 1.

brisk *a.* lively, refreshing, invigorating; see STIMULATING.

briskly *a.* energetically, quickly, brusquely, rapidly, impulsively, nimbly, agilely, dexterously, decisively, firmly, actively, promptly, readily, vigorously, in a lively manner; see also EMPHATICALLY.—*Ant.* SLOWLY, listlessly, sluggishly.

bristle *n.* hair, fiber, quill; see POINT 2.

British *a.* Anglo-Saxon, Celtic, Brit*; see ENGLISH.

brittle *a.* fragile, crisp, inelastic; see WEAK 2.

broad *a.* **1** [Physically wide] deep, extended, large, extensive, ample, spacious, expansive, immense, wide, roomy, outstretched, thick, widespread, full, stocky.—*Ant.* NARROW, thin, slender. **2** [Wide in range] cultivated, experienced, cosmopolitan; see CULTURED. **3** [Tolerant] progressive, open-minded, unbiased; see LIBERAL.

broadcast *n.* program, newscast, telecast; see PERFORMANCE.

broadcast *v.* announce, relay, telephone, send out, telegraph, radio, transmit, televise, telecast, air, put on the air, go on the air, be on the air; see also SEND 2.

broadcasting *n.* radio, announcing, television, airing, telecasting, newscasting, transmitting, reporting, cable television, cable, TV, direct TV, digital television.

broaden *v.* widen, expand, increase; see GROW 1, INCREASE.

broad-minded *a.* tolerant, progressive, unprejudiced; see LIBERAL.

brochure *n.* handout, circular, pamphlet; see ADVERTISEMENT.

broil *v.* sear, bake, roast; see COOK.

broiler *n.* oven, grill, barbecue; see APPLIANCE.

broke* *a.* bankrupt, out of money, indebted; see RUINED 3. **—go for broke*** gamble, wager, risk everything; see RISK. **—go broke*** become bankrupt, lose everything, be reduced to poverty; see FAIL 4, LOSE 2.

broken *a.* **1** [Fractured] shattered,

hurt, ruptured, burst, splintered, smashed, in pieces, collapsed, destroyed, pulverized, crumbled, mutilated, bruised, injured, damaged, rent, split, cracked, mangled, dismembered, fragmentary, disintegrated, crippled, shredded, crushed, gashed, defective, busted*.—*Ant.* WHOLE, intact, sound. **2** [Not functioning properly] defective, inoperable, in need of repair, in disrepair, out of order, busted*, gone to pot*, screwed up*, shot*, gone haywire*, on the fritz*, on the blink*, gone to pieces, out of whack*, out of commission; see also FAULTY. **3** [Discontinuous] spasmodic, erratic, intermittent; see IRREGULAR 1, 4. **4** [Incoherent; *said of speech*] muttered, unintelligible, mumbled; see INCOHERENT.

broken-down *a.* shattered, dilapidated, battered; see OLD 2.

brokenhearted *a.* despondent, crushed, grieved; see SAD 1.

brood *n.* flock, offspring, young; see FAMILY, HERD.

brood *v.* **1** [To hatch] set, cover, incubate, warm, sit; see also PRODUCE 1. **2** [To nurse one's troubles] think, meditate, grieve, fret, sulk, mope, ponder, consider, muse, deliberate, dwell upon, speculate, daydream, reflect, dream, agonize, ruminate, chafe inwardly, give oneself over to reflections, mull over, eat one's heart out; see also WORRY 2.

brook *n.* creek, stream, streamlet; see RIVER.

broom *n.* sweeper, carpet sweeper, whisk broom, mop, feather duster.

broth *n.* brew, concoction, soup, consommé, purée, bouillon, stock, chowder, gumbo, porridge, borscht, vichyssoise; see also FOOD, SOUP.

brotherhood *n.* fellowship, equality, kinship, intimacy, relationship, affiliation, association, society, fraternity, family, race, comradeship, camaraderie, friendship, amity.

brotherly *a.* kindly, humane, sympathetic; see FRIENDLY, KIND, LOVING.

browbeat *v.* bully, intimidate, frighten; see THREATEN.

brown *n.* Shades and tints of brown include the following: tan, bay, chestnut, nutbrown, copper-colored, mahogany, bronze, russet, chocolate, cinnamon, hazel, reddish-brown, sorrel, sepia, tawny, ochre, rust-colored, rust, brownish, puce, fawn, liver-colored, beige, dust, drab, coffee, khaki, maroon, cocoa, umber, brick, ginger, light brown, dark brown, auburn, buff; see also COLOR.

brown *v.* toast, scorch, sauté; see COOK, FRY.

browse *v.* skim, peruse, scan, glance at, look through, run through, flip through, look over, survey, inspect loosely, examine cursorily, glance over, check over, run over, go through carelessly, dip into, leaf through, thumb through.

bruise *n.* abrasion, wound, swelling; see BLEMISH.

bruise *v.* beat, injure, wound; see DAMAGE, HURT.

brunet *a.* dark, tawny, dusky, brown, tanned, swarthy, dark-complexioned, dark-haired, dark-skinned, Latin, Mediterranean.—*Ant.* FAIR, light-skinned, light-complexioned.

brush *n.* **1** [A brushing instrument] *Varieties include the following:* bristle, nail, clothes, rotary, paint, tooth, scrubbing, floor, toilet, hair, wire, scrub. **2** [A touch] rub, tap, stroke; see TOUCH 2. **3** [Underbrush] bush, thicket, undergrowth, secondary growth, chaparral, cover, brushwood, shrubbery, canebrake, hedge, fern, underwood, scrub, brake, sedge.

brush *v.* **1** [To cleanse by brushing] sweep, whisk, wipe; see CLEAN. **2** [To touch lightly] stroke, smooth, graze; see TOUCH 1.

brush up on *v.* reread, look over again, review; see STUDY.

brutal *a.* pitiless, harsh, unmerciful; see CRUEL.

brutality *n.* savageness, ruthlessness, harshness; see CRUELTY.

brutally *a.* ruthlessly, cruelly, callously, relentlessly, mercilessly, heartlessly, grimly, viciously, meanly, inhumanly, inhumanely, brutishly, savagely, pitilessly, barbarously, remorselessly, unkindly, wildly, fiercely, hardheartedly, murderously, ferociously, animalistically, demoniacally, diabolically, barbarically, in cold blood.—*Ant.* NICELY, kindly, gently.

bubble *n.* sac, air bubble, balloon, foam, froth, spume, effervescence, lather.

bubble *v.* froth, gurgle, gush, well, trickle, effervesce, boil, percolate, simmer, seep, eddy, ferment, erupt, issue, fester.

bucket *n.* pail, canister, can; see CONTAINER, POT 1. —**kick the bucket*** expire, lose one's life, pass away; see DIE 1.

buckle *n.* clasp, harness, fastening; see FASTENER.

buckle down *v.* apply oneself, attend to, keep one's mind on; see CONCENTRATE 2.

buck up* *v.* comfort, hearten, cheer; see ENCOURAGE.

bud *n.* shoot, embryo, germ; see FLOWER. —**nip in the bud** check, halt, stop; see PREVENT.

budding *a.* maturing, developing,

opening, blossoming, bursting forth, putting forth shoots, burgeoning, flowering, fresh, pubescent, blooming, promising, young, sprouting, germinating, aspiring, latent, embryonic, in bud; see also GROWING.

buddy* *n.* peer, companion, pal*; see ASSOCIATE, FRIEND.

budge *v.* stir, change position, shift; see MOVE 1.

budget *n.* estimates, estimated expenses, allocations, accounts, financial statement, financial plan, cost of operation, funds; see also ESTIMATE.

budget *v.* allocate expenditures, balance income and expenses, forecast, allow for, figure in, plan, estimate necessary expenditures; see also ESTIMATE.

bug *n.* 1 [An insect] beetle, pest, gnat; see INSECT. 2 [*A microbe] pathogen, microorganism, virus; see GERM. 3 [*A defect] flaw, fault, imperfection; see BLEMISH, DEFECT. 4 [*An enthusiast] devotee, zealot, fanatic; see FOLLOWER.

bug* *v.* 1 [To annoy] irritate, plague, pester; see BOTHER 2, DISTURB. 2 [To install hidden microphones] spy, overhear, listen in on, wiretap, tap; see also EAVESDROP.

build *v.* create, form, erect, frame, raise, make, construct, manufacture, put together, fit together, fabricate, contrive, assemble, put up, model, contrive, assemble, put up, model, hammer together, set up, reconstruct, mold, sculpture, fashion, compose, evolve, compile, cast, produce, forge, bring about, devise, carve, weave.—*Ant.* DESTROY, demolish, wreck. —**build up** 1 [To increase] strengthen, add to, expand; see INCREASE. 2 [To construct] make, erect, establish; see BUILD.

building *n.* edifice, construction, fabrication, house, framework, superstructure, structure, palace, mansion, apartment house, barn, castle, church, factory, home, hotel, motel, skyscraper, temple, office building, mosque, mall, store, school, stadium, arena; see also ARCHITECTURE.

built *a.* constructed, fabricated, manufactured, made, put together, produced, assembled, contrived, remodeled, completed, established, perfected, finished, realized, created; see also FORMED.

bulb *n.* globe, globule, light bulb, ball, knob, corn, tuber, protuberance, head, bunch, swelling, tumor, nodule.

bulge *n.* swelling, bunch, lump, protuberance, hump, bump, bulb, outgrowth, protrusion, nodule, sagging, growth, prominence, excess, bagginess, appendage, projection, tumor, egg, sac, knob, horn, ridge, wart, promontory.

bulge *v.* puff out, distend, protrude; see SWELL.

bulk *n.* greater part, main part, predominant part, better part, most, majority, plurality, biggest share, greater number, nearly all, body, more than half, best, gross, lion's share.—*Ant.* BIT, remnant, fraction.

bulky *a.* massive, big, huge; see HIGH 1, LARGE 1, LONG 1.

bull *n.* 1 [The male of various cattle] steer, ox, bullock; see COW. 2 [*Nonsense] balderdash, rubbish, trash; see NONSENSE 1.

bullet *n.* shell, cartridge, ball, projectile, missile, piece of ammunition, dumdum, slug, ammo*; see also SHOT 1.

bulletin *n.* release, notice, communiqué; see ANNOUNCEMENT.

bully *n.* ruffian, rowdy, tough; see RASCAL.

bully *v.* tease, domineer, harass; see THREATEN.

bum *n.* hobo, tramp, vagrant; see BEGGAR.

bump *n.* 1 [A jarring collision] knock, bang, bounce, jar, box, smash, pat, crack, jolt, crash, sideswipe, punch, hit, clap, push, shove, thrust, boost, shock, clash, impact, stroke, rap, tap, slap, clout, jab, jerk, crash, prod, slam, nudge, buffet, swat, bash*, wallop*, belt*, bat*, swipe*, thump, whack, poke*, clunk*, sock*, whop*, lick*, smack, cuff, slug*. 2 [A swelling] projection, protuberance, knob; see BULGE, LUMP.

bump *v.* 1 [To collide with] collide, run against, strike; see CRASH 4, HIT 1. 2 [To make a bumping sound] thud, whack, smack; see SOUND.

bumper *n.* cover, guard, protector; see DEFENSE 2, FENDER.

bun *n.* muffin, biscuit, roll; see BREAD, ROLL 4, PASTRY.

bunch *n.* clump, group, batch, spray, sheaf, tuft, shock, stack, thicket, group, gathering, host, galaxy, bundle, knot, accumulation, collection, mess, bouquet, oodles*.

bundle *n.* packet, parcel, pack; see PACKAGE.

bungle *v.* blunder, fumble, mishandle; see BOTCH, FAIL 1.

bungler *n.* fumbler, lout, blunderer, flounderer, muddler, numskull, featherbrain, dolt, scatterbrain, dunce, clod, ignoramus, idiot, duffer, addlebrain, butterfingers, bonehead*, blockhead, goof-off*, clumsy oaf, bull in a china shop*, harebrain*, klutz*, knucklehead*, dork*, airhead*.

bungling *a.* clumsy, unskillful, inept; see AWKWARD, INCOMPETENT.

bunk *n.* **1** [A bed] berth, cot, mattress; see BED 1. **2** [*Anything untrue, silly, or unreliable] rubbish, rot, hogwash; see NONSENSE 1.

buoy *n.* pontoon, channel marker, life preserver; see FLOAT.

burden *n.* **1** [Something carried] cargo, freight, pack; see LOAD 1. **2** [Anything hard to support or endure] encumbrance, punishment, misery; see DIFFICULTY 2, MISFORTUNE.

burden *v.* weigh down, force, hinder, encumber, overwhelm, hamper, strain, load with, lade, saddle with, handicap, obligate, tax, afflict, vex, try, trouble, pile, bog down, crush, depress, impede, overload, oppress, make heavy, press down.—*Ant.* LIGHTEN, relieve, unload.

burdensome *a.* heavy, oppressive, troublesome; see DIFFICULT 1, 2, DISTURBING.

bureau *n.* **1** [Committee] commission, authority, board; see COMMITTEE. **2** [Chest of drawers] highboy, dresser, cabinet; see CHEST 1, FURNITURE.

bureaucracy *n.* the Establishment, the authorities, the system; see GOVERNMENT 1, 2.

burglar *n.* thief, housebreaker, robber; see CRIMINAL.

burglary *n.* housebreaking, stealing, robbery; see CRIME, THEFT.

burial *n.* last rites, interment, entombment; see FUNERAL.

burn *n.* scorch, singe, scald; see BLISTER.

burn *v.* ignite, kindle, incinerate, burn up, burn down, blaze, flame, flare, burst into flame, rage, consume, enkindle, cremate, consume with flames, set a match to, set on fire, set ablaze, set afire, sear, singe, scorch, brand, fire, light, torch, char, roast, toast, heat, bake; see also COOK.—*Ant.* EXTINGUISH, put out, quench.

burned *a.* scorched, charred, seared, burnt, singed, branded, cauterized, marked, blistered, scalded. — **burned up*** angered, enraged, infuriated; see ANGRY.

burning *a.* fiery, blazing, glowing, ablaze, afire, on fire, smoking, in flames, aflame, inflamed, kindled, enkindled, ignited, scorching, turning to ashes, searing, in a blaze, blistering, red-hot, white-hot, roasting; see also PASSIONATE 2.—*Ant.* COLD, frozen, out.

burnt *a.* scorched, singed, charred; see BURNED.

burst *n.* **1** [An explosion] blowout, blast, blowup; see EXPLOSION. **2** [A

sudden spurt] rush, outburst, torrent; see FIT 2.

burst *v.* **1** [To explode] blow up, erupt, rupture; see BREAK 2, DISINTEGRATE, EXPLODE. **2** [To break] crack, split, fracture; see BREAK 1, DESTROY. —**burst into tears** weep, start crying, sob; see CRY 1.

bury *v.* **1** [To inter] lay in the grave, entomb, enshrine, deposit in the earth, to give burial to, embalm, hold funeral services for, hold last rites for, lay out. **2** [To cover] conceal, mask, stow away; see HIDE 1. **3** [To defeat] overcome, win over, conquer; see DEFEAT 2, 3.

bus *n.* coach, minibus, school bus, shuttle bus, sightseeing bus, common carrier, public conveyance, Greyhound (trademark).

bus *v.* transport, ship, convey; see CARRY.

bush *n.* shrub, bramble, thicket, hedge, shrubbery, briar bush, rose bush; see also PLANT. —**beat around the bush** speak evasively, avoid the subject, be deceptive; see EVADE.

bushy *a.* fuzzy, disordered, thick, shaggy, rough, full, tufted, fringed, woolly, nappy, fluffy, furry, crinkly, stiff, wiry, rumpled, prickly, feathery, leafy, bristly, heavy, hairy.—*Ant.* THIN, sleek, smooth.

busily *a.* diligently, actively, energetically, strenuously, eagerly, earnestly, seriously, intently, rapidly, dexterously, industriously, carefully, intently, studiously, hurriedly, briskly, purposefully, ardently, arduously, fervently, nimbly, zealously, vigorously, restlessly, enthusiastically, speedily, hastily, persistently, like hell*.—*Ant.* SLOWLY, listlessly, idly.

business *n.* **1** [Industry and trade] commerce, exchange, trade, traffic, barter, commercial enterprise, gainful occupation, buying and selling, negotiation, production and distribution, dealings, affairs, sales, contracts, transaction, bargaining, trading, banking, marketing, undertaking, speculation, market, mercantilism, wholesale and retail, capital and labor, free enterprise, game*, racket*, wheeling and dealing*. **2** [Occupation] trade, profession, vocation; see JOB 1. **3** [A person's proper concerns] affair, concern, interest; see AFFAIR 1. **4** [A commercial enterprise] firm, factory, mill, store, company, shop, corporation, concern, combine, conglomerate, cooperative, establishment, enterprise, partnership, institution, house, market, syndicate, cartel, trust, monopoly, holding company, consortium. —**do business with** deal with, trade with, patronize; see BUY, SELL, TREAT 1. — **get the business*** be mistreated, be abused, endure; see SUFFER 1. — **give the business*** mistreat, bother, victimize; see ABUSE. —**mean business*** be serious, stress, impress; see EMPHASIZE.

businesslike *a.* purposeful, systematic, methodical; see PRACTICAL.

businessman *n.* businesswoman, industrialist, capitalist, employer, tycoon, broker, retailer, stockbroker, manager, buyer, operator, backer, financier, systems expert, comptroller, accountant, investor, speculator, entrepreneur, purchasing agent, storekeeper, tradesman; see also EXECUTIVE.

busy *a.* 1 [Engaged] occupied, diligent, industrious, employed, working, in conference, in a meeting, in the field, in the laboratory, on an assignment, on duty, on the job, at work, busy with, on the run, on the road, hard-working, busy as a bee*, hustling*, up to one's ears*, hard at it*.—*Ant.* IDLE, unemployed, unoccupied. 2 [In use] employed, occupied, taken; see RENTED.

busybody *n.* meddler, tattletale, troublemaker; see GOSSIP 2.

but *conj., prep.* 1 [Indicating contrast] however, on the other hand, in contrast, nevertheless, still, yet, though, on the contrary, but then, but as you see; see also ALTHOUGH. 2 [Indicating an exception] save, disregarding, without, not including, not taking into account, let alone, aside from, with the exception of, not to mention, passing over, barring, setting aside, forgetting; see also EXCEPT. 3 [Indicating a limitation] only, merely, simply, barely, solely, purely, just, no more, exactly, no other than, without; see also ONLY 1.

butcher *v.* 1 [To slaughter for human consumption] carve, pack, dress, clean, cure, smoke, salt, cut, trim. 2 [To kill inhumanly] slaughter, slay, massacre; see KILL 1. 3 [To ruin] mess up, spoil, wreck; see BOTCH, DESTROY.

butt *n.* base, tail end, bottom, hilt, extremity, tail, tip, fundament, stump, rump, bottom, seat, posterior; see also BOTTOM.

butt *v.* hit, ram, push headfirst,

bump, batter, knock, collide with, run into, smack, strike, gore, buck, toss, crash into.

butter *n.* *Varieties of butter include the following:* creamery, sweet, dairy, cube, tub, vegetable, salted, unsalted.

button *n.* knob, catch, disk; see FASTENER. —**on the button*** correctly, precisely, accurately; see RIGHT 1.

button *v.* close, clasp, snap; see FASTEN.

buy* *n.* value, good deal, steal*; see BARGAIN 2.

buy *v.* purchase, get, bargain for, procure, gain, contract for, sign for, get in exchange, go marketing, buy and sell, order, invest in, make an investment, shop for, acquire ownership of, procure title to, pay for, redeem, pay a price for, buy into, score*. —**buy off** corrupt, influence, fix*; see BRIBE.

buyer *n.* purchasing agent, purchaser, customer, client, prospect, consumer, representative, patron, user, shopper.—*Ant.* SELLER, vendor, dealer.

buying *n.* purchasing, getting, obtaining, acquiring, paying, investing, exchange, bartering, bargaining, procuring, trafficking.—*Ant.* SELLING, vending, auctioning.

buzz *n.* murmur, buzzing, hum; see NOISE 1.

buzz *v.* drone, hum, whir; see SOUND.

buzzer *n.* siren, signal, bell; see ALARM, WARNING, WHISTLE 1.

by *prep.* 1 [Near] close to, next to, nigh; see NEAR 1, NEXT 2. 2 [By stated means] over, with, through, by means of, in the name of, at the hand of, along with, through the medium of, with the assistance of, with the aid of, on, supported by.

bylaw *n.* ordinance, local law, regulation; see LAW 3.

bypass *n.* detour, temporary route, side road; see ROAD 1.

bypass *v.* miss, evade, detour around; see AVOID.

bystander *n.* onlooker, watcher, spectator; see OBSERVER.

C

cab *n.* taxi, taxicab, hack*; see AUTOMOBILE, VEHICLE.

cabin *n.* log house, cottage, hut; see HOME 1, SHELTER.

cabinet *n.* council, advisory council, authority, bureaucracy, committee, bureau, governing body, adminis-

trators, assembly, assistants, department heads, advisors, United States Cabinet, ministry, shadow cabinet, backstairs cabinet, brain trust; see also GOVERNMENT 2.

cable *n.* cord, preformed cable, wire twist; see CHAIN, WIRE 1.

cackle *v.* chuckle, snicker, giggle; see LAUGH.

cactus *n. Cactuses include the following:* giant, saguaro, barrel, cholla, hedgehog, cochineal, nipple, night-blooming cereus, century plant, prickly pear, mescal; see also PLANT.

cad *n.* rogue, scoundrel, rake; see RASCAL.

cadence *n.* rhythm, meter, flow; see BEAT 2, MEASURE 3.

cafe *n.* cafeteria, lunchroom, coffee shop; see RESTAURANT.

cage *n.* coop, jail, crate; see ENCLOSURE 1, PEN 1.

cake *n.* **1** [A flattish, compact mass] cube, bar, loaf; see BLOCK 1. **2** [Sweet baked goods] *Kinds of cake include the following:* wedding, birthday, angel food, devil's-food, corn, caramel, German chocolate, upside-down, Martha Washington, maple, orange, white, yellow, chocolate, carrot, Bundt (trademark), lemon, walnut, almond, layer, spice, marble, Lady Baltimore cake; spongecake, fruitcake, poundcake, torte, cheesecake, cupcake, Boston cream pie, coffeecake, jellyroll, gingerbread, shortbread; see also BREAD, PASTRY. —**take the cake*** excel, outdo, win the prize; see EXCEED.

cake *v.* crust, solidify, pack; see FREEZE 1, HARDEN, THICKEN.

calamity *n.* cataclysm, distress, trial; see CATASTROPHE, DISASTER, MISFORTUNE, TRAGEDY 1.

calculate *v.* count, measure, reckon, enumerate, determine, rate, forecast, weigh, gauge, number, figure, figure up, account, compute, sum up, divide, multiply, subtract, add, work out, cipher, tally, dope out*; see also ESTIMATE.

calculation *n.* **1** [The act of calculating] adding, totaling, count; see ESTIMATE. **2** [A forecast] prediction, divination, prognostication; see FORECAST.

calendar *n.* list, program, record, timetable, schedule, annals, journal, diary, daybook, chronology, log, logbook, table, register, almanac, agenda, itinerary, docket; see also ALMANAC.

calf *n.* young cow, young bull, yearling; see COW.

calisthenics *n.* exercises, workout, aerobics; see EXERCISE 1, GYMNASTICS.

call *n.* **1** [A shout] yell, whoop, hail; see ALARM, CRY 1. **2** [Characteristic sound] twitter, tweet, shriek; see CRY 2. **3** [A brief visit] visiting, a few words, stop; see VISIT. **4** [Word of command] summons, battle cry, reveille; see ALARM, COMMAND, CRY 1. **5** [An invitation] bidding, solicitation, proposal; see INVITATION, REQUEST. —**on call** usable, ready, prepared; see AVAILABLE. —**within call** close by, approximate, not far away; see NEAR 1.

call *v.* **1** [To raise the voice] shout, call out, exclaim; see YELL. **2** [To bring a body of people together] collect, convene, muster; see ASSEMBLE 2. **3** [To address or label as] denominate, designate, term; see NAME 1. **4** [To invite] summon, request, ask; see INVITE. —**call down*** rebuke, chide, admonish; see SCOLD. —**call for** **1** [To ask] ask for, request, make inquiry about; see ASK. **2** [To need] require, want, demand; see NEED. **3** [To come to get] come for, collect, fetch; see GET 1, PICK UP 6. —**call in** [To collect] collect, remove, receive; see WITHDRAW. —**call off** cancel, postpone, cease; see HALT, STOP 2. —**call on** (or **upon**) stop in, have an appointment with, go to see; see VISIT. —**call up** **1** [To remember] recollect, recall, summon up; see REMEMBER 1. **2** [To summon] send for, bid, order; see INVITE, SUMMON. **3** [To telephone] phone, call, ring; see TELEPHONE.

called *a.* christened, termed, labeled; see NAMED 1.

calling *n.* occupation, vocation, work; see JOB 1, PROFESSION 1, TRADE 2.

callous *a.* unfeeling, hardened, insensitive; see INDIFFERENT.

calm *a.* **1** [Said especially of persons] dignified, reserved, cool, composed, collected, unmoved, levelheaded, coolheaded, impassive, detached, aloof, unconcerned, disinterested, unhurried, neutral, gentle, sedate, serene, unanxious, unexcited, contented, meek, satisfied, pleased, amiable, temperate, placid, civil, kind, moderate, confident, poised, tranquil, self-possessed, restful, relaxed, dispassionate, mild, still, patient, self-controlled, untroubled, cool as a cucumber, unflappable*; see also RESERVED 3, PATIENT 1.—*Ant.* VIOLENT, excited, furious. **2** [Said often of things] quiet, undisturbed, unruffled, comfortable, moderate, in order, soothing, at peace, placid, smooth, still, restful, harmonious, peaceful, pacific, balmy, waveless, windless, serene, motionless, slow; see also QUIET.—*Ant.* ROUGH, agitated, aroused. —**keep calm** take one's time, keep cool, be patient; see CALM DOWN, RELAX.

calm *n.* **1** [Peace] stillness, peacefulness, quiet; see PEACE 2, REST 1, SILENCE 1. **2** [Composure] serenity, tranquillity, peace of mind; see COMPOSURE, PATIENCE 1, RESTRAINT 1.

calm *v.* tranquilize, soothe, pacify; see QUIET 1. —**calm down** compose oneself, control oneself, calm oneself, keep oneself under control, keep cool, take it easy*, get organized, rest, get hold of oneself, cool it*, cool off, cool down, simmer down, keep one's shirt on*; see also RELAX.

calmly *a.* quietly, unexcitedly, tranquilly, unconcernedly, serenely, confidently, sedately, collectedly, composedly, placidly, smoothly, restfully, motionlessly, peacefully, naturally, comfortably, unhurried, without anxiety, without fuss, dully; see also EASILY, EVENLY.—*Ant.* EXCITEDLY, agitatedly, disturbed.

calmness *n.* quietness, tranquillity, calm; see COMPOSURE, PATIENCE 1, PEACE 2.

calumny *n.* slander, defamation, detraction; see LIE.

camera *n. Kinds of cameras include the following:* cinecamera, X-ray machine, microcamera, photomicroscope, photostat, spectrograph, motion-picture, television, TV, minicam, video, camcorder, press, movie, film, flash, still, electron-diffraction, box, stereo, zoom-lens, Polaroid (trademark), single-lens reflex, double-lens reflex, spectroscopic, telescopic.

camouflage *n.* dissimulation, deceit, masquerade, simulation, cloak, shade, shroud, veil, blackout, masking, paint, netting; see also DISGUISE, SCREEN 1.

camouflage *v.* cover, conceal, veil; see DECEIVE, DISGUISE, HIDE 1.

camp *n.* **1** [A temporary living place] camping ground, campground, campsite, encampment, tents, bivouac, tent city, wigwams, tepees, wickiups. **2** [Temporary living quarters] tent, lean-to, cottage, tilt, shack, hut, lodge, cabin, chalet, shed, log house, summer home, cottage. —**break camp** dismantle, depart, pack up; see LEAVE 1.

camp *v.* bivouac, stop over, make camp, encamp, dwell, nest, locate, pitch camp, pitch a tent, tent, quarter, lodge, sleep out, station, put up for the night, camp out, rough it, sleep under the stars.

campaign *n.* operations, crusade, warfare; see ATTACK, FIGHT.

campaign *v.* crusade, electioneer, run, agitate, contend for, contest, canvass for, solicit votes, lobby, barnstorm, mend fences, go to the grass roots, stump, beat the bushes*, whistle-stop; see also COMPETE.

campus *n.* seat of learning, buildings and grounds, school grounds, physical plant, alma mater, academia, quad; see also COLLEGE, UNIVERSITY.

can *n.* **1** [A container] tin can, tin (British), canister, receptacle, package, jar, bottle, quart can, bucket, gallon can, vessel; see also CONTAINER. **2** [*Jail] prison, penitentiary, stir*; see JAIL. **3** [*A toilet] lavatory, restroom, washroom; see TOILET.

can *v.* **1** [To preserve] bottle, put up, keep; see PRESERVE 3. **2** [To be able] could, may, be capable of, be equal to, be up to, have in one's power to, have within one's control, manage, can do, take care of, make it*, make the grade.

canal *n.* waterway, trench, ditch; see CHANNEL, WATER 2.

cancel *v.* repudiate, nullify, ignore, invalidate, suppress, countermand, call off, set aside, rule out, refute, rescind, remove, repeal, counteract, recall, retract, abrogate, discharge, void, make void, put an end to, abort, offset, revoke, overthrow, scratch, drop; see also ABOLISH.—*Ant.* SUSTAIN, approve, uphold.

cancellation *n.* cancelling, annulment, nullification, abrogation, dissolution, invalidation, revocation, repudiation, repeal, abolition, retraction, reversal, voiding, recall, overruling, withdrawing, abandoning, undoing; see also REMOVAL.

cancer *n.* growth, tumor, malignancy; see GROWTH 3, ILLNESS 2.

cancerous *a.* carcinogenic, virulent, mortal; see HARMFUL.

candid *a.* straightforward, sincere, open; see FRANK, HONEST 1.

candidate *n.* aspirant, possible choice, nominee, applicant, political contestant, office-seeker, successor, competitor, bidder, solicitor, petitioner; see also CONTESTANT.

candle *n.* taper, rush, torch; see LIGHT 3. —**burn the candle at both ends** dissipate, squander, use up; see WASTE 1, 2. —**not hold a candle to** be unequal to, not measure up to, be inferior to; see FAIL 1.

candlestick *n.* candelabrum, candelabra, taper holder, flat candlestick, menorah, candleholder.

candy *n.* confection, confectionery, sweetmeat, bonbon. *Varieties of candy include the following:* caramel, taffy, saltwater taffy, licorice, fondant, jelly bean, chocolate bar, fudge, cream, lemon drop, cotton candy, nougat, peanut brittle, praline, fruit roll, marshmallow, Turkish delight, lollipop, halvah, marzipan, gumdrop, divinity, toffee, after-dinner mint, butterscotch, peppermint stick, hard candy, sucker, rock candy, sourball, jawbreaker; bubble gum.

cane *n.* walking stick, staff, pole; see STICK.

canned *a.* bottled, conserved, sealed; see PRESERVED 2.

cannon *n. Types of cannon include the following:* self-propelled, muzzleloading, breech-loading, tank destroyer, turret, mountain, siege, coast defense, field, antiaircraft, railway, antitank gun, knee mortar, recoilless rifle, howitzer.

canoe *n.* kayak, dugout, outrigger; see BOAT.

canon *n.* decree, rule, church law; see COMMAND, DECLARATION, LAW 3.

canonize *v.* sanctify, saint, beatify; see BLESS, LOVE 1, WORSHIP.

canopy *n.* awning, sunshade, umbrella; see COVER 1.

canteen *n.* jug, flask, water supply; see BOTTLE, CONTAINER.

canvas *n.* **1** [A coarse cloth] tenting, awning cloth, sailcloth, duck, coarse cloth; see also CLOTH. **2** [Anything made of canvas] sail, awning, tarpaulin; see COVER 1, TENT. **3** [A painting on canvas] portrait, still life, oil; see ART, PAINTING 1.

canyon *n.* gulch, gorge, gully; see RAVINE, VALLEY.

cap *n.* beret, skullcap, tam-o'-shanter; see HAT.

capability *n.* capacity, skill, aptitude; see ABILITY, INCLINATION 1.

capable *a.* proficient, competent, fitted; see ABLE, INTELLIGENT.

capacity *n.* contents, limit, space, room, size, volume, holding power, extent, compass, magnitude, spread, expanse, scope, latitude, bulk, dimensions, measure, range, quantity, size, reach, holding ability, sweep, proportions, mass, sufficiency.

cape *n.* **1** [Land jutting into the water] headland, peninsula, foreland, point, promontory, jetty, head, tongue, neck of land, ness, mole, finger, arm. **2** [An overgarment] cloak, wrapper, mantilla, mantle, shawl, wrap, overdress, poncho; see also COAT 1.

caper *n.* prank, trick, escapade; see JOKE.

caper *v.* frolic, gambol, cavort; see PLAY 1, 2.

capital *n.* **1** [A seat of government] metropolis, principal city, capitol; see CENTER 2, CITY. **2** [Money and property] cash, assets, interests; see ESTATE, PROPERTY 1, WEALTH. **3** [A letter usually used initially] initial, uppercase, majuscule; see LETTER 1.

capitalism *n.* capitalistic system, free enterprise, private ownership; see DEMOCRACY, ECONOMICS, GOVERNMENT 2.

capitalist *n.* entrepreneur, investor, landowner; see BANKER, BUSINESSMAN, FINANCIER.

capitol *n.* statehouse, state capitol, seat of government; see CENTER 2.

capitulate *v.* surrender, submit, give up; see YIELD 1.

capsize *v.* overturn, invert, tip over; see UPSET 1.

caption *n.* inscription, title, subtitle; see HEADING.

captive *a.* restrained, incarcerated, jailed; see BOUND 1, 2, RESTRICTED.

captive *n.* hostage, convict, POW; see PRISONER.

captivity *n.* imprisonment, jail, restraint, slavery, bondage, subjection, servitude, duress, detention, incarceration, enslavement, constraint, the guardhouse, custody; see also CONFINEMENT.—*Ant.* FREEDOM, liberty, independence.

capture *n.* capturing, arrest, recovery, seizing, taking, seizure, acquisition, obtaining, securing, gaining, winning, occupation, appropriation, ensnaring, abduction, laying hold of, grasping, catching, trapping, commandeering, apprehending, confiscation, apprehension, taking into custody, fall.—*Ant.* RESCUE, liberation, setting free.

capture *v.* seize, take, apprehend; see ARREST, SEIZE 2.

captured *a.* taken, seized, arrested, apprehended, detained, grasped, overtaken, grabbed, snatched, kidnapped, abducted, netted, hooked, secured, collared*, nabbed*, bagged*; see also UNDER ARREST.—*Ant.* RELEASED, unbound, loosed.

car *n.* auto, motorcar, wheels*; see AUTOMOBILE, VEHICLE. *Types of cars include the following:* passenger car, limousine, sedan, hardtop, compact, subcompact, sports car, coupe, roadster, convertible, ragtop*, town car, ranch wagon, station wagon, taxicab, squad car, prowl car, staff car, saloon (British), SUV.

carcass *n.* corpse, cadaver, remains; see BODY 2.

card *n.* cardboard, ticket, sheet, square, Bristol board, fiberboard. *Varieties of cards include the following:* poster, window card, show card, ticket, label, badge, tally, check, billet, voucher, pass; calling card, playing card, fortunetelling cards, tarot cards, address card, visiting card, credit card, bank card, greeting card, registration card, filing card, index card, check-cashing card, FOP card, social security card, identification card, ID card; see also PAPER 1. —**in the cards** probable, predicted, possible; see LIKELY 1. —**put one's**

cards on the table reveal, tell the truth, expose; see ADMIT 2.

care *n.* 1 [Careful conduct] heed, concern, caution, consideration, regard, thoughtfulness, forethought, attention, precaution, wariness, vigilance, watchfulness, watching, diligence, nicety, pains, application, conscientiousness, thought, discrimination, exactness, exactitude, watch, concentration; see also ATTENTION, PRUDENCE.— *Ant.* CARELESSNESS, neglect, negligence. 2 [Worry] concern, anxiety, distress; see WORRY 2. 3 [Custody] supervision, administration, keeping; see CUSTODY. 4 [A cause of worry] problem, care, concern; see DISASTER, MISFORTUNE. —**take care** be careful, be cautious, beware, heed; see also MIND 3, WATCH OUT. —**take care of** protect, attend to, be responsible for; see GUARD.

care *v.* 1 [To be concerned] attend, take pains, regard; see CONSIDER. 2 [To be careful] look out for, be on guard, watch out; see MIND 3. —**care about** cherish, be fond of, hold dear; see LIKE 2, LOVE 1. —**care for** 1 [To look after] provide for, attend to, nurse; see RAISE 2, SUPPORT 3. 2 [To like] be fond of, hold dear, prize; see LIKE 2, LOVE 1. —**care to** prefer, desire, wish; see LIKE 1, WANT 1.

career *n.* occupation, vocation, work; see JOB 1, PROFESSION 1.

carefree *a.* lighthearted, cheerful, jovial; see HAPPY, CALM 1.

careful *a.* thorough, concerned, deliberate, conservative, prudent, meticulous, particular, rigorous, fussy, finicky, prim, exacting, wary, sober, vigilant, watchful, suspicious, alert, wide-awake, scrupulous, religious, hard to please, discriminating, sure-footed, precise, painstaking, exact, on one's guard, on the alert, conscientious, attentive, calculating, mindful, cautious, guarded, considerate, shy, circumspect, discreet, noncommittal, self-possessed, cool, calm, self-disciplined, solid, farsighted, frugal, thrifty, stealthy, observant, on guard, apprehensive, leery, choosy*, picky*, feeling one's way, seeing how the land lies, going to great lengths.—*Ant.* CARELESS, heedless, haphazard.

carefully *a.* 1 [Scrupulously] conscientiously, exactly, rigidly, correctly, strictly, precisely, minutely, painstakingly, faithfully, honorably, attentively, rigorously, providently, deliberately, reliably, particularly, solicitously, concernedly, meticulously, laboriously, thoroughly, dependably, in detail.—*Ant.* haphazardly, neglectfully, indifferently. 2 [Cautiously] prudently, discreetly, watchfully; see CAUTIOUSLY.

careless *a.* loose, lax, remiss, unguarded, incautious, forgetful, unthinking, unobservant, reckless, unheeding, indiscreet, inadvertent, unconcerned, wasteful, regardless, imprudent, unconsidered, hasty, inconsiderate, heedless, mindless, untroubled, negligent, neglectful, thoughtless, indifferent, casual, oblivious, absent-minded, listless, abstracted, nonchalant, blasé, undiscerning, offhand, slack, blundering; see also RASH.—*Ant.* THOUGHTFUL, attentive, careful.

carelessly *a.* heedlessly, negligently, neglectfully, thoughtlessly, nonchalantly, offhandedly, rashly, unconcernedly, at random, happen what may, incautiously, improvidently, wastefully, without caution, without care, without concern, with no attention, like crazy*.

carelessness *n.* unconcern, nonchalance, heedlessness, rashness, omission, slackness, delinquency, indolence, procrastination, dereliction, neglect, negligence, disregard, imprudence, haphazardness; see also INDIFFERENCE.—*Ant.* CARE, consideration, caution.

caress *n.* embrace, stroke, fondling; see HUG, KISS, TOUCH 2.

caress *v.* embrace, cuddle, pet; see LOVE 2, TOUCH 1.

caretaker *n.* porter, keeper, janitor; see CUSTODIAN, WATCHMAN.

cargo *n.* shipload, baggage, lading; see FREIGHT, LOAD 1.

carnal *a.* fleshly, bodily, sensuous; see LEWD 2, SENSUAL 2.

carnival *n.* sideshow, circus, fair; see ENTERTAINMENT, SHOW 1.

carol *n.* hymn, Christmas song, ballad; see SONG.

carpenter *n.* cabinetmaker, woodworker, craftsman; see LABORER, WORKMAN.

carpet *n.* wall-to-wall carpet, carpeting, linoleum, floor covering, matting; see also RUG. —**(called) on the carpet** reprimanded, censured, interrogated; see IN TROUBLE.

carriage *n.* 1 [The manner of carrying the body] walk, pace, step, attitude, aspect, presence, look, cast, gait, bearing, posture, pose, mien, demeanor, poise, air; see also BEHAVIOR. 2 [A horse-drawn passenger vehicle] buggy, surrey, coach, coach-and-four, buckboard, cart, dogcart, two-wheeler, trap, gig, sulky, hansom, coupe, four-wheeler, stagecoach, chariot, hack, hackney coach; see also WAGON.

carrier *n.* aircraft carrier, escort carrier, flattop*; see SHIP.

carry *v.* 1 [To transport] convey, move, transplant, transfer, cart, import, transmit, freight, remove, conduct, bear, take, bring, shift, haul, change, convoy, relocate, relay, lug, tote, fetch; see also SEND 1. **2** [To transmit] pass on, transfer, relay; see SEND 1. **3** [To support weight] bear, sustain, shoulder; see SUPPORT 1. **4** [To give support] corroborate, back up, confirm; see APPROVE, SUPPORT 2, STRENGTHEN. —**carried away** zealous, aroused, exuberant; see EXCITED. —**carry on 1** [To continue] keep going, proceed, persist; see ACHIEVE, CONTINUE 1, 2, ENDURE 1. **2** [To manage] conduct, engage in, administer; see MANAGE 1. **3** [To behave badly] blunder, be indecorous, raise Cain*; see MISBEHAVE. —**carry out** complete, accomplish, fulfill; see ACHIEVE, COMPLETE, SUCCEED 1. —**carry over** continue, persist, survive; see ENDURE 1.

carry (oneself) *v.* appear, seem, behave; see ACT 2, WALK 1.

carry-over *n.* holdover, vestige, remains; see REMAINDER.

cart *n.* truck, wheelbarrow, little wagon, tip cart, handcart, gig, dray, two-wheeler, pushcart, go-cart, two-wheeled cart; see also CARRIAGE 2, WAGON. —**put the cart before the horse** reverse, be illogical, err; see MISTAKE.

cartoon *n.* animation, animated film, anime; comic, comics, comic strip, funnies*.

carve *v.* create, form, hew, chisel, engrave, etch, sculpt, incise, mold, fashion, cut, shape, model, tool, block out, scrape, pattern, trim; see also CUT 1, ENGRAVE.

carved *a.* incised, graven, cut, chiseled, chased, furrowed, formed, hewn, hewed, etched, sculptured, scratched, slashed, done in relief, scrolled, grooved, sliced, scissored; see also ENGRAVED.—*Ant.* PLAIN, molded, cast.

case *n.* **1** [An example] instance, illustration, sample; see EXAMPLE 1. **2** [Actual conditions] incident, occurrence, fact; see CIRCUMSTANCE 1, EVENT, FACT 2, STATE. **3** [A legal action] suit, litigation, lawsuit; see TRIAL 2. **4** [An organized argument] argument, petition, evidence; see CLAIM, PROOF 1. **5** [A container or its contents] carton, canister, crate, crating, box, baggage, trunk, casing, chest, drawer, holder, tray, receptacle, coffer, crib, chamber, bin, bag, grip, cabinet, sheath, scabbard, wallet, safe, basket, casket; see also CONTAINER. —**in any case** in any event, anyway, however; see ANYHOW. —**in case** in the event that, provided, if it should happen that; see IF. —**in case of** in the event of,

in order to be prepared for, as a provision against; see IF.

cash *n.* money in hand, ready money, liquid assets, currency, legal tender, principal, available means, working assets, funds, payment, capital, finances, stock, resources, wherewithal, investments, savings, riches, reserve, treasure, moneys, security; ready cash, cold cash, hard cash, cash on the barrelhead; see also MONEY 1, WEALTH.

cash *v.* cash in, change, draw; see PAY 1. —**cash in** realize, change, exchange, turn into money, discharge, draw, pay.

cashier *n.* purser, treasurer, receiver; see CLERK.

cast *n.* **1** [A plaster reproduction] facsimile, duplicate, replica; see COPY, SCULPTURE. **2** [Those in a play] persons in the play, cast of characters, players, roles, parts, dramatis personae, company, troupe, producers, dramatic artists. **3** [Aspect] complexion, face, appearance; see LOOKS. **4** [A surgical dressing] plaster-of-Paris dressing, plaster cast, arm cast, leg cast, knee cast, body cast, traction, splints; see also DRESSING 3. **5** [A tinge] hue, shade, tint; see COLOR.

cast *v.* **1** [To throw] pitch, fling, hurl; see THROW 1. **2** [To form in a mold] shape, roughcast, wetcast; see FORM 1. **3** [To select actors for a play] appoint, designate, decide upon, determine, pick, give parts, detail, name; see also ASSIGN, CHOOSE. —**cast away** dispose of, reject, throw out; see ABANDON 1. —**cast off** reject, jettison, throw away; see ABANDON 1.

castle *n.* stronghold, manor, seat, villa, fortress, château, citadel, keep, fort, hold, safehold; see also FORTIFICATION.

castrate *v.* emasculate, sterilize, asexualize, mutilate, cut, spay, geld, unman, steer, caponize, effeminize, deprive of manhood; see also MAIM.

casual *a.* **1** [Accidental] chance, unexpected, unplanned; see SPONTANEOUS. **2** [Nonchalant] blasé, apathetic, unconcerned; see CARELESS, INDIFFERENT.

casually *a.* **1** [Accidentally] unintentionally, by chance, inadvertently; see ACCIDENTALLY. **2** [Nonchalantly] indifferently, coolly, unemotionally; see CARELESSLY, EASILY.

casualty *n.* fatality, loss, death toll; see LOSS 3.

cat *n.* **1** [A domestic animal] tomcat, kitten, kit, tabby, puss*, pussy*, mouser, kitty*. *House cats include the following:* Maltese, Persian, Siamese, Angora, shorthair, tortoise shell, alley, tiger, calico; see also ANIMAL. **2** [A member of the cat family] feline, lion, tiger, leopard, puma, wildcat, cheetah, lynx, bobcat, mountain lion, caracal, serval, panther, ocelot, cougar, jaguar; see also ANIMAL. **—let the cat out of the bag** expose, tell a secret, let slip; see REVEAL.

catalog n. register, file, directory, schedule, inventory, index, bulletin, syllabus, brief, slate, table, calendar, list, docket, classification, record, draft, roll, timetable, table of contents, prospectus, program, *catalogue raisonné* (French); see also LIST.

catalog v. classify, record, index; see LIST 1.

catastrophe n. calamity, mishap, mischance, misadventure, misery, accident, trouble, casualty, infliction, affliction, stroke, havoc, ravage, wreck, fatality, grief, crash, devastation, desolation, hardship, blow, ruin, reverse, emergency, scourge, convulsion, tragedy, adversity, bad luck, upheaval; see also DISASTER.

catch n. 1 [A desirable mate] match, sweetheart, fiancé; see LOVER 1. 2 [*A trick] puzzle, trick, trap; see JOKE. 3 [A hook] clasp, clamp, snap; see FASTENER.

catch v. 1 [To seize hold of] snatch, take, take hold of, snag, grab, pick, pounce on, fasten upon, snare, pluck, hook, claw, clench, clasp, grasp, clutch, grip, nab, net, bag*; see also SEIZE 2. 2 [To bring into captivity] trap, apprehend, capture; see ARREST, SEIZE 2. 3 [To come to from behind] overtake, reach, come upon; see PASS 1. 4 [To contract a disease] get, fall ill with, become infected with, incur, become subject to, be liable to, fall victim to, take, succumb to, break out with, receive, come down with.—*Ant.* ESCAPE, ward off, get over. **—catch on** 1 [To understand] grasp, comprehend, perceive; see UNDERSTAND 1. 2 [To become popular] become fashionable, become prevalent, become common, become widespread, become acceptable, grow in popularity, find favor; see also SUCCEED 1. **—catch up** catch, join, equal; see REACH 1.

catching a. contagious, communicable, transmittable, infectious, epidemic, endemic, pestilential, noxious, dangerous, pandemic; see also CONTAGIOUS.

category n. level, section, classification; see CLASS 1, DIVISION 2, KIND.

cathedral n. temple, house of God, house of prayer, holy place, basilica, minster; see also CHURCH 1. *Parts of a cathedral include the following:* altar, sanctuary, holy of holies, sacristy, sacrarium, holy table, baptistery, chancel, apse, choir, nave, aisle, transept, crypt, pew, seat, pul-

pit, confessional. *Famous cathedrals include the following:* St. Peter's (Rome), St. Paul's (London), Notre Dame (Paris), St. Matthew's, Washington National (Washington, D.C.), St. John the Divine, St. Patrick's (New York).

cattle n. stock, cows, steers, calves, herd, beef cattle, dairy cattle; see also COW.

caucus n. assembly, meeting, council; see GATHERING.

caught a. taken, seized, arrested; see CAPTURED, UNDER ARREST.

cause n. 1 [Purpose] motive, causation, object, end, explanation, inducement, incitement, prime mover, motive power, mainspring, ultimate cause, ground, matter, element, stimulation, instigation, foundation, the why and wherefore; see also BASIS, REASON 3.—*Ant.* RESULT, effect, outcome. 2 [Moving force] agent, case, condition; see CIRCUMSTANCES. 3 [A belief] principles, conviction, creed; see BELIEF, FAITH 2.

cause v. originate, provoke, generate, occasion, let, kindle, give rise to, lie at the root of, be at the bottom of, bring to pass, bring into effect, sow the seeds of; see also BEGIN.

caution n. care, heed, discretion; see ATTENTION, PRUDENCE.

caution v. forewarn, alert, advise; see WARN.

cautious a. circumspect, watchful, wary; see CAREFUL.

cautiously a. tentatively, prudently, discreetly, watchfully, wisely, sparingly, thoughtfully, heedfully, delicately, mindfully, anxiously, with care, with caution, gingerly, with forethought, slowly.

cave n. rock shelter, cavern, grotto; see HOLE.

cavern n. cave, hollow, grotto; see HOLE.

cavity n. 1 [Sunken area] pit, depression, basin; see HOLE. 2 [Hollow place in a tooth] caries, distal pit, gingival pit; see DECAY.

cease v. desist, terminate, discontinue; see HALT, STOP 1, 2.

ceaseless a. continual, endless, unending; see CONSTANT, ETERNAL.

celebrate v. 1 [To recognize an occasion] keep, observe, consecrate, hallow, dedicate, commemorate, honor, proclaim, ritualize.—*Ant.* FORGET, overlook, neglect. 2 [To indulge in celebration] feast, give a party, carouse, rejoice, kill the fatted calf, revel, go on a spree, make whoopee*, blow off steam*, let off steam*, have a party, have a ball*, kick up one's heels*, let loose*, let go, live it up*, whoop it up*, make merry, kick up a row*, party*.

celebrated *a.* renowned, well-known, noted; see FAMOUS, IMPORTANT 2.

celebration *n.* commemoration, holiday, anniversary, jubilee, inauguration, installation, coronation, presentation, carnival, revelry, spree, festivity, festival, feast, merrymaking, gaiety, frolic, hilarity, joviality, merriment, remembrance, ceremonial, observance, fete, Mardi Gras, birthday.

celebrity *n.* famous man, famous woman, hero, heroine, leader, notable, magnate, dignitary, worthy, figure, personage, famous person, person of note, someone, somebody, VIP*, luminary, lion, lioness, star, superstar, bigwig*, big gun*, big shot*, big name.

cell *n.* **1** [A unit of a living organism] corpuscle, cellule, microorganism, vacuole, spore, plastid, organism, egg, ectoplasm, protoplasm, cytoplasm, embryo, germ, follicle. **2** [A room] vault, hold, pen, cage, tower, hole, coop, keep, bastille, chamber, den, recess, retreat, alcove, manger, crypt, crib, nook, burrow, stall, closet, booth, cloister, compartment, lockup; see also ROOM 2.

cellar *n.* half basement, underground room, basement apartment; see BASEMENT.

cement *n.* glue, putty, tar, gum, mortar, paste, adhesive, rubber cement, epoxy, bond.

cement *v.* mortar, plaster, connect; see FASTEN, JOIN 1.

cemetery *n.* burial ground, memorial park, funerary grounds, churchyard, necropolis, potter's field, catacomb, mausoleum, tomb, vault, crypt, charnel house, sepulcher, graveyard, mortuary, last resting place, Golgotha, boneyard*.

censor *n.* inspector, judge, expurgator, bowdlerizer, guardian of morals; see also EXAMINER.

censor *v.* control, restrict, strike out, forbid, suppress, ban, withhold, inspect, oversee, abridge, expurgate, bowdlerize, bleep, review, criticize, exert pressure, conceal, prevent publication, blacklist, blue-pencil, cut, black out; see also RESTRICT.

censorship *n.* licensing, restriction, forbidding, controlling the press, infringing the right of freedom of speech, governmental control, security blackout, news blackout, thought control, thought police*; see also RESTRAINT.

censure *n.* criticism, reproof, admonition; see BLAME, OBJECTION.

censure *v.* **1** [To blame] criticize, judge, disapprove; see BLAME. **2** [To

scold] rebuke, reprove, attack; see SCOLD.

census *n.* statistics, enumeration, valuation, account, registration, listing, evaluation, demography, figures, statement, numbering, registering, roll call, tabulation, tally, poll, count, counting, head count, nose count; see also COUNT.

cent *n.* penny, 100th part of a dollar, red cent*; see MONEY 1.

center *a.* mid, middle, inmost, inner, midway, medial, dead-center, deepest, at the inmost, innermost, internal, interior, at the halfway point; see also CENTRAL, MIDDLE.—*Ant.* OUTSIDE, outer, exterior.

center *n.* **1** [A central point] point, middle, focus, nucleus, core, place, heart, hub, navel, point of convergence, point of concentration, focal point, midst, middle point, centrality, marrow, kernel, bull's-eye, pivot, axis, pith, dead center; see also MIDDLE. **2** [A point that attracts people] city, town, metropolis, plaza, capital, shopping center, trading center, station, hub, mart, market, crossroads, mall, social center, meeting place, club, market place. **3** [Essence] core, gist, kernel; see CHARACTER 1.

center *v.* concentrate, centralize, focus, intensify, unify, unite, combine, converge upon, join, meet, gather, close on, consolidate, bring to a focus, center round, center in, zero in, gather together, flock together, collect, draw together, bring together, focus attention, attract; see also MEET 1.—*Ant.* SPREAD, decentralize, branch off.

central *a.* middle, midway, equidistant, medial, focal, nuclear, midmost, mean, inner, median, inmost, middlemost, intermediate, interior, in the center of; see also MIDDLE.—*Ant.* OUTER, peripheral, verging on.

centrally *a.* in the middle, focal, middlemost, in the center, in the heart of; see also CENTRAL.

century *n.* 100 years, centenary, era; see AGE 3, TIME 1.

ceramics *n.* earthenware, crockery, porcelain; see POTTERY, SCULPTURE.

cereal *n.* corn, breakfast food, seed; see GRAIN 1.

ceremonial *a.* ritual, formal, stately; see CONVENTIONAL 3.

ceremony *n.* **1** [A public event] function, commemoration, services; see CELEBRATION. **2** [A rite] observance, ritual, rite, service, solemnity, formality, custom, tradition, liturgy, ordinance, sacrament, liturgical practice, conformity, etiquette, politeness, propriety, preciseness, decorum, strictness, nicety, formalism, conventionality.

certain *a.* **1** [Confident] calm,

assured, sure, positive, satisfied, self-confident, undoubting, believing, secure, untroubled, unconcerned, undisturbed, unperturbed, fully convinced, assertive, cocksure; see also CONFIDENT. **2** [Beyond doubt] indisputable, unquestionable, assured, positive, real, true, genuine, plain, clear, undoubted, guaranteed, unmistakable, sure, incontrovertible, undeniable, definite, unqualified, infallible, undisputed, unerring, sound, reliable, trustworthy, evident, conclusive, authoritative, irrefutable, unconditional, incontestable, unquestioned, absolute, unequivocal, inescapable, conclusive, in the bag*; see also TRUE 1, 3. **3** [Fixed] settled, concluded, set; see DEFINITE 1, DETERMINED 1. **4** [Specific but not named] special, definite, individual, marked, one, some, a few, a couple, several, upwards of, regular, particular, singular, precise, specific, express; see also SOME. **—for certain** without doubt, absolutely, certainly; see SURELY.

certainly *a.* positively, absolutely, unquestionably; see SURELY.

certificate *n.* declaration, warrant, voucher, testimonial, credentials, license, testament, endorsement, affidavit, certification, diploma, coupon, document, pass, ticket, warranty, guarantee, testimony, receipt, affirmation; see also RECORD 1.

certify *v.* swear, attest, state; see DECLARE, TESTIFY 2.

chain *n.* **1** [A series of links] series, train, set, string, connection, cable, link, charm bracelet, atomic ring, shackle, manacle; see also SERIES. **2** [A sequence] succession, progression, continuity; see SERIES.

chain *v.* connect, attach, secure; see FASTEN, HOLD 1.

chair *n.* **1** [A single seat] seat, place, room, space; see also FURNITURE. *Chairs include the following:* stool, throne, footstool, rocker, wing chair, armchair, easy chair, wheelchair, highchair, occasional chair, dining-room chair, desk chair, kitchen chair, deck chair, lawn chair, swivel chair, folding chair, recliner. **2** [A position of authority] throne, professorship, fellowship; see INFLUENCE.

chairman *n.* chairperson, chairwoman, chair, president, administrator, director, toastmaster, speaker, moderator, monitor, leader, principal, captain, master of ceremonies, MC, emcee; see also LEADER 2.

chalk up *v.* credit, enter, register; see ADD 1, RECORD 1, SCORE 1.

challenge *n.* dare, provocation, threat; see OBJECTION.

challenge *v.* **1** [To call to a contest, etc.] defy, confront, throw down the gauntlet; see DARE 2, THREATEN. **2** [To question] dispute, inquire, search out; see ASK, DOUBT, QUESTION.

champion *n.* vanquisher, conqueror, victor; see HERO 1, WINNER.

chance *a.* accidental, unintentional, haphazard; see AIMLESS, INCIDENTAL.

chance *n.* **1** [The powers of uncertainty] fate, fortune, hazard, casualty, lot, accident, luck, good luck, bad luck, destiny, outcome, cast, lottery, gamble, adventure, contingency, happening, future, doom, destination, occurrence, Lady Luck*, turn of the cards, heads or tails.—*Ant.* PURPOSE, aim, design. **2** [A possibility] opening, occasion, prospect; see OPPORTUNITY 1, POSSIBILITY 2. **3** [Probability; *often plural*] likelihood, feasibility, indications; see ODDS. **—by chance** by accident, as it happens, unexpectedly; see ACCIDENTALLY. **—on the off chance** in case, in the event that, supposing; see IF.

chance *v.* venture, stake, hazard, wager, jeopardize, speculate, tempt fate, tempt fortune, play with fire, take a shot*, take a leap in the dark, buy a pig in a poke, go out on a limb*, chance it, take a fling at*, put all one's eggs in one basket, skate on thin ice*, run the risk; see also RISK.

change *n.* **1** [An alteration] modification, correction, remodeling, switch, reformation, reconstruction, shift, reform, conversion, transformation, revolution, rearrangement, adjustment, readjustment, reorganization, reshaping, renovation, realignment, redirection, reprogramming, variation, addition, refinement, advance, development, diversification, turn, turnover, enlargement, revision, qualification, distortion, compression, contraction, widening, narrowing, lengthening, flattening, shortening, fitting, setting, adjusting, rounding, mutation, evolution. **2** [Substitution] switch, replacement, exchange; see SHIFT 1. **3** [Variety] diversity, novelty, variance; see DIFFERENCE 1, VARIETY 1.

change *v.* **1** [To make different] vary, turn, alternate; see ALTER 1. **2** [To become different] alter, vary, modify, evolve, be converted, turn into, resolve into, grow, ripen, mellow, mature, transform, reform, moderate, adapt, adjust, mutate, evolve; see also BECOME. **3** [To put in place of another] displace, supplant, transpose; see EXCHANGE 1, REPLACE 1, SUBSTITUTE. **4** [To change clothing] switch outfits, slip into something comfortable, undress; see DRESS 1.

changeable *a.* **1** [*Said of persons*] fickle, flighty, unreliable; see UNSTABLE 2. **2** [*Said of conditions*] variable, unsteady, unsettled; see UNCERTAIN.

changed *a.* **1** [Exchanged] substituted, replaced, traded; see RETURNED. **2** [Altered] reconditioned, modified, limited, reformed, shifted, moved, mutated, deteriorated, aged, run down, rewritten, qualified, conditioned, modernized, remodeled, reprogrammed, rescheduled, redone, done over, brought up to date, edited, censored, moderated, innovated, deviated, diverted, fluctuated, chopped, warped, passed to, re-created, converted, transfigured, metamorphosed, transmuted.—*Ant.* UNCHANGED, PERMANENT, final.

changing *a.* changeful, changeable, mobile, dynamic, alternative, unstable, inconstant, uncertain, mutable, fluid, mercurial, declining, deteriorating, degenerating, unsteady, irresolute, wavering; see also UNCERTAIN.—*Ant.* FIXED, stable, unchanging.

channel *n.* conduit, tube, canal, duct, course, gutter, furrow, trough, runway, tunnel, strait, sound, race, sewer, main, artery, vein, ditch, aqueduct, canyon; see also WAY 2.

channel *v.* route, send, direct; see SEND 1.

chant *n.* religious song, chorus, incantation; see SONG.

chant *v.* intone, chorus, carol; see SING.

chaos *n.* turmoil, anarchy, discord; see CONFUSION, DISORDER.

chaotic *a.* disorganized, disordered, uncontrolled; see CONFUSED 2.

chapel *n.* nondenominational place of worship, small church, shrine; see CHURCH 1.

chapter *n.* part, section, book; see DIVISION 2.

character *n.* **1** [The dominant quality] temper, temperament, attitude, nature, sense, complex, mood, streak, attribute, badge, tone, style, aspect, complexion, spirit, genius, humor, frame, grain, vein; see also CHARACTERISTIC. **2** [The sum of a person's characteristics] personality, reputation, constitution, repute, individuality, estimation, record, caliber, standing, type, shape, quality, habit, appearance; see also KIND 2. **3** [A symbol, especially in writing] sign, figure, emblem; see LETTER 1, MARK 1. **4** [An odd or striking person] personality, figure, personage, original, eccentric, crank*, nut*, oddball*, weirdo*, freak*,

piece of work. —**in character** consistent, usual, predictable; see CONVENTIONAL 1. —**out of character** unusual, inconsistent, unpredictable; see UNEXPECTED.

characteristic *a.* innate, fixed, essential, distinctive, distinguishing, marked, discriminative, symbolic, individualizing, representative, specific, personal, original, peculiar, individualistic, individual, idiosyncratic, unique, special, particular, symptomatic, private, exclusive, inherent, inborn, inbred, ingrained, native, indicative, inseparable, genetic; see also NATURAL 2, TYPICAL.—*Ant.* IRREGULAR, erratic, aberrant.

characteristic *n.* flavor, attribute, quality, faculty, peculiarity, individuality, style, aspect, tone, tinge, feature, distinction, manner, bearing, inclination, nature, personality, temperament, frame, originality, singularity, qualification, virtue, mark, essence, caliber, complexion, particularity, idiosyncrasy, trick, earmark, mannerism, trademark, badge, symptom, disposition, specialty, mood, character, bent, tendency, component, thing*.

characterize *v.* delineate, designate, portray; see DEFINE 2, DESCRIBE.

charge *n.* **1** [A charged sale] entry, debit, credit; see PRICE. **2** [An attack] assault, invasion, outbreak; see ATTACK. —**in charge** responsible, controlling, managing; see RESPONSIBLE 1.

charge *v.* **1** [To ask a price] require, sell for, fix the price at; see PRICE. **2** [To enter on a charge account] debit, put to account, charge to, run up an account, take on account, put on one's account, incur a debt, put down, credit, encumber, sell on credit, buy on credit, chalk up, put on the books, carry, put on the cuff*, take plastic*; see also BUY, SELL. **3** [To attack] assail, assault, invade; see ATTACK. **4** [To accuse] indict, censure, impute; see BLAME.

charged *a.* **1** [Bought but not paid for] debited, outstanding, unpaid, on credit, on time, owing, owed, on the cuff*, on the tab*; see also BOUGHT, DUE. **2** [Accused] taxed, confronted with, arraigned; see ACCUSED.

charitable *a.* openhanded, liberal, philanthropic; see GENEROUS, KIND.

charity *n.* **1** [Kindness] benevolence, magnanimity, compassion; see KINDNESS 1, TOLERANCE 1. **2** [An organization to aid the needy] charitable institution, welfare organization, foundation; see FOUNDATION 3.

charm *n.* **1** [An object thought to possess power] amulet, talisman, mojo, fetish, mascot, good-luck piece, lucky piece, rabbit's foot. **2**

[The quality of being charming] grace, attractiveness, attraction; see BEAUTY 1.

charm v. enchant, captivate, possess, enrapture, enthrall, transport, delight, please, entrance, bewitch, mesmerize; see also FASCINATE.

charmed a. enchanted, bewitched, enraptured, entranced, captivated, attracted, lured, tempted, enticed, bedazzled, hypnotized, mesmerized, under a spell, in a trance, spellbound, moonstruck, possessed, obsessed, infatuated, starstruck; see also FASCINATED.

charming a. enchanting, bewitching, entrancing, captivating, cute, fascinating, delightful, lovable, sweet, winning, irresistible, attractive, amiable, appealing, alluring, charismatic, pleasing, nice, graceful, winsome, seducing, seductive, desirable, enticing, tempting, inviting, ravishing, enrapturing, glamorous, elegant, infatuating, dainty, delicate, absorbing, tantalizing, engrossing, titillating, engaging, enthralling, rapturous, electrifying, lovely, intriguing, thrilling, fair, exquisite, likable, diverting, fetching, provocative, delectable, sexy*.—Ant. OFFENSIVE, disgusting, unpleasant.

chart n. graph, outline, diagram; see MAP, PLAN 1.

chart v. map, outline, plot; see PLAN 2.

charter n. contract, settlement, pact; see AGREEMENT 2, TREATY.

chase v. trail, track, seek; see HUNT 1, PURSUE 1.

chaste a. immaculate, unstained, clean, innocent, virginal, unblemished, unsullied, moral, modest, proper, decent, demure, virgin, celibate, platonic, controlled, unmarried, unwed, spotless, infallible, strong; see also INNOCENT 2.—Ant. WEAK, corruptible, frail.

chastise v. scold, discipline, spank; see PUNISH.

chastity n. innocence, purity, virtue, uprightness, honor, celibacy, integrity, decency, delicacy, cleanness, goodness, demureness, abstinence, morality, chasteness, modesty, sinlessness, continence, coldness, reserve, restraint, virginity, spotlessness.—Ant. LEWDNESS, adultery, licentiousness.

chat v. converse, prattle, chatter; see TALK 1.

chatter v. gossip, chat, prattle; see BABBLE.

cheap a. 1 [Low in price] inexpensive, low-priced, family-size, economy-size, budget, depreciated, slashed, cut-rate, on sale, competitive, lowered, thrifty, bargain, irregular, reduced, cut-priced, low-

cost, at a bargain, reasonable, marked down, closed-out, half-priced, popular-priced, worth the money, dime-a-dozen*, dirt-cheap*, for peanuts*, for a song*, second, bargain-basement; see also ECONOMICAL.—Ant. EXPENSIVE, dear, costly. 2 [Low in quality] inferior, ordinary, shoddy; see COMMON 1, POOR 2. 3 [Dishonest or base] dirty, tawdry, low; see DISHONEST, MEAN 3, VULGAR.

cheapen v. spoil, depreciate, demean; see CORRUPT, DAMAGE.

cheaply a. economically, inexpensively, advantageously, at a bargain price, at a good price, on sale, at cost, below cost, discounted, at a discount, reduced, at a reduced price, sacrificed, dirt-cheap*, given away*.

cheat n. rogue, cheater, confidence man, quack, charlatan, conniver, fraud, swindler, chiseler*, beguiler, fake, bluff, deceiver, inveigler, hypocrite, trickster, pretender, dodger, humbug, crook*, wolf in sheep's clothing, con artist*, shark*, four-flusher*, shill*; see also CRIMINAL.

cheat v. defraud, swindle, beguile; see DECEIVE.

cheated a. defrauded, swindled, duped, tricked, imposed upon, victimized, beguiled, trapped, foiled, lured, taken in*, bamboozled, hoodwinked; see also DECEIVED.

cheating n. lying, defrauding, deceiving; see DECEPTION, DISHONESTY.

check n. 1 [An order on a bank] money order, letter of credit, traveler's check, bank check, cashier's check, note, remittance; see also MONEY 1. 2 [A control] limit, curb, rein; see RESTRAINT 2. 3 [An examination] investigation, analysis, inquiry; see EXAMINATION 1, 3. 4 [A pattern in squares] patchwork, checkered design, checkerboard; see DESIGN. —**in check** controlled, under control, checked; see HELD.

check v. 1 [To bring under control] bridle, repress, inhibit, control, checkmate, counteract, discourage, repulse, neutralize, squelch*; see also RESTRAIN.—Ant. FREE, liberate, loose. 2 [To determine accuracy] review, monitor, inspect, test, balance the books, keep account of, correct, compare, find out, investigate, vet*, count, tell, call the roll, take account of, take stock, go through, go over with a fine-toothed comb*, keep tabs on*, keep track of; see also EXAMINE. 3 [To halt] hold, terminate, cut short; see HALT, STOP 1. —**check in** appear, sign in, come; see ARRIVE, REGISTER 4. —**check off** mark off, notice, correct; see MARK 2.

—check out depart, pay one's bill, settle up; see LEAVE 1, PAY 1. **— check up on** watch, investigate, control; see EXAMINE.

cheek *n.* jowl, gill, chop; see FACE 1.

cheer *n.* **1** [An agreeable mental state] delight, mirth, glee; see JOY. **2** [An encouraging shout] roar, applause, ovation, hurrah, hurray, college yell, approval; see also YELL.

cheer *v.* **1** [To hearten] console, inspirit, brighten; see COMFORT 1, ENCOURAGE, HELP. **2** [To support with cheers] applaud, shout, salute; see SUPPORT 2, YELL. **—cheer up** enliven, inspirit, exhilarate, inspire, brighten, rally, restore, perk up, boost, buck up*, pat on the back; see also IMPROVE 1.

cheerful *a.* **1** [*Said especially of persons*] gay, merry, joyful; see HAPPY. **2** [*Said especially of things*] bright, sunny, sparkling; see COMFORTABLE 2, PLEASANT 2.

cheerfully *a.* cheerily, gladly, willingly, happily, merrily, joyfully, lightheartedly, pleasantly, blithely, brightly, vivaciously, airily, genially, jovially, sportively, elatedly, winsomely, gleefully, gaily, mirthfully, playfully, hopefully, breezily, briskly, with good cheer.—*Ant.* SADLY, unwillingly, reluctantly.

cheers *interj.* here's to you, to your health, skoal; see TOAST 1.

cheese *n. Varieties of cheese include the following:* mild, sharp, hard, soft, semisoft, aged, ripened, fresh, blue-veined, blue, bleu, cow's-milk, sheep's-milk, goat, process, smoked cheese; American, cheddar, Monterey Jack, Edam, Roquefort (trademark), brie, mozzarella, provolone, Gorgonzola, Swiss, Camembert, Liederkranz (trademark), Neufchâtel, Gruyère, Parmesan, Stilton, Gouda, Limburger, Muenster, Port du Salut, ricotta, feta, Romano, Colby, longhorn, chèvre, havarti; cottage, pot, cream, brick cheese; see also FOOD.

chemical *a.* synthetic, artificial, ersatz; see FALSE 3.

chemical *n.* substance, synthetic, compound; see DRUG, MEDICINE 2.

chemistry *n. Branches of chemistry include the following:* pure, quantitative, qualitative, organic, inorganic, theoretical, physical, physiological, pathological, metallurgical, mineralogical, geological, applied, agricultural, pharmaceutical, sanitary, industrial, technical, engineering chemistry; biochemistry, electrochemistry, zoochemistry; see also MEDICINE 3, SCIENCE 1.

cherish *v.* treasure, value, adore; see LOVE 1, 2.

cherry *a.* ruddy, reddish, rosy; see RED, PINK.

chest *n.* **1** [A boxlike container] case, box, coffer, cabinet, strongbox, receptacle, crate, locker, bureau, coffin, casket, treasury; see also CONTAINER. **2** [The ribbed portion of the body] breast, thorax, bosom, rib cage, heart, upper trunk, pulmonary cavity, peritoneum, ribs.

chew *v.* bite, champ, munch, crunch, masticate, nibble, feast upon, gnaw, gulp, grind, rend, scrunch, ruminate; see also EAT 1.

chicken *n.* **1** [A barnyard fowl] chick, hen, rooster; see FOWL. **2** [Flesh of the chicken] white meat, dark meat, giblets; see MEAT. **3** [*A coward*] recreant, dastard, craven; see COWARD. **—count one's chickens before they are hatched** rely on, depend on, put trust in; see ANTICIPATE.

chief *a.* leading, first, foremost; see MAIN, PRINCIPAL.

chief *n.* principal, manager, overseer, governor, president, foreman, proprietor, supervisor, director, chairman, ringleader, general, master, dictator, superintendent, head, prince, emperor, duke, majesty, monarch, overlord, lord, potentate, sovereign, chieftain, ruler, captain, commander, bigwig*, prima donna*, boss, it*; see also LEADER.

chiefly *a.* mainly, particularly, in the first place; see PRINCIPALLY.

child *n.* newborn, infant, youth, adolescent, youngster, daughter, son, grandchild, stepchild, offspring, innocent, minor, juvenile, tot, cherub, papoose, moppet*, kid*, kiddie*, kiddy*, whelp*, brat*, imp, small fry; see also BOY, GIRL.—*Ant.* PARENT, forefather, adult. **—with child** carrying a child, going to have a baby, expecting*; see PREGNANT.

childbirth *n.* delivery, childbearing, parturition, childbed, labor, nativity, delivering, accouchement, lying in, confinement, reproduction, giving birth, blessed event; see also BIRTH.

childhood *n.* infancy, youth, minority, school days, adolescence, nursery days, babyhood, boyhood, girlhood, teens, puberty, immaturity, tender age.—*Ant.* AGE, maturity, senility.

childish *a.* childlike, foolish, stupid, baby, infantile, juvenile, youthful, babyish, boyish, girlish, adolescent, green, soft, immature; see also NAIVE, SIMPLE 1, YOUNG 2.—*Ant.* MATURE, adult, grown.

chill *n.* crispness, coolness, coldness; see COLD 1.

chill *v.* **1** [To reduce temperature] refrigerate, frost, make cold; see COOL, FREEZE 1. **2** [To check] dispirit, dishearten, dampen; see DEPRESS 2, DISCOURAGE.

chilly *a.* brisk, fresh, crisp; see COLD 1, COOL 1.

chime *v.* tinkle, clang, toll; see RING 2, SOUND.

chimney *n.* smokestack, fireplace, furnace, hearth, flue, vent, pipe, funnel, chimney pot, stack.

chin *n.* mentum, mandible, jawbone; see JAW.

china *n.* porcelain, pottery, crockery; see DISH.

chip *n.* **1** [A fragment] fragment, slice, wedge; see BIT 1, FLAKE, PART 1. **2** [A microcircuit] integrated circuit, semiconductor, microprocessor, microchip. **—having a chip on one's shoulder** ready to fight, disturbed, agitated; see ANGRY. **—when the chips are down** in a crisis, having trouble, in a difficult position; see IN TROUBLE.

chip *v.* slash, hew, hack, crumble, snip, fragment, incise, whittle, crack off, splinter, notch, sliver, cut off, chop, split, slice, chisel, clip, break, crack, flake, cut away, nick, shiver, reduce, shear; see also BREAK.

chip in* *v.* contribute, pay, pitch in*; see SHARE 1.

chirp *v.* twitter, warble, cheep; see SOUND.

chisel *n.* gouge, blade, edge; see KNIFE, TOOL 1.

chisel *v.* **1** [To work with a chisel] carve, hew, incise; see CUT 1. **2** [*To get by imposition] impose upon, defraud, gyp*; see DECEIVE, STEAL.

chivalrous *a.* courteous, heroic, valiant; see BRAVE, NOBLE 1, 2, POLITE.

chivalry *n.* valor, gallantry, honor; see COURTESY 1.

chock-full *a.* packed, crammed, stuffed; see FULL 1.

choice *a.* superior, fine, exceptional; see BEST 1.

choice *n.* selection, preference, alternative, election, substitute, favorite, pick, a good bet; see also OPTION 1.

choke *v.* asphyxiate, strangle, strangulate, stifle, throttle, garrote, drown, noose, smother, grab by the throat, wring the neck of, stop the breath of, gag, gasp, suffocate, choke off, be choked, die out, die by asphyxiation; see also DIE. **—choke up*** give way to one's feelings, weep, break down; see CRY 1.

choose *v.* take, pick out, draw lots, cull, prefer, make a choice of, accept, weigh, judge, sort, appoint, embrace, will, call for, fancy, take up, separate, favor, determine, resolve, discriminate, make a decision, adopt, collect, mark out for, cut out, arrange, keep, make one's choice, pick and choose, settle on,

use one's discretion, determine upon, fix on, place one's trust in, glean, single out, espouse, exercise one's option, make up one's mind, set aside, set apart, commit oneself, separate the wheat from the chaff, incline toward, opt for, burn one's bridges; see also DECIDE.—*Ant.* DISCARD, reject, refuse.

choosing *n.* selecting, picking, judging; see JUDGMENT 2.

chop *v.* fell, cut with an ax, whack; see CUT 1.

chord *n.* harmonizing tones, triad, octave; major chord, minor chord, diminished chord, augmented chord, inverted chord, broken chord; tonic chord, dominant chord, subdominant chord; tetrachord, perfect fourth, arpeggio, common chord; see also HARMONY 1, MUSIC 1.

chore *n.* task, work, errand; see JOB 2.

chorus *n.* **1** [A body of singers] choir, singing group, choristers, voices, glee club, singing society, church singers, male chorus, female chorus, mixed chorus, chorale; see also MUSIC 1. **2** [A refrain] melody, strain, tune; see SONG.

chosen *a.* picked, elected, preferred; see NAMED 2.

Christ *n.* the Saviour, Jesus, Jesus Christ, Jesus of Nazareth, the Redeemer, the Messiah, Immanuel, Emmanuel, the Anointed, the Word, the Son, the Son of Man, the Son of God, God the Son, the Son of David, the Son of Mary, the Risen, the King of Glory, the Prince of Peace, the Good Shepherd, King of the Jews, the Lamb of God, the Only Begotten, King of Kings, Lord of Lords, Christ Our Lord, the Way, the Door, the Truth, the Life, the Light of the World, Alpha and Omega, the Incarnate Word, the Word made Flesh; see also GOD 2.

christen *v.* immerse, sprinkle, name; see BAPTIZE, BLESS.

Christian *a.* pious, reverent, gentile; see HUMBLE 1, RELIGIOUS 1, 2.

Christian *n.* Protestant, Catholic, gentile; see CHURCH 3, SAINT.

Christianity *n.* **1** [A religion based upon the divinity of Christ] teachings of Christ, the Gospel, the Faith; see FAITH 2, RELIGION 2. **2** [The body of Christian people] Christendom, Christians, followers of Christ; see CHURCH 3. **3** [An attitude associated with Christianity] Christian spirit, forgiving disposition, mercy; see KINDNESS 1, TOLERANCE 1.

Christmas *n.* Xmas*, the Nativity, Yule; see HOLIDAY, WINTER.

chronic *a.* inveterate, confirmed, settled, rooted, deep-seated, continuing, persistent, stubborn, incurable, lasting, lingering, deep-rooted, perennial, fixed, continual, incessant, long-standing, recurring, continuous, of long duration, long-lived, protracted, ceaseless, sustained, lifelong, prolonged, recurrent, obstinate, inborn, inbred, ingrained, ever-present; see also CONSTANT, HABITUAL, PERMANENT.—*Ant.* TEMPORARY, acute, casual.

chronicle *n.* narrative, annals, account; see HISTORY, RECORD 1.

chronological *a.* temporal, historical, classified according to chronology, in the order of time, sequential, consecutive, properly dated, measured in time, in sequence, progressive in time, ordered, in order, in due course.

chubby *a.* plump, round, pudgy; see FAT.

chuckle *n.* chortle, snicker, giggle; see LAUGH.

chuckle *v.* giggle, chortle, snicker; see LAUGH.

chummy* *a.* affectionate, sociable, palsy-walsy*; see FRIENDLY.

chunk *n.* piece, mass, lump; see PART 1.

chunky *a.* stocky, thickset, stout; see FAT.

church *n.* 1 [A building consecrated to worship] cathedral, house of God, Lord's house, temple, synagogue, mosque, house of worship, meetinghouse, chapel, basilica, tabernacle, abbey, sanctuary, house of prayer, mission, shrine, pagoda. 2 [A divine service] rite, prayers, prayer meeting, Sunday school, worship, Mass, liturgy, Lord's Supper, sacrament, the holy sacrament, rosary, ritual, religious rite, morning service, evening service, congregational worship, fellowship, devotion, office, revival meeting, chapel service, sermon, communion; see also CEREMONY. 3 [An organized religious body] congregation, gathering, denomination, sect, chapter, body, order, communion, faith, religion, religious order, affiliation, persuasion, belief, faction, doctrine, creed, cult. *Christian churches include the following:* Methodist, Presbyterian, Episcopal, Baptist, Christian Science, Mormon, Congregational, Lutheran, Roman Catholic, Eastern Orthodox, Greek Catholic, Pentecostal, Church of England, Church of the Nazarene, Society of Friends.

churn *v.* stir, beat, agitate; see MIX 1.

cigarette *n.* fag*, smoke*, coffin nail*, weed*.

cinema *n.* film, motion pictures, the movies; see MOVIE.

circle *n.* 1 [A round closed plane figure] ring, loop, wheel, sphere, globe, orb, orbit, zodiac, bowl, vortex, hoop, horizon, perimeter, periphery, circumference, full turn, circuit, disk, meridian, equator, ecliptic, cycle, bracelet, belt, wreath. 2 [An endless sequence of events] cycle, course, succession; see PROGRESS 1, SERIES, SEQUENCE 1. —**come full circle** go through a cycle, come back, revert; see RETURN 1.

circle *v.* round, encircle, loop, tour, circumnavigate, ring, belt, embrace, encompass, wind about, revolve around, circumscribe, curve around, circuit, enclose, spiral, coil, circulate, detour, wind, roll, wheel, swing past, go round about, evade; see also SURROUND 1.—*Ant.* DIVIDE, bisect, cut across.

circuit *n.* circumference, course, circle; see ORBIT 1, REVOLUTION 1.

circular *a.* annular, spherical, cyclical; see ROUND 1.

circular *n.* handbill, flier, leaflet; see ADVERTISEMENT, PAMPHLET.

circulate *v.* 1 [To go about] move around, go about, wander; see TRAVEL, WALK 1. 2 [To send about] diffuse, report, broadcast; see DISTRIBUTE.

circulation *n.* 1 [Motion in a circle] rotation, passage, flow; see FLOW, REVOLUTION 1. 2 [Number of copies distributed] volume, apportionment, dissemination; see DISTRIBUTION.

circumference *n.* perimeter, periphery, border; see CIRCLE 1.

circumscribe *v.* encircle, encompass, girdle; see SURROUND 1.

circumstance *n.* 1 [An attendant condition] situation, condition, contingency, phase, factor, detail, item, fact, case, place, time, cause, status, element, feature, point, incident, article, stipulation, concern, matter, event, occurrence, crisis, coincidence, fate, chance, happenstance*. 2 [An occurrence] episode, happening, incident; see EVENT.

circumstances *n.* 1 [Condition in life] worldly goods, outlook, prospects, chances, means, assets, prosperity, financial condition, resources, standing, property, net worth, financial standing, credit rating, terms, way of life, rank, class, degree, capital, position, financial responsibility, footing, income, sphere, substance, stock in trade, lot, prestige, what one is worth, place on the ladder; see also STATE 2, WEALTH. 2 [Attendant conditions] situation, environment, surroundings, facts, particulars, factors, features, motives, controlling factors, governing factors, the times, occasion, basis, grounds, setting, background, needs, requirements, necessities, course of events, legal status, change, life, fluctuation, phase, case, condition, state of affairs, surrounding facts, the score*, the scene*, the story*, where it's at*, how the land lies, the lay of the land, current regime, ups and downs. —under no circumstances under no conditions, by no means, absolutely not; see NEVER. —under the circumstances conditions being what they are, for this reason, because of this; see BECAUSE.

circumstantial *a.* presumptive, inferential, inconclusive; see UNCERTAIN.

circumvent *v.* **1** [To go around] encircle, encompass, entrap; see SURROUND 1. **2** [To avoid] dodge, elude, bypass; see AVOID, EVADE.

circus *n.* carnival, spectacle, fair; see ENTERTAINMENT.

citation *n.* subpoena, charge, summons; see COMMAND.

citizen *n.* inhabitant, denizen, national, subject, cosmopolite, commoner, civilian, urbanite, taxpayer, member of the community, householder, native, occupant, settler, voter, dweller, immigrant, naturalized person, townsman, the man in the street, villager, John Q. Public; see also RESIDENT.

city *a.* metropolitan, urban, civic; see MUNICIPAL.

city *n.* town, place, municipality, capital, megalopolis, metropolis, suburb, county seat, trading center, inner city, downtown, shopping district, business district, financial district, incorporated town, village, metropolitan area, township, borough, port; see also CENTER 2.

civic *a.* civil, urban, municipal; see PUBLIC 1, 2.

civil *a.* **1** [Civic] local, civic, public; see MUNICIPAL. **2** [Polite] formal, courteous, refined; see POLITE.

civilian *n.* private citizen, noncombatant, nonmilitary person; see CITIZEN.

civilization *n.* cultivation, polish, enlightenment, refinement, civility, illumination, advancement of knowledge, elevation, edification, culture, advancement, social well-being, sophistication, literacy, material well-being, education, breeding; see also CULTURE 1, PROGRESS 1.—*Ant.* barbarism, savagery, degeneration.

civilize *v.* enlighten, cultivate, enrich, reclaim, refine, acculturate, spiritualize, humanize, edify, uplift, tame, foster, instruct, indoctrinate, idealize, elevate, educate, advance, ennoble; see also DEVELOP 1, TEACH.

civilized *a.* enlightened, refined, humanized; see CULTURED, EDUCATED.

civil rights *n.* civil liberties, equality, human rights; see CHOICE, FREEDOM 1.

claim *n.* demand, declaration, profes-

sion, entreaty, petition, suit, ultimatum, call, request, requirement, application, case, assertion, plea, right, interest, title, stake, part; see also APPEAL 1. —**lay claim to** demand, appropriate, stake out a claim to; see OWN 1.

claim *v.* **1** [To assert a claim to] demand, attach, lay claim to; see OWN 1. **2** [To assert] insist, maintain, allege; see BELIEVE, DECLARE.

clam *n.* bivalve, mollusk, shellfish; see FISH.

clammy *a.* moist, damp, sweaty; see COLD 1, WET 1.

clamor *n.* din, outcry, discord; see NOISE 2, UPROAR.

clamp *n.* vise, clasp, clip; see FASTENER, LOCK 1.

clan *n.* group, clique, tribe; see ORGANIZATION 2, RACE 2.

clang *n.* clank, clash, jangle; see NOISE 1.

clank *n.* chink, clang, clink; see NOISE 1.

clap *v.* **1** [To applaud] cheer, acclaim, applaud; see PRAISE 1. **2** [To strike] bang, slap, slam; see HIT 1.

clarification *n.* exposition, elucidation, description; see DEFINITION, EXPLANATION, INTERPRETATION.

clarify *v.* interpret, define, elucidate; see EXPLAIN.

clarity *n.* transparency, clearness, purity, limpidity, brightness, precision, explicitness, exactness, distinctness, plain speech, openness, directness, prominence, salience, conspicuousness, certainty, lucidity.—*Ant.* DARKNESS, haze, obscurity.

clash *n.* **1** [Collision] crash, jolt, impact; see COLLISION. **2** [Disagreement] opposition, conflict, argument; see DISAGREEMENT 1, DISPUTE.

clash *v.* be dissimilar, mismatch, conflict; see CONTRAST, DIFFER 1.

clasp *n.* buckle, pin, catch; see FASTENER.

clasp *v.* clamp, pin, secure; see FASTEN.

class *n.* **1** [A classification] degree, order, rank, grade, standing, genus, division, distinction, breed, type, kingdom, subdivision, phylum, subphylum, superorder, family, sect, category, rate, collection, denomination, department, sort, species, variety, branch, group, genre, range, brand, set, kind, section, domain, color, origin, character, temperament, school, designation, sphere, spirit, vein, persuasion, province, make, grain, source, name, form, selection, stamp, status, range, property, aspect, tone; see also

CLASSIFICATION. 2 [A group organized for study] lecture, seminar, study session; see SCHOOL 1. 3 [A division of society] set, caste, social level; see FAMILY. —in a class by itself unusual, different, one of a kind; see UNIQUE.

class v. identify, rank, grade; see CLASSIFY, MARK 2.

classic n. opus, masterwork, exemplar; see MASTERPIECE.

classical a. 1 [Of recognized importance] standard, first-rate, established, ideal, flawless, distinguished, paramount, aesthetic, superior, artistic, well-known; see also EXCELLENT.—Ant. POPULAR, modern, transitory. 2 [Concerning ancient Greece or Rome] humanistic, academic, classic; see OLD 3.

classification n. arrangement, assortment, grouping, ordering, allotment, organization, gradation, coordination, disposition, categorizing, apportionment, analysis, division, assignment, designation, assorting, distribution, allocation, categorization; see also CLASS 1, ORDER 3.

classified a. sorted, assorted, grouped, classed, indexed, filed, orderly, recorded, listed, registered, detailed, arranged, regulated, compiled, coordinated, ranked, distributed, cataloged, separated, labeled, numbered, systematized, tabulated, alphabetized, typed, on file, rated.—Ant. MIXED, confused, jumbled.

classify v. arrange, order, pigeonhole, tabulate, organize, distribute, categorize, systematize, coordinate, correlate, incorporate, label, alphabetize, place in a category, range, form into classes, divide, allocate, number, rate, class, rank, catalog, segregate, distinguish, allot, analyze, regiment, name, group, tag, type, put in order, break down, assort, sort, index, grade, match, size, reduce to order; see also FILE 1, LIST 1.—Ant. DISORGANIZE, disorder, disarrange.

clatter v. rattle, clash, crash; see SOUND.

clause n. 1 [A provision] condition, codicil, stipulation; see LIMITATION 2, REQUIREMENT 1. 2 [A grammatical structure] construction, sentence, word group; see GRAMMAR.

claw n. talon, hook, spur, paw, grappling iron, grappling hook, forked end, clutching hand, grapnel, crook, barb, pincers, fingernail.

claw v. tear, scratch, rip open; see BREAK 1, HURT, RIP.

clay n. earth, till, marl, kaolin, potter's clay, clayware, green pottery, terra cotta, green brick, china clay, porcelain clay, adobe; see also MUD.

clean a. 1 [Not soiled] spotless, washed, stainless, laundered, untarnished, unstained, neat, tidy, clear, fresh, pure, blank, white, unblemished, unspotted, snowy, well-kept, dustless, cleansed, immaculate, unsoiled, unpolluted, spick-and-span, clean as a whistle*.—Ant. DIRTY, soiled, stained. 2 [Not contaminated] unadulterated, antiseptic, sanitary; see PURE 2. 3 [Having sharp outlines] clear-cut, sharp, distinct; see DEFINITE 2. 4 [Thorough] complete, entire, total; see ABSOLUTE 1, WHOLE 1. 5 [Fair] reliable, decent, lawful; see FAIR 1, HONEST 1. —come clean* confess, tell the truth, own up; see ADMIT 2.

clean v. cleanse, clean up, clear up, clear out, purify, soak, shake out, wash down, scrub off, disinfect, tidy up, deodorize, swab, polish, sterilize, scrape, sweep out, scour, launder, vacuum, scald, dust, mop, cauterize, rinse, sponge, brush, comb, whisk, scrub, sweep, wipe up, clarify, rake, clean away, make clear, bathe, soap, bleach, erase, neaten, shampoo, refine, flush, blot, do up*, spruce up, slick up*; see also WASH 1, 2.—Ant. DIRTY, soil, smear.

cleaner n. detergent, disinfectant, cleaning agent; see CLEANSER, SOAP.

cleaning a. cleansing, purgative, detergent, washing, delousing, dusting, sweeping, scouring, soaking, sterilizing, laundering, vacuuming, scalding, purifying.

cleaning n. cleansing, purge, scrubbing, scouring, purification, sweeping, prophylaxis, sterilization, dry cleaning, ablution, sanitizing, shampooing, disinfection, washing, brushing, purifying, deodorizing, catharsis.

cleanliness n. cleanness, neatness, pureness, purity, tidiness, trimness, immaculateness, spotlessness, orderliness, whiteness, disinfection, sanitation.—Ant. FILTH, dirtiness, griminess.

cleanse v. 1 [To remove dirt from the surface of] launder, wash, scrub; see CLEAN. 2 [To remove impurities from within] refine, disinfect, purge; see CLEAN, PURIFY.

cleanser n. cleansing agent, cleaning agent, abrasive, lather, solvent, purgative, deodorant, fumigant, soap flakes, polish, disinfectant, antiseptic, purifier, scouring powder, spray cleaner, cleaner, detergent, soap powder, cleaning fluid, suds; see also SOAP. Cleansers include the following: water, soap and water, soap, detergent, washing soda, scouring powder, oven cleaner, naphtha, furniture polish, borax, lye, household ammonia, solvent, bluing, carbon tetrachloride, toilet-bowl cleaner, baking soda, chlorine compound, silver polish, kerosene, gasoline, vinegar, rug shampoo.

clear *a.* **1** [Open to the sight or understanding] explicit, plain, manifest; see OBVIOUS 1, 2. **2** [Offering little impediment to the vision] lucid, pure, transparent, apparent, limpid, translucent, crystal, crystalline, crystal clear.—*Ant.* OPAQUE, dark, muddy. **3** [Unclouded] sunny, bright, rainless; see FAIR 3. **4** [Freed from legal charges] free, guiltless, cleared, exonerated, blameless, innocent, dismissed, discharged, absolved; see also INNOCENT 1.—*Ant.* GUILTY, accused, blamed. **5** [Audible] loud enough to be heard, distinct, definite; see AUDIBLE. **—in the clear** guiltless, not suspected, cleared; see FREE 2, INNOCENT 1.

clear *v.* **1** [To free from uncertainty] clear up, relieve, clarify; see EXPLAIN. **2** [To free from obstacles] disentangle, unblock, unloose; see FREE, REMOVE 1. **3** [To profit] realize, net, make; see RECEIVE 1. **—clear out 1** [To remove] clean out, dispose of, get rid of; see ELIMINATE. **2** [*To leave] depart, go, remove oneself; see LEAVE 1. **—clear up 1** [To become clear; *said especially of weather*] improve, blow over, stop raining, stop snowing, run its course, die away, die down, show improvement, pick up, lift, become fair, have fair weather. **2** [To make clear] explicate, clarify, make plausible, make understandable, resolve, settle, make reasonable; see also EXPLAIN.

clear-cut *a.* precise, plain, evident; see OBVIOUS 1, 2.

cleared *a.* **1** [Emptied] cleaned, unloaded, cleared out; see EMPTY. **2** [Freed of charges] vindicated, absolved, set right; see DISCHARGED, FREE 2.

clearing *n.* **1** [The act of clearing] clearance, freeing, removing; see REMOVAL. **2** [A cleared space] open space, clearing, glade; see AREA, COURT, EXPANSE, YARD 1.

clearly *a.* **1** [Distinctly; *said of sight*] plainly, precisely, lucidly, purely, brightly, perceptibly, unmistakably, in full view, in focus, discernibly, decidedly, undoubtedly, incontestably, noticeably, before one's eyes, beyond doubt, prominently, obviously, openly, overtly, observably, certainly, apparently, manifestly, recognizably, conspicuously, in plain sight, definitely, markedly, surely, visibly, positively, seemingly, evidently, at first sight, to all appearances, on the face of it.—*Ant.* hazily, dully, cloudily. **2** [Distinctly; *said of sounds*] sharply, acutely, penetratingly, audibly, bell-like.—

Ant. indistinctly, mutteringly, unclearly.

clearness *n.* brightness, lucidity; see CLARITY.

clench *v.* grip, grasp, double up; see HOLD 1.

clergy *n.* priesthood, prelacy, pastorate; see MINISTRY 2.

clergyman *n.* cleric, pastor, preacher; see MINISTER 1, PRIEST, RABBI.

clerical *a.* **1** [Concerning clerks] stenographic, accounting, bookkeeping, secretarial, typing, written, assistant, subordinate. **2** [Concerning the clergy] ministerial, priestly, apostolic, monastic, monkish, churchly, papal, episcopal, canonical, pontifical, ecclesiastic, rabbinical, sacred, holy, ecclesiastical, in God's service, devoted to the Lord, in the Lord's work.

clerk *n.* salesgirl, saleswoman, saleslady, shopgirl, shop assistant, shopkeeper, salesclerk, salesman, salesperson, counterman, seller, auditor, bookkeeper, recorder, registrar, stenographer, timekeeper, cashier, teller, office worker, notary, controler, copyist, typist, inputter, file clerk, law clerk, switchboard operator; see also SECRETARY 2.

clever *a.* **1** [Apt, particularly with one's hands] skillful, expert, adroit; see ABLE. **2** [Mentally quick] smart, bright, shrewd; see INTELLIGENT, SLY.

cleverly *a.* neatly, skillfully, tactfully, dexterously, ingeniously, resourcefully, deftly, nimbly, agilely, adroitly, proficiently, expertly, smoothly, quickly, speedily; see also EASILY.—*Ant.* AWKWARDLY, clumsily, unskillfully.

cleverness *n.* skill, adroitness, ingenuity; see ABILITY.

cliché *n.* commonplace, platitude, stereotype, proverb, saying, slogan, trite phrase, vapid expression, triteness, banality, triviality, hackneyed phrase, trite idea; see also MOTTO.

click *n.* tick, snap, crack; see NOISE 1.

click *v.* **1** [To make a clicking sound] tick, snap, bang; see SOUND. **2** [*To be successful] match, go off well, meet with approval; see SUCCEED 1.

client *n.* customer, patient, patron; see BUYER.

cliff *n.* bluff, crag, steep rock; see HILL, MOUNTAIN 1, WALL 1.

climate *n.* characteristic weather, atmospheric conditions, aridity, humidity, temperature, weather conditions; see also COLD 1, HEAT 1, WEATHER.

climax *n.* peak, apex, highest point, culmination, acme, pinnacle, crest, zenith, summit, apogee, extremity, limit, utmost extent, highest degree, turning point, crowning point; see also MAXIMUM, TOP 1.—*Ant.* DEPRESSION, anticlimax, nadir.

climax *v.* culminate, tower, end, conclude, reach a peak, come to a head, reach the zenith, break the record; see also ACHIEVE.

climb *n.* **1** [The act of climbing] ascent, clamber, mounting; see RISE. **2** [An ascending place] slope, incline, dune; see GRADE 1, HILL.

climb *v.* scale, work one's way up, ascend gradually, scramble up, clamber up, swarm up, start up, go up, ascend, struggle up, get on, climb on, progress upward, rise, rise hand over hand, come up, creep up, escalate, surmount, shinny up, shoot up. —**climb down** step off, come down, dismount; see DESCEND.

cling *v.* adhere, clasp, hold fast; see STICK 1.

clip *v.* snip, crop, clip off; see CUT 1, DECREASE 2.

clippers *n.* shears, trimmers, barber's tools; see SCISSORS.

clique *n.* coterie, inner circle, club; see FACTION, ORGANIZATION 2.

clock *n.* timepiece, timekeeper, chronometer, timer, alarm clock, cuckoo clock, electric clock, grandfather clock, pendulum clock, atomic clock, digital clock, clock radio, hourglass, stopwatch, sundial, wristwatch; see also WATCH 1. —**around the clock** continuously, continually, twenty-four hours a day; see REGULARLY.

clock *v.* time, measure time, register speed; see MEASURE 1.

clog *v.* stop up, jam, obstruct; see CLOSE 2, HINDER.

close *a.* **1** [Nearby] neighboring, across the street, around the corner; see NEAR 1. **2** [Intimate] confidential, intimate, familiar; see PRIVATE. **3** [Compact] dense, solid, compressed; see THICK 1. **4** [Stingy] narrow, parsimonious, miserly; see STINGY. **5** [Stifling] sticky, stuffy, unventilated, heavy, motionless, uncomfortable, stale-smelling, musty, stagnant, confined, suffocating, sweltering, tight, stale, oppressive, breathless; see also UNCOMFORTABLE 2.—*Ant.* FRESH, refreshing, brisk. **6** [Similar] resembling, having common qualities, much the same; see ALIKE, LIKE.

close *n.* termination, adjournment, ending; see END 2.

close *v.* **1** [To put a stop to] conclude, finish, terminate; see END 1. **2** [To put a stopper into] shut, stop, choke off, stuff, clog, prevent passage, shut off, turn off, lock, block, bar, dam, cork, seal; see also CLOSE 2.—*Ant.* OPEN, uncork, unseal. **3** [To come together] meet, unite,

agree; see JOIN 1. **4** [To shut] slam, close down, shut, shut down, shut up, seal, fasten, bolt, bar, shutter, lock, bring to.

closed *a.* **1** [Terminated] ended, concluded, final; see FINISHED 1. **2** [Not in operation] shut down, out of order, out of service, bankrupt, closed up, padlocked, having folded up*; see also BROKEN 2. **3** [Not open] shut, fastened, sealed; see TIGHT 2.

closely *a.* approximately, similarly, exactly, nearly, strictly, intimately, jointly, in conjunction with; see also ALMOST.—*Ant.* INDIVIDUALLY, separately, one by one.

closet *n.* cabinet, recess, cupboard, buffet, locker, wardrobe, receptacle, safe, bin, vault, cold storage, armoire, cloakroom, storeroom.

clot *n.* lump, bulk, clotting, curdling, coagulation, mass, clump, coagulum, thickness, coalescence, curd.

clot *v.* coagulate, curdle, lump; see THICKEN.

cloth *n.* fabric, material, textiles; see GOODS.

clothe *v.* attire, dress up, costume; see DRESS 1.

clothed *a.* clad, invested, costumed, robed, shod, dressed, attired, decked, disguised, covered, draped, veiled.—*Ant.* NAKED, exposed, stripped.

clothes *n.* wearing apparel, raiment, clothing, garments, garb, vestments, attire, array, casual wear, informal wear, formal wear, evening clothes, work clothes, suit of clothes, costume, wardrobe, trappings, gear, underclothes, outfit, get-up*, rags*, togs*, duds*, threads*, things; see also COAT 1, DRESS 1, 2, HAT, PANTS 1, SHIRT. *Men's clothes include the following:* business suit, sport jacket, sport coat, trousers, breeches, knickers*, tuxedo, tux*, dress suit, dinner jacket, uniform, shirt, tie, necktie, bow tie, ascot, bolo tie, long underwear, long johns*, undershirt, T-shirt, briefs, undershorts. *Women's clothes include the following:* dress, evening gown, frock, shirtwaist, blouse, skirt, housecoat, negligee, nightgown, nightie*, underwear, lingerie, bra, brassiere, panties, underpants, camisole, pantyhose, nylons, stockings, tights, girdle, slip, kimono, suit, housedress, smock, miniskirt, shift, muumuu, jumper, petticoat, bonnet. *Clothes worn by both men and women include the following:* blue jeans, Levi's (trademark), shirt, turtleneck, sweat shirt, sweat pants, tank top, pajamas, pj's*, slacks, pants, sweater, cardigan, pullover, coat, raincoat, hat, gloves, socks, shoes, robe, bathrobe, slippers, shorts, cutoffs, bell-bottoms, hat, cap, beret, uniform, scarf. *Children's clothes include the following:* rompers, playsuit, coveralls, snowsuit. *Work clothes include the following:* overalls, windbreaker, blue jeans, coveralls.

clothing *n.* attire, apparel, garb; see CLOTHES, DRESS 1.

cloud *n.* haze, mist, fogginess, haziness, film, puff, billow, smoke, veil, cloud cover, overcast. *Types of clouds include the following:* cirrus, cumulus, stratus, nimbus, cirrocumulus, cirrostratus. **—in the clouds** fanciful, fantastic, romantic; see IMPRACTICAL. **—under a cloud** suspect, dubious, uncertain; see SUSPICIOUS 2.

cloudy *a.* 1 [Hazy] overcast, foggy, sunless; see DARK 1. 2 [Not clear] dense, nontransparent, murky, textiles; see also OPAQUE.

clown *n.* buffoon, fool, joker, harlequin, Punch, funnyman, humorist, jester, comedian, cutup*; see also ACTOR.

clown (around) *v.* fool around, kid around, cut up*; see JOKE.

club *n.* 1 [A social organization] association, order, society; see FACTION, ORGANIZATION 2. 2 [A heavy stick] bat, baton, blackjack; see STICK.

club *v.* batter, whack, pound; see BEAT 1, HIT 1.

clue *n.* evidence, trace, mark; see PROOF 1, SIGN 1.

clump *n.* cluster, bundle, knot; see BUNCH.

clumsily *a.* crudely, gawkily, stumblingly; see AWKWARDLY.

clumsiness *n.* crudity, ineptitude, boorishness; see AWKWARDNESS.

clumsy *a.* ungainly, gawky, inexpert; see AWKWARD.

cluster *n.* group, batch, clump; see BUNCH.

clutch *v.* grab, grasp, grip; see HOLD 1, SEIZE 1.

clutches *n.* control, grasp, keeping; see POWER 2.

clutter *n.* disarray, jumble, mess; see CONFUSION.

coach *n.* 1 [A carriage] stagecoach, chaise, victoria; see CARRIAGE 2, VEHICLE. 2 [An instructor] physical education instructor, drillmaster, mentor; see TEACHER, TRAINER.

coach *v.* train, drill, instruct; see TEACH.

coagulate *v.* curdle, clot, congeal; see THICKEN.

coal *n.* anthracite, bituminous coal, peat; see FUEL. **—haul (or rake or drag) over the coals*** reprimand, criticize, castigate; see BLAME.

coalition *n.* compact, alliance, association; see FACTION.

coarse *a.* 1 [Not fine] rough, granular, harsh; see CRUDE. 2 [Vulgar] low, common, rude; see RUDE 1, VULGAR.

coast *n.* shoreline, beach, seaboard; see SHORE.

coast *v.* glide, float, ride on the current; see DRIFT, RIDE 1.

coat *n.* 1 [An outer garment] topcoat, overcoat, cloak, suit coat, tuxedo, dinner jacket, sport coat, blazer, dress coat, fur coat, ski jacket, parka, mackintosh, raincoat, trench coat, jacket, windbreaker, peacoat, three-quarter-length coat, wrap, leather jacket, southwester, slicker, waterproof*; see also CLOTHES. 2 [The covering of an animal] protective covering, shell, scales, fleece, epidermis, pelt, membrane; see also FUR, HIDE, SKIN. 3 [An applied covering] coating, layer, wash, primer, finish, glaze, crust, painting, overlay, whitewashing, varnish, lacquer, gloss, tinge, prime coat, plaster; see also FINISH 2.

coat *v.* cover, glaze, enamel; see PAINT 2, VARNISH.

coating *n.* crust, covering, layer; see COAT 3.

coax *v.* persuade, cajole, inveigle; see INFLUENCE, URGE 2.

cocktail *n.* mixed drink, aperitif, highball. *Cocktails include the following:* Manhattan, martini, old-fashioned, champagne, margarita, pink lady, whiskey sour, screwdriver, bloody mary, daiquiri, Alexander, piña colada, mint julep; see also DRINK 2.

code *n.* body of laws, regulations, digest; see LAW 2, SYSTEM.

coerce *v.* impel, compel, constrain; see FORCE.

coercion *n.* compulsion, persuasion, constraint; see PRESSURE 2, RESTRAINT 2.

coexist *v.* exist together, coincide, be contemporary; see ACCOMPANY.

coexistence *n.* order, détente, accord; see PEACE 1, 2.

coffee *n.* caffeinated beverage, decaf*, java*; see DRINK 2. *Prepared coffee includes the following:* Turkish, Armenian, drip, percolated, vacuum, instant, French roast, coffee with cream, demitasse, espresso, café au lait, latte, cappuccino, black coffee.

coffin *n.* box, casket, sarcophagus, burial urn, funerary urn, pine box, mummy case; see also CONTAINER.

cohabit *v.* shack up with*, play house with*, be roommates; see ACCOMPANY.

coherence *n.* stickiness, viscosity, gumminess, cementation, adhesiveness, sticking together, coagulation, viscidity, adherence, fusion, sticking, union, adhesion, cohesiveness, consistency.

coherent *a.* comprehensible, sound, intelligible; see LOGICAL, UNDERSTANDABLE.

coil *n.* curl, turn, ring, wind, convolution, twist, twirl, lap, loop, curlicue, corkscrew, roll, spiral, helix, scroll; see also CIRCLE 1.

coil *v.* scroll, wind, loop, twist, fold, twine, intertwine, entwine, convolute, lap, twirl, wreathe; see also CURL.—*Ant.* UNFOLD, unwind, ravel.

coin *n.* legal tender, silver, copper; see MONEY 1.

coin *v.* **1** [To mint money] mint, strike, stamp; see MANUFACTURE. **2** [To invent a word, etc.] create, originate, make up; see INVENT 1.

coincide *v.* correspond, agree, concur, match, accord, harmonize; see also AGREE.

coincidence *n.* luck, fortune, circumstance; see ACCIDENT, CHANCE 1.

coincidental *a.* **1** [Occurring simultaneously] concurrent, concomitant, contemporaneous; see SIMULTANEOUS. **2** [Apparently accidental] chance, unpredictable, unplanned; see RANDOM.

cold *a.* **1** [*Said of the weather*] crisp, cool, icy, freezing, frosty, frigid, wintry, bleak, nippy, brisk, keen, penetrating, snowy, frozen, cutting, snappy, piercing, chill, bitter, numbing, severe, stinging, glacial, intense, Siberian, chilly, sharp, raw, nipping, arctic, polar, below zero, biting.—*Ant.* HOT, warm, heated. **2** [*Said of persons, animals, etc.*] coldblooded, frozen, clammy, stiff, chilled, frostbitten, shivering, blue from cold.—*Ant.* HOT, perspiring, thawed. **3** [*Said of temperament*] unconcerned, apathetic, distant; see INDIFFERENT, RESERVED 3. —**have (or get) cold feet** go back on one's word, hold back, back down; see FEAR, STOP 2. —**throw cold water on** dishearten, squelch, dampen; see DISCOURAGE.

cold *n.* **1** [Conditions having a cold temperature] coldness, frozenness, chilliness, frostiness, draft, frostbite, absence of warmth, want of heat, chill, shivers, coolness, goose flesh, numbness, iciness, frigidity, freeze, glaciation, refrigeration; see also WEATHER.—*Ant.* HEAT, warmth, heat wave. **2** [Head or respiratory congestion] cough, sore throat, sickness, head cold, sinus trouble, chest cold, bronchial irritation, common cold, laryngitis, hay fever, whooping cough, influenza, flu, asthma, bronchitis, strep throat, strep, sniffles*, frog in one's throat; see also ILLNESS 2. —**catch cold** come down with a

cold, become ill, get a cold; see SICKEN 1. —**leave out in the cold** ignore, slight, neglect; see ABANDON 2. —**(out) in the cold** forgotten, ignored, rejected; see NEGLECTED.

coldblooded *a.* relentless, callous, unfeeling; see CRUEL.

collaborate *v.* work together, conspire, work with; see COOPERATE.

collapse *n.* breakdown, downfall, destruction; see FAILURE 1, WRECK.

collapse *v.* break down, cave in, give way; see FALL 1, FAIL 1, 2.

collar *n.* neckband, neckpiece, dickey; see CLOTHES.

collateral *n.* security, guarantee, pledge; see INSURANCE, MONEY 1, WEALTH.

colleague *n.* partner, collaborator, teammate; see ASSOCIATE.

collect *v.* **1** [To bring into one place] amass, consolidate, convoke; see ACCUMULATE, ASSEMBLE 2, CONCENTRATE 1. **2** [To come together] congregate, assemble, flock; see GATHER. **3** [To obtain funds] solicit, raise, secure; see GET 1.

collected *a.* **1** [Composed] self-possessed, poised, cool; see CALM 1. **2** [Assembled] accumulated, amassed, compiled; see GATHERED.

collection *n.* specimens, samples, examples, extracts, gems, models, assortment, medley, accumulation, pile, stack, group, assemblage, compilation, mass, quantity, selection, treasury, anthology, miscellany, aggregation, combination, number, store, stock, digest, arrangement, concentration, finds, batch, mess, lot, heap, bunch; see also GROUP 3.

collector *n.* authority, hobbyist, fancier, serious amateur, gatherer, discoverer, curator, compiler, finder, assembler, hoarder, librarian, archivist; see also SCIENTIST, SPECIALIST.

college *n.* institute, institution, community college, liberal arts college, teachers college, junior college, state college, denominational college, nondenominational college, private college, business school, technical school, higher education, graduate school, medical school, law school, seminary; see also UNIVERSITY.

collide *v.* **1** [To come into violent contact] hit, strike, smash; see CRASH 4. **2** [To come into conflict] clash, conflict, disagree; see OPPOSE 1.

collision *n.* impact, contact, shock, accident, crash, colliding, bump, jar, jolt, sideswipe, strike, hit, slam, blow, thud, thump, knock, smash, head-on crash, fender bender*; see also DISASTER.

colonial *a.* **1** [Concerning a colony] pioneer, isolated, dependent, settled, provincial, frontier, Pilgrim, emigrant, immigrant, territorial, outland, distant, remote, early American, overseas, established. **2** [Having qualities suggestive of colonial life] hard, raw, crude, harsh, wild, unsettled, limited, uncultured, new, unsophisticated.

colonization *n.* immigration, settlement, expansion; see FOUNDATION 2.

colonize *v.* found, people, pioneer; see ESTABLISH 2, SETTLE 5.

colony *n.* settlement, dependency, subject state, colonial state, dominion, offshoot, political possession, province, group, new land, protectorate, hive, daughter country, satellite state, community, group migration; see also NATION 1.

color *n.* hue, tone, tint, shade, tinge, dye, complexion, brilliance, undertone, value, iridescence, intensity, coloration, discoloration, pigmentation, coloring, cast, glow, blush, wash, tincture. *Colors include the following—colors in the solar spectrum:* red, orange, yellow, green, blue, violet; *primary colors of the spectrum:* red, green, blue; *psychological primary colors:* red, yellow, green, blue, black, white; *primary colors of paints or pigments:* red, blue, yellow; see also BLACK 1, BLUE 1, PURPLE, BROWN, GREEN 1, ORANGE 1, PINK, RED, YELLOW. —**change color** flush, redden, become red in the face; see BLUSH. —**lose color** become pale, blanch, faint; see WHITEN 1.

color *v.* chalk, daub, gild, enamel, lacquer, suffuse, stipple, pigment, glaze, tinge, tint, stain, tone, shade, dye, wash, crayon, enliven, embellish, give color to, adorn, imbue, emblazon, illuminate, rouge; see also DECORATE, PAINT 1, 2.

colored *a.* hued, tinted, tinged, shaded, flushed, reddened, glowing, stained, dyed, washed, rouged; see also PAINTED 2.

colorful *a.* vivid, glowing, realistic; see BRIGHT 1.

colorless *a.* drab, pale, neutral; see DULL 2, TRANSPARENT 1.

colossal *a.* huge, enormous, immense; see LARGE 1.

colt *n.* foal, filly, yearling; see HORSE.

column *n.* **1** [A pillar] support, prop, shaft, monument, totem, pylon, obelisk, tower, minaret, cylinder, mast, monolith, upright, pedestal; see also POST. **2** [Journalistic commentary] article, editorial, Op-Ed; see NEWS 1.

columnist *n.* feature writer, journalist, correspondent; see REPORTER, WRITER.

coma *n.* unconsciousness, insensibility, stupor; see SLEEP.

comb *n.* pocket comb, pick, currycomb; see BRUSH 1.

comb *v.* untangle, disentangle, cleanse, scrape, arrange, straighten, part, tease, smooth.

combat *n.* struggle, warfare, conflict; see BATTLE, FIGHT.

combat *v.* battle, oppose, resist; see FIGHT.

combination *n.* **1** [The act of combining] uniting, joining, unification; see UNION 1. **2** [An association] union, alliance, federation; see ORGANIZATION 2. **3** [Something formed by combining] compound, aggregate, blend; see MIXTURE 1.

combine *v.* **1** [To bring together] connect, mix, link; see JOIN 1. **2** [To become one] fuse, merge, blend; see MIX 1, UNITE.

combined *a.* linked, mingled, connected; see JOINED.

combustion *n.* flaming, burning, oxidization; see FIRE 1.

come *v.* **1** [To move toward] close in, advance, draw near; see APPROACH 2. **2** [To arrive] appear at, reach, attain; see ARRIVE. **3** [To be available] appear, be at someone's disposal, be ready, be obtainable, be handy, be accessible, be able to be reached, show up, turn up; see also APPEAR 1. **4** [*To have an orgasm] reach sexual fulfillment, ejaculate, climax; see ACHIEVE, COPULATE. —**as good as they come** excellent, superior, fine; see BEST. —**come about** occur, take place, result; see HAPPEN 2. —**come across 1** [To find] uncover, stumble upon, notice; see DISCOVER, FIND. **2** [*To give] deliver, pay, hand over; see GIVE 1. —**come along 1** [To accompany] accompany, go with, attend; see ARRIVE, ADVANCE 1. **2** [To progress] show improvement, do well, prosper; see IMPROVE 2. —**come around 1** [To recover] improve, recuperate, rally; see RECOVER 3, REVIVE 2. **2** [*To visit] call on, stop by, drop in on; see VISIT. —**come by 1** [To pass] go by, overtake, move past; see PASS 1. **2** [To acquire] get, win, procure; see GET 1. —**come into 1** [To inherit] fall heir to, succeed to, acquire; see INHERIT, RECEIVE 1. **2** [To join] enter into, associate with, align; see JOIN 2. —**come off 1** [To become separated] be disconnected, be disengaged, be severed, be parted, be disjoined, be detached, be disunited; see also DIVIDE. **2** [To happen] occur, turn out, come about; see HAPPEN 2. —**come out 1** [To be made public] be published, be made known, be announced, be issued, be brought out, be reported, be revealed, be divulged, be disclosed, be exposed; see also APPEAR 1. **2** [To result] end, conclude, terminate; see SUCCEED 1. —**come out for** announce, state, affirm; see DECLARE, SUPPORT 1. —**come**

through 1 [To be successful] accomplish, score, triumph; see ACHIEVE, SUCCEED 1. 2 [To survive] live through, persist, withstand; see ENDURE 2. 3 [To do] accomplish, achieve, carry out; see PERFORM 1. —**come to** 1 [To recover] rally, come around, recuperate; see RECOVER 3, REVIVE 2. 2 [To result in] end in, terminate by, conclude; see HAPPEN 2, RESULT. —**come up** appear, arise, move to a higher place; see RISE 1. —**how come?*** for what reason?, how so?, what is the cause of that?; see WHY.

comeback* n. 1 [Improvement] revival, progress, betterment; see IMPROVEMENT 1, RECOVERY 1, 2. 2 [Witty answer] retort, reply, rejoinder; see ANSWER 1.

comedian n. comic, humorist, entertainer; see ACTOR, CLOWN.

comedown n. reversal, blow, defeat; see FAILURE 1.

comedy n. comic drama, tragicomedy, stand-up comedy, situation comedy, sitcom, musical comedy, farce, satire, burlesque, parody, cartoon, skit, slapstick, light entertainment; see also DRAMA.

comfort n. rest, quiet, relaxation, repose, relief, poise, well-being, cheer, abundance, sufficiency, gratification, luxury, warmth, plenty, prosperity, pleasure, happiness, contentment, convenience, restfulness, peacefulness, cheerfulness, coziness, exhilaration, complacency, bed of roses*; see also EASE 1, ENJOYMENT, SATISFACTION 2.—Ant. WEAKNESS, discomfort, uneasiness.

comfort v. 1 [To console] share with, commiserate, solace, grieve with, cheer, gladden, uphold, hearten, pat on the back, put someone in a good humor, sustain, support, help, aid, confirm, reassure, refresh; see also ENCOURAGE, PITY 1.—Ant. DISCOURAGE, be indifferent to, depress. 2 [To make easy physically] alleviate, relieve, make comfortable, assuage, soothe, mitigate, gladden, quiet someone's fears, help someone in need, lighten someone's burden, encourage, calm, revive, sustain, aid, assist, nourish, support, compose oneself, delight, divert, bolster up, invigorate, refresh, put at ease, reassure, warm, lighten, soften, remedy, release, restore, free, make well, revitalize; see also EASE 1, HELP, STRENGTHEN.—Ant. WEAKEN, make uneasy, worsen.

comfortable a. 1 [In physical ease] contented, cheerful, easy, at rest, relaxed, at ease, untroubled, healthy, rested, pleased, complacent, soothed, relieved, strengthened, restored, in comfort, at home with, without care, snug as a bug in a rug*; see also HAPPY, SATISFIED.—Ant. UNEASY, ill, disturbed. 2 [Conducive to physical ease] satisfactory, snug, cozy, warm, sheltered, convenient, protected, cared for, appropriate, useful, roomy, spacious, luxurious, rich, satisfying, restful, in comfort, well-off, well-to-do; see also PLEASANT 2.—Ant. SHABBY, rundown, uncomfortable.

comfortably a. luxuriously, in comfort, restfully, snugly, cozily, pleasantly, warmly, conveniently, adequately, with ease, competently, amply; see also EASILY.—Ant. INADEQUATELY, insufficiently, poorly.

comforting a. sympathetic, cheering, encouraging, invigorating, health-giving, warming, consoling, sustaining, reassuring, inspiring, refreshing, relieving, soothing, lightening, mitigating, alleviating, softening, curing, restoring, releasing, freeing, revitalizing, tranquilizing.—Ant. DISTURBING, distressing, upsetting.

comic a. humorous, ridiculous, ironic; see FUNNY 1.

comical a. witty, amusing, humorous; see FUNNY 1.

coming a. 1 [Approaching] advancing, drawing near, progressing, nearing, in the offing, arriving, gaining upon, pursuing, getting near, converging, coming in, close at hand, coming on, near at hand, almost upon, immediate, future, in view, preparing, to come, eventual, fated, written, hereafter, at hand, in store, due, about to happen, hoped for, deserved, close, imminent, prospective, anticipated, forthcoming, looming, threatening, certain, ordained, impending, to be, expected, near, pending, foreseen, in the cards, in the wind; see also EXPECTED, LIKELY 1.—Ant. DISTANT, going, leaving. 2 [Having a promising future] promising, advancing, probable; see ABLE, AMBITIOUS. 3 [Future] lying ahead, pending, impending; see EXPECTED, FUTURE.

coming n. approach, landing, homecoming; see ARRIVAL 1.

command n. order, injunction, direction, demand, decree, prohibition, interdiction, canon, rule, call, summons, imposition, precept, mandate, charge, behest, edict, proclamation, instruction, proscription, ban, requirement, dictate, subpoena, commandment, dictum, word of command, writ, citation, notification, will, regulation, ordinance, act, fiat, bidding, word, requisition, ultimatum, exaction, enactment, caveat, prescript, warrant; see also LAW 3, POWER 2, REQUEST.

command v. 1 [To issue an order] charge, tell, demand; see ORDER 1.

2 [To have control] rule, dominate, master; see CONTROL.

commandeer *v.* appropriate, take, confiscate; see SEIZE 2.

commander *n.* commandant, officer, head; see ADMINISTRATION 2, ADMINISTRATOR, CHIEF, LEADER 2.

commanding *a.* **1** [Ruling] leading, directing, determining, ordering, instructing, dictating, dominating, compelling, managing, checking, curbing, forcing, coercing, requiring, restraining, in command, in authority, in charge, regulating. **2** [Important] decisive, impressive, significant; see IMPORTANT 1.

commemorate *v.* solemnize, honor, memorialize; see ADMIRE, CELEBRATE 1.

commemoration *n.* recognition, remembrance, observance; see CELEBRATION, CEREMONY, CUSTOM.

commemorative *a.* dedicated to the memory of, in remembrance of, in honor of; see MEMORABLE 1.

commence *v.* start, initiate, set in motion; see BEGIN 2.

commend *v.* laud, support, acclaim; see APPROVE, PRAISE 1.

commendable *a.* praiseworthy, laudable, deserving; see EXCELLENT.

commendation *n.* tribute, approval, approbation; see HONOR, PRAISE 1.

comment *n.* report, commentary, editorial; see DISCUSSION, EXPLANATION, REMARK.

comment *v.* observe, remark, criticize, notice, state, express, pronounce, assert, affirm, mention, interject, say, note, touch upon, disclose, bring out, point out, conclude; see also MENTION, TALK 1.

commentary *n.* criticism, analysis, description; see EXPLANATION, INTERPRETATION.

commerce *n.* buying and selling, trading, marketing; see BUSINESS 1, ECONOMICS.

commercial *a.* trading, business, financial, economic, materialistic, practical, profitable, mercantile, merchandising, exchange, bartering, fiscal, monetary, trade, market, retail, wholesale, marketable, in the market, for sale, profit-making, money-making, across the counter; see also INDUSTRIAL, PROFITABLE.

commercial *n.* message from the sponsor, commercial announcement, plug*; see ADVERTISEMENT.

commercialize *v.* lower the quality of, degrade, cheapen; see ABUSE.

commission *n.* **1** [An authorization] order, license, command; see PERMISSION. **2** [A committee] commissioners, representatives, board; see COMMITTEE. **3** [A payment] percentage, fee, rake-off*; see PAY 2, PAYMENT 1. **—out of commission** dam-

aged, not working, out of order; see BROKEN 2.

commission *v.* send, appoint, authorize, charge, empower, constitute, ordain, commit, entrust, send out, dispatch, deputize, assign, engage, employ, inaugurate, invest, name, nominate, hire, enable, license, command, elect, select; see also DELEGATE 1.

commissioner *n.* administrator, magistrate, government official; see EXECUTIVE.

commit *v.* **1** [To perpetrate] do, be guilty of, carry out; see PERFORM 1. **2** [To entrust] confide, delegate, relegate to, leave to, give to do, promise, assign, turn over to, put in the hands of, charge, invest, rely upon, depend upon, confer a trust, bind over, make responsible for, put an obligation upon, employ, dispatch, send, vest in, engage, commission; see also ASSIGN.—*Ant.* DISMISS, relieve of, discharge.

commitment *n.* pledge, responsibility, agreement; see DUTY 1, PROMISE 1, GUARANTY.

committee *n.* consultants, board, bureau, council, cabinet, investigators, trustees, appointed group, board of inquiry, representatives, investigating committee, executive committee, standing committee, planning committee, ad hoc committee, special committee, referees, task force, study group, subcommittee; see also REPRESENTATIVE 2.

commodity *n.* goods, articles, stocks, merchandise, wares, materials, possessions, property, assets, belongings, things, stock in trade, consumers' goods, line, what one handles, what one is showing.

common *a.* **1** [Ordinary] universal, familiar, natural, normal, everyday, accepted, commonplace, characteristic, customary, bourgeois, conventional, passable, general, informal, wearisome, unassuming, pedestrian, lower-level, habitual, prevalent, probable, typical, prosaic, simple, current, prevailing, trite, household, second-rate, banal, unvaried, homely, colloquial, trivial, stock, oft-repeated, indiscriminate, tedious, worn-out, hackneyed, monotonous, stale, casual, undistinguished, uneducated, artless, workaday, provincial, unsophisticated, unrefined, untutored, plain, uncultured, vulgar, unadorned, ugly, obvious, average, orthodox, mediocre, humdrum, well-known, insipid, stereotyped, patent, moderate, middling, abiding, indifferent, tolerable, temperate, innocuous, undistinguished, run-of-the-mill, not too bad*, garden-variety, fair to middling*, so-so, nothing to write home about*; see also CONVENTIONAL 1, DULL 4, POPULAR 1, 3, TRADITIONAL.—*Ant.* UNIQUE, extraordinary, unnatural. **2** [Of frequent occurrence] customary, constant, usual; see FREQUENT 1, HABITUAL, REGULAR 3. **3** [Generally known] general, prevalent, well-known; see FAMILIAR, TRADITIONAL. **4** [Low] cheap, inferior, shoddy; see POOR 2, SUBORDINATE. **5** [Held or enjoyed in common] shared, joint, mutual; see COOPERATIVE, PUBLIC 2. —**in common** shared, communal, mutually held; see PUBLIC 2.

commonly *a.* usually, ordinarily, generally; see REGULARLY.

commonplace *a.* usual, hackneyed, mundane; see COMMON 1, CONVENTIONAL 1, 3.

common sense *n.* good sense, judgment, horse sense*; see SENSE 2, WISDOM.

commotion *n.* violence, tumult, uproar; see DISTURBANCE 2, FIGHT.

communal *a.* shared, cooperative, mutual; see PUBLIC 2.

commune *n.* community, collective, co-op*; see COOPERATIVE.

communicate *v.* **1** [To impart information] convey, inform, advise; see TEACH, TELL 1. **2** [To be in communication] correspond, be in touch, have access to, contact, reach, hear from, be within reach, be in correspondence with, be near, be close to, have the confidence of, associate with, establish contact with, be in agreement with, be in agreement about, confer, talk, converse, chat, speak together, deal with, write to, telephone, e-mail, wire, cable, fax, network, reply, answer, have a meeting of minds, find a common denominator; see also AGREE.—*Ant.* AVOID, withdraw, elude.

communication *n.* talk, utterance, announcing, extrasensory perception, telepathy, ESP, publication, writing, drawing, painting, broadcasting, televising, correspondence, disclosure, speaking, disclosing, conference, faxing, telephoning, wiring, e-mailing, cabling, networking, description, mention, announcement, presentation, interchange, expression, narration, relation, declaration, assertion, elucidation, transmission, reception, reading, translating, interpreting, news, ideas, statement, speech, language, warning, communiqué, briefing, bulletin, summary, information, report, account, publicity, translation, printed work, advice, tidings, conversation. *Means of communication include the following:* book, letter, newspaper, magazine, radio, TV, e-mail, proclamation, broadcast, dispatch, press-release, fax, wire, printout, telecast, telephone call, telegram, cable, broadside, circular, flier, brochure, notes, memorandum, postcard, poster, billboard; see also MAIL, NEWS 1, 2, RADIO 2, TELEPHONE, TELEVISION.

communications *n.* mail, mass media, telephone; see COMMUNICATION.

communism *n.* state socialism, Marxism, dictatorship of the proletariat, collectivism, state ownership of production; see also GOVERNMENT 2.

communist *n.* Marxist, commie*, red*; see RADICAL.

community *n.* **1** [A town] village, colony, hamlet; see CITY, TOWN 1. **2** [Society] the public, the people, the nation; see SOCIETY 2.

commute *v.* **1** [To exchange for something less severe] reduce, lessen, mitigate; see DECREASE 2. **2** [Travel] go back and forth, drive, take the train; see TRAVEL.

commuter *n.* suburbanite, city worker, daily traveler; see DRIVER, TRAVELER.

companion *n.* attendant, comrade, associate, partner, escort, chaperon, protector, guide, friend, bodyguard.

companionship *n.* fraternity, rapport, association; see BROTHERHOOD, FELLOWSHIP 1, FRIENDSHIP.

company *n.* **1** [A group of people] assembly, throng, band; see GATHERING. **2** [People organized for business] partnership, firm, corporation; see BUSINESS 4. **3** [A guest or guests] visitors, callers, overnight guests; see GUEST. —**keep (a person) company** stay with, visit, amuse; see ENTERTAIN 1. —**keep company (with)** fraternize, accompany, associate, go together, date, go with*, take up with*, hang around with*, pal around with*. —**part company** separate, part, stop associating with; see LEAVE 1.

comparable *a.* **1** [Worthy of comparison] as good as, equivalent, tantamount; see EQUAL. **2** [Capable of comparison] similar, akin, relative; see ALIKE, LIKE.

comparatively *a.* relatively, similarly, analogously; see APPROXIMATELY.

compare *v.* **1** [To liken] relate, connect, make like, notice the similarities, associate, link, distinguish between, bring near, put alongside, reduce to a common denominator, declare similar, equate, match, express by metaphor, correlate, parallel, show to be analogous, identify with, bring into meaningful relation with, collate, balance, bring into comparison, estimate relatively, set over against, compare notes, exchange observations, weigh one thing against another, set side by side, measure, place in juxtaposition, note the similarities and differences of, juxtapose, draw a parallel between, tie up, come up to, stack up with; see also DISTINGUISH 1. **2** [To examine on a comparative basis] contrast, set against, weigh; see ANALYZE, EXAMINE. **3** [To stand in relationship to another] match, vie, rival; see EQUAL, MATCH 3. — **beyond** (or **past** or **without**) **compare** incomparable, without equal, distinctive; see UNIQUE. —**compare to** (or **with**) put side by side, relate to, equate; see COMPARE 1.

comparison *n.* likening, metaphor, simile, resemblance, analogy, illustration, correspondence, relation, correlation, parable, allegory, similarity, identification, equation, measurement, example, contrast, parallel, connection, paralleling; see also ASSOCIATION 2.

compartment *n.* section, portion, subdivision; see PART 1.

compassion *n.* sympathy, consideration, clemency; see KINDNESS 1, PITY.

compassionate *a.* kind, humane, sympathetic; see MERCIFUL.

compatible *a.* agreeable, congruous, cooperative; see HARMONIOUS 2.

compel *v.* enforce, constrain, coerce; see FORCE.

compensate *v.* recompense, remunerate, requite; see PAY 1, REPAY 1.

compensation *n.* remuneration, recompense, indemnity, satisfaction, reparation, restitution, remittal, return for services, commission, gratuity, reimbursement, allowance, deserts, remittance, salary, stipend, wages, hire, earnings, settlement, honorarium, coverage, consideration, damages, repayment, fee, reckoning, bonus, premium, amends, reward, advantage, profit, benefit, gain, kickback*; see also PAY 2, PAYMENT 1.—*Ant.* LOSS, deprivation, confiscation.

compete *v.* enter competition, take part, strive, struggle, vie with, be in the running, become a competitor, enter the lists, run for, participate in, engage in a contest, oppose, wrestle, be rivals, battle, bid, spar, fence, face, clash, encounter, match wits, play, grapple, take on all comers, go in for*, lock horns, go out for; see also FIGHT.

competence *n.* capability, skill, fitness; see ABILITY.

competent *a.* fit, qualified, skilled; see ABLE.

competition *n.* race, match, contest, meet, fight, bout, boxing match, game of skill, trial, athletic event, wrestling; see also GAME 1, SPORT 1, 3. —**in competition with** opposed to, competing against, in a rivalry with; see AGAINST 1.

competitive *a.* competing, aggressive, ambitious; see RIVAL.

competitor *n.* foe, rival, antagonist; see CONTESTANT, OPPONENT 1.

compile *v.* collect, arrange, assemble; see ACCUMULATE, EDIT.

complacent *a.* self-satisfied, contented, self-righteous; see EGOTISTIC, HAPPY, SATISFIED, SMUG.

complain *v.* disapprove, accuse, deplore, criticize, denounce, differ, disagree, dissent, charge, report adversely, reproach, oppose, grumble, whine, whimper, remonstrate, fret, protest, fuss, moan, make a fuss, take exception to, object to, deprecate, enter a demurrer, demur, defy, carp, impute, indict, attack, refute, grouse*, kick*, bitch*, grouch, gripe*, grunt, beef*, bellyache*, kick up a fuss*.—*Ant.* APPROVE, sanction, countenance.

complaining *a.* objecting, lamenting, murmuring, mourning, regretting, bewailing, deploring, weeping, moaning, protesting, charging, accusing, disapproving, grumbling, fretting, whining, imputing, resenting, dissenting, registering a protest, filing a complaint, making an adverse report, kicking.—*Ant.* enjoying, appreciating, praising.

complaint *n.* **1** [An objection] charge, criticism, reproach; see ACCUSATION, OBJECTION. **2** [An illness] ailment, disease, infirmity; see ILLNESS 1.

complementary *a.* paired, mated, corresponding; see ALIKE, MATCHED.

complete *a.* **1** [Not lacking in any part] total, intact, entire; see FULL 1, WHOLE 1. **2** [Finished] concluded, terminated, ended; see FINISHED 1. **3** [Perfect] flawless, unblemished, impeccable; see PERFECT, WHOLE 2.

complete *v.* execute, consummate, perfect, accomplish, realize, perform, achieve, fill out, fulfill, equip, actualize, furnish, make up, elaborate, make good, make complete, develop, fill in, refine, effect, carry out, crown, get through, round out; see also CREATE.—*Ant.* BEGIN, start, commence.

completed *a.* achieved, ended, concluded; see BUILT, DONE 2, FINISHED 1.

completely *a.* entirely, fully, totally, utterly, wholly, perfectly, exclusively, simply, effectively, competently, solidly, absolutely, unanimously, thoroughly, en masse, exhaustively, minutely, painstakingly, extensively, conclusively, unconditionally, finally, to the utmost, ultimately, altogether, comprehensively, to the end, from beginning to end, on all counts, in all, in full measure, to the limit, to the full, in full, to completion, to the nth degree, to a frazzle*, downright, through thick and thin, down to the ground, through and through, rain or shine, in one lump, from A to Z, from head to foot; hook, line, and sinker*.—*Ant.* PARTLY, somewhat, partially.

completion n. finish, conclusion, fulfillment; see END 2.

complex a. 1 [Composed of several parts] composite, heterogeneous, conglomerate, multiple, mosaic, manifold, multiform, compound, complicated, aggregated, involved, combined, compact, compounded, miscellaneous, multiplex, multifarious, variegated; see also MIXED 1. 2 [Difficult to understand] entangled, tangled, circuitous, convoluted, puzzling, mixed, mingled, muddled, jumbled, impenetrable, inscrutable, unfathomable, indecipherable, bewildering, intricate, perplexing, complicated, involved, enigmatic, hermetic, Byzantine, hidden, knotted, meandering, winding, tortuous, snarled, rambling, twisted, disordered, devious, discursive, cryptic, inextricable, knotty, roundabout; see also CONFUSED 2, DIFFICULT 2.—*Ant.* UNDERSTANDABLE, plain, apparent.

complex n. 1 [An obsession] phobia, mania, neurosis, obsessive-compulsive disorder, repressed emotions, repressed desires; see also FEAR, INSANITY. 2 [A composite] conglomerate, syndrome, ecosystem, aggregation, association, totality; see also COLLECTION.

complexion n. tone, glow, color, coloration, general coloring, tinge, cast, flush, skin texture, tint, hue, pigmentation; see also SKIN. *Descriptions of complexions include the following:* blond, blonde, fair, pale, sallow, sickly, dark, brunet, olive, bronze, sandy, rosy, red, ruddy, brown, yellow, tan, black, peaches-and-cream*.

compliant a. obedient, pliant, acquiescent; see DOCILE.

complicate v. involve, obscure, confound, muddle, clog, jumble, interrelate, elaborate, embellish, implicate, tangle, conceal, mix up, snarl up, encumber, impede, perplex, hinder, hamper, handicap, tie up with, ball up*; see also CONFUSE, ENTANGLE.—*Ant.* SIMPLIFY, clear up, unfold.

complicated a. intricate, various, mixed; see COMPLEX 2, CONFUSED 2, DIFFICULT 2.

complication n. dilemma, complexity, development; see CONFUSION, DIFFICULTY 1, 2.

compliment n. felicitation, tribute, approval, commendation, endorsement, confirmation, sanction, applause, flattery, acclaim, adulation, notice, puff, blurb, regards, honor, appreciation, respects, blessing, ovation, veneration, admiration, congratulations, homage, good word, sentiment; see also PRAISE 2.—*Ant.* ABUSE, censure, disapproval.

compliment v. wish joy to, remember, commemorate, pay one's respects, honor, cheer, salute, hail, toast, applaud, extol, celebrate, felicitate, pay tribute to, be in favor of, commend, endorse, sanction, confirm, acclaim, pay a compliment to, sing the praises of, speak highly of, exalt, applaud, worship, eulogize, glorify, magnify, flatter, fawn upon, butter up*, puff, hand it to*; see also PRAISE 1.—*Ant.* DENOUNCE, disapprove of, censure.

complimentary a. flattering, laudatory, approving, celebrating, honoring, respectful, congratulatory, well-wishing, highly favorable, praising, singing the praises of, with highest recommendations, with high praise; see also POLITE.

compose v. 1 [To be the parts or the ingredients of] constitute, comprise*, go into the making of, make up, merge into, be a component of, be an element of, belong to, consist of, be made of; see also COMPRISE, INCLUDE 1. 2 [To create] fabricate, produce, write music, score, arrange, orchestrate, forge, discover, design, conceive, imagine, make up, turn out, draw up; see also CREATE, INVENT 1.

composed a. 1 [Made] created, made up, fashioned; see FORMED. 2 [Calm] poised, confident, cool; see CALM 1, CONFIDENT.

composer n. arranger, songwriter, musical author; see AUTHOR, MUSICIAN, POET, WRITER. *Major composers include the following—Baroque period:* Antonio Vivaldi, Henry Purcell, J.S. Bach, George Frideric Handel; *Classical period:* Joseph Haydn, Wolfgang Amadeus Mozart, Ludwig van Beethoven, Franz Schubert, Gioacchino Rossini; *Romantic period;* Hector Berlioz, Felix Mendelssohn, Frédéric Chopin, Franz Liszt, Giuseppe Verdi, Richard Wagner, Anton Bruckner, Johann Strauss, Johannes Brahms, Peter Tchaikovsky, Antonín Dvořák, Giacomo Puccini, Gustav Mahler, Claude Debussy, Sergej Rachmaninoff, Maurice Ravel; *Modern period:* Igor Stravinsky, Béla Bartók, Richard Strauss, Arnold Schönberg, Sergey Prokofiev, Jean Sibelius, Dmitri Shostakovich, Aaron Copland.

composition n. creation, making, fashioning, formation, conception, presentation, invention; novel, tale, essay, play, drama, poem, verse, stanza, symphony, concerto, quartet, song, rhapsody, melody; see also BIOGRAPHY, LITERATURE 2, MUSIC 1, POETRY, WRITING 2.

composure *n.* serenity, peace of mind, calm, calmness, self-possession, nonchalance, coolheadedness, control, self-control, balance, contentment, tranquillity, stability, harmony, assurance, self-assurance, poise, composed state of mind, even temper, equanimity, coolness, levelheadedness, fortitude, moderation, gravity, sobriety, a cool head, presence of mind, equilibrium, aplomb, self-restraint, ease, evenness, complacence, tolerance, content, quiet, command, forbearance, cool*; see also PATIENCE 1, PEACE.—*Ant.* EXUBERANCE, passion, wildness.

compound *n.* composite, union, aggregate; see MIXTURE 1.

comprehend *v.* grasp, discern, perceive; see KNOW 1, UNDERSTAND 1.

comprehension *n.* understanding, perception, cognizance; see AWARENESS, KNOWLEDGE 1.

comprehensive *a.* extensive, sweeping, complete; see ABSOLUTE 1, GENERAL 1, INFINITE, LARGE 1.

compress *v.* condense, compact, press together, consolidate, squeeze together, tighten, cramp, contract, crowd, constrict, abbreviate, shrivel, make brief, reduce, dehydrate, pack, shorten, shrink, narrow, abridge, bind tightly, wrap closely, wedge, boil down, cram; see also PRESS 1, TIGHTEN 1.—*Ant.* SPREAD, stretch, expand.

comprise *v.* comprehend, contain, embrace, include, involve, enclose, embody, encircle, encompass, sum up, cover, consist of, be composed of, be made up of, constitute, incorporate, span, hold, engross, take into account, be contained in, add up to, amount to, take in; see also COMPOSE 1, INCLUDE 1.—*Ant.* BAR, lack, exclude.

compromise *n.* covenant, bargain, give-and-take; see AGREEMENT.

compromise *v.* agree, conciliate, find a middle ground; see NEGOTIATE 1.

compulsion *n.* 1 [Force] drive, necessity, need; see REQUIREMENT 2. 2 [An obsession] preoccupation, obsession, engrossment; see REQUIREMENT 2.

compulsive *a.* driving, impelling, besetting; see PASSIONATE 2.

compulsory *a.* obligatory, required, requisite; see NECESSARY.

compute *v.* count, figure, measure; see CALCULATE.

computer *n.* electronic brain, thinking machine, calculator, data processor, word processor, electronic cir-

cuit, cybernetic device, analog computer, digital computer, terminal, workstation, console, personal computer, PC, microcomputer, minicomputer, server, mainframe, laptop, palmtop, desktop; see also MACHINE.

comrade *n.* companion, confidante, intimate; see ASSOCIATE, FRIEND.

con *a.* conversely, opposed to, in opposition; see AGAINST 1.

con* *n.* deception, swindle, fraud; see TRICK 1.

con* *v.* cheat, dupe, mislead; see DECEIVE.

concave *a.* curved, sunken, cupped; see ROUND 2.

conceal *v.* screen, secrete, cover; see HIDE 1.

concealed *a.* covered, obscured, unseen; see HIDDEN.

concealment *n.* hiding, covering, camouflage; see DISGUISE.

concede *v.* yield, grant, acknowledge; see ADMIT 2, ALLOW.

conceit *n.* arrogance, self-admiration, narcissism; see VANITY.

conceited *a.* vain, arrogant, stuck-up*; see EGOTISTIC.

conceivable *a.* understandable, credible, believable; see CONVINCING, IMAGINABLE, LIKELY 1.

conceive *v.* 1 [To form a concept or image of] consider, formulate, speculate; see IMAGINE, THINK 1. 2 [To become pregnant] be with child, get pregnant, be impregnated, be in the family way*.

concentrate *v.* 1 [To bring or come together] amass, mass, assemble, combine, consolidate, compact, condense, reduce, hoard, garner, centralize, store, bring into a small compass, bring toward a central point, embody, localize, strengthen, direct toward one object, constrict, fix, cramp, focus, reduce, intensify, crowd together, flock together, contract, muster, bunch, heap up, swarm, conglomerate, stow away, congest, narrow, compress, converge, center, collect, cluster, congregate, huddle; see also ACCUMULATE, GATHER 2, PACK 2. 2 [To employ all one's mental powers] think intensely, give attention to, meditate upon, ponder, focus attention on, direct attention, weigh, consider closely, scrutinize, regard carefully, contemplate, study deeply, examine closely, brood over, put one's mind to, to be engrossed in, be absorbed in, attend, give exclusive attention to, occupy the thoughts with, fix one's attention, apply the mind, give heed, focus one's thought, give the mind to, direct the mind upon, center, think hard, rack one's brains, be on the beam*, keep one's eye on the ball*, knuckle down, buckle down; see also ANALYZE, EXAMINE, THINK 1.—*Ant.* DRIFT, be inattentive, ignore.

concentrated *a.* **1** [Undiluted] rich, unmixed, unadulterated, straight; see also STRONG 4, THICK 1. **2** [Intense] intensive, deep, hard; see INTENSE.

concentration *n.* **1** [Attention] close attention, concern, application; see THOUGHT 1. **2** [Density] solidity, consistency, frequency; see CONGESTION, DENSITY.

concept *n.* idea, theory, notion; see THOUGHT 2.

conception *n.* **1** [The act of conceiving mentally] perception, apprehension, comprehension, imagining, speculating, meditation, dreaming, cogitating, deliberating, concentrating, meditating, realization, consideration, speculation, understanding, cognition, mental grasp, apperception, forming an idea, formulation of a principle; see also THOUGHT 1. **2** [The act of conceiving physically] inception, impregnation, insemination; see FERTILIZATION 2.

concern *n.* **1** [Affair] business, matter, interest; see AFFAIR 1. **2** [Regard] care, interest, solicitude; see ATTENTION.

concern *v.* **1** [To have reference to] refer to, pertain to, relate to, be related to, have significance for, bear on, regard, be connected with, be about, have to do with, be a matter of concern to, have a bearing on, have connections with, be applicable to, depend upon, be dependent upon, answer to, deal with, belong to, touch upon, figure in; see also INFLUENCE, TREAT 1. **2** [Concern oneself] be concerned, become involved, take pains; see BOTHER 1, CARE, WORRY 2.

concerning *prep.* respecting, touching, regarding; see ABOUT 2.

concert *n.* musicale, recital, serenade; see PERFORMANCE.

concise *a.* succinct, brief, condensed; see SHORT 1.

conclude *v.* **1** [To finish] terminate, bring to an end, complete; see ACHIEVE. **2** [To deduce] presume, reason, gather; see ASSUME.

conclusion *n.* **1** [An end] finish, termination, completion; see END 2. **2** [A decision] determination, resolve, resolution; see JUDGMENT 3. —**in conclusion** lastly, in closing, in the end; see FINALLY 1.

conclusive *a.* final, decisive, absolute; see CERTAIN 2.

concord *n.* harmony, consensus, accord; see AGREEMENT, UNITY 1.

concrete *a.* **1** [Specific] particular,

solid, precise; see DEFINITE 1, DETAILED, REAL 2. **2** [Made of concrete] cement, poured, prefabricated, precast, concrete and steel, unyielding; see also FIRM 2.

concrete *n.* cement, ferroconcrete, reinforced concrete; see CEMENT, PAVEMENT.

concur *v.* accord with, be consonant with, be in harmony with; see AGREE, APPROVE, EQUAL.

concurrent *a.* synchronous, parallel, coexisting; see SIMULTANEOUS.

concussion *n.* jolt, shock, head trauma; see FRACTURE, INJURY.

condemn *v.* doom, sentence, damn, pass sentence on, find guilty, seal the doom of, pronounce judgment, prescribe punishment; see also CONVICT, PUNISH.—*Ant.* EXCUSE, acquit, exonerate.

condemnation *n.* denunciation, disapprobation, reproach; see ACCUSATION, BLAME, OBJECTION.

condense *v.* **1** [To compress] press together, constrict, consolidate; see COMPRESS, CONTRACT 1, DECREASE 1, 2. **2** [To abridge] abbreviate, summarize, digest; see DECREASE 2.

condensed *a.* **1** [Shortened] concise, brief, succinct; see SHORT 2. **2** [Concentrated] undiluted, rich, evaporated; see THICK 3.

condescend *v.* stoop, lower oneself, agree, humble oneself, demean oneself, submit with good grace, assume a patronizing air, lower one's tone, descend, comply, oblige, favor, concede, grant, accord, accommodate to, come down a peg, come down off one's high horse*; see also PATRONIZE 2.

condescending *a.* patronizing, disdainful, superior; see EGOTISTIC.

condition *n.* **1** [A state] situation, position, status; see STATE 2. **2** [A requisite] stipulation, contingency, provision; see REQUIREMENT 1. **3** [A limitation] restriction, qualification, prohibition; see LIMITATION 2, RESTRAINT 2. **4** [State of health] fitness, tone, trim, shape; see also HEALTH. **5** [Illness] ailment, infirmity, temper; see ILLNESS 1, 2. —**in condition** physically fit, conditioned, in the pink*; see HEALTHY, STRONG 1.

condition *v.* adapt, modify, customize; see PRACTICE 1, TRAIN 1.

conditional *a.* provisional, subject, contingent, limited, restricted, relying on, subject to, restrictive, guarded, not absolute, granted on certain terms; see also DEPENDENT 3.

conditionally *a.* hypothetically, subject to a condition, with reservations, with limitations, tentatively, possibly; see also TEMPORARILY.

conditioned *a.* altered, disciplined, modified; see TRAINED.

condominium *n.* cooperative apartment dwelling, condo, commonly owned apartment house, town house, co-op*; see also APARTMENT, HOME 1.

condone *v.* pardon, excuse, overlook; see APPROVE.

conduct *n.* deportment, demeanor, manner; see BEHAVIOR.

conduct *v.* 1 [To guide] escort, convoy, attend; see ACCOMPANY, LEAD 1. 2 [To manage] administer, handle, carry on; see MANAGE 1. —**conduct oneself** comport oneself, act properly, acquit oneself well; see BEHAVE.

conductor *n.* 1 [That which conducts] conduit, conveyor, transmitter; see CHANNEL, WIRE 1, WIRING. 2 [One who conducts] orchestra leader, pilot, head; see ADMINISTRATOR, GUIDE, LEADER 2. 3 [One in charge of a car or train] trainman, railroad man, ticket taker, brakeman, streetcar conductor, motorman, bus driver; see also DRIVER.

Confederacy *n.* Confederate States of America, CSA, rebel states, the South, Dixie; see also SOUTH.

confer *v.* converse, deliberate, parley; see DISCUSS.

conference *n.* convention, consultation, meeting; see GATHERING.

conferring *a.* discussing, conversing, in conference; see TALKING.

confess *v.* acknowledge, own, concede; see ADMIT 2.

confession *n.* 1 [The act of confessing] concession, allowance, owning to, owning up, revelation, disclosure, publication, affirmation, assertion, admission, declaration, telling, exposure, narration, exposé, proclamation, making public; see also ACKNOWLEDGMENT.—*Ant.* DENIAL, concealment, disclaimer. 2 [A sacrament] absolution, contrition, penance; see SACRAMENT.

confidant *n.* comrade, intimate, associate, companion; see also FRIEND.

confide *v.* disclose, admit, divulge; see REVEAL, TELL 1.

confidence *n.* self-confidence, self-reliance, morale, fearlessness, boldness, resolution, firmness, sureness, faith in oneself, tenacity, fortitude, certainty, daring, spirit, reliance, grit, cool*, heart, backbone, nerve, moxie*, spunk*; see also COURAGE, DETERMINATION.

confident *a.* self-confident, assured, being certain, fearless, assertive, positive, sure, convinced, self-reliant, sure of oneself, dauntless, self-sufficient, bold; see also CERTAIN 1.

confidential *a.* classified, intimate, privy; see PRIVATE, SECRET 1, 3.

confidentially *a.* privately, personally, in confidence; see SECRETLY.

confidently *a.* in an assured way, with conviction, assuredly; see BOLDLY 1, POSITIVELY 1.

confine *v.* 1 [To restrain] repress, hold back, keep within limits; see HINDER, RESTRAIN. 2 [To imprison] cage, incarcerate, shut up; see ENSLAVE, IMPRISON.

confined *a.* 1 [Restricted] limited, hampered, compassed; see BOUND 1, 2, RESTRICTED. 2 [Bedridden] on one's back, ill, laid up; see SICK. 3 [In prison] behind bars, locked up, in bonds, in irons, in chains, in jail, imprisoned, jailed, immured, incarcerated, detained, under lock and key.—*Ant.* FREE, released, at liberty.

confinement *n.* restriction, limitation, constraint, repression, control, coercion, keeping, safekeeping, custody, curb, bounds, check, bonds, bondage, detention, imprisonment, incarceration; see also JAIL.—*Ant.* FREEDOM, release, independence.

confines *n.* bounds, limits, periphery; see BOUNDARY.

confining *a.* limiting, restricting, bounding, prescribing, restraining, hampering, repressing, checking, enclosing, imprisoning, incarcerating, detaining, keeping locked up, keeping behind bars.

confirm *v.* 1 [To ratify] sanction, affirm, settle; see APPROVE, ENDORSE 2. 2 [To prove] verify, authenticate, validate; see EXPLAIN, PROVE.

confirmation *n.* ratification, proving, authentication, corroboration, support, endorsement, sanction, authorization, verification, affirmation, acceptance, passage, validation, approval, attestation, assent, admission, recognition, witness, consent, testimony, agreement, evidence; see also AGREEMENT, PROOF 1.—*Ant.* CANCELLATION, annulment, disapproval.

confirmed *a.* 1 [Firmly established] proved, valid, accepted; see CERTAIN 2, ESTABLISHED 2, GUARANTEED. 2 [Inveterate] ingrained, seasoned, regular; see CHRONIC, HABITUAL.

confiscate *v.* appropriate, impound, usurp; see SEIZE 2, STEAL.

conflict *n.* struggle, strife, engagement; see BATTLE, FIGHT.

conflict *v.* clash, contrast, contend; see DIFFER 1, FIGHT, OPPOSE 1, 2.

conform *v.* comply, accord, submit, accommodate, live up to, fit, suit, acclimate, accustom, be regular, harmonize, adapt, be guided by, fit the pattern, be in fashion, reconcile, obey, grow used to, do as others do, get in line, fall in with, go by, adhere to, adjust to, keep to, keep up, keep up with the Joneses*, chime in with, join the parade, play the game, follow the beaten path, toe the line, follow suit, run with the pack, follow the crowd, adhere to the status quo, when in Rome do as the Romans do; see also AGREE, FOLLOW 2, OBEY.—*Ant.* DIFFER, CONFLICT, disagree.

conforming *a.* agreeing, in line with, in agreement; see HARMONIOUS 2.

conformist *n.* conformer, philistine, advocate; see FOLLOWER.

conformity *n.* 1 [Similarity] congruity, correspondence, resemblance; see SIMILARITY. 2 [Obedience] willingness, submission, compliance; see AGREEMENT.

confound *v.* puzzle, perplex, bewilder; see CONFUSE.

confounded *a.* confused, bewildered, disconcerted; see DOUBTFUL.

confront *v.* brave, defy, repel; see DARE 2, FACE 1.

confrontation *n.* meeting, battle, strife; see DISPUTE, FIGHT 1.

confuse *v.* upset, befuddle, mislead, misinform, puzzle, perplex, confound, fluster, bewilder, embarrass, daze, dazzle, astonish, disarrange, disorder, jumble, blend, mix, mingle, cloud, fog, stir up, disconcert, abash, agitate, amaze, worry, trouble, snarl, unsettle, muddle, clutter, complicate, involve, rattle, derange, baffle, nonplus, frustrate, perturb, dismay, distract, entangle, encumber, befog, obscure, mystify, make a mess of, throw off the scent, cross up, foul up, mix up, ball up*, lead astray, stump, rattle, make one's head swim; see also DISTURB, TANGLE.—*Ant.* CLEAR UP, clarify, untangle.

confused *a.* 1 [Puzzled in mind] disconcerted, abashed, perplexed; see DOUBTFUL. 2 [Not properly distinguished] mistaken, jumbled, snarled, deranged, bewildered, out of order, disarrayed, confounded, mixed, mixed up, chaotic, disordered, muddled, fuddled, befuddled, slovenly, untidy, messy, involved, misunderstood, blurred, obscured, topsy-turvy, balled up*, fouled up*, screwed up*, in a mess, haywire*, snafu*; see also OBSCURE 1, TANGLED.—*Ant.* DISTINGUISHED, discriminated, ordered.

confusing *a.* disconcerting, confounding, baffling, puzzling, disturbing, unsettling, upsetting, embarrassing, obscuring, blurring, befuddling, tangling, snarling, cluttering, muddling, disarranging; see also DIFFICULT 2, OBSCURE 1.—*Ant.* ORDERLY, reassuring, clear.

confusion *n.* complication, intricacy, muss, untidiness, complexity, difficulty, mistake, bewilderment, turmoil, tumult, pandemonium, commotion, stir, ferment, disarray, jumble, convulsion, bustle, trouble, row, riot, uproar, fracas, distraction, agitation, emotional upset, daze, astonishment, surprise, fog, haze, consternation, racket, excitement, chaos, turbulence, dismay, uncertainty, irregularity, maze, interruption, stoppage, clutter, entanglement, backlash, clog, break, breakdown, knot, trauma, congestion, obstruction, interference, nervousness, disorganization, muddle, mass, snarl, to-do*, hubbub, tie-up, botch, rumpus, scramble, shuffle, mess, hodgepodge, stew, going round and round, jam*, fix*, bull in a china shop; see also DISORDER.—*Ant.* ORDER, quiet, calm.

confute *v.* confound, refute, invalidate; see DENY, OPPOSE 1.

congenial *a.* kindred, agreeable, genial; see FRIENDLY, HARMONIOUS 2.

congestion *n.* profusion, crowdedness, overpopulation, press, traffic jam, gridlock, overcrowding, overdevelopment, too many, too much, concentration, surplus; see also EXCESS 1.

congratulate *v.* felicitate, wish joy to, toast; see COMPLIMENT, PRAISE 1.

congratulations *interj.* best wishes, compliments, congrats*; see COMPLIMENT.

congregate *v.* convene, meet, converge; see GATHER 1.

congregation *n.* meeting, group, assemblage; see GATHERING.

congress *n.* [*often capital C*] parliament, assembly, legislative body; see COMMITTEE, GOVERNMENT, LEGISLATURE.

congruent *a.* in agreement, harmonious, corresponding; see HARMONIOUS 2.

congruous *a.* suitable, appropriate, fitting; see HARMONIOUS 2.

conjunction *n.* 1 [Act of joining together] combination, connection, association; see UNION 1. 2 [A syntactic connecting word] *Conjunctions include the following:* and, but, if, for, or, nor, so, yet, only, that, than, before, since, then, though, when, whenever, provided, where, why, both, either, while, as, neither, although, because, unless, until.

conjure up *v.* call, invoke, materialize; see SUMMON, URGE 2.

connect *v.* 1 [To join] combine, unite, attach; see JOIN 1. 2 [To associate] relate, equate, correlate; see COMPARE 1.

connected *a.* 1 [Joined together] united, combined, coupled; [see]

JOINED. **2** [Related] associated, applicable, pertinent; see RELATED 2, RELEVANT.

connecting *a.* joining, linking, combining, uniting, associating, relating, tying, cementing, knitting, fusing, hooking, bringing together, clinching, fastening, mixing, mingling, intertwining, welding, pairing, coupling; see also JOINED.

connection *n.* **1** [Relationship] kinship, association, reciprocity; see ASSOCIATION 2, RELATIONSHIP. **2** [A junction] combination, juncture, consolidation; see UNION 1. **3** [A link] attachment, fastening, bond; see LINK. **—in connection with** in conjunction with, associated with, together with; see WITH.

connotation *n.* implication, intention, essence; see MEANING.

conquer *v.* subdue, overcome, crush; see DEFEAT 2.

conqueror *n.* vanquisher, victor, conquistador; see HERO 1, WINNER.

conquest *n.* triumph, success, conquering; see VICTORY.

conscience *n.* moral sense, inner voice, the still small voice; see DUTY 1, MORALS, SHAME 2. **—have on one's conscience** be culpable for, be responsible for, feel guilty about; see GUILTY. **—in (all) conscience** rightly, fairly, properly; see JUSTLY 1.

conscientious *a.* fastidious, meticulous, scrupulous; see CAREFUL, RELIABLE.

conscientiousness *n.* exactness, care, honor; see CARE 1, DUTY 1, HONESTY, RESPONSIBILITY 1.

conscious *a.* cognizant, aware, informed, sure, certain, assured, discerning, knowing, sensible, sensitive, acquainted, attentive, watchful, mindful, vigilant, understanding, keen, alert, alert to, alive to, sensitive to, conscious of, mindful of, cognizant of, hip to*, on to*; see also INTELLIGENT.—*Ant.* UNAWARE, insensitive, inattentive.

consciousness *n.* alertness, cognizance, mindfulness; see AWARENESS, KNOWLEDGE 1.

consecrate *v.* hallow, sanctify, anoint; see BLESS.

consecrated *a.* blessed, sanctified, hallowed; see DIVINE.

consecration *n.* making holy, sanctification, exalting; see CELEBRATION.

consecutive *a.* continuous, chronological, serial, in turn, progressive, connected, in order, in sequence, sequential, going on, continuing, one after another, one after the other, serialized, seriatim, numerical; see also CONSTANT, REGULAR 3.

consecutively *a.* following, successively, continuously; see GRADUALLY.

consensus *n.* consent, unison, accord; see AGREEMENT.

consent *n.* assent, approval, acquiescence; see PERMISSION.

consent *v.* accede, assent, acquiesce; see AGREE, ALLOW, APPROVE.

consequence *n.* **1** [Effect] outgrowth, end, outcome; see RESULT. **2** [Importance] moment, value, weight; see IMPORTANCE. **—in consequence of** because of, owing to, consequently; see BECAUSE. **—take the consequences** accept the results of one's actions, suffer, bear the burden; see ENDURE 2.

conservation *n.* maintenance, keeping, preservation, preserving, conserving, guarding, protecting, stewardship, husbandry, saving, safekeeping, storage, upkeep, economy, keeping in trust; see also PRESERVATION.—*Ant.* WASTE, misuse, destruction.

conservative *a.* conserving, preserving, unchanging, unchangeable, stable, constant, steady, traditional, reactionary, conventional, moderate, unprogressive, firm, obstinate, inflexible, opposed to change, cautious, sober, Tory, taking no chances, timid, fearful, unimaginative, right-wing, in a rut*; see also CAREFUL, MODERATE 3.—*Ant.* RADICAL, risky, changing.

conservative *n.* reactionary, right-winger, die-hard, Tory, Whig, Federalist, champion of the status quo, opponent of change, classicist, traditionalist, unprogressive, conventionalist, mossback*, old fogy, fossil*—*Ant.* RADICAL, progressive, liberal.

consider *v.* allow for, provide for, grant, take up, concede, acknowledge, recognize, favor, value, take under advisement, deal with, regard, make allowance for, take into consideration, keep in mind, reckon with, play around with*, toss around; see about; see also RECONSIDER, THINK 1.—*Ant.* REFUSE, deny, reject.

considerable *a.* **1** [Important] noteworthy, significant, essential; see IMPORTANT 1. **2** [Much] abundant, lavish, bountiful; see MUCH 2, PLENTIFUL 1.

considerate *a.* charitable, kind, solicitous; see POLITE, THOUGHTFUL 2.

consideration *n.* **1** [The state of being considerate] kindliness, thoughtfulness, attentiveness; see COURTESY 1, KINDNESS 1, TOLERANCE 1. **2** [Payment] remuneration, salary, fee; see PAYMENT 1. **3** [Something to be considered] situation, problem, judgment, notion, fancy, puzzle, proposal, difficulty, incident, evidence, new development, occurrence, taste, pass, occasion, emergency, idea, thought, trouble, plan, particulars, items, scope, extent, magnitude; see also IDEA 1, PLAN 2. —**in consideration of** because of, on account of, for; see CONSIDERING. —**take into consideration** take into account, weigh, keep in mind; see CONSIDER. —**under consideration** thought over, discussed, evaluated; see CONSIDERED.

considered *a.* carefully thought about, treated, gone into, contemplated, weighed, meditated, examined, investigated; see also DETERMINED 1.

considering *prep., conj.* in light of, in view of, in consideration of, pending, taking into account, everything being equal, inasmuch as, insomuch as, with something in view.

consign *v.* convey, dispatch, transfer; see GIVE 1, SEND 1.

consistency *n.* 1 [Harmony] union, compatibility, accord; see AGREEMENT, SYMMETRY. 2 [The degree of firmness or thickness] hardness, softness, firmness; see DENSITY, TEXTURE 1.

consistent *a.* compatible, equable, expected; see LOGICAL, RATIONAL 1, REGULAR 3.

consist of *v.* embody, contain, involve; see COMPRISE, INCLUDE 1.

consolation *n.* sympathy, compassion, support; see PITY, RELIEF 1, 4.

console *v.* solace, sympathize with, hearten; see COMFORT 1, ENCOURAGE.

consolidate *v.* connect, mix, unify; see COMPRESS, PACK 2.

consolidation *n.* alliance, association, federation; see UNION 1.

consonant *n. Linguistic terms referring to consonant sounds include the following:* voiceless, voiced, stop, fricative, semivowel, affricate, bilabial, glottal, sibilant, implosive, plosive, nasal, click, glide, continuant, trill. *In the English alphabet, consonants are represented as follows:* b,c, d,f,g,h,j,k,l,m,n,p,q,r,s,t,v,w,x,y,z; see also LETTER, SOUND 2, VOWEL.

conspicuous *a.* outstanding, eminent, distinguished, celebrated, noted, renowned, famed, notorious, important, influential, notable, illustrious, striking, prominent, well-known, arresting, remarkable, noticeable, flagrant, glaring, like a sore thumb*; see also PROMINENT 1.—*Ant.* UNKNOWN, inconspicuous, unsung.

conspiracy *n.* intrigue, collusion, connivance; see TRICK 1.

conspirator *n.* betrayer, schemer, cabalist; see TRAITOR.

conspire *v.* plot, scheme, contrive; see PLAN 1.

constant *a.* steady, uniform, perpetual, unchanging, continual, continuous, uninterrupted, unvarying, connected, even, incessant, unbroken, nonstop, monotonous, standardized, regularized; see also REGULAR 3.

constantly *a.* uniformly, steadily, invariably; see REGULARLY.

constituency *n.* the voters, constituents, electorate, body politic, electors, voting public, balloters, the people; see also VOTER.

constituent *n.* component, element, ingredient; see PART 1.

constitute *v.* 1 [To found] establish, develop, create; see ESTABLISH 2. 2 [To make up] frame, compound, aggregate; see COMPOSE 1.

constitution *n.* 1 [Health] vitality, physique, build; see HEALTH. 2 [A basic political document] legal code, written law, doctrines; see LAW 2.

constitutional *a.* lawful, safeguarding liberty, democratic; see LEGAL, DEMOCRATIC.

constrain *v.* necessitate, compel, stifle; see FORCE, URGE 2.

constraint *n.* 1 [The use of force] coercion, force, compulsion; see PRESSURE 2. 2 [Shyness] bashfulness, restraint, humility; see RESERVE 2. 3 [Confinement] captivity, detention, restriction; see ARREST, CONFINEMENT.

constrict *v.* contract, cramp, choke; see TIGHTEN 1.

construct *v.* make, erect, fabricate; see BUILD, CREATE.

construction *n.* 1 [The act of constructing] formation, manufacture, building; see ARCHITECTURE, BUILDING, PRODUCTION 1. 2 [A method of constructing] structure, arrangement, organization, system, plan, development, steel and concrete, contour, format, mold, cast, outline, type, shape, build, cut, fabric, formation, turn, framework, configuration, brick and mortar, prefab*. —**under construction** in production, in preparation, being built, going up.

constructive *a.* useful, valuable, effective; see HELPFUL 1.

construe *v.* infer, deduce, interpret; see EXPLAIN.

consult *v.* take counsel, deliberate, confer, parley, conspire with, be closeted with, compare notes about, put heads together, commune, treat, negotiate, debate, argue, talk over, call in, ask advice of, turn to, seek advice; see also ASK, DISCUSS.

consultation *n.* interview, conference, deliberation; see DISCUSSION.

consume *v.* 1 [To use] use, buy, wear out; see SPEND, USE 1. 2 [To eat or drink] absorb, feed, devour; see EAT 1.

consumer *n.* user, customer, shopper; see BUYER.

consumption *n.* using, spending, expending; see DESTRUCTION 1, USE 1, WASTE 1.

contact *n.* touch, junction, connection; see MEETING 1. —**in contact with** **1** [Contiguous] meeting, joining, connecting, bordering, adjacent, close; see also NEAR 1.—*Ant.* DISTANT, out of contact, far. **2** [Communicating with] in touch with, writing to, corresponding with, in communication with.

contact *v.* speak to, reach, make contact with; see COMMUNICATE 2, TALK 1, MEET.

contagion *n.* poison, virus, illness; see ILLNESS 1.

contagious *a.* communicable, infectious, transmittable, spreading, poisonous, epidemic, deadly, endemic, tending to spread; see also CATCHING.

contain *v.* **1** [Include] comprehend, embrace, be composed of; see INCLUDE 1. **2** [Restrict] hold, keep back, stop; see RESTRAIN.

container *n.* receptacle, basket, bin, bowl, dish, tub, holder, caldron, vessel, capsule, package, packet, chest, purse, pod, pouch, cask, sack, pot, pottery, jug, bucket, canteen, pit, box, carton, canister, crate, pail, kettle; see also BAG, CAN 1, CASE 5, JAR 1, VASE.

contaminate *v.* pollute, infect, defile; see CORRUPT, DIRTY.

contamination *n.* impurity, taint, infection; see POLLUTION.

contemplate *v.* ponder, muse, speculate on; see STUDY, THINK 1.

contemporary *a.* present, fashionable, current; see MODERN 1, 3.

contempt *n.* scorn, derision, disdain; see HATRED.

contend *v.* contest, battle, dispute; see FIGHT.

content *a.* appeased, gratified, comfortable; see HAPPY, SATISFIED.

contented *a.* happy, pleased, thankful; see HAPPY, SATISFIED.

contention *n.* **1** [A quarrel] struggle, belligerency, combat; see COMPETITION, DISPUTE, FIGHT. **2** [An assertion supported by argument] explanation, stand, charge; see ATTITUDE, DECLARATION.

contentment *n.* peace, pleasure, happiness; see COMFORT, EASE 1, SATISFACTION 2.

contents *n.* constituents, components, elements, filling, content, aspects, gist, essence, meaning, significance, intent, implication, connotation, text, subject matter, sum, substance, sum and substance, details; see also INGREDIENTS, MATTER 1.

contest *n.* trial, match, challenge; see GAME 1, SPORT 1.

contest *v.* oppose, battle, quarrel; see DARE, FIGHT.

contestant *n.* competitor, opponent, participant, rival, challenger, contester, disputant, antagonist, adversary, combatant, player, team member; see also PLAYER 1.

context *n.* connection, text, frame of reference; see MEANING.

continent *n.* mainland, continental landmass, body of land; see LAND.

continual *a.* repeated, constant, connected; see CONSECUTIVE, REGULAR 3.

continually *a.* steadily, continuously, constantly; see FREQUENTLY, REGULARLY.

continuation *n.* succession, line, extension, increase, endurance, prolongation, protraction, elongation, sustaining, preservation, perseverance, supplement, complement, new version; see also ADDITION 1, SEQUENCE 1.—*Ant.* END, pause, delay.

continue *interj.* keep on, carry on; keep going, keep talking, keep reading, etc.; keep it up.

continue *v.* **1** [To persist] persevere, carry forward, maintain, carry on, keep on, go on, run on, live on, never stop, sustain, promote, progress, uphold, forge ahead, remain, press onward, make headway, move ahead, keep the ball rolling*, leave no stone unturned, chip away at*; see also ADVANCE 1, ENDURE 1.—*Ant.* END, cease, give up. **2** [To resume] begin again, renew, begin over, return to, take up again, begin where one left off, be reestablished, be restored; see also RESUME.—*Ant.* HALT, discontinue, postpone.

continuing *a.* persevering, carrying on, progressing; see CONSTANT, REGULAR 3.

continuity *n.* continuousness, constancy, continuance, flow, succession, unity, sequence, chain, linking, train, progression, dovetailing, extension; see also CONTINUATION.—*Ant.* INTERRUPTION, stop, break.

continuous *a.* uninterrupted, unbroken, perpetual; see CONSECUTIVE, CONSTANT, REGULAR 3.

contort *v.* deform, misshape, twist; see DISTORT 2.

contortion *n.* deformity, distortion, grimace, twist, ugliness, pout, crookedness.

contour *n.* profile, silhouette, shape; see FORM 1.

contraband *n.* plunder, smuggling, illegal goods; see BOOTY.

contract *n.* agreement, compact, stipulation, contractual statement, contractual obligation, understanding, promise, pledge, covenant, obligation, guarantee, settlement, gentlemen's agreement, commitment, bargain, pact, arrangement, the papers, deal; see also AGREEMENT, TREATY.

contract v. **1** [To diminish] draw in, draw back, shrivel, weaken, shrink, become smaller, decline, fall away, subside, grow less, ebb, wane, lessen, lose, dwindle, recede, fall off, wither, waste, condense, constrict, deflate, evaporate; see also DECREASE 1.—*Ant.* STRETCH, strengthen, expand. **2** [To cause to diminish] abbreviate, narrow, condense; see COMPRESS, DECREASE 2. **3** [To enter into an agreement by contract] pledge, undertake, come to terms, make terms, adjust, dicker, make a bargain, agree on, limit, establish by agreement, engage, stipulate, consent, enter into a contractual obligation, sign the papers, negotiate a contract, accept an offer, obligate oneself, put something in writing, swear to, sign for, give one's word, sign on the dotted line, shake hands on it, initial, close; see also AGREE. **4** [To catch; *said of diseases*] get, incur, become infected with; see CATCH 4.

contraction n. shrinkage, shrinking, recession, reduction, withdrawal, consumption, condensation, omission, deflation, evaporation, constriction, shortening, compression, decrease, confinement, curtailment, omitting, abridgment, cutting down, consolidating, consolidation, lowering; see also ABBREVIATION, REDUCTION 1, SHRINKAGE.—*Ant.* INCREASE, expansion, extension.

contractor n. builder, jobber, subcontractor; see ARCHITECT.

contradict v. differ, call in question, repudiate; see DARE 2, OPPOSE 1.

contradiction n. incongruity, inconsistency, opposition; see DIFFERENCE 1, OPPOSITE.

contrary a. **1** [Opposed] antagonistic to, hostile, counter; see AGAINST 1, OPPOSED. **2** [Unfavorable] untimely, bad, unpropitious; see UNFAVORABLE. **3** [Obstinate] willful, contradictory, headstrong; see STUBBORN. —**on the contrary** conversely, antithetically, inversely, contrastingly, on the other hand, at the opposite pole, on the other side; see also NOT. —**to the contrary** in disagreement with, in opposition to, in contradiction to; see AGAINST 1, ON THE CONTRARY.

contrast n. divergence, incompatibility, variation, variance, dissimilarity, inequality, distinction, oppositeness, contradiction, diversity, disagreement, opposition; see also DIFFERENCE 1.—*Ant.* AGREEMENT, similarity, uniformity. —**in contrast to** (or **with**) as against, opposed to, contrasting; see AGAINST 3, OPPOSED.

contrast v. contradict, disagree, conflict, set off, be contrary to, diverge from, depart from, deviate from, differ from, vary, show difference, stand out; see also DIFFER 1, OPPOSE 1.—*Ant.* AGREE, concur, be identical.

contribute v. add, share, endow, supply, furnish, bestow, present, confer, commit, dispense, settle upon, grant, afford, donate, dispense, assign, give away, subscribe, devote, will, bequeath, subsidize, hand out, ante up*, chip in*, kick in*, have a hand in, get in the act*, go Dutch*; see also GIVE 1, OFFER 1, PROVIDE 1.—*Ant.* RECEIVE, accept, take.

contributing a. aiding, helpful, supporting, ancillary, secondary, subordinate, valuable, sharing, causative, forming a part of, not to be overlooked, to be considered, coming into the picture; see also HELPFUL.

contribution n. donation, present, bestowal; see GIFT 1, GRANT.

contributor n. subscriber, giver, grantor; see DONOR, PATRON.

contrive v. make, improvise, devise; see CREATE, INVENT 1.

control n. **1** [The power to direct] dominion, reign, direction; see POWER 2. **2** [A device that regulates; *often plural*] instrument, switch, dial, knob, button, key, lever, handle, toggle switch, valve, regulator, governor, instrument panel, dashboard, keyboard, keypad, remote control.

control v. **1** [To hold in check] constrain, master, repress; see CHECK 1, RESTRAIN. **2** [To direct] lead, rule, dominate, determine, master, conquer, conduct, administer, supervise, run, coach, head, dictate, manage, influence, prevail, domineer, constrain, charge, subdue, push, coerce, oblige, train, limit, officiate, drive, move, regulate, take over, rule the roost, crack the whip, call the shots*; see also GOVERN.

controlling a. ruling, supervising, regulating; see GOVERNING.

controversial a. disputable, debatable, suspect; see UNCERTAIN.

controversy n. contention, debate, quarrel; see DIFFERENCE 1, DISCUSSION.

convene v. unite, congregate, collect; see ASSEMBLE 2, GATHER 1.

convenience n. **1** [The quality of being convenient] fitness, availability, accessibility, suitability, appropriateness, decency, acceptability, receptiveness, openness, accord, consonance, adaptability, useful-

ness. 2 [An aid to ease or comfort]
ease, comfort, accommodation, help,
aid, assistance, means, support,
luxury, personal service, relief,
cooperation, promotion, advancement, satisfaction, service, benefit,
contribution, advantage, utility,
labor saver, labor-saving device,
modern convenience, time saver,
lift; see also ADVANTAGE, APPLIANCE.
—at one's convenience at one's leisure, conveniently, when convenient; see APPROPRIATELY.

convenient *a.* **1** [Serving one's con-
venience] ready, favorable, suitable,
adapted, available, fitted, suited,
adaptable, roomy, well-arranged,
appropriate, well-planned, decent,
agreeable, acceptable, useful, serviceable, assisting, aiding, beneficial,
accommodating, advantageous, conducive, comfortable, opportune,
timesaving, labor-saving; see also
HELPFUL.—*Ant.* DISTURBING, disadvantageous, unserviceable. **2**
[Near] handy, close by, easy to
reach; see NEAR 1.

convention *n.* **1** [An occasion at
which delegates assemble] assembly, convocation, meeting; see GATH-
ERING. **2** [Custom] practice, habit,
fashion; see CUSTOM.

conventional *a.* **1** [Established by
convention] accustomed, prevailing,
accepted, customary, traditional,
regular, standard, orthodox, normal, typical, expected, usual, routine, general, everyday, commonplace, ordinary, plain, current,
popular, prevalent, predominant,
expected, in established usage, well-
known, stereotypical; see also COM-
MON 1, FAMILIAR, HABITUAL.—*Ant.*
UNUSUAL, atypical, unpopular. **2**
[In accordance with convention]
established, sanctioned, correct; see
POPULAR 3. **3** [Devoted to or bound
by convention] formal, stereotyped,
orthodox, narrow, narrow-minded,
dogmatic, parochial, strict, rigid,
puritanical, inflexible, hidebound,
conservative, conforming, believing,
not heretical, literal, bigoted, obstinate, straight*, straight-laced; see
also PREJUDICED.—*Ant.* LIBERAL,
broad-minded, unconventional.

conversation *n.* talk, discussion,
communion, consultation, hearing,
conference, gossip, chat, rap*, dialogue, discourse, expression of
views, mutual exchange, questions
and answers, traffic in ideas, getting
to know one another, general conversation, talking it out, heart-to-
heart talk, powwow*, bull session*,
chitchat; see also COMMUNICATION,
SPEECH 3.

converse *n.* inverse, antithesis,
reverse; see OPPOSITE.

conversion *n.* changeover, transformation, metamorphosis; see
CHANGE 1.

convert *n.* proselyte, neophyte, disciple; see FOLLOWER.

convert *v.* **1** [To alter the form or
use] turn, transform, alter; see
CHANGE 2. **2** [To alter convictions]
persuade, proselytize, bring around;
see CONVINCE, REFORM 1.

convertible *n.* open car, sports car,
ragtop*; see AUTOMOBILE.

convey *v.* pass on, communicate,
conduct; see SEND 1, 2.

convict *n.* captive, malefactor, felon;
see CRIMINAL, PRISONER.

convict *v.* find guilty, sentence, pass
sentence on, doom, declare guilty,
bring to justice, send up; see also
CONDEMN.—*Ant.* FREE, acquit, find
not guilty.

conviction *n.* persuasion, confidence,
reliance; see BELIEF, FAITH 2.

convince *v.* prove to, persuade,
establish, refute, satisfy, assure,
demonstrate, argue into, change,
effect, overcome, turn, win over,
bring around, put across, bring to
one's senses, bring to reason, gain
the confidence of, sell a bill of goods;
see also PROVE, TEACH. **—convince
oneself** be convinced, be converted,
persuade oneself, make up one's
mind; see also BELIEVE, PROVE.

convinced *a.* converted, indoctri-
nated, talked into something; see
CHANGED 2.

convincing *a.* trustworthy, credible,
acceptable, reasonable, creditable,
plausible, probable, likely, presumable, possible, dependable, hopeful,
worthy of confidence, to be
depended on; see also RELIABLE.

convulsion *n.* paroxysm, epilepsy,
attack; see FIT 1.

cook *n.* short-order cook, chef,
caterer; see SERVANT.

cook *v.* prepare, fix, warm up, warm
over, stew, simmer, sear, braise,
scald, broil, parch, scorch, poach,
dry, chafe, fricassee, percolate,
steam, bake, microwave, sauté,
shirr, charbroil, griddle, brew, boil,
seethe, barbecue, grill, roast, pan-
fry, panbroil, deep-fry, French fry,
brown; see also FRY, HEAT 1. **—cook
up*** make up, concoct, falsify; see
ARRANGE 2, PLAN 1, 2.

cookie *n.* small cake, sweet wafer,
biscuit (British); see BREAD, CAKE 2,
PASTRY. *Common varieties of cookies
include the following:* cream, lemon,
icebox, oatmeal, vanilla, chocolate,
sugar, molasses, ginger, etc.; cookie;
gingersnap, fig bar, raisin bar,
Scotch shortbread, macaroon, tart,
fruit bar, brownie, wafer.

cooking *a.* simmering, heating,
scalding, brewing, stewing, steeping, frying, broiling, griddling, grill-

ing, browning, roasting, baking; see also BOILING.

cooking n. cookery, dish, cuisine; see FOOD.

cool a. **1** [Having a low temperature] cooling, frigid, frosty, wintry, somewhat cold, chilly, shivery, chill, chilling, refrigerated, air-conditioned, snappy, nippy, biting; see also COLD 1.—Ant. WARM, tepid, heated. **2** [Calm] unruffled, imperturbable, composed; see CALM 1. **3** [Somewhat angry or disapproving] disapproving, distant, offended; see ANGRY, INDIFFERENT. **4** [*Excellent] neat*, splendid, great*; see EXCELLENT. —**play it cool*** hold back, underplay, exercise restraint; see RESTRAIN.

cool v. lose heat, lessen, freeze, reduce, calm, chill, cool off, become cold, be chilled to the bone, become chilly, moderate, refrigerate, air-cool, air-condition, pre-cool, frost, freeze, quick-freeze; see also FREEZE 1.—Ant. BURN, warm, defrost.

cool it* v. quiet down, hold back, be sensible; see CALM DOWN.

cooperate v. unite, combine, concur, conspire, pool, join forces, act in concert, hold together, stick together, comply with, join in, go along, make common cause, unite efforts, share in, second, take part, work in unison, participate, work side by side, side with, join hands, play along, play fair, throw in with*, fall in with, be in cahoots*, chip in*, stand shoulder to shoulder, pull together; see also AGREE.—Ant. DIFFER, act independently, diverge.

cooperation n. collaboration, participation, combination, concert, union, confederacy, confederation, conspiracy, alliance, society, company, partnership, coalition, federation, clanship, unanimity, concord, harmony; see also AGREEMENT, UNITY 2.—Ant. DISAGREEMENT, discord, separation.

cooperative a. cooperating, agreeing, joining, combining, collaborating, coactive, allying, uniting, concurring, participating, in joint operation; see also HELPFUL, UNITED.

cooperative n. marketing cooperative, consumer's cooperative, communal society, kibbutz, commune, collective, co-op*; see also UNITY 2.

coordinate v. harmonize, regulate, organize; see ADJUST 1, AGREE.

coordinator n. superintendent, supervisor, organizer; see EXECUTIVE.

cope (with) v. manage, deal with, handle; see ENDURE 2, FACE 1.

copulate v. sleep with, make love, go to bed, unite, couple, cover, lie with, know*, have relations, have sexual relations, have marital relations, have extramarital relations, be carnal, have carnal knowledge of someone, unite sexually, have sexual intercourse, have intercourse, have sex, breed, cohabit, fornicate, fool around*, do it*, make it*, get it on*.—Ant. ABSTAIN, be continent, be celibate.

copulation n. coitus, intercourse, sex, sex act, sexual union, sexual congress, coupling, mating, coition, carnal knowledge, making love; see also SEX 1, 4.

copy n. imitation, facsimile, photostat, likeness, print, similarity, mimeograph sheet, fax, simulation, mirror image, spitting image, spit and image, impersonation, offprint, xerox, semblance, forgery, counterfeit, reprint, rubbing, transcript, carbon, replica, typescript, cast, tracing, counterpart, likeness, portrait, model, reflection, representation, study, photograph, carbon copy, certified copy, office copy, typed copy, pencil copy, fair copy, ditto; see also DUPLICATE, REPRODUCTION 2.

copy v. **1** [To imitate] follow, mimic, ape; see IMITATE 1. **2** [To reproduce] duplicate, counterfeit, forge, depict, portray, picture, draw, sketch, paint, sculpt, mold, engrave; see also REPRODUCE 2.

cord n. string, cordage, fiber; see ROPE.

cordial a. genial, hearty, warmhearted; see FRIENDLY.

core n. **1** [Essence] gist, kernel, heart; see ESSENCE 1. **2** [Center] hub, focus, pivot; see CENTER 1.

cork n. stopper, tap, spike; see PLUG 1.

corn n. oats, millet, maize; see FOOD, GRAIN 1.

corn bread n. corn pone, hoecake, corndodger*, corncake, hot bread, johnnycake, hush puppy, spoon bread, corn tortilla; see also BREAD, CAKE 2.

corner n. **1** [A projecting edge] ridge, sharp edge, projection; see EDGE 1, RIM. **2** [A recess] niche, nook, indentation; see HOLE 1. **3** [A sharp turn] bend, veer, shift; see CURVE, TURN 2. **4** [The angle made where ways intersect] V, Y, intersection; see ANGLE 1. **5** [*Difficulty] impediment, distress, knot; see DIFFICULTY 2. —**around the corner** immediate, imminent, next; see NEAR 1, SOON. —**cut corners** cut down, shorten, reduce; see DECREASE 2.

corner v. trap, trick, fool; see CATCH 1, DECEIVE.

corny* a. old-fashioned, trite, sentimental; see DULL 4, STUPID.

corporation n. partnership, enterprise, company; see BUSINESS 4.

corps n. troops, brigade, regiment; see ARMY 2, ORGANIZATION 2.

corpse n. carcass, remains, cadaver; see BODY 2.

correct a. 1 [Accurate] exact, true, right; see ACCURATE 2. 2 [Proper] suitable, becoming, fitting; see FIT.

correct v. better, help, remove the errors of, remove the faults of, remedy, alter, rectify, accommodate for, make right, mend, amend, fix up, do over, reform, remodel, review, reconstruct, reorganize, edit, revise, make corrections, put to rights, put in order, doctor*, touch up, polish; see also REPAIR.

corrected a. rectified, amended, reformed; see CHANGED 2.

correction n. revision, reexamination, rereading, remodeling, rectification, editing, righting, reparation, mending, fixing, amending, changing; see also REPAIR.

corrective a. restorative, curative, healing; see MEDICAL.

correctly a. rightly, precisely, perfectly; see RIGHT 1.

correctness n. 1 [Accuracy] precision, exactness, rightness; see ACCURACY, TRUTH. 2 [Propriety] decency, decorum, fitness; see PROPRIETY.

correlate v. connect, equate, associate; see COMPARE 1.

correlation n. interdependence, alternation, equivalence; see RELATIONSHIP.

correspond v. 1 [To be alike] compare, match, be identical; see RESEMBLE. 2 [To communicate with, usually by letter] write to, reply to, drop a line to; see ANSWER 1, COMMUNICATE 2. —**correspond to** be in accord with, mesh with, harmonize with; see AGREE, FIT.

correspondence n. 1 [The quality of being like] conformity, equivalence, accord; see AGREEMENT, SIMILARITY. 2 [Communication, usually by letter] messages, reports, exchange of letters; see COMMUNICATION.

corresponding a. identical, similar, coterminous; see LIKE.

corrode v. rot, degenerate, deteriorate; see RUST.

corrupt a. exploiting, underhanded, mercenary, fraudulent, crooked, nefarious, profiteering, unscrupulous, shady*, fixed*, on the take*; see also DISHONEST.

corrupt v. pervert, degrade, demean, lower, pull down, reduce, adulterate, depreciate, deprave, debauch, defile, demoralize, pollute, taint, contaminate, infect, stain, spoil, blight, blemish, undermine, impair, mar, injure, harm, hurt, damage, deface, disfigure, deform, abuse, maltreat, ill-treat, outrage, mistreat, misuse, dishonor, disgrace, violate, waste, ravage, cause to degenerate; see also RAPE, WEAKEN 2.—Ant. CLEAN, purify, restore.

corrupted a. debased, perverted, depraved; see WICKED.

corruption n. 1 [Vice] baseness, depravity, degradation; see CRIME, EVIL 1. 2 [Conduct involving graft] extortion, exploitation, fraudulence, misrepresentation, dishonesty, bribery, racketeering; see also CRIME.

cosmetic n. beauty preparation, makeup, beauty-care product, cosmetics; see also MAKEUP 1. Cosmetics include the following: hair, body, suntan, etc., oil; hair, eye, cold, cleansing, hormone, complexion, skin, hand, etc., cream; after-shave, hand, suntan, etc., lotion; talcum, face, bath, tooth, etc., powder; eyebrow pencil, mascara, eye shadow, eyeliner, lipstick, nail polish, moisturizer, blush, blusher, rouge, foundation, powder, perfume, toilet water, cologne, hair tonic, hair dye, hair bleach, mouthwash, toothpaste, shampoo, shaving soap, shaving cream, shaving foam, depilatory, deodorant, antiperspirant; see also LOTION, PERFUME, SOAP.

cosmic a. vast, empyrean, grandiose; see UNIVERSAL 1.

cosmopolitan a. metropolitan, worldly, fashionable; see INTERNATIONAL, PUBLIC 2.

cosmos n. solar system, galaxy, star system; see UNIVERSE.

cost n. payment, value, charge; see PRICE, VALUE 1. —**at all costs** by any means, in spite of difficulties, without fail; see REGARDLESS 2.

cost v. require, take, be priced at, be marked at, be valued at, be worth, amount to, be for sale at, command a price of, bring in, sell for, set one back*, go for.

costing a. as much as, to the amount of, priced at, no less than, estimated at, selling for, on sale at, reduced to, a bargain at, a steal at*.

costly a. high-priced, dear, precious; see EXPENSIVE.

costume n. attire, apparel, garb; see CLOTHES, DRESS 1.

cottage n. cabin, shack, small house; see HOME 1.

cotton n. Cotton cloth includes the following: chintz, organdy, dotted swiss, voile, cambric, calico, flannel, denim, ticking, net, muslin, crinoline, flannelette, gingham, jersey, lace, monk's cloth, poplin, velveteen, gabardine, crepe, twill, canvas, percale, terry cloth, sailcloth, cheesecloth, theatrical gauze.

couch *n.* sofa, lounge, davenport; see CHAIR 1, FURNITURE.

cough *n.* hem, hack, frog in one's throat; see COLD 2, ILLNESS 2.

cough *v.* hack, convulse, bark*; see CHOKE.

council *n.* advisory board, cabinet, directorate; see COMMITTEE.

counsel *n.* 1 [Advice] guidance, instruction, information; see ADVICE, SUGGESTION 1. 2 [A lawyer] attorney, legal adviser, barrister; see LAWYER. **—keep one's own counsel** be secretive, conceal oneself, keep quiet; see HIDE 1.

counsel *v.* give advice to, direct, inform; see ADVISE, TEACH.

counselor *n.* guide, instructor, mentor; see TEACHER.

count *n.* total, number, enumeration, account, listing, statistics, returns, figures, tabulation, tally, poll, sum, outcome; see also RESULT, WHOLE.

count *v.* compute, reckon, enumerate, number, add up, figure, count off, count up, foot up, count heads, count noses; see also ADD, TOTAL. **—count on** rely on, depend on, depend upon, lean upon, expect from, take for granted, believe in, swear by; see also TRUST 1.

counter *n.* board, shelf, ledge; see BENCH 2, TABLE 1. **—under the counter** unofficial, black-market, underhanded; see ILLEGAL.

counteract *v.* offset, check, invalidate; see HALT, HINDER, PREVENT.

counterfeit *a.* sham, spurious, fictitious; see FALSE 3.

counterfeit *v.* make counterfeit money, coin (British), make funny money*, circulate bad money; see also FORGE.

counterfeiter *n.* forger, paperhanger*, plagiarist; see CRIMINAL.

countless *a.* innumerable, incalculable, numberless; see INFINITE, MANY.

country *a.* 1 [*Said of people*] rural, homey, unpolished; see IGNORANT 2, RUDE 1. 2 [*Said of areas*] rustic, agrarian, provincial; see RURAL.

country *n.* 1 [Rural areas] farms, farmland, farming district, rural region, rural area, range, country district, backcountry, bush, forests, woodlands, backwoods, sparsely settled areas, sticks*, the boondocks*, boonies*; see also FARM, FOREST.—*Ant.* CITY, borough, municipality. 2 [A nation] government, a people, a sovereign state; see NATION 1. 3 [Land and all that is associated with it] homeland, native land, fatherland; see LAND 2.

countryside *n.* rural district, farmland, woods; see COUNTRY 1.

county *n.* province, constituency, shire; see AREA, REGION 1.

couple *n.* 1 [A pair] two, set, brace; see PAIR. 2 [*A few] two, several, a handful; see FEW.

couple *v.* unite, come together, link; see COPULATE, JOIN 1.

coupon *n.* token, box top, order blank, detachable portion, premium certificate, ticket; see also CARD, TICKET 1.

courage *n.* bravery, valor, boldness, fearlessness, spirit, audacity, audaciousness, temerity, manliness, pluck, mettle, enterprise, stoutheartedness, firmness, self-reliance, hardihood, heroism, gallantry, daring, prowess, power, resolution, dash, recklessness, defiance, the courage of one's convictions, spunk*, grit, backbone, guts*, what it takes*, moxie*, nerve; see also STRENGTH.—*Ant.* FEAR, cowardice, timidity.

courageous *a.* daring, gallant, intrepid; see BRAVE.

course *n.* 1 [A route] passage, path, way; see ROUTE 1. 2 [A prepared way, especially for racing] lap, cinder path, track; see ROAD 1. 3 [A plan of study] subject, studies, curriculum; see EDUCATION 1. 4 [A series of lessons] classes, lectures, seminar; see EDUCATION 1. **—in due course** in due time, properly, conveniently; see APPROPRIATELY. **—in the course of** during, in the process of, when; see WHILE 1. **—of course** certainly, by all means, indeed; see SURELY. **—off course** misdirected, erratic, going the wrong way; see WRONG 2. **—on course** on target, correct, going in the right direction; see ACCURATE 2.

court *n.* 1 [An enclosed, roofless area] square, courtyard, patio; see YARD 1. 2 [An instrument for administering justice] tribunal, bench, magistrate, bar, session. *Types of courts include the following:* the Supreme Court of the United States, appellate court of the United States, federal court, state supreme court, district court, county court, justice's court, magistrate's court, mayor's court, police court. 3 [A sovereign's family, attendants, etc.] lords and ladies, attendants, royal household; see GOVERNMENT 2, ROYALTY, RULER 1. 4 [An area for playing certain games] arena, rink, ring; see FIELD 2.

court *v.* attract, allure, solicit, beseech, entice, pursue, accompany, follow, plead, make love, pay court, pay attentions to, pay court to, make overtures, go courting, woo, propose, ask in marriage, set one's cap for*, pop the question*, go steady*, go together*, go with*, make a play for*; see also DATE 2.

courteous *a.* courtly, affable, cultivated; see POLITE.

courteously *a.* civilly, affably, obligingly; see POLITELY.

courtesy *n.* 1 [Courteous conduct] kindness, friendliness, affability, courteousness, gentleness, consideration, thoughtfulness, sympathy, geniality, cordiality, graciousness, tact, good manners, politeness, refinement, chivalry, gallantry, respect, deference, polished manners, good breeding; see also GENEROSITY, KINDNESS 1. 2 [Courteous act] favor, polite gesture, charitable act; see KINDNESS 2.

cousin *n.* kin, an aunt's child, an uncle's child; see RELATIVE.

cove *n.* inlet, sound, lagoon; see BAY.

cover *n.* 1 [A covering object] covering, ceiling, canopy, hood, sheath, sheet, awning, tent, umbrella, dome, stopper, lid, canvas, tarpaulin, book cover, folder, wrapper, wrapping paper, jacket, case, spread, tarp*; see also BLANKET, ENVELOPE, FOLDER, ROOF. 2 [A covering substance] paint, varnish, polish; see COAT 3, SHEET 2. 3 [Shelter] harbor, asylum, refuge; see RETREAT 2, SHELTER. **—take cover** conceal oneself, take shelter, go indoors; see HIDE 1. **—under cover** secretive, hiding, concealed; see HIDDEN.

cover *v.* 1 [To place as a covering] carpet, put on, overlay, surface, board up, superimpose, black in, black out; see also SPREAD 3. 2 [To wrap] envelop, enshroud, encase; see WRAP. 3 [To protect] shield, screen, house; see DEFEND 1, 2, SHELTER. 4 [To hide] screen, camouflage, mask; see DISGUISE, HIDE 1. 5 [To include] embrace, comprise, incorporate; see INCLUDE 1. 6 [To travel] traverse, journey over, cross; see TRAVEL. 7 [To send down in plenty] drench, engulf, overcome; see FLOOD. 8 [To report upon, especially for a newspaper] recount, narrate, relate; see BROADCAST, RECORD 3. **—cover up** lie about, keep secret, keep the lid on*; see DEFEND 1, 2, SHELTER.

covered *a.* 1 [Provided with cover] topped, lidded, roofed, wrapped, enveloped, bound, painted, varnished, coated, camouflaged, sheltered, shielded, disguised, masked, secreted, protected, concealed; see also HIDDEN.—*Ant.* OBVIOUS, revealed, exposed. 2 [Plentifully bestrewn] scattered with, sprinkled over, spattered, spangled, dotted, strewn with, starred, starry with, flowered, spotted with, sown, dusted over, powdered, spread with.—*Ant.* EMPTY, bare, unfurnished. 3 [Attended to] noted, taken note of, reported, recorded, written, included, marked, explored,

regarded, scrutinized, examined, surveyed, investigated, observed, looked to, hurdled, cared for; see also DONE 1, RECOGNIZED.—*Ant.* unheeded, unnoticed, passed over.

covering *n.* concealment, top, spread; see COVER 1.

covet *v.* desire, envy, wish for; see WANT 1.

cow *n.* heifer, milk cow, dairy cow, bovine, bossy*; see also CATTLE.

coward *n.* sneak, milksop, shirker, deserter, weakling, alarmist, slacker*, quitter*, chicken*, lily-liver*, scaredy-cat* chicken-heart*, fraidy-cat*, yellow-belly*.

cowardice *n.* cowardliness, timidity, faintheartedness, fear, weakness, quailing, lack of courage, apprehension, shyness, dread, fearfulness, yellow streak*, cold feet*; see also FEAR.—*Ant.* bravery, valor, fearlessness.

cowardly *a.* timid, frightened, afraid, fearful, shy, backward, cowering, apprehensive, nervous, anxious, dismayed, fainthearted, panicky, scared, scary*, jittery*, craven, mean-spirited, weak, soft, chicken-livered*, lily-livered*, yellow*, skulking, sneaking, cringing, trembling, shaken, crouching, running, quaking, afraid of one's own shadow, shaking like a leaf, shaking in one's boots*; see also AFRAID, WEAK 3.—*Ant.* BRAVE, fearless, open.

cowboy *n.* cowhand, hand, wrangler, rider, herder, cattle-herder, drover, gaucho, cowpuncher*, cowpoke*, buckaroo; see also RANCHER.

cower *v.* cringe, shrink, fear, run, quake, shiver, tremble, shake, snivel, flinch, quail; see also GROVEL.

coy *a.* bashful, shy, demure; see HUMBLE 1.

cozy *a.* secure, sheltered, snug; see COMFORTABLE 2, SAFE 1.

crab *n.* crayfish, crustacean, seafood; see SHELLFISH.

crack* *a.* first-rate, first-class, skilled; see ABLE, EXCELLENT.

crack *n.* 1 [An incomplete break] chink, split, cut; see HOLE 1. 2 [A crevice] cleft, fissure, rift; see HOLE 1. 3 [A blow] hit, thwack, stroke; see BLOW. 4 [*A witty or brazen comment] return, witticism, jest; see JOKE, REMARK.

crack *v.* 1 [To become cracked] cleave, burst, split; see BREAK. 2 [To cause to crack] cleave, split, sever; see BREAK. 3 [To damage] injure, hurt, impair; see DAMAGE. 4 [*To become mentally deranged] become insane, go crazy, have a nervous breakdown; see CRACK UP 2.

5 [To solve] figure out, answer, decode; see SOLVE. —**crack a joke** quip, jest, jape; see JOKE. —**crack up 1** [*To crash a vehicle] collide, be in an accident, smash up; see CRASH 4. **2** [*To fail suddenly in health, mind, or strength] go to pieces, fail, deteriorate, sicken, go insane, go crazy, become demented, freak out*, have a nervous breakdown, go out of one's mind, go off one's rocker*, blow a fuse*, go off the deep end*; see also WEAKEN 1. **3** [*To laugh] roar, howl, roll in the aisles*; see LAUGH. —**get cracking*** get going, get a move on*, start; see BEGIN 2, MOVE 1.

cracked *a.* shattered, split, fractured; see BROKEN 1.

cracker *n.* wafer, cookie, soda cracker, oyster cracker, biscuit, saltine, hardtack, sea biscuit, wheat biscuit; see also BREAD.

cradle *n.* trundle bed, crib, bassinet; see BED 1, FURNITURE.

craft *n.* **1** [Skill] proficiency, competence, aptitude; see ABILITY. **2** [Trade] occupation, career, work; see JOB 1, PROFESSION 1. **3** [Ship] vessel, aircraft, spacecraft; see BOAT, SHIP.

craftsman *n.* artisan, skilled worker, journeyman, maker, technician, manufacturer, machinist, handcraftsman, mechanic; see also ARTIST, LABORER, SPECIALIST.

crafty *a.* clever, sharp, shrewd; see INTELLIGENT.

cram *v.* **1** [To stuff] crush, jam, press; see COMPRESS, PACK. **2** [To study hurriedly] review, bone up*, burn the midnight oil; see STUDY.

cramp *n.* spasm, crick, pang; see PAIN 2.

cramped *a.* narrow, confined, restraining; see RESTRICTED, UNCOMFORTABLE 1.

cranium *n.* brain, cerebrum, cerebellum, brainpan, braincase, skull; see also HEAD 1.

crank *n.* **1** [A device for revolving a shaft] bracket, lever, handle; see ARM 2, HANDLE 1. **2** [*A person with an obsession] eccentric, fanatic, monomaniac; see CHARACTER 4. **3** [*An ill-natured person] curmudgeon, misanthrope, complainer; see GROUCH.

cranky *a.* disagreeable, cross, testy; see IRRITABLE.

crash *n.* **1** [A crashing sound] clatter, clash, din; see NOISE 1, SOUND 2. **2** [A collision] wreck, accident, shock; see COLLISION.

crash *v.* **1** [To fall with a crash] overturn, upset, break down, plunge, be hurled, pitch, smash, dive, hurtle, lurch, sprawl, tumble, fall headlong, fall flat, drop, slip, collapse; see also FALL 1. **2** [To break into pieces] shatter, shiver, splinter; see BREAK, SMASH. **3** [To make a crashing sound] clatter, bang, smash; see SOUND. **4** [To have a collision] collide, run together, run into, smash into, bang into, meet, jostle, bump, butt, knock, punch, jar, jolt, crack up; see also HIT 1. **5** [To collapse] fail, come to ruin, collapse; see FAIL 1, FALL 1, 2. **6** [*To go uninvited] disturb, gate-crash*, intrude; see INTERRUPT, MEDDLE 1.

crash program* *n.* crash project*, accelerated program, crash course*, intensive program, around-the-clock endeavor, marathon, speedup; see also EMERGENCY.

crass *a.* gross, tasteless, coarse; see IGNORANT 1, 2, VULGAR.

crate *n.* carton, box, cage; see CONTAINER, PACKAGE.

crater *n.* hollow, opening, abyss; see HOLE 1.

craving *n.* need, longing, yearning; see DESIRE 1.

crawl *v.* creep, worm along, wriggle, squirm, slither, move on hands and knees, writhe, go on all fours, worm one's way, go on one's belly; see also GROVEL, SNEAK.

crayon *n.* chalk, pastel, colored wax; see PENCIL.

craze *n.* fad, rage, fashion; see FAD.

crazily *a.* furiously, irrationally, hastily, madly, rashly, insanely, psychotically, maniacally; see also VIOLENTLY, WILDLY.

crazy *a.* crazed, demented, mad; see INSANE 1. —**go crazy** become insane, lose one's wits, get angry; see RAGE 1.

cream *n.* **1** [The fatty portion of milk] heavy cream, light cream, crème, coffee cream, whipping cream, ice cream, half-and-half, butterfat, sour cream, crème fraîche; see also MILK. **2** [A creamy substance] emulsion, salve, jelly; see COSMETIC, LOTION.

creamy *a.* smooth, buttery, creamed; see RICH 3, SOFT 1.

crease *n.* tuck, overlap, pleat; see FOLD, WRINKLE.

crease *v.* double, rumple, crimp; see FOLD 1, WRINKLE.

create *v.* make, produce, form, perform, bring into being, bring into existence, build, fashion, constitute, originate, generate, construct, discover, shape, forge, design, plan, fabricate, cause to be, conceive, give birth to; see also COMPOSE 2, INVENT 1, PRODUCE 2.

creation *n.* **1** [The process of creating] imagination, production, formulation; see CONCEPTION 1, MAKING. **2** [All that has been created] cosmos, nature, totality; see EARTH

1, UNIVERSE. **3** [A work of art] creative work, masterpiece, brainchild*; see PRODUCTION 1.

creative *a.* formative, inventive, productive; see ARTISTIC, ORIGINAL 2.

Creator *n.* First Cause, Deity, Maker; see GOD.

creature *n.* creation, being, beast; see ANIMAL, HUMAN BEING.

credential *n.* declaration, document, voucher; see CERTIFICATE, RECORD 1.

credibility *n.* likelihood, probability, trustworthiness; see POSSIBILITY 2.

credible *a.* trustworthy, dependable, sincere; see RELIABLE.

credit *n.* **1** [Belief] credence, reliance, confidence; see FAITH 1. **2** [Unencumbered funds] assets, capital, stocks, bonds, paper credit, bank account, mortgages, liens, securities, debentures, cash; see also WEALTH. **3** [Permission to defer payment] extension, borrowing power, line of credit, trust; see also LOAN. —**do credit to** bring approval to, reflect well on, do honor to; see SATISFY 1. —**give credit to** believe in, rely on, have confidence in; see TRUST 1. —**give one credit for** believe in, rely on, have confidence in; see TRUST 1. —**on credit** on loan, on a charge, charged; see UNPAID 1. —**to one's credit** good, honorable, beneficial; see WORTHWHILE.

credit card *n.* charge card, smart card, gold card, plastic*, plastic money*.

creditor *n.* lessor, lender, mortgager; see BANKER.

creed *n.* belief, doctrine, dogma; see FAITH 2.

creek *n.* stream, spring, brook; see RIVER. —**up the creek*** in difficulty, desperate, lost; see IN TROUBLE.

creep *v.* slither, writhe, worm along; see CRAWL.

creeping *a.* crawling, squirming, writhing, wriggling, crouching, cowering, slinking, skulking, inching, dragging, lagging, limping, faltering, shuffling, hobbling, sneaking, moving slowly, going at a snail's place, worming along.

crevice *n.* chasm, cleft, slit; see GAP 3.

crew *n.* **1** [Company of sailors] seafarers, sailors, hands, able seamen, ship's company, mariners, sea dogs, gobs*. **2** [A group of people organized to do a particular job] company, troupe, squad; see ORGANIZATION 2, TEAM 1.

crime *n.* transgression, misdemeanor, vice, outrage, wickedness, immorality, infringement, depravity, evil behavior, wrongdoing, misconduct, corruption, delinquency, wrong, trespass, malefaction, der-

eliction, lawlessness, domestic violence, hate crime, discrimination, harassment, arson, bigamy, killing, forgery, atrocity, felony, capital crime, offense, white-collar crime, scandal, infraction, violation, mortal sin, homicide, voluntary manslaughter, involuntary manslaughter, simple assault, aggravated assault, battery, larceny, robbery, burglary, holdup, kidnapping, swindling, fraud, defrauding, embezzlement, smuggling, extortion, bribery, mugging, date rape, statutory rape, attack, sexual molestation, breach of promise, malicious mischief, breach of the peace, libel, perjury, conspiracy, counterfeiting, inciting to revolt, sedition, mayhem, crime of passion, war crime, crime against humanity; see also CORRUPTION, EVIL 2, MURDER, RAPE, SIN, THEFT, TREASON.

criminal *a.* unlawful, felonious, illegal; see BAD 1.

criminal *n.* lawbreaker, felon, crook*. *Criminals include the following:* murderer, killer, rapist, perjurer, arsonist, mugger, desperado, thug, gangster, gang leader, burglar, safecracker, swindler, clip artist*, confidence man, con man*, thief, bandit, second-story man*, cattle rustler, horse thief, car thief, pickpocket, counterfeiter, forger, smuggler, extortionist, kidnapper, gunman, triggerman*, accomplice, informer, stool pigeon*, stoolie*, squealer*, con*, dope peddler*, pusher*.

crimson *a.* blood-red, bright red, scarlet; see COLOR *n.*, RED *n.*

cringe *v.* flinch, quail, wince; see COWER, CRAWL.

crinkle *v.* coil, wind, crease; see WRINKLE.

cripple *v.* disable, mangle, injure; see HURT.

crippled *a.* maimed, mutilated, mangled; see DEFORMED, DISABLED.

crisis *n.* straits, urgency, necessity, dilemma, puzzle, pressure, embarrassment, pinch, juncture, pass, change, contingency, situation, condition, plight, impasse, deadlock, predicament, corner, trauma, quandary, extremity, trial, crux, moment of truth, turning point, critical situation, pickle*, stew*, fix*, mess, hot water*.—*Ant.* STABILITY, normality, regularity.

crisp *a.* **1** [Fresh and firm] green, plump, firm; see FRESH 1, RIPE 1. **2** [Brisk] fresh, invigorating, bracing; see STIMULATING.

criterion *n.* basis, foundation, test, standard, rule, proof, scale, prototype, pattern, example, standard of judgment, standard of criticism, archetype, norm, precedent, fact, law, principle; see also MEASURE 2, MODEL 2.

critic *n.* 1 [One who makes adverse comments] faultfinder, censor, quibbler, detractor, slanderer, complainer, doubter, nagger, fretter, scolder, worrier, mudslinger*.—*Ant.* BELIEVER, praiser, supporter. 2 [One who endeavors to interpret and judge] commentator, reviewer, analyst, connoisseur, writer of reviews, cartoonist, caricaturist, expert; see also EXAMINER, WRITER.

critical *a.* 1 [Disapproving] faultfinding, trenchant, derogatory, disapproving, hypercritical, demanding, satirical, cynical, nagging, scolding, condemning, censuring, reproachful, disapproving, disparaging, exacting, sharp, cutting, biting; see also SARCASTIC. 2 [Capable of observing and judging] penetrating, perceptive, discerning; see DISCREET, OBSERVANT. 3 [Crucial] decisive, significant, deciding; see IMPORTANT 1.

criticism *n.* 1 [A serious estimate or interpretation] study, analysis, critique; see JUDGMENT 2, REVIEW 1. 2 [An adverse comment] blame, carping, faultfinding; see OBJECTION.

criticize *v.* 1 [To make a considered analysis] study, probe, scrutinize; see ANALYZE, EXAMINE. 2 [To make adverse comments] chastise, reprove, reprimand; see BLAME.

crook* *n.* 1 [A criminal] swindler, thief, rogue; see CRIMINAL. 2 [A bend] fork, bend, hook; see ANGLE 1.

crooked *a.* 1 [Having a crook] curved, curving, hooked, winding, bowed, spiral, serpentine, not straight, zigzag, twisted, meandering, tortuous, sinuous; see also ANGULAR, BENT, OBLIQUE.—*Ant.* STRAIGHT, unbent, direct. 2 [Dishonest] iniquitous, corrupt, nefarious; see DISHONEST.

crop *n.* harvest, yield, product, reaping, hay, fodder, grains, vintage, fruits; see also PRODUCE.

cross *a.* ill-tempered, easily annoyed, pettish; see CRITICAL, IRRITABLE.

cross *n.* 1 [Religious symbol, especially of Christianity] crucifix, Greek cross, papal cross, Maltese cross, Latin cross. 2 [A tribulation] affliction, trial, misfortune; see DIFFICULTY 2. 3 [A mixed offspring] mongrel, crossbreed, half-breed; see HYBRID, MIXTURE 1.

cross *v.* 1 [To pass over] traverse, go across, go over, pass, ford, cut across, span. 2 [To lie across] intersect, lean on, extend across; see DIVIDE. 3 [To mix breeds] hybridize, interbreed, cross-pollinate; see MIX 1.

cross-examine *v.* investigate, check, interrogate; see EXAMINE, QUESTION.

crossing *n.* 1 [A place to cross] intersection, overpass, crosswalk; see BRIDGE 1. 2 [A mixing of breeds] hybridization, interbreeding, cross-pollination; see MIXTURE 1.

crossroad *n.* intersecting road, intersection, junction; see ROAD 1.

crosswise *a.* across, cross, perpendicular, transversely, vertically, horizontally, at right angles, over, sideways, crisscross, askew, crossways; see also ANGULAR.

crotch *n.* 1 [Angle] fork, corner, elbow; see ANGLE 1, CURVE 2. 2 [Loins] pubic area, groin, pelvic girdle; see BODY 1.

crouch *v.* 1 [To stoop] dip, duck, bow; see BEND. 2 [To cower] cringe, flinch, quail; see COWER, CRAWL.

crowd *n.* host, horde, flock, mob, company, swarm, press, crush, surge, legion, group, body, pack, army, drove, party, flood, throng, troupe, deluge, multitude, congregation, cluster, assembly, crew, herd, bunch, gang; see also GATHERING.

crowd *v.* stuff, jam, squeeze; see PACK 2, PUSH 1.

crowded *a.* packed, huddled, crushed; see FULL 1.

crown *n.* diadem, headdress, tiara, coronet, circlet.

crown *v.* commission, authorize, invest, enable, sanction, inaugurate, exalt, raise, heighten, set up, ennoble, establish; see also DELEGATE 1.

crucial *a.* decisive, climactic, deciding; see IMPORTANT 1.

crude *a.* rude, rough, unpolished, in a raw state, homemade, thick, coarse, harsh, rudimentary, homespun, rough-hewn, unfashioned, unformed, undeveloped, in the rough, raw, immature, sketchy; see also UNFINISHED 1.—*Ant.* FINISHED, polished, refined.

crudely *a.* clumsily, coarsely, impudently; see RUDELY.

cruel *a.* malevolent, spiteful, depraved, wicked, vengeful, evil, sinful, degenerate, brutish, demonic, outrageous, tyrannical, gross, demoralized, evil-minded, vicious, brutal, rough, wild, bestial, ferocious, monstrous, demoniac, debased, destructive, harmful, mischievous, callous, unnatural, merciless, sadistic, unpitying, unmerciful, unyielding, remorseless, pitiless, unfeeling, inflexible, bloodthirsty, unrelenting, relentless, grim, inhuman, inhumane, atrocious, harsh, heartless, stony, unconcerned, showing no mercy, turning a deaf ear, hard as nails*.—*Ant.* MERCIFUL, kindly, compassionate.

cruelly *a.* savagely, inhumanly, viciously; see BRUTALLY.

cruelty *n.* brutality, barbarity, sadism, inhumanity, barbarism, mercilessness, wickedness, coarseness, ruthlessness, severity, malice, rancor, venom, coldness, unfeelingness, insensibility, indifference, fierceness, bestiality, ferocity, savagery, grimness, monstrousness, inflexibility, fiendishness, hardness of heart, bloodthirstiness, torture, relentlessness, persecution, harshness, heartlessness, atrocity; see also EVIL 1, 2, TYRANNY.—*Ant.* KINDNESS, benevolence, humanity.

cruise *n.* voyage, sail, jaunt; see JOURNEY.

cruise *v.* voyage, navigate, coast; see SAIL 1, TRAVEL.

cruiser *n.* cabin cruiser, boat, privateer; see SHIP.

crumb *n.* particle, scrap, morsel; see BIT 1.

crumble *v.* fall apart, decay, break up; see DISINTEGRATE.

crumbly *a.* breaking up, breaking down, falling to pieces, decayed, perishing, deteriorating, soft, corroded, rusted, rotted, worn away, fragile, brittle, friable, crisp, frail, rotten, breakable, eroded, disintegrated; see also DECAYING, GRITTY.—*Ant.* FIRM, sound, undecayed.

crumple *v.* rumple, crush, crease; see WRINKLE.

crush *v.* **1** [To break into small pieces] smash, pulverize, powder; see GRIND. **2** [To bruise severely] press, mash, bruise; see BEAT 1, BREAK 1. **3** [To defeat utterly] overwhelm, force down, annihilate; see DEFEAT 2.

crust *n.* hull, rind, pie crust; see SHELL 1.

cry *n.* **1** [A loud utterance] outcry, exclamation, clamor, shout, call, battle cry, halloo, hurrah, cheer, scream, shriek, yell, whoop, squall, groan, bellow, howl, bawl, holler, uproar, acclamation, roar; see also sense 2 and NOISE 2.—*Ant.* WHISPER, murmur, silence. **2** [A characteristic call] howl, hoot, wail, bawl, screech, bark, squawk, squeak, yelp, meow, whinny, moo, chatter, bay, cluck, crow, whine, trill, quack, cackle, caw, bellow, croak, coo, whistle, gobble, hiss, growl; see also YELL. **3** [A fit of weeping] sobbing, wailing, shedding tears, sorrowing, mourning, whimpering; see also TEARS. —**a far cry (from)** unlike, dissimilar, remote; see DIFFERENT.

cry *v.* **1** [To weep] weep, sob, wail, shed tears, snivel, sniffle, squall, lament, mourn, bewail, bemoan, moan, howl, keen, whimper, whine, weep over, complain, deplore, sorrow, grieve, fret, groan, burst into tears, choke up, cry one's eyes out, break down, break up*, blubber,

bawl.—*Ant.* LAUGH, rejoice, exult. **2** [To call; *said of other than human creatures*] howl, bark, hoot, scream, screech, squawk, squeak, yelp, grunt, roar, shriek, meow, whinny, moo, bawl, snarl, chatter, bay, cluck, crow, whine, pipe, trill, coo, whistle, caw, bellow, quack, gabble, hiss, growl, croak, cackle, twitter, tweet; see also YELL.

crying *n.* shrieking, sorrow, sobbing; see TEARS. —**for crying out loud*** for God's sake; for heaven's sake; oh, no; see CURSE, NO.

crystallize *v.* become definite, take shape, be outlined; see FORM 4.

cub *n.* young, offspring, whelp; see ANIMAL.

cube *n.* six-sided solid, hexahedron, die; see SOLID.

cuddle *v.* snuggle, huddle, curl up; see NESTLE.

cue *n.* prompt, warning signal, opening bars*; see SIGN 1.

cuff *n.* **1** [Edge of a sleeve or pants leg] French cuff, fold, wristband; see BAND 1. **2** [A blow] slap, punch, hit; see BLOW. —**off the cuff*** extemporaneous, extemporaneously, offhand; see INFORMAL. —**on the cuff*** on credit, charged, delayed; see UNPAID 1.

culminate *v.* finish, close, end up*; see END 1.

culprit *n.* offender, felon, accused; see CRIMINAL.

cult *n.* clique, sect, followers; see FACTION, RELIGION 2.

cultivate *v.* **1** [Plant] till, garden, seed; see HARVEST, PLANT. **2** [Educate] nurture, refine, improve; see TEACH.

cultivation *n.* horticulture, agriculture, gardening; see FARMING.

cultural *a.* educational, socializing, refining, refined, constructive, influential, nurturing, disciplining, enlightening, civilizing, instructive, humanizing, beneficial, learned, artistic, aesthetic, educative, polishing, enriching, elevating, uplifting, ennobling, broadening, developmental.—*Ant.* PRIMITIVE, barbaric, crude.

culture *n.* **1** [Civilizing tradition] folklore, folkways, instruction, education, study, society, family, convention, habit, inheritance, learning, arts, sciences, custom, mores, knowledge, letters, literature, poetry, painting, music, lore, architecture, history, religion, humanism, the arts and sciences; see also CIVILIZATION.—*Ant.* DISORDER, barbarism, chaos. **2** [Refinement and education] breeding, gentility, enlightenment, learning, capacity, ability, skill, science, lore, education, training, art, perception, discrimination, finish, taste, grace, dignity, politeness, savoir-faire, manners, urbanity, dress, fashion, address, tact, nobility, kindness, polish; see also COURTESY 1, ELEGANCE, EXPERIENCE.—*Ant.* IGNORANCE, crudeness, vulgarity.

cultured *a.* cultivated, educated, informed, advanced, accomplished, enlightened, polished, well-bred, genteel, elegant, courteous, intellectual, sophisticated, sensitive, intelligent, au courant, able, well-read, up-to-date, well-informed, traveled, experienced, tolerant, understanding, appreciative, civilized, literary, urbane, mannerly, gently bred, chivalrous, erudite, gallant, lettered, highbrow, high-class*; see also LIBERAL, POLITE, REFINED 2.—*Ant.* PREJUDICED, narrow, backward.

cunning *a.* clever, skillful, ingenious; see INTELLIGENT.

cup *n.* vessel, bowl, goblet, mug, tumbler, beaker, stein, bumper, teacup, coffee cup, measuring cup, chalice; see also CAN 1, CONTAINER.

cupboard *n.* closet, locker, storeroom; see FURNITURE.

curable *a.* improvable, subject to cure, not hopeless, correctable, capable of improvement, healable, restorable, mendable.

curb *n.* **1** [Restraint] hindrance, chain, check; see BARRIER, RESTRAINT 2. **2** [Edge] border, ledge, lip; see EDGE 1, RIM.

curb *v.* retard, impede, subdue; see HINDER, RESTRAIN, RESTRICT.

curdle *v.* coagulate, condense, clot; see THICKEN.

cure *n.* restorative, remedy, antidote; see MEDICINE 2.

cure *v.* make healthy, restore, make whole; see HEAL.

curfew *n.* late hour, time limit, check-in time; see LIMITATION 2.

curiosity *n.* **1** [Interest] concern, regard, inquiring mind, inquisitiveness, thirst for knowledge, a questing mind, questioning, interest, desire to know, interest in learning, scientific interest, healthy curiosity. **2** [An unusual object] oddity, rarity, marvel; see WONDER 2.

curious *a.* **1** [Strange or odd] rare, odd, unique; see UNUSUAL 2. **2** [Interested] inquiring, inquisitive, questioning; see INTERESTED 1.

curl *n.* coil, spiral, wave; see HAIR 1.

curl *v.* curve, coil, bend, spiral, crinkle, wind, twine, loop, crimp, lap, fold, roll, contort, form into a spiral, form into a curved shape, meander, ripple, buckle, zigzag, wrinkle,

twirl.—*Ant.* STRAIGHTEN, uncurl, unbend.

curly *a.* curled, kinky, wavy, coiled, crinkly, looped, winding, wound; see also ROLLED 1.

currency *n.* coin, bank notes, cash; see MONEY 1.

current *a.* prevailing, contemporary, in fashion; see FASHIONABLE, MODERN 1, POPULAR 3.

current *n.* drift, tidal motion, ebb and flow; see FLOW, TIDE.

curse *n.* oath, blasphemy, obscenity, sacrilege, anathema, ban, cursing, profanity, denunciation, damning, cuss word*, cussing*, swearword, four-letter word. *Common exclamations and curses include the following (many of which are old-fashioned):* Lord, oh God, the Devil, bless my soul, bless me, mercy, gracious, goodness, in Heaven's name, gee*, sakes alive*, darn*, hang it all*, dang*, blast*, damn it*, damn*, by golly*, for crying out loud*, Judas Priest*, hell's bells*, geez*, jeez*, shoot*, hell*, good grief, nuts*, wow.

curse *v.* blaspheme, profane, swear, use foul language, be foulmouthed, be obscene, take the Lord's name in vain, damn, turn the air blue*, abuse, revile, swear at, insult, call down curses on the head of, blast, doom, fulminate, denounce, call names, cuss*, cuss out*.

cursed *a.* blighted, doomed, confounded; see DAMNED 1.

curt *a.* brief, concise, terse; see SHORT 2.

curtain *n.* hanging, screen, shade, drape, drapery, window covering, window treatment, blind. *Kinds of curtains include the following:* draw curtain, roller shade, valance, sheer, portiere, cafe curtains, vertical blinds, Venetian blinds.

curve *n.* sweep, bow, arch, circuit, curvature, crook. *Types of curves include the following:* bell curve, bell-shaped curve, hairpin curve, S-curve, sine curve, extrapolated curve, hyperbola, parabola, normal curve, logarithmic curve, French curve, circle, ellipse, arc.

curve *v.* bow, crook, twist; see BEND.

curved *a.* bowed, arched, rounded; see BENT.

cushion *n.* mat, seat, pad; see PILLOW.

custodian *n.* superintendent, janitor, porter, cleaner, cleaning man, cleaning woman, attendant, caretaker, building superintendent, keeper, gatekeeper, night watchman; see also WATCHMAN.

custody *n.* care, guardianship, supervision, keeping, safekeeping, watch, superintendence, safeguarding; see also MANAGEMENT. —**take**

into custody capture, apprehend, seize; see ARREST.

custom *n.* habit, practice, usage, wont, fashion, routine, precedent, use, form, addiction, rule, procedure, observance, characteristic, second nature, matter of course, beaten path, rut, manner, way, mode, method, system, style, vogue, convention, formality, mold, pattern, design, type, taste, character, ritual, rite, attitude, mores, dictate of society, unwritten law, etiquette, conventionality.—*Ant.* DEPARTURE, deviation, shift.

customarily *a.* usually, commonly, generally; see REGULARLY.

customary *a.* usual, wonted, habitual; see COMMON 1, CONVENTIONAL 1, 2.

customer *n.* client, patron, consumer; see BUYER.

cut *a.* **1** [Formed] shaped, modeled, arranged; see FORMED. **2** [Reduced] lowered, debased, marked down; see REDUCED 1, 2. **3** [Severed] split, divided, sliced through; see CARVED.

cut *n.* **1** [The using of a sharp instrument] slash, thrust, dig, prick, gouge, penetrating, dividing, separation, severance, slitting, hacking, slice, carving, chop, stroke, incision, cleavage, penetration, gash, cleft, mark, nick, notch, opening, groove, furrow, slit, wound, fissure; see also HOLE 1, INJURY. **2** [A reduction] decrease, diminution, lessening; see REDUCTION 1. **3** [The shape] fashion, figure, construction; see FORM 1. **4** [A section] segment, slice, portion; see PART 1, PIECE 1. **5** [A piece of butchered meat] piece, slice, chunk; see MEAT. **6** [*An insult] indignity, offense, abuse; see INSULT. —**a cut above*** superior, higher, more capable; see BETTER 1.

cut *v.* **1** [To sever] slice, separate, slice through, cut into, cleave, mow, prune, reap, shear, dice, chop down, chop, slit, split, cut apart, hew, fell, rip, saw through, chisel, cut away, snip, chip, quarter, clip, behead,

---

scissor, bite, shave, dissect, bisect, amputate, gash, incise, truncate, lacerate, slash, notch, nick, indent, score, mark, scratch, rake, furrow, wound, gouge; see also CARVE. **2** [To cross] intersect, pass, move across; see CROSS 1. **3** [To shorten] curtail, delete, lessen; see DECREASE 2. **4** [To divide] split, break apart, separate; see DIVIDE. **5** [*To absent oneself from] shirk, avoid, stay away; see EVADE. **6** [To record electronically] make a record, make a recording, tape; see RECORD 3. —**cut back** reduce, curtail, shorten; see DECREASE 2. —**cut off** **1** [To remove] eliminate, sever, cut out; see REMOVE 1. **2** [To interrupt] intrude, break in on, cut in on; see INTERRUPT. —**cut out for** suited to, adequate, good for; see FIT. —**cut up** **1** [To chop] chop up, slice, dice; see CUT 1. **2** [*To clown] show off, play jokes, fool around*; see JOKE, PLAY 2.

cute* *a.* dainty, attractive, delightful; see CHARMING, PLEASANT 1, 2.

cycle *n.* revolution of time, period, recurrence; see AGE 3, SEQUENCE 1, SERIES.

cylinder *n.* **1** [An automobile part] compression chamber, combustion chamber, cylinder block; see AUTOMOBILE. **2** [A geometric form] circular cylinder, circular solid, barrel; see CIRCLE 1.

cynic *n.* misanthrope, misogynist, mocker, satirist, scoffer, pessimist, sarcastic person, caviler, carper, sneerer, unbeliever, egotist, man-hater, skeptic, doubter, questioner, detractor, doubting Thomas; see also CRITIC 1.—*Ant.* BELIEVER, optimist, idealist.

cynical *a.* scornful, skeptical, sneering; see SARCASTIC.

cynicism *n.* criticism, ridicule, contempt; see SARCASM.

czar *n.* emperor, autocrat, despot; see DICTATOR, KING, LEADER 2.

D

dab *n.* small quantity, fragment, lump; see BIT 1.

dab *v.* tap, pat, nudge; see TOUCH 1.

dabble *v.* trifle with, trifle, engage in superficially, amuse oneself with, dally, be an amateur, be a dilettante, have sport with, fiddle with, flirt with, toy with, putter, idle away time, work superficially, putter around, fool with*, fool around*, dip into.—*Ant.* STUDY, work at, become an expert.

dad* *n.* daddy*, male parent, pop*; see FATHER, PARENT.

dagger *n.* stiletto, short sword, blade; see KNIFE. —**look daggers at** glower at, look at with anger, scowl at; see DISLIKE.

daily *a.* diurnal, per diem, every day, occurring every day, issued every day, periodic, cyclic, day after day, once daily, by day, once a day, during the day, day by day, from day to day; see also REGULAR 3.

dainty *a.* delicate, fragile, petite, frail, thin, light, pretty, beautiful, lovely, attractive, trim, graceful, fine, neat, elegant, exquisite, precious, rare, soft, tender, airy, lacy, nice, darling*, cute*, sweet; see also CHARMING, WEAK.—*Ant.* ROUGH, coarse, gross.

dairy *n.* creamery, dairy farm, ice-cream plant, cheese factory, buttery, milk station, pasteurizing plant, cooperative; see also FARM.

dally with *v.* flirt with, trifle with, toy with; see DABBLE.

dam *n.* dike, wall, bank, embankment, gate, levee, irrigation dam, beaver dam, cofferdam; see also BARRIER.

dam *v.* hold back, check, obstruct, bar, slow, retard, restrict, stop up, close, clog, choke, block up, impede, hold, stop, block, confine; see also HINDER, RESTRAIN.—*Ant.* FREE, release, open up.

damage *n.* 1 [Injury] harm, hurt, wound, bruise, wrong, casualty, suffering, illness, stroke, affliction, accident, catastrophe, adversity, outrage, hardship, disturbance, mutilation, impairment, mishap, evil, blow, devastation, mischief, reverse, disablement, loss, collapse, vandalism; see also DISASTER, INJURY, MISFORTUNE.—*Ant.* BLESSING, benefit, boon. 2 [Loss occasioned by injury] ruin, breakage, ruined goods, wreckage, deprivation, waste, shrinkage, depreciation, pollution, corruption, blemish, contamination, defacement, degeneration, deterioration, ravage, havoc, erosion, disrepair, debasement, corrosion, atrophy, scratch, scar, erosion, decay, wear and tear, foul play; see also DESTRUCTION 2, LOSS 1.—*Ant.* IMPROVEMENT, betterment, growth.

damage *v.* ruin, wreck, tarnish, burn, scorch, dirty, rot, smash, bleach, drench, batter, discolor, mutilate, scratch, smudge, crack, bang up, abuse, maltreat, mar, deface, disfigure, mangle, contaminate, crumple, dismantle, cheapen, blight, disintegrate, pollute, ravage, sap, stain, tear, undermine, gnaw, corrode, break, split, stab, pierce, lacerate, cripple, rust, warp, maim, wound, taint, despoil, incapacitate, pervert, bruise, spoil, wear away, defile, wrong, corrupt, infect; see also BREAK, DESTROY.

damaged *a.* 1 [Injured] marred, in need of repair, in poor condition; see BROKEN 1, 2. 2 [Reduced in value because of damage] secondhand, used, faded; see CHEAP 1.

damages *n.* reparations, costs, reimbursement; see COMPENSATION, EXPENSE, EXPENSES.

damn *v.* curse, ban, doom, banish, excommunicate, sentence, convict, excoriate, cast into hell, torment, condemn to hell, condemn to eternal punishment, call down curses on; see also CONDEMN.—*Ant.* FORGIVE, bless, elevate. **—not give a damn*** not care, be indifferent, reject; see NEGLECT 1. **—not worth a damn*** useless, unproductive, valueless; see WORTHLESS.

damnation *n.* damning, condemnation, doom; see BLAME, CURSE.

damned *a.* 1 [Consigned to hell] cursed, condemned, accursed, lost, infernal, gone to blazes*; see also UNFORTUNATE.—*Ant.* BLESSED, saved, holy. 2 [*Disapproved of] bad, unwelcome, blankety-blank*, blasted*, bloody*, danged*, dog-gone*, darned*, lousy*; see also BAD 1, UNDESIRABLE.—*Ant.* WELCOMED, desirable, favorite. **—do (or try) one's damnedest*** endeavor, do one's best, give one's all; see TRY 1.

damp *a.* moist, soaked, soggy; see WET 1.

dampen *v.* sprinkle, water, rinse; see MOISTEN.

dance *n.* 1 [Rhythmic movement] dancing, choreography, caper, hop, skip. *Types of dances include the following—social:* waltz, rumba, fox trot, polka, tango, cha-cha, disco, mambo, samba, twist, jitterbug, two-step, box-step, line dance, lambada, break dancing, slam dancing, Charleston, bunny hop, hokey-pokey; *theatrical:* ballet, modern dance, tap dance, soft-shoe; *traditional:* cotillion, polonaise, quadrille, pavane, mazurka, bolero, fandango, minuet; *folk and ethnic:* sun dance, ghost dance, rain dance, sword dance, snake dance, fertility dance, Highland fling, flamenco, Irish jig, square dance, Virginia reel, tarantella, hornpipe, clog, hora, hula. 2 [A dancing party] grand ball, dress ball, reception, ball, sock hop*, hoedown, shindig*, prom; see also PARTY 1.

dance *v.* waltz, shimmy, samba, jitterbug, twist, disco, fox-trot, cha-cha, mambo, tango, polka, hop, skip, jump, leap, bob, scamper, bounce, sway, swirl, sweep, swing, cut a rug*, rock*; see also MOVE 1.

dancer *n.* ballerina, danseur, danseuse, chorus girl, showgirl, stripper*, hoofer*; ballet, tap, toe, hula, belly, go-go, folk, square, modern, flamenco, break, etc. dancer.

dandy* *a.* very good, fine, first-rate; see EXCELLENT.

danger *n.* uncertainty, risk, peril, emergency, crisis, jeopardy, threat, hazard, insecurity, instability, exposure, menace, vulnerability; see also

CHANCE 1.—*Ant.* SAFETY, security, certainty.

dangerous *a.* perilous, critical, serious, pressing, vulnerable, exposed, full of risk, threatening, alarming, urgent, hazardous, risky, menacing, ugly, nasty, formidable, terrible, deadly, insecure, precarious, ticklish, delicate, unstable, touchy, treacherous, bad, thorny, breakneck, shaky, on a collision course*, hairy*, under fire*, unhealthy, hot*; see also ENDANGERED, UNCERTAIN, UNSAFE.—*Ant.* CERTAIN, sure, secure.

dangerously *a.* desperately, precariously, severely; see SERIOUSLY 1.

dangle *v.* hover, swing, suspend; see HANG 1, 2.

dare *v.* 1 [To be courageous] take a chance, venture, adventure, undertake, try, attempt, endeavor, try one's hand, hazard, have the courage of one's convictions, take the bull by the horns*, go ahead, go for it*; see also CHANCE, RISK, TRY 1.—*Ant.* AVOID, dread, fear. 2 [To defy] meet, confront, oppose, disregard, brave, scorn, insult, resist, threaten, spurn, denounce, bully, mock, laugh at, challenge, have the nerve, face the music*, face up to, call someone's bluff; see also FACE 1.—*Ant.* AVOID, shun, evade.

daredevil *n.* stuntman, stuntwoman, gambler; see ADVENTURER.

daring *a.* bold, courageous, fearless; see BRAVE.

dark *a.* 1 [Lacking illumination] unlighted, unlit, dim, shadowy, somber, cloudy, foggy, sunless, lightless, indistinct, dull, faint, vague, dusky, dingy, murky, gloomy, obscure, pitch-dark, pitch-black, shady, shaded, clouded, darkened, overcast, opaque, without light, inky; see also BLACK 1, HAZY.—*Ant.* BRIGHT, lighted, illuminated. 2 [Dark in complexion] tan, swarthy, dark-complexioned; see BLACK 1. 3 [Evil] wicked, immoral, corrupt; see BAD 1.

dark *n.* gloom, evening, dusk; see DARKNESS 1. —**in the dark** uninformed, unaware, naive; see IGNORANT 1.

darken *v.* 1 [To grow darker] cloud up, cloud over, become dark; see SHADE 3. 2 [To make darker] cloud, shadow, blacken; see SHADE 2.

darkness *n.* 1 [Gloom] dark, dusk, murkiness, dimness, shade, blackness, pitchdarkness, twilight, eclipse, nightfall, obscurity, cloudiness; see also NIGHT 1. 2 [Evil] wickedness, sin, corruption; see EVIL 1. 3 [Secrecy] concealment, isolation, seclusion; see PRIVACY, SECRECY.

darling *n.* lover, sweetheart, dear one, beloved, dear heart, heart's

desire, dearest, pet, angel, love, sweetie pie*, sugar*, honey, precious*, sweetie*, hon*, light of my life*, baby*, one and only*.

darn *v.* mend, sew, patch; see REPAIR.

dart *n.* missile, barb, arrow; see WEAPON.

dart *v.* shoot, shoot out, speed, plunge, launch, thrust, hurtle, fling, heave, pitch, dash, spurt, spring, spring up, fly, fire off, scoot*; see also MOVE 1.—*Ant.* STOP, amble, loiter.

dash *n.* 1 [A short, swift movement] spurt, charge, rush; see RUN 1. 2 [Punctuation marking a break in thought] em, em dash, en dash, hyphen; see also MARK 1, PUNCTUATION. 3 [A little of something] a few drops, hint, sprinkle, seasoning, touch, grain, trace, suspicion, suggestion, taste; see also BIT 1, PART 1.—*Ant.* TOO MUCH, quantity, excess.

dash *v.* 1 [To discourage] dampen, dismay, dispirit; see DISCOURAGE. 2 [To sprint] race, speed, hurry; see RUN 1.

data *n.* evidence, reports, details, results, notes, documents, abstracts, testimony, facts, raw data, memorandums, memos, records, findings, numbers, statistics, figures, measurements, conclusions, information, experiments, info*, dope*; see also DECLARATION, KNOWLEDGE 1, PROOF 1.

date *n.* 1 [A specified time or period of time] epoch, period, era, generation, day, term, course, spell, duration, span, moment, minute, reign, hour, century; see also AGE 3, TIME 2, YEAR. 2 [An appointment] meeting, rendezvous, engagement, interview, call, visit; see also APPOINTMENT 2. 3 [Person with whom one has a date] partner, companion, associate; see FRIEND, LOVER 1. —**out of date** obsolete, passé, antiquated; see OLD-FASHIONED. —**to date** until now, as yet, so far; see NOW 1. —**up-to-date** modern, contemporary, current; see FASHIONABLE.

date *v.* 1 [To indicate historical time] ascertain the time of, determine, assign a time to, mark with a date, fix the date of, chronicle, isolate, carbon-date; see also DEFINE 1, MEASURE 1, RECORD 1. 2 [To court or be courted] escort, associate with, take out*, keep company with, go out with*, go together*, make a date with, go steady*; see also ACCOMPANY.

daughter *n.* female child, female offspring, descendant, stepdaughter, infant; see also CHILD, GIRL.

dawn *n.* dawning, sunrise, daybreak; see MORNING 1.

day *n.* **1** [The time of light or work] daylight, daytime, full day, working day, daylight hours, eight-hour day, sizzler*, scorcher*; good day, bad day, hot day, rainy day. **2** [A special day] feast day, celebration, festival; see HOLIDAY. **3** [A period of time] era, age, time; see AGE 3. —**call it a day*** finish, quit working, end; see STOP 1. —**day after day** continuously, daily, steadily; see REGULARLY. —**day in and day out** consistently, steadily, every day; see DAILY, REGULARLY. —**from day to day** without thought for the future, sporadically, heedlessly; see IRREGULARLY.

daydream *n.* trance, vision, fantasy; see DREAM.

daylight *n.* daytime, daylight hours, broad daylight; see DAY 1. —**scare (or beat or knock) the daylights out of*** frighten, scare, beat; see THREATEN.

daze *n.* stupor, trance, bewilderment; see CONFUSION.

dazed *a.* confused, bewildered, disoriented; see DOUBTFUL.

dead *a.* **1** [Without life] not existing, expired, deceased, perished, lifeless, inanimate, late, defunct, breathless, no longer living, devoid of life, departed, brain-dead, clinically dead, gone, no more*, done for*, gone the way of all flesh*, gone to one's reward*, gone to meet one's Maker, at rest with God*, out of one's misery*, snuffed out*, pushing up daisies*, rubbed out*, wasted*, liquidated*, erased*, gone by the board, resting in peace*.—*Ant.* ALIVE, animate, enduring. **2** [Without the appearance of life] inert, still, stagnant; see DULL 2. **3** [Numb] insensible, deadened, anesthetized; see NUMB 1, UNCONSCIOUS. **4** [*Exhausted] wearied, worn, spent; see TIRED.

deaden *v.* blunt, impair, dull, repress, slow, paralyze, freeze, anesthetize, put to sleep, numb, knock out, incapacitate, depress, stifle, benumb, smother, retard, KO*; see also HURT, WEAKEN 2.—*Ant.* EXCITE, revitalize, invigorate.

deadlock *n.* standstill, stalemate, impasse; see PAUSE.

deadly *a.* fatal, lethal, murderous, mortal, bloody, homicidal, virulent, poisonous, deadly, destructive, venomous, life-threatening, deathly, toxic, terminal, malignant, injurious, carcinogenic, suicidal, bloodthirsty, cannibalistic, harmful, violent; see also DANGEROUS.

deaf *a.* unable to hear, hearing-impaired, without hearing, deaf and dumb, deafened, stunned, hard of hearing.

deafening *a.* thunderous, overpowering, shrieking; see LOUD 1, 2.

deal *n.* **1** [An agreement] pledge, compromise, pact; see AGREEMENT, CONTRACT. **2** [A secret or dishonest agreement] swindle, robbery, graft; see CRIME, THEFT. **3** [A lot] much, abundance, superabundance; see PLENTY. —**a good** (or **great**) **deal** a lot, quite a bit, a considerable amount; see MUCH. —**make a big deal out of*** expand, magnify, blow up; see EXAGGERATE.

deal *v.* trade, bargain, barter; see BUY, SELL. —**deal with** handle, manage, have to do with; see TREAT 1.

dealer *n.* retailer, trader, vendor; see BUSINESSMAN, MERCHANT.

dealings *n.* business, trade, transactions; see BUSINESS 1, 4.

dear *a.* precious, respected, cherished; see BELOVED.

dear *n.* loved one, sweetheart, love; see DARLING, LOVER 1.

dearly *a.* **1** [In an affectionate manner] fondly, affectionately, yearningly; see LOVINGLY. **2** [To a great extent] greatly, extremely, profoundly; see VERY.

death *n.* decease, dying, demise, passing, loss of life, departure, release, parting, end of life, afterlife, other world, grave, tomb, paradise, heaven, hell, extinction, mortality, exit, end, finish, the way of all flesh*, the Grim Reaper*, eternal rest, last rest*; see also DESTRUCTION 1.—*Ant.* LIFE, birth, beginning. —**at death's door** failing, wasting away, nearly dead; see DYING 1, 2. —**to death** very much, extremely, to the extreme; see MUCH 1. —**to the death** to the end, constantly, faithfully; see LOYALLY.

debatable *a.* disputable, unsettled, up for discussion; see CONTROVERSIAL, QUESTIONABLE 1.

debate *n.* contest, argumentation, dispute; see DISCUSSION.

debate *v.* refute, oppose, question, contend, contest, reason with, wrangle, answer, differ, dispute, quarrel, bandy words with, argue the pros and cons of; see also ARGUE, DISCUSS.—*Ant.* AGREE, concur, concede.

debauched *a.* corrupted, debased, depraved; see WICKED.

debit *n.* deficit, obligation, liability; see DEBT.

debris *n.* rubbish, litter, wreckage; see TRASH 1.

debt *n.* liability, obligation, mortgage, duty, arrears, deficit, note, bill, account payable, indebtedness; see also OBLIGATION.—*Ant.* CASH, asset, capital.

debtor *n.* one that owes, borrower, mortgagor; see BUYER.

debunk *v.* uncover, disclose, demystify; see EXPOSE 1.

decadence *n.* decline, deterioration, degeneration; see DECAY, EVIL 1.

decadent *a.* immoral, wicked, degenerate; see BAD 1.

decay *n.* decline, decrease, consumption, decomposition, collapse, downfall, decadence, depreciation, corruption, spoilage, wasting away, degeneration, dry rot, putrefaction, corruption, dissolution, rottenness, spoiling, breakup, breakdown, mold, rust, atrophy, blight, mildew, deterioration, extinction, disintegration, ruin, crumbling, waste, corrosion, wear and tear.

decay *v.* corrode, rot, wither; see SPOIL 1.

decayed *a.* decomposed, putrid, spoiled; see ROTTEN 1.

decaying *a.* rotting, crumbling, spoiling, breaking down, breaking up, wasting away, deteriorating, wearing away, disintegrating, worsening, tumbling down; see also ROTTEN 1.

deceased *a.* late, lifeless, departed; see DEAD 1.

deceit *n.* fraud, trickery, duplicity; see DECEPTION, DISHONESTY.

deceitful *a.* tricky, cunning, insincere; see DISHONEST.

deceive *v.* mislead, swindle, outwit, fool, delude, rob, defraud, not play fair, play a practical joke on, victimize, betray, beguile, take advantage of, entrap, ensnare, hoodwink, dupe, fleece, con*, skin*, sucker*, string along*, screw out of*, lead astray, bamboozle*, cross up, bilk*, gouge*, clip*, fake, gyp*, put on*, burn*, sell out*, chisel*, double-cross*, shake down*, make a sucker out of*, take to the cleaners*, take for a ride*, snow*, put one over on*, take in*, pull the wool over someone's eyes*, flimflam*, give someone the runaround*, do a snow job on*, play upon*, make a monkey of*, stack the cards*; see also TRICK.

deceived *a.* duped, fooled, humbugged, hoaxed, snared, trapped, decoyed, baited, deluded, defrauded, hoodwinked, betrayed, bamboozled*, sucked in*, conned*; see also CHEATED.—*Ant.* dealt with openly, informed, freed from illusion.

deceiver *n.* conniver, swindler, impostor; see CHEAT.

decency *n.* propriety, righteousness, respectability; see HONESTY, VIRTUE 1.

decent *a.* 1 [In accordance with common standards] accepted, standard, approved; see CONVENTIONAL 3. 2 [In accordance with the moral code] proper, moral, honest, honorable, chaste, modest, pure, ethical, spotless, respectable, prudent, mannerly, virtuous, immaculate, delicate, stainless, clean, trustworthy,

upright, worthy, untarnished, unblemished, straight; see also GOOD 1.

deception *n.* trickery, double-dealing, untruth, insincerity, craftiness, treachery, treason, betrayal, mendacity, disinformation, falsehood, trickiness, lying, deceitfulness, deceit, duplicity, cunning, fast one*, snow job*, hokum*; see also DISHONESTY.—*Ant.* HONESTY, frankness, sincerity.

deceptive *a.* misleading, ambiguous, deceitful; see FALSE 2, 3.

decide *v.* settle, determine, judge, conclude, compromise, choose, terminate, vote, poll, make a decision, come to a conclusion, form an opinion, form a judgment, make up one's mind, make a selection, select, pick, make one's choice, commit oneself, come to an agreement, have the final word; see also AGREE, RESOLVE.—*Ant.* DELAY, hesitate, hedge.

decided *a.* 1 [Determined] settled, decided upon, arranged for; see DETERMINED 1. 2 [Certain] clear, emphatic, determined; see DEFINITE 1.

deciding *a.* determining, crucial, conclusive; see IMPORTANT 1, NECESSARY.

decipher *v.* interpret, translate, explain; see SOLVE.

decision *n.* resolution, result, declaration; see JUDGMENT 3, OPINION 1.

decisive *a.* final, definitive, absolute; see DEFINITE 1, DETERMINED 1.

deck *n.* 1 [The floor of a ship] level, flight, story, layer, tier, topside; see also FLOOR 1, 2. 2 [Cards sufficient for a game] pack, set, pinochle deck, playing cards, the cards; see also CARD. —**on deck*** prepared, available, on hand; see READY 2.

declaration *n.* statement, assertion, utterance, information, affirmation, profession, manifesto, document, bulletin, denunciation, proclamation, confirmation, ultimatum, notice, notification, resolution, affidavit, testimony, charge, indictment, allegation, bill of rights, constitution, creed, article of faith, presentation, exposition, communication, disclosure, explanation, revelation, publication, answer, advertisement, saying, report, oath, admission; see also ACKNOWLEDGMENT, ANNOUNCEMENT.

declare *v.* assert oneself, announce, pronounce, claim, tell, state, point out, affirm, maintain, attest to, testify to, confess, reveal, swear, disclose, impart, represent, indicate, notify, repeat, insist, contend, advance, allege, argue, demonstrate, propound, bring forward, put forward, set forth, stress, cite, advocate, pass, proclaim, acknowledge, profess, give out, certify, swear; see also REPORT 1, SAY.—*Ant.* HIDE, equivocate, withhold.

decline *n.* deterioration, dissolution, lessening; see DECAY.

decline *v.* 1 [To refuse] desist, beg to be excused, send regrets; see REFUSE. 2 [To decrease] degenerate, deteriorate, backslide; see DECREASE 1.

decompose *v.* rot, crumble, break up; see DISINTEGRATE.

decomposition *n.* dissolution, breakdown, disintegration; see DECAY.

decontaminate *v.* disinfect, purify, sterilize; see CLEAN.

decor *n.* decoration, ornamentation, adornment; see DECORATION 1.

decorate *v.* adorn, beautify, ornament, deck, paint, color, renovate, enrich, brighten, enhance, festoon, embellish, illuminate, spangle, elaborate, enamel, bead, polish, varnish, grace, garnish, finish, tile, redecorate, add the finishing touches, perfect, dress up, fix up, deck out, pretty up.

decorated *a.* adorned, ornamented, embellished; see ORNATE.

decoration *n.* 1 [The act of decorating] adornment, ornamentation, embellishment; see DESIGN, IMPROVEMENT 1. 2 [Something used for decorating] tinsel, thread work, lace, ribbon, braid, gilt, color, appliqué, scroll, wreath, glass, flourish, tooling, inlay, figure work, spangle, finery, filigree, design, ornament, extravagance; see also JEWELRY, PAINT 1. 3 [An insignia of honor] citation, medal, ribbon; see EMBLEM.

decorative *a.* embellishing, beautifying, florid; see ORNATE.

decoy *n.* imitation, bait, lure; see CAMOUFLAGE, TRICK 1.

decrease *n.* shrinkage, lessening, contraction; see DISCOUNT, REDUCTION 1.

decrease *v.* 1 [To grow less] lessen, diminish, decline, wane, deteriorate, degenerate, dwindle, sink, settle, lighten, slacken, ebb, melt, lower, moderate, subside, shrink, shrivel up, depreciate, soften, quiet, narrow, waste away, fade, run low, weaken, crumble, let up, dry up, slow down, calm down, burn away, burn down, die away, die down, decay, evaporate, slack off, wear off, wear away, wear out, wane down, slump; see also CONTRACT 1.—*Ant.* GROW, increase, multiply. 2 [To make less] cut, reduce, check, curb, restrain, quell, tame, hush, still, sober, pacify, blunt, curtail, lessen, lower, subtract, abridge, abbreviate,

condense, shorten, minimize, diminish, slash, dilute, shave, pare, prune, digest, limit, level, deflate, compress, strip, thin, make smaller, curtail, clip, lighten, trim, level off, take from, take off, roll back, hold down, step down, scale down, boil down, cut off, cut down, cut short, cut back, chisel*, wind down, knock off*; see also COMPRESS.—*Ant.* INCREASE, expand, augment.

decree *n.* edict, pronouncement, proclamation; see DECLARATION, JUDGMENT 3.

dedicate *v.* devote, apply, give, appropriate, set aside, surrender, apportion, assign, give over to, donate; see also GIVE 1.

dedication *n.* sanctification, devotion, glorification; see CONSECRATION.

deduct *v.* take away, diminish by, subtract; see DECREASE 2.

deduction *n.* 1 [The act of deducing] deducing, concluding, reasoning; see THOUGHT 1. 2 [A conclusion] result, answer, conclusion; see JUDGMENT 3, OPINION 1. 3 [A reduction] subtraction, abatement, decrease; see DISCOUNT, REDUCTION 1.

deed *n.* 1 [An action] act, feat, accomplishment; see ACTION 2. 2 [Legal title to real property] document, release, agreement, charter, title deed, record, certificate, voucher, indenture, warranty, lease; see also PROOF 1, RECORD 1, SECURITY 2. —**in deed** in fact, actually, really; see SURELY.

deep *a.* 1 [Situated or extending far down] low, below, beneath, bottomless, submerged, subterranean, submarine, inmost, deep-seated, immersed, dark, dim, impenetrable, buried, inward, underground, downreaching, of great depth, depthless, immeasurable; see also UNDER 1.—*Ant.* SHALLOW, near the surface, surface. 2 [Extending laterally or vertically] extensive, far, wide, yawning, penetrating, distant, thick, fat, spread out, to the bone*, to the hilt; see also BROAD, LONG 1.—*Ant.* NARROW, thin, shallow. 3 [Showing evidence of thought and understanding] penetrating, acute, incisive; see PROFOUND. —**go off the deep end*** 1 [To act rashly] go to extremes, go too far, rant; see EXAGGERATE, RAGE 1. 2 [To break down] collapse, lose control of oneself, become insane; see CRACK UP 2.

deepen *v.* intensify, expand, extend; see DEVELOP 1, GROW 1, INCREASE.

deeply *a.* surely, profoundly, genuinely; see SINCERELY, TRULY.

deer *n.* doe, buck, fawn, roe, stag, venison, member of the deer family, cervine animal, cervid animal. *Creatures popularly called deer include* *the following:* spotted, white-tailed, mule, red, musk deer; antelope, American elk, wapiti, moose, caribou, reindeer, roebuck.

deface *v.* disfigure, scratch, mutilate; see DESTROY.

default *n.* failure, lack, error, offense, failure to act, wrongdoing, transgression, imperfection, oversight, neglect, shortcoming, inadequacy, insufficiency, failure to appear, failure to pay, lapse, weakness, vice, blunder; see also FAILURE 1. —**in default of** lacking, absent, in the absence of; see WANTING.

defeat *n.* repulse, reverse, rebuff, conquest, rout, overthrow, subjugation, destruction, breakdown, collapse, extermination, annihilation, check, trap, ambush, breakthrough, withdrawal, setback, stalemate, ruin, blow, loss, butchery, massacre, Waterloo, beating, whipping, thrashing, fall, comedown, upset, battering*, pasting*, walloping*, whaling*, slaughter*, KO*, the old one-two*; see also LOSS 1.—*Ant.* VICTORY, triumph, conquest.

defeat *v.* **1** [To get the better of] master, subjugate, overwhelm; see OVERCOME. **2** [To worst in war] overcome, vanquish, conquer, rout, entrap, subdue, overrun, best, overthrow, crush, smash, drive off, annihilate, overwhelm, scatter, repulse, halt, reduce, outflank, finish off, encircle, slaughter, butcher, outmaneuver, ambush, demolish, sack, torpedo, sink, swamp, wipe out, decimate, obliterate, roll back, mop up*, chew up*, mow down*; see also DESTROY, RAVAGE.—*Ant.* YIELD, give up, surrender. **3** [To worst in sport or in personal combat] overpower, outplay, trounce, knock out, throw, floor, pummel, pound, flog, outhit, outrun, outjump, thrash, edge out*, clobber*, lay low, skin alive*, lick*, wallop*, clean up on*, beat up*, take*, KO*, put down*, beat the pants off*, pulverize*, steamroll*, take to the cleaners*, plow under*, smear*, cream*; see also BEAT 1.—*Ant.* FAIL, suffer, be defeated.

defeated *a.* crushed, overcome, conquered; see BEATEN 1.

defect *n.* imperfection, flaw, drawback; see FAULT 1.

defect *v.* change sides, run away, forsake; see ABANDON 2, DESERT, LEAVE 1.

defective *a.* imperfect, incomplete, inadequate; see FAULTY, POOR 2, UNFINISHED 1.

defend *v.* **1** [To keep safe from an enemy; *often used figuratively*] shield, shelter, screen; see PROTECT. **2** [To support an accused person or thing] plead for, justify, uphold, second, exonerate, back, vindicate, aid, espouse the cause of, befriend, say

in defense of, guarantee, endorse, warrant, maintain, recommend, rationalize, plead someone's cause, say a good word for, speak for, stand up for, put in a good word for, apologize for, go to bat for*, cover for*, back up, stick up for*; see also SUPPORT 2.—*Ant.* CONVICT, accuse, charge.

defendant *n.* the accused, defense, offender; see PRISONER.

defended *a.* protected, guarded, safeguarded; see SAFE 1.

defender *n.* champion, patron, sponsor; see GUARDIAN 1, PROTECTOR.

defense *n.* **1** [The act of defending] resistance, protection, safeguard, preservation, security, custody, stand, front, backing, guardianship, the defensive, precaution, inoculation, excusing, apologizing, explaining, justifying, exoneration, explanation.—*Ant.* OFFENSE, retaliation, aggression. **2** [A means or system for defending] bulwark, dike, stockade, machine-gun nest, bastion, fort, chemical or biological warfare, barricade, garrison, rampart, fence, wall, embankment, citadel, fortress, armor, antiaircraft gun, camouflage, gas mask, shield, screen, stronghold, parapet, buttress, guard; see also FORTIFICATION, TRENCH.—*Ant.* ATTACK, siege, blitzkrieg. **3** [In law, the reply of the accused] denial, plea, answer; see DECLARATION, PROOF 1, STATEMENT 1.

defensible *a.* justfiable, proper, permissible; see FIT 1, 2, LOGICAL.

defensive *a.* protecting, guarding, watchful, protective, vigilant; see also CAREFUL.

defensively *a.* protectively, guardedly, suspiciously; see CAREFULLY 1.

defer *v.* **1** [To postpone] put off, postpone, shelve; see DELAY, SUSPEND 2. **2** [To yield] submit, accede, concede; see AGREE.

deference *n.* veneration, acclaim, homage; see REVERENCE.

deferred *a.* delayed, prolonged, held up; see POSTPONED.

defiance *n.* insubordination, rebellion, insurgence; see DISOBEDIENCE.

defiant *a.* resistant, obstinate, disobedient; see REBELLIOUS.

deficiency *n.* want, need, absence; see LACK 2.

deficient *a.* insufficient, skimpy, meager; see INADEQUATE.

deficit *n.* shortage, paucity, deficiency; see LACK 2.

defile *v.* ravish, violate, molest; see HURT, RAPE.

define *v.* **1** [To set limits for] bound, confine, limit, outline, fix, settle, circumscribe, mark, set, distinguish, establish, encompass, mark the limits of, determine the boundaries of, fix the limits of, curb, edge, border, enclose, set bounds to, fence in, rim, encircle, wall in, envelop, flank, stake out; see also LIMIT.—*Ant.* CONFUSE, distort, mix. **2** [To provide a name or description for] paraphrase, give the meaning of, differentiate, gloss, determine, entitle, label, designate, characterize, elucidate, interpret, illustrate, represent, individuate, find out, clarify, construe, denote, spell out, translate, exemplify, specify, prescribe, dub; see also DESCRIBE, EXPLAIN, NAME 1.—*Ant.* MISUNDERSTAND, misconceive, mistitle.

definite *a.* **1** [Determined with exactness] fixed, exact, precise, positive, accurate, correct, decisive, absolute, clearly defined, well-defined, limited, strict, explicit, specific, settled, decided, prescribed, restricted, assigned, unequivocal, special, conclusive, categorical, particular, unerring, to the point, beyond doubt; see also CERTAIN 2, DETERMINED.—*Ant.* OBSCURE, indefinite, inexact. **2** [Clear in detail] sharp, visible, audible, tangible, distinct, vivid, unmistakable in meaning, straightforward, unambiguous, palpable, obvious, marked, plain, not vague, well-drawn, clearly defined, well-marked, well-defined, clear-cut, explicit, unmistakable, distinguishable, undistorted, crisp, bold, graphic, downright, undisguised, in plain sight, clear as day, standing out like a sore thumb*.—*Ant.* CONFUSED, vague, hazy. **3** [Positive] sure, beyond doubt, convinced; see CERTAIN 1.

definitely *a.* clearly, unmistakably, unquestionably; see SURELY.

definition *n.* meaning, terminology, sense, gloss, paraphrase, denotation, exemplification, signification, diagnosis, synonym, exposition, interpretation, explication, clue, key, translation, comment, rationale, commentary, representation, characterization, solution, answer; see also DESCRIPTION, EXPLANATION.

definitive *a.* final, ultimate, conclusive; see ABSOLUTE 1.

deflate *v.* exhaust, flatten, void; see EMPTY 1, 2.

deflect *v.* swerve, divert, curve; see TURN 3, 6.

deform *v.* disfigure, deface, injure; see DAMAGE.

deformed *a.* damaged, distorted, misshapen, disfigured, crippled, misproportioned, malformed, cramped, badly made, disjointed, ill-favored, dwarfed, hunchbacked, clubfooted, unshapely, mangled, crushed, warped, curved, contorted, gnarled, crooked, grotesque, lame, irregular; see also TWISTED 1, UGLY 1.—*Ant.* REGULAR, shapely, well-formed.

deformity *n.* malformation, deformation, disfigurement; see CONTORTION, DAMAGE 1.

defraud *v.* hoax, dupe, cheat; see DECEIVE.

defy *v.* insult, resist, confront; see DARE 2, OPPOSE 1, 2.

degenerate *a.* depraved, immoral, corrupt; see BAD.

degradation *n.* depravity, corruption, degeneration; see EVIL 1.

degrade *v.* demote, discredit, diminish; see HUMBLE.

degraded *a.* disgraced, debased, depraved; see BAD.

degree *n.* **1** [One in a series used for measurement] measure, grade, step, unit, mark, interval, space, measurement, gradation, size, dimension, shade, point, line, plane, step in a series, gauge, rung, term, tier, ratio, period, level; see also DIVISION 2. **2** [An expression of relative excellence, attainment, or the like] extent, station, order, quality, development, height, expanse, length, potency, range, proportion, compass, quantity, standing, strength, reach, intensity, scope, caliber, pitch, stage, sort, status, rate; see also RANK 3. **3** [Recognition of academic achievement] title, distinction, testimonial, honor, qualification, eminence, credit, credentials, baccalaureate, bachelor's degree, master's degree, doctorate, sheepskin*; see also DIPLOMA, GRADUATION. **—by degrees** step by step, slowly but surely, inch by inch; see GRADUALLY. **—to a degree** somewhat, partially, to an extent; see PARTLY.

dehydrate *v.* dessicate, parch, drain; see DRY 1.

dejected *a.* depressed, dispirited, cast down; see SAD 1.

delay *n.* deferment, adjournment, putting off, procrastination, suspension, moratorium, reprieve, setback, stay, stop, discontinuation, cooling-off period*, holdup*; see also PAUSE.

delay *v.* postpone, defer, retard, hold up, deter, clog, choke, slacken, keep, hold, keep back, impede, discourage, interfere with, detain, stay, stop, withhold, arrest, check, prevent, repress, curb, obstruct, inhibit, restrict, prolong, encumber, procrastinate, adjourn, block, bar, suspend, table, slow, put aside, hold back, hold off, hold everything*, bide one's time, slow up, slow down, stall, put off, restrain, put on ice*, shelve, pigeonhole; see also HINDER, INTERRUPT.—*Ant.* SPEED, accelerate, encourage.

delayed *a.* held up, slowed, put off; see LATE 1, POSTPONED.

delegate *n.* legate, emissary, proxy, deputy, substitute, appointee, consul, minister, alternate, nominee, ambassador, stand-in*, sub*, pinch hitter*; see also AGENT, REPRESENTATIVE 2.

delegate *v.* **1** [To give authority to] authorize, commission, appoint, name, nominate, select, choose, assign, license, empower, deputize, swear in, ordain, invest, elect, give someone the green light*, give someone the go-ahead*; see also APPROVE.—*Ant.* DISMISS, repudiate, reject. **2** [To give duties to another] entrust, parcel out, hold responsible for; see ASSIGN.

delegation *n.* **1** [The act of assigning to another] assignment, giving over, nomination, trust, commissioning, ordination, authorization, charge, deputation, referring, transferring; see also APPOINTMENT 1. **2** [A group with a specific mission] representatives, deputation, commission; see COMMITTEE, ORGANIZATION 2.

deliberate *a.* thought out, predetermined, conscious, advised, prearranged, fixed, with forethought, well-considered, cautious, studied, intentional, planned in advance, done on purpose, willful, considered, thoughtful, planned, reasoned, calculated, intended, purposeful, premeditated, voluntary, designed, coldblooded, cut-and-dried; see also CAREFUL.

deliberately *a.* resolutely, determinedly, emphatically, knowingly, meaningfully, voluntarily, consciously, on purpose, willfully, premeditatedly, in cold blood, with malice aforethought, advisedly, freely, independently, without any qualms, by design, intentionally, purposely, all things considered, pointedly, to that end, with eyes wide open*; see also CAREFULLY 1.

delicacy *n.* **1** [Fineness of texture] airiness, daintiness, transparency, flimsiness, softness, smoothness, subtlety, tenderness; see also LIGHTNESS 2. **2** [A rare commodity, especially for the table] tidbit, luxury, gourmet dish, gourmet food, dessert, sweet, delight, party dish, imported food, delicatessen, chef's special*; see also FOOD.

delicate *a.* **1** [Sickly] susceptible, in delicate health, feeble; see SICK, WEAK 1. **2** [Dainty] fragile, frail, fine; see DAINTY.

delicately *a.* deftly, skillfully, cautiously; see CAREFULLY 1.

delicatessen *n.* **1** [Ready-to-serve foods] *Varieties of delicatessen include the following:* cold meats, luncheon meats, salads, dairy products, salami, pastrami, bologna, wurst, sausage, frankfurters, olives, lox, corned beef, pickled peppers, pickled fish, dill pickles, sweet pickles, caviar, anchovies, pâté; see also BREAD, CHEESE, DESSERT, FISH, FRUIT, MEAT, WINE. **2** [A place that sells delicatessen] food store, butcher shop, grocery; see MARKET 1.

delicious *a.* tasty, savory, good, appetizing, choice, well-seasoned, well-done, spicy, sweet, delectable, exquisite, dainty, luscious, tempting, yummy*, fit for a king*; see also EXCELLENT, RICH 4.—*Ant.* ROTTEN, flat, stale.

delight *n.* enjoyment, joy, pleasure; see HAPPINESS.

delight *v.* fascinate, amuse, please; see ENTERTAIN 1.

delighted *a.* **1** [Greatly pleased] entranced, excited, pleasantly surprised; see HAPPY. **2** [An expression of acceptance or pleasure] thank you, by all means, to be sure, splendid, excellent, overwhelmed, charmed, so glad.

delightful *a.* charming, amusing, engaging; see PLEASANT 1.

delinquent *a.* **1** [Lax in duty] slack, behindhand, tardy, procrastinating, criminal, neglectful, faulty, blamable, negligent, derelict, remiss; see also CARELESS.—*Ant.* PUNCTUAL, punctilious, scrupulous. **2** [Not paid on time; *said especially of taxes*] owed, back, overdue; see DUE, UNPAID 1.

delinquent *n.* defaulter, tax evader, offender, dropout, reprobate, loafer, derelict, bad debtor, poor risk, felon, lawbreaker, wrongdoer, sinner, juvenile offender, juvenile delinquent, JD*, punk*, outlaw, black sheep*; see also CRIMINAL.

delirious *a.* demented, crazy, irrational; see INSANE.

deliver *v.* **1** [To free] set free, liberate, save; see FREE. **2** [To transport] pass, remit, hand over; see GIVE 1. **3** [To speak formally] present, read, give; see ADDRESS 2. **4** [To bring to birth] bring forth, be delivered of, give birth to; see PRODUCE 2. **5** [To distribute] allot, dispense, give out; see DISTRIBUTE.

delivered *a.* brought, deposited, transported, checked in, forwarded, expressed, hand-delivered, dispatched, at the door, sent out by truck, trucked; see also MAILED.

delivery *n.* **1** [Bringing goods into another's possession] consignment, carting, shipment, transfer, portage, freighting, dispatch, conveyance, mailing, special delivery, parcel post, giving over, handing over, cash on delivery, COD, free on board, FOB; see also TRANSPORTA-

TION. **2** [Delivery of a child] parturition, confinement, childbirth, labor, bringing forth, midwifery, obstetrics, cesarean section; see also BIRTH. **3** [The manner of a speaker] articulation, enunciation, accent, utterance, pronunciation, emphasis, elocution; see also ELOQUENCE.

delusion *n.* phantasm, hallucination, fancy; see ILLUSION.

deluxe *a.* elegant, expensive, grand; see LUXURIOUS.

demand *n.* **1** [A peremptory communication] order, call, charge; see COMMAND. **2** [Willingness to purchase] trade, request, sale, bid, need, requirement, interest, call for, rush, search, inquiry, desire to buy, market; see also DESIRE 1.—*Ant.* INDIFFERENCE, lack of interest, sales resistance. —**in demand** sought, needed, requested; see WANTED. —**on demand** ready, prepared, usable; see AVAILABLE.

demand *v.* charge, direct, command; see ASK.

demanding *a.* fussy, imperious, exacting; see CRITICAL.

demented *a.* crazy, bemused, unbalanced; see INSANE.

demerit *n.* bad mark, loss of points, poor grade; see FAULT 1, PUNISHMENT.

demobilize *v.* disband, disperse, withdraw; see DISARM.

democracy *n.* justice, the greatest good for the greatest number, egalitarianism, popular suffrage, individual enterprise, capitalism, laissez faire, rugged individualism, freedom of religion, freedom of speech, freedom of the press, the right to work, private ownership, emancipation, political equality, representative government, democratic spirit, the American Way*; see also EQUALITY, FREEDOM 2.—*Ant.* dictatorship, feudalism, tyranny.

democrat *n.* republican, Social Democrat, populist, civil libertarian, advocate of democracy, constitutionalist, individualist.—*Ant.* DICTATOR, Nazi, autocrat.

Democrat *n.* Southern Democrat, Jeffersonian Democrat, Dixiecrat*, Great Society Democrat*, New Dealer*, liberal, progressive; see also REPUBLICAN.—*Ant.* REPUBLICAN, Tory, Socialist.

democratic *a.* popular, constitutional, representative, free, equal, just, common, bourgeois, individualistic, communal, laissez-faire.

demolish *v.* wreck, devastate, obliterate; see DESTROY.

demolition *n.* extermination, annihilation, wrecking; see DESTRUCTION 1, EXPLOSION.

demon *n.* imp, vampire, incubus; see DEVIL.

demonstrate *v.* **1** [To prove] show, make evident, confirm; see PROVE. **2** [To present for effect] exhibit, manifest, parade; see DISPLAY.

demonstration *n.* **1** [An exhibition] showing, presentation, exhibit; see DISPLAY, SHOW 1. **2** [A mass rally] picket line, march, sit-in; see PROTEST.

demoralize *v.* weaken, unman, enfeeble; see DISCOURAGE.

demoralized *a.* unnerved, weakened, depressed; see SAD 1.

demote *v.* downgrade, lower, bust*; see DECREASE 2, DISMISS.

den *n.* **1** [The home of an animal] cavern, lair, cave; see HOLE 1. **2** [A private or secluded room] study, recreation room, workroom; see RETREAT 2, ROOM 2.

denial *n.* repudiation, disclaimer, rejection, refutation, rejecting, retraction, dismissal, renunciation, refusal to recognize, the cold shoulder*, the brushoff*; see also OPPOSITION 2.—*Ant.* ACKNOWLEDGMENT, avowal, confession.

denomination *n.* **1** [A class] category, classification, group; see CLASS 1. **2** [A religious group] creed, sect, persuasion; see CHURCH 3.

denounce *v.* condemn, threaten, charge, blame, accuse, indict, arraign, implicate, incriminate, upbraid, impugn, prosecute, revile, stigmatize, ostracize, reproach, castigate, brand, boycott, rebuke, dress down, take to task, damn, impeach, scold, reprimand, reprove, condemn openly, charge with, blacklist, expose, knock*, rip into*, blackball; see also DENY.—*Ant.* PRAISE, laud, commend.

dense *a.* **1** [Close together] solid, compact, impenetrable; see THICK 1. **2** [Slow-witted] stupid, dumb*, imbecilic; see DULL 3, IGNORANT 2.

density *n.* solidity, thickness, impenetrability, consistency, quantity, bulk, heaviness, body, compactness, denseness; see also MASS 1, WEIGHT 1.—*Ant.* LIGHTNESS, rarity, thinness.

dent *n.* indentation, depression, impression, dimple, nick, notch, dip, cavity, cut, incision, sinkhole, pit, trough, furrow, scratch; see also HOLE 1.

dent *v.* hollow, depress, indent, gouge, sink, dig, imprint, mark, dimple, pit, notch, scratch, nick, make a dent in, perforate, furrow.—*Ant.* STRAIGHTEN, bulge, make protrude.

dentist *n.* DDS, dental practitioner, orthodontist; see DOCTOR.

deny *v.* contradict, disagree with, disprove, disallow, gainsay, disavow, disclaim, negate, repudiate, controvert, revoke, rebuff, reject, renounce, discard, not admit, take exception to, disbelieve, spurn, doubt, veto, discredit, nullify, say "no" to; see also DENOUNCE, REFUSE.—*Ant.* ADMIT, accept, affirm.

deodorant *n.* disinfectant, deodorizer, fumigator; see CLEANSER, COSMETIC.

depart *v.* go, quit, withdraw; see LEAVE 1.

departed *a.* 1 [Dead] defunct, expired, deceased; see DEAD 1. 2 [Gone away] absent, disappeared, moved; see GONE 1.

department *n.* 1 [The field of one's activity] jurisdiction, activity, interest, occupation, province, bureau, business, capacity, dominion, administration, station, function, office, walk of life, vocation, specialty, field, duty, assignment, bailiwick; see also JOB 1. 2 [An organized subdivision] section, office, bureau, precinct, tract, range, quarter, area, arena, corps, agency, board, administration, circuit, territory, ward, state office, district office, force, staff, beat; see also DIVISION 2.

department store *n.* variety store, shopping center, shopper's square, mall, drygoods store, mail-order house, five-and-dime, bargain store; see also MARKET 1.

departure *n.* going, departing, separation, embarkation, taking leave, sailing, withdrawal, hegira, evacuation, passage, setting out, setting forth, parting, takeoff, taking off, becoming airborne, starting, leaving, flight, exodus, exit, walkout, getaway; see also RETREAT 1.—*Ant.* ARRIVAL, landing, invasion.

dependable *a.* trustworthy, steady, sure; see RELIABLE.

dependence *n.* reliance, servility, inability to act independently, subordination to the direction of another, subjection to control, subservience; see also NECESSITY 3.

dependent *a.* 1 [Subordinate] inferior, secondary, lesser; see SUBORDINATE. 2 [Needing outside support] helpless, poor, immature, clinging, not able to sustain itself, on a string; see also WEAK 5. 3 [Contingent] liable to, subject to, incidental to, conditioned, sustained by, unable to exist without, subordinate, accessory to, controlled by, regulated by, determined by; see also CONDITIONAL.

dependent *n.* ward, foster child, charge, orphan, minor, delinquent, protégé, hanger-on.

depending (on) *a.* contingent upon, regulated by, controlled by, determined by, in the event of, on the

condition that, subject to, providing, provided, secondary to, growing from; see also CONDITIONAL.

depend on *v.* 1 [To be contingent upon] be determined by, rest with, rest on, be subordinate to, be dependent on, be based on, be subject to, hinge on, turn on, turn upon, be in the power of, be conditioned by, revolve on, trust to, be at the mercy of. 2 [To rely on] put faith in, confide in, believe in; see TRUST 1.

depleted *a.* emptied, exhausted, spent; see WASTED.

depletion *n.* exhaustion, consumption, deficiency; see EMPTINESS.

deport *v.* exile, ship out, ship away, expel; see also BANISH, DISMISS.

deposit *v.* 1 [To lay down] drop, place, put; see INSTALL. 2 [To present money for safekeeping] invest, amass, store, keep, stock up, bank, hoard, collect, treasure, lay away, put in the bank, entrust, transfer, put for safekeeping, put aside for a rainy day, salt away*; see also ACCUMULATE, SAVE 2.—*Ant.* SPEND, withdraw, put out. **—on deposit** in safekeeping, stored, saved; see KEPT 2.

depot *n.* station, base, lot, freight depot, passenger depot, railway depot, railroad depot, terminal, railway station, railroad yards, stockyards, sidetrack, siding, loading track, ammunition dump, ticket office, waiting room, junction, central station, airport, harbor, stopping place, destination.

deprave *v.* pervert, debase, degrade; see CORRUPT.

depraved *a.* low, mean, base; see BAD.

depreciate *v.* deteriorate, lessen, worsen; see DECREASE 1.

depreciation *n.* harm, reduction, shrinkage; see LOSS 3.

depress *v.* 1 [To bring to a lower level] press down, squash, settle; see FLATTEN, PRESS 1. 2 [To bring to a lower state] reduce, dampen, dishearten, debase, degrade, abase, dismay, sadden, mock, darken, scorn, reduce to tears, deject, weigh down, keep down, cast down, beat down, chill, dull, oppress, lower in spirits, throw cold water on*; see also DISCOURAGE, DISGRACE, HUMBLE, HUMILIATE.—*Ant.* URGE, animate, stimulate.

depressed *a.* discouraged, dejected, cast down; see SAD 1.

depressing *a.* discouraging, disheartening, saddening; see DISMAL, SAD 1.

depression *n.* 1 [Something lower than its surroundings] cavity, dent, sinkhole; see HOLE 1. 2 [Low spirits] despair, despondency, sorrow, unhappiness, gloom, dejection, melancholy, misery, trouble, worry, discouragement, hopelessness, distress, desperation, desolation, dreariness, dullness, cheerlessness, darkness, bleakness, oppression, gloominess, the dumps*, blues*, doldrums; see also GRIEF, SADNESS.—*Ant.* JOY, cheer, satisfaction. **3** [Period of economic stress] decline, unemployment, slack times, hard times, bad times, inflation, crisis, economic decline, overproduction, economic stagnation, recession, panic, crash, slump; see also FAILURE 1.

deprive *v.* strip, despoil, divest; see SEIZE 2.

depth *n.* **1** [Vertical or lateral distance] lowness, deepness, drop, distance inward, downward measure; see also EXPANSE.—*Ant.* HEIGHT, shallowness, flatness. **2** [Deepness] profundity, intensity, abyss, pit, base, bottom of the sea; see also BOTTOM. **3** [Intellectual power] profundity, weightiness, acumen; see WISDOM. —**in depth** extensive, broad, thorough, thoroughly.

deputy *n.* lieutenant, appointee, aide; see ASSISTANT, DELEGATE.

derail *v.* run off the rails, be wrecked, fall off; see CRASH 1, WRECK.

derange *v.* madden, craze, unbalance; see CONFUSE, DISTURB.

deranged *a.* demented, crazy, mad; see INSANE.

deride *v.* scorn, jeer, mock; see RIDICULE.

derision *n.* scorn, mockery, disdain; see RIDICULE.

derivation *n.* root, source, etymology; see ORIGIN 3.

derive *v.* draw a conclusion, work out, conclude; see ASSUME.

derogatory *a.* belittling, faultfinding, detracting; see CRITICAL, SARCASTIC.

descend *v.* slide, settle, gravitate, slip, dismount, topple, plunge, sink, dip, pass downward, pitch, light, deplane, tumble, move downward, come down upon, slump, trip, stumble, flutter down, plummet, submerge, step down, climb down, go down, swoop down, get off; see also DIVE, DROP 1, FALL 1.—*Ant.* CLIMB, ascend, mount.

descendant *n.* offspring, kin, child; see FAMILY.

descent *n.* **1** [A downward incline] declivity, slant, slide; see HILL, INCLINATION 2. **2** [The act of descending] slump, downfall, drop, lapse, subsiding, falling, coming down, sinking, reduction, landslide, tumble, decline; see also FALL 1.—

Ant. RISE, mounting, growth. **3** [Lineal relationship] extraction, origin, lineage; see FAMILY, RELATIONSHIP.

describe *v.* delineate, characterize, portray, depict, picture, illuminate, make clear, make apparent, make vivid, give the details of, specify, give meaning to, elucidate, report, draw, paint, illustrate, limn, detail, make sense of, relate, express, narrate, label, name, call, term, write up, give the dope on*, spell out*; see also DEFINE, EXPLAIN.

description *n.* narration, story, portrayal, word picture, account, report, delineation, sketch, specifications, characterization, declaration, rehearsal, information, definition, brief, summary, depiction, explanation, write-up*; see also RECORD 1.

descriptive *a.* designating, identifying, definitive, photographic, describing, interpretive, narrative, characterizing, expressive, clear, true to life, illustrative, lifelike, vivid, picturesque, circumstantial, eloquent, detailed, pictorial, indicative, revealing; see also CHARACTERISTIC, EXPLANATORY, GRAPHIC 1, 2.—*Ant.* DULL, analytical, expository.

desert *n.* waste, sand, wastelands, wilds, barren plains, arid region, deserted region, sand dunes, lava beds, salt flats, abandoned land; see also WILDERNESS.

desert *v.* defect, be absent without leave, abandon one's post, sneak off, run away from duty, violate one's oath, leave unlawfully, go AWOL, go over the hill*; see also ABANDON 2.—*Ant.* OBEY, stay, do one's duty.

deserted *a.* left, forsaken, relinquished; see ABANDONED, EMPTY.

deserter *n.* runaway, fugitive, refugee, truant, defector, derelict, delinquent, lawbreaker, betrayer, backslider, slacker; see also CRIMINAL, TRAITOR.

desertion *n.* abandonment, flight, departure, leaving, defection, defecting, renunciation, withdrawal, avoidance, evasion, elusion, truancy, retirement, resignation, divorce, backsliding, running out on*, going back on*; see also ESCAPE.—*Ant.* LOYALTY, cooperation, union.

deserve *v.* merit, be worthy of, earn, be deserving, lay claim to, have the right to, be given one's due, be entitled to, warrant, rate*, have it coming*.—*Ant.* FAIL, be unworthy, usurp.

deserved *a.* merited, earned, justified, appropriate, suitable, equitable, right, rightful, proper, fitting, just, due, well-deserved; see also FIT.

deserving *a.* meriting, meritorious, exemplary; see WORTHY.

design *n.* pattern, layout, conception, diagram, drawing, preliminary sketch, draft, blueprint, picture, tracing, outline, depiction, chart, map, plan, perspective, treatment, idea, study; see also COMPOSITION, FORM 1, PURPOSE 1.—*Ant.* CONFUSION, jumble, mess. **—by design** on purpose, with intent, purposely; see DELIBERATELY.

design *v.* block out, outline, sketch; see PLAN 2.

designate *v.* indicate, point out, name; see CHOOSE.

designation *n.* classification, label, appellation; see CLASS 1, NAME 1.

designer *n.* planner, draftsman, creator; see ARCHITECT, ARTIST, SCULPTOR.

desirable *a.* 1 [Stimulating erotic desires] seductive, fascinating, alluring; see CHARMING. 2 [Having many good qualities] good, welcome, acceptable; see EXCELLENT.

desire *n.* 1 [The wish to enjoy] aspiration, wish, motive, will, urge, eagerness, propensity, fancy, frenzy, craze, mania, hunger, thirst, attraction, longing, yearning, fondness, liking, inclination, proclivity, craving, relish, hankering, itch*, yen*; see also AMBITION, GREED.—*Ant.* INDIFFERENCE, unconcern, apathy. 2 [Erotic wish to possess] lust, passion, hunger, appetite, fascination, infatuation, fervor, excitement, sexual love, nymphomania, libido, sensual appetite, carnal passion, eroticism, biological urge, rut, heat.—*Ant.* ABSTINENCE, coldness, frigidity.

desire *v.* 1 [To wish for] long for, crave, wish for; see NEED, WANT 1. 2 [To request] ask for, seek, solicit; see BEG. 3 [To want sexually] lust after, hunger for, have the hots for*, be turned on by*; see also WANT 1.

desk *n.* 1 [A piece of furniture] secretary, roll-top, bureau, box, lectern, frame, case, pulpit; see also FURNITURE, TABLE 1. 2 [A department of an editorial office] division, section, bureau; see DEPARTMENT.

desolate *a.* deserted, forsaken, uninhabited; see ABANDONED, ISOLATED, ALONE.

desolation *n.* bareness, barrenness, devastation, havoc, ruin, dissolution, wreck, demolition, annihilation, extinction; see also DESERT.

despair *n.* hopelessness, depression, discouragement; see DESPERATION, GLOOM.

despair *v.* lose hope, lose faith, lose heart, give up hope, abandon hope, have no hope, have a heavy heart,

abandon oneself to fate; see also ABANDON 1.

despairing *a.* hopeless, despondent, miserable; see SAD 1.

desperado *n.* outlaw, bandit, ruffian; see CRIMINAL.

desperate *a.* 1 [Hopeless] despairing, despondent, downcast; see HOPELESS, SAD 1. 2 [Reckless] incautious, frenzied, wild; see CARELESS, RASH.

desperately *a.* severely, harmfully, perilously; see CARELESSLY, SERIOUSLY 1.

desperation *n.* despondency, despair, depression, discomfort, dejection, distraction, distress, desolation, anxiety, anguish, agony, melancholy, grief, sorrow, worry, trouble, pain, hopelessness, torture, pang, heartache, concern, misery, unhappiness; see also FEAR, FUTILITY, GLOOM.—*Ant.* HOPE, hopefulness, confidence.

despicable *a.* contemptible, abject, base; see MEAN 3.

despise *v.* scorn, disdain, condemn; see HATE 1.

despite *prep.* in spite of, in defiance of, regardless of, even with.

despondent *a.* dejected, discouraged, depressed; see SAD 1.

dessert *n.* sweet, tart, cobbler, pastry, torte, custard, sherbet, mousse, cookie, trifle, soufflé, sundae, compote, fruit salad, pudding, ice cream; see also CAKE 2, CANDY, CHEESE, DELICACY 2, FRUIT, PASTRY, PIE.

destination *n.* objective, goal, aim; see PURPOSE 1.

destined *a.* fated, compulsory, foreordained, menacing, near, forthcoming, threatening, in prospect, predestined, predetermined, compelled, condemned, at hand, impending, inexorable, that is to be, in store, to come, directed, ordained, settled, sealed, closed, predesigned, in the wind, in the cards; see also DOOMED, INEVITABLE.—*Ant.* INVOLUNTARY, at will, by chance.

destiny *n.* fate, lot, fortune; see DOOM.

destitute *a.* impoverished, poverty-stricken, penniless; see POOR 1.

destroy *v.* ruin, demolish, exterminate, raze, tear down, plunder, ransack, eradicate, overthrow, root up, root out, devastate, butcher, consume, liquidate, break up, dissolve, blot out, quash, quell, level, abort, stamp out, suppress, squelch, scuttle, undo, annihilate, lay waste, overturn, impair, damage, ravish, deface, shatter, split up, crush, obliterate, knock to pieces, abolish, crash, extinguish, wreck, dismantle, upset, bomb, mutilate, smash, trample, overturn, maim, mar, end, nullify, blast, neutralize, gut, snuff out, erase, sabotage, repeal, pull down, terminate, conclude, finish, bring to ruin, put a stop to, wipe out, do in*, do away with, finish off, make short work of, total*, cream*, destruct, self-destruct, put an end to; see also DEFEAT, RAVAGE, STOP 1.—*Ant.* BUILD, construct, establish.

destroyed *a.* wrecked, annihilated, killed, lost, devastated, wasted, demolished, overturned, overwhelmed, upset, nullified, undone, put to an end, shattered, smashed, scuttled, ravished, engulfed, submerged, overrun, extinguished, eradicated, devoured, consumed, burned up, burned down, gone to pieces, razed, lying in ruins, sacked; see also BROKEN 1, DEAD 1, RUINED 1.—*Ant.* SAVED, protected, restored.

destroyer *n.* 1 [An agent of destruction] assassin, terrorist, slayer; see CRIMINAL, KILLER, WEAPON. 2 [A swift, armed surface vessel] armed ship, battleship, fighting vessel; see SHIP, WARSHIP.

destruction *n.* 1 [The act of destroying] demolition, annihilation, eradication, slaughter, liquidation, overthrow, extermination, elimination, abolition, murder, assassination, killing, disintegration, bombardment, disruption, extinction, annihilating, wreckage, dissolution, butchery, sabotage, sacking, extinguishing, eliminating, crashing, falling, felling, tearing down; see also DAMAGE 1, DISASTER.—*Ant.* PRODUCTION, formation, erection. 2 [The result of destroying] waste, ashes, annihilation, remnants, devastation, vestiges, desolation, ruins, catastrophe, overthrow, decay, loss, remains, havoc, prostration, injury, downfall, end, dissolution, disorganization; see also DAMAGE 2, WRECK.

destructive *a.* 1 [Harmful] hurtful, injurious, troublesome; see HARMFUL. 2 [Deadly] fatal, ruinous, devastating; see DEADLY, VICIOUS.

detach *v.* separate, withdraw, disengage; see DIVIDE.

detached *a.* 1 [Cut off or removed] loosened, divided, disjoined; see SEPARATED. 2 [Indifferent] apathetic, uninvolved, unconcerned; see INDIFFERENT.

detail *n.* item, portion, particular, trait, specialty, feature, aspect, article, peculiarity, fraction, specification, technicality; see also CIRCUMSTANCE, PART 1.—*Ant.* WHOLE, entirety, synthesis. —**in detail** minutely, item by item, part by part, step by step, inch by inch, systematically, intimately.—*Ant.* VAGUELY, generally, indefinitely.

detail *v.* itemize, exhibit, show, report, relate, narrate, tell, designate, catalogue, recite, specialize, depict, enumerate, mention, uncover, reveal, recount, recapitulate, analyze, set forth, produce, go into the particulars, get down to cases*; see also DESCRIBE.—*Ant.* DABBLE, summarize, generalize.

detailed *a.* enumerated, specified, explicit, specific, particularized, individual, individualized, developed, itemized, definite, minute, described, precise, full, narrow, complete, exact, fussy, particular, meticulous, point by point, circumstantial, accurate, unfolded, disclosed, elaborated, complicated, comprehensive, at length, gone into; see also ELABORATE 2.—*Ant.* GENERAL, brief, hazy.

details *n.* analysis, trivia, minutiae, particulars, itemized account, trivialities, factoids, statistics, fine points, items; see also DETAIL.

detain *v.* hold, keep, inhibit; see DELAY, RESTRAIN.

detect *v.* distinguish, recognize, identify; see DISCOVER.

detection *n.* apprehension, investigation, disclosure; see DISCOVERY, EXPOSURE.

detective *n.* agent, plainclothes man, private eye*, narcotics agent, police sergeant, police officer, FBI agent, wiretapper, investigator, criminologist, patrolman, sleuth, shadow, eavesdropper, spy, shamus*, flatfoot*, dick*, G-man*, copper*, cop*, fed, narc*; see also POLICE OFFICER.

detention *n.* custody, internment, quarantine; see ARREST, CONFINEMENT, RESTRAINT 2.

deter *v.* caution, stop, dissuade; see PREVENT, WARN.

detergent *n.* cleansing agent, disinfectant, washing substance; see CLEANSER, SOAP.

deteriorate *v.* depreciate, lessen, degenerate; see DECREASE 1.

deterioration *n.* decadence, rotting, degeneration; see DECAY.

determinable *a.* definable, discoverable, capable of being determined; see DEFINITE 2.

determination *n.* resolution, certainty, persistence, stubbornness, obstinacy, resolve, certitude, decision, assurance, conviction, boldness, fixity of purpose, hardihood, tenacity, courage, independence, self-confidence, purposefulness, fortitude, self-assurance, firmness, self-reliance, nerve, heart, bravery, fearlessness, will, energy, vigor, stamina, perseverance, strength of will, a brave front, a bold front, a stout heart, enterprise, guts*, spunk*, a stiff upper lip*; see also CONFIDENCE, FAITH 1, PURPOSE 1.

determine v. 1 [To define] limit, circumscribe, delimit; see DEFINE 1, RESTRICT. 2 [To find out the facts] ascertain, find out, learn; see DISCOVER. 3 [To resolve] fix upon, settle, conclude; see DECIDE, RESOLVE.

determined a. 1 [Already fixed or settled] decided, agreed, acted upon, agreed upon, concluded, contracted, set, ended, resolved, closed, terminated, achieved, finished, over, at an end, checked, measured, tested, budgeted, passed, given approval, given the green light*, given the go-ahead, over and done with; see also APPROVED.—*Ant.* UNFINISHED, suspended, moot. 2 [Having a fixed attitude] resolute, firm, strong-minded; see STUBBORN.

deterrent n. hindrance, impediment, obstacle; see RESTRAINT 2.

detest v. abhor, loathe, despise; see HATE.

detonate v. touch off, discharge, blast; see EXPLODE, SHOOT 1.

detour n. temporary route, alternate route, byway, back road, service road, alternate highway, secondary highway, bypass, circuit, roundabout course.

detract v. decrease, take away a part, subtract, draw away, diminish, lessen, withdraw, derogate, depreciate, discredit; see also SLANDER.

devalue v. devaluate, depreciate, mark down; see DECREASE 2.

devastate v. ravage, demolish, pillage; see DESTROY.

devastation n. destruction, ruin, waste; see DESOLATION.

develop v. 1 [To improve] enlarge, expand, extend, promote, advance, magnify, build up, refine, enrich, cultivate, elaborate, polish, finish, perfect, hone, sharpen, deepen, lengthen, heighten, intensify, fix up, shape up*; see also GROW 1, IMPROVE 1, 2, STRENGTHEN.—*Ant.* DAMAGE, disfigure, spoil. 2 [To grow] mature, evolve, advance; see GROW 1. 3 [To reveal slowly] unfold, disclose, exhibit, unravel, uncover, make known, explain, unroll, explicate, produce, detail, tell, state, recount, account for, give an account of; see also REVEAL.—*Ant.* HIDE, conceal, blurt out. 4 [To work out] enlarge upon, elaborate upon, go into detail; see EXPLAIN, INCREASE.

developed a. grown, refined, advanced; see MATURED, PERFECTED.

development n. growth, elaboration, unfolding, maturing, ripening, maturation, enlargement, addition, spread, gradual evolution, evolving,

advancement, growing, increasing, spreading, making progress, advancing; see also IMPROVEMENT 1, INCREASE, PROGRESS 1.—*Ant.* REDUCTION, decrease, lessening.

deviate v. deflect, digress, swerve, detour, vary, wander, stray, turn aside, keep aside, stay aside, go out of control, shy away, depart, break the pattern, not conform, go out of the way, take a wrong turn, veer, go off on a tangent, go haywire*, swim against the stream; see also DIFFER 1.—*Ant.* CONFORM, keep on, keep in line.

deviation n. change, deflection, alteration; see DIFFERENCE 1, VARIATION 2.

device n. 1 [An instrument] invention, contrivance, mechanism, gear, equipment, appliance, contraption, means, agent, material, implement, utensil, construction, apparatus, outfit, article, accessory, gadget, thing, whatnot, whatsit*, whatchamacallit*; see also MACHINE, TOOL 1. 2 [A shrewd method] artifice, scheme, design, trap, dodge, pattern, loophole, wile, craft, ruse, expedient, subterfuge, plan, project, plot, racket*, game, finesse, catch*; see also DISCOVERY, METHOD, TRICK 1.

devil n. Satan, fiend, the Adversary, error, sin, imp, mischief-maker, Beelzebub, fallen angel, hellhound, Mammon, Molech, Hades, Lucifer, Mephistopheles, diabolical force, the Tempter, Prince of Darkness, Lord of the Flies, Evil One; see also EVIL 1.—*Ant.* GOD, angel, Christ. —**give the devil his due** give someone credit, give credit where credit is due, recognize; see ACKNOWLEDGE 2. —**go to the devil** 1 [To decay] degenerate, fall into bad habits, go to pot; see FAIL 1. 2 [A curse] go to hell, damn you, be damned; see CURSE. —**raise the devil*** cause trouble, riot, be unruly; see DISTURB, FIGHT.

devious a. underhanded, insidious, shrewd; see DISHONEST, SLY.

devote v. apply, consecrate, give; see BLESS, DEDICATE.

devoted a. dutiful, loyal, constant; see FAITHFUL.

devotion n. allegiance, service, consecration, devotedness, adoration, piety, zeal, ardor, earnestness, faithfulness, fidelity, deference, sincerity, adherence, observance; see also LOYALTY, WORSHIP 1.—*Ant.* INDIFFERENCE, apathy, carelessness.

devotions n. religious worship, church services, prayers; see CHURCH 2, WORSHIP 1.

devour v. gulp, swallow, gorge; see EAT 1.

devout a. devoted, pious, reverent; see FAITHFUL, HOLY, RELIGIOUS 2.

diagnosis n. analysis, determination, investigation; see SUMMARY.

diagonal a. slanting, inclining, askew; see OBLIQUE.

diagram n. sketch, layout, picture; see DESCRIPTION, DESIGN, PLAN 1.

dial n. face, gauge, indicator, meter, register, measuring device, compass; see also CONTROL 2.

dialect n. idiom, accent, local speech, regional speech, social dialect, pidgin, creole, argot, standard dialect, pidgin English, brogue, lingo*, trade language, lingua franca, usage level, jargon, cant, vernacular, patois; see also LANGUAGE 1.

dialogue n. talk, exchange, remarks; see CONVERSATION.

diameter n. breadth, measurement across, broadness; see WIDTH.

diametrical a. contrary, adverse, facing; see OPPOSITE 3.

diamond n. 1 [A crystalline jewel] precious stone, solitaire, engagement ring, brilliant, crystal, ring, stone, rock*, sparkler*, glass*, ice*; see also JEWEL. 2 [Shape or figure] lozenge, quadrilateral, rhombus; see FORM 1. 3 [A baseball playing field, particularly the infield] lot, ballpark, sandlot; see FIELD 2, PARK 1.

diary n. chronicle, journal, log; see RECORD 1.

dicker v. trade, barter, bargain; see ARGUE, BUY, SELL.

dictate v. speak, deliver, give forth, compose, formulate, verbalize, record, orate, give an account; see also TALK 1.

dictator n. autocrat, despot, tyrant, czar, fascist, absolute ruler, oppressor, terrorist, master, leader, ringleader, magnate, lord, commander, chief, advisor, overlord, taskmaster, disciplinarian, headman, cock of the walk*, martinet, slave driver; see also LEADER 2, RULER 1.

dictatorial a. despotic, authoritarian, tyrannical; see ABSOLUTE 2.

dictatorship n. despotism, unlimited rule, totalitarianism; see GOVERNMENT 2, TYRANNY.

diction n. style, enunciation, expression, wording, usage, choice of words, command of language, locution, rhetoric, fluency, oratory, articulation, vocabulary, language, line*, gift of gab*; see also ELOQUENCE, SPEECH 2.

dictionary n. wordbook, word list, lexicon, thesaurus, reference work, glossary, encyclopedia, Webster*, Webster's*, vocabulary, dictionary of synonyms.

die v. 1 [To cease living] expire, pass away, pass on, depart, perish, succumb, go, commit suicide, suffocate, lose one's life, cease to exist, drown, hang, fall, meet one's death, be no more, drop dead, be done for*, rest in peace, go to one's final resting place, pass over to the great beyond, give up the ghost*, go the way of all flesh, return to dust*, be a goner*, cash in one's chips*, push up daisies*, buy the farm*, kick the bucket*, bite the dust*, lay down one's life, breathe one's last, croak*, check out*, kick off*, go by the board.—Ant. LIVE, thrive, exist. 2 [To cease existing] disappear, vanish, become extinct; see STOP 2. 3 [To decline as though death were inevitable] fade, ebb, wither; see DECAY, WEAKEN 2. —**die away** decline, go away, sink; see STOP 2. —**die down** decline, disappear, recede; see DIE 2, 3, DECREASE 1. —**die off** (or **out**) go, cease to exist, disappear; see VANISH.

die-hard n. zealot, reactionary, extremist; see CONSERVATIVE.

diet n. 1 [What one eats] menu, fare, daily bread*; see FOOD. 2 [Restricted intake of food] weight-reduction plan, fast, abstinence from food, starvation diet, bread and water*.

diet v. lose weight, go without, starve oneself, slim down, go on a diet, reduce, tighten one's belt*.

differ v. 1 [To be unlike] vary, modify, not conform, digress, take exception, turn, reverse, qualify, alter, change, diverge from, contrast with, bear no resemblance, not look like, jar with, clash with, conflict with, be distinguished from, diversify, stand apart, depart from, go off on a tangent; see also CONTRAST.—Ant. RESEMBLE, parallel, take after. 2 [To oppose] disagree, object, fight; see OPPOSE 1.

difference n. 1 [The quality of being different] disagreement, nonconformity, divergence, contrariness, deviation, opposition, antithesis, dissimilarity, inequality, diversity, departure, variance, discrepancy, separation, differentiation, distinctness, separateness, asymmetry; see also CONTRAST, VARIETY 1.—Ant. AGREEMENT, similarity, resemblance. 2 [That which is unlike in comparable things] deviation, departure, exception; see VARIATION 2. 3 [Personal dissension] discord, estrangement, dissent; see DISPUTE. —**make a difference** change, have an effect, affect; see MATTER. —**split the difference** compromise, go halfway, come to an agreement; see AGREE. —**what's the difference?*** what does it matter?, what difference does it make?, so what?*; see WHY.

different *a.* **1** [Unlike in nature] distinct, separate, not the same; see UNLIKE. **2** [Composed of unlike things] diverse, miscellaneous, assorted; see VARIOUS. **3** [Unusual] unconventional, strange, startling; see UNUSUAL 1, 2.

differentiate *v.* contrast, set apart, discriminate; see DISTINGUISH 1.

differently *a.* variously, divergently, individually, distinctively, creatively, uniquely, separately, each in his or her own way, severally, diversely, incongruously, abnormally, not normally, unusually, asymmetrically, in a different manner, with a difference, otherwise.—*Ant.* EVENLY, uniformly, invariably.

difficult *a.* **1** [Hard to achieve] laborious, hard, unyielding, strenuous, exacting, stiff, heavy, arduous, painful, labored, trying, bothersome, troublesome, demanding, burdensome, backbreaking, not easy, wearisome, onerous, rigid, crucial, uphill, challenging, exacting, formidable, ambitious, immense, tough, heavy*, no picnic*, stiff; see also SEVERE 1.—*Ant.* EASY, manageable, light. **2** [Hard to understand] intricate, involved, perplexing, abstruse, abstract, delicate, hard, knotty, thorny, troublesome, ticklish, obstinate, puzzling, mysterious, mystifying, subtle, confusing, bewildering, confounding, esoteric, unclear, mystical*, tangled, hard to explain, hard to solve, profound, rambling, loose, meandering, inexplicable, awkward, complex, complicated, deep, stubborn, hidden, formidable, enigmatic, paradoxical, incomprehensible, unintelligible, inscrutable, inexplicable, unanswerable, not understandable, unsolvable, unfathomable, concealed, unaccountable, ambiguous, equivocal, metaphysical, inconceivable, unknown, over someone's head, not making sense, too deep for someone, Greek to someone*; see also OBSCURE 1, 3.—*Ant.* CLEAR, obvious, simple.

difficulty *n.* **1** [Something in one's way] obstacle, obstruction, stumbling block, impediment, complication, hardship, adversity, misfortune, distress, deadlock, dilemma, hard job, maze, stone wall, barricade, impasse, knot, opposition, quandary, struggle, crisis, trouble, embarrassment, entanglement, mess, paradox, muddle, emergency, matter, standstill, hindrance, perplexity, bar, trial, check, predicament, hot water*, pickle*, fix*, stew*, scrape, hard nut to crack*, hitch*, dead end*, snag, monkey wrench in the works*, pinch, deep water*, jam*, the devil to pay*, hang-up*; see also sense 2 and BARRIER.—*Ant.* HELP, aid, assistance. **2** [Something mentally disturbing]

trouble, annoyance, to-do*, ado, worry, weight, complication, distress, oppression, depression, aggravation, anxiety, discouragement, touchy situation, embarrassment, burden, grievance, irritation, strife, puzzle, responsibility, frustration, harassment, misery, predicament, setback, pressure, stress, strain, charge, struggle, maze, hang-up*, mess*, pickle*, pinch, scrape; see also sense 1 and CRISIS, EMERGENCY.—*Ant.* EASE, comfort, happiness.

dig* *n.* **1** [Insult] slur, innuendo, cut; see INSULT. **2** [Excavation] digging, archaeological expedition, exploration; see EXPEDITION.

dig *v.* **1** [To stir the earth] delve, spade, mine, excavate, channel, deepen, till, drive a shaft, clean, undermine, burrow, root, dig out, gouge, dredge, scoop out, tunnel out, hollow out, clean out, grub, bulldoze; see also SHOVEL.—*Ant.* BURY, embed, fill. **2** [To remove by digging] dig up, uncover, turn up; see HARVEST. **3** [*To like] enjoy, love, appreciate; see LIKE 1, 2. **4** [*To understand] comprehend, recognize, appreciate; see UNDERSTAND 1. — **dig into** investigate, research, probe; see EXAMINE. —**dig up** find, uncover, excavate; see DIG 2, DISCOVER.

digest *n.* epitome, précis, condensation; see SUMMARY.

digest *v.* transform food, consume, absorb; see EAT 1.

digestible *a.* eatable, absorbable, good to eat; see EDIBLE.

digit *n.* figure, Arabic notation, numeral; see NUMBER.

dignified *a.* stately, somber, solemn, courtly, reserved, ornate, elegant, classic, lordly, aristocratic, majestic, formal, noble, regal, superior, magnificent, grand, eminent, sublime, august, grave, distinguished, magisterial, imposing, portly, haughty, honorable, decorous, lofty, proud, classy*, snazzy*, sober as a judge*, highbrow; see also CULTURED, REFINED 2.—*Ant.* RUDE, undignified, boorish.

dignify *v.* exalt, elevate, ennoble; see PRAISE 1.

dignity *n.* nobility, self-respect, lofty bearing, grandeur, quality, culture, distinction, stateliness, elevation, worth, worthiness, character, importance, renown, splendor, majesty, class*; see also HONOR, PRIDE 1.—*Ant.* HUMILITY, lowness, meekness.

dilemma *n.* quandary, perplexity, predicament; see DIFFICULTY 1.

diligence *n.* alertness, earnestness, quickness, perseverance, industry, vigor, carefulness, heed, intent, intensity, assiduity; see also ATTENTION, CARE 1.—*Ant.* CARELESSNESS, sloth, laziness.

dilute *v.* mix, reduce, thin; see WEAKEN 2.

dim *a.* faint, dusky, shadowy; see DARK 1.

dimensions *n.* size, measurements, extent; see HEIGHT, LENGTH 1, 2, WIDTH.

diminish *v.* lessen, depreciate, abbreviate; see DECREASE.

din *n.* clamor, commotion, hubbub; see CONFUSION, NOISE 2.

dine *v.* lunch, feast, sup; see EAT 1.

dingy *a.* grimy, muddy, soiled; see DIRTY 1.

dining room *n.* *Varieties include the following:* dining hall, breakfast nook, dinette, tea shop, lunch counter, lunchroom, luncheonette, cafeteria, cafe, ice-cream parlor, drugstore, grill, coffee shop, fast-food outlet, soda fountain, steakhouse, buffet, inn, tavern, deli, eatery, pizza shop, pizzeria, bistro, sandwich shop, diner, mess hall, galley, automat, greasy spoon*; see also RESTAURANT.

dinner *n.* feast, banquet, main meal, supper, repast; see also MEAL 2.

dip *n.* 1 [The action of dipping] plunge, immersion, soaking, ducking, drenching, sinking; see also BATH 1. 2 [Material into which something is dipped] preparation, solution, suspension, dilution, concoction, saturation, mixture; see also LIQUID. 3 [A low place] depression, slope, inclination; see HOLE 1. 4 [A swim] plunge, bath, dive; see SWIM.

dip *v.* 1 [To put into a liquid] plunge, lower, wet, slosh, submerge, irrigate, steep, drench, douse, souse, moisten, splash, slop, water, duck, bathe, rinse, baptize, dunk; see also IMMERSE, SOAK 1, WASH 2. 2 [To transfer by scooping] scoop, shovel, ladle, bale, spoon, dredge, lift, draw, dish, dip up, dip out, offer; see also SERVE.—*Ant.* EMPTY, pour, let stand. 3 [To fall] slope, decline, recede, tilt, swoop, slip, spiral, sink, plunge, bend, verge, veer, slant, settle, slump, slide, go down; see also DIVE, DROP 2, FALL 1.

diploma *n.* degree, graduation certificate, credentials, honor, award, recognition, commission, warrant, voucher, confirmation, sheepskin*; see also GRADUATION.

diplomacy *n.* artfulness, statesmanship, discretion; see TACT.

diplomat *n.* ambassador, consul, minister, legate, emissary, envoy,

agent; see also REPRESENTATIVE 2, STATESMAN.

diplomatic *a.* tactful, suave, gracious, calculating, shrewd, opportunistic, smooth, capable, conciliatory, conniving, sly, artful, wily, subtle, crafty, sharp, cunning, contriving, scheming, discreet, deft, intriguing, politic, strategic, astute, clever; see also POLITE.

dipped *a.* immersed, plunged, bathed, ducked, doused, drenched, soused, covered, dunked; see also SOAKED, WET 1.

dire *a.* dreadful, terrible, horrible; see FRIGHTFUL 1.

direct *a.* 1 [Without divergence] in a straight line, straight ahead, undeviating, uninterrupted, unswerving, shortest, nonstop, as the crow flies, straight as an arrow, in a beeline, point-blank; see also STRAIGHT 1.—*Ant.* ZIGZAG, roundabout, crooked. 2 [Frank] straightforward, outspoken, candid; see FRANK, HONEST. 3 [Immediate] firsthand, close, primary; see IMMEDIATE.

direct *v.* 1 [To show the way] conduct, show, guide; see LEAD 1. 2 [To decide the course of affairs] regulate, govern, influence; see MANAGE 1. 3 [To aim a weapon] sight, train, level; see AIM. 4 [To command] command, bid, charge; see ORDER 1.

directed *a.* supervised, controlled, conducted, sponsored, under supervision, assisted, counseled, guided, serviced, managed, orderly, purposeful, functioning; see also AIMED, ORGANIZED.

direction *n.* 1 [A position] point of the compass, objective, bearing, region, area, place, spot; see also WAY 2. 2 [Supervision] management, superintendence, control; see ADMINISTRATION 2. 3 [A tendency] bias, bent, proclivity; see INCLINATION 1.

directions *n.* instructions, advice, notification, specification, indication, orders, assignment, recommendations, summons, directive, regulation, prescription, plans.

directly *a.* instantly, at once, quickly; see IMMEDIATELY.

director *n.* manager, supervisor, executive; see LEADER 2.

directory *n.* list, syllabus, register, record, almanac, roster, dictionary, gazetteer, telephone book, Yellow Pages, city directory, social register, who's who, blue book; see also CATALOG, INDEX.

dirt *n.* 1 [Earth] soil, loam, clay; see EARTH 2. 2 [Filth] rottenness, filthiness, smut; see FILTH.

dirty *a.* 1 [Containing dirt] soiled, unclean, unsanitary, unhygienic, filthy, polluted, nasty, slovenly, dusty, messy, squalid, sloppy, disheveled, uncombed, unkempt, unsightly, untidy, straggly, unwashed, stained, tarnished, spotted, smudged, foul, fouled, grimy, greasy, muddy, mucky, sooty, smoked, slimy, rusty, unlaundered, unswept, crummy*, grubby, scuzzy*, scummy.—*Ant.* PURE, unspotted, sanitary. 2 [Obscene] pornographic, smutty, ribald; see LEWD 1, 2, SENSUAL. 3 [Nasty] mean, contemptible, disagreeable; see RUTHLESS.

dirty *v.* soil, sully, defile, pollute, foul, tarnish, spot, smear, blot, blur, smudge, smoke, spoil, sweat up, blotch, spatter, splash, stain, debase, corrupt, taint, contaminate.—*Ant.* CLEAN, cleanse, rinse.

disability *n.* feebleness, inability, incapacity; see INJURY, WEAKNESS 1.

disable *v.* incapacitate, impair, put out of action; see DAMAGE, WEAKEN 2.

disabled *a.* handicapped, incapacitated, physically challenged, injured, crippled, helpless, wrecked, stalled, maimed, wounded, mangled, lame, mutilated, run-down, worn-out, weakened, impotent, castrated, paralyzed, senile, decrepit, laid up*, done for*, done in*, cracked up*, out of action*; see also HURT, USELESS 1, WEAK 1.—*Ant.* HEALTHY, strong, capable.

disadvantage *n.* 1 [Loss] damage, harm, deprivation; see LOSS 3. 2 [A position involving difficulties] bar, obstacle, handicap, inconvenience, obstacle, drawbacks; see also RESTRAINT 2, WEAKNESS 1.

disagree *v.* 1 [To differ] dissent, object, oppose; see DIFFER 1. 2 [To have uncomfortable effect] nauseate, make ill, be hard on the stomach*; see BOTHER 2.

disagreeable *a.* 1 [Having an unpleasant disposition] difficult, obnoxious, offensive; see IRRITABLE, RUDE 2. 2 [Irritating; *said of things and conditions*] bothersome, unpleasant, upsetting; see DISTURBING, OFFENSIVE 2.

disagreement *n.* 1 [Discord] contention, strife, conflict, controversy, wrangle, dissension, animosity, ill feeling, ill will, misunderstanding, division, opposition, hostility, breach, discord, feud, clashing, antagonism, bickering, squabble, tension, split, quarreling, falling-out, break, rupture, quarrel, clash, opposition, contest, friction; see also BATTLE, COMPETITION, FIGHT. 2 [Inconsistency] discrepancy, dissimilarity, disparity; see DIFFERENCE 1. 3 [A quarrel] fight, argument, feud; see DISPUTE.

disappear *v.* cease, fade, die; see ESCAPE, EVAPORATE, VANISH.

disappearance *n.* vanishing, fading, departure, ebbing away, removal, dissipation, ceasing to exist, ceasing to appear, desertion, flight, retirement, escape, exodus, vanishing point, going, disintegration, exit, withdrawal, decline and fall, eclipse; see also ESCAPE, EVAPORATION.

disappoint *v.* fail, delude, deceive, dissatisfy, disillusion, harass, embitter, chagrin, dumbfound, fall short, cast down, frustrate, torment, tease, miscarry, abort, thwart, foil, baffle, balk, mislead, bungle, let down, leave in the lurch*, fizzle out*.

disappointed *a.* dissatisfied, discouraged, unsatisfied, despondent, depressed, objecting, complaining, distressed, hopeless, balked, disconcerted, aghast, disgruntled, disillusioned; see also SAD.—*Ant.* SATISFIED, pleased, content.

disappointing *a.* unsatisfactory, ineffective, uninteresting, discouraging, unpleasant, inferior, lame, insufficient, failing, at fault, limited, second-rate, mediocre, ordinary, unexpected, unhappy, depressing, disconcerting, disagreeable, irritating, annoying, troublesome, disheartening, unlucky, uncomfortable, bitter, distasteful, disgusting, deplorable, short of expectations; see also INADEQUATE.

disappointment *n.* 1 [The state of being disappointed] dissatisfaction, frustration, chagrin, lack of success, despondency, displeasure, distress, discouragement, disillusionment, check, disillusion, setback, adversity; see also DEFEAT, FAILURE 1, REGRET 1.—*Ant.* SUCCESS, fulfillment, realization. 2 [A person or thing that disappoints] miscarriage, misfortune, calamity, blunder, bad luck, setback, downfall, slip, defeat, mishap, error, mistake, discouragement, obstacle, miscalculation, fiasco, no go*, blind alley, washout*, lemon*, dud*, letdown, bust*; see also sense 1 and FAILURE 2.—*Ant.* ACHIEVEMENT, successful venture, success.

disapproval *n.* criticism, censure, disparagement; see OBJECTION.

disapprove *v.* blame, chastise, reprove; see DENOUNCE. —**disapprove of** object to, dislike, deplore; see COMPLAIN, OPPOSE 1.

disarm *v.* demobilize, disable, unarm, weaken, debilitate, incapacitate, muzzle, deprive of weapons, deprive of means of defense, subdue, strip, tie the hands of, clip the wings of; see also DEFEAT 2, 3.—*Ant.* ARM, outfit, equip.

disarmament *n.* arms reduction,

cease-fire, de-escalation; see PEACE 1.

disaster *n.* accident, calamity, mishap, debacle, casualty, emergency, adversity, harm, misadventure, collapse, slip, fall, collision, crash, hazard, setback, defeat, failure, woe, trouble, scourge, grief, undoing, curse, tragedy, blight, cataclysm, downfall, rainy day, bankruptcy, upset, blast, blow, wreck, bad luck, comedown, crackup, pileup*, smashup, washout*, flop*, bust*; see also CATASTROPHE, MISFORTUNE.

disastrous *a.* calamitous, ruinous, unfortunate; see HARMFUL, UNFAVORABLE.

disband *v.* scatter, disperse, dismiss; see LEAVE 1.

disbelief *n.* unbelief, skepticism, mistrust; see DOUBT.

disbeliever *n.* doubter, skeptic, agnostic; see CRITIC 1.

disburse *v.* expend, distribute, dispense; see PAY 1, SPEND.

discard *v.* reject, expel, repudiate, protest, cast aside, cast away, cast out, cast off, throw away, throw aside, throw overboard, throw out, get rid of, give up, renounce, have done with, dump, make away with, dismantle, discharge, write off, banish, eject, divorce, dispossess, dispense with, shake off, pass up, free oneself from, be free of, give away, part with, dispose of, do away with, shed, relinquish, thrust aside, sweep away, cancel, forsake, desert, cut, have nothing to do with, brush away, scotch, chuck*, drop, wash one's hands of*, junk*; see also ABANDON 1, DISMISS.—*Ant.* SAVE, retain, preserve.

discarded *a.* rejected, repudiated, cast off, thrown away, dismantled, dismissed, useless, damaged, outworn, worn-out, done with, rundown, not worth saving, abandoned, obsolete, shelved, neglected, deserted, forsaken, outmoded, out of date, out of style, out of fashion, old-fashioned, old hat*.—*Ant.* KEPT, worthwhile, modern.

discern *v.* find out, determine, discriminate; see DISCOVER.

discerning *a.* discriminating, perceptive, penetrating; see DISCREET.

discharge *v.* **1** [To unload] unpack, release, remove cargo; see EMPTY, UNLOAD. **2** [To remove] take off, send, carry away; see REMOVE 1. **3** [To cause to fire] blast, shoot off, fire; see SHOOT 1. **4** [To release] emancipate, liberate, let go; see FREE.

discharged *a.* mustered out, sent home, recalled, freed, liberated, released, let go, sent away, emancipated, expelled, ejected, dismissed,

fired, ousted, canned*, axed*; see also FREE 2, 3.

disciple *n.* adherent, pupil, believer, apostle; see also FOLLOWER. *Christ's disciples mentioned in the New Testament include:* Matthew, John, Peter, Bartholomew, Nathaniel, James, Philip, Andrew, Thaddaeus, Thomas, James the son of Alphaeus, Judas Iscariot, Jude, Simon the Canaanite.

discipline *n.* **1** [Mental self-training] preparation, development, exercise, drilling, training, regulation, self-disciplining; see also DRILL 3, EDUCATION 1. **2** [A system of obedience] conduct, regulation, drill, orderliness, restraint, limitation, curb, indoctrination, brainwashing*; see also TRAINING.

discipline *v.* chastise, correct, limit; see PUNISH.

disc jockey *n.* radio announcer, commentator, DJ; see ANNOUNCER, REPORTER.

disclose *v.* make known, confess, publish; see REVEAL.

disclosure *n.* exposé, acknowledgment, confession; see ADMISSION 3, DECLARATION.

discolor *v.* stain, rust, tarnish; see COLOR, DIRTY.

discoloration *n.* blot, blotch, splotch; see BLEMISH, STAIN.

discomfort *n.* trouble, displeasure, uneasiness; see ANNOYANCE, EMBARRASSMENT.

disconnect *v.* separate, detach, disengage; see CUT 1, DIVIDE.

disconnected *a.* broken off, detached, switched off; see SEPARATED.

discontent *n.* dissatisfaction, unease, restlessness; see REGRET 1.

discontented *a.* unhappy, disgruntled, malcontented; see SAD 1.

discontinue *v.* finish, close, cease; see END 1, STOP 2.

discontinued *a.* ended, terminated, given up; see ABANDONED.

discord *n.* **1** [Conflict] strife, contention, dissension; see DISAGREEMENT 1. **2** [Noise] din, dissonance, disharmony; see NOISE 2.

discount *n.* deduction, allowance, rebate, decrease, markdown, concession, percentage, premium, subtraction, commission, exemption, modification, qualification, drawback, depreciation, cut rate; see also REDUCTION 1.—*Ant.* INCREASE, markup, surcharge. —**at a discount** discounted, cheap, below face value; see REDUCED 2.

discount *v.* reduce, remove, redeem, diminish, depreciate, deduct from, lower, make allowance for, allow, take off, charge off, rebate, mark down, discredit, rake off*; see also

DECREASE 2.—*Ant.* RAISE, mark up, advance.

discourage *v.* repress, appall, intimidate, break someone's heart, deject, unnerve, scare, confuse, dampen, dismay, daunt, bully, demoralize, throw a wet blanket on*, throw cold water on*, dampen the spirits of, dash someone's hopes; see also DEPRESS 2, FRIGHTEN.—*Ant.* ENCOURAGE, cheer, inspire.

discouraged *a.* downcast, demoralized, depressed; see SAD 1.

discouragement *n.* **1** [Dejection] melancholy, despair, the blues*; see DEPRESSION 2, SADNESS. **2** [A restriction] constraint, hindrance, deterrent; see IMPEDIMENT 1.

discouraging *a.* **1** [Acting to discourage] depressing, disheartening, demoralizing; see DISMAL. **2** [Suggesting an unwelcome future] inopportune, disadvantageous, dissuading; see UNFAVORABLE.

discourteous *a.* boorish, crude, impolite; see RUDE 2.

discourtesy *n.* impudence, impoliteness, vulgarity; see RUDENESS.

discover *v.* invent, find out, ascertain, detect, discern, recognize, distinguish, determine, observe, explore, hear of, hear about, awake to, bring to light, uncover, ferret out, root out, trace out, unearth, look up, stumble on, stumble upon, come on, come upon, run across, fall upon, strike upon, think of, perceive, glimpse, identify, devise, catch, spot, create, make out, sense, feel, sight, smell, hear, spy, bring out, find a clue, put one's finger on, get wise to*, dig out, dig up, turn up, sniff out, come up with, happen upon, get wind of, hit upon, lay one's hands on; see also FIND, LEARN.—*Ant.* MISS, pass by, omit.

discovered *a.* found, searched out, come upon, happened on, happened upon, unearthed, ascertained, detected, revealed, disclosed, unveiled, observed, sighted, shown, exposed, traced out, made out, met with, come across, recognized, identified, laid bare, opened, presented, spotted, perceived, learned; see also REAL 2.—*Ant.* HIDDEN, unfound, lost.

discovery *n.* invention, detection, exploration, identification, discernment, distinction, determination, calculation, experimentation, feeling, hearing, sighting, strike, results, findings, formula, device, find, contrivance, design, machine, invention, process, breakthrough, data, principle, law, theorem, innovation, conclusion, method, way; see also RESULT.

discredit *v.* question, disbelieve, distrust; see DOUBT.

discreet *a.* cautious, prudent, dis-

cerning, discriminating, not rash, strategic, noncommittal, heedful, vigilant, civil, sensible, reserved, alert, awake, wary, watchful, wise, circumspect, attentive, considerate, intelligent, guarded, politic, diplomatic, tight-lipped, cagey*; see also CAREFUL, THOUGHTFUL 2.—*Ant.* RASH, indiscreet, imprudent.

discretion *n.* caution, foresight, carefulness, wariness, sound judgment, thoughtfulness, attention, heed, concern, consideration, observation, watchfulness, precaution, good sense, providence, maturity, discernment, forethought, calculation, deliberation, vigilance, discrimination, responsibility, presence of mind; see also CARE 1, PRUDENCE, TACT.—*Ant.* CARELESSNESS, rashness, thoughtlessness. **—at one's discretion** as one wishes, whenever appropriate, at one's option; see APPROPRIATELY.

discriminate *v.* **1** [To differentiate] specify, separate, tell apart; see DISTINGUISH 1. **2** [To be (racially) prejudiced] be a bigot, show prejudice, set apart, segregate; see also HATE, SEPARATE 1.

discrimination *n.* **1** [The power to make distinctions] perception, acuteness, understanding; see INTELLIGENCE 1. **2** [The act of drawing a distinction] separation, differentiation, difference; see JUDGMENT 2. **3** [Partiality] unfairness, bias, bigotry; see HATRED, PREJUDICE.

discuss *v.* argue, debate, dispute, talk of, talk about, explain, contest, confer, deal with, reason with, take up, look over, consider, talk over, talk out, take up in conference, engage in conversation, go into, think over, telephone about, have a conference on, discourse about, argue for and against, canvass, consider, handle, present, review, recite, treat of, speak of, converse, discourse, take under advisement, comment upon, have out, speak on, kick around*, toss around*, chew the fat*, jaw*, air out*, knock around*, compare notes*, chew the rag*; see also TALK 1.—*Ant.* DELAY, table, postpone.

discussed *a.* talked over, debated, argued; see CONSIDERED.

discussion *n.* exchange, consultation, interview, deliberation, argumentation, contention, dialogue, talk, conference, argument, debate, panel discussion, summit meeting, dealing with the agenda, controversy, altercation, review, reasons, rap session*, symposium, quarrel, powwow*, bull session*; see also CONVERSATION, DISPUTE.—*Ant.* AGREEMENT, decision, conclusion.

disease n. 1 [A bodily infirmity] sickness, malady, ailment; see ILLNESS 1. 2 [Any ailment] condition, disorder, infirmity; see ILLNESS 2.

diseased a. unhealthy, unsound, ailing; see SICK.

disengage v. loose, undo, disentangle; see FREE.

disengaged a. detached, unattached, disjoined; see SEPARATED.

disentangle v. disengage, untangle, untwist; see FREE.

disfavor n. displeasure, disapproval, disrespect; see DISAPPOINTMENT 1.

disfigure v. deface, mar, mutilate; see DAMAGE, HURT.

disgrace n. scandal, shame, stain, slur, slight, stigma, brand, spot, slander, dishonor, infamy, reproach, disrepute, humiliation, degradation, taint, tarnish, mark of Cain*, scarlet letter; see also INSULT.—Ant. PRIDE, praise, credit.

disgrace v. debase, shame, degrade, abase, dishonor, disparage, discredit, deride, disregard, strip of honors, dismiss from favor, disrespect, mock, humble, reduce, put to shame, tarnish, stain, blot, sully, taint, defile, stigmatize, brand, tar and feather, put down, snub, derogate, belittle, take down a peg*; see also HUMILIATE, RIDICULE, SLANDER.—Ant. PRAISE, honor, exalt.

disgraced a. discredited, in disgrace, dishonored; see ASHAMED.

disgraceful a. dishonorable, disreputable, shocking; see OFFENSIVE, SHAMEFUL 1, 2.

disguise n. mask, deceptive covering, makeup, faking, false front, deception, smoke screen, blind, concealment, counterfeit, pseudonym, costume, masquerade, veil, cover, facade, put-on*; see also CAMOUFLAGE.

disguise v. mask, conceal, camouflage, pretend, screen, cloak, shroud, cover, veil, alter, obscure, feign, counterfeit, varnish, age, redo, make up, simulate, muffle, dress up, touch up, doctor up*; see also CHANGE 2, DECEIVE, HIDE.—Ant. REVEAL, open, strip.

disguised a. cloaked, masked, camouflaged; see CHANGED 2, COVERED 1, HIDDEN.

disgust n. loathing, abhorrence, aversion; see HATRED, OBJECTION.

disgust v. repel, revolt, offend, displease, nauseate, sicken, make someone sick, fill with loathing, cause aversion, be repulsive, irk, scandalize, shock, upset, turn someone's stomach*; see also DISTURB, INSULT.

disgusted a. offended, sickened, displeased, repelled, unhappy, revolted, appalled, overwrought, outraged, having had a bellyful*, fed up*, having had it*, having had enough*; see also INSULTED, SHOCKED. —**disgusted with** repelled by, sick of*, fed up with*; see INSULTED, SHOCKED.

disgusting a. repugnant, revolting, sickening; see OFFENSIVE 2.

dish n. 1 [Plate] vessel, china, ceramic; see PLATE 3. *Table dishes include the following:* dinner plate, luncheon plate, salad plate, bread and butter plate, platter, casserole, cake plate, coffee cup, coffee mug, espresso cup, demitasse, teacup, egg cup, saucer, cereal bowl, soup bowl, gravy boat, relish tray, cruet, teapot, coffeepot, cream pitcher, water pitcher, lemonade pitcher, sugar bowl, butter dish, saltcellar, saltshaker, pepper shaker, pepper mill see also CONTAINER, CUP, POTTERY. 2 [Meal] course, serving, helping; see MEAL 2.

dishonest a. deceiving, fraudulent, double-dealing, backbiting, treacherous, deceitful, cunning, sneaky, tricky, wily, deceptive, misleading, elusive, slippery, shady*, swindling, cheating, sneaking, traitorous, villainous, sinister, underhanded, two-timing*, two-faced, double-crossing*, unprincipled, shiftless, unscrupulous, undependable, disreputable, questionable, dishonorable, counterfeit, infamous, corrupt, immoral, discredited, unworthy, shabby, mean, low, venial, self-serving, contemptible, rotten, fishy*, crooked; see also FALSE 1, LYING 1.—Ant. HONEST, irreproachable, scrupulous.

dishonesty n. infidelity, faithlessness, falsity, falsehood, deceit, trickery, duplicity, insidiousness, cunning, guile, slyness, double-dealing, trickiness, treachery, crookedness, corruption, cheating, stealing, lying, swindle, fraud, fraudulence, forgery, perjury, treason, flimflam, hocus-pocus*, hanky-panky*; see also DECEPTION, HYPOCRISY, LIE.—Ant. HONESTY, virtue, integrity.

dishonor n. shame, ignominy, abasement; see DISGRACE.

dish towel n. tea towel, kitchen towel, drying towel; see TOWEL.

disillusion v. disenchant, disabuse, embitter; see DISAPPOINT.

disinfect v. purify, fumigate, use disinfectant on; see CLEAN.

disinherit v. disown, evict, dispossess; see DISMISS, NEGLECT 2.

disintegrate v. break down, separate, divide, dismantle, break into pieces, disunite, disperse, crumble, disband, take apart, disorganize, detach, break apart, come apart, fall apart, sever, disconnect, fall to pieces, fade away, reduce to ashes;

see also DISSOLVE.—*Ant.* UNITE, put together, combine.

disinterested *a.* impartial, not involved, unconcerned; see INDIFFERENT, UNMOVED 2.

disjoint *v.* dismember, cut up, carve; see CUT 1, DIVIDE, SEPARATE 1.

disjointed *a.* disconnected, divided, unattached; see SEPARATED.

dislike *n.* opposition, aversion, distaste; see HATE, HATRED, OBJECTION.

dislike *v.* detest, condemn, deplore, regret, lose interest in, speak down to, have hard feelings toward, not take kindly to, not be able to say much for, not have the stomach for, not speak well of, not want any part of, not care for, bear a grudge, have nothing to do with, keep one's distance from, care nothing for, resent, not appreciate, not endure, be averse to, abhor, abominate, disapprove, loathe, despise, object to, shun, shrink from, mind, shudder at, scorn, avoid, be displeased by, turn up the nose at, look on with aversion, not be able to stomach, regard with displeasure, not like, take a dim view of, have it in for*, be down on*, look down one's nose at*, have a bone to pick with*; see also HATE.

dislocate *v.* disjoint, disunite, disengage; see BREAK 1, DIVIDE, SEPARATE 1.

dislocation *n.* displacement, discontinuity, luxation; see BREAK 1, DIVISION 1.

dislodge *v.* eject, evict, uproot; see OUST, REMOVE 1.

disloyalty *n.* infidelity, betrayal, bad faith; see DISHONESTY, TREASON.

dismal *a.* gloomy, monotonous, dim, melancholy, desolate, dreary, sorrowful, morbid, troublesome, horrid, shadowy, overcast, cloudy, unhappy, discouraging, hopeless, black, unfortunate, ghastly, horrible, boring, gruesome, tedious, mournful, lugubrious, dull, disheartening, regrettable, cheerless, dusky, dingy, sepulchral, joyless, funereal, comfortless, murky, wan, bleak, somber, disagreeable, creepy, spooky*, blue; see also DARK 1.—*Ant.* HAPPY, joyful, cheerful.

dismantle *v.* take apart, disassemble, break down, take down, tear down, knock down, undo, demolish, level, ruin, unrig, subvert, raze, take to pieces, fell, take apart; see also DESTROY.

dismay *n.* consternation, dread, anxiety; see FEAR.

dismember *v.* dissect, disjoint, amputate; see CUT 1, DIVIDE.

dismiss *v.* send away, discard, reject, decline, repel, let out, repudiate, disband, detach, lay off, pack off, cast off, cast out, relinquish, dispense with, disperse, remove, expel, abolish, relegate, push aside, shed, do without, have done with, dispose of, sweep away, clear, rid, chase, dispossess, boycott, exile, expatriate, banish, outlaw, deport, excommunicate, get rid of, send packing, drop, brush off*, kick out*, blackball, write off; see also OUST, REFUSE.—*Ant.* MAINTAIN, retain, keep.

dismissal *n.* deposition, displacement, expulsion; see REMOVAL.

dismissed *a.* sent away, ousted, removed; see DISCHARGED, FREE 2, 3.

disobedience *n.* insubordination, defiance, insurgence, disregard, violation, neglect, mutiny, revolt, nonobservance, strike, stubbornness, noncompliance, infraction of the rules, unruliness, sedition, rebellion, sabotage, riot; see also REVOLUTION 2.

disobedient *a.* insubordinate, refractory, defiant; see REBELLIOUS, UNRULY.

disobey *v.* balk, decline, neglect, desert, be remiss, ignore the commands of, refuse submission to, disagree, differ, evade, disregard the authority of, break rules, object, defy, resist, revolt, strike, violate, infringe, transgress, shirk, misbehave, withstand, counteract, take the law into one's own hands, not mind, pay no attention to, go counter to, not listen to; see also DARE 2, OPPOSE 1, REBEL.—*Ant.* OBEY, follow, fulfill.

disorder *n.* tumult, discord, turmoil, complication, chaos, mayhem, terrorism, rioting, mob rule, anarchy, anarchism, lawlessness, entanglement, commotion, agitation, insurrection, revolution, rebellion, strike, disorganization, riot, reign of terror, uproar, dither, static*; see also DISTURBANCE 2, TROUBLE 1.—*Ant.* ORDER, peace, tranquillity.

disorder *v.* disarrange, clutter, scatter; see CONFUSE, DISORGANIZE.

disordered *a.* displaced, misplaced, dislocated, mislaid, out of place, deranged, in disorder, out of kilter, out of hand, in confusion, in a mess, all over the place, in a jumble, upset, unsettled, disorganized, disarranged, moved, removed, shifted, tampered with, tumbled, ruffled, rumpled, jumbled, jarred, tossed, stirred up, roiled, jolted, muddled; see also CONFUSED 2, TANGLED.—*Ant.* ORDERED, arranged, settled.

disorderly *a.* **1** [Lacking orderly arrangement] confused, jumbled, undisciplined, unrestrained, scattered, dislocated, unsystematic, messy, slovenly, untidy, cluttered, unkempt, scrambled, badly managed, in confusion, untrained, disorganized, out of control, topsy-turvy, all over the place*, mixed-up; see also DISORDERED.—*Ant.* REGULAR, neat, trim. **2** [Creating a disturbance] intemperate, disruptive, rowdy; see UNRULY.

disorganization *n.* disunion, dissolution, derangement; see CONFUSION.

disorganize *v.* break up, disperse, destroy, scatter, litter, clutter, break down, put out of order, disarrange, disorder, upset, disrupt, derange, dislocate, disband, jumble, muddle, unsettle, disturb, perturb, shuffle, toss, complicate, confound, overthrow, overturn, scramble; see also CONFUSE.—*Ant.* SYSTEMATIZE, order, distribute.

disown *v.* repudiate, deny, disavow; see DISCARD.

dispatch *v.* **1** [To send something on its way] transmit, express, forward; see SEND 1. **2** [To make an end] finish, conclude, perform; see ACHIEVE.

dispel *v.* disperse, deploy, dissipate; see DISTRIBUTE, SCATTER.

dispensable *a.* removable, excessive, unnecessary; see TRIVIAL, USELESS 1.

dispense *v.* apportion, assign, allocate; see DISTRIBUTE, GIVE 1. —**dispense with** ignore, pass over, brush aside; see DISREGARD, NEGLECT 2.

dispenser *n.* vendor, tap, vending machine, spray can, spray gun, cigarette machine, Coke machine (trademark), automat, squeeze bottle.

disperse *v.* break up, separate, disband; see SCATTER.

displace *v.* **1** [To remove] replace, transpose, dislodge; see REMOVE 1. **2** [To put in the wrong place] mislay, misplace, disarrange; see LOSE 2.

display *n.* exhibition, exhibit, presentation, representation, exposition, arrangement, demonstration, performance, revelation, unveiling, procession, parade, pageant, example, appearance, waxworks, fireworks, carnival, fair, pomp, splendor, unfolding; see also SHOW 1.

display *v.* show, show off, exhibit, uncover, open up, unfold, reveal, spread, parade, unmask, present, represent, perform, flaunt, lay out, put out, set out, disclose, unveil, arrange, make known; see also EXPOSE.—*Ant.* HIDE, conceal, veil.

displayed *a.* presented, visible, on display; see ADVERTISED, SHOWN 1.

displease *v.* vex, provoke, enrage; see ANGER.

displeasure *n.* disapproval, annoyance, resentment; see ANGER.

disposal *n.* action, provision, determination, disposition, distribution, arrangement, conclusion, settlement, control, winding up; see also RESULT. —**at someone's disposal** ready, prepared, usable; see AVAILABLE.

dispose *v.* settle, adapt, arrange; see ADJUST 1, PREPARE 1. —**dispose of** relinquish, throw away, part with; see DISCARD, SELL.

disposed *a.* inclined, prone, apt; see LIKELY 4.

disposition *n.* **1** [Arrangement] decision, method, distribution; see ORGANIZATION 1, PLAN 2. **2** [Temperament] character, nature, temper; see MOOD, TEMPERAMENT.

disproportionate *a.* unbalanced, incommensurate, excessive; see IRREGULAR 4.

disprove *v.* prove false, throw out, set aside, find fault in, invalidate, weaken, overthrow, tear down, confound, expose, cut the ground from under, poke holes in; see also DENY.

disputable *a.* debatable, doubtful, dubious; see QUESTIONABLE 1, UNCERTAIN.

dispute *n.* argument, quarrel, debate, misunderstanding, conflict, strife, discussion, polemic, bickering, squabble, disturbance, feud, commotion, tiff, fracas, controversy, altercation, dissension, squall, difference of opinion, rumpus*, row, flare-up, fuss, fireworks; see also DISAGREEMENT 1.

dispute *v.* debate, contradict, quarrel; see ARGUE, DISCUSS.

disqualify *v.* preclude, disentitle, disbar; see BAR 2.

disquieting *a.* distressing, troubling, disconcerting; see DISTURBING.

disregard *v.* ignore, pass over, let pass, make light of, have no use for, laugh off, take no account of, brush aside, turn a deaf ear to, be blind to, shut one's eyes to; see also NEGLECT 1.

disrepair *n.* decrepitude, deterioration, dilapidation; see DECAY.

disreputable *a.* low, objectionable, discreditable; see OFFENSIVE 2, SHAMEFUL 1, 2.

disrespect *n.* discourtesy, insolence, irreverence; see RUDENESS.

disrespectful *a.* discourteous, impolite, impudent; see RUDE 2.

disrobe *v.* strip, divest, unclothe; see UNDRESS.

disrupt *v.* disturb, intrude, obstruct; see BREAK 1, INTERRUPT.

disruption *n.* debacle, disturbance, agitation; see CONFUSION.

dissatisfaction *n.* dislike, displeasure, disapproval; see OBJECTION.

dissatisfied *a.* displeased, unsatisfied, fed up*; see DISAPPOINTED.

dissect *v.* dismember, quarter, operate; see CUT 1, DIVIDE.

disseminate *v.* sow, propagate, broadcast; see DISTRIBUTE.

dissension *n.* difference, quarrel, trouble; see DISAGREEMENT 1, DISPUTE.

dissent *n.* nonconformity, difference, heresy; see DISAGREEMENT 1, OBJECTION, PROTEST.

dissent *v.* disagree, refuse, contradict; see DIFFER 1, OPPOSE 1.

dissenter *n.* dissident, protester, demonstrator; see NONCONFORMIST, RADICAL, REBEL.

disservice *n.* wrong, injury, outrage; see DAMAGE 1, INJUSTICE, INSULT.

dissipate *v.* 1 [To dispel] disperse, diffuse, disseminate; see SCATTER 2. 2 [To squander] use up, consume, misuse; see SPEND, WASTE 2.

dissipated *a.* 1 [Scattered] dispersed, strewn, disseminated; see SCATTERED. 2 [Wasted] squandered, spent, consumed; see EMPTY, WASTED.

dissipation *n.* 1 [Dispersion] scattering, dispersal, spread; see DISTRIBUTION. 2 [Debauchery] indulgence, intemperance, dissolution; see EVIL 1.

dissolve *v.* liquefy, melt, thaw, soften, run, defrost, waste away, cause to become liquid; see also EVAPORATE, MELT 1.—*Ant.* HARDEN, freeze, solidify.

distance *n.* 1 [A degree or quantity of space] reach, span, range; see EXPANSE, EXTENT, LENGTH 1, 2. 2 [A place or places far away] background, horizon, as far as the eye can see, sky, heavens, outskirts, foreign countries, different worlds, strange places, distant terrain, outer space, far-off lands, the ends of the earth, the country, beyond the horizon.—*Ant.* NEIGHBORHOOD, surroundings, neighbors. 3 [A measure of space] statute mile, mile, inch, rod, yard, foot, kilometer, meter, centimeter, millimeter, league, fathom, span, hand, cubit, furlong, a stone's throw. **—go the distance** finish, bring to an end, see something through; see COMPLETE. **—keep at a distance** ignore, reject, shun; see AVOID. **—keep one's distance** be aloof, ignore, shun; see AVOID.

distant *a.* afar, far off, abroad, faraway, yonder, removed, abstracted, inaccessible, unapproachable, out-of-the-way, at arm's length, stretching to, out of range, out of reach, out of earshot, out of sight, in the background, in the distance, separate, far, farther, further, far away, at a distance; see also SEPARATED.—*Ant.* CLOSE, near, next.

distaste *n.* aversion, dislike, abhorrence; see HATRED.

distasteful *a.* disagreeable, repugnant, undesirable; see OFFENSIVE 2.

distend *v.* enlarge, widen, inflate; see DISTORT 2, INCREASE, STRETCH 1, 2.

distended *a.* swollen, tumescent, bloated; see ENLARGED, INFLATED.

distill *v.* vaporize and condense, steam, precipitate; see CONCENTRATE 1, EVAPORATE.

distinct *a.* 1 [Having sharp outlines] lucid, plain, obvious; see CLEAR 2, DEFINITE 2. 2 [Not connected with another] discrete, separate, disunited; see SEPARATED. 3 [Clearly heard] clear, sharp, enunciated; see AUDIBLE.

distinction *n.* 1 [The act or quality of noticing differences] separation, differentiation, refinement; see DEFINITION. 2 [That which makes a thing distinct] distinctive feature, particular, qualification; see CHARACTERISTIC, DETAIL. 3 [A mark of personal achievement] repute, renown, prominence; see FAME.

distinctive *a.* peculiar, unique, distinguishing; see CHARACTERISTIC.

distinctly *a.* precisely, sharply, plainly; see CLEARLY 1, 2, SURELY.

distinguish *v.* 1 [To make distinctions] discriminate, differentiate, classify, specify, identify, individualize, characterize, separate, divide, collate, sort out, sort into, set apart, mark off, select, draw the line, tell from, pick and choose, separate the wheat from the chaff, separate the sheep from the goats; see also DEFINE 2. 2 [To discern] detect, discriminate, notice; see DISCOVER, SEE 1. 3 [To bestow honor upon] pay tribute to, honor, celebrate; see ACKNOWLEDGE 2, ADMIRE, PRAISE 1.

distinguishable *a.* separable, perceptible, discernible; see AUDIBLE, OBVIOUS, TANGIBLE.

distinguished *a.* 1 [Made recognizable by markings] characterized, labeled, marked, stamped, signed, signified, identified, made certain, obvious, set apart, branded, earmarked, separate, unique, differentiated, observed, distinct, conspicuous; see also SEPARATED.—*Ant.* TYPICAL, unidentified, indistinct. 2 [Notable for excellence] eminent, illustrious, venerable, renowned, honored, memorable, celebrated, well-known, noted, noteworthy, highly regarded, well-thought-of, esteemed, prominent, reputable, superior, outstanding, brilliant, glorious, extraordinary, singular, great, special, striking, unforgettable, shining, foremost, dignified, famed, talked of, first-rate, big-name*, headline*; see also FAMOUS.—*Ant.* OBSCURE, insignificant, unimportant.

distort *v.* **1** [To alter the meaning] pervert, misinterpret, misconstrue; see DECEIVE. **2** [To change shape] contort, sag, twist, slump, knot, get out of shape, buckle, writhe, melt, warp, deform, collapse; see also CHANGE 2.

distortion *n.* **1** [Deformity] twist, malformation, mutilation; see CONTORTION. **2** [Misrepresentation] perversion, misinterpretation, misuse; see LIE.

distract *v.* divert, sidetrack, occupy, amuse, entertain, draw away, call away, draw someone's attention from, lead astray, attract from; see also MISLEAD.

distracted *a.* preoccupied, inattentive, unable to concentrate; see ABSENT-MINDED.

distraction *n.* **1** [Confusion] perplexity, abstraction, complication; see CONFUSION. **2** [Diversion] amusement, pastime, preoccupation; see ENTERTAINMENT, GAME 1.

distress *n.* worry, anxiety, misery, sorrow, wretchedness, pain, dejection, irritation, suffering, ache, heartache, ordeal, desolation, anguish, affliction, woe, torment, shame, embarrassment, disappointment, tribulation, pang; see also GRIEF, TROUBLE 1.—*Ant.* JOY, happiness, jollity.

distress *v.* irritate, disturb, upset; see BOTHER 1, 2.

distribute *v.* dispense, divide, share, deal, bestow, issue, dispose, disperse, disburse, mete out, pass out, parcel out, dole out, hand out, give away, assign, allocate, ration, appropriate, pay dividends, dish out, divvy up*; see also GIVE 1.—*Ant.* HOLD, keep, preserve.

distributed *a.* delivered, scattered, shared, dealt, divided, apportioned, assigned, awarded, sown, dispensed, dispersed, appropriated, budgeted, disbursed, disseminated, returned, rationed, given away, handed out, parceled out, spread.

distribution *n.* dispersal, allotment, partitioning, partition, dividing up, deal, circulation, disposal, apportioning, prorating, arrangement, scattering, dissemination, sorting, spreading, parceling out, handing out, peddling, assorting, occurrence, frequency, ordering, pattern, combination, relationship, appearance, configuration, scarcity, number, plenty, saturation, population, demographics, spread, concentration; see also DIVISION 1, 2, ORDER 3.—*Ant.* COLLECTION, retention, storage.

distributor *n.* wholesaler, jobber, merchant; see BUSINESSMAN.

district *a.* community, provincial, territorial; see LOCAL 1.

district *n.* neighborhood, community, vicinity; see AREA.

distrust *v.* mistrust, suspect, disbelieve; see DOUBT.

distrustful *a.* distrusting, doubting, fearful; see SUSPICIOUS 1.

disturb *v.* trouble, worry, agitate, perplex, rattle, startle, shake, amaze, astound, alarm, excite, arouse, badger, plague, fuss, perturb, vex, upset, outrage, molest, grieve, depress, distress, irk, ail, tire, provoke, afflict, irritate, pain, make uneasy, harass, exasperate, pique, gall, displease, complicate, involve, astonish, fluster, ruffle, burn up*; see also BOTHER 2, CONFUSE.—*Ant.* QUIET, calm, soothe.

disturbance *n.* **1** [Interpersonal disruption] quarrel, brawl, fisticuffs; see FIGHT 1. **2** [Physical disruption] turmoil, rampage, tumult, clamor, violence, restlessness, uproar, riot, disruption, agitation, turbulence, change, bother, stir, racket, ferment, spasm, convulsion, tremor, shock, explosion, eruption, earthquake, flood, shock wave, storm, whirl; see also TROUBLE. **3** [A political or social uprising] revolt, insurrection, riot; see REVOLUTION 2.

disturbed *a.* **1** [Disturbed physically] upset, disorganized, confused; see DISORDERED. **2** [Disturbed mentally] agitated, disquieted, upset; see TROUBLED.

disturbing *a.* disquieting, upsetting, tiresome, perturbing, bothersome, unpleasant, provoking, annoying, alarming, painful, discomforting, inauspicious, foreboding, aggravating, disagreeable, troublesome, worrisome, burdensome, trying, distressing, perplexing, frightening, startling, threatening, galling, difficult, severe, hard, inconvenient, discouraging, pessimistic, gloomy, depressing, irritating, harassing, unpropitious, dismaying, troubling, irksome, sinister, embarrassing, ruffling, agitating; see also OMINOUS.

disunite *v.* dissociate, disjoin, separate; see DIVIDE.

ditch *n.* canal, moat, furrow; see CHANNEL, TRENCH.

ditch* *v.* desert, forsake, leave; see ABANDON 2, DISCARD.

dive *n.* **1** [A sudden motion downward] plunge, leap, spring, nose dive, headlong leap, pitch, ducking, swim, swoop, dip; see also FALL 1, JUMP 1. **2** [*A cheap saloon, etc.*] saloon, tavern, dump*; see BAR 2, RESTAURANT.

dive *v.* plunge, spring, jump, vault,

leap, go headfirst, plummet, sink, dip, duck, dabble, submerge, nose-dive; see also FALL 1, JUMP 1.

diver *n.* high diver, fancy diver, submarine diver, deep-sea diver, aquanaut, pearl diver, skin diver, scuba diver, swimmer, frogman; see also ATHLETE.

diverge *v.* radiate, veer, swerve; see DEVIATE.

diverse *a.* different, assorted, distinct; see VARIOUS.

diversify *v.* vary, expand, alter; see CHANGE 2, INCREASE.

diversion *n.* 1 [The act of changing a course] detour, alteration, deviation; see CHANGE 1. 2 [Entertainment] amusement, recreation, pastime; see ENTERTAINMENT, SPORT 1.

divert *v.* 1 [To deflect] turn aside, redirect, avert; see TURN 3. 2 [To distract] attract the attention of, lead away from, disturb; see DISTRACT.

diverted *a.* deflected, turned aside, redirected, perverted, averted, turned into other channels, rechanneled, taken away, made use of, taken over; see also CHANGED 2.—*Ant.* UNTOUCHED, undiverted, left.

divide *v.* part, cut up, fence off, detach, disengage, dissolve, sever, rupture, dismember, sunder, split, unravel, carve, cleave, intersect, cross, bisect, rend, tear, segment, halve, quarter, break down, divorce, dissociate, isolate, count off, pull away, chop, slash, gash, carve, splinter, pull to pieces, tear apart, break apart, segregate, fork, branch, tear limb from limb*, split off, split up; see also BREAK 1, CUT 1, SEPARATE 1.—*Ant.* UNITE, combine, connect.

dividend *n.* pay, check, coupon, proceeds, returns, quarterly dividend, annual dividend, share, allotment, appropriation, remittance, allowance, cut*, rakeoff*; see also PROFIT 2.

divine *a.* sacred, hallowed, spiritual, sacramental, ceremonial, ritualistic, consecrated, dedicated, devoted, venerable, pious, religious, sanctified, anointed, ordained, sanctioned, set apart, sacrosanct, scriptural, blessed, worshiped, revered, venerated, mystical, adored, solemn, faithful; see also HOLY.

divine *v.* predict, prophesy, prognosticate; see FORETELL.

divinity *n.* deity, godhead, higher power; see GOD, GOD.

divisible *a.* separable, distinguishable, distinct, divided, fractional, fragmentary, detachable; see also SEPARATED.—*Ant.* INSEPARABLE, indivisible, fast.

division *n.* 1 [The act or result of

dividing] separation, detachment, apportionment, partition, parting, distribution, severance, cutting, subdivision, dismemberment, distinction, distinguishing, selection, reduction, splitting, breakdown, fracture, disjuncture.—*Ant.* UNION, joining, gluing. 2 [A part produced by dividing] section, kind, sort, portion, compartment, share, split, member, subdivision, parcel, segment, fragment, department, category, branch, fraction, cross-section, dividend, degree, piece, slice, lump, wedge, cut, book, chapter, verse, class, race, clan, tribe, caste; see also PART 1. 3 [Discord or disunion] trouble, dissension, schism; see DISAGREEMENT 1, DISPUTE. 4 [A military unit] armored division, airborne division, infantry division; see ARMY 2. 5 [An organized area] state, district, province; see NATION.

divorce *n.* separation, partition, divorcement, bill of divorcement, annulment, separate maintenance, parting of the ways, dissolution, split-up.—*Ant.* MARRIAGE, betrothal, wedding.

divorce *v.* separate, annul, nullify, put away, split up; see also CANCEL.

divorced *a.* dissolved, parted, disunited, divided, split, washed-up*; see also SEPARATED.—*Ant.* MARRIED, joined, mated.

divulge *v.* disclose, impart, confess; see ADMIT 2, EXPOSE 1.

dizzy *a.* confused, lightheaded, giddy, bemused, staggering, upset, dazzled, dazed, dumb, faint, with spots before one's eyes, out of control, weak-kneed, wobbly; see also UNSTABLE 1.

DNA *n.* genetic alphabet, double helix, chromosome, gene, hereditary information, deoxyribonucleic acid, nucleic acids, genetic code.

do *v.* 1 [To discharge one's responsibilities] effect, execute, act, finish, complete, work, labor, produce, create, effect, accomplish; see also ACHIEVE, PERFORM 1, SUCCEED 1. 2 [To execute commands or instructions] carry out, complete, fulfill; see OBEY. 3 [To suffice] serve, be sufficient, give satisfaction; see SATISFY 3. 4 [To solve] figure out, work out, decipher, decode; see also SOLVE. 5 [To present a play, etc.] give, put on, produce; see PERFORM 2. 6 [To act] perform, portray, take on the role of; see ACT 3. 7 [To conduct oneself] behave oneself, comport oneself, acquit oneself, seem, appear; see also BEHAVE. **—do in*** eliminate, slay, murder; see DESTROY, KILL 1. **—do without** dispense with, get along without, forgo; see ENDURE 1, 2, NEED. **—have to do with** be related to, be connected with, bear on; see CONCERN 1. —**make do** get by, get along, manage, survive; see also ENDURE 2.

docile *a.* meek, mild, tractable, pliant, submissive, accommodating, adaptable, resigned, agreeable, willing, obliging, well-behaved, manageable, tame, yielding, teachable, easily influenced, easygoing, usable, soft, childlike; see also GENTLE 3, HUMBLE 1, OBEDIENT 1.

docility *n.* obedience, gentleness, adaptability; see HUMILITY, SHYNESS.

dock *n.* pier, wharf, lock, boat landing, marina, dry dock, embarcadero, waterfront.

dock *v.* lessen, withhold, deduct; see DECREASE 2.

doctor *n.* Doctor of Medicine, MD, physician, general practitioner, GP, surgeon, consultant, specialist, intern, house physician, resident, veterinarian, chiropractor, homeopath, osteopath, acupuncturist, faith healer, witch doctor, shaman, medicine man, quack, doc*, sawbones*. *Types of doctors include the following:* heart specialist; ear, nose, and throat specialist; inhalation therapist, anesthetist, dentist, pediatrician, gynecologist, oculist, obstetrician, psychiatrist, psychoanalyst, orthopedist, neurologist, cardiologist, pathologist, dermatologist, endocrinologist, ophthalmologist, urologist, hematologist; see also MEDICINE 3.

doctor* *v.* tamper with, change, adulterate; see ALTER 1.

doctrine *n.* principle, proposition, precept, article, concept, conviction, opinion, convention, attitude, tradition, unwritten law, natural law, common law, teachings, accepted belief, article of faith, canon, regulation, rule, pronouncement, declaration; see also LAW 2, 4.

document *n.* paper, diary, report; see RECORD 1.

dodge *n.* trick, strategy, scheme; see METHOD, PLAN 1.

dodge *v.* duck, elude, evade; see AVOID.

doer *n.* actor, performer, activist; see MEANS 1.

dog *n.* hound, bitch, puppy, pup, mongrel, stray, canine, cur, guide dog, watchdog, pooch*, mutt*. *Types and breeds of dogs include the following:* hunting dog, racing dog, boxer, shepherd, bloodhound, wolfhound, greyhound, whippet, Saint Bernard, Great Dane, German shepherd, Doberman pinscher, bulldog, Afghan, Irish wolfhound, Labrador retriever, Rottweiler, malamute, husky, collie, Old English sheep dog, Irish setter, pointer, spaniel, cocker spaniel, basset, beagle, dachshund, Dalmatian, poodle, French poodle, Pekingese, Pomeranian, Chihuahua, Airedale, schnauzer, fox terrier, wirehaired terrier, Scottie, Scottish terrier, bull terrier, Boston terrier. —**a dog's life** wretched existence, bad luck, trouble; see POVERTY 1. —**go to the dogs*** deteriorate, degenerate, weaken; see WEAKEN 1, 2. —**let sleeping dogs lie** ignore, leave well enough alone, pass over; see NEGLECT 1. —**put on the dog*** show off, entertain lavishly, put on airs; see DISPLAY. —**teach an old dog new tricks** influence, convince, change; see PERSUADE.

dogged *a.* stubborn, tenacious, firm; see STUBBORN.

dogmatic *a.* 1 [Based on an assumption of absolute truth] authoritarian, on faith, by nature; see ABSOLUTE 1. 2 [Acting as though possessed of absolute truth] dictatorial, stubborn, egotistical, bigoted, fanatical, intolerant, opinionated, overbearing, magisterial, arrogant, domineering, tyrannical, obstinate, confident, sure, downright, arbitrary, unequivocal, definite, formal, stubborn, determined, emphatic, narrow-minded, one-sided, hidebound, high and mighty*, pigheaded, bullheaded, stubborn as a mule*; see also ABSOLUTE 2.—*Ant.* LIBERAL, tolerant, dubious.

doing *n.* performing, accomplishing, achieving; see PERFORMANCE.

doings *n.* activities, conduct, dealings; see ACTION 1.

dole out *v.* share, assign, parcel out; see DISTRIBUTE.

doll *n.* manikin, model, dolly, rag doll, paper doll, kewpie doll, Barbie (trademark); see also TOY 1.

dollar *n.* coin, legal tender, dollar bill, silver dollar, currency, bank note, greenback, folding money*, buck*; see also MONEY 1.

dollop *n.* blob, touch, dab; see DASH 3, BIT 1.

doll up *v.* fix up, put on one's best clothes, primp; see DRESS 1.

dolt *n.* simpleton, nitwit, blockhead; see FOOL.

domain *n.* dominion, field, specialty; see AREA.

dome *n.* ceiling, top, vault; see ROOF.

domestic *a.* 1 [Home-loving] house-loving, domesticated, stay-at-home, settled, household, family, quiet, private, sedentary, indoor; see also CALM 1, 2, TRANQUIL.—*Ant.* UNRULY, roving, restless. 2 [Homegrown] indigenous, handcrafted, native; see HOMEMADE.

domesticate *v.* tame, breed, housebreak; see TEACH, TRAIN 2.

domesticated *a.* tamed, trained, housebroken; see TAME 1.

dominant *a.* commanding, authoritative, assertive; see AGGRESSIVE, POWERFUL 1.

dominate *v.* rule, manage, control, dictate to, subject, subjugate, tyrannize, have one's own way, have influence over, domineer, bully, walk all over*, boss*, keep under one's thumb; see GOVERN.

domination *n.* rule, control, mastery; see COMMAND, POWER 2.

domineering *a.* despotic, imperious, oppressive; see EGOTISTIC.

dominion *n.* region, district, state; see AREA, NATION 1.

donate *v.* grant, bestow, bequeath; see DISTRIBUTE, GIVE 1, PROVIDE 1.

donation *n.* contribution, offering, present; see GIFT 1.

done *a.* **1** [Accomplished] over, through, completed, realized, effected, actualized, executed, performed, fulfilled, brought to pass, brought about, perfected; see also FINISHED 1.—*Ant.* UNFINISHED, unrealized, failed. **2** [Cooked] brewed, stewed, broiled, boiled, crisped, crusted, fried, browned, roasted, grilled; see also BAKED.—*Ant.* RAW, fresh, uncooked. —**done for*** defeated, conquered, vanquished; see BEATEN 1.

Don Juan *n.* Lothario, womanizer, Romeo, libertine, philanderer, rake, seducer, lecher, wolf*.

donkey *n.* burro, mule, jackass; see HORSE.

donor *n.* benefactor, contributor, patron, humanitarian, philanthropist, giver, subscriber, altruist, good Samaritan, fairy godmother*, angel*, sugar daddy*; see also PATRON.

doom *n.* fate, lot, destiny, downfall, future, fortune, ruin, goal.

doomed *a.* ruined, cursed, sentenced, lost, condemned, unfortunate, ill-fated, foreordained, predestined, threatened, menaced, suppressed, wrecked; see also DESTROYED, FATED.

door *n.* entry, portal, hatchway, doorway, gateway, opening; see also ENTRANCE 2, GATE. —**out of doors** outside, in the air, out; see OUTDOORS. —**show someone the door** show out, ask to leave, dismiss; see OUST.

dope *n.* **1** [*A drug] narcotic, stimulant, opiate; see DRUG. **2** [*Pertinent information] details, account, developments; see INFORMATION 1, KNOWLEDGE 1, NEWS 1. **3** [*A dullwitted person] dunce, dolt, simpleton; see FOOL.

dope *v.* anesthetize, drug, put to sleep; see DEADEN.

dormitory *n.* barracks, residence hall, dorm*; see HOTEL.

dose *n.* prescription, dosage, treatment, spoonful, portion; see also QUANTITY, SHARE.

dot *n.* point, spot, speck; see MARK 1. —**on the dot*** precisely, accurately, punctually; see PUNCTUAL.

dote *v.* adore, pet, admire; see LOVE 1.

double *a.* twofold, two times, paired, coupled, binary, doubled, redoubled, duplex, renewed, dual, both one and the other, repeated, second, increased, as much again, duplicated; see also TWICE, TWIN.—*Ant.* ALONE, single, apart. —**on the double*** hastily, rapidly, hurriedly; see QUICKLY.

double *v.* **1** [To make or become double] make twice as much, duplicate, multiply; see GROW 1, INCREASE. **2** [To replace] substitute, stand in, fill in; see SUBSTITUTE. —**double back** backtrack, reverse, circle; see RETURN 1, TURN 2, 6. —**double up** combine, join, share; see JOIN 1, 2, UNITE.

double-cross *v.* cheat, defraud, trick; see DECEIVE.

double-dealing *n.* deceit, cheating, trickery; see DISHONESTY, HYPOCRISY.

doubly *a.* twofold, redoubled, increased; see AGAIN, DOUBLE, TWICE.

doubt *n.* distrust, mistrust, disbelief, suspicion, misgiving, skepticism, apprehension, agnosticism, incredulity, lack of faith, lack of confidence, jealousy, rejection, scruple, reservation, misgiving, indecision, lack of conviction, ambiguity, dilemma, reluctance, quandary, feeling of inferiority; see also UNCERTAINTY 1, 2.—*Ant.* BELIEF, conviction, certainty. —**beyond (or without) doubt** doubtless, certainly, without a doubt; see SURELY. —**no doubt** doubtless, in all likelihood, certainly; see PROBABLY, SURELY.

doubt *v.* wonder, question, query, ponder, dispute, be dubious, be uncertain, be doubtful, refuse to believe, demur, have doubts about, have one's doubts, stop to consider, have qualms, call in question, give no credit to, throw doubt upon, have no conception, not know which way to turn, not know what to make of, close one's mind, not admit, not believe, refuse to believe, not buy*, smell a rat, put no stock in; see also ASK, DENY, QUESTION 1.—*Ant.* TRUST, believe, confide.

doubter *n.* questioner, unbeliever, agnostic; see CYNIC.

doubtful *a.* **1** [Uncertain in mind] dubious, doubting, questioning, undecided, unsure, wavering, hesitant, undetermined, uncertain, unsettled, confused, disturbed, lost, puzzled, perplexed, flustered, baffled, distracted, unresolved, in a quandary, of two minds, unable to make up one's mind, troubled with doubt, having little faith, of little faith, in question, not knowing what's what, not following, up a tree*, not able to make head or tail of, going around in circles*, out of focus, up in the air, wishy-washy*, iffy*; see also SUSPICIOUS 1. **2** [Improbable] probably wrong, questionable, unconvincing; see OBSCURE 1, UNCERTAIN.

doubtless *a.* positively, certainly, unquestionably; see SURELY.

dough *n.* **1** [A soft mixture] paste, pulp, mash; see BATTER 2, MIXTURE 1. **2** [*Money] dollars, change, silver; see MONEY 1, WEALTH.

doughnut *n.* friedcake, cruller, sinker*; see CAKE 2, PASTRY.

douse *v.* submerge, splash, drench; see IMMERSE, SOAK 1.

dove *n.* peacemaker, activist, pacifier; see PACIFIST.

dowdy *a.* untidy, slovenly, frumpy; see SHABBY.

down *a., prep.* forward, headlong, bottomward, downhill, on a downward course, from higher to lower, to the bottom, to a lower position, declining, falling, descending, gravitating, slipping, sliding, sagging, slumping, dropping, sinking, earthward, groundward, downward; see also BACKWARD 1.—*Ant.* UP, upward, rising. —**down and out** ruined, defeated, finished; see BEATEN. —**down on*** against, disillusioned about, furious with; see OPPOSED.

down *n.* feathers, fluff, fur; see HAIR 1.

down *v.* put down, throw down, knock down, conquer, topple, fell, subdue, tackle, trip, overthrow, overpower, upset, overturn; see also DEFEAT 3, HIT 1.—*Ant.* RAISE, lift, elevate.

downcast *a.* discouraged, dejected, unhappy; see SAD 1.

downfall *n.* defeat, comedown, ruin; see DESTRUCTION 2.

downgrade *v.* minimize, deprecate, lower; see DECREASE 2.

downhearted *a.* dejected, downcast, despondent; see SAD 1.

downpour *n.* rain, deluge, flood, monsoon; see also STORM.

downright *a.* total, complete, utter; see ABSOLUTE 1, WHOLE 1.

downstairs *a.* down below, below decks, on the floor below; see BELOW 4, UNDER 1.

downstairs *n.* first floor, ground floor, cellar; see BASEMENT.

down-to-earth *a.* sensible, mundane, practicable; see COMMON 1, PRACTICAL, RATIONAL 1.

downtown *a.* city, central, inner-city, main, midtown, in the business district, on the main street, metropolitan, business; see also URBAN.—*Ant.* RURAL, suburban, residential.

downtown *n.* hub, crossroads, business district; see CENTER 2, CITY.

downtrodden *a.* tyrannized, subjugated, mistreated; see OPPRESSED.

downward *a.* earthward, descending, downwards; see DOWN.

downy *a.* woolly, fuzzy, fluffy; see LIGHT 5, SOFT 2.

doze *v.* nap, drowse, slumber; see SLEEP.

dozen *a.* twelve, baker's dozen, long dozen, handful, pocketful.

drab *a.* **1** [Dismal] dingy, colorless, dreary; see DULL 2, 4. **2** [Dun-colored] yellowish-brown, dull brown, dull gray; see BROWN, GRAY.

draft *n.* **1** [A preliminary sketch] plans, blueprint, sketch; see DESIGN. **2** [A breeze] current of air, gust, puff; see WIND. **3** [An order for payment] cashier's check, bank draft, money order; see CHECK 1. **4** [The selection of troops] conscription, induction, recruiting; see SELECTION 1.

draft *v.* **1** [Make a rough plan] outline, delineate, sketch; see PLAN 1, 2. **2** [Select for military service] select, conscript, choose; see RECRUIT 1.

draftsman *n.* sketcher, designer, drawer; see ARCHITECT, ARTIST.

drag *n.* **1** [A restraint] hindrance, burden, impediment; see BARRIER. **2** [*An annoying person, thing, or situation] bother, annoyance, bore; see NUISANCE 3.

drag *v.* **1** [To go slowly; *said of animate beings*] lag, straggle, dawdle; see LOITER, PAUSE. **2** [To go slowly; *said of an activity*] creep, crawl, be prolonged tediously, pass slowly; see also DELAY.—*Ant.* IMPROVE, progress, pick up. **3** [To pull an object] haul, move, transport; see DRAW 1. —**drag on** go on slowly, keep going, persist; see CONTINUE 1, ENDURE 1.

dragon *n.* mythical beast, serpent, hydra; see MONSTER 1, SNAKE.

drain *n.* duct, channel, sewer; see CHANNEL, PIPE 1. —**down the drain** wasted, ruined, gone; see LOST 1.

drain *v.* **1** [To withdraw fluid] tap, draw off, remove; see EMPTY 2. **2** [To withdraw strength] exhaust, weary, tire out; see SPEND, WEAKEN 2. **3** [To seep away] run off, run out, flow away, seep out, exude, trickle out, filter off, ooze, find an opening, percolate, diminish, leave dry; see also FLOW.

drama *n.* play, theatrical piece, theatrical production, dramatization, stage show, skit, sketch, theatre. *Types of drama include the following:* melodrama, tragicomedy, comedy of manners, burlesque, pantomime, mime, grand opera, operetta, light opera, musical comedy, musical, mystery, murder mystery, farce, classical drama, historical drama, theatre of the absurd, epic, pageant, miracle play, revival; see also ACTING, COMEDY, PERFORMANCE.

dramatic *a.* tense, climactic, moving; see EXCITING.

dramatist *n.* playwright, scriptwriter, scenario writer, screenwriter; see also AUTHOR, WRITER. *Major dramatists include the following—Great Britain:* Christopher Marlowe, Ben Jonson, William Shakespeare, William Congreve, Oscar Wilde, George Bernard Shaw, John Millington Synge, Sean O'Casey, Harold Pinter; *United States:* Eugene O'Neill, Thornton Wilder, Tennessee Williams, Arthur Miller, Edward Albee; *Greece:* Aeschylus, Sophocles, Euripides, Aristophanes; *France:* Moliere, Pierre Corneille, Jean Racine, Jean Anouilh, Eugene Ionesco, Jean Genet, Jean Cocteau; *Germany:* Wolfgang von Goethe, Friedrich Schiller, Bertolt Brecht; *other:* Anton Chekov, Henrik Ibsen, August Strindberg, Karel Capek, Luigi Pirandello.

dramatize *v.* enact, produce, execute; see PERFORM 2.

drape *v.* clothe, wrap, model; see DRESS.

drapes *n.* window covering, drapery, hanging; see CURTAIN.

drastic *a.* extravagant, exorbitant, radical; see EXTREME.

draw *v.* 1 [To move an object] pull, drag, attract, move, bring, tug, lug, tow, carry, jerk, wrench, yank, haul, extract.—*Ant.* REPEL, repulse, reject. 2 [To make a likeness by drawing] sketch, describe, etch, pencil, outline, trace, make a picture of, depict, model, portray, engrave, chart, map; see also PAINT 1. —**beat to the draw** be quicker than another, forestall, stop; see ANTICIPATE, PREVENT. —**draw away** pull away from, gain on, increase a lead; see ADVANCE 1, DEFEAT 1, LEAVE 1. —**draw back** withdraw, recede, draw in; see RETREAT. —**draw on** take from, extract from, employ; see USE 1. —**draw out** 1 [To induce to talk] make talk, lead on, interrogate; see INTERVIEW. 2 [To pull] drag, tug, attract; see DRAW 1. 3 [To extend] prolong, stretch, lengthen;

see INCREASE. —**draw up** draft, execute, prepare; see WRITE 1.

drawback *n.* detriment, hindrance, check; see LACK 1.

drawing *n.* sketching, designing, illustrating, tracing, etching, design, illustration, rendering, graphic art; see also PICTURE 3, REPRESENTATION.

dread *n.* awe, horror, terror; see FEAR.

dreadful *a.* hideous, fearful, shameful; see FRIGHTFUL 1.

dream *n.* nightmare, apparition, hallucination, image, trance, idea, impression, emotion, reverie, daydream, castle in the air, mirage, chimera, pipe dream*; see also FANTASY, ILLUSION, THOUGHT 2, VISION 3, 4.—*Ant.* REALITY, actuality, truth.

dream *v.* 1 [To have visions, usually during sleep or fever] hallucinate, fancy, visualize; see IMAGINE. 2 [To entertain or delude oneself with imagined things] fancy, imagine, conceive, have notions, conjure up, create, picture, idealize, daydream, fantasize, be in the clouds, pipe dream*; see also INVENT 1. —**dream up** devise, contrive, concoct; see IMAGINE.

dreamer *n.* visionary, idealist, romantic; see RADICAL.

dreaming *a.* thinking, daydreaming, musing; see THOUGHTFUL 1.

dreamy *a.* whimsical, fanciful, daydreaming, visionary, given to reverie, illusory, introspective, otherworldly, idealistic, mythical, utopian, romantic, starry-eyed; see also IMAGINARY, IMPRACTICAL.—*Ant.* PRACTICAL, ACTIVE, REAL.

dreary *a.* damp, raw, windy; see COLD 1, DISMAL.

dregs *n.* scum, grounds, remains; see RESIDUE.

drench *v.* wet, saturate, flood; see IMMERSE, SOAK 1.

dress *n.* 1 [Clothing] ensemble, attire, garments, outfit, garb, apparel, array, costume, wardrobe, uniform, habit, formal dress, evening clothes, trappings, things, getup*, threads*, rags*, duds*; see also CLOTHES, COAT 1, PANTS 1, SHIRT, SUIT 3, UNDERWEAR. 2 [A woman's outer garment] frock, gown, wedding dress, evening gown, formal, cocktail dress, suit, skirt, robe, shift, sundress, shirtdress, housedress, smock; see also CLOTHES.

dress *v.* 1 [To put on clothes] don, wear, garb, clothe, robe, attire, drape, array, cover, spruce up, dress up, bundle up, get into*, doll up*, dress to the nines*, slip into, dress down; see also WEAR 1. 2 [To provide with clothes] costume, outfit, clothe; see SUPPORT 3. **3** [To give medical treatment] treat, bandage, give first aid; see HEAL. —**dressed up** dressed formally, dressed to kill*, dolled up*; see FANCY, FASHIONABLE, ORNATE. —**dress up** spiff up*, spruce up, put on the dog*; see DRESS 1.

dresser *n.* dressing table, chest of drawers, bureau; see FURNITURE, TABLE 1.

dressing *n.* **1** [A food mixture] stuffing, filling, forcemeat. *Dressings include the following:* bread, giblet, oyster, chestnut, potato, prune, plum, apple, duck, turkey, chicken, fish, clam, wild rice, sage. **2** [A flavoring sauce] *Salad dressings include the following:* ranch, French, Russian, Thousand Island, blue cheese, Roquefort (trademark), Italian, Caesar, oil and vinegar; see also SAUCE. **3** [An external medical application] bandage, plaster cast, adhesive tape, Band-Aid (trademark), compress, gauze, tourniquet, pack; see also CAST 4.

dressmaker *n.* seamstress, garment worker, designer; see TAILOR.

dressy *a.* dressed up, elegant, elaborate; see FANCY, FASHIONABLE, ORNATE.

dribble *v.* trickle, spout, squirt; see DROP 1.

dried *a.* drained, dehydrated, desiccated; see DRY 1, PRESERVED 2.

drift *n.* **1** [The tendency in movement] bent, trend, tendency, end, inclination, impulse, propulsion, aim, scope, goal, push, bias, set, impetus, leaning, progress, disposition, bearing, line; see also DIRECTION 1, WAY 2. **2** [The measure or character of movement] current, deviation, flux; see FLOW.

drift *v.* float, ride, sail, wander, stray, sweep, move with the current, gravitate, tend, be carried along by the current, move toward, go with the tide, be caught in the current, move without effort, move slowly; see also FLOW, MOVE 1.—*Ant.* LEAD, steer, guide.

drill *n.* **1** [Practice] preparation, repetition, learning by doing; see PRACTICE 3. **2** [A tool for boring holes] borer, pneumatic drill, electric drill, steam drill, diamond drill, compressed-air drill, drill press, auger, corkscrew, awl, riveter, jackhammer; see also TOOL 1. **3** [Exercise, especially in military formation] training, maneuvers, marching, close-order drill, open-order drill, conditioning, survival training, guerrilla training; see also PARADE 1. **4** [Device for planting seed in holes] planter, seeder, dibble; see TOOL 1.

drill *v.* **1** [To bore] pierce, sink in, puncture; see DIG 1, PENETRATE. **2** [To train] practice, rehearse, discipline; see TEACH.

drink *n.* **1** [A draft] gulp, sip, potion, drop, bottle, glass, refreshment, shot, stiff one*, slug*, belt*, nip, swig*, spot*, nightcap*, hair of the dog*, one for the road*. **2** [Something drunk] champagne, rye, bourbon, Scotch, Irish whiskey, ale, stout, rum, liqueur, tequila, vodka, wine cooler, distilled water, mineral water, carbonated water, mixer, tonic, seltzer, iced tea, cocoa, hot chocolate, chocolate milk, milkshake, cola, float, frappé, lemonade, punch, soft drink, soda water, pop, soda, soda pop, ginger ale, ice-cream soda; orange juice, tomato juice, grapefruit juice, etc.; see also BEER, COFFEE, MILK, WATER 1, WHISKEY, WINE.

drink *v.* **1** [To swallow liquid] gulp down, take in, sip, down, guzzle, imbibe, wash down, slurp; see also SWALLOW. **2** [To consume alcoholic liquor] tipple, swill, swig, guzzle, belt*, carouse, take a nip, wet one's whistle*, booze*, hit the bottle*, go on a binge*.

drinker *n.* tippler, alcoholic, lush*; see DRUNKARD.

drip *v.* dribble, trickle, plop; see DROP 1.

drive *n.* **1** [A ride in a vehicle] ride, trip, outing, expedition, tour, excursion, jaunt, spin, Sunday drive*; see also JOURNEY. **2** [A road] approach, avenue, boulevard, entrance, street, roadway, parkway, lane, track, path, pavement; see also ROAD 1. **3** [Impelling force] energy, effort, impulse; see FORCE 2.

drive *v.* **1** [To urge on] impel, propel, instigate, incite, animate, hasten, egg on, urge on, compel, coerce, induce, force, press, stimulate, hurry, provoke, arouse, make, put up to*, motivate, inspire, prompt, rouse, work on, act upon; see also sense 2 and ENCOURAGE, PUSH 2.— *Ant.* STOP, hinder, drag. **2** [To manage a propelled vehicle] direct, operate, steer, handle, run, wheel, bicycle, bike*, cycle, transport, float, drift, dash, put in motion, start, set going, speed, roll, coast, get under way, keep going, back up, burn up the road*, go like hell*, step on it*, floor it*, gun it*, burn rubber*, give it the gas*; see also RIDE 1. —**drive a bargain** deal, close a deal, bargain; see BUY, SELL. —**drive at** allude to, indicate, signify; see MEAN 1. — **drive away** drive off, disperse, banish; see SCATTER 2.

driven *a.* blown, drifted, herded, pushed, pounded, washed, guided, steered, directed, urged on, compelled, forced, shoved, sent, hard pressed, impelled, unable to help oneself, with one's back to the wall.

driver *n.* chauffeur, motorist, licensed operator, bus driver, truck driver, cab driver, cabbie*, cabby*, trucker, designated driver.

driveway *n.* drive, entrance, approach; see DRIVE 2, ROAD 1.

drizzle *v.* spray, shower, sprinkle; see DROP 1, RAIN.

drone *n.* **1** [A continuous sound] hum, buzz, vibration; see NOISE 1. **2** [An idle person] idler, loafer, parasite; see LOAFER.

drone *v.* hum, buzz, vibrate; see SOUND.

drool *v.* drivel, slaver, slobber, drip, salivate, spit, dribble, trickle, ooze, run; see also DROP 1.

droop *v.* settle, sink, hang down; see LEAN 1.

drop *n.* **1** [Enough fluid to fall] drip, trickle, droplet, bead, teardrop, dewdrop, raindrop; see also TEAR. **2** [A lowering or falling] fall, tumble, reduction, decrease, slide, descent, slump, lapse, slip, decline, downfall, downturn, plunge, dip; see also FALL 1. **3** [A small quantity] speck, dash, dab; see BIT 1. —**at the drop of a hat** without warning, at the slightest provocation, quickly; see IMMEDIATELY.

drop *v.* **1** [To fall in drops] drip, fall, dribble, trickle, descend, leak, ooze, seep, drain, filter, sink, bleed, bead, splash, hail; see also RAIN.—*Ant.* RISE, spurt, squirt. **2** [To cause or to permit to fall] let go, give up, release, shed, relinquish, abandon, loosen, lower, floor, ground, shoot out, knock down, fell, topple; see also DUMP.—*Ant.* RAISE, elevate, send up. **3** [To discontinue] give up, quit, leave; see STOP 2. **4** [To break off an acquaintance] break with, part from, cast off; see ABANDON 1. —**drop a hint** suggest, intimate, imply; see HINT, PROPOSE 1. —**drop a line** write to, post, communicate with; see COMMUNICATE, WRITE 1. —**drop behind** slow down, worsen, decline; see FAIL 1, LOSE 3. —**drop dead*** expire, collapse, succumb; see DIE. —**drop in** call, stop, look in on; see VISIT. —**drop off 1** [*To sleep] fall asleep, doze, drowse; see SLEEP. **2** [*To deliver] leave, hand over, present; see GIVE 1. —**drop out** withdraw, cease, quit; see ABANDON 1, RETREAT.

dropout *n.* failing student, truant, quitter; see FAILURE 1.

drought *n.* dry season, hot spell, dry spell; see WEATHER.

drove *n.* flock, pack, throng; see CROWD, HERD.

drown *v.* **1** [To cover with liquid] swamp, inundate, overflow; see FLOOD. **2** [To lower into a liquid]

dip, plunge, submerge; see IMMERSE, SINK 2. **3** [To kill or die by drowning] go under, suffocate, sink; see DIE, KILL 1. —**drown out** silence, hush, muffle; see QUIET 2.

drowned *a.* suffocated, sunk, submerged; see DEAD 1, GONE 2.

drowsy *a.* sleepy, languid, tired; see LAZY 1.

drudge *n.* slave, drone, hard worker; see LABORER, WORKMAN.

drug *n.* sedative, potion, painkiller*, smelling salts, powder, tonic, opiate, pills, hard drug*, designer drug, uppers*, downers*. *Kinds of drugs include the following—general:* caffeine, alcohol, adrenalin, amphetamine, nicotine, dope*; *hallucinogens:* marijuana, pot*, grass*, weed*; peyote, mescaline, psilocybin; *D*-lysergic acid diethylamide, LSD, acid*; *stimulants:* cocaine, coke*, snow*, crack*; benzedrine, bennies*, pep pills*; dexedrine, dexies*; methedrine, meth*, speed*; Ecstasy*, poppers*; *narcotics:* opium*; morphine; heroin, H*, horse*, junk*, smack*; codeine; see also MEDICINE 2.

drug *v.* anesthetize, desensitize, dope*; see DEADEN.

drugged *a.* comatose, doped, stupefied; see UNCONSCIOUS.

druggist *n.* apothecary, chemist, registered pharmacist, licensed pharmacist, pharmacologist, proprietor, drugstore owner, merchant; see also DOCTOR.

drum *n.* snare drum, skins*, traps; see MUSICAL INSTRUMENT.

drum up *v.* attract, provide, succeed in finding; see DISCOVER, FIND.

drunk *a.* intoxicated, inebriated, befuddled, tipsy, overcome, sottish, drunken, stoned, feeling no pain*, out of it*, seeing double*, smashed*, blotto*, gassed*, plowed*, under the table*, tanked*, wiped out*, soused*, high*, pickled*, stewed*, boozed up*, tight*, plastered*, higher than a kite*; see also DIZZY.—*Ant.* SOBER, steady, temperate.

drunkard *n.* sot, inebriate, heavy drinker, tippler, alcoholic, drunken sot, drunk*, carouser, boozer*, barfly*, souse*, wino*, lush*, alky*; see also ADDICT.

drunkenness *n.* inebriety, intoxication, intemperance, insobriety, alcoholism, jag*.—*Ant.* ABSTINENCE, sobriety, temperance.

dry *a.* **1** [Having little or no moisture] arid, parched, waterless, hard, dried up, evaporated, desiccated, barren, dehydrated, drained, rainless, not irrigated, bare, thirsty, waterproof, rainproof, baked, shriveled, desert, dusty, depleted, dry as a bone*, bone-dry*; see also STERILE 2.—*Ant.* WET, moist, damp. **2** [Thirsty] parched, dehydrated, athirst*; see THIRSTY. **3** [Lacking in interest] boring, uninteresting, tedious; see DULL 4. **4** [Possessed of intellectual humor] sarcastic, cynical, biting; see FUNNY 1.

dry *v.* **1** [To become dry] dry up, shrivel, wilt; see EVAPORATE, WITHER. **2** [To cause to become dry] air-dry, condense, concentrate, dehydrate, freeze-dry, blot, sponge, parch, scorch, dry up, exhaust; see also DRAIN 1, EMPTY 2. —**dry out** (or **up**) drain, dehydrate, undergo evaporation; see DRY 1, 2.

dry goods *n.* cloth, yard goods, yardage; see COTTON, LINEN, WOOL.

dryness *n.* aridity, lack of moisture, dehydration; see THIRST.

dual *a.* binary, twofold, coupled; see DOUBLE, TWIN.

dubious *a.* **1** [Doubtful] indecisive, perplexed, hesitant; see DOUBTFUL, UNCERTAIN. **2** [Vague] ambiguous, indefinite, unclear; see OBSCURE 1.

dubiously *a.* doubtfully, doubtingly, indecisively; see SUSPICIOUSLY.

duck *n.* teal, mallard, fresh water duck, sea duck; see also BIRD. —**like water off a duck's back** ineffective, ineffectual, weak; see USELESS 1.

duck *v.* **1** [To immerse quickly] plunge, submerge, drop; see DIP 1, IMMERSE. **2** [*To avoid] dodge, escape, elude; see AVOID, EVADE.

duct *n.* tube, canal, channel; see PIPE 1.

dud* *n.* failure, flop, debacle; see FAILURE 1.

duds* *n.* garb, garments, clothing; see CLOTHES.

due *a.* payable, owed, owing, overdue, collectible, unsatisfied, unsettled, not met, receivable, to be paid, chargeable, outstanding, in arrears; see also UNPAID 1, 2. —**become** (or **fall**) **due** be owed, payable, remain unsatisfied, mature. —**due to** because of, resulting from, accordingly; see BECAUSE.

duel *n.* combat, engagement, contest; see FIGHT 1.

dues *n.* contribution, obligation, toll, duty, levy, collection, fee, assessment, tax, rates; see also PAY 1, TAX 1.

dull *a.* **1** [Without point or edge] blunt, blunted, unsharpened, pointless, unpointed, round, square, flat, nicked, broken, toothless.—*Ant.* SHARP, sharpened, keen. **2** [Lacking brightness or color] gloomy, sober, somber, drab, dismal, dark, dingy, dim, dusky, colorless, plain, obscure, tarnished, opaque, leaden, grave, grimy, faded, sooty, inky,

dead, black, coal-black, unlighted, sordid, dirty, muddy, gray, lifeless, rusty, flat.—*Ant.* BRIGHT, colorful, gleaming. **3** [Lacking intelligence; *said usually of living beings*] slow, retarded, witless; see STUPID. **4** [Lacking interest; *said usually of writing, speaking, or inanimate things*] heavy, prosaic, trite, hackneyed, monotonous, humdrum, tedious, dreary, dismal, dry, arid, colorless, insipid, boring, vapid, flat, senseless, long-winded, stupid, commonplace, ordinary, common, usual, old, ancient, stale, motheaten, out-of-date, archaic, worn-out, tiring, banal, tired, uninteresting, wooden, pointless, uninspiring, piddling, senile, proverbial, tame, routine, familiar, known, well-known, conventional, depressing, sluggish, repetitious, repetitive, soporific, tiresome, lifeless, wearying, unexciting, flat, stereotyped, stock, the usual thing, the same old thing, the same thing day after day, slow, dry as a bone*, cut and dried, dead as a doornail.—*Ant.* EXCITING, fascinating, exhilarating. **5** [Not loud or distinct] low, soft, softened; see FAINT 3. **6** [Showing little activity] still, routine, regular; see SLOW 1. **7** [Gloomy] cloudy, dim, unlit; see DARK 1.

dullness *n.* **1** [Quality of being boring] flatness, sameness, routine, evenness, tedium, aridity, depression, dreariness, commonplaceness, mediocrity, tameness, familiarity; see also BOREDOM, MONOTONY.—*Ant.* ACTION, liveliness, interest. **2** [Stupidity] nonsense, lunacy, slow-wittedness; see STUPIDITY 1.

duly *a.* rightfully, properly, appropriately; see JUSTLY 1.

dumb *a.* **1** [Unable to speak] silent, inarticulate, deaf and dumb, voiceless, speechless, having a speech impediment; see also MUTE 1, QUIET. **2** [Slow of wit] simple-minded, feebleminded, moronic; see DULL 3, STUPID.

dumbbell* *n.* blockhead, fool, dunce; see FOOL.

dummy *n.* **1** [*Fool] dolt, blockhead, oaf; see FOOL. **2** [Imitation] sham, counterfeit, duplicate; see COPY, IMITATION 2.

dump *n.* refuse heap, junk pile, garbage dump, city dump, dumping ground, junkyard, scrapheap, landfill.

dump *v.* empty, unload, deposit, unpack, discharge, evacuate, drain, eject, exude, expel, throw out, throw over, throw overboard; see also DISCARD.—*Ant.* LOAD, fill, pack.

dumps *n.* despondency, dejection, despair; see DESPERATION, GLOOM.

dunce *n.* dolt, lout, moron; see FOOL.

dune *n.* rise, knoll, ridge; see HILL.

dung *n.* offal, defecation, compost, manure, guano, fertilizer, excreta; horse dung, cow dung, etc.; chips, pellets, leavings, muck, feces, filth, garbage, sludge, slop, sewage; see also EXCREMENT, FERTILIZER.

duo *n.* couple, two, twosome; see PAIR.

duplicate *n.* double, second, mate, facsimile, replica, carbon copy, likeness, counterpart, analogue, parallel, correlate, repetition, duplication, recurrence, match, twin, Xerox (trademark), chip off the old block, clone*; see also COPY, IMITATION. — **in duplicate** duplicated, doubled, copied; see REPRODUCED.

duplicate *v.* **1** [To copy] reproduce, counterfeit, make a replica of; see COPY. **2** [To double] make twofold, multiply, make twice as much; see INCREASE. **3** [To repeat] redo, remake, rework; see REPEAT 1.

durability *n.* durableness, stamina, persistence; see ENDURANCE.

durable *a.* strong, firm, enduring; see PERMANENT.

duration *n.* span, continuation, continuance; see TERM 2.

duress *n.* compulsion, discipline, control; see PRESSURE 2, RESTRAINT 2.

during *prep.* as, at the time, at the same time as, the whole time, the time between, in the course of, in the middle of, when, in all along, pending, throughout, in the meanwhile, in the interim, all the while, for the time being; see also MEANWHILE, WHILE 1.

dusk *n.* gloom, twilight, nightfall; see NIGHT 1.

dust *n.* dirt, lint, soil, sand, flakes, ashes, cinders, grime, soot, grit, filings, sawdust; see also EARTH 2, FILTH. —**bite the dust*** be killed, fall in battle, succumb; see DIE. —**make the dust fly** move swiftly, work hard, be active; see ACT 1, MOVE 1.

dust *v.* **1** [To put a powder on] sprinkle, sift, powder; see SCATTER 2. **2** [To remove dust] wipe, whisk, brush; see CLEAN.

dusty *a.* undusted, untouched, unused; see DIRTY 1.

dutiful *a.* devoted, respectful, conscientious; see FAITHFUL, OBEDIENT 1.

duty *n.* **1** [A personal sense of what one should do] moral obligation, conscience, liability, charge, accountability, faithfulness, pledge, burden, good faith, honesty, integrity, sense of duty, call of duty; see also RESPONSIBILITY 1, 2.—*Ant.* DISHONESTY, irresponsibility, disloy-

alty. **2** [Whatever one has to do] work, task, occupation, function, business, province, part, calling, charge, office, service, mission, obligation, contract, station, trust, burden, undertaking, commission, engagement, assignment, routine, chore, pains, responsibility; see also JOB 2.—*Ant.* ENTERTAINMENT, amusement, sport. **3** [A levy, especially on goods] charge, revenue, custom; see TAX 1. —**off duty** at leisure, off work, inactive; see FREE 2. —**on duty** working, on the job, at work; see BUSY 1.

dwarf *a.* dwarfed, low, diminutive; see LITTLE 1.

dwarf *v.* minimize, overshadow, dominate, predominate over, tower over, detract from, belittle, rise over, rise above, look down upon.—*Ant.* INCREASE, magnify, enhance.

dwell *v.* live, inhabit, stay, lodge, stop, settle, remain, live in, live at, continue, go on living, rent, tenant, have a lease on, make one's home at, have one's address at, keep house, be at home, room, bunk*, crash*; see also OCCUPY 2. —**dwell on** involve oneself in, think about, be engrossed in; see CONSIDER, EMPHASIZE.

dweller *n.* tenant, inhabitant, occupant; see RESIDENT.

dwelling *n.* house, establishment, lodging; see HOME 1.

dye *n.* tinge, stain, tint; see COLOR.

dye *v.* tint, stain, impregnate with color; see COLOR.

dying *a.* **1** [Losing life] sinking, terminal, passing away, fated, going, perishing, failing, expiring, moribund, withering away, at death's door, done for*, cashing in one's chips*, with one foot in the grave; see also WEAK 2. **2** [Becoming worse or less] declining, going down, receding, retarding, decreasing, disappearing, dissolving, disintegrating, vanishing, failing, fading, ebbing, decaying, overripe, decadent, passé, doomed, neglected; see also SICK, WEAK 2.

dynamic *a.* energetic, potent, compelling, forceful, changing, progressive, productive, vigorous, magnetic, electric, effective, influential, charismatic, high-powered, peppy*, hopped up; see also ACTIVE, POWERFUL 1.

dynamite *n.* nitroglycerin, TNT, blasting powder; see EXPLOSIVE.

dynasty *n.* line, house, lineage; see FAMILY.

E

each *a.* **1** [Every] all, any, one by one, separate, particular, specific, private, several, respective, various, piece by piece, individual, personal, without exception. **2** [For each time, person, or the like] individually, proportionately, respectively, for one, per unit, singly, per capita, apiece, separately, every, without exception, by the, per, a whack*, a throw*, a shot*.

each *pron.* each one, one, each for himself or herself, each in his or her own way, every last one, one another, each other.

eager *a.* anxious, keen, fervent; see ZEALOUS.

eagerly *a.* zealously, intently, anxiously, sincerely, vigorously, readily, earnestly, willingly, heartily, strenuously, fiercely, rapidly, hungrily, thirstily, fervently, actively, enthusiastically, gladly, lovingly, with zeal, with open arms, with all the heart, from the bottom of one's heart, with delight, full tilt.—*Ant.* SLOWLY, unwillingly, grudgingly.

eagerness *n.* zest, anticipation, excitement; see ZEAL.

eagle *n.* hawk, falcon, bird of prey; see BIRD.

eagle-eyed *a.* discerning, keen-sighted, clear-sighted; see OBSERVANT.

ear *n.* outer ear, middle ear, inner ear, eardrum, labyrinth, acoustic organ, auditory apparatus. —**all ears** attentive, hearing, paying attention; see LISTENING. —**bend someone's ear*** jabber, chatter, gossip; see TALK 1. —**fall on deaf ears** be ignored, fail to attract notice, be received with indifference; see FAIL 1, WAIT 1. —**have (or keep) an ear to the ground** be aware of, observe, keep one's eyes open; see LISTEN, MIND 3. —**in one ear and out the other** ignored, forgotten, received with indifference; see NEGLECTED. —**play it by ear*** improvise, concoct, go along; see INVENT 1. —**set on its ear*** stir up, agitate, arouse; see EXCITE. —**turn a deaf ear (to)** disregard, ignore, shun; see NEGLECT 1.

earlier *a.* former, previous, prior; see PRECEDING.

early *a.* **1** [Near the beginning] recent, primitive, prime, new, brand-new, fresh, budding.—*Ant.* LATE, old, tardy. **2** [Sooner than might have been expected] quick, premature, in advance, far ahead, in the bud, preceding, advanced, immediate, unexpected, speedy,

ahead of time, direct, prompt, punctual, briefly, shortly, presently, beforehand, on short notice, on the dot*, with time to spare.—*Ant.* SLOW, late, tardy.

earmark *n.* characteristic, attribute, quality; see CHARACTERISTIC.

earmark *v.* reserve, set aside, keep back; see MAINTAIN 3.

earn *v.* **1** [To deserve as reward] win, merit, gain; see DESERVE. **2** [To receive in payment] obtain, attain, get, procure, realize, obtain a return, make money by, acquire, profit, net, clear, score, draw, gather, secure, derive, make money, bring home, bring in, collect, pick up, scrape together.—*Ant.* SPEND, consume, exhaust.

earnest *a.* ardent, zealous, warm; see ENTHUSIASTIC.

earnestly *a.* solemnly, soberly, thoughtfully; see SERIOUSLY 2.

earnings *n.* net proceeds, balance, receipts; see PAY 2.

earring *n.* pendant, ornament, jewel; see JEWELRY.

earth *n.* **1** [The world] globe, sphere, planet, *terra* (Latin), mundane world, creation, terrestrial sphere, orb, cosmos, universe, biosphere. **2** [The earthly crust] dirt, turf, loam, humus, clay, gravel, sand, land, dry land, terrain, mud, muck, soil, ground, fill, compost, topsoil, alluvium, subsoil, surface, shore, coast, deposit. —**come back (or down) to earth** be practical, be sensible, return to one's senses, quit dreaming; see also CALM DOWN, WORK 1. —**down to earth** earthly, realistic, mundane; see PRACTICAL. —**on earth** of all things, of everything, what; see WHATEVER.

earthen *a.* clay, stone, mud, dirt, rock, fictile, made of earth, made of baked clay.

earthenware *n.* crockery, ceramics, china; see POTTERY.

earthly *a.* human, mortal, global, mundane, worldly, under the sun, in all creation.—*Ant.* UNNATURAL, alien, superhuman.

earthquake *n.* tremor, temblor, aftershock, seismic activity, shock, quake, fault, slip, movement of the earth's crust, earth tremor, volcanic quake.

earthy *a.* **1** [Characteristic of earth] dusty, made of earth, muddy; see EARTHEN. **2** [Unrefined] coarse, dull, unrefined; see CRUDE.

ease *n.* **1** [Freedom from pain] comfort, rest, quietness, peace, leisure, repose, satisfaction, calm, calmness, restfulness, serenity, tranquillity, solace, consolation.—*Ant.* PAIN, discomfort, unrest. **2** [Freedom from difficulty] expertness, facility, efficiency, knack, readiness, quickness, skillfulness, dexterity, cleverness, smoothness, child's play, clear sailing*, snap*, breeze*, cinch*, pushover*.—*Ant.* DIFFICULTY, trouble, clumsiness. **—at ease** relaxed, collected, resting; see CALM 1.

ease *v.* **1** [To relieve of pain] alleviate, allay, drug, keep under sedation, tranquilize, sedate, anesthetize, reduce, mitigate, assuage, ameliorate, comfort, relieve pressure, cure, attend to, doctor, nurse, soothe.—*Ant.* HURT, injure, aggravate. **2** [To lessen pressure or tension] cheer, lift, bear, hold up, make comfortable, raise, unburden, release, soften, relieve one's mind, lighten, let up on, give rest to, relax, quiet, calm, pacify. **3** [To move carefully] induce, remove, extricate, set right, right, insert, join, slide, maneuver, handle.—*Ant.* HURRY, rush, blunder.

easily *a.* readily, with ease, in an easy manner, effortlessly, simply, with no effort, without trouble, handily, regularly, steadily, efficiently, smoothly, plainly, comfortably, calmly, coolly, surely, just like that*, with one hand tied behind one's back*.

easiness *n.* carelessness, nonchalance, facility; see ABILITY.

east *a.* **1** [Situated to the east] eastward, in the east, on the east side of, toward the sunrise, east side, eastern, easterly, easternmost. **2** [Going toward the east] eastbound, eastward, to the east, headed east, in an easterly direction, out of the west. **3** [Coming from the east] westbound, westward, to the west, headed west, in a westerly direction, out of the east.

East *n.* **1** [The eastern part of the United States] East Coast, the eastern states, the Atlantic seaboard, the Eastern seaboard, land east of the Alleghenies, east of the Appalachians, land east of the Mississippi. **2** [The eastern part of Eurasia] Asia, Asia Minor, Near East, Far East, Middle East, Siberia, Mongolia, southeast Asia, Arabia, Orient, Levant.

eastern *a.* **1** [Concerning the direction to the east] easterly, eastward, on the east side of; see EAST 1. **2** [Concerning the eastern part of the United States] East, Atlantic, Atlantic Seaboard, East Coast, Northeastern, Southeastern, New England, Middle Atlantic, South Atlantic. **3** [Concerning the Near East or Middle East] Palestinian, Egyptian, of the Holy Land, Arab,

Arabic, Israeli, Hellenic, Hebraic, in Asia Minor. **4** [Concerning the Orient] Far Eastern, East Asian, Asian, Oriental.

easy *a.* **1** [Free from constraint] secure, at ease, prosperous, leisurely, unembarrassed, spontaneous, calm, peaceful, tranquil, careless, contented, carefree, untroubled, moderate, hospitable, soft.—*Ant.* DIFFICULT, demanding, hard. **2** [Providing no difficulty] simple, facile, obvious, apparent, yielding, easily done, smooth, manageable, accessible, wieldy, slight, little, paltry, inconsiderable, nothing to it*, simple as ABC*, easy as pie*, like taking candy from a baby*.—*Ant.* HARD, difficult, complicated. **3** [Lax] lenient, indulgent, easygoing; see KIND. **—take it easy** relax, rest, slow down; see CALM DOWN.

easygoing *a.* tranquil, carefree, patient; see CALM 1.

eat *v.* **1** [To take as food] consume, bite, chew, devour, swallow, feast on, dine out, gulp, peck at, gorge, gobble up, eat up, digest, masticate, feed on, breakfast, dine, eat out, sup, lunch, feed, feast, banquet, fall to, live on, feed on, wolf down, enjoy a meal, have a bite, put away*, make a pig of oneself*, eat out of house and home*.—*Ant.* FAST, starve, diet. **2** [To reduce gradually] eat up, eat away, liquefy, melt, disappear, vanish, waste, rust away, spill, dissipate, squander, drain, gnaw, run through.—*Ant.* INCREASE, swell, build. **3** [To bother] worry, vex, disturb; see BOTHER 2.

eatable *a.* digestible, nutritious, delicious; see EDIBLE.

eating *n.* consuming, consumption, devouring, feasting on, gorging on, feeding on, biting, chewing, dining, breakfasting, lunching, eating out, overeating, dining out, eating up, having a coffee break, having a lunch break, having a bite, having a snack, breaking bread, making a pig of oneself*, stuffing oneself, swallowing, gulping down, gobbling up, gobbling down, putting on the feed bag*, eating out of house and home*.

eats* *n.* food, victuals*, meal; see FOOD.

eavesdrop *v.* overhear, wiretap, listen, listen in on, try to overhear, monitor, bug*, tap.

ebb *n.* recession, decline, outward flow, outward sweep, shrinkage, wane, waste, depreciation, reduction, lessening, ebb tide, regression, withdrawal, decrease, depreciation.—*Ant.* INCREASE, flow, rise.

ebb *v.* recede, subside, retire, flow back, sink, decline, decrease, drop off, melt, fall away, peter out*, wane, fall off, decay, abate.—*Ant.* INCREASE, flow, rise.

eccentric *a.* odd, queer, strange; see UNUSUAL 2.

eccentricity *n.* peculiarity, abnormality, idiosyncrasy; see CHARACTERISTIC.

echo *n.* repetition, imitation, reply; see ANSWER 1.

echo *v.* repeat, mimic, impersonate; see IMITATE 1.

eclipse *n.* solar eclipse, lunar eclipse, total eclipse; see DARKNESS 1.

ecologist *n.* environmentalist, conservationist, naturalist, ecological engineer, oceanographer, biologist, botanist; see also SCIENTIST.

ecology *n.* ecological engineering, environmental science, antipollution projects, pollution control, survival studies, study of ecosystems, conservation of natural resources; see also SCIENCE 1, ZOOLOGY.

economic *a.* industrial, business, financial; see COMMERCIAL.

economical *a.* **1** [Careful of expenditures] saving, sparing, careful, economizing, thrifty, prudent, frugal, miserly, stingy, mean, parsimonious, close, watchful, tight*, close-fisted, penny-pinching; see also STINGY.—*Ant.* GENEROUS, liberal, wasteful. **2** [Advantageously or reasonably priced] cheap, low-cost, low, reasonable, fair, moderate, inexpensive, marked down, on sale. **3** [Making good use of materials] practical, efficient, methodical; see EFFICIENT 1.

economics *n.* commerce, finance, business, political economy, science of wealth, economic theory, business theory, macroeconomics, microeconomics, fiscal policy, monetary policy; see also LAW 2, SCIENCE 1.

economist *n.* statistician, business analyst, efficiency expert; see SCIENTIST.

economize *v.* husband, manage, retrench, stint, conserve, scrimp, skimp, be frugal, be prudent, pinch, cut costs, cut corners, meet expenses, keep within one's means, cut down, meet a budget, make both ends meet, tighten one's belt, save for a rainy day*, pinch pennies; see also ACCUMULATE, MAINTAIN 3, SAVE 3.—*Ant.* SPEND, waste, splurge.

economy *n.* curtailment, cutback, business recession, retrenchment, rollback, reduction, layoff, wage decrease, cut in wages, moratorium.—*Ant.* INCREASE, outlay, raise.

ecstasy *n.* joy, rapture, delight; see HAPPINESS.

edge *n.* **1** [The outer portion] border, frontier, extremity, threshold, brink, boundary, end, limit, brim, rim, margin, ring, frame, side, corner, point, bend, peak, turn, crust, verge, perimeter, ledge, skirt, outskirt, lip, limb, hem, seam, fringe, frill, mouth, shore, strand, bank, beach, curb, periphery, circumference.—*Ant.* CENTER, middle, interior. **2** [Anything linear and sharp] blade, cutting edge, razor edge; see KNIFE. **3** [*Advantage] upper hand, handicap, head start; see ADVANTAGE. —**on edge** nervous, tense, uptight*; see IRRITABLE. —**set someone's teeth on edge** irritate, annoy, provoke; see BOTHER 2. —**take the edge off** weaken, subdue, dull; see SOFTEN.

edge *v.* **1** [To trim] embellish, beautify, perfect; see TRIM 2, DECORATE. **2** [*To defeat narrowly] nose out, slip past, squeeze by; see DEFEAT 3.

edgy *a.* irritable, touchy, excitable; see NERVOUS.

edible *a.* palatable, good, delicious, satisfying, fit to eat, savory, tasty, culinary, yummy*, nutritious, digestible; see also DELICIOUS.

edifice *n.* structure, architectural monument, pile; see BUILDING.

edit *v.* revise, alter, rewrite, rephrase, annotate, abridge, compose, compile, select, arrange, set up, censor, polish, finish, analyze, revise and correct, delete, condense, discard, strike out, write, proofread, cut, trim, blue-pencil, doctor up*.

edition *n.* printing, reprint, revision; see BOOK.

editor *n.* reviser, copyreader, supervisor, director, manager, editor-in-chief, proofreader, reader, editorial writer, deskman, newspaperman, newspaperwoman; see also AUTHOR, WRITER.

editorial *n.* essay, article, column; see COMPOSITION.

educate *v.* tutor, instruct, train; see TEACH.

educated *a.* trained, accomplished, skilled, well-taught, scientific, scholarly, intelligent, learned, well-informed, well-read, well-versed, well-grounded, disciplined, prepared, instructed, developed, well-trained, fitted, versed in, informed in, acquainted with, professional, expert, polished, cultured, finished, initiated, enlightened, literate, lettered, tutored, schooled.—*Ant.* IGNORANT, illiterate, unlettered.

education *n.* **1** [The process of directing learning] schooling, study, training, direction, instruction, guidance, apprenticeship, teaching, coaching, tutelage, learning, reading, discipline, preparation, adult education, book learning, information, indoctrination, brainwashing, cultivation, background, rearing. **2** [Knowledge acquired through education] learning, wisdom, scholarship; see KNOWLEDGE 1. **3** [The teaching profession] teaching, tutoring, pedagogy, instruction, training, the field of education, the educational profession, progressive education, lecturing.

educational *a.* enlightening, instructive, enriching; see CULTURAL.

educator *n.* pedagogue, instructor, tutor; see TEACHER.

eerie *a.* strange, ghostly, weird; see FRIGHTFUL 1.

effect *n.* conclusion, consequence, outcome; see RESULT. —**in effect** as a result, in fact, actually; see REALLY 1. —**take effect** work, produce results, become operative; see ACT 1. —**to the effect (that)** as a result, so that, therefore; see FOR.

effect *v.* produce, cause, make; see BEGIN 1, CAUSE.

effective *a.* efficient, serviceable, useful, operative, effectual, sufficient, adequate, productive, capable, competent, yielding, practical, valid, forceful.—*Ant.* USELESS, inoperative, inefficient.

effectively *a.* efficiently, completely, finally, expertly, conclusively, definitely, persuasively, adequately, capably, productively; see also WELL 2, 3.

effects *n.* personal property, baggage, possessions; see PROPERTY 1.

effectual *a.* adequate, efficient, qualified; see EFFECTIVE.

efficiency *n.* productivity, capability, capableness; see ABILITY.

efficient *a.* **1** [*Said of persons*] competent, businesslike, good at, apt, adequate, fitted, able, capable, qualified, skillful, clever, talented, energetic, skilled, adapted, familiar with, adept, adept, expert, experienced, equal to, practiced, practical, proficient, accomplished, active, productive, dynamic, decisive, tough, shrewd.—*Ant.* INCOMPETENT, inefficient, incapable. **2** [*Said of things*] economical, fitting, suitable, suited, effectual, effective, adequate, serviceable, useful, saving, profitable, valuable, expedient, handy, conducive, well-designed, streamlined, cost-effective.—*Ant.* INADEQUATE, unsuitable, ineffectual.

effluent *a.* emanating, issuing forth, seeping; see FLOWING.

effort *n.* attempt, enterprise, undertaking, struggle, battle, try, trial, work, venture, aim, aspiration, purpose, intention, resolution, exercise, discipline, bid, endeavor, crack*, go*, whirl*; see also ACTION 1, 2.

effortless *a.* simple, offhand, smooth; see EASY 2.

egg *n.* ovum, seed, germ, spawn, bud,

embryo, nucleus, cell. *Prepared eggs include the following:* fried, scrambled, poached, deviled, hard-boiled, soft-boiled, shirred, soufflé, raw, buttered, on toast, egg salad, ham or bacon and eggs, over easy, sunny side up. —**lay an egg*** be unsuccessful, err, make a mistake; see FAIL 1. —**put (or have) all one's eggs in one basket** chance, gamble, bet; see RISK.

egg on *v.* encourage, goad, incite; see DRIVE 1, 2, URGE 2, 3.

ego *n.* personality, individuality, self; see CHARACTER 1, 2.

egotism *n.* egoism, conceit, vanity, pride, assurance, self-love, self-confidence, self-glorification, self-worship, arrogance, insolence, overconfidence, haughtiness.—*Ant.* MODESTY, humility, meekness.

egotist *n.* conceited person, boaster, egoist; see BRAGGART.

egotistic *a.* conceited, vain, boastful, inflated, pompous, arrogant, insolent, puffed up, affected, self-centered, self-glorifying, presumptuous, blustering, showy, boisterous, haughty, snobbish, contemptuous, proud, bullying, sneering, aloof, pretentious, assuming, cocky*, brazen, impertinent, selfish, bragging, insulting, theatrical, garish, gaudy, spectacular, reckless, impudent, inflated, stiff, overbearing, domineering, bold, rash, overconfident, self-satisfied, stuck-up*, looking down one's nose*, snooty*, uppity*, wrapped up in oneself*, on one's high horse*, high and mighty*, too big for one's breeches*.—*Ant.* HUMBLE, meek, modest.

egotistically *a.* vainly, boastfully, arrogantly, haughtily, pretentiously, loftily, selfishly.

either *a., conj.* on the one hand, whether or not, unless, it could be that, it might be that.

either *pron.* one, one or the other, this one, either/or, each of two, as soon one as the other, one of two.

eject *v.* dislodge, discard, reject, run out, kick out, throw out, put out, force out, spit out, turn out, squeeze out, oust, do away with, evict, banish, throw off, vomit, excrete, dump, get rid of, send packing, give the boot*, ditch*, bounce*.

ejection *n.* eviction, expulsion, dismissal; see REMOVAL.

elaborate *a.* **1** [Ornamented] gaudy, decorated, garnished, showy, fussy, dressy, refined, flowery, flashy; see also ORNATE.—*Ant.* COMMON, ordinary, unpolished. **2** [Detailed] complicated, extensive, laborious, minute, intricate, involved, many-faceted, complex, a great many, painstaking, studied, convoluted.—*Ant.* GENERAL, usual, simple.

elaborate *v.* embellish, bedeck, deck; see DECORATE. **—elaborate upon** expand, discuss, comment upon; see EXPLAIN.

elapse *v.* transpire, pass away, slip by; see PASS 2.

elastic *a.* plastic, tempered, pliant; see FLEXIBLE.

elasticity *n.* resiliency, buoyancy, pliability; see FLEXIBILITY.

elbow *n.* joint, angle, funny bone; see BONE. **—rub elbows with** mingle with, associate with, be friends with; see JOIN 2. **—up to the elbows** (in) engaged, employed, working at; see BUSY 1.

elbowroom *n.* sweep, range, margin; see SPACE 2.

elder *n.* veteran, old lady, old man, old woman, superior, old timer, senior, gramps*, granny*, patriarch, matriarch, chief, tribal head, dignitary, counselor, father, mother, uncle, aunt, grandfather, grandmother, ancestor.

elderly *a.* declining, retired, venerable; see OLD 1.

elect *v.* choose, name, select; see CHOOSE.

elected *a.* chosen, duly elected, picked; see NAMED 2.

election *n.* poll, polls, ballot, balloting, ticket, vote, voting, vote-casting, primaries, suffrage, referendum, plebiscite, voice vote.

elective *a.* voluntary, selective, not compulsory; see OPTIONAL.

electric *a.* 1 [Electrical] magnetic, galvanic, electronic, power-driven, telegraphic, electrified, cordless, battery-operated, photoelectric, solar-powered. 2 [Thrilling] vibrating, energetic, dynamic, pulsing, electrifying.

electricity *n.* power, current, service, heat, light, ignition, spark, utilities, alternating current (AC), direct current (DC), voltage, 110 volts, 220 volts, high voltage, high tension, kilowatts, kilowatt hours, juice*.

electrify *v.* wire, charge, power, heat, light, equip, lay cables, provide service, magnetize, galvanize, energize, subject to electricity, pass an electric current through, give an electric shock to, charge with electricity.

electrocute *v.* execute, put to death, kill by electric shock, put in the electric chair, send to the hot seat*, fry*, burn*.

electron *n.* negative particle, subatomic particle, elementary particle; see ATOM.

electronic *a.* cathodic, anodic, voltaic, photoelectric, photoelectronic, thermionic, computerized, digital,

automatic, automated; see also ELECTRIC.

electronics *n.* radar, photoelectronics, cybernetics, computer electronics, thermionics, microelectronics; see also SCIENCE 1.

elegance *n.* culture, tastefulness, taste, cultivation, politeness, polish, grace, delicacy, splendor, beauty, balance, purity, grace, gracefulness, delicacy, magnificence, courtliness, nobility, charm, sophistication, propriety, style.

elegant *a.* ornate, polished, perfected, elaborate, finished, ornamented, adorned, embellished, embroidered, flowing, artistic, fancy, rich, pure, fluent, neat.—*Ant.* DULL, ill-chosen, inarticulate.

element *n.* 1 [A constitution] portion, particle, detail, component, constituent, ingredient, factor; see also PART 1. 2 [A form of matter] *The older sciences determined the following elements:* earth, air, fire, water; *modern chemistry and physics identify the following elements:* actinium (Ac), aluminum (Al), americium (Am), antimony (Sb), argon (Ar), arsenic (As), astatine (At), barium (Ba), berkelium (Bk), beryllium (Be), bismuth (Bi), bohrium (Bh), boron (B), bromine (Br), cadmium (Cd), calcium (Ca), californium (Cf) carbon (C), cerium (Ce), cesium (Cs), chlorine (Cl), chromium (Cr), cobalt (Co), copper (Cu), curium (Cm), dubnium (Db), dysprosium (Dy), einsteinium (Es), erbium (Er), europium (Eu), fermium (Fm), fluorine (F), francium (Fr), gadolinium (Gd), gallium (Ga), germanium (Ge), gold (Au), hafnium (Hf), hassium (Hs), helium (He), holmium (Ho), hydrogen (H), indium (In), iodine (I), iridium (Ir), iron (Fe), krypton (Kr), lanthanum (La), lawrencium (Lr), lead (Pb), lithium (Li), lutetium (Lu), magnesium (Mg), manganese (Mn), meitnerium (Mt), mendelevium (Md), mercury (Hg), molybdenum (Mo), neodymium (Nd), neon (Ne), neptunium (Np), nickel (Ni), niobium (Nb), nitrogen (N), nobelium (No), osmium (Os), oxygen (O), palladium (Pd), phosphorus (P), platinum (Pt), plutonium (Pu), polonium (Po), potassium (K), praseodymium (Pr), promethium (Pm), protactinium (Pa), radium (Ra), radon (Rn), rhenium (Re), rhodium (Rh), rubidium (Rb), ruthenium (Ru), rutherfordium (Rf), samarium (Sm), scandium (Sc), seaborgium (Sg), selenium (Se), silicon (Si), silver (Ag), sodium (Na), strontium (Sr), sulfur (S), tantalum (Ta), technetium (Tc), tellurium (Te), terbium (Tb), thallium (Tl), thorium (Th), thulium (Tm), tin (Sn), titanium (Ti), tungsten (W), uranium (U), vanadium (V), xenon (Xe), ytterbium (Yb), yttrium (Y), zinc (Zn), zirconium (Zr).

elementary *a.* 1 [Suited to beginners] primary, rudimentary, introductory; see EASY 2. 2 [Fundamental] foundational, essential, basic; see FUNDAMENTAL.

elements *n.* basic material, fundamentals, grammar, ABC's, initial stage, basis, beginning, first step, principles, rudiments, groundwork, brass tacks*.

elevate *v.* 1 [To lift bodily] hoist, heave, tilt; see RAISE 1. 2 [To promote] advance, appoint, further; see PROMOTE 1.

elevated *a.* aerial, towering, tall; see HIGH 2, RAISED 1.

elevation *n.* altitude, tallness, loftiness; see HEIGHT.

elevator *n.* 1 [Machine for lifting] lift, escalator, conveyor, elevator shaft, chair lift, passenger elevator, freight elevator, dumbwaiter, hoist, chute. 2 [A building handling grain] bin, storage plant, silo; see BARN.

elf *n.* brownie, sprite, leprechaun; see FAIRY.

eligibility *n.* fitness, acceptability, capability; see ABILITY.

eligible *a.* qualified, fit, suitable, suited, equal to, worthy of being chosen, capable of, fitted for, satisfactory, trained, employable, usable, likely, in the running, in line for, desirable, available.—*Ant.* UNFIT, ineligible, disqualified.

eliminate *v.* take out, wipe out, clean out, throw out, stamp out, blot out, cut out, phase out, drive out, dispose of, get rid of, do away with, put aside, set aside, exclude, eject, cast off, disqualify, oust, depose, evict, cancel, eradicate, erase, expel, discharge, dislodge, reduce, invalidate, abolish, repeal, abrogate, exterminate, annihilate, kill, murder, throw overboard, be done with, discard, dismiss, obliterate, discount, exile, banish, deport, expatriate, maroon, blackball, ostracize, fire, dump, can*, ditch*, scrap, bounce*, sack*, drop.—*Ant.* INCLUDE, accept, welcome.

elimination *n.* 1 [The act of removing] dismissal, expulsion, exclusion; see REMOVAL. 2 [The act of declining to consider] rejection, repudiation, denial, disqualification, avoidance.

elite *n.* society, nobility, celebrities; see ARISTOCRACY.

ellipse *n.* oval, conic section, closed curve; see CIRCLE 1.

elongate *v.* prolong, lengthen, extend; see STRETCH.

eloquence *n.* fluency, wit, wittiness, expression, expressiveness, appeal, ability, diction, articulation, delivery, power, force, vigor, facility, style, poise, expressiveness, flow, command of language, gift of gab*.

eloquent *a.* vocal, articulate, outspoken; see FLUENT.

elsewhere *a.* gone, somewhere else, not here, in another place, in some other place, to some other place, away, absent, abroad, hence, removed, remote, outside, formerly, subsequently.—*Ant.* HERE, at this point, in this spot.

elude *v.* dodge, shun, escape; see AVOID.

elusive *a.* slippery, fleeting, evasive; see TEMPORARY.

emaciated *a.* gaunt, famished, wasted; see THIN 2.

emanate *v.* exude, radiate, exhale; see EMIT.

emancipate *v.* release, liberate, deliver; see FREE.

emancipation *n.* liberty, release, liberation; see FREEDOM.

emasculate *v.* geld, unman, sterlize; see CASTRATE.

embalm *v.* preserve, process, freeze, anoint, wrap, mummify, prepare for burial, lay out.

embankment *n.* dike, breakwater, pier; see DAM.

embargo *n.* restriction, prohibition, impediment; see RESTRAINT 2.

embark *v.* set out, leave port, set sail; see LEAVE 1.

embarrass *v.* perplex, annoy, puzzle, vex, distress, disconcert, agitate, bewilder, confuse, chagrin, confound, upset, bother, plague, tease, worry, trouble, distract, discomfort, disturb, let down, perturb, fluster, irk, shame, stun, rattle, put on the spot*, make a monkey out of.—*Ant.* ENCOURAGE, cheer, please.

embarrassed *a.* abashed, perplexed, disconcerted; see ASHAMED.

embarrassing *a.* difficult, disturbing, confusing, distracting, bewildering, puzzling, rattling, perplexing, delicate, unbearable, distressing, disconcerting, upsetting, discomforting, ticklish, flustering, troublesome, worrisome, uncomfortable, awkward, disagreeable, helpless, unseemly, impossible, uneasy, mortifying, shameful, inconvenient, annoying, irksome, exasperating, sticky*, unmanageable.—*Ant.* COMFORTABLE, easy, agreeable.

embarrassment *n.* confusion, chagrin, mortification, discomfiture, shame, humiliation, shyness, timidity, inhibition, dilemma, puzzle, perplexity, tangle, strait, pinch, quandary, mistake, blunder, clumsiness, indebtedness, uncertainty, hindrance, poverty, destitution, distress, difficulties, involvement, obligation, indiscretion, awkward situation, predicament, plight, fix*, snag, hitch, hot seat*, hot water*, pickle*, stew.

embassy *n.* commission, mission, delegation; see COMMITTEE, DIPLOMAT.

embed *v.* plant, implant, secure; see FASTEN.

embezzle *v.* thieve, forge, pilfer; see STEAL.

embezzlement *n.* fraud, misappropriation, stealing; see THEFT.

embezzler *n.* thief, robber, defaulter; see CRIMINAL.

embitter *v.* irritate, aggravate, annoy; see BOTHER 2.

emblem *n.* symbol, figure, image, design, token, sign, insignia, banner, seal, colors, crest, coat of arms, representation, effigy, reminder, mark, badge, souvenir, keepsake, medal, memento, character, motto, hallmark, flag, pennant, banner, standard, logo, monogram, colophon.

embodiment *n.* incarnation, matter, structure; see CHARACTERISTIC, ESSENCE 1, 2.

emboss *v.* raise, design, enchase; see DECORATE.

embrace *v.* enfold, squeeze, clasp; see HUG.

embroider *v.* stitch, knit, weave; see SEW.

embryo *n.* fetus, blastula, blastocyst; see EGG.

embryonic *a.* incipient, immature, undeveloped; see EARLY 1.

emerald *n.* green beryl, valuable gem, precious stone; see JEWEL.

emerge *v.* rise, arrive, come out; see APPEAR 1.

emergence *n.* rise, evolution, appearance; see VIEW.

emergency *n.* accident, unforeseen occurrence, misadventure, strait, urgency, necessity, pressure, tension, distress, turn of events, obligation, plight, crisis, predicament, turning point, impasse, dilemma, quandary, pinch, fix*, hole*; see also DIFFICULTY 1, 2.

emigrant *n.* exile, expatriate, émigré, colonist, migrant, displaced person, D.P., traveler, foreigner, pilgrim, refugee, fugitive, wayfarer, wanderer, immigrant, alien, outcast, man without a country.

emigrate *v.* migrate, immigrate, quit; see LEAVE 1.

emigration *n.* migration, relocation, uprooting, colonization, departure, removal, leaving, expatriation, displacement, moving away, crossing, migrating, exodus, exile, trek, journey, movement, trend, march,

travel, voyage, wayfaring, wandering, shift, settling, homesteading.— *Ant.* immigration, arriving, remaining.

émigré *n.* exile, emigrant, refugee; see REFUGEE.

eminence *n.* standing, prominence, distinction; see FAME.

eminent *a.* renowned, celebrated, prominent; see DIGNIFIED, DISTINGUISHED 2.

emissary *n.* intermediary, ambassador, consul; see AGENT.

emission *n.* ejection, effusion, eruption; see RADIATION 1.

emit *v.* give off, let off, give out, let out, send forth, send out, broadcast, throw up, throw out, spill out, pour out, give forth, eject, blow, hurl, gush, secrete, spurt, shoot, erupt, squirt, shed, expel, expend, vomit, belch, excrete, issue, perspire, spew, spit, ooze, exhale, emanate; see also EMPTY 2.

emotion *n.* feelings, passion, agitation, tremor, commotion, excitement, disturbance, sentiment, feeling, tumult, turmoil, sensation. *Emotions include the following:* love, passion, ecstasy, warmth, glow, fervor, ardor, zeal, thrill, elation, joy, satisfaction, happiness, sympathy, tenderness, concern, grief, remorse, sorrow, sadness, melancholy, despondency, despair, depression, worry, disquiet, uneasiness, dread, fear, apprehension, hate, malice, resentment, conflict, jealousy, greed, anger, rage, ire, shame, pride, sensuality, lust, desire.

emotional *a.* hysterical, demonstrative, fiery, warm, zealous, sensuous, fervent, ardent, enthusiastic, passionate, excitable, impulsive, spontaneous, ecstatic, impetuous, nervous, wrought-up, overwrought, temperamental, irrational, sensitive, oversensitive, hypersensitive, sentimental, melodramatic, maudlin, overflowing, affectionate, loving, neurotic, fickle, wearing one's heart on one's sleeve, high-strung, mushy*.—*Ant.* COLD, rational, hard.

emotionalism *n.* hysteria, sentimentality, excitement; see EMOTION.

empathy *n.* vicarious emotion, insight, understanding; see PITY.

emperor *n.* monarch, sovereign, dictator; see RULER 1.

emphasis *n.* stress, accent, weight; see IMPORTANCE.

emphasize *v.* make clear, make emphatic, underline, underscore, highlight, dramatize, pronounce, enunciate, articulate, accentuate, accent, stress, point up, point out, strike, call to the attention of, reiterate, repeat, insist, maintain, impress, affirm, indicate, rub in*, pound into one's head*, drum into one's head*, labor the point, make a fuss about.

emphatic *a.* assured, strong, determined, forceful, forcible, earnest, positive, energetic, potent, powerful, dynamic, stressed, pointed, flat, definitive, categorical, dogmatic, explicit.

emphatically *a.* definitely, certainly, of course, undoubtedly, decidedly, decisively, absolutely, entirely, flatly, distinctly.—*Ant.* SLOWLY, hesitantly, indistinctly.

empire *n.* union, people, federation; see NATION 1.

employ *v.* **1** [To make use of] operate, manipulate, apply; see USE 1. **2** [To obtain services for pay] engage, contract, procure; see HIRE.

employed *a.* working, occupied, busy, laboring, gainfully employed, not out of work, in one's employ, on the job, hired, operating, active, engaged, on duty, on the payroll.—*Ant.* UNEMPLOYED, out of work, jobless.

employee *n.* worker, laborer, servant, domestic, agent, representative, hired hand, salesman, salesperson, assistant, associate, attendant, apprentice, operator, workman, workingman, breadwinner, craftsman, wage earner, hireling, lackey, underling, flunky.

employer *n.* owner, manager, proprietor, management, head, director, executive, superintendent, supervisor, president, chief, businessman, manufacturer, corporation, company, boss, front office, big shot*.

employment *n.* job, profession, vocation; see BUSINESS 1, TRADE 2, WORK 2.

emptiness *n.* void, vacuum, vacancy, gap, chasm, blankness, blank, exhaustion, hollowness.

empty *a.* hollow, bare, clear, blank, unfilled, unfurnished, unoccupied, vacated, vacant, void, vacuous, void of, devoid, lacking, wanting, barren, emptied, abandoned, exhausted, depleted, deserted, stark, deprived of, dry, destitute, negative, deflated, evacuated.—*Ant.* FULL, filled, occupied.

empty *v.* **1** [To become empty] discharge, leave, pour, flow out, ebb, run out, open into, be discharged, void, release, exhaust, leak, drain off, drain, rush out, escape.—*Ant.* ABSORB, flow in, enter. **2** [To cause to become empty] dump, dip, ladle, tap, void, pour, spill out, let out, deplete, exhaust, deflate, drain, bail out, clean out, clear out, evacuate, eject, expel, draw off, draw out, disgorge, suck dry, drink.—*Ant.* FILL, pack, stuff.

emulate *v.* challenge, contend, imitate; see COMPETE, FOLLOW 2.

enable *v.* make possible, sanction, give power to, give authority to, invest, endow, authorize, allow, let, permit, license; see also APPROVE.

enact *v.* decree, sanction, ordain, order, dictate, make into law, legislate, pass, establish, ratify, vote in, proclaim, vote favorably, determine, authorize, appoint, institute, railroad through*, get the floor, put in force, make laws, put through, constitute, fix, set, formulate.

enactment *n.* edict, decree, statute; see LAW 3.

enamel *n.* lacquer, coating, finish, polish, gloss, top coat, varnish, glaze, veneer.

enamel *v.* lacquer, glaze, gloss, paint, veneer, coat, varnish, finish, paint.

encampment *n.* village, campsite, bivouac; see CAMP 1.

enchant *v.* entrance, entice, allure; see FASCINATE.

enchanted *a.* charmed, enraptured, entranced; see FASCINATED.

encircle *v.* encompass, circle, cordon off; see SURROUND 1.

enclose *v.* insert, jail, pen, corral, impound, confine, blockade, imprison, block off, fence off, set apart, lock up, lock in, keep in, box in, close in, shut in, wall in, box off, box up, seal up, wrap.—*Ant.* FREE, liberate, open.

enclosed *a.* locked in, penned in, jailed, packed up, wrapped up, shut up, buried, encased, walled in, fenced in.

enclosure *n.* **1** [A space enclosed] pen, sty, yard, jail, garden, corral, cage, asylum, pound, park, zone, precinct, plot, court, patch, coop, den, cell, dungeon, vault, paddock, stockade, concentration camp, prison; see also BUILDING, PLACE 2, ROOM 2. **2** [Something inserted] information, check, money, circular, copy, questionnaire, forms, documents, printed matter.

encompass *v.* encircle, compass, gird; see SURROUND 1.

encounter *n.* **1** [A coming together] interview, rendezvous, appointment; see MEETING 1. **2** [Physical violence] conflict, clash, collision; see FIGHT 1.

encounter *v.* **1** [To meet unexpectedly] meet, confront, come across; see FIND. **2** [To meet in conflict] battle, attack, struggle; see FIGHT.

encourage *v.* cheer, refresh, enliven, exhilarate, inspire, cheer up, praise, restore, revitalize, gladden, fortify, console, ease, relieve, help, aid, comfort, approve, reassure, assist, befriend, uphold, reinforce, back, bolster, brace, further, favor, strengthen, side with, cheer on, back up, egg on, buck up*, root for*, pat on the back.—*Ant.* RESTRAIN, discourage, caution.

encouraged *a.* inspired, enlivened, renewed, aided, supported, hopeful, confident, enthusiastic, roused, cheered; see also HELPED.—*Ant.* SAD, discouraged, disheartened.

encouragement *n.* aid, faith, help, assistance, support, cheer, confidence, trust, advance, promotion, reward, reassurance, incentive, backing, optimism, comfort, consolation, hope, relief, pat on the back, lift, shot in the arm, vote of confidence.

encouraging *a.* bright, good, promising; see HOPEFUL 1, 2.

encyclopedia *n.* book of facts, book of knowledge, compilation, general reference work, encyclopedic reference work, cyclopedia.

encyclopedic *a.* exhaustive, broad, all-encompassing; see COMPREHENSIVE, GENERAL 1, WIDESPREAD.

end *n.* 1 [Purpose] aim, object, intention; see PURPOSE 1. 2 [The close of an action] expiration, completion, target date, termination, adjournment, final event, ending, close, finish, conclusion, finis, finale, retirement, accomplishment, attainment, determination, achievement, fulfillment, realization, period, consummation, culmination, execution, performance, last line, curtain, terminus, payoff*, last word*, wrapup*, windup, cutoff, end of the line*.—*Ant.* ORIGIN, beginning, opening. 3 [A result] conclusion, effect, outcome; see RESULT. 4 [The extremity] terminal, termination, terminus, boundary, limit, borderline, point, stub, stump, tail end, edge, tip, top, head, butt end.—*Ant.* CENTER, middle, hub. 5 [The close of life] demise, passing, doom; see DEATH. —**in the end** at length, in conclusion, as a result; see FINALLY 2. —**keep one's end up*** do one's share, join, participate; see SHARE 1. —**make ends meet** manage, get by, survive; see ENDURE 2. —**no end*** very much, extremely, greatly; see MUCH, VERY. —**on end** 1 [Endless] ceaseless, without interruption, constant; see ENDLESS. 2 [Upright] erect, vertical, standing up; see STRAIGHT 1. —**put an end to** stop, finish, cease; see END 1.

end *v.* 1 [To bring to a halt] stop, finish, quit, close, halt, shut down, ban, curtail, settle, bring to an end, make an end of, break off, break up, put an end to, discontinue, postpone, delay, conclude, interrupt, dispose of, drop, call it a day*, cut short, wind up, get done, call off, give up, wrap up*.—*Ant.* BEGIN, initiate, start. 2 [To bring to a conclusion] settle, conclude, terminate; see ACHIEVE. 3 [To come to an end] desist, cease, die; see STOP 2. 4 [To die] expire, depart, pass away; see DIE.

endanger *v.* imperil, jeopardize, expose to danger, expose to peril, be careless with, lay open, put on the spot*, leave in the middle, leave in the lurch.—*Ant.* SAVE, protect, preserve.

endangered *a.* exposed, imperiled, in a dilemma, in a predicament, jeopardized, in danger, in jeopardy, in a bad way*, on thin ice*, hanging by a thread*.

endeavor *n.* effort, try, attempt; see EFFORT.

endeavor *v.* attempt, aim, essay; see TRY 1.

ending *n.* finish, closing, terminus; see END 2.

endless *a.* infinite, interminable, untold, without end, unbounded, unlimited, immeasurable, limitless, boundless, incalculable, unfathomable.

endorse *v.* 1 [To inscribe one's name] sign, put one's signature to, put one's signature on, countersign, underwrite, sign one's name on, subscribe, notarize, add one's name to, put one's John Hancock on*, sign on the dotted line*. 2 [To indicate one's active support of] approve, confirm, sanction, ratify, guarantee, underwrite, support, stand up for, stand behind, be behind, vouch for, uphold, recommend, praise, give one's word for, OK*, back up, go to bat for*.—*Ant.* BLAME, censure, condemn.

endorsed *a.* signed, notarized, legalized, ratified, sealed, settled, approved, upheld, supported, recommended, sanctioned, advocated, backed, OK'd*.

endorsement *n.* support, sanction, permission; see SIGNATURE.

endow *v.* enrich, provide, supply; see GIVE 1.

endowment *n.* benefit, provision, bequest, gratuity, grant, pension, stipend, legacy, inheritance, subsidy, revenue, trust, nest egg.

endurable *a.* sustainable, tolerable, supportable; see BEARABLE.

endurance *n.* sufferance, fortitude, capacity to endure, long suffering, resignation, patience, tolerance, courage, perseverance, stamina, restraint, resistance, will, backbone, guts*, spunk*.—*Ant.* WEAKNESS, feebleness, infirmity.

endure *v.* 1 [To continue] persist, remain, last, continue, exist, be, stay, prevail, wear, sustain, survive, outlast, carry on, live on, go on, hold on, hang on, keep on, linger, outlive, hold out, never say die*, stick to*, ride out.—*Ant.* DIE, cease, end. **2** [To sustain adversity] suffer, tolerate, bear with, bear up, allow, permit, support, undergo, sit through, take, withstand, bear up under, stand, accustom oneself to, submit to, sustain, go through, get through, encounter, be patient with, keep up, resign oneself, weather, brave, face, put up with, live through, stand for*, swallow, stomach, never say die*, grin and bear it, take it*, brace oneself, like it or lump it*, hang on, keep one's chin up.—*Ant.* AVOID, resist, refuse.

enduring *a.* lasting, abiding, surviving; see PERMANENT.

enemy *n.* foe, rival, assailant, competitor, attacker, antagonist, opponent, adversary, public enemy, criminal, opposition, guerrilla, guerrilla force, fifth column, saboteur, spy, foreign agent, assassin, murderer, betrayer, traitor, terrorist, revolutionary, rebel, invader.—*Ant.* FRIEND, ally, supporter.

energetic *a.* industrious, vigorous, forcible; see ACTIVE.

energy *n.* **1** [One's internal powers] force, power, virility; see STRENGTH. **2** [Power developed or released by a device] horsepower, motive power, pressure, potential energy, kinetic energy, atomic energy, solar energy, high pressure, foot-pounds, magnetism, friction, voltage, kilowatt-hours, current, electricity, gravity, heat, suction, radioactivity, potential, fuel consumption.

enfold *v.* envelope, encase, enclose; see SURROUND 1, WRAP.

enforce *v.* urge, compel, impose, exert, drive, demand, carry out vigorously, put in force, dictate, exact, require, execute, coerce, oblige, insist upon, emphasize, necessitate, press, impel, make, sanction, force upon, goad, stress, spur, hound, crack down.—*Ant.* ABANDON, neglect, evade.

enforced *a.* compelled, established, exacted, required, executed, pressed, sanctioned, imposed, kept, dictated, admonished, advocated, charged, meted out.

enforcement *n.* requirement, enforcing, prescription, compulsion, constraint, coercion, pressure, duress, obligation, necessity, insistence, carrying out, fulfilling.

engage *v.* **1** [To hire] employ, contract, retain; see HIRE. **2** [To engross] absorb, captivate, bewitch; see FASCINATE. **3** [To enmesh, especially gears] interlock, mesh, connect; see FASTEN. **—engage in** take part in, participate in, undertake; see PERFORM 1.

engaged *a.* **1** [Promised in marriage] bound, pledged, betrothed, matched, spoken for.—*Ant.* FREE, unpledged, unbetrothed. **2** [Not at liberty] working, employed, occupied; see BUSY 1. **3** [In a profession, business, or the like] employed, practicing, performing, dealing in, doing, interested, absorbed in, pursuing, at work, working at, involved with, involved in, connected with; see also EMPLOYED.—*Ant.* UNEMPLOYED, out of a job, without connection.

engagement *n.* **1** [A predetermined action] meeting, rendezvous, errand; see APPOINTMENT 2. **2** [The state of being betrothed] contract, promise, match, betrothal, espousal, betrothing.

engine *n.* motor, power plant, dynamo, generator, turbine; diesel, rotary, internal-combustion, external-combustion, compound, jet, Wankel, high-compression, low-compression, piston, radial, etc. engine.

engineer *n.* **1** [A professional engineer] surveyor, designer, planner, builder. *Types of engineers include the following:* mining, civil, metallurgical, geological, electrical, architectural, chemical, construction, military, naval, flight, industrial. **2** [The operator of a locomotive] motorman, brakeman, stoker; see DRIVER.

engineering *n.* design, planning, blueprinting, structure, structures, surveying, metallurgy, architecture, shipbuilding, installations, stresses, communications.

English *a.* British, Britannic, Anglian, Anglican, England's, His Majesty's, Her Majesty's, Commonwealth, Anglo-, anglicized, English-speaking, Norman.

engrave *v.* etch, bite, stipple, lithograph, cut, burn, incise, grave, chisel, crosshatch.

engraved *a.* carved, decorated, etched, scratched, bitten into, embossed, furrowed, incised, deepened, marked deeply, lithographed.

engraving *n.* print, wood engraving, etching, aquatint, rotogravure, lithograph, cut, woodcut, illustration, impression, copy, proof.

engross *v.* absorb, busy, fill; see OCCUPY 3.

engulf *v.* swallow up, submerge, inundate; see SINK 2.

enhance *v.* heighten, magnify, amplify; see INCREASE.

enigma *n.* problem, riddle, parable; see PUZZLE 2.

enjoy *v.* **1** [To get pleasure from] relish, luxuriate in, delight in; see

LIKE 1. **2** [To have the use or benefit of] experience, partake of, share, undergo, make use of, use. —**enjoy oneself** take pleasure, celebrate, have a good time, revel in, delight in, luxuriate in, be pleased with; see also PLAY 1.

enjoyable *a.* agreeable, welcome, genial; see PLEASANT 1, 2.

enjoyment *n.* pleasure, delight, satisfaction, gratification, triumph, loving, enjoying, rejoicing, having, using, occupation, use, diversion, entertainment, luxury, sensuality, indulgence, self-indulgence, hedonism.—*Ant.* ABUSE, dislike, displeasure.

enlarge *v.* **1** [To increase] expand, spread, swell; see GROW 1. **2** [To cause to increase] extend, augment, expand; see INCREASE.

enlarged *a.* increased, augmented, expanded, enhanced, developed, exaggerated, extended, amplified, spread, added to, lengthened, broadened, widened, thickened, magnified, filled-out, inflated, swelled, swollen, stretched, heightened, intensified, blown up.

enlargement *n.* **1** [Growth or extension] augmentation, amplification, expansion; see INCREASE. **2** [An enlarged photograph] view, 8 x 10, blowup; see PHOTOGRAPH, PICTURE 2.

enlighten *v.* inform, divulge, acquaint; see TEACH, TELL 1.

enlightened *a.* instructed, learned, informed; see EDUCATED.

enlightenment *n.* wisdom, culture, education; see KNOWLEDGE 1.

enlist *v.* **1** [To enroll others] sign up, press into service, hire, retain, call up, recruit, mobilize, induct, register, list, initiate, employ, place, admit, draft, conscript, muster, call to arms.—*Ant.* REFUSE, neglect, turn away. **2** [To enroll oneself] enter, sign up, serve; see JOIN 2, REGISTER 4.

enlisted *a.* recruited, commissioned, registered; see ENROLLED.

enlistment *n.* conscription, levy, recruitment; see ENROLLMENT 1, INDUCTION 3.

en masse *a.* bodily, as one, together; see TOGETHER 2, UNIFIED.

enmity *n.* animosity, malice, rancor; see HATRED.

enormous *a.* monstrous, immense, huge; see LARGE 1.

enough *a.* **1** [Sufficient] plenty, abundant, adequate, acceptable, ample, satisfactory, complete, copious, plentiful, satisfying, unlimited, suitable.—*Ant.* INADEQUATE, deficient, insufficient. **2** [Sufficiently] satisfactorily, amply, abundantly;

see ADEQUATELY. **3** [Fully] quite, rather, just; see VERY. **4** [Just adequately] tolerably, fairly, barely; see ADEQUATELY.

enough *n.* abundance, sufficiency, adequacy; see PLENTY.

enrage *v.* anger, incite, outrage, provoke, irk, bother, annoy, tease, pester, agitate, arouse, stir, goad, bait, inflame, incense, infuriate, madden; see also INCITE.

enrich *v.* adorn, better, decorate; see IMPROVE 1.

enriched *a.* improved, bettered, embellished; see IMPROVED.

enrichment *n.* advancement, promotion, endowment; see IMPROVEMENT 1.

enroll *v.* **1** [To obtain for service] recruit, obtain, employ; see HIRE. **2** [To register oneself] enter, sign up, enlist; see JOIN 2, REGISTER 4.

enrolled *a.* joined, inducted, registered, installed, pledged, enlisted, commissioned, employed, mustered, on the roll, signed up.—*Ant.* SEPARATED, mustered out, discharged.

enrollment *n.* **1** [The act of enrolling] registering, listing, inducting, recording, enlistment, matriculation, induction, entry, enlisting, selecting, registration. **2** [The persons enrolled] group, students, student body, conscripts, volunteers, number enrolled, response, registration, entrants, subscription.

en route *a.* on the way, in transit, flying, driving, traveling, midway, in passage, on the road, making headway toward, bound, heading toward.—*Ant.* MOTIONLESS, delayed, stalled.

enslave *v.* bind, imprison, incarcerate, shut in, enclose, confine, hold under, hold, subjugate, restrain, oppress, restrict, fetter, coerce, check, subdue, capture, suppress, make a slave of, hold in bondage, compel, chain, jail, deprive, tie, shackle.

enslavement *n.* oppression, subjection, servitude; see SLAVERY 1.

ensnare *v.* entrap, trap, snare; see CATCH 1.

ensure *v.* secure, assure, warrant; see GUARANTEE.

entail *v.* require, necessitate, evoke; see NEED.

entangle *v.* ensnare, entrap, trap, implicate, complicate, involve, snarl, corner, catch, embroil, tangle, ravel, unsettle, foul up*, mess up*, goof up*.—*Ant.* FREE, liberate, disentangle.

entanglement *n.* complexity, intricacy, complication; see DIFFICULTY 1, 2.

enter *v.* invade, make an entrance, set foot in, pass into, come in, drive in, burst in, rush in, go in, break into, get in, barge in, penetrate, intrude, reenter, slip in, sneak in, infiltrate, insert, move in, fall into*, crowd in, worm oneself into.—*Ant.* LEAVE, depart, exit. —**enter into** engage in, take part in, become part of; see JOIN 2. —**enter on** (or **upon**) start, take up, make a beginning; see BEGIN 2.

entered *a.* filed, listed, posted; see RECORDED.

enterprise *n.* affair, undertaking, endeavor; see BUSINESS.

entertain *v.* **1** [To keep others amused] amuse, cheer, please, interest, enliven, delight, divert, beguile, charm, captivate, inspire, stimulate, satisfy, humor, enthrall, elate, tickle, distract, indulge, flatter, relax, comfort.—*Ant.* TIRE, bore, weary. **2** [To act as host or hostess] receive, host, invite, treat, charm, feed, dine, wine and dine, give a party, throw a party*, do the honors, welcome, give a warm reception to, receive with open arms.—*Ant.* NEGLECT, ignore, bore.

entertained *a.* amused, diverted, pleased, occupied, charmed, cheered, interested, relaxed, delighted, engrossed, enjoying oneself, happy, in good humor, in good company.—*Ant.* BORED, depressed, irritated.

entertainer *n.* performer, player, artist; see ACTOR.

entertaining *a.* diverting, amusing, engaging, enchanting, sprightly, lively, witty, clever, interesting, gay, charming, enjoyable, delightful, funny, pleasing, edifying, engrossing, compelling, rousing, cheerful, relaxing, moving, inspiring, captivating, thrilling, entrancing, stirring, poignant, impressive, soul-stirring, stimulating, absorbing, riveting, exciting, fascinating, provocative, ravishing, satisfying, seductive; see also FUNNY 1.—*Ant.* BORING, irritating, dull.

entertainment *n.* amusement, enjoyment, merriment, fun, pleasure, sport, recreation, pastime, diversion, relaxation, distraction, play, feast, banquet, picnic, show, television, the movies, treat, game, party, reception, spree.

enthused* *a.* excited, approving, eager; see ENTHUSIASTIC.

enthusiasm *n.* fervor, ardor, eagerness; see ZEAL.

enthusiast *n.* **1** [A zealous person] zealot, fanatic, partisan; see BELIEVER. **2** [One who has strong interest in something] hobbyist, supporter, freak*; see FOLLOWER.

enthusiastic *a.* interested, fascinated, willing, thrilled, feverish, concerned, passionate, raging, excited, attracted, exhilarated, anx-

ious, eager, yearning, dying to*, inflamed, absorbed, devoted, diligent, ardent, fiery, longing, desiring, spirited, zestful, fervent, ecstatic, impatient, delighted, enraptured, avid, wild about*, crazy about*, mad about*, hot for*, gung-ho*, aching to*.—*Ant.* OPPOSED, reluctant, apathetic.

entice *v.* lure, allure, attract; see FASCINATE.

enticement *n.* lure, bait, promise; see ATTRACTION.

entire *a.* complete, untouched, undamaged; see WHOLE 1, 2.

entirely *a.* **1** [Completely] totally, fully, wholly; see COMPLETELY. **2** [Exclusively] uniquely, solely, undividedly; see ONLY 1.

entirety *n.* total, aggregate, sum; see WHOLE.

entitle *v.* authorize, empower, qualify; see ALLOW.

entity *n.* item, article, something; see THING 1.

entourage *n.* retinue, associates, followers; see FOLLOWING.

entrails *n.* viscera, guts, insides; see INTESTINES.

entrance *n.* **1** [The act of coming in] arrival, entry, passage, approach, induction, initiation, admission, admittance, appearance, introduction, penetration, trespass, debut, enrollment, baptism, invasion, immigration.—*Ant.* ESCAPE, exit, issue. **2** [The opening that permits entry] gate, door, doorway, vestibule, entry, gateway, portal, port, inlet, opening, passage, staircase, porch, hall, hallway, path, way, entry way, passageway, threshold, lobby, corridor, approach, way in.

entrance *v.* charm, captivate, hypnotize; see FASCINATE.

entrap *v.* catch, ensnare, decoy; see CATCH 1.

entrapment *n.* snare, ambush, ruse; see TRAP 1.

entree *n.* main course, main dish, meat dish; see MEAL.

entrepreneur *n.* owner, capitalist, employer; see BUSINESSMAN.

entrust *v.* deposit with, trust to, leave with; see TRUST 4.

entry *n.* approach, hall, lobby, foyer, door, gate; see also ENTRANCE 2.

enumerate *v.* list, mention, identify; see RECORD 1.

enumeration *n.* inventory, catalog, register; see RECORD 1.

envelop *v.* encompass, contain, hide; see SURROUND 1.

envelope *n.* receptacle, pouch, pocket, bag, container, box, covering, case, wrapper, enclosure, cover, sheath, casing.

enviable *a.* welcome, good, superior; see EXCELLENT.

envious *a.* covetous, desirous, resentful, desiring, wishful, longing for, aspiring, greedy, grasping, craving, begrudging, green-eyed, hankering, green with envy; see also JEALOUS.—*Ant.* GENEROUS, trustful, charitable.

environment *n.* conditions, living conditions, circumstances, surroundings, scene, external conditions, background, milieu, setting, habitat, ecosystem, situation.

envoy *n.* emissary, ambassador, intermediary; see AGENT.

envy *n.* jealousy, ill will, spite, rivalry, opposition, grudge, malice, prejudice, malevolence, covetousness, enviousness, backbiting, maliciousness, the green-eyed monster.

envy *v.* begrudge, covet, lust after, crave, be envious of, feel ill toward, have hard feelings toward, feel resentful toward, have a grudge against, object to.

eon *n.* eternity, cycle, time; see AGE 3.

epic *a.* heroic, classic, grand; see IMPORTANT 1.

epic *n.* narrative poem, saga, legend; see POEM, STORY.

epidemic *n.* plague, scourge, pestilence; see ILLNESS 1.

epidermis *n.* cuticle, dermis, hide; see SKIN.

episode *n.* happening, occurrence, incident; see EVENT.

epoch *n.* era, period, time; see AGE 3.

equal *a.* even, regular, like, same, identical, similar, uniform, invariable, fair, unvarying, commensurate, just, impartial, unbiased, to the same degree, on a footing with, without distinction, equitable, one and the same, level, parallel, corresponding, equivalent, proportionate, comparable, tantamount.—*Ant.* IRREGULAR, unequal, uneven. — **equal to** adequate, capable, qualified; see ABLE.

equal *n.* parallel, match, counterpart, complement, peer, fellow, twin, double, likeness, companion, copy, duplicate, rival, competitor, opposite number.

equal *v.* match, equalize, rank with, be the same, rival, equate, approach, live up to, come up to, amount to, consist of, comprise, be composed of, be made of, measure up to, even off, break even, come to, compare, square with, tally with, agree, correspond, be tantamount to, be identical, keep pace with, be commensurate, meet, rise to.

equality *n.* balance, parity, uniformity, sameness, likeness, identity, evenness, equalization, equilibrium, impartiality, fairness, civil rights, equivalence, tolerance, all for one and one for all*, even-steven*, fair shake.—*Ant.* INJUSTICE, inequality, unfairness.

equalize *v.* make even, make equal, balance, equate, match, level, adjust, establish equilibrium, even up.

equally *a.* evenly, symmetrically, proportionately, coordinately, equivalently, on a level, both, impartially, justly, fairly, across the board, on even terms, as well as, the same for one as for another.

equate *v.* **1** [To equalize] make equal, average, balance; see EQUALIZE. **2** [To compare] match, link, relate; see COMPARE 1.

equation *n.* mathematical statement, formal statement of equivalence, chemical statement. *Kinds of equations include the following:* linear, quadratic, cubic, quartic, polynomial, balanced, unbalanced, chemical.

equator *n.* middle, circumference of the earth, tropics; see JUNGLE.

equatorial *a.* tropical, in the Torrid Zone, central; see HOT 1.

equilibrium *n.* stability, center of gravity, steadiness; see BALANCE 2.

equip *v.* furnish, outfit, supply; see PROVIDE 1.

equipment *n.* material, materiel, tools, facilities, implements, utensils, apparatus, furnishings, appliances, paraphernalia, belongings, devices, outfit, accessories, attachments, extras, conveniences, articles, tackle, rig, machinery, fittings, trappings, fixtures, contraptions, supplies, accompaniments, gear, fixings, stuff, gadgets, things; see also MACHINE, PART 3.

equipped *a.* outfitted, furnished, supplied, rigged up, fitted out, arrayed, dressed, accoutered, assembled, readied, provided, implemented, decked, bedecked, appareled, completed, supplemented, set up.

equitable *a.* impartial, just, moral; see FAIR 1.

equity *n.* investment, owner's interest, capital; see PROPERTY 1.

equivalent *a.* commensurate, comparable, similar; see EQUAL.

era *n.* epoch, period, date; see AGE 3, TIME 2.

eradicate *v.* eliminate, exterminate, annihilate; see DESTROY.

eradication *n.* extermination, annihilation, elimination; see DESTRUCTION 1.

erase *v.* delete, expunge, omit, obliterate, cut, clean, nullify, eradicate; see also CANCEL.

erect *a.* upright, vertical, perpendicular; see STRAIGHT 1.

erect *v.* construct, raise, fabricate; see BUILD.

erected *a.* constructed, completed, raised; see BUILT.

erection *n.* building, erecting, constructing; see CONSTRUCTION 2.

erode *v.* decay, corrode, consume; see DISINTEGRATE.

erosion *n.* wearing away, decrease, carrying away; see DESTRUCTION 1, 2.

erotic *a.* amorous, stimulating, carnal; see SENSUAL 1, 2.

err *v.* misjudge, blunder, be mistaken; see FAIL 1.

errand *n.* mission, task, commission; see DUTY 2.

erratic *a.* **1** [Wandering] nomadic, rambling, roving; see WANDERING 1. **2** [Strange] eccentric, queer, irregular; see UNUSUAL 2. **3** [Variable] inconsistent, unpredictable, variable; see IRREGULAR 1.

erring *a.* mistaken, faulty, blundering; see WRONG 1.

erroneous *a.* untrue, inaccurate, incorrect; see FALSE 2.

error *n.* blunder, mistake, fault, oversight, inaccuracy, omission, deviation, faux pas, solecism, typo*, fall, slip, wrong, lapse, miss, failure, slight, misunderstanding, misstatement, misstep, flaw, boner*, bad job, blooper*, muff, boo-boo*, botch. **—in error** mistakenly, inaccurately, by mistake; see BADLY 1, WRONG 2, WRONGLY.

ersatz *a.* artificial, synthetic, imitation; see FALSE 3.

erupt *v.* go off, eject, emit; see EXPLODE.

eruption *n.* burst, outburst, flow; see EXPLOSION.

escalate *v.* heighten, intensify, make worse; see INCREASE.

escalation *n.* intensification, growth, acceleration; see INCREASE, RISE 2.

escapade *n.* caper, adventure, prank; see JOKE.

escape *n.* flight, retreat, disappearance, evasion, avoidance, leave, departure, withdrawal, liberation, deliverance, desertion, abdication, break, rescue, freedom, release.—*Ant.* IMPRISONMENT, retention, bondage.

escape *v.* flee, fly, leave, depart, elude, avoid, evade, shun, run off, run away, make off, disappear, vanish, steal off, steal away, flow out, get away, break out, break away, wriggle out, desert, slip away, run out, go scot-free, take flight, elope, duck out*, get clear of, break loose, cut and run, worm out of, clear out*, bail out, crawl out of, save one's

neck, scram*, make a break*.—*Ant.* RETURN, come back, remain.

escaped *a.* out, at liberty, liberated; see FREE 2.

escort *n.* guide, attendant, guard; see COMPANION.

escort *v.* go with, attend, take out*; see ACCOMPANY, DATE 2.

esophagus *n.* gullet, food tube, neck; see THROAT.

especially *a.* **1** [To an unusual degree] particularly, unusually, abnormally, extraordinarily, uncommonly, peculiarly, unexpectedly, pre-eminently, eminently, notably, supremely, remarkably, strangely, curiously, uniquely, singularly, to a marked degree, above all. **2** [For one more than for others] chiefly, mainly, primarily; see PRINCIPALLY.

espionage *n.* undercover work, reconnaissance, spying; see INFORMATION 1.

espouse *v.* advocate, adopt, uphold; see SUPPORT 2.

essay *n.* dissertation, treatise, article; see WRITING 2.

essence *n.* **1** [Basic material] pith, core, kernel, spirit, gist, root, nature, basis, being, essential quality, reality, constitution, substance, nucleus, vital part, base, quintessence, primary element, germ, heart, marrow, backbone, soul, bottom, life, grain, structure, principle, character, fundamentals. **2** [Distinctive quality] principle, nature, essential quality; see CHARACTERISTIC. **—in essence** ultimately, fundamentally, basically; see ESSENTIALLY.

essential *a.* **1** [Necessary] imperative, required, indispensable; see NECESSARY. **2** [Rooted in the basis or essence] basic, primary, quintessential; see FUNDAMENTAL.

essentially *a.* basically, fundamentally, radically, at bottom, at heart, centrally, originally, intimately, chiefly, naturally, inherently, permanently, necessarily, primarily, significantly, importantly, at the heart of, in effect, in essence, materially, in the main, at first, characteristically, intrinsically, substantially, typically, approximately, precisely, exactly, actually, truly, really; see also PRINCIPALLY.

establish *v.* **1** [To set up in a formal manner] institute, found, authorize; see ORGANIZE 2. **2** [To work or settle in a permanent place] build up, set up, install, build, erect, plant, root, place, settle, practice, live, stay, start.—*Ant.* LEAVE, break up, depart. **3** [To prove] verify, authenticate, confirm; see PROVE.

established *a.* **1** [Set up to endure] endowed, founded, organized, instituted, set up, originated, chartered, incorporated, settled, begun, initiated, realized, codified, produced, completed, finished; see also FINISHED 1, CERTAIN.—*Ant.* TEMPORARY, insolvent, unsound. **2** [Conclusively proved] approved, verified, guaranteed, endorsed, demonstrated, determined, confirmed, substantiated, assured, concluded, authenticated, ascertained, certain, achieved, upheld, validated, identified, proved, undeniable.—*Ant.* FALSE, invalidated, untrue.

establishment *n.* **1** [A business, organization, or the like] company, corporation, enterprise; see BUSINESS 4. **2** [The act of proving] verification, substantiation, demonstration; see PROOF 1.

estate *n.* property, bequest, inheritance, fortune, endowment, wealth, legacy, heritage, belongings, effects, earthly possessions, personal property, private property.

esteem *n.* regard, respect, appreciation; see ADMIRATION.

esteem *v.* prize, respect, appreciate; see ADMIRE.

estimate *n.* evaluation, assessment, valuation, guess, appraisal, estimation, calculation, gauging, rating, survey, measure, reckoning; see also JUDGMENT 2.

estimate *v.* rate, value, measure, calculate, appraise, assess, account, compute, evaluate, count, number, reckon, guess, guesstimate*, expect, judge, figure, plan, outline, run over, rank, furnish an estimate, set a value on, set a figure, appraise, assay, consider, predict, suppose, suspect, reason, think through, surmise, determine, decide, budget.

estimated *a.* supposed, approximated, guessed at; see LIKELY 1.

estimation *n.* opinion, appraisal, valuation; see JUDGMENT 2.

et cetera (etc.) *a.* and so forth, and so on, and others; see AND.

etching *n.* print, cut, work of art; see ENGRAVING.

eternal *a.* endless, interminable, continual, unbroken, continuous, continued, unceasing, ceaseless, constant, unending, incessant, relentless, undying, enduring, persistent, always, uninterrupted, everlasting, perpetual, indestructible, unconquerable, never-ending, indefinite, permanent, ageless, boundless, timeless, immortal, forever, indeterminable, immeasurable, having no limit, imperishable, to one's dying day, for ever and ever.—*Ant.* TEMPORARY, finite, ending.

eternally *a.* endlessly, continually, perpetually; see REGULARLY.

eternity *n.* endlessness, forever, infinite, duration, timelessness, world without end, the future, infinity, all eternity, other world, afterlife, life after death, for ever and ever.—*Ant.* INSTANT, moment, second.

ethical *a.* humane, moral, respectable; see DECENT 2, HONEST, NOBLE 1, 2.

ethics *n.* conduct, morality, mores, decency, integrity, moral conduct, social values, moral code, principles, right and wrong, natural law, honesty, goodness, honor, social laws, human nature, the Golden Rule.

etiquette *n.* conduct, manners, social graces; see BEHAVIOR.

Eucharist *n.* sacrament, Host, Communion; see SACRAMENT.

eulogize *v.* laud, extol, applaud; see PRAISE 1.

eulogy *n.* tribute, glorification, commendation; see PRAISE 2.

euphoria *n.* joy, delight, glee; see HAPPINESS.

European *a.* Continental, old-country, old-world, Eurasian, Indo-European, West European, East European.

evacuate *v.* **1** [To empty] void, exhaust, deplete; see REMOVE 1. **2** [To abandon] vacate, desert, leave; see ABANDON 1.

evacuation *n.* **1** [Removal] draining, depletion, exhaustion; see REMOVAL. **2** [Withdrawal] abandonment, removal, retreat; see DEPARTURE.

evade *v.* lie, prevaricate, dodge, shun, put off, avoid, elude, trick, baffle, quibble, shift, mystify, cloak, cover, conceal, deceive, screen, veil, hide, drop the subject, pretend, confuse, equivocate, hedge, dodge the issue, beat around the bush, give someone the runaround*, throw off the scent*, lead on a merry chase, pass up, put off, get around, lie out of, take the Fifth*; see also AVOID.—*Ant.* EXPLAIN, make clear, elucidate.

evaluate *v.* appraise, judge, assess; see DECIDE, ESTIMATE.

evangelical *a.* pious, fervent, spiritual; see RELIGIOUS 2.

evangelist *n.* preacher, missionary, revivalist; see MINISTER 1.

evangelize *v.* proselytize, instruct, convert; see PREACH.

evaporate *v.* diffuse, vanish, fade, dissolve, dissipate, steam, steam away, boil away, burn off, fume, distill, turn to steam, rise in a mist.

evaporation *n.* drying, dehydration, vanishing, steaming away, boiling away, vaporization, distillation, dissipation, disappearance, vanishing into thin air.

evasion *n.* quibble, subterfuge, equivocation; see LIE, TRICK 1.

evasive a. elusive, fugitive, shifty; see SLY.

eve n. evening before, night preceding, evening; see NIGHT 1.

even a. **1** [Lying in a smooth plane] smooth, level, surfaced; see FLAT 1. **2** [Similar] uniform, unbroken, homogeneous; see ALIKE, REGULAR 3. **3** [Equal] commensurate, equivalent, tied; see EQUAL. **4** [In addition] also, too, as well; see AND. — **break even** make nothing, tie, neither win nor lose; see BALANCE 2.

evening n. twilight, dusk, gloaming; see NIGHT 1.

evenly a. **1** [On an even plane] smoothly, regularly, without bumps, without lumps, uniformly, placidly, unvaryingly, steadily, constantly, fluently, on an even keel, without variation, neither up nor down; **2** [Equally proportioned or distributed] exactly, justly, fairly, precisely, equally, impartially, identically, equitably, symmetrically, proportionately, correspondingly, synonymously, analogously, tied, alike, fifty-fifty*, squarely.—Ant. WRONGLY, unfairly.

evenness n. smoothness, similarity, likeness; see REGULARITY.

event n. occurrence, happening, episode, incident, circumstance, affair, phenomenon, development, function, transaction, experience, appearance, turn, tide, shift, phase, accident, chance, pass, situation, story, case, matter, occasion, catastrophe, mishap, mistake, experience, parade, triumph, coincidence, miracle, adventure, holiday, wonder, marvel, celebration, crisis, predicament, misfortune, situation, calamity, emergency, something to write home about*; see also DISASTER, HOLIDAY, WONDER 2. —**in any event** anyway, no matter what happens, however; see ANYHOW. —**in the event of** (or that) in case of, if it should happen that, if there should happen to be; see IF.

eventful a. momentous, memorable, signal; see IMPORTANT 1.

eventual a. inevitable, ultimate, consequent; see LAST 1.

eventually a. in the end, at last, ultimately; see FINALLY 2.

ever a. eternally, always, at all times; see REGULARLY. —**for ever and a day** always, for ever and ever, perpetually; see FOREVER.

evergreen n. coniferous tree, ornamental shrub, fir; see PINE, TREE.

everlasting a. permanent, unending, perpetual; see ETERNAL.

every a. each one, all, without exception; see EACH 1. —**every now and then** sometimes, occasionally, once in a while; see FREQUENTLY: also **every so often***.

everybody n. each one, every one, all, the public, old and young; men, women, and children; the people, the populace, the voters; the buying public, the voting public; generality, anybody, all sorts, the masses, the man in the street, you and I; see also MAN 1.—Ant. NOBODY, no one, not a one.

everyday a. commonplace, normal, plain; see COMMON 1.

everyone pron. all, each person, whoever; see EVERYBODY.

everything pron. all, all things, the universe, the whole complex, the whole, many things, all that, every little thing, the whole kit and caboodle*; lock, stock, and barrel, the whole shebang*, the works*, the lot*.

everywhere a. everyplace, here and there, at all points, wherever one turns, at each point, without exception, universally, ubiquitously, pervasively, at all times and places; here, there and everywhere; in every direction, on all hands, all over the place, throughout, to the four winds, in all creation, to hell and back*, inside and out, from beginning to end, high and low, all around, the world over.

evict v. remove, expel, oust; see DISMISS.

eviction n. ouster, ejection, dispossession; see REMOVAL.

evidence n. testimony, data, confirmation; see PROOF 1. —**in evidence** evident, visible, manifest; see OBVIOUS 1, 2.

evident a. apparent, visible, manifest; see OBVIOUS 1.

evidently a. seemingly, obviously, so far as one can see; see APPARENTLY.

evil n. **1** [The quality of being evil] sin, wickedness, depravity, crime, sinfulness, corruption, vice, immorality, iniquity, perversity, badness, vileness, baseness, meanness, malevolence, indecency, hatred, viciousness, wrong, debauchery, lewdness, wantonness, grossness, foulness, degradation, obscenity.—Ant. VIRTUE, good, goodness. **2** [A harmful or malicious action] ill, harm, mischief, misfortune, scandal, calamity, pollution, contamination, catastrophe, blow, disaster, plague, outrage, foul play, ill wind*, crying shame*, double cross*, raw deal*.

evil a. immoral, sinful, corrupt; see BAD.

evildoer n. malefactor, sinner, wrongdoer; see CRIMINAL.

evoke v. summon forth, call out, invoke; see SUMMON.

evolution n. growth, unfolding, natural process; see DEVELOPMENT.

evolve v. result, unfold, emerge; see DEVELOP 3, GROW 2.

exact a. 1 [Accurate] precise, correct, perfect; see ACCURATE 2, DEFINITE 1. 2 [Clear] sharp, distinct, clear-cut; see DEFINITE 2.

exacting a. precise, careful, critical; see DIFFICULT 1, 2.

exactly a. precisely, specifically, correctly; see DETAILED.

exactness n. precision, nicety, scrupulousness; see ACCURACY.

exaggerate v. overestimate, overstate, misrepresent, falsify, magnify, expand, amplify, pile up, heighten, intensify, distort, enlarge on, stretch, overdo, misquote, go to extremes, give color to, misjudge, elaborate, romance, embroider, color, make too much of, lie, fabricate, corrupt, paint in glowing colors, carry too far*, lay it on thick*, make a mountain out of a molehill, build up, make much of, make the most of.—*Ant.* UNDERESTIMATE, tell the truth, minimize.

exaggerated a. colored, magnified, overwrought, extravagant, preposterous, impossible, fabulous, sensational, spectacular, melodramatic, out of proportion, fantastic, high-flown, far-fetched, false, distorted, fabricated, strained, artificial, glaring, pronounced, unrealistic, whopping*, too much.—*Ant.* ACCURATE, exact, precise.

exaggeration n. overestimation, misrepresentation, extravagance, elaboration, coloring, flight of fancy, fantasy, fancy, stretch of the imagination, figure of speech, yarn, making a mountain out of a molehill, tall story*, whopper*.—*Ant.* TRUTH, accuracy, understatement.

exalt v. commend, glorify, laud; see PRAISE 1.

exaltation n. rapture, elation, rhapsody; see HAPPINESS.

examination n. 1 [The act of seeking evidence] search, research, survey, scrutiny, investigation, inquiry into, inspection, observation, checking, exploration, analysis, audit, study, questioning, testing program, inquest, test, trial, cross-examination, the third degree*. 2 [A formal test] experiment, review, questionnaire, battery, quiz, exam, makeup*, midterm*, final, blue book, orals, writtens*; see also TEST. 3 [A medical checkup] checkup, physical examination, physical; see TEST.

examine v. 1 [To inspect with care] inspect, analyze, criticize, scrutinize, investigate, go into, inquire into, scan, probe, sift, explore, reconnoiter, audit, take stock of, take note of, make an inventory of, consider, canvass, find out, search out, review, assay, check, check out, check up on, reexamine, go back over, concentrate on, give one's attention to, look at, look into, look over, conduct research on, run checks on, put to the test, sound out, feel out, subject to scrutiny, peer into, look into, pry into, hold up to the light, finger, pick over, sample, experiment with, give the once-over*, size up*, smell around, see about, see into, poke into, nose around, look up and down, go over with a fine-toothed comb, dig into*. 2 [To test] question, interrogate, cross-examine; see TEST.

examined a. checked, tested, inspected; see INVESTIGATED.

examiner n. tester, questioner, observer; see INSPECTOR.

example n. 1 [A representative] illustration, representation, warning, sample, citation, case in point, concrete example, case, prototype, archetype, stereotype, original, copy, instance, quotation. 2 [Something to be imitated] standard, pattern, sample; see MODEL 2. —**for example** for instance, as a model, as an example, to illustrate, to cite an instance, to give an illustration, a case in point, like. —**set an example** instruct, behave as a model, set a pattern; see TEACH.

excavate v. shovel, empty, hollow out; see DIG 1.

excavation n. cavity, hollow, pit; see HOLE 1, TUNNEL.

exceed v. excel, outdo, overdo, outdistance, pass, outrun, beat, get the better of, go beyond, surpass, transcend, eclipse, rise above, pass over, run circles around*, get the edge on*, excel in, have it all over someone*, get the drop on*, beat to the draw*, break the record, have the best of, have the jump on*, be ahead of the game, have the advantage, gain the upper hand.

exceedingly a. greatly, remarkably, in a marked degree; see VERY.

excel v. surpass, transcend, improve upon; see EXCEED.

excellence n. superiority, worth, distinction; see PERFECTION.

excellent a. first-class, premium, choice, first, choicest, prime, high, the best obtainable, select, exquisite, high-grade, very fine, finest, good, desirable, admirable, distinctive, attractive, great, highest, superior, exceptional, unique, striking, superb, supreme, custom-made, incomparable, surprising, transcendent, priceless, rare, invaluable, highest priced, magnificent, wonderful, skillful, above par, superlative, worthy, refined, well-done, cultivated, competent, skilled, notable, first-rate, terrific*, sensational*, sharp*, groovy*, all right, A-1*, grade A*, classy*, top-notch*, tops*.—*Ant.* POOR, inferior, imperfect.

excellently *a.* perfectly, exquisitely, splendidly; see WELL 2.

except *prep.* excepting, excluding, rejecting, omitting, barring, save, but, with the exception of, other than, if not, not for, without, outside of, aside from, leaving out, exempting, minus*.

except *v.* exclude, reject, leave out; see BAR 1.

exception *n.* exclusion, omission, making an exception of, rejection, barring, reservation, leaving out, segregation, limitation, exemption, elimination, expulsion, excusing. —**take exception (to)** 1 [To differ] object, disagree, demur; see DIFFER 1. 2 [To dislike] resent, be offended, take offense; see DISLIKE.

exceptional *a.* uncommon, extraordinary, rare; see UNUSUAL 1, 2.

exceptionally *a.* unusually, particularly, abnormally; see ESPECIALLY 1.

excerpt *n.* selection, extract, citation; see QUOTATION.

excess *n.* 1 [More than is needed] profusion, abundance, surplus, remainder, too much, too many, exorbitance, waste, wastefulness, luxuriance, lavishness, oversupply, overstock, surfeit, plenty, bellyful*, too much of a good thing*.—*Ant.* LACK, dearth, deficiency. 2 [Conduct that is not temperate] prodigality, dissipation, intemperance; see GREED, WASTE 1. —**in excess of** additional, surplus, more than; see EXTRA. —**to excess** too much, excessively, extravagantly; see EXTREME.

excessive *a.* immoderate, extravagant, exorbitant; see EXTREME.

excessively *a.* extravagantly, extremely, unreasonably; see VERY.

exchange *n.* 1 [The act of replacing one thing with another] transfer, substitution, replacement, change, rearrangement, shift, revision, sleight-of-hand. 2 [The act of giving and receiving reciprocally] reciprocity, barter, correspondence, interdependence, buying and selling, negotiation, transaction, commerce, trade, give and take. 3 [A substitution] change, shift, swap*, trade, interchange, replacing, shuffle, reciprocation, replacement, switch.

exchange *v.* 1 [To replace one thing with another] substitute, transfer, replace, go over to, give in exchange, remove, pass to, reverse, provide a replacement, shuffle, shift, revise, rearrange, change, interchange, transact, reset, change hands, rob

Peter to pay Paul, swap*. 2 [To give and receive reciprocally] reciprocate, barter, trade with, buy and sell, deal with, do business with, correspond, swap*.

exchanged *a.* restored, traded, brought back; see RETURNED.

excitable *a.* sensitive, high-strung, impatient; see NERVOUS.

excite *v.* stimulate, inflame, arouse, anger, delight, move, tease, worry, infuriate, madden, stir up, fire up, work up, goad, taunt, mock, provoke, incite, astound, amaze, annoy, jolt, fan the flames, carry away, warm, irritate, offend, bother.

excited *a.* aroused, stimulated, inflamed, agitated, hot, annoyed, seething, wrought up, frantic, flushed, overwrought, restless, feverish, apprehensive, roused, disturbed, perturbed, flustered, upset, angry, tense, discomposed, embarrassed, hurt, angered, distracted, distraught, edgy, furious, beside oneself, delighted, eager, enthusiastic, frenzied, troubled, ruffled, moved, avid, hysterical, passionate, provoked, quickened, inspired, wild, nervous, animated, ill at ease, jumpy, jittery, turned on*, hyped up*, hopped up, worked up, in a tizzy*, uptight*, all nerves*, blue in the face*, on fire*.—*Ant.* CALM, reserved, self-confident.

excitedly *a.* tensely, apprehensively, hysterically; see EXCITED.

excitement *n.* confusion, disturbance, tumult, enthusiasm, rage, turmoil, stir, excitation, agitation, movement, feeling, exhilaration, emotion, stimulation, drama, melodrama, activity, commotion, fuss, hullabaloo, bother, dither, hubbub, bustle, to-do*.—*Ant.* PEACE, calm, quiet.

exciting *a.* stimulating, moving, animating, provocative, arousing, arresting, stirring, thrilling, dangerous, breathtaking, overwhelming, interesting, new, mysterious, overpowering, inspiring, impressive, soul-stirring, sensational, astonishing, bracing, appealing, bloodcurdling, racy, hair-raising, mindblowing*.—*Ant.* DULL, pacifying, tranquilizing.

exclaim *v.* cry out, call out, burst out, assert, shout, call aloud, say loudly; see also YELL.

exclamation *n.* yell, clamor, vociferation; see CRY 1.

exclude *v.* shut out, reject, ban; see BAR 1, 2.

exclusion *n.* keeping out, rejection, elimination, prohibition, nonadmission, omission, segregation, isolation, blockade, repudiation, separation, eviction, dismissal, suspension,

refusal, expulsion, barring.—*Ant.*
WELCOME, invitation, inclusion.

exclusive *a.* restricted, restrictive, fashionable, aristocratic, preferential, privileged, particular, licensed, select, private, segregated, prohibitive, clannish, independent, swank*.—*Ant.* FREE, inclusive, unrestricted.

exclusively *a.* particularly, solely, completely; see ONLY 1.

excommunicate *v.* expel, curse, oust; see DISMISS.

excommunication *n.* expulsion, dismissal, suspension; see REMOVAL.

excrement *n.* excretion, stool, fecal matter, offal, droppings, discharge, dung, manure, urine, effluvium, feces, sweat, perspiration, excreta, poop*.

excrete *v.* remove, eliminate, eject, defecate, urinate, discharge, secrete, go to the bathroom, go to the toilet, answer a call of nature, pass, expel, exude, perspire, sweat, squeeze out, give off, dump*, poop*.

excretion *n.* eliminating, elimination, urinating, discharging, secreting, secretion, defecation, ejecting, ejection, passing off.

excruciating *a.* torturing, intense, agonizing; see PAINFUL 1.

excursion *n.* jaunt, ramble, tour; see JOURNEY.

excusable *a.* pardonable, forgivable, understandable, justifiable, reasonable, defensible, permissible, trivial, passable, slight, plausible, allowable, explainable, not excessive, not fatal, not too bad, not inexcusable, not injurious, moderate, temperate, all right, fair, within limits, OK*.

excuse *n.* apology, reason, defense; see EXPLANATION. —**a poor excuse for** inferior, poor, unsatisfactory; see INADEQUATE. —**make one's excuses** regret, apologize, offer an explanation; see APOLOGIZE, EXPLAIN.

excuse *v.* pardon, forgive, justify, discharge, vindicate, apologize for, release from, dispense with, free, set free, overlook, purge, exempt, rationalize, acquit, condone, appease, reprieve, absolve, exonerate, clear, give absolution to, pass over, give as an excuse, make excuses for, make allowances for, make apologies for, grant amnesty to, provide with an alibi, plead ignorance, whitewash, let off easy, let go scot-free, wink at*, wipe the slate clean, shrug off, take the rap for*. —**excuse me** pardon me, forgive me, begging your pardon, I'm sorry.

excused *a.* forgiven, freed, permitted; see PARDONED.

execute *v.* 1 [To carry out instruc-

tions] act, do, effect; see PERFORM 1. 2 [To put to death] electrocute, hang, behead; see KILL 1.

executed *a.* 1 [Performed] completed, done, carried out; see FINISHED 1. 2 [Formally put to death] killed, hanged, sent to the gallows, electrocuted, gassed, shot at sunrise, sent before a firing squad, beheaded, guillotined, crucified, sent to the chair*, fried*, lethally injected.

execution *n.* punishment, capital punishment, killing, electrocution, hanging, gassing, beheading, decapitation, guillotining, crucifixion, martyrdom.

executive *a.* administrative, governing, ruling; see MANAGING.

executive *n.* businessman, businesswoman, president, vice-president, secretary, treasurer, supervisor, chairman, chairwoman, chairperson, chair, CEO, dean, head, chief, superintendent, bureaucrat, leader, governor, controller, organizer, commander, director, boss, big shot*, official, manager; see also BUSINESSMAN, LEADER 2.

exemplify *v.* illustrate, give an example, represent; see EXPLAIN.

exempt *a.* freed, cleared, liberated, privileged, excused, absolved, not subject to, released from, not responsible for, not responsible for, set apart, excluded, released, not liable, unrestrained, unbound, uncontrolled, unrestricted, not restricted by, not restricted to, outside.—*Ant.* RESPONSIBLE, liable, subject.

exempt *v.* free, liberate, pass by; see EXCUSE.

exemption *n.* exception, immunity, privilege; see FREEDOM.

exercise *n.* 1 [Action undertaken for training] practice, exertion, drill, drilling, gymnastics, sports, calisthenics, workout. 2 [The means by which training is promoted] performance, action, activity; see ACTION. 3 [Use] application, employment, operation; see USE 1.

exercise *v.* 1 [To move the body] stretch, bend, pull, tug, hike, work, promote muscle tone, labor, strain, loosen up, discipline, drill, execute, perform exercises, practice, take a walk, work out, limber up, warm up; see also TRAIN 1. 2 [To use] employ, practice, exert, apply, operate, execute, handle, utilize, devote, put in practice; see also USE 1. 3 [To train] drill, discipline, give training to; see TEACH, TRAIN 1.

exert *v.* put forth, bring to bear, exercise; see USE 1. —**exert oneself** strive, attempt, endeavor; see TRY 1.

exertion *n.* struggle, attempt, endeavor; see EFFORT.

exhalation *n.* emanation, vapor, air; see BREATH.

exhaust *v.* 1 [To consume strength] debilitate, tire, wear out, wear down; see also WEAKEN 1, 2, WEARY 1, 2. 2 [To use entirely] use up, take the last of, deplete; see WEAR 3.

exhausted *a.* 1 [Without further physical resources] debilitated, wearied, worn; see TIRED, WEAK 1. 2 [Having nothing remaining] all gone, consumed, used; see EMPTY.

exhaustion *n.* weariness, fatigue, depletion; see FATIGUE.

exhibit *n.* show, performance, presentation; see DISPLAY.

exhibit *v.* show, present, manifest; see DISPLAY.

exhibited *a.* shown, presented, advertised; see SHOWN 1.

exhibition *n.* exposition, fair, carnival; see SHOW 1.

exile *n.* 1 [Banishment] expulsion, deportation, expatriation, ostracism, displacement, separation. 2 [An outcast] fugitive, outlaw, man without a country; see REFUGEE.

exile *v.* ostracize, outlaw, cast out; see BANISH.

exist *v.* 1 [To have being] breathe, live, survive; see BE 1. 2 [To carry on life] be alive, endure, go on; see SURVIVE 1.

existence *n.* 1 [The carrying on of life] being, actuality, reality; see LIFE 1. 2 [The state of being] presence, actuality, permanence; see REALITY.

existing *a.* for the time being, temporary, just now; see PRESENT 1.

exit *n.* 1 [A means of egress] way out, outlet, opening; see DOOR. 2 [The act of leaving] going, farewell, exodus; see DEPARTURE.

exorbitant *a.* excessive, extravagant, too much; see WASTEFUL.

exotic *a.* 1 [Foreign] imported, not native, extrinsic; see FOREIGN. 2 [Peculiar] strange, fascinating, different; see FOREIGN, UNUSUAL 2.

expand *v.* extend, augment, dilate; see GROW 1.

expanse *n.* breadth, width, length, extent, reach, stretch, distance, area, belt, space, field, territory, span, spread, room, scope, range, compass, sphere, margin, sweep, radius, wilderness, region, immensity.

expansion *n.* enlargement, augmentation, extension; see INCREASE.

expatriate *n.* exile, emigrant, outcast; see REFUGEE.

expatriate *v.* exile, ostracize, deport; see BANISH.

expect *v.* 1 [To anticipate] await, look for, look forward to, count on, plan on, assume, suppose, lean on, feel it in one's bones*, wait for, hope

for; see also ANTICIPATE. 2 [To require] demand, insist upon, exact; see REQUIRE 2. 3 [To assume] presume, suppose, suspect; see ASSUME.

expectancy *n.* hope, prospect, likelihood; see ANTICIPATION.

expectant *a.* 1 [Characterized by anticipation] expecting, hoping, hopeful, waiting, awaiting, in anticipation, watchful, vigilant, eager, ready, prepared, in suspense, gaping, wide-eyed, on edge, itching.—*Ant.* INDIFFERENT, UNPREPARED, nonchalant. 2 [Anticipating birth] pregnant, parturient, expecting; see PREGNANT.

expectation *n.* hope, belief, prospect; see ANTICIPATION.

expected *a.* looked for, counted upon, contemplated, looked forward to, hoped for, relied upon, foreseen, predictable, predetermined, foretold, prophesied, planned for, prepared for, budgeted, within normal expectations, in the works, in the cards, coming up, in the bag*; see also LIKELY.

expecting *a.* expectant, due, about to become a mother; see PREGNANT.

expediency *n.* advantageousness, efficiency, profitableness; see USEFULNESS.

expedient *a.* profitable, useful, convenient; see PRACTICAL.

expedition *n.* 1 [Travel undertaken] excursion, voyage, campaign; see JOURNEY. 2 [That which undertakes travel] party, hunters, explorers, pioneers, traders, soldiers, scouts, archaeologists, tourists, sightseers, caravan, posse; see also CROWD.

expel *v.* 1 [To eject] get rid of, cast out, dislodge; see EJECT. 2 [To dismiss] suspend, discharge, oust; see DISMISS.

expend *v.* pay out, write checks for, lay out; see SPEND.

expenditure *n.* outgo, investment, payment; see EXPENSE.

expense *n.* expenditure, responsibility, obligation, loan, mortgage, lien, debt, liability, investment, insurance, upkeep, alimony, debit, account, cost, price, outlay, charge, payment, outgo, value, worth, sum, amount, risk, capital, rate, tax, carrying charges, budgeted items, cost of materials, overhead, time, payroll, investment.—*Ant.* PROFIT, income, receipts. —**at the expense of** paid by, at the cost of, charged to; see OWED.

expenses *n.* living expenses, costs, lodging, room and board, incidentals, carrying charges.

expensive *a.* dear, precious, valuable, invaluable, rare, high-priced,

pricey*, costly, prized, choice, rich, priceless, high, too high, unreasonable, exorbitant, extravagant, at a premium, out of sight*, at great cost, sky-high, steep*, stiff*.—*Ant.* CHEAP, inexpensive, low.

experience *n.* background, skill, knowledge, wisdom, practice, maturity, judgment, practical knowledge, sense, patience, caution, know-how*, savvy*; see also BACKGROUND 2.

experience *v.* undergo, feel, live through; see ENDURE 2, FEEL 2.

experienced *a.* skilled, practiced, instructed, accomplished, versed, qualified, able, skillful, knowing, savvy*, trained, wise, expert, veteran, mature, with a good background, rounded, knowing the score*, knowing the ropes*, having all the answers, having been around*, having been through the mill*, broken in*.—*Ant.* NEW, apprentice, beginning.

experiment *n.* analysis, essay, examination, trial, inspection, search, organized observation, research, scrutiny, speculation, check, proof, operation, test, exercise, quiz, investigation.

experiment *v.* analyze, investigate, probe, search, venture, explore, test, rehearse, try out, sample, subject to discipline, prove, conduct an experiment, research, study, examine, scrutinize, weigh, play around with, fool with*.

experimental *a.* tentative, trial, temporary, test, provisional, preliminary, preparatory, under probation, on approval, on trial, pending verification, hypothetical, momentary, primary, beginning, in its first stage.—*Ant.* PERMANENT, tried, tested.

expert *a.* skillful, practiced, proficient; see ABLE.

expert *n.* authority, professional, master; see SPECIALIST.

expiration *n.* close, closing, finish; see END 2.

expire *v.* stop, finish, quit; see END 1.

explain *v.* interpret, explicate, account for, elucidate, illustrate, clarify, illuminate, make clear, describe, expound, teach, reveal, point out, demonstrate, tell, read, translate, paraphrase, put in other words, define, justify, untangle, unravel, make plain, come to the point, put across, throw light upon, comment on, remark upon, remark on, offer an explanation of, resolve, clear up, get right, set right, put someone on the right track, spell out, go into detail, get to the bottom of, figure out, cast light upon, get across, get through, bring out, work out, solve, put in plain English*.—*Ant.* CONFUSE, puzzle, confound.

explainable *a.* explicable, accountable, intelligible; see UNDERSTANDABLE.

explained *a.* made clear, interpreted, elucidated; see KNOWN 2, OBVIOUS 2.

explanation *n.* information, answer, account, reason, illustration, description, comment, justification, narrative, story, tale, footnote, anecdote, example, analysis, criticism, exegesis, key, commentary, note, summary, report, brief, the details, budget, breakdown; see also PROOF 1.

explanatory *a.* expository, illustrative, informative, allegorical, interpretative, instructive, guiding, descriptive, analytical, graphic, critical.

explicit *a.* express, sure, plain; see DEFINITE 1, UNDERSTANDABLE.

explode *v.* blow up, blow out, break out, erupt, go off, detonate, discharge, backfire, shatter, fracture, split, collapse, blow off, blast, blow to smithereens*; see also RAGE 1.

exploit *n.* deed, venture, escapade; see ACHIEVEMENT.

exploit *v.* utilize, take advantage of, employ; see USE 1.

exploited *a.* taken advantage of, utilized, worked; see USED.

exploration *n.* investigation, research, search; see EXAMINATION 1.

explore *v.* search, investigate, seek; see EXAMINE.

explorer *n.* adventurer, traveler, pioneer, wayfarer, pilgrim, voyager, space traveler, astronaut, cosmonaut, seafarer, mountaineer, mountain climber, scientist, navigator, colonist.

explosion *n.* detonation, blast, burst, discharge, blowout, blowup, eruption, combustion, outburst, firing, ignition, backfire.

explosive *a.* stormy, fiery, incendiary, forceful, raging, wild, violent, uncontrollable, vehement, sharp, hysterical, frenzied, savage.—*Ant.* MILD, gentle, uneventful.

explosive *n.* mine, gunpowder, ammunition, TNT, plastic explosive, dynamite, nitroglycerine, bomb, missile, blockbuster*, warhead, grenade, charge, shell, Molotov cocktail, firecracker; see also AMMUNITION, WEAPON.

export *n.* shipping, trading, overseas shipment, commodity, international trade, foreign trade.

export *v.* send out, sell abroad, trade abroad, ship, transport, consign, dump.

expose *v.* 1 [To uncover] disclose,

smoke out, show up, present, prove, reveal, air, exhibit, unmask, lay open, lay bare, bring to light, open, dig up, give away, bring into view, unfold, let the cat out of the bag, drag through the mud, put the finger on*. 2 [To endeavor to attract attention] show, show off, bare; see DISPLAY. 3 [To open to danger] lay open to, subject to, imperil; see ENDANGER.

exposed *a*. disclosed, defined, revealed, divulged, made public, laid bare, dug up, brought to light, solved, resolved, discovered, found out, seen through.—*Ant.* HIDDEN, concealed, disguised.

exposition *n*. 1 [The process of making clear] elucidation, delineation, explication; see EXPLANATION. 2 [A popular exhibition] exhibit, showing, performance; see DISPLAY.

ex post facto *a*. subsequently, retroactively, retrospectively; see FINALLY 2.

exposure *n*. disclosure, betrayal, display, exhibition, publication, showing, revelation, confession, unveiling, acknowledgment, exposé, giveaway, bombshell, stink*.—*Ant.* SECRECY, protection, concealment.

express *a*. 1 [Explicit] definite, specific, exact; see DEFINITE 1. 2 [Nonstop] fast, direct, high-speed; see FAST 1.

express *v*. declare, tell, signify; see UTTER.

expression *n*. 1 [Significant appearance] look, cast, character; see LOOKS. 2 [Putting into understandable form] representation, art product, interpretation, invention, narration, creation, utterance, declaration, commentary, diagnosis, definition, explanation, illustration; see also COMPOSITION, WRITING 1. 3 [A traditional form of speech] locution, idiom, speech pattern; see PHRASE, WORD 1. 4 [Facial cast] grimace, smile, smirk, sneer, pout, grin; see also SMILE.

expressionless *a*. wooden, dull, vacuous; see BLANK.

expressive *a*. eloquent, demonstrative, revealing, indicative, representative, dramatic, stirring, sympathetic, articulate, touching, significant, meaningful, pathetic, spirited, emphatic, strong, forcible, energetic, lively, tender, passionate, warm, colorful, vivid, picturesque, brilliant, stimulating.—*Ant.* INDIFFERENT, impassive, dead.

expulsion *n*. ejection, suspension, purge; see REMOVAL.

exquisite *a*. fine, scrupulous, precise; see DAINTY.

extemporaneous *a*. spontaneous, impromptu, unprepared; see AUTOMATIC, IMMEDIATE, IMMEDIATELY.

extend *v*. 1 [To make larger] lengthen, enlarge, prolong; see INCREASE. 2 [To occupy space to a given point] continue, go as far as, spread; see REACH 1.

extended *a*. 1 [Outspread] spread, widespread, expansive; see WIDESPREAD. 2 [Very long] elongated, drawn-out, lengthened; see LONG 1.

extending *a*. reaching, continuing, continual, perpetual, ranging, stretching, spreading, spanning, going on, running to, drawn out to, lengthening; see also ENDLESS.

extension *n*. section, branch, extra time; see ADDITION 2.

extensive *a*. wide, broad, long; see LARGE 1.

extensively *a*. widely, broadly, greatly; see WIDELY.

extent *n*. degree, limit, span, space, area, measure, size, bulk, length, compass, scope, reach, sweep, wideness, width, range, amount, expanse, magnitude, intensity; see also EXPANSE.

exterior *a*. outer, outlying, outermost; see OUTSIDE.

exterior *n*. surface, covering, visible portion; see OUTSIDE 1.

exterminate *v*. annihilate, eradicate, abolish; see DESTROY.

external *a*. surface, visible, outside; see OBVIOUS 1.

extinct *a*. dead, ended, terminated, exterminated, deceased, lost, unknown, no longer known.

extinction *n*. abolition, extermination, extirpation; see DESTRUCTION 1, MURDER.

extinguish *v*. smother, choke, quench, douse, put out, snuff out, drown out, blow out, stifle, suffocate.

extort *v*. extract, wrench, force; see STEAL.

extortion *n*. fraud, stealing, blackmail; see THEFT.

extortionist *n*. thief, blackmailer, oppressor; see CRIMINAL.

extra *a*. additional, in addition, other, one more, spare, reserve, supplemental, increased, another, new, auxiliary, added, adjunct, besides, also, further, more, beyond, over and above, plus, supplementary, accessory, unused.—*Ant.* LESS, short, subtracted.

extract *n*. distillation, infusion, concentration; see ESSENCE 1.

extract *v*. evoke, derive, secure; see OBTAIN 1.

extradite *v*. obtain, apprehend, bring to justice; see ARREST.

extraordinarily *a*. remarkably, notably, peculiarly; see VERY.

extraordinary *a.* remarkable, curious, amazing; see UNUSUAL 1.

extravagance *n.* improvidence, lavishness, conspicuous consumption; see WASTE 1.

extravagant *a.* lavish, prodigal, immoderate; see WASTEFUL.

extravagantly *a.* expensively, beyond one's means, without restraint; see RASHLY, WASTEFULLY.

extreme *a.* radical, intemperate, immoderate, imprudent, excessive, inordinate, extravagant, flagrant, outrageous, unreasonable, irrational, improper, preposterous, thorough, far, fanatical, desperate, severe, intense, drastic, sheer, total, advanced, violent, sharp, acute, unseemly, beyond control, fantastic, to the extreme, exaggerated, monstrous, absurd, foolish.—*Ant.* RESTRAINED, cautious, moderate.

extreme *n.* height, apogee, apex; see END 4, LIMIT 2. —**go to extremes** be excessive, overreact, act rashly; see EXCEED. —**in the extreme** to the highest degree, inordinately, extremely; see MUCH.

extremely *a.* greatly, remarkably, notably; see MUCH.

extremist *n.* zealot, fanatic, diehard; see RADICAL.

exuberance *n.* fervor, eagerness, exhilaration; see ZEAL.

exuberant *a.* ardent, vivacious, passionate; see ZEALOUS.

eye *n.* 1 [The organ of sight] instrument of vision, eyeball, compound eye, simple eye, naked eye, optic, orb, peeper*, lamp*. *Parts of the eye include the following:* eyeball, pupil, retina, iris, cornea, eye muscles, optic nerve, white, lens, conjunctiva, aqueous humor, vitreous humor. 2 [Appreciation] perception, taste, discrimination; see TASTE 1, 3. 3 [A center] focus, core, heart; see CENTER 1. —**private eye*** detective, investigator, gumshoe*; see POLICE OFFICER. —**all eyes*** attentive, aware, perceptive; see OBSERVANT. —**an eye for an eye** punishment, retaliation, vengeance; see REVENGE 1. —**catch one's eye** attract one's attention, cause notice, stand out; see FASCINATE. —**easy on the eyes*** attractive, appealing, pleasant to look at; see BEAUTIFUL. —**give someone the eye*** attract, charm, invite; see SEDUCE. —**have an eye for** appreciate, be interested in, desire; see WANT 1. —**have an eye to** watch out for, be mindful of, attend to; see WATCH OUT. —**have eyes for*** appreciate, be interested in, desire; see WANT 1. —**in a pig's eye*** under no circumstances, impossible, no way; see NEVER. —**in the public eye** well-known, renowned, celebrated; see FAMOUS. —**keep an eye on** look after, watch over, protect; see GUARD. —**keep an eye out for** watch for, be mindful of, attend to; see WATCH OUT. —**keep one's eyes open (or peeled)** be aware, be watchful, look out; see WATCH. —**lay eyes on** look at, stare, survey; see SEE 1. —**make eyes at** attract, charm, invite; see SEDUCE. —**open someone's eyes** make aware, inform, apprise; see TELL 1. —**shut one's eyes to** refuse, reject, ignore; see REFUSE. —**with an eye to** considering, mindful of, aware of; see OBSERVANT.

eyesight *n.* vision, sense of seeing, visual perception; see SIGHT 1.

eyesore *n.* ugly thing, distortion, blot; see UGLINESS.

eyewitness *n.* onlooker, passerby, observer; see WITNESS.

F

fable *n.* allegory, tale, parable; see STORY.

fabled *a.* mythical, fanciful, unreal; see LEGENDARY.

fabric *n.* textile, cloth, material; see GOODS.

fabricate *v.* 1 [To construct] erect, make, form; see BUILD, MANUFACTURE. 2 [To misrepresent] make up, contrive, prevaricate; see LIE 1.

fabulous *a.* remarkable, amazing, immense; see UNUSUAL 1.

facade *n.* face, appearance, look; see FRONT 3.

face *n.* 1 [The front of the head] visage, countenance, appearance, features, silhouette, profile, front, mug*. 2 [An outer or front surface] front, surface, finish; see PLANE 1. 3 [Prestige] status, standing, social position; see REPUTATION 2. —**face to face** eye to eye, cheek by jowl, facing; see OPPOSITE 3. —**make a face** distort one's face, grimace, scowl; see FROWN. —**on the face of it** to all appearances, seemingly, according to the evidence; see APPARENTLY. —**pull (or wear) a long face** look sad, scowl, pout; see FROWN. —**show one's face** be seen, show up, come; see APPEAR 1. —**to one's face** candidly, openly, frankly; see BOLDLY 1.

face *v.* 1 [To confront conflict or trouble] confront, oppose, defy, meet, dare, brave, challenge, withstand, encounter, risk, tolerate, endure, sustain, suffer, bear, tell to someone's face, make a stand, meet face to face, cope with, allow, stand, submit, abide, go up against, swallow, stomach, take, take it.—*Ant.* EVADE, elude, shun. **2** [To put a face on a building] refinish, front, redecorate; see COVER 1, PAINT 2. **3** [To look out on] front, border, be turned toward; see LIE 2.

facet *n.* aspect, face, side; see PLANE 1.

facetious *a.* humorous, whimsical, ridiculous; see FUNNY 1.

facile *a.* simple, obvious, apparent; see EASY 2.

facilitate *v.* promote, aid, make easy; see HELP.

facility *n.* **1** [Material means; *usually plural*] tools, plant, buildings; see EQUIPMENT. **2** [Administrative agency] department, bureau, agency; see OFFICE 3.

facsimile *n.* duplicate, reproduction, likeness; see COPY.

fact *n.* **1** [A reliable generality] certainty, truth, appearance, experience, matter, the very thing, not an illusion, what has really happened, something concrete, what is the case, matter of fact, hard evidence, actuality, naked truth, gospel, reality, law, basis, state of being, hard facts*.—*Ant.* FANCY, fiction, imagination. **2** [An individual reality] circumstance, detail, factor, case, evidence, event, action, deed, happening, occurrence, creation, conception, manifestation, being, entity, experience, affair, episode, performance, proceeding, phenomenon, incident, thing done, act, plain fact, accomplishment, accomplished fact, *fait accompli* (French).—*Ant.* error, illusion, untruth. **—in** (or **as a matter of**) **fact** in reality, in fact, actually; see REALLY 1.

faction *n.* cabal, combine, party, conspiracy, plot, gang, crew, wing, block, junta, clique, splinter group, set, clan, club, lobby, camp, inner circle, sect, coterie, partnership, cell, unit, mob, side, machine, band, team, knot, circle, concern, guild, schism, outfit, crowd*, bunch*.

factor *n.* portion, constituent, determinant; see PART 1, 3.

factory *n.* manufactory, plant, shop, industry, workshop, machine shop, mill, laboratory, assembly plant, foundry, forge, loom, mint, carpenter shop, brewery, sawmill, supply house, processing plant, works, workroom, firm, packing plant.

factual *a.* exact, specific, true; see ACCURATE 1.

faculty *n.* **1** [A peculiar aptitude] ability, strength, forte; see ABILITY. **2** [A group of specialists, usually engaged in instruction or research] staff, teachers, research workers, personnel, instructors, university, college, institute, teaching staff, research staff, teaching assistants, professoriate, society, body, organization, mentors, professors, assistant professors, associate professors, docents, tutors, foundation, department, pedagogues, lecturers, advisors, masters, scholars, fellows, profs*.

fad *n.* fancy, style, craze, fashion, humor, prank, quirk, kink, eccentricity, popular innovation, vogue, fantasy, whimsy, passing fancy, latest word, all the rage, the latest thing, the last word*; see also FASHION 2.—*Ant.* CUSTOM, convention, practice.

fade *v.* **1** [To lose color or light] bleach, tone down, wash out, blanch, tarnish, dim, discolor, pale, grow dim, neutralize, become dull, lose brightness, lose luster, lose color.—*Ant.* COLOR, brighten, glow. **2** [To diminish in sound] hush, quiet, sink; see DECREASE 1.

faded *a.* used, washed-out, shopworn; see DULL 2.

fail *v.* **1** [To be unsuccessful] fall short, miss, back out, abandon, desert, neglect, slip, lose ground, come to naught, come to nothing, falter, flounder, blunder, break down, get into trouble, abort, fault*, come down, fall flat, go amiss, go astray, fall down, get left, be found lacking, go down, go under, not hold a candle to, fold up, go on the rocks*, not have it in one, miss the boat*, not measure up, lose out, give out, fall short of, not make the grade*, miss the mark, lose control, fall down on the job*, go wrong, be out of it*, blow it*, fizzle out*, hit rock bottom, go up in smoke, bomb*, not get to first base*, get hung up*, get bogged down*, flunk out*, flop*, conk out*, peter out*.—*Ant.* WIN, succeed, triumph. **2** [To prove unsatisfactory] lose out, come short of, displease; see DISAPPOINT. **3** [To grow less] lessen, worsen, sink; see DECREASE 1. **4** [To become insolvent] go bankrupt, go out of business, go broke*; see sense 1. **—without fail** constantly, dependably, reliably; see REGULARLY 1.

failing *a.* declining, feeble, faint; see WEAK 1.

failure *n.* **1** [An unsuccessful attempt] fiasco, misadventure, abortion, bankruptcy, miscarriage, frustration, misstep, faux pas, breakdown, checkmate, stoppage, collapse, defeat, overthrow, downfall, total loss, stalemate, flop*, bust*, dud*, washout*, sinking ship*, mess.—*Ant.* SUCCESS, accomplishment, triumph. **2** [An unsuccessful person] incompetent, underachiever, bankrupt, derelict, dropout, loser*, lemon*, bum*, dud*.—*Ant.* SUCCESS, winner, star.

faint *a.* **1** [Having little physical strength] shaky, faltering, dizzy; see WEAK 1. **2** [Having little light or color] vague, thin, hazy; see DULL 2. **3** [Having little volume of sound] whispered, breathless, murmuring, inaudible, indistinct, low, stifled, dull, hoarse, soft, heard in the distance, quiet, low-pitched, muffled, hushed, distant, subdued, gentle, softened, from afar, deep, rumbling, far-off, out of earshot.—*Ant.* LOUD, audible, raucous.

faint *v.* lose consciousness, become unconscious, fall, go into a coma, drop, collapse, succumb, pass out, go out like a light*, keel over*, black out.—*Ant.* RECOVER, awaken, come to.

fair *a.* **1** [Just] forthright, impartial, plain, scrupulous, upright, candid, generous, frank, open, sincere, straightforward, honest, lawful, clean, legitimate, decent, honorable, virtuous, righteous, temperate, unbiased, reasonable, civil, courteous, blameless, uncorrupted, square, equitable, fair-minded, dispassionate, uncolored, objective, unprejudiced, evenhanded, good, principled, moderate, praiseworthy, aboveboard, trustworthy, due, fit, appropriate, on the level*, on the up-and-up*, fair and square*, straight*.—*Ant.* UNFAIR, unjust, biased. **2** [Moderately satisfactory] average, pretty good, not bad, up to standard, ordinary, mediocre, usual, common, all right, commonplace, fair to middling*, so-so, OK*; see also COMMON 1.—*Ant.* POOR, bad, unsatisfactory. **3** [Not stormy or likely to storm] clear, pleasant, sunny, bright, calm, placid, tranquil, favorable, balmy, mild.—*Ant.* STORMY, threatening, overcast. **4** [Of light complexion] blond, blonde, light-colored, light-complexioned, pale, white, white-skinned, flaxen, fair-haired, snow-white, snowy, whitish, light, lily-white, faded, neutral, platinum blonde, peroxide blonde, bleached blond*, pale-faced, white as a sheet, white as a ghost.—*Ant.* DARK, brunet, black.

fair *n.* exposition, county fair, state fair, world's fair, carnival, bazaar, exhibition, display, festival, market, exchange, centennial, observance, celebration.

fairly *a.* **1** [In a just manner] honestly, reasonably, honorably; see JUSTLY 1. **2** [A qualifying word] somewhat, moderately, reasonably; see ADEQUATELY.

fairness *n.* decency, honesty, uprightness, truth, integrity, charity, impartiality, justice, tolerance, honor, moderation, consideration, good faith, decorum, propriety, courtesy, reasonableness, rationality, humanity, equity, justness, goodness, measure for measure, give-and-take, fair-mindedness, open-mindedness, just dealing, good sense, fair treatment, evenhanded justice, due, accuracy, scrupulousness, correctness, virtue, duty, dutifulness, legality, rightfulness, lawfulness, square deal*, fair play, fair shake*.—*Ant.* INJUSTICE, unfairness, partiality.

fairy *n.* spirit, sprite, good fairy, elf, goblin, hobgoblin, nymph, pixie, brownie, gremlin, Puck, fay, dryad, will-o'-the-wisp, mermaid, siren, bogy, genie, imp, enchantress, witch, warlock, banshee, werewolf, ogre, demon, succubus, devil, ghoul, Harpy, poltergeist, troll, gnome, leprechaun, satyr, fiend, Fate, Weird Sister.

fairy tale *n.* folk tale, children's story, romance; see STORY.

faith *n.* **1** [Complete trust] confidence, trust, credence, credit, assurance, acceptance, troth, dependence, conviction, sureness, fidelity, loyalty, certainty, allegiance, reliance.—*Ant.* DOUBT, suspicion, distrust. **2** [A formal system of beliefs] creed, doctrine, dogma, tenet, revelation, credo, gospel, profession, conviction, canon, principle, church, worship, teaching, theology, denomination, cult, sect. **—bad faith** insincerity, duplicity, infidelity; see DISHONESTY. **—break faith** be disloyal, abandon, fail; see DECEIVE. **—good faith** sincerity, honor, trustworthiness; see HONESTY. **—in faith** indeed, in fact, in reality; see REALLY 1. **—keep faith** be loyal, adhere, follow; see SUPPORT 2.

faithful *a.* reliable, genuine, dependable, incorruptible, straight, honest, upright, honorable, scrupulous, firm, sure, unswerving, conscientious, enduring, unchanging, steady, staunch, attached, obedient, steadfast, sincere, resolute, on the level*, devoted, true, dutiful; see also LOYAL.—*Ant.* FALSE, fickle, faithless.

faithfully *a.* trustingly, conscientiously, truly; see LOYALLY.

faithfulness *n.* trustworthiness, care, duty; see DEVOTION.

fake *a.* pretended, fraudulent, bogus; see FALSE 3.

fake *n.* deception, counterfeit, sham, copy, cheat, imitation, charlatan, fraud, make-believe, pretense, fabrication, forgery, cheat, humbug, trick, swindle, phony*, gyp*, put-on*, flimflam.—*Ant.* FACT, original, reality.

fake *v.* feign, simulate, disguise; see PRETEND 1.

fall *n.* **1** [The act of falling] drop, decline, lapse, collapse, breakdown, tumble, spill, downfall, overthrow, defeat, degradation, humiliation, descent, plunge, slump, recession, ebb.—*Ant.* RISE, elevation, ascent. **2** [That which falls] rainfall, snowfall, precipitation; see RAIN 1, SNOW. **3** [The season after summer] autumn, harvest, September, October, November, harvest time. —**ride for a fall** endanger oneself, take chances, act indiscreetly; see RISK.

fall *v.* **1** [To pass quickly downward] sink, topple, drop, settle, droop, stumble, trip, plunge, tumble, descend, totter, break down, cave in, make a forced landing, decline, subside, collapse, drop down, pitch, be precipitated, fall down, fall flat, fall in, fold up, keel over, tip over, slip, recede, ebb, diminish, flop.—*Ant.* RISE, ascend, climb. **2** [To be overthrown] submit, yield, surrender, succumb, be destroyed, be taken, bend, defer to, obey, resign, capitulate, back down, fall to pieces, break up.—*Ant.* ENDURE, prevail, resist. —**fall for** become infatuated with, desire, flip over*; see FALL IN LOVE (WITH) at LOVE. —**fall in** get into line, form ranks, take a place; see LINE UP. —**fall off** decline, lessen, wane; see DECREASE 1. —**fall out** argue, disagree, fight; see QUARREL. —**fall short** fail, be deficient, be lacking; see NEED.

fallacy *n.* inconsistency, quibbling, evasion, fallacious reasoning, illogical reasoning, mistake, deceit, deception, subterfuge, inexactness, perversion, bias, prejudice, preconception, ambiguity, paradox, miscalculation, quirk, flaw, irrelevancy, erratum, heresy; see also ERROR.—*Ant.* LAW, theory, reason.

fallible *a.* liable to err, faulty, deceptive, frail, imperfect, ignorant, uncertain, erring, unpredictable, unreliable, in question, prone to error, untrustworthy, questionable; see also WRONG 2.

falling *a.* dropping, sinking, descending, plunging, slipping, sliding, declining, settling, toppling, tumbling, tottering, diminishing, weak-

ening, decreasing, ebbing, subsiding, collapsing, crumbling, dying.—*Ant.* INCREASING, improving, mounting.

fallow *a.* unplowed, unplanted, unproductive; see VACANT 2.

false *a.* **1** [Said of persons] faithless, treacherous, unfaithful, disloyal, dishonest, lying, foul, hypocritical, double-dealing, malevolent, mean, malicious, deceitful, underhanded, corrupt, wicked, unscrupulous, untrustworthy, dishonorable, two-faced.—*Ant.* FAITHFUL, true, honorable. **2** [Said of statements or supposed facts] untrue, spurious, fanciful, lying, untruthful, fictitious, deceptive, fallacious, incorrect, misleading, delusive, imaginary, illusive, erroneous, invalid, inaccurate, deceiving, fraudulent, trumped up.—*Ant.* ACCURATE, correct, established. **3** [Said of things] sham, counterfeit, fabricated, manufactured, synthetic, bogus, spurious, make-believe, assumed, unreal, copied, forged, pretended, faked, made-up, simulated, pseudo, hollow, mock, feigned, bastard, alloyed, artificial, contrived, colored, disguised, deceptive, adulterated, so-called, fake, phony*, shoddy, not what it's cracked up to be*.—*Ant.* REAL, genuine, authentic.

falsehood *n.* deception, prevarication, story*; see LIE.

falsely *a.* traitorously, treacherously, deceitfully, foully, faithlessly, behind one's back, disloyally, underhandedly, maliciously, malevolently, unfaithfully, dishonestly, unscrupulously, dishonorably.—*Ant.* TRULY, justly, honorably.

falsify *v.* adulterate, counterfeit, misrepresent; see DECEIVE.

falter *v.* waver, fluctuate, be undecided; see HESITATE.

fame *n.* renown, glory, distinction, eminence, honor, celebrity, esteem, name, estimation, public esteem, credit, note, greatness, dignity, rank, splendor, position, standing, preeminence, superiority, regard, character, station, place, degree, popularity.

familiar *a.* everyday, well-known, customary, frequent, homely, humble, usual, intimate, habitual, accustomed, common, ordinary, informal, unceremonious, plain, simple, matter-of-fact, workaday, prosaic, commonplace, homespun, natural, native, unsophisticated, old hat*, garden-variety.—*Ant.* UNUSUAL, exotic, strange. —**familiar with** well-acquainted with, acquainted with, aware of, informed of, on speaking terms with, having some connections with, cognizant of, attuned to.—*Ant.* UNAWARE, UNKNOWN, unacquainted with.

familiarity *n.* 1 [Acquaintance with people] friendliness, acquaintanceship, fellowship; see FRIENDSHIP. 2 [Acquaintance with things] the feel of, being at home with, comprehension; see AWARENESS, EXPERIENCE.

familiarize (oneself with) *v.* accustom, acquaint, habituate, make the acquaintance of, get acquainted with, gain the friendship of, make friends with, awaken to, come to know, become aware of.

family *n.* kin, folk, clan, relationship, relations, tribe, dynasty, breed, house, kith and kin, blood, blood tie, progeny, offspring, descendants, forebears, heirs, race, ancestry, parents, ancestors, relatives, pedigree, genealogy, descent, parentage, extraction, paternity, inheritance, kinship, lineage, line, one's own flesh and blood, strain, siblings, in-laws, people.

famine *n.* starvation, want, misery; see HUNGER.

famished *a.* starving, hungering, starved; see HUNGRY.

famous *a.* eminent, foremost, famed, preeminent, acclaimed, illustrious, celebrated, noted, conspicuous, prominent, honored, reputable, renowned, recognized, notable, important, well-known, of note, notorious, exalted, remarkable, extraordinary, great, powerful, noble, grand, mighty, imposing, towering, influential, leading, noteworthy, talked of, outstanding, distinguished, excellent, memorable, elevated, in the spotlight, in the limelight.—*Ant.* UNKNOWN, obscure, humble.

fan *n.* 1 [An instrument for creating currents of air] ventilator, agitator, blower, forced draft, vane, air conditioner, propeller, electric fan, Japanese fan, windmill. 2 [*Supporter] supporter, enthusiast, devotee; see FOLLOWER.

fanatic *n.* devotee, bigot, enthusiast; see ZEALOT.

fanatical *a.* obsessed, passionate, devoted; see ZEALOUS.

fanaticism *n.* bigotry, intolerance, obsession, prejudice, hatred, superstition, narrow-mindedness, injustice, obstinacy, stubbornness, bias, unfairness, partiality, devotion, violence, immoderation, zeal, willfulness, single-mindedness, infatuation, dogma, arbitrariness, unruliness, enthusiasm, frenzy, passion, rage.—*Ant.* INDIFFERENCE, tolerance, moderation.

fanciful *a.* unreal, incredible, whimsical; see FANTASTIC.

fancy *a.* elegant, embellished, rich,

adorned, ostentatious, gaudy, showy, intricate, baroque, lavish; see also ELABORATE, ORNATE.

fancy *n.* 1 [The mind at play] whimsy, frolic, caprice, banter, sport, diversion, whim, notion, quip, prank, wit, buffoonery, fooling, facetiousness, merriment, levity, humor. 2 [The product of a playful mind] whim, notion, impulse; see IDEA. 3 [Inclination] wishes, will, preference; see DESIRE 1.

fang *n.* tusk, prong, venom duct; see TOOTH.

fantastic *a.* whimsical, capricious, extravagant, freakish, strange, odd, queer, quaint, peculiar, outlandish, far-fetched, wonderful, comical, humorous, foreign, exotic, extreme, ludicrous, ridiculous, preposterous, grotesque, absurd, vague, hallucinatory, high-flown, affected, artificial, out of sight*.—*Ant.* COMMON, conventional, routine.

fantasy *n.* vision, appearance, illusion, flight, figment, fiction, romance, mirage, nightmare, fairyland.

far *a.* 1 [Distant from the speaker] removed, faraway, remote; see DISTANT. 2 [To a considerable degree] extremely, incomparably, notably; see VERY. —**as far as** to the extent that, to the degree that, up to the time that, insofar as. —**by far** very much, considerably, to a great degree; see MUCH 1, VERY. —**few and far between** scarce, sparse, in short supply; see RARE 2. —(**in**) **so far as** to the extent that, to the degree that, to the point that; see CONSIDERING. —**so far** thus far, until now, up to this point; see NOW 1. —**so far, so good** all right, favorable, going well; see SUCCESSFUL.

farce *n.* travesty, burlesque, horseplay; see FUN.

fare *n.* 1 [A fee paid, usually for transportation] ticket, charge, passage, passage money, toll, tariff, expenses, transportation, check, token. 2 [Served food] menu, rations, meals; see FOOD.

fare *v.* prosper, prove, turn out; see HAPPEN 2.

farewell *n.* goodbye, valediction, parting; see DEPARTURE.

far-fetched *a.* forced, strained, unbelievable; see FANTASTIC.

farm *n.* plantation, ranch, homestead, claim, holding, field, kibbutz, pasture, meadow, grassland, truck farm, estate, land, acres, freehold, cropland, soil, acreage, garden, patch, vegetable garden, orchard, nursery, vineyard.

farm *v.* cultivate land, produce crops, cultivate, till, garden, work, run, ranch, crop, graze, homestead, produce, pasture, till the soil. —**farm**

out lease, rent, allot; see DISTRIBUTE, RENT 1.

farmer *n.* planter, grower, livestock breeder, stockman, tenant farmer, husbandman, cultivator, sower, hydroponist, feeder, agriculturist, rancher, dirt farmer, lessee, homesteader, producer, tiller of the soil, peasant, peon, herdsman, plowman, sharecropper, hired man, cropper, grazer, cattleman, sheepman, harvester, truck gardener, gardener, nurseryman, horticulturist, settler, sodbuster*, farm hand, hired hand.

farming *n.* agriculture, tillage, cultivation, husbandry, farm management, soil culture, ranching, sharecropping, homesteading, horticulture, agronomy, grazing, livestock raising, taking up a claim, hydroponics, growing, crop-raising.

farmyard *n.* barnyard, yard, farmstead; see FARM.

far-off *a.* far, remote, strange; see DISTANT.

farsighted *a.* aware, perceptive, sagacious; see INTELLIGENT.

farther *a.* at a greater distance, more distant, beyond, further, more remote, remoter, longer.

farthest *a.* remotest, ultimate, last; see FURTHEST.

fascinate *v.* charm, entrance, captivate, enchant, bewitch, ravish, enrapture, delight, overpower, please, attract, compel, lure, seduce, entice, tempt, draw, engage, excite, stimulate, overwhelm, provoke, arouse, intoxicate, thrill, stir, kindle, absorb, tantalize, win, interest, enthrall, influence, capture, coax, tease, lead on, knock dead*, cast a spell over, catch one's eye, carry away, invite attention.—*Ant.* DISGUST, repel, horrify.

fascinated *a.* enchanted, captivated, bewitched, dazzled, attracted, seduced, enraptured, charmed, hypnotized, delighted, infatuated, thrilled, spellbound; see also CHARMED.—*Ant.* DISGUSTED, repelled, disenchanted.

fascinating *a.* engaging, attractive, delightful; see CHARMING.

fascination *n.* charm, power, enchantment; see ATTRACTION.

fascism *n.* dictatorship, totalitarianism, Nazism; see GOVERNMENT 2.—*Ant.* DEMOCRACY, self-government, socialism.

fascist *n.* reactionary, Nazi, rightist; see RADICAL.

fashion *n.* 1 [The manner of behavior] way, custom, convention, style, vogue, mode, tendency, trend, formality, formula, procedure, practice, device, usage, observance, new look. 2 [Whatever is temporarily in vogue] craze, sport, caprice, whim, hobby, innovation, custom, amusement, eccentricity, rage. —**after (or in) a fashion** somewhat, to some extent, in a way; see MODERATELY. —**in fashion** stylish, modish, chic; see FASHIONABLE, POPULAR 1.

fashion *v.* model, shape, form; see CREATE.

fashionable *a.* in fashion, in style, in vogue, being done, well-liked, favored, smart, stylish, chic, hot*, in*, trendy*, up to the minute.

fashioned *a.* molded, shaped, intended; see FORMED.

fast *a.* 1 [Rapid] swift, fleet, quick, speedy, brisk, accelerated, hasty, nimble, active, electric, agile, ready, quick as lightning, like a flash, racing, like a bat out of hell*, like a house afire*.—*Ant.* SLOW, sluggish, tardy. 2 [Firmly fixed] secure, attached, immovable; see FIRM 1.

fast *n.* abstinence, day of fasting, Lent; see ABSTINENCE.

fast *v.* not eat, go hungry, observe a fast; see ABSTAIN.

fasten *v.* lock, fix, tie, lace, close, bind, tighten, make firm, attach, secure, anchor, grip, zip up, hold, screw up, screw down, clasp, clamp, pin, nail, tack, bolt, rivet, set, weld, cement, glue, hold fast, make secure, make fast, cinch, catch, buckle, bolt, bar, seal up.—*Ant.* RELEASE, loosen, unfasten.

fastened *a.* locked, fixed, tied; see TIGHT 2.

fastener *n.* buckle, hook, hasp, lock, clamp, tie, stud, vise, grappling iron, clasp, snap, bolt, bar, lace, cinch, pin, safety pin, nail, rivet, tack, thumbtack, screw, dowel, binder, binding, button, padlock, catch, bond, band, mooring, rope, cable, anchor, chain, harness, strap, thong, girdle, latch, staple, zipper.

fastening *n.* catch, clasp, hook; see FASTENER.

fat *a.* portly, stout, obese, corpulent, fleshy, potbellied, beefy, brawny, solid, plumpish, plump, burly, bulky, unwieldy, heavy, husky, puffy, on the heavy side, in need of reducing, swollen, inflated, ponderous, lumpish, fat as a pig, tubby.—*Ant.* THIN, lean, skinny.

fat *n.* blubber, lard, oil; see GREASE. —**chew the fat*** chat, gossip, confer; see TALK 1.

fatal *a.* inevitable, mortal, lethal; see DEADLY.

fatality *n.* casualty, dying, accident; see DEATH.

fate *n.* fortune, destiny, luck; see DOOM.

fated *a.* condemned, destined, elected; see DOOMED.

fateful *a.* 1 [Momentous] portentous, critical, decisive; see IMPOR-

TANT 1. **2** [Fatal] destructive, ruinous, lethal; see DEADLY.

father *n.* **1** [A male parent] sire, progenitor, procreator, forebear, ancestor, head of the household, papa, dad*, daddy*, pa*, the old man*, pappy*, pop*. **2** [An originator] founder, inventor, promoter; see AUTHOR. **3** [A priest, especially a Catholic priest] pastor, clergyman, parson; see PRIEST.

Father *n.* Supreme Being, Creator, Author; see GOD 1.

father-in-law *n.* spouse's father, parent, in-law*; see RELATIVE.

fatherland *n.* mother country, homeland, native land; see NATION 1.

fatherly *a.* paternal, patriarchal, benevolent; see KIND.

fatigue *n.* weariness, lassitude, exhaustion, weakness, feebleness, faintness, battle fatigue, nervous exhaustion, dullness, heaviness, listlessness, tiredness.

fatness *n.* plumpness, obesity, weight, flesh, heaviness, grossness, corpulence, bulkiness, girth, breadth, largeness, protuberance, flabbiness, chubbiness, portliness, fleshiness, stoutness, heftiness*.

fatten *v.* feed, stuff, prepare for market, plump, cram, fill, round out.—*Ant.* STARVE, reduce, constrict.

fatty *a.* greasy, blubbery, containing fat; see OILY 1.

faucet *n.* tap, fixture, petcock, drain, spigot, plumbing, hot-water faucet, cold-water faucet.

fault *n.* **1** [A moral delinquency] misdemeanor, weakness, offense, wrongdoing, transgression, crime, sin, impropriety, juvenile delinquency, misconduct, malpractice, failing; see also MISTAKE. **2** [An error] blunder, mistake, misdeed; see ERROR. **3** [Responsibility] liability, accountability, blame; see RESPONSIBILITY 2. —**at fault** culpable, blamable, in the wrong; see GUILTY. —**find fault (with)** complain about, carp at, criticize; see BLAME.

faulty *a.* imperfect, flawed, blemished, deficient, distorted, weak, tainted, leaky, defective, damaged, unsound, spotted, cracked, warped, injured, broken, wounded, hurt, impaired, worn, battered, frail, crude, botched, insufficient, inadequate, incomplete, out of order, below par, incorrect, unfit; see also UNSATISFACTORY.—*Ant.* WHOLE, perfect, complete.

favor *n.* **1** [Preference] help, support, partiality; see ENCOURAGEMENT. **2** [A kindness] service, courtesy, boon; see KINDNESS 2. —**find favor** please, suit, become welcome; see SATISFY 1. —**in favor** liked, esteemed, wanted; see FAVORITE. —

in favor of approving, endorsing, condoning; see FOR. —**in one's favor** to one's advantage, on one's side, creditable; see FAVORABLE 3.

favor *v.* prefer, like, approve, sanction, praise, regard favorably, be in favor of, pick, choose, lean toward, incline toward, value, prize, esteem, think well of, set great store by, look up to, think the world of, be partial to, grant favors to, promote, play favorites, show consideration for, spare, make an exception for, pull strings for; see also PROMOTE 1.—*Ant.* HATE, dislike, disesteem.

favorable *a.* **1** [Friendly] well-disposed, kind, well-intentioned; see FRIENDLY. **2** [Displaying suitable or promising qualities] propitious, convenient, beneficial; see HOPEFUL 2. **3** [Commendatory] approving, commending, assenting, complimentary, well-disposed toward, in favor of, agreeable, in one's favor.

favorably *a.* approvingly, agreeably, kindly, helpfully, fairly, willingly, heartily, cordially, genially, graciously, courteously, receptively, in an approving manner, positively, without prejudice.—*Ant.* UNFAVORABLY, adversely, discouragingly.

favorite *a.* liked, beloved, favored, intimate, to one's taste, to one's liking, choice, pet, desired, wished-for, preferred, adored.—*Ant.* UNPOPULAR, unwanted, unwelcome.

favorite *n.* darling, pet, idol, ideal, favored one, mistress, love, favorite son, favorite child, fair-haired boy*, teacher's pet, odds-on favorite, apple of one's eye.

favoritism *n.* bias, partiality, inequity; see INCLINATION 1.

fawn *n.* baby deer, baby doe, baby buck; see DEER.

faze *v.* bother, intimidate, worry; see DISTURB.

fear *n.* fright, terror, horror, panic, dread, dismay, awe, scare, revulsion, aversion, tremor, mortal terror, cowardice, timidity, misgiving, trembling, anxiety, phobia, foreboding, despair, agitation, hesitation, worry, concern, suspicion, doubt, qualm, funk*, cold feet*, cold sweat.—*Ant.* COURAGE, intrepidity, dash. —**for fear of** avoiding, lest, in order to prevent, out of apprehension concerning.

fear *v.* be afraid, shun, avoid, falter, lose courage, be alarmed, be frightened, be scared, live in terror, dare not; have qualms about, cower, flinch, shrink, quail, cringe, turn pale, tremble, break out in a sweat*.—*Ant.* DARE, outface, withstand.

fearful *a.* timid, shy, apprehensive; see COWARDLY.

fearfully *a.* apprehensively, shyly,

with fear and trembling, for fear of, in fear.

fearless *a.* bold, daring, courageous; see BRAVE.

feasible *a.* **1** [Suitable] fit, expedient, worthwhile; see CONVENIENT 1. **2** [Likely] probable, practicable, attainable; see LIKELY 1.

feast *n.* banquet, entertainment, festival, treat, merrymaking, fiesta, barbecue, picnic; see also DINNER.

feat *n.* act, effort, deed; see ACHIEVEMENT.

feather *n.* quill, plume, plumage, down, tuft, crest, fringe. **—in fine (or high or good) feather** well, in good humor, in good health; see HAPPY.

feature *n.* **1** [Anything calculated to attract interest] innovation, highlight, prominent part, drawing card, main bout, specialty, special attraction, featured attraction. **2** [Matter other than news published in a newspaper] article, editorial, feature story; see STORY. **3** [A salient quality] point, peculiarity, trait; see CHARACTERISTIC.

features *n.* lineaments, looks, appearance; see FACE 1.

featuring *a.* presenting, showing, recommending, calling attention to, giving prominence to, emphasizing, making much of, pointing up, drawing attention to, turning the spotlight on, centering attention on, starring.

feces *n.* excretion, waste, dung; see EXCREMENT.

federal *a.* general, central, governmental; see NATIONAL 1.

federation *n.* confederacy, alliance, combination; see ORGANIZATION 2.

fee *n.* remuneration, salary, charge; see PAY 2.

feeble *a.* fragile, puny, strengthless; see WEAK 1, 2.

feed *n.* provisions, supplies, fodder, food for animals, pasture, forage, roughage. *Common feeds include the following:* grain, small grain, corn, oats, barley, rye, wheat, peanuts, hay, clover, sweet clover, alfalfa, sorghum, kale, soybeans, beets, straw, grass, bran.

feed *v.* feast, give food to, satisfy the hunger of, nourish, supply, support, satisfy, fill, stuff, cram, gorge, banquet, dine, nurse, maintain, fatten, provide food for, cater to, stock, furnish, nurture, sustain, encourage, serve.—*Ant.* STARVE, deprive, quench.

feel *n.* touch, quality, air; see FEELING 2.

feel *v.* **1** [To examine by touch] finger, explore, stroke, palm, caress, handle, manipulate, press, squeeze, fondle, tickle, paw, feel for, fumble,

grope, grasp, grapple, grip, clutch, clasp, run the fingers over, pinch, poke, contact. **2** [To experience] sense, perceive, receive, be aware of, observe, be moved by, respond, know, acknowledge, appreciate, accept, be affected, be impressed, be excited by, have the experience of, take to heart.—*Ant.* IGNORE, be insensitive to, be unaware of. **3** [To believe] consider, hold, know; see THINK 1. **4** [To give an impression through touch] appear, exhibit, suggest; see SEEM.

feeler *n.* hint, tentative proposal, trial balloon; see TEST.

feeling *n.* **1** [The sense of touch] tactile sensation, tactility, power of perceiving by touch, touch. **2** [State of the body, or of a part of it] sense, sensation, sensibility, feel, sensitiveness, sensory response, perception, perceptivity, susceptibility, activity, consciousness, receptivity, responsiveness, excitability, excitement, awareness, enjoyment, sensuality, pain, pleasure, reaction, motor response, reflex, excitation.—*Ant.* INDIFFERENCE, apathy, numbness. **3** [A personal reaction] opinion, thought, outlook; see ATTITUDE. **4** [Sensitivity] taste, emotion, passion, tenderness, discrimination, delicacy, discernment, sentiment, sentimentality, refinement, culture, cultivation, capacity, faculty, judgment, sympathy, imagination, intelligence, intuition, spirit, soul, appreciation, response, affection.—*Ant.* RUDENESS, crudeness, coldness.

feign *v.* simulate, imagine, fabricate; see PRETEND 1.

feigned *a.* imagined, fictitious, simulated; see IMAGINARY.

fell *v.* pull down, knock down, cause to fall; see CUT 1.

fellow *n.* **1** [A young man] youth, lad, boy, person, teenager, stripling, novice, cadet, apprentice, adolescent, juvenile, youngster, guy*, kid*, squirt*. **2** [An associate] peer, associate, colleague; see FRIEND.

fellowship *n.* **1** [Congenial social feeling] comradeship, conviviality, sociability, intimacy, acquaintance, friendliness, familiarity, good-fellowship, amity, affability, camaraderie, togetherness.—*Ant.* RUDENESS, unsociability, surliness. **2** [Subsistence payment to encourage study] stipend, scholarship, honorarium, subsidy, teaching fellowship, assistantship.

felon *n.* outlaw, delinquent, convict; see CRIMINAL.

felony *n.* major crime, offense, transgression; see CRIME.

female *a.* womanly, sensitive, childbearing, of the female gender.—*Ant.*

MALE, masculine, of the male gender.

feminine *a.* female, distaff, soft, womanly, delicate, gentle, ladylike, matronly, maidenly, tender, fair; see also WOMANLY.—*Ant.* MALE, masculine, virile.

fence *n.* **1** [That which surrounds an enclosure] picket fence, wire fence, board fence, barbed-wire fence, rail fence, chain-link fence, iron fence, hedge, backstop, rail, railing, barricade, net, barrier, wall, dike. **2** [A receiver of stolen goods] accomplice, front*, uncle*; see CRIMINAL. — **mend one's fences** renew contacts, look after one's political interests, solicit votes; see CAMPAIGN. —**on the fence** undecided, uncommitted, indifferent; see UNCERTAIN.

fender *n.* guard, mudguard, shield, apron, buffer, mask, cover, frame, protector, bumper.

fend for oneself *v.* take care of oneself, stay alive, eke out an existence; see SURVIVE 1.

fend off *v.* keep off, ward off, repel; see DEFEND 1.

ferment *v.* effervesce, sour, foam, froth, bubble, seethe, fizz, sparkle, boil, work, ripen, dissolve, evaporate, rise.

fermentation *n.* souring, foaming, seething; see FROTH.

fern *n.* greenery, bracken, lacy plant; see PLANT.

ferocious *a.* fierce, savage, wild; see FIERCE.—*Ant.* GENTLE, meek, mild.

ferocity *n.* fierceness, brutality, barbarity; see CRUELTY.

ferry *n.* boat, barge, packet; see BOAT.

fertile *a.* fruitful, rich, productive, fat, teeming, yielding, arable, flowering.—*Ant.* STERILE, barren, desert.

fertility *n.* fecundity, richness, fruitfulness, potency, virility, pregnancy, productiveness, productivity, generative capacity.

fertilization *n.* **1** [The enrichment of land] manuring, dressing, mulching; see PREPARATION 1. **2** [Impregnation of the ovum] insemination, impregnation, pollination, implantation, breeding, propagation, generation, procreation.

fertilize *v.* **1** [To enrich land] manure, dress, lime, mulch, cover, treat, enrich. **2** [To impregnate] breed, make pregnant, generate, germinate, pollinate, inseminate, propagate, procreate, get with child, beget, knock up*.

fertilizer *n.* manure, chemical fertilizer, plant food, compost, humus, mulch. *Common fertilizers include the following:* barnyard manure, guano, sphagnum, peat moss, phosphate, dung, crushed limestone, bone dust, kelp, bone meal, nitrogen, ammonium sulfate, legumes, potash.

fervent *a.* zealous, eager, ardent; see ENTHUSIASTIC.

fervor *n.* fervency, ardor, enthusiasm; see ZEAL.

fester *v.* rankle, putrefy, rot; see SPOIL.

festival *n.* festivity, feast, entertainment; see CELEBRATION.

festive *a.* merry, gay, joyful; see HAPPY.

festivity *n.* revelry, pleasure, amusement; see ENTERTAINMENT.

fetch *v.* bring, get, retrieve; see CARRY 1.

fete *n.* festival, entertainment, ball; see CELEBRATION, PARTY 1.

fetish *n.* fixation, craze, mania; see OBSESSION.

fetus *n.* developing organism, embryo, the young of an animal in the uterus.

feud *n.* quarrel, strife, bickering; see FIGHT.

fever *n.* abnormal temperature and pulse, febrile disease, high body temperature; see ILLNESS 1.

feverish *a.* burning, above normal, running a temperature; see HOT 1.

few *a.* not many, scarcely any, less, sparse, scanty, thin, widely spaced, inconsiderable, negligible, infrequent, not too many, some, any, scarce, rare, few and far between.— *Ant.* MANY, numerous, innumerable.

few *pron.* not many, a small number, a handful, scarcely any, not too many, several, a scattering, three or four, a sprinkling.—*Ant.* MANY, a multitude, a great many. —**quite a few** several, some, a large number; see MANY.

fiancé *n.* intended, betrothed, person engaged to be married; see LOVER.

fib *n.* prevarication, fabrication, misrepresentation; see LIE.

fiber *n.* thread, cord, string, strand, tissue, filament, vein, hair, strip, shred. *Some common fibers include the following:* vegetable fiber, animal fiber, synthetic fiber, silk, linen, hemp, cotton, wool, jute, rayon, nylon, orlon, polyester, acetate.

fibrous *a.* veined, hairy, coarse; see STRINGY.

fickle *a.* capricious, whimsical, mercurial; see CHANGING.

fiction *n.* novel, tale, romance; see STORY.

fictitious *a.* made-up, untrue, counterfeit; see FALSE 1, 2.

fiddle* *n.* violin, stringed instrument, cornstalk fiddle*; see MUSICAL INSTRUMENT. —**fit as a fiddle**

healthy, strong, sound; see WELL 1.
—**play second fiddle (to)** defer to, be inferior to, be less successful than; see FAIL 1.

fidelity *n.* fealty, constancy, devotion; see LOYALTY.

fidget *v.* stir, twitch, worry; see WIGGLE.

fidgety *a.* nervous, uneasy, apprehensive; see RESTLESS.

field *n.* 1 [Open land] grainfield, hayfield, meadow, pasture, range, acreage, plot, patch, garden, cultivated ground, grassland, green, ranchland, arable land, plowed land, cleared land, cropland, tract, vineyard. 2 [An area devoted to sport] diamond, gridiron, track, rink, court, course, racecourse, golf course, racetrack, arena, stadium, theater, amphitheater, playground, park, turf, green, fairground. 3 [An area devoted to a specialized activity] airfield, airport, flying field, battlefield, battleground, sector, field of fire, terrain, no man's land, theater of war, field of battle, field of honor, parade ground, range. —**play the field** experiment, explore, look elsewhere; see DISCOVER, EXAMINE, TRY 1.

fielder *n.* infielder, outfielder, center fielder; see BASEBALL PLAYER.

fiend *n.* 1 [A wicked or cruel person] monster, barbarian, brute; see BEAST. 2 [*An addict] fan, aficionado, monomaniac; see ADDICT.

fiendish *a.* diabolical, demoniac, infernal; see BAD.

fierce *a.* ferocious, wild, furious, enraged, raging, impetuous, untamed, angry, passionate, savage, primitive, brutish, animal, raving, outrageous, terrible, vehement, frightening, awful, horrible, venomous, bold, malevolent, malign, brutal, uncivilized, feral, menacing, fearsome, cruel, hostile, rabid, merciless, monstrous, severe, rough, rude, vicious, dangerous, frenzied, mad, insane, desperate, ravening, frantic, wrathful, irate, fanatical, bestial, boisterous, violent, threatening, stormy, thunderous, howling, tumultuous, turbulent, uncontrolled, storming, blustering, cyclonic, torrential, frightful, fearful, devastating, hellish, rip-roaring*.—*Ant.* MILD, moderate, calm.

fiercely *a.* ferociously, violently, wildly, terribly, vehemently, angrily, threateningly, frighteningly, awfully, horribly, mightily, passionately, impetuously, boldly, irresistibly, furiously, riotously, brutally, monstrously, forcibly, forcefully, convulsively, hysterically, severely, roughly, rudely, viciously, dangerously, madly, insanely, desperately, outrageously, savagely, frantically, wrathfully,

irately, virulently, relentlessly, turbulently, overpoweringly, strongly, deliriously, fanatically, with rage, in a frenzy, tooth and nail.—*Ant.* PEACEFULLY, mildly, reasonably.

fiesta *n.* festival, holiday, feast; see CELEBRATION.

fifty *a.* half a hundred, half a century, two score and ten, many, five times ten, a considerable number.

fight *n.* 1 [A violent physical struggle] strife, contention, feud, quarrel, contest, encounter, row, dispute, disagreement, battle, confrontation, controversy, brawl, bout, match, fisticuffs, round, fracas, difficulty, altercation, bickering, wrangling, riot, argument, debate, competition, rivalry, conflict, skirmish, clash, scuffle, collision, brush, action, engagement, combat, exchange of blows, blow, wrestling match, squabble, game, discord, estrangement, fuss, tussle, scrap*, free-for-all, ruckus*, run-in*, tiff, flare-up, go*, set-to*, difference of opinion. 2 [Willingness or eagerness to fight] mettle, hardihood, boldness; see COURAGE.

fight *v.* strive, war, struggle, resist, assert oneself, challenge, meet, contend, attack, carry on war, withstand, give blow for blow, do battle, war against, persevere, force, go to war, exchange blows, encounter, oppose, tussle, grapple, flare up, engage with, combat, wrestle, box, spar, skirmish, quarrel, bicker, dispute, have it out, squabble, come to grips with, row, light into*, tear into*, mix it up with*.—*Ant.* RETREAT, submit, yield. —**fight back** defend oneself, resist, retaliate; see OPPOSE 2. —**fight off** defend from, hold back, resist; see DEFEND 1.

fighter *n.* 1 [One who fights] contestant, disputant, contender, party to a quarrel, warrior, soldier, combatant, belligerent, assailant, aggressor, antagonist, rival, opponent, champion, bully, competitor, controversialist, scrapper*. 2 [A professional pugilist] boxer, prizefighter, pug*, bruiser*.

fighting *a.* combative, battling, brawling, unbeatable, argumentative, angry, ferocious, quarrelsome, ready to fight, belligerent, boxing, wrestling, warlike, contending, up in arms.

fighting *n.* combat, struggle, strife; see FIGHT.

figurative *a.* not literal, metaphorical, allegorical; see ILLUSTRATIVE.

figure *n.* 1 [A form] shape, mass, structure; see FORM 1. 2 [The human torso] body, frame, torso, shape, form, configuration, build, appearance, outline, posture, attitude, pose, carriage. **3** [A representation of quantity] sum, total, symbol; see NUMBER. **4** [Price] value, worth, terms; see PRICE.

figure *v.* **1** [To compute] reckon, number, count; see CALCULATE. **2** [To estimate] set a figure, guess, fix a price; see ESTIMATE. **3** [*To come to a conclusion] suppose, think, opine; see DECIDE. **4** [To figure out] solve, master, reason; see DISCOVER.

figure of speech *n. Varieties include the following:* image, comparison, metaphor, simile, trope, metonymy, synecdoche, personification, hyperbole, litotes, allegory, parable, allusion, euphemism, analogue, parallel, irony, satire, understatement, paradox.

file *n.* **1** [An orderly collection of papers] card index, card file, portfolio, record, classified index, list, register, dossier, notebook. **2** [Steel abrasive] rasp, steel, sharpener. *Types of files include the following:* flat, rat-tail, triangular, fingernail, wood. **3** [A line] rank, row, column; see LINE 1. **—on file** filed, cataloged, registered; see RECORDED.

file *v.* **1** [To arrange in order] classify, index, deposit, categorize, catalog, record, register, list, arrange. **2** [To use an abrasive] abrade, rasp, scrape, smooth, rub down, level off, finish, sharpen.

fill *n.* enough, capacity, satiety; see PLENTY.

fill *v.* **1** [To pour to the capacity of the container] pack, stuff, replenish, furnish, supply, satisfy, blow up, fill up, pump up, fill to capacity, fill to overflowing, brim over, swell, charge, inflate.—*Ant.* EMPTY, exhaust, drain. **2** [To occupy available space] take up, pervade, overflow, stretch, bulge out, distend, brim over, stretch, swell, blow up, run over at the top, permeate, take over. **—fill in** **1** [To insert] write in, answer, sign; see ANSWER. **2** [To substitute] replace, act for, represent; see SUBSTITUTE. **—fill out** **1** [To enlarge] swell out, expand, round out; see GROW 1. **2** [To insert] fill in, sign, apply; see ANSWER. **—fill up** saturate, pack, stuff; see FILL 1.

filled *a.* finished, completed, done; see FULL 1.

filling *n.* stuffing, dressing, contents, mixture, center, layer, filler, fill, sauce, insides, lining, wadding, padding, cement, innards*, guts*.

film *n.* **1** [Thin, membranous matter] gauze, tissue, fabric, sheet, membrane, layer, transparency, foil, fold, skin, coat, coating, scum, veil, cobweb, web, mist, cloud. **2** [A preparation containing a light-sensitive emulsion] negative, positive, microfilm, color film. **3** [A moving picture] motion picture, cinema, photoplay; see MOVIE.

film *v.* record, take, shoot; see PHOTOGRAPH.

filter *v.* **1** [To soak slowly] seep, penetrate, percolate; see SOAK 1. **2** [To clean by filtering] strain, purify, sift, sieve, refine, clarify, clean, separate.

filth *n.* dirt, dung, feces, contamination, corruption, pollution, foul matter, sewage, muck, manure, slop, squalor, trash, grime, mud, smudge, silt, garbage, carrion, slush, slime, sludge, foulness, filthiness, excrement, dregs, lees, sediment, rottenness, impurity.—*Ant.* CLEANLINESS, purity, spotlessness.

filthy *a.* foul, squalid, nasty; see DIRTY 1.

fin *n.* membrane, paddle, propeller, balance, guide, blade, ridge, organ, spine, pectoral fin, ventral fin, dorsal fin, caudal fin, pelvic fin, fish's tail, flipper.

final *a.* terminal, concluding, ultimate; see LAST 1.

finalized *a.* concluded, decided, completed; see FINISHED 1.

finally *a.* **1** [As though a matter were settled] with finality, with conviction, settled, in a final manner, certainly, officially, irrevocably, decisively, definitely, beyond recall, permanently, for all time, conclusively, assuredly, done with, once and for all, for good, beyond the shadow of a doubt.—*Ant.* TEMPORARILY, momentarily, for the time being. **2** [After a long period] at length, at last, in the end, subsequently, in conclusion, lastly, after all, after a while, eventually, ultimately, at long last, at the final point, at the last moment, at the end, tardily, belatedly, when all is said and done, in spite of all, at the eleventh hour.

finance *n.* business, commerce, financial affairs; see ECONOMICS.

finance *v.* fund, support, provide funds for; see PAY FOR.

finances *n.* revenue, capital, funds; see WEALTH.

financial *a.* economic, business, monetary; see COMMERCIAL.

financier *n.* capitalist, banker, investor; see EXECUTIVE.

find *n.* fortunate discovery, findings, acquisition; see DISCOVERY.

find *v.* discover, detect, notice, observe, perceive, arrive at, discern, hit upon, encounter, uncover, recover, expose, stumble on, happen upon, come across, track down, dig up, turn up, scare up*, run across, run into, lay one's hands on, bring to light, spot; see also SEE 1.—*Ant.* LOSE, mislay, miss. **—find out** rec-

ognize, learn, identify; see DIS-
COVER.

finder *n.* acquirer, discoverer, search
party; see OWNER.—*Ant.* LOSER,
seeker, failure.

finding *n.* verdict, decision, sentence;
see JUDGMENT 3.

findings *n.* data, discoveries, conclusions; see SUMMARY.

fine *a.* **1** [Not coarse] light, powdery,
granular; see LITTLE 1. **2** [Of superior quality] well-made, supreme,
fashionable; see EXCELLENT. **3**
[Exact] precise, distinct, strict; see
ACCURATE 2, DEFINITE 2.

fine *n.* penalty, damage, forfeit; see
PUNISHMENT.

fine *v.* penalize, exact, tax, confiscate, levy, seize, extort, alienate,
make pay; see also PUNISH.

finger *n.* digit, organ of touch, tactile
member, forefinger, thumb, index
finger, extremity, pointer, feeler,
tentacle, middle finger, ring finger,
little finger, pinkie. —**have (or
keep) one's fingers crossed*** wish,
aspire to, pray for; see HOPE. —**lift a
finger** make an effort, attempt,
endeavor; see TRY 1. —**put one's finger on** indicate, ascertain, detect;
see DISCOVER. —**put the finger on***
inform on, turn in, fink on*; see
TELL 1.

finger *v.* **1** [To feel] handle, touch,
manipulate; see FEEL 1. **2** [To
choose or specify] appoint, point out,
name; see CHOOSE.

fingernail *n.* nail, talon, matrix; see
CLAW.

finish *n.* **1** [The end] close, termination, ending; see END 2. **2** [An
applied surface] shine, polish, glaze,
surface. *Finishes include the following:* shellac, oil, plastic, turpentine,
lacquer, stain, varnish, polish, wallpaper, wash, whitewash, paint,
casein paint, enamel, gold leaf, wax,
veneer, cement, stucco, luster.

finish *v.* **1** [To bring to an end] complete, end, perfect; see ACHIEVE. **2**
[To develop a surface] polish, wax,
stain; see COVER 1, PAINT 2. **3** [To
come to an end] cease, close, end;
see STOP.

finished *a.* **1** [Completed] done,
accomplished, perfected, achieved,
ended, performed, executed, dispatched, concluded, complete,
through, fulfilled, closed, over,
decided, brought about, ceased,
stopped, resolved, settled, made,
worked out, rounded out, discharged, satisfied, disposed of, realized, finalized, effected, put into
effect, all over with, attained, done
with, made an end of, brought to a
close, said and done, sewed up*,
wound up.—*Ant.* UNFINISHED,
imperfect, incomplete. **2** [Given a
finish] polished, coated, varnished;
see PAINTED 2.

fire *n.* **1** [Burning] flame, conflagration, blaze, campfire, coals, flame
and smoke, blazing fire, hearth,
burning coals, tinder, bonfire, bed of
coals, embers, source of heat,
sparks, heat, glow, warmth, luminosity, combustion, pyre, signal fire,
flare, inferno. **2** [The discharge of
ordnance] artillery attack, bombardment, rounds, barrage, explosions,
bombings, curtain of fire, volley,
sniping, mortar attack, salvos,
shells, pattern of fire, fire superiority, crossfire, machine-gun fire, rifle
fire, small-arms fire, antiaircraft
fire; see also ATTACK. —**catch (on)
fire** begin burning, ignite, flare up;
see BURN. —**on fire 1** [Burning]
flaming, fiery, hot; see BURNING. **2**
[Excited] full of ardor, enthusiastic,
zealous; see EXCITED. —**open fire**
start shooting, shoot, attack; see
SHOOT 1. —**play with fire** gamble,
endanger one's interests, do something dangerous; see RISK. —**set fire
to** ignite, oxidize, make burn; see
BURN. —**set the world on fire**
achieve, become famous, excel; see
SUCCEED 1. —**under fire** criticized,
censured, under attack; see
ATTACKED.

fire *v.* **1** [To set on fire] kindle,
enkindle, ignite, inflame, light,
burn, set fire to, put a match to,
start a fire, set burning, touch off,
rekindle, relight.—*Ant.* EXTINGUISH,
smother, quench. **2** [To shoot] discharge, shoot off, blast; see SHOOT 1.
3 [To dismiss] discharge, let go,
eject; see DISMISS.

fired *a.* **1** [Subjected to fire] set on
fire, burned, baked, ablaze, afire, on
fire, aflame, burning, incandescent,
scorched, glowing, kindled, enkindled, smoking, smoldering, heated.
2 [Discharged] dropped, let go, given
one's walking papers*; see DIS-
CHARGED.

fireman *n.* **1** [One who extinguishes
fires] firefighter, engineman, lad-
derman, fire chief. **2** [One who
fuels engines or furnaces] stoker,
engineer's helper, railroad man,
trainman, attendant.

fireplace *n.* hearth, chimney, hearth-
side, stove, furnace, blaze, bed of
coals, grate.

fireproof *a.* flameproof, fire-retard-
ant, noncombustible, nonflammable,
fire-resistant, incombustible, concrete and steel, asbestos.

fireworks *n.* rockets, Roman can-
dles, sparklers; see EXPLOSIVE.

firm *a.* **1** [Stable] fixed, solid, rooted,
immovable, fastened, motionless,
secured, steady, substantial,
durable, rigid, bolted, welded, riv-
eted, soldered, embedded, nailed,
tightened, fast, secure, sound,
immobile, unmovable, mounted, sta-

tionary, set, settled.—*Ant.* LOOSE, movable, mobile. **2** [Firm in texture] solid, dense, compact, hard, stiff, impenetrable, impervious, rigid, hardened, inflexible, unyielding, thick, compressed, substantial, heavy, close, condensed, impermeable.—*Ant.* SOFT, porous, flabby. **3** [Settled in purpose] determined, steadfast, resolute; see CONSTANT. —**stand (or hold) firm** be steadfast, endure, maintain one's resolution; see FIGHT, RESOLVE.

firmly *a.* **1** [Not easily moved] immovably, solidly, rigidly, stably, durably, enduringly, substantially, securely, heavily, stiffly, inflexibly, soundly, strongly, thoroughly.—*Ant.* LIGHTLY, tenuously, insecurely. **2** [Showing determination] resolutely, steadfastly, doggedly, stolidly, stubbornly, tenaciously, determinedly, staunchly, constantly, intently, purposefully, persistently, obstinately, unwaveringly, through thick and thin.

firmness *n.* stiffness, hardness, toughness, solidity, impenetrability, durability, imperviousness, temper, impermeability, inflexibility.

first *a.* beginning, original, primary, prime, primal, antecedent, initial, virgin, earliest, opening, introductory, primeval, leading, in the beginning, front, head, rudimentary.—*Ant.* LAST, ultimate, final. —**in the first place** firstly, initially, to begin with; see FIRST.

first aid *n.* emergency medical aid, emergency relief, field dressing; see MEDICINE 2, TREATMENT 2.

first-class *a.* superior, supreme, choice; see EXCELLENT.

first-rate *a.* prime, very good, choice; see EXCELLENT.

fiscal *a.* monetary, economic, financial; see COMMERCIAL.

fish *n.* seafood, panfish, denizen of the deep. *Types of fish include the following:* shark, skate, ray, manta, catfish, pickerel, pike, perch, trout, flounder, sucker, sunfish, bass, crappy, mackerel, cod, salmon, carp, minnow, eel, bullhead, herring, shad, barracuda, swordfish, marlin, grouper, piranha, goldfish, gar, dogfish, flyingfish, whitefish, tuna, pompano, haddock, hake, halibut, mullet, loach, muskellunge, muskie, sardine, smelt, anchovy, angelfish, neon tetra, swordtail, molly; see also SHELLFISH. —**drink like a fish** drink heavily, get drunk, become inebriated; see DRINK 2. —**like a fish out of water** out of place, alien, displaced; see UNFAMILIAR 1.

fish *v.* go fishing, troll for, net, shrimp, bait the hook, trawl, angle, cast one's net. —**fish for** hint at, elicit, try to evoke; see HINT.

fisherman *n.* angler, fisher, harpooner, sailor, seaman, whaler, fish catcher.

fishing *n.* angling, casting, trawling; see SPORT 1.

fishy* *a.* improbable, dubious, implausible; see UNLIKELY.

fist *n.* clenched hand, clenched fist, hand, clutch, clasp, grasp, grip, hold.

fit *a.* **1** [Appropriate by nature] suitable, proper, fitting, likely, expedient, appropriate, convenient, timely, opportune, feasible, practicable, wise, advantageous, favorable, preferable, beneficial, desirable, adequate, tasteful, becoming, agreeable, seasonable, due, rightful, decent, equitable, legitimate, harmonious, pertinent, according, relevant, in keeping, consistent, applicable, compatible, admissible, concurrent, to the point, adapted, fitted, suited, calculated, prepared, qualified, competent, matched, readymade, accommodated, right, happy, lucky, cut out for*.—*Ant.* unfit, unseemly, inappropriate. **2** [In good physical condition] trim, in good health, robust; see HEALTHY.

fit *n.* **1** [Sudden attack of disease] muscular convulsion, spasm, seizure, stroke, epileptic attack, paroxysm, spell*; see also ILLNESS 1. **2** [Transitory spell of action or feeling] impulsive action, burst, rush, outbreak, torrent, tantrum, mood, outburst, whimsy, huff, rage, spell. —**have (or throw) a fit*** become angry, lose one's temper, give vent to emotion; see RAGE 1.

fit *v.* **1** [To be suitable in character] agree, suit, accord, harmonize, apply, belong, conform, consist, fit right in, be in keeping, parallel, relate, concur, match, correspond, be comfortable, respond, have its place, answer the purpose, meet, click*.—*Ant.* OPPOSE, disagree, clash. **2** [To make suitable] arrange, alter, adapt; see ADJUST 1.

fitness *n.* appropriateness, suitability, propriety, expediency, convenience, adequacy, correspondence, decency, decorum, harmony, keeping, consistency, applicability, compatibility, rightness, timeliness, adaptation, qualification, accommodation, competence.

fix *v.* **1** [To make firm] plant, implant, secure; see FASTEN. **2** [To prepare a meal] prepare, heat, get ready; see COOK. **3** [To put in order] correct, improve, settle, put into shape, reform, patch, rejuvenate, touch up, revive, refresh, renew, renovate, rebuild, make compatible, clean, align, adapt, mend, adjust. —

fix up* fix, mend, rehabilitate; see REPAIR.

fixed *a.* **1** [Firm] solid, rigid, immovable; see FIRM 1. **2** [Repaired] rebuilt, in order, timed, synchronized, adjusted, settled, mended, rearranged, adapted, corrected, restored, renewed, improved, patched up, put together, in working order. **3** [*Prearranged] predesigned, put-up*, set up*; see PLANNED.

fixings *n.* parts, components, constituents; see INGREDIENTS.

fixture *n.* convenience, gas appliance, electric appliance; see APPLIANCE.

fizz *n.* hissing, sputtering, bubbling; see NOISE 1.

fizzle* *n.* disappointment, fiasco, defeat; see FAILURE 1.

flabby *a.* flaccid, slack, soft; see FAT.

flag *n.* banner, standard, colors; see EMBLEM.

flag *v.* signal, wave, give a sign to; see SIGNAL.

flagrant *a.* notorious, disgraceful, infamous; see OUTRAGEOUS.

flair *n.* talent, aptitude, gift; see ABILITY.

flake *n.* scale, cell, sheet, wafer, peel, skin, slice, sliver, layer, leaf, shaving, plate, section, scab.

flake *v.* scale, peel, sliver, shed, drop, chip, slice, pare, trim, wear away.

flamboyant *a.* baroque, bombastic, ostentatious; see ORNATE.

flame *n.* blaze, flare, flash; see FIRE 1.

flame *v.* blaze, oxidize, flare up; see BURN.

flaming *a.* blazing, ablaze, fiery; see BURNING.

flannel *n.* light woolen cloth, cotton flannel, flannelette; see WOOL.

flap *n.* fold, tab, lapel, fly, cover, pendant, drop, tail, appendage, tag, accessory, apron, strip.

flap *v.* flutter, flash, swing; see WAVE 1.

flare *n.* glare, brief blaze, spark; see FLASH.

flare *v.* blaze, glow, burn; see FLASH. —**flare up 1** [*Said of persons*] lose one's temper, rant, seethe; see RAGE 1. **2** [*Said of fire*] glow, burst into flame, blaze; see BURN.

flash *n.* glimmer, sparkle, glitter, glisten, gleam, beam, blaze, flicker, flame, glare, burst, impulse, vision, dazzle, shimmer, shine, glow, twinkle, twinkling, phosphorescence, reflection, radiation, ray, luster, spark, streak, stream, illumination, incandescence.

flash *v.* glimmer, sparkle, glitter, glisten, gleam, beam, blaze, flame, glare, dazzle, shimmer, shine, glow,

twinkle, reflect, radiate, shoot out beams, flicker; see also SHINE 1, 2.

flashlight *n.* electric lantern, spotlight, torch (British); see LIGHT 1.

flashy *a.* gaudy, showy, ostentatious; see ORNATE.

flask *n.* decanter, jug, canteen; see BOTTLE.

flat *a.* **1** [Lying in a smooth plane] level, even, smooth, spread out, extended, prostrate, horizontal, low, on a level, fallen, level with the ground, prone.—*Ant.* ROUGH, raised, uneven. **2** [Lacking savor] unseasoned, insipid, flavorless; see TASTELESS 1.

flatten *v.* level off, even out, smooth, spread out, depress, squash, smash, level, even, knock down, wear down, beat down, fell, floor, ground, roll out, straighten, deflate.—*Ant.* RAISE, elevate, inflate.

flattened *a.* leveled, depressed, smoothed; see FLAT 1.

flatter *v.* overpraise, adulate, glorify; see PRAISE 1.

flatterer *n.* parasite, toady, sycophant, flunky, slave, puppet, groveler, sniveler, yes man*, bootlicker*, apple polisher*, doormat*.

flattering *a.* pleasing, favorable, unduly favorable; see COMPLIMENTARY.

flattery *n.* adulation, compliments, blandishment, sycophancy, false praise, applause, commendation, tribute, gratification, pretty speeches, soft words, fawning, blarney, soft soap*, hokum*, mush*.—*Ant.* HATRED, criticism, censure.

flaunt *v.* vaunt, display, brandish; see BOAST.

flaunting *a.* gaudy, ostentatious, pretentious; see ORNATE.

flavor *n.* taste, savor, tang, relish, smack, twang, gusto, piquancy, zest, aftertaste. *Individual flavors include the following:* tartness, sweetness, acidity, saltiness, spiciness, pungency, piquancy, astringency, bitterness, sourness, pepperiness, hotness, gaminess, greasiness, fishy taste.

flavor *v.* season, salt, pepper, spice, give a tang to, make tasty, bring out a flavor in, put in flavoring.

flavoring *n.* essence, extract, seasoning, spice, additive, condiment, sauce, relish; see also HERB, SPICE.

flavorless *a.* insipid, flat, bland; see TASTELESS 1.

flaw *n.* defect, imperfection, stain; see BLEMISH.

flawless *a.* faultless, sound, impeccable; see PERFECT.

flea *n.* dog flea, sand flea, flea beetle; see INSECT.

fleck *n.* mite, speck, dot; see BIT 1.

flee *v.* desert, escape, run; see RETREAT.

fleet *n.* armada, naval force, task force; see NAVY.

flesh *n.* meat, fat, muscle, brawn, tissue, cells, flesh and blood, protoplasm, body parts, heart, insides*. —one's (own) flesh and blood family, kindred, kin; see RELATIVE.

fleshy *a.* obese, plump, corpulent; see FAT.

flexibility *n.* pliancy, plasticity, flexibleness, pliableness, suppleness, elasticity, extensibility, limberness, litheness.

flexible *a.* limber, lithe, supple, plastic, elastic, bending, malleable, pliable, soft, spongy, tractable, moldable, yielding, formable, bendable, impressionable, like putty, like wax, adjustable, stretchable, resilient, rubbery, springy.—*Ant.* STIFF, hard, rigid.

flicker *v.* sparkle, twinkle, glitter; see FLASH, SHINE 1.

flight *n.* 1 [Act of remaining aloft] soaring, winging, flying, journey by air. 2 [Travel by air] aerial navigation, aeronautics, flying, gliding, space flight, air transport, aviation. 3 [Act of fleeing] fleeing, running away, retreating; see RETREAT 1. 4 [Stairs] steps, staircase, stairway; see STAIRS.

flighty *a.* capricious, fickle, whimsical; see CHANGING.

flimsy *a.* slight, infirm, frail, weak, unsubstantial, inadequate, defective, wobbly, fragile, makeshift, decrepit; see also POOR 2.

flinch *v.* start, shrink back, blench; see COWER.

fling *n.* indulgence, party, good time; see CELEBRATION.

fling *v.* toss, sling, dump; see THROW 1.

flippancy *n.* impertinence, impudence, sauciness; see RUDENESS.

flippant *a.* impudent, saucy, smart*; see RUDE 2.

flirt *n.* coquette, tease, wolf*; see LOVER.

flirt *v.* coquet, make advances, make eyes at; see SEDUCE.

float *n.* buoy, air cell, air cushion, pontoon, bobber, cork, raft, diving platform, life preserver.

float *v.* waft, stay afloat, swim; see DRIFT.

floating *a.* buoyant, hollow, unsinkable, lighter-than-water, light, swimming, inflated, sailing, soaring, volatile, loose, free.—*Ant.* HEAVY, submerged, sunk.

flock *n.* group, pack, drove; see HERD.

flock *v.* throng, congregate, crowd; see GATHER 1.

flood *n.* deluge, surge, tide, high tide, flash flood, overflow, torrent, wave, flood tide, tidal flood, tidal flow, inundation.

flood *v.* inundate, swamp, overflow, deluge, submerge, immerse, brim over.

floor *n.* 1 [The lower limit of a room] floorboards, deck, flagstones, tiles, planking, ground, carpet, rug, linoleum. 2 [The space in a building between two floors] story, stage, landing, level, basement, cellar, ground floor, ground story, lower story, first floor, mezzanine, upper story, downstairs, upstairs, loft, attic, garret, penthouse.

flooring *n.* floors, woodwork, oak flooring, hardwood flooring, tile, flagstones, boards, cement, floor covering, linoleum.

flop *v.* 1 [To move with little control] wobble, teeter, stagger, flounder, wriggle, squirm, stumble, tumble, totter, flounce, quiver, flap. 2 [To fall without restraint] tumble, slump, drop; see FALL 1. 3 [*To be a complete failure] founder, fall short, bomb*; see FAIL 1.

flounder *v.* struggle, wallow, blunder; see FLOP 1, TOSS 2.

flour *n.* meal, pulp, powder, grit, bran, starch, wheat germ, white flour, wheat flour, rye flour, potato flour, barley meal, cornmeal, oatmeal, cake flour, pancake flour, soy flour, unbleached flour, semolina, rice flour, all-purpose flour.

flourish *v.* thrive, increase, wax; see SUCCEED 1.

flourishing *a.* thriving, doing well, growing; see RICH 1, SUCCESSFUL.

flow *n.* current, movement, progress, stream, tide, run, river, flood, ebb, surge, influx, outpouring, effusion, gush, spurt, spout, leakage, dribble, oozing, flux, overflow, issue, discharge, drift, course, draft, downdraft, up-current, wind, breeze.

flow *v.* stream, course, slide, slip, glide, move, progress, run, pass, float, sweep, rush, whirl, surge, roll, swell, ebb, pour out, spurt, squirt, flood, spout, rush, gush, well up, drop, drip, seep, trickle, overflow, spill, spew, brim, leak, run out, ooze, splash, pour forth, bubble.

flower *n.* blossom, bud, spray, cluster, shoot, posy*, herb, vine, annual, perennial, flowering shrub, potted plant; see also FRUIT. *Common flowers include the following:* daisy, violet, cowslip, jack-in-the-pulpit, goldenrod, orchid, primrose, bluebell, salvia, geranium, begonia, pansy, calendula, forsythia, daffodil, jonquil, crocus, dahlia, zinnia, tulip, iris, lily, petunia, gladiolus, gladiola, aster, rose, peony, nasturtium, chrysanthemum, poppy, morning-glory, lily of the valley, clematis, buttercup, bougainvillea, dandelion, fuchsia, bridal wreath, lilac, stock, bachelor's button, sweet william, tuberose, bleeding heart, phlox.

flower v. open, blossom, bud; see BLOOM.

flowery a. elaborate, ornamented, rococo; see ORNATE.

flowing a. sweeping, sinuous, spouting, gushing, pouring out, rippling, issuing, fluid, tidal, running.

fluctuate v. vacillate, waver, falter; see HESITATE.

fluctuation n. vacillation, variation, rise and fall; see CHANGE 1.

fluency n. facility of speech, volubility, command of language; see ELOQUENCE.

fluent a. eloquent, voluble, glib, wordy, smooth, talkative, smooth-spoken, garrulous, verbose, chatty, argumentative, articulate, vocal, cogent, persuasive, silver-tongued, having the gift of gab*.—Ant. DUMB, tongue-tied, stammering.

fluffy a. fleecy, fuzzy, lacy; see SOFT 1.

fluid a. liquid, fluent, flowing, running, watery, molten, liquefied, juicy.—Ant. STIFF, solid, frozen.

fluid n. water, vapor, solution; see LIQUID.

flunk* v. miss, drop, have to repeat; see FAIL 1.

flute n. pipe, piccolo, wind instrument, fife, panpipe, recorder; see also MUSICAL INSTRUMENT.

flutter v. flap, ripple, tremble; see WAVE 1, 3.

fly n. 1 [An insect] housefly, bluebottle, bug, winged insect, gnat, horsefly, fruit fly, tsetse fly. 2 [A ball batted into the air] infield fly, high fly, fly ball, fungo, pop fly. 3 [A hook baited artificially] lure, fish lure, dry fly, wet fly, spinner, trout fly, bass fly, minnow.

fly v. 1 [To pass through the air] wing, soar, float, glide, remain aloft, take flight, take wing, hover, sail, swoop, dart, drift, flutter, circle. 2 [To move swiftly] rush, dart, flee; see SPEED. 3 [To flee from danger] retreat, hide, withdraw; see ESCAPE. 4 [To manage a plane in the air] pilot, navigate, control, take off, operate, glide, climb, dive, manipulate, maneuver.

flyer n. aviator, navigator, airman; see PILOT 1.

flying a. floating, passing through the air, on the wing, soaring, gliding, winging, swooping, darting, plummeting, drifting, rising, airborne, in midair.

foam n. fluff, bubbles, lather; see FROTH.

focus n. focal point, locus, point of convergence; see CENTER 1. —**in focus** distinct, obvious, sharply defined; see CLEAR 2. —**out of focus** indistinct, unclear, blurred; see OBSCURE 1.

focus v. 1 [To draw toward a center] concentrate, converge, convene; see CENTER. 2 [To make an image clear] adjust, bring out, get detail; see SHARPEN 2.

foe n. opponent, antagonist, adversary; see ENEMY.

fog n. mist, haze, cloud, film, steam, wisp, smoke, smog, soup*, pea soup*.

foggy a. dull, misty, gray; see HAZY.

fold n. lap, pleat, lapel, tuck, folded portion, part turned over, part turned back, doubled material, crease, turn, folded edge, crimp, wrinkle.

fold v. 1 [To place together, or lay in folds] double, crease, curl, crimp, wrinkle, ruffle, pucker, gather, lap, overlap, overlay.—Ant. UNFOLD, straighten, expand. 2 [*To fail] become insolvent, declare itself bankrupt, close; see FAIL 4.

folder n. 1 [A folded sheet of printed matter] circular, pamphlet, paper, bulletin, advertisement, enclosure, brochure, throwaway, insert. 2 [A light, flexible case] envelope, binder, portfolio, Manila folder.

folk n. race, nation, community, tribe, society, nationality, population, state, culture group, people, culture, ethnic group, clan, confederation.

folklore n. traditions, lore, fables, folk tales, oral tradition, folk wisdom, oral literature, ballad lore, customs, superstitions, legends, folkways, folk wisdom, traditional lore; see also MYTH.

folks* n. relatives, relations, kin; see FAMILY.

follow v. 1 [To be later in time] come next, ensue, postdate; see SUCCEED 2. 2 [To regulate one's action] conform, observe, imitate, copy, take after, match, mirror, reflect, follow the example of, do as, mimic, follow suit, do like, tag along, obey, abide by, adhere to, comply, be in keeping, be consistent with.—Ant. NEGLECT, disregard, depart from. 3 [To observe] heed, regard, keep an eye on; see WATCH. 4 [To understand] comprehend, catch, grasp; see UNDERSTAND 1. 5 [To result] proceed from, happen, ensue; see RESULT. —**as follows** as explained below, as stated in what follows, thus; see FOLLOWING.

follower *n.* henchman, attendant, hanger-on, companion, lackey, helper, partisan, recruit, disciple, pupil, protégé, imitator, apostle, adherent, supporter, zealot, backer, upholder, participant, sponsor, witness, devotee, believer, advocate, member, admirer, patron, promoter, copycat*, yes man*, groupie*.—*Ant.* OPPONENT, deserter, heretic.

following *a.* succeeding, next, ensuing, subsequent, later, after a while, by and by, later on, a while later, then, henceforth, afterwards, presently, afterward, coming after, directly after, in the wake of, pursuing, in pursuit of, in search of, resulting, latter, rear, back.—*Ant.* PRECEDING, former, earlier.

following *n.* group, clientele, public, audience, train, adherents, supporters, hangers-on, patrons.

fond *a.* enamored, attached, affectionate; see LOVING.

fondness *n.* partiality, attachment, kindness; see AFFECTION.

food *n.* victuals, foodstuffs, meat and drink, meat, drink, nutriment, refreshment, edibles, table, comestibles, provisions, stores, sustenance, subsistence, rations, board, cooking, cookery, cuisine, nourishment, fare, grub*, vittles*, eats*, chow*; see also MEAL 2. For food in the menu, see also BREAD, BUTTER, CAKE 2, CANDY, CHEESE, COFFEE, COOKIE, DELICATESSEN 1, DESSERT, DRESSING 1, 2, DRINK 2, EGG, FISH, FLAVORING, FOWL, FRUIT, HERB, JAM 1, JELLY, MEAT, MILK, NUT 1, PASTRY, PICKLE 1, PIE, RELISH 1, ROLL 4, SALAD, SANDWICH, SOUP, SPICE, STEW, TEA, VEAL, VEGETABLE, WINE.

fool *n.* nitwit, simpleton, dunce, oaf, ninny, cretin, nincompoop, dolt, idiot, jackass, ass, buffoon, blockhead, numskull, boob*, goose, ignoramus, imbecile, moron, clown, loon, dullard, fathead*, half-wit, bonehead*, dope*, sap*, birdbrain*, meathead*, lamebrain*, airhead*, ditz*, knucklehead*, dimwit*.—*Ant.* PHILOSOPHER, sage, scholar. —**no** (or **nobody's**) **fool** shrewd, calculating, capable; see ABLE, INTELLIGENT. —**play the fool** be silly, show off, clown; see JOKE.

fool *v.* trick, dupe, mislead; see DECEIVE. —**fool around*** waste time, idle, dawdle; see PLAY 1, 2, WASTE 1, 2.

fooled *a.* tricked, duped, deluded; see DECEIVED.

fooling *a.* joking, jesting, humorous, deceitful, gay, witty, smart, frivolous, flippant, laughable, insincere, misleading, absurd, clever, playful, merry, kidding*, spoofing*.—*Ant.* SERIOUS, grave, earnest.

foolish *a.* silly, simple, half-witted; see STUPID.

foolishly *a.* stupidly, irrationally, idiotically, insanely, imprudently, ineptly, mistakenly, illogically, unwisely, ill-advisedly, crazily, thoughtlessly, carelessly, senselessly, irresponsibly, absurdly, preposterously, ridiculously, with bad judgment, without good sense.

foolishness *n.* folly, weakness, silliness; see STUPIDITY 1.

foot *n.* **1** [A unit of measurement] twelve inches, running foot, front foot, board foot, square foot, cubic foot. **2** [End of the leg] pedal extremity, hoof, paw, pad, dog*, tootsy*. **3** [A foundation] footing, base, pier; see FOUNDATION 2. **4** [A metrical unit in verse] measure, accent, interval, meter, duple meter, triple meter. *Metrical feet include the following:* iamb, dactyl, spondee, trochee, anapest, pyrrhic. —**on foot** running, hiking, moving; see WALKING. —**on one's feet 1** [Upright] standing, erect, vertical; see STRAIGHT. **2** [Established] sound, settled, secure; see ESTABLISHED 1. —**on the wrong foot** unfavorably, ineptly, incapably; see WRONGLY. —**put one's best foot forward*** do one's best, appear at one's best, try hard; see DISPLAY. —**put one's foot down*** be firm, act decisively, determine; see RESOLVE. —**under foot** on the ground, at one's feet, in the way; see UNDER 1.

football *n.* American football, Canadian football, association football, soccer, gridiron pastime.

football player *n.* *In the United States, football players include the following:* end, flanker, tight end, split end, wide receiver, wideout, tackle, guard, center, quarterback, halfback, fullback, running back, blocking back, tailback, H-back, wingback, slotback, linebacker, cornerback, nose guard, free safety, strong safety, punter, place kicker.

foothold *n.* ledge, footing, niche; see STEP 2.

footing *n.* basis, substructure, support; see FOUNDATION 2.

footprint *n.* trace, trail, spoor; see TRACK 2.

footstep *n.* trace, trail, evidence; see TRACK 2. —**follow in someone's footsteps** emulate, succeed, resemble a predecessor; see IMITATE 1.

for *prep.* toward, to, in favor of, intended to be given to, in order to get, under the authority of, in the interest of, during, in order to, in the direction of, to go to, to the amount of, in place of, in exchange for, as, in spite of, supposing, concerning, with respect to, with regard to, notwithstanding, with a view to, for the sake of, in consideration of, in the name of, on the part of.

for *conj.* as, since, seeing that; see BECAUSE.

forbid *v.* prohibit, debar, embargo, restrain, inhibit, preclude, oppose, cancel, hinder, obstruct, bar, prevent, censor, outlaw, declare illegal, withhold, restrict, deny, block, check, disallow, deprive, exclude, ban, taboo, say no to, put under an injunction.—*Ant.* APPROVE, recommend, authorize.

forbidden *a.* denied, taboo, kept back; see REFUSED.

forbidding *a.* unpleasant, offensive, repulsive; see GRIM 1.

force *n.* 1 [Force conceived as a physical property] power, might, energy; see STRENGTH. 2 [Force conceived as part of one's personality] forcefulness, dominance, competence, energy, persistence, willpower, drive, determination, effectiveness, efficiency, authority, impressiveness, ability, capability, potency, sapience, guts*.—*Ant.* INDIFFERENCE, impotence, incompetence. 3 [An organization] group, band, army; see ORGANIZATION 2, POLICE. —**in force** 1 [Powerfully] in full strength, totally, all together; see ALL 2. 2 [In operation] operative, valid, in effect; see WORKING.

force *v.* compel, coerce, press, drive, make, impel, constrain, oblige, obligate, necessitate, require, enforce, demand, order, command, inflict, burden, impose, insist, exact, put under obligation, contract, charge, restrict, limit, pin down, pressure, bring pressure to bear upon, bear down, ram down someone's throat*, high-pressure*, strong-arm*, put the squeeze on*.

forced *a.* compelled, coerced, constrained; see BOUND 2.

forceful *a.* commanding, dominant, electric; see POWERFUL 1.

forcefully *a.* forcibly, stubbornly, willfully; see VIGOROUSLY.

foreboding *n.* premonition, dread, presentiment; see ANTICIPATION.

forecast *n.* prediction, guess, estimate, prognosis, divination, forethought, foresight, prescience, foreknowledge, conjecture, prophecy, calculation, foreseeing.

forecast *v.* predetermine, predict, guess; see FORETELL.

forefather *n.* ancestor, progenitor, forebear; see ANCESTOR.

foregoing *a.* prior, former, previous; see PRECEDING.

foreground *n.* face, forefront, frontage, facade, neighborhood, proximity, nearness, adjacency, range, reach, view.—*Ant.* BACKGROUND, shadow, perspective.

forehead *n.* brow, countenance, temples; see FACE 1.

foreign *a.* remote, exotic, strange, far, distant, inaccessible, unaccustomed, different, unknown, alien, imported, borrowed, immigrant, outside, expatriate, exiled, from abroad, overseas, coming from another land, not native, not domestic, nonresident, alienated, faraway, far-off, outlandish.—*Ant.* LOCAL, national, indigenous.

foreigner *n.* stranger, immigrant, newcomer; see ALIEN.

foreknowledge *n.* foresight, prescience, premonition; see FEELING 4, FORECAST.

foreman *n.* overseer, manager, supervisor, superintendent, head, head man, shop foreman, boss.

foremost *a.* fore, original, primary; see FIRST.

forerunner *n.* herald, harbinger, precursor; see ANCESTOR, MESSENGER.

foresee *v.* prophesy, understand, predict; see FORETELL.

foreseen *a.* anticipated, predictable, prepared for; see EXPECTED, LIKELY 1.

foreshadow *v.* imply, presage, suggest; see FORETELL.

foresight *n.* economy, carefulness, preparedness; see PRUDENCE.

forest *n.* wood, woods, jungle, timber, growth, stand of trees, grove, woodland, park, greenwood, cover, clump, forested area, shelter, brake, backwoods, tall timber; see also TREE.

forestall *v.* thwart, prevent, preclude; see HINDER.

forestry *n.* forest management, horticulture, dendrology, woodcraft, forestation, reclamation, woodmanship; see also CONSERVATION.

foretell *v.* predict, prophesy, divine, foresee, announce in advance, prognosticate, augur, portend, foreshadow.—*Ant.* RECORD, confirm, recount.

forethought *n.* judgment, planning, foresight; see PRUDENCE.

forever *a.* everlastingly, permanently, immortally, on and on, ever, perpetually, always, in perpetuity, *in perpetuum* (Latin), world without end, eternally, interminably, infinitely, enduringly, unchangingly, durably, ever and again, indestructibly, endlessly, forevermore, for good, till hell freezes over*, for keeps*, for always, now and forever, for life, till death do us part.—*Ant.* TEMPORARILY, for a time, at present.

forewarn *v.* alert, advise, caution; see WARN.

forfeit v. sacrifice, give up, relinquish; see ABANDON 1.

forge v. falsify, counterfeit, fabricate, trump up, invent, feign, make, fashion, design, imitate, copy, duplicate, reproduce, trace.

forger n. falsifier, counterfeiter, con man*; see CRIMINAL.

forgery n. imitation, copy, counterfeit, fake, fabrication, sham, phony*.—Ant. ORIGINAL, real thing, real article.

forget v. lose consciousness of, put out of one's head, fail to remember, be forgetful, have a short memory, overlook, ignore, omit, neglect, slight, disregard, lose sight of, pass over, skip, think no more of, close one's eyes to, not give another thought to, draw a blank*, dismiss from the mind; see also NEGLECT 2.—Ant. REMEMBER, recall, recollect. —**forget oneself** offend, go astray, lose control; see MISBEHAVE.

forgetful a. inattentive, neglectful, heedless; see CARELESS.

forgetfulness n. negligence, neglect, inattention; see CARELESSNESS.

forgivable a. venial, trivial, pardonable; see EXCUSABLE.

forgive v. pardon, forgive and forget, let pass, excuse, condone, remit, forget, relent, bear no malice, exonerate, exculpate, let bygones be bygones, let it go, kiss and make up, bury the hatchet, turn the other cheek, make allowance, write off.—Ant. HATE, resent, retaliate.

forgiven a. absolved, taken back, excused; see PARDONED.

forgiveness n. absolution, pardon, acquittal, exoneration, remission, dispensation, reprieve, justification, amnesty, respite.

forgiving a. charitable, openhearted, generous; see KIND.

forgo v. quit, relinquish, waive; see ABANDON 1.

forgotten a. not remembered, not recalled, not recollected, lost, out of one's mind, erased from one's consciousness, beyond recollection, relegated to oblivion, past recall, not recoverable, blanked out, lapsed; see also ABANDONED.

fork n. 1 [A forked implement] table fork, hayfork, pitchfork, salad fork, cooking fork, trident, prong. 2 [A branch of a road or river] bend, turn, crossroad, tributary, byway, junction, branch, stream, confluence.

form n. 1 [Shape] figure, appearance, plan, arrangement, design, outline, configuration, formation, structure, style, construction, fashion, mode, scheme, framework, contour, stance, profile, silhouette, skeleton, anatomy. 2 [The human form] body, frame, torso, build; see FIGURE 2. 3 [The approved procedure] manner, mode, custom; see METHOD. 4 [Anything intended to give form] pattern, model, die; see MOLD 1. 5 [A standard letter or blank] duplicate, form letter, data sheet, information blank, chart, card, reference form, order form, questionnaire, application; see also COPY.

form v. 1 [To give shape to a thing] mold, pattern, model, arrange, make, block out, fashion, construct, devise, plan, design, contrive, produce, invent, frame, scheme, plot, compose, erect, build, cast, cut, carve, chisel, hammer out, put together, whittle, assemble, conceive, create, outline, trace, develop, cultivate, work, complete, finish, perfect, fix, regulate, establish, sculpt, sculpture, bend, twist, knead, set, determine, arrive at, reach.—Ant. DESTROY, demolish, shatter. 2 [To give character to a person] instruct, rear, breed; see TEACH. 3 [To comprise] constitute, figure in, act as; see COMPOSE 1. 4 [To take form] accumulate, condense, harden, set, congeal, accrete, settle, rise, appear, take shape, grow, develop, unfold, mature, materialize, become a reality, take on character, become visible, shape up*, fall into place, get into shape*.—Ant. DISAPPEAR, dissolve, waste away.

formal a. 1 [Notable for arrangement] orderly, precise, set; see REGULAR 3. 2 [Concerned with etiquette and behavior] reserved, distant, stiff; see CONVENTIONAL 3, POLITE. 3 [Official] prescribed, directed, lawful; see APPROVED, LEGAL. 4 [In evening clothes] full dress, black-tie, dressed up; see SOCIAL.

formation n. arrangement, composition, constitution, crystallization, deposit, accumulation, development, fabrication, generation, production, creation, genesis.—Ant. DESTRUCTION, dissolution, annihilation.

formed a. shaped, molded, patterned, modeled, carved, outlined, developed, cultivated, completed, finished, built, forged, created, invented, concocted, designed, accomplished, manufactured, produced, born, perfected, fixed, established, arrived at, solidified, hardened, set, determined.—Ant. SHAPELESS, formless, nebulous.

former a. earlier, previous, past; see PRECEDING.

formerly a. before now, some time ago, once, once upon a time, already, in former times, previously, earlier, in the early days, eons ago, centuries ago, in the past, in the olden days, used to be, long ago, before this, in time past, heretofore, a while back.—*Ant.* RECENTLY, immediately, subsequently.

formula *n.* specifications, prescription, recipe; see METHOD.

formulate *v.* express, give form to, set down; see FORM 1.

fornication *n.* adultery, incontinence, carnality, lechery, illicit sex, lewdness, licentiousness, unfaithfulness, fooling around*, promiscuity, debauchery, libertinism, prostitution.

forsake *v.* desert, leave, quit; see ABANDON 2.

forsaken *a.* destitute, deserted, rejected; see ABANDONED.

fort *n.* fortress, citadel, stockade; see FORTIFICATION.

forth *a.* first, out, into; see AHEAD. —**and so forth** and so on, similarly, and the like; see OTHER.

forthcoming *a.* expected, inevitable, anticipated, future, impending, pending, resulting, awaited, destined, fated, predestined, approaching, in store, at hand, inescapable, imminent, in prospect, prospective, in the wind, in preparation, in the cards.

forthright *a.* at once, straightaway, directly; see IMMEDIATELY.

fortification *n.* fort, fortress, defense, dugout, trench, entrenchment, gun emplacement, barricade, battlement, stockade, outpost, citadel, support, wall, barrier, earthwork, castle, pillbox, bastion, bulwark, breastwork, blockhouse, fortalice*.

fortified *a.* defended, guarded, safeguarded, protected, manned, garrisoned, barricaded, armed, barbed, secured, entrenched, strong, covered, strengthened, supported, surrounded, fortressed, walled, enclosed, stockaded, armored, dug in, hidden, camouflaged.—*Ant.* OPEN, unprotected, unguarded.

fortify *v.* 1 [To strengthen against attack] barricade, entrench, buttress; see DEFEND 1, SUPPORT 1. 2 [To strengthen physically or emotionally] sustain, invigorate, toughen; see STRENGTHEN, SUPPORT 2.

fortitude *n.* firmness, resolution, persistence; see DETERMINATION.

fortunate *a.* lucky, blessed, prosperous, successful, having a charmed life, in luck, favored, well-to-do, happy, triumphant, victorious, overcoming, affluent, thriving, flourishing, healthy, wealthy, well-fixed*, well-heeled*, born with a silver spoon in one's mouth.—*Ant.* UNFORTUNATE, unlucky, cursed.

fortunately *a.* luckily, happily, in good time, auspiciously, favorably,

prosperously, in the nick of time.—*Ant.* UNFORTUNATELY, unluckily, unhappily.

fortune *n.* 1 [Chance] luck, fate, uncertainty; see CHANCE 1. 2 [Great riches] possessions, inheritance, estate; see WEALTH. —**a small fortune** a high price, a great expense, a large amount of money; see PRICE.

forward *a.* 1 [Going forward] advancing, progressing, ahead, leading, progressive, onward, propulsive, in advance.—*Ant.* BACKWARD, retreating, regressive. 2 [Bold] presumptuous, impertinent, fresh; see RUDE 2.

forwarded *a.* shipped, expressed, dispatched; see DELIVERED.

fossil *n.* remains, reconstruction, specimen, skeleton, relic, find, impression, trace, petrified deposit; see also RELIC.

foster *v.* cherish, nurse, nourish; see RAISE 2.

foul *a.* 1 [Disgusting] nasty, vulgar, coarse; see OFFENSIVE 2. 2 [Unfair] vicious, inequitable, unjust; see DISHONEST.

foul *v.* 1 [To make dirty] defile, pollute, sully; see DIRTY. 2 [To become dirty] soil, spot, stain; see DIRTY.

found *a.* unearthed, revealed, detected; see DISCOVERED.

found *v.* establish, endow, set up; see ESTABLISH 2.

foundation *n.* 1 [An intellectual basis] reason, justification, authority; see BASIS. 2 [A physical basis] footing, base, foot, basement, pier, groundwork, bed, ground, bottom, substructure, wall, underpinning, solid rock, infrastructure, pile, roadbed, support, prop, stand, shore, post, pillar, skeleton, column, shaft, pedestal, buttress, framework, scaffold, beam. 3 [That which has been founded] institution, organization, endowment, institute, society, establishment, company, guild, corporation, association, charity, scholarship fund, trust.

founded *a.* organized, endowed, set up; see ESTABLISHED 1.

founder *n.* originator, sponsor, prime mover; see ANCESTOR, AUTHOR.

fountain *n.* 1 [A jet of water] jet, stream, gush, spout, geyser, spurt, spring, pond, basin, pool; see also WATER 1, 2. 2 [A source] origin, font, wellspring; see ORIGIN 2.

fowl *n.* barnyard fowl, wild fowl, poultry, chicken, duck, goose, turkey, cock, hen, Cornish hen, pheasant, partridge, prairie chicken, grouse, capon, ptarmigan, swan; see also BIRD.

fox *n.* 1 [A clever person] cheat,

trickster, con man*; see RASCAL. **2** [An animal] red fox, gray fox, silver fox; see DOG.

fraction *n.* section, portion, part; see DIVISION 2.

fractional *a.* partial, sectional, fragmentary; see UNFINISHED 1.

fracture *n.* rupture, wound, crack, cleavage, shattering, breach, fragmentation, displacement, dislocation, broken bone, shearing, severing, separating, dismembering.

fragile *a.* brittle, frail, delicate; see DAINTY, WEAK 1, 2.

fragment *n.* piece, scrap, remnant; see BIT 1.

fragrance *n.* perfume, aroma, odor; see SMELL 1.

fragrant *a.* aromatic, sweet, perfumed; see SWEET 3.

frail *a.* feeble, breakable, tender; see DAINTY.

frailty *n.* brittleness, delicacy, feebleness; see WEAKNESS 1.

frame *n.* **1** [The structural portion] skeleton, scaffold, framework, scaffolding, casing, framing, support, substructure, infrastructure, stage, groundwork, organization, fabric, anatomy, architecture, enclosure, span, block, window frame, doorjamb. **2** [A border intended as an ornament] margin, fringe, hem, flounce, trim, trimming, outline, mounting, molding.

frame *v.* **1** [To make] construct, erect, raise; see BUILD. **2** [To enclose in a frame] mount, border, enclose; see SUPPORT 1. **3** [To act as a frame] encircle, confine, enclose; see SURROUND 1. **4** [*To cause a miscarriage of justice] set up*, double-cross, entrap; see DECEIVE.

framed *a.* mounted, enclosed, bordered, encircled, fringed, enveloped, outlined, confined, enclosed, wrapped, clasped.

frame-up* *n.* deception, fraud, conspiracy; see TRICK 1.

framework *n.* skeleton, structure, core; see FRAME.

frank *a.* candid, sincere, free, easy, familiar, open, direct, unreserved, uninhibited, downright, ingenuous, unsophisticated, unaffected, plain, aboveboard, forthright, outspoken, tactless, guileless, straightforward, plain-spoken, natural, blunt, matter-of-fact.—*Ant.* DISHONEST, insincere, secretive.

frankfurter *n.* wiener, wiener sausage, weenie*, hot dog*, frank*, dog*, link.

frankly *a.* freely, honestly, candidly; see OPENLY 1.

frankness *n.* openness, sincerity, candidness; see HONESTY.

frantic *a.* distracted, mad, wild, frenetic, furious, raging, raving, frenzied, violent, agitated, deranged, crazy, delirious, insane, angry; see also EXCITED.—*Ant.* CALM, composed, subdued.

fraternity *n.* brotherhood, club, fellowship; see ORGANIZATION 2.

fraud *n.* **1** [Deceit] trickery, duplicity, guile; see DECEPTION. **2** [An impostor] pretender, charlatan, fake; see CHEAT.

fraudulent *a.* deceitful, tricky, swindling; see DISHONEST.

freak *n.* monstrosity, monster, rarity, malformation, freak of nature, oddity, aberration, curiosity, hybrid, anomaly, mutation; see also MONSTER.

freckle *n.* mole, patch, blotch; see BLEMISH.

free *a.* **1** [Not restricted politically] sovereign, independent, autonomous, democratic, self-ruling, self-governing, released, unconstrained, liberated, at liberty, freed.—*Ant.* RESTRICTED, enslaved, subject. **2** [Not restricted in space; *said of persons*] unconfined, at large, cast loose, escaped, let out, scot-free, free as air, free to come and go, unfettered, footloose and fancy-free, free-wheeling*, on the loose.—*Ant.* CONFINED, imprisoned, restrained. **3** [Not restricted in space; *said of things*] unimpeded, unobstructed, unhampered, unattached, loose, not attached, clear, unentangled, unengaged, disengaged, unfastened.—*Ant.* FIXED, fastened, rooted. **4** [Given without charge] gratuitous, gratis, for nothing, without charge, free of cost, complimentary, for free*, on the house.—*Ant.* PAID, charged, costly. —**set free** release, liberate, emancipate; see FREE.

free *v.* release, discharge, deliver, save, emancipate, manumit, rescue, extricate, loosen, loosen, unbind, disengage, undo, set free, let out, let loose, bail out, cut loose, relieve, absolve, acquit, dismiss, pardon, clear, ransom, redeem, unbind, unchain, disentangle, untie, let go, unlock, unhand, let out of prison, open the cage, turn loose, unfetter, unshackle.—*Ant.* SEIZE, capture, incarcerate.

freedom *n.* **1** [Political liberty] independence, sovereignty, self-government, autonomy, democracy, citizenship, representative government, self-determination; see also LIBERTY 4.—*Ant.* SLAVERY, bondage, regimentation. **2** [Exemption from necessity] privilege, immunity, license, indulgence, facility, range, latitude, scope, play, own accord, free rein, leeway, plenty of rope*.—*Ant.* RESTRAINT, constraint, hindrance. **3** [Natural ease and facility] readiness, forthrightness, spontaneity; see EASE 2.

freeing *n.* emancipation, releasing, salvation; see RESCUE.

freely *a.* 1 [Without physical restriction] loosely, without encumbrance, without restraint, unhindered, as one pleases, easily, smoothly.—*Ant.* with difficulty, uneasily, stressfully. 2 [Without mental restriction] voluntarily, willingly, fancy-free, of one's own accord, at will, at pleasure, of one's own free will, purposely, deliberately, intentionally, advisedly, spontaneously, frankly, openly.—*Ant.* UNWILLINGLY, under compulsion, hesitantly.

freeway *n.* turnpike, superhighway, toll road; see HIGHWAY, ROAD 1.

freeze *v.* 1 [To change to a solid state] congeal, harden, solidify, ice, quick-freeze, glaciate, chill, benumb, cool, ice up.—*Ant.* MELT, thaw, liquefy. 2 [To suspend] seal, terminate, immobilize; see HALT, SUSPEND 2.

freezing *a.* frosty, wintry, frigid; see COLD 1.

freight *n.* burden, load, contents, weight, bulk, encumbrance, bales, shipment, cargo, shipping, consignment, goods, tonnage, packages, ware.

freighter *n.* tanker, transport, cargo ship; see SHIP.

French *a.* Gallic, Latin, Frenchified, Parisian.

frenzy *n.* rage, craze, furor; see EXCITEMENT, INSANITY.

frequency *n.* recurrence, number, reiteration; see REGULARITY.

frequent *a.* 1 [Happening often] repeated, numerous, common, habitual, monotonous, profuse, incessant, continual, customary, intermittent, familiar, commonplace, expected, various.—*Ant.* RARE, infrequent, occasional. 2 [Happening regularly] recurrent, usual, periodic; see REGULAR 3.

frequent *v.* visit often, go to, be seen at daily, attend regularly, be at home in, be often in, be accustomed to, hang around*, hang out at*; see also VISIT.

frequently *a.* often, regularly, usually, commonly, successively, many times, in many instances, all the time, notably, repeatedly, intermittently, generally, at times, not infrequently, often enough, not seldom, periodically, at regular intervals; see also REGULARLY.—*Ant.* SELDOM, infrequently, rarely.

fresh *a.* 1 [Newly produced] new, green, crisp, raw, recent, current, late, this season's, factory-fresh, garden-fresh, farm-fresh, brand-new, newborn, immature, young, beginning, hot off the press*, just

out, newfangled.—*Ant.* OLD, stale, musty. 2 [Not preserved] unsalted, uncured, unsmoked, unpickled, uncanned. 3 [Unspoiled] uncontaminated, green, not stale, good, undecayed, well-preserved, odor-free, in good condition, unblemished, unspotted, preserved, new, virgin, unimpaired.—*Ant.* DECAYED, spoiled, contaminated. 4 [Not faded] colorful, vivid, sharp; see BRIGHT 1, DEFINITE 2. 5 [Not salt; *said of water*] potable, drinkable, cool, clear, pure, clean, sweet, fit to drink, safe.—*Ant.* DIRTY, brackish, briny. 6 [Refreshed] restored, rested, rehabilitated, like new, unused, new, relaxed, stimulated, relieved, freshened, revived.—*Ant.* TIRED, worn-out, exhausted. 7 [Inexperienced] green, untried, unskilled; see INEXPERIENCED.

freshman *n.* beginner, novice, underclassman; see AMATEUR.

fret *v.* disturb, agitate, vex; see BOTHER 2.

friar *n.* brother, padre, father; see MONK.

friction *n.* 1 [The rubbing of two bodies] attrition, abrasion, erosion; see GRINDING. 2 [Trouble between individuals or groups] animosity, conflict, discord; see HATRED.

fried *a.* grilled, deep-fried, French-fried, sautéed, pan-fried, stir-fried, browned; see also DONE 2.

friend *n.* familiar, schoolmate, playmate, best friend, roommate, companion, intimate, confidant, comrade, mate, amigo, compadre, fellow, pal*, chum*, crony*, goombah*, buddy*, sidekick*.—*Ant.* ENEMY, foe, stranger. —**make** or **be friends with** befriend, stand by, become familiar with; see ASSOCIATE 1.

friendless *a.* deserted, alone, forlorn; see ABANDONED.

friendliness *n.* kindness, amiability, geniality; see FRIENDSHIP.

friendly *a.* kind, kindly, helpful, sympathetic, well-disposed, neighborly, well-intentioned, sociable, civil, peaceful, loving, affectionate, fond, warmhearted, attentive, brotherly, agreeable, genial, amiable, amicable, affable, benevolent, accommodating, unoffensive, pleasant, tender, companionable, with open arms, cordial, familiar, intimate, close, devoted, dear, attached, loyal, faithful, steadfast, true, responsive, understanding, congenial, approachable, cheerful, convivial, good-humored, good-natured, generous, gracious, cooperative, wholehearted, bighearted, arm in arm, chummy*, folksy*, thick*.—*Ant.* UNFRIENDLY, antagonistic, spiteful.

friendship *n.* harmony, friendliness, brotherly love; see FELLOWSHIP 1.

fright *n.* panic, dread, horror; see FEAR.

frighten *v.* scare, scare away, scare off, dismay, terrify, cow, shock, intimidate, threaten, badger, petrify, panic, demoralize, disrupt, give cause for alarm, terrorize, horrify, astound, awe, perturb, disturb, startle, frighten out of one's wits, take someone's breath away, chill to the bone, make someone's hair stand on end, make someone's blood run cold, make someone's flesh creep, scare one stiff*, curdle the blood.

frightened *a.* terrorized, scared, startled; see AFRAID.

frightful *a.* 1 [Causing fright] fearful, horrifying, dreadful; see TERRIBLE 1, 2. 2 [Very unpleasant] calamitous, shocking, terrible; see OFFENSIVE 2.

frigid *a.* 1 [Thermally cold] freezing, frosty, refrigerated; see COLD 1. 2 [Unresponsive] unloving, distant, chilly; see COLD 2, INDIFFERENT.

fringe *n.* hem, trimming, border; see EDGE 1.

frisky *a.* spirited, dashing, playful; see ACTIVE.

frivolity *n.* silliness, levity, folly; see FUN.

frivolous *a.* superficial, petty, trifling; see TRIVIAL.

frog *n.* amphibian, tree frog, toad, bullfrog, horned frog, horned toad, polliwog.

from *prep.* in distinction to, out of, beginning with; see OF.

front *a.* fore, forward, frontal, foremost, head, headmost, leading, in the foreground.—*Ant.* BACK, rear, hindmost.

front *n.* 1 [The forward part or surface] exterior, forepart, anterior, bow, foreground, face, head, breast, frontal area.—*Ant.* REAR, posterior, back. 2 [The fighting line] front line, no man's land, advance position, line of battle, vanguard, outpost, field of fire, advance guard. 3 [The appearance one presents before others] mien, demeanor, aspect, countenance, face, presence, expression, figure, exterior. —**in front of** before, preceding, leading; see AHEAD.

frontier *n.* hinterland, remote districts, outskirts; see COUNTRY 1.

frost *n.* frozen dew, permafrost, rime; see ICE.

frosting *n.* icing, topping, finish, covering, coating.

frosty *a.* frigid, freezing, chilly; see COLD 1.

froth *n.* bubbles, scum, fizz, effervescence, foam, ferment, head, lather, suds, spray.

frothy *a.* fizzing, bubbling, foaming, soapy, sudsy, bubbly, fizzy, foamy, having a head.

frown *n.* scowl, grimace, wry face, gloomy countenance, forbidding aspect, dirty look.

frown *v.* scowl, grimace, pout, glare, sulk, glower, gloom, look stern.—*Ant.* SMILE, laugh, grin.

frozen *a.* chilled, frosted, iced; see COLD 1, 2.

frugal *a.* thrifty, prudent, parsimonious; see CAREFUL.

frugality *n.* carefulness, conservation, management; see ECONOMY.

fruit *n.* berry, grain, nut, root; see also VEGETABLE. *Common fruits include the following:* apple, pear, peach, plum, nectarine, tangerine, orange, grapefruit, citron, banana, pineapple, watermelon, cantaloupe, honeydew melon, papaya, mango, guava, kiwi, coconut, grape, lime, lemon, persimmon, kumquat, pomegranate, raspberry, blackberry, blueberry, cranberry, loganberry, huckleberry, date, fig, apricot, cherry, raisin, avocado, gooseberry, strawberry.

fruitful *a.* prolific, productive, fecund; see FERTILE.

fruitless *a.* vain, unprofitable, empty; see FUTILE.

frustrate *v.* defeat, foil, balk; see PREVENT.

frustration *n.* disappointment, impediment, failure; see DEFEAT.

fry *v.* sauté, sear, singe, brown, grill, pan-fry, deep-fry, French-fry, sizzle; see also COOK. —**small fry** children, infants, toddlers; see BABY, CHILD.

fudge *n.* penuche, chocolate fudge, divinity; see CANDY.

fuel *n.* propellant, combustible, firing material. *Fuels include the following:* coal, gas, oil, coke, charcoal, anthracite, propane, bituminous coal, peat, slack, stoker coal, lignite, carbon, turf, cordwood, firewood, log, kindling, timber, diesel oil, crude oil, fuel oil, natural gas, gasoline, kerosene, wax.

fuel *v.* fill up, tank up*, gas up*; see FILL 1.

fugitive *n.* outlaw, refugee, truant, runaway, exile, vagabond, waif, stray, derelict, outcast, recluse, hermit.

fulfill *v.* accomplish, effect, complete; see ACHIEVE.

fulfilled *a.* accomplished, completed, achieved, realized, effected, finished, obtained, perfected, concluded, attained, reached, actualized, executed, brought about, performed, carried out, put into effect, made good, brought to a close.—*Ant.*

DISAPPOINTED, unfulfilled, unrealized.

fulfillment *n.* attainment, accomplishment, realization; see ACHIEVEMENT.

full *a.* 1 [Filled] running over, abundant, weighted, satisfied, saturated, crammed, packed, stuffed, jammed, glutted, gorged, loaded, chock-full, stocked, satiated, crowded, stuffed to the gills*, jampacked*, crawling with*, to the brim, packed like sardines*.—*Ant.* EMPTY, exhausted, void. 2 [Well-supplied] abundant, complete, copious, ample, plentiful, sufficient, adequate, competent, lavish, extravagant, profuse.—*Ant.* INADEQUATE, scanty, insufficient. 3 [Not limited] broad, unlimited, extensive; see ABSOLUTE 1, 2. —**in full** 1 for the entire amount, fully, thoroughly; see COMPLETELY. 2 complete, entire, inclusive; see WHOLE 1.

fully *a.* entirely, thoroughly, wholly; see COMPLETELY.

fumble *n.* mistake, blunder, dropped ball; see ERROR.

fumble *v.* mishandle, bungle, mismanage; see BOTCH.

fun *n.* play, game, sport, jest, amusement, relaxation, pastime, diversion, frolic, mirth, entertainment, solace, merriment, pleasure, caper, foolery, joke, absurdity, playfulness, laughter, festivity, carnival, tomfoolery, ball*, escapade, antic, romp, prank, comedy, teasing, celebration, holiday, rejoicing, good humor, joking, enjoyment, gladness, good cheer, delight, glee, treat, lark, recreation, joy, time of one's life, blast*, big time*, picnic*, riot*.—*Ant.* UNHAPPINESS, tedium, sorrow. —**for** (or **in**) **fun** for amusement, not seriously, playfully; see HAPPILY. —**make fun of** mock, satirize, poke fun at; see RIDICULE.

function *n.* employment, capacity, faculty; see USE 1.

function *v.* perform, run, work; see OPERATE 2.

functional *a.* occupational, utilitarian, useful; see PRACTICAL.

fund *n.* endowment, trust fund, capital; see GIFT 1.

fundamental *a.* basic, underlying, primary, first, rudimentary, elemental, supporting, elementary, cardinal, organic, theoretical, structural, sustaining, central, original.—*Ant.* SUPERFICIAL, incidental, consequent.

fundamentally *a.* basically, radically, centrally; see ESSENTIALLY.

funds *n.* capital, wealth, cash, collateral, money, assets, currency, savings, revenue, wherewithal, proceeds, hard cash, stocks and bonds, money on hand, money in the bank,

accounts receivable, property, means, affluence, belongings, resources, securities, stakes, earnings, winnings, possessions, profits, dividends, nest egg; see also MONEY.

funeral *n.* interment, last rites, burial, burial ceremony, entombment, requiem, cremation.

fungus *n.* mushroom, mold, rust; see DECAY, PARASITE 1.

funnel *n.* duct, shaft, conduit; see PIPE 1.

funny *a.* 1 [Stirring to laughter] laughable, comic, comical, whimsical, amusing, entertaining, diverting, humorous, witty, jesting, jocular, waggish, droll, facetious, clever, mirthful, ludicrous, jolly, risible, madcap, absurd, ridiculous, sly, sportive, playful, merry, joyful, joyous, good-humored, glad, gleeful, hilarious, jovial, farcical, joking, sidesplitting.—*Ant.* SAD, serious, melancholy. 2 [*Out of the ordinary] curious, odd, unusual; see SUSPICIOUS 2.

fur *n.* pelt, hide, hair, coat, brush. *Types of fur include the following:* sable, mink, chinchilla, karakul, seal, muskrat, ermine, monkey, beaver, skunk, otter, marten, stone marten, weasel, squirrel, leopard, raccoon, wolverine; white fox, blue fox, red fox, etc.; sheepskin, bearskin, calfskin, rabbit, coney. —**make the fur fly*** fight, bicker, stir up trouble; see EXCITE.

furious *a.* enraged, raging, fierce; see ANGRY.

furnace *n.* heater, heating system, boiler, hot-air furnace, steam furnace, hot-water furnace, oil burner, gas furnace, electric furnace, kiln, blast furnace, open-hearth furnace, stove, forge.

furnish *v.* fit out, equip, stock; see PROVIDE 1.

furnished *a.* supplied, provided, fitted out; see EQUIPPED.

furniture *n.* movables, household goods, home furnishings. *Furniture includes the following—home:* table, chair, rug, carpeting, drapes, sofa, davenport, love seat, settee, ottoman, couch, cabinet, picture, chest, bureau, buffet, cupboard, bed, dresser, mirror, commode, chiffonier, tapestry, footstool, secretary, highboy, sideboard, clock, bookcase; *office:* desk, filing cabinet, stool, chair, table, counter, workstation, printer stand.

furor *n.* tumult, excitement, stir; see DISTURBANCE 2.

further *a.* more, at a greater distance, in addition; see DISTANT.

furthermore *a.* moreover, too, in addition; see BESIDES.

furthest *a.* most remote, most distant, remotest, farthest, uttermost, outermost, ultimate, extreme, outmost.

fury *n.* wrath, fire, rage; see ANGER.

fuse *n.* wick, tinder, kindling; see FUEL. **—blow a fuse*** become angry, lose one's temper, rant; see RAGE 1.

fuss *n.* trouble, complaint, bother; see DISTURBANCE 2.

fuss *v.* whine, whimper, object; see COMPLAIN.

fussy *a.* fastidious, particular, meticulous; see CAREFUL.

futile *a.* vain, useless, in vain, fruitless, hopeless, impractical, worthless, unprofitable, to no effect, not successful, to no purpose, unneeded, unsatisfactory, unsatisfying, ineffective, ineffectual, unproductive, idle, empty, hollow, unreal.—*Ant.* HOPEFUL, practical, effective.

futility *n.* uselessness, falseness, hollowness, frivolity, idleness, emptiness, fruitlessness, hopelessness, worthlessness, illusion, folly, unimportance, carrying water in a sieve, wild-goose chase, running around in circles, carrying coals to Newcastle.—*Ant.* IMPORTANCE, fruitfulness, significance.

future *a.* coming, impending, imminent, destined, fated, prospective, to come, in the course of time, expected, inevitable, approaching, eventual, ultimate, planned, scheduled, budgeted, booked, looked toward, likely, coming up, in the cards.—*Ant.* PAST, completed, recorded.

future *n.* infinity, eternity, world to come, subsequent time, coming time, events to come, prospect, tomorrow, the hereafter, by and by.—*Ant.* PAST, historic ages, recorded time. **—in the future** eventually, sometime, in due time; see FINALLY 2, SOMEDAY.

fuzz *n.* nap, fluff, fur; see HAIR 1.

fuzzy *a.* 1 [Like or covered with fuzz] hairy, woolly, furry; see HAIRY. 2 [Not clear] blurred, indistinct, out of focus, hazy, imprecise, foggy; see also OBSCURE 1, HAZY.

G

gab* *n.* gossip, idle talk, prattle; see NONSENSE 1. **—gift of (the) gab*** loquacity, volubility, verbal ability; see ELOQUENCE.

gab* *v.* gossip, jabber, chatter; see BABBLE.

gadget *n.* mechanical contrivance, object, contraption; see DEVICE 1.

gag *v.* 1 [To stop the mouth] choke, muzzle, muffle, obstruct, stifle, throttle, tape up, deaden. 2 [To retch] be nauseated, sicken, choke; see VOMIT.

gaiety *n.* jollity, mirth, exhilaration; see HAPPINESS.

gaily *a.* showily, brightly, vivaciously, spiritedly, brilliantly, splendidly, gaudily, expensively, colorfully, extravagantly, garishly, in a sprightly manner.—*Ant.* PEACEFULLY, quietly, modestly.

gain *n.* increase, accrual, accumulation; see ADDITION 1.

gain *v.* 1 [To increase] augment, expand, enlarge; see GROW 1, INCREASE. 2 [To advance] progress, overtake, move forward; see ADVANCE 1. 3 [To achieve] attain, realize, reach; see SUCCEED 1.

gainful *a.* lucrative, productive, useful; see PROFITABLE.

gainfully *a.* productively, profitably, usefully; see PROFITABLY.

gait *n.* walk, run, motion, step, tread, stride, pace, tramp, march, carriage, movements.

galaxy *n.* cosmic system, star cluster, nebula; see STAR.

gale *n.* hurricane, windstorm, typhoon; see STORM, WIND.

gall *n.* effrontery, insolence, impertinence; see RUDENESS.

gall *v.* annoy, irk, irritate; see BOTHER 2.

gallant *a.* bold, intrepid, courageous; see BRAVE.

gallantry *n.* heroism, valor, bravery; see COURAGE.

gallery *n.* 1 [An elevated section of seats] mezzanine, upstairs, balcony; see UPSTAIRS. 2 [Onlookers, especially from the gallery] spectators, audience, public; see LISTENER. 3 [A room for showing works of art] salon, museum, exhibition room, studio, hall, exhibit, showroom.

gallon *n.* 3.78 liters, half a peck, four quarts, eight pints.

gallop *v.* run, spring, leap, jump, go at a gallop, bound, hurdle, swing, stride, lope, canter, amble, trot.

galoshes *n.* overshoes, rubbers, boots; see SHOE.

gamble *n.* chance, lot, hazard; see CHANCE 1.

gamble *v.* game, wager, bet, play, plunge, play at dice, bet against, speculate, back, lay money on, lay odds on, try one's luck, go for broke*, shoot craps; see also RISK.

gambler *n.* backer, sharper, card-sharp*, speculator, confidence man, bettor, bookmaker, croupier, banker, player, sport*, highroller*, shark*, shill*, bookie*, con man*.

gambling *n.* betting, staking, venturing, gaming, laying money on, speculating.

game *a.* spirited, hardy, resolute; see BRAVE.

game *n.* 1 [Entertainment] *Card games include the following:* poker, rummy, gin rummy, pinochle, whist, euchre, bridge, contract bridge, duplicate bridge, five hundred, casino, war, seven-up, cribbage, solitaire, patience, canasta, old maid, hearts, twenty-one, blackjack, baccarat. *Children's games include:* hide-and-seek, tag, hopscotch, jacks, ball, fox and geese, marbles, crack the whip, statues, London Bridge, ring around the roses, drop the handkerchief, blindman's buff, follow the leader, Simon says, catch, post office, favors, musical chairs, mumbletypeg, cops and robbers, soldier, cowboys and Indians, mother-may-I, spin the bottle. *Board games include:* chess, checkers, Chinese checkers, backgammon, go, pachisi, Monopoly, Ouija (trademarks). 2 [Sport] play, recreation, merry-making; see SPORT 1. 3 [Wild meat, fish, or fowl] quarry, prey, wildlife; see FISH, FOWL, MEAT. —**ahead of the game*** winning, doing well, thriving; see SUCCESSFUL. —**play the game*** behave properly, act according to custom, do what is expected; see BEHAVE.

gang *n.* horde, band, troop; see ORGANIZATION 2.

gangster *n.* gunman, underworld leader, racketeer; see CRIMINAL.

gang up on* *v.* combat, overwhelm, join forces against; see ATTACK.

gap *n.* 1 [A breach] cleft, break, rift; see HOLE 1. 2 [A break in continuity] hiatus, recess, lull; see PAUSE. 3 [A mountain pass] way, chasm, hollow, cleft, ravine, gorge, arroyo, canyon, passageway, notch, gully, gulch.

garage *n.* parking space, parking garage, parking, parking lot, carport.

garbage *n.* refuse, waste, rubbish; see TRASH 1.

garden *n.* vegetable patch, melon patch, cultivated area, truck garden, enclosure, field, plot, bed, herb garden, rock garden, rose garden, formal garden, kitchen garden, hotbed, greenhouse, patio, terrace, backyard, nursery, flower garden, garden spot, oasis.

gardener *n.* vegetable grower, caretaker, landscaper; see FARMER.

gargantuan *a.* enormous, huge, immense; see LARGE 1.

gargle *v.* swash, rinse the mouth, use a mouthwash; see CLEAN.

garish *a.* showy, gaudy, ostentatious; see ORNATE.

garment *n.* dress, attire, apparel; see CLOTHES.

garnish *v.* embellish, beautify, deck; see DECORATE.

gas *n.* 1 [A state of matter] vapor, volatile substance, fumes, aeriform fluid, gaseous mixture. 2 [Gasoline] propellant, petrol (British), motor fuel; see GASOLINE. 3 [Poisonous gas] systemic poison, mustard gas, tear gas; see POISON. 4 [An anesthetic] ether, general anesthetic, chloroform, nitrous oxide, laughing gas. 5 [A fuel] natural gas, propane, bottled gas, acetylene, coal gas; see also FUEL. —**step on the gas*** drive faster, hasten, move fast; see HURRY 1.

gaseous *a.* vaporous, effervescent, in the form of gas; see LIGHT 5.

gash *n.* slash, slice, wound; see CUT.

gasoline *n.* petrol, motor fuel, propellant, gas, juice*, low-octane gasoline, high-octane gasoline, ethyl gasoline, gasohol.

gasp *v.* labor for breath, gulp, have difficulty in breathing, pant, puff, wheeze, blow, snort.

gate *n.* entrance, ingress, passage, way, bar, turnstile, revolving door, barrier; see also DOOR.

gather *v.* 1 [To come together] assemble, meet, gather around, congregate, flock in, pour in, rally, crowd, throng, come together, convene, collect, unite, reunite, associate, hold a meeting, hold a reunion, swarm, huddle, draw in, group, converge, accrete, concentrate.—*Ant.* SCATTER, disperse, part. 2 [To bring together] collect, aggregate, amass; see ACCUMULATE, ASSEMBLE 2. 3 [To conclude] infer, deduce, find; see ASSUME.

gathered *a.* assembled, met, congregated, joined, rallied, crowded together, thronged, collected, united, associated, swarmed, huddled, grouped, massed, amassed, accumulated, picked, garnered, harvested, stored, combined, brought together, convened, convoked, summoned, compiled, mobilized, lumped together, raked up, concentrated, heaped, stacked, piled, stowed away.—*Ant.* SCATTERED, dispersed, separated.

gathering *n.* assembly, meeting, conclave, caucus, parley, council, conference, band, congregation, company, rally, crowd, throng, bunch, collection, union, association, society, committee, legislature, house, senate, parliament, swarm, huddle, group, powwow*, body, mass, herd, turnout, flock, coven, combination, convention, discussion, panel, reunion, meet, congress, attendance, multitude, audience, horde, mob, crush, party, social gathering, crew, gang, school, bevy, troop, drove, concentration, convocation, get-together, bull session*.

gaudy *a.* showy, flashy, tawdry; see ORNATE.

gauge *n.* scale, criterion, standard; see MEASURE 2.

gauge *v.* check, weigh, calibrate, calculate; see also MEASURE 1.

gaunt *a.* emaciated, scraggy, skinny; see THIN 2.

gauze *n.* veil, bandage, cheesecloth; see DRESSING 3.

gawk *v.* stare, ogle, gaze; see LOOK 2.

gay *a.* **1** [Happy] cheerful, merry, vivacious; see HAPPY. **2** [Homosexual] homophile, homoerotic, lesbian; see HOMOSEXUAL.

gaze *v.* stare, watch, gape; see LOOK 2.

gear *n.* **1** [Equipment] material, tackle, things; see EQUIPMENT. **2** [A geared wheel] cog, cogwheel, pinion, toothed wheel, sprocket. **—in gear** usable, efficient, productive; see WORKING 1. **—out of gear** inefficient, not working, broken; see USELESS 1.

gem *n.* **1** [A jewel] precious stone, bauble, ornament; see JEWEL. *Types of gems include the following:* diamond, emerald, ruby, pearl, brilliant, aquamarine, amethyst, topaz, turquoise, jade, opal, sapphire, garnet, carnelian, jacinth, beryl, cat's-eye, chrysoprase, chalcedony, agate, bloodstone, moonstone, onyx, sard, lapis lazuli, chrysolite, carbuncle, coral. **2** [Anything excellent, especially if small and beautiful] jewel, pearl of great price, paragon, ace, nonpareil, perfection, ideal.

gender *n.* sexuality, sort, variety; see KIND 2, SEX 3.

genealogy *n.* derivation, lineage, extraction; see FAMILY.

general *a.* **1** [Having wide application] comprehensive, comprehending, widespread, universal, limitless, unlimited, extensive, ecumenical, all-embracing, ubiquitous, unconfined, broad, taken as a whole, not particular, not specific, blanket, inclusive, wide, catholic, infinite, worldwide, endless.—*Ant.* SPECIAL, particular, limited. **2** [Of common occurrence] usual, customary, prevailing; see COMMON 1. **3** [Not specific] indefinite, uncertain, imprecise; see VAGUE 2. **—in general** gen-

erally, usually, ordinarily; see REGULARLY.

generality *n.* abstraction, universality, sweeping statement; see LAW 4.

generalize *v.* theorize, speculate, postulate; see UNDERSTAND.

generally *a.* usually, commonly, ordinarily; see REGULARLY.

generate *v.* form, make, beget, create; see also PRODUCE 1.

generation *n.* **1** [The act of producing offspring] procreation, reproduction, breeding; see BIRTH. **2** [One cycle in the succession of parents and children] age, stage, crop, rank, age group; Silent Generation, baby boomers, boomers*, Generation X, Generation Y. **3** [The time required for a generation] span, 30 years, period; see AGE 3.

generic *a.* universal, general, nonproprietary; see UNIVERSAL 3, GENERAL 1.

generosity *n.* hospitality, benevolence, charity, liberality, philanthropy, altruism, unselfishness; see also KINDNESS 2.—*Ant.* GREED, miserliness, stinginess.

generous *a.* **1** [Openhanded] bountiful, liberal, charitable, altruistic, munificent, freehanded, beneficent, unselfish, hospitable, philanthropic, prodigal, lavish, profuse, unsparing, unstinting.—*Ant.* STINGY, close, tightfisted. **2** [Considerate] kindly, magnanimous, reasonable; see KIND.

generously *a.* **1** [With a free hand] bountifully, liberally, lavishly, unsparingly, unstintingly, in full measure, handsomely, freely, profusely, abundantly, munificently, charitably, copiously, with open hands.—*Ant.* SELFISHLY, grudgingly, sparingly. **2** [With an open heart] charitably, liberally, magnanimously, wholeheartedly, unreservedly, nobly, majestically, royally, honestly, candidly, enthusiastically, unselfishly, disinterestedly, chivalrously, benevolently, genially, warmly.—*Ant.* SELFISHLY, coldly, heartlessly.

genetic *a.* sporogenous, hereditary, genic, patrimonial; see also HISTORICAL.

genetics *n.* heredity, inheritance, eugenics; see HEREDITY.

genial *a.* cordial, kind, warmhearted; see FRIENDLY.

genitals *n.* organs, sexual organs, genitalia, private parts, reproductive organs, privates.

genius *n.* **1** [The highest degree of intellectual capacity] ability, talent, intellect, brains, intelligence, inspiration, imagination, gift, aptitude, wisdom, astuteness, penetration, grasp, discernment, acumen, acuteness, perspicacity, power, capability, accomplishment, sagacity, understanding, reach, enthusiasm, creative gift, knack, bent, turn. 2 [One having genius] gifted person, prodigy, Einstein; see ARTIST, AUTHOR, PHILOSOPHER, POET, WRITER.

gentility *n.* decorum, propriety, refinement; see BEHAVIOR.

gentle *a.* 1 [Soft] tender, smooth, sensitive; see FAINT 3, SOFT 2, 3. 2 [Kind] tender, considerate, benign; see KIND. 3 [Tamed] domesticated, housebroken, disciplined, educated, trained, civilized, tractable, biddable, pliable, taught, cultivated, tame.—*Ant.* WILD, savage, untamed.

gentleman *n.* man of honor, man of his word, sir, cavalier, don, nobleman, gentleman and a scholar.

gentlemanly *a.* polite, polished, gallant; see REFINED 2.

gentleness *n.* tenderness, softness, delicacy, smoothness, fragility, sweetness.—*Ant.* ROUGHNESS, hardness, imperviousness.

gently *a.* considerately, tenderly, benevolently; see GENEROUSLY 2.

genuine *a.* 1 [Authentic; *said of things*] real, true, actual, original, veritable, unadulterated, official, whole, accurate, proved, tested, good, bona fide, natural, unimpeachable, pure, unquestionable, authenticated, existent, essential, substantial, factual, palpable, exact, precise, positive, valid, literal, sound, plain, certain, legitimate, legit*, for real*, honest-to-goodness*.—*Ant.* VULGAR, spurious, sham. 2 [Sincere] unaffected, unquestionable, certain, absolute, unimpeachable, definite, incontrovertible, well-established, known, reliable, bona fide, staunch, trustworthy, valid, positive, frank, honest, candid.

geographical *a.* terrestrial, geographic, geophysical; see PHYSICAL 1, WORLDLY.

geography *n.* earth science, geology, topography, economic geography, political geography, geopolitics, geopolitical study, physiography, geochemistry, geophysics, natural history, cartography; see also SCIENCE 1.

geometrical *a.* square, regular, even, proportional, many-sided, multilateral, bilateral, triangular, trilateral, quadrilateral.

germ *n.* microbe, antibody, bacterium, disease germ, microorganism, virus, pathogen, retrovirus, prion, infectious agent, toxin, bug*.

German *a.* Germanic, Teutonic, Prussian, Saxon, Bavarian.

germinate *v.* generate, sprout, develop; see GROW 1.

gesture *n.* gesticulation, indication, signal; see SIGN 1.

gesture *v.* make a sign, motion, signal, pantomime, act out, use sign language, use one's hands, indicate, signalize, point, nod; see also MOVE 1.

get *v.* 1 [To obtain] gain, procure, occupy, reach, capture, recover, take, grab, accomplish, attain, win, secure, achieve, collect, purchase, earn, receive, realize, possess, get possession of, take title to, acquire. 2 [To become] grow, develop into, go; see BECOME. 3 [To receive] be given, take, accept; see RECEIVE 1. 4 [To induce] persuade, talk into, compel; see URGE 2. 5 [*To overcome] beat, vanquish, overpower; see DEFEAT 2, 3. 6 [To prepare] make, arrange, dress; see PREPARE 1. 7 [To contract; *said of bodily disorders*] catch, succumb to, get sick; see CATCH 4. 8 [To learn] acquire, gain, receive; see LEARN. 9 [*To understand] comprehend, perceive, know; see UNDERSTAND 1. 10 [*To irritate] annoy, provoke, vex; see BOTHER 2. 11 [To arrive] come to, reach, land; see ARRIVE. —**get away** flee, run away, elude; see ESCAPE. —**get by** * manage, get along, do well enough; see SURVIVE 1. —**get it** * 1 [To understand] comprehend, perceive, know; see UNDERSTAND 1. 2 [To be punished] suffer, get what is coming to one, be reprimanded, suffer for, catch it*, get in trouble. —**get off** 1 [To go away] depart, escape, go; see LEAVE 1. 2 [To dismount] alight, dismount, disembark; see DESCEND. —**get on** 1 [To mount] go up, mount, scale; see CLIMB. 2 [To succeed] manage, do well enough, get along; see SUCCEED 1. 3 [To age] grow older, advance in years, approach retirement; see AGE. —**get out** 1 [To leave] go, depart, take one's leave; see LEAVE 1. 2 [To escape] break out, run away, flee; see ESCAPE. —**get over** overcome, recuperate from, survive; see RECOVER 3. —**get through** 1 [To complete] discharge, enact, finish; see ACHIEVE. 2 [To endure] live through, survive, subsist; see ENDURE 1, 2. —**get together** 1 [To gather] collect, accumulate, congregate; see ASSEMBLE 2. 2 [To reach an agreement] come to terms, settle, make a bargain; see AGREE. —**get up** 1 [To climb] ascend, mount, go up; see CLIMB. 2 [To arise] get out of bed, rise, turn out; see ARISE 1.

getting *n.* taking, obtaining, gaining, catching, earning, winning, seizing, securing, capturing, mastering, confiscating, appropriating.

ghastly *a.* 1 [Terrifying] hideous, horrible, frightening; see FRIGHT-

FUL. **2** [*Unpleasant] repulsive, disgusting, abhorrent; see OFFENSIVE 2.

ghost *n.* vision, specter, apparition, spirit, demon, shade, phantom, phantasm, poltergeist, appearance, spook; see also DEVIL.

giant *a.* monstrous, colossal, enormous; see LARGE 1.

giant *n.* ogre, Cyclops, Titan, colossus, Goliath, Hercules, Atlas, mammoth, behemoth, monster, whale, elephant, leviathan, mountain, hulk; see also MONSTER 1.

gibberish *n.* jargon, chatter, claptrap; see NONSENSE 1.

giddy *a.* high, towering, lofty; see STEEP.

gift *n.* **1** [A present] presentation, donation, grant, gratuity, alms, endowment, bequest, bounty, charity, favor, legacy, award, reward, offering, souvenir, token, remembrance, courtesy, bonus, subsidy, tribute, subvention, contribution, subscription, relief, ration, benefit, tip, allowance, handout. **2** [An aptitude] faculty, capacity, capability; see ABILITY. —**look a gift horse in the mouth** carp, criticize, be ungrateful; see JUDGE.

gifted *a.* smart, skilled, talented; see ABLE.

gigantic *a.* massive, immense, huge; see LARGE 1.

giggle *n.* titter, chuckle, snicker; see LAUGH.

gild *v.* varnish, whitewash, paint in rosy colors; see PAINT 2.

gimmick* *n.* catch*, deceptive device, method; see TRICK.

girder *n.* truss, rafter, mainstay; see BEAM 1.

girdle *n.* belt, cincher, sash; see UNDERWEAR.

girdle *v.* encircle, enclose, clasp; see SURROUND 1.

girl *n.* young woman, schoolgirl, miss, lass, coed, damsel, maid, mademoiselle (French), *señorita* (Spanish), maiden, tomboy, chick*, filly*, skirt*, dame*, babe*.

girlish *a.* juvenile, naive, unsophisticated, fresh, unaffected; see also YOUNG 1.—*Ant.* MATURE, matronly, sophisticated.

girth *n.* circumference, distance around, bigness; see SIZE 2.

gist *n.* substance, essence, significance; see BASIS, SUMMARY.

give *v.* **1** [To transfer] grant, bestow, confer, impart, present, endow, bequeath, award, dispense, subsidize, contribute, hand out, dole out, hand in, hand over, deliver, let have, tip, pass down, convey, deed, sell, will, make over to, put into the hands of, contribute to, consign, relinquish, cede, lease, invest, dispose of, part with, lay upon, turn over, come through with*, come across with*, shell out*, fork over*, kick in*, palm off*.—*Ant.* MAINTAIN, withhold, take. **2** [To yield under pressure] give way, retreat, collapse, fall, contract, shrink, recede, open, relax, sag, bend, flex, crumble, yield.—*Ant.* RESIST, remain rigid, stand firm. **3** [To allot] assign, dispense, deal; see DISTRIBUTE. **4** [To pass on] communicate, transmit, transfer; see SEND 1. **5** [To administer] minister, provide with, dispense; see PROVIDE 1. —**give away** **1** [*To reveal] betray, divulge, disclose; see REVEAL. **2** [To give] bestow, award, present; see GIVE 1. —**give back** return, refund, reimburse; see REPAY 1. —**give in** capitulate, submit, surrender; see ADMIT 2, YIELD 1. —**give out** **1** [To emit] emanate, expend, exude; see EMIT, SMELL 1. **2** [To distribute] dole out, hand out, pass out; see DISTRIBUTE. **3** [To publish] proclaim, make known, announce; see ADVERTISE, DECLARE. **4** [To weaken] faint, fail, break down; see TIRE 1, WEAKEN 1. —**give up** **1** [To surrender] stop fighting, cede, hand over; see YIELD 1. **2** [To stop] quit, halt, cease; see END 1.

given *a.* granted, supplied, donated, bestowed, presented, awarded, bequeathed, dispensed, handed out, contributed, offered.—*Ant.* KEPT, taken, withheld.

giver *n.* provider, supplier, donator; see DONOR.

giving *n.* donating, granting, supplying, awarding, presenting, dispensing, passing out, handing out, contributing, conferring, distributing, remitting, transferring, consigning, yielding, giving up, furnishing, allowing, expending, offering, tipping, parting with, pouring forth, discharging, emitting.—*Ant.* GETTING, taking, appropriating.

glacial *a.* icy, frozen, polar; see COLD 1.

glacier *n.* ice floe, floe, iceberg, berg, glacial mass, snow slide, icecap, ice field, ice stream, glacial table.

glad *a.* exhilarated, animated, jovial; see HAPPY.

gladly *a.* joyously, happily, gaily, blithely, cheerfully, ecstatically, blissfully, contendedly, readily, gratefully, enthusiastically, merrily, heartily, willingly, zealously, pleasantly, pleasurably, zestfully, complacently, delightfully, gleefully, cheerily, warmly, passionately, ardently, lovingly, cordially, genially, sweetly, joyfully, with relish, with satisfaction, with full agreement, with full approval, with delight.—*Ant.* SADLY, unwillingly, gloomily.

gladness *n.* cheer, mirth, delight; see HAPPINESS.

glamorous *a.* fascinating, alluring, captivating, bewitching, dazzling; see also CHARMING.

glamour *n.* allurement, charm, attraction; see BEAUTY 1.

glance *n.* glimpse, sight, fleeting impression; see LOOK 3.

glance *v.* 1 [To look] see, peep, glimpse; see LOOK 2. 2 [To ricochet] skip, slide, rebound; see BOUNCE.

gland *n.* endocrine organ, pancreas, kidney, liver, testicle, spleen. *Kinds of glands include the following:* simple, compound, tubular, sacular, ductless, adrenal, carotid, endocrine, lymphatic, parathyroid, parotid, pineal, pituitary, thyroid, thymus, sweat, lacrimal, salivary, mammary, seminal, prostate.

glare *v.* 1 [To shine fiercely] beam, glow, radiate; see SHINE 1, 2. 2 [To stare fiercely] pierce, glower, scowl; see FROWN, LOOK 2.

glaring *a.* 1 [Shining] blinding, dazzling, blazing; see BRIGHT 1. 2 [Obvious] evident, conspicuous, obtrusive; see OBVIOUS 2.

glass *n. Objects called glass include the following:* tumbler, goblet, beaker, chalice, cup, looking glass, mirror, barometer, thermometer, hourglass, windowpane, watch crystal, monocle, telescope, microscope, spyglass, burning glass, eye-glass, lens, optical glass.

glasses *n.* spectacles, eyeglasses, bifocals, trifocals, aviator glasses, sunglasses, goggles, field glasses, opera glasses, contact lenses, specs*.

glassware *n.* crystal, glasswork, glass; see GLASS. *Types of common glassware include the following:* tumbler, jug, decanter, bottle, fruit jar, tableware, glass ovenware, vase, flower bowl, goblet, sherbet glass, wine glass, liqueur glass, champagne glass, cocktail glass, highball glass, old-fashioned glass, brandy snifter, shot glass, parfait glass, beer mug.

glassy *a.* vitreous, lustrous, polished; see SMOOTH 1.

glaze *n.* enamel, polish, varnish; see FINISH 2.

glaze *v.* coat, enamel, gloss over; see SHINE 3.

glazed *a.* glassy, translucent, transparent, enameled, varnished, filmed over, shiny, encrusted, burnished, lustrous, smooth.—*Ant.* ROUGH, fresh, unglazed.

glee *n.* joviality, merriment, mirth; see HAPPINESS.

gleeful *a.* joyous, jolly, merry; see HAPPY.

glide *n.* floating, continuous motion, smooth movement, flow, slide, drift, swoop, skimming, flight, soaring, slither.

glide *v.* float, slide, drift, waft, skim, skip, trip, fly, coast, flit, wing, soar, coast along, slide along, skim along.—*Ant.* HIT, rattle, lurch.

glimmer *n.* gleam, flash, flicker; see LIGHT 1.

glimpse *n.* flash, impression, sight; see LOOK 3.

glisten *v.* sparkle, shimmer, flicker; see SHINE 1.

glitter *n.* sparkle, twinkle, gleam; see LIGHT 1.

glitter *v.* twinkle, shimmer, sparkle; see SHINE 1.

globe *n.* balloon, orb, spheroid; see BALL 1.

gloom *n.* woe, sadness, depression, dejection, melancholy, melancholia, dullness, despondency, misery, sorrow, morbidity, pessimism, foreboding, low spirits, cheerlessness, heaviness of mind, weariness, apprehension, misgiving, distress, affliction, despair, anguish, grief, horror, mourning, bitterness, chagrin, discouragement, the blues*, the dumps*.—*Ant.* HAPPINESS, optimism, gaiety.

gloomy *a.* dreary, depressing, discouraging; see DISMAL.

glorify *v.* laud, commend, acclaim; see PRAISE 1.

glorious *a.* famous, renowned, famed, well-known, distinguished, splendid, excellent, noble, exalted, grand, illustrious, notable, celebrated, esteemed, honored, eminent, remarkable, brilliant, great, heroic, memorable, apotheosized, immortal, time-honored, admirable, praiseworthy, remarkable; see also FAMOUS.—*Ant.* UNIMPORTANT, inglorious, ignominious.

glory *n.* 1 [Renown] honor, distinction, reputation; see FAME. 2 [Splendor] grandeur, radiance, majesty, brilliance, richness, beauty, fineness.—*Ant.* tawdriness, meanness, baseness.

glossy *a.* shining, reflecting, lustrous; see BRIGHT 1.

glove *n.* mitten, mitt, gauntlet; see CLOTHES.

glow *n.* warmth, shine, ray; see HEAT 1, LIGHT 1.

glow *v.* gleam, redden, radiate; see BURN, SHINE 1.

glowing *a.* gleaming, lustrous, phosphorescent; see BRIGHT 1.

glue *n.* paste, mucilage, cement; see ADHESIVE.

glue *v.* paste, bond, cement; see REPAIR.

glum *a.* moody, morose, sullen; see SAD 1.

glut *n.* oversupply, overabundance, excess; see EXCESS 1.

glut *v.* 1 [To oversupply] overwhelm, overstock, fill; see FLOOD 1. 2 [To overeat] stuff, cram, gorge, eat one's fill, gobble up, eat out of house and home*, fill, feast, wolf, bolt, devour, eat like a horse*.—*Ant.* DIET, starve, fast.

glutton *n.* gourmand, overeater, pig; see BEAST 2.

gluttony *n.* voracity, piggishness, intemperance; see GREED.

gnarled *a.* knotted, twisted, contorted; see BENT.

gnaw *v.* crunch, chomp, masticate; see BITE, CHEW.

go *v.* 1 [To leave] quit, withdraw, take leave, depart, move, set out, go away, take off, start, leave, vanish, retire, vacate, flee, get out, fly, run along, say goodbye, escape, run away, abandon, abdicate, clear out*, pull out, push off*, scram*, split*, blow*, beat it*, take a powder*, get along*, fade away; see LEAVE 1. 2 [To proceed] travel, progress, proceed; see ADVANCE 1, MOVE 1. 3 [To function] work, run, perform; see OPERATE 2. 4 [To fit or suit] conform, accord, harmonize; see AGREE, FIT 1. 5 [To extend] stretch, cover, spread; see REACH 1. 6 [To elapse] be spent, waste away, transpire; see PASS 2. 7 [To fail] diminish, stop working, die; see FAIL 1. 8 [To continue] maintain, carry on, persist; see CONTINUE 1. 9 [To die] pass away, depart, succumb; see DIE. 10 [To end] terminate, finish, conclude; see STOP 2. 11 [To endure] persevere, go on, persist; see ENDURE 1. —**as people** (or **things**) **go** in comparison with others, by all standards, according to certain criteria; see ACCORDING TO. —**from the word "go"** from the outset, at the start, beginning with; see FIRST. —**go after** 1 [To chase] seek, try to catch, hunt; see PURSUE 1. 2 [To follow in time] come after, supersede, supplant; see SUCCEED 2. —**go against** be opposed to, contradict, counteract; see OPPOSE 1, 2. —**go ahead** move on, proceed, progress; see ADVANCE 1. —**go back on** desert, be unfaithful, forsake; see ABANDON 2. —**go by** move onward, make one's way, proceed; see PASS 1. —**go down** 1 [To sink] descend, decline, submerge; see SINK 1. 2 [To lose] be defeated, submit, succumb; see FAIL 1, LOSE 3. 3 [To decrease] fall, decline, lessen; see DECREASE 1. —**go for** 1 [To reach for] try to get, aim at, clutch at; see REACH 2. 2 [*To attack] rush upon, run at, spring at; see ATTACK. 3 [*To like]

be fond of, fancy, care for; see LIKE 2. —**go in for** 1 [To advocate] endorse, favor, back; see PROMOTE 1. 2 [To like] care for, be fond of, fancy; see LIKE 1. —**go off** 1 [To leave] quit, depart, part; see LEAVE 1. 2 [To explode] blow up, detonate, discharge; see EXPLODE. —**go on** 1 [To act] execute, behave, conduct; see ACT 1, 2. 2 [To happen] occur, come about, take place; see HAPPEN 2. 3 [To persevere] persist, continue, bear; see ENDURE 1. 4 [*To talk] chatter, converse, speak; see TALK 1. —**go out** cease, die, darken, flicker out, flash out, become dark, become black, burn out, stop shining. —**go over** 1 [To rehearse] repeat, say something repeatedly, practice; see REHEARSE 3. 2 [To examine] look at, investigate, analyze; see EXAMINE, STUDY. —**go through** 1 [To inspect] search, audit, investigate; see EXAMINE. 2 [To undergo] withstand, survive, suffer; see ENDURE 1. 3 [To spend] consume, deplete, expend; see SPEND. —**go through with** fulfill, finish, follow through with; see ACHIEVE, COMPLETE. —**go together** 1 [To harmonize] be suitable, match, fit; see AGREE. 2 [To keep company] go steady*, escort, go with; see DATE 2, KEEP COMPANY (WITH). —**go under** 1 [Drown] sink, drown, suffocate; see DIE. 2 [To become bankrupt] default, go broke, go bankrupt; see LOSE 2. —**go with** 1 [*To keep company with] escort, attend, be with; see ACCOMPANY, DATE 2, KEEP COMPANY (WITH) at COMPANY. 2 [To be appropriate to] match, correspond, not clash, go well with, harmonize, complement, fit; see also AGREE. —**have a go at*** attempt, endeavor, try one's hand at; see TRY 1. —**let go** set free, give up, release; see ABANDON 1. —**let oneself go** be unrestrained, free oneself, have fun; see RELAX. —**no go*** impossible, worthless, without value; see USELESS 1. —**on the go*** in constant motion, moving, busy; see ACTIVE.

goad *v.* prod, urge, prick, prompt, spur, drive, whip, press, push, impel, force, stimulate, provoke, tease, excite, needle*, nag, noodge*, instigate, arouse, animate, encourage, bully, coerce; see also URGE 2.—*Ant.* RESTRAIN, curb, rein in.

goal *n.* object, aim, intent; see END 2, PURPOSE 1.

goat *n.* nanny goat, buck, kid; see ANIMAL. —**get one's goat*** annoy, irritate, anger; see BOTHER 2.

gobble *v.* bolt, cram, stuff; see EAT 1.

go-between *n.* middleman, referee, mediator; see AGENT, MESSENGER.

god *n.* deity, divinity, divine being, spirit, numen, power, demigod, oversoul, prime mover, godhead, omnipotence, world soul, universal life force, infinite spirit. *Greek gods and their Roman counterparts include:* Zeus or Jupiter or Jove, Phoebus or Apollo, Ares or Mars, Hermes or Mercury, Poseidon or Neptune, Hephaestus or Vulcan, Dionysius or Bacchus, Hades or Pluto or Dis, Faunus or Pan, Kronos or Saturn, Eros or Cupid. *Norse gods include:* Balder, Bragi, Tyr, Frey, Loki, Odin or Woden or Wotan, Thor. *Egyptian gods include:* Ra, Amon, Amon-Re, Bes, Horus, Osiris, Ptah, Set, Thoth. *Hindu gods include:* Ganesha, Indra, Kama, Krishna, Rama, Vishnu, Siva, Shakti, Skanda, Varuna, Hanuman. *Babylonian and Semitic gods include:* Bel, Marduk, Shamash, Baal, Dagon, Molech. *Other gods include:* Mithras (Persian), Ashur (Assyrian), Tiki (Polynesian), Quetzalcoatl (Aztec). For specific female deities see also GODDESS.

God *n.* **1** [The Judeo-Christian deity] Lord, Jehovah, Yahweh, the Almighty, the King of Kings, the Godhead, the Creator, the Maker, the Supreme Being, the Ruler of Heaven, Our Father in Heaven, Almighty God, God Almighty, the Deity, the Divinity, Providence, the All-knowing, the Infinite Spirit, the First Cause, the Lord of Lords, the Supreme Soul, the All-wise, the All-merciful, the All-powerful; the Trinity, the Holy Trinity, Threefold Unity; Father, Son, and Holy Spirit; God the Son, Jesus Christ, Christ, Jesus, Jesus of Nazareth, the Nazarene, the Messiah, the Savior, the Redeemer, the Son of God, the Son of Man, the Son of Mary, the Lamb of God, Immanuel, Emmanuel, the King of the Jews, the Prince of Peace, the Good Shepherd, the Way, the Door, the Truth, the Life, the Light, the Christ Child, the Holy Spirit, the Spirit of God. **2** [The supreme deity of other religions] Allah (Islam); Brahma (Hinduism); Buddha (Buddhism); Mazda or Ormazd (Zoroastrianism).

goddess *n.* female deity, she-god, beauty; see GOD. *Greek goddesses and their Roman counterparts include the following:* Hera or Juno, Ceres or Demeter, Proserpina or Persephone, Tellus or Gaea, Vesta or Hestia, Artemis or Diana, Minerva or Athena, Aphrodite or Venus. *Hindu and Brahmanic goddesses include:* Devi, Maya, Kali, Parvati, Sarasvati. *Norse goddesses include:* Freya, Frigg, Idun, the Norns. *Other goddesses include:* the Goddess; Isis, Hather (Egyptian); Ashtoreth, Astarte (Semitic).

godly *a.* righteous, devout, pious; see HOLY 1.

going *a.* flourishing, thriving, profit-

able; see SUCCESSFUL. —**be going to** shall, be intending to, be prepared to; see WILL 3. —**get someone going*** annoy, excite, enrage; see BOTHER 2. —**have something going for one*** have an advantage, be talented, have opportunity; see SUCCEED 1. —**keep going** progress, promote, proceed; see ADVANCE 1, IMPROVE 2. —**going strong*** flourishing, surviving, thriving; see SUCCESSFUL.

gold *n.* **1** [A color] dark yellow, bright yellow, tawny; see COLOR, GOLD *a.* **2** [A precious metal] green gold, white gold, red gold, gold foil, gold leaf, gold plate, filled gold, commercial gold, gold alloy, cloth of gold, gold thread, gold wire; see also METAL. —**as good as gold*** very good, valuable, secure; see EXCELLENT.

gold *a.* yellow, golden, gold-colored, red-gold, greenish gold, flaxen, wheat-colored, deep tan, tawny.

golf *n.* match play, medal play, open tournament, skins game, Scotch doubles, nine holes, eighteen holes, front nine, back nine, game; see also SPORT 1.

gone *a.* **1** [Having left] gone out, gone away, moved, removed, traveling, transferred, displaced, shifted, withdrawn, retired, left, taken leave, departed, deserted, abandoned, quit, disappeared, not here, no more, flown, run off, decamped.—*Ant.* HERE, returned, remained. **2** [Being no longer in existence] dead, vanished, dissipated, disappeared, dissolved, burned up, disintegrated, decayed, rotted away, extinct. —**far gone** **1** advanced, deeply involved, absorbed; see INTERESTED 2. **2** crazy, mad, eccentric; see INSANE.

good *a.* **1** [Moral] upright, just, honest, worthy, respectable, noble, ethical, fair, guiltless, blameless, pure, truthful, decent, kind, conscientious, honorable, charitable. **2** [Kind] considerate, tolerant, generous; see KIND. **3** [Proper] suitable, becoming, desirable; see FIT 1. **4** [Reliable] trustworthy, dependable, loyal; see RELIABLE. **5** [Sound] safe, solid, stable; see RELIABLE. **6** [Pleasant] agreeable, satisfying, enjoyable; see PLEASANT 1, 2. **7** [Qualified] suited, competent, suitable; see ABLE. **8** [Of approved quality] choice, select, high-grade; see EXCELLENT. **9** [Healthy] sound, normal, vigorous; see HEALTHY. **10** [Obedient] dutiful, tractable, well-behaved; see OBEDIENT 1. **11** [Genuine] valid, real, sound; see GENUINE 1. **12** [Delicious] tasty, flavorful, tasteful; see DELICIOUS. **13** [Considerable] great, big, immeasurable; see LARGE 1, MUCH. **14** [Favorable] approving, commendatory, commending; see FAVORABLE 3. **—as good as** in effect, virtually, nearly; see ALMOST. **—for good** permanently, for all time, henceforth; see FOREVER. **—good for 1** [Helpful] useful, beneficial, salubrious; see HELPFUL 1. **2** [Financially sound] safe, creditworthy, sound; see VALID 2. **—make good 1** [To repay] compensate, adjust, reimburse; see PAY 1, REPAY 1. **2** [To justify] maintain, support, uphold; see SUPPORT 2. **3** [To succeed] arrive, pay off, prove oneself; see PAY 2, SUCCEED 1.

good *n.* **1** [A benefit] welfare, gain, asset; see ADVANTAGE. **2** [That which is morally approved] ethic, merit, ideal; see VIRTUE 1. **—come to no good** come to a bad end, get into trouble, have difficulty; see FAIL 1. **—no good** useless, valueless, unserviceable; see WORTHLESS. **—to the good** favorable, advantageous, beneficial; see PROFITABLE.

goodbye *interj.* farewell, fare you well, God bless you and keep you, God be with you, adieu, adios, ciao*, so long, bye, bye-bye*, see you later, take it easy*, have a nice day.

good humor *n.* cordiality, levity, geniality; see HAPPINESS.

good-looking *a.* clean-cut, attractive, impressive; see BEAUTIFUL, HANDSOME.

good-natured *a.* cordial, kindly, amiable; see FRIENDLY.

goodness *n.* decency, morality, honesty; see VIRTUE 1, 2.

goods *n.* **1** [Effects] equipment, personal property, possessions; see PROPERTY 1. **2** [Commodities] merchandise, materials, wares; see COMMODITY.

goodwill *n.* benevolence, charity, kindness, cordiality, sympathy, tolerance, helpfulness, altruism.—*Ant.* HATRED, malevolence, animosity.

goof* *v.* err, make a mistake, flub*; see FAIL 1.

goose *n.* gray goose, snow goose, Canada goose; see BIRD.

gorge *n.* chasm, abyss, crevasse; see RAVINE.

gorge *v.* glut, devour, stuff oneself; see EAT 1, FILL 1.

gorgeous *a.* superb, sumptuous, impressive; see BEAUTIFUL, GRAND.

gory *a.* blood-soaked, bloodstained, bloody; see OFFENSIVE 2.

gospel *n.* **1** [A record of Christ] New Testament, Christian Scripture, Evangel; see BIBLE. **2** [Belief or statement supposedly infallible] creed, certainty, dogma; see DOCTRINE, FAITH 2, TRUTH.

gossip *n.* **1** [Idle talk] babble, chatter, meddling, small talk, malicious talk, hearsay, rumor, scandal, news, slander, defamation, injury, blackening, skinny*, the grapevine. **2** [One who indulges in gossip] snoop*, busybody, meddler, tattler, newsmonger, scandalmonger, muckraker, backbiter, chatterbox, talkative person, babbler.

gossip *v.* tattle, prattle, tell tales, talk idly, chat, chatter, rumor, report, tell secrets, blab, babble, repeat.

gouge *v.* scoop, chisel, channel; see DIG 1.

govern *v.* command, administer, reign, rule, legislate, oversee, assume command, hold office, administer the laws, exercise authority, be in power, supervise, direct, dictate, tyrannize.

governed *a.* commanded, administered, under authority, supervised, directed, dictated to, conducted, guided, piloted, mastered, led, driven, subjugated, subordinate, determined, guided, influenced, swayed, inclined, regulated, directed, ordered, dependent, obedient, under someone's jurisdiction.—*Ant.* UNRULY, self-determined, capricious.

governing *a.* commanding, administrative, executive, authoritative, supervisory, regulatory, controlling, directing, overseeing, dictatorial, conducting, guiding, mastering, dominating, dominant, determining, supreme, influential, presidential, absolute, ruling, checking, curbing, inhibiting, limiting.—*Ant.* SUBORDINATE, powerless, tributary.

government *n.* **1** [The process of governing] rule, control, command, regulation, direction, dominion, sway, authority, jurisdiction, sovereignty, direction, power, management, authorization, mastery, supervision, superintendence, supremacy, domination, influence, politics, state, political practice; see also ADMINISTRATION 2. **2** [The instrument of governing] administration, assembly, legislature, congress, cabinet, executive power, bureaucracy, authority, party, council, parliament, senate, department of justice, soviet, synod, convocation, convention, court, house. *Types of government include the following:* absolute monarchy, dictatorship, empire, tyranny, fascism, imperialism, colonialism, despotism, constitutional monarchy, oligarchy, aristocracy, theocracy, republic, democracy, popular government, representative government, social democracy, communism, socialism, party government. *Divisions of government include:* state, province, kingdom, territory, colony, dominion, commonwealth, soviet, republic, shire, city, county, town, village, township, municipality, borough, commune, canton, ward, district, department, parish.

governmental *a.* political, administrative, executive, regulatory, bureaucratic, legal, supervisory, sovereign, presidential, official, gubernatorial, national.

governor *n.* director, leader, head, presiding officer, ruler; see also LEADER 2.

gown *n.* garb, garment, clothes; see DRESS 2.

grab *v.* clutch, grasp, take; see SEIZE 1, 2.

grace *n.* **1** [The quality of being graceful] suppleness, ease of movement, nimbleness, agility, pliancy, smoothness, form, poise, dexterity, symmetry, balance, style, harmony.—*Ant.* AWKWARDNESS, stiffness, maladroitness. **2** [Mercy] forgiveness, love, charity; see MERCY. —**in the bad graces of** in disfavor, rejected, disapproved; see HATED. — **in the good graces of** favored, accepted, admired; see APPROVED.

graceful *a.* **1** [*Said of movement*] supple, agile, lithe, pliant, nimble, elastic, springy, easy, dexterous, adroit, smooth, controlled, light-footed, athletic, willowy, poised, practiced, skilled, rhythmic, sprightly, elegant.—*Ant.* AWKWARD, fumbling, stiff. **2** [*Said of objects*] elegant, neat, well-proportioned, trim, balanced, symmetrical, dainty, pretty, harmonious, beautiful, comely, seemly, handsome, fair, delicate, tasteful, slender, decorative, artistic, exquisite, statuesque.—*Ant.* UGLY, shapeless, cumbersome. **3** [*Said of conduct*] cultured, seemly, becoming; see POLITE.

gracefully *a.* lithely, agilely, harmoniously, daintily, nimbly, elegantly, trimly, symmetrically, beautifully, delicately, tastefully, artistically, easily, dexterously, smoothly, skillfully, fairly, adroitly, handsomely, rhythmically, exquisitely, neatly, delightfully, charmingly, imaginatively, becomingly, suitably, pleasingly, appropriately, happily, decoratively, prettily.—*Ant.* AWKWARDLY, insipidly, grotesquely.

gracious *a.* **1** [Genial] amiable, courteous, condescending; see POLITE. **2** [Merciful] tender, loving, charitable; see KIND.

grade *n.* **1** [An incline] slope, inclined plane, gradient, slant, inclination, pitch, ascent, descent, ramp, upgrade, downgrade, climb, elevation, height; see also HILL. **2** [An embankment] fill, causeway, dike; see DAM. **3** [Rank or degree] class, category, classification; see DEGREE 2. **4** [A division of a school] standard, form, rank; see GATHERING. —

make the grade win, prosper, achieve; see SUCCEED 1.

grade *v.* rate, assess, assort; see RANK 3.

gradual *a.* creeping, regular, continuous; see REGULATED.

gradually *a.* step by step, by degrees, steadily, increasingly, slowly, regularly, a little at a time, little by little, bit by bit, inch by inch, by installments, in small doses, continually, continuously, progressively, successively, sequentially, constantly, unceasingly, imperceptibly, deliberately.—*Ant.* QUICKLY, haphazardly, by leaps and bounds.

graduate *n.* recipient of a degree, recipient of a certificate, recipient of a diploma, alumnus, alumna, former student, holder of a degree, bearer of a degree, holder of a certificate, bearer of a certificate, baccalaureate, grad*, alum*.

graduate *v.* receive a degree, receive a certificate, receive a diploma, be awarded a degree, be awarded a certificate, be awarded a diploma, earn a degree, earn a certificate, earn a diploma, become an alumna, become an alumnus, get out, finish one's schooling; get a B.A., M.A., Ph.D., M.D., etc.; get a sheepskin*.

graduated *a.* **1** [Granted a degree] certified, ordained, passed; see OFFICIAL 1. **2** [Arranged or marked according to a scale] graded, sequential, progressive; see ORGANIZED.

graduation *n.* commencement, convocation, granting of diplomas, promotion, bestowal of honors, commissioning.

grain *n.* **1** [Seeds of domesticated grasses] cereals, corn, small grain, seed. *Varieties of grain include the following:* rice, wheat, oats, barley, maize, corn, rye, millet, Indian corn, hybrid corn, popcorn. **2** [Character imparted by fiber] texture, warp and woof, warp and weft, tendency, fabric, tissue, current, direction, tooth, nap. —**against the grain** disturbing, irritating, bothersome; see OFFENSIVE 2.

grammar *n.* syntax, morphology, structure, syntactic structure, sentence structure, language pattern, sentence pattern, linguistic science, generative grammar, stratificational grammar, transformational grammar, universal grammar, tagmemics, synthetic grammar, inflectional grammar, analytic grammar, traditional grammar, structural linguistics; see also LANGUAGE. *Terms in grammar include the following:* tense, mood, voice, person, gender, number, word, phrase, clause, aspect, case, modification, incorporation, inflection, concord, agreement, sentence, nexus, coordination, subordination, structure, phrase structure, phoneme, phonemics, string, head word, morpheme, transform.

grammatical *a.* 1 [Having to do with grammar] linguistic, syntactic, morphological, logical, philological, analytic, analytical. 2 [Conforming to rules of grammar] grammatically correct, conventional, accepted; see CONVENTIONAL 1.

grand *a.* lofty, stately, dignified, elevated, high, regal, noble, illustrious, sublime, great, ambitious, august, majestic, solemn, grave, preeminent, extraordinary, monumental, stupendous, huge, chief, commanding, towering, overwhelming, impressive, imposing, awe-inspiring, mighty, terrific*.—*Ant.* POOR, low, mediocre.

grandeur *n.* splendor, magnificence, pomp, circumstance, impressiveness, eminence, distinction, fame, glory, brilliancy, richness, luxury, stateliness, beauty, ceremony, importance, celebrity, solemnity, fineness, majesty, sublimity, nobility, scope, dignity, elevation, preeminence, height, greatness, might, breadth, immensity, amplitude, vastness.

grandfather *n.* elder, forefather, ancestor, patriarch, grandpa*, gramps*, granddaddy*, grandpappy*.

grandmother *n.* matriarch, dowager, ancestor, nana*, grandma*, gram*, granny*.

grant *n.* gift, boon, reward, present, allowance, stipend, donation, matching grant, benefaction, gratuity, endowment, concession, bequest, privilege, subsidy.—*Ant.* DISCOUNT, deprivation, deduction.

grant *v.* 1 [To permit] yield, cede, impart; see ALLOW. 2 [To accept as true] concede, accede, acquiesce; see ACKNOWLEDGE 2.

granted *a.* 1 [Awarded] conferred, bestowed, awarded; see GIVEN. 2 [Allowed] accepted, admitted, acknowledged; see ASSUMED. **—take for granted** accept, presume, consider settled; see ASSUME.

grape *n.* wine grape, raisin, Concord grape; see FRUIT.

graph *n.* diagram, chart, linear representation; see DESIGN, PLAN 1.

graphic *a.* 1 [Pictorial] visible, illustrated, descriptive, photographic, visual, depicted, limned, seen, drawn, portrayed, traced, sketched, outlined, pictured, painted, engraved, etched, chiseled, penciled, printed.—*Ant.* UNREAL, imagined, chimerical. 2 [Vivid] forcible, telling, picturesque, intelligible, comprehensible, clear, explicit, striking, definite, distinct, precise, expressive, eloquent, moving, stirring, concrete, energetic, colorful, strong, figurative, poetic.—*Ant.* OBSCURE, ambiguous, abstract.

grasp *v.* 1 [To clutch] grip, enclose, clasp; see SEIZE 1, 2. 2 [To comprehend] perceive, apprehend, follow; see UNDERSTAND 1.

grasp *n.* hold, clutch, cinch; see GRIP 2.

grass *n.* 1 [Plant for food, grazing, etc.] *Wild grasses include the following:* Johnson grass, salt grass, bluegrass, foxtail, buffalo grass, sandbur, crab grass, deer grass, bunch grass, meadow grass, fescue, orchard grass, pampas grass, June grass, redtop, river grass, ribbon grass, sweet grass, cattail, wild rice. 2 [Grassed area] grassland, meadow, lawn, sward, turf, pasture, prairie, hayfield; see also FIELD 1, YARD 1. 3 [*A drug] marijuana, cannabis, pot*; see DRUG.

grassy *a.* grass-grown, verdant, green, reedy, lush, matted, tangled, carpeted, sowed, luxuriant, deep.

grate *v.* rasp, grind, abrade; see RUB 1.

grateful *a.* appreciative, pleased, obliged; see THANKFUL.

gratefully *a.* appreciatively, thankfully, obligingly, delightedly, responsively, admiringly.—*Ant.* RUDELY, ungratefully, thanklessly.

gratitude *n.* thankfulness, appreciation, acknowledgment, response, sense of indebtedness, feeling of obligation, responsiveness, thanks, praise, recognition, honor, thanksgiving, grace.—*Ant.* INDIFFERENCE, ingratitude, thanklessness.

grave *a.* 1 [Important] momentous, weighty, consequential; see IMPORTANT 1. 2 [Dangerous] critical, serious, ominous; see DANGEROUS. 3 [Solemn] serious, sober, earnest; see SOLEMN.

grave *n.* vault, sepulcher, tomb, pit, crypt, mausoleum, catacomb, long home*, six feet of earth, final resting place, place of interment, mound, burial place, charnel house, last home*. **—make one turn (over) in one's grave** do something shocking, sin, err; see MISBEHAVE.

gravel *n.* sand, pebbles, shale, macadam, screenings, crushed rock, washings, alluvium, tailings.

graveyard *n.* burial ground, necropolis, churchyard; see CEMETERY.

gravity *n.* 1 [Weight] heaviness, pressure, force; see PRESSURE 1. 2 [Importance] seriousness, concern, significance; see IMPORTANCE.

gravy *n.* sauce, dressing, brown gravy, white gravy, milk gravy, pan gravy, chicken gravy, meat gravy.

gray *a.* neutral, dusky, silvery, dingy, somber, shaded, drab, leaden, grayish, ashen, grizzled. *Shades of gray include the following:* blue-gray, silver-gray, smoke-gray, slate, charcoal, mouse-colored, iron-gray, lead, ash-gray, pepper-and-salt, dusty, smoky.

gray *n.* shade, drabness, dusk; see COLOR.

graze *v.* 1 [To touch or score lightly] brush, scrape, rub; see TOUCH 1. 2 [To pasture] browse, feed, crop, gnaw, nibble, bite, uproot, pull grass, forage, eat, munch, ruminate, chew cud.

grazing *a.* cropping, feeding, gnawing, nibbling, biting, uprooting, pasturing, pulling grass, foraging, eating, munching, ruminating, chewing cud.

grease *n.* oil, wax, lubricant, salve, petrolatum, petroleum jelly, animal fat, lard, shortening, suet, hydrogenated oil, axle grease, suint; see also OIL 1.

grease *v.* oil, lubricate, smear, salve, coat with oil, cream, pomade, grease the wheels, anoint, swab.

greasy *a.* creamy, oleaginous, fatty; see OILY 1.

great *a.* 1 [Eminent] noble, grand, majestic, dignified, exalted, commanding, famous, renowned, widely acclaimed, famed, celebrated, distinguished, noted, conspicuous, elevated, prominent, high, stately, honorable, magnificent, glorious, regal, royal, kingly, imposing, preeminent, unrivaled, fabulous, fabled, legendary, storied.—*Ant.* OBSCURE, retired, anonymous. 2 [Large] numerous, big, vast; see LARGE 1. 3 [*Excellent] exceptional, first-rate, top-notch*; see EXCELLENT.

greatly *a.* exceedingly, considerably, hugely; see VERY.

greatness *n.* 1 [Eminence] prominence, renown, importance; see FAME. 2 [Size] bulk, extent, largeness; see SIZE 2.

greed *n.* greediness, selfishness, eagerness, voracity, excess, gluttony, piggishness, indulgence, hoggishness, niggardliness, acquisitiveness, intemperance, covetousness, desire.—*Ant.* GENEROSITY, liberality, kindness.

greedy *a.* avid, grasping, rapacious, selfish, miserly, parsimonious, close, closefisted, tight, tightfisted, niggardly, exploitative, grudging, devouring, ravenous, omnivorous, intemperate, gobbling, indulging one's appetites, mercenary, stingy, covetous, grabby*, penny-pinching.—*Ant.* GENEROUS, munificent, bountiful.

Greek *a.* Grecian, Hellenic, Hellenis-

tic, Minoan, Dorian, Attic, Athenian, Spartan, Peloponnesian, Ionian, Corinthian, Thessalian, Boeotian, Homeric, ancient, classic; see also CLASSICAL 2.

Greek *n.* 1 [A citizen of Greece] Hellene, Athenian, Spartan; see EUROPEAN. 2 [The Greek language] Hellenic, Ionic, koine; see LANGUAGE 1.

green *a.* 1 [Of the color green] *Tints and shades of green include the following:* emerald, blue-green, sage, aquamarine, chartreuse, lime, kelly, bronze-green, yellow-green, bottle-green, pea-green, sea-green, apple-green, grass-green, forest-green, moss-green, spinach-green, pine-green, olive-green, jade. 2 [Verdant] growing, leafy, grassy, flourishing, lush. 3 [Immature] young, growing, unripe, sprouting, maturing, developing, half-formed, fresh.—*Ant.* MATURE, ripe, gone to seed. 4 [Inexperienced] youthful, callow, raw; see INEXPERIENCED.

green *n.* greenness, verdure, virescence; see COLOR.

greet *v.* welcome, speak to, salute, address, hail, recognize, embrace, shake hands, nod, receive, call to, stop, acknowledge, bow to, approach, give one's love, hold out one's hand, herald, bid good day, bid hello, bid welcome, exchange greetings, usher in, attend, pay one's respects.—*Ant.* IGNORE, snub, slight.

greeting *n.* welcome, address, notice, speaking to, ushering in, acknowledgment, one's compliments, regards. *Common greetings include the following:* hello, how do you do, how are you, good morning, good day, good afternoon, good evening, hi*, hey*, yo*.

grey *a.* dun, drab, grayish; see GRAY.

grief *n.* sorrow, sadness, regret, melancholy, mourning, misery, trouble, anguish, despondency, pain, worry, harassment, anxiety, woe, heartache, malaise, disquiet, discomfort, affliction, gloom, unhappiness, desolation, despair, agony, torture, purgatory.—*Ant.* HAPPINESS, exhilaration, pleasure.

grievance *n.* complaint, injury, case; see OBJECTION.

grieve *v.* lament, bewail, sorrow for; see MOURN.

grill *v.* roast, sauté, barbecue; see COOK.

grim *a.* 1 [Sullen] sour, crusty, gloomy, sulky, morose, churlish, forbidding, glum, grumpy, scowling, grouchy, crabby, glowering, stubborn, cantankerous.—*Ant.* HAPPY, cheerful, gay. 2 [Stern] austere, strict, harsh; see SEVERE 1. 3

[Relentless] unrelenting, implacable, inexorable; see SEVERE 2.

grimace n. smirk, smile, sneer; see EXPRESSION 4.

grime n. soil, smudge, dirt; see FILTH.

grimy a. begrimed, dingy, soiled; see DIRTY 1.

grin n. smirk, simper, delighted look; see SMILE.

grin v. smirk, simper, beam; see SMILE.

grind v. crush, powder, mill, grate, granulate, disintegrate, rasp, scrape, file, abrade, pound, reduce to fine particles, crunch, roll out, pound out, chop up, crumble.—*Ant.* ORGANIZE, mold, solidify.

grinding a. abrasive, crushing, pulverizing, grating, rasping, rubbing, milling, powdering, cracking, bone-crushing, crunching, splintering, shivering, smashing, crumbling, scraping, chopping, wearing away, eroding.

grip n. 1 [The power and the application of the power to grip] grasp, hold, manual strength, clutch, clasp, catch, cinch, vise, clench, clinch, embrace, handhold, fist, handshake, anchor, squeeze, wrench, grab, fixing, fastening, crushing, clamp, vicelike grip, jaws. 2 [Something suited to grasping] knocker, knob, ear; see HANDLE 1. 3 [A traveling bag] valise, suitcase, satchel; see BAG. —**come to grips** engage, encounter, cope with; see FIGHT, TRY 1.

grip v. clutch, grasp, clasp; see SEIZE 1.

gripe* n. complaint, grievance, beef*; see OBJECTION.

gripe* v. grumble, mutter, fuss; see COMPLAIN.

grit n. sand, dust, crushed rock; see GRAVEL.

gritty a. rough, abrasive, sandy, rasping, lumpy, gravelly, muddy, dusty, powdery, granular, crumbly, loose, scratchy.

groan n. moan, sob, grunt; see CRY 1.

groan v. moan, murmur, keen; see CRY 1.

groceries n. food, edibles, produce, comestibles, foodstuffs, perishables, vegetables, staples, green groceries, fruits, dairy products, processed foods, frozen foods, freeze-dried foods, dried foods, packaged foods, canned foods.

grocery n. food store, vegetable market, supermarket; see MARKET 1.

groggy a. sleepy, dizzy, reeling; see TIRED.

groom n. bridegroom, married man, newlywed; see HUSBAND.

groom v. rub down, comb, brush; see PREPARE 1.

groove n. channel, trench, gouge, depression, scratch, canal, valley, notch, furrow, rut, incision, slit, gutter, ditch, crease. —**in the groove*** efficient, skillful, operative; see WORKING 1.

grope v. fumble, touch, feel blindly; see FEEL 1.

gross a. 1 [Fat] corpulent, obese, huge; see FAT. 2 [Obscene] foul, swinish, indecent; see LEWD 1, 2. 3 [Without deduction] in sum, total, entire; see WHOLE 1.

gross n. total, aggregate, total amount; see WHOLE.

gross v. earn, bring in, take in; see EARN 2.

grotesque a. malformed, ugly, distorted; see DEFORMED.

grouch n. complainer, grumbler, growler, bear*, sourpuss*, sorehead*, crab*, crank*, bellyacher*.

grouch v. mutter, grumble, gripe*; see COMPLAIN.

grouchy a. surly, ill-tempered, crusty; see IRRITABLE.

ground n. 1 [Soil] sand, dirt, clay; see EARTH 2. 2 [An area] spot, terrain, territory; see AREA. —**break ground** begin construction, initiate, commence; see BEGIN 1. —**cover ground** move, go on, progress; see ADVANCE 1. —**from the ground up** thoroughly, wholly, entirely; see COMPLETELY. —**gain ground** move, go on, progress; see ADVANCE 1. —**get off the ground** start, commence, come into being; see BEGIN 2. —**hold** (or **stand**) **one's ground** maintain one's position, defend, sustain; see ENDURE 2. —**lose ground** lag, fall behind, drop back; see LAG. —**run into the ground*** exaggerate, do too much, press; see OVERDO 1.

ground v. 1 [To bring to the ground] floor, bring down, prostrate; see TRIP 2. 2 [To restrict] punish, take away priveleges, force to stay home; see RESTRICT. 3 [To instruct in essentials] train, indoctrinate, educate; see TEACH.

grounds n. 1 [Real estate] lot, environs, territory; see PROPERTY 2. 2 [Basis] reasons, arguments, proof; see BASIS. 3 [Sediment] dregs, lees, leavings; see RESIDUE.

groundwork n. background, base, origin; see BASIS, FOUNDATION 2.

group n. 1 [A gathering of persons] assembly, assemblage, crowd; see GATHERING. 2 [Collected things] accumulation, assortment, combination; see COLLECTION. 3 [An organized body of people] association, club, society; see ORGANIZATION 2.

group v. file, assort, arrange; see CLASSIFY.

grovel v. crawl, beg, sneak, stoop,

kneel, crouch before, kowtow to, sponge, cower, snivel, beseech, wheedle, flatter, cater to, humor, pamper, curry favor with, court, act up to, play up to, beg for mercy, prostrate oneself, be a toady, soft-soap*, butter up*, make up to, kiss someone's feet*, lick someone's boots*, knuckle under, polish the apple*, eat dirt*, brown-nose*.—*Ant.* HATE, spurn, scorn.

grow *v.* **1** [To become larger] increase, expand in size, swell, inflate, wax, thrive, gain, enlarge, advance, dilate, stretch, mount, build, burst forth, burgeon, spread, multiply, develop, mature, flourish, grow up, rise, sprout, shoot up, jump up, start up, spring up, spread like wildfire.—*Ant.* WITHER, lessen, shrink. **2** [To change slowly] become, develop, alter, tend, pass, evolve, flower, shift, flow, progress, advance; get bigger, larger, etc.; wax, turn into, improve, mellow, age, better, ripen into, blossom, open out, resolve itself into, mature. **3** [To cultivate] raise, nurture, tend, nurse, foster, produce, plant, breed.—*Ant.* HARM, impede, neglect.

growing *a.* increasing, ever-widening, expanding, budding, germinating, maturing, waxing, enlarging, amplifying, swelling, developing, mushrooming, spreading, thriving, flourishing, stretching, living, sprouting, viable, organic, animate, spreading like wildfire.—*Ant.* CONTRACTION, withering, shrinking.

growl *n.* snarl, gnarl, moan, bark, woof, bellow, rumble, roar, howl, grumble, grunt.

growl *v.* snarl, bark, gnarl; see CRY 2.

grown *a.* of age, adult, grown up; see MATURE.

grown-up *n.* adult, grown person, big person, grown man, grown woman.

growth *n.* **1** [The process of growing] extension, organic development, germination; see INCREASE. **2** [The result of growing] completion, adulthood, fullness; see MAJORITY 2. **3** [A swelling] tumor, cancer, mole, lump, cyst, sty, neoplasm, goose egg*, outgrowth, thickening.

grubby *a.* dirty, sloppy, grimy; see DIRTY 1.

grudge *n.* spite, rancor, animosity; see HATRED.

grudge *v.* begrudge, resent, give reluctantly; see ENVY.

grueling *a.* exhausting, tiring, fatiguing; see DIFFICULT 1, 2.

gruesome *a.* grim, grisly, horrible*; see FRIGHTFUL, OFFENSIVE 2.

gruff *a.* harsh, grating, rough; see HOARSE.

grumble *v.* whine, protest, fuss; see COMPLAIN.

grumpy *a.* sullen, grouchy, morose; see IRRITABLE.

grunt *v.* snort, squawk, squeak; see CRY 2.

guarantee *v.* attest, testify, vouch for, declare, assure, answer for, be responsible for, pledge, give bond, go bail, wager, stake, give a guarantee, stand behind, back, sign for, become surety for, endorse, secure, notarize, make certain, warrant, insure, witness, prove, reassure, support, affirm, confirm, cross one's heart.

guaranteed *a.* warranted, certified, bonded, secured, endorsed, insured, pledged, confirmed, assured, approved, attested, sealed, certificated, protected, affirmed, sure-fire*.—*Ant.* ANONYMOUS, unsupported, unendorsed.

guaranty *n.* warrant, warranty, bond, contract, certificate, charter, testament, security.

guard *n.* sentry, sentinel, protector; see WATCHMAN. **—off one's guard** unaware, unprotected, defenseless; see UNPREPARED. **—on one's guard** alert, mindful, vigilant; see READY 2.

guard *v.* watch, observe, protect, patrol, picket, police, look out, look after, see after, tend, keep in view, keep an eye on, attend, overlook, hold in custody, stand over, babysit, care for, see to, chaperone, oversee, ride herd on*, keep tabs on*;—*Ant.* NEGLECT, disregard, forsake.

guarded *a.* **1** [Protected] safeguarded, secured, defended; see SAFE 1. **2** [Cautious] circumspect, attentive, overcautious; see CAREFUL.

guardian *n.* **1** [One who regulates or protects] overseer, safeguard, curator, guard, protector, preserver, trustee, custodian, keeper, patrol, warden, defender, supervisor, babysitter, sponsor, superintendent, sentinel. **2** [A foster parent] adoptive parent, legal guardian, nanny; see FATHER 1, MOTHER 1.

guerrilla *a.* clandestine, underground, independent; see FIGHTING.

guerrilla *n.* irregular soldier, underground resistance fighter, revolutionary; see SOLDIER.

guess *n.* conjecture, surmise, supposition, theory, hypothesis, presumption, opinion, postulate, estimate, suspicion, guesswork, guesstimate*, view, belief, assumption, speculation, fancy, inference, conclusion, deduction, induction, shot in the dark*.

guess *v.* conjecture, presume, infer, suspect, speculate, imagine, surmise, theorize, hazard a guess, suggest, figure, venture, suppose, presume, imagine, think likely, reckon*, calculate. —**guess at** reckon*, calculate, survey; see ESTI-MATE.

guessing *n.* guesswork, supposition, imagination, fancy, inference, deduction, presupposition, reckoning, surmise, theorizing, taking for granted, postulating, assuming, presuming, jumping to conclusions.

guest *n.* visitor, caller, house guest, dinner guest, luncheon guest, visitant, company.

guidance *n.* direction, leadership, supervision; see ADMINISTRATION 2.

guide *n.* pilot, captain, pathfinder, scout, escort, courier, director, explorer, guru, conductor, pioneer, leader, superintendent.

guide *v.* conduct, escort, show the way; see LEAD 1.

guilt *n.* culpability, blame, error, fault, crime, sin, offense, liability, criminality, sinfulness, misconduct, misbehavior, malpractice, delinquency, transgression, indiscretion, weakness.—*Ant.* INNOCENCE, blamelessness, honor.

guilty *a.* found guilty, guilty as charged, guilty as sin*, condemned, sentenced, criminal, censured, impeached, incriminated, indicted, liable, condemned, convictable, judged, damned, doomed, at fault, sinful, to blame, in the wrong, in error, wrong, blamable, reproachable, chargeable.—*Ant.* INNOCENT, blameless, right.

gulch *n.* gully, ditch, gorge; see RAVINE.

gulf *n.* 1 [Chasm] abyss, gap, depth; see RAVINE. 2 [An arm of the sea] inlet, sound, cove; see BAY.

gullible *a.* innocent, trustful, simple; see NAIVE.

gully *n.* ditch, chasm, crevasse; see RAVINE.

gulp *v.* swig, choke down, chug*; see SWALLOW.

gum *n.* resin, glue, pitch, tar, pine tar, amber, wax. *Commercial gums include the following:* chewing gum, sealing wax, rosin, mucilage, chicle, latex, gum arabic.

gummy *a.* sticky, cohesive, viscid; see STICKY.

gun *n. Types include the following:* rifle, automatic rifle, repeating rifle, repeater, recoilless rifle, air rifle, BB gun, shotgun, sawed-off shotgun, musket, handgun, assault rifle, semiautomatic pistol, squirrel gun, carbine, long rifle, laser gun, revolver, pistol, rod*; see also MACHINE GUN. —**jump the gun*** start too soon, act inappropriately, give oneself away; see BEGIN 1, HURRY 1.

gunfire *n.* bombardment, artillery support, air support, air strike, mortar fire, heavy arms attack, explosion, shooting, shot, report, artillery, volley, discharge, detonation, blast, firing, burst, barrage, cannonade, fire superiority, salvo, firepower.

gunman *n.* killer, assassin, hit man*; see CRIMINAL.

gunner *n.* machine gunner, turret gunner, ball-turret gunner, tail gunner, rocketeer, missile launcher, bazooka launcher, sniper, sharpshooter, aerial gunner, artilleryman, cannoneer.

gurgle *v.* ripple, murmur, pour; see FLOW.

gush *v.* pour, well, spew; see FLOW.

gusto *n.* fervor, vigor, ardor; see ZEAL.

gut *n.* small intestine, large intestine, duodenum; see INTESTINES.

guts *n.* 1 [Bowels] viscera, insides, belly; see INTESTINES. 2 [*Fortitude] pluck, hardihood, effrontery; see COURAGE. —**hate someone's guts*** detest, loathe, despise; see HATE.

gutter *n.* canal, gully, sewer, watercourse, channel, dike, drain, moat, trough; see also TRENCH.

guttural *a.* throaty, gruff, deep; see HOARSE.

guy* *n.* chap, lad, person; see FELLOW 1, MAN 2, PERSON 1.

guzzle *v.* swill, quaff, swig; see DRINK 1.

gymnasium *n.* health center, recreation center, playing floor, exercise room, sports center, field house, court, athletic club, arena, coliseum, theater, circus, stadium, ring, rink, pit, gym*.

gymnast *n.* acrobat, tumbler, jumper; see ATHLETE.

gymnastics *n.* trapeze performance, floor exercises, acrobatics, aerobatics, therapeutics, body-building exercises, tumbling, vaulting; work on the rings, parallel bars, balance beam, horse, etc.

gyp* *n.* cheat, fraud, trick; see FAKE, TRICK 1.

gypsy *n.* tramp, wanderer, itinerant; see TRAVELER.

H

habit *n.* **1** [A customary action] mode, wont, routine, rule, characteristic, practice, disposition, way, fashion, manner, propensity, bent, turn, proclivity, predisposition, susceptibility, weakness, bias, persuasion, second nature; see also CUSTOM. **2** [An obsession] addiction, fixation, hang-up*; see OBSESSION.

habitat *n.* locality, territory, natural surroundings; see ENVIRONMENT, HOME 1, POSITION 1.

habitual *a.* ingrained, confirmed, frequent, periodic, continual, routine, mechanical, automatic, seasoned, permanent, perpetual, fixed, rooted, systematic, recurrent, repeated, periodical, methodical, disciplined, practiced, accustomed, established, set, repetitious, cyclic, reiterated, settled, trite, stereotyped, in a groove, in a rut.—*Ant.* DIFFERENT, exceptional, extraordinary.

hack *n.* **1** [A literary drudge] pulpstory writer, ghostwriter, propagandist, commercial writer, popular novelist; see also WRITER. **2** [*Commercial driver, especially of a taxicab] cab driver, chauffeur, cabby*; see DRIVER. **3** [A cut] notch, nick, cleavage; see CUT 1.

hack *v.* chop, whack, mangle; see CUT 1.

hag *n.* crone, witch, withered old woman, shrew, ogress, hellcat, fishwife, harridan, old bag*, battle-ax*; see also WITCH.

haggle *v.* deal, wrangle, argue; see BUY, SELL.

hail *n.* hailstorm, sleet, ice pellets, icy rain; see also RAIN 1.

hail *v.* cheer, welcome, honor; see GREET. **—hail from** come from, be born in, be a native of; see BEGIN 2.

hair *n.* **1** [Threadlike growth] locks, wig, moustache, whiskers, eyebrow, eyelash, sideburn, mane, fluff; see also BEARD, FUR. **2** [Anything suggesting the thickness of a hair] a hairbreadth, a narrow margin, hair trigger, hairspring, splinter, shaving, sliver; see also BIT 1. **—get in one's hair*** irritate, annoy, disturb; see BOTHER 2. **—let one's hair down*** be informal, have fun, let oneself go; see RELAX. **—make one's hair stand on end** terrify, scare, horrify; see FRIGHTEN.

haircut *n.* trim, trimming, bob, crew cut, flattop*, pageboy, pigtails, French roll, bun, ponytail, braid, feathercut, bangs, butch*, buzz cut*.

hairdo *n.* coiffure, hairdressing, hair style; see HAIRCUT.

hairless *n.* cleanshaven, beardless, smooth-faced; see BALD, SMOOTH 3.

hairpin *n.* bobby pin, hair clip, barrette; see FASTENER.

hairsplitting *a.* unimportant, scrupulous, subtle; see TRIVIAL, IRRELEVANT, UNIMPORTANT.

hairy *a.* bristly, shaggy, woolly, unshorn, downy, fleecy, whiskered, tufted, unshaven, bearded, bewhiskered, furry, fuzzy, hirsute, fluffy.—*Ant.* BALD, hairless, smooth.

half *a.* partial, divided by two, equally distributed in halves, mixed, divided, halved, bisected; see also HALFWAY.—*Ant.* FULL, all, whole.

half *n.* equal share, moiety, fifty percent; see SHARE. **—by half** considerably, many, very much; see MUCH. **—in half** into halves, split, divided; see HALF. **—not the half of it** not all of it, partial, incomplete; see UNFINISHED.

halfback *n.* running back, rusher, offensive back; see FOOTBALL PLAYER.

half dollar *n.* fifty cents, fifty-cent piece, four bits*; see MONEY 1.

halfhearted *a.* lukewarm, indecisive, wishy-washy*; see INDIFFERENT.

halfway *a.* midway, half the distance, in the middle, incomplete, unsatisfactory, partially, fairly, imperfectly, in part, partly, nearly, insufficiently, to a degree, to some extent, comparatively, moderately, at half the distance, in some measure, middling; see also HALF.—*Ant.* COMPLETELY, wholly, entirely.

hall *n.* **1** [A large public or semipublic building or room] legislative chamber, assembly room, meeting place, banquet hall, town hall, concert hall, dance hall, music hall, arena, ballroom, clubroom, church, salon, lounge, chamber, stateroom, gymnasium, dining hall, armory, amphitheater, council chamber, reception room, waiting room, lecture room, gallery, gym*, mess hall. **2** [An entranceway] foyer, corridor, hallway; see ENTRANCE 2, ROOM 2.

hallelujah *interj.* alleluia, praise God, praise the Lord; see YELL.

hallmark *n.* symbol, seal, certification; see EMBLEM.

hallowed *a.* sacred, sacrosanct, consecrated; see DIVINE.

hallway n. foyer, entranceway, corridor; see ENTRANCE 2.

halt v. pull up, check, terminate, suspend, put an end to, interrupt, break into, block, cut short, adjourn, hold off, cause to halt, stem, deter, bring to a standstill, stall, bring to an end, curb, stop, restrict, arrest, hold in check, defeat, thwart, hamper, frustrate, suppress, clog, intercept, extinguish, blockade, obstruct, repress, inhibit, hinder, barricade, impede, overthrow, vanquish, override, dam, upset, stand in the way of, baffle, contravene, overturn, reduce, counteract, quell, prohibit, outdo, put down, finish, forbid, oppose, crush, nip in the bud, break it up, put on the brakes*, hold on*, throw a wet blanket on*, throw a monkey wrench in the works*, clip someone's wings*, tie someone's hands*, take the wind out of someone's sails, squelch*.—*Ant.* BEGIN, start, instigate.

halter n. leash, bridle, rein; see ROPE.

halve v. split, bisect, cut in two; see DIVIDE.

ham n. 1 [Smoked pork thigh] sugar-cured ham, Virginia ham, picnic ham; see MEAT. 2 [*An incompetent actor] one who overacts, hambone*, one who chews the scenery*; see AMATEUR.

hamburger n. ground round, ground beef, burger; see MEAT.

hammer n. maul, mallet, mace, ballpeen hammer, sheet-metal hammer, tack hammer, claw hammer, meat tenderizer, gavel, triphammer, jackhammer, sledge; see also STICK, TOOL 1.

hammer v. strike, bang, pound away at; see BEAT 1, HIT.

hamper v. impede, thwart, embarrass; see HINDER.

hand n. 1 [The termination of the arm] fingers, palm, grip, grasp, hold, knuckles, paw*; see also FIST. 2 [A workman] helper, worker, hired hand; see LABORER. 3 [Handwriting] chirography, script, penmanship; see HANDWRITING. 4 [Aid] help, guidance, instruction; see HELP 1. 5 [Applause] ovation, reception, handclapping; see PRAISE 2. 6 [Round of cards] deal, round, trick; see GAME 1. —**at hand** immediate, approximate, close by; see NEAR 1. —**by hand** handcrafted, handmade, manual; see HOMEMADE. —**change hands** transfer, pass on, shift; see GIVE 1. —**from hand to hand** shifted, given over, changed; see TRANSFERRED. —**from hand to mouth** from day to day, by necessity, in poverty; see POOR 1. —**hand in hand** closely associated, working together, related; see TOGETHER 2,

UNITED. —**in hand** under control, in order, all right; see MANAGED 2. —**join hands** unite, associate, agree; see JOIN 1. —**keep one's hand in** carry on, continue, stay in practice; see PRACTICE 1. —**lay hands on** get, acquire, grasp; see SEIZE 1, 2. —**lend a hand** assist, aid, succor; see HELP. —**not lift a hand** do nothing, be lazy, not try; see NEGLECT 1, 2. —**off one's hands** out of one's responsibility, no longer one's concern, not accountable for; see IRRESPONSIBLE. —**on hand** ready, close by, usable; see AVAILABLE. —**on one's hands** in one's care or responsibility, chargeable to one, accountable to; see RESPONSIBLE 1. —**on the other hand** otherwise, conversely, from the opposite position; see OTHERWISE 1, 2. —**out of hand** out of control, wild, unmanageable; see UNRULY. —**take in hand** take responsibility for, take over, handle; see TRY 1. —**throw up one's hands** give up, resign, quit; see YIELD 1. —**wash one's hands of** be done with, reject, refuse to take responsibility for; see DENOUNCE.

hand v. deliver, give to, return; see GIVE 1. —**hand around** hand out, pass around, allot; see DISTRIBUTE, GIVE 1. —**hand in** deliver, submit, return; see GIVE 1, OFFER 1. —**hand out** give to, deliver, distribute; see GIVE 1, PROVIDE 1. —**hand over** deliver, surrender, give up; see GIVE 1, YIELD 1.

handbag n. lady's pocketbook, bag, clutch purse; see PURSE.

handbook n. textbook, vade mecum, guidebook; see BOOK.

handful n. a small quantity, some, a sprinkling; see FEW.

handicap n. 1 [A disadvantage] hindrance, obstacle, block; see BARRIER. 2 [A physical injury] impairment, affliction, disability; see IMPEDIMENT 2, INJURY.

handicapped a. thwarted, crippled, disabled, impeded, burdened, hampered, obstructed, encumbered, put at a disadvantage, checked, blocked, limited, restrained, wounded, curbed, put behind; see also DISABLED, RESTRICTED.—*Ant.* HELPED, aided, supported.

handily a. skillfully, smoothly, deftly; see CLEVERLY, EASILY.

handiwork n. handicraft, creation, handwork; see WORKMANSHIP.

handkerchief n. kerchief, hankie*, snotrag*; see TOWEL.

handle n. 1 [A holder] handhold, hilt, grasp, crank, knob, stem, grip, arm; see also HOLDER. 2 [*A title] nickname, designation, moniker*; see NAME 1, TITLE 3. —**fly off the handle** become angry, lose one's temper, blow off steam*; see RAGE 1.

handle v. 1 [To deal in] retail, market, offer for sale; see SELL. 2 [To touch] finger, check, examine; see FEEL 1, TOUCH 1. **3** [To deal with] treat, manage, operate; see MANAGE 1.

handling *n.* treatment, approach, styling; see MANAGEMENT.

handmade *a.* made by hand, handicraft, handcrafted; see HOMEMADE.

hand-me-down *n.* secondhand article, discard; old clothes, etc.; see SECONDHAND.

handout *n.* contribution, donation, aid; see GIFT 1, GRANT.

handsome *a.* smart, impressive, stately, good-looking, attractive, athletic, personable, strong, muscular, robust, well-dressed, sharp*; see also BEAUTIFUL.—*Ant.* UGLY, homely, unsightly.

hand-to-hand *a.* face-to-face, facing, *mano a mano* (Spanish); see NEAR 1.

handwriting *n.* penmanship, hand, chirography, writing, cursive, script, longhand, scrawl, scribble, manuscript, calligraphy, scratching*, chicken scratch*.

handwritten *a.* in writing, in longhand, not typed; see REPRODUCED, WRITTEN 2.

handy *a.* **1** [Near] nearby, at hand, close by; see NEAR 1. **2** [Useful] beneficial, advantageous, gainful; see HELPFUL 1, PROFITABLE, USABLE.

hang *v.* **1** [To suspend] dangle, attach, drape, hook up, hang up, nail to the wall, put on a clothesline, fix, pin up, tack up, drape on the wall, fasten up; see also FASTEN.—*Ant.* DROP, throw down, let fall. **2** [To be suspended] overhang, wave, flap, be loose, droop, flop, be in midair, swing, dangle, be fastened, hover, stay up.—*Ant.* FALL, come down, drop. **3** [To kill by hanging] execute, lynch, string up*; see KILL 1. **—hang around*** associate with, get along with, have relations with; see KEEP COMPANY (WITH) at COMPANY. **—hang on** persist, remain, continue; see ENDURE 1, 2. **—hang out*** loiter, spend time, haunt; see VISIT.

hanged *a.* lynched, strung up*, brought to the gallows; see EXECUTED 2.

hanger *n.* coat hook, nail, peg, coat hanger, clothes hanger, holder, clothes rod, wire hanger, collapsible hanger; see also HOLDER.

hanging *a.* dangling, swaying, swinging, overhanging, projecting, suspended, fastened to, pendulous, drooping.

hang-up* *n.* problem, phobia, qualm; see DIFFICULTY 1, 2.

haphazard *a.* offhand, casual, random, careless, slipshod, incidental, unthinking, unconscious, uncoordinated, reckless, unconcerned, unpremeditated, loose, indiscriminate, unrestricted, irregular, blind, purposeless, unplanned, hit-or-miss, willy-nilly; see also AIMLESS.—*Ant.* CAREFUL, studied, planned.

happen *v.* **1** [To be by chance] come up, come about, turn up, crop up, chance, occur unexpectedly, come face to face with, befall, be just one's luck. **2** [To occur] take place, come to pass, arrive, ensue, befall, come after, arise, take effect, come into existence, recur, come into being, spring, proceed, follow, come about, fall, repeat, appear, go on, turn out, become known, be found, come to mind, transpire, come off, go down*; see also RESULT.

happening *n.* incident, affair, event; see EVENT.

happily *a.* joyously, gladly, joyfully, cheerily, gaily, laughingly, smilingly, jovially, merrily, brightly, vivaciously, hilariously, with pleasure, peacefully, blissfully, cheerfully, gleefully, playfully, heartily, lightheartedly, lightly, to one's delight, optimistically, with all one's heart, with relish, with good will, in a happy manner, with zeal, with open arms, sincerely, willingly, freely, graciously, tactfully, lovingly, agreeably.—*Ant.* SADLY, morosely, dejectedly.

happiness *n.* mirth, merrymaking, cheer, merriment, joyousness, vivacity, laughter, delight, gladness, good spirits, hilarity, playfulness, exuberance, gaiety, cheerfulness, goodwill, rejoicing, exhilaration, glee, geniality, good cheer, lightheartedness, joy, pleasure, contentment; see also JOY.

happy *a.* joyous, joyful, merry, mirthful, glad, gleeful, delighted, cheerful, gay, laughing, contented, genial, satisfied, enraptured, congenial, cheery, jolly, hilarious, sparkling, enchanted, transported, rejoicing, blissful, jovial, delightful, delirious, exhilarated, pleased, gratified, peaceful, comfortable, intoxicated, debonair, light, bright, ecstatic, charmed, pleasant, hearty, overjoyed, lighthearted, radiant, vivacious, sunny, smiling, content, animated, lively, spirited, exuberant, good-humored, elated, jubilant, rollicking, playful, thrilled, fun-loving, carefree, at peace, in good spirits, in high spirits, happy as a lark, in ecstasy, beside oneself, bubbling over, tickled pink*, tickled to death*, tickled silly*, happy-go-lucky, in seventh heaven.—*Ant.* SAD, sorrowful, melancholy.

happy-go-lucky *a.* cheerful, easygoing, carefree; see IRRESPONSIBLE.

harass *v.* tease, vex, irritate; see BOTHER 2.

harbinger *n.* indication, sign, signal; see MESSENGER, SIGNAL.

harbor *n.* port, pier, inlet; see DOCK.

harbor *v.* 1 [To protect] shelter, provide refuge, secure; see DEFEND 2. 2 [To consider] entertain, cherish, regard; see CONSIDER.

hard *a.* 1 [Solid] unyielding, thick, heavy, strong, impermeable, tough, tempered, hardened, dense; see also FIRM 2. 2 [Difficult] arduous, tricky, impossible, trying, tedious, complex, abstract, puzzling, troublesome, laborious; see also DIFFICULT 1, 2. 3 [Cruel] perverse, unrelenting, vengeful; see CRUEL. 4 [Severe] harsh, exacting, grim; see SEVERE 1, 2. 5 [With difficulty] strenuously, laboriously, with great effort; see CAREFULLY 1, VIGOROUSLY. —**be hard on** treat severely, be harsh toward, be painful to; see ABUSE. —**hard of hearing** almost deaf, having a hearing problem, in need of a hearing aid; see DEAF. —**hard up*** poverty-stricken, in trouble, strapped*; see POOR 1.

hard-core *a.* dedicated, steadfast, unwavering; see FAITHFUL.

harden *v.* steel, temper, solidify, precipitate, crystallize, freeze, coagulate, clot, granulate, make firm, make compact, make tight, make hard, petrify, starch, cure, bake, dry, flatten, cement, compact, concentrate, sun, fire, fossilize, vulcanize, toughen, concrete, encrust; see also STIFFEN.—*Ant.* SOFTEN, unloose, melt.

hardened *a.* 1 [Made hard] compacted, stiffened, stiff; see FIRM 2. 2 [Inured to labor or hardship] accustomed, conditioned, tough; see HABITUAL.

hardening *n.* thickening, crystallization, setting; see SOLIDIFICATION.

hardheaded *a.* willful, stubborn, headstrong; see STUBBORN.

hardhearted *a.* cold, unfeeling, heartless; see CRUEL.

hardly *a.* scarcely, barely, just, merely, imperceptibly, not noticeably, gradually, not markedly, no more than, not likely, not a bit, almost not, only just, with difficulty, with trouble, by a narrow margin, not by a great deal, seldom, almost not at all, but just, in no manner, by no means, little, infrequently, somewhat, not quite, here and there, simply, not much, rarely, slightly, sparsely, not often, once in a blue moon*, by the skin of one's teeth*; see also ONLY.—*Ant.* EASILY, without difficulty, readily.

hard-nosed *a.* stubborn, unyielding, hardheaded; see OBSTINATE, RESOLUTE.

hardship *n.* trial, sorrow, worry; see DIFFICULTY 2, GRIEF.

hardware *n.* domestic appliances, fixtures, metal manufactures, casting, plumbing, metalware, implements, tools, housewares, fittings, aluminum ware, cutlery, house furnishings, kitchenware, household utensils, equipment.

hardy *a.* tough, toughened, in good shape, in good condition, hardened, resistant, solid, staunch, seasoned, capable of endurance, able-bodied, physically fit, well-equipped, acclimatized, rugged, mighty, well, fit, robust, hearty, sound, fresh, hale, brawny, able, vigorous, powerful, firm, sturdy, solid, substantial; see also STRONG.—*Ant.* WEAK, unaccustomed, unhabituated.

harm *n.* 1 [Injury] hurt, damage, impairment; see INJURY. 2 [Evil] wickedness, outrage, foul play; see ABUSE, EVIL 1, WRONG.

harm *v.* injure, wreck, cripple; see HURT.

harmed *a.* damaged, injured, wounded; see HURT.

harmful *a.* injurious, detrimental, hurtful, noxious, evil, mischievous, ruinous, adverse, sinister, subversive, incendiary, virulent, cataclysmic, corroding, toxic, baleful, painful, wounding, crippling, bad, malicious, malignant, sinful, pernicious, unwholesome, corrupting, menacing, dire, prejudicial, damaging, corrupt, vicious, insidious, treacherous, catastrophic, disastrous, wild, murderous, destructive, unhealthy, killing, fatal, mortal, serious, dangerous, fraught with evil, doing harm, doing evil, sore, distressing, diabolic, brutal, unhealthful, satanic, grievous, lethal, venomous, cruel, unfortunate, disadvantageous, felonious, objectionable, fiendish, unlucky, malign, devilish, corrosive.

harmless *a.* pure, innocent, painless, powerless, controllable, manageable, safe, sure, reliable, trustworthy, sanitary, germproof, sound, sterile, disarmed.—*Ant.* HARMFUL, injurious, poisonous.

harmonica *n.* mouth organ, mouth harp, harp*; see MUSICAL INSTRUMENT.

harmonious *a.* 1 [In tune musically] melodious, tuneful, musical, rhythmical, melodic, symphonic, in tune. 2 [Congruous] agreeable to, corresponding, suitable, adapted, similar, like, peaceful, cooperative, in step, in accordance with, in concord with, in favor with, in harmony with, on a footing with, friendly, conforming, well-matched, evenly balanced, symmetrical, congruent; see also FIT.—*Ant.* OPPOSED, incongruous, incompatible.

harmonize *v.* blend, arrange, put to

harmony, adapt, set, orchestrate, tune, sing a duet, sing in harmony.

harmony *n.* **1** [Musical concord] chord, consonance, accord, symphony, harmonics, counterpoint, concert, music, chorus, blending, unity, accordance, chime, overtone, musical pattern, musical blend. **2** [Social concord] compatibility, equanimity, unanimity; see AGREEMENT 1, PEACE 2.

harness *n.* tackle, gear, yoke, apparatus, bridle, rigging, fittings; see also EQUIPMENT.

harness *v.* fetter, saddle, yoke, outfit, bridle, hold in leash, hitch up, control, limit, cinch, strap, collar, put in harness, rig up, rig out, tie, secure, rein in, curb, check, constrain.

harp *n.* lyre, psaltery, zither; see MUSICAL INSTRUMENT.

harp on *v.* repeat, pester, nag; see COMPLAIN, TALK 1.

harsh *a.* discordant, jangling, cacophonous, grating, rusty, dissonant, strident, creaking, clashing, sharp, jarring, jangled, clamorous, cracked, hoarse, out of tune, unmelodious, rasping, screeching, earsplitting, disturbing, noisy, flat, sour, out of key, tuneless, unmusical, off-key; see also SHRILL.

harshly *a.* sternly, powerfully, grimly; see BRUTALLY, FIRMLY 2, LOUDLY, SERIOUSLY 1, 2.

harshness *n.* crudity, brutality, roughness; see ANGER, CRUELTY, TYRANNY.

harvest *n.* reaping, yield, produce; see CROP, FRUIT, GRAIN 1, VEGETABLE.

harvest *v.* gather, accumulate, pile up, collect, garner, crop, cut, pluck, pick, cull, take in, draw in, glean, gather in the harvest, hoard, mow.—*Ant.* SOW, plant, seed.

hash *n.* ground meat and vegetables, leftovers, casserole; see MEAT, STEW.

hash over* *v.* debate, argue about, review; see DISCUSS.

hassle* *n.* quarrel, squabble, row; see DISPUTE.

hassle* *v.* pester, annoy, harass; see BOTHER 2.

haste *n.* hurry, scramble, bustle, scurry, precipitation, flurry, hurly-burly, impetuosity, rashness, dispatch, impetuousness, foolhardiness, want of caution, hustling, press, recklessness, rush, hastiness, carelessness, irrationality, rashness, giddiness, impatience, heedlessness, plunge, testiness, excitation, abruptness, anticipation.—*Ant.* PRUDENCE, caution, attention. —**in haste** hastening, in a hurry, moving fast; see FAST. —**make haste** hasten, act quickly, speed up; see HURRY 1.

hasten *v.* **1** [To make haste] rush,

fly, sprint; see HURRY 1. **2** [To expedite] accelerate, speed up, advance, move up, quicken, stimulate, hurry up, push, make short work of, urge, goad, press, agitate, push ahead, put into action, get started, drive on, set in motion, take in hand, blast off, gear up; see also SPEED.—*Ant.* DELAY, defer, put off.

hastily *a.* **1** [Rapidly] hurriedly, speedily, fast; see QUICKLY. **2** [Carelessly] thoughtlessly, recklessly, rashly; see CARELESSLY.

hasty *a.* **1** [Hurried] quick, speedy, swift; see FAST 1. **2** [Careless] ill-advised, precipitate, foolhardy; see CARELESS, RASH.

hat *n.* headgear, millinery, headpiece, helmet, chapeau, bonnet. *Coverings for the head include the following—for men:* cap, yarmulke, derby, straw hat, felt hat, sombrero, cowboy hat, top hat, bowler, Panama hat, fedora, beret, turban; *for women:* hood, snood, cowl, kerchief, beret, bandanna, cloche, boater, bonnet, turban, pillbox, scarf, babushka. —**take one's hat off to** salute, cheer, congratulate; see PRAISE 1. —**talk through one's hat*** chatter, talk nonsense, make foolish statements; see BABBLE. —**throw one's hat into the ring** enter a contest, run for office, enter politics; see CAMPAIGN. —**under one's hat*** confidential, private, hidden; see SECRET 1.

hatch *v.* bear, lay eggs, bring forth; see PRODUCE 1.

hate *n.* ill will, animosity, enmity; see HATRED.

hate *v.* **1** [To detest] abhor, abominate, loathe, scorn, despise, have an aversion toward, look at with loathing, spit upon, curse, dislike intensely, shudder at, not care for, have enough of, be repelled by, feel repulsion for, have no use for, object to, bear a grudge against, shun, denounce, resent, curse, be sick of, be tired of, reject, revolt against, deride, have no stomach for, disfavor, look down upon, hold in contempt, be disgusted with, view with horror, be down on*, have it in for*.—*Ant.* LOVE, adore, worship. **2** [To dislike; *often used with infinitive or participle*] object to, shudder at, not like; see DISLIKE.

hated *a.* despised, loathed, abhorred, detested, disliked, cursed, unpopular, avoided, shunned, out of favor, condemned; see also UNDESIRABLE.

hateful *a.* odious, detestable, repugnant; see OFFENSIVE 2, UNDESIRABLE.

hater *n.* despiser, racist, antagonist; see BIGOT, ENEMY.

hatred *n.* abhorrence, loathing, rancor, detestation, antipathy, repugnance, repulsion, disgust, contempt, intense dislike, scorn, abomination, distaste, disapproval, horror, hard feelings, displeasure, ill will, bitterness, antagonism, animosity, pique, grudge, malice, malevolence, revulsion, prejudice, spite, revenge, hate, venom, envy, spleen, coldness, hostility, alienation, bad blood, chip on one's shoulder*, grudge; see also ANGER.—*Ant.* DEVOTION, friendship, affection.

haughty *a.* arrogant, disdainful, proud; see EGOTISTIC.

haul *n.* **1** [A pull] tug, lift, wrench; see PULL 1. **2** [The distance something is hauled] trip, voyage, yards; see DISTANCE 3. **3** [*Something obtained, especially loot] find, spoils, take; see BOOTY.

haul *v.* pull, drag, bring; see DRAW 1.

haunt *v.* **1** [To frequent persistently] habituate, visit often, hang around; see LOITER. **2** [To prey upon] recur in someone's mind, obsess, torment, beset, possess, trouble, weigh on someone's mind, craze, madden, hound, terrify, plague, vex, harass, prey on, pester, worry, tease, terrorize, frighten, annoy, cause regret, cause sorrow, molest, appall, agitate, drive someone nuts*; see also BOTHER 2, DISTURB.

haunted *a.* frequented, visited by, preyed upon; see TROUBLED.

haunting *a.* eerie, unforgettable, seductive; see FRIGHTFUL, REMEMBERED.

have *v.* **1** [To be in possession of] possess, keep, retain, guard, use, maintain, control, treasure, keep title to, hold; see also OWN 1. **2** [To bear] beget, give birth to, bring forth; see PRODUCE 1. **3** [*To have sexual intercourse with] seduce, sleep with*, deflower; see COPULATE. —**have on** be clothed in, be wearing, try on; see WEAR 1. —**have something on someone** be able to expose, have special knowledge of, be able to control; see CONVICT, KNOW 1. —**have to** be compelled to, be forced to, should, ought, be someone's duty to, be up to, have got to; see also MUST.

haven *n.* port, harbor, roadstead; see REFUGE 1, SHELTER.

having *a.* owning, possessing, enjoying, holding; see also COMMANDING.

havoc *n.* devastation, plunder, ruin; see DESTRUCTION 2.

hawk *n.* **1** [A member of the Accipitridae] bird of prey, osprey, falcon; see BIRD. **2** [A warlike person] militarist, chauvinist, warmonger; see CONSERVATIVE, RADICAL.

hay *n.* fodder, roughage, forage, feed; see also GRASS 1. *Hay includes the following:* red clover, wild hay, timothy, alsike, sweet clover, swamp hay, alfalfa, oat hay, millet. —**hit the hay*** go to bed, rest, recline; see SLEEP.

hazard *n.* risk, peril, jeopardy; see DANGER.

hazard *v.* stake, try, guess; see CHANCE, GAMBLE, RISK.

hazardous *a.* perilous, uncertain, precarious; see DANGEROUS.

haze *n.* mist, smog, cloudiness; see FOG.

hazy *a.* cloudy, foggy, murky, misty, unclear, overcast, steaming, filmy, gauzy, vaporous, smoky, dim, dull, indistinct, smoggy, fumy, crepuscular, bleary, nebulous, shadowy, dusky, obscure, thick, opaque, frosty, veiled, blurred, semitransparent, blurry, faint; see also DARK 1.—*Ant.* CLEAR, bright, cloudless.

he *pron.* this one, the male, the above-named, this man, this boy, that man, that boy, this male animal, that male animal, third person masculine singular.

head *n.* **1** [The skull] brainpan, scalp, crown, bean*, noggin*, noodle*. **2** [A leader or supervisor] commander, commanding officer, ruler; see LEADER 2. **3** [The top] summit, peak, crest; see TOP 1. **4** [*The beginning] front, start, source; see ORIGIN 2. **5** [An attachment] cap, bottle top, cork; see COVER 1. **6** [*Intelligence] brains, foresight, ingenuity; see JUDGMENT 1. **7** [*Drug addict] habitual user of drugs, acidhead*, pothead*; see ADDICT. —**come to a head** culminate, reach a crisis, come to a climax; see CLIMAX. —**get it through one's head** learn, comprehend, see; see UNDERSTAND 1. —**go to someone's head** stir mentally, stimulate, intoxicate; see EXCITE. —**hang (or hide) one's head** repent, be sorry, grieve; see REGRET 1. —**head off** block off, interfere with, intervene; see STOP 1. —**head over heels** entirely, precipitately, unreservedly; see COMPLETELY. —**keep one's head** remain calm, keep one's self-control, hold one's emotions in check; see RESTRAIN. —**lose one's head** become excited, become angry, rave; see RAGE 1. —**make head or tail of** comprehend, apprehend, see; see UNDERSTAND 1. —**one's head off** greatly, extremely, considerably; see MUCH. —**on (or upon) someone's head** burdensome, taxing, strenuous; see DIFFICULT 1. —**out of (or off) one's head*** crazy, raving, delirious; see INSANE. —**over someone's head** incomprehensible, not understandable, hard; see DIFFICULT 2.

head *v.* direct, oversee, supervise; see COMMAND 2, MANAGE 1.

headache *n.* **1** [A pain in the head] migraine, sick headache, neuralgia; see PAIN 2. **2** [*A source of vexation and difficulty] problem, jumble, mess; see DIFFICULTY 1, 2, TROUBLE 1.

headed *a.* in transit, in motion, en route, going, directed, started, aimed, slated for, on the way to, pointed toward, consigned to, on the road to.

heading *n.* headline, subtitle, address, caption, legend, head, banner head, subject, capital, superscription, headnote, display line, preface, prologue, streamer, preamble, topic, designation, specification.

headless *a.* **1** [Unthinking] witless, fatuous, brainless; see DULL 3, STUPID. **2** [Without a head] decapitated, lifeless, truncated; see DEAD 1.

headlight *n.* searchlight, beacon, spotlight; see LIGHT 3.

headline *n.* heading, caption, title; see HEADING.

headquarters *n.* main office, home office, chief office, central station, central place, distribution center, police station, meeting place, meeting house, manager's office, quarters, base, military station, military town, post, center of operations, base of operations, HQ.

headstone *n.* gravestone, marker, stone; see GRAVE.

headstrong *a.* determined, strongminded, obstinate; see STUBBORN.

headway *n.* advance, increase, promotion; see PROGRESS 1.

heal *v.* restore, renew, treat, attend, make healthy, return to health, fix, repair, regenerate, bring around, cure, nurse, care for, take care of, renovate, set right, make better, ease, remedy, purify, rejuvenate, medicate, make clean, dress a wound, rebuild, revive, rehabilitate, work a cure, cause to heal, resuscitate, salve, help to get well, ameliorate, doctor*, put someone on his or her feet again, breathe new life into*.—*Ant.* EXPOSE, make ill, infect.

healing *a.* restorative, invigorating, medicinal; see HEALTHFUL.

health *n.* vigor, wholeness, good condition, healthfulness, good health, fitness, bloom, soundness of body, physical fitness, tone, hardiness, well-being, stamina, energy, full bloom, rosy cheeks*, good shape*, clean bill of health*; see also STRENGTH.

healthful *a.* nutritious, restorative, sanitary, hygienic, salutary, invigorating, tonic, stimulating, bracing,

197   ◀ **hearing**

salubrious, wholesome, beneficial, health-giving, nutritive, nourishing, energy-giving, fresh, pure, clean, corrective, cathartic, sedative, regenerative, substantial, sustaining, benign, healthy, good for someone, desirable, harmless, innocuous, healing, preventive, disease-free, unpolluted, unadulterated, favorable.—*Ant.* UNHEALTHY, sickly, unwholesome.

healthy *a.* sound, trim, all right, normal, robust, hale, vigorous, well, hearty, athletic, rosy-cheeked, hardy, able-bodied, virile, muscular, blooming, sturdy, safe and sound, in good condition, in full possession of one's faculties, in good health, full of pep*, never feeling better, fresh, whole, firm, lively, undecayed, flourishing, good, physically fit, clear-eyed, in fine fettle, youthful, free from disease, fine, fine and dandy*, hunky-dory*, in the pink*, rugged, fit as a fiddle; see also SANE 1, STRONG 1.—*Ant.* UNHEALTHY, ill, diseased.

heap *n.* pile, mass, stack; see QUANTITY.

heap *v.* pile, add, lump; see LOAD 1, PACK 2.

hear *v.* **1** [To perceive by ear] listen to, give attention, attend to, make out, become aware of, catch, apprehend, take in, eavesdrop, detect, perceive by the ear, overhear, take cognizance of, keep one's ears open, have the sense of hearing, read loud and clear, strain one's ears, listen in, get an earful*. **2** [To receive information aurally] overhear, eavesdrop, find out; see LISTEN. **3** [To hold a hearing] preside over, put on trial, summon to court; see JUDGE. —**hear from** get word from, be informed, learn through; see RECEIVE 1. —**hear of** know about, be aware of, discover; see KNOW 1, 3. —**not hear of** not allow, refuse to consider, reject; see FORBID.

heard *a.* perceived, witnessed, caught, made out, understood, heeded, noted, made clear.

hearer *n.* listener, bystander, witness; see LISTENER.

hearing *n.* **1** [An opportunity to be heard] audition, interview, test, fair hearing, tryout, conference, audit, notice, performance, consultation, council, reception, presentation, audience, attention; see also TRIAL 2. **2** [The act of hearing] detecting, recording, distinguishing; see LISTENING. **3** [The faculty for hearing] ear, auditory faculty, perception, listening ear, sense of hearing, audition, act of perceiving sound, acoustic sensation. **4** [Range of hearing] earshot, hearing distance, reach, sound, carrying distance, range, auditory range; see also EXTENT.

hearsay *n.* noise, scandal, report; see GOSSIP 1, RUMOR.

heart *n.* 1 [The pump in the circulatory system] vital organ, vascular organ, blood pump, cardiac organ, ticker*; see also ORGAN 2. 2 [Feeling] response, sympathy, sensitivity; see EMOTION, FEELING 4, PITY. 3 [The center] core, middle, pith; see CENTER 1. 4 [The most important portion] gist, essence, root; see SOUL 1. 5 [Courage] fortitude, gallantry, spirit; see COURAGE, MIND 1, SOUL 2. —**after one's own heart** suitable, pleasing, lovable; see PLEASANT 2. —**break someone's heart** grieve, disappoint, pain; see HURT. —**by heart** from memory, memorized, learned; see REMEMBERED. —**change of heart** change of mind, reversal, alteration; see CHANGE 1. —**do someone's heart good** please, make content, delight; see SATISFY 1. —**eat one's heart out** worry, regret, nurse one's troubles; see BROOD 2. —**from (the bottom of) one's heart** deeply, honestly, frankly; see SINCERELY. —**have a heart** be kind, empathize, take pity; see SYMPATHIZE. —**lose one's heart to** love, cherish, adore; see FALL IN LOVE (WITH) at LOVE. —**set someone's heart at rest** calm, placate, soothe; see COMFORT 1. —**set one's heart on** long for, need, desire; see WANT 1. —**take to heart** think about, take into account, believe; see CONSIDER. —**wear one's heart on one's sleeve** disclose, divulge, confess; see REVEAL. —**with all one's heart** honestly, deeply, frankly; see SINCERELY.

heartache *n.* sorrow, despair, anguish; see GRIEF, REGRET.

heartbeat *n.* pulsation, throb of the heart, cardiovascular activity; see BEAT 1.

heartbreaking *a.* unbearable, deplorable, joyless; see PITIFUL, TRAGIC.

heartbroken *a.* melancholy, sorrowful, doleful; see SAD 1.

heartburn *n.* indigestion, nervous stomach, stomach upset; see ILLNESS 2.

hearth *n.* 1 [A fireplace] grate, fireside, hearthstone; see FIREPLACE. 2 [Home] dwelling, abode, residence; see HOME 1.

heartily *a.* enthusiastically, earnestly, cordially; see SERIOUSLY 2, SINCERELY.

heartless *a.* unkind, unthinking, insensitive; see CRUEL, RUTHLESS.

hearty *a.* warm, zealous, sincere, cheery, cheerful, jovial, wholehearted, neighborly, well-meant, animated, jolly, ardent, genial, glowing, enthusiastic, genuine, avid, passionate, deep, intense, exuberant, profuse, eager, devout, deep-felt, unfeigned, fervent, warmhearted, authentic, impassioned, heartfelt, responsive; see also FRIENDLY.—*Ant.* FALSE, mock, sham.

heat *n.* 1 [Warmth] torridity, high temperature, hot wind, heat wave, fever, hot weather, temperature, hotness, warmness, sultriness, white heat, torridness, tropical heat, dog days; see also WARMTH.—*Ant.* COLD, frost, frigidity. 2 [Fervor] ardor, passion, excitement; see DESIRE 2. 3 [Sources of heat] flame, radiation, solar energy; see ENERGY 2, FIRE 1, 2.

heat *v.* 1 [To make hot] warm, fire, heat up, inflame, kindle, enkindle, subject to heat, put on the fire, make hot, make warm, scald, thaw, boil, char, roast, chafe, seethe, toast, oxidize, set fire to, melt, cauterize, reheat, steam, incinerate, sear, singe, scorch, fry, turn on the heat; see also BURN, COOK, IGNITE.—*Ant.* COOL, freeze, chill. 2 [To become hot] glow, warm up, rise in temperature, grow hot, blaze, flame, seethe, burst into flame, kindle, ignite, thaw, swelter, perspire.

heated *a.* 1 [Warmed] cooked, fried, burnt; see BAKED, BURNED. 2 [Fervent] fiery, ardent, avid; see EXCITED, PASSIONATE 2.

heater *n.* radiator, car heater, electric heater; see FURNACE.

heathen *n.* infidel, non-Christian, atheist; see BARBARIAN.

heave *n.* throw, hurl, fling, cast, wing, toss; see also PITCH 2.

heave *v.* rock, bob, pitch, go up and down, lurch, roll, reel, sway, swell, expand, be raised, swirl, throb, ebb and flow, wax and wane, slosh, wash; see also WAVE 3.—*Ant.* REST, lie still, quiet.

heaven *n.* 1 [The sky; *often plural*] firmament, stratosphere, heights, atmosphere, azure, beyond, heavenly spheres, upstairs*. 2 [The abode of the blessed] Paradise, the Great Beyond, Elysian fields, bliss, the Abode of the Dead, the Home of the Gods, Heavenly Home, God's Kingdom, Valhalla, the Holy City, Nirvana, the throne of God, the New Jerusalem, the afterworld, the heavenly city, the city of God, our eternal home, the Kingdom of Heaven, the next world, the world to come, our Father's house, the world beyond the grave, the happy hunting grounds*, the eternal rest*, Kingdom Come, the hereafter.—*Ant.* HELL, underworld, inferno. 3 [A state of great comfort] bliss, felicity, harmony; see HAPPINESS.

heavenly *a.* 1 [Concerning heaven]

divine, celestial, supernal; see ANGELIC, HOLY 1. **2** [*Much approved of or liked*] blissful, sweet, enjoyable; see EXCELLENT, PLEASANT 1, 2.

heavily *a.* laboriously, tediously, weightily, massively, ponderously, gloomily, with difficulty, wearily, profoundly, densely; see also GRADUALLY.—*Ant.* LIGHTLY, gently, easily.

heaviness *n.* burden, denseness, ballast; see DENSITY, MASS 1, WEIGHT 1.

heavy *a.* **1** [*Weighty*] bulky, massive, unwieldy, ponderous, huge, overweight, top-heavy, of great weight, burdensome, weighty, stout, big, hard to carry, dense, fat, substantial, ample, hefty*, chunky; see also LARGE 1.—*Ant.* LIGHT, buoyant, feather-light. **2** [*Burdensome*] troublesome, oppressive, vexatious; see DIFFICULT 1, DISTURBING. **3** [*Dull*] listless, slow, apathetic; see DULL 4, INDIFFERENT. **4** [*Gloomy*] dejected, cloudy, overcast; see DARK 1, DISMAL, SAD 1.

heavy-handed *a.* oppressive, harsh, coercive; see CRUEL, SEVERE 2.

heckle *v.* torment, disturb, pester; see BOTHER 2, RIDICULE.

hectic *a.* unsettled, boisterous, restless; see CONFUSED 2, DISORDERED.

hedge *n.* shrubbery, bushes, thicket; see PLANT.

heel *n.* **1** [*Hind part of the foot*] hock, back of the foot, Achilles tendon; see FOOT 2. **2** [*The portion of the shoe under the heel*] low heel, high heel, stacked heel; see BOTTOM, FOUNDATION 2, SHOE. **3** [*A worthless individual*] scamp, skunk*, trickster; see RASCAL. —**down at the heel(s)** shabby, seedy, rundown; see WORN 2. —**kick up one's heels** be lively, have fun, enjoy oneself; see PLAY 1, 2. —**on** (or **upon**) **the heels of** close behind, in back of, behind; see FOLLOWING. —**take to one's heels** run away, flee, take flight; see ESCAPE.

heel *v.* follow, stay by someone's heel, attend; see OBEY.

hefty* *a.* sturdy, husky, stout, beefy, strapping, substantial, massive; see also STRONG 1.

heifer *n.* yearling, baby cow, calf; see ANIMAL, COW.

height *n.* elevation, extent upward, prominence, loftiness, highness, perpendicular distance, upright distance, tallness, stature; see also EXPANSE, EXTENT, LENGTH 1.—*Ant.* DEPTH, breadth, width.

heighten *v.* **1** [*Increase*] sharpen, redouble, emphasize; see INCREASE, STRENGTHEN. **2** [*Raise*] lift, elevate, uplift; see RAISE 1.

heir *n.* future possessor, legal heir, heir apparent, successor, descend-

ant, one who inherits, heiress, beneficiary, inheritor, crown prince.

heiress *n.* female inheritor, crown princess, wealthy girl; see HEIR.

heirloom *n.* inheritance, legacy, bequest; see GIFT 1.

held *a.* grasped, controlled, occupied, guarded, taken, gripped, clutched, defended, stuck, detained, sustained, believed.—*Ant.* LOST, released, freed.

hell *n.* **1** [*Place of the dead, especially of the wicked dead; often capitalized*] underworld, inferno, place of departed spirits, the lower world, the grave, infernal regions, abyss, Satan's Kingdom, purgatory, nether world, hellfire, Hades, bottomless pit, perdition, place of the lost, place of torment, limbo, the hereafter.—*Ant.* HEAVEN, earth, paradise. **2** [*A condition of torment*] trial, agony, ordeal; see CRISIS, DIFFICULTY 1, 2, EMERGENCY. —**catch** (or **get**) **hell*** get into trouble, be punished, receive punishment; see GET IT 2. —**for the hell of it*** for no reason, for the fun of it, playfully; see LIGHTLY. —**hell of a*** helluva*, extremely, very bad or good; see POOR 2, EXCELLENT. —**hell on*** hard on, prejudiced against, strict with; see CRUEL, HARMFUL.

hellish *a.* diabolical, fiendish, destructive; see BAD 1.

hello *interj.* how do you do?, greetings, welcome, how are you?, good morning, good day, hi*, hey*, howdy*, hi there*, hi-ya*, *bonjour* (French), *buenos dias* (Spanish), ciao*, shalom*, how goes it?.—*Ant.* GOODBYE, farewell, so long.

helmet *n.* football helmet, diver's helmet, hard hat; see HAT.

help *n.* **1** [*Assistance*] advice, comfort, aid, favor, support, gift, reward, charity, encouragement, advancement, subsidy, service, relief, care, endowment, cooperation, guidance. **2** [*Employees*] aides, representatives, hired help; see ASSISTANT, FACULTY 2, STAFF 2. **3** [*Physical relief*] maintenance, sustenance, nourishment; see RELIEF 4, REMEDY.

help *v.* assist, uphold, advise, encourage, stand by, cooperate, intercede for, befriend, accommodate, work for, back up, maintain, sustain, benefit, bolster, lend a hand, do a service, see through, do one's part, give a hand, be of use, come to the aid of, be of some help, help along, do a favor, promote, back, advocate, abet, stimulate, further, stick up for*, take under one's wing, go to bat for*, side with, give a lift, boost, pitch in*; see also SUPPORT 2.—*Ant.* OPPOSE, rival, combat. —**cannot**

help but be obliged to, cannot fail to, have to; see MUST. —**cannot help oneself** be compelled to, have a need to, be the victim of habit; see MUST. —**help oneself** aid oneself, promote oneself, further oneself, live by one's own efforts, get on, get along. —**help oneself to** take, grab, pick up; see SEIZE 1, 2, STEAL. —**so help me (God)** as God is my witness, by God, I swear; see OATH 1.

helped a. aided, maintained, supported, advised, befriended, relieved, assisted, sustained, nursed, encouraged, accompanied, taken care of, subsidized, upheld.—Ant. HURT, impeded, harmed.

helpful a. 1 [Useful] valuable, important, significant, crucial, essential, cooperative, symbiotic, serviceable, profitable, advantageous, favorable, convenient, suitable, practical, operative, usable, applicable, conducive, improving, bettering, of service, all-purpose, desirable, instrumental, contributive, good for, to someone's advantage, at someone's command; see also CONVENIENT 1.—Ant. USELESS, ineffective, impractical. 2 [Curative] healthy, salutary, restorative; see HEALTHFUL. 3 [Obliging] accommodating, considerate, neighborly; see KIND.

helping a. aiding, assisting, cooperating, collaborating, synergistic, working, being assistant to, being consultant to, in cooperation with, in combination with, contributing to, accessory to, going along with, in cahoots with*, thick as thieves*; see also HELPFUL 1.

helping n. serving, plateful, portion; see FOOD, MEAL 2, SHARE.

helpless a. 1 [Dependent] feeble, unable, invalid; see DEPENDENT 2, DISABLED, WEAK 1, 5. 2 [Incompetent] incapable, unfit, inexpert; see INCOMPETENT.

helplessness n. 1 [Disability] poor health, frailty, convalescence; see ILLNESS 1, WEAKNESS 1. 2 [Incompetence] incapacity, disorder, failure; see WEAKNESS 1.

hem n. border, skirting, edging; see EDGE 1, FRINGE, RIM.

hemisphere n. half of the globe, Western Hemisphere, Eastern Hemisphere, Northern Hemisphere, Southern Hemisphere, territory; see also EARTH 1.

hemorrhage n. discharge, bleeding, blood flow; see ILLNESS 1, INJURY.

hen n. female chicken, pullet, egger*; see BIRD, FOWL.

hence a. 1 [Therefore] consequently, for that reason, on that account; see SO 2, THEREFORE. 2 [From now]

henceforth, henceforward, from here; see HEREAFTER.

henpeck v. bully, nag, intimidate; see BOTHER 2, THREATEN.

henpecked a. dominated by a wife, subjected to nagging, browbeaten, intimidated, passive, constrained, compliant, in bondage, yielding, without independence, acquiescent, in subjection, subject, resigned, submissive, docile, meek, cringing, unresisting, unassertive, led by the nose, under someone's thumb, at someone's beck and call, tied to someone's apron strings, nagged, in harness; see also OBEDIENT 1.

herb n. seasoning, flavoring, spice, medicine. *Herbs include the following:* ginger, peppermint, spearmint, thyme, savory, mustard, chives, cardamom, sweet basil, parsley, anise, cumin, fennel, caraway, rosemary, tarragon, oregano, wintergreen, coriander, cilantro, wormwood, marjoram, bay leaf, dill, sage, lavender, borage, camomile, chervil, digitalis, chicory; see also SPICE.

herd n. flock, drove, pack, brood, swarm, lot, bevy, covey, gaggle, nest, flight, school, clan; see also GATHERING.

herdsman n. shepherd, herder, sheepherder; see COWBOY, RANCHER.

here a. in this place, hereabout, in this direction, on this spot, over here, up here, down here, right here, on hand, on board, on deck*, within reach. —**here and there** often, in various places, sometimes; see EVERYWHERE, SCATTERED.

hereafter a. hence, henceforth, from now on, after this, in the future, hereupon, in the course of time.

hereafter n. underworld, abode of the dead, the Great Beyond; see HEAVEN 2, HELL 1.

hereby a. with these means, with this, thus, herewith.

hereditary a. inherited, maternal, paternal; see GENETIC.

heredity n. inheritance, ancestry, hereditary transmission, genetics, eugenics.

heresy n. nonconformity, dissidence, protestantism, dissent, heterodoxy, sectarianism, agnosticism, schism, unorthodoxy, secularism.

heretic n. schismatic, apostate, sectarian; see CYNIC.

heritage n. 1 [Inheritance] legacy, birthright, heirloom, ancestry, right, dowry; see also DIVISION 2, HEREDITY, SHARE. 2 [Tradition] convention, endowment, cultural inheritance; see CULTURE 1, CUSTOM, FASHION 2, METHOD, SYSTEM.

hermit n. holy man, ascetic, anchorite, solitary, recluse, eremite, anchoress, pillar saint.

hero n. 1 [One distinguished for

action] brave man, model, conqueror, victorious general, god, martyr, champion, prize athlete, master, brave, warrior, saint, man of courage, star, popular figure, great man, knight-errant, a man among men, man of the hour; see also HEROINE 1. **2** [Principal male character in a literary composition] protagonist, male lead, leading man; see ACTOR.

heroic *a.* valiant, valorous, fearless; see BRAVE, NOBLE 1, 2.

heroine *n.* **1** [A female hero] brave woman, champion, goddess, ideal, intrepid woman, courageous woman, woman of heroic character, woman of the hour; see also HERO 1. **2** [Leading female character in a literary composition] protagonist, leading lady, female lead; see ACTOR.

heroism *n.* rare fortitude, valor, bravery; see COURAGE, STRENGTH.

hesitancy *n.* wavering, delaying, procrastination; see DELAY, PAUSE.

hesitant *a.* **1** [Doubtful] skeptical, unpredictable, irresolute; see DOUBTFUL, UNCERTAIN. **2** [Slow] delaying, wavering, dawdling; see LAZY 1, SLOW 2.

hesitantly *a.* dubiously, falteringly, shyly; see CAUTIOUSLY.

hesitate *v.* falter, fluctuate, vacillate, pause, stop, hold off, hold back, be dubious, be uncertain, flounder, alternate, ponder, think about, defer, delay, think it over, change one's mind, recoil, not know what to do, pull back, catch one's breath, weigh, consider, hang back, swerve, debate, shift, wait, deliberate, linger, balance, think twice, drag one's feet*, hem and haw, blow hot and cold, dillydally, straddle the fence, leave up in the air.—*Ant.* RESOLVE, decide, conclude.

hesitation *n.* **1** [Doubt] equivocation, skepticism, irresolution; see DOUBT, UNCERTAINTY 2. **2** [Delay] wavering, delaying, dawdling; see DELAY, PAUSE.

hey *interj.* you there, say, hey there, hi*, hi there*; see also HALT, HELLO.

heyday *n.* adolescence, bloom, prime of life; see YOUTH 1.

hibernate *v.* sleep through the winter, lie dormant, hole up*; see SLEEP.

hidden *a.* secluded, out of sight, covert, concealed, undercover, occult, in the dark, in a haze, in a fog, in darkness, masked, screened, veiled, cloaked, obscured, disguised, invisible, clouded, sealed, unobserved, blotted, impenetrable, unseen, eclipsed, camouflaged, shrouded, shadowy, unknown, buried, undetected, deep, unsuspected, inscrutable, illegible, puzzling, unobserved, out of view, dim, clan-

---

201 ◀ **high**

---

destine, subterranean, cloistered, suppressed, dark, inward, underground, unrevealed, withheld, surreptitious, underhand, kept in the dark, under wraps; see also PRIVATE.—*Ant.* OBVIOUS, open, apparent.

hide *n.* pelt, rawhide, pigskin, horsehide, cowhide, suede, kidskin, chamois, bearskin, goatskin, jacket, sheepskin, sealskin, snakeskin, alligator skin, calfskin; see also FUR, LEATHER, SKIN.—**neither hide nor hair** nothing whatsoever, no indication, not at all; see NOTHING.

hide *v.* **1** [To conceal] shroud, curtain, veil, camouflage, cover, mask, cloak, not give away, screen, blot out, bury, suppress, withhold, keep underground, stifle, keep secret, hush up, shield, eclipse, not tell, lock up, put out of sight, put out of the way, hold back, keep from, secrete, smuggle, shadow, conceal from sight, keep out of sight, stow away, protect, hoard, store, seclude, reserve, tuck away, cache, harbor, envelop, closet, conceal, hush, obscure, wrap, shelter, throw a veil over, keep in the dark, keep under one's hat*, seal one's lips*, put the lid on*, salt away*; see also DISGUISE.—*Ant.* EXPOSE, lay bare, uncover. **2** [To keep oneself concealed] disguise oneself, change one's identity, cover one's traces, keep out of sight, go underground, lie in ambush, sneak, travel incognito, take refuge, disappear, prowl, burrow, skulk, avoid notice, lie in wait, hibernate, lie concealed, lie low, conceal oneself, lurk, shut oneself up, seclude oneself, lie hidden, keep out of the way, stay in hiding, hide out*, cover up, duck*, keep in the background; see also DECEIVE.

hideous *a.* ghastly, grisly, frightful; see UGLY 1.

hiding *a.* concealing, in concealment, out of sight; see HIDDEN.

hierarchy *n.* regime, bureaucracy, chain of command; see GOVERNMENT 1, 2.

high *a.* **1** [Tall] towering, gigantic, big, colossal, tremendous, great, giant, huge, formidable, immense, tall, long, steep, sky-high; see also LARGE 1.—*Ant.* SHORT, diminutive, undersized. **2** [Elevated] lofty, uplifted, soaring, aerial, high-reaching, flying, hovering, overtopping, jutting; see also RAISED 1.—*Ant.* LOW, depressed, underground. **3** [Exalted] eminent, leading, powerful; see DISTINGUISHED 2, NOBLE 1, 2. **4** [Expensive] high-priced, costly, precious; see EXPENSIVE. **5** [To an unusual degree] great, extraordinary, special; see UNUSUAL 1, 2. **6** [Shrill] piercing, sharp, penetrating;

see LOUD 1, SHRILL. **7** [*Drunk]
intoxicated, tipsy, inebriated; see
DRUNK. **8** [*Under the influence of
drugs] stoned*, freaked out*,
wasted*, turned on*, on a trip*,
tripping*, hyped-up*, spaced-out*,
zonked out*. **—high and low** in
every nook and corner, in all possible places, exhaustively; see COM-
PLETELY, EVERYWHERE.

higher *a.* taller, more advanced,
superior to, over, larger than,
ahead, surpassing, bigger, greater;
see also ABOVE 1, BEYOND.—*Ant.*
SHORTER, smaller, inferior.

highest *a.* topmost, superlative,
supreme, maximal, most, top, maximum, head, preeminent, capital,
chief, paramount, tiptop, top-
notch*.

highly *a.* extremely, profoundly,
deeply; see VERY.

highness *n.* **1** [Quality of being
high] length, tallness, loftiness; see
HEIGHT. **2** [Term of respect, usually
to royalty; *often capitalized*] majesty, lordship, ladyship; see ROY-
ALTY.

high-pressure *a.* forceful, potent,
compelling; see POWERFUL 1.

high school *n.* public school, secondary school, preparatory school, prep
school, private academy, military
school, upper grades, trade school,
seminary, junior high school, senior
high school, vocational school; see
also SCHOOL 1.

high-spirited *a.* daring, dauntless,
reckless; see BRAVE.

high-strung *a.* nervous, tense, impatient; see RESTLESS.

highway *n.* roadway, parkway,
superhighway, freeway, turnpike,
toll road, state highway, thruway,
expressway, interstate; see also
ROAD 1.

hijack *v.* highjack, skyjack, capture;
see SEIZE 2.

hike *n.* trip, backpacking, tour; see
JOURNEY, WALK 3.

hike *v.* **1** [To tramp] take a hike,
tour, explore; see TRAVEL, WALK 1. **2**
[*To raise] lift, advance, pull up; see
INCREASE.

hiking *a.* hitchhiking, backpacking,
exploring; see WALKING.

hilarious *a.* amusing, lively, witty;
see ENTERTAINING, FUNNY 1.

hill *n.* mound, knoll, butte, bluff,
promontory, precipice, cliff, range,
rising ground, headland, upland,
mesa, hillock, acropolis, downgrade,
inclination, descent, slope, ascent,
slant, grade, incline, height, highland, rise, foothill, dune, climb,
elevation, ridge, heap, hillside,
upgrade, hilltop, vantage point, gradient, summit; see also MOUNTAIN 1.

hillside *n.* grade, gradient, acclivity;
see HILL.

hilltop *n.* peak, height, elevation; see
HILL, TOP 1.

hilly *a.* steep, sloping, rugged; see
MOUNTAINOUS, ROUGH 1.—*Ant.*
LEVEL, even, regular.

hinder *v.* impede, obstruct, interfere
with, check, retard, fetter, block,
thwart, bar, clog, encumber, burden,
cripple, handicap, cramp, preclude,
inhibit, shackle, interrupt, arrest,
curb, resist, oppose, baffle, deter,
hamper, frustrate, outwit, stop,
counteract, offset, neutralize, tie up,
hold up, embarrass, delay, postpone,
keep back, set back, dam, close, box
in, end, terminate, shut out, choke,
intercept, bottleneck, defeat, trap,
control, conflict with, deadlock, hold
back, clash with, be an obstacle to,
cross, exclude, limit, shorten, go
against, prohibit, withhold, slow
down, stall, bring to a standstill,
smother, disappoint, spoil, gag,
annul, silence, invalidate, detain,
stalemate, taboo, suspend, set
against, clip someone's wings*, tie
someone's hands*, get in the way of,
throw a monkey wrench into the
works*, knock the props from
under*.—*Ant.* HELP, assist, aid.

hindrance *n.* obstacle, intervention,
trammel; see BARRIER, INTERFER-
ENCE 1.

hinge *n.* hook, pivot, juncture,
articulation, link, elbow, ball-and-
socket joint, knee, butt hinge, strap
hinge, articulated joint, flap; see
also JOINT 1.

hinge *v.* connect, add, couple; see
JOIN 1.

hint *n.* allusion, inkling, insinuation,
implication, reference, advice,
observation, reminder, communication, notice, information, announcement, inside information, tip, clue,
token, idea, omen, scent, cue, trace,
notion, whisper, taste, suspicion,
evidence, innuendo, symptom, sign,
bare suggestion, impression, suggestion, premonition, broad hint, gentle hint, word to the wise, indication, tip-off, pointer*; see also SUG-
GESTION 1.

hint *v.* touch on, allude to, intimate,
inform, hint at, imply, foreshadow,
remind, impart, bring up, recall,
cue, prompt, insinuate, indicate,
wink, advise, cause to remember,
make an allusion to, jog the
memory, give a hint of, suggest,
make mention of, remark in passing, drop a hint, whisper, give an
inkling of, tip off*.—*Ant.* HIDE, conceal, cover. **—hinted at** signified,
intimated, referred to; see IMPLIED,
SUGGESTED.

hip* *a.* aware, informed, enlightened;
see MODERN 1, OBSERVANT.

hip *n.* side, hipbone, pelvis; see BONE.

hippie n. bohemian, nonconformist, flower child*; see RADICAL.

hire v. engage, sign up, draft, obtain, secure, enlist, give a job to, take on, put to work, bring in, occupy, use, fill a position, appoint, delegate, authorize, empower, retain, commission, book, utilize, select, pick, contract, procure, fill an opening, find help, find a place for, exploit, make use of, use another's services, add to the payroll.—Ant. DISMISS, discharge, fire.

hired a. signed up, given work, contracted; see BUSY, EMPLOYED, ENGAGED 3.

hiring n. engaging, contracting, employing; see EMPLOYER.

hiss n. buzz, sibilance, escape of air; see NOISE 1.

hiss v. sibilate, fizz, seethe; see SOUND.

historical a. factual, traditional, chronicled; see OLD 3, PAST 1.

history n. annals, records, archives, recorded history, chronicle, historical knowledge, historical writings, historical evidence, oral history, genealogy, narrative; see also RECORD 1, SOCIAL SCIENCE. **—make history** accomplish, do something important, achieve; see SUCCEED 1.

hit a. shot, struck, slugged, cuffed, slapped, smacked, clouted*, punched, boxed, slammed, knocked, beaten, whipped, poked, pounded, thrashed, spanked, banged, smashed, tapped, rapped, whacked, thumped, kicked, swatted, mugged, knocked out; see also HURT.—Ant. UNTOUCHED, unhurt, unscathed.

hit n. **1** [A blow] slap, rap, punch; see BLOW. **2** [A popular success] favorite, sellout*, smash; see SUCCESS 2. **3** [In baseball, a batted ball that cannot be fielded] base hit or single, two-base hit or double, three base-hit or triple, home run, Texas leaguer*, two-bagger*, three-bagger*, homer*.

hit v. **1** [To strike] knock, sock*, slap, jostle, butt, knock against, scrape, bump, run against, thump, collide with, bump into, punch, punish, hammer, strike down, bang, whack, jab, tap, smack, kick at, pelt, flail, thrash, cuff, kick, rap, clout*, club, bat around, lash out at, hit at, hit out at, let have it, crack, pop*, bash*; see also BEAT 1. **2** [To fire in time; *said of an internal combustion motor*] catch, go, run; see OPERATE 2. **3** [In baseball, to hit safely] make a hit, get on, get on base. **—hit it off** get along well, become friends, become friendly; see AGREE, LIKE 1, 2. **—hit upon** realize, come upon, stumble on; see DISCOVER, FIND, RECOGNIZE 1. **—hit or miss** at random, uncertainly, sometimes; see SCATTERED.

hit-and-run a. leaving without offering assistance, fugitive, illegally departed; see ILLEGAL.

hitch n. **1** [A knot] loop, noose, yoke; see KNOT 1, TIE 1. **2** [A difficulty] block, obstacle, tangle; see DIFFICULTY.

hitch v. tie up, strap, hook; see FASTEN, JOIN 1.

hitchhike v. take a lift, hitch a ride, thumb a ride; see RIDE 1, TRAVEL.

hive n. apiary, swarm, beehive; see COLONY.

hoard v. store up, acquire, keep; see ACCUMULATE, SAVE 3.

hoarse a. grating, rough, uneven, harsh, raucous, discordant, gruff, husky, thick, growling, croaking, cracked, guttural, dry, piercing, scratchy, indistinct, squawking, jarring, rasping.—Ant. PURE, sweet, mellifluous.

hoax n. falsification, fabrication, deceit; see DECEPTION, LIE.

hobby n. avocation, pastime, diversion, side interest, leisure-time activity, specialty, whim, fancy, whimsy, labor of love, play, craze, sport, amusement, craft, fun, art, game, sideline; see also ENTERTAINMENT.

hobo n. vagrant, vagabond, tramp; see BEGGAR.

hock* v. sell temporarily, pledge, deposit; see PAWN, SELL.

hockey n. ice hockey, field hockey, hockey game; see GAME 1, SPORT 3.

hodgepodge n. jumble, combination, mess; see MIXTURE 1.

hoe n. digger, scraper, garden hoe; see TOOL 1.

hog n. **1** [A pig] swine, sow, boar, shoat, razorback, wild boar, wart hog, peccary, porker, piggy, pork; see also ANIMAL. **2** [A person whose habits resemble a pig's] pig, glutton, filthy person; see SLOB. **—high on (or off) the hog*** luxuriously, extravagantly, richly; see EXPENSIVE.

hogtie v. fetter, shackle, tie up; see BIND.

hogwash n. foolishness, absurdity, ridiculousness; see NONSENSE 1.

hoist n. crane, lift, derrick; see ELEVATOR 1.

hold v. **1** [To have in one's grasp] grasp, grip, clutch, carry, embrace, cling to, detain, enclose, restrain, confine, check, take hold of, contain, hold down, hold on to, not let go, hang on, squeeze, press, hug, handle, have in hand, keep in hand, retain, keep, clasp, hold fast, hold tight, keep a firm hold on, tie, take, catch; see also SEIZE 1.—Ant. DROP, let fall, release. **2** [To have in one's possession] keep, retain, possess;

see HAVE 1. **3** [To remain firm] resist, persevere, keep staunch; see CONTINUE 1, ENDURE 2. **4** [To adhere] attach, cling, take hold; see FASTEN, STICK 1. **5** [To be valid] exist, continue, operate; see BE 1.— *Ant.* STOP, expire, be out of date. **6** [To contain] have the capacity for, carry, accommodate; see INCLUDE 1. **7** [To support; *often used with "up"*] sustain, brace, buttress, prop, lock, stay, shoulder, uphold, bear up; see also SUPPORT 1. —**hold back 1** [To restrain] inhibit, control, curb; see CHECK 1, PREVENT, RESTRAIN. **2** [To refrain] desist, hesitate, forbear; see ABSTAIN, AVOID. —**hold fast** clasp, lock, clamp; see FASTEN, STICK 1. —**hold off** be above, keep aloof, stave off; see AVOID, PREVENT. —**hold out 1** [To offer] proffer, tempt with, grant; see GIVE 1, OFFER 1. **2** [To endure] suffer, hold on, withstand; see CONTINUE 1, ENDURE 2. —**hold out for*** persist, go on supporting, stand firmly for; see CONTINUE 1. —**hold over** do again, show again, play over; see REPEAT 1. —**hold up 1** [To show] exhibit, raise high, elevate; see DISPLAY. **2** [To delay] stop, delay, interfere with; see HINDER, INTERRUPT. **3** [To rob at gunpoint] waylay, burglarize, steal from; see ROB. **4** [To support] brace, prop, shoulder; see HOLD 7, SUPPORT 1.

holder n. **1** [Something used in holding] sheath, container, holster, bag, sack, clip, handle, rack, knob, stem; see also CONTAINER, FASTENER. **2** [An owner or occupant] leaseholder, renter, dweller; see OWNER, RESIDENT, TENANT.

holdings n. lands, possessions, security; see ESTATE, PROPERTY 1.

holdover n. remnant, relic, surplus; see REMAINDER.

holdup n. robbery, burglary, stickup*; see CRIME, THEFT.

hole n. **1** [A perforation or cavity] notch, puncture, slot, eyelet, keyhole, porthole, buttonhole, peephole, loophole, air hole, window, crack, rent, split, tear, cleft, opening, fissure, gap, gash, rift, rupture, fracture, break, leak, aperture, space, chasm, breach, slit, nick, cut, chink, incision, orifice, eye, crater, mouth, gorge, throat, gullet, cranny, dent, opening, depression, indentation, impression, corner, pockmark, pocket, dimple, dip, drop, gulf, depth, pit, abyss, hollow, chasm, crevasse, mine, shaft, chamber, valley, ravine, burrow, rift, cell, niche. **2** [A cave] burrow, den, lair; see sense 1. **3** [*Serious difficulty]* impasse, tangle, mess; see CRISIS, DIFFICULTY 1, EMERGENCY. —**in a hole*** in trouble, suffering, caught; see ABANDONED. —**in the hole***

broke*, without money, in debt; see POOR 1.

holiday n. feast day, fiesta, legal holiday, holy day, festival, centennial, carnival, jubilee, red-letter day; see also ANNIVERSARY, CELEBRATION. *Common holidays include the following:* Sunday, Independence Day, Patriot's Day, Canada Day, Veterans Day, Memorial Day, Mardi Gras, New Year's Day, Saint Valentine's Day, Christmas, Easter, Boxing Day (British), Thanksgiving Day, May Day, Washington's Birthday, Lincoln's Birthday, Presidents' Day, Martin Luther King Day, Columbus Day, Labor Day, Halloween, Election Day, Cinco de Mayo (Mexican); *Jewish:* Passover, Purim, Shavuot, Yom Kippur, Rosh Hashana, Hanukkah.

holiness n. devoutness, humility, saintliness; see DEVOTION, WORSHIP 1.

hollow a. **1** [Concave] curving inward, bell-shaped, curved, carved out, sunken, depressed, arched, vaulted, cup-shaped, excavated, hollowed-out, indented, cupped; see also BENT, ROUND 2.—*Ant.* RAISED, convex, elevated. **2** [Sounding as though from a cave] cavernous, echoing deep, resonant, booming, roaring, rumbling, reverberating, muffled, dull, resounding, sepulchral, vibrating, low, ringing, deeptoned, thunderous; see also LOUD 1.—*Ant.* DEAD, mute, silent.

hollow n. dale, bowl, basin; see VALLEY.

hollow (out) v. excavate, indent, remove earth; see DIG 1, SHOVEL.

holy a. **1** [Sinless] devout, pious, blessed, righteous, moral, just, good, angelic, godly, reverent, venerable, immaculate, pure, spotless, clean, humble, saintly, innocent, godlike, saintlike, perfect, faultless, undefiled, untainted, chaste, upright, virtuous, revered, sainted, heavensent, believing, profoundly good, sanctified, devotional, spiritual, unstained, pure in heart, dedicated, unspotted; see also FAITHFUL, RELIGIOUS 2.—*Ant.* BAD, wicked, sinful. **2** [Concerned with worship] devotional, religious, ceremonial; see DIVINE.

Holy Spirit n. Holy Ghost, the Dove, third person of the Trinity; see GOD.

homage n. respect, adoration, deference; see DEVOTION, REVERENCE, WORSHIP 1.

home a. in one's home, at ease, at rest, homely, domestic, familiar, homey, in the bosom of one's family, down home, in one's element; see also COMFORTABLE 1.

home n. **1** [A dwelling place] house, dwelling, residence, habitation, tenement, abode, lodging, quarters, homestead, domicile, dormitory, apartment house, flat*, living quarters, chalet, shelter, asylum, hut, cabin, cottage, mansion, castle, summer home, rooming house, place, address, hovel, lodge, hotel, inn, farmhouse, tent, pad*, hangout*, digs*, nest; see also APARTMENT. **2** [An asylum] orphanage, sanatorium, mental hospital; see HOSPITAL. —**at home** relaxed, at ease, familiar; see COMFORTABLE 1, HOME. —**bring home to** make clear to, convince, impress upon; see EMPHASIZE. —**come home** come back, return home, go back; see RETURN 1. —**leave home** run off, play truant, depart; see LEAVE 1.

homeless *a.* desolate, outcast, destitute, vagrant, wandering, itinerant, friendless, banished, derelict, without a country, exiled, having no home, vagabond, forsaken, unsettled, unwelcome, dispossessed, disinherited, left to shift for oneself, without a roof over one's head; see also ABANDONED, POOR 1.—*Ant.* ESTABLISHED, at home, settled.

homely *a.* **1** [Unpretentious] snug, simple, cozy; see MODEST 2. **2** [Illfavored] plain, unattractive, not good-looking; see UGLY 1.

homemade *a.* homespun, domestic, do-it-yourself, self-made, made at home, home, not foreign.

home run *n.* four-base hit, roundtripper*, homer*; see SCORE 1.

homesick *a.* nostalgic, pining, yearning for home, ill with longing, unhappy, alienated, rootless; see also LONELY.

homesickness *n.* nostalgia, isolation, unhappiness; see LONELINESS.

homespun *a.* handcrafted, domestic, handspun; see HOMEMADE.

homestead *n.* house, ranch, estate; see HOME 1, PROPERTY 2.

homeward *a.* toward home, back home, on the way home, homewards, home, homeward bound, to one's family, to one's native land.

homework *n.* outside assignment, study, preparation; see EDUCATION 1.

homey *a.* enjoyable, livable, familiar; see COMFORTABLE 2, PLEASANT 2.

homosexual *a.* gay, same-sex, bisexual, lesbian, Sapphic, homoerotic, epicene.

homosexual *n.* lesbian, gay, gay man, bisexual, Sapphist.

honest *a.* **1** [Truthful] true, trustworthy, correct, exact, verifiable, undisguised, candid, straightforward, aboveboard, just, frank, impartial, respectful, factual, sound, reasonable, unimpeachable, legitimate, unquestionable, realistic, true-to-life, naked, plain, square, honest as the day is long*, on the level*, kosher*, fair and square*, straight.—*Ant.* deceptive, false, misleading. **2** [Frank] candid, straightforward, aboveboard; see sense 1 and FRANK. **3** [Fair] just, equitable, impartial; see FAIR 1.

honestly *a.* **1** [In an honest manner] uprightly, fairly, genuinely; see JUSTLY 1, SINCERELY. **2** [Really] indeed, truly, naturally; see REALLY 1.

honesty *n.* honor, fidelity, scrupulousness, trustworthiness, self-respect, straightforwardness, confidence, soundness, right, principle, truthfulness, candor, frankness, openness, morality, goodness, responsibility, loyalty, faithfulness, good faith, probity, courage, moral strength, virtue, reliability, character, conscience, worth, conscientiousness, trustiness, faith, justice.—*Ant.* DISHONESTY, deception, deceit.

honey *n.* comb honey, extracted honey, wild honey; see FOOD.

honk *n.* croak, quack, blare; see NOISE 1.

honk *v.* blare, trumpet, bellow; see SOUND.

honor *n.* **1** [Respect] reverence, esteem, worship, adoration, veneration, high regard, trust, faith, confidence, recognition, praise, attention, deference, notice, consideration, renown, reputation, elevation, credit, tribute, popularity; see also ADMIRATION.—*Ant.* DISGRACE, disrepute, opprobrium. **2** [Integrity] courage, character, truthfulness; see HONESTY. —**do the honors** act as host or hostess, present, host; see SERVE. —**on** (or **upon**) **one's honor** by one's faith, on one's word, staking one's good name; see SINCERELY.

honor *v.* **1** [To treat with respect] worship, sanctify, venerate; see PRAISE 1. **2** [To recognize worth] esteem, value, look up to; see ADMIRE. **3** [To recognize as valid] clear, pass, accept; see ACKNOWLEDGE 2.

honorable *a.* upright, reputable, creditable; see DISTINGUISHED 2, FAMOUS, NOBLE 2, 3.

honorably *a.* nobly, fairly, virtuously; see JUSTLY 1.

honored *a.* respected, revered, decorated, privileged, celebrated, reputable, well-known, esteemed, eminent, distinguished, dignified, noble, recognized, highly regarded, venerated; see also FAMOUS.—*Ant.* CORRUPT, disgraced, shamed.

hood *n.* **1** [Covering worn over the head] cowl, shawl, bonnet, protector, veil, capuchin, kerchief, mantle; see also HAT. **2** [A covering for vehicles and the like] engine cover, bonnet (British), canopy; see COVER 1. **3** [*A criminal] gangster, hoodlum, crook*; see CRIMINAL.

hoodlum *n.* outlaw, gangster, crook*; see CRIMINAL.

hoof *n.* ungula, animal foot, paw; see FOOT 2.

hook *n.* latch, catch, clasp; see FASTENER.

hook *v.* **1** [To curve in the shape of a hook] angle, crook, curve; see ARCH. **2** [To catch on a hook] pin, catch, secure; see FASTEN. **—hooked up** connected, linked together, attached; see JOINED. **—hook up** combine, connect, attach; see JOIN 1, UNITE.

hookup *n.* attachment, connection, consolidation; see LINK, UNION 1.

hoop *n.* loop, band, circlet; see CIRCLE 1.

hoot *n.* howl, whoop, boo; see CRY 2.

hop *n.* spring, bounce, leap; see JUMP 1.

hop *v.* leap, skip, jump on one leg; see BOUNCE, JUMP 1.

hope *n.* **1** [Reliance upon the future] faith, expectation, confidence; see ANTICIPATION, OPTIMISM 2. **2** [The object of hope] wish, goal, dream; see DESIRE 1, END 2, PURPOSE 1.

hope *v.* be hopeful, lean on, wish, desire, live in hope, rely, depend, count on, aspire to, doubt not, keep one's fingers crossed, hope for the best, be of good cheer, pray, cherish the hope, look forward to, await, dream, presume, watch for, bank on, foresee, promise oneself, suppose, deem likely, believe, suspect, surmise, hold, be assured, feel confident, anticipate, be prepared for, make plans for, have faith, rest assured, be sure of, be reassured, take heart, hope to hell*, knock on wood*; see also EXPECT 1, TRUST 1.

hopeful *a.* **1** [Optimistic] expectant, assured, sanguine, buoyant, enthusiastic, trustful, reassured, emboldened, full of hope, cheerful, anticipating, expecting, in hopes of, forward-looking, lighthearted, serene, calm, poised, comfortable, eager, elated, looking through rose-colored glasses; see also CONFIDENT, TRUSTING. **2** [Encouraging] promising, reassuring, favorable, bright, cheering, flattering, gracious, opportune, timely, fortunate, propitious, auspicious, well-timed, fit, suitable, convenient, beneficial, fair, uplifting, heartening, inspiring, exciting, pleasing, fine, lucky, stirring, making glad, helpful, rose-colored, rosy, animating, attractive, satisfactory, refreshing, probable, good, conducive, advantageous, pleasant, of promise, happy, cheerful.—*Ant.*

UNFORTUNATE, discouraging, unfavorable.

hopefully *a.* **1** [Optimistically] confidently, expectantly, with confidence, with hope, trustingly, naively, with some reassurance, trustfully; see also BOLDLY 1, POSITIVELY 1, SURELY.—*Ant.* HOPELESSLY, doubtfully, gloomily. **2** [Probably] conceivably, expectedly, feasibly; see PROBABLY.

hopeless *a.* unfortunate, threatening, bad, sinister, unyielding, incurable, past hope, past cure, vain, irreversible, irreparable, without hope, with no hope, down in the mouth*, impracticable, ill-fated, disastrous, menacing, foreboding, unfavorable, dying, worsening, past saving, tragic, fatal, desperate, helpless, lost, to no avail, gone, empty, idle, useless, pointless, worthless; see also ABANDONED, IMPOSSIBLE.—*Ant.* FAVORABLE, heartening, cheering.

hopelessly *a.* cynically, pessimistically, despondently, dejectedly, desperately, emptily, darkly, gloomily, dismally, desolately; see also SADLY.—*Ant.* HOPEFULLY, confidently, expectantly.

horde *n.* pack, throng, swarm; see CROWD, GATHERING.

horizon *n.* range, border, limit; see BOUNDARY, EXTENT.

horizontal *a.* **1** [Level] plane, aligned, parallel to the horizon; see FLAT 1, LEVEL 3, STRAIGHT 1. **2** [Even] flush, uniform, regular; see FLAT 1, SMOOTH 1.

horn *n.* **1** [A wind instrument] *Horns include the following:* bugle, trombone, saxophone, cornet, clarinet, bassoon, pipe, fife, flute, picolo, oboe, English horn, French horn, tuba, sousaphone, baritone, alphorn, shofar, ram's horn, hunting horn; see also MUSICAL INSTRUMENT. **2** [Hard process protruding from the head of certain animals] antler, outgrowth, pronghorn, frontal bone, spine, spike, point; see also BONE. **— horn in (on)*** intrude, impose upon, get in on; see ENTER, MEDDLE 1. **— lock horns** disagree, conflict, defy; see OPPOSE 1.

horny *a.* **1** [Callous] hard, firm, bony; see TOUGH 2. **2** [*Sexually excited] sensual, aroused, lecherous; see EXCITED, LEWD 2.

horrendous *a.* horrible, frightful, terrifying; see POOR 2, TERRIBLE 1.

horrible *a.* **1** [Offensive] repulsive, dreadful, disgusting; see OFFENSIVE 2. **2** [Frightful] shameful, shocking, awful; see FRIGHTFUL, TERRIBLE 1.

horrid *a.* hideous, disturbing, shameful; see OFFENSIVE 2, PITIFUL.

horror *n.* awe, terror, fright; see FEAR.

horse *n.* nag, draft animal, plow

horse, racer, saddle horse, steed, mount, charger, pony, mustang, bronco, quarter horse, piebald, pinto, palomino, Arabian, stallion, gelding, hack, mare, Thoroughbred, pacer, trotter, courser; see also ANIMAL. —**from the horse's mouth*** originally, from an authority, according to the original source of the information; see OFFICIALLY 1. —**hold one's horses*** curb one's impatience, slow down, relax; see RESTRAIN. —**horse around*** fool around, cavort, cause trouble; see MISBEHAVE, PLAY 2. —**on one's high horse*** arrogant, haughty, disdainful; see EGOTISTIC.

horseman *n.* equestrian, rider, jockey; see COWBOY.

horseplay *n.* clowning, play, fooling around; see FUN, JOKE.

horsepower *n.* strength, pull, power; see ENERGY 2.

hose *n.* **1** [Stocking] stockings, socks, pantyhose; see HOSIERY. **2** [A flexible conduit] garden hose, fire hose, line, tubing; see also PIPE 1, TUBE 1.

hosiery *n.* stockings, nylons, hose, seamless hose, full-fashioned hose, socks, anklets, tights, pantyhose, knee socks, bobby socks*, sport socks, sox, support hose.

hospitable *a.* cordial, courteous, open; see FRIENDLY.

hospital *n.* clinic, infirmary, sanatorium, sanitarium, dispensary, mental hospital, army hospital, city hospital, public hospital, veterans' hospital, teaching hospital, university hospital, treatment center, rehabilitation center, surgery center, maternity hospital, medical center, lying-in hospital, health service, outpatient ward, sick bay.

hospitality *n.* good cheer, companionship, good fellowship; see ENTERTAINMENT, WELCOME.

host *n.* **1** [A person who entertains] man of the house, woman of the house, entertainer, toastmaster, master of ceremonies, hostess, emcee. **2** [A large group] throng, multitude, army; see CROWD, GATHERING. **3** [Organism on which a parasite subsists] victim, host body, animal; see PARASITE 1.

host *v.* receive, treat, wine and dine; see ENTERTAIN 2.

hostage *n.* security, captive, victim of a kidnapping; see PRISONER.

hostess *n.* society lady, socialite, clubwoman, social leader, entertainer, lady of the house, toastmistress, mistress of ceremonies.

hostile *a.* antagonistic, hateful, opposed; see UNFRIENDLY.

hostility *n.* abhorrence, aversion, bitterness; see HATRED.

hot *a.* **1** [Having a high temperature] torrid, burning, fiery, flaming, blazing, very warm, baking, roasting, smoking, scorching, blistering, searing, sizzling, tropical, warm, broiling, red-hot, grilling, piping hot, white-hot, scalding, parching, sultry, on fire, at a high temperature, incandescent, smoldering, thermal, toasting, simmering, blazing hot*, boiling hot*, like an oven*, hotter than blazes*; see also BOILING, COOKING, MOLTEN.—*Ant.* COLD, frigid, chilly. **2** [Aroused] furious, ill-tempered, indignant; see ANGRY. **3** [*Erotic] spicy, salacious, carnal; see SENSUAL 2. —**get hot*** become excited, become enthusiastic, burn with fervor, get angry, rave; see also RAGE 1. —**hot under the collar*** furious, mad, resentful; see ANGRY. —**make it hot for*** create discomfort for, cause trouble for, vex; see DISTURB.

hotel *n.* stopping place, inn, lodging house, bed-and-breakfast, boardinghouse, hostel, motel, motor hotel, resort, tavern, spa, rooming house, boatel, flophouse*.

hotheaded *a.* unmanageable, wild, reckless; see RASH, UNRULY.

hound *n.* greyhound, bloodhound, beagle; see ANIMAL, DOG.

hound *v.* badger, provoke, annoy; see BOTHER 2.

hour *n.* time unit, sixty minutes, man-hour, horsepower hour, class hour, supper hour, study hour, rush hour; see also TIME 1. —**hour after hour** continually, steadily, on and on; see REGULARLY.

hourly *a.* each hour, every hour, every sixty minutes; see FREQUENTLY, REGULARLY.

house *n.* **1** [A habitation] dwelling, apartment house, residence; see APARTMENT, HOME 1. **2** [A family] line, family tradition, ancestry; see FAMILY. **3** [A legislative body] congress, council, parliament; see LEGISLATURE. —**bring down the house*** receive applause, create enthusiasm, please; see EXCITE. —**clean house** arrange, put in order, tidy up; see CLEAN. —**keep house** manage a home, run a house, be a housekeeper; see MANAGE 1. —**like a house on fire** (or afire) actively, vigorously, energetically; see QUICKLY. —**on the house** without expense, gratis, complimentary; see FREE 4.

household *n.* family unit, house, domestic establishment; see FAMILY, HOME 1.

housekeeper *n.* homemaker, caretaker, serving woman; see SERVANT.

housewife *n.* mistress, lady of the house, housekeeper, home economist, homemaker, family manager, wife and mother; see also WIFE.

housework *n.* housecleaning, spring cleaning, chores, window-washing, sweeping, cooking, baking, dusting, dishwashing, vacuuming, tidying up, putting things away, discarding trash, tending plants, minor repairs, recycling, mopping, washing, laundering, bed-making, sewing, ironing, mending; see also JOB 2.

housing *n.* habitation, home construction, housing development, low-cost housing, house-building program, sheltering, installation, abode, domicile, house, accommodations, quarters, roof, dwelling, lodging, pad*, residence, headquarters; see also HOME 1, SHELTER.

hover *v.* float, flutter, be in midair; see FLY 1, HANG 2.

how *a., conj.* in what way, to what degree, by what method, in what manner, according to what specifications, from what source, by whose help, whence, wherewith, by virtue of what, whereby, through what agency, by what means.

however *a.* still, yet, nevertheless, in spite of this, despite that, nonetheless, notwithstanding, without regard to that.

howl *n.* wail, lament, shriek; see CRY 1, YELL.

howl *v.* bawl, wail, lament; see CRY 1, YELL.

hub *n.* core, heart, middle; see CENTER 1.

hubbub *n.* turmoil, fuss, disorder; see CONFUSION, NOISE 2, UPROAR.

huddle *v.* crouch, press close, crowd, bunch, draw, together, mass, cluster, throng, nestle, cuddle, hug, curl up, snuggle.

hue *n.* color, shade, dye; see TINT.

huff *n.* annoyance, offense, perturbation; see ANGER, RAGE 1.

huffy *a.* offended, piqued, huffish; see ANGRY, INSULTED, IRRITABLE.

hug *n.* embrace, squeeze, tight grip, caress, clinch*, bearhug; see also TOUCH 2.

hug *v.* embrace, squeeze, clasp, press, love, hold, be near to, cling, fold in the arms, clutch, seize, envelop, enfold, nestle, welcome, cuddle, press to the bosom, snuggle.

huge *a.* tremendous, enormous, immense; see LARGE 1.

hulk *n.* bulk, hunk, lump; see MASS 1, PART 1.

hull *n.* 1 [The body of a vessel] framework, covering, main structure; see FRAME 1. 2 [A shell] peel, husk, shuck; see SHELL 1.

hullabaloo *n.* tumult, chaos, clamor; see CONFUSION, NOISE 2, UPROAR.

hum *v.* buzz, drone, murmur, sing low, hum a tune, croon, sing without words, moan, make a buzzing sound, whir, vibrate, purr.

human *a.* anthropoid, animal, biped, civilized, man-made, anthropomorphic, manlike, humanlike, of mankind, belonging to mankind, mortal, humanistic, individual, man's, personal, humane; see also ANIMAL.—*Ant.* DIVINE, bestial, nonhuman.

human being *n.* being, human, mortal; see MAN 1, PERSON 1, WOMAN 1.

humane *a.* benevolent, sympathetic, understanding, pitying, compassionate, kindhearted, human, tenderhearted, forgiving, gracious, charitable, gentle, tender, friendly, generous, lenient, tolerant, democratic, good-natured, liberal, open-minded, broad-minded, altruistic, philanthropic, helpful, magnanimous, amiable, genial, cordial, unselfish, warmhearted, bighearted, softhearted, good; see also KIND.—*Ant.* CRUEL, barbaric, inhuman.

humanitarian *n.* altruist, philanthropist, benefactor; see PATRON.

humanity *n.* 1 [The human race] human beings, mankind, human race; see MAN 1, PERSON 1, WOMAN 1. 2 [An ideal of human behavior] tolerance, sympathy, understanding; see KINDNESS 1, VIRTUE 1, 2.

humble *a.* 1 [Meek] lowly, submissive, gentle, quiet, unassuming, diffident, simple, retiring, bashful, shy, timid, reserved, deferential, self-conscious, soft-spoken, sheepish, mild, withdrawn, unpretentious, hesitant, fearful, tentative, poor in spirit, sedate, unpresuming, manageable, ordinary, unambitious, commonplace, free from pride, without arrogance, peaceable, obedient, passive, tame, restrained, unostentatious, unimportant, gentle as a lamb, resigned, subdued, tolerant, eating humble pie; see also MODEST 2.—*Ant.* PROUD, haughty, conceited. 2 [Lowly] unpretentious, unassuming, modest, seemly, becoming, homespun, natural, low, proletarian, servile, undistinguished, pitiful, sordid, shabby, underprivileged, meager, beggarly, commonplace, unimportant, insignificant, small, poor, rough, hard, base, meek, little, of low birth, obscure, inferior, plain, common, homely, simple, uncouth, miserable, scrubby, ordinary, humdrum, trivial, vulgar.—*Ant.* NOBLE, upper-class, privileged.

humble *v.* shame, mortify, chasten, demean, demote, lower, crush, bring low, put to shame, silence, reduce, humiliate, embarrass, degrade, overcome, strike dumb, put down, pull down, bring down, snub, discredit, deflate, upset, make ashamed, take down a peg, pull rank on*, squelch*, squash*.—*Ant.* PRAISE, exalt, glorify.

humbly *a.* meekly, submissively, simply, obscurely, apologetically.

humbug *n.* lie, fraud, faker; see DECEPTION, NONSENSE 1.

humdrum *a.* monotonous, tedious, uninteresting; see DULL 4.

humid *a.* stuffy, sticky, muggy; see CLOSE 5, WET 1.

humidity *n.* moisture, wetness, dampness, mugginess, dankness, heaviness, sogginess, thickness, fogginess, wet, sultriness, steaminess, steam, evaporation, dewiness, stickiness, moistness; see also RAIN 1.

humiliate *v.* debase, chasten, mortify, make a fool of, put to shame, humble, degrade, crush, shame, confuse, snub, confound, lower, dishonor, depress, fill with shame, break, demean, bring low, conquer, make ashamed, vanquish, take down a peg; see also DISGRACE, EMBARRASS.

humiliation *n.* chagrin, mortification, degradation; see DISGRACE, EMBARRASSMENT, SHAME 1.

humility *n.* meekness, timidity, submissiveness, servility, reserve, subservience, subjection, humbleness, submission, obedience, passiveness, nonresistance, resignation, bashfulness, shyness, inferiority complex.—*Ant.* PRIDE, vainglory, conceit.

humor *n.* **1** [Comedy] amusement, jesting, raillery, joking, merriment, clowning, farce, facetiousness, whimsy, black humor; see also ENTERTAINMENT, FUN. **2** [An example of humor] witticism, pleasantry, banter; see JOKE. **3** [The ability to appreciate comedy] sense of humor, wittiness, high spirits, jolliness, gaiety, joyfulness, playfulness, happy frame of mind.

humor *v.* indulge, pamper, baby, play up to, gratify, please, pet, coddle, spoil, comply with, appease, placate, soften, be playful with; see also COMFORT 1.—*Ant.* ANGER, provoke, enrage.

humorous *a.* comical, comic, entertaining; see FUNNY 1.

humorously *a.* comically, ridiculously, playfully, absurdly, ludicrously, amusingly, jokingly, ironically, satirically, facetiously, merrily, genially, jovially, in a comical manner, in an amusing manner, just for fun.

hump *n.* protuberance, mound, bump, swelling, camel hump, humpback, hunchback, hummock, protrusion, knob, prominence, eminence,

projection, swell, hunch, lump, dune.

hunch *n.* idea, notion, feeling, premonition, forecast, presentiment, instinct, expectation, anticipation, precognition, prescience, forewarning, clue, foreboding, hint, portent, apprehension, misgiving, qualm, suspicion, inkling, glimmer; see also THOUGHT 2.

hundred *n.* ten tens, five score, century; see NUMBER.

hung *a.* suspended, swaying, dangling; see HANGING. —**hung up*** **1** [Troubled] disturbed, distressed, confused; see TROUBLED. **2** [Intent] absorbed, engrossed, preoccupied; see THOUGHTFUL 1.

hunger *n.* craving, longing, yearning, mania, lust, desire for food, famine, starvation, ravenousness, appetite, hungriness, panting, drought, want, greediness, void, sweet tooth*.—*Ant.* SATISFACTION, satiety, glut.

hungry *a.* starved, famished, ravenous, desirous, hankering, unsatisfied, unfilled, starving, insatiate, voracious, half-starved, omnivorous, piggish, hoggish, on an empty stomach*, hungry as a wolf*, empty*.—*Ant.* FULL, satisfied, fed.

hunk *n.* lump, large piece, good-sized bit, portion, a fair quantity, a good bit, chunk, bunch, mass, clod, a pile, thick slice, morsel, a lot, slice, gob, nugget, block, loaf, wad; see also PIECE 1.

hunt *n.* chase, shooting, field sport; see HUNTING, SPORT 3.

hunt *v.* **1** [To pursue with intent to kill] follow, give chase, stalk, hound, trail, dog, seek, capture, kill, shoot, track, heel, shadow, chase, hunt out, snare, look for, fish, fish for, poach, gun for*, go gunning for*; see also TRACK 1. **2** [To try to find] investigate, probe, look for; see SEEK.

hunted *a.* pursued, followed, tracked, sought, trailed, chased, stalked, hounded, tailed, wanted, driven out, searched for.

hunter *n.* huntsman, stalker, chaser, sportsman, pursuer, big-game hunter, gunner, poacher, horsewoman, huntress, horseman, archer, trapper, deerstalker, angler, fisherman, bowman, shooter.

hunting *n.* the chase, the hunt, sporting, shooting, stalking, preying, trapping, big-game hunting, deer hunting, fox hunting, pheasant shooting, angling, fishing, steeplechase, riding to hounds; see also SPORT 3.

hurdle *n.* barricade, obstacle, blockade; see BARRIER.

hurdle *v.* jump over, scale, leap over; see JUMP 1.

hurl *v.* cast, fling, heave; see THROW 1.

hurrah *interj.* three cheers, hurray, yippee; see CHEER 2, CRY 1, ENCOURAGEMENT, YELL 1.

hurricane *n.* typhoon, tempest, monsoon; see STORM.

hurry *interj.* run, hasten, move, hustle, get a move on*, on the double*.

hurry *n.* dispatch, haste, rush; see SPEED.

hurry *v.* **1** [To act quickly] hasten, be quick, make haste, scurry, scuttle, fly, tear, dash, sprint, be in a hurry, lose no time, move quickly, move rapidly, bolt, bustle, rush, make short work of, scoot*, work at high speed, dash on, hurry about, hurry off, hurry up, run off, waste no time, plunge, skip, gallop, zoom, dart, spring, make good time, whip, go by forced marches, speed, work under pressure, run like mad*, go at full tilt, make strides, act on a moment's notice, step on the gas*, floor it*, get cracking*, step on it*, shake a leg*.—*Ant.* DELAY, lose time, procrastinate. **2** [To move rapidly] fly, bustle, dash off; see RACE 1, RUN 1, 2. **3** [To urge others] push, spur, goad; see DRIVE 1, URGE 2.

hurrying *a.* speeding, in a hurry, running; see FAST.

hurt *a.* injured, damaged, harmed, marred, wounded, in critical condition, impaired, shot, struck, bruised, stricken, battered, mauled, hit, stabbed, mutilated, disfigured, bleeding, burned, in pain, suffering, distressed, tortured, unhappy, grazed, scratched, nicked, winged; see also WOUNDED.

hurt *n.* **1** [A wound] blow, gash, ache; see INJURY, PAIN 1. **2** [Damage] ill-treatment, harm, persecution; see DAMAGE 1, DISASTER, MISFORTUNE.

hurt *v.* **1** [To cause pain] cramp, squeeze, cut, bruise, tear, torment, afflict, kick, puncture, do violence to, slap, abuse, flog, whip, torture, gnaw, stab, pierce, maul, cut up, harm, injure, wound, lacerate, sting, bite, inflict pain, burn, crucify, tweak, thrash, punch, pinch, spank, punish, trounce, scourge, lash, cane, switch, work over*, wallop*, slug*.—*Ant.* EASE, comfort, soothe. **2** [To harm] maltreat, injure, spoil; see DAMAGE 1, DESTROY. **3** [To give a feeling of pain] ache, throb, sting; see sense 1.

hurtful *a.* aching, injurious, bad; see DANGEROUS, DEADLY, HARMFUL.

husband *n.* spouse, married man, mate, bedmate, helpmate, consort, bridegroom, breadwinner, provider, man, common-law husband, hubby*, lord and master*, the man of the house, old man*, groom, cuckold; see also MAN 2.

hush *interj.* quiet, be quiet, pipe down*; see SHUT UP 1.

hush *n.* peace, stillness, quiet; see SILENCE 1.

hush *v.* silence, gag, stifle; see QUIET 2. —**hush (up)** cover, conceal, suppress; see HIDE 1.

husk *n.* shuck, covering, outside; see COVER 1, SHELL 1.

husky *a.* **1** [Hoarse] throaty, growling, gruff; see HOARSE. **2** [Strong] muscular, sinewy, strapping; see STRONG 1.

hustle* *v.* act quickly, rush, push; see HURRY 1, RACE 1, RUN 1, SPEED.

hustler* *n.* **1** [A professional gambler] gamester, bookmaker, plunger*; see GAMBLER. **2** [A prostitute] whore, harlot, call girl; see PROSTITUTE. **3** [An energetic worker] dynamo, go-getter, workaholic; see EXECUTIVE, ZEALOT.

hut *n.* shanty, lean-to, shack, bungalow, bunkhouse, refuge, lodge, dugout, hovel, cottage, cabin, hogan, tepee, log cabin, wigwam, dump*; see also HOME 1, SHELTER.

hybrid *a.* crossed, alloyed, crossbred, interbred, mongrel, cross, half-blooded, heterogeneous, intermingled, half-and-half.

hybrid *n.* crossbreed, cross, mixture, composite, half-blood, combination, mestizo, outcross; see also MIXTURE 1.

hydrant *n.* fire hydrant, fireplug, spigot; see FAUCET.

hydraulics *n.* science of liquids in motion, hydrodynamics, hydrology; see SCIENCE 1.

hygiene *n.* cleanliness, hygienics, preventive medicine, public health, sanitary measures; see also HEALTH, CLEANLINESS.

hygienic *a.* healthful, sanitary, clean; see PURE 2, STERILE 3.

hymn *n.* chant, psalm, spiritual; see SONG.

hyperbole *n.* overstatement, figure of speech, distortion; see EXAGGERATION.

hypnosis *n.* trance, anesthesia, lethargy; see SLEEP.

hypnotic *a.* sleep-inducing, narcotic, anesthetic, soporific, sleep-producing, soothing, calmative, trance-inducing.

hypnotism *n.* bewitchment, suggestion, hypnotherapy, deep sleep, self-hypnosis, autohypnosis, hypnotic suggestion, charm, fascination.

hypnotize *v.* mesmerize, lull to sleep, dull the will, hold under a spell, bring under one's control, stupefy, drug, soothe, fascinate, anesthetize, subject to suggestion, make drowsy.

hypnotized *a.* entranced, mesmerized, enchanted; see CHARMED.

hypochondria *n.* anxiety, imagined ill-health, neurosis; see PRETENSE 1.

hypochondriac *n.* worrier, neurotic, self-tormentor; see FAKE.

hypocrisy *n.* affectation, deception, bad faith, hollowness, display, lip service, bigotry, sham, fraud, pretense of virtue, quackery, empty ceremony, sanctimony, cant; see also DISHONESTY, LIE.—*Ant.* VIRTUE, devotion, piety.

hypocrite *n.* pretender, fraud, faker, deceiver, charlatan, bigot, quack, pharisee, sham, actor, cheat, informer, trickster, confidence man, malingerer, humbug, impostor, swindler, informer, rascal, traitor, wolf in sheep's clothing, masquerader, four-flusher*, two-timer*, two-face*; see also FAKE.

hypocritical *a.* deceptive, double-dealing, insincere; see DISHONEST.

hypothesis *n.* supposition, theory, assumption; see GUESS, OPINION 1.

hypothetical *a.* 1 [Supposed] imagined, uncertain, vague; see ASSUMED, LIKELY 1. 2 [Characterized by hypothesis] postulated, academic, philosophical; see LOGICAL.

hysteria *n.* delirium, agitation, feverishness; see CONFUSION, EXCITEMENT, NERVOUSNESS.

hysterical *a.* convulsed, uncontrolled, raving, delirious, unnerved, neurotic, emotional, rabid, emotionally disordered, distracted, fuming, distraught, unrestrained, possessed, fanatical, irrepressible, convulsive, carried away, seething, beside oneself, rampant, out of one's wits, mad, uncontrollable, agitated, raging, frenzied, spasmodic, confused, tempestuous, maddened, crazy, impetuous, crazed, furious, violent, impassioned, panic-stricken, nervous, vehement, overwrought, fiery, passionate, jittery*, wild-eyed, on a crying jag*; see also ANGRY, EXCITED, TROUBLED.

I

I *pron.* myself, yours truly*, first person; see CHARACTER 2.

ICBM *n.* Intercontinental Ballistic Missile, guided missile, nuclear weapon; see ROCKET, WEAPON.

ice *n.* crystal, hail, floe, glacier, icicle, ice cube, cube ice, dry ice, black ice, white ice, crushed ice, iceberg, permafrost; see also FROST. —**break the ice** make a start, initiate, commence; see BEGIN 1. —**on ice*** in reserve, held, in abeyance; see SAVED 2. —**on thin ice*** in a dangerous situation, imperiled, insecure; see ENDANGERED.

ice *v.* frost, coat, mist; see FREEZE 1.

iceberg *n.* ice field, berg, floe; see ICE.

icebox *n.* cooler, freezer, fridge*; see REFRIGERATOR.

ice cream *n.* frozen dessert, ice, ice milk, frozen custard, soft serve, sherbet, sorbet, frozen yogurt, gelato, *glace* (French), spumoni, sundae, parfait; see also DESSERT.

icy *a.* frozen over, iced, freezing, glacial, frostbound, frosted, frosty, smooth as glass; see also SLIPPERY.

idea *n.* 1 [A concept] conception, plans, view, fancy, impression, image, understanding, observation, belief, feeling, opinion, guess, inference, theory, hypothesis, supposition, assumption, intuition, conjecture, design, approach, mental impression, notion. 2 [Fancy] whimsy, whim, fantasy; see FANCY 1, IMAGINATION. 3 [Meaning] sense, import, purport; see MEANING.

ideal *a.* 1 [Typical] prototypical, model, archetypical; see TYPICAL. 2 [Perfect] supreme, fitting, exemplary; see EXCELLENT, PERFECT.

ideal *n.* paragon, goal, prototype; see MODEL 1.

idealism *n.* principle, conscience, philosophy; see ETHICS.

idealistic *a.* lofty, utopian, exalted; see IMPRACTICAL, NOBLE 1.

idealize *v.* romanticize, glorify, put on a pedestal; see ADMIRE, DREAM 2.

identical *a.* like, twin, indistinguishable; see ALIKE.

identification *n.* 1 [The act of identifying] classifying, naming, cataloging; see CLASSIFICATION, DESCRIPTION. 2 [Means of identifying] credentials, letter of introduction, testimony, letter of credit, badge, papers, ID; see also PASSPORT.

identify *v.* classify, catalog, analyze; see DESCRIBE, NAME 1, 2.

identity *n.* identification, character, individuality, uniqueness, antecedents, true circumstances, parentage, status, citizenship, nationality, connections; see also NAME 1.

ideology *n.* beliefs, ideas, philosophy; see CULTURE 2, ETHICS.

idiot *n.* simpleton, nincompoop, booby; see FOOL.

idiotic *a.* thickwitted, dull, moronic; see STUPID.

idle *a.* unoccupied, fallow, vacant, deserted, not in use, barren, void, empty, abandoned, still, quiet, motionless, inert, dead, rusty, dusty, out of action, out of a job, out of work, resting; see also UNEMPLOYED.—*Ant.* ACTIVE, busy, engaged.

idle *v.* slack, shirk, slow down; see LOAF.

idleness *n.* loitering, time-killing, dawdling, inertia, inactivity, indolence, sluggishness, unemployment, dormancy, lethargy, stupor, loafing.—*Ant.* ACTION, industry, occupation.

idol *n.* graven image, god, effigy, false god, figurine, fetish, totem, golden calf, pagan deity.

idolatry *n.* infatuation, fervor, transport; see ZEAL.

idolize *v.* glorify, adore, canonize; see WORSHIP.

if *conj.* provided that, with the condition that, supposing that, conceding that, on the assumption that, granted that, assuming that, whenever, wherever. —*as if* as though, assuming that, in a way; see AS IF at AS.

iffy *a.* unsettled, doubtful, not sure; see UNCERTAIN.

ignite *v.* kindle, light, strike a light, start up, burst into flames, touch off, touch a match to, set off; see also BURN.

ignition *n.* 1 [Igniting] combustion, bursting into flame, kindling; see FIRE 1. 2 [A system for igniting] distributor, firing system, wiring system; see ENGINE, MACHINE, MOTOR.

ignorance *n.* unconsciousness, incomprehension, bewilderment, incapacity, inexperience, disregard, illiteracy, denseness, stupidity, dumbness, empty-headedness, unintelligence, rawness, blindness, simplicity, insensitivity, shallowness, fog, vagueness, half-knowledge, lack of education, a little learning.—*Ant.* ABILITY, learning, erudition.

ignorant *a.* 1 [Unaware] unconscious of, uninformed, unknowing, uninitiated, inexperienced, unwitting, unmindful, disregardful, misinformed, unsuspecting, unaware of, unmindful of, mindless, witless, not conversant with, unintelligent, obtuse, thick, dense, unscientific, birdbrained*, lowbrow*, sappy*, green; see also sense 2 and DULL 3, SHALLOW 2, STUPID.—*Ant.* INTELLIGENT, alert, aware. 2 [Untrained] illiterate, uneducated, unlettered, untaught, uninstructed, uncultivated, unenlightened, untutored, unschooled, unread, benighted, shallow, superficial, gross, coarse,

vulgar, crude, green, knowing nothing, misinformed, misguided, just beginning, apprenticed, unbriefed; see also INEXPERIENCED, NAIVE, UNAWARE.—*Ant.* LEARNED, cognizant, tutored.

ignore *v.* disregard, overlook, pass over; see DISCARD, NEGLECT 2.

ill *a.* 1 [Bad] harmful, evil, noxious; see BAD 1. 2 [Sick] unwell, ailing, unhealthy; see SICK. —**ill at ease** anxious, uneasy, uncomfortable; see DOUBTFUL, RESTLESS, SUSPICIOUS 1, 2.

ill *n.* depravity, misfortune, mischief; see EVIL 2, INSULT, WRONG.

illegal *a.* illicit, unlawful, contraband, unwarranted, banned, unconstitutional, actionable, outside the law, extralegal, outlawed, not legal, unauthorized, unlicensed, lawless, illegitimate, prohibited, forbidden, criminal, against the law, not approved, uncertified, smuggled, bootlegged, hot*.—*Ant.* LEGAL, lawful, authorized.

illegible *a.* faint, unintelligible, difficult to read; see CONFUSED 2, OBSCURE 1.

illegibly *a.* faintly, unintelligibly, indistinctly; see CONFUSED 2.

illegitimate *a.* 1 [Unlawful] contraband, wrong, illicit; see BAD 1, ILLEGAL. 2 [Born of unmarried parents] born out of wedlock, unlawfully begotten, fatherless; see BASTARD.

illicit *a.* unlawful, prohibited, unauthorized; see BAD 1, ILLEGAL, WRONG 1.

illiteracy *n.* lack of education, inability to read and write, inadequacy; see IGNORANCE.

illiterate *a.* uneducated, unenlightened, unlettered; see IGNORANT 2.

ill-mannered *a.* impolite, uncouth, rough; see RUDE 2.

illness *n.* 1 [Poor health] sickness, failing health, seizure, ailing, disease, ailment, infirmity, disorder, relapse, attack, fit, convalescence, complaint, delicate health, collapse, breakdown, confinement, disturbance, ill health; see also WEAKNESS 1. 2 [A particular disease] sickness, ailment, malady, ache, infection, stroke, allergy; see also COLD 2, IMPEDIMENT 2, PAIN 2.

illogical *a.* irrational, unreasonable, absurd, fallacious, specious, incorrect, inconsistent, false, unscientific, contradictory, untenable, unsound, preposterous, invalid, self-contradictory, unproved, groundless, implausible, hollow, irrelevant, inconclusive, prejudiced, biased, unconnected, without foundation, not following, without rhyme or reason; see also WRONG 2.—*Ant.* LOGICAL, sound, reasonable.

ill-suited *a.* inappropriate, not harmonious, mismatched; see UNSUITABLE.

ill-tempered *a.* cross, touchy, querulous; see IRRITABLE, SULLEN.

illuminate *v.* **1** [To make light(er)] lighten, irradiate, illume; see BRIGHTEN 1, LIGHT 1. **2** [To explain] interpret, elucidate, clarify; see EXPLAIN.

illumination *n.* **1** [A light] gleam, flame, brilliance, lighting; see also FLASH, LIGHT 1, 3. **2** [Instruction] teaching, education, elucidation; see KNOWLEDGE 1.

illusion *n.* fancy, hallucination, mirage, apparition, ghost, delusion, figment of the imagination, image, trick of vision, myth, make-believe; see also DREAM.

illustrate *v.* picture, represent, portray, depict, imitate; see also DRAW 2, PAINT 1.

illustrated *a.* pictorial, decorated, portrayed; see DESCRIPTIVE.

illustration *n.* engraving, tailpiece, frontispiece, cartoon, vignette, etching, inset picture, news photo; see also PICTURE 3.

illustrative *a.* symbolic, representative, pictorial; see DESCRIPTIVE, EXPLANATORY, GRAPHIC 1, 2.

ill will *n.* malevolence, dislike, hostility; see BLAME, HATRED, OBJECTION.

image *n.* **1** [Mental impression] concept, conception, perception; see IDEA 1, THOUGHT 2. **2** [Representation] effigy, form, drawing, model, illustration, portrait, photograph, reproduction, copy, likeness, facsimile, counterpart, replica; see also PICTURE 2.

imagery *n.* illustration, metaphor, representation; see COMPARISON.

imaginable *a.* conceivable, comprehensible, credible, thinkable, possible, plausible, believable, reasonable, feasible; see also LIKELY 1.—*Ant.* UNBELIEVABLE, unimaginable, inconceivable.

imaginary *a.* fancied, illusory, visionary, shadowy, dreamy, dreamlike, hypothetical, theoretical, deceptive, imagined, hallucinatory, whimsical, fabulous, nonexistent, apocryphal, fantastic, mythological, fictitious, legendary, imaginative; see also UNREAL.—*Ant.* REAL, factual, existing.

imagination *n.* intelligence, wit, thoughtfulness, inventiveness, conception, mental agility, sensitivity, fancy, visualization, realization, cognition, awareness, dramatization, insight; see also MIND 1.

imaginative *a.* creative, inventive, resourceful; see ARTISTIC, ORIGINAL 2.

imagine *v.* conceive, picture, conjure up, envisage, envision, see in one's mind, invent, fabricate, formulate,

devise, think of, make up, conceptualize, dream, dream up*, perceive, dramatize, create.

imagined *a.* not real, insubstantial, thought-up; see FALSE 1, 2, 3, IMAGINARY.

imbalance *n.* lack of balance, disproportion, inequality; see IRREGULARITY.

imbibe *v.* ingest, sip, guzzle; see DRINK 1, SWALLOW.

imitate *v.* **1** [To mimic] impersonate, mirror, copy, mime, ape, simulate, duplicate, act, repeat, echo, parody, emulate, do like*, reflect, pretend, play a part, take off*. **2** [To copy] duplicate, counterfeit, falsify; see COPY, REPRODUCE 2. **3** [To resemble] be like, simulate, parallel; see RESEMBLE.

imitated *a.* copied, duplicated, mimicked, mocked, aped, counterfeited, caricatured, parodied.

imitation *a.* copied, feigned, bogus; see FALSE 3.

imitation *n.* **1** [The act of imitating] simulation, counterfeiting, copying, duplication, patterning after, picturing, representing, mimicry, aping, impersonation, echoing, matching, mirroring, paralleling; see also COPY. **2** [An object made by imitating] counterfeit, imitation, sham, fake, picture, replica, echo, reflection, match, parallel, resemblance, transcription, image, mockery, take-off*, caricature, parody, satire, substitution, forgery; see also COPY.—*Ant.* ORIGINAL, novelty, pattern.

imitative *a.* forged, sham, deceptive; see FALSE 2, 3.

imitator *n.* follower, copier, impersonator, mime, mimic, pretender, counterfeiter, forger, copycat.

immaculate *a.* unsullied, spotless, stainless; see BRIGHT 1, CLEAN 1.

immature *a.* youthful, sophomoric, half-grown; see NAIVE.

immaturity *n.* imperfection, incompleteness, childlike behavior; see INSTABILITY.

immediate *a.* instant, instantaneous, quick, direct, fast, on the moment, at this moment, at the present time, next, prompt; see also FOLLOWING.—*Ant.* SOMEDAY, later, any time.

immediately *a.* at once, without delay, instantly, directly, right away, at the first opportunity, at short notice, now, this instant, speedily, quickly, promptly, on the spot, on the dot, rapidly, instantaneously, shortly, on the double*, in a jiffy*; see also URGENTLY.—*Ant.* LATER, in the future, in a while.

immense *a.* gigantic, tremendous, enormous; see LARGE 1.

immensity *n*. infinity, vastness, greatness; see EXTENT.

immerse *v*. submerge, dip, douse, plunge, sink, cover with water, drown, bathe, steep, drench, dunk, souse; see also SOAK 1.

immersed *a*. drowned, plunged, bathed; see DIPPED, SOAKED, WET 1.

immigrant *n*. newcomer, naturalized citizen, adoptive citizen; see ALIEN, EMIGRANT.

immigrate *v*. migrate, resettle, seek political asylum; see ENTER.

immigration *n*. colonization, settlement, migration; see ENTRANCE 1.

imminent *a*. approaching, in store, about to happen; see COMING 1, DESTINED.

immodest *a*. brazen, shameless, bold; see EGOTISTIC, RUDE 2.

immoral *a*. sinful, corrupt, shameless; see BAD 1.

immorality *n*. vice, depravity, dissoluteness; see EVIL 1.

immorally *a*. sinfully, wickedly, unrighteously; see WRONGLY.

immortal *a*. **1** [Deathless] undying, permanent, imperishable, endless, timeless, everlasting, death-defying, unfading, never-ending, perennial, constant, ceaseless, indestructible, enduring; see also ETERNAL.—*Ant.* MORTAL, perishable, corrupt. **2** [Illustrious] celebrated, eminent, glorious; see FAMOUS.

immortality *n*. deathlessness, everlasting life, permanence, endlessness, timelessness, divinity, indestructibility, continuity, perpetuation, endless life, unlimited existence, perpetuity; see also ETERNITY.—*Ant.* DEATH, mortality, decease.

immovable *a*. solid, stable, fixed; see FIRM 1.

immune *a*. free, unaffected by, hardened to, unsusceptible, privileged, not liable, excused; see also SAFE 1.

immunity *n*. **1** [Exemption] favor, privilege, license; see FREEDOM 2. **2** [Freedom from disease] resistance, immunization, protection, active immunity, passive immunity; see also SAFETY 1.

impact *n*. shock, impression, contact; see COLLISION.

impair *v*. spoil, injure, hurt; see BREAK 2, DAMAGE, DESTROY.

impart *v*. **1** [To give] bestow, grant, present; see ALLOW, GIVE 1. **2** [To make known] tell, announce, divulge; see ADMIT 2, REVEAL.

impartial *a*. unbiased, unprejudiced, disinterested; see EQUAL, FAIR 1.

impartiality *n*. objectivity, candor, justice; see EQUALITY, FAIRNESS.

impasse *n*. deadlock, standstill, cessation; see PAUSE.

impatience *n*. agitation, restlessness, anxiety; see EXCITEMENT, NERVOUSNESS.

impatient *a*. anxious, eager, feverish; see RESTLESS.

impeach *v*. criticize, charge, arraign, denounce, indict, discredit, reprimand, accuse, incriminate, try, bring charges against, question; see also BLAME.—*Ant.* FREE, acquit, absolve.

impediment *n*. **1** [An obstruction] hindrance, obstacle, difficulty; see BARRIER. **2** [An obstruction in speech] speech impediment, speech difficulty, stutter, stammer, lisp, halting, cleft palate.

impending *a*. in the offing, threatening, menacing; see OMINOUS.

impenetrable *a*. **1** [Dense] impervious, hard, compact; see FIRM 2, THICK 3. **2** [Incomprehensible] unintelligible, inscrutable, unfathomable; see OBSCURE 1.

imperative *a*. **1** [Necessary] inescapable, compelling, crucial; see IMPORTANT 1, NECESSARY, URGENT 1. **2** [Authoritative] masterful, commanding, dominant; see AGGRESSIVE, POWERFUL 1.

imperfect *a*. flawed, incomplete, deficient; see FAULTY.

imperfection *n*. fault, flaw, stain; see BLEMISH.

imperialism *n*. empire, international domination, power politics; see POWER 2.

impersonal *a*. detached, disinterested, cold; see INDIFFERENT.

impersonate *v*. mimic, portray, act out, pose as, pass for, double for, put on an act, pretend to be, act the part of, take the part of, act a part, dress as, represent; see also IMITATE 1.

impersonation *n*. imitation, role, enactment; see PERFORMANCE.

impertinence *n*. impudence, insolence, disrespect; see RUDENESS.

impertinent *a*. saucy, insolent, impudent; see RUDE 2.

impervious *a*. impenetrable, watertight, sealed; see TIGHT 2.

impetus *n*. force, cause, stimulus; see INCENTIVE, PURPOSE 1, REASON 3.

impious *a*. sinful, profane, blasphemous; see BAD 1.

implant *v*. stick in, insert, root; see PLANT.

implement *n*. utensil, instrument, device; see EQUIPMENT, MACHINE, TOOL 1.

implicate *v*. connect, cite, associate, tie up with, charge, link, catch up in, relate, compromise; see also BLAME.

implicated *a.* under suspicion, suspected, suspected, known to have been involved; see GUILTY, INVOLVED, SUSPICIOUS 1, 2.

implication *n.* **1** [Assumption] hint, indication, suggestion; see ASSUMPTION 1, GUESS. **2** [A link] connection, involvement, entanglement; see JOINT 1, LINK, UNION 1.

implicit *a.* unquestionable, certain, absolute; see DEFINITE 1, INEVITABLE.

implied *a.* implicit, indicated, foreshadowed, involved, tacit, signified, figured, intended, meant, alluded to, latent, hidden, insinuated, hinted at, understood, symbolized, potential, indirectly meant, undeclared; see also SUGGESTED.

imply *v.* **1** [To indicate] intimate, hint at, suggest; see HINT, MENTION, REFER 2. **2** [To mean] import, indicate, signify; see INTEND 2, MEAN 1.

impolite *a.* discourteous, moody, churlish; see IRRITABLE, RUDE 2, SULLEN.

import *v.* introduce, bring in, buy abroad; see CARRY 1, SEND 1.

importance *n.* import, force, consequence, bearing, denotation, gist, effect, distinction, influence, usefulness, moment, weightiness, momentousness, emphasis, standing, stress, accent, weight, concern, attention, interest, seriousness, point, substance, relevance, sum and substance; see also MEANING.— *Ant.* INSIGNIFICANCE, triviality, emptiness.

important *a.* **1** [Weighty; *said usually of things*] significant, considerable, momentous, essential, great, decisive, critical, major, chief, paramount, primary, foremost, principal, influential, marked, of great consequence, ponderous, of importance, never to be overlooked, of note, valuable, crucial, substantial, vital, serious, grave, relevant, pressing, far-reaching, extensive, conspicuous, heavy, big-league*, big; see also NECESSARY.—*Ant.* TRIVIAL, inconsequential, unimportant. **2** [Eminent; *said usually of persons*] illustrious, well-known, influential; see FAMOUS. **3** [Relevant] material, influential, significant; see FIT 1, RELATED 2, RELEVANT.

imported *a.* shipped in, produced abroad, exotic, alien; see also FOREIGN.—*Ant.* NATIVE, domestic, made in America.

impose *v.* force upon, inflict, foist; see FORCE. —**impose on** (or **upon**) intrude, interrupt, presume; see BOTHER 2, DISTURB.

imposing *a.* stirring, exciting, overwhelming; see IMPRESSIVE.

imposition *n.* demand, restraint,

encumbrance; see COMMAND, PRESSURE 2.

impossibility *n.* hopelessness, impracticality, impracticability, difficulty, unworkability, unlikelihood, failure; see also FUTILITY.

impossible *a.* inconceivable, vain, unachievable, unattainable, out of the question, too much, insurmountable, useless, inaccessible, unworkable, preposterous, unimaginable, unobtainable, not to be thought of, hardly possible, like finding a needle in a haystack*, a hundred to one*; see also FUTILE, HOPELESS.— *Ant.* REASONABLE, possible, likely.

impostor *n.* pretender, charlatan, quack; see CHEAT.

impotence *n.* **1** [Sterility] unproductiveness, frigidity, infecundity; see EMPTINESS. **2** [Weakness] inability, feebleness, infirmity; see WEAKNESS 1.

impotent *a.* **1** [Weak] powerless, inept, infirm; see UNABLE, WEAK 1. **2** [Sterile] barren, frigid, unproductive; see STERILE 1.

impound *v.* appropriate, take, usurp; see SEIZE 2.

impounded *a.* kept, seized, confiscated; see HELD, RETAINED 1.

impoverish *v.* make poor, bankrupt, exhaust; see DESTROY.

impoverished *a.* poverty-stricken, bankrupt, broke*; see POOR 1, RUINED 3.

impractical *a.* unreal, unrealistic, unworkable, improbable, illogical, unreasonable, absurd, wild, abstract, impossible, idealistic, unfeasible, out of the question.— *Ant.* PRACTICAL, logical, reasonable.

impregnate *v.* **1** [To permeate] fill up, pervade, overflow; see FILL 2, SOAK 1. **2** [To beget] procreate, inseminate, reproduce; see FERTILIZE 2.

impregnated *a.* **1** [Full] saturated, shot through, full of; see FULL 1. **2** [Pregnant] expecting*, in a family way*, with child; see PREGNANT.

impress *v.* **1** [To make an impression] indent, emboss, imprint; see DENT, MARK 1, PRINT 2. **2** [To attract attention] stand out, be conspicuous, cause a stir, create an impression, make an impression on, direct attention to, make an impact upon, engage the thoughts of, engage the attention of, be listened to, find favor with, make a hit*, make a dent in; see also FASCINATE.

impressed *a.* aroused, awakened, awed; see AFFECTED 1, EXCITED.

impression *n.* **1** [An imprint] print, footprint, fingerprint, dent, mold, indentation, depression, cast, form, track, pattern; see also MARK 1. **2**

[An effect] response, consequence, reaction; see RESULT. **3** [A notion based on scanty evidence] theory, conjecture, supposition; see GUESS, OPINION 1.

impressionable *a.* susceptible, suggestible, receptive; see AFFECTED 1.

impressive *a.* stirring, moving, inspiring, effective, affecting, eloquent, impassioned, thrilling, exciting, intense, well-done, dramatic, absorbing, deep, profound, penetrating, remarkable, extraordinary, notable, important, momentous, vital; see also PROFOUND.—*Ant.* DULL, uninteresting, common.

imprint *n.* **1** [A printed identification] firm name, banner, trademark, heading; see also EMBLEM, SIGNATURE. **2** [An impression] dent, indentation, print; see MARK 1.

imprint *v.* print, stamp, designate; see MARK 1, 2.

imprison *v.* jail, lock up, confine, incarcerate, immure, impound, detain, keep in, hold, intern, shut in, lock in, box in, fence in, cage, send to prison, keep as captive, hold captive, hold hostage, enclose, keep in custody, put behind bars, put away*.—*Ant.* FREE, liberate, release.

imprisoned *a.* arrested, jailed, incarcerated; see CONFINED 3.

imprisonment *n.* captivity, isolation, incarceration, duress, bondage; see also CONFINEMENT.—*Ant.* FREEDOM, liberty, emancipation.

improbable *a.* not likely, doubtful, not to be expected; see UNLIKELY.

improper *a.* ill-advised, unsuited, incongruous, out of place, ludicrous, incorrect, preposterous, unwarranted, undue, imprudent, abnormal, irregular, inexpedient, unseasonable, inadvisable, untimely, inopportune, unfit, malapropos, unfitting, inappropriate, unbefitting, ill-timed, awkward, inharmonious, inapplicable, odd; see also UNSUITABLE.

improperly *a.* poorly, inappropriately, clumsily; see AWKWARDLY, BADLY 1, INADEQUATELY.

improve *v.* **1** [To make better] mend, update, refine; see CHANGE 1, REPAIR. **2** [To become better] regenerate, advance, progress, renew, augment, gain strength, develop, get better, grow better, grow, make progress, widen, increase, mellow, mature, come along, get on, look up, shape up*, pick up, perk up, come around, make headway, snap out of*; see also CHANGE 2, RECOVER 3.—*Ant.* WEAKEN, worsen, grow worse. —**improve on** (or **upon**) make better, develop, refine; see CORRECT, REPAIR.

improved *a.* corrected, bettered, amended, mended, reformed, elaborated, refined, modernized, brought up-to-date, enhanced, repaired, bolstered, rectified, remodeled, reorganized, made over, better for, doctored up*, polished up*; see also CHANGED 2.

improvement *n.* **1** [The process of becoming better] amelioration, betterment, rectification, change, alteration, reformation, progression, advance, advancement, development, growth, rise, civilization, gain, cultivation, increase, enrichment, promotion, elevation, regeneration, recovery, renovation, reorganization, amendment, reform, revision, elaboration, refinement, modernization, enhancement, remodeling.—*Ant.* DECAY, deterioration, retrogression. **2** [That which has been improved] addition, supplement, repair, extra, attachment, correction, reform, remodeling, refinement, luxury, advance, latest thing, last word*; see also CHANGE 1.

improving *a.* reconstructing, repairing, elaborating, bettering, correcting, developing, remodeling, fixing, on the mend.

impudence *n.* insolence, impertinence, effrontery; see RUDENESS.

impudent *a.* forward, insolent, shameless; see RUDE 2.

impugn *v.* question, attack, challenge, call into question, contradict, assail, knock*; see also DOUBT.

impulse *n.* **1** [A throb] surge, pulse, pulsation; see BEAT 1. **2** [A sudden urge] fancy, whim, caprice, motive, motivation, spontaneity, drive, appeal, notion, inclination, disposition, wish, whimsy, inspiration, hunch, flash, thought.

impulsive *a.* offhand, unpremeditated, extemporaneous; see AUTOMATIC, SPONTANEOUS.

impulsively *a.* imprudently, hastily, abruptly; see CARELESSLY, RASHLY.

impure *a.* **1** [Adulterated] not pure, loaded, weighted, salted, diluted, debased, contaminated, mixed, watered down, polluted, corrupted, tainted, cut, adulterated, doctored*, tampered with; see also UNCLEAN. **2** [Not chaste] unclean, unchaste, corrupt; see BAD 1, LEWD 2.

impurity *n.* **1** [Lewdness] indecency, profligacy, pornography; see LEWDNESS. **2** [Filth] dirt, defilement, excrement; see FILTH, POLLUTION.

in *prep.* **1** [Within] surrounded by, in the midst of, within the boundaries of, in the area of, within the time of, concerning the subject of, as a part of, inside, inside of, enclosed in, not out of; see also WITHIN. **2** [Into] to the center of, to the midst of, in the direction of, within the extent of, under, near, against; see also INTO,

TOWARD. **3** [While engaged in] in the act of, during the process of, while occupied with; see DURING, MEANWHILE, WHILE 1. **—have it in for*** wish to harm, be out to destroy, detest; see HATE 1.

inability *n.* **1** [Lack of competence] incapacity, incompetence, shortcoming; see FAILURE 1, WEAKNESS 1. **2** [A temporary lack] disability, failure, frailty; see LACK 2, NECESSITY 2.

inaccessible *a.* unobtainable, out of reach, unworkable; see AWAY, BEYOND, DIFFICULT 2, DISTANT, RARE 2, REMOTE 1, SEPARATED.

inaccuracy *n.* exaggeration, mistake, deception; see ERROR.

inaccurate *a.* fallacious, in error, incorrect; see MISTAKEN 1, WRONG 2.

inactive *a.* dormant, stable, still; see IDLE, MOTIONLESS 1.

inadequacy *n.* **1** [Inferiority] ineptitude, incompetence, insufficiency; see WEAKNESS 1. **2** [A defect] flaw, drawback, shortcoming; see BLEMISH, DEFECT, LACK 2.

inadequate *a.* lacking, scanty, short, insufficient, meager, failing, unequal, not enough, sparing, stinted, stunted, feeble, sparse, too little, small, thin, deficient, incomplete, inconsiderable, spare, bare, niggardly, miserly, scarce, barren, depleted, low, weak, impotent, unproductive, sterile, imperfect, defective, lame, skimpy*; see also UNSATISFACTORY.—*Ant.* ENOUGH, adequate, sufficient.

inadequately *a.* insufficiently, not enough, partly, partially, incompletely, scantily, deficiently, perfunctorily, ineffectively, inefficiently, ineptly, not up to standards, not up to specifications, not up to requirements, meagerly, not in sufficient quantity, not of sufficient quality, to a limited degree, below par, not up to snuff*; see also BADLY 1.

inadvisable *a.* unsuitable, inappropriate, inconvenient; see IMPROPER, WRONG 2.

inane *a.* pointless, foolish, ridiculous; see ILLOGICAL, SILLY, STUPID.

inanimate *a.* dull, inert, inoperative; see IDLE, MOTIONLESS 1.

inappropriate *a.* improper, irrelevant, inapplicable; see UNSUITABLE.

inarticulate *a.* **1** [Mute] reticent, wordless, mute; see DUMB 1. **2** [Indistinct] unintelligible, inaudible, vague; see OBSCURE 1.

inasmuch as *conj.* in view of, the fact that, seeing that, while; see also BECAUSE, SINCE 1.

inattentive *a.* indifferent, preoccupied, negligent; see CARELESS, DIVERTED.

inaudible *a.* low, indistinct, silent; see OBSCURE 1, VAGUE.

inaugurate *v.* introduce, initiate, originate; see BEGIN 1.

inauguration *n.* initiation, commencement, introduction; see INSTALLATION 1.

inborn *a.* innate, intrinsic, inbred; see NATIVE 1.

inbred *a.* innate, inborn, ingrained; see NATIVE 1.

incalculable *a.* unpredictable, unforeseen, unfixed; see UNCERTAIN.

incandescent *a.* radiant, glowing, brilliant; see BRIGHT 1.

incapable *a.* unsuited, poor, inadequate; see INCOMPETENT, INEXPERIENCED, NAIVE.

incapacity *n.* inadequacy, insufficiency, inability; see WEAKNESS 1.

incense *n.* scent, fragrance, essence; see PERFUME.

incentive *n.* spur, inducement, motive, stimulus, stimulation, impetus, provocation, enticement, temptation, bait, consideration, excuse, rationale, urge, influence, lure, persuasion, inspiration, encouragement, insistence, instigation, incitement, reason why; see also PURPOSE 1.

incessant *a.* ceaseless, continuous, monotonous; see CONSTANT.

incessantly *a.* steadily, monotonously, perpetually; see REGULARLY.

inch *n.* **1** [Twelfth of a foot] fingerbreadth, 2.54 centimeters, 1/36 yard; see MEASURE 1. **2** [Small degree] jot, little bit, iota; see BIT 2. **—by inches** slowly, by degrees, step by step; see GRADUALLY. **—every inch** in all respects, thoroughly, entirely; see COMPLETELY.

inch *v.* creep, barely move, make some progress; see CRAWL.

inchoate *a.* incipient, rudimentary, preliminary, beginning; see also UNFINISHED 1.

incident *n.* episode, happening, occurrence; see EVENT.

incidental *a.* subsidiary, relative to, contributing to; see RELATED 2, SUBORDINATE.

incidentally *a.* subordinately, by chance, by the way, as a side effect, as a byproduct, unexpectedly, not by design, remotely; see also ACCIDENTALLY.

incidentals *n.* minor needs, incidental expenses, per diem; see EXPENSES, NECESSITY 2.

incinerate *v.* cremate, parch, burn up; see BURN.

incise *v.* engrave, chisel, carve; see CUT 1.

incision *n.* gash, slash, surgery; see CUT 1, HOLE 1.

incite v. arouse, rouse, impel, stimulate, instigate, provoke, excite, spur, goad, persuade, influence, induce, taunt, activate, animate, inspirit, coax, stir up, motivate, prompt, urge on, inspire, force, work up*, talk into*, egg on, fan the flame*; see also URGE 2.—Ant. DISCOURAGE, dissuade, check.

incited a. driven, pushed, motivated; see URGED 1.

inclination n. 1 [A tendency] bias, bent, propensity, predilection, penchant, attachment, capability, capacity, aptness, leaning, fondness, disposition, liking, preference, movement, susceptibility, weakness, drift, trend, turn, slant, impulse, attraction, affection, desire, temperament, whim, idiosyncrasy, urge, persuasion. 2 [A slant] pitch, slope, incline, angle, ramp, bank, list; see also GRADE 1.

incline n. slope, inclined plane, approach; see GRADE 1, INCLINATION 2.

incline v. 1 [To lean] bow, nod, bend; see LEAN 1. 2 [To tend toward] prefer, be disposed, be predisposed; see FAVOR.

inclined a. prone, tending, willing; see LIKELY 4.

include v. 1 [To contain] hold, admit, cover, embrace, involve, consist of, take in, entail, incorporate, constitute, accommodate, comprise, be comprised of*, be composed of, embody, be made up of, number among, carry, bear; see also COMPOSE 1.—Ant. BAR, omit, stand outside of. 2 [To place into or among] enter, introduce, take in, incorporate, make room for, build in, work in, inject, interject, add on, insert, combine, make a part of, make allowance for, give consideration to, count in.—Ant. DISCARD, exclude, reject.

included a. counted, numbered, admitted, covered, involved, constituted, embodied, inserted, entered, incorporated, combined, placed, fused, merged; see also WITHIN.—Ant. REFUSED, excluded, left out.

including a. together with, along with, as well as, in conjunction with, not to mention, to say nothing of, among other things, with the addition of, in addition to, comprising, containing, counting, made up of, incorporating.—Ant. BESIDES, not counting, aside from.

incoherence n. unintelligibility, dissimilarity, incongruity; see INCONSISTENCY.

incoherent a. mumbling, stammering, confused, speechless, puzzling, indistinct, faltering, stuttering, unintelligible, muttered, mumbled,

jumbled, gasping, breathless, tongue-tied, muffled, indistinguishable, incomprehensible, disconnected, muddled.—Ant. CLEAR, eloquent, distinct.

incoherently a. inarticulately, unclearly, illogically, drunkenly, confusedly, chaotically, randomly, ineptly, unsystematically, aimlessly, casually, sloppily, ambiguously, equivocally, illegibly, incomprehensibly, unrecognizably, uncertainly, inaudibly; see also WILDLY.

income n. earnings, salary, wages, returns, profit, dividends, assets, proceeds, benefits, receipts, gains, commission, rent, royalty, honorarium, net income, gross income, taxable income, cash, take; see also PAY 2.—Ant. EXPENSE, expenditures, outgo.

incomparable a. unequaled, exceptional, superior; see EXCELLENT, PERFECT.

incompatibility n. variance, conflict, animosity; see DISAGREEMENT 1.

incompatible a. inconsistent, contrary, clashing, inappropriate, contradictory, disagreeing, inconstant, unadapted, opposite, jarring, discordant, incoherent, inadmissible; see also OPPOSED, UNSUITABLE.

incompetence n. inadequacy, inexperience, ineptitude; see WEAKNESS 1.

incompetent a. incapable, inefficient, unskillful, not qualified, inadequate, unfit, unskilled, bungling, inexpert, ineffectual, unsuitable, untrained, raw, green, inexperienced, not equal to, amateurish; see also UNABLE.—Ant. ABLE, fit, qualified.

incomplete a. rough, half-done, under construction; see UNFINISHED 1.

inconceivable a. unimaginable, fantastic, incredible; see IMPOSSIBLE.

inconclusive a. indecisive, unresolved, unsettled; see INADEQUATE, UNSATISFACTORY.

incongruous a. uncoordinated, unconnected, contradictory; see ILLOGICAL, UNSUITABLE.

inconsequential a. unimportant, immaterial, insignificant; see IRRELEVANT, TRIVIAL, UNNECESSARY.

inconsiderate a. boorish, impolite, discourteous; see RUDE 2, THOUGHTLESS 2.

inconsistency n. discrepancy, disagreement, dissimilarity, disparity, variance, incongruity, inequality, divergence, deviation, disproportion, paradox; see also DIFFERENCE 1.—Ant. SIMILARITY, consistency, congruity.

inconsistent a. contradictory, illogical, incoherent; see ILLOGICAL.

inconspicuous a. concealed, indistinct, retiring; see HIDDEN, OBSCURE 1, 3, SECRETIVE.

inconspicuously *a.* secretly, surreptitiously, not openly; see SLYLY.

inconvenience *n.* bother, trouble, awkward detail; see DIFFICULTY 1.

inconvenient *a.* bothersome, awkward, badly arranged; see DISTURBING.

incorporate *v.* add, combine, fuse; see INCLUDE 2, JOIN 1.

incorporated *a.* entered, placed, fused; see INCLUDED, JOINED.

incorporation *n.* embodiment, adding, fusion; see ADDITION 1.

incorrect *a.* inaccurate, not trustworthy, false; see MISTAKEN 1, UNRELIABLE, WRONG 2.

incorrectly *a.* mistakenly, inaccurately, clumsily; see BADLY 1, WRONGLY.

increase *n.* development, spread, enlargement, expansion, escalation, elaboration, swelling, addition, incorporation, inflation, extension, heightening, dilation, multiplication, rise, broadening, advance, intensification, deepening, swell, amplification, progression, improvement, boost, hike*, jump, boom; see also PROGRESS 1.—*Ant.* REDUCTION, decline, decrease. —**on the increase** growing, developing, spreading; see INCREASING.

increase *v.* extend, enlarge, expand, dilate, broaden, widen, thicken, deepen, heighten, build, lengthen, magnify, add on to, augment, escalate, let out, branch out, further, mark up, sharpen, build up, raise, enhance, amplify, reinforce, supplement, annex, double, triple, stretch, multiply, intensify, exaggerate, prolong, redouble, boost, step up, rev up*.—*Ant.* DECREASE, reduce, abridge.

increased *a.* marked up, raised, heightened, elevated, added on to, doubled.

increasing *a.* developing, maturing, multiplying, broadening, widening, intensifying, heightening, growing, dominant, advancing, growing louder, sharpening, accentuating, aggravating, emphasizing, accelerating, deepening, flourishing, rising, expanding, enlarging, accumulating, piling up, shooting up, getting big, swelling, on the rise, on the increase, booming; see also GROWING.

increasingly *a.* with continuing acceleration, more and more, with steady increase; see MORE 1, 2.

incredible *a.* unbelievable, improbable, ridiculous; see IMPOSSIBLE.

incriminate *v.* implicate, blame, charge; see IMPLICATE.

incriminating *a.* damning, damaging, accusatory; see SUSPICIOUS 2.

inculcate *v.* instill, implant, impress upon; see TEACH.

incurable *a.* fatal, serious, hopeless; see DEADLY.

indebted *a.* obligated, grateful, appreciative; see RESPONSIBLE 1, THANKFUL.

indebtedness *n.* deficit, responsibility, obligation; see DEBT.

indecency *n.* impurity, immodesty, vulgarity, impropriety, obscenity, raciness, four-letter word, lewdness, foulness; see also EVIL 1.—*Ant.* CHASTITY, purity, delicacy.

indecent *a.* immoral, shocking, shameless; see BAD 1, LEWD 2, SHAMEFUL 1, 2.

indecision *n.* hesitation, question, irresolution; see DOUBT, UNCERTAINTY 2.

indecisive *a.* irresolute, unstable, wishy-washy*; see DOUBTFUL.

indeed *a.* in fact, of course, certainly; see REALLY 1, SURELY.

indeed *interj.* really?, honestly?, is that so?; see OH.

indefensible *a.* bad, unforgivable, unpardonable; see WRONG 1.

indefinite *a.* unsure, unsettled, loose; see UNCERTAIN, VAGUE 2.

indefinitely *a.* **1** [Vaguely] loosely, unclearly, ambiguously, indistinctly, incoherently, obscurely, indecisively, incompletely, lightly, briefly, momentarily, generally; see also VAGUELY.—*Ant.* POSITIVELY, clearly, exactly. **2** [Without stated limit] endlessly, continually, considerably; see FREQUENTLY, REGULARLY.

indelible *a.* ingrained, enduring, strong; see PERMANENT.

indent *v.* make a margin, paragraph, space inward; see ORDER 3.

indentation *n.* imprint, recession, depression; see DENT.

independence *n.* sovereignty, autonomy, license; see FREEDOM 1, 2.

independent *a.* self-ruling, autonomous, sovereign; see FREE 1.

independently *a.* alone, autonomously, unilaterally, without support, separately, exclusively, individually, by oneself, on one's own*; see also FREELY 2.

indestructible *a.* unchangeable, durable, immortal; see PERMANENT.

index *n.* **1** [An indicator] formula, rule, average; see MODEL 2. **2** [An alphabetical arrangement] tabular matter, book index, guide to publications, bibliography, contents, catalog, card file, book list, appendix, end list, directory, dictionary; see also FILE 1, LIST, RECORD 1.

index v. alphabetize, arrange, tabulate; see FILE 1, LIST 1, RECORD 1.

Indian a. Native American, pre-Columbian, Amerindian; see INDIAN, n. 1.

Indian n. 1 [An indigenous person of the Americas] Native American, American aborigine, American Indian, red man*. *Terms for Indian groups having had historical or social importance include the following—United States and Canada: Arctic Indians:* Eskimo, Inuit, Aleut; *Eastern Woodlands Indians:* Iroquois or Six Nations, Mohawk, Oneida, Onondaga, Tuscarora, Seneca, Cayuga, Huron, Algonquin, Mahican, Delaware, Ojibwa or Chippewa, Sauk, Fox, Potawatomi, Seminole, Cherokee, Choctaw, Chickasaw, Creek, Natchez, Winnebago; *Plains Indians:* Sioux or Dakota, Oglala, Mandan, Iowa, Omaha, Comanche, Crow, Osage, Kiowa, Arapaho, Cheyenne, Pawnee, Blackfoot; *Great Basin Indians:* Ute, Paiute, Shoshone, Bannock; *West Coast Indians:* Athabascan, Costanoan, Chinook, Nez Percé, Tlingit, Flathead, Kwakiutl, Bella Coola, Klamath, Luiseño, Pomo; *Southwest Indians:* Navajo, Apache, Hopi, Pueblo, Zuni; *Mexico and Central America:* Maya, Aztec, Toltec, Nahuatl; *South America:* Inca, Quechua, Carib, Tupí, Arawak. 2 [A native of India] South Asian, Asian Indian, Dravidian, Hindu, Muslim, Buddhist, Jain, Sikh.

indicate v. 1 [To signify] symbolize, betoken, intimate; see MEAN 1. 2 [To designate] show, point to, register; see NAME 2.

indication n. evidence, sign, implication; see HINT, SUGGESTION 1.

indicator n. notice, pointer, symbol; see SIGN 1.

indict v. charge, face with charges, arraign; see BLAME.

indictment n. detention, censure, incrimination; see BLAME.

indifference n. unconcern, nonchalance, aloofness, coldness, insensitivity, callousness, alienation, disregard, neutrality, isolationism, heedlessness, detachment, dullness, sluggishness, stupor, coldbloodedness, disdain, cool*.

indifferent a. listless, cold, cool, unemotional, unsympathetic, heartless, unresponsive, unfeeling, uncommunicative, nonchalant, impassive, detached, callous, uninterested, stony, reticent, remote, reserved, distant, unsocial, scornful, apathetic, heedless, unmoved, not inclined toward, neutral, uncaring, aloof, silent, disdainful, haughty, condescending, arrogant, not caring about; see also UNMOVED 2.—*Ant.* EXCITED, aroused, warm.

indifferently a. 1 [Rather badly] poorly, not very well done, in a mediocre manner; see BADLY 1, INADEQUATELY. 2 [In an indifferent manner] nonchalantly, coolly, detachedly; see CALMLY.

indigestible a. inedible, rough, hard, unripe, green, tasteless, unhealthy, unhealthful, putrid, heavy, unwholesome, undercooked, raw, poisonous, toxic, moldy, bad-smelling, rotten, uneatable, icky*.—*Ant.* DELICIOUS, appetizing, tasty.

indigestion n. heartburn, nausea, acid indigestion; see ILLNESS 1, PAIN 2.

indignant a. upset, displeased, piqued; see ANGRY.

indirect a. roundabout, out-of-the-way, tortuous, twisting, long, complicated, devious, erratic, sidelong, zigzag, crooked, backhanded, obscure, sinister, rambling, long-winded, secondary, implied, oblique.—*Ant.* DIRECT, straight, immediate.

indirectly a. by implication, by indirection, in a roundabout way, secondhand, from a secondary source, not immediately, discursively, obliquely.—*Ant.* IMMEDIATELY, primarily, directly.

indiscreet a. naive, inopportune, misguided; see RASH, TACTLESS.

indiscretion n. recklessness, tactlessness, rashness; see CARELESSNESS.

indiscriminate a. random, confused, chaotic; see AIMLESS.

indispensable a. required, needed, essential; see NECESSARY.

indisputable a. undoubted, undeniable, unquestionable; see CERTAIN 2.

indistinct a. vague, confused, indefinite; see OBSCURE 1.

indistinguishable a. 1 [Identical] like, same, equivalent; see ALIKE, EQUAL. 2 [Indistinct] vague, invisible, dull; see OBSCURE 1, UNCERTAIN.

individual a. specific, personal, special, proper, own, particular, definite, lone, alone, solitary, original, distinct, distinctive, personalized, individualized, exclusive, select, single, only, reserved, separate, sole; see also PRIVATE, SPECIAL.—*Ant.* PUBLIC, collective, social.

individual n. human being, self, somebody; see CHILD, MAN 2, PERSON 1, WOMAN 1.

individuality n. personality, distinctiveness, particularity, separateness, dissimilarity, singularity, air, manner, habit, eccentricity, way of doing things; see also ORIGINALITY.

individually a. separately, severally,

one by one, one at a time, personally, exclusively, singly, by oneself, alone, independently, without help, distinctively, apart; see also ONLY 1.—*Ant*. TOGETHER, collectively, cooperatively.

indoctrinate *v*. inculcate, imbue, implant; see CONVINCE, INFLUENCE, TEACH.

indoctrination *n*. propagandism, instruction, brainwashing; see EDUCATION 1, TRAINING.

indoors *a*. in the house, at home, under a roof; see INSIDE 2, WITHIN.

induce *v*. produce, effect, make; see BEGIN 1.

induced *a*. **1** [Brought about] effected, achieved, caused; see FINISHED 1. **2** [Inferred] thought, concluded, reasoned; see CONSIDERED, DETERMINED 1.

induct *v*. conscript, initiate, draft; see ENLIST 1, RECRUIT 1.

inducted *a*. conscripted, called up, drafted; see INITIATED 2.

induction *n*. **1** [Logical reasoning] inference, rationalization, conclusion, judgment, conjecture; see also REASON 2. **2** [The process of electrical attraction] electric induction, magnetic induction, electromagnetic action; see ELECTRICITY. **3** [The process of being initiated] initiation, introduction, ordination, consecration, entrance into service.

indulge *v*. **1** [To humor] pamper, spoil, coddle; see ENTERTAIN 1, HUMOR. **2** [To take part in] go in for, revel, give way to; see JOIN 2.

indulgence *n*. **1** [Humoring] coddling, pampering, petting, fondling, babying, spoiling, placating, pleasing, toadying, favoring, kowtowing, gratifying. **2** [Revelry] intemperance, overindulgence, self-indulgence; see GREED, WASTE 1.

indulgent *a*. fond, considerate, tolerant; see KIND.

industrial *a*. manufacturing, manufactured, mechanized, automated, industrialized, in industry, factory-made, machine-made, modern, streamlined, technical; see also MECHANICAL 1.—*Ant*. HOMEMADE, handmade, domestic.

industrious *a*. intent, involved, diligent; see ACTIVE, BUSY 1.

industriously *a*. diligently, energetically, busily; see CAREFULLY 1, VIGOROUSLY.

industry *n*. **1** [Attention to work] activity, persistence, application, patience, intentness, perseverance, enterprise, hard work, zeal, energy, dynamism, pains, inventiveness; see also ATTENTION.—*Ant*. LAZINESS, lethargy, idleness. **2** [Business as a division of society] big business, management, corporate officers, shareholders, high finance, entre-

preneurs, capital, private enterprise, monied interests, stockholders.

inebriated *a*. intoxicated, tipsy, plastered*; see DRUNK.

ineffective *a*. not effective, worthless, neutralized; see INCOMPETENT, WEAK 1, 2.

inefficiency *n*. incompetence, incapability, wastefulness; see FAILURE 1, WEAKNESS 1.

inefficient *a*. extravagant, prodigal, improvident; see WASTEFUL.

ineligible *a*. unsuitable, inappropriate, unavailable; see INCOMPETENT, UNFIT.

ineluctable *a*. certain, inescapable, unavoidable; see INEVITABLE.

inept *a*. clumsy, gauche, ungraceful; see AWKWARD.

inequality *n*. disparity, dissimilarity, irregularity; see CONTRAST, DIFFERENCE 1, VARIATION 2.

inert *a*. still, dormant, inactive; see IDLE.

inertia *n*. passivity, indolence, inactivity; see LAZINESS.

inevitable *a*. fated, sure, unavoidable, impending, inescapable, necessary, unpreventable, irresistible, destined, assured, unalterable, compulsory, obligatory, binding, irrevocable, inexorable, without fail, undeniable, fateful, doomed, determined, decreed, fixed, ordained, foreordained, decided, sure as shooting*, in the cards, come rain or shine*.—*Ant*. DOUBTFUL, contingent, indeterminate.

inevitably *a*. unavoidably, inescapably, surely; see NECESSARILY.

inexcusable *a*. unpardonable, reprehensible, indefensible; see WRONG 1.

inexpensive *a*. thrifty, low-priced, modest; see CHEAP 1, ECONOMICAL 2.

inexperience *n*. naiveté, inability, greenness; see IGNORANCE.

inexperienced *a*. unused to, unaccustomed, unadapted, unskilled, unlicensed, untried, youthful, undeveloped, naive, amateur, untrained, untutored, inefficient, fresh, ignorant, innocent, uninformed, unacquainted, undisciplined, new, immature, tender, wet behind the ears*, soft, raw, green.—*Ant*. EXPERIENCED, seasoned, hardened.

inexplicable *a*. unexplainable, incomprehensible, puzzling; see OBSCURE 1.

infallibility *n*. supremacy, impeccability, consummation; see PERFECTION.

infallible *a*. perfect, reliable, unquestionable; see ACCURATE 1, 2, CERTAIN 2.

infamous *a*. shocking, disgraceful,

heinous; see OFFENSIVE 2, SHAME-FUL 2.

infancy *n.* cradle, babyhood, early childhood; see CHILDHOOD.

infant *n.* small child, tot, little one; see BABY, CHILD.

infantile *a.* babyish, childlike, juvenile; see CHILDISH.

infantry *n.* foot soldiers, infantrymen, combat troops; see ARMY 1, 2.

infect *v.* defile, taint, spoil; see POISON.

infection *n.* 1 [The spread of disease] contagion, communicability, epidemic, taint, corruption; see also POLLUTION. 2 [Disease] virus, impurity, germs; see GERM.

infectious *a.* transferable, diseased, communicable; see CATCHING, CONTAGIOUS, DANGEROUS.

infer *v.* reason, gather, reach the conclusion that; see ASSUME, UNDERSTAND 1.

inference *n.* deduction, conclusion, answer; see JUDGMENT 3, RESULT.

inferior *a.* mediocre, common, second-rate; see POOR 2.

inferiority *n.* deficiency, mediocrity, inadequacy; see FAILURE 1, WEAKNESS 1.

infest *v.* 1 [To contaminate] pollute, infect, defile; see CORRUPT, DIRTY. 2 [To swarm] overrun, swarm about, crowd, press, harass, teem, fill, flood, throng, flock, be thick as flies*; see also SWARM.

infested *a.* 1 [Overrun] swarming with, full of, overwhelmed; see FULL 1. 2 [Diseased] wormy, having parasites, ill; see SICK.

infielder *n.* first baseman, second baseman, third baseman; see BASEBALL PLAYER.

infiltrate *v.* permeate, pervade, penetrate; see JOIN 2.

infinite *a.* incalculable, unbounded, boundless, unconfined, countless, interminable, measureless, inexhaustible, bottomless, without end, limitless, tremendous, immense, having no limit, never-ending, immeasurable; see also ENDLESS, UNLIMITED.—*Ant.* RESTRICTED, limited, bounded.

infinite *n.* boundlessness, infinity, the unknown; see ETERNITY, SPACE 1.

infinitely *a.* extremely, very much, unbelievably; see VERY.

infinity *n.* boundlessness, endlessness, the beyond, limitlessness, expanse, extent, continuum, continuity, eternity, infinite space; see also SPACE 1.

infirmary *n.* clinic, sickroom, sick bay; see HOSPITAL.

infirmity *n.* frailty, deficiency, debility; see WEAKNESS 1.

inflame *v.* 1 [To arouse emotions] incense, irritate, disturb; see EXCITE. 2 [To cause physical soreness] redden, chafe, swell; see HURT 1. 3 [To burn] kindle, set on fire, scorch; see BURN, IGNITE.

inflamed *a.* 1 [Stirred to anger] aroused, incited, angered; see ANGRY. 2 [Congested] raw, blistered, swollen; see HURT, PAINFUL 1, SORE 1.

inflammable *a.* flammable, combustible, burnable, liable to burn, risky, unsafe, hazardous, dangerous.—*Ant.* SAFE, fireproof, nonflammable.

inflammation *n.* congestion, soreness, infection; see PAIN 2, SORE.

inflate *v.* 1 [To fill with air or gas] pump up, expand, swell; see FILL 1. 2 [To increase] exaggerate, bloat, cram, expand, balloon, distend, swell up, widen, augment, spread out, enlarge, magnify, exalt, build up, raise, maximize, overestimate; see also STRETCH 1, SWELL.

inflated *a.* distended, swollen, extended, dilated, puffed, filled, grown, stretched, spread, enlarged, amplified, augmented, pumped up, exaggerated, bloated, crammed, magnified, overestimated, pompous, verbose.—*Ant.* REDUCED, deflated, minimized.

inflation *n.* 1 [Increase] expansion, extension, buildup; see INCREASE. 2 [General rise in price levels] financial crisis, boom, rising prices; see RISE 3.

inflection *n.* pronunciation, enunciation, intonation; see ACCENT, SOUND 2.

inflexibility *n.* stability, toughness, rigidity, stiffness, ossification, fossilization, solidity, crystallization; see also FIRMNESS.

inflexible *a.* rigid, hardened, taut; see FIRM 2, STIFF 1.

inflict *v.* deliver, strike, dispense; see CAUSE.

influence *n.* control, weight, authority, supremacy, command, domination, esteem, political influence, monopoly, rule, fame, prominence, prestige, character, reputation, force, importance, money, power behind the throne*, pull*, clout*; see also LEADERSHIP, POWER 2.

influence *v.* sway, affect, impress, carry weight, be influential, determine, make oneself felt, have influence over, lead to believe, bring pressure to bear, bribe, seduce, talk someone into, alter, change, act upon, act on, lead, brainwash, direct, modify, regulate, rule, compel, urge, incite, bias, prejudice, train, channel, mold, form, shape, exert influence, get at*, be recognized, induce, convince, cajole, persuade, motivate, have an in*, pull strings, have a finger in the pie*, lead by the nose*, fix*.

influenced *a.* changed, swayed, persuaded; see AFFECTED 1.

influential *a.* prominent, substantial, powerful; see FAMOUS.

influx *n.* introduction, penetration, coming in; see ENTRANCE 1.

inform *v.* instruct, apprise, teach; see TELL 1.

informal *a.* intimate, relaxed, frank, open, straightforward, ordinary, everyday, inconspicuous, habitual, free, extemporaneous, spontaneous, easygoing, unrestrained, unconventional; see also FRIENDLY.—*Ant.* RESTRAINED, ceremonial, ritualistic.

informality *n.* casualness, familiarity, ease; see COMFORT.

information *n.* **1** [Derived knowledge] acquired facts, evidence, knowledge, reports, details, results, notes, documents, testimony, facts, figures, statistics, measurements, conclusions, deductions, plans, field notes, lab notes, learning, erudition; see also KNOWLEDGE 1. **2** [News] report, notice, message; see NEWS 1, 2.

informative *a.* instructive, enlightening, accurate; see DETAILED.

infraction *n.* nonobservance, infringement, breach; see VIOLATION.

infrastructure *n.* foundation, basic structure, base; see FOUNDATION 2.

infrequent *a.* sparse, occasional, scarce; see RARE 2.

infrequently *a.* occasionally, rarely, hardly ever; see SELDOM.

infringe *v.* transgress, violate, trespass; see MEDDLE 1.

infuriate *v.* irritate, enrage, provoke; see ANGER.

infuriated *a.* furious, enraged, incensed; see ANGRY.

ingenious *a.* resourceful, skillful, gifted; see ABLE, INTELLIGENT.

ingenuity *n.* inventiveness, imagination, productiveness; see ORIGINALITY.

ingrained *a.* congenital, inborn, indelible; see NATIVE 1.

ingratitude *n.* disloyalty, ungratefulness, callousness, boorishness, lack of appreciation, inconsiderateness, thoughtlessness; see also RUDENESS.—*Ant.* GRATITUDE, appreciation, consideration.

ingredient *n.* constituent, component, element; see FUNDAMENTAL.

ingredients *n.* parts, elements, additives, constituents, pieces, components, makings, fixings*.

inhabit *v.* occupy, stay in, live in; see DWELL.

inhabitant *n.* occupant, dweller, settler, denizen, lodger, permanent resident, roomer, boarder, occupier, householder, addressee, inmate, tenant, settler, colonist, squatter, native; see also CITIZEN, RESIDENT.—*Ant.* ALIEN, transient, nonresident.

inhabited *a.* settled, owned, lived in, dwelt in, sustaining human life, peopled, occupied, colonized, developed, pioneered.

inhale *v.* breathe in, smell, sniff; see BREATHE.

inherent *a.* innate, inborn, inbred; see NATURAL 1, NATIVE 1.—*Ant.* SUPERFICIAL, incidental, extrinsic.

inherently *a.* naturally, intrinsically, by birth; see ESSENTIALLY.

inherit *v.* succeed to, acquire, receive, obtain, get one's inheritance, fall heir to, come into, come in for*, take over, receive an endowment; see also GET 1.—*Ant.* LOSE, be disowned, miss.

inheritance *n.* bequest, legacy, heritage; see GIFT 1.

inhibit *v.* repress, frustrate, hold back; see HINDER, RESTRAIN.

inhibition *n.* prevention, restraint, hindrance; see BARRIER, INTERFERENCE 1.

inhuman *a.* mean, heartless, coldblooded; see CRUEL, FIERCE, RUTHLESS.

inhumanity *n.* savagery, barbarity, brutality; see CRUELTY, EVIL 1, TYRANNY.

initial *a.* basic, primary, elementary; see FIRST, FUNDAMENTAL.

initially *a.* at first, in the beginning, originally; see FIRST.

initiate *v.* open, start, inaugurate; see BEGIN 1.

initiated *a.* **1** [Introduced into] sponsored, originated, entered, brought into, admitted, put into, instituted; see also PROPOSED. **2** [Having undergone initiation] installed, inducted, confirmed, grounded, instructed, approved, admitted, passed, made part of, made a member of, received, introduced, acknowledged, accepted, drafted, called up.

initiation *n.* baptism, induction, indoctrination; see INTRODUCTION 3.

initiative *n.* action, enterprise, first step; see RESPONSIBILITY 1.

inject *v.* inoculate, introduce, mainline*; see VACCINATE.

injection *n.* dose, vaccination, inoculation; see TREATMENT 2.

injure *v.* harm, damage, wound; see HURT 1.

injured *a.* spoiled, damaged, harmed; see HURT, WOUNDED.

injurious *a.* detrimental, damaging, bad; see DANGEROUS, DEADLY, HARMFUL, POISONOUS.

injury *n.* harm, sprain, damage, mutilation, blemish, cut, gash, twinge, contusion, puncture, break, scrape, scratch, stab, impairment, bite, fracture, hemorrhage, sting, bruise, sore, cramp, trauma, abrasion, burn, lesion, swelling, wound, scar, laceration, affliction, deformation; see also PAIN 1.

injustice *n.* wrongdoing, malpractice, offense, crime, villainy, injury, unfairness, miscarriage of justice, infringement, violation, abuse, criminal negligence, transgression, grievance, inequality, tort, outrage, maltreatment, bum rap*, breach, damage, infraction, a crying shame*; see also EVIL 1, WRONG.— *Ant.* RIGHT, just decision, fairness.

ink *n.* dye, paint, watercolor; see COLOR.

inkling *n.* indication, clue, suspicion; see HINT, SUGGESTION 1.

inland *a.* toward the interior, backcountry, backland, hinterland, interior, midland, provincial, domestic, inward; see also CENTRAL.—*Ant.* FOREIGN, international, outlying.

inmate *n.* patient, convict, captive; see PRISONER.

inn *n.* tavern, hostel, bed-and-breakfast; see BAR 2, HOTEL, MOTEL, RESORT 2.

inner *a.* innate, inherent, essential, inward, internal, interior, inside, nuclear, central, spiritual, private, personal, inmost, intimate, subconscious, intrinsic, deep-seated, deep-rooted, intuitive.—*Ant.* OUTER, surface, external.

innocence *n.* 1 [Freedom from guilt] guiltlessness, blamelessness, integrity, clear conscience, faultlessness, clean hands*; see also HONESTY.— *Ant.* GUILT, culpability, dishonesty. 2 [Freedom from guile] frankness, candidness, sincerity, plainness, forthrightness, inoffensiveness; see also SIMPLICITY 1. 3 [Lack of experience] purity, virginity, naiveté; see CHASTITY, IGNORANCE, VIRTUE 1.

innocent *a.* 1 [Guiltless] blameless, not guilty, impeccable, faultless, safe, upright, free of guilt, uninvolved, above suspicion, clean*; see also HONEST 1.—*Ant.* GUILTY, culpable, blameworthy. 2 [Without guile] open, fresh, guileless; see FRANK, CHILDISH, NAIVE, NATURAL 3, SIMPLE 1. 3 [Morally pure] sinless, unblemished, pure, unsullied, undefiled, spotless, wholesome, upright, unimpeachable, clean, virtuous, virginal, immaculate, impeccable, righteous, uncorrupted, irreproachable, stainless, unstained, moral, angelic.— *Ant.* DISHONEST, sinful, corrupt. 4 [Harmless] innocuous, powerless, inoffensive; see HARMLESS, SAFE 1.

innocently *a.* without guilt, with good intentions, ignorantly, with the best of intentions; see also POLITELY.

innovation *n.* modernization, alteration, addition; see CHANGE 1.

innuendo *n.* aside, intimation, insinuation; see HINT, SUGGESTION 1.

inoculate *v.* immunize, inject, vaccinate; see TREAT 3.

inoculation *n.* vaccination, injection, shot; see TREATMENT 2.

inoffensive *a.* innocuous, pleasant, peaceable; see CALM 1, FRIENDLY.

input *n.* information, knowledge, facts; see DATA.

inquire *v.* make an inquiry, probe, interrogate; see ASK, QUESTION.

inquiry *n.* probe, analysis, hearing; see EXAMINATION.

inquisitive *a.* curious, inquiring, speculative, questioning, meddling, searching, probing, intrusive, challenging, analytical, scrutinizing, prying, presumptuous, impertinent, snoopy*, nosy*; see also INTERESTED 1.—*Ant.* INDIFFERENT, unconcerned, aloof.

insane *a.* 1 [Deranged] crazy, crazed, wild, raging, frenzied, lunatic, balmy, schizophrenic, psychotic, psychopathic, delusional, paranoid, maniacal, raving, demented, rabid, unhinged, mentally unsound, mentally ill, suffering from hallucinations, daft, possessed, stark mad, out of one's mind, obsessed, touched, cracked*, screwy*, nutty*, nuts*, schizo*, loco*, wacko*, wacky*, haywire*, batty*, bonkers*, unglued*, off one's rocker*, not all there*; see also SICK.—*Ant.* SANE, rational, sensible. 2 [Utterly foolish] madcap, daft, idiotic; see STUPID.

insanely *a.* furiously, psychopathically, fiercely; see CRAZILY, VIOLENTLY, WILDLY.

insanity *n.* mental derangement, delusions, hysteria, obsession, compulsion, madness, dementia, lunacy, psychosis, neurosis, mania, phobia.—*Ant.* SANITY, reason, normality.

inscription *n.* engraving, epitaph, legend; see WRITING 2.

insect *n.* bug, beetle, mite, vermin, arthropod, cootie*; see also PEST 1. *Creatures commonly called insects include the following:* spider, ant, bee, flea, fly, mosquito, gnat, silverfish, hornet, leafhopper, squash bug, earwig, mayfly, walking stick, dragonfly, termite, cicada, aphid, mantis, beetle, butterfly, moth, wasp, locust, bedbug, caterpillar, grasshopper, cricket, bumblebee, honeybee, cockroach, potato bug, corn borer, ladybug, boll weevil, stinkbug, firefly, Japanese beetle, yellow jacket; see also FLY 1, SPIDER.

insecticide *n.* bug spray*, insect poison, pesticide; see POISON.

insecure *a.* anxious, vague, uncertain; see TROUBLED.

insecurity *n.* **1** [Anxiety] vacillation, indecision, instability; see DOUBT, UNCERTAINTY 2. **2** [Danger] risk, hazard, vulnerability; see CHANCE 1, DANGER.

inseparable *a.* indivisible, as one, tied up, intertwined, integrated, integral, interwoven, entwined, whole, connected, attached, conjoined, united; see also JOINED, UNIFIED.—*Ant.* DIVISIBLE, separable, apart.

insert *n.* supplement, advertisement, new material; see ADDITION 1.

insert *v.* introduce, inject, place inside; see INCLUDE 2.

inserted *a.* introduced, added, stuck in; see INCLUDED.

insertion *n.* insert, injection, inclusion; see ADDITION 1.

inside *a.* **1** [Within] inner, in, within the boundaries of, bounded, surrounded by; see also INNER, UNDER.—*Ant.* BEYOND, after, outside. **2** [Within doors] indoors, under a roof, in the privacy of one's own home, out of the open, behind closed doors, under a shelter; see also WITHIN.—*Ant.* OUTSIDE, out-of-doors, in the open.

inside *n.* inner wall, sheathing, plaster, facing, stuffing, wadding; see also LINING.

insides *n.* interior, inner portion, bowels, recesses, belly, gut, womb, heart, soul, breast; see also CENTER 1, STOMACH.

insight *n.* intuition, acuteness, perspicacity; see JUDGMENT 1.

insignia *n.* ensign, logo, symbol; see EMBLEM.

insignificance *n.* unimportance, worthlessness, indifference, triviality, nothingness, smallness, pettiness, matter of no consequence, nothing to speak of, nothing particular, trifling matter, drop in the bucket*, molehill.

insignificant *a.* inconsequential, petty, trifling; see TRIVIAL, UNIMPORTANT.

insincere *a.* deceitful, pretentious, shifty; see DISHONEST, FALSE 1, HYPOCRITICAL, SLY.

insincerity *n.* deceit, treachery, mendacity; see DECEPTION, DISHONESTY, HYPOCRISY.

insinuate *v.* imply, suggest, purport;

see HINT, MENTION, PROPOSE 1, REFER 2.

insinuation *n.* implication, veiled remark, innuendo; see HINT, SUGGESTION 1.

insistence *n.* persistence, perseverance, obstinacy; see DETERMINATION.

insistent *a.* persistent, obstinate, continuous; see STUBBORN.

insist upon *v.* expect, demand, order; see ASK.

insolvent *a.* bankrupt, failed, broke*; see RUINED 3.—*Ant.* RUNNING, solvent, in good condition.

inspect *v.* scrutinize, probe, investigate; see EXAMINE.

inspected *a.* tested, checked, authorized; see APPROVED, INVESTIGATED.

inspection *n.* inventory, investigation, inquiry; see EXAMINATION 1.

inspector *n.* police inspector, chief detective, investigating officer, customs officer, immigration inspector, government inspector, checker, FBI agent, narc*, postal inspector; see also POLICE OFFICER.

inspiration *n.* **1** [An idea] notion, hunch, whim; see FANCY 1, IMPULSE 2, THOUGHT 2. **2** [A stimulant to creative activity] stimulus, motivation, influence; see INCENTIVE.

inspire *v.* fire, be the cause of, start off, urge, stimulate, cause, put one in the mood, give one the idea for, motivate, give an impetus.

inspired *a.* roused, animated, motivated, stimulated, energized, stirred, excited, exhilarated, influenced, set going, started, activated, moved; see also ENCOURAGED.

inspiring *a.* illuminating, encouraging, revealing; see EXCITING, STIMULATING.

instability *n.* inconstancy, changeability, immaturity, variability, inconsistency, irregularity, imbalance, unsteadiness, restlessness, anxiety, fluctuation, alternation, disquiet, fitfulness, impermanence, transience, vacillation, hesitation, oscillation, volatility, flightiness, capriciousness, wavering, fickleness; see also CHANGE 1, UNCERTAINTY 2.

install *v.* set up, establish, build in, put in, place, invest, introduce, inaugurate, furnish with, fix up.

installation *n.* **1** [The act of installing] placing, induction, ordination, inauguration, launching, coronation, establishment. **2** [That which has been installed] machinery, wiring, lighting, insulation, power, operating system, heating system, furnishings, foundation, base.

installed *a.* set up, started, put in; see ESTABLISHED 1, FINISHED 1.

installment *n.* periodic payment, down payment, tranche; see PART 1, PAYMENT 1.

instance *n.* case, situation, occurrence; see EXAMPLE. —**for instance** as an example, by way of illustration, case in point; see FOR EXAMPLE.

instant *n.* short while, second, flash, split second, wink of the eye, jiffy*; see also MOMENT 1. —**on the instant** instantly, without delay, right now; see IMMEDIATELY.

instantly *a.* directly, at once, without delay; see IMMEDIATELY.

instead *a.* in place of, as a substitute, as an alternative, on second thought, in lieu of, on behalf of, alternatively; see also RATHER 2. —**instead of** rather than, in place of, as a substitute for, in lieu of, as an alternative for.

instill *v.* inject, infiltrate, inoculate, impregnate, inseminate, implant, inspire, impress, brainwash*, introduce, inculcate, indoctrinate, impart, insert, cultivate, imbue, put into someone's head*; see also TEACH.—*Ant.* REMOVE, draw out, extract.

instinct *n.* drive, sense, intuition; see FEELING 4.

instinctive *a.* spontaneous, reflex, normal; see NATURAL 2.

instinctively *a.* inherently, intuitively, by instinct; see NATURALLY 2.

institute *v.* found, organize, launch; see ESTABLISH 2.

institution *n.* system, company, association; see BUSINESS 4, OFFICE 3, UNIVERSITY.

institutionalize *v.* standardize, incorporate into a system, make official; see ORDER 3, REGULATE 2, SYSTEMATIZE.

instruct *v.* educate, give lessons, guide; see TEACH.

instructed *a.* advised, informed, told; see EDUCATED, LEARNED 1.

instruction *n.* guidance, preparation, direction; see EDUCATION 1.

instructions *n.* orders, plans, directive; see ADVICE, DIRECTIONS.

instructor *n.* professor, tutor, lecturer; see TEACHER.

instrument *n.* means, apparatus, implement; see CONTROL 2, DEVICE 1, MACHINE, TOOL 1.

instrumental *a.* partly responsible for, contributory, conducive; see EFFECTIVE, HELPFUL 1, NECESSARY.

insubordinate *a.* disobedient, dissident, defiant; see REBELLIOUS.

insubordination *n.* disobedience, defiance, disregard; see DISOBEDIENCE.

insubstantial *a.* petty, slight, inadequate; see FLIMSY, POOR 2.

insufficient *a.* skimpy, meager, thin; see INADEQUATE, UNSATISFACTORY.

insufficiently *a.* barely, incompletely, partly; see BADLY 1, INADEQUATELY.

insulate *v.* protect, coat, treat, apply insulation, tape up, glass in, pad, caulk, weatherstrip, paint.

insulation *n.* nonconductor, protector, covering, packing, lining, resistant material, weatherproofing, padding, caulking.

insult *n.* indignity, offense, affront, abuse, outrage, impudence, insolence, blasphemy, mockery, derision, impertinence, discourtesy, invective, disrespect, slight, slander, libel, slap in the face; see also RUDENESS.—*Ant.* PRAISE, tribute, homage.

insult *v.* revile, libel, offend, outrage, vilify, humiliate, mock, vex, tease, irritate, annoy, aggravate, provoke, taunt, ridicule, abuse, deride, jeer, step on one's toes; see also CURSE, SLANDER.

insulted *a.* slandered, libeled, reviled, disgraced, defamed, vilified, cursed, dishonored, mocked, ridiculed, jeered at, humiliated, mistreated, offended, hurt, outraged, affronted, slighted, shamed; see also HURT.—*Ant.* PRAISED, admired, extolled.

insulting *a.* outrageous, offensive, degrading, humiliating, debasing, embarrassing, humbling, deriding, contemptuous.—*Ant.* RESPECTFUL, complimentary, honoring.

insurance *n.* indemnity, assurance, warrant, backing, allowance, safeguard, protection, coverage, support, something to fall back on*; see also SECURITY 2.

insure *v.* warrant, protect, cover; see GUARANTEE.

insured *a.* safeguarded, defended, warranteed; see GUARANTEED, PROTECTED.

insurmountable *a.* unconquerable, unbeatable, hopeless; see IMPOSSIBLE.

insurrection *n.* riot, revolt, rebellion; see DISORDER, REVOLUTION 2.

intact *a.* together, entire, uninjured; see WHOLE 2.

intake *n.* **1** [Contraction] alteration, shortening, constriction; see ABBREVIATION, REDUCTION 1. **2** [Profit] harvest, gain, accumulation; see PROFIT 2.

intangible *a.* indefinite, unsure, hypothetical; see UNCERTAIN, VAGUE 2.

integrate *v.* unify, combine, desegregate; see MIX 1, UNITE.

integrated *a.* nonsegregated, not segregated, for both black and white, interracial, nonracial, for all races, diverse, multicultural, combined; see also FREE 1, 2, OPEN 3.

integration *n.* unification, combination, cooperation; see ALLIANCE 1, MIXTURE 1, UNION 1.

integrity *n.* uprightness, honor, probity; see HONESTY.

intellect *n.* intelligence, brain, mentality; see MIND 1.

intellectual *a.* mental, cerebral, rarefied; see INTELLIGENT, LEARNED 1.

intellectual *n.* genius, philosopher, academician, highbrow, member of the intelligentsia, egghead*, brain*, Einstein*; see also ARTIST, PHILOSOPHER, SCIENTIST, WRITER.

intelligence *n.* **1** [Understanding] perspicacity, discernment, comprehension; see JUDGMENT 1. **2** [Secret information] report, statistics, facts, inside information, classified information, info*; see also KNOWLEDGE 1, NEWS 1, SECRET. **3** [The mind] intellect, brain, mentality; see MIND 1.

intelligent *a.* clever, bright, exceptional, gifted, astute, smart, brilliant, perceptive, well-informed, resourceful, profound, penetrating, original, keen, imaginative, inventive, reasonable, capable, able, ingenious, knowledgeable, creative, responsible, understanding, alert, quick-witted, clearheaded, quick, sharp, witty, ready, perspicacious, calculating, comprehending, discerning, discriminating, knowing, intellectual, studious, contemplative, having a head on his or her shoulders*, talented, apt, wise, shrewd, smart as a whip*, on the ball*, on the beam*, not born yesterday*.—*Ant.* DULL, slow-minded, shallow.

intelligently *a.* skillfully, admirably, reasonably, logically, judiciously, capably, diligently, sharply, astutely, discerningly, knowingly, knowledgeably, farsightedly, sensibly, prudently, alertly, keenly, resourcefully, aptly, discriminatingly; see also EFFECTIVELY.—*Ant.* BADLY, foolishly, stupidly.

intelligible *a.* plain, clear, obvious; see UNDERSTANDABLE.

intend *v.* **1** [To propose] plan, purpose, aim, expect, be resolved, be determined to, aspire to, have in mind, hope to, contemplate, think, aim at, take into one's head. **2** [To destine for] design, mean, devote to, reserve, appoint, set apart, aim at, aim for; see also ASSIGN, DEDICATE. **3** [To mean] indicate, signify, denote; see MEAN 1.

intended *a.* designed, advised, expected, predetermined, calculated, dedicated, prearranged, predestined, meant; see also PLANNED, PROPOSED.

intense *a.* intensified, deep, profound, extraordinary, exceptional, heightened, marked, vivid, ardent, powerful, passionate, impassioned, diligent, hard, full, great, exaggerated, violent, excessive, acute, keen, piercing, cutting, bitter, severe, concentrated, intensive, forceful, sharp, biting, stinging, shrill, high-pitched, strenuous, fervent, earnest, zealous, vehement, harsh, strong, brilliant.

intensely *a.* deeply, profoundly, strongly; see VERY.

intensify *v.* heighten, sharpen, emphasize, augment, enhance; see also STRENGTHEN, INCREASE.

intensity *n.* strain, force, concentration, power, vehemence, passion, fervor, ardor, severity, acuteness, depth, deepness, forcefulness, high pitch, sharpness, emphasis, magnitude.

intensive *a.* accelerated, sped up, hard; see FAST 1, SEVERE 1, 2.

intention *n.* aim, end, plan; see PURPOSE 1.

intentional *a.* intended, meditated, prearranged; see DELIBERATE.

intentionally *a.* specifically, purposely, willfully; see DELIBERATELY.

intently *a.* hard, with concentration, keenly; see CLOSELY.

intercept *v.* cut off, stop, ambush, block, catch, take away, appropriate, hijack, head off; see also PREVENT.

interception *n.* seizing, stopping, interposing; see INTERFERENCE 1.

interchange *n.* **1** [The act of giving and receiving reciprocally] barter, trade, reciprocation; see EXCHANGE 1. **2** [A highway intersection] cloverleaf, intersection, off-ramp; see HIGHWAY, ROAD 1.

intercourse *n.* **1** [Communication] association, dealings, interchange; see COMMUNICATION. **2** [Sex act] coitus, coition, sexual relations; see COPULATION, SEX 4.

interest *n.* **1** [Concern] attention, curiosity, excitement; see ATTENTION. **2** [Advantage] profit, benefit, gain; see ADVANTAGE. **3** [Money charged for a loan, etc.] cost of borrowing, cost of money*, finance charges; see EXPENSE. **—in the interest(s) of** for the sake of, on behalf of, in order to promote; see FOR.

interest *v.* intrigue, amuse, please; see ENTERTAIN 1, FASCINATE.

interested *a.* **1** [Having one's interest aroused] stimulated, attentive, curious, drawn, touched, moved, affected, inspired, sympathetic to, responsive, struck, impressed, roused, awakened, stirred, open to suggestion, all for, all wrapped up in.—*Ant.* BORED, tired, annoyed. **2**

[Concerned with or engaged in] occupied, engrossed, partial, prejudiced, biased, taken, obsessed with, absorbed in; see also INVOLVED.—*Ant.* INDIFFERENT, impartial, disinterested.

interesting.

interesting *a.* pleasing, pleasurable, fine, satisfying, fascinating, arresting, engaging, readable, absorbing, compelling, riveting, stirring, affecting, exotic, unusual, impressive, attractive, captivating, enchanting, beautiful, inviting, winning, magnetic, delightful, amusing, genial, refreshing; see also EXCITING.—*Ant.* DULL, shallow, boring.

interfere *v.* intervene, interpose, interlope; see MEDDLE 1.

interference *n.* 1 [Taking forcible part in the affairs of others] meddling, interruption, prying, trespassing, tampering, barging in, back-seat driving; see also INTERRUPTION. 2 [That which obstructs] obstruction, check, obstacle; see BARRIER, RESTRAINT 2.

interior *a.* inner, internal, inward; see CENTRAL, INSIDE 2.

interior *n.* 1 [Inside] inner part, lining, heart; see CENTER 1, INSIDE. 2 [The inside of a building] rooms, halls, stairway, vestibule, lobby, chapel, choir, gallery, basement, inner sanctum, sanctum sanctorum.

interjection *n.* 1 [Insertion] interpolation, insinuation, inclusion; see ADDITION 1. 2 [Exclamation] utterance, ejaculation, exclamation; see CRY 1.

intermediate *a.* mean, between, medium, halfway, compromising, neutral, standard, median, moderate, average; see also CENTRAL, COMMON 1, MIDDLE.

intermission *n.* interim, break, interlude; see PAUSE, RECESS 1.

intermittent *a.* periodic, coming and going, recurrent; see CHANGING, IRREGULAR 1.

internal *a.* 1 [Within] inside, inward, interior, private, intrinsic, innate, inherent, under the surface, intimate, subjective, enclosed, circumscribed; see also INNER.—*Ant.* OUTER, external, outward. 2 [Within the body] intestinal, physiological, physical, neurological, abdominal, visceral.—*Ant.* FOREIGN, alien, external.

internally *a.* within, beneath the surface, inwardly, deep down, spiritually, mentally, invisibly, out of sight; see also INSIDE 1, WITHIN.

international *a.* worldwide, global, worldly, world, intercontinental, between nations, all over the world, universal, all-embracing, foreign, cosmopolitan; see also UNIVERSAL

3.—*Ant.* DOMESTIC, national, internal.

internationally *a.* cooperatively, globally, universally, around the world, not provincial; see also ABROAD, EVERYWHERE.

interpret *v.* give one's impression of, render, play, perform, depict, delineate, enact, portray, make sense of, read into, improvise on, reenact, mimic, gather from, view as, give one an idea about, make something of*; see also DEFINE, DESCRIBE.

interpretation *n.* account, rendition, exposition, statement, diagnosis, description, representation, definition, presentation, argument, answer, solution, take*; see also EXPLANATION.

interpreter *n.* commentator, writer, journalist, talking head, member of the chattering classes, artist, editor, reviewer, biographer, analyst, scholar, spokesman, delegate, speaker, exponent, demonstrator, philosopher, professor, translator, linguist, language expert.

interrogate *v.* cross-examine, grill, give the third degree*; see EXAMINE, QUESTION.

interrogation *n.* inquiry, query, investigation; see EXAMINATION 1.

interrupt *v.* intrude, intervene, cut in on, break into, interfere, infringe, cut off, break someone's train of thought, come between, butt in*, burst in.

interrupted *a.* stopped, checked, held up, obstructed, delayed, interfered with, disordered, hindered, suspended, cut short.

interruption *n.* check, break, gap, hiatus, suspension, intrusion, obstruction; see also DELAY, INTERFERENCE 1.

intersect *v.* cut across, come together, run through; see DIVIDE.

interstate *a.* between two states, among the states, national; see NATIONAL 2.

interval *n.* period, interlude, interim; see PAUSE.

intervene *v.* step in, intercede, mediate; see NEGOTIATE 1, RECONCILE 2.

intervention *n.* 1 [The act of intervening] intercession, interruption, breaking in; see INTERFERENCE 1, INTRUSION. 2 [Armed interference] invasion, military occupation, armed aggression; see ATTACK.

interview *n.* meeting, audience, conference; see COMMUNICATION, CONVERSATION.

interview *v.* converse with, get someone's opinion, consult with, interrogate, hold an inquiry, give an oral examination to, get something for the record.

intestines *n.* entrails, bowels, viscera, vitals, digestive organs, guts; see also INSIDES.

intimacy *n.* closeness, familiarity, confidence; see AFFECTION, FRIENDSHIP.

intimate *a.* familiar, confidential, trusted; see PRIVATE, SECRET 1, SPECIAL.

intimate *n.* associate, constant companion, close friend; see FRIEND, LOVER 1.

intimate *v.* suggest, imply, hint; see HINT.

intimately *a.* closely, personally, informally, familiarly, confidentially, without reserve, privately; see also LOVINGLY, SECRETLY.—*Ant.* OPENLY, unreservedly, publicly.

into *prep.* inside, in the direction of, through, to, to the middle of; see also IN 1, 2, TOWARD, WITHIN.

intolerable *a.* insufferable, unendurable, unbearable; see IMPOSSIBLE, OFFENSIVE 2, PAINFUL 1, UNDESIRABLE.

intolerance *n.* racism, chauvinism, bigotry; see FANATICISM, PREJUDICE.

intolerant *a.* dogmatic, narrow, bigoted; see PREJUDICED, STUPID.

intoxicant *n.* **1** [Alcohol] alcoholic drink, liquor, booze*; see DRINK 2. **2** [Drug] narcotic, hallucinogen, dope*; see DRUG.

intoxicate *v.* befuddle, inebriate, muddle; see CONFUSE.

intoxicated *a.* inebriated, high*, stoned*; see DIZZY, DRUNK.

intoxication *n.* infatuation, inebriation, intemperance; see DRUNKENNESS.

intricacy *n.* complication, elaborateness, complexity; see CONFUSION, DIFFICULTY 1, 2.

intricate *a.* involved, tricky, abstruse; see COMPLEX 2, DIFFICULT 1, 2, OBSCURE 1.

intrigue *n.* scheme, conspiracy, ruse; see TRICK 1.

intrigue *v.* delight, please, attract; see CHARM, ENTERTAIN 1, FASCINATE.

intrigued *a.* attracted, delighted, pleased; see CHARMED, ENTERTAINED, FASCINATED.

intriguing *a.* engaging, attractive, delightful; see BEAUTIFUL, CHARMING, HANDSOME, PLEASANT 1.

introduce *v.* **1** [To bring in] import, carry in, transport; see CARRY, SEND 1. **2** [To present] set forth, submit, advance; see OFFER 1, PROPOSE 1. **3** [To make strangers acquainted] present, give an introduction, make known, put on speaking terms with, do the honors, break the ice, hook up*. **4** [To insert] put in, add, enter; see INCLUDE 2.

introduced *a.* **1** [Brought in] made known, put on the market,

advanced, proposed, offered, imported, popularized; see also RECEIVED. **2** [Made acquainted] acquainted with, befriended, acknowledged, recognized, on speaking terms, not unknown to one another; see also FAMILIAR WITH.

introduction *n.* **1** [The act of bringing in] admittance, initiation, installation; see ENTRANCE 1. **2** [The act of making strangers acquainted] presentation, debut, meeting, formal acquaintance, preliminary encounter. **3** [Introductory knowledge] first acquaintance, elementary statement, first contact, start, awakening, first taste, baptism, preliminary training, basic principles; see also KNOWLEDGE 1. **4** [An introductory explanation] preface, preamble, foreword, prologue, prelude, overture; see also EXPLANATION. **5** [A work supplying introductory knowledge] primer, manual, handbook; see BOOK.

introductory *a.* initial, opening, early, prior, starting, beginning, preparatory, primary, original, provisional.—*Ant.* PRINCIPAL, substantial, secondary.

intrude *v.* interfere, interrupt, interpose; see MEDDLE 1.

intruder *n.* prowler, thief, burglar, unwelcome guest, meddler, invader, snooper, interloper, unwanted person, interferer, interrupter, trespasser; see also ROBBER, TROUBLE 1.

intrusion *n.* interruption, forced entrance, trespass, intervention, meddling, encroachment, invasion, infraction, overstepping, transgression, nose-in*, horn-in*, muscle-in*; see also INTERFERENCE 1.

intuition *n.* presentiment, foreknowledge, inspiration; see FEELING 4.

intuitive *a.* prescient, emotional, instinctive; see AUTOMATIC, NATURAL 1, SPONTANEOUS.

invade *v.* **1** [To enter with armed force] lay siege to, penetrate, fall on; see ATTACK. **2** [To encroach upon] infringe on, trespass, interfere with; see MEDDLE 1.

invader *n.* trespasser, alien, attacking force; see ATTACKER, ENEMY.

invalid *a.* irrational, unreasonable, fallacious; see ILLOGICAL, WRONG 2.

invalid *n.* disabled person, incurable, paralytic, chronically ill person, valetudinarian, crippled person; see also PATIENT.

invalidate *v.* annul, refute, nullify; see CANCEL.

invaluable *a.* priceless, expensive, dear; see VALUABLE.

invariable *a.* unchanging, uniform, static; see CONSTANT, REGULAR 3.

invariably a. perpetually, constantly, habitually; see CUSTOMARILY, REGULARLY.

invasion n. forced entrance, intrusion, aggression; see ATTACK.

invent v. 1 [To create or discover] originate, devise, fashion, form, project, design, find, improvise, contrive, execute, come upon, conceive, author, plan, think up, make up, bear, turn out, forge, make, hatch, dream up*, cook up*. 2 [To fabricate] misrepresent, fake, make believe; see LIE 1.

invention n. contrivance, contraption, design; see DISCOVERY.

inventive a. productive, imaginative, fertile; see ARTISTIC, ORIGINAL 2.

inventor n. author, originator, creator; see ARCHITECT, ARTIST.

inventory n. 1 [A list] stock book, itemization, register; see INDEX 2, LIST, RECORD 1. 2 [The act of taking stock] inspection, examination, investigation; see SUMMARY.

inventory v. take stock of, count, audit; see FILE 1, LIST 1, RECORD 1.

invert v. 1 [To upset] overturn, turn upside-down, tip; see UPSET 1. 2 [To reverse] change, rearrange, transpose; see EXCHANGE.

invest v. lay out, spend, put one's money into, provide capital for, give money over, buy stocks, make an investment, buy into, sink money in*, put up the dough*; see also BUY.

investigate v. look into, interrogate, review; see EXAMINE, STUDY.

investigated a. examined, tried, tested, inspected, searched, questioned, probed, considered, measured, checked, studied, researched, made the subject of an investigation, worked on, thought out, thought through, scrutinized, put to the test, gone over, gone into, cross-examined.

investigation n. inquiry, search, research; see EXAMINATION 1.

investigator n. reviewer, examiner, auditor; see DETECTIVE, INSPECTOR.

investment n. grant, loan, expenditure, expense, backing, speculation, financing, finance, purchase, advance, bail, interest. *Types of investment include the following:* stocks, bonds, shares, securities, property, real estate, mortgage, capital, mutual funds, hedge funds, debentures, futures, precious metals, gems.

invigorate v. stimulate, freshen, exhilarate; see ANIMATE, EXCITE.

invigorating a. refreshing, exhilarating, bracing; see STIMULATING.

invincible a. unconquerable, insuperable, impregnable; see POWERFUL 1, STRONG 1, 2.

invisibility n. obscurity, concealment, camouflage, indefiniteness, seclusion, cloudiness, haziness, fogginess, mistiness, duskiness, darkness, gloom, intangibility, disappearance, vagueness, indefiniteness.

invisible a. imperceptible, out of sight, microscopic, beyond the visual range, unseen, undisclosed, vaporous, gaseous.—*Ant.* REAL, substantial, material.

invisibly a. imperceptibly, out of sight, undetectably; see VAGUELY.

invitation n. note, card, message, encouragement, proposition, proposal, call, petition, overture, offer, solicitation, temptation, attraction, lure, prompting, urge, pressure, reason, motive, ground.

invite v. bid, request, beg, suggest, encourage, entice, solicit, pray, petition, persuade, insist, press, ply, propose, appeal to, implore, call upon, ask, have over, have in, formally invite, send an invitation to; see also ASK.

invited a. asked, requested, solicited, persuaded, bade, summoned; see also WELCOME.

inviting a. appealing, alluring, tempting, attractive, captivating, agreeable, open, encouraging, delightful, pleasing, persuasive, magnetic, fascinating, provocative, bewitching.—*Ant.* PAINFUL, unbearable, insufferable.

involuntary a. unintentional, uncontrolled, instinctive; see AUTOMATIC, HABITUAL.

involve v. draw into, compromise, implicate, entangle, embroil, link, connect, incriminate, associate, relate, suggest, prove, comprise, point to, commit, bring in.

involved a. brought into difficulties, entangled in a crime, incriminated, embarrassed, embroiled, caught up in; see also INCLUDED.

involvement n. 1 [Difficulty] quandary, predicament, embarrassment; see DIFFICULTY 1, 2. 2 [Engrossment] intentness, study, preoccupation; see REFLECTION 1.

invulnerable a. strong, invincible, secure; see SAFE 1.

inward a. 1 [Moving into] penetrating, ingoing, through, incoming, entering, inbound, infiltrating, inflowing. 2 [Placed within] inside, internal, interior; see IN 1, WITHIN. 3 [Private] spiritual, meditative, intimate; see PRIVATE, RELIGIOUS 2.

inwardly a. from within, fundamentally, basically; see NATURALLY, WITHIN.

iota n. grain, particle, speck; see BIT 1.

irate a. enraged, furious, incensed; see ANGRY.

Irish *a.* Celtic, Gaelic, Hibernian*; see EUROPEAN.

irk *v.* annoy, harass, disturb; see BOTHER 1, 2.

iron *a.* ferrous, ironclad, hard, robust, strong, unyielding, dense, inflexible, heavy; see also FIRM 2, THICK 3.

iron *n.* pig iron, cast iron, wrought iron, sheet iron, coke; see also METAL.

iron *v.* use a steam iron on, press, mangle, roll, finish, smooth out; see also SMOOTH. **—iron out** compromise, settle differences, smooth over; see AGREE, NEGOTIATE 1.

ironic *a.* contradictory, twisted, ridiculous, mocking, satiric, sardonic, paradoxical, critical, derisive, exaggerated, caustic, biting, incisive, scathing, satirical, bitter; see also SARCASTIC.

irony *n.* satire, wit, ridicule, mockery, quip, banter, derision, criticism, paradox, twist, humor, reproach, repartee, back-handed compliment; see also SARCASM.

irrational *a.* **1** [Illogical] unreasonable, specious, fallacious; see ILLOGICAL, WRONG 2. **2** [Stupid] senseless, silly, ridiculous; see STUPID.

irrationally *a.* illogically, unreasonably, stupidly; see FOOLISHLY.

irregular *a.* **1** [Not even] uneven, spasmodic, fitful, uncertain, random, unsettled, inconstant, unsteady, fragmentary, unsystematic, occasional, infrequent, fluctuating, wavering, intermittent, sporadic, changeable, capricious, variable, erratic, unmethodical, shifting, jerky, up and down.—*Ant.* REGULAR, even, punctual. **2** [Not customary] unique, extraordinary, abnormal; see UNUSUAL 2. **3** [Questionable] strange, overt, debatable; see QUESTIONABLE 2, SUSPICIOUS 2. **4** [Not regular in form or in outline] not uniform, uneven, unsymmetrical, asymmetrical, unequal, craggy, hilly, saw-toothed, broken, jagged, notched, eccentric, bumpy, meandering, variable, wobbly, lumpy, off balance, off center, lopsided, pockmarked, scarred, bumpy, sprawling, out of proportion; see also BENT.

irregularity *n.* peculiarity, singularity, abnormality, strangeness, uniqueness, exception, excess, malformation, deviation, allowance, exemption, privilege, nonconformity, innovation, oddity, eccentricity, anomaly, rarity; see also CHARACTERISTIC.—*Ant.* CUSTOM, regularity, rule.

irregularly *a.* periodically, at irregular intervals, intermittently, fitfully, off and on; see also UNEXPECTEDLY.

irrelevant *a.* inapplicable, impertinent, off the topic, inappropriate, inapt, unrelated, extraneous, unconnected, inapropos, off the point, foreign, beside the question, out of order, out of place, pointless, beside the point, not pertaining to, without reference to, out of the way, remote, neither here nor there; see also TRIVIAL, UNNECESSARY.

irreparable *a.* incurable, hopeless, irreversible; see BROKEN 1, RUINED 1, DESTROYED.

irresistible *a.* compelling, overpowering, invincible; see OVERWHELMING, POWERFUL 1.

irresponsible *a.* untrustworthy, capricious, flighty, fickle, thoughtless, rash, undependable, unstable, loose, lax, immoral, shiftless, unpredictable, wild, devil-may-care; see also UNRELIABLE.—*Ant.* RESPONSIBLE, trustworthy, dependable.

irrevocable *a.* permanent, indelible, set in stone; see CERTAIN 2, INEVITABLE.

irrigate *v.* water, pass water through, inundate; see FLOOD.

irrigation *n.* watering, flooding, inundation; see FLOOD.

irritability *n.* anger, peevishness, impatience; see ANGER, ANNOYANCE.

irritable *a.* sensitive, touchy, testy, peevish, ill-tempered, huffy, petulant, tense, resentful, fretting, carping, crabbed, hypercritical, quick-tempered, easily offended, glum, complaining, brooding, dissatisfied, snarling, grumbling, surly, gloomy, ill-natured, morose, moody, snappish, waspish, in bad humor, cantankerous, fretful, hypersensitive, annoyed, piqued, cross, churlish, grouchy, sulky, sullen, high-strung, thin-skinned, grumpy; see also ANGRY.—*Ant.* PLEASANT, agreeable, good-natured.

irritant *n.* bother, burden, nuisance; see ANNOYANCE.

irritate *v.* **1** [To bother] provoke, exasperate, pester; see BOTHER 1, CONFUSE, DISTURB. **2** [To inflame] redden, chafe, swell, erupt, pain, sting; see also BURN, HURT 1, ITCH.

irritated *a.* disturbed, upset, bothered; see TROUBLED.

irritating *a.* annoying, bothersome, trying; see DISTURBING.

irritation *n.* **1** [The result of being irritated] soreness, tenderness, rawness; see FEELING 4. **2** [A disturbed mental state] excitement, upset, provocation; see ANGER, ANNOYANCE.

is *v.* lives, breathes, subsists, transpires, happens, amounts to, equals, comprises, signifies, means.

island *n.* **1** [Land surrounded by

water] isle, sandbar, archipelago; see LAND 1. **2** [An isolated spot] haven, retreat, sanctuary; see REFUGE 1, SHELTER.

isolate v. confine, detach, seclude; see DIVIDE.

isolated a. secluded, apart, backwoods, insular, provincial, segregated, confined, withdrawn, rustic, separate, lonely, forsaken, hidden, remote, out-of-the-way, lonesome, Godforsaken, rare, infrequent; see also ALONE, PRIVATE, SOLITARY.

isolation n. detachment, solitude, loneliness, seclusion, segregation, confinement, separation, self-sufficiency, obscurity, retreat, privacy; see also WITHDRAWAL.

issue n. **1** [Question] point, matter, problem, concern, point in question, argument; see also MATTER. **2** [Result] upshot, culmination, effect; see RESULT. **3** [Edition] number, copy, impression; see COPY. **—at issue** in dispute, unsettled, controversial; see CONTROVERSIAL. **—take issue** differ, disagree, take a stand against; see OPPOSE 1.

issue v. **1** [To emerge] flow out, proceed, come forth; see APPEAR 1. **2** [To be a result of] rise from, spring, originate; see BEGIN 2, RESULT. **3** [To release] circulate, announce, send out; see ADVERTISE, DECLARE, PUBLISH 1.

issued a. circulated, broadcast, televised, made public, announced, published, sent out, disseminated, spread; see also DISTRIBUTED.

it pron. such a thing, that which, that object, this thing, the subject; see also THAT, THIS.

Italian a. Latin, Etruscan, Roman, Florentine, Milanese, Venetian, Neapolitan, Sicilian.

italicize v. stress, underline, print in italic type, draw attention to; see also DISTINGUISH 1, EMPHASIZE.

itch n. tingling, prickling, crawling, creeping sensation, rawness, psoriasis, scabbiness.

itch v. creep, prickle, be irritated, crawl, tickle; see also TINGLE.

item n. piece, article, matter; see DETAIL, PART 1.

itemize v. inventory, enumerate, number; see DETAIL, LIST 1.

itemized a. counted, particularized, enumerated; see DETAILED.

itinerant a. roving, nomadic, peripatetic; see VAGRANT, WANDERING 1.

itinerant n. nomad, wanderer, vagrant; see TRAMP 1.

itinerary n. course, travel plans, route; see PATH, PLAN 2, PROGRAM 2, WAY 2.

J

jab n. poke, punch, hit; see BLOW.

jabber v. gibber, babble, mutter; see MURMUR 1, SOUND.

jack n. automobile jack, pneumatic jack, hydraulic jack; see DEVICE 1, TOOL 1. **—jack up** lift, add to, hike*; see INCREASE, RAISE 1.

jacket n. tunic, jerkin, parka; see CAPE 2, CLOTHES, COAT 1.

jackknife n. clasp knife, case knife, pocket knife; see KNIFE.

jack-of-all-trades n. handyman, factotum, versatile person; see LABORER, WORKMAN.

jackpot n. bonanza, find, winnings; see LUCK 1, PROFIT 2, SUCCESS 2.

jagged a. serrated, ragged, rugged; see IRREGULAR 4, ROUGH 1.

jail n. penitentiary, cage, cell, dungeon, bastille, pound, reformatory, stockade, detention camp, gaol (British), concentration camp, penal institution, house of detention, lockup, the big house*, pen*, stir*, clink*, jug*, can*; see also PRISON.

jail v. confine, lock up, incarcerate, sentence, impound, detain, arrest, put behind bars, put in the clink*, throw away the keys*; see also IMPRISON. **—Ant.** FREE, liberate, discharge.

jailed a. arrested, incarcerated, in jail; see CONFINED 3, HELD, UNDER ARREST.

jam n. **1** [Preserves] conserve, fruit butter, spread, marmalade; blackberry jam, plum jam, strawberry jam, etc.; see also JELLY. **2** [*A troublesome situation] fix*, dilemma, problem; see DIFFICULTY 1.

jam v. **1** [To force one's way] jostle, squeeze, crowd, throng, press, thrust, pack; see also PUSH 1. **2** [To compress] bind, squeeze, push; see COMPRESS, PACK 2, PRESS 1.

jammed a. **1** [Stuck fast] wedged, caught, frozen; see TIGHT 2. **2** [Thronged] crowded, busy, congested; see FULL 1.

janitor n. building custodian, watchman, doorman; see ATTENDANT, CUSTODIAN.

jar n. **1** [A glass or earthen container] crock, pot, fruit jar, can, vessel, basin, beaker, jug, cruet, vat, decanter, pitcher, bottle, flagon, flask, vial, vase, chalice, urn; see also CONTAINER. 2 [A jolt] jounce, thud, thump; see BUMP 1.

jar v. jolt, bounce, bump; see CRASH 4, HIT 1.

jargon n. 1 [Trite speech] banality, patter, hackneyed terms, overused words, commonplace phrases, shopworn language, trite vocabulary, hocus-pocus; see also LANGUAGE 1. 2 [Specialized vocabulary or pronunciation, etc.] argot, patois, lingo, broken English, idiom, pidgin English, vernacular, colloquialism, coined words, localism, rhyming slang, doubletalk, officialese, newspeak, journalese; see also DIALECT, SLANG.

jarring a. 1 [Discordant] unharmonious, grating, rasping; see HARSH, LOUD 1, 2, SHRILL. 2 [Jolting] bumpy, rough, uneven; see UNSTABLE 1.

jaunt n. excursion, trip, tour; see JOURNEY, WALK 3.

jaw n. jawbone, muzzle, jowl, mandible, maxilla, chops; see also BONE.

jaywalk v. cross against a light, cut across, cross illegally.

jazz n. Dixieland, ragtime, modern jazz, traditional jazz, improvisation, hot music, bop, bebop, hard bop, mainstream, fusion, free jazz, swing, big-band, cool jazz, boogie-woogie; see also MUSIC 1.

jealous a. possessive, demanding, monopolizing, envious, watchful, resentful, mistrustful, doubting, apprehensive; see also SUSPICIOUS 1.—Ant. TRUSTING, confiding, believing.

jealousy n. resentment, possessiveness, suspicion; see DOUBT, ENVY.

jell v. set, crystallize, condense; see FREEZE 1, HARDEN, STIFFEN, THICKEN.

jelly n. jell, extract, preserve, gelatin; apple jelly, currant jelly, raspberry jelly, etc.; see also JAM 1.

jellyfish n. medusa, coelenterate, hydrozoan; see FISH.

jeopardize v. imperil, expose, venture; see ENDANGER, RISK.

jeopardy n. risk, peril, exposure; see CHANCE 1, DANGER.

jerk n. 1 [A twitch] tic, shrug, wiggle, shake, quiver, flick, jiggle; see also BUMP 1. 2 [*A contemptible person] scoundrel, rat*, creep*; see FOOL, RASCAL.

jerk v. 1 [To undergo a spasm] have a convulsion, quiver, shiver; see SHAKE 1, TWITCH 2. 2 [To move an object with a quick tug] snatch, grab, flick; see SEIZE 1, 2.

jester n. comedian, buffoon, joker; see ACTOR, CLOWN, FOOL.

jet n. 1 [A stream of liquid or gas] spray, stream, spurt; see FOUNTAIN 1. 2 [A jet-propelled airplane]

turbojet, turboprop, SST; see PLANE 3. *Types of jets include the following:* 737, 747, 757, 767, 777, DC-10, MD-80, Concorde.

jet v. 1 [To gush out in a stream] spout, squirt, spurt; see FLOW. 2 [To travel by jet airplane] take a jet, go by jet, fly; see TRAVEL.

Jew n. Hebrew, Israelite, Semite.

jewel n. bauble, gem, trinket; see DIAMOND. *Jewels include the following:* emerald, amethyst, sapphire, opal, pearl, jade, aquamarine, moonstone, agate, ruby, turquoise, topaz, garnet, jasper, coral, peridot, lapis lazuli, bloodstone, onyx, zircon.

jeweler n. goldsmith, diamond setter, lapidary; see ARTIST, CRAFTSMAN, SPECIALIST.

jewelry n. gems, jewels, baubles, trinkets, adornments, frippery, ornaments, costume jewelry, bangles; see also JEWEL.

Jewish a. Hebrew, Semitic, Yiddish.

jibe* v. agree, match, correspond; see RESEMBLE, AGREE.

jiggle v. shake, twitch, wiggle; see JERK 2.

jingle n. tinkle, jangle, clank; see NOISE 1.

jingle v. tinkle, clink, rattle; see SOUND.

jinx* n. evil eye, hex, curse, spell; see also CHANCE 1.

job n. 1 [Gainful employment] situation, place, position, appointment, operation, task, line, calling, vocation, career, craft, pursuit, office, function, livelihood; see also BUSINESS 1, PROFESSION 1, TRADE 2, WORK 2. 2 [Something to be done] task, business, action, act, mission, assignment, affair, concern, obligation, enterprise, undertaking, project, chore, errand, care, matter in hand, commission, function, responsibility, office, tour of duty, operation; see also DUTY 1. 3 [The amount of work done] assignment, day's work, output; see DUTY 1. — **odd jobs** miscellaneous duties, chores, occasional labor; see WORK 2. —**on the job** busy, engaged, occupied; see BUSY 1.

jog n. 1 [A slow run] trot, amble, pace; see RUN 1. 2 [A bump] nudge, poke, shake; see BLOW, BUMP 1. — **jog someone's memory** bring up, recall, suggest; see REMIND.

jog v. run, do roadwork, trot; see RUN 1.

join v. 1 [To unite] put together, blend, combine, bring in contact with, touch, connect, couple, mix, assemble, bind together, fasten, attach, annex, pair with, link, yoke, marry, wed, copulate, cement, weld, clasp, fuse, lock, grapple, clamp, entwine; see also UNITE.—*Ant.* SEPARATE, sunder, sever. **2** [To enter the company of] go to, seek, associate with, join forces, go to the aid of, place by the side of, follow, register, team up with, take up with, be in, sign on, sign up, go in with, fall in with, consort, enlist, fraternize, throw in with*, pair with, affiliate, side with, make one of, take part in, seek a place among, advance toward, seek reception, hook up*, go to meet.—*Ant.* DESERT, leave, abandon. **3** [*To adjoin] lie next to, neighbor, border, fringe, verge upon, be adjacent to, open into, be close to, bound, lie beside, be at hand, touch, skirt, parallel, rim, hem.

joined *a.* linked, yoked, coupled, allied, akin, intertwined, blended, connected, united, federated, banded, wedded, married, mixed, tied together, combined, touching, cemented, welded, fused, locked, clipped together, accompanying, associated, confederated, mingled, spliced, affixed, attached, joint, incorporated, involved, inseparable, affiliated, related, pieced together, coupled with, bound up with; see also UNIFIED.—*Ant.* SEPARATED, disparate, apart.

joint *n.* **1** [A juncture] union, coupling, hinge, tie, swivel, link, connection, point of union, bond, splice, bend, hyphen, junction, bridge; see also BOND 1. **2** [A section] piece, unit, portion; see LINK, PART 3. **3** [*A cheap bar, restaurant, etc.] hangout*, dive*, hole in the wall*; see BAR 2, RESTAURANT. **4** [*A marijuana cigarette] roach*, doobie*, reefer*, stick*; see also DRUG. **—out of joint** dislocated, disjointed, wrong; see DISORDERED.

jointly *a.* conjointly, mutually, combined; see TOGETHER.

joke *n.* prank, put-on*, game, sport, frolic, practical joke, jest, pun, witticism, play on words, quip, pleasantry, banter, drollery, retort, repartee, crack*, wisecrack*, clowning, caper, mischief, escapade, tomfoolery, play, antic, spree, farce, monkeyshine*, shenanigan*, horseplay, stunt, gag*; see also TRICK 1.

joke *v.* jest, quip, banter, laugh, raise laughter, poke fun, play, frolic, play tricks, pun, twit, trick, fool, make merry, play the fool, wisecrack*, pull someone's leg*.

joking *a.* humorous, facetious, not serious; see FUNNY 1.

jokingly *a.* facetiously, amusingly, not seriously; see HUMOROUSLY.

jolly *a.* gay, merry, joyful; see HAPPY.

jolt *n.* **1** [A bump] jar, punch, bounce; see BLOW, BUMP 1. **2** [A surprise] jar, start, shock; see SURPRISE 2, WONDER 1.

jostle *v.* nudge, elbow, shoulder; see PRESS 1, PUSH 1.

jot *v.* scribble, indicate, list; see RECORD 1, WRITE 1.

journal *n.* **1** [A daily record] diary, almanac, chronicle; see RECORD 1. **2** [A periodical] publication, annual, daily; see MAGAZINE, NEWSPAPER.

journalism *n.* reportage, news coverage, the fourth estate; see WRITING 3.

journalist *n.* investigative reporter, correspondent, columnist, stringer; see also ANNOUNCER, REPORTER, WRITER.

journey *n.* trip, visit, run, passage, tour, excursion, jaunt, pilgrimage, voyage, crossing, expedition, patrol, beat, venture, adventure, drive, flight, cruise, course, route, sojourn, travels, trek, migration, caravan, roaming, quest, safari, exploration, hike, airing, outing, march, picnic, survey, mission, ride.

journey *v.* tour, jaunt, take a trip; see TRAVEL.

jovial *a.* affable, amiable, merry; see HAPPY.

jowl *n.* dewlap, chin, cheek; see JAW.

joy *n.* mirth, cheerfulness, delight, pleasure, gratification, treat, diversion, sport, refreshment, revelry, frolic, playfulness, gaiety, geniality, good humor, merriment, merry-making, levity, rejoicing, liveliness, high spirits, good spirits, jubilation, celebration, ecstasy; see also LAUGHTER.—*Ant.* COMPLAINING, weeping, wailing.

joyful *a.* joyous, cheery, glad; see HAPPY.

joyous *a.* blithe, glad, gay; see HAPPY.

Judaism *n.* Jewish religion, Hebraism, Zionism; see RELIGION 2.

Judas *n.* betrayer, fraud, informer; see HYPOCRITE, TRAITOR.

judge *n.* **1** [A legal official] justice, executive judge, magistrate, justice of the peace, chief justice, associate justice, judiciary, circuit judge, county judge, judge of the district court, appellate judge. **2** [A connoisseur] expert, arbiter of taste, master of discernment; see CRITIC 2, SPECIALIST.

judge *v.* adjudge, adjudicate, rule on, pass on, sit in judgment, sentence, give a hearing to, hold the scales; see also CONDEMN, CONVICT.

judged *a.* found guilty or innocent, convicted, settled; see DETERMINED 1, GUILTY.

judgment *n.* **1** [Discernment] discrimination, taste, shrewdness, sapience, understanding, knowledge, wit, keenness, sharpness, critical faculty, rational faculty, reason, rationality, intuition, mentality, acuteness, intelligence, awareness, experience, profundity, depth, brilliance, sanity, intellectual power, capacity, comprehension, mother wit, quickness, readiness, grasp, apprehension, perspicacity, soundness, genius, good sense, common sense, astuteness, prudence, wisdom, gray matter*, brains, savvy*, horse sense*.—*Ant.* STUPIDITY, simplicity, naïveté. 2 [The act of judging] decision, appraisal, consideration, examination, weighing, sifting the evidence, determination, inspection, assessment, estimate, estimation, probing, appreciation, evaluation, review, contemplation, analysis, inquiry, inquisition, inquest, search, quest, pursuit, scrutiny, exploration, close study, observation, exhaustive inquiry; see also EXAMINATION 1. 3 [A pronouncement] conclusion, appraisal, estimate, opinion, report, view, summary, belief, idea, conviction, inference, resolution, deduction, induction, determination, decree, fiat, *fatwa* (Arabic), supposition, commentary, finding, recommendation; see also VERDICT.

Judgment Day *n.* doomsday, Day of Judgment, retribution, visitation, chastisement, correction, castigation, mortification, end of the world, last day, day of reckoning; see also JUDGMENT 1, 2.

judicial *a.* juridical, court-ordered, equitable; see LAWFUL.

judiciary *n.* justices, bench, bar; see COURT 2.

judicious *a.* well-advised, prudent, sensible; see DISCREET, RATIONAL 1.—*Ant.* RASH, ill-advised, hasty.

jug *n.* crock, flask, pitcher; see CONTAINER.

juggle *v.* 1 [To keep in the air by tossing] toss, keep in motion, bobble; see BALANCE 2. 2 [To alter, usually so as to deceive] shuffle, trick, delude; see DECEIVE.

juice *n.* sap, extract, fluid; see LIQUID.

juicy *a.* 1 [Succulent] moist, wet, watery, humid, dewy, sappy, dank, dripping, sodden, soaked, liquid, oily, syrupy; see also WET.—*Ant.* DRY, dehydrated, bone-dry. 2 [*Full of interest] spicy, piquant, intriguing, racy, risqué, fascinating, colorful. 3 [*Profitable] lucrative, remunerative, fruitful; see PROFITABLE.

jumble *n.* clutter, mess, hodgepodge; see CONFUSION, MIXTURE 1.

jumbo *a.* immense, mammoth, gigantic; see LARGE 1.

jump *n.* 1 [A leap up or across] skip, hop, rise, pounce, lunge, jumping, broad jump, high jump, vault,

bounce, hurdle, spring, bound, caper. 2 [A leap down] plunge, plummet, fall; see DIVE, DROP 2. 3 [Distance jumped] leap, stretch, vault; see HEIGHT, LENGTH 1. 4 [*An advantage] upper hand, edge, head start; see ADVANTAGE. 5 [A sudden rise] ascent, spurt, spike; see INCREASE, RISE 3.

jump *v.* 1 [To leap across or up] vault, leap over, spring, lurch, lunge, pop up, bound, hop, skip, high-jump, broad-jump, hurdle, top. 2 [To leap down] drop, plummet, plunge; see DIVE, FALL 1. 3 [To pass over] skip, traverse, remove, nullify; see also CANCEL, CROSS 1. 4 [*To accost belligerently] attack suddenly, assault, mug*; see ATTACK.

jumping *a.* vaulting, hopping, skipping; see ACTIVE.

jumpy *a.* sensitive, restless, nervous; see EXCITED.

junction *n.* 1 [A meeting] joining, coupling, reunion; see JOINT 1, UNION 1. 2 [A place of meeting, especially of roads] crossroads, crossing, intersection; see ROAD 1.

jungle *n.* wilderness, rain forest, tropical forest; see FOREST.

junior *a.* subordinate, lesser, lower; see SUBORDINATE.

junk *n.* waste, garbage, filth; see TRASH 1.

junk* *v.* dump, scrap, wreck; see DISCARD.

junkie* *n.* drug addict, dope addict*, doper*; see ADDICT.

jurisdiction *n.* authority, range, supervision, control, discretion, province, commission, scope, arbitration, reign, domain, bailiwick, extent, empire, sovereignty.

jurist *n.* legal scholar, justice, judge; see LAWYER.

jury *n.* tribunal, panel, board; see COURT 2.

just *a.* 1 [Precisely] exactly, correctly, perfectly; see ACCURATE. 2 [Hardly] barely, scarcely, by very little; see HARDLY. 3 [Only] merely, simply, no more than; see ONLY 2. 4 [Recently] just a while ago, lately, a moment ago; see RECENTLY. 5 [Fair] impartial, equitable, righteous; see FAIR 1. —**just the same** nevertheless, however, in spite of that; see BUT 1.

justice *n.* 1 [Fairness] right, truth, equity; see FAIRNESS. 2 [Lawfulness] legality, equity, prescriptive right, statutory right, established right, legitimacy, sanction, legalization, constitutionality, authority, code, charter, decree, rule, legal process, authorization; see also CUSTOM, LAW 1, POWER 2.—*Ant.* WRONG, illegality, illegitimacy. 3 [The administration of law] adjudication, settlement, arbitration, hearing, legal process, due process, judicial procedure, jury trial, trial by jury, regulation, decision, pronouncement, review, appeal, sentence, consideration, taking evidence, litigation, prosecution; see also JUDGMENT 2, LAW 1, TRIAL 2.—*Ant.* DISORDER, lawlessness, despotism. **4** [A judge] magistrate, umpire, chancellor; see JUDGE 1. —**do justice to** esteem, pay tribute to, honor; see ADMIRE, CONSIDER, RESPECT 2. —**do oneself justice** be fair to oneself, give oneself credit, behave in a worthy way; see APPROVE.

justifiable *a.* proper, suitable, probable; see FIT 1, LOGICAL.

justification *n.* excuse, defense, rationale; see APPEAL 1, EXPLANATION.

justify *v.* **1** [To vindicate] absolve, acquit, clear; see EXCUSE. **2** [To give reasons for] support, apologize for, excuse; see DEFEND, EXPLAIN.

justly *a.* **1** [Honorably] impartially, honestly, frankly, candidly, reasonably, straightforwardly, fairly, moderately, temperately, evenhandedly, rightly, equitably, tolerantly, charitably, respectably, lawfully, legally, legitimately, rightfully, properly, duly, in justice, as it ought to be. **2** [Exactly] properly, precisely, rationally; see ACCURATELY.

jut *v.* extend, bulge, stick out; see PROJECT 1.

juvenile *a.* youthful, adolescent, teenage; see YOUNG 1.

K

keen *a.* **1** [Sharp] pointed, edged, acute; see SHARP 1. **2** [Astute] bright, clever, shrewd; see INTELLIGENT. **3** [Eager] ardent, interested, intent; see ZEALOUS.

keenly *a.* acutely, sharply, penetratingly; see CLEARLY 1, 2, VERY, VIGOROUSLY.

keep *v.* **1** [To hold] retain, grip, own, possess, have, take, seize, save, grasp; see also HOLD 1. **2** [To maintain] preserve, conserve, care for; see MAINTAIN 3. **3** [To continue] persist in, carry on, sustain; see CONTINUE 1, ENDURE 1. **4** [To operate] administer, run, direct; see MANAGE 1. **5** [To tend] care for, minister to, attend; see TEND 1. **6** [To remain] stay, continue, abide; see SETTLE 5, 6. **7** [To store] deposit, hoard, retain, preserve, reserve, put away, conserve, warehouse, stash away*, put away, cache; see also SAVE 3, STORE. **8** [To prevent; *used with* "from"] stop, block, avert; see HINDER, PREVENT. **9** [To stay in good condition] not spoil, last, hold up; see PRESERVE 3. —**for keeps*** permanently, always, perpetually; see FOREVER. —**keep after** **1** [To pursue] track, trail, follow; see PURSUE 1. **2** [To nag] push, remind, pester; see BOTHER 2, DISTURB. —**keep at** persist, persevere, endure; see CONTINUE 1. —**keep away** **1** [To remain] stay away, hold back, keep one's distance; see WAIT 1. **2** [To restrain] keep off, hold back, defend oneself from; see HINDER, PREVENT, RESTRICT. —**keep back** **1** [To delay] check, hold, postpone; see DELAY, HINDER, SUSPEND. **2** [To restrict] enclose, inhibit, oppose; see FORBID, RESTRICT. —**keep down** reduce,

deaden, muffle; see SOFTEN, DECREASE 2. —**keep from** **1** [To abstain] desist, refrain, avoid; see ABSTAIN. **2** [To prevent] prohibit, forestall, impede; see HINDER, PREVENT. —**keep on** finish, repeat, pursue; see CONTINUE 1, ENDURE 1. —**keep to oneself** be a recluse, be a hermit, cultivate solitude, avoid human companionship, stay away, keep one's own counsel; see also HIDE. —**keep up** support, care for, safeguard; see SUSTAIN 2. —**keep up with** keep step with, keep pace with, run with; see COMPETE.

keeper *n.* guard, official, attendant; see WARDEN, WATCHMAN.

keeping *n.* care, custody, guard; see PROTECTION 2. —**in keeping with** similar to, much the same as, in conformity with; see ALIKE.

keepsake *n.* memento, token, souvenir; see REMINDER.

keg *n.* cask, drum, vat; see BARREL, CONTAINER.

kennel *n.* doghouse, den, pound; see ENCLOSURE 1, PEN 1.

kept *a.* **1** [Preserved] put up, pickled, stored; see PRESERVED 2. **2** [Retained] maintained, withheld, held, reserved, guarded, watched over, on file, at hand; see also SAVED 2. **3** [Observed] obeyed, honored, continued, discharged, maintained, carried on; see also FULFILLED.—*Ant.* ABANDONED, dishonored, forgotten.

kernel *n.* nut, core, heart; see GRAIN 1, SEED.

ketchup *n.* tomato sauce, catsup, condiment; see RELISH.

kettle *n.* caldron, saucepan, stewpot; see POT 1.

key *n.* **1** [Instrument to open a lock] latchkey, opener, master key, passkey, skeleton key. **2** [A means of solution] clue, code, indicator; see ANSWER 2.

keyboard *n.* keypad, console, row of keys; see CONTROL 2.

keyed up *a.* stimulated, spurred on, nervous; see EXCITED.

keynote *a.* main, leading, official; see IMPORTANT 1, PRINCIPAL.

kick *n.* **1** [A blow with the foot] boot, swift kick, jolt, jar, hit; see also BLOW. **2** [In sports, a kicked ball] punt, drop kick, placekick; see sense 1. **3** [*Pleasant reaction] joy, pleasant sensation, refreshment; see ENJOYMENT.

kick *v.* **1** [To give a blow with the foot] boot, jolt, punt, drop-kick, placekick, kick off; see also BEAT 1, HIT 1. **2** [*To object] make a complaint, criticize, carp; see COMPLAIN, OPPOSE 1. —**kick around** (or **about**) mistreat, treat badly, misuse; see ABUSE. —**kick off** start, open, get under way; see BEGIN 1. —**kick out** reject, throw out, eject; see DISMISS, REMOVE 1.

kickoff *n.* opening, beginning, launching; see ORIGIN 2.

kid *n.* **1** [The young of certain animals] young goat, young antelope, yearling; see ANIMAL. **2** [*A child] son, daughter, tot; see BOY, CHILD, GIRL.

kid* *v.* tease, pretend, fool; see BOTHER 2, JOKE.

kidnap *v.* abduct, ravish, capture, steal, rape, carry away, hold for ransom, shanghai, carry off, make off with, make away with, grab, spirit away, pirate, snatch*, bundle off.— *Ant.* RESCUE, ransom, release.

kidnapped *a.* made off with, abducted, ravished, stolen, carried away, held for ransom, shanghaied, waylaid, manhandled, seized, held under illegal restraint; see also CAPTURED.—*Ant.* FREE, rescued, freed.

kidney *n.* excretory organ, urinary organ, abdominal organ; see ORGAN 2.

kill *v.* **1** [To deprive of life] slay, slaughter, murder, assassinate, massacre, butcher, hang, lynch, electrocute, dispatch, execute, knife, sacrifice, shoot, strangle, poison, choke, smother, suffocate, asphyxiate, drown, behead, guillotine, crucify, dismember, decapitate, disembowel, quarter, tear limb from limb, destroy, give the death blow, give the coup de grâce, put to death, deprive of life, put an end to, exterminate, stab, cut the throat of, shoot down, mangle, cut down, bring down, mow down, machine-gun, liquidate, put someone out of his or her misery, starve, do away with,

commit murder, bump off*, rub out*, wipe out*, do in*, knock off*, finish off*, blow someone's brains out*, put to sleep*, brain*, whack*, zap*.—*Ant.* RESCUE, resuscitate, animate. **2** [To cancel] annul, nullify, counteract; see CANCEL. **3** [To turn off] turn out, shut off, stop; see HALT, TURN OFF. **4** [To veto] cancel, prohibit, refuse; see FORBID.

killer *n.* murderer, manslayer, gunman, gangster, shooter, butcher, executioner, hit man*, homicide, poisoner, exterminator, hangman, assassin, slayer, sniper, cutthroat, thug, Cain; see also CRIMINAL.

killing *a.* mortal, lethal, fatal; see DEADLY.

killing *n.* slaying, assassination, slaughter; see CRIME.

kin *n.* blood relation, member of the family, sibling; see FAMILY, RELATIVE.

kind *a.* tender, well-meaning, considerate, charitable, loving, pleasant, amiable, soft, softhearted, compassionate, sympathetic, understanding, solicitous, sweet, generous, helpful, obliging, neighborly, accommodating, indulgent, delicate, tactful, gentle, tenderhearted, kindhearted, good-natured, inoffensive, benevolent, altruistic, lenient, easygoing, patient, tolerant, mellow, genial, sensitive, courteous, agreeable, thoughtful, well-disposed.— *Ant.* ROUGH, brutal, harsh.

kind *n.* **1** [Class] classification, species, genus; see CLASS 1. **2** [Type] sort, variety, description, stamp, character, tendency, gender, habit, breed, set, tribe, denomination, persuasion, manner, connection, designation. —**kind of** somewhat, rather, sort of*; see MODERATELY.

kindergarten *n.* class for small children, pre-elementary grade, preschool; see SCHOOL 1.

kindhearted *a.* amiable, generous, good; see HUMANE, KIND.

kindle *v.* light, catch fire, set fire; see BURN, IGNITE.

kindling *n.* firewood, tinder, twigs; see FUEL, WOOD 2.

kindly *a.* generous, helpful, good; see HUMANE, KIND.

kindness *n.* **1** [The quality of being kind] tenderness, good intentions, consideration, sympathy, sweetness, helpfulness, tact, benignity, mildness, courtesy, thoughtfulness, humanity, courteousness, understanding, compassion, unselfishness, altruism, warmheartedness, softheartedness, politeness, kindliness, clemency, benevolence, goodness, philanthropy, charity, friendliness, affection, lovingkindness, cordiality, amiability, forbearance, mercy, graciousness, kindheartedness, virtue.—*Ant.* CRUELTY, brutality, selfishness. **2** [A kindly act] relief, charity, benevolence, philanthropy, favor, good deed, good turn, self-sacrifice, mercy, lift, boost; see also HELP 1.—*Ant.* INJURY, transgression, wrong.

kindred *n.* kin, relations, relatives; see FAMILY.

king *n.* **1** [A male sovereign] monarch, tyrant, prince, autocrat, czar, tsar, potentate, caesar, lord, emperor, overlord, crowned head, imperator, majesty, highness, mogul, *rex* (Latin), sultan, caliph, shah, rajah, maharajah; see also RULER 1.—*Ant.* SERVANT, slave, subordinate. **2** [A very superior being] lord, chief, head; see LEADER 2.

kingdom *n.* realm, domain, country, empire, lands, possessions, principality, state, dominions, monarchy, nation, subject territory.

kingship *n.* supremacy, sovereignty, majesty; see POWER 2, ROYALTY.

king-size *a.* big, large-size, giant; see BROAD 1, LARGE 1.

kink *n.* **1** [A twist] tangle, crimp, crinkle; see CURL, CURVE. **2** [A difficulty] hitch, defect, complication; see DIFFICULTY 1.

kinky *a.* **1** [Full of kinks] fuzzy, curled, crimped; see CURLY. **2** [*Bizarre] weird, odd, sick*; see UNUSUAL 2.

kinship *n.* affiliation, affinity, cohesion, unity, familiarity, intimacy, connection, alliance; see also FAMILY, RELATIONSHIP.

kiss *n.* embrace, endearment, touch of the lips, caress, French kiss, smooch*, smack*, peck*; see also TOUCH 2.

kiss *v.* salute, osculate, make love, play post office*, smack*, smooch*, pet*, neck*, make out*, blow a kiss*; see also LOVE 2.

kit *n.* **1** [Equipment] material, tools, outfit; see EQUIPMENT. **2** [A pack] backpack, knapsack, satchel; see BAG, CONTAINER.

kitchen *n.* scullery, galley, canteen, cook's room, kitchenette, mess.

kite *n.* box kite, Chinese kite, tailless kite; see TOY 1.

kitten *n.* pussycat, kitty, baby cat; see ANIMAL, CAT.

knack *n.* trick, skill, faculty; see ABILITY.

knapsack *n.* backpack, kit, rucksack; see BAG, CONTAINER.

knead *v.* work, mix, squeeze; see PRESS 1.

knee *n.* knee joint, crook, bend, hinge, kneecap, articulation of the femur and the tibia; see also BONE.

kneel *v.* bend the knee, rest on the knees, genuflect, bend, stoop, bow down, curtsy.

knickknack *n.* gadget, bric-a-brac, curio, ornament, trifle, bauble, trinket, plaything, showpiece, gewgaw*; see also TOY 1.

knife *n.* blade, cutter, sword, bayonet, cutting edge, dagger, stiletto, lance, machete, poniard, scalpel, edge, dirk, sickle, scythe, saber, scimitar, broadsword, point, pigsticker*, shiv*; see also RAZOR. *Knives include the following:* carving, chopping, table, dinner, dessert, grapefruit, fish, pocket, hunting, Bowie, butcher, skinning, surgical, paper, pruning, oyster, putty, palette, bread, cake, serving, Boy Scout, Swiss Army.

knife *v.* **1** [To stab] slash, lance, thrust through; see HURT 1, KILL 1, STAB. **2** [*To injure in an underhanded way] trick, give a coward's blow, strike below the belt; see DECEIVE.

knight *n.* cavalier, champion, knight-errant; see ARISTOCRAT.

knit *v.* **1** [To form by knitting] crochet, purl, spin, web, loop; see also SEW, WEAVE 1. **2** [To combine or join closely] intermingle, connect, affiliate; see JOIN 1.

knitted *a.* knit, purled, crocheted; see WOVEN.

knob *n.* **1** [A projection] hump, bulge, knot, node, bump, protuberance; see also LUMP. **2** [A door handle] doorknob, latch, door latch; see HANDLE 1.

knobby *a.* knobbed, lumpy, bumpy; see BENT, CROOKED 1.

knock *n.* rap, thump, whack; see BEAT 1, BLOW, INJURY.

knock *v.* tap, rap, thump; see BEAT 2, HIT 1, HURT 1. —**knock down** thrash, drub, kayo*; see BEAT 1, HIT 1, KNOCK OUT 2. —**knock off** **1** [To kill] murder, stab, shoot; see KILL 1. **2** [To accomplish] complete, finish, eliminate; see ACHIEVE, SUCCEED 1. **3** [To stop] quit, leave, halt; see STOP 2. —**knock oneself out*** slave, labor, do one's utmost; see WORK 1. —**knock out** **1** [To anesthetize] etherize, put to sleep, drug; see DEADEN. **2** [To strike down] strike senseless, render unconscious, knock someone out of his or her senses, knock cold*, kayo*, knock for a loop*, put out like a light*. —**knock up*** impregnate, make pregnant, inseminate; see FERTILIZE 2.

knockout *n.* **1** [A blow that knocks unconscious] knockout punch, final blow, kayo*; see BLOW. **2** [*A success] excellent thing, sensation, perfection; see SUCCESS 1.

knot *n.* **1** [An arrangement of strands] tie, clinch, hitch, splice, ligature, bond. **2** [A hard or twisted portion] snarl, gnarl, snag, bunch, coil, entanglement, tangle, twist.

knot *v.* bind, tie, hitch; see FASTEN.

knotted *a.* tied, twisted, tangled, snarled, entangled, bunched, clustered, looped, hitched, spliced, fastened, bent, warped, clinched, banded, lassoed, braided, linked, involved.—*Ant.* FREE, loose, separate.

know *v.* **1** [To possess information] be cognizant, be acquainted, be informed, be in possession of the facts, have knowledge of, be schooled in, be versed in, understand, appreciate, be conversant with, recognize, know full well, have at one's fingertips, know by heart, know inside out*, be instructed, awaken to, keep up on, have information about, know what's what*, know all the answers, have someone's number*, have the jump on*, have down cold*, know one's stuff*, know the score*, know the ropes*.—*Ant.* NEGLECT, be oblivious to, overlook. **2** [To understand] comprehend, apprehend, see into; see UNDERSTAND 1. **3** [To recognize] perceive, discern, be familiar with, have the friendship of, acknowledge, be accustomed to, associate with, get acquainted. —**know how** be able, have the necessary background, be trained; see UNDERSTAND 1.

know-how* *n.* skill, background, wisdom; see ABILITY, EXPERIENCE, KNOWLEDGE 1.

knowing *a.* sharp, clever, acute; see INTELLIGENT, REASONABLE 1.

knowingly *a.* intentionally, purposely, consciously; see DELIBERATELY.

knowledge *n.* **1** [Information] lore, learning, scholarship, facts, wisdom, instruction, book learning, erudition, culture, data, enlightenment, expertise, intelligence, light, theory, science, principles, philosophy, awareness, insight, education, substance, store of learning, know-how*; see also INFORMATION 1.—*Ant.* IGNORANCE, emptiness, pretension. **2** [Culture] tradition, cultivation, learning; see EXPERIENCE, REFINEMENT 2.

known *a.* **1** [Open] discovered, disclosed, revealed; see OBVIOUS 1, PUBLIC 1. **2** [Established] well-known, published, recognized, notorious, received, accepted, noted, proverbial, certified, down pat*; see also FAMILIAR.

knuckle under *v.* give in, give up, acquiesce; see YIELD 1.

kook* *n.* eccentric, crackpot*, loony*, cuckoo*, ding-a-ling*, nut*, screwball*, crazy*, weirdo*, wacko*, flake*, dingbat*.

kudos *n.* credit, glory, fame; see PRAISE 2, HONOR 1.

L

label *n.* tag, marker, mark, stamp, hallmark, insignia, design, number, identification, description, sticker, emblem, ticket; see also NAME 1.

label *v.* specify, mark, identify; see NAME 1, 2.

labeled *a.* identified, tagged, stamped; see MARKED 1, 2.

labor *n.* **1** [The act of doing work] activity, toil, operation; see WORK 2. **2** [Work to be done] task, employment, undertaking; see JOB 2. **3** [Exertion required in work] exertion, energy, industry, diligence, strain, stress, drudgery; see also EFFORT, EXERCISE 1. **4** [The body of workers] laborers, workers, workingmen, workingwomen, wage earners, proletariat, work force, labor force, working people, employees.—*Ant.* EMPLOYER, capitalist, businessman. **5** [Childbirth] parturition, giving birth, labor pains; see BIRTH.

labor *v.* toil, strive, get cracking*; see WORK 1.

laboratory *n.* workroom, lab*, research facility, testing room; see also OFFICE 3.

laborer *n.* day laborer, unskilled worker, hand, manual laborer, ranch hand, farmhand, worker, blue-collar worker, serf, apprentice, hired man, transient worker, toiler, seasonal laborer, ditch digger, pick-and-shovel man, roustabout, stevedore, miner, street cleaner, wage slave, robot, peon, flunky, lackey, hireling, hack, beast of burden*.

labor union *n.* organized labor, American Federation of Labor and Congress of Industrial Organizations (AFL-CIO), craft union, industrial union, trade union, local, labor party; see also ORGANIZATION 2.

lace *n.* **1** [Ornamental threadwork] tatting, crocheted lace, edging; see DECORATION 2. **2** [Material for binding through openings] thong, cord, band; see ROPE.

lace *v.* strap, bind, close; see FASTEN, TIE 2.

lacing *n.* bond, hitch, tie; see FASTENER, KNOT 1.

lack *n.* **1** [The state of being lacking] destitution, absence, need, shortage, paucity, deprivation, deficiency, scarcity, insufficiency, inadequacy, privation, poverty, distress, scantiness.—*Ant.* PLENTY, sufficiency, abundance. **2** [That which is lacking] need, decrease, want, loss, depletion, shrinkage, shortage, defect, inferiority, paucity, stint, curtailment, reduction; see also NECESSITY 2.—*Ant.* WEALTH, overflow, satisfaction.

lack *v.* want, require, have need of; see NEED.

lacking *a.* needed, deprived of, missing; see WANTING.

lacy *a.* sheer, thin, gauzy; see TRANSPARENT 1.

lad *n.* fellow, youth, stripling; see BOY, CHILD.

ladder *n. Ladders include the following:* stepladder, rope ladder, ship's ladder, aerial ladder, extension ladder, step stool, gangway, fire escape; see also STAIRS.

ladle *n.* skimmer, scoop, dipper; see SILVERWARE.

lady *n.* **1** [A woman] female, adult, matron; see WOMAN 1. **2** [A woman of gentle breeding] gentlewoman, well-bred woman, woman of quality, cultured woman, highborn lady, mistress of an estate, noblewoman, titled lady; see also WOMAN 1.

ladylike *a.* womanly, cultured, well-bred; see POLITE, REFINED 2.

lag *n.* slackness, slowness, tardiness, falling behind, sluggishness, backwardness.—*Ant.* PROGRESS, progression, advance.

lag *v.* dawdle, linger, fall back, loiter, tarry, straggle, get behind, slacken, slow up, fall behind, procrastinate, plod, trudge, lounge, shuffle, falter, stagger, limp, get no place fast*; see also DELAY.—*Ant.* HURRY, hasten, keep pace with.

lagoon *n.* inlet, sound, pool; see BAY, LAKE.

lair *n.* cave, home, den; see PEN 1.

lake *n.* pond, creek, loch, pool, lagoon, inland sea; see also SEA. *Famous lakes include the following:* Geneva, Lucerne, Great Salt, Superior, Huron, Michigan, Erie, Ontario, Champlain, Finger Lakes, Tahoe, Tanganyika, Nyasa, Loch Lomond, Victoria, Baikal, Great Slave, Titicaca, Great Bear, Loch Ness, Caspian Sea, Aral Sea.

lamb *n.* young sheep, young one, yeanling; see ANIMAL.

lame *a.* **1** [Forced to limp] crippled, unable to walk, halt, weak, paralyzed, impaired, handicapped, limping; see also DEFORMED, DISABLED. **2** [Weak; *usually used figuratively*] inefficient, ineffective, faltering; see UNSATISFACTORY, WANTING.

lamp *n.* light, light bulb, lighting device; see LIGHT 3. *Types and forms of lamps include the following:* wick, oil, gas, electric, table, hanging, safety, gooseneck, three-way, floor, miner's, arc, incandescent, halogen, fluorescent; sunlamp, streetlamp, night light, flashlight, chandelier, lantern.

lampoon *n.* satire, pasquinade, travesty, parody, burlesque.

land *n.* **1** [The solid surface of the earth] ground, soil, dirt, clay, loam, gravel, subsoil, clod, sand, rock, mineral, pebble, stone, dry land, valley, desert, hill, bank, seaside, shore, beach, crag, cliff, boulder, ledge, peninsula, delta, promontory; see also EARTH 2, MOUNTAIN 1, PLAIN.—*Ant.* SEA, stream, ocean. **2** [Land as property] estate, tract, ranch, farm, home, lot, real estate; see also AREA, PROPERTY 2. **3** [A country] state, province, region; see NATION 1.

land *v.* **1** [To come into port; *said of a ship*] dock, berth, moor, make port, tie up, come to land, drop anchor, put in; see also ARRIVE.—*Ant.* LEAVE, weigh anchor, cast off. **2** [To go ashore] disembark, come ashore, arrive, alight, leave the boat or ship, go down the gangplank, hit the beach*. **3** [To bring an airplane to earth] touch down, ground, take down, alight, come in, settle, level off, come down, descend, make a forced landing, crash-land, nose over, overshoot, splash down, check in, undershoot, pancake, settle her down hot*, fishtail down; see also ARRIVE.

landing *n.* **1** [The act of reaching shore] arriving, docking, making port, anchoring, mooring, dropping anchor; see also ARRIVAL 1. **2** [The place where landing on the shore is possible] marina, pier, wharf; see DOCK. **3** [The act of reaching the earth] setting down, grounding, getting in, arriving, reaching an airport, splashing down, completing a mission, settling, splashdown.

landlady *n.* homeowner, apartment manager, innkeeper; see OWNER, LANDLORD.

landlord *n.* homeowner, apartment manager, realtor, landowner, lessor, property owner, innkeeper; see also OWNER.

landmark *n.* **1** [A notable relic] remnant, vestige, historic structure; see MONUMENT 1, RELIC. **2** [A point from which a course may be taken] vantage point, mark, blaze, guide, marker, stone, tree, hill, mountain, bend, promontory.

landscape n. scene, scenery, panorama; see VIEW.

landscape v. lay out a garden or yard, finish up, put in the lawn and shrubbery; see DECORATE.

landslide n. slide, avalanche, rock slide; see DESCENT 2.

lane n. way, alley, passage; see PATH, ROAD 1.

language n. 1 [A means of communication] voice, utterance, expression, vocalization, sound, phonation, tongue, mother tongue, articulation, metalanguage, physical language; language of diplomacy, language of chemistry, language of flowers, etc.; accent, word, sign, signal, pantomime, gesture, vocabulary, diction, dialect, idiom, local speech, broken English, pidgin English, patois, vernacular, lingua franca, gibberish, pig Latin; see also DIALECT, JARGON 2, WRITING 1, 2. 2 [The study of language] semantics, psycholinguistics, morphology, phonology, phonemics, morphemics, phonics, phonetics, letters, linguistic studies, history of language, etymology, dialectology, linguistic geography; see also GRAMMAR, LINGUISTICS, LITERATURE 1. *Indo-European languages include the following—Germanic:* Old English or Anglo-Saxon, English, German, Yiddish, Dutch, Afrikaans, Old Norse, Danish, Swedish, Norwegian; *Celtic:* Welsh or Cymric, Irish or Erse, Gaelic or Scots Gaelic; *Italic:* Latin; *Romance:* Portuguese, Spanish, Provençal, French, Italian, Romanian; *Greek:* Attic, Ionic, Doric, Koine; *Slavic:* Russian, Belorussian, Ukrainian, Polish, Czech, Slovak, Slovenian, Macedonian, Serbo-Croatian, Bulgarian; *Baltic:* Lithuanian, Latvian; *Iranian:* Old Persian, Avestan, Pehlevi, Kurdish, Persian, Pashto or Afghan; *Indic:* Sanskrit, Pali, Prakrits, Hindi, Bengali, Gujarati, Hindustani, Urdu; *other branches:* Albanian, Armenian. *Other Eurasian languages include the following—Uralic:* Finnish, Estonian, Hungarian; *Altaic:* Turkish, Mongolian. *African and Asian languages include the following—Afro-Asiatic or Haimo-Semitic:* Aramaic, Phoenician, Hebrew, Arabic, Egyptian, Coptic; *Niger-Congo:* Bantu, Yoruba, Swahili, Zulu, Xhosa, Swazi; *other languages:* Masai, Bushman-Hottentot. *Asian and Malayo-Polynesian languages include the following—Japanese, Korean; *Sino-Tibetan:* Burmese, Tibetan, Mandarin, Cantonese; *Kadai:* Thai, Siamese, Laotian, Lao; *Malayao-Polynesian:* Malay, Indonesian, Javanese, Tagalog, Filipino, Papuan. *North American Indian languages include the following—*Nahuatl, Dakota, Zapotec, Navajo, Caddo, Cherokee, Choc-

taw, Arapaho. —**speak the same language** understand one another, communicate, get along; see AGREE.

languor n. lethargy, listlessness, lassitude; see INDIFFERENCE, LAZINESS.

lanky a. lean, bony, rangy; see THIN 2.

lap n. 1 [That portion of the body that is formed when one sits down] knees, legs, thighs, front. 2 [The portion that overlaps] extension, overlap, fold; see FLAP. 3 [Part of a race] circuit, round, loop; see DISTANCE 3, RACE 3. —**drop into someone's lap** transfer responsibility, shift blame, pass the buck*; see GIVE 1. —**in the lap of luxury** very wealthy, living elegantly, prospering; see RICH 1.

lapse n. slip, mistake, failure; see ERROR.

lapse v. slip, deteriorate, decline; see WEAKEN 1.

larceny n. burglary, thievery, robbery; see CRIME, THEFT.

large a. 1 [Of great size] huge, wide, grand, great, considerable, substantial, vast, massive, immense, spacious, bulky, colossal, gigantic, mountainous, immeasurable, plentiful, copious, populous, ample, abundant, liberal, comprehensive, lavish, swollen, bloated, puffy, obese, monstrous, towering, mighty, magnificent, enormous, giant, tremendous, monumental, stupendous, voluminous, cumbersome, ponderous, gross, immoderate, extravagant, super*, booming, bumper, whopping*; see also BIG 1, BROAD 1, DEEP 2, EXTENSIVE, HIGH 1.—*Ant.* LITTLE, small, tiny. 2 [Involving great plans] extensive, extended, considerable; see GENERAL 1.

largely a. 1 [In large measure] mostly, mainly, chiefly; see PRINCIPALLY. 2 [In a large way] extensively, abundantly, comprehensively; see WIDELY.

largeness n. magnitude, proportion, breadth; see MEASURE 1, MEASUREMENT 2, QUANTITY, SIZE.

lariat n. lasso, tether, line; see ROPE.

lark n. songbird, warbler, skylark; see BIRD.

larva n. maggot, grub, caterpillar; see WORM.

lash v. cane, scourge, strap; see BEAT 1, HIT 1.

lass n. young woman, damsel, maiden; see GIRL, WOMAN.

lasso n. tether, lariat, noose; see ROPE.

last a. 1 [Final] ultimate, utmost, lowest, meanest, least, end, extreme, remotest, furthest, outermost, farthest, uttermost, concluding, hindmost, far, far-off, ulterior, once and for all, definitive, after all others, ending, at the end, terminal, eventual, settling, resolving, decisive, crowning, climactic, closing, finishing, irrefutable.—*Ant.* FIRST, foremost, beginning. **2** [Most recent] latest, newest, current, freshest, immediate, in the fashion, modish, the last word*, trendy*; see also FASHIONABLE, MODERN 1.—*Ant.* OLD, stale, outmoded.

last *n.* tail end, last one, ending; see END 4. —**at (long) last** after a long time, in the end, ultimately; see FINALLY 2. —**see the last of** see for the last time, dispose of, get rid of; see END 1.

last *v.* **1** [To endure] remain, carry on, survive, hold out, suffer, stay, overcome, persist, stick it out*, stick with it*, go on; see also CONTINUE 1, ENDURE 1, 2. **2** [To be sufficient] hold out, be adequate, be enough, serve, do, accomplish the purpose, answer; see also SATISFY 3.

lasting *a.* enduring, abiding, constant; see PERMANENT.

latch *n.* catch, hook, bar; see FASTENER, LOCK 1.

latch *v.* lock, cinch, close up; see CLOSE 4, FASTEN.

late *a.* **1** [Tardy] too late, held up, overdue, stayed, postponed, put off, not on time, belated, behind time, lagging, delayed, backward, not in time; see also SLOW 2, 3.—*Ant.* EARLY, punctual, on time. **2** [Recently dead] defunct, deceased, departed; see DEAD 1. **3** [Recent] new, just out, recently published; see FRESH 1. **4** [Far into the night] nocturnal, night-loving, advanced, tardy, toward morning, after midnight. —**of late** lately, in recent times, a short time ago; see RECENTLY.

lately *a.* a short time ago, in recent times, of late; see RECENTLY.

lateness *n.* belatedness, procrastination, hesitation, tardiness, protraction, prolongation, slowness, backwardness, advanced hour, late date.—*Ant.* ANTICIPATION, earliness, promptness.

latent *a.* underdeveloped, potential, dormant, inactive.

later *a.* succeeding, next, more recent; see FOLLOWING.

lateral *a.* oblique, sidelong, side by side; see SIDE.

latest *a.* most recent, immediately prior, just finished; see LAST 1, 2.

lather *n.* suds, foam, bubbles; see FROTH.

Latin *a.* **1** [Pertaining to ancient Rome or to its language] of Rome, classical, Italic; see ROMAN. **2** [Pertaining to southwestern Europe] Roman, Mediterranean, speaking Romance languages; see EUROPEAN.

Latin *n.* language of Rome, classical Latin, church Latin; see LANGUAGE 2.

latitude *n.* meridional distance, degree, measure, degrees of latitude; see also MEASURE 1.

latter *a.* late, last, recent; see FOLLOWING, LAST 1.

laugh *n.* mirth, merriment, amusement, rejoicing, shout, chuckle, chortle, cackle, peal of laughter, horselaugh, guffaw, titter, snicker, giggle, roar, snort; see also LAUGHTER.—*Ant.* CRY, sob, whimper. —**have the last laugh** defeat finally, beat in the end, overcome all obstacles; see WIN 1.

laugh *v.* chuckle, chortle, guffaw, laugh off, snicker, titter, giggle, burst out laughing, shriek, roar, beam, grin, smile, smirk, shout, die laughing*, break up*, crack up*, howl, roll in the aisles*, be in stitches; see also SMILE.—*Ant.* CRY, sob, weep. —**laugh at** deride, taunt, make fun of; see RIDICULE. —**no laughing matter** serious, grave, significant; see IMPORTANT 1.

laughable *a.* ludicrous, comic, comical; see FUNNY 1.

laughing *a.* chortling, giggling, chuckling; see HAPPY.

laughter *n.* chortling, chuckling, guffawing, tittering, giggling, shouting, roaring, howling, snorting; see also LAUGH.—*Ant.* CRY, weeping, wailing.

launch *v.* **1** [To initiate] originate, start, set going; see BEGIN 1. **2** [To send off] set in motion, propel, thrust, fire off, send forth, eject; see also DRIVE 1, 2, PROPEL.

launched *a.* started, sent, set in motion; see BEGIN, DRIVEN.

launder *v.* cleanse, do the wash, wash and iron; see CLEAN, WASH 2.

laundry *n.* ironing, washing, clothes; see WASH 1.

lavatory *n.* restroom, bathroom, washroom; see BATH 2, TOILET.

lavender *a.*, *n.* lilac, pale purple, bluish-red; see COLOR, PURPLE.

lavish *a.* generous, unstinted, unsparing; see PLENTIFUL 1, 2.

lavish *v.* scatter freely, give generously, squander; see SPEND, WASTE 2.

lavishly *a.* profusely, richly, expensively; see CARELESSLY, FOOLISHLY, WASTEFULLY.

law *n.* **1** [The judicial system] judicial procedure, legal process, the legal authorities, the police, due process, precept, summons, notice, warrant, search warrant, warrant of arrest, subpoena. **2** [Bodies of law] code, constitution, criminal law, statute law, civil law, martial law, military law, commercial law, probate law, statutory law, statutes, civil code, ordinances, equity, cases, common law, canon law, decisions, unwritten law, natural law. **3** [An enactment] statute, edict, decree, ordinance, judicial decision, ruling, injunction, summons, act, enactment, requirement, demand, canon, regulation, bylaw, commandment, mandate, dictate, instruction, legislation; see also COMMAND, ORDER 1. **4** [A principle] foundation, fundamental, origin, source, ultimate cause, truth, axiom, maxim, ground, base, rule, theorem, guide, precept, usage, postulate, proposition, generalization, assumption, hard and fast rule; see also REASON 3. **5** [Officers appointed to enforce the law] sheriff, state police, city police; see JUDGE 1, LAWYER, POLICE. —**lay down the law** establish rules, command, prohibit; see ORDER 1.

lawbreaker *n.* felon, offender, violator; see CRIMINAL.

lawful *a.* legalized, legitimate, statutory, passed, decreed, judged, rightful, just, valid, authorized, licit, commanded, ruled, ordered, constitutional, legislated, enacted, official, enforced, protected, vested, within the law, legitimized, established; see also LEGAL, PERMITTED.—*Ant.* ILLEGAL, unlawful, illegitimate.

lawfully *a.* licitly, in accordance with the law, by law; see LEGALLY.

lawless *a.* **1** [Without law] wild, untamed, uncivilized, savage, barbarous, fierce, violent, tempestuous, disordered, agitated, disturbed, warlike; see also UNCONTROLLED.—*Ant.* CULTURED, cultivated, controlled. **2** [Not restrained by law] riotous, insubordinate, disobedient; see UNRULY.

lawlessness *n.* irresponsibility, terrorism, chaos; see DISORDER, DISTURBANCE 2.

lawmaker *n.* lawgiver, member of Congress, councilman; see LEGISLATOR.

lawn *n.* green, grassplot, grassland; see GRASS 2, YARD 1.

lawsuit *n.* action, prosecution, suit; see CLAIM, TRIAL 2.

lawyer *n.* legal advisor, defense attorney, jurist, member of the bar, public defender, defender, prosecuting attorney, prosecutor, attorney, solicitor, counsel, counselor, counselor-at-law, barrister, advocate, professor of law, attorney at law, attorney general, district attorney, DA, Philadelphia lawyer*, legal eagle*, shyster*, mouthpiece*.

lax *a.* slack, remiss, soft; see CARELESS, INDIFFERENT.

laxative *n.* physic, purgative,

diuretic, cathartic, purge, remedy, cure, dose; see also MEDICINE 1. *Common laxatives include the following:* castor oil, mineral oil, agar, cascara sagrada, flaxseed, milk of magnesia, croton oil, epsom salts, cascarin compound.

lay *v.* **1** [To knock down] trounce, defeat, club; see BEAT 1, HIT 1. **2** [To place] put, locate, settle, deposit, plant, lodge, store, stow, situate, deposit; see also SET 1. **3** [To put in order] arrange, organize, systematize; see ORDER 3. —**lay aside 1** [To place] deposit, put, place; see SET 1. **2** [To save] lay away, collect, keep; see SAVE 3, STORE. —**lay away** lay aside, keep, collect; see STORE. —**lay down 1** [To declare] assert, state, affirm; see DECLARE, REPORT 1, SAY. **2** [To bet] game, put up, wager; see BET, GAMBLE. —**lay off 1** [To discharge employees, usually temporarily] fire, discharge, let go; see DISMISS, OUST. **2** [*To stop] cease, halt, desist; see END 1, STOP 2. —**lay out** lend, put out at interest, put up; see INVEST, SPEND. —**lay over** delay, stay over, break a journey; see STOP 1. —**lay up 1** [To save] conserve, preserve, hoard; see SAVE 3, STORE. **2** [To disable] injure, harm, beat up*; see HURT.

layer *n.* thickness, fold, band, overlay, lap, overlap, seam, floor, story, tier, zone, stripe, coating, flap, panel.

layman *n.* nonprofessional, novice, layperson; see AMATEUR, RECRUIT.

laymen *n.* laity, converts, congregation, neophytes, parish, parishioners, the faithful, communicants, members, believers; see also FOLLOWING.

layout *n.* arrangement, design, draft; see ORGANIZATION 2, PLAN 1, PURPOSE 1.

layover *n.* break, stop, rest; see DELAY, PAUSE.

lazily *a.* indolently, nonchalantly, slackly; see GRADUALLY, SLOWLY.

laziness *n.* indolence, sloth, lethargy, inactivity, slackness, sluggishness, dullness, heaviness, inertia, drowsiness, passivity, listlessness, laxness, negligence, sleepiness, dreaminess, weariness, apathy, indifference, tardiness, shiftlessness, procrastination; see also IDLENESS.—*Ant.* ACTION, promptitude, agility.

lazy *a.* **1** [Indolent] idle, remiss, sluggish, lagging, apathetic, loafing, dallying, passive, asleep on the job, procrastinating, neglectful, indifferent, dilatory, tardy, slack, inattentive, careless, flagging, weary, tired.—*Ant.* ACTIVE, businesslike, indefatigable. **2** [Slow] slothful, inactive, lethargic; see SLOW 1, 2.

lead *a.* leading, head, foremost; see BEST, FIRST, PRINCIPAL.

lead *n.* 1 [The position at the front] head, advance, first place, point, edge, front rank, first line, scout, outpost, scouting party, patrol, advance position, forerunner; see also FRONT.—*Ant.* END, rear, last place. 2 [Leadership] direction, guidance, headship; see LEADERSHIP. 3 [A clue] evidence, trace, hint; see PROOF 1, SIGN 1. 4 [A leading role] principal part, important role, chief character; see ROLE. —**in the lead** ahead, winning, leading; see TRIUMPHANT. —**take the lead** direct, guide, head; see LEAD 1.

lead *n.* metallic lead, galena, blue lead; see ELEMENT 2, METAL.

lead *v.* 1 [To conduct] guide, steer, pilot, show the way, point the way, show in, point out, escort, accompany, protect, guard, safeguard, watch over, drive, discover the way, find a way through, be responsible for.—*Ant.* FOLLOW, be conveyed, be piloted. 2 [To exercise leadership] direct, command, supervise; see MANAGE 1. 3 [To extend] traverse, pass along, span; see REACH 1. —**lead on** lure, entice, intrigue; see DECEIVE. —**lead up to** prepare for, introduce, make preparations for; see BEGIN 2, PROPOSE 1.

leaden *a.* 1 [Made of lead] plumbous, pewter, galena; see METALLIC 1. 2 [Heavy] burdensome, oppressive, weighty; see HEAVY 1. 3 [Lead-colored] dull, pewter, blue-gray; see GRAY.

leader *n.* 1 [A guide] conductor, lead, pilot; see GUIDE. 2 [One who provides leadership] general, commander, director, manager, head, officer, captain, master, mistress, chieftain, governor, ruler, admiral, chief, administrator, chairman, chairperson, chair, president, boss, supervisor, executive director, brains*; see also EXECUTIVE.

leadership *n.* authority, control, administration, effectiveness, superiority, supremacy, skill, initiative, foresight, energy, capacity; see also INFLUENCE, POWER 2.

leading *a.* foremost, chief, dominant; see BEST, PRINCIPAL.

leaf *n.* leaflet, needle, blade, stalk, scale, floral leaf, seed leaf, sepal, petal. —**turn over a new leaf** make a new start, redo, begin again; see CHANGE 2.

leaflet *n.* handbill, circular, broadside; see PAMPHLET.

leafy *a.* leafed out, in leaf, shaded; see SHADY.

league *n.* band, group, unit; see ORGANIZATION 2.

leak *n.* 1 [Loss through leakage] leakage, loss, flow, seepage, escape, falling off, expenditure, decrease; see also WASTE 1. 2 [An aperture through which a leak may take place] puncture, chink, crevice; see HOLE 1. 3 [Surreptitious news] news leak, exposé, slip; see NEWS 1, 2.

leak *v.* 1 [To escape by leaking] drip, ooze, seep; see FLOW. 2 [To permit leakage] be cracked, be split, have a fissure, be out of order, have a slow leak.

leaky *a.* punctured, cracked, split; see BROKEN 1, OPEN 4.

lean *a.* 1 [Thin] lank, slender, slim; see THIN 2. 2 [Containing little fat] fibrous, muscular, sinewy, meaty, free from fat, all-meat, protein-rich.

lean *v.* 1 [To incline] slope, slant, sag, sink, decline, list, tip, bow, roll, veer, droop, drift, pitch, be slanted, be off; see also BEND, TILT. 2 [To tend] favor, be disposed, incline; see TEND 2. —**lean on** 1 [To be supported by] rest on, be held up by, bear on, put one's weight on, hang on, fasten on; see also LEAN 1. 2 [To rely upon] believe in, count on, put faith in; see TRUST 1.

leaning *a.* inclining, tilting, out of perpendicular; see OBLIQUE.

lean-to *n.* shelter, shanty, cabin; see HUT.

leap *v.* spring, vault, bound; see BOUNCE, JUMP 1.

learn *v.* acquire, receive, get, take in, drink in, pick up, read, master, ground oneself in, pore over, gain information, ascertain, determine, unearth, hear, find out, learn by heart, memorize, be taught a lesson, improve one's mind, build one's background, get up on*, get the signal*; see also STUDY.

learned *a.* 1 [Having great learning; *said of people*] scholarly, erudite, academic, accomplished, conversant with, lettered, instructed, collegiate, well-informed, bookish, pedantic, professorial; see also CULTURED, EDUCATED.—*Ant.* IGNORANT, incapable, illiterate. 2 [Showing evidence of learning; *said of writings*] deep, sound, solemn; see PROFOUND.

learning *n.* lore, scholarship, training; see EDUCATION 1, KNOWLEDGE 1.

lease *n.* rental agreement, permission to rent, charter; see CONTRACT, RECORD 1.

lease *v.* let, charter, rent out; see RENT 1.

leash *n.* cord, chain, strap; see ROPE.

least *a.* 1 [Smallest] tiniest, infinitesimal, microscopic; see MINUTE 1. 2 [Least important] slightest, piddling, next to nothing; see TRIVIAL, UNIMPORTANT. 3 [In the lowest degree] minimal, most inferior, bottom; see LOWEST, MINIMUM. —**at**

(the) least in any event, with no less than, at any rate; see ANYHOW. —
not in the least not at all, in no way, not in the slightest degree; see NEVER.

leather n. tanned hide, parchment, calfskin, horsehide, buckskin, deerskin, vellum, suede, kid, patent leather, buffalo hide, goatskin, sheepskin, rawhide, cowhide, snakeskin, sharkskin, lizard, shoe leather, glove leather, chamois, alligator hide; see also HIDE, SKIN.

leave n. 1 [Permission] consent, dispensation, allowance; see PERMISSION. 2 [Authorized absence] leave of absence, holiday, furlough; see VACATION. —**on leave** away, gone, on a vacation; see ABSENT. —**take one's leave** go away, depart, remove oneself; see LEAVE 1.

leave v. 1 [To go away] go, depart, take leave, withdraw, move, set out, come away, go forth, take off, start, step down, quit a place, part company, defect, vanish, walk out, walk away, get out, get away, slip out, slip away, break away, break out, ride off, ride away, go off, go out, go away, move out, move away, vacate, abscond, flee, flit, migrate, fly, run along, embark, say goodbye, emigrate, clear out*, cut out*, pull out, push off*, cast off*, scram*, split*, sign out, check out, beat it*, take a powder*, pull up stakes*.—*Ant.* ARRIVE, get to, reach. 2 [To abandon] back out, forsake, desert; see ABANDON 2. 3 [To allow to remain] let stay, leave behind, let continue, let go, drop, lay down, omit, forget; see also NEGLECT 1, 2.—*Ant.* SEIZE, take away, keep. 4 [To allow to fall to another] bequeath, hand down, transmit; see GIVE 1. —**leave out** cast aside, reject, dispose of; see DISCARD, ELIMINATE. —**leave to** bequeath, hand down, pass on; see GIVE 1.

leavings n. remains, residue, garbage; see TRASH 1.

lecture n. 1 [A speech] discourse, instruction, lesson; see SPEECH 3. 2 [A reprimand] rebuke, talking-to, dressing-down.

lecture v. 1 [To give a speech] talk, instruct, expound; see ADDRESS 2, TEACH. 2 [To rebuke] reprimand, admonish, give a going-over*, give a piece of one's mind*; see also SCOLD.

led a. taken, escorted, guided; see ACCOMPANIED.

ledge n. shelf, mantel, strip, bar, step, ridge, reef, rim, bench, edge, walk.

leech n. 1 [A parasite] tapeworm, hookworm, bloodsucker; see PARASITE 1. 2 [Dependent] parasite, hanger-on, sponger*; see WEAKLING.

leeward a. protected, screened, safe; see CALM 2.

leeway n. space, margin, latitude; see EXTENT.

left a. 1 [Opposite to right] leftward, left-hand, near, sinister, larboard, port, portside.—*Ant.* RIGHT, right-hand, starboard. 2 [Remaining] staying, continuing, over; see EXTRA. 3 [Radical] left-wing, liberal, progressive; see RADICAL 2, REVOLUTIONARY 1. 4 [Departed] gone out, absent, lacking; see GONE 1. —**left out** omitted, neglected, removed; see LOST 1.

left n. left hand, left side, left part, port, not the right, not the center; see also POSITION 1.

leftist n. socialist, anarchist, communist; see LIBERAL, RADICAL.

leftover a. remaining, unwanted, unused, residual, uneaten, unconsumed, untouched, perfectly good; see also EXTRA.

leftovers n. leavings, scraps, debris; see FOOD, TRASH 1.

left-wing a. leftist, not conservative, reform; see LIBERAL, RADICAL 2.

leg n. part, member, lower appendage, hind leg, foreleg, back leg, front leg, left leg, right leg, shank; see also LIMB 2. —**not have a leg to stand on*** be unreasonable, make rash statements, have no defense; see MISTAKE. —**on one's (or its) last legs*** decaying, not far from breakdown, old; see DYING 2, WORN 2. —**pull someone's leg*** make fun of, fool, play a trick on; see DECEIVE.

legal a. constitutional, permissible, allowable, allowed, proper, legalized, sanctioned, legitimate, right, just, justifiable, justified, fair, authorized, accustomed, due, rightful, warranted, admitted, sound, granted, acknowledged, equitable, within the law, protected, enforced, judged, decreed, statutory, contractual, customary, chartered, clean*, legit*, straight*, on the up and up*; see also LAWFUL, PERMITTED.—*Ant.* ILLEGAL, unlawful, prohibited.

legality n. legitimacy, lawfulness, authority; see LAW 1.

legalize v. authorize, formulate, sanction; see APPROVE.

legally a. lawfully, legitimately, permissibly, licitly, enforcibly, allowably, admittedly, constitutionally, with due process of law, by statute, by law, in the eyes of the law, in accordance with law, in accordance with the constitution; see also RIGHTFULLY.—*Ant.* illegally, illicitly, unconstitutionally.

legend n. folk tale, saga, fable; see MYTH, STORY.

legendary a. fabulous, mythical, mythological, fanciful, imaginative, created, invented, allegorical, apocryphal, improbable, dubious, not historical, doubtful, romantic, storied, unverifiable; see also IMAGINARY.

legerdemain *n.* deceit, trickery, sleight of hand; see DECEPTION, TRICK 1.

legible *a.* distinct, readable, plain; see CLEAR 2.

legion *n.* multitude, body, group; see CROWD, GATHERING.

legislate *v.* make laws, pass, constitute; see ENACT.

legislation *n.* bill, enactment, act; see LAW 3.

legislative *a.* lawmaking, enacting, decreeing, ordaining, lawgiving, congressional, parliamentary, senatorial, by the legislature.

legislator *n.* lawmaker, lawgiver, assemblyman, representative, member of congress, congressman, congresswoman, senator, member of parliament, floor leader, councilman, councilwoman, alderman; see also EXECUTIVE.

legislature *n.* lawmakers, congress, parliament, chamber, assembly, senate, house, elected representatives, soviet, plenum, lawmaking body, voice of the people.

legitimate *a.* 1 [In accordance with legal provisions] licit, statutory, authorized; see LAWFUL, LEGAL. 2 [Logical] reasonable, probable, consistent; see LOGICAL, UNDERSTANDABLE. 3 [Authentic] verifiable, valid, reliable; see GENUINE 1, 2.

leisure *n.* freedom, free time, spare time, spare moments, relaxation, recreation, ease, recess, holiday, leave of absence, convenience, idle hours, opportunity; see also REST 1, VACATION.—*Ant.* WORK, toil, travail. —**at leisure** idle, at rest, not busy; see RESTING 1. —**at one's leisure** when one has time, at one's convenience, at an early opportunity; see WHENEVER.

leisurely *a.* slow, unhurried, deliberate, calm, taking one's time, gradual, lethargic, sluggish, indolent.—*Ant.* FAST, rapid, hasty.

lemon *n.* citrus fruit, juicy fruit, food; see FRUIT.

lend *v.* advance, provide with, let out, furnish, permit to borrow, trust with, lend on security, extend credit, entrust, accommodate.—*Ant.* BORROW, repay, pay back.

lender *n.* moneylender, bank, loan company; see BANKER, DONOR.

length *n.* 1 [Linear distance] space, measure, span, reach, range, longitude, remoteness, magnitude, compass, portion, dimension, unit, radius, diameter, longness, mileage, stretch, extensiveness, spacious-

ness, distance, height, expansion; see also EXPANSE, EXTENT.—*Ant.* NEARNESS, shortness, closeness. 2 [Duration] period, interval, season, year, month, week, day, minute, limit; see also TIME 1. —**at length** 1 [Finally] after a while, at last, in the end; see FINALLY 2. 2 [Fully] in full, extensively, without omission; see COMPLETELY.

lengthen *v.* 1 [To make longer] extend, stretch, protract; see INCREASE. 2 [To grow longer] extend itself, increase, expand; see GROW 1.

lengthwise *a.* longitudinally, the long way, along, endlong*, from end to end, from stem to stern, overall, from head to foot, from top to bottom; see also ALONGSIDE.

lengthy *a.* tedious, not brief, long; see DULL 4.

lenient *a.* soft, mild, tolerant; see KIND.

lens *n.* microscope, camera, spectacles; see GLASS.

leopard *n.* panther, hunting leopard, jaguar; see ANIMAL, CAT 2.

lesbian *n.* gay, Sapphist, homosexual woman; see HOMOSEXUAL.

less *a.* smaller, lower, lesser, minor, fewer, reduced, in decline, depressed, inferior, secondary, subordinate, beneath, minus, deficient, diminished, shortened, limited, not so much as, not as much; see also SHORTER.—*Ant.* MORE, more than, longer.

lessen *v.* 1 [To grow less] diminish, dwindle, decline; see DECREASE 1. 2 [To make less] reduce, diminish, lower; see DECREASE 2.

lessening *a.* decreasing, declining, waning, dropping, diminishing, abating, slowing down, dwindling, sinking, sagging, subsiding, moderating, slackening, ebbing, lowering, shrinking, drying up, shriveling up, softening, weakening, decaying, narrowing down, drooping, wasting, running low, running down, dying away, dying down, wearing off, wearing out, wearing away, wearing down, falling off, slacking off, growing less and less, losing momentum, slumping, plunging, plummeting, going down, in reverse, getting worse, growing slower.

lesser *a.* inferior, minor, secondary; see SUBORDINATE.

lesson *n.* drill, assignment, reading; see JOB 2.

let *v.* 1 [To permit] suffer, give permission, condone, approve, authorize, consent, permit, tolerate; see also ALLOW. 2 [To rent] lease, hire, sublet; see RENT 1. —**let down** disappoint, disillusion, not support; see ABANDON 2, FAIL 1. —**let in** admit, allow to enter, give admission to;

see RECEIVE 4. —**let off** leave, excuse, let go, remove; see also ABANDON 1. —**let on*** imply, indicate, suggest; see HINT. —**let out** liberate, let go, eject; see FREE. —**let up** cease, release, slow down; see SLOW 1, STOP 2.

letdown *n.* frustration, setback, disillusionment; see DISAPPOINTMENT 1.

lethal *a.* fatal, mortal, malignant; see DEADLY, HARMFUL, POISONOUS.

letter *n.* **1** [A unit of the alphabet] capital, upper-case letter, lower-case letter, small letter, digraph, rune; see also CONSONANT, VOWEL. **2** [A written communication] note, epistle, missive, message, memorandum, report, line. *Types of letters include the following:* business, form, circular, chain, cover, fan, love, thank-you, registered, airmail, open, personal; billet-doux, postcard, e-mail, fax, letter of resignation, invitation, direct mail advertising, junk mail*. —**to the letter** just as directed, accurately, precisely; see PERFECTLY.

letup *n.* interval, recess, respite; see PAUSE.

level *a.* **1** [Smooth] polished, rolled, planed; see FLAT 1, SMOOTH 1. **2** [Of an even height] regular, equal, uniform, flush, of the same height, same, constant, straight, balanced, steady, stable, trim, precise, exact, matched, unbroken, on a line, lined up, aligned, uninterrupted, continuous; see also SMOOTH 1.—*Ant.* IRREGULAR, uneven, crooked. **3** [Horizontal] plane, leveled, lying prone, in the same plane, on one plane; see also FLAT 1. —**one's level best*** one's best, the best one can do, all one's effort; see BEST. —**on the level*** fair, sincere, truthful; see HONEST 1.

level *v.* **1** [To straighten] surface, bulldoze, equalize; see SMOOTH, STRAIGHTEN. **2** [To demolish] ruin, waste, wreck; see DESTROY. **3** [*To be honest with] be frank with, come to terms, be open and aboveboard; see DECLARE. —**level off** level out, find a level, reach an equilibrium; see DECREASE 1, STRAIGHTEN.

levelheaded *a.* wise, practical, prudent; see RATIONAL 1, REASONABLE 1.

lever *n.* lifter, pry, leverage, pry bar, pinch bar, crowbar, handspike, arm, advantage; see also TOOL 1.

leverage *n.* purchase, lift, hold; see SUPPORT 2.

levied *a.* exacted, taken, collected; see TAXED 1.

levy *n.* toll, duty, customs; see TAX 1.

lewd *a.* **1** [Suggestive of lewdness] ribald, smutty, indecent; see sense 2 and SENSUAL 2. **2** [Inclined to lewdness] lustful, wanton, lascivious, libidinous, licentious, lecherous,

profligate, dissolute, carnal, sensual, debauched, depraved, unchaste, corrupt, unbridled, ruttish, nymphomaniacal, prurient, concupiscent, incontinent, incestuous, goatish, raunchy*, horny*, in heat*; see also VULGAR.—*Ant.* PURE, chaste, modest.

lewdly *a.* wantonly, shockingly, indecently, lasciviously, lecherously, libidinously, unchastely, carnally, dissolutely, immodestly, voluptuously, sensually, incontinently, indelicately, in a lewd manner, with lewd gestures, in a suggestive manner.

lewdness *n.* indecency, unchastity, incontinence, vulgarity, lechery, wantonness, lasciviousness, sensuality, licentiousness, voluptuousness, lecherousness, profligacy, dissoluteness, lustfulness, prurience, ribaldry, concupiscence, obscenity, scurrility, coarseness, carnal passion, grossness, sensuous desire, salaciousness, pornography, lust, depravity, carnality, nymphomania, corruption, raunchiness*, dirtiness, incest, indelicacy, eroticism, erotism, smut, impurity, debauchery.—*Ant.* MODESTY, continence, decency.

liability *n.* obligation, indebtedness, answerability; see RESPONSIBILITY 2.

liable *a.* **1** [Responsible] answerable, subject, accountable; see RESPONSIBLE 1. **2** [Likely] tending, apt, inclined; see LIKELY 4.

liar *n.* prevaricator, false witness, deceiver, perjurer, trickster, misleader, falsifier, storyteller*, equivocator, fibber, fabricator; see also CHEAT.

libel *n.* calumny, slander, lying; see LIE.

liberal *a.* tolerant, receptive, nonconformist, progressive, advanced, left, radical, leftist, reformist, broadminded, understanding, permissive, indulgent, impartial, unprejudiced, reasonable, rational, unbiased, detached, dispassionate, unconventional, avant-garde, left-wing, objective, magnanimous; see also FAIR 1.—*Ant.* PREJUDICED, intolerant, biased.

liberal *n.* individualist, insurgent, rebel, revolutionary, nonconformist, progressive, leftist, independent, believer in civil rights, reformer, socialist, eccentric, freethinker, left-winger; see also RADICAL.

liberate *v.* set free, loose, release; see FREE.

liberation *n.* release, freedom, deliverance; see RESCUE 1.

liberty *n.* **1** [Freedom from bondage] deliverance, emancipation, enfranchisement; see RESCUE 1. **2** [Freedom from activity or obligation] rest, leave, relaxation; see FREEDOM 2, LEISURE, RECREATION. **3** [Freedom to choose] permission, alternative, decision; see CHOICE, SELECTION 1. **4** [The rights supposedly natural to human beings] freedom, independence, power of choice; see DEMOCRACY. **—at liberty** unrestricted, unlimited, not confined; see FREE 1, 2. **—take liberties** be impertinent, act too freely, use carelessly; see ABUSE.

librarian *n.* keeper, caretaker, curator; see EXECUTIVE.

library *n.* books, book collection, manuscripts, manuscript collection, archives, institution, public library, private library, book room, lending library, reference collection, museum, treasury, memorabilia, rare books, reading room.

license *n.* **1** [Unbridled use of freedom] looseness, excess, immoderation; see FREEDOM 2. **2** [A formal permission] permit, form, identification, tag, card, consent, grant; see also PERMISSION.

license *v.* permit, authorize, accredit; see ALLOW.

lick *v.* **1** [To pass the tongue over] stroke, rub, touch, pass over, pass across, caress, wash, graze, brush, glance, tongue, fondle. **2** [To play over; *said of flames*] rise and fall, fluctuate, leap; see BURN, DART, WAVE 3. **3** [*To beat*] whip, trim*, thrash; see BEAT 1. **4** [*To defeat*] overcome, vanquish, frustrate; see DEFEAT 3.

lid *n.* cap, top, roof; see COVER 1, HOOD 1.

lie *n.* falsehood, untruth, fiction, inaccuracy, misstatement, myth, fable, deceptiveness, misrepresentation, lying, prevarication, falsification, falseness, defamation, tall story*, fabrication, deception, slander, aspersion, tale, perjury, libel, forgery, distortion, fib, white lie, fish story*, whopper*.—*Ant.* TRUTH, veracity, truthfulness.

lie *v.* **1** [To utter an untruth] falsify, prevaricate, tell a lie, deceive, mislead, misinform, exaggerate, distort, concoct, equivocate, be untruthful, be a liar, break one's word, bear false witness, go back on, say one thing and mean another, misrepresent, dissemble, perjure oneself, delude, invent.—*Ant.* DECLARE, tell the truth, be honest. **2** [To be situated] extend, be on, be beside, be located, be fixed, be established, be placed, be seated, be set, be level, be smooth, be even, exist in space, stretch along, reach along, spread along. **3** [To be prostrate] be flat, be prone, sprawl, loll, be stretched out; see also REST 1.—*Ant.* STAND, be

upright, sit. **4** [To assume a prostrate position] lie down, recline, stretch out, go to bed, turn in, retire, take a nap, take a siesta, hit the sack*, hit the hay*; see also REST 1, SLEEP.—*Ant.* RISE, get up, arise. **—take lying down** submit, surrender, be passive; see YIELD 1.

life *n.* **1** [The fact or act of living] being, entity, growth, animation, endurance, survival, presence, living, consciousness, breath, continuance, flesh and blood, viability, metabolism, vitality, vital spark; see also EXPERIENCE.—*Ant.* DEATH, discontinuance, nonexistence. **2** [The sum of one's experiences] life experience, conduct, behavior, way of life, reaction, response, participation, enjoyment, joy, suffering, happiness, tide of events, circumstances, realization, knowledge, enlightenment, attainment, development, growth, personality. **3** [A biography] life story, memoir, memorial; see BIOGRAPHY, STORY. **4** [Duration] lifetime, one's natural life, period of existence, duration of life, endurance, continuance, span, history, career, course, era, epoch, century, decade, days, generation, time, period, life span, season, cycle, record; see also TIME 1. **5** [One who promotes gaiety] animator, entertainer, life of the party; see HOST 1, HOSTESS. **6** [Vital spirit] vital force, vital principle, *élan vital* (French); see EXCITEMENT, ZEAL. **—as large (or big) as life** actually, really, in actual fact; see TRULY. **—for dear life** intensely, desperately, for all one is worth; see STRONGLY. **—for life** for the duration of one's life, for a long time, as long as one lives; see FOREVER. **—for the life of me*** by any means, as if one's life were at stake, whatever happens; see ANYHOW. **—life or death** decisive, necessary, critical; see IMPORTANT 1. **—matter of life and death** crisis, grave concern, something vitally important; see IMPORTANCE. **—not on your life*** by no means, certainly not, never; see NO. **—take one's own life** kill oneself, die by one's own hand, commit suicide. **—true to life** true to reality, realistic, real; see GENUINE 1.

lifeless *a.* **1** [Without life] inert, inanimate, departed; see DEAD 1. **2** [Lacking spirit] lackluster, listless, heavy; see DULL 3, 4, SLOW 2.

lifelike *a.* simulated, exact, imitative; see GRAPHIC 1, 2.

lifetime *a.* lifelong, continuing, enduring; see PERMANENT.

lifetime *n.* existence, endurance, continuance; see LIFE 4, RECORD 2.

lift *n.* **1** [The work of lifting] pull, lifting, ascension, raising, weight, foot-pounds, elevation, escalation, ascent, mounting. **2** [A ride] transportation, drive, passage; see JOURNEY. **3** [Aid] encouragement, assistance, support; see HELP 1.

lift *v.* hoist, elevate, heave; see RAISE 1.

light *a.* **1** [Having illumination] illuminated, radiant, luminous; see BRIGHT 1. **2** [Having color] vivid, rich, bright; see CLEAR 2. **3** [Having little content] superficial, slight, frivolous; see TRIVIAL, UNIMPORTANT. **4** [Having gaiety and spirit] lively, merry, animated; see ACTIVE. **5** [Having little weight] airy, fluffy, feathery, slender, downy, floating, lighter than air, light as air, floatable, light as a feather, frothy, buoyant, dainty, thin, sheer, insubstantial, ethereal, graceful, weightless.—*Ant.* HEAVY, ponderous, weighty. **6** [Digestible] slight, edible, moderate; see EATABLE. **7** [Small in quantity or number] wee, small, tiny, minute, thin, inadequate, insufficient, hardly enough, not much, hardly any, not many, slender, scanty, slight, sparse, fragmentary, fractional; see also FEW.—*Ant.* LARGE, great, immense. — **make light of** make fun of, mock, belittle; see NEGLECT 1, RIDICULE.

light *n.* **1** [The condition opposed to darkness] radiance, brilliance, splendor, glare, brightness, clearness, lightness, incandescence, shine, luster, sheen, sparkle, glitter, glimmer, flood of light, blare, radiation, gleam.—*Ant.* DARKNESS, blackness, blankness. **2** [Emanations from a source of light] radiation, stream, blaze; see FLASH, RAY. **3** [A source of light] lamp, lantern, match, candle, sun, planet, star, moon, lightning, torch, flashlight, chandelier, spotlight, light bulb, halo, corona. **4** [Day] daylight, sun, sunrise; see DAY 1. **5** [Aspect] point of view, condition, standing; see CIRCUMSTANCES 2. —**in (the) light of** with knowledge of, because of, in view of; see CONSIDERING. —**see the light (of day) 1** come into being, exist, begin; see BE. **2** comprehend, realize, be aware; see UNDERSTAND 1.

light *v.* **1** [To provide light] illuminate, illumine, lighten, give light to, shine upon, furnish with light, light up, turn on the electricity, make visible, provide adequate illumination, switch on a light, floodlight, make bright, flood with light, fill with light; see also BRIGHTEN 1.—*Ant.* SHADE, put out, darken. **2** [To cause to ignite] set fire to, spark, kindle; see BURN, IGNITE. **3** [To become ignited] take fire, become inflamed, flame; see BURN, IGNITE. **4** [To come to rest from flight or travel] descend, come down, stop; see ARRIVE. —**light into*** rebuke, blame, assault; see SCOLD.

lighted *a.* **1** [Illuminated] brilliant, alight, glowing; see BRIGHT 1. **2** [Burning] blazing, flaming, aflame; see BURNING.

lighten *v.* unburden, make lighter, reduce the load of, lessen the weight of, uplift, buoy up, alleviate, take off a load, remove, take from, pour out, throw overboard, reduce, cut down, put off, make buoyant, take off weight, eradicate, shift, change; see also UNLOAD.—*Ant.* LOAD, burden, overload.

lighter *n.* cigarette lighter, igniter, flame; see LIGHT 3, MATCH 1.

lightheaded *a.* **1** [Giddy] inane, fickle, frivolous; see SILLY. **2** [Faint] tired, delirious, dizzy; see WEAK 1.

lighthearted *a.* gay, joyous, cheerful; see HAPPY.

lighting *n.* brilliance, flame, brightness; see FLASH, LIGHT 1, 3.

lightly *a.* delicately, airily, buoyantly, daintily, readily, gently, subtly, mildly, softly, tenderly, carefully, leniently, effortlessly, smoothly, blandly, sweetly, comfortably, restfully, peacefully, quietly; see also EASILY.—*Ant.* HEAVILY, ponderously, roughly.

lightness *n.* **1** [Illumination] sparkle, blaze, shine; see FLASH, LIGHT 1, 3. **2** [The state of being light] airiness, etherealness, downiness, thinness, sheerness, fluffiness. **3** [Agility] balance, deftness, nimbleness; see AGILITY, GRACE 1.

lightning *n.* electrical discharge, bolt, streak of lightning, fireball, thunderbolt; see also ELECTRICITY.

likable *a.* agreeable, amiable, attractive; see FRIENDLY.

like *a.* similar, same, alike, near, close, matching, equaling, not unlike, akin, related, analogous, twin, corresponding, allied, much the same, in the same form, of the same form, comparable, identical, parallel, homologous, consistent, approximating.—*Ant.* UNLIKE, different, unrelated.

like *prep.* similar to, same as, near to, resembling, alike to, in the manner of; see also LIKE, *a.*

like *n.* counterpart, resemblance, equal; see SIMILARITY. —**and the like** and so forth, and so on, similar kinds; see OTHERS. —**more like it*** acceptable, good, improved; see BETTER 1. —**nothing like** dissimilar, contrasting, opposed; see UNLIKE. — **something like** similar, resembling, akin; see LIKE *a.*

like *v.* **1** [To enjoy] take delight in, relish, derive pleasure from, be keen on, be pleased by, revel in, indulge in, rejoice in, find agreeable, find appealing, be gratified by, take satisfaction in, savor, fancy, dote on, take an interest in, develop interest for, delight in, regard with favor, have a liking for, love, have a taste for, care to, get a kick out of*, be tickled by, eat up*, go in for*.—*Ant.* ENDURE, detest, dislike. **2** [To be fond of] have a fondness for, admire, take a fancy to, feel affectionately toward, adore, prize, esteem, hold dear, care about, care for, approve of, be pleased with, take to, have a soft spot in one's heart for, hanker for, dote on, have a yen for*, become attached to, be sweet on*, have eyes for*; see also LOVE 1.—*Ant.* HATE, disapprove, dislike. **3** [To be inclined] choose, feel disposed, wish, desire, have a preference for, prefer, fancy, feel like, incline toward, want.

liked *a.* popular, loved, admired; see BELOVED, HONORED.

likely *a.* **1** [Probable] apparent, probable, seeming, credible, possible, feasible, presumable, conceivable, reasonable, workable, attainable, achievable, believable, rational, thinkable, imaginable, ostensible, plausible, anticipated, expected, imminent.—*Ant.* IMPOSSIBLE, doubtful, questionable. **2** [Promising] suitable, apt, assuring; see FIT 1, HOPEFUL 2. **3** [Believable] plausible, true, acceptable; see CONVINCING. **4** [Apt] inclined, tending, disposed, predisposed, prone, liable, subject to, on the verge of, in the habit of, given to, in favor of, having a weakness for.

likeness *n.* **1** [Similarity] resemblance, correspondence, affinity; see SIMILARITY. **2** [A representation] portrait, image, effigy; see COPY, PICTURE 3.

likewise *a.* in like manner, furthermore, moreover; see BESIDES.

liking *n.* desire, fondness, devotion; see AFFECTION, LOVE 1.

limb *n.* **1** [A tree branch] arm, bough, offshoot; see BRANCH 2. **2** [A bodily appendage] part, wing, fin, flipper, member; see also ARM 1, LEG.

limber *a.* nimble, spry, deft; see AGILE, GRACEFUL 1.

limit *n.* **1** [The boundary] end, frontier, border; see BOUNDARY. **2** [The ultimate] utmost, farthest point, farthest reach, destination, goal, conclusion, extremity, eventuality, termination, absolute, the bitter end, deadline, cutoff point; see also END 4.—*Ant.* ORIGIN, start.

limit *v.* bound, confine, curb; see DEFINE 1, RESTRICT.

limitation *n.* **1** [The act of limiting] restriction, restraint, control; see ARREST, INTERFERENCE 1, INTERRUP-

TION, PREVENTION. **2** [That which limits] condition, definition, qualification, reservation, control, curb, check, injunction, bar, obstruction, stricture, taboo, inhibition, modification; see ARREST, BARRIER, BOUNDARY, REFUSAL, RESTRAINT 2.—*Ant.* FREEDOM, latitude, liberty. **3** [A shortcoming] inadequacy, insufficiency, deficiency, shortcoming, weakness, want, blemish, defect, lack, imperfection, failing, frailty, flaw; see also FAULT 1.—*Ant.* STRENGTH, perfection, ability.

limited *a.* **1** [Restricted] confined, checked, curbed; see BOUND 1, 2, RESTRICTED. **2** [Having only moderate capacity] cramped, insufficient, short; see FAULTY, INADEQUATE, POOR 2, UNSATISFACTORY.

limitless *a.* unending, boundless, immeasurable; see ENDLESS, INFINITE, UNLIMITED.

limp *a.* pliant, soft, flaccid, flabby, supple, pliable, limber, relaxed, flexible, droopy, unsubstantial, bending readily, plastic, yielding, lax, slack, loose, flimsy.—*Ant.* STIFF, rigid, wooden.

limp *v.* walk lamely, proceed slowly, shuffle, lag, stagger, totter, dodder, hobble, falter.

line *n.* **1** [A row] array, list, rank, file, catalog, order, group, arrangement, ridge, range, seam, series, sequence, succession, procession, chain, train, string, column, formation, division, queue, channel, furrow, scar, trench, groove, mark, thread, fissure, crack, straight line. **2** [A mark] outline, tracing, stroke; see MARK 1. **3** [A rope] string, cable, towline; see ROPE, WIRE 1. **4** [Lineal descent] ancestry, pedigree, lineage; see FAMILY, HEREDITY. **5** [A borderline] border, mark, limit; see BOUNDARY, EDGE 1. **6** [Matter printed in a row of type] row, words, letters; see COPY. **7** [A military front] disposition, formation, position; see FRONT 2. **8** [A transportation system] trunk line, bus line, steamship line, railroad line, airline. **9** [Goods handled by a given company] wares, merchandise, produce; see MATERIAL 2. **10** [*Talk intended to influence another] rhetoric, lecture, propaganda, advertising; see also CONVERSATION, SPEECH 3. **—all along the line** at every turn, completely, constantly; see EVERYWHERE. **—bring (or come or get) into line** align, make uniform, regulate; see ORDER 3. **—draw the (or a) line** set a limit, prohibit, restrain; see RESTRICT. **—get a line on*** find out about, investigate, expose; see DISCOVER. **—in line** agreeing, conforming, uniform; see REGULAR 3. **—in line for** being considered for, ready, thought about; see CONSIDERED. **—in line with** similar to, in accord with, consonant; see HARMONIOUS 2, FIT 1. —**lay (or put) it on the line** speak frankly, define, clarify; see EXPLAIN. —**on a line** straight, even, level; see DIRECT 1, STRAIGHT 1. —**out of line** misdirected, not uniform, not even; see IRREGULAR 1, 4. —**read between the lines** read meaning into, discover a hidden meaning, figure out; see UNDERSTAND 1.

line v. **1** [To provide a lining] interline, stuff, wad, panel, pad, quilt, fill. **2** [To provide lines] trace, delineate, outline; see DRAW 2, MARK 1. **3** [To be in a line] border, edge, outline, rim, bound, fall in, fall into line, fringe, follow. **4** [To arrange in a line] align, queue, marshal, arrange, range, array, group, set out, bring into a line with others, fix, place, draw up; see also LINE UP.—*Ant.* SCATTER, disarrange, disperse. —**line up** fall in, form in line, take one's proper place in line, queue up, form ranks, get in line, get set, get into formation.

linear a. long, elongated, successive; see DIRECT 1, STRAIGHT 1.

lined a. interlined, stuffed, coated; see FULL 1.

linen n. material, sheeting, linen cloth; see GOODS. *Articles called linens include the following:* handkerchiefs, towels, bedding, sheets, pillowcases, underwear, comforters, dishtowels, tablecloths, napkins, doilies.

lineup n. starters, entrants, first string; see LIST.

linger v. tarry, saunter, lag, hesitate, trail, vacillate, delay, plod, trudge, falter, dawdle, procrastinate, stay, shuffle, crawl, loll, take one's time, wait, putter, be tardy, dillydally, sit around, hang around*; see also LOITER.—*Ant.* HURRY, hasten, speed.

lingerie n. women's underwear, undergarmets, unmentionables*; see CLOTHES, UNDERWEAR.

linguist n. student of language, language expert, philologist, lexicographer, polyglot, translator, grammarian, etymologist; see also SCIENTIST.

linguistics n. grammar, semantics, phonology, etymology, prosody, morphology, syntax, philology; see also GRAMMAR, LANGUAGE 2.

liniment n. ointment, cream, lotion; see MEDICINE 2, SALVE.

lining n. interlining, inner coating, inner surface, filling, quilting, stuffing, wadding, padding, sheathing, covering, wall, reinforcement, partition, paneling.

link n. ring, loop, coupling, coupler, section, seam, weld, bond, hitch, intersection, copula, connective, connection, fastening, splice, knot, interconnection, junction, joining,

ligature, articulation; see also JOINT 1.

link v. connect, associate, combine; see JOIN 1.

linked a. connected, combined, associated; see JOINED.

linking a. combining, joining, associating; see CONNECTING.

lint n. thread, fluff, fiber; see DUST.

lion n. king of beasts, king of the jungle, lioness; see ANIMAL, CAT 2.

lip n. edge of the mouth, liplike part, labium; see MOUTH 1. —**keep a stiff upper lip*** take heart, be encouraged, remain strong; see ENDURE 2.

liquid a. **1** [In a state neither solid nor gaseous] watery, molten, damp, moist, aqueous, liquefied, dissolved, melted, thawed; see also FLUID, WET 1. **2** [Having qualities suggestive of fluids] flowing, running, splashing, thin, moving, viscous, sappy, diluting; see also FLUID, JUICY.

liquid n. liquor, fluid, juice, sap, extract, secretion, flow; see also WATER 1.

liquidate v. **1** [To change into money] sell, convert, change; see EXCHANGE. **2** [To abolish] annul, cancel, destroy; see ABOLISH, ELIMINATE.

liquor n. whiskey, booze*, alcohol; see COCKTAIL, DRINK 2.

lisp v. mispronounce, sputter, stutter; see UTTER.

lissome a. lithe, supple, flexible; see AGILE, FLEXIBLE.

list n. roll, record, schedule, agenda, arrangement, enrollment, slate, draft, panel, brief, invoice, register, memorandum, inventory, account, outline, tally, bulletin, directory, roster, subscribers, subscription list, muster, poll, ballot, table of contents, menu, dictionary, thesaurus, glossary, lexicon, vocabulary, docket.

list v. **1** [To enter in a list] set down, arrange, bill, catalogue, schedule, enter, note, add, place, file, record, insert, enroll, register, tally, inventory, index, draft, enumerate, tabulate, book, take a census, poll, slate, keep count of, run down, call the roll.—*Ant.* REMOVE, wipe out, obliterate. **2** [To lean] pitch, slant, incline; see LEAN 1.

listed a. filed, cataloged, indexed; see RECORDED.

listen v. attend, keep one's ears open, be attentive, listen in, pick up, overhear, monitor, tap, give attention to, give ear, listen to, pay attention, hear, tune in*, lend an ear*, strain one's ears*.—*Ant.* IGNORE, be deaf to, turn a deaf ear to.

listener n. spy, student, monitor,

spectator, audience, eavesdropper, witness.

listening *a.* hearing, paying attention, interested, involved, attentive, heeding, overhearing, straining to hear, receiving, lending an ear*.— *Ant.* INDIFFERENT, giving no attention, inattentive.

listless *a.* passive, sluggish, lifeless; see INDIFFERENT, SLOW 2.

lit *a.* illuminated, resplendent, lighted; see BRIGHT 1, BURNING.

literacy *n.* scholarship, ability to read and write, verbal competence; see EDUCATION 1, KNOWLEDGE 1.

literal *a.* true, verbatim, exact; see ACCURATE 2.

literally *a.* really, actually, precisely, exactly, completely, indisputably, correctly, strictly, to the letter, faithfully, rigorously, straight, unmistakably, truly, not metaphorically, not figuratively, word for word, verbatim, letter by letter.— *Ant.* FREELY, figuratively, fancifully.

literary *a.* scholarly, bookish, literate; see LEARNED 1.

literate *a.* informed, scholarly, able to read and write; see EDUCATED, INTELLIGENT, LEARNED 1.

literature *n.* 1 [Artistic production in language] letters, lore, belles-lettres, literary works, literary productions, the humanities, classics, books, writings. 2 [Written matter treating a given subject] article, discourse, composition, treatise, dissertation, thesis, paper, treatment, essay, discussion, research, observation, comment, critique, findings, abstract, report, summary, précis.

litter *n.* 1 [Trash] rubbish, debris, waste; see TRASH 1. 2 [The young of certain animals] piglets, puppies, kittens; see OFFSPRING.

litter *v.* scatter, discard, spread; see DIRTY.

litterbug *n.* slob*, pig, polluter; see SLOB.

little *a.* 1 [Small in size] minute, diminutive, small, tiny, wee, undersized, stubby, truncated, stunted, limited, cramped, imperceptible, light, slight, microscopic, short, runty, shriveled, toy, miniature, puny, pygmy, dwarfed, bantam, half pint*, pocket-sized, pint-sized.— *Ant.* LARGE, big, huge. 2 [Inadequate] wanting, deficient, insufficient; see INADEQUATE. 3 [Few in number] scarce, not many, hardly any; see FEW. 4 [Brief] concise, succinct, abrupt; see SHORT 2. 5 [Small in importance] trifling, shallow, petty, superficial, frivolous, irrelevant, meaningless, slight, paltry, insignificant, inconsiderable; see also TRIVIAL, UNIMPORTANT. 6 [Small in character] base, weak,

shallow, small-minded, prejudiced, bigoted, low, sneaky, mean, petty; see also VULGAR. 7 [Weak] stunted, runty, undersized; see WEAK 1. — **make little of** make fun of, mock, abuse; see RIDICULE.

little *n.* some, a few, trifle; see BIT 1.

livable *a.* habitable, endurable, inhabitable; see BEARABLE, COMFORTABLE 2.

live *a.* 1 [Active] energetic, lively, dynamic; see ACTIVE. 2 [Not dead] aware, conscious, existing; see ALIVE. 3 [Not taped or filmed] broadcast direct, unrehearsed, on stage; see REAL 2.

live *v.* 1 [To have life] exist, continue, subsist, prevail, survive, breathe, be alive; see also BE 1. 2 [To enjoy life] relish, savor, experience, love, delight in, make every moment count, experience life to the fullest, live it up*, make the most of life, have a meaningful existence, take pleasure in, get a great deal from life.— *Ant.* SUFFER, endure pain, be discouraged. 3 [To dwell] live in, inhabit, settle; see DWELL. 4 [To gain subsistence] earn a living, support oneself, earn money, get ahead, provide for one's needs, make ends meet, subsist, maintain oneself; see also SURVIVE 1. 5 [To persist in human memory] remain, be remembered, last; see ENDURE 1. —**live and let live** be tolerant, accept, ignore; see ALLOW. —**live at** inhabit, reside, occupy; see DWELL. —**live down** overcome, endure, outgrow; see ENDURE 2. —**live on** be supported, earn, subsist on; see LIVE 4. —**live up to** meet expectations, do well, give satisfaction; see SATISFY 3. —**where one lives*** personally, in a vulnerable area, at one's heart; see PERSONALLY 2.

livelihood *n.* career, occupation, job; see PROFESSION 1.

lively *a.* vigorous, brisk, industrious; see ACTIVE.

livestock *n.* cows, sheep, domestic animals; see CATTLE, HERD.

living *a.* 1 [Alive] existing, breathing, having being; see ALIVE. 2 [Vigorous] awake, brisk, alert; see ACTIVE.

living *n.* 1 [A means of survival] existence, sustenance, maintenance; see SUBSISTENCE 2. 2 [Those not dead; *usually used with "the"*] the world, everyone, people; see ANIMAL, PERSON, PLANT.

living room *n.* lounge, front room, den; see ROOM 2.

load *n.* 1 [A physical burden] weight, encumbrance, truckload, carload, wagonload, shipload, cargo, haul, bale, charge, pack, mass, payload, shipment, contents, capacity, bundle.— *Ant.* LIGHTNESS, buoyancy, weightlessness. 2 [Responsibility]

charge, obligation, trust; see DUTY 1.
3 [A charge; *said especially of firearms*] shot, clip, round; see AMMUNITION. **4** [A measure] quantity, portion, amount; see MEASUREMENT 2, QUANTITY.

load *v.* **1** [To place a load] arrange, stow away, store, burden, stuff, put goods in, put goods on, containerize, pile, heap, fill, cram, put aboard, stack, pour in, take on cargo; see also PACK 1.—*Ant.* UNLOAD, unpack, take off cargo. **2** [To overload] encumber, saddle, weigh down; see BURDEN. **3** [To charge; *said especially of firearms*] insert a clip, ready, make ready to fire; see SHOOT 1.

loaded *a.* **1** [Supplied with a load] laden, burdened, weighted; see FULL 1. **2** [Ready to discharge; *said of firearms*] charged, primed, ready to shoot. **3** [*Intoxicated] inebriated, drunken, under the influence; see DRUNK.

loaf *n.* roll, bun, pastry; see BREAD, CAKE 2.

loaf *v.* idle, trifle, lounge, kill time, be inactive, be slothful, be lazy, take it easy, not lift a finger, putter, rest, dally, let down, slack off, vegetate, loll, malinger, drift, relax, slack, shirk, waste time, slow down, evade, dillydally, stand around, dream, goof off, goof around, goldbrick*, bum*, stall, piddle.

loafer *n.* idler, lounger, lazy person, ne'er-do-well, good-for-nothing, lazybones, malingerer, waster, slacker, shirker, wanderer, bum*, goldbrick*, deadbeat*.

loafing *a.* careless, apathetic, shirking; see LAZY 1.

loan *n.* lending, advance, giving credit, mortgage, time payment, installment loan, student loan, car loan, home equity loan, personal loan.

loan *v.* provide with, share, furnish; see LEND.

loaned *a.* lent, advanced, invested, granted, furnished, put out at interest, let, risked, leased; see also GIVEN.—*Ant.* BORROWED, rented, taken.

lobby *n.* vestibule, entryway, foyer; see HALL 1, ROOM 2.

lobby *v.* induce, put pressure on, promote; see INFLUENCE.

local *a.* **1** [Associated with a locality] sectional, divisional, territorial, district, provincial, neighborhood, town, civic, small-town, grass-roots, parochial, geographical; see also REGIONAL. **2** [Restricted to a locality] limited, confined, bounded; see RESTRICTED.

locale *n.* vicinity, territory, district; see AREA, REGION 1.

locality *n.* **1** [Area] district, section,

sector; see AREA, REGION 1. **2** [Position] spot, location, site; see POSITION 1. **3** [Neighborhood] block, vicinity, district; see NEIGHBORHOOD.

locally *a.* regionally, sectionally, provincially, in the neighborhood, in the town, close by, nearby.

locate *v.* **1** [To determine a location] discover, search out, find, come across, position, ferret out, stumble on, discover the location of, get at, hit upon, come upon, lay one's hands on, track down, unearth, establish, determine, station, place; see also FIND. **2** [To take up residence] settle down, establish oneself, inhabit; see DWELL, SETTLE 5.

located *a.* **1** [Discovered] traced, found, detected; see DISCOVERED. **2** [Situated] positioned, seated, fixed; see PLACED.

location *n.* **1** [A position] place, spot, section; see POSITION 1. **2** [A site] zone, place, scene; see AREA, NEIGHBORHOOD.

lock *n.* **1** [A device for locking] hook, catch, latch, bolt, deadbolt, bar, hasp, fastening, padlock, safety catch, clamp, clasp, tumblers, barrier, device, fixture, grip; see also FASTENER. **2** [A tuft of hair] tress, ringlet, curl; see HAIR 1. —**under lock and key** locked up, imprisoned, in jail; see CONFINED 3.

lock *v.* bolt, bar, secure; see FASTEN. —**lock up** confine, put behind bars, shut up; see IMPRISON.

locked *a.* secured, padlocked, closed; see TIGHT 2.

locker *n.* cabinet, footlocker, cupboard; see CLOSET, FURNITURE.

locket *n.* memento case, pendant, keepsake; see JEWELRY, NECKLACE.

lockup *n.* prison, jail, penitentiary; see JAIL.

lodge *n.* inn, hostel, ski lodge; see HOTEL, MOTEL, RESORT 2.

lodge *v.* **1** [To become fixed] catch, stay, remain; see STICK 1. **2** [To take (temporary) residence] room, stay over, stop over; see DWELL.

lodger *n.* guest, roomer, resident; see TENANT.

lodging *n.* **1** [Place of protection] sanctuary, retreat, asylum; see REFUGE 1, SHELTER. **2** [A (temporary) living place; *usually plural*] room, apartment, suite; see HOTEL, MOTEL, RESORT 2.

lofty *a.* tall, elevated, towering; see HIGH 2, RAISED 1.

log *n.* **1** [The main stem of a fallen or cut tree] timber, trunk, lumber; see WOOD 2. **2** [The record of a voyage] journal, account, diary; see RECORD 1.

logic *n.* reasoning, deduction, induction; see THOUGHT 1, PHILOSOPHY 1.

logical *a.* coherent, consistent, probable, sound, valid, pertinent, germane, legitimate, cogent, relevant, congruent with, as it ought to be; see also REASONABLE 1.

logically *a.* rationally, by reason, inevitably; see REASONABLY 1, 2.

logy* *a.* dull, sluggish, drowsy; see LAZY 1.

loiter *v.* saunter, stroll, dawdle, delay, lag, shuffle, waste time, procrastinate, tarry, fritter away time, loll, loaf, dabble, wait, pause, dillydally, hang back, trail, drag, ramble, idle; see also LINGER.—*Ant.* HURRY, hasten, stride along.

lone *a.* solitary, lonesome, deserted; see ALONE.

loneliness *n.* detachment, separation, solitude, desolation, isolation, aloneness, lonesomeness, forlornness.

lonely *a.* abandoned, homesick, forlorn, forsaken, friendless, deserted, desolate, homeless, left, lone, lonesome, solitary, empty, companionless, without company, unwanted, withdrawn, renounced, secluded, unattended, by oneself, apart, reclusive, single, rejected, unaccompanied; see also ALONE.—*Ant.* ACCOMPANIED, escorted, associated.

lonesome *a.* solitary, forlorn, alone; see HOMESICK, LONELY.

long *a.* 1 [Extended in space] lengthy, extended, outstretched, elongated, interminable, boundless, endless, unending, limitless, stretching, great, high, deep, drawn out, enlarged, expanded, spread, tall, lofty, towering, lengthened, stringy, rangy, lanky, gangling, far-reaching, distant, running, faraway, far-off, remote; see also LARGE 1.—*Ant.* SHORT, small, stubby. 2 [Extended in time] protracted, prolonged, enduring, unending, meandering, long-winded, spun out, lengthy, for ages, delayed, tardy, dilatory, without end, perpetual, forever and a day, lasting, continued, long-lived, sustained, lingering, day after day, hour after hour, etc.—*Ant.* SHORT, brief, fleeting. 3 [Tedious] hard, boring, prolonged; see DULL 4, 4 [Having (a certain commodity) in excess] rich, profuse, abundant; see PLENTIFUL 1. —**as (or so) long as** seeing that, provided, since; see BECAUSE. —**before long** in the near future, immediately, shortly; see SOON. —**long and short of it** gist, totality, outcome; see RESULT, WHOLE.

long *v.* desire, yearn for, wish; see WANT 1.

longing *n.* yearning, pining, hunger; see DESIRE 1, WISH.

long-lived *a.* long-lasting, perpetual, enduring; see PERMANENT.

look *n.* 1 [Appearance] features, demeanor, shape; see EXPRESSION 4, LOOKS. 2 [An effort to see] gaze, stare, gander, scrutiny, inspection, examination, contemplation, speculation, attending, noticing, regarding, marking, observation, reconnaissance, keeping watch, once-over*, look-see*; see also ATTENTION. 3 [A quick use of the eyes] glance, survey, squint, glimpse, peek, peep, leer, flash.

look *v.* 1 [To appear] seem to be, look like, resemble; see SEEM. 2 [To endeavor to see] seem, gaze, glance at, scan, stare, behold, contemplate, watch, survey, scrutinize, regard, inspect, discern, spy, observe, attend, examine, mark, gape, give attention, peer, ogle, have an eye on, study, peep, look at, take a gander at*, get a load of*; see also SEE 1. —**it looks like** probably, it seems that there will be, it seems as if; see SEEM. —**look after** look out for, support, watch; see GUARD. —**look into** investigate, study, probe; see EXAMINE. —**look up** come upon, research, find; see DISCOVER, SEARCH, SEEK. —**look up to** respect, idolize, honor; see ADMIRE.

lookout *n.* 1 [A place of vantage] watchtower, tower, observatory, patrol station, post, crow's-nest, observation tower. 2 [One stationed at a lookout] observer, sentinel, scout; see WATCHMAN.

looks* *n.* appearance, countenance, aspect, manner, demeanor, face, expression, features, form, shape, posture, bearing, presence.

loom *v.* 1 [To appear] come into view, come on the scene, arrive; see APPEAR 1. 2 [To appear large or imposing] menace, overshadow, hulk, emerge, shadow, top, tower, impress, hang over, emanate, seem huge, be near, hover, approach, come forth; see also THREATEN.

loop *n.* ring, orbit, circuit; see CIRCLE 1. —**knock (or throw) for a loop*** confuse, disturb, startle; see SHOCK 2.

loop *v.* curve, connect, tie together; see BEND.

loophole *n.* avoidance, means of escape, escape clause; see LIE, TRICK 1.

loose *a.* 1 [Unbound] unfastened, undone, untied, insecure, relaxed, unattached, unconnected, disconnected, untethered, unbuttoned, unclasped, unhooked, unsewed, unstuck, slack, loosened, baggy, unconfined, unlatched, unlocked, unbolted, unscrewed, unhinged, worked free; see also FREE 3.—*Ant.*

TIGHT, confined, bound. **2** [Movable] unattached, free, wobbly; see MOVABLE. **3** [Vague] disconnected, random, detached; see OBSCURE 1, VAGUE 2. **4** [Wanton] dissolute, licentious, disreputable; see LEWD 2. **—on the loose*** unconfined, unrestrained, wild; see FREE. **—set (or turn) loose** set free, release, untie; see FREE.

loosen v. **1** [To make loose] extricate, untie, unbind, undo, disentangle, let go, unlock, release, unfix; see also FREE. **2** [To become loose] relax, slacken, work free, break up, let go, become unstuck.—*Ant.* TIGHTEN, tighten up, become rigid.

loot n. spoils, plunder, take*; see BOOTY.

loot v. plunder, thieve, pilfer; see ROB, STEAL.

lop v. trim, prune, chop; see CUT 1.

lopsided a. uneven, unbalanced, crooked; see IRREGULAR 4.

lord n. **1** [A master] ruler, governor, prince; see LEADER 2. **2** [A member of the nobility] nobleman, count, peer; see ARISTOCRAT, ROYALTY.

Lord n. Divinity, the Supreme Being, Jehovah; see GOD 1.

lordly a. grand, dignified, honorable; see NOBLE 1, 2, 3.

lore n. enlightenment, wisdom, learning; see KNOWLEDGE 1.

lose v. **1** [To bring about a loss] mislay, misfile, misplace, disturb, disorder, confuse, mix, scatter, mess, muss, disorganize, forget, be careless with. **2** [To incur loss] suffer, miss, be deprived of, fail to keep, suffer loss, be impoverished from, become poorer by, let slip through the fingers*; see also WASTE 1.—*Ant.* PROFIT, improve, gain. **3** [To fail to win] suffer defeat, be defeated, go down in defeat, succumb, fall, be the loser, miss, have the worst of it, be humbled, take defeat at the hands of, be outdistanced; see also FAIL 1.—*Ant.* WIN, triumph, be victorious. **4** [To suffer financially] squander, expend, deplete; see SPEND, WASTE 2.

loser n. sufferer, victim, prey, failure, defeated, vanquished, dispossessed, underdog, disadvantaged, underprivileged, fallen.—*Ant.* WINNER, victor, conqueror.

losing a. **1** [Said of one who loses] failing, having the worst of it, on the way out; see RUINED 1. **2** [Said of an activity in which one must lose] futile, desperate, lost; see HOPELESS.

loss n. **1** [The act or fact of losing] ruin, destruction, mishap, misfortune, giving up, ill fortune, accident, calamity, trouble, disaster, sacrifice, catastrophe, trial, failure. **2** [Damage caused by losing something]

hurt, injury, wound; see DAMAGE 1, 2. **3** [The result of unprofitable activity] privation, want, bereavement, deprivation, need, destitution, being without, lack, waste, deterioration, impairment, degeneration, decline, disadvantage, wreck, wreckage, undoing, annihilation, bane, end, undoing, disorganization, breaking up, suppression, relapse.—*Ant.* ADVANTAGE, advancement, supply. **—at a loss** confused, puzzled, unsure; see UNCERTAIN.

losses n. casualties, damage, deaths; see DESTRUCTION 2.

lost a. **1** [Not to be found] misplaced, mislaid, missing, hidden, obscured, gone astray, nowhere to be found, strayed, lacking, wandered off, absent, forfeited, vanished, wandering, without, gone out of one's possession.—*Ant.* FOUND, come back, returned. **2** [Ignorant of the way] perplexed, bewildered, ignorant; see DOUBTFUL 1. **3** [Destroyed] demolished, devastated, wasted; see DESTROYED, RUINED 1. **4** [No longer to be gained] gone, passed, costly; see UNPROFITABLE. **5** [Helpless] feeble, sickly, disabled; see WEAK 1, 3. **—get lost*** go away, leave, begone.

lot n. **1** [A small parcel of land] parcel, part, division, patch, clearing, piece of ground, plat, plot, field, tract, block, portion, parking lot, piece, property, acreage. **2** [A number of individual items, usually alike] batch, group, set; see LOAD 1. **3** [Destiny] doom, fortune, fate; see CHANCE 1. **4** [*A great quantity] large amount, abundance, plenty, considerable amount, great numbers, bundle, bunch, cluster, group, pack, large numbers, very much, very many, quite a lot, quite a bit, a good deal, a whole bunch*, loads*, oodles*; see also PLENTY.

lotion n. liniment, hand lotion, cream, moisturizer, after-shave; see also COSMETIC, MEDICINE 2, SALVE.

loud a. **1** [Having volume of sound] deafening, ringing, ear-piercing, earsplitting, booming, intense, resounding, piercing, blaring, sonorous, resonant, crashing, deep, full, powerful, emphatic, thundering, heavy, big, deep-toned, thunderous, roaring, enough to wake the dead*; see also SHRILL.—*Ant.* SOFT, faint, feeble. **2** [Producing loud sounds] clamorous, noisy, uproarious, blatant, vociferous, turbulent, tumultuous, blustering, lusty, loud-voiced, boisterous, bombastic, raucous; see also HARSH.—*Ant.* QUIET, soft-voiced, calm. **3** [*Lacking manners and refinement] loudmouthed, brash, offensive; see RUDE 2, VULGAR. **4** [*Lacking good taste, especially in colors] garish, flashy, gaudy; see ORNATE.

loudly *a.* audibly, fully, powerfully, crashingly, shrilly, deafeningly, piercingly, resonantly, emphatically, vehemently, thunderingly, thunderously, in full cry, clamorously, noisily, uproariously, blatantly, at the top of one's lungs.

loudspeaker *n.* speaker, amplifier, public address system, PA, high-fidelity speaker, high-frequency speaker, low-frequency speaker, tweeter, woofer, bullhorn.

lounge *v.* idle, repose, kill time; see LOAF, REST 1.

lousy *a.* 1 [Having lice] infested with lice, crawling with lice, pediculous, pedicular; see also CREEPING. 2 [*Bad] horrible, miserable, faulty; see OFFENSIVE 2.

lovable *a.* adorable, sweet, lovely; see FRIENDLY.

love *n.* 1 [Passionate and tender devotion] attachment, devotedness, passion, infatuation, yearning, flame, rapture, enchantment, ardor, emotion, sentiment, fondness, tenderness, adoration, puppy love, crush*; see also AFFECTION.—*Ant.* HATE, aversion, antipathy. 2 [Affection based on esteem] respect, regard, appreciation; see ADMIRATION. 3 [A lively and enduring interest] involvement, concern, enjoyment; see DEVOTION. 4 [A beloved] dear one, loved one, cherished one; see LOVER 1. **—fall in love (with)** become enamored, lose one's heart, take a fancy to, have eyes for, take a liking to, become attached to, become fond of, fancy. **—for the love of** for the sake of, with fond concern for, because of; see FOR. **—in love** enamored, infatuated, charmed; see LOVING. **—make love** fondle, embrace, sleep with; see COPULATE, LOVE 2. **—not for love or money** under no conditions, by no means, no; see NEVER.

love *v.* 1 [To be passionately devoted] adore, be in love with, care for, hold dear, choose, fancy, be enchanted by, be passionately attached to, have affection for, dote on, glorify, idolize, prize, be fascinated by, hold high, think the world of, treasure, prefer, yearn for, be fond of, admire, long for, flip over*, fall for*, be nuts about*, be crazy about*, go for*.—*Ant.* HATE, detest, loathe. 2 [To express love by caresses] cherish, fondle, kiss, make love to, embrace, cling to, clasp, hug, take into one's arms, hold, pet, stroke, draw close, bring to one's side; see also KISS.—*Ant.* REFUSE, reject, spurn. 3 [To possess a deep and abiding interest] enjoy, delight in, relish; see ADMIRE, LIKE 1.

loved *a.* desired, cherished, adored; see BELOVED.

loveliness *n.* appeal, charm, fairness; see BEAUTY 1.

lovely *a.* 1 [Beautiful] attractive, pretty, gorgeous; see sense 2 and BEAUTIFUL, HANDSOME. 2 [Charming] engaging, enchanting, captivating; see CHARMING. 3 [*Very pleasing] nice, splendid, delightful; see PLEASANT 1, 2.

lover *n.* 1 [A suitor] sweetheart, admirer, escort, paramour, fiancé, fiancée, gentleman friend, significant other, flame, boyfriend*, girlfriend*, steady*. 2 [A willing student or practitioner] enthusiast, fan, hobbyist; see ZEALOT. 3 [An epithet for a beloved] beloved, sweetheart, dear; see DARLING.

loving *a.* admiring, respecting, valuing, liking, fond, tender, kind, enamored, attached, devoted, appreciative, attentive, thoughtful, passionate, ardent, amiable, warm, amorous, affectionate, anxious, concerned, sentimental, earnest, benevolent, cordial, caring, considerate, loyal, generous.

lovingly *a.* tenderly, devotedly, adoringly, warmly, ardently, fervently, zealously, earnestly, loyally, generously, kindly, thoughtfully, dotingly, fondly, affectionately, passionately, longingly, rapturously, admiringly, respectfully, reverently, with love, attentively.

low *a.* 1 [Close to the earth] squat, flat, level, low-lying, prostrate, crouched, below, not far above the horizon, low-hanging, knee-high, beneath, under, depressed, sunken, inferior, lying under.—*Ant.* HIGH, lofty, elevated. 2 [Quiet] muffled, hushed, soft; see FAINT 3. 3 [Low in spirits] dejected, moody, blue; see SAD 1. 4 [Vulgar] base, mean, coarse; see VULGAR. 5 [Ill] faint, dizzy, feeble; see SICK, WEAK 1. 6 [Inexpensive] economical, affordable, low-priced; see CHEAP 1. **—lay low** bring to ruin, overcome, kill; see DESTROY. **—lie low** wait, conceal oneself, take cover; see HIDE 2.

lower *a.* beneath, inferior, under; see LOW 1.

lower *v.* bring low, cast down, depress; see DECREASE 1, 2, DROP 2.

lowest *a.* shortest, littlest, smallest, slightest, least, rock-bottom, ground, base; see also MINIMUM.

low-key *a.* subdued, relaxed, laid-back*; see CALM.

lowly *a.* unpretentious, unassuming, meek; see HUMBLE 2.

loyal *a.* true, dependable, firm; see FAITHFUL.

loyally *a.* faithfully, conscientiously, truly, devotedly, constantly, sincerely, obediently, resolutely, ear-

loyalty *n.* allegiance, faithfulness, fidelity, trustworthiness, constancy, integrity, attachment, sincerity, adherence, bond, tie, honor, reliability, good faith, conscientiousness, dependability, commitment, support, zeal, ardor, earnestness, resolution, obedience, duty, honesty, truthfulness; see also DEVOTION.— *Ant.* INDIFFERENCE, disloyalty, faithlessness.

lubricant *n.* cream, ointment, oil; see GREASE.

lubricate *v.* oil, put grease on or in, lube*; see GREASE.

luck *n.* **1** [Good fortune] good luck, prosperity, wealth, streak of luck, windfall, success, advantage, profit, triumph, victory, win, happiness, blessings, godsend, opportunity, lucky break, break, the breaks*.— *Ant.* FAILURE, ill-fortune, bad luck. **2** [Chance] unforeseen occurrence, happenstance*, fate; see ACCIDENT, CHANCE 1. —**good luck** prosperity, fortune, affluence; see SUCCESS 2. —**in luck** lucky, successful, prosperous; see FORTUNATE. —**out of luck** unlucky, in misfortune, in trouble; see UNFORTUNATE. —**press (or push) one's luck** gamble, take risks, chance; see RISK. —**try one's luck** attempt, risk, endeavor; see TRY 1.

luckily *a.* opportunely, happily, favorably; see FORTUNATELY.

lucky *a.* **1** [Enjoying good luck] blessed, wealthy, victorious, happy, favored, winning, in luck, successful, prosperous; see also FORTUNATE. **2** [Supposed to bring good luck] providential, propitious, auspicious; see MAGIC.

lucrative *a.* fruitful, productive, gainful; see PROFITABLE.

ludicrous *a.* comical, odd, absurd; see FUNNY 1.

lug *v.* carry, tug, lift; see DRAW 1.

luggage *n.* trunks, bags, suitcases; see BAGGAGE.

lukewarm *a.* cool, tepid, room-temperature; see WARM 1.

lull *n.* quiet, stillness, calm; see SILENCE 1, PAUSE.

lull *v.* calm, quiet down, bring repose; see QUIET 1, 2.

lullaby *n.* good-night song, bedtime song, cradlesong; see SONG.

lumber *n.* cut timber, logs, sawed timber, forest products, boards, hardwood, softwood, lumbering products; see also WOOD 2.

luminescence *n.* fluorescence, incandescence, radiance; see LIGHT 1.

luminous *a.* lighted, glowing, radiant; see BRIGHT 1.

lump *n.* handful, protuberance, bunch, bump, hump, block, bulk, chunk, piece, portion, section; see also HUNK.

lumpy *a.* knotty, clotty, uneven; see IRREGULAR 4, THICK 1, 3.

lunacy *n.* madness, dementia, mania; see INSANITY.

lunatic *a.* **1** [Insane] demented, deranged, psychotic; see INSANE. **2** [Foolish] irrational, idiotic, senseless; see STUPID.

lunatic *n.* crazy person, psychotic, insane person; see MADMAN.

lunch *n.* meal, luncheon, brunch, refreshment, sandwich, snack, high tea.

lunch *v.* dine, have lunch, take a lunch break; see EAT 1.

lunge *v.* surge, lurch, bound; see JUMP 1.

lurch *v.* stagger, weave, lunge; see TOTTER.

lure *n.* bait, decoy, fake; see CAMOUFLAGE, TRICK 1.

lure *v.* enchant, bewitch, allure; see CHARM, FASCINATE.

lurid *a.* **1** [Shocking] startling, ghastly, sensational; see UNUSUAL, OFFENSIVE 2. **2** [Vivid] distinct, extreme, deep; see INTENSE.

lurk *v.* wait, crouch, conceal oneself; see HIDE 2.

lurking *a.* hiding out, sneaking, hidden; see HIDDEN.

luscious *a.* sweet, tasty, palatable; see DELICIOUS.

lush *a.* **1** [Green] verdant, dense, grassy; see GREEN 2. **2** [Delicious] rich, juicy, succulent; see DELICIOUS. **3** [Elaborate] extensive, luxurious, ornamental; see ELABORATE 1, ORNATE.

lust *n.* appetite, passion, sensuality; see DESIRE 2.

lust (after) *v.* long for, desire, hunger for; see WANT 1.

luster *n.* glow, brilliance, radiance; see LIGHT 1.

lustrous *a.* shiny, radiant, glowing; see BRIGHT 1.

lusty *a.* hearty, robust, vigorous; see HEALTHY.

luxuriant *a.* lush, dense, abundant; see GREEN 2.

luxurious *a.* comfortable, easy, affluent; see EXPENSIVE, RICH 2.

luxury *n.* **1** [Indulgence of the senses, regardless of the cost] gratification, costliness, expensiveness, richness, idleness, leisure, high living, lavishness; see also INDULGENCE 1.—*Ant.* POVERTY, deprivation, lack. **2** [An indulgence beyond one's means] extravagance, exorbitance, wastefulness; see EXCESS 1, WASTE 1.

lying *a.* **1** [In the act of lying] falsifying, prevaricating, swearing falsely, committing perjury, fibbing, equivocating, inventing, misrepresenting.—*Ant.* FRANK, truthful, honest. **2** [Given to lying] deceitful, unreliable, double-dealing; see DISHONEST. **3** [Not reliable] unsound, tricky, treacherous; see FALSE 2. **4** [Prostrate] supine, reclining, rest-

ing, horizontal, reposing, recumbent, flat, fallen, prone, powerless.

lynch *v.* hang, string up*, murder; see KILL 1.

lyric *n.* **1** [Verses set to music] the words, the lyrics, the verse; see POEM. **2** [A short, songlike poem] lyrical poem, ode, sonnet, hymn, nursery rhyme; see also POETRY, SONG, VERSE 1.

M

ma* *n.* mama*, mommy*, mom*; see MOTHER 1.

machine *n.* instrument, appliance, vehicle, computer, mechanism, implement, gadget; see also DEVICE 1, ENGINE, MOTOR, TOOL 1.

machine gun *n.* submachine gun, automatic rifle, semiautomatic rifle, tommy gun, burp gun*, Gatling gun, assault rifle, Uzi, M16, AK-47; see also GUN, WEAPON.

machinery *n.* appliances, implements, tools; see APPLIANCE, DEVICE 1, ENGINE, MACHINE, MOTOR.

mad *a.* **1** [Insane] demented, deranged, psychotic; see INSANE. **2** [Angry] provoked, enraged, exasperated; see ANGRY. **3** [Afflicted with rabies] rabid, hydrophobic, foaming at the mouth; see SICK. —**get mad** lose one's temper, become angry, rant and rave; see GET ANGRY.

madden *v.* annoy, infuriate, enrage; see ANGER.

maddening *a.* annoying, infuriating, offensive; see DISTURBING.

made *a.* fashioned, shaped, finished; see BUILT, FORMED, MANUFACTURED. —**have (or have got) it made*** succeed, be assured, be prosperous; see SUCCEED 1.

made-up *a.* **1** [False] invented, concocted, devised, fabricated, exaggerated, prepared, fictitious; see also FALSE 2, 3, UNREAL. **2** [Marked by the use of makeup] rouged, powdered, painted, colored, freshened, reddened.

madhouse *n.* mental hospital, asylum, bedlam; see HOSPITAL.

madly *a.* rashly, crazily, hastily; see VIOLENTLY, WILDLY.

madman *n.* lunatic, psychopath, maniac, insane person, deranged person, psychiatric patient, nut*, screwball*, oddball*, psycho*, loony*, wacko*, schizo*, cuckoo*.

madness *n.* derangement, aberration, delusion; see INSANITY.

magazine *n.* publication, pamphlet, booklet, manual, circular, journal, periodical, weekly, monthly, quarterly, annual, bulletin, transactions, review, supplement, gazette, report, brochure, pulp, zine, glossy*, slick*.

maggot *n.* grub, slug, larva; see PARASITE 1, WORM.

magic *a.* magical, mystic, diabolic, Satanic, necromantic, fiendish, demoniac, malevolent, shamanist, voodooistic, conjuring, spellbinding, enchanting, fascinating, cryptic, transcendental, supernatural, alchemistic, spooky, ghostly, haunted, weird, uncanny, eerie, disembodied, immaterial, astral, spiritualistic, psychic, supersensory, otherworldly, fairylike, mythical, mythic, charmed, spellbound, enchanted, under a spell, bewitched, entranced, cursed, prophetic, telepathic, clairvoyant, telekinetic, parapsychological; see also MYSTERIOUS 2.

magic *n.* **1** [The controlling of supernatural powers] occultism, legerdemain, necromancy, incantation, spell, wizardry, alchemy, superstition, enchantment, sorcery, prophecy, divination, astrology, taboo, witchcraft, black magic, voodooism, fire worship; see also WITCHCRAFT. **2** [An example of magic] incantation, prediction, soothsaying, fortunetelling, foreboding, exorcism, ghost dance.

magical *a.* occult, enchanting, mystic; see MAGIC, MYSTERIOUS 2.

magician *n.* enchanter, necromancer, conjurer, seer, soothsayer, diviner, sorcerer, wizard, warlock, medicine man, shaman, exorcist; see also PROPHET, WITCH.

magnet *n.* lodestone, magnetite, magnetic iron ore, natural magnet, artificial magnet, bar magnet, electromagnet, horseshoe magnet.

magnetic *a.* irresistible, captivating, fascinating; see CHARMING.

magnetism *n.* lure, influence, charm; see ATTRACTION.

magnificence *n.* grandeur, majesty, stateliness, nobleness, glory, radiance, grace, beauty, style, flourish, luxuriousness, glitter, nobility, greatness, lavishness, brilliance, splendor, richness, pomp; see also

GRANDEUR.—*Ant.* DULLNESS, simplicity, unostentatiousness.

magnificent *a.* exalted, great, majestic; see GRAND.

magnify *v.* amplify, blow up, expand; see INCREASE.

magnitude *n.* **1** [Size] extent, breadth, dimension; see MEASURE 1, MEASUREMENT 2, QUANTITY, SIZE. **2** [Importance] greatness, consequence, significance; see DEGREE 2, IMPORTANCE.

maid *n.* **1** [A female servant] maid-servant, nursemaid, housemaid, chambermaid, domestic, cleaning lady; see also SERVANT. **2** [A girl] child, maiden, schoolgirl; see GIRL, WOMAN 1.

maiden *a.* earliest, beginning, initial; see FIRST.

maiden name *n.* family name, inherited name, surname; see NAME 1.

mail *n.* letter, missive, snail mail, communication, correspondence, airmail letters, postal card, junk mail, postcard, printed matter, e-mail; see also LETTER 2.

mail *v.* post, send by mail, drop into a mailbox; see SEND 1.

mailed *a.* posted, sent by post, delivered, in the mail, shipped, consigned, dispatched, sent by mail, dropped in a mailbox, e-mailed; see also SENT.

maim *v.* mutilate, disable, disfigure; see DAMAGE, HURT.

main *a.* **1** [Principal] chief, dominant, first, authoritative, significant, most important, superior, foremost, central, leading; see also MAJOR 1. **2** [Only] utter, pure, simple; see ABSOLUTE.

mainland *n.* shore, beach, dry land; see LAND 1, REGION 1.

mainly *a.* chiefly, largely, essentially; see PRINCIPALLY.

maintain *v.* **1** [To uphold] hold up, advance, keep; see SUPPORT 2, SUSTAIN 1. **2** [To assert] state, affirm, attest; see DECLARE, REPORT 1, SAY. **3** [To keep ready for use] preserve, keep, conserve, repair, withhold, renew, reserve, defer, hold back, have in store, care for, save, put away, set aside, store up, keep for, lay aside, lay away, set by, keep on hand, keep in reserve, set apart, keep up, keep aside, control, hold over, manage, direct, have, own, sustain, secure, stick to, stand by; see also KEEP 1.—*Ant.* WASTE, neglect, consume. **4** [To continue] carry on, persevere, keep on; see CONTINUE 1. **5** [To support] provide for, take care of, keep; see SUPPORT 3, SUSTAIN 2.

maintenance *n.* sustenance, livelihood, resources; see PAY 1, 2, SUBSISTENCE 2.

majestic *a.* dignified, sumptuous, exalted; see GRAND, NOBLE 1, 3.

majesty *n.* **1** [Grandeur] splendor, magnificence, greatness; see GRANDEUR. **2** [A form of address; *usually capital*] Lord, King, Emperor, Prince, Royal Highness, Highness, Sire, Eminence, Queen.

major *a.* **1** [Greater] higher, larger, dominant, primary, upper, exceeding, extreme, ultra, over, above; see also SUPERIOR. **2** [Important] significant, main, influential; see IMPORTANT 1, PRINCIPAL.

majority *n.* **1** [The larger part] bulk, more than half, preponderance, most, best, gross, lion's share, greater number. **2** [Legal maturity] legal age, adulthood, voting age; see MANHOOD 1.

make *v.* **1** [To manufacture] construct, fabricate, assemble, fashion, form, shape, mold, compose, compile, create, effect, produce; see also BUILD, MANUFACTURE. **2** [To total] add up to, come to, equal; see AMOUNT TO. **3** [To create] originate, actualize, effect, generate, compose, plan, devise, construct, cause, conceive; see also COMPOSE 2, CREATE, INVENT 1, PRODUCE 1. **4** [To acquire] gain, get, secure; see GET 1. **5** [To force] constrain, compel, coerce; see FORCE. **6** [To cause] start, effect, initiate; see BEGIN 1, CAUSE. **7** [To wage] carry on, conduct, engage in; see ACT 2. **8** [To prepare] get ready, arrange, fix; see COOK, PREPARE 1. — **make believe** feign, simulate, counterfeit; see DREAM 2, PRETEND 1, 2. —**make do** get by, manage, accept; see ENDURE 2, SURVIVE 1, USE 1. —**make it*** achieve, triumph, accomplish; see SUCCEED 1. —**make off with** abduct, rob, kidnap; see STEAL. —**make out 1** [To understand] perceive, recognize, see; see UNDERSTAND 1. **2** [To succeed] accomplish, achieve, prosper; see SUCCEED 1. **3** [To see] discern, perceive, detect; see DISCOVER, SEE 1. — **make over 1** [To improve] amend, correct, restore; see IMPROVE 1, REDECORATE, REMODEL. **2** [To rebuild] renovate, reconstruct, refurbish; see REPAIR, RESTORE 3. — **make up 1** [To compose] compound, combine, mingle; see JOIN 1, MIX 1. **2** [To constitute] comprise, belong to, go into the making of, be contained in, be an element of, be a portion of, include, consist of; see also COMPOSE 1. **3** [To invent] fabricate, devise, fashion; see COMPOSE 2, CREATE, INVENT 1. **4** [To reconcile] conciliate, pacify, accommodate; see RECONCILE 2. **5** [To apply cosmetics] apply face powder, apply lipstick, apply eye shadow, etc.; powder, beautify, do up*, put one's face on. —**make up one's mind** choose, pick, elect; see DECIDE, RESOLVE.

make-believe *a.* fraudulent, pretended, acted; see FALSE 3, FANTASTIC, UNREAL.

make-believe *n.* sham, unreality, fairy tale; see FANTASY, PRETENSE 2.

makeshift *a.* substitute, alternative, stopgap; see TEMPORARY.

makeup *n.* 1 [Cosmetics] greasepaint, mascara, eyeliner, powder, foundation, eye shadow, lipstick, lip gloss, rouge, blush, war paint*; see also COSMETIC. 2 [Composition] construction, structure, arrangement; see COMPOSITION, DESIGN, FORMATION.

making *n.* performing, conception, formulation, devising, producing, constituting, causation, fashioning, building, origination, shaping, forging, designing, planning, fabrication, composition; see also PRODUCTION 1.

male *a.* manlike, virile, macho; see MASCULINE.

male *n.* fellow, man, guy; see BOY, FATHER 1.

malformed *a.* distorted, grotesque, abnormal; see DEFORMED, TWISTED 1.

malfunction *n.* slip, bad performance, glitch*; see FAILURE 1.

malice *n.* spite, animosity, resentment; see EVIL 1, HATRED.

malicious *a.* wicked, spiteful, hateful; see BAD 1.

malignant *a.* 1 [Diseased] cancerous, lethal, poisonous; see DEADLY. 2 [Harmful] deleterious, corrupt, subversive; see DANGEROUS, HARMFUL.

malpractice *n.* negligence, misbehavior, neglect; see CARELESSNESS, VIOLATION.

mama* *n.* mom*, ma*, mommy*; see MOTHER 1.

mammal *n.* quadraped, suckler, beast; see ANIMAL.

man *n.* 1 [The human race] mankind, human beings, humanity, human species, human nature, persons, mortals, individuals, earthlings, men and women, civilized society, creatures, fellow creatures, people, folk, society, *Homo sapiens* (Latin). 2 [An adult male] he, gentleman, Sir, Mr., fellow, mister, master, chap*, guy*; see also BOY. 3 [Anyone] human being, an individual, fellow creature; see PERSON 1. 4 [An employee] hand, worker, representative; see EMPLOYEE. 5 [Husband] married man, spouse, partner; see HUSBAND. —**as a (or one) man** in unison, united, all together; see UNANIMOUSLY. —**be one's own man** be independent, stand alone,

be free; see ENDURE 1. —**to a man** all, everyone, with no exception; see EVERYBODY.

man *v.* garrison, protect, fortify; see DEFEND 1, GUARD.

manage *v.* 1 [To direct] lead, oversee, instruct, mastermind, engineer, show, dominate, execute, handle, watch, guide, supervise, conduct, pilot, steer, run, minister, regulate, administer, delegate, manipulate, officiate, superintend, preside, control, operate, maneuver, maintain, care for, take over, take care of, carry on, watch over, have in one's charge, look after, see to, run the show*, call the shots*, run a tight ship*.—*Ant.* OBEY, follow, take orders. 2 [To contrive] accomplish, bring about, effect; see ACHIEVE, SUCCEED 1. 3 [To get along] bear up, survive, get by; see ENDURE 2.

manageable *a.* controllable, docile, compliant, governable, teachable, tractable, willing, obedient, submissive, yielding, adaptable, flexible, dutiful, humble, meek, easy; see also GENTLE 3, OBEDIENT 1, WILLING.—*Ant.* REBELLIOUS, unwilling, defiant.

managed *a.* 1 [Trained] handled, guided, persuaded, influenced, driven, counseled, urged, taught, instructed, coached, groomed, primed; see also EDUCATED, TRAINED.—*Ant.* WILD, undisciplined, unrestrained. 2 [Governed] ruled, controlled, dominated, commanded, directed, swayed, mastered, run, regulated, ordered, compelled, supervised, piloted, cared for, taken care of; see also GOVERNED.—*Ant.* FREE, ungoverned, unsupervised.

management *n.* 1 [Direction] command, supervision, superintendence, government, guidance, conduct, organization, handling, policy, order, power, control; see also COMMAND. 2 [Those who undertake management; *usually preceded by "the"*] directors, administrators, executives; see ADMINISTRATION 2.

manager *n.* director, handler, superintendent, supervisor; see also EXECUTIVE.

managing *n.* directing, supervising, governing, superintending, advising, overseeing, controlling, taking charge of, caring for, administering, executing, organizing, regulating, leading, piloting, steering, handling, charging, manipulating; see also OPERATING.

mandate *n.* command, decree, order; see COMMAND.

mandatory *a.* compulsory, forced, obligatory; see NECESSARY.

man-eating *a.* cannibal, carnivorous, omnivorous; see DANGEROUS, DEADLY.

maneuver *n.* 1 [A movement, usually military] stratagem, movement, procedure; see PLAN 2, TACTICS. **2** [A trick] subterfuge, finesse, ruse; see TRICK 1. **3** [Extensive practice in arms; *plural*] imitation war, exercise, war games; see DRILL 3, EXERCISE 1, PARADE 1.

maneuver *v.* plot, scheme, move, manage, contrive, design, devise, trick, cheat, conspire, finesse, angle for; see also PLAN 1.

mangle *v.* tear, lacerate, wound, injure, cripple, maim, rend, disfigure, cut, slit, butcher, hack, slash, slice, carve, bruise, mutilate; see also HURT 1.

manhandle *v.* damage, maul, mistreat; see ABUSE, BEAT 1.

manhood *n.* **1** [Male maturity] legal age, coming of age, prime of life, middle age, voting age, majority, adulthood. **2** [Manly qualities] virility, resoluteness, honor, gallantry, nobility, forcefulness, daring, boldness, tenacity, self-reliance, potency.

mania *n.* craze, lunacy, madness; see DESIRE 1, INSANITY, OBSESSION.

maniac *n.* lunatic, insane person, crazy person; see MADMAN.

manipulate *v.* handle, shape, mold; see FORM 1, MANAGE 1, PLAN 1.

manipulation *n.* guidance, use, direction; see MANAGEMENT 1.

mankind *n.* humanity, human race, society; see MAN 1.

manly *a.* masculine, courageous, fearless, firm, noble, valiant, intrepid, gallant, resolute, bold, confident, dauntless, self-reliant; see also MASCULINE.—*Ant.* COWARDLY, timid, effeminate.

man-made *a.* manufactured, artificial, synthetic, unnatural, counterfeit, not organic, ersatz, false, not genuine.

manner *n.* **1** [Personal conduct] mien, deportment, demeanor; see BEHAVIOR. **2** [Customary action] use, way, practice; see CUSTOM, HABIT 1. **3** [Method] mode, fashion, style; see METHOD. —**in a manner of speaking** in a way, so to speak, so to say; see RATHER.

mannerism *n.* idiosyncrasy, pretension, peculiarity; see CHARACTERISTIC, QUIRK.

mannerly *a.* polished, considerate, charming; see POLITE.

manners *n.* **1** [Personal behavior] conduct, deportment, bearing; see BEHAVIOR. **2** [Culture] etiquette, decorum, refinement; see COURTESY 1, CULTURE, ELEGANCE.

manpower *n.* workers, laborers, work force; see LABOR 4.

mansion *n.* villa, stately home, hall; see ESTATE, HOME 1.

manslaughter *n.* killing, homicide, slaying; see CRIME, MURDER.

mantel *n.* fireplace, mantelpiece, chimney piece; see SHELF 2.

manual *a.* hand-operated, not automatic, by hand; see OLD-FASHIONED.

manual *n.* guidebook, reference book, textbook; see BOOK.

manufacture *n.* fashioning, forming, assembling; see PRODUCTION 1.

manufacture *v.* make, construct, fabricate, produce, form, fashion, carve, mold, cast, frame, put together, turn out, stamp out, print out, cut out, have in production, have on the assembly line, mass-produce, print, shape, execute, accomplish, complete, tool, machine, mill, make up; see also BUILD.—*Ant.* DESTROY, demolish, tear down.

manufactured *a.* made, produced, constructed, fabricated, erected, fashioned, shaped, forged, turned out, mass-produced, tooled, executed, done, assembled, ready for the market, in shape, complete, completed; see also BUILT, FORMED.

manufacturer *n.* maker, producer, fabricator, constructor, builder, operator, craftsman, corporation, entrepreneur, company, business.

manufacturing *n.* fabrication, building, construction, assembling, preparing for market, putting in production, continuing production, keeping in production, forging, formation, mass production, composition, accomplishment, completion, finishing, doing, turning out; see also PRODUCTION 1.—*Ant.* DESTRUCTION, wreck, demolition.

manure *n.* guano, plant-food, compost; see DUNG, FERTILIZER.

manuscript *n.* composition, parchment, tablet, paper, document, original, copy, typescript, translation, facsimile, book, script; see also WRITING 2.

many *a.* numerous, multiplied, manifold, multitudinous, multifarious, diverse, sundry, profuse, innumerable, multiple, numberless, a world of, countless, uncounted, alive with, teeming, in heaps, several, of every description, prevalent, no end of, no end to, everywhere, crowded, common, usual, plentiful, abundant, galore; see also VARIOUS.—*Ant.* FEW, meager, scanty.

many *n.* a great number, abundance, thousands*; see PLENTY. —**a good** (or **great**) **many** a great number, abundance, thousands*; see PLENTY. —**as many** as much as, an equal number, a similar amount; see SAME.

many-sided *a.* **1** [Multilateral] polyhedral, geometric, trilateral, quadrilateral, tetrahedral; see also GEO-METRICAL. **2** [Gifted] endowed, talented, adaptable; see ABLE, VERSATILE.

map *n.* chart, graph, plat, sketch, delineation, drawing, picture, portrayal, draft, tracing, outline, projection. —**put on the map** make famous, bring fame to, glorify; see ESTABLISH 2. —**wipe off the map** eliminate, put out of existence, ruin; see DESTROY.

map *v.* outline, draft, chart; see PLAN 2.

mar *v.* **1** [To damage slightly] harm, bruise, scratch; see BREAK 2, DAMAGE. **2** [To impair] deform, deface, warp; see DESTROY.

marble *a.* petrified, granitelike, unyielding; see ROCK *n.* 1, STONE.

marble *n.* **1** [Metamorphic limestone] *Marbles include the following:* Parian, Pentelic, Carrian, Serpentine, Algerian, Tecali (onyx marbles), Tuscan, Gibraltar, Vermont, Georgia, fire, black, ophicalcite; see also STONE. **2** [A piece of carved marble] carving, figurine, figure; see ART, SCULPTURE, STATUE. **3** [A ball used in marbles] cat's-eye, shooter*, aggie; see TOY 1.

march *n.* **1** [The act of marching] progression, movement, advancing, advancement, countermarch, hike, parade, trudge; see also STEP 1, WALK 3. **2** [The distance or route marched] walk, trek, hike; see JOURNEY. **3** [Music for marching] martial music, wedding march, processional; see MUSIC. —**on the march** proceeding, advancing, tramping; see MOVING 1.

march *v.* move, advance, step out, go on, proceed, step, tread, tramp, patrol, prowl, parade, trudge, file, range, strut, progress, go ahead, forge ahead.—*Ant.* PAUSE, halt, retreat.

mare *n.* female horse, filly, jenny; see ANIMAL, HORSE.

margin *n.* border, lip, shore; see BOUNDARY, EDGE 1.

marginal *a.* rimming, borderline, peripheral; see BORDERING.

marijuana *n.* weed*, grass*, pot*; see DRUG.

marine *a.* maritime, of the sea, oceanic; see MARITIME, NAUTICAL.

marital *a.* conjugal, connubial, nuptial; see MARRIED.

maritime *a.* naval, marine, oceanic, seagoing, hydrographic, seafaring, aquatic, pelagic, Neptunian; see also NAUTICAL.

mark *n.* **1** [The physical result of marking] brand, stamp, blaze, imprint, impression, line, trace, check, stroke, streak, dot, point,

nick. **2** [A target] butt, prey, bull's-eye. **3** [Effect] manifestation, consequence, value; see RESULT. —**hit the mark** achieve, accomplish, do well; see SUCCEED 1. —**make one's mark** accomplish, prosper, become famous; see SUCCEED 1. —**miss the mark** be unsuccessful, err, mistake; see FAIL 1.

mark *v.* **1** [To make a mark] brand, stamp, imprint, blaze, print, check, chalk, label, sign, identify, check off, trace, stroke, streak, dot, point, nick, x, underline. **2** [To designate] earmark, point out, stake out, indicate, check off, mark off, signify, denote; see also MEAN 1. **3** [To distinguish] characterize, demarcate, qualify; see DISTINGUISH 1. **4** [To put prices upon] ticket, label, tag; see PRICE. —**mark down** reduce, put on sale, cut the price of; see PRICE. —**mark time** put off, postpone, kill time; see DELAY, WAIT 1. —**mark up** raise the price, adjust, add to; see INCREASE.

marked *a.* **1** [Carrying a mark] branded, signed, sealed, stamped, imprinted, inscribed, characterized by, distinguished by, recognized by, identified by. **2** [Priced] labeled, price-marked, marked down, marked up, ticketed, priced, tagged; see also COSTING.

marker *n.* **1** [A label] ticket, price mark, seal, brand, stamp, boundary mark, tombstone; see also LABEL. **2** [A writing instrument] pencil, pen, felt tip pen; see PEN 2.

market *n.* **1** [A place devoted to sale] trading post, mart, shopping mall, emporium, exchange, city market, public market, supermarket, meat market, fish market, stock market, stock exchange, fair, dime store, drugstore, discount store, department store, variety store, bazaar, warehouse, warehouse club, flea market, business, delicatessen; see also SHOP, STORE. **2** [The state of trade] supply and demand, market, sales; see BUSINESS 1, 4, DEMAND 1. —**be in the market (for)** want to buy, be willing to purchase, need; see WANT 1. —**on the market** salable, ready for purchase, available; see FOR (or ON or UP FOR) SALE.

market *v.* trade, exchange, barter; see SELL.

markup *n.* raise, margin, gross profit; see INCREASE, PROFIT 2.

marriage *n.* wedding, ceremony, nuptials, pledging, mating, matrimony, conjugality, union, match, arrangement, wedlock, wedded state, wedded bliss, holy matrimony, sacrament.

married *a.* wedded, espoused, mated, united, given in marriage, pledged in marriage, living in the married state, in the state of matrimony, hitched*.—*Ant.* SINGLE, unwedded, unmarried.

marry *v.* **1** [To take a spouse] wed, enter the matrimonial state, take wedding vows, pledge in marriage, mate, lead to the altar, take the vows, become one, tie the knot*, get hitched*.—*Ant.* DIVORCE, separate, reject. **2** [To join in wedlock] unite, give, join in matrimony, pronounce man and wife, pair up with, couple; see also JOIN 1.—*Ant.* DIVORCE, annul, separate.

marsh *n.* morass, bog, quagmire; see SWAMP.

marshy *a.* swampy, wet, sloppy; see MUDDY 1, 2.

martial *a.* warlike, soldierly, combative; see AGGRESSIVE.

martyr *n.* sufferer, offering, scapegoat; see SAINT, VICTIM.

martyrdom *n.* agony, suffering, ordeal; see TORTURE.

marvel *n.* miracle, phenomenon, curiosity; see WONDER 2.

marvel *v.* stare, stand in awe, stare with open mouth; see WONDER 1.

marvelous *a.* fabulous, astonishing, spectacular; see UNUSUAL 1.

masculine *a.* brawny, macho, male, virile, potent, vigorous, forceful, aggressive, muscular, powerful; see also MANLY.

masculinity *n.* virility, power, manliness; see MANHOOD 2, STRENGTH.

mash *n.* mix, pulp, paste; see FEED, MIXTURE 1.

mash *v.* crush, bruise, squash, chew, masticate, smash, pound, reduce, squeeze, brew, pulverize; see also GRIND, PRESS 1.

mashed *a.* crushed, pressed, mixed, pulpy, battered, pounded, smashed, macerated, squashed, softened, reduced, spongy, pasty, pulverized, masticated, chewed, bruised; made into a powder, made into a paste, etc.—*Ant.* WHOLE, hard, uncrushed.

mask *n.* **1** [A disguise] cover, false face, veil, hood, costume, domino; see also CAMOUFLAGE, DISGUISE. **2** [A protection] gas mask, catcher's mask, face mask, fencing mask, fireman's mask, respirator; see also PROTECTION 2. **3** [A masquerade] revel, party, carnival; see PARTY 1.

mask *v.* cloak, conceal, veil; see DISGUISE, HIDE 1.

masquerade *n.* masque, masked ball, Mardi Gras; see DANCE 1, ENTERTAINMENT, PARTY 1.

mass *n.* **1** [A body of matter] lump, bulk, piece, portion, section, batch, block, body, core, clot, coagulation, wad, gob; see also HUNK. **2** [A considerable quantity] heap, volume, crowd; see QUANTITY, SIZE 2. **3** [Size] magnitude, volume, span; see EXTENT, SIZE 2. **—the masses** the

proletariat, the rank and file, the multitude; see PEOPLE 3.

Mass *n.* eucharistic rite, Catholic service, Eucharist, Lord's Supper, Holy Communion, ceremony, liturgy; High Mass, Low Mass, Solemn High Mass, Requiem Mass, Votive Mass; see also CELEBRATION, WORSHIP 1.

massacre *n.* butchering, killing, slaughter; see MURDER.

massacre *v.* exterminate, decimate, annihilate; see KILL 1.

massage *v.* stimulate, caress, rub down; see RUB 1.

massive *a.* huge, heavy, cumbersome; see LARGE 1.

mass production *n.* automation, mass-producing, assembly-line methods; see MANUFACTURING, PRODUCTION 1.

mast *n.* spar, pole, flagstaff, post, timber, trunk; see also POST.

master *a.* leading, supreme, main; see EXCELLENT, MAJOR 1, PRINCIPAL.

master *n.* **1** [One who directs others] chief, director, boss; see EXECUTIVE, LEADER 2. **2** [A teacher] instructor, preceptor, mentor; see TEACHER. **3** [One who possesses great skill] genius, maestro, sage, past master, champion, prima donna, connoisseur, fellow, doctor; see also ARTIST.—*Ant.* DISCIPLE, beginner, undergraduate.

master *v.* **1** [To conquer] subdue, rule, humble; see SUCCEED 1. **2** [To become proficient in] gain mastery in, understand, comprehend; see LEARN, STUDY.

masterful *a.* commanding, expert, skillful; see EXCELLENT.

masterpiece *n.* model, standard, classic, gem, showpiece, cream of the crop, masterwork, magnum opus, *chef-d'oeuvre* (French).

mastery *n.* **1** [Control] dominance, sovereignty, government; see COMMAND, POWER 2. **2** [Ability to use to the full] skill, capacity, proficiency; see ABILITY, EDUCATION 1.

mat *n.* covering, floor covering, doormat, place mat, runner, doily, table mat, place setting, web, mesh, cloth, straw mat; see also COVER 1, RUG.

mat *v.* braid, tangle, snarl; see TWIST, WEAVE 1.

match *n.* **1** [An instrument to produce fire] safety match, sulphur match, matchstick, fusee*; see also LIGHT 3. **2** [An article that is like another] peer, equivalent, mate, analogue, counterpart, approximation; see also EQUAL. **3** [A formal contest] race, event, rivalry; see COMPETITION, SPORT 3.

match *v.* **1** [To find or make equals] equalize, liken, equate, make equal, pair, coordinate, level, even, match up, balance, mate, marry, unite; see also EQUAL. **2** [To be alike] harmonize, suit, be twins, be counterparts, be doubles, check with, go together, go with, rhyme with, take after; see also AGREE, RESEMBLE.—*Ant.* DIFFER, be unlike, bear no resemblance. **3** [To meet in contest] equal, keep pace with, compete with; see COMPETE.

matched *a.* doubled, similar, equated, evened, coordinated, harmonized, paired, mated; see also ALIKE, BALANCED 1.—*Ant.* UNLIKE, unequal, different.

matching *a.* comparable, analogous, parallel; see EQUAL.

mate *n.* **1** [One of a pair] complement, analogue, counterpart; see MATCH 2. **2** [A companion] playmate, classmate, buddy; see FRIEND. **3** [A marriage partner] spouse, bride, groom, bedmate, the old man*, the old lady*; see also HUSBAND, WIFE.

material *a.* palpable, sensible, corporeal; see PHYSICAL 1, REAL 2, TANGIBLE.

material *n.* **1** [Matter] body, corporeality, substance; see ELEMENT 2, MATTER 1. **2** [Unfinished matter; *often plural*] raw material, stuff, stock, staple, ore, stockpile, crop, supply, accumulation; see also ALLOY, ELEMENT 2, GOODS, METAL, MINERAL, PLASTIC, ROCK 1, WOOL.

materialistic *a.* possessive, acquisitive, opportunistic; see GREEDY, WORLDLY.

materialize *v.* be realized, take on form, become real, actualize, become concrete, metamorphose, reintegrate; see also BECOME.—*Ant.* DISSOLVE, disintegrate, disperse.

maternal *a.* parental, sympathetic, protective; see MOTHERLY.

maternity *n.* parenthood, motherhood, motherliness; see PARENT.

mathematical *a.* arithmetical, numerical, digital; see NUMERICAL.

mathematics *n.* science of real numbers, science of numbers, computation, reckoning, calculation, new math, math. *Types of mathematics include the following:* arithmetic, algebra, plane geometry, solid geometry, spherical geometry, trigonometry, trig*, analytical geometry, calculus, differential calculus, integral calculus, applied mathematics, statistics, topology, geodesy, Fourier analysis, game theory, set theory, number theory, systems analysis, quadratics.

matriarch *n.* female ruler, dowager, matron; see QUEEN.

matrimony *n.* conjugality, wedlock, union; see MARRIAGE.

matron *n.* lady, wife, mother; see WOMAN 1.

matronly *a.* middle-aged, dignified, sedate; see MATURE, MOTHERLY.

matted *a.* snarled, rumpled, disordered; see TANGLED, TWISTED 1.

matter *n.* **1** [Substance] body, material, substantiality, corporeality, constituents, stuff, object, thing, physical world; see also ELEMENT 2.—*Ant.* NOTHING, nothingness, immateriality. **2** [Subject] interest, focus, resolution; see SUBJECT, THEME 1. **3** [An affair] undertaking, circumstance, concern; see AFFAIR 1. **—as a matter of fact** in fact, in actuality, truly; see REALLY 1. **—for that matter** in regard to that, as far as that is concerned, concerning that; see AND. **—no matter** it does not matter, it is of no concern, regardless of; see REGARDLESS 2.

matter *v.* signify, be substantive, carry weight, weigh, be important, have influence, import, imply, express, be of consequence, involve, be worthy of notice; see also MEAN 1.

matter-of-fact *a.* objective, prosaic, feasible; see PRACTICAL.

mattress *n.* innerspring, springs, box spring, bedding, cushion, crib mattress; see also BED.

mature *a.* full-grown, middle-aged, grown, grown-up, of age, in full bloom, womanly, manly, matronly, developed, prepared, settled, cultivated, cultured, sophisticated; see also EXPERIENCED.—*Ant.* YOUNG, adolescent, immature.

mature *v.* grow up, become a man, become a woman, come of age, become experienced, settle down, ripen, reach perfection, attain majority, culminate, become wise, become perfected, grow skilled, fill out; see also AGE, DEVELOP 1.

matured *a.* grown, full-grown, aged; see FINISHED.

maturity *n.* **1** [Mental competence] development, sophistication, cultivation, culture, civilization, advancement, mental power, capability. **2** [Physical development] prime of life, post-pubescence, adulthood; see MAJORITY 2. **3** [Ripeness] readiness, mellowness, sweetness; see DEVELOPMENT.

maul *v.* mangle, manhandle, batter; see BEAT 1, HIT 1.

maxim *n.* aphorism, adage, epithet; see PROVERB, SAYING.

maximum *a.* supreme, highest, greatest; see BEST.

maximum *n.* supremacy, height, pinnacle, preeminence, culmination, matchlessness, preponderance, apex, acme, peak, greatest number, highest degree, summit; see also CLIMAX.—*Ant.* MINIMUM, foot, bottom.

may *v.* **1** [Grant permission] be permitted to, be allowed to, can, be privileged to, be authorized to, be at liberty to. **2** [Concede possibility] will, shall, be going to, should, be conceivable, be possible, be practicable, be within reach, be obtainable; see also WILL 3.

maybe *a.* perhaps, possibly, it might be, it could be, maybe so, as it may be, conceivably, God willing.—*Ant.* HARDLY, scarcely, probably not.

mayor *n.* magistrate, Lord Mayor, burgomaster, His Honor, Her Honor, president of a city council, civil administrator, civil judge, city father; see also EXECUTIVE.

maze *n.* tangle, entanglement, twist, winding, convolution, intricacy, confusion, meandering, labyrinth, puzzle.—*Ant.* ORDER, disentanglement, simplicity.

meadow *n.* grass, pasture, lea, mead*, mountain meadow, upland pasture, meadowland, bottom land, bottoms, pasturage; hay meadow, clover meadow, bluegrass meadow, etc.; salt marsh, steppe, heath, pampa, savanna; see also FIELD 1.

meager *a.* lank, lanky, gaunt, starved, emaciated, lean, bony, slender, slim, spare, little, bare, scant, stinted, lacking, wanting, scrawny, withered, lithe, narrow, tenuous, skinny; see also THIN 2.—*Ant.* FAT, plump, stout.

meal *n.* **1** [Ground feed] bran, farina, grits, fodder, provender, forage; see also FEED, FLOUR, GRAIN 1. *Types of meal include the following:* corn meal, corn grits, hominy, corn starch, barley meal, oatmeal, soybean meal, soybean flour. **2** [The quantity of food taken at one time] repast, feast, refreshment, mess, eats*, grub*, chow*, spread*, square meal*, snack. *Meals include the following:* breakfast, dinner, lunch, banquet, brunch, snack; tea, high tea (British), picnic, luncheon, dessert, midnight supper; see also BREAKFAST, DINNER, LUNCH.

mean *a.* **1** [Small-minded] base, low, debased; see VULGAR 2. **2** [Of low estate] servile, pitiful, shabby; see HUMBLE 2. **3** [Vicious] spiteful, malicious, cruel, unkind, shameless, dishonorable, degraded, contemptible, evil, infamous, treacherous, crooked, faithless, unfaithful, ill-tempered, bad-tempered, dangerous, despicable, degenerate, knavish, unscrupulous, hard as nails.

mean *n.* middle, median, midpoint; see AVERAGE, CENTER 1.

mean *v.* **1** [To have as meaning] indicate, spell, denote, signify, add up, determine, symbolize, imply, involve, speak of, touch on, stand for, drive at, point to, connote, suggest, express, designate, intimate,

betoken, purport. **2** [To have in mind] anticipate, propose, expect; see INTEND 1. **3** [To design for] destine for, aim at, set apart; see INTEND 2.

meander *v.* twist and turn, zigzag, snake; see RAMBLE 2, WIND 3, WALK 1.

meaning *n.* sense, import, purport, purpose, definition, object, implication, application, intent, suggestion, denotation, connotation, aim, drift, context, significance, essence, worth, intrinsic value, interest.—*Ant.* NONSENSE, aimlessness, absurdity.

meaningful *a.* significant, exact, essential; see IMPORTANT 1.

meaningless *a.* vague, absurd, insignificant; see TRIVIAL, UNIMPORTANT.

meanness *n.* **1** [The quality of being mean] small-mindedness, debasement, degradation, degeneracy, unscrupulousness, stinginess, disrepute, malice, unworthiness, ill-temper, unkindness, covetousness, avarice, miserliness; see also GREED.—*Ant.* GENEROSITY, nobility, worthiness. **2** [A mean action] belittling, defaming, groveling, cheating, sneaking, quarreling, scolding, taking advantage of, deceiving, coveting, grudging, dishonoring, defrauding, shaming, degrading, stealing.

means *n.* **1** [An instrumentality or instrumentalities] machinery, mechanism, agency, organ, channel, medium, factor, agent, power, organization; see also METHOD, SYSTEM. **2** [Wealth] resources, substance, property; see WEALTH. **—by all means** of course, certainly, indeed; see SURELY, YES. **—by any means** in any way, at all, somehow; see ANYHOW. **—by means of** with the aid of, somehow, through; see BY 2. **—by no (manner of) means** in no way, not possible, definitely not; see NEVER, NO.

meanwhile *a.* meantime, during the interval, in the interim, ad interim (Latin), for the time being, until, till, up to, in the meantime, when; see also DURING.

measurable *a.* weighable, definite, limited, determinable, knowable, recognizable, detectable, calculable, real, present, fathomable, assessable.

measure *n.* **1** [A unit of measurement] dimension, capacity, weight, volume, distance, degree, quantity, area, mass, frequency, density, intensity, rapidity, speed, caliber, bulk, sum, duration, magnitude, amplitude, size, pitch, ratio, depth, scope, height, strength, breadth, amplification. *Common units of* *measure include the following—linear:* inch, foot, yard, rod, mile, millimeter, centimeter, meter, kilometer; *surface:* square inch, square foot, square yard, acre, square rod, square mile, hectare; *volume:* fluid ounce, fluid dram, pint, quart, gallon, milliliter, liter; *weight:* ounce, pound, ton, milligram, gram, kilogram; *relationship:* horsepower, baud, revolutions per minute (rpm), miles per hour (mph), feet per second (fps), per second per second, erg, foot-pound, kilowatt-hour, acre-foot, decibel, man-hour, ohm, watt, volt, octane number. **2** [Anything used as a standard] rule, test, trial, example, standard, yardstick, norm, pattern, type, model; see also CRITERION. **3** [A beat] rhythm, tempo, time, step, throb, stroke, accent, meter, cadence, tune, melody, stress, vibration, division; see also BEAT 2. **—for good measure** added, as a bonus, additionally; see EXTRA. **—in full measure** completely, sufficiently, amply; see ADEQUATELY. **—take measures** take action, do things to accomplish a purpose, take steps; see ACT 1.

measure *v.* **1** [To apply a standard of measurement] rule, weigh, mark, lay out, grade, graduate, gauge, sound, pitch, beat, stroke, time, mark off, scale, rank, even, level, gradate, line, align, line out, regulate, portion, set a standard, average, equate, square, calibrate, block in, survey, map. **2** [To contain by measurement] hold, cover, contain; see INCLUDE 1.

measured *a.* **1** [Steady] orderly, systematic, deliberate; see REGULAR 3. **2** [Determined] checked, evaluated, calculated; see DETERMINED 1.

measurement *n.* **1** [The act of measuring] estimation, analysis, computation; see JUDGMENT 2. **2** [The result of measuring] distance, dimension, weight, degree, pitch, time, height, depth, density, volume, area, length, measure, thickness, quantity, magnitude, extent, range, scope, reach, amount, capacity, frequency, intensity, pressure, speed, caliber, grade, span, step, strength, mass. **3** [A set of measures] inch, foot, yard; see MEASURE 1.

meat *n.* beef, pork, flesh, veal, mutton, lamb, chicken, turkey, goose, duck, rabbit, venison, horsemeat; see also FOOD. *Cuts and forms of meat include the following:* roast, cutlet, steak, filet, leg, shoulder, loin, sirloin, tenderloin, rib, round, chuck, brisket, shank, rump, flank, chop, liver, brains, kidneys, heart, bacon, tripe, shank, sausage, frankfurter, ground meat, chipped meat,

dried meat, salted meat, pickled meat.

mechanic *n.* machinist, technician, skilled worker; see WORKMAN.

mechanical *a.* **1** [Concerning machinery] engineering, production, manufacturing, tooling, tuning, implementing, fabricating, forging, machining, building, construction, constructing. **2** [Like a machine] made to a pattern, machinelike, stereotyped, standardized, without variation, robotic, unchanging, monotonous.—*Ant.* ORIGINAL, varied, changing. **3** [Operated by the use of machinery] power-driven, involuntary, programmed; see AUTOMATED, AUTOMATIC.

mechanically *a.* automatically, unreasoningly, unchangeably; see REGULARLY.

mechanism *n.* working parts, mechanical action, the works; see DEVICE 1, TOOL 1.

mechanize *v.* equip, computerize, industrialize, motorize, automate, put on the assembly line, make mechanical, robotize, introduce machinery into.

medal *n.* award, commemoration, badge; see DECORATION 3.

medallion *n.* ornament, emblem, necklace; see JEWELRY.

meddle *v.* **1** [To interfere in others' affairs] interfere, obtrude, interlope, intervene, pry, snoop, nose, impose oneself, infringe, break in upon, make it one's business, abuse one's rights, push in, chime in, force an entrance, encroach, intrude, be officious, obstruct, impede, hinder, encumber, busy oneself with, come uninvited, tamper with, inquire, be curious, kibitz*, stick one's nose in*, monkey with*, bust in*, muscle in*, barge in, have a finger on*, butt in*, horn in*; see also INTERRUPT.—*Ant.* NEGLECT, ignore, let alone. **2** [To handle others' things] tamper, molest, pry, fool with, trespass, use improperly.

meddlesome *a.* obtrusive, interfering, officious, meddling, intrusive, impertinent, interposing, interrupting, obstructive, impeding, hindering, encumbering, curious, tampering, prying, snooping, troublesome, snoopy*, nosy*, kibitzing*, chiseling*.

meddling *n.* interfering, interrupting, snooping; see INTERFERENCE 1, RUDENESS.

media *n.* radio, television, newspapers, magazines, journalism, news, reporters, reportage, *paparazzi* (Italian), the networks, cable, programming, audiovisual devices.

medic* *n.* physician, practitioner, surgeon; see DOCTOR, MEDICINE 1.

medical *a.* healing, medicinal, curative, therapeutic, restorative, prophylactic, preventive, alleviating, medicating, pharmaceutical, sedative, narcotic, tonic, disinfectant, corrective, pathological, cathartic, health-bringing, demulcent, balsamic, emollient.—*Ant.* HARMFUL, destructive, disease-giving.

medication *n.* remedy, pill, vaccination; see MEDICINE 2.

medicinal *a.* curative, healing, therapeutic; see HEALTHFUL.

medicine *n.* **1** [The healing profession] healers, practitioners, doctors, physicians, nurses, EMT's, medics*, surgeons, osteopaths, homeopaths, chiropractors. **2** [A medical preparation] drug, dose, dosage, potion, prescription, pill, tablet, caplet, capsule, draft, patent medicine, remedy, cure, antipoison, antibiotic, medication, vaccination, inoculation, injection, draught, herb, specific, nostrum, elixir, tonic, balm, salve, lotion, ointment, emetic, shot. **3** [The study and practice of medicine] medical science, physic, healing art, medical profession. *Branches of medicine include the following:* surgery, therapy, therapeutics, anesthesiology, internal medicine, family practice, general practice, psychiatry, psychotherapy, ophthalmology, obstetrics, gynecology, pediatrics, sports medicine, audiology, orthopedics, neurology, cardiology, dermatology, pathology, endocrinology, immunology, hematology, urology, inhalation therapy, diagnostics, radiotherapy, geriatrics, veterinary medicine.

medieval *a.* pertaining to the Middle Ages, feudal, antiquated; see OLD 3.

mediocre *a.* **1** [Ordinary] average, typical, unexceptional; see COMMON 1. **2** [Low in quality] not good enough, inferior, second-rate; see POOR 2.

mediocrity *n.* **1** [Ordinariness] commonplaceness, commonness, averageness; see REGULARITY. **2** [Substandard quality] inferiority, triviality, second-rateness.

meditate *v.* **1** [To muse] ponder, study, contemplate, muse over, revolve, say to oneself, reflect, view, brood over, dream; see also THINK 1. **2** [To think over] weigh, consider, speculate; see THINK 1.

meditation *n.* musing, contemplation, reflection; see REFLECTION 1, THOUGHT 1.

medium *a.* commonplace, average, ordinary; see COMMON 1.

medium *n.* **1** [A means] mechanism, means, agent; see MEANS 1, PART 3. **2** [A means of expression] symbol, sign, token, interpretation, manifestation, revelation, evidence, mark, statement; see also COMMUNICATION, SPEECH 2. **3** [A supposed

channel of supernatural knowledge] oracle, seer, spiritualist; see PROPHET.

medley *n.* mingling, assortment, conglomeration; see MIXTURE 1, VARIETY 1.

meek *a.* **1** [Humble] unassuming, plain, mild; see HUMBLE 1, MODEST 2. **2** [Long-suffering] passive, resigned, uncomplaining; see PATIENT 1. **3** [Lacking spirit] submissive, compliant, subdued; see DOCILE, RESIGNED.

meekness *n.* submissiveness, mildness, timidity; see HUMILITY.

meet *n.* match, athletic event, tournament; see EVENT, COMPETITION.

meet *v.* **1** [To come together] converge, assemble, crowd, rally, convene, collect, associate, unite, swarm, get together, enter in; see also GATHER 1. **2** [To go to a place of meeting] resort, be present at, gather together, convene, congregate, muster, appear; see also ASSEMBLE 1, ATTEND.—*Ant.* LEAVE, disperse, scatter. **3** [To touch] reach, coincide, adhere; see JOIN 1. **4** [To become acquainted] make the acquaintance of, be presented to, be introduced, present oneself to, make oneself known to, get next to*, come to know; see also FAMILIARIZE (ONESELF WITH). **5** [To fulfill] answer, fit, suffice; see SATISFY 3. **6** [To encounter] fall in with, come upon, meet by accident, come across, meet face to face, face up to, bump into, touch shoulders with, meet at every turn, engage, join, battle, match, push, brush against, shove; see also FACE 1, FIGHT.—*Ant.* ABANDON, turn one's back on, leave. —**meet with** observe, experience, suffer; see FIND.

meeting *n.* **1** [The act of coming together] encounter, juxtaposition, joining, juncture, unifying, unification, adherence, convergence, confrontation, contacting, connection, conflict, accord, agreement.—*Ant.* SEPARATION, departure, dispersal. **2** [A gathering, usually of people] conference, assemblage, rally; see GATHERING.

melancholy *a.* depressed, unhappy, dispirited; see SAD 1.

melancholy *n.* unhappiness, wistfulness, despair; see DEPRESSION 2, GRIEF, SADNESS.

meld *v.* blend, merge, unite; see MIX 1, UNITE.

mellow *a.* **1** [Ripe] sweet, soft, perfected; see RIPE 1. **2** [Culturally mature] cultured, fully developed, broad-minded; see MATURE.

mellowed *a.* mature, ripened, softened; see RIPE 1, SOFT 3.

melodious *a.* agreeable, pleasing,

resonant; see HARMONIOUS 1, MUSICAL 1.

melodrama *n.* play, theater, sitcom*; see DRAMA.

melodramatic *a.* artificial, spectacular, sensational; see EXAGGERATED.

melody *n.* 1 [The quality of being melodious] concord, euphony, resonance; see HARMONY 1. 2 [A melodious arrangement] air, lyric, strain; see SONG.

melon *n.* watermelon, cantaloupe, muskmelon; see FOOD, FRUIT.

melt *v.* 1 [To liquefy] thaw, fuse, blend, merge, soften, flow, run, disintegrate, waste away; see also DISSOLVE.—*Ant.* FREEZE, harden, coagulate. 2 [To relent] forgive, show mercy, become lenient; see YIELD 1. 3 [To decrease] vanish, pass away, go; see DECREASE 1.

melted *a.* softened, thawed, liquefied, dwindled, blended, merged, wasted away, disintegrated, vanished, decreased, diminished, tempered, relaxed.

melting *a.* softening, liquefying, reducing; see SOFT 2.

member *n.* 1 [A person or group] constituent, charter member, active member, member in good standing, honorary member, affiliate, brother, sister, comrade, chapter, post, branch, lodge, district, company, battalion, regiment, division. 2 [A part] portion, segment, fragment; see DIVISION 1, PART 1. 3 [A part of the body] organ, arm, leg; see LIMB 2.

membership *n.* club, society, association; see MEMBER 1.

memorable *a.* 1 [Historic] momentous, critical, unforgettable, crucial, famous, illustrious, distinguished, great, notable, significant, decisive, enduring, lasting, monumental, eventful, interesting; see also FAMOUS. 2 [Unusual] remarkable, exceptional, singular; see sense 1 and UNUSUAL 1.

memorandum *n.* notice, record, memo; see NOTE 2, REMINDER.

memorial *a.* dedicatory, remembering, commemorative; see REMEMBERED.

memorial *n.* remembrance, testimonial, tablet, slab, pillar, tombstone, headstone, column, monolith, mausoleum, record, memento, inscription, statue; see also CELEBRATION, CEREMONY 2, MONUMENT.

memorize *v.* fix in the memory, record, commemorate, memorialize, retain, commit to memory, imprint in one's mind, bear in mind, give word for word, get down pat*, have in one's head*, have at one's fingertips, learn by heart; see also LEARN,

REMEMBER 2.—*Ant.* NEGLECT, forget, fail to remember.

memory *n.* 1 [The power to call up the past] recollection, retrospection, reminiscence, thought, consciousness, subconsciousness, unconscious memory, retentive memory, photographic memory, visual memory, auditory memory; see also MIND 1. 2 [That which can be recalled] mental image, picture, vision; see THOUGHT 2. —**in memory** in commemoration, in honor, in memoriam; see REMEMBERED.

menace *n.* 1 [A threat] caution, intimidation, foretelling; see WARNING. 2 [An imminent danger] hazard, peril, threat; see DANGER.

menace *v.* intimidate, portend, loom; see THREATEN.

menacing *a.* imminent, impending, threatening; see DANGEROUS, OMINOUS, SINISTER.

mend *v.* 1 [To repair] heal, patch, fix; see REPAIR. 2 [To improve] aid, remedy, cure; see CORRECT.

mended *a.* restored, put in shape, patched, patched up, renovated, refreshed, renewed, corrected, helped, bettered, lessened, remedied, cured, relieved, rectified, rejuvenated, remodeled, altered, changed, fixed, regulated, rebuilt, regenerated, reorganized, revived, touched up, doctored*; see also REPAIRED.

menial *a.* common, servile, abject; see HUMBLE 1, 2.

mental *a.* 1 [Concerning the mind] reasoning, cerebral, thinking; see RATIONAL 1, THOUGHTFUL 1. 2 [Existing only in the mind] subjective, subliminal, subconscious, telepathic, psychic, clairvoyant, imaginative; see also IMAGINARY.—*Ant.* OBJECTIVE, BODILY, SENSUAL.

mentality *n.* intellect, comprehension, reasoning; see MIND 1.

mentally *a.* rationally, psychically, intellectually; see REASONABLY 1.

mention *n.* notice, naming, specifying; see REMARK. —**not to mention** in addition, too, without even mentioning; see ALSO.

mention *v.* notice, specify, cite, introduce, state, declare, quote, refer to, discuss, touch on, instance, intimate, notify, communicate, suggest, make known, point out, bring up, speak of, throw out, toss off; see also TELL 1.—*Ant.* OVERLOOK, take no notice of, disregard.

mentioned *a.* noticed, cited, specified, named, quoted, introduced, referred to, discussed, declared, revealed, brought up, considered, communicated, made known, spoken of; see also TOLD.

menu *n.* bill of fare, cuisine, food; see LIST.

merchandise n. wares, commodities, stock; see COMMODITY.

merchandise v. market, distribute, promote; see SELL.

merchant n. trader, storekeeper, retailer, shopkeeper, wholesaler, exporter, shipper, dealer, jobber, tradesman; see also BUSINESSMAN.

merciful a. lenient, feeling, compassionate, softhearted, mild, tolerant, kindly, indulgent; see also KIND.—*Ant.* CRUEL, pitiless, unsparing.

merciless a. pitiless, unsparing, relentless; see CRUEL, FIERCE, RUTHLESS.

mercy n. leniency, lenience, softheartedness, mildness, clemency, amnesty, pardon, tenderness, gentleness, compassion, ruth*; see also GENEROSITY, TOLERANCE 1.—*Ant.* INDIFFERENCE, intolerance, selfishness. —**at the mercy of** in the power of, vulnerable to, controlled by; see SUBJECT.

mere a. small, minor, insignificant; see LITTLE 1, POOR 2.

merely a. slightly, solely, simply; see HARDLY, ONLY 3.

merge v. fuse, join, blend; see MIX 1, UNITE.

merger n. amalgamation, consolidation, alliance; see ORGANIZATION 2.

merit n. 1 [Worth] credit, benefit, advantage; see QUALITY 3, VALUE 3. 2 [A creditable quality] worthiness, excellence, honor; see CHARACTER 2, VIRTUE 1.

merit v. be worth, warrant, justify; see DESERVE.

merited a. earned, proper, fitting; see DESERVED, FIT 1.

merrily a. joyfully, gleefully, genially; see CHEERFULLY, HAPPILY.

merriment n. joy, cheerfulness, gaiety; see HAPPINESS, HUMOR 3.

merry a. festive, joyous, mirthful; see HAPPY. —**make merry** frolic, revel, enjoy; see PLAY 1.

mesa n. plateau, table, tableland, butte, table mountain; see also HILL, MOUNTAIN 1.

mesh v. coincide, suit, coordinate; see AGREE, FIT 1.

mess n. 1 [A mixture] combination, compound, blend; see MIXTURE 1. 2 [A confusion] jumble, muss, chaos, clutter, clog, congestion, snag, scramble, complexity, mayhem, shambles, hodgepodge; see also CONFUSION, DISORDER.

message n. news, information, intelligence; see ADVICE, BROADCAST, COMMUNICATION, DIRECTIONS. —**get the message*** get the hint, comprehend, perceive; see UNDERSTAND 1.

messenger n. bearer, minister, herald, carrier, courier, runner, crier, gopher*, errand boy, intermediary,

envoy, emissary, angel, prophet, nuncio, go-between; see also AGENT.

Messiah n. Saviour, Redeemer, Son of Man, Jesus Christ; see also CHRIST, GOD 1.

mess up v. spoil, ruin, foul up*, damage; see also BOTCH, DESTROY.

messy a. rumpled, untidy, slovenly; see DIRTY, DISORDERED.

metal n. element, native rock, ore deposit, free metal, refined ore, smelted ore. *Types of metal include the following:* gold, silver, copper, iron, aluminum, manganese, nickel, lead, cobalt, platinum, zinc, tin, barium, cadmium, chromium, tungsten, mercury, molybdenum, sodium, potassium, radium, magnesium, calcium, titanium, uranium, gallium, rubidium, vanadium.

metallic a. 1 [Made of metal] hard, rocklike, iron, leaden, silvery, golden, metallurgic, mineral, geologic. 2 [Suggestive of metal; *said especially of sound*] ringing, resounding, resonant, bell-like, tinny, clanging.

metaphor n. trope, simile, figure of speech; see COMPARISON.

metaphorical a. figurative, symbolical, allegorical; see DESCRIPTIVE, GRAPHIC 1, 2.

metaphysical a. mystical, abstract, spiritual; see DIFFICULT 2.

meteor n. falling star, shooting star, meteorite, fireball, meteoroid.

meteorology n. weather science, climatology, aerology; see CLIMATE, SCIENCE 1, WEATHER.

meter n. measure, rhythm, tempo, metrical feet, common meter, long meter, ballad meter, tetrameter, pentameter, sprung rhythm, dipodic rhythm.

method n. mode, style, standard operating procedure, fashion, way, means, process, proceeding, adjustment, disposition, practice, routine, technique, attack, mode of operation, manner of working, ways and means, habit, custom, manner, formula, course, MO*, rule; see also SYSTEM.

methodical a. well-regulated, systematic, exact; see ORDERLY 2, REGULAR 3.

métier n. forte, area of expertise, occupation; see JOB 1, PROFESSION 1.

metropolis n. capital, megalopolis, municipality; see CENTER 2, CITY.

metropolitan a. city, municipal, cosmopolitan; see MODERN 2, URBAN.

microbe n. microorganism, bacterium, bacillus; see GERM.

microphone n. sound transmitter, receiver, pickup instrument, mike*, bug*, wire*, walkie-talkie.

microscope *n.* lens, magnifying glass, optical instrument, scope. *Microscopes include the following:* high-powered, compound, photographic, electron, electronic.

microscopic *a.* diminutive, tiny, infinitesimal; see LITTLE 1, MINUTE 1.

middle *a.* mean, midway, medial, average, equidistant; see also CENTRAL, HALFWAY, INTERMEDIATE.

middle *n.* mean, core, nucleus, heart, navel, midst, marrow, pivot, axis, medium, halfway point, midpoint; see also CENTER 1.

middle age *n.* adulthood, prime, maturity; see MAJORITY 2.

middle-aged *a.* in midlife, in one's prime, matronly; see MATURE.

middle-class *a.* white-collar, bourgeois, substantial; see COMMON 1, POPULAR 3, 4.

midget *n.* pygmy, dwarf, little person, Lilliputian.

midnight *n.* dead of night, stroke of midnight, twelve o'clock, twelve midnight, noon of night, witching hour; see also NIGHT 1. **—burn the midnight oil** stay up late, work late, keep late hours; see STUDY, WORK 1.

midst *n.* midpoint, nucleus, middle; see CENTER 1. **—in the midst of** in the course of, engaged in, in the middle of; see AMONG, CENTRAL.

midway *a.* in an intermediate position, halfway, in the middle of the way; see CENTRAL, INTERMEDIATE, MIDDLE.

might *n.* power, force, vigor; see STRENGTH.

mightily *a.* energetically, strongly, forcibly; see POWERFULLY, VIGOROUSLY.

mighty *a.* 1 [Strong] powerful, stalwart, muscular; see STRONG 1. 2 [Powerful through influence] great, all-powerful, omnipotent; see POWERFUL 3. 3 [Imposing] great, extensive, impressive, gigantic, magnificent, towering, dynamic, notable, extraordinary, grand, considerable, monumental, tremendous; see also LARGE 1.—*Ant.* PLAIN, unimpressive, ordinary. 4 [*To a high degree] exceedingly, greatly, extremely; see VERY.

migrate *v.* move, emigrate, immigrate; see LEAVE 1.

migration *n.* emigration, immigration, trek; see DEPARTURE, JOURNEY, MOVEMENT 2.

migratory *a.* wandering, migrant, vagrant; see TEMPORARY.

mild *a.* 1 [Gentle; *said especially of persons*] meek, easygoing, patient; see KIND. 2 [Temperate; *said especially of weather*] bland, untroubled, tropical, peaceful, summery, tepid,

cool, balmy, breezy, gentle, soft, lukewarm, clear, moderate, mellow, fine, uncloudy, sunny, warm.—*Ant.* ROUGH, COLD, STORMY. 3 [Easy; *said especially of burdens or punishment*] soft, light, tempered; see MODERATE 4. 4 [Not irritating] bland, soothing, soft, smooth, gentle, moderate, emollient, easy, mellow, delicate, temperate.

mildly *a.* gently, meekly, calmly, genially, tranquilly, softly, lightly, moderately, tenderly, compassionately, tolerantly, patiently, temperately, indifferently, quietly.—*Ant.* VIOLENTLY, harshly, roughly.

mildness *n.* tolerance, tenderness, gentleness; see KINDNESS 1.

mile *n.* 5,280 feet, 1.6 kilometers, statute mile, geographical mile, nautical mile, Admiralty mile; see also DISTANCE 3, MEASURE 1.

militant *a.* combative, belligerent, offensive; see AGGRESSIVE.

militant *n.* rioter, violent objector, demonstrator; see RADICAL.

military *a.* armed, martial, soldierly; see AGGRESSIVE.

militia *n.* military force, civilian army, National Guard; see ARMY 1.

milk *n.* fluid, juice, sap; see LIQUID. *Types of milk include the following:* whole, skim, low-fat, raw, pasteurized, homogenized, certified; loose, condensed, dried, evaporated, powdered; two-percent, four-percent, etc.; goat's, mare's, mother's; cream, half-and-half, buttermilk, baby formula, kefir. **—cry over spilt milk** mourn, lament, sulk; see REGRET.

milky *a.* opaque, pearly, cloudy; see WHITE 1.

mill *n.* 1 [A factory] manufactory, plant, millhouse; see FACTORY. 2 [A machine for grinding, crushing, pressing, etc.] *Types of mills include the following:* flour, coffee, cotton, weaving, spinning, powder, rolling, cider, cane, lapidary, sawmill, gristmill, coin press.

millionaire *n.* person of means, capitalist, tycoon, billionaire, magnate, plutocrat, Croesus, nabob, Midas, robber baron, fat cat*.—*Ant.* BEGGAR, poor person, pauper.

mimic *n.* mime, impersonator, comedian; see ACTOR, IMITATOR.

mimic *v.* 1 [To imitate] copy, simulate, impersonate; see IMITATE. 2 [To mock] make fun of, burlesque, caricature; see RIDICULE.

mimicry *n.* mime, pretense, mockery; see IMITATION 2.

mind *n.* 1 [Intellectual potentiality] soul, spirit, intellect, brain, consciousness, thought, mentality, intuition, perception, conception, intelligence, intellectuality, capacity, judgment, understanding, wisdom, genius, talent, reasoning, instinct, wit, mental faculties, intellectual faculties, creativity, ingenuity, intellectual powers, gray matter*, brainpower. 2 [Purpose] intention, inclination, determination; see PURPOSE 1. —**bear (or keep) in mind** heed, recollect, recall; see REMEMBER 1. —**be in one's right mind** be mentally well, be rational, be sane; see SANE. —**be of one mind** have the same opinion, concur, be in accord; see AGREE. —**call to mind** recall, recollect, bring to mind; see REMEMBER 1. —**change one's mind** alter one's opinion, change one's views, decide against, modify one's ideas. —**give someone a piece of one's mind** rebuke, chide, criticize; see SCOLD. —**have a good mind to** be inclined to, propose, intend to; see INTEND 1. —**have half a mind to** be inclined to, propose, intend to; see INTEND 1. —**have in mind** 1 [To remember] recall, recollect, think of; see REMEMBER 1, THINK 1. 2 [To intend] expect, plan on, propose; see ANTICIPATE, INTEND 1. —**know one's own mind** know oneself, be deliberate, have a plan; see KNOW 1. —**make up one's mind** form a definite opinion, choose, finalize; see DECIDE. —**meeting of the minds** concurrence, unity, harmony; see AGREEMENT 1. —**on one's mind** occupying one's thoughts, causing concern, worrying one; see IMPORTANT 1. —**out of one's mind** mentally ill, raving, mad; see INSANE. —**take one's mind off** turn one's attention from, divert, change; see DISTRACT.

mind v. 1 [To obey] be under the authority of, heed, do as one is told; see BEHAVE, OBEY. **2** [To give one's attention] heed, regard, be attentive to; see ATTEND. **3** [To be careful] tend, watch out for, take care, be wary, be concerned for, mind one's p's and q's*; see also CONSIDER.—*Ant.* NEGLECT, ignore, be careless. **4** [*To remember] recollect, recall, bring to mind; see REMEMBER 1. **5** [To dislike] object to, take exception, be opposed to; see DISLIKE. —**never mind** forget it, it doesn't matter, ignore it, don't bother, let it go, drop it*; see also STOP.

minded a. disposed, inclined, leaning toward; see WILLING.

mindful a. attentive, heedful, watchful; see CAREFUL.

mindless a. 1 [Careless] inattentive, oblivious, neglectful; see CARELESS, INDIFFERENT, RASH. **2** [Stupid] foolish, senseless, unintelligent; see STUPID.

mine n. 1 [A source of natural wealth] pit, well, shaft, diggings, excavation, workings, quarry, deposit, vein, lode, ore bed, placer, pay dirt, bonanza, strip mine, open-pit mine, surface mine, hard-rock

mine. **2** [An explosive charge] land mine, ambush, trap; see BOMB, EXPLOSIVE, WEAPON.

mine v. excavate, work, quarry; see DIG 1.

mine pron. my own, belonging to me, possessed by me, mine by right, owned by me, left to me, from me, by me; see also OUR.

miner n. excavator, digger, driller, dredger, mine worker, prospector, mucker, driller, placer miner, hard-rock miner, mine superintendent, mining engineer, sourdough*, fortyniner*; see also LABORER, WORKMAN.

mineral a. geologic, rock, metallurgic; see METALLIC 1.

mineral n. geologic rock, rock deposit, ore deposit, igneous rock, metamorphic rock, magma, petroleum, crystal; see also METAL, ROCK 1. *Common minerals include the following:* quartz, feldspar, mica, basalt, coal, hornblende, pyroxene, olivine, calcite, dolomite, pyrite, chalcopyrite, barite, garnet, diopside, gypsum, staurolite, tourmaline, obsidian, malachite, azurite, limonite, galena, aragonite, magnetite, ilmenite, serpentine, epidote, fluorite, cinnabar, talc, bauxite, corundum, cryolite, spinel, sheelite, wolframite, graphite, diatomite, pitchblende.

mingle v. combine, blend, merge; see MIX 1.

miniature a. diminutive, small, tiny; see LITTLE 1, MINUTE 1.

minimize v. lessen, depreciate, reduce; see DECREASE 2.

minimum a. smallest, tiniest, merest, lowest, least.

minimum n. smallest, least, lowest, narrowest, atom, molecule, particle, dot, jot, iota, spark, shadow, gleam, grain, scruple.

mining n. excavating, hollowing, opening, digging, boring, drilling, delving, burrowing, tunneling, honeycombing, placer mining, hard-rock mining, prospecting.

minister n. 1 [One authorized to conduct Christian worship] pastor, parson, preacher, clergyman, rector, monk, abbot, prelate, canon, curate, vicar, deacon, chaplain, servant of God, shepherd, churchman, cleric, padre, ecclesiastic, bishop, archbishop, confessor, reverend, diocesan, divine, missionary; see also PRIEST.—*Ant.* LAYMAN, church member, parishioner. **2** [A high servant of the state] ambassador, consul, liaison officer; see DIPLOMAT, REPRESENTATIVE 2, STATESMAN.

minister to v. administer to, tend to, wait on; see HELP.

ministry n. 1 [The functions of the

clergy] preaching, prayer, spiritual leadership; see RELIGION 2. **2** [The clergy] the cloth, clergymen, ecclesiastics, clerics, the clerical order, priesthood, clericals, prelacy, vicarage. **3** [A department of state] bureau, agency, executive branch; see DEPARTMENT.

minor *a.* secondary, lesser, insignificant; see TRIVIAL, UNIMPORTANT.

minor *n.* person under eighteen or twenty-one, underage person, boy, girl, child, infant, little one, lad, schoolboy, schoolgirl; see also YOUTH 3.

minority *n.* **1** [An outnumbered group] opposition, less than half, the outvoted, the few, the outnumbered, ethnic minority, religious minority, the losing side, splinter group. **2** [The time before one is of legal age] childhood, immaturity, adolescence; see YOUTH 1.

mint *v.* strike, coin, issue; see PRINT 2.

minus *a.* diminished, negative, deficient; see LESS.

minute *a.* **1** [Extremely small] microscopic, diminutive, wee, tiny, atomic, subatomic, miniature, puny, microbic, molecular, exact, precise, fine, inconsiderable, teeny*, weeny*, teeny-weeny*, teensy*, itty-bitty*, invisible; see also LITTLE 1.—*Ant.* LARGE, huge, immense. **2** [Trivial] immaterial, nonessential, paltry; see TRIVIAL, UNIMPORTANT. **3** [Exact] particular, circumstantial, specialized; see DETAILED, ELABORATE 2.

minute *n.* sixty seconds, unit of time, moment, short time, second, flash, twinkling, breath, jiffy*, bat of an eye*; see also TIME 1.—*Ant.* FOREVER, eternity, long time. **—in a minute** before long, shortly, presently; see SOON. **—the minute that** as soon as, the second that, at the time that; see WHEN 2. **—up to the minute** modern, contemporary, up-to-date; see FASHIONABLE, NEW 1, 2.

miracle *n.* marvel, revelation, supernatural occurrence; see WONDER 2.

miraculous *a.* **1** [Caused by divine intervention] supernatural, marvelous, superhuman, beyond understanding, phenomenal, awesome, unimaginable, stupendous, wondrous; see also MYSTERIOUS.—*Ant.* NATURAL, familiar, imaginable. **2** [So unusual as to suggest a miracle] extraordinary, freakish, monstrous; see UNUSUAL 1, 2.

mirage *n.* phantasm, delusion, hallucination; see FANTASY, ILLUSION.

mirror *n.* looking glass, speculum, reflector, polished metal, hand glass, pier glass, mirroring surface,

hand mirror, full-length mirror; see also GLASS.

mirth *n.* frolic, jollity, entertainment; see FUN.

misbehave *v.* do wrong, sin, fail, trip, blunder, offend, trespass, behave badly, misdo, misstep, err, lapse, be delinquent, be at fault, be culpable, be guilty, be bad, forget oneself, be dissolute, be indecorous, carry on*, be naughty, go astray, sow one's wild oats, cut up*.—*Ant.* BEHAVE, be good, do well.

miscalculate *v.* blunder, miscount, err; see MISTAKE.

miscarriage *n.* malfunction, defeat, mistake; see FAILURE 1.

miscellaneous *a.* **1** [Lacking unity] diverse, disparate, unmatched; see UNLIKE. **2** [Lacking order] mixed, muddled, scattered; see CONFUSED 2, DISORDERED.

mischief *n.* troublesomeness, harmfulness, prankishness, playfulness, impishness, misbehavior, misconduct, fault, transgression, wrongdoing, misdoing, naughtiness, mischief-making, friskiness.—*Ant.* DIGNITY, demureness, sedateness.

mischievous *a.* playful, roguish, prankish; see NAUGHTY, RUDE 2.

misconception *n.* delusion, blunder, fault; see ERROR, MISTAKE 2, MISUNDERSTANDING 1.

misconduct *n.* misbehavior, offense, wrongdoing; see EVIL 2, MISCHIEF.

misdemeanor *n.* misconduct, misbehavior, misdeed; see CRIME.

miser *n.* extortioner, usurer, misanthropist, stingy person, skinflint, Scrooge, money-grubber.—*Ant.* BEGGAR, spendthrift, waster.

miserable *a.* distressed, afflicted, sickly, ill, wretched, sick, ailing, unfortunate, uncomfortable, suffering, hurt, wounded, tormented, tortured, in pain, strained, injured, convulsed; see also TROUBLED.—*Ant.* HELPED, aided, comfortable.

miserably *a.* poorly, unsatisfactorily, imperfectly; see BADLY 1, INADEQUATELY.

miserly *a.* covetous, parsimonious, closefisted; see STINGY.

misery *n.* **1** [Pain] distress, suffering, agony; see PAIN 2. **2** [Dejection] worry, despair, desolation; see DEPRESSION 2, GRIEF, SADNESS.

misfit *n.* maladjusted person, maverick, loner, dropout, nonconformist, oddball*, sociopath.

misfortune *n.* misadventure, ill luck, ill fortune, disadvantage, mischance, disappointment, adversity, discomfort, burden, annoyance, nuisance, unpleasantness, inconvenience, worry, anxiety; see also DIFFICULTY 1.—*Ant.* ADVANTAGE, good fortune, stroke of fortune.

misgiving *n.* apprehension, qualm, reservation; see DOUBT, UNCERTAINTY 2.

misguided *a.* misled, deceived, benighted; see MISTAKEN 1.

mishap *n.* accident, mischance, misadventure; see CATASTROPHE, DISASTER, MISFORTUNE.

misinform *v.* mislead, report inaccurately to, misstate; see DECEIVE, LIE.

misinterpret *v.* falsify, distort, miscalculate; see MISTAKE, MISUNDERSTAND.

misinterpretation *n.* distortion, misreckoning, delusion; see MISTAKE 2, MISUNDERSTANDING 1.

misjudge *v.* 1 [To make a wrong judgment, usually of a person] be overcritical, be unfair, come to a hasty conclusion; see MISUNDERSTAND. 2 [To make an inaccurate estimate] miss, miscalculate, misconceive, misthink, misconstrue, overestimate, underestimate, bark up the wrong tree*; see also MISTAKE.—*Ant.* UNDERSTAND, estimate, calculate.

misjudgment *n.* miscalculation, misinterpretation, misconception; see MISTAKE 2.

mislay *v.* lose, disarrange, displace; see MISPLACE.

mislead *v.* delude, cheat, defraud, bilk, take in, outwit, trick, entangle, advise badly, victimize, lure, beguile, hoax, dupe, bait, misrepresent, bluff, give a bum steer*, throw off the scent*, bamboozle, hoodwink, put on*; see also DECEIVE.

misled *a.* misguided, deluded, wronged; see DECEIVED, MISTAKEN 1.

mismanage *v.* bungle, blunder, mess up, foul up*; see also FAIL 1.

mismatched *a.* incompatible, discordant, inconsistent; see UNFIT.

misplace *v.* mislay, displace, shuffle, disarrange, remove, disturb, take out of its place, confuse, mix, scatter, unsettle, disorganize; see also LOSE 2.—*Ant.* FIND, LOCATE, place.

misplaced *a.* displaced, mislaid, out of place; see LOST 1.

mispronounce *v.* falter, misspeak, mumble; see HESITATE, STAMMER.

misrepresent *v.* distort, falsify, misstate; see DECEIVE, LIE 1, MISLEAD.

misrepresentation *n.* untruth, deceit, disguise; see DECEPTION, LIE.

miss *n.* 1 [A failure] slip, blunder, mishap; see MISTAKE 2. 2 [A young woman] lass, young lady, female; see GIRL.

miss *v.* 1 [To feel a want] desire, crave, yearn; see NEED, WANT 1. 2 [To fail to catch] snatch at, drop, fumble, have butterfingers*, muff*, boot*.—*Ant.* CATCH, grab, hold. 3 [To fail to hit] miss one's aim, miss the mark, be wide of the mark, over-

shoot, undershoot, fan the air*.—*Ant.* HIT, shoot, get.

missed *a.* 1 [Not found or noticed] gone, misplaced, mislaid, forgotten, unrecalled, unnoticed, not in sight, put away, in hiding, hidden, strayed, moved, removed, unseen; see also LOST 1.—*Ant.* REMEMBERED, found, located. 2 [Longed for] needed, desired, wished for, pined for, wanted, yearned for, clung to, craved for, hungered for.—*Ant.* HATED, disliked, unwanted.

misshapen *a.* distorted, disfigured, twisted; see DEFORMED.

missile *n.* cartridge, projectile, ammunition; see BULLET, SHOT 1, WEAPON. *Terms for types of missiles include the following:* Polaris, Poseidon, RPV or remotely piloted vehicle, Minuteman, guided missile, cruise missile, ICBM or intercontinental ballistic missile, ABM or antiballistic missile, MIRV or multiple independently targeted reentry vehicle.

missing *a.* disappeared, lacking, removed; see ABSENT, LOST 1.

mission *n.* aim, resolution, goal; see PURPOSE 1.

missionary *n.* apostle, evangelist, preacher; see MESSENGER, MINISTER 1.

misspent *a.* wasted, squandered, thrown away; see WASTED.

mist *n.* cloud, rain, haze; see FOG.

mistake *n.* 1 [A blunder] false step, blunder, slip, error, omission, failure, confusion, wrongdoing, sin, crime, goof*; see also ERROR. 2 [A misunderstanding] misapprehension, confusion, muddle, misconception, delusion, illusion, overestimation, underestimation, impression, confounding, misinterpretation, perversion, perplexity, bewilderment, misjudgment; see also EXAGGERATION, MISUNDERSTANDING 1.—*Ant.* KNOWLEDGE, certainty, interpretation.

mistake *v.* err, blunder, slip, lapse, miss, overlook, omit, underestimate, overestimate, substitute, misjudge, misapprehend, misconceive, misunderstand, confound, misinterpret, confuse, botch, bungle, have the wrong impression, tangle, snarl, slip up, make a mess of*, miss the boat*, put one's foot in one's mouth*.—*Ant.* SUCCEED, know, explain.

mistaken *a.* 1 [In error] misinformed, deceived, confounded, confused, having the wrong impression, deluded, misinformed, misguided, at fault, off the track; see also WRONG 2. 2 [Ill-advised] unadvised, duped, fooled, misled, tricked, unwarranted; see also DECEIVED. 3 [Taken for another] wrongly identified, unrecognized, confused with, taken for, in a case of mistaken identity, misnamed, misconstrued.

mister *n.* Mr., man, sir, *monsieur* (French), *Herr* (German), *signor* (Italian), *señor* (Spanish).

mistreat *v.* harm, injure, wrong; see ABUSE.

mistress *n.* **1** [A woman in authority] housekeeper, chaperone, manager; see LADY 2. **2** [An illicit lover] courtesan, paramour, kept woman; see PROSTITUTE.

mistrust *v.* suspect, distrust, be skeptical of; see DOUBT.

misty *a.* dim, foggy, hazy, murky, shrouded, obscure; see also DARK 1.

misunderstand *v.* err, misconceive, misinterpret, miscomprehend, misjudge, miscalculate, misconstrue, be perplexed, be bewildered, be confused, be confounded, have the wrong impression, fail to understand, misapprehend, overestimate, underestimate, be misled, be unfamiliar with, have the wrong slant on*, have something not register; see also MISTAKE.—*Ant.* UNDERSTAND, grasp, apprehend.

misunderstanding *n.* **1** [Misapprehension] delusion, miscalculation, confusion, misinterpretation, confounding; see also MISTAKE 2.—*Ant.* UNDERSTANDING, conception, apprehension. **2** [Disagreement] debate, dissension, quarrel; see DISAGREEMENT 1, DISPUTE.

misunderstood *a.* misinterpreted, badly interpreted, misconceived; see MISTAKEN 1, WRONG 2.

mitigate *v.* alleviate, lessen, moderate; see DECREASE, RELIEVE 2.

mitten *n.* mitt, gauntlet, glove; see CLOTHES.

mix *v.* **1** [To blend] fuse, merge, coalesce, brew, unite, combine, cross, interbreed, amalgamate, incorporate, alloy, mingle, marry, compound, intermingle, weave, interweave, throw together, adulterate, infiltrate, twine, knead, stir, suffuse, instill, transfuse, synthesize, stir around, infuse, saturate, season. **2** [To confuse] mix up, jumble, tangle; see CONFUSE. **3** [To associate] fraternize, get along, consort; see JOIN 2.

mixed *a.* **1** [Commingled] blended, fused, mingled, compounded, combined, amalgamated, united, brewed, merged, transfused, crossed, assimilated, married, woven, kneaded, incorporated.—*Ant.* SEPARATED, severed, raveled. **2** [Various] miscellaneous, unselected, diverse; see VARIOUS. **3** [Confused] mixed up, jumbled, disordered; see CONFUSED 2.

mixer *n.* blender, food processor, juicer, eggbeater, cake mixer, food mixer, cocktail shaker, converter, carburetor, cement mixer, paint mixer; see also MACHINE.

mixture *n.* **1** [A combination] blend, compound, composite, amalgam, miscellany, mishmash, mingling, medley, marriage, pastiche, mix, potpourri, alloy, fusion, jumble, brew, merger, hybrid, crossing, infiltration, transfusion, infusion, mélange, saturation, assimilation, incorporation, hodgepodge. **2** [A mess] mix-up, muddle, disorder; see CONFUSION.

mix-up *n.* turmoil, chaos, commotion; see CONFUSION, DISORDER.

moan *n.* plaint, groan, wail; see CRY 1.

moan *v.* groan, wail, whine; see CRY 1.

mob *n.* **1** [A disorderly crowd of people] swarm, rabble, throng, press, multitude, populace, horde, riot, rout, host, lawless element; see also CROWD, GATHERING. **2** [The lower classes] bourgeoisie, plebeians, proletariat; see PEOPLE 3.

mob *v.* throng, crowd, swarm; see ATTACK, REBEL.

mobile *a.* unstationary, loose, free; see MOVABLE.

mobility *n.* changeability, versatility, flow; see MOVEMENT 1.

mobilize *v.* assemble, muster, gather; see ENLIST 1.

moccasin *n.* heelless shoe, slipper, sandal; see SHOE.

mock *a.* counterfeit, sham, pretended; see FALSE 3, UNREAL.

mock *v.* **1** [To ridicule] deride, scorn, taunt; see RIDICULE. **2** [To mimic] mime, burlesque, caricature; see IMITATE.

mockery *n.* disparagement, imitation, sham; see RIDICULE.

model *n.* **1** [A person worthy of imitation] archetype, prototype, exemplar, role model, paradigm, ideal, good man, good woman, good example, hero, demigod, saint. **2** [Anything that serves as a copy] original, text, guide, copy, tracing, facsimile, duplicate, pattern, template, design, gauge, ideal, shape, form, specimen, mold, principle, basis, standard, sketch, painting, precedent, archetype, prototype; see also CRITERION. **3** [A duplicate on a small scale] miniature, image, illustration, representation, reduction, statue, figure, figurine, effigy, mock-up, skeleton, portrait, photograph, relief, print, engraving; see also COPY, DUPLICATE. **4** [One who poses professionally] poser, sitter, mannequin; see NUDE.

model *v.* **1** [To form] shape, mold, fashion; see CREATE, FORM 1. **2** [To imitate a model] trace, duplicate, sketch, reduce, represent, print, counterfeit, caricature, parody; see also ILLUSTRATE, PAINT 1. **3** [To serve as a model] sit, be a role model, set an example; see POSE 2. **4** [To demonstrate] show off, wear, parade in; see DISPLAY.

moderate *a.* **1** [Not expensive] inexpensive, low-priced, reasonable; see CHEAP 1, ECONOMICAL 2. **2** [Not violent] modest, cool, tranquil; see CALM 1, RESERVED 3. **3** [Not radical] tolerant, judicious, nonpartisan, liberal, middle-of-the-road, unopinionated, undogmatic, not given to extremes, measured, low-key, evenly balanced, neutral, impartial, centrist, conventional, in the mean, average, restrained, sound, cautious, respectable, middle-class, compromising; see also CONSERVATIVE.—*Ant.* RADICAL, unbalanced, partial. **4** [Not intemperate] pleasant, gentle, soft, balmy, inexpensive, tepid, easy, not rigorous, not severe, temperate, favorable, tolerable, bearable, tame, untroubled, unruffled, monotonous, even; see also FAIR 3, MILD 2.—*Ant.* SEVERE, rigorous, bitter. **5** [Not indulgent] sparing, frugal, abstemious, regulated, self-denying, abstinent, non-indulgent, self-controlled, disciplined, careful, on the wagon*, sworn off*, teetotalling; see also SOBER.—*Ant.* WASTEFUL, excessive, self-indulgent.

moderate *v.* abate, modify, decline; see DECREASE 1.

moderately *a.* tolerantly, tolerably, temperately, somewhat, to a degree, enough, to some extent, to a certain extent, a little, to some degree, fairly, not exactly, in moderation, within reason, within bounds, within reasonable limits, as far as could be expected, within the bounds of reason, in reason; see also REASONABLY 2, SLIGHTLY.—*Ant.* MUCH, extremely, remarkably.

moderation *n.* **1** [Restraint] toleration, steadiness, sobriety, coolness, the golden mean, quiet, temperance, patience, fairness, justice, constraint, forbearance, poise, balance; see also RESTRAINT 1. **2** [The act of moderating] mediation, regulation, limitation; see RESTRAINT 2.

modern *a.* **1** [Up-to-date] stylish, modish, chic, smart, up-to-the-minute, current, recent, of the present, prevailing, prevalent, faddish, avant-garde, present-day, latest, most recent, advanced, modernistic, streamlined, breaking with tradition, new, newest, untraditional, contemporary, in vogue, in use, common, newfangled, just out, cool*, sharp*, smooth*, state-of-the-art, mod, trendy*; see also FASHIONABLE.—*Ant.* OLD-FASHIONED, out-of-date, out-of-style. **2** [Having the comforts of modern life] high-tech,

modernized, renovated, functional, with modern conveniences, done over, having modern improvements; see also CONVENIENT 1, IMPROVED. **3** [Concerning recent times] contemporary, contemporaneous, recent, concurrent, present-day, coincident, twentieth-century, twenty-first-century, latter-day, mechanical, of the Machine Age, of the Space Age, of the Computer Age, automated, of modern times; see also NEW 1, 2, NOW 1.—*Ant.* OLD, medieval, primordial.

modest *a.* **1** [Humble] unassuming, meek, diffident; see also HUMBLE 1, RESIGNED. **2** [Not showy] unpretentious, plain, unostentatious, unobtrusive, demure, quiet, seemly, proper, decorous, simple, natural, unassuming, humble, tasteful, unadorned, unaffected, homely. **3** [Moderate] reasonable, inexpensive, average; see CHEAP 1, ECONOMICAL 2. **4** [Proper] pure, chaste, seemly; see DECENT 2, HONEST 1. **5** [Lowly] plain, simple, unaffected; see HUMBLE 2.

modestly *a.* unobtrusively, retiringly, quietly, unpretentiously, diffidently, bashfully, unassumingly, chastely, virtuously, purely, shyly, demurely.—*Ant.* BOLDLY, boastfully, pretentiously.

modesty *n.* **1** [Unassuming or humble attitude] humility, delicacy, reticence, unobtrusiveness, meekness; see also COURTESY 1, DIGNITY, RESTRAINT 1.—*Ant.* VANITY, conceit, egotism. **2** [Shyness] inhibition, timidity, diffidence; see SHYNESS. **3** [Chastity] decency, innocence, celibacy; see CHASTITY, VIRTUE 1.

modicum *n.* trifle, fraction, particle; see BIT.

modification *n.* qualification, alteration, correction; see ADJUSTMENT, CHANGE 2.

modified *a.* varied, mutated, adjusted; see CHANGED 2.

modify *v.* **1** [To change] alter, modify, vary; see BECOME, CHANGE 2. **2** [To moderate] mitigate, restrain, curb; see DECREASE 2, RESTRICT.

moist *a.* humid, dank, moistened; see WET 1.

moisten *v.* sprinkle, dampen, saturate, drench, waterlog, steep, sog, sop, dip, rinse, wash over, wet down, water down, squirt, shower, rain on, splash, splatter, bathe, steam, spray, sponge.

moisture *n.* precipitation, mist, drizzle; see FOG, WATER 1.

mold *n.* **1** [A form] matrix, cavity, shape, frame, pattern, design, template, die, cast, cup, image, kind, molding, casting, reproduction, form, pottery, shell, core. **2** [A parasitic growth] mildew, rust, parasite, fungus, lichen; see also DECAY.

mold *v.* **1** [To give physical shape to] make, round into, fashion; see FORM 1. **2** [To decay through the action of mold] rot, mildew, rust; see SPOIL.

moldy *a.* musty, mildewed, dank; see ROTTEN 1.

mole *n.* flaw, birthmark, blotch; see BLEMISH.

molecular *a.* miniature, microscopic, atomic; see LITTLE 1, MINUTE 1.

molecule *n.* particle, fragment, unit; see ATOM, BIT 1.

molest *v.* bother, interrupt, break in upon, intrude, encroach upon, annoy, worry, irritate, plague, badger, bait, pester, hinder, tease, irk, vex, trouble, harass, assault, assault sexually, confuse, perturb, frighten, terrify, scare; see also BOTHER 2.

mollycoddle *v.* pamper, coddle, spoil, overindulge; see also BABY.

molten *a.* heated, melted, fused, liquefied, running, fluid, seething; see also HOT 1.—*Ant.* COLD, cool, solid.

moment *n.* **1** [A brief time] minute, instant, millisecond, trice, second, bit, while, flash, jiffy*; see also MINUTE. **2** [Importance] significance, note, consequence; see IMPORTANCE.

momentarily *a.* immediately, right now, instantly; see NOW 1.

momentary *a.* fleeting, quick, passing, flitting, flashing, transient, impermanent, shifting, ephemeral, vanishing, cursory, temporary, dreamlike, in the blink of an eye, in the wink of an eye.—*Ant.* ETERNAL, continual, ceaseless.

momentum *n.* impulse, force, drive; see ENERGY 2.

mommy *n.* mom*, female parent, mama*; see MOTHER 1, PARENT.

monarch *n.* hereditary ruler, sovereign, autocrat; see KING 1.

monarchy *n.* kingship, sovereignty, command; see POWER 2.

monastery *n.* abbey, priory, religious community; see CHURCH 1.

monetary *a.* pecuniary, financial, fiscal; see COMMERCIAL.

money *n.* **1** [A medium of monetary exchange] gold, silver, cash, currency, check, bills, notes, specie, legal tender, Almighty Dollar*, gravy*, wampum*, shekels*, dough*, long green*, coins*, lucre, folding money*, wad*, bucks*, hard cash*, bread*. *Money includes the following:* dollar, pound, franc, lira, peso, ruble, krone, yuan, yen, euro, schilling, real, deutsche mark, drachma, rupee, shekel, won, sol, złoty, escudo, rand, peseta. **2** [Wealth] funds, capital, property; see WEALTH. **3** [Merged interest] financiers, corporate interests, capitalists; see BUSINESS 4. **4** [Pay] payment, salary, wages; see PAY 2. —**for one's money*** for one's choice, in one's opinion, to one's mind; see PERSONALLY 2. —**in the money*** wealthy, flush*, loaded*; see RICH 1. —**make money** gain profits, become wealthy, earn; see PROFIT 2. —**one's money's worth** full value, gain, benefit; see VALUE 1, 3. —**put money into** invest in, support, underwrite; see INVEST.

mongrel *n.* mutt*, cur, crossbreed, mixed breed.

monk *n.* hermit, religious, ascetic, solitary, recluse, abbot, prior; see also PRIEST.

monkey *n.* *Monkeys include the following:* marmoset, tamarin, capuchin; squirrel, proboscis, howler, spider, woolly, etc. monkey; macaque, baboon, mandrill, colobus.

monkey* *v.* pry, fool around, tamper with; see MEDDLE 2.

monkey business* *n.* deceit, conniving, misconduct; see DECEPTION, LIE.

monolithic *a.* solid, unified, inflexible, unyielding; see also FIRM 1, UNITED.

monologue *n.* talk, speech, discourse; see ADDRESS 1.

monopolize *v.* engross, acquire, exclude, own exclusively, absorb, consume, manage, have, hold, corner, restrain, patent, copyright, corner the market.—*Ant.* INCLUDE, give, invite.

monopoly *n.* trust, syndicate, cartel; see BUSINESS 1.

monotonous *a.* **1** [Tiresome] tedious, wearisome, wearying; see DULL 4. **2** [Having but one tone] monotonic, unvarying, lacking variety, in one key, unchanged, reiterated, recurrent, single, uniform.—*Ant.* VARIOUS, varying, multiple.

monotony *n.* invariability, likeness, tediousness, tedium, similarity, continuity, continuance, oneness, evenness, levelness, flatness, the same old thing; see also BOREDOM.—*Ant.* VARIETY, difference, variability.

monsoon *n.* typhoon, hurricane, tempest; see STORM.

monster *n.* **1** [A great or imaginary beast] beastlike creature, centaur, monstrosity, sphinx, chimera, unicorn, dragon, griffin, cyclops, phoenix, mermaid, sea serpent, rhinoceros, elephant, werewolf. **2** [An unnatural creation] abnormality, monstrosity, malformation; see FREAK. **3** [An inhuman person] brute, beast, cruel person; see CRIMINAL, RASCAL.

monstrous *a.* **1** [Huge] stupendous,

prodigious, enormous; see LARGE 1.
2 [Unnatural] abnormal, preposterous, uncanny; see UNNATURAL 1, UNUSUAL 2.

month *n.* measure of time, thirty days, one-twelfth of a year, four weeks. *Months of the year are the following:* January, February, March, April, May, June, July, August, September, October, November, December.

monthly *a.* once a month, every month, from month to month, menstrual, recurrent, cyclic, cyclical, repeated, rhythmic; punctually, steadily, methodically, periodically; see also REGULARLY.

monument *n.* **1** [Anything erected to preserve a memory] tomb, shaft, column, pillar, headstone, tombstone, gravestone, mausoleum, obelisk, shrine, statue, building, tower, monolith, tablet, slab, stone; see also MEMORIAL. **2** [A landmark in the history of creative work] work of art, magnum opus, permanent contribution; see ACHIEVEMENT, MASTERPIECE.

monumental *a.* lofty, impressive, majestic; see GRAND, GREAT 1.

mood *n.* **1** [A state of mind] state, condition, frame of mind, temper, humor, disposition, inclination, caprice, whim, fancy, pleasure, freak, wish, desire, bent, propensity, tendency; see also ATTITUDE. **2** [Grammatical mode] aspect, inflection, mode. *Moods in English grammar include the following:* indicative, subjunctive, imperative.

moody *a.* pensive, unhappy, low-spirited; see SAD 1.

moon *n.* celestial body, heavenly body, planet, planetoid, satellite, crescent, new moon, half-moon, full moon, old moon, Luna*, Diana*, moon goddess, harvest moon, blue moon.

moonlight *n.* effulgence, radiance, luminescence; see LIGHT 3.

moonshine *n.* **1** [Moonlight] effulgence, radiance, luminosity; see LIGHT 3. **2** [Whiskey distilled illicitly] mountain dew*, hooch*, white lightning*; see WHISKEY.

moot *a.* unsettled, debatable, disputable; see UNCERTAIN.

mop *n.* swab, duster, sweeper; see BROOM.

mop *v.* swab, wipe, rub, dab, pat, polish, wash, dust, wipe up; see also CLEAN. **—mop up*** finish off, dispatch, clean up; see DEFEAT 2, ELIMINATE.

mope *v.* fret, pine away, grieve, sorrow, sink, lose heart, brood, pine, yearn, despair, grumble, chafe, lament, regret, look glum, sulk, pull a long face*.—*Ant.* CELEBRATE, revive, cheer up.

moral *a.* **1** [Characterized by conventional virtues] trustworthy, kindly, courteous, respectable, proper, scrupulous, conscientious, good, truthful, decent, just, honorable, honest, high-minded, saintly, pure, worthy, correct, seemly, aboveboard, dutiful, principled, conscientious, chaste, ethical; see also NOBLE 1, 2, RELIABLE.—*Ant.* LYING, DISHONEST, unscrupulous. **2** [Having to do with approved relationships between the sexes] virtuous, immaculate, decent; see CHASTE, INNOCENT 2.

morale *n.* assurance, resolve, spirit; see CONFIDENCE.

morality *n.* righteousness, uprightness, ethics; see VIRTUE 1.

morally *a.* **1** [In accordance with accepted standards of conduct] conscientiously, truthfully, honestly, honorably, appropriately, respectably, courteously, scrupulously, ethically, correctly, in a principled manner, uprightly, righteously, trustworthily, decently, properly, in a manner approved by society; see also JUSTLY 1, SINCERELY.—*Ant.* WRONGLY, worthlessly, dishonorably. **2** [In a chaste manner] chastely, virtuously, purely; see MODESTLY.

morals *n.* ideals, customs, standards, mores, policies, beliefs, dogmas, social standards, principles; see also ETHICS.

morbid *a.* **1** [Diseased] sickly, unhealthy, ailing; see SICK. **2** [Pathological] gloomy, depressed, melancholic; see SAD 1.

more *a.* **1** [Additional] some more, over and above, more than that, in addition, further, besides, added; see also EXTRA.—*Ant.* LESS, less than, subtracted from. **2** [Greater in quantity, amount, degree, or quality] more numerous, exceeding, many more, much more, extra, expanded, augmented, increased, major, extended, enhanced, added to, larger, higher, wider, deeper, heavier, stronger, above the mark.—*Ant.* weaker, lessened, decreased.

moreover *a.* further, by the same token, furthermore; see BESIDES.

morning *n.* **1** [Dawn] morn, daybreak, break of day, first blush of morning, daylight, cockcrow, sunup, the wee small hours*, crack of dawn*. **2** [The time before noon] forenoon, morningtide*, after midnight, before noon, breakfast time, before lunch. **—good morning** good day, good morrow*, greetings; see HELLO.

mornings *a.* in the morning, every

morning, before noon; see DAILY, REGULARLY.

moron *n.* imbecile, idiot, goose, simpleton, dullard, dolt, blockhead, cretin, dunce, dunderhead*, numskull, loony*, dummy*; see also FOOL.—*Ant.* PHILOSOPHER, sage, scientist.

moronic *a.* foolish, slow, dumb*; see STUPID.

morsel *n.* bite, chunk, piece; see BIT 1, PART 1.

mortal *a.* **1** [Causing death] malignant, fatal, lethal; see DEADLY, POISONOUS. **2** [Subject to death] human, transient, temporal, passing, frail, impermanent, perishable, fading, passing away, momentary; see also TEMPORARY.—*Ant.* ETERNAL, perpetual, everlasting.

mortal *n.* creature, being, human; see ANIMAL, MAN 1.

mortality *n.* dying, extinction, ending; see DEATH, DESTRUCTION 1.

mortgage *n.* lease, title, debt; see CONTRACT.

mortuary *n.* morgue, funeral parlor, funeral home; see FUNERAL.

moss *n.* lichen, Iceland moss, peat moss; see PLANT.

mossy *a.* tufted, velvety, plushy, downy, smooth, fresh, damp, moist, resilient, soft, covered, overgrown.—*Ant.* DRY, bare, prickly.

most *a.* nearly all, all but, not quite all, maximum, greatest, utmost, in the majority. **—at the most** in toto, not more than, at the outside; see MOST. **—make the most of** exploit, utilize, take advantage of; see USE 1.

mostly *a.* **1** [Frequently] often, many times, in many instances; see FREQUENTLY. **2** [Largely] chiefly, essentially, for the most part; see PRINCIPALLY.

motel *n.* motor inn, inn, cabins, stopping place, roadhouse, court, motor court; see also HOTEL, RESORT 2.

moth *n.* silkworm moth, gypsy moth, clothes moth; see INSECT.

mother *n.* **1** [A female parent] parent, matriarch, dam*, mama, mammy*, mum*, ma*, mom*, mommy*, maw*, mater*; see also PARENT, RELATIVE. **2** [The source] fountainhead, source, beginning; see ORIGIN 2.

mother-in-law *n.* spouse's mother, mother by marriage, in-law*; see RELATIVE.

motherly *a.* maternal, devoted, careful, watchful, kind, warm, gentle, tender, sympathetic, supporting, protective, nurturing, caretaking; see also LOVING.

motion *n.* **1** [A movement] change, act, action; see MOVEMENT 2. **2** [The state of moving] passage, translating, changing; see MOVEMENT 1. **3** [An act formally proposed] suggestion, consideration, proposition; see PLAN 2. **—in motion** traveling, going, under way; see MOVING 1.

motionless *a.* **1** [Not moving] still, unmoving, dead, deathly still, inert, stock-still, stagnant, quiet.—*Ant.* MOVING, CHANGING, shifting. **2** [Firm] unmovable, fixed, stationary; see FIRM 1.

motion picture *n.* moving picture, cinema, film; see MOVIE.

motivate *v.* impel, inspire hope, stimulate, incite, propel, spur, goad, move, induce, prompt, arouse, whet, instigate, fire up*, provoke, cause, touch off, egg on, trigger; see also DRIVE 1, EXCITE, URGE 2.

motive *n.* cause, purpose, idea; see REASON 3.

motor *n.* machine, device, instrument; see ENGINE. *Types of motors include the following:* internal-combustion engine, diesel engine, steam engine, external-combustion engine; radial, airplane, automobile, truck, AC electric, DC electric.

motorboat *n.* speedboat, putt-putt*, powerboat, racer; see also BOAT. *Types of motorboats include the following:* open, outboard, electric-powered, gasoline-powered, cruiser, runabout.

motorcycle *n.* motorized two-wheeled vehicle, cycle, hog*, bike*, chopper*; see also VEHICLE.

motorist *n.* automobile operator, traveler, car pool member; see DRIVER.

motorized *a.* motor-driven, motor-powered, electric-driven, gasoline-driven, oil-driven, motor-equipped, motor-operated.

motto *n.* maxim, adage, saw, epigram, aphorism, sentiment, slogan, catchword, axiom; see also PROVERB, SAYING. *Familiar mottoes include the following:* in God we trust, *e pluribus unum* (Latin), time flies, seize the day, make hay while the sun shines, rest in peace, peace be with you, one for all and all for one, home sweet home, God bless our home, don't tread on me, give me liberty or give me death, all or nothing, you can't take it with you, all men are created equal, for God and country, what's worth doing is worth doing well, don't give up the ship, don't fire until you see the whites of their eyes; remember the Alamo, remember the Maine, remember Pearl Harbor, etc.; my country, right or wrong; praise the Lord and pass the ammunition, put your trust in God and keep your powder dry; abandon hope, all ye who enter here; to err is human, to forgive, divine; liberty, equality, fraternity; I came, I saw, I conquered; Pikes Peak or bust*.

mound *n*. pile, heap, knoll; see HILL.

mount *v*. **1** [To rise] ascend, arise, uprise; see RISE 1. **2** [To climb] ascend, scale, clamber; see CLIMB.

mountain *n*. **1** [A lofty land mass] mount, elevation, peak, sierra, butte, hill, alp, range, ridge, pike, bluff, headland, volcano, crater, tableland, mesa, plateau, height, crag, precipice, cliff, earth mass.— *Ant*. VALLEY, ravine, flatland. *Famous chains of mountains include the following:* Alps, Himalayas, Caucasus, Urals, Pyrenees, Andes, Rockies, Canadian Rockies, Appalachians, Cascades, Adirondacks, White Mountains, Sierra Nevada, Sierra Madre, Ozarks, Smokies, Cordilleras, Apennines. *Famous peaks include the following:* Mont Blanc, Mt. Etna, Vesuvius, the Matterhorn, Pikes Peak, Mt. Whitney, Mt. Shasta, Mt. Washington, Mt. McKinley, Krakatau, Pelée, Popocatépetl, Mt. Everest, Annapurna, Mount of Olives, Mt. Sinai, Fuji, Mt. Kilimanjaro, Mt. St. Helens, Mt. Rainier, K2. **2** [A pile] mass, mound, glob; see HEAP.

mountaineer *n*. mountain man, mountain dweller, hillman, highlander, uplander, native of mountains, mountain climber, rock climber, mountain guide, mountain scaler, hillbilly*.

mountainous *a*. mountainlike, with mountains, difficult, barbarous, wild, untamed, strange, remote, uncivilized, rude, unpopulated, solitary, unfamiliar, isolated, steep, lofty, hilly, alpine, upland, elevated, volcanic, towering, craggy, rugged.—*Ant*. LOW, small, flat.

mounted *a*. **1** [On horseback] seated, riding, in the saddle, cavalry, horsed*, up.—*Ant*. AFOOT, unhorsed, dismounted. **2** [Firmly fixed] supported, set, attached; see FIRM 1. **3** [Backed] pasted on, set off, strengthened; see REINFORCED.

mourn *v*. deplore, grieve, fret, sorrow, rue, regret, bemoan, sigh, long for, miss, droop, languish, yearn, pine, anguish, complain, agonize, weep, suffer, wring one's hands, be brokenhearted, be in distress, be sad.—*Ant*. CELEBRATE, rejoice, be happy.

mourner *n*. lamenter, griever, keener, weeper, wailer, sorrower, pallbearer, friend of the deceased, member of the family.

mournful *a*. sorrowful, mourning, unhappy; see SAD 1.

mourning *n*. **1** [The act of expressing grief] sorrowing, grieving, yearning, sorrow, lamentation, pining, sighing, regretting, deploring, weeping over, wailing, crying, moaning, murmuring, complaining, sobbing; see also DEPRESSION 2,

GRIEF, SADNESS.—*Ant*. CELEBRATION, rejoicing, being glad. · **2** [Symbols of mourning] black, sackcloth and ashes, arm band, mourning veil, widow's weeds, black suit, black tie.

mouse *n*. rodent, vermin, rat; see ANIMAL.

mouth *n*. **1** [The principal facial opening] *Parts of the mouth include the following:* lips, roof, floor, tongue, jaws, gums, teeth, soft palate, alveolar ridge, hard palate, uvula. **2** [Any opening resembling a mouth] orifice, entrance, aperture; see ENTRANCE 2. **3** [The end of a river] estuary, firth, delta, portal, harbor, roads, sound, tidewater. — **down in** (or **at**) **the mouth*** depressed, discouraged, unhappy; see SAD 1. —**have a big mouth*** talk loudly, exaggerate, brag; see TALK 1.

mouthful *n*. portion, piece, morsel; see BITE 1.

movable *a*. not fastened, portable, adjustable, adaptable, not fixed, transportable, ambulatory, mobile, detachable, turnable, removable, separable, transferable, loose, unfastened, free, unattached, in parts, in sections, knocked down, on wheels.—*Ant*. FIXED, fastened, stationary.

move *n*. action, transit, progress; see MOVEMENT 1, 2. —**get a move on*** go faster, start moving, get cracking*; see HURRY 1. —**on the move*** moving, busy, acting; see ACTIVE.

move *v*. **1** [To be in motion] go, walk, run, glide, travel, drift, budge, stir, shift, pass, cross, roll, flow, march, travel, progress, proceed, traverse, drive, ride, fly, hurry, head for, bustle, climb, crawl, leap, hop to it*, get a move on*, scooch*, get going, get cracking*; see also ADVANCE 1.—*Ant*. STOP, remain stationary, stay quiet. **2** [To set in motion] impel, actuate, propel; see PUSH 2. **3** [To arouse the emotions of] influence, stir, instigate, stimulate, touch, play on, sway, induce, rouse, prevail upon, work upon, strike a sympathetic chord; see also DRIVE 1, ENCOURAGE, EXCITE.—*Ant*. QUIET, lull, pacify. **4** [To take up another residence] pack up, move out, move in; see LEAVE 1. **5** [To propose an action formally] suggest, introduce, submit; see PROPOSE 1. — **move up** go forward, do well, get ahead; see ADVANCE 1, RISE 1.

moved *a*. **1** [Transported] conveyed, carried, taken, shifted, transferred, reassigned, changed, flown, driven, drawn, pushed, lifted, elevated, lowered, let down, displaced, withdrawn, replaced, sent abroad, trucked, hauled, dragged; see also SENT. **2** [Gone to a different residence] emigrated, migrated, vacated, removed, departed, gone away, changed residences, left, gone for good; see also GONE 1.—*Ant.* RESIDENT, remaining, still here. **3** [Proposed] recommended, submitted, introduced; see PROPOSED, SUGGESTED. **4** [Excited] disturbed, stimulated, upset; see EXCITED.

movement *n.* **1** [The act of moving] move, transit, passage, progress, journey, advance, mobility, change, shift, alteration, ascension, descent, propulsion, flow, flux, action, flight, wandering, journeying, voyaging, migration, emigration, immigration, transplanting, evolving, shifting, changing, locomotion, drive, evolution, undertaking, regression.—*Ant.* QUIET, rest, fixity. **2** [An example of movement] journey, trip, immigration, migration, march, crusade, patrol, sweep, emigration, evolution, unrest, transition, change, transfer, displacement, withdrawal, ascension, descent, progression, regression, transportation, removal, departure, shift, flight, slip, slide, step, footfall, stride, gesture, act, action, pilgrimage, expedition, locomotion. **3** [A trend] drift, tendency, bent; see INCLINATION 1.

movie *n.* moving picture, motion picture, photoplay, cinema, film, show, screenplay, cartoon, animated cartoon, serial, comedy, foreign film, travelogue, short, documentary, feature film, videotape, flick*; see also DRAMA.

movies *n.* **1** [A showing of a moving picture] motion picture, film, photoplay; see MOVIE. **2** [The motion picture industry] moving pictures, the cinematic industry, Hollywood, the screen world, the silver screen*, the industry*, pictures*, the flicks*, celluloids*.

moving *a.* **1** [In motion] going, changing, progressing, advancing, shifting, evolving, withdrawing, rising, going down, descending, ascending, getting up, traveling, journeying, on the march, moving up, starting, proceeding, flying, climbing, up-tempo, on the jump*, going great guns*. **2** [Going to another residence] migrating, emigrating, vacating, removing, departing, leaving, going away, changing residences. **3** [Exciting] affecting, emotional, touching; see EXCITING.

mow *v.* scythe, reap, cut; see HARVEST.

much *a.* **1** [To a great degree or extent] considerably, greatly, vastly, enormously, significantly, notably, remarkably; see also ESPECIALLY 1. **2** [Great in amount or degree] abundant, satisfying, enough, sufficient, adequate, considerable, substantial, ample, everywhere, copious, voluminous, plentiful, profuse, complete, lavish, generous, immeasurable, endless, countless, extravagant, hell of a lot*.—*Ant.* INADEQUATE, insufficient, limited. —**as much as** practically, virtually, in effect; see ALMOST, EQUAL. —**too much** excess, waste, extravagance, overabundance, superfluity, preposterousness, overcharge, ever so much, more than can be used, vastness, prodigiousness, immensity; see also EXCESS 1.—*Ant.* LACK, want, shortage.

much *n.* a great quantity, abundance, quantities, a great deal, riches, wealth, volume, very much, breadth, plentifulness, fullness, completeness, lavishness, a lot*, lots*, quite a bit*, gobs*, thousands*, tons*, oodles*; see also PLENTY.—*Ant.* LITTLE, penury, scarcity. —**make much of** treat as of great importance, expand, exaggerate; see OVERDO 1. —**not much of a** inferior, mediocre, unsatisfactory; see POOR 2.

muck *n.* refuse, dung, waste; see TRASH 1.

mucus *n.* phlegm, slime, expectoration, spit, snot*.

mud *n.* dirt, muck, clay, mire, slush, silt, muddiness, stickiness, ooze, bog, marsh, swamp.

muddle *n.* trouble, disarrangement, disarray; see CONFUSION, DISORDER.

muddle *v.* stir up, disarrange, entangle, foul, mix, jumble, derange, shake up, mess, botch, clutter, snarl, complicate, disorder; see also CONFUSE.

muddled *a.* uncertain, addled, perplexed; see CONFUSED 2.

muddy *a.* **1** [Containing sediment] stirred, dull, dark, cloudy, murky, indistinct, roiled, roily, confused, obscure, opaque; see also DIRTY 1.—*Ant.* CLEAR, translucent, pellucid. **2** [Deep with mud] sloppy, swampy, soggy, sodden, slushy, watery, boggy, soaked.—*Ant.* DRY, barren, parched.

muffle *v.* deaden, mute, stifle; see DECREASE 2, SOFTEN.

muffled *a.* suppressed, stifled, indistinct; see OBSCURE 1.

muffler *n.* chest protector, scarf, neckpiece, babushka, neckerchief, kerchief, neckband, neckcloth, Ascot, choker, mantle, stole; see also CLOTHES.

mug *n.* vessel, stein, flagon; see CUP.

muggy *a.* damp, humid, moist; see WET 1.

mule *n.* hinny, donkey, burro; see ANIMAL.

mull *v.* reflect, meditate, ponder; see THINK 1.

multiple *a.* **1** [Various] complicated,

more than one, many, manifold, compound, having many uses, multifold, multitudinous, aggregated, many-sided, versatile, increased, varied, compound, added; see also VARIOUS.—*Ant.* SIMPLE, UNITED, centralized. **2** [Repeated] recurring, repetitious, duplicated; see MULTIPLIED.

multiplication *n.* duplication, reproduction, addition, increase, repetition, compounding, recurrence, amplification, making more, reproducing, repeating, augmenting; see also MATHEMATICS.—*Ant.* REDUCTION, subtraction, decrease.

multiplied *a.* compounded, added, reproduced, amplified, repeated, augmented, duplicated, reduplicated, made many.—*Ant.* REDUCED, divided, decreased.

multiply *v.* **1** [To increase] add, augment, double; see INCREASE. **2** [To bring forth young] generate, produce, populate; see REPRODUCE 3. **3** [To employ multiplication as an arithmetical process] square, cube, raise to a higher power; see INCREASE.

multitude *n.* throng, drove, mob; see CROWD, GATHERING, PEOPLE 3.

mumble *v.* mutter, utter, whine, whimper, grumble, murmur, maunder, ramble on, whisper, speak indistinctly, say to oneself; see also HESITATE, STAMMER.—*Ant.* SAY, articulate, enunciate.

mumbo jumbo *n.* gibberish, double talk, drivel; see NONSENSE 1.

munch *v.* crunch, bite, crush; see CHEW, EAT.

mundane *a.* normal, ordinary, everyday; see WORLDLY.

municipal *a.* self-governing, metropolitan, city, town, community, local, civil, incorporated, corporate; see also PUBLIC.—*Ant.* PRIVATE, national, state.

municipality *n.* district, village, borough; see CITY, TOWN 1.

munitions *n.* materiel, weapons, ordnance; see AMMUNITION, BOMB, BULLET, CANNON, EXPLOSIVE, GUN, MACHINE GUN, ROCKET, SHOT 1.

murder *n.* killing, homicide, death, destruction, annihilation, carnage, terrorism, mayhem, dispatching, putting an end to, slaying, shooting, knifing, assassination, lynching, crime, felony, killing with malice aforethought, murder in the first degree, first-degree murder, contract killing, murder in the second degree, murder in the third degree, massacre, genocide, butchery, patricide, parricide, matricide, infanticide, fratricide, genocide, suicide, foul play. **—get away with murder*** escape punishment, take flight, avoid punishment; see EVADE.

murder *v.* **1** [To kill unlawfully] slay, assassinate, butcher; see KILL 1. **2** [*To ruin, especially by incompetence] spoil, mar, misuse; see BOTCH, DESTROY, FAIL 1.

murdered *a.* killed, assassinated, massacred; see DEAD 1.

murderer *n.* slayer, assassin, butcher; see CRIMINAL, KILLER.

murderous *a.* killing, cruel, criminal; see DEADLY.

murky *a.* dim, dusky, dingy; see DARK 1, DIRTY 1.

murmur *v.* **1** [To make a low, continuous sound] ripple, moan, trickle, burble, babble, tinkle, gurgle, meander, flow gently; see also HUM, WHISPER.—*Ant.* SOUND, peal, clang. **2** [To mutter] mumble, rumble, growl; see MUTTER 2.

muscle *n.* fiber, flesh, tissue, brawn, beef*.

muscular *a.* brawny, powerful, husky; see STRONG 1.

muse *v.* ponder, meditate, reflect; see THINK 1.

museum *n.* institution, building, hall, place of exhibition, foundation, art gallery, library, picture gallery, archives, treasury, storehouse, repository, vault, aquarium, menagerie, zoological garden, zoo, botanical garden, herbarium, arboretum.

mush *n.* **1** [Boiled meal] Indian meal, hasty pudding, hominy, cereal, grain; see also FOOD. **2** [*Sentimentality] sentimentalism, excessive sentiment, mawkishness, affectation, superficiality, romanticism, puppy love, hearts and flowers*, sob story*.

mushroom *n.* toadstool, fungus, *champignon* (French); see FOOD, PLANT.

mushroom *v.* augment, spread, sprout; see GROW 1, INCREASE.

mushy *a.* **1** [Soft] pulpy, gooey*, muddy; see SOFT 2. **2** [*Sentimental] romantic, maudlin, effusive; see EMOTIONAL, SENTIMENTAL.

music *n.* **1** [A combination of tone and rhythm] melody, tune, air, strain, harmonics, song, measure, refrain, phrasing; see also BEAT 2, HARMONY 1. *Terms used in music include the following:* scale, clef, note, tone, pitch, sharp, flat, major, minor, key, mode, bridge, theme, movement, orchestration, instrumentation, variation, improvisation, rhythm, accent, beat, down-beat, up-beat, off-beat, chord, counterpoint, timbre, volume, resonance; see also SONG. *Musical forms for instruments include the following:* symphony, concerto, suite; trio, quartet, quintet, etc.; overture, prelude, sonata, mass, scherzo, nocturne, fugue, étude, tone poem, variations, rhapsody, serenade, ballade, march; see also OVERTURE 2. *Musical dance forms include the following:* waltz, tango, foxtrot, rhumba, polka, minuet, ballet; see also DANCE 1. *General styles of music include the following:* classical, longhair*, serious, medieval, modern, folk, primitive, popular, national, sacred, baroque, romantic, jazz, blues, rhythm-and-blues, gospel, fusion, boogie-woogie, folk-rock, heavy metal, acid rock, rock-and-roll, pop, bebop, bop, soul, ragtime, swing, funk, rap, hip-hop, punk, New Age, minimalist, serial, country; see also JAZZ. 2 [Responsiveness to music] music appreciation, sensitivity, aesthetic sense; see APPRECIATION 2, FEELING 4. —**face the music*** accept the consequences of one's actions, suffer, undergo; see ENDURE 2.

musical *a.* 1 [Having the qualities of music] tuneful, sweet, pleasing, agreeable, symphonic, lyric, mellow, vocal, choral, consonant, rhythmical; see also HARMONIOUS 1.—*Ant.* HARSH, tuneless, discordant. 2 [Having aptitude for music] having perfect pitch, talented, musically inclined; see ARTISTIC.

musical *n.* musicale, musical comedy, burlesque; see PERFORMANCE, SHOW 1.

musical instrument *n.* *Types of musical instruments include the following:* recorder, grand piano, spinet, lyre, bells, flute, piccolo, violin, fiddle*, oboe, clarinet, bassoon, fife, English horn, maracas, sousaphone, alpenhorn, shofar, bagpipe, trombone, French horn, tuba, cornet, trumpet, saxophone, dulcimer, harpsichord, harmonica, organ, harp, tambourine, ukelele, guitar, electric guitar, banjo, mandolin, lute, viola, cello, double bass, xylophone, marimba, cymbal, drum, balalaika, accordion, concertina, tom-tom, sitar, calliope.

musician *n.* player, performer, composer; see ARTIST. *Musicians include the following:* singer, instrumentalist, soloist, soprano, alto, contralto, coloratura, mezzo-soprano, countertenor, tenor, baritone, bass, conductor, director, leader, basso profundo, folk singer, drummer, pianist, violinist, cellist, guitarist, bassist, keyboardist, organist, saxophonist, woodwind player, percussionist, brass player, jazzman.

muss* *n.* chaos, disarrangement, mess; see CONFUSION, DISORDER.

muss *v.* rumple, tousle, dishevel, ruffle, crumple, jumble, disarrange, disturb, mess up; see also TANGLE.

mussy* *a.* messy, chaotic, rumpled; see TANGLED.

must* *n.* requirement, need, obligation; see NECESSITY 2.

must *v.* ought to, should, have to, have got to, be compelled to, be obliged to, be required to, be destined to, be ordered to, be made to, have no choice but to, have as one's fate; see also NEED.

mustache *n.* mustachio, handlebar*, soup strainer*; see BEARD, WHISKERS.

muster *v.* gather, marshal, summon; see ASSEMBLE 1.

musty *a.* moldy, fusty, rank; see ROTTEN 1.

mutation *n.* deviation, modification, variation; see CHANGE 1, VARIETY 1, 2.

mute *a.* 1 [Without power of speech] tongueless, deaf-mute, aphasic, inarticulate, voiceless, tongue-tied; see also DUMB 1, QUIET.—*Ant.* VOCAL, noisy, unimpaired. 2 [Suddenly deprived of speech] speechless, wordless, silent; see BEWILDERED, SURPRISED.

mutilate *v.* 1 [To maim] cut, batter, scratch; see WEAKEN 2. 2 [To damage] injure, deface, ravage; see DAMAGE, HURT 1.

mutilated *a.* disfigured, distorted, maimed; see DEFORMED.

mutiny *n.* insurrection, revolt, resistance; see REVOLUTION 2.

mutter *v.* 1 [To make a low, mumbling sound] rumble, growl, snarl; see SOUND. 2 [To speak as if to oneself] murmur, grunt, grumble, sputter, whisper, speak inarticulately, speak indistinctly, speak in an undertone, swallow one's words*; see also MUMBLE, MURMUR 1. 3 [To complain] grumble, moan, groan; see COMPLAIN.

mutual *a.* 1 [Reciprocal] interchangeable, two-sided, give-and-take; see COMPLEMENTARY. 2 [Common] joint, shared, belonging equally to each; see COMMON 5.

mutually *a.* commonly, cooperatively, jointly, reciprocally, in combination, by common consent, in conjunction; see also TOGETHER 2.

muzzle *v.* 1 [To fasten a muzzle upon] wrap, muffle, enclose; see BIND 1, GAG 1. 2 [To silence] gag, restrain, restrict, repress, suppress, check, stop, stop someone's mouth, hush, still, shush*; see also QUIET 2.

myriad *a.* variable, infinite, innumerable; see ENDLESS, MULTIPLE 1.

myself *pron.* me, me personally, the speaker, the writer, etc.; on my own authority, on my own responsibility, yours truly*, me myself.

mysterious *a.* 1 [Puzzling] enigmatic, uncanny, strange; see DIFFICULT 2, OBSCURE 1, UNNATURAL 1. 2

[Concerning powers beyond those supposedly natural] mystic, occult, dark, mystifying, transcendental, abstruse, arcane, inscrutable, metaphysical, mystical, magical, dark, veiled, strange, astrological, unknowable, unfathomable, esoteric, cryptic, oracular, incredible; see also MAGIC. 3 [Not generally known] obscure, hidden, ambiguous; see SECRET 1.

mystery *n.* 1 [The quality of being mysterious] inscrutability, occultism, abstruseness; see MAGIC 1, 2, STRANGENESS. 2 [Something difficult to know] riddle, conundrum, enigma; see DIFFICULTY 2, PUZZLE 1. 3 [A trick] sleight-of-hand, magic trick, magic; see TRICK 1. 4 [A mystery story] detective story, mystery play, mystery movie; see STORY.

mystic *a.* occult, transcendental, spiritual; see MYSTERIOUS 2, SECRET 1.

mysticism *n.* occultism, cabala, quietism, orphism.

mystify *v.* perplex, trick, hoodwink; see DECEIVE, LIE 1.

mystique *n.* attitude, complex, nature; see CHARACTER 1, TEMPERAMENT.

myth *n.* fable, folk tale, legend, lore, saga, folk ballad, allegory, parable, tale; see also STORY.

mythical *a.* mythological, fabricated, fictitious; see FALSE 3, UNREAL.

mythological *a.* whimsical, fictitious, chimerical; see FANTASTIC, IMAGINARY.

mythology *n.* belief, tradition, stories of gods and heroes; see RELIGION 1.

N

nab* *v.* grab, take, snatch; see SEIZE 2.

nag *v.* vex, annoy, pester; see BOTHER 2.

nail *n.* brad, pin, peg, stud, spike; see also TACK 1.

nail *v.* 1 [To hammer] drive, pound, spike; see HIT 1. 2 [To fasten with nails] secure, hold, clinch; see FASTEN. 3 [*To arrest] capture, detain, apprehend; see ARREST, SEIZE 2. —**hard as nails** callous, unfeeling, remorseless; see CRUEL. —**hit the nail on the head*** say what is exactly right, be accurate, come to the point; see DEFINE 2.

naive *a.* unaffected, childish, childlike, plain, artless, innocent, untrained, countrified, callow, natural, unschooled, ignorant, untaught, unworldly, provincial, unsophisticated, guileless, spontaneous, instinctive, impulsive, simpleminded, innocuous, unsuspecting, unsuspicious, harmless, gullible, credulous, trusting, original, fresh, unpolished, rude, primitive, ingenuous, sincere, open, candid, forthright, aboveboard, romantic, fanciful, unpretentious, transparent, straightforward, uncomplicated, easily imposed upon; see also INEXPERIENCED.—*Ant.* EXPERIENCED, sophisticated, complicated.

naively *a.* childishly, innocently, stupidly; see FOOLISHLY, OPENLY 1.

naiveté *n.* simplicity, childishness, inexperience; see INNOCENCE 2.

naked *a.* 1 [Nude] unclothed, undressed, stripped, unclad, unrobed, disrobed, leafless, hairless, bare, undraped, exposed, having nothing on, unappareled, denuded, unveiled, uncovered, uncloaked, stark naked, topless, bald, in one's birthday suit*, in the buff, peeled*, without a stitch, in the raw. 2 [Unadorned] plain, simple, artless; see MODEST 2, NATURAL 3.

nakedness *n.* nudity, bareness, undress, exposure, the raw, nudism.

name *n.* 1 [A title] proper name, Christian name, given name, cognomen, appellation, designation, first name, family name, title, denomination, surname, last name, middle name, confirmation name, moniker*, sign, handle*. 2 [Reputation] renown, honor, repute; see FAME. 3 [An epithet] nickname, pen name, pseudonym, sobriquet, stage name, nom de plume, nom de guerre, pet name, fictitious name, alias. 4 [A famous person] star, hero, a person of renown; see CELEBRITY. —**call names** swear at, insult, slander; see SCOLD. —**in the name of** by authority of, in reference to, as representative of; see FOR. —**know only by name** be familiar with, not know personally, have heard of; see KNOW 3. —**to one's name** belonging to one, in one's possession, possessed by one; see OWNED.

name *v.* 1 [To give a name] call, christen, baptize, style, term, label, identify, designate, classify, denominate, title, entitle, nickname, characterize, label, dub; see also DESCRIBE, DEFINE. 2 [To indicate by name] refer to, specify, signify, denote, single out, mark, suggest, connote, point to, note, remark, index, list, cite; see also MENTION. 3

[To appoint] elect, nominate, select; see DELEGATE 1.

named *a.* 1 [Having as a name] called, designated, entitled, titled, termed, specified, styled, denominated, christened, baptized, nicknamed, labeled, tagged*, dubbed. 2 [Chosen] appointed, commissioned, delegated, authorized, nominated, elected, invested, vested, assigned, ordained, entrusted, picked, selected, decided upon, settled on, picked out, preferred, favored, supported, approved, certified, called, anointed, consecrated, sanctioned, drafted, opted, declared, announced, singled out.

nameless *a.* inconspicuous, undistinguished, obscure; see UNKNOWN 2.

namely *a.* specifically, to wit, that is to say, particularly, by way of explanation, strictly speaking, in other words, in plain English.

nap *n.* 1 [A short sleep] siesta, cat nap, doze; see SLEEP. 2 [The finish of certain goods, especially fabric] pile, shag, surface; see GRAIN 2, OUTSIDE 1, TEXTURE 1.

napkin *n.* paper napkin, serviette*, table linen; see TOWEL.

narcotic *n.* depressant, sedative, opiate; see DRUG.

narrate *v.* detail, describe, depict; see REPORT 1, TELL 1.

narrative *a.* storylike, historical, sequential; see CHRONOLOGICAL.

narrow *a.* 1 [Lacking breadth] close, cramped, tight, confined, shrunken, compressed, slender, fine, linear, threadlike, tapering, tapered, slim, scant, scanty, lanky, small, meager; see also THIN 1.—*Ant.* BROAD, wide, extensive. 2 [Lacking tolerance] dogmatic, narrow-minded, parochial; see CONSERVATIVE, CONVENTIONAL 3, PREJUDICED. 3 [Lacking a comfortable margin] close, near, precarious; see DANGEROUS, ENDANGERED, UNSAFE.

narrowly *a.* nearly, closely, by a narrow margin; see ALMOST.

narrow-minded *a.* bigoted, biased, provincial; see CONSERVATIVE, CONVENTIONAL 3, PREJUDICED.

narrowness *n.* 1 [A physical restriction] confinement, thinness, restriction; see BARRIER, INTERFERENCE 1. 2 [A mental restriction] intolerance, bigotry, bias; see PREJUDICE, STUBBORNNESS.

nasty *a.* 1 [Offensive to the senses] foul, gross, revolting; see OFFENSIVE 2, VULGAR. 2 [Indecent] immoral, immodest, smutty; see LEWD 1, SHAMEFUL 1. 3 [Unkind] sarcastic, critical, mean; see CRUEL, FIERCE, RUTHLESS.

nation *n.* 1 [An organized state] realm, country, commonwealth, republic, democracy, state, monarchy, dominion, body politic, land, domain, empire, kingdom, principality, sovereignty, colony; see also GOVERNMENT 1. 2 [A people having some unity] populace, community, public; see POPULATION, RACE 2, SOCIETY 2.

national *a.* 1 [Concerning a nation] ethnic, political, sovereign, state, social, civic, civil, societal, communal, royal, imperial, federal; see also GOVERNMENTAL, PUBLIC 2. 2 [Operative throughout a nation] nationwide, countrywide, interstate, internal, social, widespread, sweeping; see also GENERAL 1.

nationalism *n.* provincialism, chauvinism, allegiance; see LOYALTY, PATRIOTISM.

nationality *n.* native land, country, citizenship; see ORIGIN 2.

nationally *a.* politically, governmentally, as a state, as a country, publicly, of the people, throughout the country, transcending state boundaries, for the general welfare.

native *a.* 1 [Natural] innate, inherent, inborn, implanted, inbred, ingrained, congenital, fundamental, hereditary, inherited, essential, constitutional; see also NATURAL 1.—*Ant.* UNNATURAL, foreign, alien. 2 [Characteristic of a region] aboriginal, indigenous, original, primitive, primary, primeval, vernacular, domestic, local, found locally; see also REGIONAL.—*Ant.* IMPORTED, brought in, transplanted.

native *n.* 1 [Aborigine] original inhabitant, indigenous inhabitant, tribesman; see MAN 1. 2 [Citizen] national, inhabitant, occupant; see CITIZEN, RESIDENT.

natural *a.* 1 [Rooted in nature] intrinsic, original, essential, true, fundamental, inborn, ingrained, inherent, instinctive, implanted, innate, inbred, incarnate, subjective, inherited, congenital, genetic; see also NATIVE 1.—*Ant.* FOREIGN, alien, acquired. 2 [To be expected] normal, typical, characteristic, usual, customary, habitual, accustomed, involuntary, spontaneous, uncontrolled, uncontrollable, familiar, common, universal, prevailing, prevalent, general, probable, uniform, constant, consistent, ordinary, logical, reasonable, anticipated, looked for, hoped for, counted on, relied on; see also REGULAR 3.—*Ant.* UNKNOWN, unexpected, unheard-of. 3 [Not affected] ingenuous, simple, artless, innocent, unstudied, spontaneous, impulsive, childlike, unfeigned, open, frank, candid, unsophisticated, unpolished, homey, unpretentious, forthright, sincere, straightforward, being oneself, unsuspecting, credulous, trusting, plain, direct, rustic; see also NAIVE.—*Ant.* ORNATE, pretentious, sophisticated. **4** [Concerning the physical universe] actual, tangible, according to nature; see PHYSICAL 1, REAL.

naturalist *n.* botanist, zoologist, biologist; see SCIENTIST.

naturally *a.* **1** [In an unaffected manner] artlessly, spontaneously, innocently, candidly, openly, honestly, disingenuously, impulsively, freely, readily, easily, without restraint, directly; see also SIMPLY, SINCERELY.—*Ant.* AWKWARDLY, restrainedly, clumsily. **2** [As a matter of course] casually, according to expectation, as anticipated, characteristically, typically, normally, commonly, usually, ordinarily, habitually, by nature, instinctively, intuitively, by birth, uniformly, generally, consistently; see also REGULARLY.—*Ant.* STRANGELY, astonishingly, amazingly.

naturally *interj.* certainly, absolutely, of course; see SURELY, YES.

nature *n.* **1** [The external universe] cosmos, creation, macrocosm; see UNIVERSE. **2** [The complex of essential qualities] characteristics, quality, constitution; see CHARACTER 1, ESSENCE 1. **3** [Natural surroundings] outside world, out-of-doors, scenery, natural setting, view, seascape, landscape, the outdoors, natural scenery, the great outdoors; see also ENVIRONMENT, REALITY. **4** [Natural forces] natural law, natural order, underlying cause, cosmic process, physical energy, kinetic energy, potential energy, water power, fission, fusion, atomic power, the sun, radiation, rays; see also ENERGY 2. **5** [Vital forces in an organism] creation, generation, regeneration; see LIFE 1, 2, STRENGTH. **6** [Kind] species, sort, type; see KIND 2, VARIETY 1, 2. —**by nature** inherently, by birth, as a matter of course; see NATURALLY 2. —**of** (or **in**) **the nature of** similar to, having the essential character of, as compared to; see LIKE.

naughty *a.* wayward, disobedient, mischievous, impish, fiendish, badly behaved, roguish, bad, unmanageable, ungovernable, insubordinate, froward, wanton, recalcitrant; see also RUDE 2, UNRULY.

nausea *n.* motion sickness, queasiness, vomiting; see ILLNESS 2.

nauseate *v.* sicken, offend, repulse; see BOTHER 2, DISGUST, DISTURB.

nauseous* *a.* queasy, ill, squeamish; see SICK.

nautical *a.* oceangoing, marine, naval, oceanic, deep-sea, aquatic, sailing, seafaring, seaworthy, seagoing, boating, yachting, cruising, whaling, oceanographic, rowing, navigating; see also MARITIME.

naval *a.* seagoing, marine, aquatic; see MARITIME, NAUTICAL.

navel *n.* bellybutton*, depression, umbilicus; see CENTER 1.

navigable *a.* passable, deep enough, open; see SAFE 1.

navigate *v.* pilot, steer, cruise, sail, head out for, ride out, lay a course, operate; see also DRIVE 2.

navigation *n.* navigating, seamanship, yachting, piloting, aeronautics, flying, sailing, seafaring, ocean travel, exploration, voyaging, shipping, cruising, plotting a course, boating, pilotage, dead reckoning.

navigator *n.* seaman, explorer, mariner; see PILOT 1, SAILOR.

navy *n.* fleet, carrier group, squadron, flotilla, armada, task force, submarine force, ships, amphibious force, coast guard.

near *a.* **1** [Not distant in space] close, nigh*, proximate, adjacent, adjoining, neighboring, not remote, close at hand, contiguous, handy, nearby, next door to, at close quarters, beside, side by side, in close proximity; see also BORDERING.—*Ant.* DISTANT, removed, far off. **2** [Not distant in relationship] touching, close, akin; see FRIENDLY, RELATED 3. **3** [Not distant in time] at hand, approaching, next; see COMING 1, EXPECTED.

nearly *a.* practically, just about*, approximately; see ALMOST.

nearness *n.* **1** [Nearness in time or space] closeness, proximity, vicinity, approximation, approach, intimacy, close quarters, resemblance, likeness, handiness, imminence, immediacy, threat, menace.—*Ant.* DISTANCE, remoteness, difference. **2** [Nearness in feeling] familiarity, affection, intimacy; see ADMIRATION, FRIENDSHIP.

neat *a.* **1** [Clean and orderly] tidy, trim, prim, spruce, dapper, smart, correct, shipshape, methodical, regular, orderly, systematic, spotless, nice, meticulous, elegant, spick-and-span, immaculate, chic, well-groomed, exact, precise, proper, neat as a pin, in good order, spruced up; see also CLEAN 1.—*Ant.* DISORDERED, messy, slovenly. **2** [Clever] dexterous, deft, skillful, expert, proficient, apt, ready, artful, nimble, quick, agile, adept, speedy, finished, practiced, easy, effortless; see also ABLE.—*Ant.* AWKWARD, clumsy, fumbling.

neatly *a.* **1** [So as to present a neat appearance] tidily, systematically, methodically, correctly, exactly, uniformly, levelly, flatly, smoothly, regularly, precisely, immaculately;

see also EVENLY 1, ORGANIZED. **2** [In an adroit manner] skillfully, deftly, agilely; see CLEVERLY, EASILY.

neatness *n.* cleanness, tidiness, orderliness; see CLEANLINESS.

necessarily *a.* vitally, fundamentally, importantly, indispensably, unavoidably, undeniably, certainly, as a matter of course, inescapably, irresistibly, inevitably, assuredly, significantly, undoubtedly, indubitably, positively, unquestionably, no doubt, without fail, of necessity, of course, beyond someone's control, come what may, by its own nature, from within, by definition; see also SURELY.

necessary *a.* important, needed, requisite, expedient, needful, indispensable, required, urgent, wanted, imperative, prerequisite, pressing, vital, fundamental, quintessential, cardinal, significant, momentous, compulsory, mandatory, basic, paramount, obligatory, essential, compelling, binding, incumbent upon someone, all-important, specified, unavoidable, decisive, crucial, elementary, chief, principal, prime, intrinsic, fixed, constant, permanent, inherent, ingrained, innate, without choice.

necessitate *v.* compel, constrain, oblige; see FORCE.

necessity *n.* **1** [The state of being required] need, essentiality, indispensability; see REQUIREMENT 2. **2** [That which is needed] need, want, requisite, vital part, essential, demand, imperative, fundamental, claim; see also LACK 2. **3** [The state of being forced by circumstances] exigency, pinch, stress, urgency, destitution, extremity, privation, obligation, matter of life and death; see also EMERGENCY, POVERTY 1. —**of necessity** inevitably, importantly, surely; see NECESSARILY.

neck *n.* **1** [The juncture of the head and the trunk] cervical vertebrae, nape, scruff; see THROAT. **2** [The part of a dress at the neck] neckband, neckline, collar; see DRESS 1, 2. —**risk one's neck** endanger oneself, gamble, take a chance; see RISK. —**stick one's neck out** endanger oneself, take a chance, gamble; see RISK.

necklace *n.* ornament, accessory, string of beads, jewels, chain, neckband, pearls, diamonds, choker; see also JEWELRY.

necktie *n.* neckwear, cravat, ascot; see TIE 2.

need *n.* **1** [Poverty] want, destitution, pennilessness; see POVERTY 1. **2** [Lack] insufficiency, shortage, inadequacy; see LACK 1, 2. **3** [A requirement] obligation, necessity, urgency; see REQUIREMENT 2. —**if need be** if it is required, if the occasion demands, if necessary; see IF.

need *v.* lack, require, feel the necessity for, be in need of, suffer privation, be in want, be destitute, be short, be inadequate, have occasion for, have use for, miss, be without, do without, be needy, be poor, be deficient in, go hungry, live from hand to mouth, feel the pinch*, be down and out*, be hard up*, be up against it*; see also WANT 2.—*Ant.* OWN, have, hold. —**have need to** have to, be obligated to, have reason to; see MUST.

needed *a.* wanted, required, desired; see NECESSARY.

needle *n.* awl, spike, hypodermic needle, syringe, phonograph needle, stylus, electric needle, probe, skewer, pin, darning needle, sewing needle, knitting needle.

needle* *v.* provoke, goad, tease; see BOTHER 2.

needless *a.* unwanted, excessive, groundless; see UNNECESSARY, USELESS 1.

needy *a.* destitute, indigent, penniless; see POOR 1.

negate *v.* repeal, retract, nullify; see CANCEL.

negation *n.* opposition, contradiction, repudiation; see DENIAL, REFUSAL.

negative *a.* **1** [Involving a refusal] denying, contradictory, contrary, disavowing, contravening, rejecting, disallowing.—*Ant.* FAVORABLE, encouraging, accepting. **2** [Lacking positive qualities] absent, removed, neutralizing, counteractive, annulling, invalidating.—*Ant.* EMPHATIC, validating, affirmative.

negative *n.* **1** [A refusal] contradiction, disavowal, refutation; see DENIAL, REFUSAL. **2** [A negative image] film, plate, developed film; see IMAGE 2, PICTURE 2.

neglect *n.* **1** [The act of showing indifference to a person] slight, disregard, thoughtlessness, disrespect, carelessness, scorn, oversight, heedlessness, inattention, unconcern, inconsideration, disdain, coolness; see also INDIFFERENCE. **2** [The act of neglecting responsibilities] negligence, slovenliness, neglectfulness; see CARELESSNESS.

neglect *v.* **1** [To treat with indifference] slight, scorn, overlook, disregard, disdain, detest, rebuff, affront, despise, ignore, depreciate, spurn, underestimate, undervalue, shake off, make light of, laugh off, keep one's distance, pass over, pass up, have nothing to do with, let alone, let go, not care for, pay no attention to, pay no heed, leave alone, not give a darn*, leave well enough alone, let it ride*, keep at arm's length.—*Ant.*

CONSIDER, appreciate, value. **2** [To fail to attend to responsibilities] pass over, defer, procrastinate, suspend, dismiss, discard, let slip, miss, skip, omit, skimp, gloss over, be remiss, be derelict, ignore, trifle, postpone, lose sight of, look the other way, let it go, not trouble oneself with, evade, be careless, be irresponsible.—*Ant.* WATCH, care for, attend to.

neglected *a.* slighted, disregarded, scorned, disdained, despised, affronted, overlooked, ignored, spurned, omitted, undervalued, deferred, dismissed, passed over, postponed, evaded, deteriorated, underestimated, declined, lapsed, uncared-for, unwatched, unheeded, depreciated, unconsidered, shaken off, unused, unwanted, tossed aside, abandoned, forgotten, out in the cold, dropped, put on the shelf.—*Ant.* CONSIDERED, cared for, heeded.

negligence *n.* disregard, inconsideration, disrespect; see CARELESSNESS, INDIFFERENCE, NEGLECT 1.

negligent *a.* indifferent, inattentive, neglectful; see CARELESS.

negotiate *v.* **1** [To make arrangements for] arrange, bargain, confer, consult, parley, transact, mediate, make peace, contract, settle, adjust, conciliate, accommodate, arbitrate, referee, umpire, compromise, bring to terms, make terms, make the best of, treat with, moderate, work out, dicker*, haggle, bury the hatchet*. **2** [To transfer] barter, allocate, transmit; see ASSIGN, SELL.

negotiation *n.* compromise, intervention, mediation; see AGREEMENT.

Negro *n.* black, African, African-American, Afro-American, Afro-Asian, black person, person of color.

neighbor *n.* acquaintance, companion, associate, next-door neighbor, nearby resident; see also FRIEND.

neighborhood *n.* environs, block, vicinity, locality, proximity, district, area, parish, ward, precinct, community, region, zone, section, suburb, tract. **—in the neighborhood of** * about, approximately, close to; see NEAR 1.

neighboring *a.* adjacent, adjoining, contiguous; see BORDERING, NEAR 1.

neighborly *a.* sociable, hospitable, helpful; see FRIENDLY.

neither *a.*, *conj.* nor yet, also not, not either, not, not at all.

neither *pron.* not one or the other, not either one, no one, nobody, neither one, not this one, nor this nor that, no one of two, not the one, not any one; see also NONE 1, NOTHING.

nephew *n.* brother's son, sister's son, grandnephew*, great-nephew, brother-in-law's son, sister-in-law's

son, nephew by marriage; see also NIECE, RELATIVE.

nerve *n.* **1** [The path of nervous impulses] nerve fiber, nerve tissue, nerve cells, neurons, nerve endings. *Types of nerves include the following:* motor, sensory, efferent, afferent; effector, receptor. **2** [Courage] resolution, spirit, mettle; see COURAGE. **3** [*Impudence] temerity, audacity, effrontery; see RUDENESS.

nerve-racking *a.* exhausting, horrible, wearisome; see DIFFICULT 1, PAINFUL 1.

nerves *n.* strain, tension, hysteria, stress, butterflies*; see also NERVOUSNESS. **—get on someone's nerves** * exasperate, irritate, annoy; see BOTHER 2.

nervous *a.* **1** [Excitable] sensitive, irritable, impatient, moody, peevish, restless, uneasy, impulsive, rash, hasty, reckless, touchy, readily upset, high-strung, neurotic; see also UNSTABLE 2. **2** [Excited] agitated, bothered, annoyed; see EXCITED.

nervousness *n.* stimulation, agitation, animation, intoxication, sensitivity, delirium, excitability, irascibility, impulsiveness, impetuosity, moodiness, anger, elation, discomfiture, hastiness, vehemence, impatience, feverishness, stage fright, butterflies in the stomach*, the jitters*, the shakes*; see also EMBARRASSMENT, EXCITEMENT.—*Ant.* REST, calm, relaxation.

nest *n.* den, cradle, incubator; see RETREAT 2.

nest egg * *n.* personal savings, personal property, money, something for a rainy day*; see also MONEY 1, SAVINGS.

nestle *v.* cuddle, snuggle, settle down, take shelter, lie close, make oneself snug, huddle, move close to, lie against, curl up to.

net *a.* clear, final, remaining, exclusive, irreducible, undeductible.

net *n.* screen, mesh, fabric; see WEB. *Varieties of nets include the following:* fishing, seine, gill, mosquito, tennis, ping-pong, volleyball, basketball, hockey, bird, butterfly, drift, hand, scoop; hairnet, dragnet.

net *v.* make, clear, gain above expenses; see PROFIT 2.

network *n.* **1** [System of channels] tracks, circuitry, channels, system, labyrinth, arrangement; see also CHAIN, WIRING. **2** [Netting] fiber, weave, mesh; see GOODS, WEB.

neurosis *n.* compulsion, instability, mental disorder; see NERVOUSNESS, OBSESSION.

neurotic *a.* disturbed, unstable, high-strung; see TROUBLED.

neurotic *n.* paranoid, compulsive person, victim of depression; see ILLNESS 1.

neutral *a.* 1 [Not fighting] noncombatant, nonpartisan, on the sidelines, nonparticipating, inactive, disengaged, uninvolved, standing by, inert, on the fence.—*Ant.* ENGAGED, involved, active. 2 [Without opinion] unbiased, open-minded, impartial; see INDIFFERENT. 3 [Without distinctive color] drab, indeterminate, vague; see DULL 2.

never *a.* not ever, at no time, not at any time, not in the least, not in any way, in no way, not at all, not under any condition, nevermore, never again, no way*.

nevertheless *a.* however, nonetheless, notwithstanding; see BUT 1, ALTHOUGH.

new *a.* 1 [Recent] current, brand-new, newborn, young, newfangled*, latest, just out; see also FRESH 1. 2 [Modern] modish, popular, faddish, up to the minute, contemporary, latest; see also FASHIONABLE, MODERN 1. 3 [Novel] unique, original, bizarre; see UNUSUAL 1, 2. 4 [Different] unlike, dissimilar, distinct; see UNLIKE. 5 [Additional] further, increased, supplementary; see EXTRA. 6 [Inexperienced] green, unseasoned, raw; see INCOMPETENT, INEXPERIENCED. 7 [Recently] of late, newly, lately; see RECENTLY.

newcomer *n.* immigrant, outsider, foreigner, tenderfoot, maverick*, Johnny-come-lately*; see also ALIEN, STRANGER.

newfangled* *a.* novel, unique, new; see FASHIONABLE, MODERN 1.

newly *a.* lately, anew, afresh; see RECENTLY.

newlywed *n.* bride, bridegroom, honeymooner; see HUSBAND, WIFE.

newness *n.* uniqueness, modernity, recentness; see ORIGINALITY.

news *n.* 1 [Information] intelligence, tidings, advice, discovery, recognition, the scoop*, the goods*, headlines, front-page news; see also DATA, KNOWLEDGE 1. 2 [A specific report] telling, narration, recital, account, description, message, copy, communication, release, communiqué, telegram, cable, radiogram, broadcast, telecast, bulletin, dispatch, news story, scoop*, big news*, eye opener*; see also ANNOUNCEMENT. —**make news** become famous, accomplish, create events; see EXPOSE, REVEAL.

newscast *n.* news broadcasting, telecast, newscasting; see ANNOUNCEMENT, NEWS 2.

newscaster *n.* news analyst, commentator, broadcaster, anchor; see also REPORTER, WRITER.

newspaper *n.* publication, daily paper, journal, press, fourth estate, public press, sheet, tabloid, gazette; see also RECORD 1. *Varieties of newspapers include the following:* daily, weekly, biweekly, metropolitan, rural, national, tabloid, alternative, trade, provincial, community. *Parts of newspapers include the following:* front page, editorial page, local news, national news, state news, international news, magazine, comics pages, TV listings, ads, classified advertising, columnists, sports pages, business section, society page, entertainment, obituaries, arts, living, food, women's section, boilerplate.

newspaperman *n.* newsperson, journalist, member of the editorial department; see AUTHOR, EDITOR, REPORTER, WRITER.

next *a.* 1 [Following in order] succeeding, resulting, subsequent, ensuing; see also FOLLOWING. 2 [Adjacent] beside, close, alongside, on one side, on the side, adjoining, neighboring, meeting, touching, bordering on, cheek by jowl, side by side, attached, abutting, back to back, to the left, to the right; see also NEAR 1.

nibble *n.* morsel, peck, cautious bite; see BIT 1, BITE 1.

nibble *v.* nip, gnaw, snack; see BITE 1, EAT 1.

nice *a.* 1 [Approved] likable, superior, admirable; see EXCELLENT. 2 [Behaving in a becoming manner] pleasing, agreeable, winning, refined, cultured, amiable, delightful, charming, inviting, pleasant, cordial, courteous, considerate, kind, kindly, helpful, gracious, obliging, genial, gentle, unassuming, modest, demure; see also FRIENDLY.—*Ant.* RUDE, indecorous, crude.

nicely *a.* 1 [In a welcome manner] pleasantly, perfectly, pleasingly, amiably, winningly, creditably, acceptably, excellently, distinctively, happily, admirably, desirably, pleasurably, attractively, likably, enjoyably, beautifully, graciously; see also AGREEABLY.—*Ant.* BADLY, unfortunately, unsuccessfully. 2 [In a becoming manner] charmingly, winsomely, invitingly; see MODESTLY, POLITELY.

niceness *n.* discernment, taste, refinement; see CARE 1, DISCRETION, KINDNESS 1.

niche *n.* cranny, corner, cubbyhole; see HOLE 1.

nick *n.* indentation, notch, slit; see CUT 1, DENT.

nick *v.* indent, notch, slit; see CUT 1, DENT.

nickel *n.* 1 silvery metal, chemical element, plating material; see

ELEMENT 2, METAL, MINERAL. **2** [A coin made of nickel] five-cent piece, coin, five cents; see MONEY 1.

niece *n.* sister's daughter, brother's daughter, niece by marriage, grand-niece, great-niece, sister-in-law's daughter, brother-in-law's daughter; see also NEPHEW, RELATIVE.

niggling *a.* trifling, petty, piddling; see TRIVIAL, UNIMPORTANT.

night *n.* **1** [The diurnal dark period] after dark, evening, from dusk to dawn, nightfall, after nightfall, twilight, nighttime, midnight, before dawn, the dark hours, dead of night. **2** [The dark] blackness, duskiness, gloom; see DARKNESS 1. —**good night** sleep well, have a good evening, nighty-night*; see GOODBYE.

nightclub *n.* casino, discotheque, cabaret; see BAR 2, RESTAURANT.

nightly *a.* nocturnal, in the hours of night, every twenty-four hours, during the hours of darkness, at night, each night, every night, by night; see also REGULAR, REGULARLY.—*Ant.* DAILY, by day, diurnal.

nightmare *n.* bad dream, horror, incubus; see DREAM.

nighttime *n.* darkness, bedtime, dark of night; see NIGHT 1.

nimble *a.* **1** [Agile] quick, spry, active; see AGILE, GRACEFUL 1. **2** [Alert] quick-witted, bright, clever; see INTELLIGENT.

nip *v.* nibble, snap, munch; see BITE 1, PINCH.

nipple *n.* mamilla, mammary gland, teat; see BREAST 2.

nitwit *n.* blockhead, dummy*, dimwit*; see FOOL.

no *a., interj.* absolutely not, not at all, by no means, the answer is in the negative, not by any means, none, nay, not, not a, not one, not any, *non*(French), *nein* (German), *nyet* (Russian), nix*; see also NEGATIVE 2, NEITHER, NEVER.

nobility *n.* [*Usually used with "the"*] ruling class, gentry, peerage; see ARISTOCRACY, ROYALTY.

noble *a.* **1** [Possessing an exalted mind and character] generous, princely, magnanimous, magnificent, courtly, lofty, elevated, splendid, excellent, supreme, eminent, lordly, dignified, great, good, superior, greathearted, high-minded, honorable, distinguished, liberal, tolerant, gracious, humane, benevolent, charitable, sympathetic, bounteous, brilliant, extraordinary, remarkable, devoted, heroic, resolute, valorous; see also WORTHY.—*Ant.* CORRUPT, low, ignoble. **2** [Possessing excellent qualities or properties] meritorious, virtuous, worthy, valuable, useful, first-rate, refined, cultivated, chivalrous,

trustworthy, candid, liberal, gracious, princely, magnanimous, generous, sincere, truthful, constant, faithful, upright, honest, warmhearted, true, incorruptible, distinctive, reputable, respectable, admirable, good, aboveboard, fair, just, estimable; see also EXCELLENT, PERFECT 2.—*Ant.* POOR, inferior, second-rate. **3** [Belonging to the nobility] titled, aristocratic, patrician, highborn, well-born, blue-blooded, of gentle birth, imperial, lordly, highbred, princely, of good breed, kingly; see also ROYAL.—*Ant.* COMMON, plebeian, lowborn. **4** [Grand] stately, impressive, imposing; see GRAND.

nobly *a.* **1** [Majestically] aristocratically, illustriously, royally; see GENEROUSLY 2, POLITELY. **2** [Honorably] fairly, respectably, honestly; see JUSTLY 1.

nobody *n.* **1** [No one at all] no person, no one, not anybody; see NONE 1. **2** [A person of little importance] upstart, cipher, nonentity, whippersnapper, no great shakes*, nix*, zero*.

nocturnal *a.* at night, night-loving, nighttime; see LATE 4, NIGHTLY.

nod *n.* slight bow, aknowledgement, gesture of agreement; see GREETING.

nod *v.* **1** [To make a nodding movement] assent, signal, greet, bend, curtsy, incline the head, bow, nod yes, acquiesce, consent, respond, concur, acknowledge, recognize; see also AGREE, APPROVE.—*Ant.* DENY, dissent, disagree. **2** [To become sleepy or inattentive] drowse, nap, drift off; see SLEEP.

noise *n.* **1** [A sound] sound, something heard, impact of sound waves. *Kinds of noises include the following*—*brief, loud noises:* bang, boom, crash, thud, blast, roar, bellow, blat, shout, peal, cry, yelp, squawk, blare, clang, ring, shot, sonic boom, jangle, eruption, explosion, detonation; *brief, faint noises:* peep, squeak, squawk, cackle, cluck, tweet, clink, tinkle, pop, whisper, stage whisper, sigh, splash, swish, sob, whine, whimper, plunk, plop, ping, rustle, murmur, stirring; *continuing noises:* reverberation, ringing, tone, tune, clanging, tinkling, resonance, cacophony, rattle, whir, whistle, dissonance, discord, shouting, roaring, bellowing, rumble, rumbling, grunting, murmuring, drone, droning, purr, thundering, whine, screeching, screaming, banging, clanging, hum, humming, laughing, chuckle, swishing, rustling, ripple, strumming, beating, pattering, clattering, trilling, whinneying, neighing, cawing, cackling,

2 [Clamor] racket, fracas, din; see UPROAR.

noiseless *a.* **1** [Containing no noise] silent, still, soundless; see QUIET. **2** [Making no noise] voiceless, speechless, wordless; see DUMB 1, MUTE 1.

noiselessly *a.* inaudibly, quietly, without a sound; see SILENTLY.

noisy *a.* clamorous, vociferous, boisterous; see LOUD 1, 2.

nomad *n.* wanderer, migrant, vagabond; see TRAVELER.

nominal *a.* professed, pretended, in name only; see GIVEN, NAMED 1.

nominate *v.* propose as a candidate, designate for election, put up; see CHOOSE, DECIDE.

nominated *a.* designated, called, suggested; see APPROVED, NAMED 2.

nomination *n.* naming, designation, proposal; see APPOINTMENT 1.

nonchalance *n.* apathy, disregard, insouciance; see INDIFFERENCE.

nonchalant *a.* **1** [Cool and casual] uncaring, unconcerned, untroubled, apathetic, unfeeling, impassive, imperturbable, easygoing, listless, lackadaisical, unruffled, lukewarm, composed, collected, aloof, detached, calm, serene, placid, disinterested, easy, effortless, light, smooth, neutral, laid-back*.—*Ant.* WARM, ardent, enthusiastic. **2** [Careless] neglectful, negligent, trifling; see CARELESS.

nonchalantly *a.* coolly, indifferently, casually; see CALMLY.

nonconformist *n.* rebel, eccentric, maverick, iconoclast, loner, malcontent, dissenter, demonstrator, hippie, protester, dissident, a different breed; see also RADICAL.

nonconformity *n.* dissent, opposition, difference; see INDIVIDUALITY.

none *pron.* **1** [No person or persons] no one, not one, not anyone, no one at all, not a person, not a soul, neither one nor the other; see also NEITHER.—*Ant.* MANY, some, a few. **2** [No thing or things] not a thing, not anything, not any; see NOTHING.

nonetheless *a.* nevertheless, in spite of that, anyway; see ALTHOUGH, BUT 1.

nonexistent *a.* missing, unsubstantial, fictitious; see IMAGINARY, UNREAL.

no-nonsense *a.* matter-of-fact, serious, purposeful, dedicated, resolute; see also PRACTICAL.

nonpartisan *a.* unprejudiced, unbiased, independent; see NEUTRAL 1.

nonpayment *n.* failure, delinquency, bankruptcy; see DEFAULT.

nonproductive *a.* unproductive, futile, ineffectual; see IDLE, USELESS 1.

nonprofit *a.* charitable, public-service, not-for-profit; see GENEROUS.

nonresident *a.* absentee, out-of-state, living abroad; see FOREIGN.

nonsense *n.* **1** [Matter that has no meaning] balderdash, rubbish, trash, scrawl, inanity, senselessness, buncombe, bunkum*, idle chatter, prattle, rant, bombast, claptrap, bull*, baloney*, hooey*, bunk*, poppycock*, guff*, hot air*. **2** [Frivolous behavior] unsteadiness, flightiness, stupidity, thoughtlessness, fickleness, foolishness, giddiness, extravagance, rashness, infatuation, imprudence, madness, irrationality, senselessness, inconsistency, shallowness.—*Ant.* CONSIDERATION, steadiness, thoughtfulness. **3** [Pure fun] absurdity, antics, monkey business*; see FUN.

nonstop *a.* uninterrupted, unbroken, continuous; see CONSTANT.

nonviolent *a.* pacifist, engaging in passive resistance, without violence; see CALM 1, QUIET.

nook *n.* niche, cubbyhole, cranny; see HOLE 1.

noon *n.* noontime, noontide, noonday, midday, twelve noon, meridian, noon hour; see also TIME 1, 2.

no one *pron.* no person, not anybody, nobody; see NEITHER, NONE 1.

noose *n.* loop, running knot, lasso; see KNOT 1, ROPE.

nor *conj.* and not, not any, not either, not one, nor yet; see also NEITHER.

normal *a.* **1** [Usual] ordinary, run-of-the-mill, typical; see COMMON 1, CONVENTIONAL 1, 3. **2** [Regular] routine, orderly, methodical; see REGULAR 3. **3** [Sane] lucid, wholesome, right-minded; see RATIONAL, REASONABLE, SANE 1. **4** [Showing no abnormal bodily condition] in good health, whole, sound; see HEALTHY.

normally *a.* usually, commonly, ordinarily; see FREQUENTLY, REGULARLY.

north *a.* **1** [Situated to the north] northward, northern, in the north, on the north side of, northerly, northmost, northernmost, toward the North Pole. **2** [Moving toward the north] northerly, northbound, northward, to the north, headed north, in a northerly direction; see also SOUTH 2. **3** [Coming from the north] northerly, southbound, headed south, out of the north, moving toward the equator, moving toward the South Pole; see also SOUTH 3. **4** [Associated with the north] polar, frozen, boreal; see COLD 1.

north *n.* tundra, northern section, northland, Northern Hemisphere, the north country, the north woods, arctic regions, polar regions, the frozen north, land of ice and snow; see also DIRECTION 1.

northeast a. NE, northeastern, northeasterly, northeastward, north-northeast, northeast by east, northeast by north; see also DIRECTION 1.

northerly a. boreal, northern, polar; see NORTH 2.

northern a. northerly, arctic, polar; see NORTH 1.

northwest a. NW, northwestern, northwesterly, northwestward, north-northwest, northwest by west, northwest by north; see also DIRECTION 1.

nose n. 1 [The organ of smell] nasal organ, nasal cavity, nares, nasal passages, nostrils, olfactory nerves, snoot*, schnoz*, beak*, bill; see also ORGAN 2. 2 [A projection] snout, nozzle, muzzle; see BEAK. —**by a nose** by a very small margin, too close for comfort, barely; see ALMOST. —**look down one's nose at*** disdain, snub, be disgusted by; see ABUSE. —**on the nose*** precisely, to the point, correctly; see ACCURATE. —**turn up one's nose at** sneer at, refuse, scorn; see ABUSE. —**under one's (very) nose** in plain sight, visible, at one's fingertips; see OBVIOUS 1.

nostalgia n. remorse, wistfulness, sentimentality; see LONELINESS.

nostalgic a. lonesome, regretful, sentimental; see HOMESICK, LONELY.

nosy* a. meddlesome, snooping*, unduly curious; see INQUISITIVE, INTERESTED 2.

not a. no, in no manner, to no degree, non-, un-, in-; see also NEGATIVE 2.

notable a. distinguished, important, striking; see FAMOUS, UNUSUAL 1.

notch n. indentation, nick, indent; see CUT 1, DENT, GROOVE.

notch v. indent, nick, chisel; see CUT 1, DENT.

notched a. nicked, jagged, sawtoothed; see IRREGULAR 4, ROUGH 1.

note n. 1 [A representation] sign, figure, mark; see REPRESENTATION. 2 [A brief record] notation, jotting, scribble, reminder, scrawl, annotation, agenda, entry, memorandum, journal, inscription, calendar, diary; see also NOTES, SUMMARY. 3 [A brief communication] dispatch, word, announcement; see LETTER 2. 4 [A musical tone, or its symbol] tone, key, pitch, whole note, half note, quarter note, eighth note, sixteenth note, grace note, triplet, interval, degree, step, sharp, flat, natural; see also MUSIC 1.

note v. 1 [To notice] remark, heed, perceive; see REGARD 1, SEE 1. 2 [To record] write down, enter, transcribe; see RECORD 1, WRITE.

notebook n. memorandum book, record book, diary; see JOURNAL 1, RECORD 1.

noted a. well-known, celebrated, notorious; see FAMOUS.

notes n. commentary, interpretation, explanation, findings, recordings, field notes, observations; see also DATA, RECORDS. —**compare notes** exchange views, confer, go over; see DISCUSS.

nothing n. nonexistence, emptiness, nothingness, inexistence, nonbeing, nullity, zero, extinction, oblivion, obliteration, annihilation, nonentity, trifle.

nothing pron. no thing, not anything, naught, trifle, no part, no trace. —**for nothing** 1 gratis, without cost, unencumbered; see FREE 4. 2 in vain, for naught, emptily; see UNNECESSARY. —**have nothing on** have no evidence, be without proof, be only guessing; see GUESS. —**in nothing flat*** in almost no time at all, speedily, rapidly; see QUICKLY. —**think nothing of** minimize, underplay, disregard; see NEGLECT 1.

nothingness n. 1 [Void] vacuum, blank, hollowness; see EMPTINESS, NOTHING. 2 [Worthlessness] pettiness, unimportance, smallness; see INSIGNIFICANCE.

notice n. 1 [A warning] note, notification, intimation; see SIGN 1, WARNING. 2 [An announcement] remark, comments, information; see DECLARATION, ANNOUNCEMENT, REPORT 1. —**serve notice** give warning, notify, announce; see DECLARE. —**take notice** observe, become aware, pay attention; see SEE 1.

notice v. mark, remark, look at; see SEE 1.

noticeable a. observable, appreciable, conspicuous; see OBVIOUS 1.

noticed a. observed, remarked, seen; see RECORDED.

notify v. declare, announce, inform; see ADVERTISE, COMMUNICATE, TELL 1.

notion n. 1 [Opinion] idea, sentiment, assumption; see OPINION 1, THOUGHT 2. 2 [Conception] concept, insight, impression; see AWARENESS, KNOWLEDGE 1.

notoriety n. repute, renown, name; see FAME.

notorious a. ill-famed, infamous, disreputable; see BAD 1.

notwithstanding a., prep. despite, in spite of, in any case; see ALTHOUGH, BUT 1.

noun n. substantive, common noun, proper noun; see LABEL, NAME 1.

nourish v. feed, supply, sustain; see PROVIDE 1, SUPPORT 3.

nourishing a. healthy, nutritious, full of vitamins; see HEALTHFUL.

nourishment n. nurture, nutriment, provender; see FOOD.

novel a. new, odd, strange; see UNIQUE, UNUSUAL 1, 2.

novel n. narrative, bestseller, fiction; see BOOK, STORY. *Types of novels include the following:* romance, detective story, love story, novella, adventure story, ghost story, mystery, western, science fiction, fantasy; historical, regional, naturalistic, Gothic, biographical, psychological, pornographic, satirical, epistolary, experimental, adventure, etc., novel; thriller, porn*.

novelist n. fiction writer, storyteller, narrative writer, writer of novels, writer of prose fiction, hack, genre writer, pulp writer; see also AUTHOR, WRITER.

novelty n. 1 [The quality of being novel] recentness, modernity, freshness; see ORIGINALITY. 2 [Something popular because it is new] innovation, origination, creation; see FAD.

novice n. beginner, learner, neophyte; see AMATEUR.

now a. 1 [At the present] at this time, right now, at the moment, just now, momentarily, this day, these days, here and now. 2 [In the immediate future] promptly, in a moment, in a minute; see SOON. 3 [Immediately] at once, momentarily, instantly; see IMMEDIATELY. —**now and then** (or **again**) sometimes, infrequently, occasionally; see SELDOM.

nowadays a. in these days, in this age, at the present time; see NOW 1.

noway a. not at all, on no account, by no means, not a bit of it, nowhere near, in no respect.

nowhere a. not anywhere, not in any place, not at any place, nowhere at all, in no place, to no place.

nozzle n. spout, outlet, vent; see END 4.

nuance n. subtlety, refinement, distinction; see DIFFERENCE 1.

nub* n. gist, crux, core, nitty-gritty*; see also ESSENCE 1.

nuclear bomb n. nuclear warhead, hydrogen bomb, H-bomb, atomic bomb, A-bomb, neutron bomb, atomic weapon, nuclear weapon; see also ARMS.

nucleus n. 1 [Essence] core, gist, kernel; see ESSENCE 1, MATTER 1. 2 [Center] hub, focus, pivot; see CENTER 1.

nude a. stripped, unclothed, bare; see NAKED 1.

nude n. naked body, naked man, naked woman, nudist, pinup,

artist's model, sculpture, sketch, painting, stripper*, peeler*.

nudge n. tap, poke, shove; see BUMP 1, PUSH, TOUCH 2.

nudge v. poke, bump, tap; see PUSH 1, TOUCH 1.

nudity n. bareness, nudeness, undress; see NAKEDNESS.

nugget n. lump, bullion, chunk; see GOLD, ROCK 1.

nuisance n. 1 [A bother] annoyance, vexation, bore; see TROUBLE 2. 2 [An offense against the public] breach, infraction, affront; see CRIME. 3 [An unpleasant or unwelcome person] problem child, frump, bother, holy terror*, bad egg*, insect*, louse*, pain in the neck*, poor excuse*, bum*; see also TROUBLE 1.

null a. invalid, vain, unsanctioned; see VOID.

numb a. 1 [Insensible] deadened, dead, unfeeling, numbed, asleep, senseless, anesthetized, comatose; see also PARALYZED. 2 [Insensitive] apathetic, lethargic, callous; see INDIFFERENT.

numb v. paralyze, stun, dull; see DEADEN.

number n. amount, sum total, totality, aggregate, whole, whole number, product, measurable quantity, estimate, the lot, plenty, abundance; see also QUANTITY. —**get** (or **have**) **someone's number*** find out about, discover someone's true character, come to know someone; see UNDERSTAND 1. —**someone's number is up*** someone's time to die has arrived, someone's time has come, someone's destiny is fulfilled; see DOOMED. —**without number** too numerous to be counted, innumerable, countless; see MANY.

number v. count, calculate, enumerate; see ADD 1, TOTAL.

numbered a. designated, enumerated, checked, specified, indicated; see also MARKED 1.

numbness n. deadness, anesthesia, dullness, insensitivity, insensibility, paralysis, loss of sensation.

numeral n. character, cipher, digit; see NUMBER.

numerical a. arithmetical, statistical, fractional, exponential, logarithmic, differential, integral, digital, mathematical, binary.

numerous a. copious, various, diverse; see INFINITE, MANY.

nun n. sister, religious, ascetic, anchorite, prioress, mother superior, abbess; see also MINISTRY.

nuptials n. wedding, matrimony, marriage ceremony; see MARRIAGE.

nurse n. 1 [One who cares for the sick] attendant, male nurse, licensed practical nurse, LPN, private nurse, registered nurse, RN, floor nurse, night nurse, day nurse, doctor's assistant, student nurse, nurse's aide, therapist, Red Cross nurse, Florence Nightingale*. **2** [One who cares for the young] nursemaid, babysitter, nanny; see ATTENDANT.

nurse *v.* attend to, aid, medicate; see HEAL, SUSTAIN 2, TEND 1, TREAT 2.

nursery *n.* **1** [A place for children] child's room, playroom, nursery school; see SCHOOL 1. **2** [A place for plants] hothouse, potting shed, greenhouse; see BUILDING.

nurture *v.* nourish, care for, provide for; see FEED, SUSTAIN 2.

nut *n.* **1** [The dry fruit] seed, kernel, stone; see FRUIT. *Common nuts include the following:* acorn, beechnut, peanut, hazelnut, black walnut, English walnut, almond, pecan, filbert, pistachio, cashew, hickory nut,

chestnut, butternut, pine nut, pignolia, kola nut, Brazil nut, betel nut. **2** [A threaded metal block] bolt nut, screw nut, lock nut, cap, ratchet nut; see also BOLT. **3** [*An eccentric or insane person] eccentric, fanatic, maniac; see ZEALOT.

nutriment *n.* nourishment, provisions, sustenance; see FOOD.

nutrition *n.* diet, nourishment, victuals; see FOOD, SUBSISTENCE 1.

nutritive *a.* edible, wholesome, nutritious; see HEALTHFUL.

nuts* *a.* crazy, deranged, ridiculous; see INSANE, UNUSUAL 2.

nuzzle *v.* caress, cuddle, nudge; see NESTLE.

nylon *n.* synthetic, polyamide product, synthetic fiber; see PLASTIC.

nymph *n.* nature goddess, sprite, mermaid; see FAIRY.

O

oak *n.* **1** [An oak tree] white oak, pin oak, cork oak; see TREE. **2** [Oak wood] hardwood, oaken wood, oak paneling; see WOOD 2.

oar *n.* pole, paddle, scull; see TOOL 1.

oasis *n.* green area, fertile area, irrigated land, watered tract, garden spot, desert garden, water hole, watering place, desert resting place; see also REFUGE 1, RETREAT 2.

oath *n.* **1** [An attestation of the truth] affirmation, declaration, affidavit, vow, sworn statement, testimony, word, contract, pledge; see also PROMISE 1.—*Ant.* DENIAL, disavowal, lie. **2** [The name of the Lord taken in vain] malediction, swearword, blasphemy; see CURSE.

obedience *n.* docility, submission, compliance; see WILLINGNESS.

obedient *a.* **1** [Dutiful] loyal, law-abiding, governable, resigned, devoted, respectful, controllable, attentive, obliging, willing, tractable, deferential, under control, at one's command, at one's beck and call, on a string*, wrapped around one's little finger*; see also FAITHFUL.—*Ant.* UNRULY, disobedient, undutiful. **2** [Docile] pliant, acquiescent, compliant; see DOCILE.

obediently *a.* dutifully, submissively, loyally; see WILLINGLY.

obese *a.* corpulent, plump, stout; see FAT.

obey *v.* submit, answer to, respond, act upon, act on, bow to, surrender, yield, perform, do, carry out, attend to orders, do what one is told, accept, consent, do what is expected of one, do one's duty, do as one says,

serve, concur, assent, conform, acquiesce, mind, take orders, do one's bidding, comply, fulfill; see also AGREE.—*Ant.* REBEL, disobey, mutiny.

obfuscate *v.* obscure, make unclear, bewilder; see MUDDLE, CONFUSE.

object *n.* **1** [A corporeal body] article, something, gadget; see THING 1. **2** [A purpose] objective, aim, wish; see PURPOSE 1. **3** [One who receives] recipient, target, victim; see RECEIVER.

object *v.* protest, take exception to, dispute; see COMPLAIN.

objection *n.* disapproval, scruple, hesitation, question, criticism, complaint, charge, accusation, reprimand, exception, admonition, reproach, dispute, opposition, adverse comment, rejection, ban, countercharge, grievance, contradiction, censure, abuse, scolding, denunciation, lecture, disagreement, difference, disdain, insistence, condemnation, grumbling, faultfinding, reproof, dissent, insinuation, complaining, frown, blame, sarcasm, wail, groan, murmur, lament, regret, aspersion, beef*, gripe*, demurring, reluctance, unwillingness, rejection, dislike, dissatisfaction, discontent, displeasure, low opinion, abhorrence, dubiousness; see also DOUBT.—*Ant.* PERMISSION, acceptance, desire.

objectionable *a.* **1** [Revolting] gross, repugnant, abhorrent; see OFFENSIVE 2. **2** [Undesirable] unacceptable, unsatisfactory, inexpedient; see UNDESIRABLE.

objective *a.* 1 [Existing independently of the mind] actual, external, material, scientific, sure, extrinsic, measurable, extraneous, reified, tactile, corporeal, bodily, palpable, physical, sensible, outward, outside, determinable, unchangeable, invariable; see also REAL 2.—*Ant.* MENTAL, subjective, introspective. 2 [Free from personal bias] detached, impersonal, unbiased; see ACCURATE 2, FAIR 1.

objective *n.* goal, aim, aspiration; see PURPOSE 1.

objectively *a.* impartially, indifferently, neutrally, open-mindedly, dispassionately, justly, equitably, detachedly, soberly, accurately, candidly, considerately, not subjectively, with objectivity, with impartiality, with consideration, with good judgment, without prejudice, without bias, without partiality, without passion.

obligate *v.* bind, restrict, constrain; see FORCE.

obligation *n.* responsibility, burden, debt; see DUTY 1.

obligatory *a.* required, essential, binding; see NECESSARY.

oblige *v.* 1 [To accommodate] assist, aid, contribute; see ACCOMMODATE 1, HELP. 2 [To require] compel, coerce, bind; see FORCE, REQUIRE 2.

obliged *a.* compelled, obligated, required; see BOUND 2.

obliging *a.* amiable, accommodating, helpful; see KIND.

obligingly *a.* helpfully, thoughtfully, graciously; see AGREEABLY.

oblique *a.* inclined, inclining, diverging, leaning, sloping, angled, askew, asymmetrical, turned, twisted, awry, askance, distorted, off level, sideways, slanted, tipping, tipped, at an angle, on the bias; see also BENT, CROOKED 1.—*Ant.* STRAIGHT, vertical, perpendicular.

oblivion *n.* nonexistence, obscurity, void; see EMPTINESS, NOTHING.

oblivious *a.* abstracted, preoccupied, absorbed; see ABSENT-MINDED, DREAMY.

oblong *a.* elongated, rectangular, oval, elliptical, egg-shaped.—*Ant.* SQUARE, round, circular.

obnoxious *a.* annoying, disagreeable, displeasing; see OFFENSIVE 2.

obscene *a.* indecent, smutty, pornographic; see LEWD 2.

obscenity *n.* vulgarity, impropriety, smut; see INDECENCY, LEWDNESS.

obscure *a.* 1 [Vague] indistinct, ambiguous, indefinite, indecisive, unintelligible, impenetrable, inscrutable, unfathomable, unclear, vague, undefined, intricate, illegible, incomprehensible, hazy, dark, dim, inexplicable, inconceivable, unbelievable, incredible, complicated, illogical, unreasoned, mix-edup, doubtful, questionable, dubious, inexact, unreasoned, loose, ill-defined, unidentified, invisible, undisclosed, perplexing, cryptic, escaping notice, mystical, secret, enigmatic, concealed, mysterious, esoteric, puzzling, lacking clarity, unreadable, contradictory, out of focus, unrelated, clear as mud*, over one's head, deep, far out*; see also COMPLEX 2, CONFUSED 2, CONFUSING, DIFFICULT 2.—*Ant.* CLEAR, definite, distinct. 2 [Dark] cloudy, dense, hazy; see DARK 1. 3 [Little known] unknown, rare, hidden, covered, remote, reticent, secretive, seldom seen, unseen, inconspicuous, humble, invisible, mysterious, deep, cryptic, enigmatic, esoteric, arcane, undisclosed, dark; see also DISTANT, IRRELEVANT, PROFOUND.

obscure *v.* 1 [To dim] shadow, cloud, screen; see SHADE 2. 2 [To conceal] cover, veil, wrap up; see DISGUISE, HIDE 1.

obscurely *a.* dimly, darkly, indistinctly; see VAGUELY.

obscurity *n.* vagueness, dimness, fuzziness; see UNCERTAINTY 1, 2.

observable *a.* perceptible, noticeable, discernible; see OBVIOUS 1.

observance *n.* 1 [A custom] ritual, practice, rite; see CUSTOM. 2 [Attention] awareness, observation, notice; see ATTENTION.

observant *a.* keen, alert, penetrating, wide-awake, discerning, perceptive, sharp, eager, interested, discovering, detecting, discriminating, judicious, searching, understanding, questioning, deducing, sensitive, surveying, considering, clear-sighted, comprehending, bright, on the ball*, on one's toes*; see also INTELLIGENT.—*Ant.* THOUGHTLESS, unobservant, insensitive.

observation *n.* 1 [The power of observing] seeing, recognizing, perception; see SIGHT 1. 2 [A remark] comment, note, commentary; see REMARK, SPEECH 3.

observe *v.* 1 [To watch] scrutinize, inspect, examine; see SEE, WATCH. 2 [To comment] note, remark, mention; see COMMENT. 3 [To commemorate] dedicate, solemnize, keep; see CELEBRATE 1. 4 [To abide by] conform to, comply, adopt; see FOLLOW 2, OBEY.

observed *a.* 1 [Noticed] seen, noted, marked; see RECOGNIZED. 2 [Commemorated] kept, celebrated, recalled; see REMEMBERED.

observer *n.* watcher, watchman, sentinel, lookout, sentry, guard, detective, policeman, policewoman, spy, spectator, eyewitness, beholder, onlooker, bystander, passerby, meddler, peeper, voyeur, prying person, peeping Tom*; see also WITNESS.

obsess *v.* dominate, possess, hound; see HAUNT 2.

obsessed *a.* haunted, beset, controlled; see TROUBLED.

obsession *n.* fixation, fascination, passion, fancy, craze, delusion, mania, infatuation, fixed idea, compulsion, bee in one's bonnet*, hang-up*; see also FANTASY.

obsolete *a.* antiquated, archaic, out-of-date; see OLD 1, 2, OLD-FASHIONED.

obstacle *n.* restriction, obstruction, hindrance; see BARRIER.

obstinate *a.* firm, headstrong, opinionated; see STUBBORN.

obstinately *a.* doggedly, bullheadedly, persistently; see STUBBORNLY.

obstruct *v.* stop, interfere, bar; see HINDER, PREVENT.

obstruction *n.* difficulty, trouble, roadblock; see BARRIER, IMPEDIMENT 1.

obtain *v.* 1 [To gain possession of] take, acquire, seize; see GET 1. 2 [To pertain] be pertinent to, appertain to, bear upon; see CONCERN 1.

obtainable *a.* ready, attainable, achievable; see AVAILABLE.

obvious *a.* 1 [Clearly apparent to the eye] clear, visible, apparent, public, transparent, observable, perceptible, exposed, noticeable, plain, conspicuous, overt, glaring, prominent, standing out, light, bright, open, unmistakable, evident, recognizable, discernible, in evidence, in view, in sight, perceivable, discoverable, distinguishable, palpable, distinct, clear as a bell*, clear as day*, hitting one in the face*; see also DEFINITE 2.—*Ant.* OBSCURE, hidden, indistinct. 2 [Clearly apparent to the mind] lucid, apparent, conclusive, explicit, understood, intelligible, comprehensible, self-evident, indisputable, unquestionable, undeniable, proverbial, aphoristic, reasonable, broad, unambiguous, on the surface, as plain as the nose on someone's face*, going without saying*, staring someone in the face*, open-and-shut; see also UNDERSTANDABLE.—*Ant.* PROFOUND, ambiguous, equivocal.

obviously *a.* without doubt, unmistakably, certainly; see CLEARLY 1, 2.

obviously *interj.* of course, yes, evidently; see SURELY.

occasion *n.* 1 [An event] occurrence, incident, happening; see EVENT. 2 [An opportunity] chance, excuse, opening; see OPPORTUNITY 1, POSSIBILITY 2. —**on occasion** once in a while, sometimes, occasionally; see HARDLY, SELDOM.

occasional *a.* 1 [Occurring at odd times] sporadic, random, infre-

quent; see IRREGULAR 1. 2 [Intended for special use] uncommon, particular, specific; see EXCLUSIVE, SPECIAL.

occasionally *a.* infrequently, at random, irregularly; see HARDLY, SELDOM.

occult *a.* secret, magical, supernatural; see MYSTERIOUS 2.

occupancy *n.* possession, occupation, title; see DEED 2, OWNERSHIP.

occupant *n.* lessee, inhabitant, renter; see RESIDENT, TENANT.

occupation *n.* 1 [The act of occupying] seizure, entering, invasion; see ATTACK, CAPTURE. 2 [A vocation] calling, craft, chosen work; see JOB 1, PROFESSION 1, TRADE 2.

occupational *a.* professional, career, vocational, technical, workaday, official, industrial.

occupied *a.* 1 [Busy] engaged, working, engrossed; see BUSY 1. 2 [Full] in use, leased, taken; see RENTED.

occupy *v.* 1 [To take possession of] conquer, take over, invade; see GET 1, SEIZE 2. 2 [To fill space] remain, tenant, reside, live in, hold, take up, pervade, keep, own, command, be in command, extend, control, maintain, permeate; see also FILL 2.—*Ant.* EMPTY, remove, move. 3 [To absorb attention] engage, engross, monopolize, interest, arrest, absorb, take up, utilize, involve, keep busy, busy; see also FASCINATE.

occupying *a.* 1 [Filling a place] holding, remaining, situated, posted, assigned to, tenanting, residing, living in, taking up, possessing, pervading, covering, settled on, controlling, maintaining, commanding, sitting, staying, established in, established at, owning, set up*; see also PLACED.—*Ant.* GONE, leaving, removing. 2 [Engaging attention] absorbing, engrossing, monopolizing, engaging, arresting, working at, attracting, focusing, drawing, exacting, requiring; see also EXCITING, INTERESTING.

occur *v.* take place, transpire, befall; see HAPPEN 1, 2. —**occur to** come to mind, present itself, offer itself, suggest itself, spring, issue, rise, appear, catch one's attention, strike one, pass through one's mind, impress one, enter one's mind, cross one's mind, crop up.

occurrence *n.* happening, incident, episode; see EVENT.

ocean *n.* great sea, high seas, salt water, seashore, seaside, shores, the mighty deep, the main, the great waters, the seven seas; see also SEA.—*Ant.* EARTH, lake, river. *Oceans include the following:* Atlantic, Pacific, Arctic, Antarctic, Indian.

oceanic *a.* marine, aquatic, pelagic; see MARITIME, NAUTICAL.

odd *a.* **1** [Unusual] peculiar, unique, strange; see UNUSUAL 2. **2** [Miscellaneous] fragmentary, different, varied; see VARIOUS. **3** [Single] unpaired, sole, unmatched; see ALONE. **4** [Not even] remaining, over and above, leftover; see IRREGULAR 1, 4.

oddly *a.* curiously, ridiculously, inexplicably; see STRANGELY, FOOLISHLY.

odds *n.* **1** [An advantage] allowance, edge, benefit, difference, superiority, place money*, show money*; see also ADVANTAGE. **2** [A probability] favor, superiority, chances; see CHANCE 1. —**at odds** disagreeing, at variance, discordant; see QUARRELSOME.

odds and ends *n.* miscellany, scraps, particles; see REMNANTS.

odor *n.* perfume, fragrance, aroma; see SMELL 1, 2.

odorless *a.* flat, scentless, unaromatic, unperfumed, unscented, without odor, odor-free, unfragrant, lacking fragrance.

odorous *a.* **1** [Having an offensive odor] smelly, stinking, putrid; see OFFENSIVE 2, ROTTEN 1. **2** [Having a pleasant odor] spicy, sweet-smelling, fragrant; see SWEET 3.

of *prep.* from, out of, out from, away from, proceeding from, coming from, going from, about, concerning, as concerns, appropriate to, pertaining to, peculiar to, attributed to, characterized by, regarding, as regards, in regard to, referring to, in reference to, belonging to, related to, having relation to, native to, consequent to, based on, akin to, connected with; see also ABOUT 2.

off *a.*, *prep.* **1** [Situated at a distance] ahead, behind, up front, to one side, divergent, beside, aside, below, beneath, above, far, absent, not here, removed, apart, in the distance, at a distance, gone, away; see also DISTANT.—*Ant.* HERE, at hand, present. **2** [Moving away] into the distance, away from, farther away, disappearing, vanishing, removing, turning aside; see also AWAY.—*Ant.* APPROACHING, returning, coming. **3** [Started] initiated, commenced, originated; see BEGUN. **4** [Mistaken] erring, in error, confused; see MISTAKEN 1, WRONG 2. **5** [*Crazy] odd, peculiar, strange; see INSANE. **6** [*Not employed] not on duty, on vacation, gone; see UNEMPLOYED.

off and on *a.* now and then, sometimes, occasionally; see SELDOM.

off-color *a.* racy, spicy, indelicate; see RISQUÉ.

offend *v.* annoy, affront, outrage; see BOTHER 2.

offended *a.* vexed, provoked, exasperated; see ANGRY, INSULTED.

offense *n.* **1** [A misdeed] misdemeanor, malfeasance, transgression; see CRIME, SIN. **2** [An attack] assault, aggression, sally; see ATTACK. *Styles of offense in football include the following:* running attack, ground attack, passing attack, aerial attack, shotgun, T formation, wishbone, razzle-dazzle, T, I formation, I, wing T, run and shoot, pro, red zone, goal line, tight end, H-back, West Coast. **3** [Resentment] umbrage, pique, indignation; see ANGER.

offensive *a.* **1** [Concerned with an attack] assaulting, attacking, invading; see AGGRESSIVE. **2** [Revolting] disgusting, horrid, repulsive, shocking, gross*, dreadful, detestable, repugnant, obnoxious, hideous, horrible, displeasing, disagreeable, repellent, nauseating, invidious, nauseous*, distasteful, unspeakable, accursed, unutterable, terrible, grisly, ghastly, bloody, gory, hateful, low, foul, corrupt, bad, indecent, nasty, dirty, unclean, filthy, sickening, malignant, rancid, putrid, vile, impure, beastly, monstrous, coarse, loathsome, abominable, stinking, reeking, obscene, smutty, damnable, distressing, irritating, unpleasant, contaminated, frightful, unattractive, forbidding, repelling, incompatible, unsavory, intolerable, unpalatable, unpleasing, dissatisfactory, unsuited, objectionable, beneath contempt, icky*, lousy*; see also REVOLTING.—*Ant.* PLEASANT, agreeable, likable. **3** [Insolent] impertinent, impudent, insulting; see RUDE 2.

offensive *n.* position of attack, invasion, assault; see ATTACK.

offer *n.* proposal, presentation, proposition; see SUGGESTION 1.

offer *v.* **1** [To present] proffer, tender, administer, donate, put forth, advance, extend, submit, hold out, grant, allow, award, volunteer, accord, place at someone's disposal, lay at someone's feet, put up; see also CONTRIBUTE, GIVE 1.—*Ant.* REFUSE, withhold, keep. **2** [To propose] suggest, submit, advise; see PROPOSE 1.

offering *n.* contribution, donation, present; see GIFT 1.

offhand *a.* at the moment, unprepared, impromptu, improvised, by ear, informal, extemporaneous, extemporary, spontaneous, unpremeditated, unstudied, unrehearsed.

office *n.* **1** [A position involving responsibility] position, post, occupation; see JOB 1, PROFESSION 1, TRADE 2. **2** [A function] performance, province, service; see DUTY 1. **3** [A place in which office work is done] room, office building, factory, bureau, agency, warehouse, facility, school building; see also BUILDING, DEPARTMENT. *Types of offices include the following:* government, principal's, counseling, secretarial, insurance, data processing, real estate, brokerage, law, bank, foreign, consular, doctor's, dentist's; advertising agency, booking office, box office. —**hold office** be in office, direct, rule; see GOVERN, MANAGE 1.

officer *n.* 1 [An executive] manager, director, president; see EXECUTIVE, LEADER 2. 2 [One who enforces the law] magistrate, military police, deputy; see POLICE OFFICER. 3 [One holding a responsible post in the armed forces] *American officers include the following — Army commissioned and special officers:* Commander in Chief, Five-star General, Four-star General, Three-star General, Two-star General, General of the Army, Lieutenant General, Major General, Brigadier General, Colonel, Lieutenant Colonel, Major, Captain, First Lieutenant, Second Lieutenant, Chief of Staff; *Navy commissioned officers:* Admiral of the Fleet, Fleet Admiral, Admiral, Rear Admiral, Vice Admiral, Captain, Commander, Lieutenant Commander, Lieutenant; Lieutenant, junior grade; Ensign; *Army noncommissioned officers:* Chief Warrant Officer; Warrant Officer, junior grade; Master Sergeant, First Sergeant, Technical Sergeant, Staff Sergeant, Sergeant, Corporal.

official *a.* 1 [Having to do with one's office] formal, fitting, suitable, precise, established, according to precedent, according to protocol, proper, correct, accepted, recognized, customary; see also CONVENTIONAL 1, 3, FIT 1.—*Ant.* INFORMAL, ill-fitting, unceremonious. 2 [Authorized] ordered, endorsed, sanctioned; see APPROVED. 3 [Reliable] authoritative, authentic, trustworthy; see CERTAIN 3, GENUINE 1, RELIABLE.

official *n.* 1 [Administrator] controller, director, manager; see EXECUTIVE, LEADER 2. 2 [A sports official] referee, judge, linesman; see UMPIRE.

officially *a.* 1 [In an official manner] regularly, formally, in an orderly manner, suitably, according to form, ceremoniously, in set form, precisely, according to precedent, conventionally, in an established manner, as prescribed, according to protocol, all in order, correctly, properly, customarily. 2 [With official approval] authoritatively, with authorization, sanctioned; see APPROVED.

offset *v.* counterbalance, compensate, allow for; see BALANCE 2.

offspring *n.* progeny, issue, descend-

297 ◀ **old**

ants, children, kids, siblings, lineage, generation, brood, seed, family, heirs, offshoots, succession, successors, next generation; see also BABY, CHILD.

often *a.* usually, many times, oftentimes; see FREQUENTLY.

oh *interj.* indeed, oh-oh, oops; oh, no; oh, yes; see also NO, YES.

oil *n.* 1 [Liquid, greasy substance] melted fat, unction, lubricant; see GREASE. *Common oils include the following:* vegetable, animal, mineral, saturated, polyunsaturated, volatile, essential, machine, crude, lubricating, cottonseed, olive, castor, palm, corn, safflower, coconut, whale, canola, peanut, tung, wintergreen, linseed, drying, nondrying, soybean, sesame, cod-liver, fish; lard, tallow, oleo, lanolin, turpentine. 2 [Liquid substance used for power or illumination] petroleum, kerosene, coal oil, crude oil, liquid coal, fossil oil; see also FUEL.

oil *v.* lubricate, smear, coat with oil; see GREASE.

oily *a.* 1 [Rich with oil] fatty, greasy, buttery, oil-soaked, rich, lardy, oleaginous, soapy, soothing, creamy, oil-bearing.—*Ant.* DRY, dried, gritty. 2 [Having a surface suggestive of oil] oiled, waxy, sleek, slippery, polished, lustrous, bright, brilliant, gleaming, glistening, shining; see also SMOOTH 1, 2.—*Ant.* ROUGH, dull, unpolished. 3 [Unctuous] fulsome, suave, flattering; see AFFECTED 2, TREACHEROUS.

ointment *n.* unguent, lotion, cream; see MEDICINE 2.

OK* *interj.* all right, correct, surely; see YES.

OK* *n.* approval, endorsement, affirmation; see PERMISSION.

OK* *v.* confirm, condone, notarize; see APPROVE, ENDORSE 2.

old *a.* 1 [No longer vigorous] aged, elderly, patriarchal, matriarchal, mature, gray, venerable, not young, of long life, past one's prime, far advanced in years, matured, having lived long, full of years, seasoned, infirm, inactive, enfeebled, decrepit, superannuated, exhausted, tired, impaired, broken-down, wasted, doddering, senile, ancient, having one foot in the grave, gone to seed.—*Ant.* YOUNG, fresh, youthful. 2 [Worn] time-worn, worn-out, thin, patched, ragged, faded, used, in holes, rubbed off, mended, broken-down, fallen to pieces, fallen in, given way, out of use, rusted, crumbled, dilapidated, battered, shattered, shabby, castoff, decayed, decaying, stale, useless, tattered, in rags, torn, moth-eaten.—*Ant.* FRESH, new, unused. 3 [Ancient] archaic, time-honored, prehistoric, bygone, early, antique, forgotten, immemorial, antediluvian, olden, remote, past, distant, former, of old, gone by, classic, medieval, in the Middle Ages, out of the dim past, primordial, primeval, before history, dateless, unrecorded, handed down, of earliest time, of the old order, ancestral, traditional, time out of mind, in the dawn of history, old as the hills; see also senses 1, 2.—*Ant.* MODERN, recent, late.

older *a.* elder, senior, former, preceding, prior, more aged, less young, not so new, earlier, first, firstborn, having come before, more ancient, lower, of an earlier time, of an earlier vintage, of a former period; see also OLD 3.—*Ant.* YOUNG, newer, of a later vintage.

oldest *a.* most aged, initial, primeval; see FIRST, ORIGINAL 1.

old-fashioned *a.* antiquated, out-of-date, obsolete, obsolescent, outmoded, *démodé* (French), unfashionable, traditional, unstylish, passé, Victorian, not modern, old-time, time-honored, not current, antique, ancient, no longer prevailing, bygone, archaic, grown old, primitive, quaint, amusing, odd, neglected, outworn, of long standing, unused, past, behind the times, gone by, of the old school, extinct, out, gone out, out of it*; see also OLD 3.—*Ant.* MODERN, fashionable, stylish.

old lady* *n.* female spouse, woman, female relative; see MOTHER 1, PARENT, WIFE.

old man* *n.* head of the house, male spouse, man; see FATHER 1, HUSBAND, PARENT.

Old Testament *n.* Torah, Hebrew Scripture, Jewish Law; see BIBLE.

old-time *a.* outmoded, ancient, obsolete; see OLD-FASHIONED.

Old World *n.* Europe, Asia, Eastern Hemisphere; see EAST 2.

Olympics *n.* Olympic Games, world championships, international amateur athletic competion; see COMPETITION, SPORT 3.

omen *n.* portent, augury, indication; see SIGN 1.

ominous *a.* threatening, forbidding, foreboding, menacing, dark, suggestive, fateful, premonitory, dire, grim, gloomy, haunting, perilous, ill-starred, ill-fated, impending, fearful, prophetic; see also DANGEROUS, DISMAL, DOOMED.—*Ant.* FAVORABLE, encouraging, auspicious.

omission *n.* 1 [The act of omitting] overlooking, missing, leaving out; see CARELESSNESS, EXCLUSION, NEGLECT 1.—*Ant.* ADDITION, mention, insertion. 2 [Something omit-

ted] need, want, imperfection; see LACK 2.

omit *v.* 1 [To fail to include] leave out, reject, exclude; see BAR 2, DISMISS, ELIMINATE. 2 [To neglect] ignore, slight, overlook; see DISREGARD, NEGLECT 2.

omitted *a.* unmentioned, left out, overlooked; see LOST 1, MISSED 1, NEGLECTED.

on *a.*, **prep.** 1 [Upon] above, in contact with, touching, supported by, situated upon, resting upon, on top of, about, held by, moving across, moving over, covering; see also UPON 1.—*Ant.* UNDER, underneath, below. 2 [Against] in contact with, close to, leaning on; see NEXT 2. 3 [Toward] in the direction of, to, at; see APPROACHING, TOWARD. 4 [Forward] onward, ahead, advancing; see FORWARD 1. 5 [Near] beside, close to, adjacent to; see BORDERING, NEAR 1. **—and so on** and so forth, also, in addition; see AND.

on and off *a.* now and then, sometimes, infrequently; see SELDOM.

once *a.* 1 [One time] this time, but once, once only, before, one time before, just this once, not more than once, never again, a single time, one time previously, on one occasion, only one time.—*Ant.* FREQUENTLY, twice, many times. 2 [Formerly] long ago, previously, earlier; see FORMERLY. **—all at once** simultaneously, all at the same time, unanimously; see TOGETHER 2. **—at once** now, quickly, this moment; see IMMEDIATELY. **—for once** for at least one time, once only, uniquely; see ONCE 1. **—once and for all** with finality, permanently, unalterably; see FINALLY 1. **—once in a while** sometimes, occasionally, on occasion; see SELDOM.

once-over* *n.* look, inspection, checkup; see EXAMINATION 1.

oncoming *a.* impending, expected, imminent; see APPROACHING.

one *a.* individual, peculiar, lone, specific, separate, single, singular, odd, one and only, precise, definite, sole, uncommon; see also SPECIAL, UNIQUE, UNUSUAL 2.—*Ant.* COMMON, several, imprecise.

one *n.* unit, 1, whole, person, thing, identity, ace, integer, item, example, digit, singleness, individual, individuality, individuation.—*Ant.* MANY, plural, several. **—all one** making no difference, insignificant, of no importance; see UNIMPORTANT. **—at one** in accord, agreeing, of the same opinion; see UNITED. **—tie one on*** go on a drinking spree, get drunk, imbibe; see DRINK 2.

oneness *n.* integrity, harmony, indivisibility; see UNITY 1.

one-sided *a.* 1 [Unilateral] single, uneven, partial; see IRREGULAR 4. 2

[Prejudiced] biased, partial, narrow-minded; see PREJUDICED, UNFAIR.

one-way *a.* directional, with no return, restricted; see NARROW 1.

ongoing *a.* open-ended, continuous, in process; see REGULAR 3.

only *a.* **1** [Solely] exclusively, uniquely, wholly, entirely, particularly, and no other, and no more, and nothing else, nothing but, totally, utterly, first and last, one and only; see also SINGLY. **2** [Merely] just, simply, plainly, barely, solely; see also HARDLY. **3** [Sole] single, companionless, without another, by oneself, isolated, apart, unaccompanied, exclusive, unique; see also ALONE.

onset *n.* incipience, opening, start; see ORIGIN 2.

onto *a., prep.* **1** [To] toward, in contact with, adjacent; see AGAINST 1. **2** [Upon] over, out upon, above; see UPON 1.

onward *a.* on ahead, beyond, in front of; see FORWARD 1, MOVING 1.

ooze *n.* slime, fluid, mire; see MUD.

ooze *n.* seep, exude, leak; see FLOW.

opaque *a.* not transparent, dim, dusky, darkened, murky, gloomy, smoky, thick, misty, cloudy, clouded, shady, muddy, dull, blurred, frosty, filmy, foggy, sooty, dirty, dusty, coated over, covered.—*Ant.* CLEAR, transparent, translucent.

open *a.* **1** [Not closed] unclosed, accessible, clear, open to view, uncovered, disclosed, divulged, introduced, initiated, begun, full-blown, unfurled, susceptible, ajar, gaping, wide, rent, torn, spacious, unshut, expansive, extensive, spread out, revealed; see also senses 2, 4.—*Ant.* CLOSED, tight, shut. **2** [Not obstructed] made passable, unlocked, unbarred, unbolted, unblocked, unfastened, cleared away, unsealed, unobstructed, unoccupied, vacated, unburdened, emptied; see also sense 1.—*Ant.* TAKEN, barred, blocked. **3** [Not forbidden] free of entrance, unrestricted, allowable, free of access, public, welcoming; see also PERMITTED.—*Ant.* REFUSED, forbidden, restricted. **4** [Not protected] insecure, unsafe, unguarded, unsecluded, liable, exposed, uncovered, apart, unshut, unroofed, conspicuous, unhidden, unconcealed, subject to, sensitive; see also sense 1 and UNSAFE.—*Ant.* SAFE, secluded, secure. **5** [Not decided] in question, up for discussion, debatable; see QUESTIONABLE 1, UNCERTAIN. **6** [Frank] plain, candid, straightforward; see FRANK.

open *v.* **1** [To begin] start, inaugurate, initiate; see BEGIN 1, 2. **2** [To move aside a prepared obstruction] unbar, unlock, unclose, clear, admit,

reopen, open the lock, lift the latch, free, loosen, disengage, unfasten, undo, unbolt, turn the key, turn the knob.—*Ant.* CLOSE, shut, lock. **3** [To make an opening] force an entrance, breach, cut in, tear down, push in, shatter, destroy, burst in, break open, cave in, burst out from, penetrate, pierce, force one's way into, smash, punch a hole into, slit, puncture, crack, muscle in*, jimmy*; see also FORCE, REMOVE 1.—*Ant.* REPAIR, seal, mend. **4** [To make available] make accessible, put on sale, put on view, open to the public, make public, put forward, free, make usable, prepare, present, make ready.—*Ant.* REMOVE, put away, lock up. **5** [To expose to fuller view] unroll, unfold, uncover; see EXPOSE 1, REVEAL.

opened *a.* unlocked, made open, not closed; see FREE 3, OPEN 2.

open-ended *a.* going on, without specified limits, optional; see CONSTANT, UNCERTAIN.

opening *a.* initial, beginning, primary; see FIRST.

opening *n.* **1** [A hole] break, crack, tear; see HOLE 1. **2** [An opportunity] chance, availability, occasion; see OPPORTUNITY 1, POSSIBILITY 2.

openly *a.* **1** [Frankly] naturally, simply, artlessly, naively, unsophisticatedly, out in the open, candidly, aboveboard, straightforwardly, honestly, unreservedly, fully, readily, willingly, without restraint, plainly, without reserve, to one's face, in public, face to face; see also SINCERELY.—*Ant.* SECRETLY, furtively, surreptitiously. **2** [Shamelessly] immodestly, brazenly, not caring, regardlessly, insensibly, unconcernedly, crassly, insolently, flagrantly, wantonly, unblushingly, notoriously, without pretense, in defiance of the law; see also CARELESSLY, LEWDLY.—*Ant.* CAREFULLY, prudently, discreetly.

open-minded *a.* tolerant, fair-minded, just; see FAIR 1, LIBERAL.

opera *n.* musical drama, libretto, score, operetta, grand opera, light opera, comic opera, rock opera, opera performance; see also PERFORMANCE.

operate *v.* **1** [To keep in operation] manipulate, conduct, administer; see MANAGE 1. **2** [To be in operation] function, work, serve, carry on, run, revolve, act, behave, fulfill, turn, roll, spin, pump, lift, perform, burn, move, progress, advance, proceed, go, contact, engage, transport, convey, click*, tick*.—*Ant.* STOP, stall, break down. **3** [To produce an effect] react, act on, influence, bring about, determine, turn, bend, contrive, work, accomplish, fulfill, finish, complete, benefit, compel, promote, concern, enforce, take effect, have effect, work on, succeed, get results, get across; see also ACHIEVE, PRODUCE 1. **4** [To perform a surgical operation] remove diseased tissue, amputate, transplant; see TREAT 2.

operated *a.* conducted, handled, run, carried on, regulated, ordered, maintained, supervised, superintended, governed, administered, transacted, performed, conveyed, transported, moved, determined, achieved, contrived, accomplished, fulfilled, promoted, enforced, worked, served, guided, executed, sustained, used, practiced, put into effect, finished, driven, brought about, bent, manipulated, negotiated; see also DIRECTED, MANAGED 2.

operating *a.* managing, conducting, directing, executing, manipulating, administering, ordering, regulating, supervising, running, wielding, transacting, guiding, putting into effect, sustaining, maintaining, performing, practicing, revolving, promoting, determining, moving, turning, spinning, driving, contriving, fulfilling, accomplishing, finishing, effecting, bringing about, serving, enforcing, in operation, at work; see also USING.

operation *n.* **1** [The act of causing to function] execution, guidance, superintendence, carrying out, ordering, order, control, maintenance, handling, administration, manipulating, manipulation, supervision, agency, enforcement, advancement, regulating, running, supervising, directing, transacting, conducting; see also MANAGEMENT 1, REGULATION 1. **2** [An action] performance, act, employment, labor, service, carrying on, transaction, deed, doing, proceeding, handiwork, workmanship, enterprise, movement, progress, development, engagement, undertaking; see also ACTION 1, WORK 2. **3** [A method] process, formula, procedure; see METHOD, PLAN 2. **4** [Surgical treatment] surgery, transplant, amputation, dismemberment, vivisection, dissection, biopsy, emergency operation, acupuncture, exploratory operation, section, resection, incision, excision, removal, tonsillectomy, appendectomy, hysterectomy, plastic surgery, cesarean section, coronary bypass, rhinoplasty, keratotomy, laparotomy, mastectomy, tracheotomy, open-heart surgery, abortion, autopsy, the knife*; see also MEDICINE 3.

operator *n.* **1** [One who operates a machine] engineer, worker, skilled employee; see LABORER, WORKMAN. *Kinds of operators include the following:* telephone, computer, switchboard, PBX, information, long-distance, emergency. **2** [One who operates workable property] executive, supervisor, director; see EXECUTIVE. **3** [*Manipulator] speculator, scoundrel, fraud; see RASCAL.

opinion *n.* **1** [A belief] notion, view, point of view, sentiment, conception, idea, surmise, impression, inference, conjecture, inclination, fancy, imagining, supposition, suspicion, assumption, guess, theory, thesis, theorem, postulate, hypothesis, persuasion, presumption, presupposition, mind; see also BELIEF. **2** [A considered judgment] estimation, estimate, view, summary, belief, idea, resolution, determination, recommendation, finding, conviction, conclusion; see also JUDGMENT 3, VERDICT.

opinionated *a.* bigoted, stubborn, unyielding; see OBSTINATE, PREJUDICED.

opium *n.* opiate, soporific, dope*; see DRUG.

opponent *n.* **1** [A rival] competitor, contender, challenger, candidate, equal, entrant, the opposition, aspirant, bidder.—*Ant.* SUPPORTER, defender, abettor. **2** [An opposing contestant] antagonist, contestant, litigant; see PLAYER 1. **3** [An enemy] foe, adversary, assailant; see ENEMY.

opportunity *n.* **1** [Favorable circumstances] chance, occasion, happening, event, excuse, suitable circumstance, probability, good fortune, luck, break; see also POSSIBILITY 2. **2** [A suitable time] occasion, moment, right time; see TIME 2.

oppose *v.* **1** [To hold a contrary opinion] object, disapprove, debate, dispute, disagree, contradict, argue, deny, run counter to, protest, defy, cross, speak against, confront, thwart, neutralize, reverse, turn the tables, be opposed to, oppose change, not have any part of, face down, interfere with, disapprove of, cry out against, disagree with, not conform, run against, run counter to, come in conflict with, go contrary to, frown at, not accept, call into question, conflict with, grapple with, doubt, be against, be unwilling, reject, dislike, take exception, repudiate, question, probe, resist, confound, confute, refute, buck*; turn thumbs down*; see also sense 2 and DARE 2, FACE 1.—*Ant.* AGREE, approve, accept. **2** [To fight] resist, battle, encounter, assault, attack, assail, storm, protest, clash, meet, skirmish, engage, contest, face, restrain, go against, turn against, uphold, defend, rebel, revolt, mutiny, strike back, combat, run counter to, defy, snub, grapple with, fight off, withstand, repel, guard, counterattack, struggle, outflank, antagonize, retaliate, impede, overpower, take on all comers*, lock horns with; see also FIGHT.

opposed *a.* antagonistic to, averse, adverse, opposite, contrary, hostile to, at odds, counter to, at cross purposes, up against, against the grain; see also OPPOSITE 2.

opposing *a.* **1** [In the act of opposition] conflicting, unfriendly, clashing; see OPPOSED. **2** [Situated opposite] face to face with, facing, fronting; see OPPOSITE 3.

opposite *a.* **1** [Contrary] antithetical, diametric, reversed; see UNLIKE. **2** [In conflict] adverse, inimical, antagonistic, rival, unfavorable, averse, argumentative, contradictory, hostile; see also AGAINST 1. **3** [So situated as to seem to oppose] facing, fronting, in front of, on different sides of, on opposite sides, in opposition to, contrasting, on the other side of, contrary, over against, front to front, back to back, nose to nose, face to face, on the farther side, opposing, diametrical, eyeball to eyeball*.—*Ant.* MATCHED, on the same side, side by side.

opposite *n.* contradiction, contrary, converse, direct opposite, opposition, vice versa, antithesis, antonym, counter term, counterpart, inverse, reverse, adverse, the opposite pole, the other extreme, the other side, the opposite idea.—*Ant.* EQUAL, like, similar thing.

opposition *n.* **1** [The act of opposing] hostilities, conflict, combat; see BATTLE, FIGHT 1. **2** [The attitude suggestive of opposition] dislike, disagreement, hostility, antagonism, defiance, antipathy, abhorrence, aversion, constraint, restriction, restraint, hindrance, discord, distaste, disfavor, dissatisfaction, discontent, displeasure, irritation, offense, chagrin, humiliation, anger, loathing, disapproval, complaint, repugnance; see also HATRED, RESENTMENT.—*Ant.* SUPPORT, enthusiasm, accord. **3** [The individual or group that opposes] antagonist, disputant, adversary; see ENEMY, OPPONENT 1.

oppress *v.* suppress, harass, maltreat; see ABUSE, BOTHER 2.

oppressed *a.* misused, downtrodden, enslaved; see HURT.

oppression *n.* tyranny, hardness, domination, coercion, dictatorship, fascism, persecution, severity, harshness, abuse, conquering, subjugation, subduing, torture, compulsion, force, torment, martial law;

see also CRUELTY.—*Ant.* FREEDOM, liberalism, voluntary control.

opt (for) *v.* select, vote, pick; see CHOOSE, DECIDE.

optical *a.* ocular, seeing, visible; see VISUAL.

optimism *n.* **1** [Belief in the essential goodness of the universe] confidence, philosophy of goodness, belief in progress; see FAITH 1. **2** [An inclination to expect or to hope for the best] cheerfulness, hope, hopefulness, confidence, assurance, encouragement, happiness, brightness, enthusiasm, good cheer, trust, calmness, elation, expectancy, expectation, anticipation, certainty.—*Ant.* GLOOM, despair, melancholy.

optimist *n.* Pollyanna, dreamer, positivist.

optimistic *a.* cheerful, sanguine, assured; see CONFIDENT, HOPEFUL 1, TRUSTING.

option *n.* **1** [A choice] selection, alternative, dilemma; see CHOICE. **2** [A privilege to purchase] right, prerogative, grant, claim, license, lease, franchise, advantage, security, immunity, benefit, title, prior claim, dibs*.

optional *a.* discretionary, elective, noncompulsory, free, unrestricted, arbitrary, not required, with no strings attached*, take it or leave it*; see also VOLUNTARY.—*Ant.* NECESSARY, compulsory, enforced.

or *conj.* **1** [A suggestion of choice] and as an alternative, and as a substitute, and on the other hand; see EITHER.—*Ant.* NOR, neither, without choice. **2** [A suggestion of correction] or not, or not exactly, but on the contrary, or rather; see also INSTEAD.

oral *a.* vocal, verbal, uttered, voiced, unwritten, phonetic, sounded, articulated, pronounced, not written, by word of mouth; see also SPOKEN.—*Ant.* WRITTEN, PRINTED, unspoken.

orange *a.* reddish, ocherous, glowing; see ORANGE, *n.* 2.

orange *n.* **1** [Color] red-yellow, apricot, tangerine, burnt orange, peach, coral, salmon; see also COLOR. **2** [Fruit] citrus fruit, tropical fruit, juice orange; see FOOD, FRUIT.

orbit *n.* **1** [Path described by one body revolving around another] ellipse, circle, ring, circuit, apogee, course, perigee, lap, round, cycle, curve, flight path; see also REVOLUTION 1. **2** [Range of activity or influence] range, field, boundary; see AREA.

orbit *v.* **1** [To revolve around another body] encircle, encompass, ring, move in a circuit, go around, revolve; see also CIRCLE. **2** [To put into orbit] fire, blast off, project; see LAUNCH 2.

orbited *a.* sent into orbit, put up, rocketed; see DRIVEN, SENT.

orchard *n.* fruit trees, fruit farm, apple orchard; see FARM.

orchestra *n.* musical ensemble, symphony, instrumental ensemble, chamber orchestra; see also BAND.

ordain *v.* **1** [To establish] install, institute, appoint; see ENACT. **2** [To destine] determine, foreordain, predestine; see INTEND 2. **3** [To invest with priestly functions] install, confer holy orders upon, consecrate, anoint, delegate, invest; see also BLESS.

ordained *a.* **1** [Ordered] commanded, determined, established by law; see ESTABLISHED 2, ORDERED 2. **2** [Invested into the ministry] consecrated, anointed, received into the ministry; see NAMED 2.

ordeal *n.* tribulation, distress, suffering; see DIFFICULTY 1, 2.

order *n.* **1** [A command] direction, demand, decree, rule, edict, charge, requirement, ordinance, act, warrant, mandate, injunction; see also COMMAND, LAW 3. **2** [Sequence] progression, succession, procession; see LINE 1, SEQUENCE 1, SERIES. **3** [Orderly arrangement] regulation, plan, disposition, management, establishment, method, distribution, placement, scale, rule, computation, adjustment, adaptation, ordering, ranging, standardizing, lining up, trimming, grouping, composition, assortment, disposal, scheme, form, routine, array, procedure, index, regularity, uniformity, symmetry, harmony, layout, lineup, setup; see also CLASSIFICATION, SYSTEM.—*Ant.* CONFUSION, disarray, displacement. **4** [Organization] society, sect, company; see ORGANIZATION 2. **5** [A formal agreement to purchase] reserve, application, requisition, request, stipulation, booking, layaway, arrangement; see also BUYING, RESERVATION 1. **6** [Kind] rank, hierarchy, degree; see CLASS 1, CLASSIFICATION. **7** [Customary method] ritual, rite, plan; see CUSTOM. —**in order** working, efficient, operative; see EFFECTIVE. —**in order to** so as to, as a means to, so that; see FOR. —**in short order** rapidly, without delay, soon; see QUICKLY. —**on order** requested, on the way, sent for; see ORDERED 1. —**out of order** broken-down, defective, faulty; see BROKEN 2.

order *v.* **1** [To give a command] direct, command, instruct, bid, tell, demand, impose, give directions,

dictate, decree; see also REQUIRE 2. **2** [To authorize a purchase] secure, reserve, request; see BUY, OBTAIN 1. **3** [To put in order] arrange, plan, furnish, regulate, establish, manage, systematize, space, file, put away, classify, distribute, alphabetize, regularize, pattern, formalize, settle, fix, locate, dress up, sort out, index, put to rights, set guidelines for, adjust, adapt, set in order, assign, place, align, standardize, group; see also ORGANIZE 1.—*Ant.* CONFUSE, disarrange, disarray.

ordered *a.* **1** [On order] requested, requisitioned, sent for, spoken for, engaged, booked, arranged for, retained, written for, telephoned for; see also RESERVED 1. **2** [Commanded] directed, ordained, charged, dictated, regulated, decreed, ruled, enjoined, stipulated, bidden, imposed, authorized, exacted, forbidden, required, as ordered, under someone's jurisdiction, by order; see also APPROVED, REQUESTED.—*Ant.* NEGLECTED, omitted, revoked. **3** [Put in order] arranged, regulated, placed; see CLASSIFIED, ORGANIZED.

orderly *a.* **1** [Ordered; *said of objects and places*] well-kept, tidy, arranged; see CLEAN 1, NEAT 1. **2** [Methodical; *said of persons*] systematic, correct, formal, businesslike, exact, tidy, neat, thorough, precise; see also CAREFUL.—*Ant.* IRREGULAR, inaccurate, unmethodical.

ordinance *n.* direction, mandate, authorization; see LAW 3.

ordinarily *a.* usually, generally, habitually; see FREQUENTLY, REGULARLY.

ordinary *a.* **1** [In accordance with a regular order or sequence] customary, normal, regular, constant, usual, habitual, routine, mundane, everyday; see also COMMON 1, POPULAR 1, 3, TRADITIONAL. **2** [Lacking distinction] average, mediocre, familiar, natural, everyday, accepted, typical, commonplace, characteristic, prosaic, simple, banal, bland, trite, monotonous, stale, tedious, plain, normal; see also COMMON 1, CONVENTIONAL 3, DULL 4. —**out of the ordinary** extraordinary, uncommon, special; see UNUSUAL 2.

ore *n.* unrefined rock, ore bed, native mineral; see MINERAL.

organ *n.* **1** [An instrument] medium, means, way; see TOOL 1. **2** [A part of an organism having a specialized use] vital part, vital structure, process; see GLAND. *Human organs include the following:* brain, heart, eye, ear, nose, tongue, lung, kidney, stomach, intestine, pancreas, gallbladder, liver, spleen, bladder, colon, reproductive organ, genitals. **3** [A musical instrument] wind instrument, keyboard instrument, calliope, hurdy-gurdy, pipe organ, harmonium, electronic organ, accordion, harmonica, mouth organ, synthesizer; see also MUSICAL INSTRUMENT.

organic *a.* basic, vital, essential; see FUNDAMENTAL, NATURAL 1.

organically *a.* by nature, inevitably, wholly; see ESSENTIALLY, NATURALLY 2.

organism *n.* person, organic structure, physiological individual; see ANIMAL, BODY 1, PLANT.

organization *n.* **1** [The process or manner of organizing] establishment, plan, planning, ordering, creation, grouping, design, provision, working out, assembling, construction, regulation, systematization, system, method, coordination, adjustment, harmony, unity, correlation, standard, standardization, settlement, arrangement, disposition, alignment, institution, foundation, preparation, direction, structure, situation, formation, association, uniformity; see also CLASSIFICATION, ORDER 3.—*Ant.* CONFUSION, bedlam, chance. **2** [An organized body] aggregation, association, federation, combine, corporation, union, institute, trust, cartel, confederation, monopoly, combination, machine, business, industry, company, society, league, club, fraternity, sorority, house, order, alliance, party, cooperative, guild, profession, trade, coalition, syndicate, fellowship, lodge, brotherhood, sisterhood, confederacy, affiliation, body, band, team, squad, crew, clique, circle, set, troupe, group; see also SYSTEM.

organize *v.* **1** [To put in order] arrange, fix, straighten, standardize, compose, combine, systematize, methodize, coordinate, adjust, put in order, line up, regulate; see also CLASSIFY, ORDER 3. **2** [To form an organization] establish, build, found; see PLAN 2.

organized *a.* established, methodized, coordinated, systematized, systematic, constituted, directed, adjusted, assigned, distributed, grouped, fixed up, standardized, in order, in succession, in good form, placed, put away, orderly, in sequence, arranged, prepared, made ready, constructed, settled, composed, framed, planned, ranked, put in order, ordered, regulated, ranged, disposed, formulated, formed, fashioned, shaped, made, projected, designed, harmonized, related, correlated, founded, associated; see also CLASSIFIED.

Orient *n.* **1** [Eastern Asia] Far East,

Asia, China, India, Japan, Vietnam, Thailand, Laos, Hong Kong, Cambodia, Korea, Myanmar, the mysterious East, land of the rising sun.—*Ant.* Occident, Europe, West. **2** [Southwestern Asia] Near East, Middle East, Levant, Egypt, Fertile Crescent, Turkey, Syria, Lebanon, Israel, Jordan, Iraq, Iran, Persia, Muslim world, Arabia, the Golden Crescent; see also EAST 2.

orientation *n.* familiarization, bearings, introduction; see ADJUSTMENT, INTRODUCTION 3, 4.

origin *n.* **1** [The act of beginning] rise, start, foundation; see BIRTH. **2** [The place or time of beginning] source, spring, issue, fountain, inlet, derivation, root, stem, shoot, twig, sapling, portal, door, gate, gateway, fountainhead, wellspring, font, fount, birthplace, cradle, nest, womb, reservoir, infancy, babyhood, childhood, youth.—*Ant.* RESULT, outcome, issue. **3** [Cause] seed, germ, stock, parentage, ancestry, parent, ancestor, egg, sperm, embryo, principle, element, nucleus, first cause, author, creator, prime mover, producer, causation, source, influence, generator, occasion, root, spring, antecedent, motive, inspiration; see also CAUSE.—*Ant.* RESULT, consequence, conclusion.

original *a.* **1** [Pertaining to the source] primary, primeval, primordial, rudimentary, elementary, inceptive, in embryo, fundamental, primitive, initial, beginning, commencing, starting, opening, dawning, incipient; see also FIRST.—*Ant.* LATE, recent, developed. **2** [Creative] originative, productive, causal, causative, generative, imaginative, inventive, thoughtful, ingenious, innovative, unconventional, clever, fresh, nonconformist, formative, resourceful, ready, quick, seminal, envisioning, sensitive, archetypal, inspiring, devising, conceiving, fertile, fashioning, molding.—*Ant.* STUPID, imitative, unproductive. **3** [Not copied] primary, principal, first, genuine, new, firsthand, uncopied, fresh, novel, independent, one, sole, lone, single, solitary, authentic, unique, pure, rare, unusual, not translated, not copied, not imitated, real, absolute.—*Ant.* IMITATED, copied, repeated.

originality *n.* creativeness, inventiveness, creative spirit, creativity, nonconformity, modernity, intellectual, independence, innovation, invention, ingenuity, conception, authenticity, novelty, freshness, newness, individuality, brilliance; see also IMAGINATION.

originally *a.* **1** [In an original manner] imaginatively, creatively, ingeniously, inventively, startlingly, freshly, in a new fashion, independently, artistically. **2** [In the beginning] first, incipiently, basically; see FORMERLY.

originate *v.* start, introduce, found; see BEGIN 1.

originated *a.* introduced, started, commenced; see BEGUN.

ornament *n.* embellishment, adornment, beautification; see DECORATION 2.

ornamental *a.* **1** [Intended for ornament] fancy, luxurious, showy; see ELABORATE 1, ORNATE. **2** [Beautiful] delicate, exquisite, lovely; see BEAUTIFUL.

ornate *a.* showy, gaudy, sumptuous, lavish, bright, colored, tinseled, jeweled, embroidered, burnished, glossy, polished, gorgeous, pompous, stylish, magnificent, adorned, trimmed, gilded, embellished, inlaid, garnished, flowered, glowing, vivid, radiant, fine, alluring, dazzling, sparkling, shining, flashing, glistening, glamorous, artificial, pretentious, baroque, rococo, tawdry, flashy; see also ELABORATE 1.

orphan *n.* foundling, ragamuffin, parentless child, orphaned child, waif, stray; see also CHILD.

orphanage *n.* orphans' home, institution, foundling home; see SCHOOL 1.

orthodox *a.* customary, standard, doctrinal; see CONSERVATIVE, CONVENTIONAL 1, 3.

ostentatious *a.* showy, pretentious, pompous; see EGOTISTIC.

ostracize *v.* exile, expel, outlaw; see BANISH.

other *a.* being one of two, remaining, another, the other, some other, former, recent, future, besides, additional, different, separate, distinct, opposite, across from; see also EXTRA.

other *pron.* one of two, another one, some other, the one remaining, the part remaining, the alternate, the alternative; see also ANOTHER.— *Ant.* THIS, that, the first choice.

others *pron.* unnamed persons, the remainder, some, a few, any others, a number, a handful, a small number, not many, hardly any, two or three, more than one, many, a great number, a great many, they, folks, the rest; see also EVERYBODY.—*Ant.* NONE, no one, not any.

otherwise *a.* **1** [In another way] in a different way, contrarily, in an opposed way, under other conditions, in different circumstances, on the other hand, in other respects, in other ways.—*Ant.* LIKE, so, in like manner. **2** [Introducing an alterna-

tive threat] unless you do, with this exception, except on these conditions, barring this, in any other circumstances, except that, without this, unless ... then, other than; see also UNLESS.—*Ant.* THEREFORE, hence, as a result.

ought (to) *v.* should, have to, need to, had better, might, will, shall; it is necessary, is fitting, is becoming, is expedient, behooves, is reasonable, is logical, is natural, requires, is in need of; see also MUST.

ounce *n.* measure, troy ounce, avoirdupois ounce, fluid ounce, one sixteenth of a pound (avoirdupois), one sixteenth of a pint, one twelfth of a pound (troy); see also MEASURE 1.

our *poss. pronominal adj.* of our own, belonging to us, owned by us, used by us, due to us, a part of us, of interest to us, done by us, accomplished by us, in our employ, with us, near us, of us.

ourselves *pron.* us, the speakers, individually, personally, privately, without help, our own selves*; see also WE.

oust *v.* eject, discharge, dispossess, evict, dislodge, remove, deprive, expel, drive out, force out, show the door, chase out, cast out, depose, dethrone, disinherit, banish, boot out*, bundle off, send packing*, give the gate*, pack off*.

ousted *a.* deposed, fired, defeated; see BEATEN 1, DISCHARGED.

out *a., prep.* **1** [In motion from within] out of, away from, from, from within, out from, out toward, outward, on the way.—*Ant.* IN, in from, into. **2** [Not situated within] not inside, not within, on the outer side, on the surface, external, extrinsic, outer, outdoors, out-of-doors, unconcealed, open, exposed, in the open; see also OUTSIDE, WITHOUT.—*Ant.* WITHIN, inside, on the inner side. **3** [Beyond] distant, removed, removed from; see AWAY, BEYOND. **4** [Continued to the limit or near it] ended, accomplished, fulfilled; see DONE 1, FINISHED 1. **5** [Not at home or at one's office] not in, away, busy, on vacation, at lunch, gone, left; see also ABSENT.—*Ant.* IN, receiving, not busy. **6** [*Unconscious] insensible, out cold, blotto*; see UNCONSCIOUS. **7** [Wanting] lacking, missing, without; see WANTING 1. **—all out*** wholeheartedly, with great effort, entirely; see COMPLETELY. **—out of 1** [Having none in stock] not having any of, without, needing to reorder; see SOLD OUT. **2** [From] out from, away from, from within; see FROM. **3** [Beyond] outside, on the outskirts, on the border of; see BEYOND.

out* *n.* means of escape, way out, excuse; see ESCAPE, EXPLANATION.

outage *n.* interruption of service, blackout, dimout, brownout, failure of electrical service; see also INTERRUPTION.

out-and-out *a.* complete, entire, total; see COMPLETELY.

outbid *v.* offer higher than, raise the price, bid something up; see PAY 1.

outbreak *n.* **1** [A sudden violent appearance] eruption, explosion, outburst, disruption, burst, bursting forth, detonation, thunder, commotion, rending, break, breaking out, breaking forth, gush, gushing forth, outpouring, pouring forth, tumult, discharge, blast, blowup, crash, roar, earthquake, squall, paroxysm, spasm, convulsion, fit, effervescence, boiling, flash, flare, crack.—*Ant.* PEACE, tranquillity, quiet. **2** [Sudden violence] fury, mutiny, brawl; see DISORDER, REVOLUTION 2.

outburst *n.* discharge, upheaval, eruption; see DISTURBANCE 2, OUTBREAK 1.

outcast *a.* vagabond, driven out, hounded, untouchable, rejected, thrown aside, pushed aside, disgraced, hunted, not accepted by society, cast out, degraded, expelled, outlawed, cast away, exiled, expatriated, serving a life sentence, having a price on one's head.

outcast *n.* fugitive, pariah, untouchable; see REFUGEE.

outcome *n.* issue, upshot, consequence; see END 2, RESULT.

outcrop *n.* bared soil, exposed surface, projecting land mass; see EARTH 2, LAND 1.

outcry *n.* complaint, clamor, scream; see OBJECTION.

outdated *a.* outmoded, out of fashion, antiquated; see OLD 3.

outdo *v.* surpass, best, beat; see EXCEED.

outdone *a.* defeated, bettered, improved upon; see BEATEN 1.

outdoor *a.* outside, airy, out-of-doors, open-air, out of the house, out in the open, free, unrestricted, rustic, free and easy, healthful; see OUTDOORS.—*Ant.* interior, indoor, in the house.

outdoors *a.* out-of-doors, outdoor, without, out of the house, outside, on the outside, in the yard, in the open, in the garden, into the street.

outdoors *n.* the out-of-doors, natural scenery, fresh air, garden, patio, woods, hills, mountains, stream, Mother Nature, the great outdoors, countryside, the country, environment, nature.—*Ant.* INSIDE, domestic matters, household concerns.

outer *a.* outward, without, external, exterior, foreign, alien to, beyond, exposed; see also OUTSIDE.—*Ant.* INNER, inward, inside.

outer space *n.* infinity, the heavens, the universe; see SPACE 1.

outfield *n.* left field, deep left, center field, deep center, right field, deep right; see also BASEBALL, FIELD 2.

outfielder *n.* right fielder, center fielder, left fielder; see BASEBALL PLAYER.

outfit *n.* trappings, paraphernalia, gear; see EQUIPMENT.

outfit *v.* equip, fit out, supply; see PROVIDE 1.

outflank *v.* bypass, surround, outmaneuver; see DEFEAT 2, PASS 1.

outgo *n.* costs, losses, outflow; see EXPENSES.

outgoing *a.* sociable, civil, kind; see FRIENDLY.

outgrowth *n.* end result, outcome, effect; see END 2, RESULT.

outhouse *n.* latrine, privy, shed; see TOILET.

outing *n.* excursion, airing, drive; see VACATION.

outlandish *a.* odd, strange, foreign; see UNUSUAL.

outlast *v.* outlive, outwear, remain; see ENDURE 1, SURVIVE 1.

outlaw *n.* fugitive, bandit, desperado; see CRIMINAL.

outlaw *v.* make illegal, stop, ban; see BANISH, CONDEMN.

outlawed *a.* stopped, banned, prevented; see ILLEGAL.

outlet *n.* **1** [An opening] break, crack, exit; see HOLE 1. **2** [An electric terminal] socket, double socket, triple socket, wall plug, floor plug, electric service connection.

outline *n.* **1** [A skeletonized plan] frame, sketch, framework; see PLAN 1. **2** [The line surrounding an object; *often plural*] contour, side, boundary; see EDGE 1, FRAME 2. **3** [A shape seen in outline] silhouette, profile, configuration, shape, figure, formation, aspect, appearance; see also FORM 1.

outline *v.* **1** [To draw] sketch, paint, describe; see DRAW 2. **2** [To plan] block out, draft, sketch; see PLAN 2.

outlined *a.* **1** [Marked in outline] bounded, edged, bordered, circumscribed, marked, delineated, surrounded, banded, configurated. **2** [Given in summary] charted, summarized, surveyed; see PLANNED.

outlive *v.* live longer than, outlast, survive; see ENDURE 1.

outlook *n.* **1** [Point of view] scope, vision, standpoint; see VIEWPOINT. **2** [Apparent future] prospects, likelihood, possibility, chances, opportunity, appearances, probable future, openings, normal course of events, probabilities, risk, law of averages.

outlying a. afar, far-off, external; see DISTANT.

outnumbered a. exceeded, bested, overcome; see BEATEN 1.

out-of-date a. obsolete, passé, antiquated; see OLD-FASHIONED.

out-of-the-way a. far-off, secluded, isolated; see DISTANT.

outplay v. overcome, surpass, beat; see DEFEAT 3.

outpost n. forward position, listening post, point of attack; see BOUNDARY, POSITION 1.

output n. yield, amount, crop; see PRODUCE.

outrage n. indignity, abuse, affront; see INSULT.

outrage v. offend, wrong, affront; see ABUSE, INSULT.

outrageous a. wanton, notorious, shameless, disgraceful, brazen, barefaced, gross, scandalous, disorderly, insulting, affronting, abusive, oppressive, dishonorable, injurious, glaring, offensive, heinous, intolerable, execrable, unspeakable, shameful, horrifying, immoderate, extreme, flagrant, contemptible, ignoble, malevolent, odious, monstrous, atrocious, nefarious, vicious, iniquitous, wicked, shocking, violent, unbearable, villainous, infamous, corrupt, degenerate, criminal, sinful, vile, abominable.—Ant. EXCELLENT, laudable, honorable.

outright a. out-and-out, unmitigated, unconditional; see COMPLETELY, OBVIOUS 1.

outset n. start, beginning, source; see ORIGIN 2.

outside a. extreme, outermost, farthest, apart from, external, away from, farther; see also OUTER.—Ant. INNER, inside, interior.

outside n. 1 [An outer surface] exterior, outer side, surface, skin, cover, covering, topside, upper side, front side, face, appearance, outer aspect, seeming.—Ant. INSIDE, interior, inner side. 2 [The limit] outline, border, bounds; see BOUNDARY, EDGE 1, END 4. —at the outside at the most, at the absolute limit, not more than; see MOST.

outsider n. foreigner, stranger, refugee; see ALIEN.

outskirts n. border, suburbs, limits; see BOUNDARY, EDGE 1.

outspoken a. blunt, candid, artless; see FRANK.

outspread a. spread out, expanded, extended; see WIDESPREAD.

outstanding a. conspicuous, leading, notable; see DISTINGUISHED 2.

outward a. 1 [In an outward direction] out, toward the edge, from within; see OUTER, OUTSIDE. 2 [To outward appearance] on the surface, visible, to the eye; see OBVIOUS 1, OPEN 1.

outwear v. remain after, last longer than, outlast; see CONTINUE 1, ENDURE 1, SURVIVE 1.

outweigh v. 1 [To exceed in weight] overbalance, overweigh, weigh more than, go beyond; see also BURDEN. 2 [To exceed in importance] excel, surpass, outrun; see EXCEED.

outwit v. baffle, trick, bewilder; see CONFUSE, DECEIVE.

outwitted a. tricked, outsmarted, taken*; see DECEIVED.

oval a. egg-shaped, elliptical, ellipsoid; see OBLONG.

oven n. baking compartment, toaster oven, broiler; see FURNACE, STOVE.

over a., prep. 1 [Situated above] aloft, overhead, up beyond, covering, roofing, protecting, upper, higher than, farther up, upstairs, in the sky, straight up, high up, up there, in the clouds, among the stars, in heaven, just over, up from, outer, on top of; see also ABOVE.—Ant. under, below, beneath. 2 [Passing above] overhead, aloft, up high; see ACROSS. 3 [Again] once more, afresh, another time; see AGAIN. 4 [Beyond] past, farther on, out of sight; see BEYOND. 5 [Done] accomplished, ended, completed; see DONE 1, FINISHED 1. 6 [*In addition] over and above, extra, additionally; see BESIDES. 7 [Having authority] superior to, in authority, above; see HIGHER, SUPERIOR.

overabundance n. surplus, profusion, superfluity; see EXCESS 1.

overall a. complete, thorough, comprehensive; see GENERAL 1.

overalls n. protective garment, jumpsuit, coveralls; see CLOTHES, PANTS 1.

overbearing a. despotic, tyrannical, dictatorial; see ABSOLUTE 3.

overblown a. excessive, magnified, overdone; see EXAGGERATED.

overboard a. over the side, out of the boat, into the water; see WET 1. —go overboard* go to extremes, get carried away, go off the deep end*; see OVERDO 1.

overcast a. cloudy, gloomy, not clear or fair; see DARK 1.

overcoat n. topcoat, greatcoat, raincoat; see CLOTHES, COAT 1.

overcome a. conquered, overwhelmed, overthrown; see BEATEN 1.

overcome v. overwhelm, best, vanquish, conquer, outdo, surpass, overpower, overwhelm, beat, trounce, subdue, master; see also DEFEAT 2, 3, WIN 1.

overconfident a. reckless, imprudent, heedless; see CARELESS, RASH.

overcritical a. domineering, harsh, hypercritical; see SEVERE 1, 2.

overcrowd v. crowd, stuff, fill; see PACK 2, PRESS 1.

overcrowded a. congested, overbuilt, overpopulated; see FULL 1.

overdo v. 1 [To do too much] magnify, amplify, overestimate, overreach, stretch, go too far, overrate, exaggerate, go to extremes, overstate, enlarge, enhance, exalt, bite off more than one can chew*, run into the ground*, do to death, go overboard*, burn the candle at both ends, lay it on*, have too many irons in the fire; see also EXCEED.—*Ant.* NEGLECT, underdo, slacken. 2 [To overtax oneself physically] tire, fatigue, exhaust; see WEARY 2.

overdone a. excessive, too much, pushed too far; see EXAGGERATED.

overdose n. excessive dose, too much, overtreatment; see EXCESS 1.

overdrawn a. exhausted, depleted, all paid out; see GONE 2.

overdue a. delayed, belated, tardy; see LATE 1.

overeat v. overindulge, stuff, gorge; see EAT 1.

overemphasize v. exaggerate, make a big thing of*, make something out of nothing*; see EMPHASIZE, EXCEED.

overestimate v. overvalue, overprice, overrate; see EXAGGERATE, EXCEED.

overflow n. 1 [The act of overflowing] redundancy, inundation, overproduction; see FLOOD. 2 [That which overflows] superfluity, surplus, extra quantity; see EXCESS 1.

overflow v. 1 [To flow over the top, or out at a vent] spill over, run over, pour out, cascade, spout forth, jet, spurt, drain, leak, squirt, spray, shower, gush, shoot, issue, rush, wave, surge, brim over, bubble over; see also LEAK 1. 2 [To flow out upon] inundate, water, wet; see FLOOD.

overflowing a. abundant, in plenty, bountiful; see PLENTIFUL 2.

overgrown a. disproportionate, excessive, huge; see LARGE 1.

overgrowth n. growth, abundance, luxuriance; see EXCESS 1.

overhang v. jut, be suspended, dangle over; see PROJECT 1.

overhaul v. modernize, fix, renew; see REPAIR.

overhead a. above, aloft, hanging; see OVER 1.

overhear v. hear intentionally, hear unintentionally, catch; see EAVESDROP, HEAR 1.

overheard a. listened to, recorded, discovered; see HEARD.

overheat v. heat too much, bake, blister; see HEAT 2.

overindulgence n. overeating,

drinking to excess, eating or drinking too much; see DRUNKENNESS, EATING, GREED.

overjoyed a. enraptured, transported, thrilled; see EXCITED, HAPPY.

overlap n. extension, overlay, addition; see FLAP.

overlap v. overlie, overhang, lap over, fold over, extend alongside, project over, overlay; see also PROJECT 1.

overload v. oppress, weigh down, encumber; see BURDEN, LOAD 1.

overlook v. 1 [To occupy a commanding height] look over, top, survey, inspect, watch over, look out, view, give upon, give on, front on, command. 2 [To ignore deliberately] slight, make light of, disdain; see NEGLECT 1. 3 [To fail to see] miss, leave out, neglect; see NEGLECT 2.

overlooked a. missed, left out, forgotten; see NEGLECTED.

overlooking a. 1 [Providing a view] looking over, looking out on, commanding; see SEEING. 2 [Disregarding] missing, neglecting, forgetting.

overnight a. one night, lasting one night, during the night; see LATE 4.

overpass n. span, footbridge, skywalk; see BRIDGE 1.

overpower v. overwhelm, master, subjugate; see DEFEAT 2, 3.

overpowering a. irresistible, uncontrollable, overriding; see OVERWHELMING, INTENSE.

overproduction n. excess, excessive production, overstock; see PRODUCTION 1.

overrate v. build up, magnify, overestimate; see EXAGGERATE, EXCEED.

overrated a. not very good, overblown, not satisfactory; see POOR 2, UNSATISFACTORY.

overreact v. make too much of, blow out of proportion, go overboard*; see EXAGGERATE.

override v. 1 [To dismiss] pass over, not heed, take no account of; see DISREGARD, NEGLECT 1. 2 [To thwart] make void, reverse, annul; see CANCEL, REVOKE.

overrule v. invalidate, rule against, override; see CANCEL, REVOKE.

overrun v. 1 [To defeat] overwhelm, invade, occupy; see DEFEAT 2. 2 [To infest] ravage, invade, overwhelm; see INFEST 2.

overseas a. away, across the ocean, in foreign countries; see ABROAD.

oversee v. superintend, supervise, look after; see MANAGE 1.

overseer n. supervisor, manager, superintendent; see FOREMAN.

overshadow v. domineer, tower above, predominate; see DOMINATE.

overshoot v. overreach, overdo, overact; see EXCEED.

oversight n. failure, omission, mistake; see ERROR.

oversleep v. sleep late, miss the alarm, stay in bed; see SLEEP.

overspecialize v. limit oneself, specialize too much, be a specialist; see RESTRAIN, RESTRICT.

overstay v. stay too long, tarry, stop, outstay one's welcome; see also REMAIN 1.

overstep v. violate, encroach, trespass; see EXCEED, MEDDLE 1.

overt a. apparent, out in the open, patent; see OBVIOUS.

overtake v. overhaul, catch up with, get to; see REACH 1.

overtaken a. caught up with, reached, apprehended; see BEATEN 1, CAPTURED.

overthrow v. overcome, overrun, overpower; see DEFEAT 2.

overthrown a. overcome, overwhelmed, vanquished; see BEATEN 1.

overtime n. extra pay, additional wages, late hours; see PAY 2.

overtone n. tone, implication, hint; see MEANING, SUGGESTION 1.

overture n. 1 [Preliminary negotiations; *sometimes plural*] approach, offer, tender; see SUGGESTION 1. 2 [A musical introduction] prelude, prologue, *Vorspiel* (German), voluntary, proem, preface; see also INTRODUCTION 3.

overturn v. reverse, upturn, overthrow; see UPSET 1.

overweight a. ample, fat, obese; see HEAVY 1.

overwhelm v. 1 [To defeat] overcome, overthrow, conquer; see DEFEAT 2, 3, WIN 1. 2 [To astonish] puzzle, bewilder, confound; see CONFUSE, SURPRISE.

overwhelmed a. beaten, worsted, submerged; see BEATEN 2.

overwhelming a. overpowering, ruinous, overthrowing, crushing, smashing, extinguishing, invading, ravaging, overriding, upsetting, inundating, drowning, deluging, surging, obliterating, dissolving, wrecking, erasing, effacing, expunging, burying, immersing, engulfing, engrossing, covering; see also HARMFUL, TRIUMPHANT.

overwork n. extra work, overtime, exhaustion; see ABUSE.

overwork v. overdo, exhaust, wear out; see BURDEN, WEARY 1.

overworked a. overburdened, too busy, worked too hard; see TIRED.

overwrought a. nervous, agitated, high-strung; see EXCITED.

owe v. be under obligation, be indebted to, be obligated to, have an obligation, be bound, get on credit, feel bound, be bound to pay, be contracted to, be in debt for, have signed a note for, have borrowed, have lost.

owed a. owing, becoming due, outstanding; see DUE, UNPAID 1.

owl n. bird of prey, night bird, nocturnal bird; see BIRD.

own a. personal, individual, owned, very own*; see also PRIVATE.

own n. one's own possession, something personal, what belongs to one. —**come into one's own** receive what one deserves, gain proper recognition, thrive; see PROFIT 2. —**of one's own** personal, private, belonging to one; see OWNED. —**on one's own** by oneself, acting independently, singly; see INDEPENDENTLY.

own v. 1 [To possess] hold, have, enjoy, fall heir to, have title to, have rights to, be master of, occupy, control, dominate, have a claim upon, reserve, retain, keep, have in hand, have a deed for.—*Ant.* LACK, want, need. 2 [To acknowledge] assent to, grant, recognize; see ADMIT 2, DECLARE.

owned a. possessed, had, bought, held, purchased, kept, inherited, enjoyed, in hand, bound over, in the possession of, among the possessions of.

owner n. one who has, keeper, buyer, purchaser, heir, heiress, proprietor, landlord, landlady, sharer, partner, title holder, master, heir apparent.

ownership n. possession, having, holding, claim, deed, title, control, buying, purchasing, proprietorship, occupancy, use, residence, tenancy, dominion.

oyster n. bivalve, mollusk, seafood; see FISH, SHELLFISH.

P

pa* *n.* male parent, papa*, dad*; see FATHER 1, PARENT.

pace *n.* step, velocity, movement; see SPEED. —**change of pace** variation, alteration, diversity; see CHANGE 1. —**keep pace (with)** go at the same speed, maintain the same rate of progress, keep up with; see EQUAL. —**set the pace** begin, initiate, establish criteria; see LEAD 1.

pace *v.* determine, pace off, step off; see MEASURE 1.

pacifist *n.* dove, peace lover, conscientious objector; see RADICAL, RESISTER.

pacify *v.* conciliate, appease, placate; see QUIET 1.

pack *n.* **1** [A package] bundle, parcel, load; see PACKAGE. **2** [Kit] outfit, baggage, luggage; see EQUIPMENT. **3** [A group] number, gang, mob; see CROWD. **4** [A medical dressing] application, hot pack, ice pack; see DRESSING 3. **5** [A set of cards] bridge deck, pinochle deck, set; see DECK 2.

pack *v.* **1** [To prepare for transportation] prepare, gather, collect, ready, get ready, put in order, stow away, tie, bind, brace, fasten.—*Ant.* UNDO, untie, take out. **2** [To stow compactly] stuff, squeeze, bind, compress, condense, arrange, ram, cram, jam, insert, press, contract, put away.—*Ant.* SCATTER, loosen, fluff up.

package *n.* parcel, packet, burden, load, kit, bunch, sheaf, pack, batch, bag, case, roll, wrapped object, box, carton, crate, bundle, bale, can, tin, sack, bottle; see also CONTAINER.

packed *a.* **1** [Ready for storage or shipment] prepared, bundled, wrapped; see READY 2. **2** [Pressed together] compact, compressed, pressed down; see FULL 1.

packet *n.* pack, receptacle, parcel; see CONTAINER, PACKAGE.

packing *n.* preparation, arrangement, compression, consignment, disposal, disposition, sorting, grading, laying away.

pact *n.* settlement, compact, bargain; see TREATY.

pad *n.* **1** [Material for writing] scratchpad, scratch paper, notepad, stationery, notepaper, legal pad; see also PAPER 4, TABLET 2. **2** [An article that cushions] cushion, support, pallet; see PILLOW, MAT. **3** [*A residence] room, apartment, living quarters; see HOME.

pad *v.* **1** [To stuff] pack, fill out, pad out; see FILL 1. **2** [To increase]

inflate, build up, falsify; see DECEIVE, INCREASE.

padded *a.* stuffed, filled, quilted; see FULL 1.

padding *n.* stuffing, wadding, waste; see FILLING.

paddle *n.* oar, pole, scull; see TOOL 1.

paddle *v.* **1** [To propel by paddling] scull, boat, cruise, drift, navigate, shoot rapids, run rapids; see also DRIVE 2. **2** [To beat, usually rather lightly] spank, thrash, rap; see BEAT 1, PUNISH.

padlock *n.* latch, fastener, catch; see LOCK 1.

pagan *a.* unchristian, non-Christian, polytheistic, pantheistic, idolatrous, heathenish.

pagan *n.* pantheist, heathen, doubter, scoffer, unbeliever, atheist, polytheist, nonbeliever, non-Christian, non-Jew, non-Muslim.

paganism *n.* heathenism, agnosticism, idolatry; see ATHEISM.

page *n.* leaf, sheet, folio, side, surface, recto, verso.

page *v.* **1** [To call] hunt for, seek for, call the name of; see SUMMON. **2** [To mark the pages] number, check, paginate; see CHECK 2.

pageant *n.* exhibition, celebration, pomp; see PARADE 1.

paid *a.* rewarded, paid off, reimbursed, indemnified, remunerated, solvent, unindebted, unowed, recompensed, salaried, hired, out of debt, refunded; see also REPAID.

pail *n.* pot, receptacle, bucket; see CONTAINER.

pain *n.* **1** [Suffering, physical or mental] hurt, anguish, distress, discomfort, agony, misery, martyrdom, wretchedness, shock, torture, torment, passion; see also INJURY.—*Ant.* HEALTH, well-being, ease. **2** [Suffering, usually physical] ache, twinge, catch, throe, spasm, cramp, torture, malady, sickness, laceration, soreness, fever, burning, torment, distress, agony, affliction, discomfort, hurt, wound, strain, sting, burn, crick; see also ILLNESS 1, INJURY. **3** [Suffering, usually mental] despondency, worry, anxiety; see DEPRESSION 2, GRIEF, SADNESS. —**feeling no pain*** intoxicated, inebriated, stoned*; see DRUNK. —**take pains** make an effort, care, endeavor; see TRY 1.

pain *v.* distress, grieve, trouble; see HURT 1.

painful *a.* **1** [Referring to physical anguish] raw, aching, throbbing, burning, torturing, hurtful, biting, piercing, sharp, severe, caustic, tormenting, smarting, extreme, grievous, stinging, bruised, sensitive, tender, irritated, distressing, inflamed, burned, unpleasant, ulcerated, abscessed, uncomfortable; see also SORE 1.—*Ant.* HEALTHY, comfortable, well. **2** [Referring to mental anguish] worrying, depressing, saddening; see DISTURBING.

paint *n.* **1** [Pigment] coloring material, chroma, chlorophyll; see COLOR. *Paints and colorings include the following—artist's materials:* oil, acrylic, pastel, crayon, charcoal, watercolor, tempera; *architectural finishes:* house paint, enamel, varnish, redwood stain, oil, wax, whitewash, latex, polyurethane, luminous paint, plastic paint, cold-water paint, flat paint, high-gloss paint, metallic paint, barn paint, interior paint, exterior paint, white lead. **2** [Covering] overlay, varnish, lacquer; see FINISH 2.

paint *v.* **1** [To represent by painting] portray, paint in oils, sketch, outline, picture, depict, limn, catch a likeness, design, shade, tint, wash; see also DRAW 2. **2** [To protect or decorate by painting] coat, decorate, apply, brush, tint, touch up, ornament, gloss over, swab, daub, slap on; see also COVER 1, SPREAD 3.

painted *a.* **1** [Portrayed] outlined, pictured, drawn, sketched, designed, depicted. **2** [Finished] coated, enameled, covered, decorated, ornamented, brushed over, tinted, washed, daubed, touched up, smeared; see also FINISHED 1.

painter *n.* **1** [House painter] interior decorator, dauber, paint-slinger*; see WORKMAN. **2** [An artist] craftsman, artisan, illustrator, draftsman, sketcher, limner, cartoonist, watercolorist, painter in oils, fresco painter, portrait painter, landscape painter; see also ARTIST. *Major painters include the following:* Giotto, Sandro Botticelli, Jan van Eyck, Albrecht Dürer, Hieronymus Bosch, Pieter Brueghel (the elder), Leonardo da Vinci, Raphael, Michelangelo, Titian, Tintoretto, El Greco, Peter Paul Rubens, Anthony Van Dyck, Rembrandt van Rijn, Jan Vermeer, Sir Joshua Reynolds, Thomas Gainsborough, J.M.W. Turner, Diego Velázquez, Francisco Goya, Eugène Delacroix, Auguste Renoir, Edgar Degas, James Whistler, Winslow Homer, John Singer Sargent, Edouard Manet, Claude Monet, Paul Cézanne, Vincent van Gogh, Paul Gauguin, Henri de Toulouse-Lautrec, Pablo Picasso, Henri Matisse, Paul Klee, Salvador Dali, Jackson Pollock.

painting *n.* **1** [A work of art] oil painting, watercolor, abstract design, landscape, sketch, picture, likeness, artwork, canvas, mural, fresco, depiction, delineation; see also ART. **2** [The act of applying paint] enameling, covering, coating; see ART.

pair *n.* couple, mates, two, two of a kind, twosome, twins, fellows, duality, brace.

pair *v.* combine, match, balance; see JOIN 1, 2.

pajamas *n.* nightwear, lounging pajamas, lounging robe, pj's*, jammies*, nightie*; see also CLOTHES.

pal* *n.* chum*, bosom friend, buddy*; see FRIEND.

palace *n.* royal residence, manor, mansion; see CASTLE.

pale *a.* **1** [Wan] pallid, sickly, anemic, bloodless, ghastly, cadaverous, haggard, deathlike, ghostly; see also DULL 2. **2** [Lacking color] white, colorless, bleached; see DULL 2.

pale *v.* grow pale, lose color, blanch; see WHITEN 1.

paleness *n.* whiteness, anemia, colorlessness; see ILLNESS 1.

paltry *a.* small, insignificant, trifling; see UNIMPORTANT.

pamper *v.* spoil, indulge, pet, cater to, humor, gratify, yield to, coddle, overindulge, please, spare the rod and spoil the child*.

pamphlet *n.* booklet, brochure, pocketbook, chapbook, leaflet, bulletin, circular, broadside, handbill; see also ANNOUNCEMENT.

pan *n.* vessel, container, pail, bucket, baking pan, gold pan; see also CONTAINER. *Kitchen pans include the following:* kettle, stewpan, saucepan, double boiler, roaster, casserole, cake pan, bread pan, pie pan, cookie sheet, frying pan, skillet, dishpan.

pan* *v.* criticize, review unfavorably, jeer at; see BLAME. —**pan out*** turn out, work, be a success; see SUCCEED 1.

panacea *n.* relief, cure, elixir; see REMEDY 2.

pancake *n.* flapjack, hot cake, griddlecake; see FOOD.

pandemonium *n.* uproar, anarchy, riot; see CONFUSION.

pane *n.* window glass, stained glass, mirror; see GLASS.

panel *n.* ornament, tablet, inset; see DECORATION 2.

pang *n.* throb, sting, bite; see PAIN 2.

panhandle* *v.* solicit, ask alms, bum*; see BEG.

panhandler* *n.* vagrant, bum*, mendicant; see BEGGAR.

panic *n.* dread, alarm, fright; see FEAR.

panic-stricken *a.* terrified, hysterical, fearful; see AFRAID.

panorama *n.* spectacle, scenery, prospect; see VIEW.

pant *v.* wheeze, throb, breathe heavily; see BREATHE, GASP.

panties *n.* pants, underpants, briefs; see UNDERWEAR.

pantomime *n.* sign, sign language, dumb show*, mimicry, play without words, acting without speech, charade, mime.

pantry *n.* storeroom, larder, cupboard; see CLOSET, ROOM 2.

pants *n.* **1** [Trousers] breeches, britches*, slacks, jeans, overalls, cords, shorts, corduroys, pantaloons, bell-bottoms, riding breeches, chaps, short pants, knee pants, knickers, bloomers, sweat pants, jodhpurs, dungarees, harem pants, stretch pants, leggings; see also CLOTHES. **2** [Underclothing] shorts, briefs, panties; see CLOTHES, UNDERWEAR.

papa* *n.* dad*, daddy*, male parent; see FATHER 1, PARENT.

paper *n.* **1** [A piece of legal or official writing] document, official document, legal paper; see RECORD 1. *Papers include the following:* abstract, affidavit, bill, certificate, citation, contract, credentials, data, deed, diploma, indictment, grant, orders, passport, visa, plea, records, safe-conduct, subpoena, summons, testimony, voucher, warrant, will, warranty, decree, writ, receipt. **2** [A newspaper] journal, daily, weekly; see NEWSPAPER. **3** [A piece of writing] essay, article, thesis; see WRITING 2. **4** [A manufactured product] *Paper products include the following—writing material:* typing paper, typewriter paper, stationery, bond paper, letterhead, personal stationery, ruled paper, second sheet, handmade paper, parchment, vellum, onionskin, carbon paper, notepad, notecard, tablet, file card, computer paper, notebook; *printing paper:* coated stock, poster, linen finish, vellum, parchment, India; 50-pound, 60-pound, etc.; *newsprint; miscellaneous:* rice, crepe, butcher's, wrapping, tissue, brown, tar, roofing, tracing, graph, filter, toilet, wax, waxed, blotting, scrap, photographic, etc. paper; cardboard, paper bag, wallpaper, cellophane, paper towel, cleansing tissue. **—on paper 1** recorded, signed, official; see WRITTEN 1. **2** in theory, assumed to be feasible, not yet in practice; see THEORETICAL.

paper *v.* hang, paste up, plaster; see COVER 1.

paperback *n.* softcover, pocket book, reprint; see BOOK.

papers *n.* **1** [Evidence of identity or authorization] naturalization papers, identification card, ID; see

IDENTIFICATION 2, PASSPORT. **2** [Documentary materials] writings, documents, effects; see RECORD 1.

paperwork *n.* office work, desk work, keeping one's desk clear, keeping records, filing, preparing reports, writing, editing, research, letter writing, billing, filling out forms, taking dictation, typing, keeping books.

papery *a.* flimsy, insubstantial, slight; see POOR 2.

par *n.* standard, level, norm; see MODEL 2.

parable *n.* fable, moral story, allegory; see STORY.

parachute *n.* chute, seat pack parachute, lap pack parachute, harness and pack, umbrella*, silk*.

parachute *v.* fall, bail out, hit the silk*; see DIVE.

parade *n.* **1** [A procession] march, motorcade, spectacle, ceremony, demonstration, review, line of floats, line of march, pageant, ritual. **2** [An ostentatious show] show, ostentation, ceremony; see DISPLAY.

parade *v.* demonstrate, display, exhibit; see MARCH.

paradise *n.* **1** [Heaven] kingdom come, celestial home, the other world; see HEAVEN. **2** [The home of Adam and Eve] Garden of Eden, Eden, the Garden.

paradox *n.* seeming contradiction, enigma, ambiguity; see PUZZLE 1.

paragon *n.* ideal, perfection, best; see MODEL 1.

paragraph *n.* passage, section, division of thought, topic, statement, verse, article, item, notice.

parallel *a.* **1** [Equidistant at all points] side by side, never meeting, running parallel, coextending, lateral, laterally, in the same direction, extending equally. **2** [Similar in kind, position, or the like] identical, equal, conforming; see ALIKE.

parallel *n.* resemblance, likeness, correspondence; see SIMILARITY.

parallel *v.* match, correspond, correlate; see EQUAL.

paralysis *n.* insensibility, loss of motion, loss of sensation; see ILLNESS 2.

paralytic *a.* inactive, paralyzed, immobile; see DISABLED, SICK.

paralytic *n.* paralysis victim, disabled person, paralyzed person; see PATIENT.

paralyze *v.* strike with paralysis, make inert, take away sensation; see DEADEN.

paralyzed *a.* insensible, benumbed, stupefied, inert, inactive, unmoving, helpless, torpid; see also DISABLED.

paranoid *a.* affected by paranoia, unreasonably distrustful, overly suspicious, having a persecution complex.

paraphernalia *n.* gear, material, apparatus; see EQUIPMENT.

parasite *n.* **1** [A plant or animal living on another] bacteria, bacterium, parasitoid, saprophyte, epiphyte. **2** [A hanger-on] dependent, freeloader*, sponger*; see SLAVE.

parcel *n.* bundle, packet, carton; see PACKAGE.

parch *v.* dessicate, dehydrate, dry up; see DRY 1.

parched *a.* burned, withered, dried; see DRY 1.

parchment *n.* vellum, goatskin, sheepskin; see PAPER 4.

pardon *n.* **1** [The reduction or removal of punishment] absolution, grace, remission, amnesty, exoneration, discharge; see also MERCY.—*Ant.* PUNISHMENT, condemnation, conviction. **2** [Forgiveness] excusing, forbearance, conciliation; see FORGIVENESS, KINDNESS 1.

pardon *v.* **1** [To reduce punishment] exonerate, clear, absolve, reprieve, acquit, set free, liberate, discharge, rescue, justify, suspend charges, put on probation, grant amnesty to; see also FREE, RELEASE.—*Ant.* PUNISH, chastise, sentence. **2** [To forgive] condone, overlook, exculpate; see EXCUSE, FORGIVE.

pardoned *a.* forgiven, freed, excused, released, granted amnesty, given a pardon, reprieved, granted a reprieve, acquitted, let off, sprung*; see DISCHARGED, FREE 1.—*Ant.* ACCUSED, convicted, condemned.

pare *v.* peel, trim, scrape; see CUT 1, SHAVE, SKIN.

parent *n.* immediate forebear, procreator, progenitor, stepparent, foster parent; see also FATHER 1, MOTHER 1.

parental *a.* paternal, maternal, familial; see GENETIC.

parentheses *n.* brackets, braces, punctuation marks; see PUNCTUATION.

parish *n.* archdiocese, congregation, diocese; see AREA, CHURCH 3.

park *n.* **1** [A place designated for outdoor recreation] square, plaza, lawn, green, village green, promenade, tract, recreational area, national park, national monument, enclosure, woodland, meadow. **2** [A place designed for outdoor storage] car park*, parking space, lot; see GARAGE, PARKING LOT.

parked *a.* standing, left, put, lined up, in rows, by the curb, in the parking lot, stored, halted, unmoving.

parking lot *n.* lot, space, parking space, parking garage, parking area, parking facility, parking slot, off-street parking.

Parliament *n.* national legislative body of Great Britain, House of Commons, House of Lords; see GOVERNMENT 1, LEGISLATURE.

parliamentary *a.* congressional, administrative, lawmaking; see GOVERNMENTAL, LEGISLATIVE.

parochial *a.* provincial, insular, sectional; see LOCAL 1, REGIONAL.

parody *n.* travesty, burlesque, mimicry; see JOKE.

parody *v.* mimic, copy, caricature; see IMITATE 1, JOKE.

parole *v.* discharge, let out, liberate; see FREE, RELEASE.

parrot *n.* **1** [A bird] parakeet, lovebird, cockatoo; see BIRD. **2** [One who copies others] plagiarist, mimic, ape, impersonator, impostor, mocker, copycat; see also IMITATOR.

parson* *n.* clergyman, cleric, preacher; see MINISTER 1.

part *n.* **1** [A portion] piece, fragment, fraction, section, sector, member, segment, division, allotment, apportionment, ingredient, element, slab, subdivision, particle, installment, component, constituent, bit, slice, scrap, chip, chunk, lump, sliver, splinter, shaving, molecule, atom, electron, proton, neutron; see also SHARE.—*Ant.* WHOLE, total, aggregate. **2** [A part of speech] grammatical form, word class, function word; see NOUN, VERB. **3** [A machine part] molding, casting, fitting, lever, shaft, cam, spring, band, belt, chain, pulley, clutch, spare part, replacement; see also BOLT, GEAR, MACHINE, WHEEL 1. **4** [A character in a drama] hero, heroine, character; see ROLE. —**for the most part** mainly, mostly, to the greatest extent; see MOST. —**in part** partially, somewhat, to some extent; see PARTLY, UNFINISHED 1. —**on one's part** privately, as far as one is concerned, coming from one; see PERSONALLY 2. —**play a part** share, join, take part; see PARTICIPATE 1. —**take part** associate, cooperate, follow; see JOIN 2, PARTICIPATE 1, SHARE 2.

part *v.* **1** [To put apart] separate, break, sever; see DIVIDE. **2** [To depart] withdraw, take leave, part company; see LEAVE 1. —**part from** separate, part, break up with; see LEAVE 1. —**part with** let go of, suffer loss, give up; see LOSE 2.

partake *v.* participate, divide, take; see SHARE 2.

parted *a.* divided, severed, sundered; see SEPARATED.

partial *a.* **1** [Not complete] not total, incomplete, half done; see UNFINISHED 1. **2** [Showing favoritism] unfair, influenced, biased; see PREJUDICED.

partiality *n.* fondness, inclination, preference; see AFFECTION.

partially *a.* to some degree, somewhat, in part; see PARTLY.

participant *n.* member, partner, sharer; see ASSOCIATE.

participate *v.* **1** [To take part in] share, partake, aid, cooperate, join in, come in, associate with, be a party to, have a hand in, concur, take an interest in, take part in, enter into, have to do with, get into the act*, go into, chip in*; see also JOIN 2.—*Ant.* RETIRE, withdraw, refuse. **2** [To engage in a contest] play, strive, engage; see COMPETE.

participation *n.* joining in, sharing, support, aid, assistance, encouragement, seconding, help, standing by, taking part; see also PARTNERSHIP.

particle *n.* jot, scrap, atom, molecule, fragment, piece, shred; see also BIT 1.

particular *a.* **1** [Specific] distinct, singular, appropriate; see SPECIAL. **2** [Accurate] precise, minute, exact; see ACCURATE 2.

particular *n.* fact, specification, item; see DETAIL. —**in particular** particularly, expressly, individually; see ESPECIALLY 1.

particularly *a.* unusually, individually, expressly; see ESPECIALLY 1.

parting *n.* leavetaking, goodbye, farewell; see DEPARTURE.

partisan *n.* adherent, supporter, disciple; see FOLLOWER.

partition *n.* **1** [Division] apportionment, separation, severance; see DISTRIBUTION. **2** [That which divides or separates] bar, obstruction, divider; see BARRIER, WALL 1.

partly *a.* in part, partially, to a degree, measurably, somewhat, noticeably, notably, in some part, incompletely, insufficiently, inadequately, up to a certain point, so far as possible, not entirely, as much as could be expected, to some extent, within limits, slightly, to a slight degree, in some ways, only in details, in a general way, not strictly speaking, in bits and pieces, by fits and starts, at best, at worst, at most, at least, at the outside.—*Ant.* COMPLETELY, wholly, entirely.

partner *n.* co-worker, ally, comrade; see ASSOCIATE.

partnership *n.* alliance, cooperation, company, combination, corporation, connection, brotherhood, society, lodge, club, fellowship, fraternity, confederation, band, body, crew, clique, gang, ring, faction, party, community, conjunction, joining, companionship, friendship, sisterhood, sorority; see also ALLIANCE 1, UNION 1.

part of speech *n.* grammatical form, word class, function word; see ADJECTIVE, GRAMMAR, PRONOUN, VERB, WORD 1.

partway *a.* started, toward the middle, somewhat; see BEGUN, SOME.

party *n.* **1** [A social affair] at-home, tea, luncheon, dinner party, dinner, cocktail hour, surprise party, house party, social, reception, banquet, feast, affair, gathering, function, fete, ball, recreation, amusement, entertainment, festive occasion, carouse, diversion, performance, high tea, binge*, spree*, blowout*, bash*. **2** [A group of people] multitude, mob, company; see CROWD, GATHERING. **3** [A political organization] organized group, body, electorate, combine, combination, bloc, ring, junta, partisans, cabal; see also FACTION. **4** [*A specified but unnamed individual] party of the first part, someone, individual; see PERSON 1, SOMEBODY.

pass *n.* **1** [An opening through mountains] gorge, ravine, crossing, track, way, path, passageway; see also GAP 3. **2** [A document assuring permission to pass] ticket, permit, passport, visa, order, admission, furlough, permission, right, license. **3** [In sports, the passing of the ball from one player to another] toss, throw, fling; see PITCH 2. **4** [*An advance] approach, sexual overture, proposition; see SUGGESTION 1.

pass *v.* **1** [To move past] go by, run by, run past, flit by, come by, shoot ahead of, catch, come to the front, go beyond, roll on, fly past, reach, roll by, cross, flow past, go in opposite directions; see also MOVE 1. **2** [To elapse] transpire, slip away, slip by, pass away, pass by, fly, fly by, run out, drag. **3** [To complete a course successfully] satisfy the requirements, be graduated, pass with honors; see SUCCEED 1. **4** [To hand to others] transfer, relinquish, hand over; see GIVE 1. **5** [To enact] legislate, establish, vote in; see ENACT. **6** [To become enacted] carry, become law, become valid, be ratified, be established, be ordained, be sanctioned. **7** [To exceed] excel, transcend, go beyond; see EXCEED. **8** [To spend time] fill, occupy oneself, while away; see SPEND. **9** [To proceed] progress, get ahead, move on, go on; see also ADVANCE 1. **10** [To emit] give off, send forth, exude; see EMIT. —**bring to pass** bring about, initiate, start; see CAUSE. —**come to pass** occur, develop, come about; see HAPPEN 2. —**pass away** depart, expire, pass on; see DIE. —**pass by** travel, move past, depart from; see LEAVE 1, PASS 1. —**pass off** pass for, make a pretense of, palm

off*; see PRETEND 1. **—pass on**
expire, depart, succumb; see DIE. **—pass out** 1 [To faint] swoon, lose consciousness, black out; see FAINT. 2 [To distribute] hand out, circulate, deal out; see DISTRIBUTE, GIVE 1. **—pass over** dismiss, overlook, neglect; see DISREGARD. **—pass up*** dismiss, let go by, reject; see DENY, REFUSE.

passable a. open, fair, penetrable, navigable, accessible, traveled, easy, broad, graded; see also AVAILABLE.

passage n. 1 [A journey] voyage, crossing, trek; see JOURNEY. 2 [A passageway] way, exit, entrance; see ENTRANCE 2. 3 [A reading] section, portion, paragraph; see QUOTATION 1.

passé a. obsolete, out-of-date, outmoded; see OLD-FASHIONED.

passenger n. commuter, tourist, traveler; see RIDER 1.

passerby n. witness, viewer, bystander; see OBSERVER.

passing a. 1 [In the act of going past] crossing, going by, gliding by, flashing by, speeding by, going in opposite directions, passing in the night; see also MOVING 1. 2 [Of brief duration] fleeting, transitory, transient; see TEMPORARY.

passion n. lust, craving, sexual excitement; see DESIRE 2, EMOTION.

passionate a. 1 [Excitable] vehement, hotheaded, tempestuous; see sense 2. 2 [Ardent] intense, impassioned, loving, fervent, moving, inspiring, dramatic, melodramatic, romantic, poignant, enthusiastic, tragic, stimulating, wistful, stirring, thrilling, warm, burning, glowing, vehement, deep, affecting, eloquent, spirited, fiery, expressive, forceful, heated, hot. 3 [Intense] strong, vehement, violent; see INTENSE.

passive a. 1 [Being acted upon] receptive, stirred, influenced; see AFFECTED 1. 2 [Not active] inactive, inert, lifeless; see IDLE.

passport n. pass, license, permit, safe-conduct, visa, travel permit, authorization, warrant, credentials; see also IDENTIFICATION 2.

password n. countersign, signal, phrase, secret word, watchword, identification, open sesame.

past a. 1 [Having occurred previously] former, preceding, gone by, foregoing, elapsed, anterior, antecedent, prior. 2 [No longer serving] ex-, retired, earlier; see PRECEDING.

past prep. through, farther than, behind; see BEYOND.

past n. 1 [Past time] antiquity, long ago, the past, past times, old times, years ago, good old days, ancient times, former times, days gone by, auld lang syne, days of old, yester-

day.—Ant. FUTURE, tomorrow, the present. 2 [Past events] memories, happenings, events; see HISTORY.

paste n. adhesive, glue, mucilage; see CEMENT.

paste v. glue, fix, affix, repair, patch; see also STICK 1.

pastime n. recreation, amusement, sport; see ENTERTAINMENT, HOBBY.

pastor n. priest, rector, member of the clergy; see MINISTER 1.

pastry n. baked goods, dainty, delicacy, goodies*, cake; see also BREAD. *Pastries include the following:* French, Danish, tart, pie, turnover, torte, cream puff, éclair, strudel, puff pastry, phyllo, brioche, napoleon, croissant, quiche Lorraine, petit four, roll, bun, baklava, patty shell, patisserie, Linzer torte, Cornish pasty, empanada, calzone, sweet roll.

pasture n. grazing land, pasturage, hayfield; see FIELD 1, MEADOW.

pasty a. wan, pallid, sickly, ashen, anemic; see also PALE 1, DULL 2.

pat v. 1 [To strike lightly] tap, beat, slap; see HIT 1. 2 [To strike lightly and affectionately] stroke, pet, rub; see TOUCH 2.

patch n. piece, bit, scrap, spot, application.

patch v. darn, mend, cover; see REPAIR. **—patch up** appease, adjust, compensate; see SETTLE 7.

patchwork n. jumble, hodgepodge, muddle; see CONFUSION, DISORDER.

patent n. patent right, protection, concession, control, limitation, license, copyright, privilege; see also RIGHT 1.

patent v. license, secure, control, limit, monopolize, safeguard, exclude, copyright.

patented a. copyrighted, patent applied for, trademarked, under patent, under copyright, patent pending; see also RESTRICTED.

paternal a. patrimonial, fatherly, protective, benevolent.

paternity n. progenitorship, parenthood, fatherhood; see FATHER 1.

path n. trail, way, track, shortcut, footpath, crosscut, footway, roadway, cinder track, byway, pathway, bridle path; see also ROUTE 1.

pathetic a. touching, affecting, moving; see PITIFUL.

patience n. 1 [Willingness to endure] forbearance, fortitude, composure, submission, endurance, nonresistance, self-control, passiveness, bearing, serenity, humility, yielding, poise, sufferance, long-suffering, moderation, leniency; see also RESIGNATION 1.—Ant. NERVOUSNESS, fretfulness, restlessness. 2 [Ability to continue] submission, perseverance, persistence; see ENDURANCE.

patient a. **1** [Enduring without complaint] submissive, meek, forbearing, mild-tempered, composed, tranquil, serene, long-suffering, unruffled, imperturbable, passive, easygoing, tolerant, gentle, unresentful; see also RESIGNED.—*Ant.* IRRITABLE, violent, resentful. **2** [Quietly persistent in an activity] steady, dependable, calm, stable, composed, unwavering, quiet, serene, unimpassioned, enduring; see also RELIABLE.—*Ant.* RESTLESS, irrepressible, feverish.

patient n. case, inmate, victim, sufferer, sick person, medical case, surgical case, outpatient, bed patient, emergency ward patient, convalescent, hospital case, hospitalized person, subject.

patiently a. **1** [Suffering without complaint] enduringly, bravely, impassively, resignedly, numbly, forbearingly, tolerantly, submissively, meekly; see also CALMLY. **2** [Continuing without impatience] steadily, firmly, unabatingly; see REGULARLY.

patio n. porch, courtyard, square; see YARD 1.

patriarch n. male ruler, head of family, ancestor; see CHIEF.

patriot n. lover of one's country, good citizen, statesman, nationalist, volunteer, loyalist, jingoist, chauvinist.

patriotic a. devoted, zealous, public-spirited, consecrated, dedicated, jingoistic, chauvinistic.

patriotism n. love of country, public spirit, good citizenship, nationality, nationalism; see also LOYALTY.

patrol n. guard, watch, protection; see ARMY 2.

patrol v. watch, walk, inspect; see GUARD.

patrolman n. police, police officer, constable; see POLICE OFFICER.

patron n. philanthropist, benefactor, helper, protector, encourager, champion, backer, advocate, defender, guide, leader, friend, ally, sympathizer, well-wisher, partisan, buyer, angel*, sugar daddy*, booster.—*Ant.* ENEMY, obstructionist, adversary.

patronage n. **1** [Trade] commerce, trading, shopping; see BUSINESS 1. **2** [Condescension] patronization, deference, toleration; see PRIDE 2.

patronize v. **1** [To trade with] frequent, buy from, shop with; see BUY, SELL. **2** [To assume a condescending attitude] talk down to, be overbearing, stoop, be gracious to, favor, pat on the back, play the snob, snub, lord it over; see also CONDESCEND.

patronizing a. condescending, snob-

bish, stooping; see EGOTISTIC, POLITE.

pattern n. original, guide, copy; see MODEL 2.

pauper n. poor person, indigent, destitute person; see BEGGAR.

pause n. lull, rest, stop, halt, truce, stay, respite, standstill, stand, deadlock, stillness, intermission, suspension, discontinuance, breathing space, hitch, hesitancy, interlude, hiatus, interim, lapse, cessation, stopover, interval, rest period, gap, stoppage.

pause v. delay, halt, rest, catch one's breath, cease, hold back, reflect, deliberate, suspend, think twice, discontinue, interrupt; see also HESITATE.

pave v. lay concrete, lay asphalt, macadamize; see COVER 1.

paved a. hard-surfaced, flagged, cobblestone, asphalt, concrete, brick, bricked, surfaced with wood blocks; see also COVERED 1.

pavement n. hard surface, paving, paving stone, paving tile, flagging. *Road surfaces include the following:* concrete, asphalt, blacktop, stone, brick, tile, macadam, gravel, cobblestone, wood blocks, flagstone.

paving n. hard surface, concrete, paved highway; see PAVEMENT.

paw n. forefoot, talon, hand; see CLAW.

paw v. **1** [To strike wildly] clutch, grasp, smite; see HIT 1. **2** [To scrape with the front foot] scratch, rake, claw; see DIG 1.

pawn v. deposit, pledge, hock*; see SELL.

pawned a. deposited, pledged, hocked*; see SOLD OUT.

pay n. **1** [Monetary return] profit, proceeds, interest, return, recompense, indemnity, reparation, rakeoff*, reward, consideration, defrayment.—*Ant.* EXPENSE, disbursement, outlay. **2** [Wages] compensation, salary, payment, hire, remuneration, commission, fee, stipend, earnings, settlement, consideration, reimbursement, reward, time, time and a half, double time, overtime.

pay v. **1** [To give payment] pay up, compensate, recompense, make payment, reward, remunerate, discharge, pay a bill, foot the bill*, refund, settle, get even with, reckon with, put down, make restitution, make reparation, hand over, repay, liquidate, handle, take care of, give, confer, bequeath, defray, meet, disburse, clear, adjust, satisfy, reimburse, kick in*, plunk down*, put up*, pay as you go, fork out*, fork over*, ante up*, even the score*, chip in*.—*Ant.* DECEIVE, swindle, victimize. **2** [To produce a profit] return, pay off, pay out, show profit, yield profit, show gain, pay dividends.—*Ant.* FAIL, lose, become bankrupt. **3** [To retaliate] repay, punish, requite; see REVENGE. —**pay for** atone for, make amends for, do penance for, compensate for, make up for, make satisfaction for, expiate, make reparation for, give satisfaction for, pay the penalty for, make compensation for.

payment *n.* **1** [The act of paying] recompense, reimbursement, restitution, subsidy, return, redress, refund, remittance, reparation, disbursement, money down, amends, cash, salary, wage, sum, payoff, repayment, defrayment, retaliation; see also PAY 1. **2** [An installment] portion, part, amount; see DEBT.

payoff *n.* settlement, conclusion, reward; see PAY 1, PAYMENT 1.

payroll *n.* employees, workers, pay list; see FACULTY 2, STAFF 2.

peace *n.* **1** [The state of being without war] armistice, pacification, conciliation, order, concord, amity, union, unity, reconciliation, brotherhood, love, unanimity; see also AGREEMENT 1, FRIENDSHIP.—*Ant.* WAR, warfare, battle. **2** [State of being without disturbance] calm, repose, quiet, tranquillity, harmony, lull, hush, congeniality, equanimity, silence, stillness; see also REST 1.—*Ant.* FIGHT, noisiness, quarrel. **3** [Mental or emotional calm] calmness, repose, harmony, concord, contentment, sympathy; see also COMPOSURE, RESERVE 2, TRANQUILLITY.—*Ant.* DISTRESS, disturbance, agitation. —**at peace** peaceful, quiet, tranquil; see CALM 1, 2. —**hold** (or **keep**) **one's peace** be silent, keep quiet, not speak; see SHUT UP 1. —**make peace** end hostilities, settle, reconcile; see QUIET 1.

peaceable *a.* conciliatory, pacific, peaceful; see FRIENDLY.

peaceful *a.* **1** [At peace] quiet, tranquil, serene; see CALM 1, 2. **2** [Inclined toward peace] well-disposed, sociable, amiable; see FRIENDLY.

peacefully *a.* **1** [Calmly] tranquilly, quietly, composedly; see CALMLY. **2** [Without making trouble] harmoniously, placatingly, inoffensively, temperately, civilly; see also MODESTLY.

peak *n.* **1** [A mountain] summit, top, crown; see MOUNTAIN 1. **2** [The maximum] zenith, highest point, greatest quantity; see HEIGHT, TIP 1, TOP 1.

peaked *a.* pointed, topped, triangle-topped; see SHARP 1.

pearl *n.* nacre, gem, cultured pearl; see JEWEL.

peasant *n.* small farmer, farm laborer, farm worker; see FARMER, LABORER, WORKMAN.

pebble *n.* small stone, gravel, cobblestone; see ROCK 1, STONE.

peck *n.* **1** [A slight, sharp blow] pinch, tap, rap; see BLOW. **2** [One fourth of a bushel] eight quarts, quarter-bushel, large amount; see MEASURE 1, QUANTITY.

peck *v.* nip, pick, tap; see BITE 1, PINCH.

peculiar *a.* **1** [Unusual] wonderful, singular, outlandish; see STRANGE, UNUSUAL 2. **2** [Characteristic of only one] strange, uncommon, eccentric; see CHARACTERISTIC, UNIQUE.

peculiarity *n.* distinctiveness, singularity, unusualness; see CHARACTERISTIC.

pedal *n.* treadle, foot lever, accelerator; see LEVER.

peddle *v.* hawk, vend, trade; see SELL.

peddler *n.* hawker, vendor, seller; see BUSINESSMAN.

pedestal *n.* stand, foundation, footstall, plinth; see also COLUMN 1, SUPPORT 2.

pedestrian *n.* traveler on foot, walker, hiker; see WALKING *a.*

peek *n.* peep, glimpse, glance; see LOOK 3.

peek *v.* glance, peep, glimpse; see SEE 1.

peel *n.* husk, bark, shell; see SKIN.

peel *v.* pare, strip, tear off, pull off, flay, uncover; see also SKIN.

peeling *n.* paring, strip, sliver; see SKIN.

peep *n.* **1** [A peek] glimpse, glance, sight; see LOOK 3. **2** [A peeping sound] cheep, chirp, squeak; see CRY 2.

peep *v.* **1** [To look cautiously] peek, glimpse, glance; see SEE 1. **2** [To make a peeping sound] cheep, chirp, squeak; see CRY 2.

peer *n.* match, rival, companion; see EQUAL.

peer *v.* gaze, inspect, scrutinize; see SEE 1.

peer group *n.* equals, social group, one's peers; see ASSOCIATE, EQUAL.

peeve* *v.* irritate, annoy, anger; see BOTHER 2.

peeved *a.* sullen, irritated, upset; see ANGRY.

peevish *a.* cross, fretful, fretting; see ANGRY.

peg *n.* pin, tack, fastener; see NAIL. —**take down a peg** humiliate, criticize, diminish; see HUMBLE.

pellet *n.* pill, bead, grain; see STONE.

pell-mell *a.* impetuously, hurriedly, indiscreetly; see FOOLISHLY.

pelt *n.* skin, hair, wool; see HIDE.

pen *n.* **1** [An enclosed place] coop, cage, corral, sty, close; see also ENCLOSURE 1. **2** [A writing instrument] *Pens include the following:* fountain, desk, drawing, ruling, artist's, reed, quill, steel, ballpoint, felt-tip. **3** [*A place of confinement] penitentiary, prison, concentration camp; see JAIL.

pen *v.* **1** [To enclose] close in, confine, coop up*; see ENCLOSE. **2** [To write] compose, indite, commit to writing; see WRITE 1, 2.

penalize *v.* scold, chasten, castigate; see PUNISH.

penalty *n.* fine, sentence, discipline; see PUNISHMENT.

penance *n.* mortification, purgation, repentance, retribution, compensation, atonement, fasting, suffering, sackcloth and ashes, hair shirt, reparation; see also PUNISHMENT.

pencil *n.* *Types of pencils include the following:* lead, mechanical, colored, drawing, indelible, charcoal, grease, eyebrow, cosmetic, drafting; chalk, crayon, stylus.

pendant *n.* earring, locket, lavaliere; see DECORATION 2, JEWELRY.

pending *a.* continuing, indeterminate, unfinished; see OMINOUS.

pendulum *n.* swing, pendant, suspended body; see DEVICE, MACHINE.

penetrable *a.* permeable, receptive, open, passable, accessible; see also POROUS.

penetrate *v.* bore, perforate, enter, insert, go through, make an entrance, stick into, jab, thrust, stab, force, make a hole, run through, punch, puncture, drive into, stick, drill, eat through, spear, impale, wound, gore, sting, sink into, knife, go through, pass through.—*Ant.* LEAVE, withdraw, turn aside.

penetrating *a.* **1** [Entering] piercing, going through, puncturing; see SHARP 1. **2** [Mentally keen] astute, shrewd, sharp; see INTELLIGENT.

penetration *n.* **1** [Act of entering] insertion, invasion, perforation; see ENTRANCE 1. **2** [Mental acuteness] discernment, perception, keensightedness; see INTELLIGENCE 1.

peninsula *n.* point, promontory, cape; see LAND 1.

penitentiary *n.* reformatory, penal institution, pen*; see JAIL, PRISON.

penniless *a.* poverty-stricken, lacking means, indigent; see POOR 1.

penny *n.* cent, copper, red cent*; see MONEY 1.

pension *n.* annuity, premium, payment, grant, social security, gift,

subsidy, fixed income, reward; see also ALLOWANCE.

pent-up *a.* held in check, repressed, unexpressed; see HELD, RESTRICTED.

people *n.* **1** [Humankind] humanity, mankind, the human race; see MAN 1. **2** [A body of persons having racial or social ties] nationality, tribe, community; see RACE 2. **3** [The middle and lower classes of society] folk, proletariat, rabble, masses, the multitude, the majority, crowd, common people, common herd, rank and file, the underprivileged, the public, the man in the street, bourgeoisie, riffraff, the herd*, the many, the great unwashed*, hoi polloi, John Q. Public, Jane Q. Public. **4** [Family] close relatives, kin, siblings; see FAMILY. **5** [Society in general] they, anybody, the public; see EVERYBODY.

peopled *a.* lived in, dwelt in, sustaining human life; see INHABITED.

pep* *n.* energy, vigor, liveliness; see ACTION 1.

per *prep.* to each, for each, contained in each, according to*, through, by, by means of.

perceive *v.* **1** [See] observe, note, notice; see LOOK 2, SEE 1. **2** [Understand] comprehend, sense, grasp; see UNDERSTAND 1.

perceived *a.* seen, felt, touched; see UNDERSTOOD 1.

percent *a.* by the hundred, per hundred, in a hundred, percentile.

percentage *n.* percent, rate, rate per cent, portion, section, allotment, proportion, duty, discount, commission, winnings, cut*, rake-off*, payoff, slice*; see also DIVISION 2.

perceptible *a.* perceivable, discernible, cognizable; see OBVIOUS 1.

perception *n.* **1** [The act of perceiving] realizing, understanding, apprehending; see ATTENTION, JUDGMENT 2. **2** [The result of perceiving] insight, knowledge, observation; see ATTITUDE, OPINION 1, VIEWPOINT.

perceptive *a.* alert, incisive, keen; see CONSCIOUS, OBSERVANT.

perch *n.* seat, pole, landing place, resting place.

perch *v.* roost, settle down, land; see REST 1, SIT.

perfect *a.* **1** [Having all necessary qualities] complete, sound, entire; see ABSOLUTE 1, WHOLE 1, 2. **2** [Without defect] excelling, faultless, flawless, impeccable, immaculate, unblemished, foolproof, untainted, unspotted, absolute, classic, stainless, spotless, crowning, culminating, sublime, supreme, ideal, beyond all praise, beyond compare; see also EXCELLENT, PURE 2, WHOLE 2.—*Ant.*

RUINED, damaged, faulty. **3** [Exact] precise, sharp, distinct; see ACCURATE 2.

perfect *v.* fulfill, realize, develop; see ACHIEVE, COMPLETE.

perfected *a.* completed, developed, mature, conclusive, full, elaborate, thorough; see also FINISHED 1, FULFILLED.

perfection *n.* completion, fulfillment, finishing, consummation, supremacy, ideal, ending, realization; see also ACHIEVEMENT.—*Ant.* RUIN, destruction, neglect.

perfectly *a.* excellently, supremely, ideally, fitly, correctly, flawlessly, faultlessly.—*Ant.* BADLY, poorly, incorrectly.

perforate *v.* drill, slit, stab; see PENETRATE.

perforation *n.* break, aperture, slit; see HOLE 1.

perform *v.* **1** [To accomplish an action] do, make, achieve, accomplish, fulfill, execute, transact, carry out, carry through, discharge, effect, enforce, administer, complete, consummate, operate, finish, realize, go about, go through with, put through, work out, devote oneself to, come through, be engrossed in, be engaged in, see to it, bring about, engage in, concern oneself with, have an effect, fall to, do justice to, do one's part, make a move, follow through, apply oneself to, deal with, do something, look to, take measures, act on, lose oneself in, make it one's business, dispose of, bring to pass, do what is expected of one, put into effect, occupy oneself with, take action, address oneself to, put in action, lift a finger*, keep one's hand in*, pull off*. **2** [To present a performance] give, present, enact, play, offer, impersonate, show, exhibit, display, act out, dramatize, execute, put on the stage, produce, act the part of, act one's part.

performance *n.* appearance, rehearsal, exhibition, offering, representation, spectacle, review, revue, opera, play, concert, display, show; see also DRAMA.

perfume *n.* scent, fragrance, aroma, odor, sweetness, bouquet, incense;. see also SMELL 1. *Perfumes include the following:* attar of roses, sandalwood, bay, rosemary, bay rum, frankincense, myrrh, eau de Cologne, musk, toilet water, potpourri, patchouli, spice, sachet, lavender, rose geranium.

perhaps *a.* conceivably, possibly, reasonably; see MAYBE.

perilous *a.* precarious, unsafe, uncertain; see DANGEROUS.

perimeter *n.* margin, outline, border; see BOUNDARY, EDGE 1.

period *n.* **1** [A measure of time] epoch, time, era; see AGE 3. **2** [An end] limit, conclusion, close; see END 2. **3** [A mark of punctuation] point, full stop, full pause, dot; see also PUNCTUATION.

periodic *a.* rhythmic, intermittent, recurrent; see REGULAR 3.

periodical *n.* review, number, publication; see MAGAZINE, NEWSPAPER.

periodically *a.* rhythmically, systematically, annually; see REGULARLY.

peripheral *a.* external, outer, surface; see OUTSIDE.

periphery *n.* covering, perimeter, border; see OUTSIDE 1.

perish *v.* pass away, be lost, depart; see DIE.

perjure *v.* prevaricate, swear falsely, lie on the stand; see LIE 1.

perjury *n.* false statement, violation of an oath, willful falsehood; see LIE.

perk up *v.* **1** [Be refreshed] revive, recuperate, liven up; see RECOVER 3. **2** [Cheer or refresh] invigorate, animate, enliven; see RENEW 1, REVIVE 1.

permanence *n.* continuity, dependability, durability; see STABILITY 1.

permanent *a.* durable, enduring, abiding, uninterrupted, stable, continuing, lasting, firm, hard, tough, strong, hardy, robust, sound, sturdy, steadfast, imperishable, surviving, living, long-lived, longstanding, invariable, persevering, unyielding, persisting, resistant, impenetrable, recurring, constant, changeless, persistent, perennial.

permanently *a.* for all time, enduringly, lastingly; see FOREVER.

permeate *v.* pervade, saturate, fill; see FILTER 1.

permissible *a.* allowable, sanctioned, authorized; see PERMITTED.

permission *n.* leave, liberty, consent, assent, acceptance, letting, approbation, agreement, license, permit, authority, tolerance, toleration, authorization, approval, acknowledgment, admission, verification, recognition, concurrence, promise, avowal, support, corroboration, guarantee, guaranty, visa, encouragement, ratification, grace, authority, sanction, confirmation, endorsement, affirmation, assurance, empowering, legalization, grant, indulgence, trust, concession, adjustment, settlement, accord, nod*, OK*, rubber stamp*, the go-ahead*, high sign, green light*.—*Ant.* DENIAL, injunction, interdiction.

permissive *a.* allowing, lenient, agreeable; see KIND.

permit *n.* license, grant, consent; see PERMISSION.

permit v. sanction, tolerate, let; see ALLOW.

permitted a. granted, allowed, licensed, authorized, legalized, tolerated, empowered, sanctioned, conceded, consented, favored, suffered, chartered, accorded, let, indulged, privileged; see also APPROVED.— *Ant.* REFUSED, denied, prohibited.

perpendicular a. vertical, plumb, upright; see STRAIGHT 1.

perpetrate v. commit, act, do; see PERFORM 1.

perpetual a. 1 [Never stopping] continuous, unceasing, constant; see ENDLESS. 2 [Continually repeating] repetitious, repeating, recurrent; see CONSTANT.

perpetually a. enduringly, permanently, unceasingly; see FOREVER.

perplex v. puzzle, confound, bewilder; see CONFUSE.

perplexed a. troubled, uncertain, bewildered; see DOUBTFUL.

perplexing a. bewildering, confusing, mystifying; see DIFFICULT 2.

per se a. as such, intrinsically, alone, singularly, fundamentally, in essence, in itself, by itself, virtually; see also ESSENTIALLY.

persecute v. afflict, harass, victimize; see ABUSE.

persecution n. torture, torment, teasing, provoking; see also ABUSE.

perseverance n. grit, resolution, pluck; see DETERMINATION.

persevere v. persist, remain, pursue; see ENDURE 1.

persist v. persevere, keep on, insist; see CONTINUE 1, ENDURE 1.

persistence n. constancy, resolution, stamina; see ENDURANCE.

persistent a. tenacious, steadfast, determined; see RESOLUTE.

person n. 1 [An individual] human being, child, adult, someone, somebody, self, oneself, I, me, soul, spirit, character, individuality, personage, personality, identity; see also MAN 2, WOMAN 1. 2 [An individual enjoying distinction] distinguished person, personality, success; see CHARACTER 4. 3 [Bodily form] physique, frame, form; see BODY 1. **—in person** personally, in the flesh, present; see NEAR 1.

personable a. agreeable, pleasant, attractive; see CHARMING.

personage n. human being, someone, individual; see MAN 2, PERSON 1.

personal a. 1 [Private] secluded, secret, intimate; see PRIVATE. 2 [Individual] own, peculiar, particular; see INDIVIDUAL, SPECIAL. 3 [Pertaining to one's person] fleshly, corporeal, corporal; see BODILY.

personality n. 1 [The total of one's

nature] self, oneself, being; see CHARACTER 2. 2 [Individual characteristics] disposition, nature, temper; see CHARACTER 1. 3 [A notable person] celebrity, star, personage; see CHARACTER 4.

personally a. 1 [Viewed in a personal manner] individually, privately, by oneself. 2 [From the point of view of the speaker] for me, myself, for myself, for my part, as I see it, according to my opinion; see also INDIVIDUALLY.—*Ant.* CERTAINLY, objectively, scientifically.

personify v. 1 [To impersonate] represent, live as, act out; see IMPERSONATE. 2 [To represent] copy, symbolize, exemplify; see REPRESENT 3.

personnel n. workers, employees, group; see STAFF 2.

perspective n. aspect, attitude, outlook; see VIEWPOINT.

perspiration n. water, exudation, beads of moisture; see SWEAT.

perspire v. secrete, exude, lather; see SWEAT.

persuade v. convince, move, induce, assure, cajole, incline, talk someone into something, win over, bring around, lead to believe, lead to do something, gain the confidence of, prevail upon, overcome another's resistance, wear down, bring a person to his or her senses, win an argument, make one's point, gain the confidence of, make someone see the light; see also INFLUENCE.—*Ant.* NEGLECT, dissuade, dampen.

persuaded a. convinced, won over, moved to, influenced, motivated, lured, impelled, wheedled, having succumbed to pressure, brought to see the light.

persuasion n. 1 [The act of persuading] inducing, influencing, enticing; see INFLUENCE. 2 [A belief] creed, tenet, religion; see FAITH.

persuasive a. convincing, alluring, luring, seductive, influential, winning, enticing, impelling, moving, actuating, efficient, effective, effectual, compelling, touching, forceful, potent, powerful, pointed, strong, energetic, forcible, plausible, inveigling; see also CONVINCING.

pertain v. relate to, belong to, refer to; see CONCERN 1.

pertaining to a. belonging to, appropriate to, connected with, having to do with.

pertinence n. consistency, congruity, relevance; see IMPORTANCE.

pertinent a. appropriate, suitable, related; see RELEVANT.

perturb v. pester, worry, irritate; see BOTHER 2.

perturbed a. uneasy, anxious, restless; see TROUBLED.

pervade v. suffuse, permeate, spread through; see PENETRATE.

perverse a. wayward, delinquent, capricious; see BAD 1.

perversion n. 1 [A distortion] involution, regression, abuse; see CONTORTION. 2 [Sexual deviation] corruption, debasement, depravity, wickedness, depredation, degeneration, degradation, bestiality, vice; see also LEWDNESS.

pervert n. sex maniac, sex criminal, rapist, molester, sodomizer, deviant, pederast, lecher.

pervert v. ruin, vitiate, divert; see CORRUPT.

perverted a. distorted, deviating, corrupt; see BAD 1.

pessimism n. doubt, cynicism, lack of hope; see DEPRESSION 2, GRIEF, SADNESS.

pessimistic a. 1 [Discouraging] worrisome, bleak, troubling; see DISMAL. 2 [Inclined to a discouraging view] hopeless, gloomy, cynical; see SAD 1.

pest n. 1 [Anything destructive] virus, germ, insect, bug, harmful bird, bird of prey, destructive animal. *Common pests include the following:* housefly, mosquito, flea, louse, mite, gnat, bedbug, tick, aphid, Japanese beetle, corn borer, boll weevil, squash bug, gypsy moth, cutworm, ant, wasp, meal moth, slug, snail, skunk, mouse, rat, gopher, prairie dog, woodchuck, groundhog, rabbit, mole, weasel, coyote, hawk. 2 [A nuisance] bore, tease, annoyance; see TROUBLE 1.

pester v. annoy, harass, provoke; see BOTHER 2.

pestilence n. epidemic, plague, sickness; see ILLNESS 1.

pet n. 1 [A term of endearment] lover, dear, love; see DARLING. 2 [Favorite] darling, idol, adored one; see FAVORITE. 3 [A creature kept as an object of affection] *Common pets include the following:* pony, dog, cat, horse, goldfish, rabbit, hamster, guinea pig, mouse, canary, parrot, parakeet, tropical fish, turtle, gerbil.

pet v. 1 [To caress] fondle, cuddle, pat; see TOUCH 1. 2 [*To make love] embrace, hug, neck*; see CARESS, KISS, LOVE 2.

petal n. flower part, bract, colored leaflike structure; see FLOWER.

petition n. prayer, request, supplication; see APPEAL 1.

petrified a. stone, hardened, mineralized; see FIRM 2.

petrify v. mineralize, clarify, solidify; see HARDEN.

petroleum n. crude oil, fuel, oil; see OIL.

petty a. small, insignificant, frivolous; see TRIVIAL, UNIMPORTANT.

phantom n. apparition, specter, shade; see GHOST.

phase n. condition, stage, appearance, point, aspect; see also STATE 2.

phase out v. slowly get rid of, gradually dispose of, weed out*; see ELIMINATE.

phenomenal a. extraordinary, unique, remarkable; see UNUSUAL 1.

phenomenon n. fact, experience, happening; see EVENT.

philanthropic a. kindhearted, benevolent, humanitarian; see HUMANE, KIND.

philosopher n. logician, wise person, wise man, thinker, scholar, sage, savant, Sophist, Solon. *Major philosophers include the following:* Socrates, Epicurus, Plato, Aristotle, Marcus Aurelius, Plotinus, St. Augustine, St. Thomas Aquinas, Thomas Hobbes, René Descartes, Baruch Spinoza, Gottfried Wilhelm von Leibniz, John Locke, George Berkeley, David Hume, Jean Jacques Rousseau, Immanuel Kant, G.W.F. Hegel, Arthur Schopenhauer, John Stuart Mill, Søren Kierkegaard, Karl Marx, Friedrich Nietzsche, William James, Martin Heidegger, Ludwig Wittgenstein, Jean-Paul Sartre.

philosophical a. 1 [Given to thought] reflective, cogitative, rational; see THOUGHTFUL 1. 2 [Embodying deep thought] erudite, thoughtful, deep; see LEARNED 1, PROFOUND.

philosophize v. ponder, weigh, deliberate; see THINK 1.

philosophy n. 1 [The study of knowledge] theory, reasoned doctrine, explanation of phenomena, logical concept, systematic view, theory of knowledge, early science, natural philosophy; see also KNOWLEDGE 1. *Fields of philosophy include the following:* aesthetics, logic, ethics, metaphysics, cosmology, epistemology, axiology, ontology. *Philosophic attitudes include the following:* idealism, realism, empiricism, existentialism, nihilism, transcendentalism, mechanism, naturalism, determinism, intuitionism, utilitarianism, nominalism, conceptualism, pragmatism, Kantianism, Hegelianism, absolutism, logical positivism. 2 [A fundamental principle] truth, axiom, conception; see BASIS, LAW 4, THEORY 1. 3 [A personal attitude or belief] outlook, view, position; see BELIEF, OPINION 1, VIEWPOINT.

phlegm n. spittle, sputum, mucus; see SALIVA.

phobia n. fear, neurosis, aversion; see HATRED, RESENTMENT.

phone n. pay phone, home phone,

wall phone, desk phone, car phone, cellular phone, cellphone, cordless phone, speakerphone, fax; see also TELEPHONE.

phony* a. counterfeit, imitation, artificial; see FALSE 3.

photograph n. photo, print, portrait, image, likeness, snapshot, microcopy, microfilm, radiograph, X-ray, photomontage, photomural, electronic image, shot, pic*, close-up, candid; see also PICTURE 2, 3.

photograph v. take a picture, get a likeness, film, copy, reproduce, illustrate, make an exposure, make a picture, record, make a movie, microfilm, snap, shoot, get a close-up.

photographer n. picture-taker, cameraman, cinematographer; see ARTIST.

photographic a. **1** [Of photography] camera, video, film, cinematographic. **2** [Precise] exact, accurate, detailed; see GRAPHIC 1.

photography n. picture-taking, portrait photography, landscape photography, aerial photography, tactical photography, candid photography, microphotography, digital photography, photomicrography, videotaping.

phrase n. group of words, expression, slogan, catchword, maxim, word group. *Grammatical phrases include the following:* prepositional, participial, infinitive, noun, adjective, adverb, verb, restrictive, nonrestrictive.

phraseology n. style, manner, idiom; see DICTION.

physical a. **1** [Concerning matter] material, corporeal, visible, tangible, environmental, palpable, substantial, natural, concrete; see also REAL 2. **2** [Concerning the body] corporal, corporeal, fleshly; see BODILY. **3** [Concerning physics] mechanical, motive, electrical, sonic, vibratory, vibrational, thermal, radioactive, atomic, relating to matter, dynamic.

physical n. examination, physical examination, exam, checkup.

physically a. corporally, really, actually; see BODILY.

physician n. practitioner, doctor of medicine, osteopath; see DOCTOR.

physicist n. biophysicist, geophysicist, nuclear physicist; see SCIENTIST.

physics n. natural philosophy, science of the material world, science of matter and motion; see SCIENCE 1. *Divisions of physics include the following:* electronics, thermodynamics, acoustics, mechanics, dynamics, kinetics, optics, geophysics, spectroscopy, pneumatics, hydraulics, aerophysics, astrophys-

ics, nuclear physics, theoretical physics, chaos theory.

physiology n. study of bodily processes, study of organic functions, biology; see SCIENCE 1.

physique n. build, structure, frame; see BODY 1.

pianist n. keyboardist, piano player, virtuoso; see MUSICIAN.

piano n. grand, baby grand, upright, pianoforte, concert grand, spinet, clavichord, harpsichord, keyboard, electric piano, synthesizer, player piano; see also MUSICAL INSTRUMENT.

picayune a. trivial, petty, small; see TRIVIAL, UNIMPORTANT.

pick n. **1** [An implement for picking] pickax, mattock, ice pick; see TOOL 1. **2** [A blow with a pointed instrument] peck, nip, dent; see BLOW. **3** [A selection] choice, election, preference; see CHOICE.

pick v. **1** [To choose] select, pick out, separate; see CHOOSE. **2** [To gather] pluck, pull, harvest; see ACCUMULATE. **3** [To use a pointed instrument] dent, indent, strike; see HIT 1. —**pick a fight** provoke, start, foment; see FIGHT. —**pick off** knock out, get, shoot; see KILL 1. —**pick out** select, make a choice of, notice; see CHOOSE. —**pick up** **1** [To acquire incidentally] happen upon, find, secure; see GET 1. **2** [To take up in the hand or arms] lift, elevate, hold up; see RAISE 1. **3** [To receive] get, take, acquire; see RECEIVE 1. **4** [To increase] improve, do better, grow; see INCREASE. **5** [To improve physically] get better, get well, recover health; see RECOVER 3. **6** [*To call for] stop for, bring along, go to get, accompany, get; see also INVITE.

picked a. elite, special, exclusive; see EXCELLENT.

picket n. **1** [A stake] stake, pole, pillar; see POST. **2** [A watchman] patrolman, guard, union member, scout, lookout, sentry.

picket v. **1** [To strike] walk out, blockade, boycott; see STRIKE 2. **2** [To enclose] imprison, fence, corral; see ENCLOSE.

pickings n. profits, earnings, proceeds; see BOOTY.

pickle n. **1** [A relish] *Varieties of pickles include the following:* cucumber, beet, green tomato, dill, bread-and-butter, sweet, gherkin, kosher, mustard, garlic, sour, pickled peppers, pickled beans, pickled apricots, pickled watermelon rind, piccalilli, chutney, spiced currants, beet relish, chili sauce, catsup, ketchup, pickle relish, kimchi. **2** [*A troublesome situation] disorder, dilemma, evil plight; see DIFFICULTY 2.

pickpocket *n.* petty criminal, thief, purse snatcher; see CRIMINAL, ROBBER.

picnic *n.* barbecue, cookout, fish fry; see MEAL 2.

pictorial *a.* **1** [Having the quality of a picture] picturesque, scenic, striking; see GRAPHIC 1. **2** [Making use of pictures] detailed, embellished, illustrated; see DESCRIPTIVE.

picture *n.* **1** [A scene before the eye or the imagination] spectacle, panorama, pageant; see VIEW. **2** [A human likeness] portrait, representation, photo, photograph, snapshot, cartoon, image, sketch, caricature, effigy, statue, statuette, figure, icon, figurine, close-up. **3** [A pictorial representation] illustration, engraving, etching, woodcut, outline, cartoon, draft, hologram, fax, graph, halftone, still, ad*, crayon sketch, pastel, watercolor, poster, oil, chart, map, mosaic, blueprint, advertisement, facsimile, animation, tracing, photograph, lithograph, print; see also DESIGN, DRAWING, PAINTING 1. *Types of pictures, as works of art, include the following:* landscape, seascape, genre painting, cityscape, historical work, religious work, battle scene, triumphal entry, detail, icon, illumination, miniature, portrait, illustration, self-portrait, nude, fresco, mural, collage, cameo, figure, still life, photomural, poster, photomontage. **4** [A motion picture] cinema, film, show; see MOVIE. **5** [A description] depiction, delineation, portrayal; see DESCRIPTION. **6** [Adequate comprehension; *usually with* "the"] idea, understanding, survey; see KNOWLEDGE 1.

picture *v.* **1** [To depict] sketch, delineate, portray; see DRAW 2. **2** [To imagine] envision, think of, conceive; see IMAGINE.

picturesque *a.* pictorial, scenic, graphic, striking, arresting.

pie *n. Varieties of pies include the following—meat pies:* fish, chicken pot, lamb, pork, beef, steak-and-kidney, shepherd's; pasty; *Other savory pies:* spinach pie, calzone, pizza, quiche; *dessert pies:* apple, banana cream, chiffon, apricot, peach, pumpkin, raisin, custard, coconut cream, pecan, chess, rhubarb, chocolate cream, lemon meringue, key lime, mince, mincemeat, cherry, blueberry, strawberry, strawberry cream, butterscotch, plum; see also DESSERT. **—as easy as pie*** not difficult, simple, uncomplicated; see EASY 2.

piece *n.* **1** [Part] portion, share, section; see PART 1. **2** [Work of art] study, composition, creation; see ART. **3** [Musical, literary, or theatrical composition] suite, orchestra-

tion, production, opus, aria, song, study, arrangement, treatise, exposition, sketch, play, novel, discourse, discussion, treatment, essay, article, paper, memoir, homily, poem, theme, monograph, commentary, review, paragraph, critique, play, drama, melodrama, pageant, monologue, opera, overture, prelude, étude, ballet. **—go to pieces 1** come apart, break up, fail; see BREAK DOWN 2. **2** quit, collapse, lose control; see CRY 1, WORRY 2. **—in pieces** shattered, damaged, busted*; see BROKEN 1, DESTROYED, RUINED 1, 2. **—piece together** combine, make, create; see ASSEMBLE 2. **—speak one's piece** air one's opinions, talk, reveal; see TELL 1.

pier *n.* wharf, landing, quay; see DOCK.

pierce *v.* break into, stab, intrude; see PENETRATE.

piercing *a.* **1** [Shrill] deafening, ear-splitting, sharp; see LOUD 1, SHRILL. **2** [Penetrating] entering, boring, puncturing; see SHARP 1.

piety *n.* reverence, duty, zeal; see DEVOTION.

pig *n.* piglet, sow, shoat; see ANIMAL, HOG 1.

pigeon *n.* dove, homing pigeon, turtledove; see BIRD.

piggish *a.* selfish, dirty, ravenous; see GREEDY.

pigheaded *a.* recalcitrant, insistent, obstinate; see STUBBORN.

pigment *n.* paint, coloring matter, dye; see COLOR.

pigskin* *n.* regulation football, the ball, the sphere*; see FOOTBALL.

pigtail *n.* plait, hairdo, braid; see HAIR 1.

piker* *n.* tightwad*, skinflint, cheapskate*; see MISER.

pile *n.* heap, mass, quantity; see COLLECTION.

pile *v.* heap, stack, gather; see ACCUMULATE, STORE.

pilgrim *n.* wayfarer, wanderer, sojourner; see TRAVELER.

pilgrimage *n.* travel, wayfaring, trip; see JOURNEY.

pill *n.* **1** [A tablet] capsule, gelcap, caplet; see MEDICINE 2. **2** [*A contraceptive tablet; usually with* "the"] birth control pill, oral contraceptive, preventive; see DRUG.

pillage *v.* plunder, loot, rob; see DESTROY, STEAL.

pillar *n.* **1** [A column] pedestal, mast, shaft; see COLUMN 1, POST. **2** [A support] mainstay, reinforcement, buttress; see SUPPORT 2.

pillow *n.* feather pillow, down pillow, foam rubber cushion, pad, padding, rest, cushion, support, headrest.

pillowcase *n.* pillowslip, pillow casing, pillow cover; see COVER 1.

pilot *n.* 1 [Flier] airman, fighter pilot, commercial pilot, bomber pilot, automatic pilot, navigator. 2 [Guide] scout, leader, director; see GUIDE.

pilot *v.* guide, conduct, manage; see LEAD 1.

pimp *n.* procurer, whoremonger, pander; see CRIMINAL.

pimple *n.* pustule, swelling, acne, whitehead, blackhead, inflammation, bump, lump, boil, carbuncle, blister, zit*; see also BLEMISH.

pin *n.* 1 [A device for fastening things by piercing or clasping] clip, catch, needle, bodkin, peg, clasp, nail, tack; see also FASTENER. *Pins include the following:* common, safety, straight, bobby, cotter pin; hatpin, hairpin, clothespin, push-pin. 2 [A piece of jewelry] tiepin, stickpin, brooch, badge, stud, sorority pin, fraternity pin, school pin; see also JEWELRY.

pin *v.* close, clasp, bind; see FASTEN.

pinch *n.* squeeze, compression, nip, nipping, grasp, grasping, pressure, cramp, contraction, confinement, limitation, hurt, torment. —**in a pinch** if necessary, in an emergency, under stress; see UNFORTUNATELY.

pinch *v.* 1 [To squeeze] nip, grasp, compress, press, cramp, grab, contract, confine, limit, torment; see also HURT 1. 2 [*To steal] take, rob, pilfer; see STEAL. 3 [*To arrest] apprehend, detain, hold; see ARREST.

pinch-hit *v.* replace, act for, succeed; see SUBSTITUTE.

pine *n. Pines include the following:* white, jack, bristlecone, nut, loblolly, ponderosa, red, yellow, pitch, sugar, longleaf, lodgepole, Scotch pine; balsam fir, piñon; see also TREE, WOOD 2.

pink *a.* rosy, reddish, pinkish, pale-red, salmon-colored, flesh-colored, flushed, ruddy.

pink *n.* rose, red, blush-rose, salmon, shocking pink, blushing pink; see also COLOR.

pinnacle *n.* zenith, crest, summit; see CLIMAX.

pioneer *a.* pioneering, initial, untried; see BRAVE, EARLY 1, EXPERIMENTAL.

pioneer *n.* 1 [One who prepares the way] pathfinder, scout, explorer; see GUIDE. 2 [One in the vanguard of civilization] early settler, colonist, pilgrim, immigrant, colonizer, homesteader, squatter.

pioneer *v.* discover, explore, found; see COLONIZE, ESTABLISH 2, SETTLE 1.

pious *a.* divine, holy, devout; see RELIGIOUS 2.

pipe *n.* 1 [A tube] pipeline, drain-

pipe, sewer, conduit, culvert, water pipe, aqueduct, trough, passage, duct, canal, vessel. 2 [A device for smoking] *Varieties of smoking pipes include the following:* meerschaum, corncob, Missouri meerschaum, bulldog pipe, briar pipe, clay pipe, hookah, water pipe, churchwarden, calabash, calumet, hash pipe*. 3 [A musical instrument] fife, flute, piccolo; see MUSICAL INSTRUMENT.

pipe down *v.* become quiet, hush, speak lower; see STOP 2.

piracy *n.* pillage, holdup, robbery; see CRIME, THEFT.

pirate *n.* thief, freebooter, plunderer, pillager, marauder, privateer, soldier of fortune, buccaneer, sea rover; see also CRIMINAL, ROBBER.

pistol *n.* revolver, automatic, six-shooter*, rod*, six-gun*, Saturday night special*, iron*, forty-five, thirty-eight; see also GUN, WEAPON.

pit *n.* abyss, cavity, depression; see HOLE 1.

pitch *n.* 1 [Slope] slant, incline, angle; see GRADE 1, INCLINATION 2. 2 [A throw] toss, fling, hurl, heave, cast, pitched ball, ball, strike, delivery, offering. 3 [Musical frequency] frequency of vibration, rate of vibration, tone; see SOUND 2. 4 [A viscous liquid] resin, gum resin, coal tar; see GUM, TAR.

pitch *v.* 1 [To throw] hurl, fling, toss; see THROW 1. 2 [To fall forward] plunge, flop, vault; see DIVE, FALL 1. 3 [To slope abruptly] rise, fall, tilt; see BEND, LEAN 1. —**pitch in*** volunteer, work, aid; see HELP. —**pitch into*** assault, blame, scold; see ATTACK, FIGHT.

pitcher *n.* 1 [A utensil for pouring liquid] cream pitcher, milk pitcher, water pitcher, ewer, jar, carafe, jug, vessel, amphora; see also CONTAINER. 2 [In baseball, one who pitches to the batter] right-hand pitcher, right-hander, left-hand pitcher, left-hander, southpaw*, lefty*, righty*, reliever*, fireballer*, hurler*, ace*.

pitchfork *n.* fork, hayfork, three-tined fork; see TOOL 1.

pitfall *n.* snare, pit, blind; see TRAP 1.

pitiful *a.* miserable, mournful, sorrowful, woeful, distressed, distressing, deplorable, cheerless, joyless, pitiable, piteous, forlorn, wretched, comfortless, dismal, touching, pathetic, affecting, stirring, lamentable, poignant, heartbreaking, human, dramatic, impressive, tearful, gratifying, heart-rending, depressing, afflicted, suffering, moving, vile; see also SAD 1.—*Ant.* HAPPY, cheerful, joyful.

pitiless *a.* unfeeling, heartless, cold; see INDIFFERENT.

pitter-patter *n.* thump, patter, tap; see NOISE 1.

pity *n.* sympathy, compassion, charity, softheartedness, tenderness, goodness, understanding, forbearance, mercy, kindness, warmheartedness, kindliness, brotherly love, unselfishness, benevolence, favor, condolence, commiseration, clemency, humanity.—*Ant.* HATRED, severity, ferocity. —**have** (or **take**) **pity on** show pity to, spare, pardon; see FORGIVE, PITY 2.

pity *v.* **1** [To feel pity] feel for, sympathize with, commiserate, be sorry for, bleed for, be sympathetic to, show sympathy for, grieve with, weep for; see also COMFORT, SYMPATHIZE. **2** [To be merciful to] spare, take pity on, show pity to, show forgiveness to, be merciful to, give quarter, pardon, reprieve, grant amnesty to; see also FORGIVE.—*Ant.* DESTROY, condemn, accuse.

pivot *v.* whirl, swivel, rotate; see TURN 1.

place *n.* **1** [Position] station, point, spot; see POSITION 1. **2** [Space] room, compass, stead, void, distance, area, seat, volume, berth, reservation, accommodation; see also EXTENT. **3** [Locality] spot, locus, site, community, district, suburb, country, section, habitat, home, residence, abode, house, quarters; see also AREA, NEIGHBORHOOD, REGION 1. **4** [Rank] status, position, station; see RANK 3. —**go places*** attain success, achieve, advance; see SUCCEED 1. —**in place** in order, timely, appropriate; see FIT 1. —**in place of** as a substitute for, instead of, taking the place of; see INSTEAD. —**out of place** inappropriate, unsuitable, not fitting; see IMPROPER. —**put someone in his (or her) place** humiliate, reprimand, shame; see HUMBLE. —**take place** occur, come into being, be; see HAPPEN 2. —**take the place of** replace, act in one's stead, serve as proxy for; see SUBSTITUTE.

place *v.* **1** [To put in a place] locate, assign, deposit; see PUT 1. **2** [To put in order] fix, arrange, group; see ORDER 3.

placed *a.* established, settled, fixed, located, rated, deposited, lodged, quartered, planted, set, arranged, stowed, stored, installed, situated, implanted, set up, ordered.

placement *n.* situation, position, arrangement; see ORGANIZATION 1.

plagiarism *n.* literary theft, forgery, fraud; see THEFT.

plague *n.* epidemic, pestilence, disease; see ILLNESS 2.

plague *v.* disturb, trouble, irk; see BOTHER 2.

plain *a.* **1** [Obvious] open, manifest, clear; see OBVIOUS 1, 2, UNDERSTANDABLE. **2** [Simple] unadorned, unostentatious, unpretentious; see MODEST 2. **3** [Ordinary] everyday, average, commonplace; see COMMON 1. **4** [Homely] plain-featured, coarse-featured, unattractive; see UGLY 1. **5** [In blunt language] outspoken, candid, impolite; see RUDE 2.

plain *n.* prairie, steppe, pampas, expanse, open country, lowland, flat, level land, mesa, savanna, moorland, moor, heath, tundra, veldt, downs; see also FIELD 1, MEADOW.

plainly *a.* obviously, evidently, visibly; see CLEARLY 1, 2.

plan *n.* **1** [A preliminary sketch] draft, diagram, map, chart, timeline, design, outline, representation, form, drawing, view, projection, blueprint, rough draft, road map. **2** [A proposed sequence of action] plans, scheme, project, flowchart, outline, idea, handling, projection, undertaking, method, design, tactics, procedure, treatment, intention, policy, course of action, plot, conspiracy, expedient, strategy, stratagem, arrangement, way of doing things, angle*, the picture; see also PROGRAM 2, PURPOSE 1. **3** [Arrangement] layout, method, disposition; see ORDER 3. —**lay plans (for)** draft, design, think out; see FORM 1, INTEND 1, PLAN 2.

plan *v.* **1** [To plot an action in advance] prepare, scheme, devise, invent, outline, project, contrive, shape, design, map, plot a course, form a plan, think out, concoct, engineer, figure on, intrigue, conspire, frame, steer one's course, establish guidelines, set parameters, work up, work out, line up, plan an attack, come through, calculate on, make arrangements, take measures, bargain for, cook up*, put on ice*. **2** [To arrange in a preliminary way] outline, draft, sketch, lay out, map out, preprint, organize, prepare a sketch, chart, map, draw, trace, design, illustrate, depict, delineate, represent, shape, chalk out, rough in, block out, block in. **3** [To have in mind] propose, think, contemplate; see INTEND 1.

plane *n.* **1** [A plane surface] level, extension, horizontal, flat, face, stratum. **2** [A tool for smoothing wood] electric planer, jointer, block plane; see TOOL 1. **3** [An airplane] aircraft, airliner, aeroplane, airship, heavier-than-air craft, shuttle, jet, jet plane. *Kinds of planes include the following:* propeller, jet, rocket, scout, observation, reconnaissance, transport, commercial, passenger;

biplane, triplane, monoplane, racer, glider, bomber, seaplane, hydroplane, fighter, fighter-bomber, interceptor, turbojet, stratojet, helicopter, gunship, amphibian, sailplane.

plane *v.* finish, smooth, level; see FLATTEN.

planet *n.* celestial body, heavenly body, luminous body, wandering star, planetoid, asteroid, star*. *The known planets are as follows:* Mercury, Venus, Earth, Mars, Jupiter, Saturn, Uranus, Neptune, Pluto, the asteroids.

plank *n.* board, planking, sheet; see LUMBER.

planned *a.* projected, budgeted, in the budget, provided for, on the drawing board, programmed, in the making, under consideration, on the docket, prospective, cut and dried, under advisement, prepared.

plant *n.* shrub, weed, bush, slip, shoot, cutting, sprout, seedling, plantlet, bulb, flower, tree, herb, grass, mushroom, fungus, moss, alga, seaweed.

plant *v.* put in the ground, sow, farm, set out, pot, start, transplant, seed, stock, colonize, settle, establish, locate.

plantation *n.* hacienda, estate, ranch; see FARM.

planted *a.* cultivated, sown, seeded, stocked, implanted, strewn, drilled.

plaster *n.* mortar, binding, plaster of Paris; see CEMENT.

plaster *v.* coat, bind, cement; see COVER 1.

plastic *a.* substitute, synthetic, cellulose; see SYNTHETIC.

plastic *n.* synthetic, artificial product, substitute, plastic material, processed material, polymerized substance, thermoplastic, cellophane, polyester, polystyrene, acrylic, polyethylene, acetate, celluloid, melamine, vinyl, nylon, PVC. *Trademarked plastics:* Neoprene, Orlon, Plexiglas, Lucite, Formica, Teflon, Styrofoam.

plate *n.* 1 [A flat surface] lamina, slice, stratum; see PLANE 1. 2 [A full-page illustration] photograph, lithograph, etching; see ILLUSTRATION, PICTURE 3. 3 [A flattish dish] dinner plate, soup plate, salad plate, casserole, dessert plate, platter, trencher, china, serving dish; see also DISH 1. 4 [Food served on a plate] helping, serving, course; see MEAL 2. 5 [In baseball, the base immediately in front of the catcher] home base, home plate, home; see BASE 4.

plate *v.* laminate, stratify, layer, scale, flake, overlay, gild, nickel, bronze, chrome, silver, enamel, encrust, cover.

plateau *n.* tableland, mesa, elevation; see HILL, PLAIN.

platform *n.* 1 [A stage] dais, pulpit, speaker's platform, rostrum, stand, floor, staging, terrace. 2 [A program] principles, policies, the party planks*; see PROGRAM 2.

platoon *n.* detachment, military unit, company; see ARMY 2.

platter *n.* tray, serving dish, meat platter; see DISH 1, PLATE 3.

plausible *a.* probable, credible, believable; see LIKELY 1.

play *n.* 1 [Amusement] enjoyment, diversion, pleasure; see ENTERTAINMENT. 2 [Recreation] relaxation, game, sport; see ENTERTAINMENT. 3 [Fun] frolic, happiness, sportiveness; see FUN. 4 [A drama] performance, musical, show; see DRAMA. 5 [Sport] exhibition, match, competition; see SPORT 1, 3. 6 [Action] activity, movement, working; see ACTION 1. —**make a play for*** make advances to, court, try to attract; see TRY 1.

play *v.* 1 [To amuse oneself] entertain oneself, revel, make merry, carouse, play games, rejoice, have a good time, idle away, horse around*.—*Ant.* MOURN, grieve, sulk. 2 [To frolic] frisk, sport, cavort, dance, play games, make jokes, be a practical joker, show off, jump about, skip, gambol, caper.—*Ant.* DRAG, mope, droop. 3 [To produce music] perform, execute, work, cause to sound, finger, pedal, bow, plunk, tinkle, pipe, toot, blow, pump, fiddle, sound, strike, scrape, twang, pound, thump, shake, beat, pluck, clash. 4 [To engage in sport] participate, engage, practice; see COMPETE. 5 [To pretend] imagine, suppose, think; see PRETEND 1. —**play down** belittle, hold back, minimize; see RESTRAIN.

player *n.* 1 [One who takes part in a game] team member, athlete, sportsman, sportswoman, amateur, professional, gymnast, acrobat, swimmer, diver, trackman, champ*, pro*, semipro*, jock*; see also CONTESTANT. 2 [An actor] performer, entertainer, thespian; see ACTOR, ACTRESS.

playful *a.* joking, whimsical, comical; see FUNNY 1.

playground *n.* playing field, park, school ground, municipal playground, yard, schoolyard, diamond, gridiron.

playmate *n.* schoolmate, neighbor, companion; see FRIEND.

plaything *n.* gadget, amusement, trinket; see DOLL, GAME 1, TOY 1.

playwright *n.* scriptwriter, dramatist, tragedian; see AUTHOR, WRITER.

plea *n.* 1 [An appeal] overture, request, supplication; see APPEAL 1. 2 [A form of legal defense] pleading, argument, case; see DEFENSE 2.

plead *v.* 1 [To beg] implore, beseech, solicit; see ASK, BEG. 2 [To enter a plea] present, allege, cite; see DECLARE. —**plead guilty** confess, repent, concede; see ADMIT 1.

pleading *a.* imploring, supplicating, desirous.

pleasant *a.* 1 [Affable] agreeable, attractive, obliging, charming, mild, amusing, kindly, mild-mannered, gracious, genial, amiable, polite, urbane, cheerful, sympathetic, civil, cordial, engaging, social, bland, diplomatic, civilized, good-humored, good-natured, soft, fun, delightful, jovial, jolly.—*Ant.* SULLEN, unsympathetic, unkind. 2 [Giving pleasure; *said of occasions, experiences, and the like*] gratifying, pleasurable, agreeable, cheering, amusing, welcome, refreshing, satisfying, all right, satisfactory, adequate, acceptable, comfortable, diverting, fascinating, adorable, enjoyable, delightful, sociable, lively, exciting, glad, festive, cheerful, entertaining, relaxing, joyous, joyful, merry, happy, pleasing, favorable, bright, sunny, brisk, sparkling, enlivening, colorful, light, humorous, comforting.—*Ant.* SAD, disagreeable, unhappy.

pleasantly *a.* pleasingly, charmingly, welcomely; see AGREEABLY.

please *interj.* if you please, if it pleases you, may it please you, by your leave.

please *v.* 1 [To give pleasure] gratify, satisfy, make up to; see ENTERTAIN. 2 [To desire] wish, demand, command; see WANT 1. —**if you please** if you will, if I may, by your leave; see PLEASE *interj.*

pleased *a.* gratified, satisfied, charmed; see HAPPY.

pleasing *a.* charming, agreeable, delightful; see PLEASANT 1.

pleasure *n.* 1 [Enjoyment] bliss, delight, ease; see HAPPINESS. 2 [Will] want, preference, wish; see DESIRE 1.

pleat *n.* pleating, tuck, crease; see FOLD.

pleat *v.* ruffle, crease, gather; see FOLD.

pledge *n.* guarantee, token, agreement; see PROMISE 1.

pledge *v.* swear, vow, declare; see PROMISE.

plentiful *a.* 1 [Bountiful] prolific, fruitful, profuse, lavish, liberal, unsparing, inexhaustible, replete, generous, abundant, extravagant, improvident, excessive, copious, superabundant, overliberal, superfluous, overflowing, flowing.—*Ant.* STINGY, niggardly, skimpy. 2 [Existing in plenty] sufficient, abundant, copious, ample, overflowing, large, chock-full, teeming, unlimited, well-provided, flowing, full, flush, lush with, pouring, fruitful, swarming, swimming, abounding.—*Ant.* POOR, scant, scanty.

plenty *n.* abundance, fruitfulness, fullness, lavishness, deluge, torrent, bounty, profusion, adequacy, flood, avalanche, limit, capacity, adequate stock, enough and to spare, everything, all kinds of, all one wants, all one can eat and drink, more than one knows what to do with, too much of a good thing, a good bit, all one needs, all one can use, a great deal, a lot*, lots*, oodles*.

pliable *a.* limber, supple, plastic; see FLEXIBLE.

pliant *a.* limber, supple, plastic; see FLEXIBLE.

pliers *n.* pinchers, wrench, pincers, tongs, forceps, tweezers.

plod *v.* trudge, hike, plug; see WALK 1.

plop *v.* thump, thud, bump; see SOUND.

plot *n.* 1 [An intrigue] conspiracy, scheme, artifice; see TRICK 1. 2 [The action of a story] plan, scheme, outline, design, development, progress, unfolding, movement, climax, events, incidents, suspense, structure, buildup, scenario. 3 [A piece of ground] parcel, land, division; see AREA, LOT 1.

plot *v.* 1 [To devise an intrigue] frame, contrive, scheme; see PLAN 1. 2 [To plan] sketch, outline, draft; see PLAN 2.

plow *n. Plows include the following:* moldboard, gang, steam, tractor, double, straddle, sulky, wheel, shovel, hand; lister, hoe plow or horse-hoe, garden plow or wheel hoe, (corn) cultivator; see also TOOL 1.

plow *v.* 1 [To use a plow] break, furrow, cultivate, turn, plow up, turn over, till, ridge, break ground, do the plowing; see also FARM. 2 [To act like a plow] smash into, rush through, shove apart; see DIG 1, PUSH 1.

plug *n.* 1 [An implement to stop an opening] cork, stopper, stopple, filling, bung, lid, wedge. 2 [An electrical fitting] attachment plug, fitting, connection, wall plug, floor plug, plug fuse. 3 [A large pipe with a discharge valve] water plug, fire hydrant, fire plug; see PIPE 1.

plug *v.* stop, fill, obstruct, secure, ram, make tight, drive in; see also STOP 2.

plum *n. Plums and plumlike fruits*

include the following: freestone, damson, greengage, Reine Claude, sugarplum, French prune, Stanley prune; see also FRUIT.

plumber *n.* steamfitter, metalworker, handyman; see WORKMAN.

plumbing *n.* pipes, water pipes, sewage pipes, heating pipes, bathroom fixtures, sanitary provisions; see also PIPE 1.

plummet *v.* plunge, fall, nose-dive; see DIVE, FALL 1.

plump *a.* obese, stout, fleshy; see FAT.

plunder *v.* burn, steal, lay waste; see RAID, RAVAGE.

plunge *v.* fall, throw oneself, rush; see DIVE, JUMP 1.

plural *a.* more than one, a number of, abundant; see MANY.

plurality *n.* majority, advantage in votes cast, greater amount; see LEAD 1, MAJORITY 1.

plus *a., prep.* added to, additional, additionally, increased by, with the addition of, surplus, positive; see also EXTRA.—*Ant.* LESS, minus, subtracted from.

plush* *a.* elegant, luxurious, sumptuous; see RICH 2.

PM or **P.M.** *abbrev.* post meridiem, postmeridian, after noon, afternoon, evening, before midnight, shank of the evening, sunset.

pneumonia *n.* pneumonitis, lung inflammation, lung infection; see ILLNESS 2.

poach *v.* filch, pilfer, smuggle; see STEAL.

pock *n.* flaw, hole, mark; see BLEMISH, SCAR.

pocket *a.* small, tiny, miniature; see LITTLE 1, MINUTE 1.

pocket *n.* **1** [A cavity] hollow, opening, air pocket; see HOLE 1. **2** [A pouch sewn into a garment] pouch, bag, sac, pod. *Kinds of pockets include the following:* patch, slash, inset, watch, coin, invisible, pants, jacket, coat, vest, inner, outer, shirt. **3** [Small area] isolated group, enclave, survival; see AREA. —**in someone's pocket*** controlled, under control, regulated; see MANAGED.

pocket *v.* conceal, hide, enclose; see STEAL.

pocketbook *n.* wallet, pouch, coin purse; see BAG, PURSE.

pod *n.* seed vessel, bean pod, pea pod; see SEED.

poem *n.* poetry, lyric, sonnet, ballad, verse, quatrain, blank verse, free verse, song, composition, creation; see also WRITING 2.

poet *n.* writer, bard, versifier, minstrel, troubadour, maker of verses, lyrist, author of the lyric, dramatic poet, dramatist, lyric poet, writer of

lyrics, lyricist, poetaster; see also ARTIST, WRITER. *Major poets include the following:—British:* Geoffrey Chaucer, Edmund Spenser, William Shakespeare, John Donne, George Herbert, John Milton, Andrew Marvell, John Dryden, Alexander Pope, Robert Burns, William Blake, William Wordsworth, Samuel Taylor Coleridge, Lord Byron, John Keats, Percy Bysshe Shelley, John Clare, Alfred, Lord Tennyson, Robert Browning, Gerard Manley Hopkins, A.E. Housman, William Butler Yeats, T.S. Eliot, W.H. Auden, Dylan Thomas, Philip Larkin; *American:* Edgar Allan Poe, Walt Whitman, Emily Dickinson, Edwin Arlington Robinson, Robert Frost, Carl Sandburg, Ezra Pound, Wallace Stevens, E.E. Cummings, Robert Lowell, Marianne Moore; *Classical Greek:* Homer, Pindar, Aeschylus, Sophocles, Euripides; *Latin:* Virgil, Lucretius, Ovid, Horace, Catullus, Juvenal, Martial; *European:* Dante Alighieri, Petrarch, Ludovico Ariosto, François Villon, Jean de La Fontaine, Charles Baudelaire, Stéphane Mallarmé, Paul Verlaine, Arthur Rimbaud, Victor Hugo, Pedro Calderón, Federico García Lorca, Pablo Neruda, Luis Vaz de Camões, Wolfgang von Goethe, Friedrich Schiller, Heinrich Heine, Rainer Maria Rilke, Bertolt Brecht, Alexander Pushkin, Aleksandr Blok, Anna Akhmatova, Osip Mandelstam, Vladimir Mayakovski.

poetic *a.* poetical, lyric, lyrical, metrical, tuneful, elegiac, romantic, dramatic, iambic, dactylic, spondaic, trochaic, anapestic, imaginative, epic, rhapsodic.

poetry *n.* poem, song, versification, metrical composition, rime, rhyme, poesy, stanza, rhythmical composition, poetical writings. *Forms of verse include the following:* sonnet, Shakespearean sonnet, Petrarchan sonnet, Italian sonnet, Miltonic sonnet, Wordsworthian sonnet, Chaucerian stanza, Spenserian stanza, heroic couplet, Alexandrine, iambic pentameter, rhyme royal, ottava rima, couplet, distich, ode, epode, triolet, rondeau, rondel, rondelet, tanka, haiku, ballade, sestine, villanelle, limerick, blank verse, free verse, strophic verse, stanzaic verse, accentual verse, alliterative verse.

pogrom *n.* slaughter, mass murder, massacre, genocide; see also MURDER.

point *n.* **1** [A position or spot having no measurable extent] location, spot, locality; see POSITION 1. **2** [A sharp, tapered end] end, pointed end, needle point, pinpoint, barb, spur, spike, snag, spine, claw, tooth, calk, sticker; see also TIP 1. **3** [Anything having a point] sword, dagger, stiletto; see KNIFE, NEEDLE. **4** [Purpose] aim, object, intent; see PURPOSE 1. **5** [Meaning] force, drift, import; see MEANING. **6** [A detail] case, feature, point at issue; see CIRCUMSTANCE 1, DETAIL. **—at** (or **on**) **the point of** on the verge of, close to, almost; see NEAR 1. **—beside the point** immaterial, not pertinent, not germane; see IRRELEVANT. **—make a point of** stress, emphasize, make an issue of; see DECLARE. **—to the point** pertinent, apt, exact; see RELEVANT.

point v. **1** [To indicate] show, designate, denote; see NAME 2. **2** [To direct] guide, steer, influence; see LEAD 1. **—point out** indicate, show, denote; see NAME 2.

pointed a. **1** [Sharp] fine, keen, spiked; see SHARP 1. **2** [Biting or insinuating] caustic, tart, trenchant; see SARCASTIC.

pointer n. **1** [A pointing instrument] hand, rod, wand, baton, indicator, dial, gauge, index, mark, signal needle, register. **2** [A variety of dog] hunting dog, gun dog, game dog; see DOG. **3** [*A hint] clue, tip, warning; see HINT.

pointless a. **1** [Dull] uninteresting, prosaic, not pertinent; see IRRELEVANT, TRIVIAL, UNNECESSARY. **2** [Blunt] worn, obtuse, rounded; see DULL 1. **3** [Ineffective] useless, powerless, impotent; see INCOMPETENT, WEAK 1, 2.

point of view n. outlook, position, approach; see ATTITUDE.

poise n. balance, gravity, equilibrium; see COMPOSURE, DIGNITY.

poison n. virus, bane, toxin, infection, germ, bacteria, venom, oil, vapor, gas. *Poisons include the following:* rattlesnake, copperhead, black-widow-spider, tarantula venom; smallpox, yellow-fever, common-cold, flu virus; poison oak, poison ivy; carbon monoxide gas, cooking gas; arsenic, lead, strychnine; oxalic, sulfuric, hydrochloric, nitric, carbolic, prussic, hydrocyanic acid; cantharides, caustic soda, lye, belladonna, aconite, lead arsenate, blue vitriol or copper sulfate, nicotine.

poison v. infect, injure, kill, murder, destroy, corrupt, pervert, undermine, defile, harm, taint, make ill, cause violent illness in.—*Ant.* HELP, benefit, purify.

poisoned a. **1** [Suffering from poisoning] ill, indisposed, diseased; see SICK. **2** [Dying of poison] expiring, beyond recovery, succumbing; see DYING 1. **3** [Polluted with poison] contaminated, tainted, defiled, corrupted, venomous, virulent,

impure, malignant, noxious, deadly, toxic; see also POISONOUS.—*Ant.* PURE, fresh, untainted.

poisonous a. bad, noxious, hurtful, dangerous, malignant, infective, venomous, virulent, vicious, corrupt, morbid, fatal, pestilential, toxic, deadly, destructive; see also HARMFUL.—*Ant.* HEALTHY, wholesome, nourishing.

poke n. jab, thrust, punch; see BLOW.

poke v. jab, punch, crowd; see PUSH 1.

polar a. glacial, frozen, frigid; see COLD 1.

pole n. shaft, flagpole, flagstaff; see POST.

police n. law enforcement body, FBI, police officers, policemen, policewomen, police force, detective force, military police, Royal Canadian Mounted Police, New York's Finest*.

police v. watch, control, patrol; see GUARD.

police officer n. patrolman, patrolwoman, policeman, policewoman, officer, magistrate, process server, constable, cop*, copper*, flatfoot*, the fuzz*, the Man*, speed cop*, bobby*, pig*. *Police officers include the following:* beat patrolman, mounted police, motorcycle police, traffic police, squad-car police, municipal police, state police, highway patrol, detective, federal agent, federal investigator, fed*, narc*, FBI agent, prefect, inspector, member of the homicide squad, member of the vice squad.

police state n. dictatorship, autocracy, authoritarian government; see TYRANNY.

policy n. course, procedure, method, system, strategy, tactics, administration, management, theory, doctrine, behavior, scheme, design, arrangement, organization, plan, order.

polish n. shine, burnish, glaze; see FINISH 2.

polish v. buff, burnish, finish; see SHINE 3.

polished a. **1** [Bright] glossy, shining, gleaming; see BRIGHT 1. **2** [Refined] polite, well-bred, cultured; see REFINED 2.

polite a. obliging, thoughtful, mannerly, attentive, pleasant, gentle, mild, nice, concerned, considerate, solicitous, bland, condescending, honey-tongued, amiable, gracious, cordial, considerate, good-natured, sympathetic, interested, smooth, diplomatic, kindly, kind, kindly disposed, affable, agreeable, civil, ladylike, respectful, amenable, gallant, genteel, gentlemanly, mannered, sociable, ingratiating, neighborly,

friendly, respectful.—*Ant.* EGOTIS-
TIC, insolent, pompous.

politely *a.* thoughtfully, considerately, attentively, solicitously, cordially, graciously, kindheartedly,
amiably, compassionately, gently,
urbanely, affably, agreeably, civilly,
gallantly, sociably, elegantly, gracefully, charmingly, ingratiatingly,
winningly, tactfully, in good humor,
with good grace; see also RESPECT-
FULLY.

politeness *n.* refinement, culture,
civility; see COURTESY 1.

political *a.* legislative, executive,
administrative; see GOVERNMENTAL.

politician *n.* officeholder, office
seeker, party member, partisan, legislator, congressman, member of
parliament, politico.

politics *n.* practical government,
functional government, statesmanship, diplomacy, domestic affairs,
internal affairs, foreign affairs, matters of state, campaigning, getting
votes, seeking nomination, election-
eering, being up for election, running for office.

poll *n.* **1** [A census] vote, consensus,
ballot; see CENSUS. **2** [A voting
place; *usually plural*] ballot box,
voting machines, polling place, polling area.

poll *v.* question, register, survey; see
EXAMINE, LIST 1.

pollute *v.* contaminate, soil, stain;
see DIRTY, POISON.

polluted *a.* corrupted, defiled,
poisoned; see DIRTY 1.

pollution *n.* corruption, defilement,
adulteration, blight, soiling, fouling,
foulness, taint, tainting, polluting,
decomposition, desecration, profa-
nation, abuse, deterioration, rottenness, impairment, misuse, infection,
besmearing, besmirching, smirch-
ing. *Some common pollutants of the
air and water include the following:*
sewage, soapsuds, garbage, factory
waste, detergent, carbon monoxide,
automobile or bus or truck exhaust,
pesticides, factory smoke.

poltergeist *n.* spirit, spook, supernatural visitant; see GHOST.

polygamy *n.* polyandry, plural marriage, polygyny; see MARRIAGE.

pomp *n.* grandeur, affectation,
splendor; see MAGNIFICENCE.

pompous *a.* arrogant, haughty,
proud; see EGOTISTIC.

pond *n.* fishpond, millpond, lily
pond; see LAKE, POOL 1.

ponder *v.* meditate, deliberate, consider; see THINK 1.

ponderous *a.* dull, weighty, lifeless;
see HEAVY.

pony *n.* Shetland pony, bronco, mustang; see HORSE.

poodle *n.* French poodle, show dog,
fancy dog; see DOG.

pool *n.* **1** [Small body of liquid, usually water] puddle, mud puddle,
pond, fishpond, millpond, swimming
pool; see also LAKE. **2** [Supply]
resources, supplies, amount available; see FUNDS. **3** [Game] snooker,
eight ball, billiards; see GAME 1.

pool *v.* combine, merge, blend; see
JOIN 1.

poor *a.* **1** [Lacking worldly goods]
indigent, penniless, moneyless,
homeless, impecunious, destitute,
needy, poverty-stricken, underprivileged, fortuneless, starved, pinched,
reduced, beggared, empty-handed,
meager, scanty, insolvent, ill-pro-
vided, ill-furnished, in want, suffering privation, in need, poor as a
church mouse*, broke*, hard up*,
down and out.—*Ant.* WEALTHY, well-
to-do, affluent. **2** [Lacking excel-
lence] pitiful, paltry, contemptible,
miserable, pitiable, dwarfed, insignificant, diminutive, ordinary, common, mediocre, trashy, shoddy,
worthless, sorry, base, mean,
coarse, vulgar, inferior, imperfect,
smaller, lesser, below par, subnormal, below average; second-rate,
third-rate, fourth-rate, etc.;
reduced, defective, deficient, lower,
subordinate, minor, secondary,
humble, secondhand, pedestrian,
beggarly, tawdry, petty, unimportant, bad, cheap, flimsy, threadbare,
badly made, less than good,
unwholesome, lacking in quality,
dowdy, second-class, shabby, gaudy,
mass-produced, squalid, trivial,
sleazy, trifling, unsuccessful, sec-
ond-best, tasteless, insipid, rustic,
crude, odd, rock-bottom, garish,
flashy, showy, loud, unsightly,
affected, ramshackle, tumbledown,
glaring, artificial, newfangled, out-
of-date, crummy*, junky*, two-bit*,
raunchy*, corny*, cheesy*; see also
INADEQUATE, UNSATISFACTORY. **3**
[Lacking strength] puny, feeble,
infirm; see WEAK 1. **4** [Lacking vigor
or health] indisposed, impaired,
imperfect; see SICK. **5** [Lacking fer-
tility] infertile, unproductive, barren; see STERILE 1, 2, WORTHLESS.

poor *n.* the needy, forgotten man,
the unemployed, the homeless,
underdogs, the underprivileged,
beggars, paupers, the impoverished
masses, second-class citizen, have-
nots; see also PEOPLE 3.

poorly *a.* defectively, crudely, unsuccessfully; see BADLY 1, INAD-
EQUATELY.

pop *n.* **1** [A slight explosive sound]
report, burst, shot; see NOISE 1. **2** [A
carbonated drink] soda pop, ginger
ale, cola, tonic, root beer, soda, soda

water, beverage, soft drink; see also DRINK 2.

pop v. dart, leap, protrude; see JUMP 1.

Pope n. Pontiff, bishop of Rome, the Holy Father; see PRIEST.

poppy n. bloom, blossom, herb; see DRUG, FLOWER.

populace n. masses, citizenry, multitude; see MAN 1, PEOPLE 3.

popular a. 1 [Generally liked] favorite, well-liked, approved, pleasing, suitable, well-received, fashionable, stylish, beloved, likable, lovable, attractive, praised, promoted, recommended, in the public eye, celebrated, noted, admired, famous, run after*.—Ant. UNKNOWN, in disrepute, out of favor. 2 [Cheap] lowpriced, inexpensive, marked down; see CHEAP 1, ECONOMICAL 2. 3 [Commonly accepted] general, familiar, in demand, prevalent, prevailing, current, in use, widespread, ordinary, adopted, embraced, having caught on, in the majority; see also FASHIONABLE, MODERN 1. 4 [Pertaining to the common people] proletarian, accessible, neighborly; see DEMOCRATIC, REPUBLICAN.

popularity n. approval, general esteem, widespread acceptance, following, prevalence, universality, repute, fame, demand, fashionableness, the rage*.

popularly a. commonly, usually, ordinarily; see REGULARLY.

populated a. crowded, teeming, populous, peopled, urban, occupied, filled; see also INHABITED.

population n. inhabitants, dwellers, citizenry, natives, group, residents, culture, community, state, populace; see also SOCIETY 2.

porch n. entrance, doorstep, stoop; see ENTRANCE 2.

pore n. opening, foramen, orifice, vesicle; see also HOLE 1.

pork n. ham, bacon, chops; see MEAT.

pornographic a. immoral, dirty, obscene; see LEWD 2.

pornography n. vulgarity, obscenity, smut; see LEWDNESS.

porous a. pervious, permeable, acceptable; see OPEN 1.

port n. haven, anchorage, gate; see DOCK.

portable a. transportable, transferable, compact; see MOVABLE.

portal n. gateway, opening, ingress; see DOOR, ENTRANCE 2, GATE.

portfolio n. 1 [A flat container] briefcase, attaché case, folder; see BAG, CONTAINER. 2 [Assets, especially stocks and bonds] holdings, securities, documents; see WEALTH.

portion n. section, piece, part; see DIVISION 2, SHARE.

portrait n. likeness, portraiture, representation; see PAINTING 1, PICTURE 4.

portray v. depict, characterize, reproduce; see DESCRIBE, REPRESENT 2.

portrayal n. depiction, replica, likeness; see DESCRIPTION, IMITATION 2.

pose n. artificial position, affectation, mannerism; see FAKE, PRETENSE 1.

pose v. 1 [To pretend] play a part, claim falsely, make believe; see ACT 1, PRETEND 1. 2 [To assume a pose for a picture] model, adopt a position, adopt a stance; see SIT.

posh* a. elegant, stylish, opulent; see RICH 2, FASHIONABLE.

position n. 1 [A physical position] location, locality, spot, seat, ground, environment, post, whereabouts, bearings, station, point, stand, space, surroundings, situation, site, geography, region, tract, district, scene, setting; see also AREA, PLACE 3. 2 [An intellectual position] view, belief, attitude; see JUDGMENT 3, OPINION 1. 3 [An occupational position] office, employment, occupation; see JOB 1, PROFESSION 1. 4 [A social position] station, state, status; see RANK 3. 5 [Posture] pose, carriage, bearing; see POSTURE 1.

positive a. 1 [Definite] decisive, actual, concrete; see DEFINITE 1, REAL 2. 2 [Emphatic] peremptory, assertive, obstinate; see EMPHATIC, RESOLUTE. 3 [Certain] sure, convinced, confident; see CERTAIN 1.

positively a. 1 [In a positive manner] assertively, uncompromisingly, dogmatically, arbitrarily, stubbornly, obstinately, emphatically, dictatorially, imperatively, absolutely, insistently, authoritatively, assuredly, confidently, unhesitatingly, with conviction. 2 [Without doubt] undoubtedly, unmistakably, undeniably; see SURELY.

posse n. detachment, armed band, police force; see POLICE.

possess v. hold, occupy, control; see MAINTAIN 3, OWN 1.

possessed a. 1 [Insane] mad, crazed, violent; see INSANE. 2 [Owned] kept, enjoyed, in one's possession; see HELD, OWNED.

possession n. 1 [Ownership] proprietary rights, hold, mastery; see OWNERSHIP. 2 [Property] personal property, real estate, something possessed; see PROPERTY 1, 2.

possessions n. belongings, goods, effects; see ESTATE, PROPERTY 1.

possessor n. holder, proprietor, occupant; see OWNER.

possibility n. 1 [The condition of being possible] plausibility, feasibility, workableness; see CHANCE 2. **2** [A possible happening] hazard, chance, occasion, circumstance, hope, occurrence, hap, happening, outside chance, incident, instance; see also EVENT, OPPORTUNITY 1.

possible *a.* **1** [Within the realm of possibility] conceivable, imaginable, thinkable; see LIKELY 1. **2** [Acceptable] expedient, desirable, welcome; see PLEASANT 2. **3** [Contingent upon the future] indeterminate, fortuitous, adventitious; see LIKELY 1, UNCERTAIN.

possibly *a.* perhaps, by chance, potentially; see LIKELY 1, MAYBE, PROBABLY.

post *n.* prop, support, pillar, pedestal, stake, stud, upright, doorpost; see also COLUMN 1, MAST.

postcard *n.* postal card, note, picture postcard; see LETTER 2.

poster *n.* placard, bill, sign, banner, sheet, billboard, handbill, broadside; see also ADVERTISEMENT.

posterior *a.* **1** [Subsequent] coming after, succeeding, next; see FOLLOWING. **2** [Behind] in back, last, after; see BACK.

posterity *n.* descendants, offspring, children; see FAMILY, OFFSPRING.

postman *n.* mailman, letter carrier, postal employee; see WORKMAN.

post office *n.* postal substation, postal service, PO; see MAIL.

postpone *v.* defer, put off, hold over; see DELAY, SUSPEND 2.

postponed *a.* deferred, delayed, put off, set for a later time, to be done later, withheld, shelved, tabled, adjourned, suspended; see also LATE 1.

postponement *n.* respite, suspension, adjournment; see DELAY, PAUSE.

posture *n.* **1** [Stance] pose, carriage, demeanor, aspect, presence, condition. **2** [Attitude] way of thinking, point of view, sentiment; see ATTITUDE.

postwar *a.* peacetime, post-bellum, after the war, peaceful.

pot *n.* **1** [Container] vessel, kettle, saucepan, pan, jug, jar, mug, tankard, cup, can, crock, canister, receptacle, bucket, urn, pitcher, bowl, caldron, crucible, melting pot; see CONTAINER. **2** [*Marijuana] *cannabis sativa* (Latin), grass*, weed*; see DRUG.—**go to pot** deteriorate, go to ruin, fall apart; see SPOIL.

potato *n.* tuber, white potato, sweet potato, yam, new potato, redskin potato, spud*, tater*.

potency *n.* **1** [Strength] power, energy, vigor; see MANHOOD 2, STRENGTH. **2** [Authority] influence, control, dominion; see COMMAND, POWER 2.

potent *a.* **1** [Strong] vigorous, robust, sturdy; see STRONG 1, 2. **2** [Powerful] mighty, great, influential; see POWERFUL 1.

potential *a.* implied, inherent, dormant; see LIKELY 1.

potentially *a.* conceivably, imaginably, possibly; see LIKELY 1, MAYBE, PROBABLY.

potion *n.* dose, draft, liquor; see DRINK 1, LIQUID, MEDICINE 2.

pottery *n.* ceramics, porcelain, crockery, earthenware, clayware; see also UTENSILS.

pouch *n.* sack, receptacle, poke*; see BAG, CONTAINER.

poultry *n.* domesticated birds, pullets, barnyard fowls; see FOWL.

pounce *v.* bound, surge, dart; see DIVE, JUMP 1.

pound *n.* **1** [Measure of weight] sixteen ounces, Troy pound, avoirdupois pound, commercial pound, pint; see also MEASURE 1, WEIGHT 1. **2** [Kennel] coop, doghouse, cage; see PEN 1. **3** [British monetary unit] pound sterling, 100 pence, 20 shillings (formerly), quid*; see also MONEY 1.

pound *v.* strike, crush, pulverize; see BEAT 1, HIT 1.

pour *v.* **1** [To flow] discharge, emit, issue; see DRAIN 3, FLOW. **2** [To allow to flow] replenish with, spill, splash; see EMPTY 2. **3** [To rain heavily] stream, flood, drench; see RAIN.

pouring *a.* streaming, gushing, spouting, rushing, raining, flooding, showering, discharging, emitting, issuing, escaping, emanating, welling out, spurting, spilling, shedding, draining, running down, running out; see also FLOWING.

pout *v.* mope, brood, sulk; see FROWN.

poverty *n.* **1** [Want of earthly goods] destitution, pennilessness, penury, indigence, pauperism, want, need, insufficiency, starvation, famine, privation, insolvency, broken fortune, straits, scantiness, deficiency, meagerness, aridity, sparingness, stint, depletion, emptiness, vacancy, deficit, debt, wolf at the door*, pinch*, bite*, tough going*; see also LACK 1.—*Ant.* WEALTH, prosperity, comfort. **2** [Want of any desirable thing] shortage, inadequacy, scarcity; see LACK 1.

poverty-stricken *a.* penniless, broke, bankrupt; see POOR 1, WANTING 1.

powder *n.* particles, film, powderiness, explosive powder, medicinal powder, cosmetic powder; see also COSMETIC, EXPLOSIVE, MEDICINE 2.

powdery *a.* sandy, gravelly, dusty; see GRITTY.

power *n.* 1 [Strength] vigor, energy, stamina; see STRENGTH. 2 [Controlling sway] authority, command, jurisdiction, dominion, ascendency, superiority, domination, dominance, mastery, control, sway, sovereignty, hegemony, prerogative, prestige, omnipotence, supreme authority, the last word, rule, law, warrant, supremacy, legal sanction, government, say-so*; see also INFLUENCE, LEADERSHIP. 3 [Ability; *often plural*] skill, endowment, capability; see ABILITY. 4 [Force] compulsion, coercion, duress; see PRESSURE 2, RESTRAINT 2. 5 [Energy] horsepower, potential, dynamism; see ENERGY 2. —**in power** ruling, authoritative, commanding; see POWERFUL 1. —**(the) powers that be** management, higher authorities, higher-ups*; see ADMINISTRATION 2.

powerful *a.* 1 [Wielding power] mighty, all-powerful, almighty, superhuman, omnipotent, overpowering, great, invincible, dominant, influential, authoritative, overruling, potent, forceful, forcible, compelling, ruling, prevailing, preeminent, commanding, supreme, highest, important, authoritarian, ruthless, having the upper hand, in control.—*Ant.* WEAK, incompetent, impotent. 2 [Strong] robust, stalwart, sturdy; see STRONG 1, 2. 3 [Effective] efficacious, effectual, convincing; see PERSUASIVE.

powerfully *a.* forcibly, forcefully, effectively, severely, intensely, with authority; see also VIGOROUSLY.

powerless *a.* impotent, feeble, infirm; see WEAK 1, 2.

practical *a.* matter-of-fact, pragmatic, unimaginative, practicable, feasible, workable, functional, useful, sound, unromantic, soundthinking, down-to-earth, realistic, sensible, sane, reasonable, rational, to one's advantage, operative, utilitarian, possible, usable, serviceable, efficient, effective, working, in action, in operation, with both feet on the ground.—*Ant.* UNREAL, imaginative, impractical.

practically *a.* 1 [In a practical manner] unimaginatively, pragmatically, efficiently, functionally, sensibly, rationally, reasonably, realistically, with regard to use, feasibly; see also EFFECTIVELY. 2 [Virtually] for ordinary purposes, nearly, just about; see ALMOST.

practice *n.* 1 [A customary action] usage, use, wont; see CUSTOM. 2 [A method] mode, manner, fashion; see METHOD, SYSTEM. 3 [Educational repetition] exercise, drill, repetition, iteration, rehearsal, recitation,

recounting, relating, tuneup*, prepping*. 4 [A practitioner's customers] clientele, patients, clients; see BUSINESS 4.

practice *v.* 1 [To seek improvement through repetition] drill, train, exercise, study, rehearse, repeat, recite, iterate, put in practice, make it one's business, work at, accustom oneself, polish up*, sharpen up*, build up. 2 [To employ one's professional skill] function, work at, employ oneself in; see WORK 2.

practiced *a.* trained, expert, exercised; see ABLE.

pragmatic *a.* realistic, utilitarian, logical; see PRACTICAL.

prairie *n.* steppe, savanna, grassland; see FIELD 1, MEADOW, PLAIN.

praise *n.* 1 [The act of praising] applause, approval, appreciation; see ADMIRATION. 2 [An expression of praise] laudation, eulogy, regard, applause, recommendation, handclapping, hurrahs, bravos, ovation, cheers, cries, whistling, tribute, compliment, acclaim, flattery, blessing, benediction, boost, rave.—*Ant.* BLAME, censure, condemnation.

praise *v.* 1 [To commend] recommend, applaud, cheer, acclaim, endorse, sanction, admire, eulogize, adulate, elevate, smile on, cajole, give an ovation to, clap, pay tribute to, do credit to, have a good word for, make much of, extend credit, advocate, compliment, appreciate, admire, celebrate, honor, congratulate, flatter, rave over, boost, give a big hand; see also APPROVE. 2 [To speak or sing in worship] glorify, adore, reverence; see WORSHIP.

praised *a.* admired, helped, flattered, worshiped, glorified, exalted, blessed, celebrated, paid tribute to, magnified.

prance *v.* cavort, frisk, gambol; see DANCE.

prank *n.* game, escapade, caper; see JOKE.

pray *v.* 1 [To ask or beg] importune, petition, plead; see ASK, BEG. 2 [To call upon God] hold communion with God, supplicate, implore, petition, entreat, bless.

prayer *n.* 1 [An earnest request] entreaty, request, petition; see APPEAL 1. 2 [An address to a deity] invocation, act of devotion, supplication, devotions, benediction, litany. *Prayers include the following:* Lord's Prayer, Our Father, Hail Mary, Pater Noster, Ave Maria, grace, kaddish, matins, vespers, Angelus, general confession, Miserere, collects, hours, stations of the cross, evensong.

prayer book *n.* liturgy, mass book, missal, missalette, hymnal, breviary, holy text, guide; see also BIBLE.

preach v. exhort, proselytize, evangelize, witness, moralize, teach, lecture, talk, harangue, inform, address.

preacher n. missionary, parson, clergyman; see MINISTER 1.

preamble n. prelude, preface, foreword; see INTRODUCTION 4.

precarious a. doubtful, uncertain, risky; see DANGEROUS.

precaution n. anticipation, forethought, regard; see CARE 1. —**take precautions** foresee, mind, be careful; see PREPARE 1, WATCH OUT.

precede v. go before, come first, be ahead of, move ahead of, take precedence over, preface, introduce, usher in, ring in, herald, forerun, head, lead, go ahead, scout, light the way, go in advance, come before, come to the front, forge ahead, head up.—*Ant.* SUCCEED, come after, come last.

precedence n. preference, precession, the lead; see ADVANTAGE.

precedent n. authoritative example, exemplar, pattern; see EXAMPLE 1, MODEL 1.

preceding a. antecedent, precedent, previous, other, prior, aforesaid, ahead of, earlier, former, forerunning, past, foregoing, above-mentioned, above-named, above-cited, aforementioned, before-mentioned, above, before, prefatory, front, forward, anterior, preliminary, preparatory, introductory, aforeknown, already indicated, previously mentioned.

precious a. 1 [Valuable] high-priced, costly, dear; see EXPENSIVE, VALUABLE. 2 [Beloved] cherished, inestimable, prized; see BELOVED, FAVORITE. 3 [Refined and delicate] overrefined, overnice, fragile; see DAINTY.

precipice n. crag, cliff, bluff; see HILL, MOUNTAIN.

precipitate v. accelerate, press, hurry; see HASTEN 2, SPEED.

precipitation n. 1 [Carelessness] rashness, presumption, impetuosity; see CARELESSNESS, RUDENESS. 2 [Condensation] hail, rain, snow; see STORM.

precise a. 1 [Exact] decisive, well-defined, strict; see ACCURATE 2, DEFINITE 1, 2. 2 [Fussily or prudishly careful] rigid, inflexible, uncompromising; see CAREFUL, SEVERE 1.

precisely a. correctly, exactly, definitely; see ACCURATE 2.

precision n. exactness, correctness, sureness; see ACCURACY.

preconception n. prejudice, bias, assumption; see INCLINATION 1.

predatory a. voracious, carnivorous, bloodthirsty; see GREEDY, HUNGRY.

predecessor n. antecedent, forerunner, ancestor; see PARENT.

predicament n. strait, quandary, plight, puzzle, perplexity, dilemma, scrape, corner, hole, impasse, tight situation, state, condition, position, lot, circumstance, mess, muddle, deadlock, pinch, crisis, bind*, fix*, pickle*, hot water*, jam*, spot*; see also DIFFICULTY 1, 2.

predicate n. verbal phrase, part of speech, verb; see VERB.

predicate v. assert, declare, state; see MEAN 1.

predict v. prophesy, prognosticate, divine; see FORETELL.

predictable a. anticipated, foreseen, prepared for; see EXPECTED, LIKELY 1.

prediction n. prophecy, foresight, prognostication; see GUESS.

predominance n. supremacy, superiority, control; see COMMAND, POWER 2.

predominant a. 1 [Supreme in power] mighty, almighty, supreme; see POWERFUL 1. 2 [Of first importance] transcendent, surpassing, superlative; see PRINCIPAL.

predominate v. dominate, prevail, rule; see GOVERN, MANAGE 1.

prefab* n. prefabricated building, modular structure, standardized housing; see BUILDING.

prefabricate v. fabricate, preform, set up, coordinate, pre-assemble; see also ASSEMBLE 2.

preface n. prelude, prolegomenon, preliminary; see EXPLANATION, INTRODUCTION 4.

preface v. introduce, commence, precede; see BEGIN 1.

prefer v. single out, fix upon, fancy; see FAVOR.

preferable a. more eligible, more desirable, better; see EXCELLENT.

preferably a. by preference, by choice, by selection, in preference, first, sooner, before, optionally, at pleasure, willingly, at will; see also RATHER 2.

preference n. favorite, election, option, decision, selection, pick; see also CHOICE.

preferred a. chosen, selected, fancied, adopted, picked out, taken, elected, liked, favored, set apart, handpicked, singled out, endorsed, settled upon, sanctioned, decided upon.—*Ant.* NEGLECTED, unpreferred, overlooked.

pregnant a. gestating, gravid, fruitful, with child, big with child, hopeful, anticipating, in a family way*, expecting*, knocked up*.

prehistoric a. ancient, primeval, earliest; see OLD 3.

prejudge *v.* presuppose, forejudge, presume; see DECIDE.

prejudice *n.* partiality, unfairness, spleen, bias, detriment, enmity, prejudgment, dislike, disgust, aversion, antipathy, racism, bigotry, apartheid, misjudgment, pique, coolness, animosity, contemptuousness, bad opinion, displeasure, repugnance, revulsion, preconception, quirk, warp, twist.—*Ant.* ADMIRATION, appreciation, good opinion.

prejudiced *a.* preconceived, prepossessed, biased, directed against, influenced, inclined, leaning, conditioned, presupposing, predisposed, dogmatic, opinionated, partisan, extreme, hidebound, narrow, intolerant, canting, racist, sexist, chauvinistic, bigoted, blind, partial, narrow-minded, parochial, provincial, one-sided, not seeing an inch beyond one's nose, squinteyed, intolerant of, disliking, having a predilection, closed against, judging on slight knowledge, smug.—*Ant.* GENEROUS, open-minded, receptive.

preliminary *a.* preparatory, preceding, prefatory; see INTRODUCTORY.

prelude *n.* preface, prologue, overture; see INTRODUCTION 3.

premarital *a.* prenuptial, before marriage, during courtship; see BEFORE.

premature *a.* unanticipated, precipitate, rash; see EARLY 2, UNTIMELY.

prematurely *a.* too early, rash, precipitately; see EARLY 2, UNTIMELY.

premiere *n.* first night, beginning, opening; see PERFORMANCE.

premise *n.* proposition, principle, assumption; see BASIS, PROOF 1.

premises *n.* bounds, real estate, land; see PROPERTY 2.

premium *a.* prime, superior, select; see EXCELLENT.

premium *n.* remuneration, bonus, installment; see PRIZE.

premonition *n.* omen, portent, forewarning; see SIGN 1, WARNING.

preoccupation *n.* absorption, daydreaming, obsession; see FANTASY, THOUGHT 1.

preoccupied *a.* engrossed, distracted, absorbed; see ABSENT-MINDED, RAPT.

preparation *n.* 1 [The act of preparing] preparing, fitting, making ready, manufacture, readying, putting in order, establishment, compounding, adapting, rehearsal, incubation, gestation, formation, maturing, development, evolution, construction, building, furnishing, anticipation, buildup*. 2 [The state of being prepared] preparedness, readiness, fitness, adaptation, suitability, capacity, qualification, background, ripeness, mellowness, maturity, training, education, equipment. 3 [Something that is prepared] arrangement, product, compound; see MIXTURE 1.

prepare *v.* 1 [To make oneself ready] get ready, foresee, arrange, make preparations, make arrangements, fit, adapt, qualify, put in order, adjust, set one's house in order, prime, fix, settle, fabricate, appoint, furnish, elaborate, perfect, develop, prepare the ground, lay the foundations, block out, smooth the way, man, arm, cut out, warm up, lay the groundwork, contrive, devise, make provision, put in readiness, build up, provide for, provide against, make snug, be ready; see also ANTICIPATE, PLAN 1. 2 [To make other persons or things ready] outfit, equip, fit out; see PROVIDE 1. 3 [To cook and serve] concoct, dress, brew; see COOK, SERVE.

prepared *a.* 1 [Fitted] adapted, qualified, adjusted; see ABLE, FIT 1. 2 [Subjected to a special process or treatment] frozen, precooked, processed; see PRESERVED 2. 3 [Ready] available, on hand, in order; see READY 2.

prepossessing *a.* pleasing, captivating, attractive; see CHARMING, PLEASANT 1.

prerequisite *n.* essential, necessity, need; see REQUIREMENT 2.

prerogative *n.* privilege, advantage, exemption; see RIGHT 1.

prescribe *v.* guide, order, give directions; see ORDER 1.

prescription *n.* direction, medicinal recipe, formula; see MEDICINE 2.

presence *n.* 1 [The fact of being present] occupancy, occupation, residence, inhabitance, habitancy; see also ATTENDANCE 1. 2 [The vicinity of a person] propinquity, nearness, closeness; see NEIGHBORHOOD. 3 [One's appearance and behavior] carriage, port, demeanor; see APPEARANCE 1, BEHAVIOR.

presence of mind *n.* sensibility, alertness, acumen; see ATTENTION.

present *a.* 1 [Near in time] existing, being, in process, in duration, begun, started, commenced, going on, under consideration, at this time, contemporary, immediate, instant, prompt, at this moment, at present, today, nowadays, these days, already, even now, but now, just now, ongoing, for the time being, for the occasion; see also NOW 1.—*Ant.* PAST, over, completed. 2 [Near in space] in view, at hand, within reach; see NEAR 1.

present *n.* 1 [The present time] instant, this time, present moment; see TODAY. 2 [A gift] grant, donation, offering; see GIFT 1.

present *v.* 1 [To introduce] make

known, acquaint with, give an introduction; see INTRODUCE 3. 2 [To submit] donate, proffer, put forth; see OFFER 1. 3 [To give] grant, bestow, confer; see GIVE 1. 4 [To give a play, etc.] put on, do, offer; see ACT 3, PERFORM 2.

presentable *a.* attractive, prepared, satisfactory; see FIT 1.

presentation *n.* 1 [The act of presenting] bestowal, donation, delivering; see GIVING. 2 [Something presented] present, offering, remembrance; see GIFT 1.

presented *a.* bestowed, granted, conferred; see GIVEN.

presently *a.* directly, without delay, shortly; see IMMEDIATELY, SOON.

preservation *n.* security, safety, protection, conservation, maintenance, saving, keeping, storage, curing, tanning, freezing, freeze-drying, sugaring, pickling, evaporation, canning, refrigeration.

preserve *v.* 1 [To guard] protect, shield, save; see DEFEND 2. 2 [To maintain] keep up, care for, conserve; see MAINTAIN 3. 3 [To keep] can, conserve, process, save, put up, put down, store, cure, bottle, do up, season, salt, pickle, put in brine, put in vinegar, pot, tin, dry, smoke, corn, dry-cure, smoke-cure, freeze, freeze-dry, quick freeze, keep up, cold-pack, refrigerate, dehydrate, seal up, kipper, marinate, evaporate, embalm, mummify, mothball, fill.—*Ant.* WASTE, allow to spoil, let spoil.

preserved *a.* 1 [Saved] rescued, guarded, secured; see SAVED 1. 2 [Prepared for preservation] canned, corned, dried, freeze-dried, dehydrated, evaporated, smoked, seasoned, pickled, salted, brined, put up, conserved, cured, marinated, tinned, potted, bottled, embalmed, mummified.

preserves *n.* spread, marmalade, conserve; see JAM 1, JELLY.

preside *v.* direct, lead, emcee; see ADVISE, MANAGE 1.

presidency *n.* office of the president, chairmanship, position; see ADMINISTRATION 2.

president *n.* presiding officer, chief executive, prez*; see EXECUTIVE.

presidential *a.* official, regulatory, of the chief executive; see MANAGING.

press *n.* 1 [The pressure of circumstances] rush, confusion, strain; see HASTE. 2 [Publishing as a social institution] the fourth estate, publishers, publicists, newsmen, newspapermen, journalists, journalistic writers, editors, correspondents, political writers, columnists, periodicals, papers, newspapers, the media.

press *v.* 1 [To subject to pressure]

thrust, crowd, bear upon, bear down on, squeeze, hold down, pin down, force down, crush, drive, weight, urge; see also PUSH 1.—*Ant.* RAISE, release, relieve. 2 [To smooth, usually by heat and pressure] finish, mangle, roll; see IRON, SMOOTH.

press conference *n.* interview, question-and-answer session, briefing; see ANNOUNCEMENT, HEARING 1.

pressing *a.* importunate, constraining, distressing; see IMPORTANT 1, URGENT 1.

pressure *n.* 1 [Physical pressure] force, burden, mass, load, encumbrance, stress, thrust, tension, squeeze; see also WEIGHT 1.—*Ant.* RELEASE, relief, deliverance. 2 [Some form of social pressure] compulsion, constraint, urgency, persuasion, stress, affliction, coercion, trouble, hardship, humiliation, misfortune, necessity, repression, confinement, unnaturalness, obligation, discipline.—*Ant.* AID, assistance, encouragement.

pressure *v.* press, compel, constrain; see URGE 2, 3.

prestige *n.* renown, effect, influence; see FAME.

presumably *a.* in all probability, credibly, likely; see PROBABLY.

presume *v.* consider, suppose, take for granted; see ASSUME.

presumption *n.* 1 [An assumption] conjecture, guess, hypothesis; see ASSUMPTION 1. 2 [Impudence] arrogance, audacity, effrontery; see RUDENESS.

pretend *v.* 1 [To feign] affect, simulate, claim falsely, imitate, counterfeit, sham, make as if, make as though, mislead, beguile, delude, pass off for, cheat, dupe, hoodwink, be deceitful, bluff, falsify, be hypocritical, fake, put on*, let on*, go through the motions, keep up appearances; see also DECEIVE. 2 [To make believe] mimic, fill a role, take a part, represent, portray, put on a front, play, make believe, act the part of, put on an act*, act a part, put on airs*, playact.

pretended *a.* feigned, counterfeit, assumed, affected, shammed, bluffing, simulated, lying, falsified, put on, concealed, covered, masked, cheating; see also FALSE 3.

pretense *n.* 1 [The act of pretending] affectation, misrepresentation, falsification, act, deceit, fabrication, trickery, double-dealing, misstatement, falsifying, simulation, excuse, insincerity, profession, ostentation, assumption, dissimulation, evasion, equivocation, prevarication, egotism, brazenness, arrogance, dandyism, foppery, servility, complacency, smugness, prudishness, coyness, formality, stiffness, blind, smoke screen; see also DISHONESTY, IMITATION.—*Ant.* HONESTY, candor, sincerity. **2** [Something pretended] falsehood, lie, falseness, affectation, mask, cloak, show, excuse, subterfuge, pretext, fraud, appearance, seeming, semblance, wile, ruse, sham, airs, claim, mannerism; see also DECEPTION, IMITATION 2.

prettily *a.* pleasingly, gently, daintily; see POLITELY.

pretty *a.* **1** [Attractive] comely, lovely, good-looking; see BEAUTIFUL. **2** [Pleasant] delightful, cheerful, pleasing; see PLEASANT 2. **3** [*Considerable] ample, sizable, notable; see LARGE 1, MUCH 1, 2. **4** [Somewhat] rather, tolerably, a little; see MODERATELY.

prevalence *n.* dissemination, occurrence, currency; see REGULARITY.

prevalent *a.* widespread, accepted, commonplace; see COMMON 1.

prevent *v.* preclude, obviate, forestall, anticipate, block, arrest, stop, thwart, repress, interrupt, halt, impede, check, avert, frustrate, balk, foil, retard, obstruct, counter, countercheck, counteract, inhibit, restrict, block off, limit, hold back, hold off, stop from, deter, intercept, override, circumvent, bar, ward off, keep from happening, nip in the bud, put a stop to, stave off, keep off, turn aside; see also HINDER, RESTRAIN.—*Ant.* HELP, aid, encourage.

prevented *a.* obviated, stopped, interfered with; see INTERRUPTED.

prevention *n.* anticipation, forestalling, arresting, obviating, bar, debarring, halt, impeding, retardation, repression, restraint, restriction, inhibition, interception, overriding, circumvention, hindering, counteraction, obstruction, opposition, stopping, thwarting, blocking, warding off, staving off, keeping off; see also REFUSAL.—*Ant.* AID, encouragement, help.

preventive *a.* deterrent, precautionary, prophylactic, averting, defensive.

previous *a.* antecedent, prior, former; see PRECEDING.

previously *a.* long ago, earlier, beforehand; see BEFORE.

prey *n.* quarry, hunted, game; see VICTIM.

prey on *v.* **1** [To destroy] seize, plunder, victimize; see DESTROY. **2** [To eat] feed on, devour, consume; see EAT 1.

price *n.* expenditure, outlay, expense, cost, value, worth, figure, dues, tariff, valuation, quotation, fare, hire, wages, return, disbursement, rate, appraisal, reckoning, equivalent, payment, demand, barter, consideration, amount, sticker price, asking price, estimate, output, ransom, reward, pay, par value, money's worth, price ceiling, ceiling; see also VALUE 1. —**at any price** whatever the cost, expense no object, anyhow; see REGARDLESS 2.

price *v.* fix the price of, appraise, assess; see RATE, VALUE 2.

priced *a.* valued, estimated, worth; see COSTING.

priceless *a.* invaluable, inestimable, without price; see VALUABLE.

prick *n.* puncture, stab, stick; see CUT.

prick *v.* pierce, puncture, stick; see CUT, HURT 1.

prickly *a.* thorny, pointed, spiny; see SHARP 1.

pride *n.* **1** [The quality of being vain] conceit, vainglory, vanity, hubris, egoism, egotism, self-esteem, self-love, self-exaltation, self-glorification, self-admiration, pretension.—*Ant.* HUMILITY, self-effacement, unpretentiousness. **2** [Conduct growing from pride or conceit] haughtiness, vanity, disdain, condescension, patronizing, patronage, snobbery, superiority; see also sense 1. **3** [Sense of personal satisfaction] self-respect, self-satisfaction, self-sufficiency; see HAPPINESS. **4** [A source of satisfaction] treasure, jewel, pride and joy; see SATISFACTION 2.

pride oneself on *v.* take pride in, flatter oneself that, be proud of; see BOAST.

priest *n.* Names for priests in various sects include the following: father confessor, spiritual father, priest-vicar, high priest, minor canon, pontiff, vicar, bishop, monsignor, clergyman, rector, preacher, presbyter, elder, rabbi, lama, imam, monk, friar; see also MINISTER 1.

priesthood *n.* clergy, Holy Orders, monasticism; see MINISTRY 2.

priestly *a.* ecclesiastic, episcopal, ministerial; see CLERICAL 2.

prim *a.* stiff, formal, precise, demure, decorous, nice, orderly, tidy, cleanly, dapper, trim, spruce, pat; see also POLITE.

primarily *a.* mainly, fundamentally, in the first place; see PRINCIPALLY.

primary *a.* **1** [Earliest] primitive, initial, first; see ORIGINAL 1. **2** [Fundamental] elemental, basic, central; see FUNDAMENTAL. **3** [Principal] chief, prime, main; see PRINCIPAL.

primate *n.* gorilla, chimpanzee, orangutan, gibbon, great ape, lemur; see also MAN 1, MONKEY.

prime *a.* **1** [Principal] main, first, chief; see PRINCIPAL. **2** [Excellent] top, choice, superior; see EXCELLENT.

primitive *a.* 1 [Simple] rudimentary, elementary, first; see FUNDAMENTAL. 2 [Ancient] primeval, archaic, primordial; see OLD 3. 3 [Uncivilized] crude, rough, simple, rude, atavistic, uncivilized, savage, uncultured, natural, barbaric, barbarous, barbarian, fierce, untamed, uncouth, ignorant, undomesticated, wild, brutish, raw, untaught, green, unlearned, untutored, underdeveloped.

prince *n.* sovereign, ruler, monarch, potentate; see also ROYALTY.

princely *a.* 1 [Royal] sovereign, regal, august; see ROYAL. 2 [Suited to a prince] lavish, sumptuous, luxurious; see EXPENSIVE, HANDSOME, RICH 1, 2.

princess *n.* sovereign, monarch, infanta; see ROYALTY.

principal *a.* leading, chief, first, head, prime, main, foremost, cardinal, essential, capital, important, preeminent, highest, supreme, prominent, dominant, predominant, controlling, superior, prevailing, paramount, greatest, incomparable, unapproachable, peerless, matchless, unequaled, unrivaled, maximum, crowning, unparalleled, sovereign, second to none.—*Ant.* UNIMPORTANT, secondary, accessory.

principal *n.* chief, head, headmaster, master; see also EXECUTIVE.

principally *a.* chiefly, mainly, essentially, substantially, materially, eminently, preeminently, superlatively, supremely, vitally, especially, particularly, peculiarly, notably, importantly, fundamentally, dominantly, predominantly, basically, largely, first and foremost, in large measure, first of all, to a great degree, prevalently, generally, universally, mostly, above all, in the first place, for the most part, for the greatest part, before anything else, in the main.—*Ant.* SLIGHTLY, somewhat, tolerably.

principle *n.* 1 [A fundamental law] underlying truth, basic doctrine, postulate; see LAW 4. 2 [A belief or set of beliefs; *often plural*] system, canon, teaching; see BELIEF, FAITH 2, POLICY.

print *n.* 1 [Printed matter] impression, reprint, issue; see COPY. 2 [A printed picture] engraving, lithograph, photograph; see PICTURE 3, SKETCH. —**in print** printed, available, obtainable; see PUBLISHED. —**out of print** OP, unavailable, remaindered; see SOLD OUT.

print *v.* 1 [To make an impression] impress, imprint, indent; see MARK 1. 2 [To reproduce by printing] run off, print up, issue, reissue, reprint, bring out, go to press, set type, compose, start the presses; see also PUBLISH 1.—*Ant.* TALK, write, inscribe.

3 [To simulate printing] letter, hand-letter, calligraph; see WRITE 2.

printed *a.* impressed, imprinted, engraved, stamped, embossed, lithographed, multilithed, xeroxed, printed by photo-offset, silkscreened; see also REPRODUCED.

printer *n.* typesetter, compositor, linotype operator; see WORKMAN.

printing *n.* 1 [A process of reproduction] typography, composition, typesetting, presswork. 2 [Printed matter] line, page, sheet; see PAGE. 3 [Publication] issuing, issue, distribution; see PUBLICATION 1.

prior *a.* antecedent, above-mentioned, foregoing; see PRECEDING.

priority *n.* superiority, preference, precedence; see ADVANTAGE.

prison *n.* penitentiary, reformatory, prison house, guardhouse, stockade; see also JAIL.

prisoner *n.* captive, convict, culprit, jailbird*, detainee, escapee, hostage, con*; see also DEFENDANT.

prisoner of war *n.* captive person, captured person, interned person, person in captivity, POW; see also PRISONER.

privacy *n.* seclusion, solitude, retreat, isolation, separateness, aloofness, separation, concealment; see also SECRECY.

private *a.* special, separate, retired, secluded, withdrawn, removed, not open, behind the scenes, off the record, privy, clandestine, single; see also INDIVIDUAL, OWN.—*Ant.* PUBLIC, open, exposed. —**in private** privately, personally, not publicly; see SECRETIVE, SECRETLY.

private *n.* enlisted man, infantryman; private first class, private second class, etc.; see also SAILOR, SOLDIER.

privately *a.* confidentially, clandestinely, alone; see PERSONALLY 1, SECRETLY.

private parts *n.* genitals, organs of reproduction, privates; see GENITALS.

privilege *n.* 1 [A customary concession] due, perquisite, prerogative; see RIGHT 1. 2 [An opportunity] chance, fortunate happening, event; see OPPORTUNITY 1.

privileged *a.* 1 [Wealthy] well-to-do, favored, affluent; see RICH 1. 2 [Confidential] classified, not public, top-secret; see SECRET 1.

prize *n.* reward, advantage, privilege, possession, honor, inducement, premium, bounty, bonus, spoil, booty, plunder, pillage, loot, award, accolade, recompense, requital, acquisitions, laurel, decoration, medal, trophy, palm, crown, citation, scholarship, fellowship, feather in one's cap, title, championship, first place, blue ribbon, *prix* (French), payoff*, cake*, plum.

prize v. regard highly, value, esteem; see VALUE 2.

probability n. likelihood, possibility, chance; see CHANCE, POSSIBILITY 2.

probable a. seeming, presumable, feasible; see LIKELY 1.

probably a. presumably, seemingly, apparently, believably, reasonably, imaginably, feasibly, practicably, expediently, plausibly, most likely, everything being equal, as like as not, in all likelihood, as the case may be, one can assume, like enough, no doubt, to all appearances, in all probability.—*Ant.* UNLIKELY, doubtfully, questionably.

problem n. 1 [A difficulty] dilemma, quandary, obstacle; see DIFFICULTY 1, 2. 2 [A question to be solved] query, intricacy, enigma; see PUZZLE 1.

procedure n. fashion, style, mode; see METHOD, SYSTEM.

proceed v. move, progress, continue; see ADVANCE 1.

proceeding n. [*Often plural*] process, transaction, deed, experiment, performance, measure, step, course, undertaking, venture, adventure, occurrence, incident, circumstance, happening, movement, operation, procedure, exercise, maneuver; see also ACTION 1.

proceeds n. gain, profit, yield; see RETURN 3.

process n. means, rule, manner; see METHOD. —**in (the) process of** while, when, in the course of; see DURING.

process v. treat, make ready, put through; see PREPARE 1.

processed a. treated, handled, fixed; see PRESERVED 2.

prod v. provoke, goad, shove; see PUSH 1.

prodigy n. marvel, portent, miracle, monster, enormity, spectacle, freak, curiosity, phenom*; see also WONDER 2. —**child prodigy** genius, gifted child, boy or girl wonder; see ARTIST, MUSICIAN, SCIENTIST, WRITER.

produce n. product, harvest, result, crop, return, effect, consequence, amount, profit, outcome, outgrowth, aftermath, gain, realization; see also BUTTER, CHEESE, CREAM 1, FOOD, FRUIT, GRAIN 1, MILK, VEGETABLE.

produce v. 1 [To bear] yield, bring forth, give birth to, propagate, bring out, come through, blossom, flower, deliver, generate, engender, breed, contribute, give, afford, furnish, return, render, fetch, bring in, present, offer, provide, contribute, sell for, bear fruit, accrue, allow, admit, proliferate, be delivered of, bring to birth, reproduce, foal, lamb, drop, calve, fawn, whelp, litter, hatch, usher into the world, spawn. 2 [To create by mental effort] originate, author, procreate, bring forth, conceive, concoct, engender, write, design, fabricate, imagine, turn out, churn out, devise; see also COMPOSE 2, CREATE, INVENT 1. 3 [To cause] effect, occasion, bring about; see BEGIN 1. 4 [To show] exhibit, present, unfold; see DISPLAY. 5 [To make] assemble, build, construct; see MANUFACTURE. 6 [To present a performance] present, play, put on; see ACT 3, PERFORM 2.

produced a. 1 [Created] originated, composed, made; see FORMED. 2 [Presented] performed, acted, put on; see SHOWN 1. 3 [Caused] occasioned, propagated, begot, bred, engendered, generated, hatched, induced.

product n. 1 [A result] output, outcome, outgrowth; see RESULT. 2 [Goods produced; *often plural*] stock, commodity, merchandise; see GOODS 1.

production n. 1 [The act of producing] origination, creation, authoring, reproduction, giving, bearing, rendering, giving forth, putting out, issuing, increasing, return, procreation, generation, engendering, blooming, blossoming; see also MAKING. 2 [The amount produced] crop, result, stock; see QUANTITY.

productive a. rich, fruitful, prolific; see FERTILE.

productivity n. richness, potency, fecundity; see FERTILITY.

profanity n. abuse, cursing, swearing; see CURSE.

profession n. 1 [A skilled or learned occupation] calling, business, avocation, vocation, career, employment, occupation, engagement, office, situation, position, lifework, chosen work, role, service, pursuit, undertaking, concern, post, berth, craft, sphere, field, walk of life; see also JOB 1, TRADE 2. 2 [A declaration] pretense, avowal, vow; see DECLARATION, OATH 1.

professional a. 1 [Skillful] expert, learned, adept; see ABLE. 2 [Well-qualified] acknowledged, known, licensed; see ABLE.

professional n. expert, trained personnel, specially trained person; see SPECIALIST.

professor n. educator, faculty member, sage; see TEACHER. *Teachers popularly called professors include the following:* full professor, associate professor, assistant professor, instructor, lecturer, graduate assistant, teaching assistant, tutor, school principal, fellow, teaching fellow, master docent.

proficiency *n.* learning, skill, knowledge; see ABILITY.

proficient *a.* skilled, expert, skillful; see ABLE.

profile *n.* silhouette, shape, figure; see FORM 1, OUTLINE 3.

profit *n.* 1 [Advantage] avail, good, value; see ADVANTAGE. 2 [Excess of receipts over expenditures] gain, returns, proceeds, receipts, take*, gate, acquisition, rake-off*, windfall, accumulation, saving, interest, remuneration, earnings.—*Ant.* LOSS, debits, costs.

profit *v.* 1 [To be of benefit] benefit, assist, avail; see HELP. 2 [To derive gain] benefit, capitalize on, cash in on, realize, clear, gain, reap profits, make a profit, be in the black, recover, thrive, prosper, harvest, make money.—*Ant.* LOSE, lose out on, miss out on.

profitable *a.* lucrative, useful, sustaining, aiding, remunerative, beneficial, gainful, advantageous, paying, successful, favorable, assisting, productive, serviceable, valuable, instrumental, practical, pragmatic, effective, to advantage, effectual, sufficient, paying its way, bringing in returns, making money, paying well, paying out, in the black; see also HELPFUL 1.—*Ant.* UNPROFITABLE, UNSUCCESSFUL, unproductive.

profitably *a.* lucratively, remuneratively, gainfully, usefully, advantageously, successfully, favorably, for money, productively, practically, effectively, effectually, sufficiently, sustainingly.

profiteer *n.* exploiter, chiseler, gouger*; see CHEAT.

profound *a.* 1 [Physically deep] fathomless, bottomless, subterranean; see DEEP 1. 2 [Intellectually deep] heavy, erudite, scholarly, mysterious, sage, serious, sagacious, penetrating, discerning, knowing, wise, knowledgeable, intellectual, enlightened, thorough, informed; see also LEARNED 1, SOLEMN.—*Ant.* SUPERFICIAL, shallow, flighty. 3 [Emotionally deep] heartfelt, deepfelt, great; see INTENSE.

profoundly *a.* deeply, extremely, thoroughly; see VERY.

program *n.* 1 [A list of subjects] schedule, menu, printed program; see LIST. 2 [A sequence of events] happenings, schedule, agenda, order of business, calendar, plans, business, affairs, details, arrangements, catalogue, curriculum, order of the day, series of events, itinerary, appointments, things to do, chores, preparations, meetings, getting and spending, all the thousand and one things; see also PLAN 2. 3 [An entertainment] performance, show, presentation; see PERFORMANCE.

program *v.* 1 [To schedule] slate,

book, bill; see sense 2. 2 [To work out a sequence to be performed] feed in, activate a computer, compute, reckon, figure, calculate, estimate, enter, compile, feed, edit, process, extend, delete, add.

programmed *a.* scheduled, slated, lined up; see PLANNED.

progress *n.* 1 [Movement forward] progression, advance, headway, impetus, forward course, development, velocity, pace, tempo, momentum, motion, rate, step, stride, current, flow, tour, circuit, transit, journey, voyage, march, expedition, locomotion, passage, course, procession, process, march of events, course of life, movement of the stars, motion through space.—*Ant.* STOP, stay, stand. 2 [Improvement] advancement, development, growth; see IMPROVEMENT 1. —**in progress** advancing, going on, continuing; see MOVING 1.

progress *v.* proceed, move onward, move on; see ADVANCE 1.

progressive *a.* 1 [In mounting sequence] advancing, mounting, rising; see MOVING 1. 2 [Receptive to new ideas] tolerant, lenient, open-minded; see LIBERAL.

prohibit *v.* interdict, ban, obstruct; see FORBID, PREVENT.

prohibited *a.* forbidden, restricted, proscribed; see ILLEGAL, REFUSED.

project *n.* outline, design, scheme; see PLAN 2.

project *v.* 1 [To thrust out] protrude, hang over, extend, jut, bulge, stick out, hang out, jut out, be prominent, be conspicuous.—*Ant.* WITHDRAW, regress, revert. 2 [To throw] pitch, heave, propel; see THROW 1.

projection *n.* 1 [Bulge] prominence, jut, protuberance, step, ridge, rim; see also BULGE. 2 [Forecast] prognostication, prediction, guess; see GUESS.

prolong *v.* continue, hold, draw out; see INCREASE.

prolonged *a.* extended, lengthened, continued; see DULL 4.

prominence *n.* 1 [A projection] jut, protrusion, bump; see BULGE, PROJECTION 1. 2 [Notability] renown, influence, distinction; see FAME.

prominent *a.* 1 [Physically prominent] protuberant, extended, jutting, conspicuous, protruding, projecting, noticeable, rugged, rough, obtrusive, standing out, sticking out, hilly, raised, relieved, rounded.—*Ant.* HOLLOW, depressed, sunken. 2 [Socially prominent] notable, preeminent, leading; see FAMOUS. 3 [Conspicuous] remarkable, striking, noticeable; see CONSPICUOUS.

promiscuity *n.* lechery, looseness, sexual immorality; see LEWDNESS.

promiscuous *a.* indiscriminate, sexually immoral, loose; see LEWD 2.

promise *n.* 1 [A pledge] assurance, agreement, pact, oath, engagement, covenant, consent, warrant, affirmation, swearing, plight, word, troth, vow, profession, guarantee, insurance, obligation, commitment, betrothal, espousal, plighted faith, marriage contract, giving one's word, gentleman's agreement, word of honor. 2 [Hope] outlook, good omen, potential; see ENCOURAGEMENT.

promise *v.* engage, declare, agree, vow, swear, consent, affirm, profess, undertake, pledge, covenant, contract, bargain, espouse, betroth, assure, guarantee, warrant, give assurance, give warranty, insure, cross one's heart, plight one's troth, bind oneself, commit oneself, obligate oneself, make oneself answerable, give security, underwrite, subscribe, lead someone to expect, answer for, pledge one's honor.— *Ant.* DECEIVE, deny, break faith.

promised *a.* pledged, sworn, vowed, agreed, covenanted, as agreed upon, undertaken, professed, consented, affirmed, insured, warranted, vouched for, underwritten, subscribed, stipulated, assured, ensured; see GUARANTEED.

promising *a.* likely, assuring, encouraging; see HOPEFUL 2.

promote *v.* 1 [To further] forward, urge, encourage, profit, patronize, help, aid, assist, develop, support, boom, back, uphold, champion, advertise, market, merchandise, sell, advocate, cultivate, improve, push, bolster, develop, speed, foster, nourish, nurture, subsidize, befriend, mentor, benefit, subscribe to, favor, expand, improve, better, cooperate, get behind, boost.—*Ant.* DISCOURAGE, weaken, enfeeble. 2 [To advance in rank] raise, advance, elevate, graduate, move up, exalt, aggrandize, magnify, prefer, favor, increase, better, dignify.—*Ant.* HUMBLE, demote, reduce.

promotion *n.* 1 [Advancement in rank] preferment, elevation, raise, improvement, advance, lift, betterment, ennobling, favoring.—*Ant.* REMOVAL, demotion, lowering. 2 [Improvement] advancement, progression, development; see IMPROVEMENT 1, INCREASE.

prompt *a.* early, timely, precise; see PUNCTUAL.

prompt *v.* 1 [To instigate] arouse, provoke, inspire; see INCITE, URGE 2. 2 [To suggest] bring up, indicate, imply; see PROPOSE 1.

promptly *a.* on time, punctually, hastily; see IMMEDIATELY, QUICKLY.

prone *a.* inclined, predisposed, disposed; see LIKELY 4.

prong *n.* spine, spur, spike; see FASTENER.

pronoun *n.* *Pronouns include the following:* personal, possessive, demonstrative, relative, definite, indefinite, interrogative, intensive, reflexive, reciprocal, compound, emphatic, negative, universal.

pronounce *v.* 1 [To speak formally] proclaim, say, assert; see DECLARE. 2 [To articulate] enunciate, say phonetically, vocalize; see UTTER.

pronounced *a.* notable, noticeable, clear; see DEFINITE 2, OBVIOUS 1, 2, UNUSUAL 1.

pronouncement *n.* report, declaration, statement; see ANNOUNCEMENT.

pronunciation *n.* articulation, utterance, voicing; see DICTION.

proof *n.* 1 [Evidence] demonstration, verification, case, reasons, exhibits, credentials, data, warrant, confirmation, substantiation, attestation, corroboration, affidavit, facts, witness, testimony, deposition, trace, record, criterion. 2 [Process of proving] test, attempt, assay; see TRIAL 2.

prop *n.* aid, assistance, strengthener; see POST.

propaganda *n.* promotion, publicity, advertisement, plug*, evangelism, proselytism, ballyhoo, disinformation, spin, PR.

propel *v.* impel forward, move, thrust; see DRIVE 2.

propellant *n.* charge, gunpowder, combustible; see EXPLOSIVE, FUEL.

propeller *n.* *Propellers include the following:* screw, Archimedean, fishtail, variable-pitch, feathering, marine, airplane, two-bladed, three-bladed, four-bladed, weedless, pusher, pulling.

propensity *n.* talent, capacity, competence; see ABILITY.

proper *a.* 1 [Suitable] just, decent, fitting; see FIT 1. 2 [Conventional] customary, usual, decorous; see CONVENTIONAL 1, 3. 3 [Prudish] prim, precise, strait-laced; see PRUDISH.

properly *a.* correctly, fitly, suitably; see WELL 3.

property *n.* 1 [Possessions] belongings, lands, assets, holdings, inheritance, capital, equity, investments, goods and chattels, earthly possessions, real property, personal property, taxable property, resources, private property, public property, wealth; see also BUSINESS 4, ESTATE, FARM, HOME 1. 2 [A piece of land] section, quarter section, subdivision, site, estate, tract, part, farm, park, ranch, homestead, yard, grounds, frontage, acres, acreage, premises, campus, grant, field, claim, holding, real estate, plot; see also LOT 1.

prophecy n. prediction, prognostication, augury; see IDEA 1.

prophesy v. predict, prognosticate, divine; see FORETELL.

prophet n. seer, oracle, soothsayer, prophetess, seeress, clairvoyant, wizard, augur, sibyl, sorcerer, predictor, forecaster, prognosticator, diviner, medium, witch, palmist, fortuneteller, magus, astrologer, horoscopist, channeler, spiritualist, table-rapper*.

prophetic a. predictive, occult, clairvoyant, oracular, sibylline.

propitious a. 1 [Favorable] auspicious, encouraging, promising; see HOPEFUL 2. 2 [Kindly] benignant, helpful, generous; see KIND.

proponent n. defender, advocate, champion; see PROTECTOR.

proportion n. relationship, dimension, share; see BALANCE 2, PART 1.

proportional a. proportionate, equivalent, comparable; see EQUAL.

proposal n. 1 [Offer] overture, recommendation, proposition; see SUGGESTION 1. 2 [Plan] scheme, program, prospectus; see PLAN 2.

propose v. 1 [To make a suggestion] suggest, offer, put forward, move, set forth, come up with, state, proffer, advance, propound, introduce, put to, contend, assert, tender, recommend, advise, counsel, lay before, submit, affirm, volunteer, press, urge upon, hold out, make a motion, lay on the line.—*Ant.* OPPOSE, dissent, protest. 2 [To mean] purpose, intend, aim; see MEAN 1. 3 [To propose marriage] offer marriage, ask in marriage, make a proposal, ask for the hand of, pop the question*.

proposed a. projected, prospective, scheduled, expected, arranged, advanced, suggested, advised, moved, put forward, submitted, recommended, urged, volunteered, pressed, intended, determined, anticipated, designed, schemed, purposed, considered, referred to, contingent; see also PLANNED.

proposition n. proposal, scheme, project; see PLAN 1.

proprietor n. owner, superintendent, operator; see MANAGER.

propriety n. aptness, suitability, advisability, accordance, agreeableness, compatibility, correspondence, consonance, appropriateness, congruity, modesty, seemliness, good breeding, decorum, rightness, dignity, concord, harmony, expedience; see also FITNESS.—*Ant.* INCONSISTENCY, incongruity, inappropriateness.

prose n. fiction, nonfiction, composition; see LITERATURE 1, 2, STORY, WRITING 2.

prosecute v. contest, indict, try; see SUE.

prosecution n. state, government, prosecuting attorney, state's attorney; see also LAWYER.

prospect n. 1 [A view] sight, landscape, vista; see VIEW. 2 [A probable future] expectancy, promise, hope; see OUTLOOK 2. 3 [A possible candidate] possibility, likely person, interested party; see CANDIDATE.

prospective a. considered, hoped for, promised; see PLANNED, PROPOSED.

prosper v. become rich, become wealthy, be enriched, thrive, turn out well, fare well, do well, be fortunate, have good fortune, flourish, get on, rise in the world, fatten, increase, bear fruit, bloom, blossom, flower, make money, make a fortune, benefit, advance, gain, make good, do well by oneself*, make one's mark, roll in the lap of luxury*, come along, do wonders; see also SUCCEED 1.

prosperity n. accomplishment, victory, successfulness; see SUCCESS 2.

prosperous a. flourishing, well-off, well-to-do; see RICH 1.

prostitute n. harlot, strumpet, lewd woman, whore, bawd, streetwalker, loose woman, fallen woman, courtesan, lady of the evening, sex worker, concubine, hustler, call girl, B-girl, tramp*, slut*, tart*, hooker*; see also CRIMINAL.

prostitution n. hustling, harlotry, hooking*, the life*; see also LEWDNESS.

protagonist n. leading character, lead, combatant; see HERO 1, IDOL.

protect v. shield, guard, preserve; see DEFEND 1, 2.

protected a. shielded, safeguarded, cared for, watched over, preserved, defended, guarded, secured, kept safe, sheltered, harbored, screened, fostered, cherished, curtained, shaded, disguised, camouflaged; see also COVERED 1, SAFE 1.—*Ant.* WEAK, insecure, unsheltered.

protection n. 1 [A covering] shield, screen, camouflage; see SHELTER. 2 [A surety] certainty, safeguard, safekeeping, assurance, invulnerability, reassurance, security, stability, strength; see also GUARANTY.—*Ant.* WEAKNESS, insecurity, frailty.

protector n. champion, defender, patron, sponsor, safeguard, benefactor, supporter, advocate, padrone, guardian angel, guard, shield, savior, standby, promoter, mediator, mentor, counsel, second, backer, upholder, sympathizer, big brother, big sister, angel*, cover*, front*, goombah*; see also GUARDIAN.

protest n. mass meeting, rally, demonstration, riot, clamor, tumult, turmoil, moratorium, sit-in, agitation, strike, sit-down strike, wildcat strike, work slowdown, work stoppage, job action, sickout, blue flu*.

protest v. demur, disagree, object; see OPPOSE 1.

Protestant n. Protestant denominations include the following: Evangelicals, Adventists, Baptists, Congregationalists, Anglicans, Episcopalians, Lutherans, Methodists, Presbyterians, Amish, Mennonites, Brethren, Christian Scientists, Jehovah's Witnesses, Quakers, Pentecostalists, United Church of Christ, Moravians, Reformed churches.

protester n. demonstrator, dissident, rebel; see RADICAL.

protrude v. come through, stick out, jut out; see PROJECT 1.

proud a. 1 [Having a creditable self-respect] self-respecting, self-sufficient, self-satisfied, ambitious, spirited, vigorous, high-spirited, great-hearted, fiery, dignified, honorable, stately, lordly, lofty-minded, high-minded, impressive, imposing, fine, splendid, looking one in the eye, on one's high horse*, high and mighty*, holding up one's head.—Ant. HUMBLE, unpretentious, unassuming. 2 [Egotistic] egotistical, vain, vainglorious; see EGOTISTIC. —**do oneself proud*** achieve, prosper, advance; see SUCCEED 1.

proudly a. boastfully, haughtily, conceitedly; see ARROGANTLY.

prove v. justify, substantiate, authenticate, corroborate, testify, explain, attest, show, warrant, uphold, determine, settle, fix, certify, back, sustain, validate, bear out, affirm, confirm, make evident, convince, evidence, be evidence of, witness, declare, have a case, manifest, demonstrate, document, establish, settle once and for all.

proved a. confirmed, established, demonstrated; see ESTABLISH 3.

proverb n. maxim, adage, aphorism, precept, saw, saying, motto, dictum, text, witticism, repartee, axiom, truism, byword, epigram, moral, folk wisdom, platitude.

proverbial a. current, general, unquestioned; see COMMON 1, DULL 4.

provide v. 1 [To supply] furnish, equip, grant, replenish, provide with, accommodate, care for, indulge with, favor with, contribute, give, outfit, stock, store, minister, administer, render, procure, afford, present, bestow, cater, rig up, fit out, fit up, provision, ration, implement.—Ant. REFUSE, take away, deny. 2 [To yield] render, afford, give; see PRODUCE 1. —**provide for** (or **against**) prepare for, arrange, plan ahead; see PREPARE 1.

provided (**that**) conj. on the assumption that, in the event, in the case that; see IF, SUPPOSING.

providence n. divine guidance, God's gifts, Nature's bounty; see GOD.

providing conj. provided, in the event that, on the assumption that; see IF, SUPPOSING.

providing n. provision, supplying, furnishing, equipping, replenishing, replenishment, contributing, outfitting, stocking, filling, procurement, affording, presenting, preparing, preparation, arrangement, planning, putting by, laying in, putting in readiness, granting, bestowing, giving, offering, tendering, accumulating, storing, saving.

province n. area, region, hinterland; see TERRITORY 2.

provincial a. rude, unpolished, narrow-minded; see RURAL.

provision n. 1 [Arrangement] preparation, outline, procurement; see PLAN 2. 2 [Supplies; usually plural] stock, store, emergency; see EQUIPMENT. 3 [A proviso] stipulation, prerequisite, terms; see REQUIREMENT 1.

provisional a. transient, passing, ephemeral; see TEMPORARY.

provisionally a. conditionally, on certain conditions, for the time being; see TEMPORARILY.

provocation n. incitement, stimulus, inducement; see INCENTIVE.

provocative a. alluring, arousing, controversial; see INTERESTING.

provoke v. 1 [To vex] irritate, put out, aggravate; see BOTHER 2. 2 [To incite] stir, rouse, arouse; see INCITE. 3 [To cause] make, produce, bring about; see BEGIN 1.

provoked a. exasperated, incensed, enraged; see ANGRY.

prowl v. slink, lurk, rove; see SNEAK.

proxy n. substitute, broker, representative; see AGENT, DELEGATE.

prude n. prig, puritan, old maid, prudish person, priss*, bluenose*, stick-in-the-mud*, spoilsport, wet blanket*, goody-goody*.

prudence n. caution, circumspection, judgment, providence, considerateness, judiciousness, deliberation, wisdom, foresight, forethought, care, carefulness, frugality, watchfulness, precaution, heedfulness, heed, economy, husbandry, concern, conservatism, conservation, discrimination, cunning, vigilance, coolness, calculation, presence of mind.—*Ant.* CARELESSNESS, imprudence, rashness.

prudent *a.* **1** [Cautious and careful] cautious, circumspect, wary; see CAREFUL, DISCREET. **2** [Sensible and wise] discerning, sound, reasonable; see CAREFUL.

prudish *a.* narrow-minded, illiberal, bigoted, prissy*, priggish, overrefined, fastidious, stiff, smug, stuffy, conventional, straitlaced, demure, narrow, puritanical, affected, artificial, scrupulous, pedantic, pretentious, strict, rigid, rigorous, simpering, finicking, finicky, squeamish, repressed, inhibited, uptight*, like a maiden aunt, like an old maid; see also PRIM.—*Ant.* SOCIABLE, broadminded, genial. ·

pry *v.* **1** [To move, with a lever] push, lift, raise, pull, move, tilt, hoist, heave, uplift, upraise, elevate, turn out, jimmy; see also FORCE, OPEN 2. **2** [To endeavor to discover; *often used with "into"*] search, ferret out, seek, reconnoiter, peep, peer, peek, snoop, gaze, look closely, spy, stare, gape, nose, be curious, inquire; see also MEDDLE 1.

pseudo *a.* imitation, faux, sham; see FALSE 3.

psyche *n.* subconscious, mind, ego; see CHARACTER 2.

psychiatrist *n.* analyst, therapist, shrink*; see DOCTOR.

psychiatry *n.* psychiatric medicine, psychotherapy, psychoanalysis; see MEDICINE 1, SCIENCE 1.

psychic *a.* **1** [Mental] analytic, intellectual, psychological; see MENTAL 2. **2** [Spiritual] telepathic, mystic, immaterial; see SUPERNATURAL.

psycho* *a.* mad, crazy, psychopathic; see INSANE.

psychological *a.* emotional, mental, cognitive; see MENTAL 2.

psychologist *n.* psychiatrist, analyst, therapist; see DOCTOR, SCIENTIST.

psychology *n.* science of mind, study of personality, medicine, psychotherapy; see also SCIENCE 1, SOCIAL SCIENCE. *Divisions and varieties of psychology include the following:* rational, existential, functionalism, structural, self, dynamic, cognitive, developmental, physiological, abnormal, differential, Gestalt, Freudian, Adlerian, Jungian, analytic, comparative, child, animal, industrial or occupational, individual, social, family therapy, behaviorism, parapsychology.

psychopath *n.* lunatic, antisocial personality, sociopath; see MADMAN.

psychotic *a.* insane, mad, psychopathic; see INSANE 1.

puberty *n.* sexual development, pubescence, adolescence; see YOUTH 1.

public *a.* **1** [Available to the public] free to all, without charge, open, unrestricted, not private, known; see also FREE 4. **2** [Owned by the public] governmental, government, civil, civic, common, communal, publicly owned, municipal, metropolitan, state, federal, county, city.—*Ant.* PRIVATE, personal, restricted.

public *n.* society, the community, the masses; see PEOPLE 3. —**in public** candidly, plainly, aboveboard; see OPENLY 1.

publication *n.* **1** [The act of making public] writing, printing, broadcasting, announcement, notification, promulgation, issuing, statement, advertisement, communication, revelation, disclosure, discovery, making current, making available. **2** [Something published] news, tidings, information; see BOOK, MAGAZINE, NEWSPAPER.

publicity *n.* **1** [Public awareness] notoriety, currency, public relations; see DISTRIBUTION. **2** [Free advertising] PR copy, press release, proclamation; see PROPAGANDA. **3** [Activity intended to advertise] promotion, publicizing, advertising, PR; see also ADVERTISEMENT.

publicize *v.* announce, broadcast, promulgate; see ADVERTISE.

publicly *a.* candidly, plainly, aboveboard; see OPENLY 1.

public relations *n.* promotion, public image, favorable climate of opinion; see ADVERTISEMENT, PROPAGANDA, PUBLICITY 3.

public-spirited *a.* humanitarian, altruistic, openhanded; see GENEROUS 1.

publish *v.* **1** [To print and distribute] reprint, issue, reissue, get into print, hit the newsstands, e-publish, self-publish, distribute, bring out, write, do publishing, become a publisher, get out, put to press, put forth, be in the newspaper business, be in the book business, own a publishing house, send forth, give out; see also PRINT 2. **2** [To make known] announce, promulgate, disseminate; see ADVERTISE.

published *a.* written, printed, made public, circulated, proclaimed, promulgated, propagated, divulged, made current, made known, broadcast, circulated, spread abroad, disseminated, gotten out, appeared, released, presented, offered, voiced, noised abroad, brought before the public; see also ADVERTISED, ISSUED.—*Ant.* UNKNOWN, unpublished, unwritten.

pudding *n.* mousse, custard, tapioca; see DESSERT.

puddle *n.* plash, mud puddle, rut; see POOL 1.

pudgy *a.* chubby, chunky, stout; see FAT.

puff *n.* whiff, sudden gust, quick blast; see WIND.

puff *v.* distend, enlarge, swell; see FILL 1, 2.

puffy *a.* 1 [Windy] airy, gusty, breezy; see WINDY. 2 [Swollen] distended, expanded, blown; see FULL 1.

puke* *v.* throw up, retch, upchuck*; see VOMIT.

pull *n.* 1 [The act of pulling] tow, drag, haul, jerk, twitch, wrench, extraction, drawing, rending, tearing, uprooting, weeding, row, paddle. 2 [Exerted force] work, strain, tug; see STRENGTH. 3 [*Influence] having friends in high places, knowing the right people, juice*; see INFLUENCE.

pull *v.* 1 [To exert force] tug, pull at, draw in; see WORK 1. 2 [To move by pulling] draw, ease, drag, lift, stretch, move, jerk, haul, tear, rend, gather; see also DRAW 1. 3 [To incline] slope, tend, move toward; see LEAN 1. —**pull away** depart, pull off, go; see LEAVE 1. —**pull off** 1 [To remove] detach, separate, yank off*; see REMOVE 1. 2 [*To achieve] accomplish, manage, succeed; see ACHIEVE. —**pull oneself together** recover, revive, get on one's feet; see IMPROVE 2. —**pull out** go, depart, stop participating; see LEAVE 1, STOP 2. —**pull through*** revive, get over something, triumph; see SURVIVE 1. —**pull up** 1 [To remove] dislodge, elevate, dig out; see REMOVE 1. 2 [To stop] arrive, come to a stop, get there; see STOP 1.

pulley *n.* sheave, block, lift, lifter, crowbar, lever, crow, pry; see also TOOL 1.

Pullman *n.* railroad sleeping car, chair car, sleeper, first-class accommodation, *wagon-lit* (French).

pulp *n.* pap, mash, sponge, paste, dough, batter, curd, jam, poultice.

pulpit *n.* 1 [The ministry] priesthood, clergy, ecclesiastics; see MINISTRY 2. 2 [A platform in a church] desk, rostrum, stage; see PLATFORM 1.

pulpy *a.* smooth, thick, pasty; see SOFT 1.

pulse *n.* pulsation, vibration, throb; see BEAT 1.

pump *n.* air pump, vacuum pump, jet pump; see MACHINE, TOOL 1.

pump *v.* elevate, draw out, tap; see DRAW 1.

pun *n.* witticism, quip, play on words; see JOKE.

punch *n.* thrust, knock, stroke; see BLOW.

punch *v.* 1 [To hit] strike, knock, thrust against; see HIT. 2 [To perforate] pierce, puncture, bore; see PENETRATE.

punched *a.* perforated, dented, pierced, punctured, needled, stamped, imprinted, bored, wounded, bitten, tapped, impaled, spiked, gored, speared, stabbed, stuck.

punctual *a.* prompt, precise, particular, on time, on schedule, exact, timely, seasonable, regular, cyclic, dependable, recurrent, constant, steady, scrupulous, punctilious, meticulous, on the nose*.—*Ant.* CARELESS, unreliable, desultory.

punctuation *n. Marks of punctuation include the following:* period, colon, semicolon, comma, question mark, exclamation mark, parentheses, dash, brackets, apostrophe, hyphen, quotation marks, braces, ellipsis.

puncture *n.* punctured tire, flat tire, flat; see HOLE, TROUBLE 1.

puncture *v.* prick, perforate, pierce; see PENETRATE.

punish *v.* correct, discipline, chasten, chastise, sentence, reprove, lecture, penalize, fine, incarcerate, expel, execute, ostracize, exile, behead, hang, electrocute, dismiss, debar, whip, spank, paddle, trounce, switch, cuff, inflict a penalty, come down on, make an example of, rap on the knuckles, attend to, crack down on, make it hot for*, pitch into*, lay into*, give a dressing-down*, lower the boom on*, ground*, throw the book at*, blacklist, blackball; see also BEAT 1, IMPRISON, KILL 1, SCOLD.

punished *a.* corrected, disciplined, chastened, penalized, sentenced, reproved, chastised, castigated, lectured, scolded, imprisoned, incarcerated, expelled, exiled, dismissed, disbarred, defrocked, whipped, switched, cuffed, cracked down on, pitched into*, grounded*, given one's just deserts; see also BEATEN 1, CONFINED 3, EXECUTED 2.—*Ant.* RELEASED, cleared, exonerated.

punishment *n.* correction, discipline, reproof, penalty, infliction, suffering, deprivation, unhappiness, trial, penance, retribution, mortification, disciplinary action, fine, reparation, forfeiture, forfeit, confiscation, rap on the knuckles.—*Ant.* FREEDOM, exoneration, release.

puny *a.* feeble, inferior, diminutive; see WEAK 1.

pup *n.* puppy, whelp, young dog; see ANIMAL, DOG.

pupil *n.* schoolboy, schoolgirl, learner; see STUDENT.

puppet *n.* manikin, figurine, moppet; see DOLL.

puppy *n.* pup, whelp, young dog; see ANIMAL, DOG.

purchase *n.* **1** [The act of buying] procurement, getting, obtaining, shopping, installment buying, bargaining, marketing, investing; see also BUYING. **2** [Something bought] buy, order, goods, shipment, acquisition, invoice, packages, delivery, articles, property, possession, gain, booty, acquirement, investment; see also BARGAIN, GOODS.

purchase *v.* obtain, acquire, buy up; see BUY.

purchaser *n.* shopper, consumer, procurer; see BUYER.

pure *a.* **1** [Not mixed] unmixed, unadulterated, unalloyed, unmingled, simple, clear, genuine, undiluted, classic, real, true, fair, bright, unclouded, transparent, lucid, straight, neat; see also CLEAR 2, GENUINE 1, SIMPLE 1.—*Ant.* MIXED, mingled, blended. **2** [Clean] immaculate, spotless, stainless, unspotted, germ-free, unstained, unadulterated, unblemished, untarnished, unsoiled, disinfected, sterilized, uncontaminated, sanitary, unpolluted, purified, refined.—*Ant.* DIRTY, sullied, contaminated. **3** [Chaste] virgin, continent, celibate; see CHASTE. **4** [Absolute] sheer, utter, complete; see ABSOLUTE 1.

purely *a.* entirely, totally, essentially; see COMPLETELY.

purification *n.* purifying, cleansing, purgation; see CLEANING.—*Ant.* POLLUTION, defilement, contamination.

purify *v.* cleanse, clear, refine, wash, disinfect, fumigate, deodorize, clarify, sublimate, purge, filter; see also CLEAN.

purity *n.* **1** [The state of being pure] pureness, cleanness, cleanliness, immaculateness, stainlessness, whiteness, clearness. **2** [Innocence] artlessness, guilelessness, blamelessness; see INNOCENCE 2. **3** [Chastity] abstemiousness, continence, self-command; see CHASTITY, VIRTUE 1.

purple *a.* purpled, reddish-blue, bluish-red; see COLOR. *Tints and shades of purple include the following:* lilac, violet, mauve, heliotrope, magenta, orchid, grape, puce, plum, lavender, pomegranate, royal purple, wine.

purpose *n.* **1** [Aim] intention, end, goal, mission, objective, idea, design, hope, resolve, meaning, view, scope, desire, dream, expectation, ambition, intent, destination, direction, scheme, prospective, proposal, target, aspiration; see also PLAN 2. **2** [Resolution] tenacity, constancy, persistence; see CONFI-

DENCE, DETERMINATION, FAITH 1. — **on purpose** purposefully, intentionally, designedly; see DELIBERATELY. —**to the purpose** to the point, pertinent, apt; see RELEVANT.

purpose *v.* aim, plan, propose; see INTEND 1.

purposeful *a.* obstinate, stubborn, persistent; see RESOLUTE.

purr *v.* hum, drone, sigh; see SOUND.

purse *n.* pouch, pocketbook, receptacle, moneybag, wallet, pocket, coin purse, billfold, money belt, sack, vanity case.

pursue *v.* **1** [To chase] seek, hound, track down, dog, shadow, search for, search out, stalk, run after, go after, hunt down, trail, follow close upon, move behind, scout out, nose around, poke around, keep on foot, follow up. **2** [To seek] strive for, aspire to, attempt; see TRY 1. **3** [To continue] persevere, proceed, carry on; see CONTINUE 1.

pursuit *n.* chase, race, pursuance; see HUNT.

pus *n.* infection, discharge, mucus; see MATTER 1.

push *n.* shove, force, bearing, propulsion, drive, inertia, exertion, weight, straining, shoving, thrusting, forcing, driving, inducement, mass, potential, reserve, impact, blow; see also PRESSURE.

push *v.* **1** [To press against] thrust, shove, butt, crowd, gore, ram, crush against, jostle, push out of one's way, shoulder, elbow, struggle, strain, exert, set one's shoulder to, rest one's weight on, put forth one's strength; see also FORCE. **2** [To move by pushing] impel, accelerate, drive onward, launch, start, set in motion, push forward, shift, start rolling, budge, stir, shove along; see also DRIVE 2. **3** [To promote] advance, expedite, urge; see PROMOTE 1.

pushover *n.* sucker*, easy pickings, fool; see VICTIM.

pussyfoot *v.* evade, avoid, dodge, sidestep, tiptoe, dance around, hedge; see also AVOID, EVADE.

put *v.* **1** [To place] set, locate, deposit, plant, lodge, store, situate, fix, put in a place, pin down, seat, settle. **2** [To establish] install, quarter, fix; see ESTABLISH 2. **3** [To deposit] invest in, insert, embed; see PLANT. —**put aside** deposit, save, hoard; see STORE. —**put down** silence, repress, crush; see DEFEAT 2, 3. —**put off** postpone, defer, retard; see DELAY. —**put on 1** [To pretend] feign, sham, make believe; see PRETEND 1. **2** [*To deceive] trick, confuse, confound; see DECEIVE. —**put through** do, manage, finish; see ACHIEVE. —**put up**

1 [To preserve] can, smoke, pickle; see see PRESERVE 2. **2** [To build] erect, fabricate, construct; see BUILD. —**put up with** undergo, tolerate, stand; see ENDURE 2.

put-down* *n.* insult, slight, demeaning remark; see INSULT.

put-on* *n.* deception, device, conjob*; see TRICK 1.

putrid *a.* spoiled, decayed, putrified; see ROTTEN 1.

putter *v.* dawdle, fritter, poke; see LOITER.

puzzle *n.* **1** [A problem] tangle, bafflement, question, frustration, intricacy, maze, issue, enigma, baffler, brainteaser, puzzler, query, mystery, dilemma, muddle, secret, riddle, ambiguity, difficulty, perplexity, confusion, entanglement, stickler*, paradox.—*Ant.* ANSWER, solution, key. **2** [A problem to be worked for amusement] *Varieties include the following:* riddle, cryptogram, crossword puzzle, jigsaw puzzle, anagram, acrostic, rebus, Chinese puzzle, palindrome.

puzzle *v.* **1** [To perplex] obscure, bewilder, complicate; see CONFUSE. **2** [To wonder] marvel, be surprised, be astonished; see WONDER 1. —**puzzle out** figure out, work out, decipher; see SOLVE.

puzzled *a.* perplexed, bewildered, mystified; see DOUBTFUL.

puzzling *a.* **1** [Obscure] uncertain, ambiguous, mystifying; see CONFUSING, OBSCURE 1. **2** [Difficult] perplexing, abstruse, hard; see DIFFICULT 2.

pyramid *n.* tomb, shrine, mausoleum; see MONUMENT 1.

Q

quack *a.* fraudulent, unprincipled, dissembling; see DISHONEST.

quack *n.* rogue, charlatan, humbug; see CHEAT, IMPOSTOR.

quadrangle *n.* geometrical four-sided figure, parallelogram, square; see RECTANGLE.

quadrangular *a.* quadrilateral, four-sided, rectangular; see ANGULAR, SQUARE.

quadruped *n.* four-legged animal, quadrupedal animal, mammal; see ANIMAL.

quadruple *a.* fourfold, four-way, four times as great, consisting of four parts, quadruplex, four-cycle, four-ply, quadruplicate.

quaff *v.* gulp, swallow, guzzle; see DRINK 1, SWALLOW.

quaint *a.* fanciful, cute, pleasing, captivating, curious, antique, whimsical, picturesque, enchanting, baroque, Victorian, French Provincial, Early American, Colonial; see also CHARMING.—*Ant.* MODERN, up-to-date, fashionable.

quake *n.* temblor, tremor, shock; see EARTHQUAKE.

quake *v.* tremble, shrink, cower; see SHAKE 1.

qualification *n.* need, requisite, essential; see REQUIREMENT 1.

qualifications *n.* endowments, acquirements, attainments; see EXPERIENCE.

qualified *a.* **1** [Limited] conditional, modified, confined; see RESTRICTED. **2** [Competent] fitted, adequate, equipped; see ABLE.

qualify *v.* **1** [To limit] reduce, restrain, temper; see ALTER 1. **2** [To fulfill requirements] fit, suit, pass, pass muster, have the requisites, meet the demands, be endowed by nature for, measure up, meet the specifications.—*Ant.* FAIL, become unfit, be unsuited.

quality *n.* **1** [A characteristic] attribute, trait, endowment; see CHARACTERISTIC. **2** [Essential character] nature, essence, genius; see CHARACTER 2. **3** [Grade] class, kind, caliber, state, condition, merit, worth, excellence, stage, step, variety, standing, rank, group, place, position, repute.

qualm *n.* indecision, scruple, suspicion; see DOUBT, UNCERTAINTY 2.

quantity *n.* amount, number, bulk, mass, measure, extent, abundance, volume, capacity, lot, deal, pile, multitude, portion, carload, sum, profusion, mountain, load, barrel, shipment, consignment, bushel, supply, ton, ocean, flood, sea, flock, the amount of, score, swarm, quite a few, army, host, pack, crowd, bunch, heap*, mess*, slew*, gob*, batch, all kinds of*, all sorts of*; see also SIZE 2.

quarantined *a.* shut up, under quarantine, hospitalized, restrained, separated; see also ISOLATED.

quarrel *n.* **1** [An angry dispute] wrangle, squabble, dissension; see DISAGREEMENT 1, DISPUTE. **2** [Objection] complaint, disapproval, disagreement; see OBJECTION.

quarrel *v.* wrangle, dispute, contend, fight, squabble, row, clash, altercate, dissent, bicker, struggle, strive, contest, object, complain, disagree, argue, charge, feud, engage in blows, mix it up with*, step on someone's toes, get tough with*, lock horns, have words with, have a brush with, have it out*, fall out with, break with*, hassle*; see also OPPOSE 1.—*Ant.* AGREE, concur, harmonize.

quarrelsome *a.* factious, irritable, combative, pugnacious, turbulent, unruly, passionate, violent, contentious, disputatious, fiery, cross, irascible, snappish, waspish, peevish, petulant, argumentative, litigious, churlish, cantankerous, thin-skinned, touchy, huffy, pettish, peppery, impassioned, hotheaded, excitable, hasty, tempestuous, with a chip on one's shoulder*.—*Ant.* AGREEABLE, CALM, peaceful.

quart *n.* two pints, thirty-two ounces, one-fourth gallon; see MEASURE 1.

quarter *n.* **1** [One of four equal parts] fourth, one-fourth part, portion, quadrant, division, three months, 90 days, school term, quarter of an hour, quarter section; see also PART 1. **2** [One quarter of a dollar; *United States*] twenty-five cents, one-fourth of a dollar, coin, two bits*; see also MONEY 1. **3** [A section of a community] neighborhood, district, section; see AREA. —**at close quarters** at close range, cramped, restricted; see NEAR 1.

quarter *v.* **1** [To divide into quarters] cleave, dismember, cut up; see CUT 1, DIVIDE. **2** [To provide living quarters] lodge, shelter, house; see SHELTER.

quarterly *a.* by quarters, once every three months, periodically; see REGULARLY.

quarters *n.* lodgings, housing, living quarters, accommodations, house, apartment, room, barracks, tent, lodge, cabins, cottage, car trailer.

quartet *n.* four persons, four voices, four musicians, string quartet.

quartz *n. Types of quartz include the following:* amethyst, chalcedony, rock crystal, rose quartz, smoky quartz, bloodstone, agate, onyx, sardonyx, carnelian, chrysoprase, prase, flint, jasper; see also ROCK 1.

quasi *a.* supposedly, to a certain extent, apparently; see ALMOST.

queasy *a.* squeamish, sick, uneasy; see UNCOMFORTABLE 1.

queen *n.* ruler, female ruler, female sovereign, empress, woman monarch, queen mother, regent, wife of a king, consort, queen consort, queen dowager, queen regent, fairy queen, May Queen, matriarch.

queer *a.* **1** [Odd] strange, peculiar, uncommon; see UNUSUAL 2. **2** [*Suspicious] doubtful, questionable, curious; see SUSPICIOUS 2.

quench *v.* **1** [To satisfy] slake, glut,

gorge; see DRINK 1. **2** [To smother] stifle, dampen, douse; see MOISTEN.

quest *n.* journey, search, crusade; see EXAMINATION 1.

question *n.* **1** [A query] inquiry, interrogatory, interrogation, inquisition, interrogate, feeler, inquest, rhetorical question, burning question, crucial question, leading question, academic question.—*Ant.* ANSWER, solution, reply. **2** [A puzzle] enigma, mystery, problem; see PUZZLE 1. **3** [A subject] issue, topic, discussion; see SUBJECT. —**beside the question** not germane, beside the point, unnecessary; see IRRELEVANT. —**beyond question** beyond dispute, without any doubt, sure; see CERTAIN 2. —**in question** open for discussion, in debate, at issue; see CONTROVERSIAL, QUESTIONABLE 1, UNCERTAIN. —**out of the question** not to be considered, by no means, no; see IMPOSSIBLE.

question *v.* **1** [To ask] inquire, interrogate, query, quest, seek, search, sound out, petition, solicit, ask about, catechize, show curiosity, pry into, debrief, ask a leading question, challenge, raise a question, make inquiry, quiz, cross-examine, probe, investigate, grill, put to the question, bring into question; see also ASK. **2** [To doubt] distrust, suspect, dispute; see DOUBT.

questionable *a.* **1** [Justifying doubt] doubtful, undefined, equivocal, disputable, obscure, occult, indecisive, controversial, vague, unsettled, open to doubt, indeterminate, debatable, unconfirmed, problematical, cryptic, apocryphal, hypothetical, mysterious, enigmatic, ambiguous, indefinite, contingent, provisional, paradoxical, under advisement, under examination, open to question, up for discussion, in question, to be decided, hard to believe, incredible, iffy*, fishy*; see also UNCERTAIN.—*Ant.* DEFINITE, undoubted, credible. **2** [Having a poor appearance or reputation] dubious, disreputable, notorious, of ill repute, unsatisfactory, of little account, thought ill of, under a cloud, ill-favored, unpopular, disagreeable, evil-looking, illegitimate, discreditable, unreliable, dishonest, untrustworthy, fly-by-night, shady*, fishy*; see also SUSPICIOUS 2.—*Ant.* HONORED, esteemed, liked.

questionnaire *n.* set of questions, inquiry, survey; see CENSUS.

quick *a.* **1** [Rapid] swift, expeditious, fleet; see FAST 1. **2** [Almost immediate] posthaste, prompt, instantaneous; see IMMEDIATE. **3** [Hasty] impetuous, mercurial, quick-tempered; see RASH. **4** [Alert] ready, sharp, vigorous; see ACTIVE.

quicken v. 1 [To hasten] speed, hurry, make haste; see HASTEN 2. 2 [To cause to hasten] expedite, urge, promote; see HASTEN 2.

quickly a. speedily, swiftly, fleetly, flying, wingedly, with dispatch, scurrying, hurrying, rushing, shooting, bolting, darting, flashing, dashing, suddenly, in haste, in a hurry, just now, this minute, in a moment, in an instant, right away, at a greater rate, without delay, against the clock, racing, galloping, loping, sweeping, light-footedly, briskly, at once, like a bat out of hell*, on the double*, in a flash*, in a jiffy*, to beat the band*, at full blast, hellbent for leather*, hand over fist*, like mad*, by leaps and bounds, like a house on fire, full steam ahead*.—Ant. SLOWLY, sluggishly, creepingly.

quick-tempered a. temperamental, quarrelsome, irascible; see IRRITABLE.

quiet a. calm, peaceful, hushed, muffled, noiseless, still, stilled, mute, muted, mum, soundless, dumb, quieted, speechless, unspeaking, quiescent, taciturn, reserved, reticent, not excited, not anxious, not disturbed, silent, unexpressed, closemouthed, close, tight-lipped, uncommunicative, secretive.

quiet n. 1 [Rest] calm, tranquillity, relaxation; see PEACE 2. 2 [Silence] hush, stillness, speechlessness; see SILENCE 1.

quiet v. 1 [To make calm] calm, comfort, ease, cool, relax, compose, tranquilize, satisfy, please, pacify, mollify, console, subdue, reconcile, gratify, calm down, soften, moderate, smooth, ameliorate, lull, appease, restrain, sober, slacken, soothe.—Ant. EXCITE, stimulate, agitate. 2 [To make silent] still, deaden, silence, lower the sound level, muffle, mute, stop, check, restrain, suppress, break in, gag, muzzle, eliminate, repress, refute, confound, answer, quell, put the lid on*, button up*, choke off*, put the stopper on*.—Ant. SOUND, ring, cause to sound. —**quiet down** grow silent, be hushed, hush, be subdued, be suppressed, become speechless, fall quiet, break off, clam up*.

quietly a. 1 [Calmly] peacefully, serenely, confidently; see CALMLY. 2 [Almost silently] noiselessly, speechlessly, as quietly as possible; see SILENTLY. 3 [Without attracting attention] humbly, unostentatiously, simply; see MODESTLY.

quilt n. bed covering, coverlet, comforter, duvet, feather bed, puff, down puff, patchwork quilt, pieced quilt, bedspread, pad; see also COVER 1.

quip n. jest, witticism, one-liner; see JOKE.

quirk n. vagary, whim, caprice, fancy, whimsy, oddity, humor, turn, twist, knack, peculiarity, idiosyncrasy, foible, eccentricity, kink, crotchet, bee in one's bonnet*; see also CHARACTERISTIC, IRREGULARITY.

quit v. 1 [Abandon] surrender, renounce, relinquish; see ABANDON 1. 2 [To cease] discontinue, cease, halt, pause, stop, end, desist; see also STOP 2. 3 [To leave] go away from, depart, vacate; see LEAVE 1. 4 [To resign] leave, stop work, walk out, change jobs, cease work, give notice; see also RESIGN 2.

quite a. 1 [Completely] entirely, wholly, totally; see COMPLETELY. 2 [Really] truly, positively, actually; see REALLY 1. 3 [To a considerable degree] pretty, more or less, considerably; see VERY.

quitter n. shirker, dropout, deserter, goldbrick*, piker*, slacker.

quiver n. shudder, shiver, tremble; see VIBRATION.

quiver v. vibrate, shudder, shiver; see WAVE 3.

quiz n. test, questioning, exam; see EXAMINATION 2.

quiz v. question, test, cross-examine; see EXAMINE.

quorum n. enough to transact business, majority of the membership, legal minimum; see MEMBER.

quota n. portion, allowance, ration; see SHARE.

quotation n. 1 [Quoted matter] excerpt, passage, citation, cite*, citing, extract, recitation, repetition, sentence, quote, plagiarism. 2 [A quoted price] market price, current price, published price; see PRICE.

quote v. 1 [To repeat verbatim] recite, excerpt, extract; see SAY. 2 [To state a price] name a price, request, demand; see PRICE, VALUE 2.

quoted a. 1 [Repeated from someone else] recited, excerpted, extracted, cited, instanced, copied. 2 [Offered or mentioned at a stated price] asked, stated, announced, published, named, marked, given, priced, ticketed, tagged.

R

rabbi *n.* Jewish teacher, teacher, Hebrew theologian; see PRIEST.

rabbit *n.* hare, pika, bunny, Easter bunny; see also ANIMAL, RODENT. *Kinds of rabbits include the following:* jack rabbit, cottontail, snowshoe rabbit, coney.

rabble *n.* mob, masses, riffraff; see CROWD, PEOPLE 3.

rabid *a.* **1** [Fanatical] obsessed, zealous, extremist; see RADICAL 2. **2** [Insane] mad, raging, deranged; see INSANE. **3** [Affected with rabies] attacked by a mad dog, hydrophobic, foaming at the mouth; see SICK.

rabies *n.* canine madness, hydrophobia, lyssa; see ILLNESS 2.

race *n.* **1** [A major division of mankind] species, culture, variety, type, kind, strain, breed, family, cultural group, color; see also MAN 1. **2** [Roughly, people united by blood or custom] nationality, caste, sect, culture, variety, type, the people, mankind, tribe, group, ethnic stock, human race, class, kind, nation, folk, gene pool, pedigree, lineage, community, inhabitants, population, populace, public, clan, breeding population; see also HEREDITY, SOCIETY 2. **3** [A contest, usually in speed] competition, run, sprint, clash, meet, event, engagement, relay, footrace, horse race, competitive action, pursuit, rush, steeplechase, handicap, chase, match, derby, regatta, sweepstakes, marathon, heat, time trial; see also SPORT 3.

race *v.* **1** [To move at great speed] speed, hurry, run, pursue, chase, tear, bustle, spurt, post, zoom, press on, run swiftly, hasten, trip, fly, hustle, dash, rush, sprint, swoop, scuttle, dart, scamper, haste, plunge ahead, whiz, bolt, scramble, whisk, shoot, run like mad, burn up the road*, gun the motor*, skedaddle*. **2** [To compete] run a race, compete in a race, contend in running, follow a course, engage in a contest of speed, contend, sprint, enter a competition.

racial *a.* lineal, hereditary, ancestral, genetic, ethnic, genealogical, ethnological, phylogenic, national.

racism *n.* racial prejudice, racial bias, bigotry, racial discrimination, apartheid, segregation; see also PREJUDICE.

racist *a.* supremacist, discriminatory, bigoted; see CONSERVATIVE, PREJUDICED.

racist *n.* supremacist, believer in racism, racialist; see BIGOT, CONSERVATIVE.

rack *n.* holder, receptacle, framework, stand, shelf, ledge, perch, frame, bracket, whatnot, arbor, box, counter, trestle, hat rack, clothes rack, bottle rack, gun rack, feed rack; see also FRAME 1.

racket *n.* **1** [Disturbing noise] uproar, clatter, din; see DISTURBANCE 2, NOISE 2. **2** [Confusion accompanied by noise] disturbance, squabble, scuffle, fracas, clash, row, wrangle, agitation, babel, pandemonium, turbulence, clamor, outcry, hullabaloo, tumult, hubbub, commotion, blare, turmoil, stir, noisy fuss, uproar, clatter, babble, roar, shouting, rumpus, riot, squall, brawl, fight, pitched battle, free-for-all, to-do*, fuss. **3** [*A means of extortion] illegitimate business, confidence game, con game*; see CORRUPTION 2, CRIME, THEFT.

racketeer *n.* gang leader, mobster, gangster; see CRIMINAL.

racy *a.* **1** [Full of zest] spicy, sharp, spirited; see EXCITING. **2** [Not quite respectable] indecent, erotic, suggestive; see LEWD 2, SENSUAL 2.

radar *n.* radio detecting and ranging, radiolocation, Loran; see ELECTRONICS.

radial *a.* branched, outspread, radiated; see SPIRAL, SPREADING.

radiance *n.* brightness, brilliance, effulgence; see LIGHT 1.

radiant *a.* shining, luminous, beaming; see BRIGHT 1.

radiate *v.* **1** [To send forth from a center] scatter, shed, diffuse, spread, disperse, shoot in all directions, irradiate, emit in straight lines, transmit, disseminate, broadcast, dispel, strew, sprinkle, circulate, send out in rays from a point, throw out. **2** [To shed light or heat] shine, beam, light up, illumine, heat, warm, circulate, expand, widen, brighten, illuminate, irradiate, glitter, glisten, glow, glare, gleam, glimmer, flare, blaze, flicker, sparkle, flash, shimmer, reflect.

radiation *n.* **1** [Dissemination] propagation, dissipation, polarization, scattering, spread, diffraction, transmission, broadcast, emission, diffusion, dispersion, circulation, divergence, dispersal; see also DISTRIBUTION, EXTENT. **2** [Fallout] nuclear particles, radioactivity, radiant energy; see ENERGY 2.

radical *a.* **1** [Fundamental] original, basic, native; see FUNDAMENTAL,

ORGANIC. **2** [Advocating violent change] extremist, fanatical, insurgent, revolutionary, iconoclastic, advanced, forward, progressive, abolitionist, militant, recalcitrant, mutinous, seditious, riotous, lawless, racist, insubordinate, anarchistic, unruly, nihilistic, communistic, liberal, leftist, left-wing, immoderate, freethinking, ultra, avant-garde, pink*, red; see also REBELLIOUS.—*Ant.* CONSERVATIVE, gradualist, reformist. **3** [Believing in violent political and social change] leftist, communistic, militant; see REVOLUTIONARY 1.

radical *n.* militant, rebel, agitator, insurgent, objector, revolutionist, revolutionary, insurrectionist, leftist, Bolshevik, anarchist, socialist, communist, nihilist, traitor, mutineer, firebrand, renegade, extremist, crusader, individualist, fascist, Nazi, misfit, iconoclast, eccentric, freethinker, rightist, hippie*, fanatic, demonstrator, rioter, fifth columnist, nonconformist, leftwinger, right-winger, pinko*, red*.

radically *a.* **1** [Completely] wholly, thoroughly, entirely; see COMPLETELY. **2** [Originally] basically, primitively, firstly; see ESSENTIALLY, FORMERLY.

radio *n.* **1** [The study and practice of wireless communication] radio transmission, radio reception, signaling; see BROADCASTING, COMMUNICATION. **2** [A receiving device] wireless, ship's radio, radio set, tuner, receiver, car radio, dish, transistor radio, transistor, portable radio, pocket radio, walkie-talkie, cellular phone, cellphone; see also ELECTRONICS.

radioactive *a.* active, energetic, dangerous, hot*; see also POISONOUS.

radioactivity *n.* radiant energy, radioactive particles, Roentgen rays; see ENERGY 2.

radius *n.* space, sweep, range; see BOUNDARY, EXPANSE.

raffle *n.* sweepstakes, pool, lottery; see GAMBLING.

raft *n.* flatboat, barge, float, catamaran, life raft, swimming raft, rubber raft; see also BOAT.

rag *n.* remnant, cloth, dishrag, discarded material, hand rag, tatter, shred; see also GOODS 1. —**chew the rag*** chat, converse, have a talk; see TALK 1.

rage *n.* **1** [A fit of anger] frenzy, tantrum, uproar, hysterics, storm, outburst, spasm, convulsion, eruption, furor, excitement, extreme agitation, madness, vehemence, fury, rampage, huff, wrath, raving, violent anger, ire, resentment, bitterness, gall, irritation, animosity, exasperation, passion, indignation, heat, temper, blowup*, fireworks, hissy*, conniption fit*. **2** [The object of enthusiasm and imitation] style, mode, fashion, vogue, craze, mania, the last word, the latest; see also FAD.

rage *v.* **1** [To give vent to anger] rant, fume, rave, foam, splutter, yell, scream, roar, rail at, boil over, shake, quiver, seethe, shout, scold, go into a tantrum, have a fit, run amok, run riot, fly apart, flare up, carry on, show violent anger, bluster, storm, be furious, fret, lose one's temper, go berserk, go into a tailspin, blow one's top*, gnash one's teeth, raise Cain*, raise the devil*, raise hell*, take on*, throw a fit*, fly off the handle*, explode, vent one's spleen, snap at, blow up*, blow a fuse*, cut loose*, have a hemorrhage*, make a fuss over, kick up a row*, have a nervous breakdown, let off steam*, get oneself into a lather*, lose one's head.—*Ant.* CRY, be calm, pout. **2** [To be out of control] explode, flare, roar; see BURN, RUN 1.

ragged *a.* tattered, in shreds, patched, badly worn, rough, worn out, broken, worn to rags, frayed, frazzled, threadbare, shoddy, out at the seams, shredded, battered, the worse for wear, worn to a thread, down at the heel, moth-eaten, full of holes, torn, badly dressed; see also SHABBY, WORN 2.—*Ant.* WHOLE, new, unworn.

raging *a.* furious, irate, enraged; see ANGRY.

raid *n.* **1** [A predatory attack] invasion, assault, forced entrance; see ATTACK. **2** [An armed investigation] seizure, surprise entrance, police raid, roundup, bust*; see also ARREST, CAPTURE.

raid *v.* assail, storm, assault; see ATTACK.

raider *n.* bandit, thief, looter; see CRIMINAL, PIRATE, ROBBER.

rail *n.* **1** [A polelike structure] post, railing, barrier, picket, rail fence, siding, banister, paling, rest, hand rail, guardrail, brass rail; see also BAR 1, FENCE. **2** [A track; *often plural*] railway, monorail, railroad track; see RAILROAD.

railroad *n.* track, line, railway, trains, rails, elevated, underground, subway, commuter line, sidetrack, siding, passing track, loading track, feeder line, main line, double track, single track, trunk line, transcontinental railroad, el*; see also TRAIN.

railway *n.* track, line, route; see RAILROAD.

rain *n.* **1** [Water falling in drops] drizzle, mist, sprinkle, sprinkling, damp day, spring rain, rainfall, shower, precipitation, wet weather.

2 [A rainstorm] thunderstorm, thundershower, cloudburst; see STORM.

rain *v.* pour, drizzle, drop, fall, shower, sprinkle, mist, teem, spit, precipitate, patter, rain cats and dogs*, come down in bucketfuls; see also STORM.

raincoat *n.* trench coat, slicker, mackintosh; see COAT 1, CLOTHES.

rainy *a.* moist, coastal, drizzly; see STORMY, WET 2.

raise *n.* increase, salary increment, advance; see PROMOTION 1.

raise *v.* **1** [To lift] uplift, upraise, upheave, pull up, lift up, hold up, stand up, heave, set upright, put on its end, shove, boost, rear, mount, pry.—*Ant.* LOWER, bring down, take down. **2** [To nurture] bring up, rear, nurse, suckle, nourish, wean, breed, cultivate, train, foster; see also PROVIDE 1, SUPPORT 3. **3** [To collect or make available] gather, borrow, have ready; see ACCUMULATE, APPROPRIATE 2. **4** [To erect] construct, establish, put up; see BUILD. **5** [To ask] bring up, suggest, put; see ASK, PROPOSE 1. **6** [To advance in rank] exalt, elevate, honor; see PROMOTE 2. —**raise hell*** carry on*, celebrate, carouse; see DRINK 2.

raised *a.* **1** [Elevated] lifted, hoisted, built high, heightened, set high, in relief, erected, constructed, set up; see also BUILT.—*Ant.* REDUCED, lowered, taken down. **2** [Nurtured] reared, brought up, trained, prepared, educated, fostered, bred, nourished, nursed. **3** [Produced] harvested, cultivated, grown; see MADE.

rake *n.* **1** [A debauched person] lecher, philanderer, profligate; see DRUNKARD, RASCAL. **2** [A pronged implement] *Rakes include the following:* clam, lawn, garden, moss, hay, stubble, weeding, oyster, horse, revolving; leaf sweeper; see also TOOL 1.

rake *v.* **1** [To use a rake] clear up, collect, scratch, gather, scrape, clean up, weed, clear, grade, level. **2** [To sweep with gunfire] strafe, machine-gun, blister; see SHOOT 1.

rally *n.* assembly, mass meeting, demonstration; see GATHERING.

rally *v.* unite against, renew, redouble; see RETURN 1, REVENGE.

ram *n.* **1** [An object used to deliver a thrust] plunger, pump, beam, prow, hammerhead, weight, pole, shaft, lever, spike, battering ram, pile driver, tamping iron, punch, sledge hammer, rammer, tamper, monkey, bat, maul, hydraulic ram, spar, piston, drop weight, bow; see also BAR 1, HAMMER. **2** [A male sheep] buck, tup, bighorn; see ANIMAL.

ram *v.* **1** [To strike head-on] bump,

collide, slam; see BUTT, HIT 1. **2** [To pack forcibly] cram, jam, stuff; see PACK 2.

ramble *v.* **1** [To saunter] stroll, promenade, roam; see WALK 1. **2** [To speak or write aimlessly] drift, stray, diverge, meander, gossip, talk nonsense, chatter, babble, digress, maunder, get off the subject, go on and on, expatiate, protract, enlarge, be diffuse, dwell on, amplify, go astray, drivel, rant and rave, talk off the top of one's head, go off on a tangent, beat around the bush.

rambling *a.* **1** [Strolling] hiking, roaming, roving; see WALKING, WANDERING 1. **2** [Incoherent] discursive, disconnected, confused; see INCOHERENT. **3** [Covering considerable territory without much plan] spread out, strewn, straggling, trailing, random, here and there, at length, unplanned, sprawling, gangling; see also SCATTERED.—*Ant.* PLANNED, closely formed, compact.

ramp *n.* incline, slope, grade; see HILL, INCLINATION 2.

rampant *a.* raging, uncontrolled, growing without check, violent, vehement, impetuous, rank, turbulent, wild, luxuriant, tumultuous, profuse, epidemic, pandemic, fanatical, plentiful, unruly, wanton, rife, prevalent, dominant, predominant, excessive, impulsive, impassioned, intolerant, unrestrained, extravagant, overabundant, sweeping the country, like wildfire.—*Ant.* MODEST, mild, meek.

ranch *n.* plantation, grange, farmstead, ranchland, ranch house, ranch buildings, hacienda, dude ranch, rancho, spread; see also FARM, PROPERTY 2.

rancher *n.* ranch owner, ranchman, stockman, breeder, cattle farmer, cowherder, shepherd, drover, stock breeder, horse trainer, herdsman, herder, ranchero, broncobuster*, granger, cattleman, cowboy, cowpoke*, ranch hand, cattle baron; see also FARMER.

rancid *a.* tainted, stale, bad; see ROTTEN 1.

random *a.* haphazard, chance, purposeless, thoughtless, careless, blind, casual, fickle, erratic, aleatory, hit-or-miss, eccentric, unpredictable, accidental; see also AIMLESS, IRREGULAR 1. —**at random** haphazardly, by chance, aimlessly; see ACCIDENTALLY.

range *n.* **1** [Distance] reach, span, horizontal projection; see EXPANSE. **2** [Extent] length, area, expanse; see EXTENT. **3** [A series of mountains] highlands, alps, sierras; see MOUNTAIN 1. **4** [Land open to grazing] pasture, grazing land, field; see

COUNTRY 1. **5** [A kitchen stove] gas range, electric range, oven; see APPLIANCE, STOVE.

range v. **1** [To vary] differ, fluctuate, diverge from; see VARY. **2** [To traverse wide areas] encompass, reach, pass over, cover, stray, stroll, wander, ramble, explore, scour, search, traverse, roam, rove; see also CROSS 1, TRAVEL. **3** [To place in order] line up, classify, arrange; see ORDER 3.

rank a. **1** [Having luxurious growth] wild, dense, lush; see GREEN 2, THICK 1. **2** [Having a foul odor] smelly, fetid, putrid, stinking, rancid, disagreeable, smelling, offensive, sour, foul, noxious, stale, tainted, gamy, musty, strong, rotten, moldy, turned, high, ill-smelling, nauseating, obnoxious, disgusting, reeking, malodorous, nasty, strong-smelling.—Ant. SWEET, fragrant, fresh.

rank n. **1** [A row] column, file, string; see LINE 1. **2** [Degree] seniority, standing, station; see DEGREE 2. **3** [Social eminence] station, position, distinction, note, nobility, caste, privilege, standing, reputation, quality, situation, esteem, condition, state, place in society, status, circumstance, footing, grade, blood, family, pedigree, ancestry, stock, parentage, birth. —**pull (one's) rank on*** take advantage of, exploit, abuse subordinates; see GOVERN, HUMILIATE.

rank v. **1** [To arrange in a row or rows] put in line, line up, place in formation; see ORDER 3. **2** [To evaluate comparatively] place, put, regard, judge, assign, give precedence to, fix, establish, settle, estimate, value, valuate, include, list, rate; see also CLASSIFY. **3** [To possess relative evaluation] be worth, stand, be at the head, have a place, go ahead of, come first, forerun, antecede, have supremacy over, have the advantage of, precede, outrank, take the lead, take precedence over, belong, count among, be classed, stand in relationship.

ranked a. ordered, piled, neatly stacked; see ORGANIZED.

ransack v. **1** [To search thoroughly] rummage, explore, turn upside down, look all over, look high and low, leave no stone unturned, scour, seek everywhere, sound, spy, peer, look around, pry, scan, probe, look into, investigate, scrutinize; see also SEARCH. **2** [To loot] pillage, plunder, ravish, raid, rape, strip, rifle, forage, maraud, make off with, take away, seize, appropriate, spoil, poach, gut, rustle, lift*, thieve, ravage, pilfer, rob, steal, filch, pinch*.

ransom n. redemption money, compensation, payoff*; see BRIBE.

ransom v. release, rescue, deliver; see FREE.

rant v. rave, fume, rail; see RAGE 1, YELL.

rap n. knock, thump, slap; see BLOW. —**beat the rap*** avoid punishment, evade, be acquitted; see ESCAPE. —**bum rap*** unfair sentence, blame, frame-up*; see PUNISHMENT. —**take the rap*** be punished, suffer, take the blame; see PAY FOR.

rap v. **1** [To tap sharply] knock, strike, whack; see BEAT 1, HIT 1. **2** [*To talk, often compulsively] chatter, jabber, discuss; see BABBLE, TALK 1.

rape n. seduction, violation, deflowering, criminal attack, assault, abduction, statutory offense, defilement, abuse, molestation, maltreatment, forcible violation of a woman, date rape; see also CRIME.

rape v. violate, seize, compromise, force a woman, molest, ravish, attack, assault, defile, wrong, debauch, ruin, corrupt, seduce, maltreat, abuse.

rapid a. speedy, accelerated, hurried; see FAST 1.

rapidly a. fast, swiftly, posthaste; see IMMEDIATELY, QUICKLY.

rapist n. raper, ravager, ravisher; see RASCAL.

rapt a. enraptured, entranced, enchanted; see HAPPY.

rapture n. pleasure, enchantment, euphoria; see HAPPINESS.

rare a. **1** [Uncommon] exceptional, singular, extraordinary; see UNUSUAL 1, 2. **2** [Scarce] sparse, few, scanty, meager, limited, short, expensive, precious, out of circulation, off the market, in great demand, occasional, uncommon, isolated, scattered, infrequent, deficient, almost unobtainable, few and far between; see also UNIQUE.—Ant. CHEAP, profuse, abounding. **3** [Choice] select, matchless, superlative; see EXCELLENT. **4** [Lightly cooked] not cooked, undercooked, not done, seared, braised, not overdone, nearly raw, underdone, red, moderately done, not thoroughly cooked; see also RAW 1.

rarely a. unusually, occasionally, once in a great while; see SELDOM.

rascal n. scoundrel, rogue, rake, knave, villain, robber, fraud, scamp, hypocrite, sneak, shyster*, cad, trickster, charlatan, swindler, grafter, cheat, black sheep, ruffian, tough, rowdy, bully, scalawag, mountebank, liar, blackguard, wretch, quack, tramp, beggar, bum*, idler, wastrel, prodigal, hooligan*, ne'er-do-well, reprobate, misdoer, felon, sinner, delinquent, recreant, malefactor, profligate, loafer, renegade, impostor, opportunist, vagrant, pretender, gambler, mischief-maker, sharper, faker, skunk*, bastard*, fink*, rat*, rotten egg*, con man*, con artist*, flimflammer*, dirty dog*, good-for-nothing, worm, two-timer*, stool pigeon*, double-dealer*, phony*, four-flusher*, slicker*; see also CRIMINAL.—*Ant.* HERO, GENTLEMAN, philanthropist.

rash *a.* impetuous, impulsive, foolish, hotheaded, thoughtless, reckless, headstrong, bold, careless, determined, audacious, heedless, madcap, unthinking, headlong, incautious, wild, precipitant, overhasty, unwary, injudicious, venturous, foolhardy, imprudent, venturesome, adventurous, daring, jumping to conclusions, insuppressible, breakneck, irrational, fiery, furious, frenzied, passionate, immature, hurried, aimless, excited, feverish, tenacious, frantic, indiscreet, quixotic, ill-advised, unconsidered, without thinking, imprudent, unadvised, irresponsible, brash, precipitous, premature, sudden, harebrained, harum-scarum, devil-may-care, daredevil; see also RUDE 1.—*Ant.* CALM, cool, levelheaded.

rashly *a.* brashly, impulsively, unwisely, abruptly, foolishly, impetuously, incautiously, carelessly, precipitately, imprudently, recklessly, boldly, indiscreetly, inadvisedly, ill-advisedly, thoughtlessly, unthinkingly, furiously, hurriedly, heedlessly, boldly, unpreparedly, excitedly, overhastily, wildly, frantically, irrepressibly, without due consideration, without thinking, without forethought, in a hasty manner, passionately, fiercely, feverishly, headily; see also RUDELY.

rashness *n.* frenzy, recklessness, foolhardiness; see CARELESSNESS.

rasping *a.* hoarse, grating, grinding; see HARSH.

rat *n.* **1** [A rodent] mouse, muskrat, vermin; see PEST 1, RODENT. **2** [*A betrayer] informer, turncoat, fink*; see DESERTER, TRAITOR.

rate *n.* **1** [Ratio] proportion, degree, standard, incidence, frequency, scale, fixed amount, quota, relation, relationship, comparison, relative weight, percentage, numerical progression; see also MEASURE 1, 2. **2** [Price] valuation, charge, cost; see PRICE. **3** [Speed] velocity, pace, tempo; see SPEED.

rate *v.* **1** [To rank] judge, estimate, evaluate, grade, relate to a standard, fix, tag, calculate, assess, class, determine, appraise, guess at; see also MEASURE 1, PRICE, RANK 2. **2** [*To be well-thought-of] be a favorite, merit, rank; see SUCCEED 1.

rated *a.* ranked, classified, graded, classed, appraised, estimated,

thought of, given a rating, weighted, measured; see also PLACED.

rather *a.* **1** [To some degree] fairly, somewhat, a little; see MODERATELY, REASONABLY 2. **2** [By preference] first, by choice, in preference, sooner, more readily, willingly, much sooner, just as soon, as a matter of choice; see also PREFERABLY.

rather *interj.* I should say, certainly, of course, by all means, most assuredly, no doubt about it, and how*, you're telling me*.

ratification *n.* acceptance, confirmation, sanction; see PERMISSION.

ratify *v.* sanction, establish, substantiate; see APPROVE, ENDORSE 2.

rating *n.* grade, relative standing, evaluation; see CLASS 1, DEGREE 2, RANK 2.

ratio *n.* proportion, quota, quotient; see DEGREE 1, RATE 1.

ration *n.* allotment, portion, quota; see DIVISION 2, SHARE.

ration *v.* proportion, allot, apportion; see DISTRIBUTE.

rational *a.* **1** [Acting in accordance with reason] stable, calm, cool, deliberate, discerning, discriminating, levelheaded, collected, logical, thoughtful, knowing, sensible, of sound judgment, having good sense, impartial, exercising reason, intelligent, wise, reasoning, prudent, circumspect, intellectual, reflective, philosophic, objective, farsighted, enlightened, well-advised, judicious, analytical, deductive, synthetic, conscious, balanced, sober, systematic; see also REASONABLE 1.—*Ant.* RASH, reckless, wild. **2** [Of a nature that appeals to reason] intelligent, sensible, wise; see REASONABLE 1. **3** [Sane] normal, lucid, responsible; see SANE 1.

rationalize *v.* explain away, vindicate, reconcile; see EXPLAIN.

rationally *a.* sensibly, normally, intelligently; see REASONABLY 1.

rattle *n.* clatter, noise, racket; see NOISE 1.

rattle *v.* **1** [To make a rattling sound] drum, clack, knock; see SOUND. **2** [To talk with little meaning] chatter, gush, prattle; see BABBLE. **3** [To disconcert] bother, put out, unnerve; see CONFUSE, DISTURB, EMBARRASS.

raucous *a.* hoarse, loud, gruff; see HARSH.

raunchy* *a.* lustful, sexy*, suggestive; see LEWD 2.

ravage *v.* pillage, overrun, devastate, destroy, crush, desolate, despoil, overspread, wreck, waste, disrupt, disorganize, demolish, annihilate, overthrow, overwhelm, break up, pull down, smash, shatter, scatter, batter down, exterminate, extinguish, trample down, dismantle, stamp out, lay waste, lay in ruins, sweep away, raze, ruin, plunder, strip, impair, sack, consume, spoil, harry, ransack, maraud, prey, rape, rob, raid, pirate, seize, capture, gut, loot; see also DAMAGE.—*Ant.* BUILD, improve, rehabilitate.

rave *v.* **1** [To babble] gabble, jabber, rattle on; see BABBLE. **2** [To rage] storm, splutter, rail; see RAGE 1.

ravel *v.* untwist, come apart, wind out, untangle, disentangle, unsnarl, unbraid, untwine, unweave, unravel, fray, make plain; see also FREE, LOOSEN 2.

ravenous *a.* voracious, omnivorous, starved; see HUNGRY.

ravine *n.* gully, gorge, canyon, gulch, arroyo, valley, gap, chasm, abyss, break, crevice, crevasse, coulee.

raving *a.* violent, shouting, fuming; see INSANE.

raw *a.* **1** [Uncooked] fresh, rare, hard, unprepared, undercooked, underdone, fibrous, coarsegrained, unpasteurized, unbaked, unfried; see also RARE 4.—*Ant.* BAKED, cooked, fried. **2** [Unfinished] natural, untreated, crude, rough, newly cut, unprocessed, unrefined, coarse, untanned, newly mined, uncut, virgin; see also UNFINISHED 2.—*Ant.* REFINED, manufactured, processed. **3** [Untrained] immature, new, fresh; see INEXPERIENCED. **4** [Cold] biting, windy, bleak; see COLD 1. **5** [Without skin] peeled, skinned, dressed, galled, scraped, blistered, cut, wounded, pared, uncovered, chafed, bruised.—*Ant.* COVERED, coated, healed. **6** [Nasty] low, dirty, unscrupulous; see MEAN 3, VULGAR. —**in the raw** nude, bare, unclothed; see NAKED 1.

ray *n.* beam, flash, light, stream, gleam, blaze, sunbeam, wave, moonbeam, radiation, flicker, spark, emanation, radiance, streak, shaft, pencil, patch, blink, glimmer, glitter, glint, sparkle.

razor *n.* shaving instrument, cutting edge, blade; see KNIFE. *Razors include the following:* double-edged, single-edged, disposable, straightback, safety, hollow-ground, electric; electric shaver.

reach *n.* compass, range, scope, grasp, stretch, extension, orbit, horizon, gamut; see also ABILITY.

reach *v.* **1** [To extend to] touch, span, encompass, pass along, continue to, roll on, stretch, go as far as, attain, equal, approach, lead, stand, terminate, end, overtake, join, come up to, sweep; see also SPREAD 2. **2** [To extend a part of the body] lunge, strain, move, reach out, feel for, come at, make contact with, shake hands, throw out a limb, make for, put out, touch, strike, seize, grasp; see also STRETCH 1. **3** [To arrive] get to, come to, enter; see ARRIVE.

reaching *a.* **1** [Extending to a point] going up to, ending at, stretching, encompassing, taking in, spanning, spreading to, embracing, joining, sweeping on to. **2** [Arriving] coming to, landing, touching down; see LANDING 1. **3** [Extending a part of the body] stretching, straining, lunging; see EXTENDING.

react *v.* **1** [To act in response] reciprocate, respond, act; see ANSWER 1. **2** [To feel in response] be affected, be impressed, be involved; see FEEL 2.

reaction *n.* reply, rejoinder, reception, receptivity, response, return, feeling, opinion, reflection, backlash, attitude, retort, reciprocation, repercussion, result, reflex; see also ANSWER 1, OPINION 1. *Reactions to stimuli include the following:* contraction, expansion, jerk, knee jerk, cognition, shock, relapse, exhaustion, stupor, anger, disgust, revulsion, fear, illness, joy, laughter, wonder.

reactionary *a.* rigid, retrogressive, ultraconservative; see CONSERVATIVE.

reactionary *n.* die-hard, right-winger, untraconservative; see CONSERVATIVE.

read *a.* examined, gone over, scanned; see UNDERSTOOD 1.

read *v.* **1** [To understand by reading] comprehend, go through, peruse, scan, glance over, go over, gather, see, know, skim, perceive, apprehend, grasp, learn, flip through the pages, dip into, scratch the surface, bury oneself in; see also UNDERSTAND 1. **2** [To interpret] view, render, translate, decipher, make out, unravel, express, explain, expound, construe, paraphrase, restate, put; see also INTERPRET.

readable *a.* **1** [Capable of being read] clear, legible, coherent, distinct, intelligible, lucid, comprehensible, decipherable, unmistakable, plain, regular, orderly, fluent, tidy, flowing, precise, graphic, explicit, understandable, unequivocal, straightforward, simple. **2** [Likely to be read with pleasure] interesting, absorbing, fascinating, pleasurable, engrossing, satisfying, amusing, entertaining, enjoyable, rewarding, gratifying, pleasing, worth reading, pleasant, inviting, engaging, eloquent, well-written, smooth, exciting, attractive, clever, brilliant, ingenious, relaxing, stimulating, riveting, appealing.—*Ant.* DULL, dreary, depressing.

reader *n.* **1** [One who reads habitually] bookworm, bibliophile, scholar; see WRITER. **2** [A book intended for the study of reading] primer, graded text, selected readings; see BOOK.

readily *a.* quickly, immediately, promptly; see EAGERLY, EASILY, WILLINGLY.

readiness *n.* aptness, predisposition, eagerness; see WILLINGNESS, ZEAL.

reading *n.* **1** [Interpretation] version, treatment, commentary; see INTERPRETATION, TRANSLATION. **2** [A selection from written matter] excerpt, passage, section; see QUOTATION. **3** [A version] account, paraphrase, rendering; see LITERATURE 2, INTERPRETATION.

ready *a.* **1** [Prompt] quick, spontaneous, alert, wide-awake, swift, fleet, fast, sharp, immediate, instant, animated; see also ACTIVE, OBSERVANT, PUNCTUAL.—*Ant.* SLOW, dull, lazy. **2** [Prepared] fit, apt, skillful, ripe, handy, in readiness, waiting, on call, in line for, in position, on the brink of, equipped to do the job, open to, fixed for, on the mark, equal to, expectant, available, at hand, anticipating, in order, all systems go*, all squared away*, in a go condition*.—*Ant.* UNPREPARED, unready, unavailable. **3** [Enthusiastic] eager, willing, ardent; see ZEALOUS. —**make ready** put in order, prepare for something, equip; see PREPARE 1.

ready-made *a.* instant, prefabricated, built; see PRESERVED 2.

real *a.* **1** [Genuine] true, authentic, original; see GENUINE 1. **2** [Having physical existence] actual, solid, firm, substantive, material, live, substantial, existent, tangible, existing, present, palpable, factual, sound, concrete, corporal, corporeal, bodily, incarnate, embodied, physical, sensible, stable, in existence, perceptible, evident, undeniable, irrefutable, practical, true, true to life.—*Ant.* UNREAL, unsubstantial, hypothetical. **3** [*Very much] exceedingly, exceptionally, uncommonly; see VERY. —**for real*** actually, in fact, certainly; see REALLY 1.

real estate *n.* land, property, realty; see BUILDING, ESTATE, FARM, HOME 1.

realism *n.* authenticity, naturalness, actuality; see REALITY.

realist *n.* pragmatist, naturalist, scientist; see PHILOSOPHER.

realistic *a.* **1** [Practical] pragmatic, sensible, rational; see PRACTICAL. **2** [Lifelike] true-to-life, faithful, representative; see GENUINE 1.

reality *n.* authenticity, factual basis, truth, actuality, realness, substantiality, existence, substance, materiality, being, presence, actual existence, sensibility, corporeality, solid-

ity, perceptibility, true being, absoluteness, tangibility, palpability. —**in reality** in truth, truly, honestly; see REALLY 1.

realization *n.* understanding, comprehension, consciousness; see AWARENESS.

realize *v.* **1** [To bring to fulfillment] perfect, make good, actualize; see COMPLETE. **2** [To understand] recognize, apprehend, discern; see UNDERSTAND 1. **3** [To receive] acquire, make a profit from, obtain; see EARN 2, PROFIT 2, RECEIVE 1.

realized *a.* **1** [Fulfilled] completed, accomplished, done; see FINISHED 1. **2** [Earned] gained, gotten, acquired, received, accrued, made, reaped, harvested, gathered, inherited, profited, taken, cleared, obtained, gleaned, netted.

really *a.* **1** [In fact] actually, indeed, genuinely, certainly, surely, absolutely, positively, veritably, in reality, authentically, upon my honor, legitimately, precisely, literally, indubitably, unmistakably, in effect, undoubtedly, categorically, in point of fact, I assure you, be assured, believe me, as a matter of fact, of course, honestly, truly, admittedly, nothing else but, beyond any doubt, in actuality, unquestionably, as sure as you're alive*, no buts about it*, without a doubt. **2** [To a remarkable degree] surprisingly, remarkably, extraordinarily; see VERY.

really *interj.* indeed, honestly, for a fact, yes, is that so, are you sure, no fooling, cross your heart and hope to die, on your honor, you don't say*, ain't it the truth*, you said it*, do tell*, no kidding*.

realm *n.* domain, area, sphere; see DEPARTMENT, EXPANSE, REGION 1.

reappear *v.* come again, reenter, crop up again; see APPEAR 1, REPEAT 2.

rear *n.* hind part, back seat, rear end, tail, tail end, posterior, rump, butt*; see also BACK 1.

rear *v.* lift, elevate, bring up; see RAISE 1, SUPPORT 1.

rearrange *v.* do over, reorganize, shift; see ORDER 3, PREPARE 1.

reason *n.* **1** [The power of reasoning] intelligence, mind, sanity; see JUDGMENT 1. **2** [A process of reasoning] logic, dialectics, speculation, generalization, rationalism, argumentation, inference, induction, deduction, analysis, rationalization. **3** [A basis for rational action] end, object, rationale, intention, motive, ulterior motive, basis, wherefore, aim, intent, cause, design, ground, impetus, idea, motivation, root, incentive, goal, purpose, the why and wherefore; see also PURPOSE 1.

4 [The mind] brain, mentality, intellect; see MIND 1. —**by reason of** because of, for, by way of; see BECAUSE. —**in** (or **within**) **reason** in accord with what is reasonable, rationally, understandably; see REASONABLY 1. —**stand to reason** be feasible, seem all right, be logical; see CONVINCE. —**with reason** understandably, soundly, plausibly; see REASONABLY 1.

reason *v.* **1** [To think logically] reflect, deliberate, contemplate; see THINK 1. **2** [To seek a reasonable explanation] suppose, gather, conclude; see ASSUME. **3** [To discuss persuasively] argue, contend, debate; see DISCUSS.

reasonable *a.* **1** [Rational] sane, logical, levelheaded, intelligent, clear-cut, tolerant, endowed with reason, conscious, cerebral, thoughtful, reflective, capable of reason, reasoning, cognitive, percipient, discerning, discriminating, commonsense, consistent, broad-minded, liberal, generous, sensible, unprejudiced, unbiased, flexible, agreeable; see also RATIONAL 1.—*Ant.* PREJUDICED, intolerant, biased. **2** [Characterized by justice] fair, right, just; see HONEST 1. **3** [Likely to appeal to the reason] feasible, sound, plausible; see UNDERSTANDABLE. **4** [Moderate in price] inexpensive, reduced, fair; see CHEAP 1.

reasonably *a.* **1** [In a reasonable manner] rationally, sanely, logically, understandably, plausibly, sensibly, soundly, persuasively, fairly, justly, honestly, wisely, judiciously, plainly, intelligently, soberly, agreeably, in reason, within reason, within the limits of reason, as far as possible, as far as could be expected, as much as good sense dictates, within reasonable limitations, with due restraint. **2** [To a moderate degree] mildly, prudently, fairly, moderately, inexpensively, temperately, evenly, calmly, gently, leniently, sparingly, frugally, indulgently, tolerantly, within bounds.

reasoning *n.* thinking, rationalizing, drawing conclusions; see THOUGHT 1.

reassure *v.* convince, console, give confidence; see COMFORT 1, ENCOURAGE, GUARANTEE.

rebel *n.* insurrectionist, revolutionist, revolutionary, agitator, insurgent, traitor, seditionist, mutineer, subversive, subverter, anarchist, overthrower, nihilist, guerrilla, member of the uprising, rioter, terrorist, demagogue, revolter, separatist, malcontent, schismatic, dissenter, deserter, apostate, turncoat, counterrevolutionary, renegade, secessionist, underground worker; see also RADICAL.

rebel *v.* rise up, resist, revolt, turn against, defy, resist lawful authority, fight in the streets, strike, boycott, break with, overturn, mutiny, riot, take up arms against, start a confrontation, secede, renounce, combat, oppose, be insubordinate, be treasonable, upset, overthrow, dethrone, disobey, raise hell*, run amok*.—*Ant.* OBEY, be contented, submit.

rebellion *n.* insurrection, revolt, defiance; see DISOBEDIENCE, REVOLUTION 2.

rebellious *a.* revolutionary, insurgent, counterrevolutionary, terrorist, warring, stubborn, contemptuous, insolent, scornful, intractable, unyielding, recalcitrant, insurrectionary, attacking, rioting, mutinous, dissident, factious, fractious, seditious, treasonable, traitorous, disobedient, refractory, defiant, resistant, riotous, insubordinate, sabotaging, treacherous, bellicose, seditious, disloyal, disaffected, alienated, ungovernable, restless, threatening, anarchistic, iconoclastic, individualistic, radical, independent-minded, quarrelsome.—*Ant.* CALM, DOCILE, peaceful.

rebirth *n.* resurrection, rejuvenation, rehabilitation; see REVIVAL 1.

rebound *v.* bounce back, ricochet, spring back; see BOUNCE.

rebuild *v.* **1** [To repair] touch up, patch, fix; see REPAIR. **2** [To restore] overhaul, replace, remake; see RECONSTRUCT.

rebuke *n.* condemnation, reproof, reprimand; see INSULT.

rebuke *v.* reprove, reprimand, censure; see OPPOSE 1.

recall *v.* **1** [To call to mind] recollect, think of, revive; see REMEMBER 1. **2** [To remove from office] discharge, disqualify, suspend; see DISMISS. **3** [To summon again] call back, reconvene, reassemble; see SUMMON.

recalled *a.* **1** [Remembered] recollected, brought to mind, summoned up; see REMEMBERED. **2** [Relieved of responsibility] stripped of office, dismissed, cast out, displaced, fired, replaced, ousted, suspended, laid off, cashiered, pensioned, let out, let go, removed, retired, impeached, kicked upstairs*, canned*, busted*, washed out*; see also DISCHARGED.

recapture *v.* regain, reobtain, reacquire; see RECOVER 1.

recede *v.* **1** [To go backward] fall back, shrink from, withdraw; see RETREAT. **2** [To sink] ebb, drift away, lower, turn down, abate, decline, go away, drop, fall off, lessen; see also DECREASE 1, FALL 2.—*Ant.* RISE, ascend, increase.

receipt *n.* **1** [The act of receiving] receiving, acquisition, acquiring, accession, acceptance, taking, arrival, getting, admitting, reception; see also ADMISSION 1.—*Ant.* DELIVERY, shipment, giving. **2** [An acknowledgement of receipt] letter, voucher, release, cancellation, slip, sales slip, signed notice, stub, discharge, declaration, paid bill; see also CERTIFICATE.

receive *v.* **1** [To take into one's charge] accept, be given, admit, get, gain, inherit, acquire, gather up, collect, obtain, reap, procure, derive, appropriate, seize, take possession, redeem, pocket, pick up, hold, come by, earn, take in, assume, draw, win, secure, come into, come in for, catch, get from; see also GET 1.—*Ant.* DISCARD, abandon, refuse. **2** [To endure] undergo, experience, suffer; see ENDURE 2. **3** [To support] bear, sustain, prop; see SUPPORT 1. **4** [To make welcome] accommodate, initiate, induct, install, make welcome, shake hands with, admit, permit, welcome home, accept, entertain, invite in, show in, usher in, let through, make comfortable, bring as a guest into, introduce, give a party, give access to, allow entrance to, roll out the red carpet for*, give the red-carpet treatment to*, get out the welcome mat for*; see also GREET.—*Ant.* VISIT, be a guest, call.

received *a.* taken, gotten, acquired, obtained, honored, brought in, signed for, admitted, collected, gathered; see also ACCEPTED, ACKNOWLEDGED.—*Ant.* GIVEN, disbursed, delivered.

receiver *n.* **1** [One who receives] customer, recipient, beneficiary; see HEIR. **2** [A device for receiving] telephone, cellphone, television, radio, satellite dish, radio telescope, walkie-talkie, headphone, car phone, beeper, pager, mission control, control center, listening device, transceiver, bug*.

recent *a.* **1** [Lately brought into being] fresh, novel, newly born; see MODERN 1, UNUSUAL 1, 2. **2** [Associated with modern times] contemporary, up-to-date, current; see MODERN 1, 3.

recently *a.* lately, in recent times, just now, just a while ago, not long ago, a short while ago, of late, newly, freshly, new, the other day, within the recent past.—*Ant.* ONCE, long ago, formerly.

receptacle *n.* box, wastebasket, holder; see CONTAINER.

reception *n.* **1** [The act of receiving] acquisition, acceptance, accession; see RECEIPT 2. **2** [The manner of receiving] greeting, encounter, meeting, reaction, response, introduction, welcome, salutation, induc-

tion, admission, disposition; see also GREETING. **3** [A social function] gathering, party, soiree; see GATHERING.

receptive *a.* responsive, sensitive, perceptive; see OBSERVANT, SYMPATHETIC.

recess *n.* **1** [An intermission] respite, rest, pause, interlude, break, cessation, stop, suspension, interval, coffee break, intervening period, halt, breather*. **2** [An indentation] break, dent, corner; see HOLE 1. **3** [A recessed space] cell, cubicle, nook; see ROOM 2.

recession *n.* unemployment, inflation, decline; see DEPRESSION 3.

recipe *n.* formula, receipt, instructions, prescription, cooking instructions, directions, method, procedure, compound.

recipient *n.* receiver, beneficiary, legatee; see HEIR.

recital *n.* presentation, concert, musical; see PERFORMANCE.

recitation *n.* **1** [The act of reciting] delivery, speaking, playing, narrating, reading, recounting, discoursing, declaiming, soliloquizing, discussion, holding forth, performance, recital, rehearsal, monologue, discourse. **2** [A compositon used for recitation] reading selection, performance piece, monologue; see SPEECH 3, WRITING 2.

recite *v.* **1** [To repeat formally] declaim, address, read, render, discourse, hold forth, enact, dramatize, deliver from memory, interpret, soliloquize. **2** [To report on a lesson] answer, give a report, explain; see DISCUSS, REPORT 1. **3** [To relate in detail] enumerate, enlarge, report, account for, give an account for, impart, convey, quote, communicate, utter, describe, relate, state, tell, mention, narrate, recount, retell, picture, delineate, portray; see also EXPLAIN, TELL 1.

reckless *a.* thoughtless, foolish, wild; see RASH.

recklessly *a.* dangerously, heedlessly, with abandon; see BRAVELY, CARELESSLY.

reckon *v.* consider, evaluate, judge; see ESTIMATE.

reclaim *v.* **1** [To bring into usable condition] restore, regenerate, redeem; see RECOVER 1. **2** [To reform] rehabilitate, improve, mend; see REFORM 3.

reclamation *n.* redemption, repair, repossession; see RECOVERY 3.

recognition *n.* **1** [The act of recognizing] recalling, remembering, identifying, perceiving, verifying, apprehending, acknowledging, noticing, recollection, memory, identification, recall, reidentification, cognizance, remembrance, realization. **2** [Tangible evidence of recognition] greeting, acknowledgment, identification, perception, admission, verification, comprehension, appreciation, renown, esteem, notice, attention, acceptance, regard, honor, credit.

recognize *v.* **1** [To know again] be familiar with, make out, distinguish, verify, recollect, sight, diagnose, place, espy, descry, recall, remember, see, perceive, admit knowledge of, notice; see also KNOW 1. **2** [To acknowledge] admit, appreciate, realize; see ALLOW. **3** [To acknowledge the legality of a government] exchange diplomatic representatives with, have diplomatic relations with, sanction, approve, extend formal recognition to; see also ACKNOWLEDGE 2.

recognized *a.* sighted, caught, realized, acknowledged, perceived, known, appreciated, admitted, recalled, remembered.

recoil *v.* turn away, shrink from, draw back; see RETREAT.

recollect *v.* recall, bring to mind, look back on; see REMEMBER 1.

recollection *n.* remembrance, reminiscence, consciousness; see MEMORY 1.

recommend *v.* **1** [To lend support or approval] agree to, sanction, hold up, commend, extol, compliment, applaud, advocate, celebrate, praise, speak highly of, acclaim, eulogize, confirm, laud, second, favor, back, stand by, magnify, glorify, exalt, think highly of, think well of, be satisfied with, esteem, value, prize, uphold, justify, endorse, go on record for, be all for, vouch for, front for, go to bat for*.—*Ant.* DENOUNCE, censure, renounce. **2** [To make a suggestion or prescription] prescribe, suggest, counsel; see ADVISE, URGE 2.

recommendation *n.* **1** [The act of recommending] guidance, counsel, direction; see ADVICE, SUGGESTION 1. **2** [A document that vouches for character or ability] certificate, testimonial, reference, letter of introduction, character reference, credentials, letter of recommendation, letter in support; see also LETTER 2.

recommended *a.* advocated, endorsed, suggested; see APPROVED.

reconcile *v.* **1** [To adjust] adapt, arrange, regulate; see ADJUST 1, 2. **2** [To bring into harmony] conciliate, assuage, pacify, propitiate, mitigate, make up, mediate, arbitrate, intercede, bring together, accustom oneself to, harmonize, accord, dictate peace, accommodate, appease,

reunite, make peace between, bring to terms, bring into one's camp, win over, bury the hatchet, patch up, kiss and make up; see also SETTLE 7.—*Ant.* BOTHER, irritate, alienate.

reconciled *a.* settled, regulated, arranged; see DETERMINED 1.

reconciliation *n.* conciliation, settlement, rapprochement; see ADJUSTMENT, AGREEMENT 1.

reconsider *v.* reevaluate, think over, rearrange, consider again, recheck, reexamine, correct, amend, revise, retrace, rework, replan, review, withdraw from consideration, reweigh, amend one's judgment; see also CONSIDER.

reconstruct *v.* rebuild, remodel, construct again, make over, re-create, revamp, recondition, reconstitute, reestablish, restore, reproduce, refashion, reorganize, replace, overhaul, renovate, modernize, rework, construct from the original, copy, remake; see also BUILD, REPAIR.

reconstruction *n.* rebuilding, rehabilitation, restoration; see REPAIR.

record *n.* **1** [Documentary evidence] manuscript, inscription, transcription, account, history, legend, story, writing, written material, document. *Types of records include the following:* register, catalog, list, inventory, memo, memorandum, registry, schedule, chronicle, docket, scroll, archive, note, contract, statement, will, testament, petition, calendar, log, letter, memoir, reminiscence, dictation, confession, deposition, inscription, official record, sworn document, evidence, license, bulletin, gazette, newspaper, magazine, annual report, journal, *Congressional Record*, transactions, debates, bill, annals, presidential order, state paper, white paper, blue book, budget, report, entry, book, publication, autograph, signature, vital statistics, deed, paper, diary, stenographic notes, ledger, daybook, almanac, proceedings, minutes, description, affidavit, certificate, transcript, dossier, roll, tape, disk, microfilm, microfiche, floppy disk, CD. **2** [One's past] career, experience, work; see LIFE 2. **3** [A device for the reproduction of sound] recording, disk, phonograph record, LP, transcription, compact disc, CD, laserdisc, canned music*, cut, take, platter*. **—go on record** assert, attest, state; see DECLARE. **—off the record** confidential, unofficial, secret; see PRIVATE. **—on the record** recorded, stated, official; see PUBLIC 1.

record *v.* **1** [To write down] register, write in, jot down, set down, take down, put on record, transcribe, list, note, file, mark, inscribe, log, catalog, tabulate, put in writing, put in black and white, chronicle, keep accounts, keep an account of, make a written account of, matriculate, enroll, journalize, put on paper, preserve, make an entry in, chalk up, write up, enter, report, book, post, copy, document, insert, enumerate; see also WRITE 1. **2** [To indicate] point out, register, show; see NAME 2. **3** [To record electronically] tape, cut, photograph, make a record of, make a tape, tape-record, film, videotape, cut a record.

recorded *a.* listed, filed, on file, in black and white, in writing, inscribed, put down, registered, documented, entered, written, published, noted down, described, reported, cataloged, mentioned, certified, kept, chronicled, booked.

recorder *n.* dictaphone, recording instrument, cassette; see TAPE RECORDER.

recording *n.* documentation, recounting, reporting; see RECORD 1.

records *n.* documents, chronicles, archives, public papers, registers, annals, memorabilia, memoranda, lists, returns, statistics, diaries, accounts.

recover *v.* **1** [To obtain again] redeem, salvage, retrieve, rescue, reclaim, recoup, find again, recapture, repossess, bring back, win back, reacquire, obtain, regain, rediscover, resume, catch up; see also GET 1.—*Ant.* LOSE, let slip, fall behind. **2** [To improve one's condition] gain, increase, better; see IMPROVE 2, PROFIT 2.—*Ant.* FAIL, go bankrupt, give up. **3** [To regain health] rally, come around, come to, come out of it, get out of danger, improve, convalesce, heal, get the better of, overcome, start anew, be restored, mend, revive, be oneself again, perk up, gain strength, recuperate, get well, get over, get better, get through, return to form, make a comeback, get back in shape, snap out of it, pull through*.—*Ant.* DIE, fail, become worse.

recovered *a.* renewed, found, replaced, reborn, rediscovered, reawakened, retrieved, redeemed, reclaimed, regained, revived, returned, resumed; see also DISCOVERED.—*Ant.* LOST, missed, dropped.

recovery *n.* **1** [The act of returning to normal] reestablishment, resumption, restoration, reinstatement, return, rehabilitation, reconstruction, reformation, re-creation, replacement, readjustment, improving, getting back to normal; see also sense 2, IMPROVEMENT 1. **2** [The process of regaining health] convalescence, recuperation, revival, rebirth, renaissance, resurgence, resurrection, regeneration, cure, improvement, reawakening, resus-

citation, renewal, rejuvenation, rehabilitation, return of health, comeback, physical improvement, healing, betterment. **3** [The act of regaining possession] repossession, retrieval, reclamation, redemption, indemnification, reparation, compensation, recapture, recouping, return, restoration, remuneration, reimbursement, retaking, recall.

recreation *n.* amusement, relaxation, diversion, play, fun, entertainment, enjoyment, festivity, hobby, holiday, vacation, pastime, pleasure, game, avocation, refreshment; see also SPORT 1.

recruit *n.* new person, novice, beginner, selectee, draftee, trainee, volunteer, enlisted person, serviceman, servicewoman, soldier, sailor, marine, rookie*; see also SOLDIER.

recruit *v.* **1** [To raise troops] draft, call up, select, supply, muster, deliver, sign up, induct, take in, find manpower, call to arms, bring into service; see also ENLIST 1. **2** [To gather needed resources] restore, store up, replenish; see GET 1.

rectangle *n.* geometrical figure, square, box, oblong, four-sided figure, right-angled parallelogram; see also FORM 1.

rectangular *a.* square, four-sided, right-angled; see ANGULAR.

rectitude *n.* integrity, trustworthiness, responsibility; see HONESTY.

recuperate *v.* heal, pull through, get back on one's feet; see RECOVER 3.

recur *v.* return, reappear, crop up again; see HAPPEN 2, REPEAT 1.

recurrent *a.* reoccurring, repetitive, habitual; see REPEATED 1.

recycle *v.* start over, start again, restart; see BEGIN 1, RESUME.

red *n.* *Tints and shades of red include the following:* scarlet, carmine, vermilion, crimson, cerise, cherry red, ruby, garnet, maroon, brick red, claret, rust, red gold, magenta, pink, fuchsia, coral red, blood red, russet, terra cotta, Chinese red, Congo red, Turkey red, aniline red, chrome red, rose, rose blush, old rose, fire engine red; see also COLOR. **—in the red** in debt, losing money, going broke*; see RUINED 3. **—see red*** become angry, lose one's temper, get mad; see RAGE 1.

red-blooded *a.* robust, vigorous, hearty; see HEALTHY.

redden *v.* flush, rouge, color, blush.

reddish *a.* flushed, somewhat red, rose; see RED, *n.*

redecorate *v.* refurbish, refresh, renew, paint, repaint, repaper, restore, recondition, remodel, renovate, revamp, reaarrange, touch up, patch up, plaster, refurnish, wallpaper, clean up, carpet, do over*, fix up*; see also DECORATE.

redeem *v.* **1** [To recover through a payment] buy back, repay, purchase; see GET 1. **2** [To save] liberate, set free, deliver; see RESCUE 1. —**redeem oneself** atone, give satisfaction, make amends; see PAY FOR.

redeemer *n.* rescuer, deliverer, liberator; see PROTECTOR.

redemption *n.* regeneration, salvation, rebirth; see RESCUE 1.

redheaded *a.* auburn-haired, red-haired, sandy-haired, titian-haired, strawberry-blonde, carrot-topped.

red-hot *a.* **1** [Burning] heated, sizzling, scorching; see BURNING, HOT 1. **2** [Raging] vehement, violent, furious; see EXTREME. **3** [Newest] latest, most recent, hippest*; see MODERN 1.

redo *v.* start over, redesign, rethink, go back to the drawing board, revamp, do over again, redecorate, remodel; see also REPEAT.

redone *a.* done over, refinished, fixed up; see IMPROVED.

redress *n.* compensation, reparation, amends; see PAYMENT 1.

red tape *n.* **1** [Delay] wait, roadblock, holdup; see DELAY. **2** [Bureaucracy] paperwork, inflexible routine, officialdom; see GOVERNMENT 1, 2.

reduce *v.* **1** [To make less] lessen, diminish, cut down; see DECREASE 2. **2** [To defeat] conquer, overcome, subdue; see DEFEAT 2, 3. **3** [To humble] degrade, demote, abase; see HUMBLE, HUMILIATE.

reduced *a.* **1** [Made smaller] lessened, decreased, diminished, shortened, abridged, abbreviated, condensed, miniaturized, transistorized, compressed, economized, cut down, shrunk, subtracted, contracted, melted, boiled down.—*Ant.* SPREAD, enlarged, stretched. **2** [Made lower] lowered, abated, sunk, deflated, leveled, marked down, discounted, cheapened, weakened, debilitated, humbled, demoted, degraded, downgraded.—*Ant.* RAISED, heightened, elevated.

reduction *n.* **1** [The process of making smaller] contraction, abatement, reducing, refinement, diminution, lowering, lessening, shortening, condensation, decrease, loss, compression, depression, subtraction, discount, shrinkage, atrophy, constriction, modification, curtailment, abbreviation, miniaturization, abridgment, mitigation, remission, decline.—*Ant.* INCREASE, increasing, enlargement. **2** [An amount that constitutes reduction] decrease, rebate, cut; see DISCOUNT.

redundant *a.* wordy, bombastic, verbose; see DULL 3, 4.

reeducate *v.* reinstruct, readjust, rehabilitate; see TEACH.

reef *n.* ridge, shoal, sand bar; see ROCK 2.

reek *n.* stench, stink, smell; see SMELL 2.

reek *v.* give off an odor, emit a stench, stink; see SMELL 1.

reel *n.* spool, bobbin, spindle; see ROLL 2.

reexamine *v.* go back over, review, check thoroughly; see EXAMINE.

refer *v.* **1** [To concern] regard, relate, have relation, have to do with, apply, be about, answer to, involve, connect, be a matter of, have a bearing on, correspond with, bear upon, comprise, include, belong, pertain, have reference, take in, cover, point, hold, encompass, incorporate, touch, deal with; see also CONCERN 1. **2** [To mention] allude to, bring up, direct a remark, make reference, ascribe, direct attention, attribute, cite, quote, hint at, point to, notice, indicate, speak about, suggest, touch on, give as an example, associate, exemplify, instance, excerpt, extract; see also MENTION. **3** [To direct] send to, put in touch with, relegate, commit, submit to, assign, give a recommendation to, introduce, designate; see also LEAD 1. —**referred to 1** [Mentioned] brought up, alluded to, spoken about; see MENTIONED, SUGGESTED. **2** [Directed] recommended, sent on, introduced to; see PROPOSED.

referee *n.* arbitrator, conciliator, judge; see UMPIRE.

reference *n.* **1** [An allusion] mention, citation, implication; see HINT. **2** [A book of reference] original text, source, informant; see BOOK, DICTIONARY. **3** [A person vouching for another] associate, employer, patron; see FRIEND.

refine *v.* **1** [To purify] clarify, strain, filter; see CLEAN, PURIFY. **2** [To improve] perfect, polish, hone; see EXPLAIN.

refined *a.* **1** [Purified] cleaned, cleansed, aerated, strained, washed, clean, rarefied, boiled down, distilled, clarified, processed, tried, drained; see also PURE.—*Ant.* RAW, crude, unrefined. **2** [Genteel] cultivated, civilized, polished, elegant, well-bred, gracious, enlightened, gentlemanly, ladylike, restrained, gentle, mannerly, high-minded, suave, urbane, courteous; see also POLITE.

refinement *n.* **1** [The act of refining] cleansing, clearing, purification; see CLEANING. **2** [Culture] civilization, cultivation, sophistication, breeding, enlightenment, wide knowledge, lore, erudition, science, scholarship, learning; see also CULTURE 1. **3** [Genteel feelings and behavior] elegance, politeness, polish, good manners, suavity, savoir-faire, courtesy, grace, gentleness, tact, cultivation, graciousness, civility, affability, taste, discrimination, fineness, delicacy, dignity, urbanity; see also CULTURE 2.

refinished *a.* redone, remodeled, fixed up; see CHANGED 2, REPAIRED.

reflect *v.* **1** [To contemplate] speculate, concentrate, weigh; see CONSIDER, THINK 1. **2** [To throw back] echo, reecho, repeat, match, take after, return, resonate, reverberate, copy, resound, reproduce, reply, be resonant, emulate, imitate, follow, catch, rebound, bounce. **3** [To throw back an image] mirror, shine, produce, show up on, flash, cast back, return, give forth.

reflection *n.* **1** [Thought] consideration, absorption, imagination, observation, thinking, contemplation, rumination, speculation, musing, deliberation, study, pondering, meditation, concentration, cogitation; see also THOUGHT 1. **2** [An image] impression, rays, light, shine, glitter, appearance, idea, reflected image, likeness, shadow, duplicate, picture, echo, representation, reproduction; see also COPY, IMAGE 2.

reflector *n.* shiny metal, glass, looking glass; see MIRROR.

reflex *a.* mechanical, unthinking, habitual; see AUTOMATIC, SPONTANEOUS.

reform *n.* reformation, betterment, new law; see IMPROVEMENT 2.

reform *v.* **1** [To change into a new form] reorganize, remodel, revise, repair, reconstruct, rearrange, transform, ameliorate, redeem, rectify, better, rehabilitate, improve, correct, cure, remedy, convert, mend, amend, restore, rebuild, reclaim, revolutionize, regenerate, refashion, renovate, renew, rework, reconstitute, make over, remake; see also CORRECT, REPAIR.—*Ant.* CORRUPT, degrade, botch. **2** [To correct evils] amend, clean out, give a new basis, abolish, repeal, uplift, ameliorate, rectify, regenerate, give new life to, remedy, stamp out, make better, standardize, bring up to code; see also IMPROVE 1. **3** [To change one's conduct for the better] resolve, mend, regenerate, uplift, make amends, make a new start, make resolutions, turn over a new leaf, go straight*, clean up one's act*, swear off; see also sense 2.

Reformation *n.* Renaissance, Lutheranism, Protestantism, Puritanism, Calvinism, Anglicanism,

Unitarianism, Counter Reformation, Protestant Movement; see also REVOLUTION 2.

reformed *a.* **1** [Changed] altered, transformed, shifted, reconstituted, reorganized, shuffled, reestablished, revolutionized, rectified, amended, reset, reworked, renewed, regenerated, redone, rejiggered; see also CHANGED 2, IMPROVED.—*Ant.* preserved, degenerated, deteriorated. **2** [Changed for the better in behavior] converted, improved, redeemed, born-again, gone straight*, turned over a new leaf; see also POLITE, RIGHTEOUS 1.

refrain *n.* undersong*, theme, strain; see MUSIC 1, SONG.

refrain *v.* cease, avoid, forbear; see ABSTAIN.

refresh *v.* invigorate, animate, exhilarate; see RENEW 1.

refreshing *a.* invigorating, rousing, exhilarating; see STIMULATING.

refreshment *n.* snack, light meal, treat; see DRINK 1, FOOD.

refrigerate *v.* chill, make cold, freeze; see COOL.

refrigeration *n.* cooling, chilling, freezing; see PRESERVATION.

refrigerator *n.* fridge*, icebox, cooler, refrigerator car, cooling apparatus, refrigeration equipment, deep freezer, freezer, deepfreeze.

refuge *n.* **1** [A place of protection] shelter, asylum, sanctuary, covert, home, retreat, anchorage, nunnery, convent, monastery, poorhouse, safe place, hiding place, game preserve, safe haven, safe house, harbor, haven, fortress, stronghold, hideaway*, hide-out*. **2** [A means of resort] alternative, resource, last resort; see ESCAPE.

refugee *n.* exile, expatriate, fugitive, emigrant, renegade, foreigner, castaway, derelict, defector, homeless person, leper, pariah, outlaw, prodigal, displaced person, alien, outcast.

refund *n.* return, reimbursement, repayment, remuneration, compensation, allowance, payment for expenses, rebate, discount, settlement, retribution, satisfaction, consolation, money back; see also PAYMENT 1.

refund *v.* pay back, reimburse, remit, return, repay, relinquish, make good, balance, recoup, adjust, reward, restore, redeem, make repayment to, compensate, recompense, make amends, redress, remunerate, give back, settle, honor a claim, kick back*, make good*, make up for; see also PAY 1.

refunded *a.* repaid, reimbursed, discharged; see PAID, RETURNED.

refusal *n.* repudiation, renunciation,

rebuff, snub, rejection, nonacceptance, denial, disavowal, noncompliance, opposition, forbidding, veto, interdiction, proscription, ban, writ, exclusion, negation, repulse, withholding, disclaimer, nonconsent, unwillingness, regrets, declination, repulsion, reversal, dissent, prohibition, disfavor, disapproval, curb, restraint.

refuse *n.* leavings, remains, residue; see TRASH 1.

refuse *v.* dissent, desist, repel, rebuff, scorn, pass up, reject, disallow, have no plans to, not anticipate, demur, protest, withdraw, hold back, withhold, shun, turn thumbs down on, evade, dodge, ignore, spurn, regret, turn down, turn from, beg to be excused, send regrets, not budge, cut out of the budget, not budget, not care to, refuse to receive, dispense with, not be at home to, say no, make excuses, disapprove, set aside, turn away, beg off, brush off*, not buy*, hold off, turn one's back on, turn a deaf ear to; see also DENY.—*Ant.* ALLOW, admit, consent.

refused *a.* declined, rejected, rebuffed, vetoed, repudiated, forbidden, denied, disowned, disavowed, forsaken, blocked, repelled, closed to, dismissed, turned down, not budgeted, not in the budget.—*Ant.* PERMITTED, allowed, consented to.

refute *v.* disprove, answer, prove false; see DENY.

regain *v.* recapture, retrieve, reacquire; see RECOVER 1.

regard *n.* 1 [A look] gaze, glance, once-over*; see LOOK 3. 2 [A favorable opinion] esteem, respect, honor, favor, liking, interest, fondness, attachment, deference, opinion, sympathy, estimation, appreciation, reverence, consideration, love, affection, value, devotion; see also ADMIRATION.

regard *v.* 1 [To look at] observe, notice, mark; see SEE 1. 2 [To have an attitude] surmise, look upon, view; see CONSIDER, THINK 1. 3 [To hold in esteem] respect, esteem, value; see ADMIRE.

regarding *a., prep.* concerning, with reference to, in relation to, as regards; see also ABOUT 2. **—as regards** concerning, regarding, respecting; see ABOUT 2. **—in regard to** as to, concerning, with regard to; see ABOUT 2, REGARDING.

regardless *a.* 1 [Indifferent] negligent, careless, unobservant, unheeding, inattentive, inconsiderate, reckless, inadvertent, unfeeling, deaf, blind, heedless, neglectful, mindless, insensitive, lax, listless, uninterested, unconcerned.—*Ant.* OBSERVANT, alert, vigilant. 2 [In spite of; *usually used with "of"*] despite, aside from, distinct from, without regard to, without considering, notwithstanding, at any cost, leaving aside; see also ALTHOUGH, BUT 1.

regards *n.* best wishes, compliments, greetings, salutations, remembrances, respects, love, deference, one's best, commendation, love and kisses*; see also GREETING.

regenerate *v.* restore, re-create, renew; see PRODUCE 2, REVIVE 1.

regeneration *n.* rebuilding, rehabilitation, renovation; see REPAIR.

regime *n.* administration, management, political system; see GOVERNMENT 2.

regiment *n.* corps, soldiers, military organization; see ARMY 2.

regimentation *n.* discipline, strictness, collectivization, organization, planned economy, standardization, regulation, uniformity, arrangement, mechanization, institutionalization, classification, division, lining up, adjustment, harmonization, grouping, ordering; see also RESTRAINT 2.

region *n.* 1 [An indefinite area] country, district, territory, section, sector, province, zone, realm, vicinity, quarter, locale, locality, environs, precinct, county, neighborhood, terrain, domain, range. 2 [A limited area] precinct, ward, block; see AREA. 3 [Scope] sphere, province, realm; see FIELD 3.

regional *a.* provincial, territorial, local, environmental, positional, geographical, parochial, sectional, topical, locational, insular, topographic.

register *n.* 1 [A list] file, registry, roll; see LIST, RECORD 1. 2 [A heating regulator] grate, hot-air vent, radiator; see APPLIANCE.

register *v.* 1 [To record] check in, enroll, file; see LIST 1, RECORD 1. 2 [To indicate] point to, designate, record; see NAME 2. 3 [To show] express, disclose, manifest; see DISPLAY. 4 [To enlist or enroll] go through registration, check into, make an entry, sign up for, check in, sign in, join.

registration *n.* 1 [The act of registering] enrolling, signing up, certification, matriculation, recording, listing, filing, cataloging, booking, noting down, stamping, authorizing, notarization; see also ENROLLMENT 1. 2 [Those who have registered] enrollment, turnout, registrants, voters, hotel guests, students, student body, delegation.

regress *v.* backslide, relapse, revert; see RETREAT, SINK 1.

regressive *a.* conservative, reverse, reactionary; see BACKWARD 1.

regret *n.* 1 [Remorse] concern, compunction, worry, repentance, self-reproach, self-condemnation, self-disgust, misgiving, regretfulness, nostalgia, self-accusation, contrition, qualm, scruple, penitence, bitterness, disappointment, dissatisfaction, uneasiness, discomfort, annoyance, spiritual disturbance; see also CARE 2.—*Ant.* COMFORT, satisfaction, ease. 2 [Grief] sorrow, pain, anxiety; see GRIEF.

regret *v.* 1 [To be sorry for] mourn, bewail, lament, cry over, rue, grieve, repent, have compunctions about, look back upon, feel conscience-stricken, moan, have a bad conscience, have qualms about, weep over, be disturbed over, feel uneasy about, laugh out of the other side of one's mouth*, kick oneself*, bite one's tongue*, cry over spilt milk*.—*Ant.* CELEBRATE, be satisfied with, be happy. 2 [To disapprove of] deplore, be opposed to, deprecate; see DENOUNCE, DISLIKE.

regular *a.* 1 [In accordance with custom] customary, usual, routine; see CONVENTIONAL 1, 3. 2 [In accordance with law] normal, legitimate, lawful; see LEGAL. 3 [In accordance with an observable pattern] orderly, methodical, routine, symmetrical, precise, exact, systematic, arranged, organized, patterned, constant, congruous, consonant, consistent, invariable, formal, regulated, rational, rhythmic, periodic, measured, classified, in order, unconfused, harmonious, normal, natural, cyclic, successive, alternating, probable, recurrent, general, usual, expected, serial, automatic, mechanical, hourly, daily, monthly, weekly, annual, seasonal, yearly, diurnal, quotidian, anticipated, hoped for, counted on, generally occurring, in the natural course of events, punctual, steady, uniform.—*Ant.* IRREGULAR, sporadic, erratic.

regularity *n.* evenness, steadiness, uniformity, routine, constancy, consistency, invariability, recurrence, system, congruity, punctuality, homogeneity, rhythm, periodicity, rotation, conformity, proportion, symmetry, balance, cadence, harmony.

regularly *a.* customarily, habitually, punctually, unchangingly, systematically, as a rule, usually, commonly, as a matter of course, tirelessly, conventionally, ordinarily, repeatedly, frequently, faithfully, religiously, mechanically, automatically, normally, periodically, evenly, methodically, exactly, monotonously, rhythmically, typically, steadily, continually, like clockwork, cyclically, constantly, always, cease-

lessly, time and time again, invariably, redundantly, hourly, incessantly, daily, 24/7*, perpetually, over and over again, weekly, monthly, annually, exactly; day in, day out.—*Ant.* IRREGULARLY, unevenly, brokenly.

regulate *v.* 1 [To control] rule, legislate, direct; see GOVERN, MANAGE 1. 2 [To adjust] arrange, methodize, classify, systematize, put in order, fix, settle, adapt, standardize, coordinate, allocate, readjust, reconcile, rectify, correct, improve, temper, set; see also ADJUST 1.

regulated *a.* fixed, adjusted, arranged, directed, controlled, supervised, methodized, systematized, settled, adapted, coordinated, reconciled, improved, standardized, tempered, ruled; see also CLASSIFIED, MANAGED 2, ORGANIZED.—*Ant.* CONFUSED, disarranged, upset.

regulation *n.* 1 [The act of regulating] handling, direction, control; see MANAGEMENT 1. 2 [A rule] principle, statute, ordinance; see COMMAND, LAW 3.

regulator *n.* control, thermostat, valve; see MACHINE.

rehabilitate *v.* restore, improve, reestablish; see RENEW 1.

rehabilitation *n.* rebuilding, reestablishment, remaking; see IMPROVEMENT 1, REPAIR.

rehearsal *n.* recitation, recital, trial performance, practice performance, experiment, test flight, reading, dress rehearsal, call; see also PERFORMANCE, PRACTICE 3.

rehearse *v.* 1 [To tell] describe, recount, relate; see TELL 1, 2. 2 [To repeat] tell again, retell, do over, recapitulate, reenact; see also REPEAT 3. 3 [To practice for a performance] drill, experiment, hold rehearsals, speak from a script, run through, hold a reading, learn one's part; see also PRACTICE 1.

reign *v.* hold power, sit on the throne, wear the crown; see GOVERN, MANAGE 1.

reimburse *v.* repay, compensate, make reparations; see PAY 1, REFUND.

reimbursement *n.* compensation, restitution, recompense; see PAYMENT 1.

rein *n.* bridle strap, line, control; see ROPE. —**give (free) rein to** authorize, permit, condone; see ALLOW. —**keep a rein on** control, check, have authority over; see MANAGE 1.

reincarnation *n.* incarnation, transmigration of souls, rebirth; see BIRTH, RETURN 2.

reinforce *v.* buttress, bolster, augment; see STRENGTHEN.

reinforced *a.* supported, assisted, strengthened, augmented, buttressed, fortified, backed, built-up, stiffened, thickened, cushioned, lined; see also STRONG 2.

reinforcement *n.* **1** [Support] coating, concrete block, pillar; see SUPPORT 2. **2** [Military aid; *usually plural*] fresh troops, additional materiel, new ordnance; see HELP 1.

reject *v.* **1** [To refuse] repudiate, decline, renounce; see DENY, REFUSE. **2** [To discard] cast out, throw out, expel; see DISCARD.

rejected *a.* returned, given back, denied; see REFUSED.

rejection *n.* repudiation, denial, dismissal; see REFUSAL.

rejoice *v.* exult, enjoy, revel; see CELEBRATE 2.

rejuvenate *v.* reinvigorate, renew, refresh; see STRENGTHEN.

rejuvenation *n.* reinvigoration, stimulation, revivification; see REVIVAL 1.

relapse *n.* reversion, recidivism, return; see LOSS 3.

relapse *v.* lapse, retrogress, fall, backslide, revert, regress, suffer a relapse, deteriorate, degenerate, fall from grace, fall off, weaken, sink back, fall into again, slip back, slide back, be overcome, give in to again.

relate *v.* **1** [Tell] recount, recite, retell; see DESCRIBE, REPORT 1. **2** [Connect] bring into relation, associate, correlate; see COMPARE 1. — **relate to** be associated with, be connected with, affect; see CONCERN 1, REFER 1.

related *a.* **1** [Told] described, narrated, recounted; see TOLD. **2** [Connected] associated, in touch, with, linked, tied up, knit together, allied, affiliated, complementary, analogous, correspondent, akin, alike, like, parallel, correlated, intertwined, interrelated, similar, mutual, dependent, interdependent, interwoven, of that ilk, in the same category, reciprocal, interchangeable. **3** [Akin] kindred, of the same family, germane, fraternal, cognate, consanguine, of one blood; see also sense 2.

relation *n.* **1** [Relationship] connection, association, similarity; see RELATIONSHIP. **2** [A relative] family connection, sibling, kin; see RELATIVE. — **in relation to** concerning, with reference to, about; see REGARDING.

relationship *n.* relation, connection, tie, association, affinity, likeness, link, kinship, bond, dependence, relativity, proportion, rapport, analogy, homogeneity, interrelation, correlation, nearness, alliance, relevance, accord, hookup*, contact; see also SIMILARITY.—*Ant.* DIFFERENCE, dissimilarity, oppositeness.

relative *a.* dependent, contingent, applicable; see RELATED 2, RELEVANT. —**relative to** with respect to, concerning, relating to; see ABOUT 2.

relative *n.* kin, family connection, relation, member of the family, blood relation, next of kin, sibling, kinsman, kinswoman. *Relatives include the following:* mother, father, parent, grandmother, grandfather, grandparent, grandchild, grandson, granddaughter, great-grandmother, great-grandfather, ancestor, aunt, uncle, great-aunt, great-uncle, cousin, first cousin, second cousin, distant cousin, wife, husband, spouse, daughter, son, child, stepchild, stepparent, half brother, half sister, stepfather, stepmother, biological parent, adoptive parent, descendant, nephew, niece, brother, sister, kinsman, kinswoman, in-law*, mother-in-law, father-in-law, brother-in-law, sister-in-law.

relatively *a.* comparatively, approximately, nearly; see ALMOST.

relax *v.* repose, recline, settle back, make oneself at home, breathe easy*, take one's time, take a break, sit around*, stop work, lie down, unbend, be at ease, take a breather*; see also REST 1.

relaxation *n.* repose, reclining, loosening; see REST 1.

relaxed *a.* untroubled, carefree, at ease; see COMFORTABLE 1.

relay *v.* communicate, transfer, send forth, transmit, hand over, hand down, turn over, deliver, pass on; see also CARRY 1, SEND 1.

release *n.* **1** [Freedom] liberation, discharge, freeing; see FREEDOM 2. **2** [That which has been released; *usually, printed matter*] news story, publicity, news flash; see PROPAGANDA, STORY.

release *v.* liberate, let go, acquit; see FREE.

released *a.* **1** [Freed] discharged, dismissed, liberated; see FREE 1, 2. **2** [Announced] broadcast, stated, made public; see PUBLISHED.

relent *v.* soften, comply, relax; see YIELD 1.

relentless *a.* unmerciful, vindictive, hard; see RUTHLESS.

relevance *n.* connection, significance, pertinence; see IMPORTANCE.

relevant *a.* suitable, appropriate, fit, proper, pertinent to, becoming, pertaining to, apt, applicable, important, fitting, congruous, cognate, related, conforming, concerning, compatible, accordant, referring, harmonious, correspondent, consonant, congruent, consistent, correlated, associated, allied, relative, connected, to the point, bearing on the question, having direct bearing, having to do with, related to, on the nose.—*Ant.* IRRELEVANT, WRONG, not pertinent.

reliability *n.* dependability, trustworthiness, constancy, loyalty, faithfulness, sincerity, devotion, honesty, authenticity, steadfastness, fidelity, safety, security.

reliable *a.* firm, unimpeachable, sterling, strong, positive, stable, dependable, sure, solid, staunch, decisive, unequivocal, steadfast, definite, conscientious, constant, steady, trustworthy, faithful, loyal, good, true, devoted, tried, trusty, honest, honorable, candid, truehearted, responsible, high-principled, sincere, altruistic, determined, reputable, careful, proved, respectable, righteous, decent, incorrupt, truthful, upright, regular, all right, kosher*, OK*, on the up and up*, true-blue, safe, sound, guaranteed, certain, substantial, secure, unquestionable, conclusive, irrefutable, incontestable, unfailing, infallible, authentic, competent, assured, workable, foolproof, surefire.—*Ant.* DANGEROUS, insecure, undependable.

reliably *a.* assuredly, presumably, certainly; see PROBABLY, SURELY.

reliance *n.* confidence, trust, hope; see FAITH 1.

relic *n.* **1** [Something left from an earlier time] vestige, trace, survival, heirloom, antique, souvenir, keepsake, curio, memento, curiosity, token, testimonial, evidence, monument, trophy, remains, artifact, remembrance, bric-a-brac. **2** [A ruin] remnant, residue, remains, broken stone; see also DESTRUCTION 2, RUIN 2.

relief *n.* **1** [The act of bringing succor] alleviation, softening, comforting; see COMFORT. **2** [Aid] assistance, support, maintenance; see HELP 1. **3** [A relieved state of mind] satisfaction, relaxation, ease, release, happiness, contentment, cheer, restfulness, a load off one's mind; see also COMFORT. **4** [The person or thing that brings relief] diversion, relaxation, consolation, solace, reinforcement, supplies, food, shelter, clothing, release, respite, remedy, nursing, medicine, medical care, redress, reparations, indemnities, variety, change, cure; see also HELP 1. **5** [The raised portions of a sculptural decoration or map] projection, contour, configuration; see DECORATION 2.

relieve *v.* **1** [To replace] discharge, throw out, force to resign; see DISMISS. **2** [To lessen; *said especially of pain*] assuage, alleviate, soothe,

comfort, allay, divert, free, ease, lighten, soften, diminish, mitigate, console, cure, aid, assist; see also DECREASE 2, HELP.

relieved *a.* **1** [Eased in mind] comforted, solaced, consoled, reassured, satisfied, soothed, relaxed, put at ease, restored, reconciled, appeased, placated, alleviated, mollified, disarmed, pacified, adjusted, propitiated, breathing easy*; see also COMFORTABLE 1.—*Ant.* SAD, worried, distraught. **2** [Deprived of something, or freed from it] replaced, dismissed, separated from, disengaged, released, made free of, rescued, delivered, supplanted, superseded, succeeded, substituted for, interchanged, exchanged. **3** [Lessened; *said especially of pain*] mitigated, palliated, softened, assuaged, eased, abated, diminished, salved, soothed, lightened, alleviated, drugged, anesthetized.

religion *n.* **1** [All that centers about human beings' belief in or relationship with a superior being or beings] belief, devotion, piety, spirituality, persuasion, godliness, sense of righteousness, morality, theology, faithfulness, devoutness, creed, myth, superstition, doctrine, cult, denomination, mythology, communion, sect, fidelity, conscientiousness, religious bent, ethical standard; see also FAITH 2. **2** [Organized worship or service of a deity] veneration, adoration, consecration, sanctification, prayer, rites, holy sacrifice, incantation, holiday, observance, orthodoxy; see also CEREMONY 2. *Religions include the following:* Christianity, Buddhism, Zen Buddhism, Hinduism, Islam, Judaism, Zoroastrianism, Shintoism, Confucianism, Taoism, Jainism, Bahaism, nature worship, Wicca, paganism, Sikhism, monotheism, ancestor worship, voodoo, Santeria, deism, theism, polytheism, dualism; see also CHURCH 3. —**get religion*** become converted, believe, change; see REFORM 2, 3.

religious *a.* **1** [Pertaining to religion] ethical, spiritual, moral, ecclesiastical, clerical, theological, canonical, divine, supernatural, holy, sacred, churchly, theistic, deistic, priestly, pontifical, pastoral, ministerial.—*Ant.* WORLDLY, secular, earthly. **2** [Devout] pious, puritanical, sanctimonious, pietistic, godly, god-fearing, orthodox, reverend, reverential, believing, faithful, fanatic, evangelistic, revivalistic, churchgoing; see also HOLY 1. **3** [Scrupulous] methodical, minute, thorough; see CAREFUL.

relish *n.* **1** [A condiment] flavoring, accent, pickle. *Relishes include the*

following: catsup or ketchup, piccalilli, cucumber relish, pickle relish,
mincemeat, pickled pears, pickled
peaches, chutney, chili sauce, hot
sauce, cranberry sauce. **2** [Obvious
delight] gusto, joy, great satisfaction; see ZEAL.

relish *v.* enjoy, fancy, be fond of; see
LIKE 1, 2.

reluctance *n.* disinclination, qualm,
hesitation; see DOUBT.

reluctant *a.* disinclined, loath,
unwilling, averse, opposed, tardy,
backward, adverse, laggard, remiss,
slack, squeamish, demurring,
grudging, involuntary, uncertain,
hanging back, hesitant, hesitating,
diffident, with bad grace, indisposed, disheartened, discouraged,
queasy.—*Ant.* WILLING, eager, disposed.

rely on (or **upon**) *v.* hope, have faith
in, count on; see TRUST 1.

remain *v.* **1** [To stay] linger, abide,
reside; see SETTLE 5. **2** [To endure]
keep on, go on, prevail; see CON-
TINUE 1, ENDURE 1. **3** [To be left]
remain standing, endure, outlast;
see SURVIVE 1.

remainder *n.* remaining portion,
leftovers, residue, remains, relic,
remnant, dregs, surplus, leavings,
balance, residuum, excess, overplus,
scrap, fragment, small piece, carry-
over, rest, residual portion, average,
salvage.

remains *n.* corpse, cadaver, relics;
see BODY 2.

remake *v.* change, revise, alter; see
CORRECT.

remark *n.* statement, saying, utterance, annotation, note, mention,
reflection, illustration, point, conclusion, consideration, talk, observation, expression, comment, assertion, witticism.

remark *v.* say, mention, observe; see
SAY, TALK 1.

remarkable *a.* exceptional, extraordinary, uncommon; see UNUSUAL 1.

remarkably *a.* exceptionally, singularly, notably; see ESPECIALLY,
VERY.

remedy *n.* **1** [A medicine] antidote,
pill, drug; see MEDICINE 2, TREAT-
MENT 2. **2** [Effective help] relief,
cure, redress, support, improvement, solution, plan, panacea, cure-
all, assistance, counteraction; see
also RELIEF 4.

remedy *v.* cure, help, aid; see HEAL.

remember *v.* **1** [To recall] recollect,
recognize, summon up, relive, dig
into the past, refresh one's memory,
be reminded of, think of, revive,
bring to mind, call to mind, think
over, think back, look back, brood
over, conjure up, call up, carry one's

thoughts back, look back upon, have
memories of, commemorate, memorialize, reminisce.—*Ant.* LOSE, forget, neglect. **2** [To bear in mind]
keep in mind, memorize, know by
heart, learn, master, get, have
impressed upon one's mind, fix in
the mind, retain, treasure, hold
dear, dwell upon, brood over, keep
forever.—*Ant.* NEGLECT, ignore, disregard.

remembered *a.* thought of, recalled,
recollected, rewarded, summoned
up, brought to mind, memorialized,
haunting one's thoughts, commemorated, dug up.—*Ant.* LOST, forgotten, overlooked.

remembrance *n.* **1** [Memory] recall,
recollection, recognition; see
MEMORY 1. **2** [A gift] memento,
token, keepsake; see GIFT 1.

remind *v.* **1** [To bring into the
memory] bring back, make one
think of, intimate; see HINT. **2** [To
call the attention of another] caution, point out, jog the memory of,
mention to, call attention to, bring
up, prompt, prod, stress, emphasize,
note, stir up, put a bug in one's ear*,
give a cue; see WARN.

reminded *a.* warned, cautioned,
prompted, put in mind of, made
aware, advised, forewarned, noti-
fied, awakened, prodded.

reminder *n.* warning, notice, admonition, note, memorandum, memo,
hint, suggestion, memento, token,
keepsake, trinket, remembrance,
souvenir.

remit *v.* make payment, forward, dispatch; see PAY 1.

remittance *n.* transmittal, money
sent, enclosure; see PAYMENT 1.

remnant *n.* residue, leavings, what
is left; see EXCESS 1, REMAINDER.

remnants *n.* scraps, odds and ends,
leftovers, particles, surplus, vestiges, remains, leavings; see also
EXCESS 1, REMAINDER.

remodel *v.* renovate, refurnish,
refurbish, readjust, reconstruct,
readapt, rearrange, redecorate,
refashion, improve, reshape, recast,
rebuild, modernize, repaint; see also
REPAIR.

remodeled *a.* refurnished, redeco-
rated, rebuilt; see CHANGED 2.

remorse *n.* compunction, contrition,
self-reproach; see GRIEF, REGRET 1.
—without remorse cruel, pitiless,
relentless; see RUTHLESS.

remorseful *a.* contrite, penitent,
repentant; see SORRY 1.

remorseless *a.* unyielding, unforgiving, vindictive; see SEVERE 1, 2.

remote *a.* **1** [Distant] far-off, faraway, out-of-the-way, removed,
beyond, secluded, inaccessible, isolated, unknown, alien, foreign,
undiscovered, off the beaten track,

over the hills and far away, God-forsaken; see also DISTANT.—*Ant.* NEAR, close, accessible. 2 [Ancient] forgotten, past, aged; see OLD 3. 3 [Separated] unrelated, irrelevant, unconnected; see SEPARATED.

removal *n.* dismissal, discharge, expulsion, exile, deportation, banishment, elimination, extraction, dislodgment, evacuation, ejection, transference, eradication, extermination, replacement, the bounce*, the gate*.—*Ant.* ENTRANCE, induction, introduction.

remove *v.* 1 [To move physically] cart away, clear away, carry away, take away, tear away, brush away, transfer, transport, dislodge, uproot, excavate, displace, unload, discharge, lift up, doff, raise, evacuate, shift, switch, lift, push, draw away, draw in, withdraw, separate, extract, cut out, dig out, tear out, pull out, take out, smoke out, rip out, take down, tear off, draw off, take off, carry off, cart off, clear off, strike off, cut off, rub off, scrape off. 2 [To eliminate] get rid of, do away with, exclude; see ELIMINATE. 3 [To dismiss] discharge, displace, discard; see DISMISS.

removed *a.* 1 [Taken out] dislodged, extracted, eliminated, withdrawn, evacuated, ejected, pulled out, amputated, excised, expunged, extirpated.—*Ant.* LEFT, established, ignored. 2 [Distant] faraway, out-of-the-way, far-off; see DISTANT. 3 [Dismissed] banished, relieved of office, retired; see DISCHARGED, RECALLED 2.

rend *v.* rip, sever, tear; see BREAK 1.

render *v.* 1 [To give] present, hand over, distribute; see GIVE 1. 2 [To perform, especially a service] do, carry out, execute; see PERFORM 1. 3 [To interpret; *said especially of music*] play, perform, portray; see INTERPRET.

rendition *n.* interpretation, version, reading; see TRANSLATION.

renew *v.* 1 [To refresh] reawaken, regenerate, reestablish, rehabilitate, reinvigorate, replace, rebuild, reconstitute, remake, refinish, refurbish, redo, repeat, invigorate, exhilarate, restore, resuscitate, recondition, overhaul, replenish, go over, freshen, stimulate, recreate, remodel, revamp, redesign, modernize, rejuvenate, give new life to, recover, renovate, reintegrate, make a new beginning, bring up to date, do over, make like new; see also REVIVE 1. 2 [To repeat] resume, reiterate, recommence; see REPEAT 1. 3 [To replace] replenish, supplant, take over; see SUBSTITUTE.

renewal *n.* resurrection, new start, renovation; see REVIVAL 1.

renewed *a.* revived, readapted, refitted; see REPAIRED.

renounce *v.* disown, disavow, give up; see DENY, DISCARD.

renovate *v.* make over, remake, rehabilitate; see RENEW 1.

renovated *a.* renewed, remodeled, redone; see CLEAN 1, REPAIRED.

renovation *n.* remodeling, repair, restoration; see IMPROVEMENT 1.

rent *v.* 1 [To sell the use of property] lease, lend, let, make available, allow the use of, take in roomers, sublet, put on loan. 2 [To obtain use by payment] hire, pay rent for, charter, contract, sign a contract for, engage, borrow, pay for services; see also PAY 1. —**for rent** on the market, renting, for hire, available, offered, advertised, to let.

rented *a.* leased, lent, hired, contracted, engaged, let, chartered, taken, on lease, out of the market.

reopen *v.* revive, reestablish, begin again; see OPEN 2, RENEW 1.

reorganization *n.* reestablishment, reconstitution, reorientation; see CHANGE 2, IMPROVEMENT 1.

reorganize *v.* rebuild, restructure, rearrange; see RECONSTRUCT.

repaid *a.* paid back, reimbursed, refunded; see PAID.

repair *n.* reconstruction, substitution, reformation, rehabilitation, new part, patch, restoration, restored portion, replacement; see also IMPROVEMENT 1, 2.—*Ant.* BREAK, tear, fracture.

repair *v.* fix, adjust, improve, correct, put into shape, reform, patch, rejuvenate, refurbish, retread, touch up, put in order, revive, refresh, renew, mend, darn, sew, revamp, rectify, ameliorate, renovate, reshape, rebuild, work over, fix up*.—*Ant.* WRECK, damage, smash.

repaired *a.* fixed, rearranged, adjusted, adapted, settled, remodeled, rectified, mended, corrected, righted, restored, renewed, remedied, improved, renovated, retouched, in working order, patched up, put together, put back into shape, sewn, reset, stitched up.—*Ant.* DAMAGED, worn, torn.

reparation *n.* indemnity, retribution, amends; see PAYMENT 1.

repay *v.* 1 [To pay back] reimburse, recompense, refund, return, indemnify, give back, make amends, requite, compensate, square oneself*, settle up; see also PAY 1. 2 [To retaliate] get even with, square accounts, reciprocate; see REVENGE.

repayment *n.* compensation, indemnity, restitution; see PAYMENT 1.

repeal *n.* annulment, cancellation, abolition; see WITHDRAWAL.

repeal v. annul, abolish, abrogate; see CANCEL.

repeat v. 1 [To do again] redo, remake, do over, rehash, reciprocate, return, rework, re-form, refashion, recast, reduplicate, renew, reconstruct, re-erect, go over again and again. 2 [To happen again] reoccur, recur, reappear, occur again, come again, return; see also HAPPEN 2. 3 [To say again] reiterate, restate, reissue, republish, reutter, echo, recite, reecho, rehearse, retell, go over, play back, recapitulate, drum into, rehash, come again; see also SAY.

repeated a. 1 [Done again] redone, remade, copied, imitated, reworked, refashioned, recast, done over, reciprocated, returned, reduplicated. 2 [Said again] reiterated, restated, reannounced, reuttered, recited, reproduced, seconded, paraphrased, reworded, retold.

repeatedly a. again and again, many times, time and again; see FREQUENTLY, REGULARLY.

repel v. 1 [To throw back] rebuff, resist, stand up against, oppose, check, repulse, put to flight, keep at bay, knock down, drive away, drive back, beat back, hold back, force back, push back, ward off, chase off, stave off, fight off.—Ant. FALL, fail, retreat. 2 [To cause aversion] nauseate, offend, revolt; see DISGUST. 3 [To reject] disown, dismiss, cast aside; see REFUSE.

repent v. be sorry, have qualms, be penitent; see APOLOGIZE, REGRET 1.

repentance n. sorrow, remorse, self-reproach; see REGRET 1.

repentant a. penitent, regretful, contrite; see SORRY 1.

repercussion n. consequence, reaction, effect; see RESULT.

repetition n. recurrence, reoccurrence, reappearance, reproduction, copy, rote, duplication, renewal, recapitulation, reiteration, return; see also WORDINESS.

repetitious a. boring, wordy, repeating; see DULL 4.

replace v. 1 [To supply an equivalent for] replenish, repay, compensate for; see RECONSTRUCT, RENEW 1, REPAIR. 2 [To take the place of] take over, supplant, displace; see SUBSTITUTE. 3 [To put back in the same place] restore, reinstate, put back; see RETURN 2.

replaced a. 1 [Returned to the same place] restored, reinstated, reintegrated, recovered, recouped, reacquired, regained, repossessed, resumed, rewon, retrieved. 2 [Having another in one's place; said of persons] dismissed, cashiered, dislodged; see RECALLED 2. 3 [Having another in its place; said of things] renewed, interchanged, replenished; see CHANGED 1.

replica n. copy, likeness, model; see DUPLICATE, IMITATION 2.

reply n. response, return, retort; see ANSWER 1.

reply v. retort, rejoin, return; see ANSWER 1.

report n. 1 [A transmitted account] tale, narrative, description; see NEWS 1, 2, STORY. 2 [An official summary] statement, bulletin, release; see RECORD 1, SUMMARY. 3 [A loud, explosive sound] detonation, bang, blast; see NOISE 1.

report v. 1 [To deliver information] describe, recount, narrate, provide the details of, give an account of, set forth, inform, advise, communicate, retail, wire, cable, telephone, broadcast, notify, relate, state; see also TELL 1. 2 [To make a summary statement] summarize, publish, proclaim; see sense 1. 3 [To present oneself] be at hand, check in, come; see ARRIVE. 4 [To record] take minutes, take notes, note down; see RECORD 1.

reported a. stated, recited, recounted, narrated, described, set forth, announced, broadcast, made known, rumored, noted, expressed, proclaimed, according to rumor, revealed, communicated, disclosed, imparted, divulged, recorded, in the air, all over town*.—Ant. UNKNOWN, verified, certain.

reporter n. newspaperman, newspaperwoman, news writer, columnist, journalist, newsman, newswoman, anchorman, anchorwoman, anchor, newscaster, stringer, correspondent, interviewer, cub reporter, star reporter, news gatherer; see also WRITER.

represent v. 1 [To act as a delegate] be an agent for, serve, hold office, be deputy for, be attorney for, steward, act as broker, sell for, buy for, do business for, be spokesperson for, serve in a legislature for, be ambassador for, exercise power of attorney for. 2 [To present as a true interpretation] render, depict, portray; see ENACT. 3 [To serve as an equivalent of] copy, imitate, reproduce, symbolize, exemplify, typify, signify, substitute for, stand for, impersonate, personify.

representation n. description, narration, delineation; see COPY.

representative n. 1 [An emissary] deputy, salesman, messenger; see AGENT, DELEGATE. 2 [One who is elected to the lower legislative body] congressman, congresswoman, congressperson, assemblyman, assemblywoman, councilman, councilwoman, member of parliament, deputy, legislator, councilor; see also DIPLOMAT.

represented *a.* 1 [Depicted] portrayed, interpreted, pictured; see MADE. 2 [Presented] rendered, exhibited, displayed; see SHOWN 1.

repress *v.* control, curb, check; see HINDER, RESTRAIN.

reprimand *v.* reproach, denounce, criticize; see SCOLD.

reproach *n.* discredit, censure, rebuke; see BLAME.

reproach *v.* condemn, censure, scold; see BLAME.

reproduce *v.* 1 [To make an exact copy] photograph, print, xerox; see COPY. 2 [To make a second time] repeat, duplicate, recreate, recount, revive, reenact, redo, reawaken, relive, remake, reflect, follow, mirror, echo, reecho, represent. 3 [To multiply] procreate, engender, breed, generate, propagate, fecundate, hatch, father, beget, impregnate, bear, sire, repopulate, multiply, give birth.

reproduced *a.* copied, printed, traced, duplicated, transcribed, dittoed, recorded, multiplied, repeated, made identical, typed, set up, set in type, in facsimile, faxed, transferred, photographed, blueprinted, photostated, xeroxed, mimeographed, engraved, photoengraved, photocopied; see also MANUFACTURED.

reproduction *n.* 1 [A copy] imitation, print, offprint; see COPY. 2 [A photographic reproduction] photostat, photoengraving, rotogravure, telephoto, wirephoto, X-ray, candid photo, closeup, pic, pix, blowup, facsimile, fax.

reproductive *a.* generative, creative, conceptive; see GENETIC.

reptile *n.* serpent, lizard, turtle; see SNAKE.

republic *n.* democracy, democratic state, constitutional government, commonwealth, self-government, representative government; see also GOVERNMENT 2.

republican *a.* democratic, constitutional, popular; see CONSERVATIVE, DEMOCRATIC.

Republican *n.* registered Republican, GOP, Old Guard, Young Republican, Old Line Republican; see also CONSERVATIVE.

repudiate *v.* retract, repeal, revoke; see ABANDON 1.

repulse *v.* 1 [To throw back] set back, overthrow, resist; see REPEL 1. 2 [To rebuff] spurn, repel, snub; see REFUSE.

repulsion *n.* 1 [Rejection] rebuff, denial, snub; see REFUSAL. 2 [Aversion] hate, disgust, resentment; see HATRED.

repulsive *a.* 1 [Capable of repelling]

offensive, resistant, unyielding, stubborn, opposing, retaliating, insurgent, counteracting, attacking, counterattacking, defensive, combative, aggressive, pugnacious; see also STUBBORN.—*Ant.* YIELDING, surrendering, capitulating. 2 [Disgusting] odious, forbidding, horrid; see OFFENSIVE 2.

reputable *a.* 1 [Enjoying a good reputation] distinguished, celebrated, honored; see IMPORTANT 2. 2 [Honorable] trustworthy, honest, worthy; see BRAVE, NOBLE 1, 2.

reputation *n.* 1 [Supposed character] reliability, trustworthiness, respectability, dependability, credit, esteem, estimation; see also CHARACTER 2. 2 [Good name] standing, prestige, regard, favor, account, respect, privilege, acceptability, social approval; see also HONOR 1. 3 [Fame] prominence, eminence, notoriety; see FAME.

request *n.* call, inquiry, petition, question, invitation, offer, solicitation, supplication, prayer, requisition, suit, entreaty, demand; see also APPEAL 1. —**by request** asked for, sought for, wanted; see REQUESTED.

request *v.* 1 [To ask] demand, inquire, call for; see ASK. 2 [To solicit] beseech, entreat, sue; see BEG.

requested *a.* asked, demanded, popular, wished, desired, sought, hunted, needed, solicited, requisitioned, in demand; see also WANTED.

require *v.* 1 [To need] want, lack, have need for; see NEED. 2 [To demand] exact, insist upon, expect; see ASK.

required *a.* requisite, imperative, essential; see NECESSARY.

requirement *n.* 1 [A prerequisite] preliminary condition, essential, imperative, element, requisite, provision, terms, necessity, stipulation, fundamental, first principle, precondition, reservation, specification, proviso, qualification, vital part, *sine qua non* (Latin); see also BASIS. 2 [A need] necessity, necessary, lack, want, demand, claim, obsession, preoccupation, prepossession, extremity, exigency, pinch, obligation, pressing concern, urgency, compulsion, exaction.

rescue *n.* 1 [The act of rescuing] deliverance, saving, release, extrication, liberation, ransom, redemption, freeing, salvation, reclamation, reclaiming, emancipation, disentanglement, recovering, heroism. 2 [An instance of rescue] action, deed, feat, performance, exploit, accomplishment, heroics; see also ACHIEVEMENT.

rescue v. 1 [To save] preserve, recover, redeem, recapture, salvage, retain, hold over, keep back, safeguard, ransom, protect, retrieve, withdraw, take to safety; see also SAVE 1.—*Ant.* LOSE, let slip from one's hands, relinquish. 2 [To free] deliver, liberate, release; see FREE.

research n. investigation, analysis, experimentation; see EXAMINATION 1, STUDY.

research v. read up on, do research, look up; see EXAMINE, STUDY.

resemblance n. likeness, correspondence, coincidence; see SIMILARITY.

resemble v. be like, look like, seem like, sound like, follow, take after, parallel, match, coincide, relate, mirror, approximate, give indication of, remind someone of, bring to mind, have all the signs of, be the very image of, be similar to, come close to, appear like, bear a resemblance to, come near, pass for, have all the earmarks of, echo, compare with, be comparable to, smack of*, be the spit and image of*, be a dead ringer for*; see also AGREE.—*Ant.* DIFFER, contradict, oppose.

resent v. frown on, be vexed by, be insulted by; see DISLIKE.

resentment n. exasperation, annoyance, irritation; see ANGER.

reservation n. 1 [The act of reserving] restriction, limitation, withholding; see RESTRAINT 2. 2 [An instrument for reserving] card, pass, license; see TICKET 1. 3 [The space reserved] seat, car, room, bus, train, plane, box, stall, place, parking spot, table, berth, compartment.

reserve n. 1 [A portion kept against emergencies] savings, insurance, resources, reserved funds, store, provisions, assets, supply, hoard, backlog, nest egg, something in the sock*, something for a rainy day; see also SECURITY 2. 2 [Calmness] backwardness, restraint, reticence, modesty, unresponsiveness, uncommunicativeness, caution, inhibition, coyness, demureness, aloofness. — **in reserve** withheld, out of circulation, stored away; see KEPT 2, RETAINED 1, SAVED 2.

reserve v. 1 [To save] store up, set aside, put away; see MAINTAIN 3, SAVE 3. 2 [To retain] keep, possess, have; see HOLD 1, OWN 1.

reserved a. 1 [Held on reservation] preempted, claimed, booked; see SAVED 2. 2 [Held in reserve] saved, withheld, kept aside, preserved, conserved, stored away, put in a safe, on ice*.—*Ant.* USED, spent, exhausted. 3 [Restrained] shy, modest, backward, reticent, secretive, quiet, composed, retiring, private, controlling oneself, mild, gentle, peaceful, soft-spoken, sedate, collected, serene, placid.—*Ant.* LOUD, ostentatious, boisterous.

reserves n. enlisted personnel, reinforcements, volunteers; see ARMY 2.

reservoir n. storage place, tank, reserve, store, pool, cistern, water supply.

reside v. dwell, stay, lodge; see OCCUPY 2.

residence n. house, habitation, living quarters; see APARTMENT, HOME 1.

resident n. house dweller, citizen, suburbanite, tenant, inhabitant, native, denizen, occupant, inmate, homeowner, renter, householder, dweller.

residual a. left over, remaining, surplus, continuing, extra, enduring, lingering.

residue n. residual, remainder, leavings, scraps, parings, shavings, debris, sewage, dregs, silt, slag, soot, scum; see also TRASH 1.

resign v. 1 [To relinquish] surrender, capitulate, give up; see ABANDON 1, YIELD 1. 2 [To leave one's employment] quit, separate oneself from, retire, step down, drop out, stand down, sign off, end one's services, leave, hand in one's resignation, cease work, give notice, walk.

resignation n. 1 [Mental preparation for something unwelcome] submission, humility, passivity, patience, deference, docility, submissiveness, abandonment, renunciation, acquiescence, endurance, compliance.—*Ant.* RESISTANCE, immovability, unwillingness. 2 [The act of resigning] retirement, departure, leaving, quitting, giving up, abdication, surrender, withdrawal, relinquishment, vacating, tendering one's resignation, giving up office.

resigned a. quiet, peaceable, docile, tractable, submissive, yielding, relinquishing, gentle, obedient, manageable, willing, agreeable, ready, amenable, pliant, compliant, easily managed, genial, cordial, satisfied, well-disposed, patient, unresisting, tolerant, calm, reconciled, adjusted, adapted, accommodated, tame, nonresisting, passive, philosophical, renouncing, unassertive, subservient, deferential.—*Ant.* REBELLIOUS, recalcitrant, resistant.

resilience n. elasticity, snap, recoil; see FLEXIBILITY.

resilient a. rebounding, elastic, springy; see FLEXIBLE.

resin n. pine tar, pitch, gum; see GUM.

resist v. withstand, remain, endure, bear, continue, persist, stay, be strong, be immune, brook, suffer, abide, tolerate, persevere, last, oppose, bear up against, stand up to, put up a struggle, hold off, repel, remain firm, die hard.—*Ant.* STOP, desist, cease.

resistance *n.* **1** [A defense] stand, holding, withstanding, warding off, rebuff, obstruction, defiance, striking back, coping, check, halting, protecting, protection, safeguard, shield, screen, cover, watch, fight, impeding, blocking, opposition; see also DEFENSE 1.—*Ant.* WITHDRAWAL, withdrawing, retirement. **2** [The power of remaining impervious to an influence] unsusceptibility, immunity, immovability, hardness, imperviousness, endurance, fixedness, fastness, stability, stableness, permanence. **3** [The power of holding back another substance] friction, attrition, impedance; see RESERVE 1. **4** [An opposition] underground movement; anti-Fascist, anti-Communist, anti-American, etc., movement; boycott, strike, walkout, slowdown, front, stand, guerrilla movement; see also REVOLUTION 2.

resister *n.* adversary, antagonist, opponent; see OPPOSITION 2.

resolute *a.* steadfast, firm, courageous; see DETERMINED 1.

resolutely *a.* with all one's heart, bravely, with a will; see FIRMLY 1, 2.

resolution *n.* **1** [Fixedness of mind] fortitude, perseverance, resolve; see DETERMINATION. **2** [A formal statement of opinion] verdict, decision, recommendation, analysis, elucidation, interpretation, exposition, presentation, declaration, recitation, assertion, judgment.

resolve *v.* determine, settle on, conclude, purpose, propose, choose, fix upon, make up one's mind, take a firm stand, take one's stand, take a decisive step, make a point of, pass upon, decree, elect, remain firm, take the bull by the horns; see also DECIDE.

resort *n.* **1** [A relief in the face of difficulty] expedient, shift, makeshift, stopgap, substitute, surrogate, resource, device, refuge, recourse, hope, relief, possibility, opportunity. **2** [A place for rest or amusement] *Resorts include the following:* seaside, mountain, rest, camping, skiing, sports, winter, lake, summer, gambling; amusement park, nightclub, spa, health spa, restaurant, dance hall, club; see also HOTEL, MOTEL. —**as a last resort** in desperation, lastly, in the end; see FINALLY 1, 2.

resort to *v.* turn to, refer to, apply, go to, use, try, employ, utilize, have recourse to, benefit by, put to use, fall back on, make use of, take up.

resource *n.* reserve, supply, support,

source, stock, store, means, expedient, stratagem, relief, resort, recourse, artifice, device, refuge.

resourceful *a.* original, ingenious, capable; see ACTIVE, INTELLIGENT.

resources *n.* means, money, stocks, bonds, products, revenue, riches, assets, belongings, effects, capital, collateral, credit, land, holdings, real estate, investments, income, savings; see also PROPERTY 1, RESERVE 1, WEALTH.

respect *n.* esteem, honor, regard; see ADMIRATION. —**pay one's respects** wait upon, show regard, be polite; see VISIT.

respect *v.* **1** [To esteem] regard, value, look up to; see ADMIRE. **2** [To treat with consideration] heed, notice, consider, note, recognize, defer to, do honor to, be kind to, show courtesy to, spare, take into account, attend, regard, uphold; see also APPRECIATE 1.—*Ant.* RIDICULE, mock, scorn.

respectability *n.* integrity, propriety, decency; see HONESTY, VIRTUE 1.

respectable *a.* upright, presentable, fair, moderate, mediocre, tolerable, passable, ordinary, virtuous, modest, honorable, worthy, estimable, decorous, seemly, admirable, correct, reputable, proper; see also DECENT 2, HONEST 1.

respected *a.* regarded, appreciated, valued; see HONORED.

respectful *a.* deferential, considerate, appreciative, courteous, admiring, reverent, attending, upholding, regarding, valuing, venerating, recognizing, deferring to, showing respect; see also POLITE.—*Ant.* RUDE, impudent, contemptuous.

respectfully *a.* deferentially, reverentially, decorously, ceremoniously, attentively, courteously, considerately, with all respect, with due respect, with the highest respect, in deference to; see also POLITELY.—*Ant.* RUDELY, disrespectfully, impudently.

respecting *a.* regarding, concerning, in relation to; see ABOUT 2.

respiration *n.* inhalation, exhalation, breathing; see BREATH.

respite *n.* reprieve, postponement, pause; see DELAY.

respond *v.* reply, retort, acknowledge; see ANSWER 1.

response *n.* statement, reply, acknowledgment; see ANSWER 1.

responsibility *n.* **1** [State of being reliable] trustworthiness, reliability, trustiness, dependability, loyalty, faithfulness, capableness, capacity, efficiency, competency, uprightness, firmness, steadfastness, stability, ability; see also HON-

ESTY. **2** [State of being accountable] answerability, accountability, liability, subjection, engagement, pledge, contract, constraint, restraint; see also DUTY 1.—*Ant.* FREEDOM, exemption, immunity. **3** [Anything for which one is accountable] obligation, trust, contract; see DUTY 1.

responsible *a.* **1** [Charged with responsibility] accountable, answerable, liable, subject, bound, under obligation, constrained, tied, fettered, bonded, censurable, chargeable, obligated, obliged, compelled, contracted, hampered, held, pledged, sworn to, bound to, beholden to, under contract, engaged; see also BOUND 2.—*Ant.* FREE, unconstrained, unbound. **2** [Capable of assuming responsibility] trustworthy, trusty, reliable, capable, efficient, loyal, faithful, dutiful, dependable, tried, self-reliant, able, competent, qualified, effective, upright, firm, steadfast, steady, stable; see also ABLE.—*Ant.* IRRESPONSIBLE, capricious, unstable.

rest *n.* **1** [Repose] quiet, quietness, quietude, ease, tranquillity, slumber, calm, calmness, peace, peacefulness, relaxation, sleep, recreation, coffee break, rest period, siesta, doze, nap, somnolence, dreaminess, comfort, breathing spell, lounging period, loafing period, vacation, lull, leisure, respite, composure; see also sense 2. **2** [State of inactivity] intermission, cessation, stillness, stop, stay, standstill, lull, discontinuance, interval, hush, silence, dead calm, stagnation, fixity, immobility, inactivity, motionlessness, pause, full stop, deadlock, recess, noon hour; see also sense 1, PEACE 2.—*Ant.* ACTIVITY, continuance, endurance. **3** [Anything upon which an object rests] support, prop, pillar; see FOUNDATION 2. **4** [*The remainder] residue, surplus, remnant; see REMAINDER. **5** [Death] release, demise, mortality; see DEATH. —**at rest** in a state of rest, immobile, inactive; see RESTING 1. —**lay to rest** inter, assign to the grave, entomb; see BURY 1.

rest *v.* **1** [To take one's rest] sleep, slumber, doze, repose, lie down, lounge, let down, ease off, recuperate, rest up, take a rest, take a break, break the monotony, lean, recline, relax, unbend, settle down, dream, drowse, take one's ease, be comfortable, stretch out, nap, nod, snooze*. **2** [To depend upon] be supported, be seated on, be based on; see DEPEND ON 2.

restaurant *n.* café, eatery, cafeteria, diner, hamburger stand. *Types of*

restaurants include the following; café, hotel, dining room, inn, coffee shop, coffeehouse, chophouse, tearoom, luncheonette, lunch wagon, lunchroom, fast-food place, diner, takeout place, pizzeria, lunch bar, soda fountain, juice bar, sushi bar, raw bar, bar, tavern, steakhouse, hot-dog stand, snack bar, automat, rotisserie, cabaret, nightclub, cafeteria, grill, oyster house, barbecue, spaghetti house, canteen, food court, dining car, wine bar, private club, wine cellar, bistro, ethnic restaurant, ice-cream parlor.

rested *a.* restored, refreshed, relaxed, strengthened, renewed, unwearied, unfatigued, untired, awake, revived, recovered, brought back, reanimated, revitalized, reintegrated, unworn.—*Ant.* TIRED, wearied, fatigued.

restful *a.* untroubling, untroubled, tranquil, tranquilizing, calm, peaceful, quiet, reposeful, serene, comfortable, easy, placid, mild, still, soothing, relaxing, restoring, refreshing, renewing, revitalizing, reviving.—*Ant.* LOUD, irritating, agitating.

resting *a.* **1** [Taking rest] relaxing, unwinding, reposing, composing oneself, reclining, lying down, sleeping, stretched out, at ease, quiet, dormant, comfortable, lounging, loafing, taking a breather*, enjoying a lull, sleeping, dozing, drowsing, napping, taking a siesta, recessing, taking a vacation, having a holiday. **2** [Situated] located, settled on, seated; see OCCUPYING 1, PLACED.

restitution *n.* compensation, return, restoration; see PAYMENT 1, REPARATION.

restless *a.* fidgety, skittish, feverish, sleepless, jumpy, nervous, unquiet, disturbed, uneasy, anxious, up in arms, discontented, vexed, agitated, angry, disaffected, estranged, alienated, resentful, recalcitrant, fractious, insubordinate, flurried, roving, transient, wandering, discontented, unsettled, roaming, nomadic, moving, straying, ranging, footloose, itinerant, gallivanting, meandering, traipsing, restive, peeved, annoyed, impatient, flustered, twitching, trembling, tremulous, rattled*, jittery*; see also ACTIVE, EXCITED, REBELLIOUS.—*Ant.* QUIET, sedate, calm.

restlessness *n.* uneasiness, discomfort, excitability; see EXCITEMENT, NERVOUSNESS.

restoration *n.* **1** [The act of restoring] revival, return, renewal; see RECOVERY 1. **2** [The act of reconstructing] rehabilitation, reconstruction, refurbishing; see REPAIR.

restore *v.* **1** [To give back] make restitution, replace, put back; see

RETURN 2. **2** [To re-create] reestablish, revive, recover; see RENEW 1. **3** [To rebuild in a form supposed to be original] rebuild, alter, rehabilitate; see RECONSTRUCT, REPAIR. **4** [To bring back to health] refresh, cure, make healthy; see HEAL.

restrain *v.* check, control, curb, bridle, rein in, hem in, keep in, handle, regulate, keep in line, guide, direct, keep down, repress, harness, muzzle, hold in leash, govern, inhibit, hold, bind, deter, hold back, hamper, constrain, restrict, stay, gag, limit, impound, bottle up, tie down, pin down, pull back, contain, sit on*, come down on.

restrained *a.* under control, in check, on a leash; see HELD.

restraint *n.* **1** [Control over oneself] control, self-control, reserve, reticence, constraint, withholding, caution, coolness, forbearance, silence, secretiveness, stress, repression, self-restraint, stiffness, abstinence, self-denial, unnaturalness, self-repression, constrained manner, abstention, self-discipline, self-censorship; see also ATTENTION.—*Ant.* LAZINESS, slackness, laxity. **2** [An influence that checks or hinders] repression, deprivation, limitation, hindrance, reduction, abridgment, decrease, prohibition, confinement, check, barrier, obstacle, obstruction, restriction, bar, curb, blockade, order, command, instruction, coercion, impediment, compulsion, duress, force, violence, deterrence, determent, discipline, definition, moderation, tempering, qualifying.—*Ant.* FREEDOM, liberty, license.

restrict *v.* delimit, limit, circumscribe, assign, contract, shorten, narrow, decrease, enclose, keep in, keep within bounds, define, encircle, surround, shut in, tether, chain, diminish, reduce, moderate, modify, temper, qualify, come down on, pin down.—*Ant.* INCREASE, extend, expand.

restricted *a.* limited, confined, restrained, circumscribed, curbed, bound, prescribed, checked, bounded, inhibited, hampered, marked, defined, delimited, encircled, surrounded, shut in, hitched, tethered, chained, fastened, bridled, secured, held back, held down, reined in, controlled, governed, deterred, impeded, stayed, stopped, suppressed, repressed, prevented, fettered, deprived, manacled, obstructed, barred, blocked, dammed, clogged, frustrated, foiled, shrunken, narrowed, shortened, decreased, diminished, reduced, moderated, tempered, modified, qualified, out of bounds; see also BOUND 1, 2.

restriction *n.* constraint, limitation, stipulation; see RESTRAINT 2.

result *n.* consequence, issue, event, effect, outcome, finish, termination, consummation, completion, after-effect, aftermath, upshot, sequel, sequence, fruit, fruition, eventuality, proceeds, emanation, outgrowth, returns, backwash, backlash, repercussion, settlement, determination, decision, arrangement, payoff*; see also END 2, 4.—*Ant.* ORIGIN, source, root.

result *v.* issue, grow from, spring from, rise from, proceed from, emanate from, germinate from, flow from, accrue from, arise from, derive from, come from, originate in, become of, spring, emerge, rise, ensue, emanate, effect, produce, follow, happen, occur, come about, come forth, come out, pan out, work out, end, finish, terminate, conclude.

resume *v.* take up again, reassume, begin again, recommence, reoccupy, go on with, renew, recapitulate, return, keep on, carry on, keep up; see also CONTINUE 2.—*Ant.* STOP, cease, discontinue.

résumé *n.* curriculum vitae, vita, CV, synopsis, abstract, précis, work history, biography; see also SUMMARY.

resurrection *n.* return to life, reanimation, reawakening, salvation, rebirth; see also RENEWAL.

retain *v.* **1** [To hold] cling to, grasp, clutch; see HOLD 1. **2** [To reserve services] employ, maintain, engage; see HIRE. **3** [To remember] recall, recollect, recognize; see REMEMBER 1.

retained *a.* **1** [Kept] had, held, possessed, owned, enjoyed, secured, saved, preserved, maintained, restrained, confined, curbed, detained, contained, received, admitted, included, withheld, put away, treasured, sustained, celebrated, remembered, commemorated; see also KEPT 2.—*Ant.* LOST, wasted, refused. **2** [Employed] hired, engaged, contracted for; see EMPLOYED.

retaliate *v.* fight back, return, repay; see REVENGE.

retaliation *n.* vengeance, reprisal, punishment; see REVENGE 1.

retard *v.* postpone, delay, impede; see HINDER.

retarded *a.* **1** [*Said of persons*] backward, slow, developmentally disabled; see DULL 3. **2** [*Said of activities*] delayed, slowed down, held back; see SLOW 1, 2, 3.

retire *v.* **1** [To draw away] withdraw, part, retreat; see LEAVE 1. **2** [To go to bed] lie down, turn in, rest; see SLEEP. **3** [To cease active life] resign, give up work, sever one's connections, leave active service, stop working, make vacant, lay down, hand over, lead a quiet life, sequester oneself, reach retirement age.

retired *a.* resigned, in retirement, emeritus, emerita, on a pension, on Social Security, having reached retirement age, laid down, handed over, removed, retreated, withdrawn, leading a quiet life, secluding oneself, separating oneself, aloof.—*Ant.* ACTIVE, working, busy.

retirement *n.* **1** [The act of retiring] removal, vacating, separation; see RESIGNATION 2. **2** [The state of being retired] seclusion, aloofness, apartness, separateness, privacy, concealment, solitude, solitariness, isolation, remoteness, loneliness, quiet, retreat, tranquillity, refuge, serenity, inactivity; see also SILENCE 1.—*Ant.* EXPOSURE, activity, association.

retort *n.* counter, repartee, response; see ANSWER 1.

retort *v.* reply, respond, snap back; see ANSWER 1.

retract *v.* withdraw, take back, take in; see REMOVE 1.

retraction *n.* denial, revocation, disowning; see DENIAL, CANCELLATION.

retreat *n.* **1** [The act of retreating] retirement, removal, evacuation, departure, escape, withdrawal, drawing back, reversal, retrogression, backing out, flight, recession, going, running away, eluding, evasion, avoidance, recoil.—*Ant.* ADVANCE, progress, progression. **2** [A place to which one retreats] seclusion, solitude, privacy, shelter, refuge, asylum, safe place, defense, sanctuary, security, cover, ark, harbor, port, haven, place of concealment, hiding place, hideaway*, resort, haunt, habitat, hermitage, cell, convent, cloister, abbey, monastery, home, cabin, lodge.—*Ant.* FRONT, exposed position, van.

retreat *v.* recede, retrograde, back out, retract, go, depart, recoil, shrink, quail, run, draw back, reel, start back, reverse, seclude oneself, keep aloof, hide, separate from, regress, resign, relinquish, lay down, hand over, withdraw, backtrack, leave, back off*, back down, chicken out*.—*Ant.* STAY, remain, continue.

retribution *n.* vengeance, reprisal, retaliation; see REVENGE 1.

retrieve *v.* regain, bring back, reclaim; see RECOVER 1.

return *a.* coming back, repeat, repeating, repetitive, recurring, reappearing, sent back, answering, replying, retorting, rotating, turning, rebounding, recurrent, intermittent, round-trip; see also REPEATED 1.

return *n.* **1** [The act of coming again] homecoming, arrival, reappearance; see sense 2. **2** [The fact or process of being returned] restoration, restitution, rejoinder, recompense, acknowledgment, answer, reaction, reversion, repetition, reverberation, reappearance, rotation, recurrence, resurgence, renewal, recovery, replacement, reoccurrence, rebound, recoil, reconsideration. **3** [Proceeds] profit, income, results, gain, avail, revenue, advantage, yield, accrual, accruement, interest.—*Ant.* FAILURE, loss, disadvantage. —**in return** in exchange, as payment, as an equivalent, as a reward, back, in response.

return *v.* **1** [To go back] come again, come back, recur, reappear, reoccur, repeat, revert, reconsider, reenter, reexamine, reinspect, bounce back, retrace one's steps, turn, rotate, revolve, renew, revive, recover, regain, rebound, circle back, double back, move back, turn back, reverberate, recoil, retrace, revisit, retire, retreat.—*Ant.* MOVE, advance, go forward. **2** [To put or send something back] bring back, toss back, roll back, hand back, give back, restore, replace, render, reseat, reestablish, reinstate, react, recompense, refund, repay, make restitution.—*Ant.* HOLD, keep, hold back. **3** [To answer] reply, respond, retort; see ANSWER 1. **4** [To repay] reimburse, recompense, refund; see REPAY 1. **5** [To yield a profit] pay off, show profit, pay dividends; see PAY 2. **6** [To reflect] echo, sound, mirror; see REFLECT 2, 3.

returned *a.* restored, given back, gone back, sent back, brought back, turned back, come back, repeated, reentered, rotated, revolved, rebounded, reverberated, refunded, acknowledged, answered, repaid, yielded; see also REFUSED.—*Ant.* KEPT, held, retained.

reunion *n.* reuniting, meeting again, rejoining, reconciliation, reconcilement, homecoming, restoration, harmonizing, bringing together, healing the breach, get-together.

reunite *v.* meet again, reassemble, reconvene, join, rejoin, become reconciled, have a reconciliation, be restored to one another, remarry, heal the breach, get together, patch it up, make up.—*Ant.* SEPARATE, go separate ways, be disrupted.

reveal *v.* disclose, betray a confidence, divulge, make known, confess, impart, publish, lay bare, betray, avow, admit, bring to light, acknowledge, give utterance to, bring out, let out, give out, make public, unfold, communicate, announce, declare, inform, notify, utter, make plain, break the news, broadcast, announcement, concede, come out with, explain, bring into the open, affirm, report, let the cat out of the bag, blab*, talk, rat*, stool*, make a clean breast of, put one's cards on the table, bring to light, show one's colors, get something out of one's system, give the low-down*, let on*, squeal*, blow the whistle*; see also TELL 1.

revelation n. 1 [A disclosure] divulgence, announcement, betrayal; see RECORD 1. 2 [Revealed divine truth] divine word, God's word, revealed truth; see DOCTRINE, FAITH 2.

revenge n. 1 [The act of returning an injury] vengeance, requital, reprisal, measure for measure, repayment, sortie, retaliation, retribution, avenging, counterinsurgency, getting even; see also ATTACK, FIGHT 1.—Ant. PARDON, forgiveness, excusing. 2 [The desire to obtain revenge] vindictiveness, rancor, malevolence; see HATRED.

revenge v. retaliate, vindicate, requite, take revenge, breathe vengeance, have accounts to settle, have one's revenge, pay back, make reprisal, get even with, punish for, repay, return like for like, retort, match, reciprocate, square accounts, settle up, take an eye for an eye, turn the tables on, get back at*, fight back, hit back at, be out for blood, give and take, give someone his or her just deserts, even the score, get*, fix*, get square with, return the compliment.—Ant. FORGIVE, condone, pardon.

revenue n. 1 [Income] return, earnings, result, yield, wealth, receipts, proceeds, resources, funds, credits, dividends, interest, salary, profits, means, fruits, rents; see also INCOME, PAY 1, 2.—Ant. EXPENSES, outgo, obligations. 2 [Governmental income] wealth, taxes, taxation; see INCOME, TAX 1. *Types of revenue include the following:* direct tax, indirect tax, bonds, loans, customs, duties, tariff, tax surcharge, excise, property tax, income tax, inheritance and death tax, land tax, poll tax, gasoline tax, school tax, franchise, license, grants, rates, bridge and road tolls, harbor dues, special taxation, patent stamps, stamp duties, registration duties, internal revenue, tax on spirits, tobacco tax, sin tax, lease of land, sale of land, subsidy.

revere v. venerate, regard with deep respect, respect; see ADMIRE.

reverence n. respect, admiration, love, regard, approval, approbation, esteem, deference, awe, fear, veneration, honor, devotion, adoration; see also PRAISE 2.—Ant. HATRED, contempt, disdain.

reverent a. venerating, esteeming, honoring; see RESPECTFUL.

reversal n. renunciation, repudiation, repeal; see CANCELLATION, REFUSAL, WITHDRAWAL.

reverse n. 1 [The opposite] converse, other side, contrary; see OPPOSITE. 2 [A defeat] downfall, catastrophe, setback; see DEFEAT.

reverse v. 1 [To turn] go back, shift, invert; see TURN 2. 2 [To alter] turn around, modify, convert; see CHANGE 2. 3 [To annul] nullify, invalidate, repeal; see CANCEL. 4 [To exchange] transpose, rearrange, shift; see EXCHANGE 1.

reversed a. turned around, turned back, backward, end for end, inverted, contrariwise, out of order, regressive, retrogressive, undone, unmade.—Ant. ORDERED, established, in proper order.

revert v. go back, reverse, relapse; see RETURN 1.

review n. 1 [A reexamination] reconsideration, second thought, revision, retrospection, second view, reflection, study, survey, retrospect. 2 [A critical study] survey, critique, criticism; see EXAMINATION 1. 3 [A summary] synopsis, abstract, outline; see SUMMARY. 4 [A formal inspection] parade, inspection, dress parade, drill, march, procession, cavalcade, column, file, military display; see also DISPLAY.

review v. 1 [To correct] criticize, revise, reedit; see CORRECT. 2 [To inspect] analyze, reexamine, check thoroughly; see EXAMINE.

revise v. reconsider, rewrite, correct; see EDIT.

revised a. corrected, edited, amended, overhauled, improved, altered, changed, rectified, polished, redone, rewritten, reorganized, restyled, emended.

revision n. reexamination, correction, editing; see CORRECTION.

revival n. 1 [The act of reviving] renewal, renascence, renaissance, refreshment, arousal, awakening, rebirth, reversion, resurrection, enkindling, restoration, invigoration, vivification, resuscitation, reawakening, improvement, freshening, recovery, cheering, consolation. 2 [An evangelical service] tent meeting, prayer meeting, camp meeting; see CEREMONY.

revive v. 1 [To give new life] enliven, enkindle, refresh, renew, vivify, animate, reanimate, resuscitate, recondition, rejuvenate, bring to, bring around, wake up, resurrect, make whole, exhilarate, energize, invigorate, breathe new life into, regenerate, restore, touch up, repair.—Ant. DECREASE, wither, lessen. **2** [To take on new life] come around, come to, freshen, improve, recover, flourish, awake, reawaken, rouse, strengthen, overcome, come to life, grow well, be cured.—*Ant.* DIE, faint, weaken.

revoke *v.* recall, retract, disclaim; see CANCEL.

revolt *n.* uprising, mutiny, sedition; see REVOLUTION 2.

revolt *v.* **1** [To rebel] mutiny, rise up, resist; see REBEL. **2** [To repel] sicken, offend, nauseate; see DISGUST.

revolting *a.* awful, loathsome, repulsive; see OFFENSIVE 2, SHAMEFUL 1, 2.

revolution *n.* **1** [A complete turn or motion around something] turning, rotation, spin, turn, revolving, circuit, round, whirl, gyration, circumvolution, cycle, roll, reel, twirl, swirl, pirouette. **2** [An armed uprising] revolt, rebellion, mutiny, insurrection, riot, anarchy, outbreak, coup, coup d'état, destruction, overturn, upset, overthrow, reversal, rising, crime, violence, bloodshed, turbulence, insubordination, disturbance, reformation, underground activity, plot, guerrilla activity, public unrest, upheaval, tumult, disorder, turmoil, uproar, uprising, row, strife, strike, putsch, subversion, breakup, secession.—*Ant.* LAW, order, control.

revolutionary *a.* **1** [Concerned with a revolution] rebellious, mutinous, insurrectionary, destructive, anarchistic, subverting, insurgent, overturning, upsetting, destroying, reformist, subversive, seceding, riotous, agitating, disturbing, working underground, treasonable.—*Ant.* PATRIOTIC, loyal, constructive. **2** [New and unusual] novel, advanced, radical; see UNUSUAL 2.

revolutionary *n.* reformer, traitor, insurrectionist; see REBEL.

revolutionize *v.* recast, remodel, refashion; see REFORM 1.

revolve *v.* spin, rotate, twirl; see TURN 1.

revolver *n.* automatic, gun, rod*; see PISTOL.

reward *n.* **1** [Payment] compensation, remuneration, recompense; see PAY 1, 2. **2** [A prize] premium, bonus, award; see PRIZE.

reward *v.* compensate, repay, remunerate; see PAY 1.

rewrite *v.* rework, revise, cut; see EDIT.

rhyme *n.* verse, rhyming verse, similarity of vowel sounds; see POETRY.

rhythm *n.* swing, accent, rise and fall; see BEAT 2.

rhythmic *a.* patterned, measured, balanced; see MUSICAL 1, REGULAR 3.

rib *n.* **1** [One part of the bony frame of the thorax] true rib, false rib, floating rib; see BONE. **2** [A rod] girder, bar, strip; see ROD 1, SUPPORT 2. **3** [A ridge] fin, nervure, vaulting; see sense 2.

ribbon *n.* strip, trimming, decoration; see BAND 1.

rich *a.* **1** [Possessed of wealth] wealthy, moneyed, affluent, well-to-do, well provided for, worth a million, well-off, well-fixed*, in clover, swimming in gravy*, in the money*.—*Ant.* POOR, poverty-stricken, destitute. **2** [Sumptuous] luxurious, magnificent, resplendent, lavish, embellished, ornate, costly, expensive, splendid, superb, elegant, gorgeous, valuable, precious, extravagant, grand; see also BEAUTIFUL.—*Ant.* CHEAP, plain, simple. **3** [Fertile] exuberant, lush, copious, plentiful, generous, fruitful, profuse, luxuriant, teeming, abundant, prolific, productive, fruit-bearing, propagating, yielding, breeding, superabounding, prodigal; see also FERTILE.—*Ant.* STERILE, unfruitful, barren. **4** [Having much butter, cream, sugar, seasoning, etc.] heavy, luscious, sweet, fatty, oily, creamy, buttery, juicy, succulent, fattening, filling, cloying, spicy, satisfying; see also DELICIOUS.—*Ant.* light, plain, low-fat.

riches *n.* fortune, possessions, money; see WEALTH.

richness *n.* copiousness, bounty, abundance; see PLENTY.

rickety *a.* infirm, shaky, fragile; see WEAK 2.

ricochet *v.* bounce off, rebound, glance off; see BOUNCE.

rid *a.* relieved, freed, delivered; see FREE 2. **—be rid of** be freed from, be relieved of, have done with; see ESCAPE. **—get rid of 1** get free from, slough off, shed; see FREE. **2** eject, expel, remove; see ELIMINATE.

rid *v.* clear, relieve, disencumber; see FREE.

riddle *n.* problem, question, knotty question, doubt, quandary, entanglement, dilemma, perplexity, enigma, confusion, complication, complexity, intricacy, strait, labyrinth, predicament, plight, distraction, bewilderment; see also PUZZLE 1.—*Ant.* SIMPLICITY, clarity, disentanglement.

ride *n.* drive, trip, transportation; see JOURNEY.

ride *v.* **1** [To be transported] be carried, travel in or on a vehicle, tour, journey, motor, drive, go for an airing, bicycle, go by automobile. **2** [To control a beast of burden by riding] manage, guide, handle; see DRIVE 1.

3 [To tease harshly] ridicule, bait, harass; see BOTHER 2.

rider *n.* **1** [One who rides] driver, fare, passenger, motorist, horseman, horsewoman, hitchhiker. **2** [An additional clause or provision, usually not connected with the main body of the document] amendment, appendix, supplement; see ADDITION 1.

ridge *n.* **1** [A long, straight, raised portion] raised strip, rib, seam; see RIM. **2** [A long, narrow elevation of land] mountain ridge, range, elevation; see HILL.

ridged *a.* crinkled, furrowed, ribbed, corrugated.

ridicule *n.* scorn, contempt, mockery, disdain, derision, jeer, leer, disparagement, sneer, flout, fleer, twit, taunt, burlesque, caricature, satire, parody, travesty, irony, sarcasm, persiflage, farce, buffoonery, horseplay, foolery, razz*, rib*, roast*, raspberry*, horselaugh.—*Ant.* PRAISE, commendation, approval.

ridicule *v.* scoff at, sneer at, laugh at, rail at, mock, taunt, banter, mimic, jeer, twit, disparage, flout, deride, scorn, make sport of, make fun of, rally, burlesque, caricature, satirize, parody, cartoon, travesty, run down, put down*, razz*, rib*, pull someone's leg*, roast*, pan*.—*Ant.* ENCOURAGE, approve, applaud.

ridiculous *a.* ludicrous, absurd, preposterous; see FUNNY 1, UNUSUAL 2.

rife *a.* **1** [Widespread] prevalent, extensive, common; see WIDESPREAD. **2** [Abundant] copious, abounding, profuse; see PLENTIFUL 1.

riffraff *n.* mob, masses, rabble; see PEOPLE 3.

rifle *n.* repeating rifle, carbine, automatic rifle; see GUN, MACHINE GUN.

rift *n.* fissure, breach, rupture; see FRACTURE.

rig *n.* tackle, apparatus, gear; see EQUIPMENT.

right *a.* **1** [Correct] true, precise, exact, sure, certain, determined, proven, factual, correct; see also ACCURATE 2, VALID 1. **2** [Just] lawful, legitimate, honest; see FAIR 1. **3** [Suitable] apt, proper, appropriate; see FIT 1. **4** [Sane] reasonable, rational, sound; see SANE. **5** [Justly] fairly, evenly, equitably, honestly, decently, sincerely, legitimately, lawfully, conscientiously, squarely, impartially, objectively, reliably, dispassionately, without bias, without prejudice; see also JUSTLY 1. **6** [Straight] directly, unswervingly, immediately; see DIRECT 1. **7** [Opposite to left] dexter, dexter, right-handed, clockwise, on the right.—*Ant.* LEFT, sinistral, counterclockwise. —**right away**

at once, directly, without delay; see IMMEDIATELY, NOW.

right *n.* **1** [Power or privilege] prerogative, immunity, exemption, license, benefit, advantage, favor, franchise, preference, priority; see also FREEDOM 2. **2** [Justice] equity, freedom, liberty, independence, emancipation, enfranchisement, self-determination; see also FAIRNESS. **3** [The part opposite the left] right hand, right side, starboard, right part. —**by rights** properly, justly, suitably; see RIGHTLY. —**in one's own right** individually, acting as one's own agent, by one's own authority; see INDEPENDENTLY. —**in the right** correct, true, accurate; see VALID 1.

right *v.* **1** [To make upright] set up, make straight, balance; see STRAIGHTEN, TURN 2. **2** [To repair an injustice] adjust, correct, restore, vindicate, do justice, recompense, reward, remedy, rectify, mend, amend, set right; see also REPAIR.—*Ant.* WRONG, hurt, harm.

righteous *a.* **1** [Virtuous] just, upright, good, honorable, honest, worthy, exemplary, noble, right-minded, good-hearted, dutiful, trustworthy, equitable, scrupulous, conscientious, ethical, fair, impartial, fair-minded, commendable, praiseworthy, guiltless, blameless, sinless, peerless, sterling, matchless, deserving, laudable, creditable, charitable, philanthropic, having a clear conscience; see also RELIABLE.—*Ant.* CORRUPT, sinful, profligate. **2** [Religious] godly, devout, pious, saintly, humble, prayerful, God-fearing, observant, unworldly, angelic, devoted, reverent, reverential, faithful, fervent, strict, rigid, devotional, zealous, spiritual; see also HOLY 1, RELIGIOUS 2.—*Ant.* BAD, impious, irreligious. **3** [Conscious of one's own virtue] self-righteous, hypocritical, self-centered; see EGOTISTIC.

righteousness *n.* **1** [Justice] uprightness, nobility, fairness; see HONOR 1. **2** [Devotion to a sinless life] piety, saintliness, godliness; see DEVOTION.

rightful *a.* proper, just, honest; see FAIR 1, LEGAL, PERMITTED.

rightfully *a.* lawfully, justly, fairly, properly, truly, equitably, honestly, impartially, fittingly, legitimately, in all conscience, in equity, by right, by reason, objectively, fair and square*, on the level*, by rights; see also LEGALLY.

rightly *a.* justly, properly, correctly; see WELL 2.

right-wing *a.* traditional, reactionary, Tory; see CONSERVATIVE.

rigid *a.* 1 [Stiff] unyielding, inflexible, solid; see FIRM 1. 2 [Strict] exact, rigorous, firm; see SEVERE 1, 2. 3 [Fixed] set, unmoving, solid; see DEFINITE 1, DETERMINED.

rigorous *a.* harsh, austere, uncompromising; see SEVERE 1.

rile *v.* irritate, provoke, annoy; see BOTHER 2, ENRAGE.

rim *n.* edge, border, verge, brim, lip, brink, top, margin, line, outline, band, ring, strip, brow, curb, ledge, skirt, fringe, hem, limit, confines, end, terminus.—*Ant.* CENTER, interior, middle.

rind *n.* peel, hull, shell, surface, coating, crust, bark, cortex, integument; see also SKIN.—*Ant.* INSIDE, center, interior.

ring *n.* 1 [A circle] circlet, girdle, brim; see CIRCLE 1, RIM. 2 [A circlet of metal] hoop, band, circle; see JEWELRY. *Rings include the following:* finger, wedding, engagement, signet, organization, class, friendship, graduation, pinkie, ankle, nose, key, harness, napkin; bracelet, earring, ear drop. 3 [A close association, often corrupt] cabal, combine, party, bloc, faction, group, gang, monopoly, cartel, junta, band, clique, pool, trust, syndicate, gang*; string; see also ORGANIZATION 2. 4 [Pugilism] prizefighting, boxing, professional fighting; see SPORT 3. 5 [A ringing sound] clank, clangor, jangle; see NOISE 1. —**give someone a ring** call, call up, phone; see TELEPHONE. —**run rings around** * excel, overtake, beat; see PASS 1.

ring *v.* 1 [To encircle] circle, rim, surround, encompass, girdle, enclose, move around, loop, gird, belt, confine, hem in. 2 [To sound or cause to sound] clap, clang, bang, beat, toll, strike, pull, punch, buzz, play, resound, reverberate, peal, chime, tinkle, jingle, jangle, vibrate, clang, sound the brass*; see also SOUND. 3 [To call by ringing] give a ring, buzz, ring up; see SUMMON.

rinse *v.* clean, flush, dip in water; see SOAK 1, WASH 2.

riot *n.* confusion, uproar, tumult; see DISORDER, DISTURBANCE 2, PROTEST. —**run riot** revolt, riot, fight; see REBEL.

riot *v.* revolt, stir up trouble, fight in the streets; see REBEL.

rip *n.* rent, cleavage, split; see TEAR.

rip *v.* rend, split, cleave, rive, tear, shred; see also CUT 1.

ripe *a.* 1 [Ready to be harvested] fully grown, fully developed, ruddy, red, yellow, plump, filled out, matured, ready.—*Ant.* GREEN, undeveloped, half-grown. 2 [Improved by time and experience] mellow, wise, perfected; see MATURE. 3

[Ready] prepared, seasoned, consummate, perfected, finished, usable, fit, conditioned, prime, available, on the mark, complete; see also READY 2.—*Ant.* UNFIT, unready, unprepared.

ripen *v.* develop, evolve, advance; see GROW 2.

ripple *v.* undulate, curl, waver; see WAVE 1, 3.

rise *n.* 1 [The act of rising] ascent, mount, lift; see CLIMB. 2 [An increase] augmentation, growth, enlargement, multiplication, heightening, intensifying, stacking up, piling up, distention, addition, accession, inflation, acceleration, doubling, advance; see also INCREASE.—*Ant.* REDUCTION, lessening, decrease. 3 [Source] start, beginning, commencement; see ORIGIN 2. —**get a rise out of*** get a response from by teasing, provoke, annoy; see BOTHER 2. —**give rise to** initiate, begin, start; see CAUSE.

rise *v.* 1 [To move upward] ascend, mount, climb, scale, soar, tower, rocket, sweep upward, lift, bob up, move up, push up, reach up, come up, go up, surge, sprout, grow, rear, uprise, blast off, curl upward; see also FLY 1.—*Ant.* FALL, drop, come down. 2 [To get out of bed] get up, rise up, wake; see ARISE 1. 3 [To increase] grow, swell, intensify, mount, enlarge, spread, expand, extend, augment, heighten, enhance, distend, inflate, pile up, stack up, multiply, accelerate, speed up, add to, wax, advance, raise, double; see also INCREASE.—*Ant.* DECREASE, lessen, contract. 4 [To begin] spring, emanate, issue; see BEGIN 2. 5 [To improve one's station] prosper, flourish, thrive; see IMPROVE 1. 6 [To be built] stand, be placed, be located, be put up, go up, be founded, have foundation, be situated; see also STAND 1. 7 [To swell; *said usually of dough or batter*] inflate, billow, bulge; see SWELL.

rising *a.* climbing, ascending, going aloft, moving up, surging up, spiraling up, slanting up, inclining up, mounting, accelerating, on the rise, in ascension, upcoming, upswinging; see also GROWING.

risk *n.* 1 [Danger] hazard, peril, jeopardy; see DANGER 1. 2 [The basis of a chance] contingency, opportunity, prospect; see CHANCE 1, UNCERTAINTY 3. —**run a risk** take a chance, gamble, venture; see RISK, *v.*

risk *v.* gamble, hazard, venture, run the risk, do at one's own peril, hang by a thread, play with fire, go out of one's depth, go beyond one's depth, bell the cat*, make an investment, take the liberty, lay oneself open to, pour money into, go through fire and water, leave to luck, leap before one looks, fish in troubled waters, skate on thin ice*, defy danger, live in a glass house.

risky *a.* perilous, precarious, hazardous; see DANGEROUS, UNSAFE.

risqué *a.* indelicate, spicy, suggestive; see LEWD 2.

rite *n.* observance, service, ritual; see CEREMONY 2, CUSTOM.

ritual *n.* observance, rite, act; see CEREMONY 2, CUSTOM.

rival *a.* competing, striving, combatant, combatting, emulating, vying, opposing, disputing, contesting, contending, conflicting, battling, equal.—*Ant.* HELPFUL, aiding, assisting.

rival *n.* emulator, competitor, antagonist; see OPPONENT 1.

rival *v.* approach, match, compare with; see EQUAL.

rivalry *n.* competition, emulation, striving, contest, vying, struggle, battle, contention, opposition, dispute; see also FIGHT 1.—*Ant.* COOPERATION, combination, conspiracy.

river *n.* stream, flow, course, current, tributary, branch, estuary, waters, run, rivulet, river system, creek, brook, watercourse. *Famous rivers include the following:* Seine, Rhone, Thames, Po, Tiber, Rubicon, Danube, Rhine, Elbe, Don, Volga, Amur, Nile, Euphrates, Tigris, Jordan, Ganges, Indus, Congo, Zambezi, Niger, Mekong, Chang (Yangtze), Huang (Yellow), St. Lawrence, Yukon, Mackenzie, Mississippi, Missouri, Ohio, Platte, Delaware, Columbia, Colorado, Snake, Hudson, Rio Grande, Potomac, Tennessee, Brazos, Amazon, Orinoco.

riveting *a.* gripping, engrossing, captivating; see INTERESTING.

road *n.* 1 [A strip prepared for travel] path, way, highway, roadway, street, avenue, thoroughfare, boulevard, high road, drive, terrace, parkway, byway, lane, alley, alleyway, crossroad, viaduct, subway, paving, slab, turnpike, trail, post road, secondary road, market road, national highway, state highway, county road, interstate, military road, Roman road, freeway, the main drag*. 2 [A course] scheme, way, plans; see PLAN 2. **—on the road** on tour, traveling, on the way; see EN ROUTE. **—one for the road*** cocktail, nightcap, toast; see DRINK 2.

roam *v.* ramble, range, stroll, rove, walk, traverse, stray, straggle, meander, prowl, tramp, saunter, knock around*, bat around*, scour, gallivant, struggle along, traipse*, hike; see also TRAVEL.

roar *n.* bellow, shout, boom, thunder, howl, bay, bawl, yell, bluster,

uproar, din, clash, detonation, explosion, barrage, reverberation, rumble; see also CRY 1, 2, NOISE 1.—*Ant.* SILENCE, whisper, sigh.

roar *v.* bellow, shout, boom, thunder, howl, bay, bawl, yell, rumble, drum, detonate, explode, reverberate, resound, reecho; see also CRY 2, SOUND.

roast *v.* toast, broil, barbecue; see COOK.

rob *v.* thieve, take, burglarize, strip, plunder, deprive of, withhold from, defraud, cheat, swindle, pilfer, break into, hold up, stick up*, purloin, filch, lift*, abscond with, embezzle, pillage, sack, loot, snitch*, pinch*, swipe*, cop*; see also STEAL.

robber *n.* thief, burglar, cheat, plunderer, pillager, bandit, pirate, raider, thug, desperado, forger, holdup man*, second-story man*, privateer, buccaneer, swindler, highwayman, bank robber, pilferer, shoplifter, cattle thief, housebreaker, pickpocket, freebooter, marauder, brigand, pickpurse*, sharper, safecracker, fence, rustler*, crook*, con man*, clip artist*, chiseler*, paperhanger*, stickup man*; see also CRIMINAL, RASCAL.

robbery *n.* burglary, larceny, thievery; see CRIME.

robe *n.* gown, dress, garment, mantle, cloak, vestment, cassock, caftan, peignoir, wrapper, costume, covering, cape, dressing gown, bathrobe, negligee, tea gown, kimono, housecoat; see also CLOTHES.

robot *n.* 1 [A mechanical person] automaton, android, Frankenstein, mechanical monster, humanoid, thinking machine. 2 [A person who resembles a machine] slave, menial, scullion; see LABORER.

robust *a.* hale, hearty, sound; see HEALTHY.

rock *n.* 1 [A solidified form of earth] stone, mineral mass, dike, mineral body, earth crust; see also METAL, MINERAL. *Rocks include the following:* igneous, sedimentary, metamorphic; gypsum, limestone, freestone, sandstone, conglomerate, marble, dolomite, chalk, soapstone, slate, shale, granite, pumice, basalt, obsidian, rhyolite, gneiss, tufa, schist, talc, chert, jasper, flint, tuff, coal, quartzite, salt, phyllite, amphibolite, diorite, gabbro, marl, puddingstone, breccia, travertine, peridotite, andesite. 2 [A piece of rock] stone, boulder, cobblestone, pebble, fieldstone, cliff, crag, promontory, scrap, escarpment, reef, chip, flake, sliver, building stone, paving block, slab. 3 [Anything firm or solid] defense, support, Rock of Gibraltar; see FOUNDATION. **4** [Lively dance music] rock-and-roll, popular music, rhythm and blues; see DANCE 1, MUSIC 1. **—on the rocks*** **1** bankrupt, poverty-stricken, impoverished; see POOR 1, RUINED 3. **2** over ice cubes, undiluted, straight; see STRONG 4.

rock *v.* sway, vibrate, reel, totter, swing, move, push and pull, agitate, roll, shake, shove, jolt, jiggle, quake, convulse, tremble, undulate, oscillate, quiver, quaver, wobble; see also WAVE 3.

rock-bottom *a.* lowest, hopeless, way down; see POOR 2, WORST. **—hit rock bottom** drop, not succeed, plunge; see FAIL 1, FALL 1.

rocket *n.* projectile, missile, retrorocket, flying missile. *Kinds of rockets include the following:* air-to-air, air-to-surface, ground-to-ground, surface-to-surface, air-to-ground, surface-to-air, ground-to-air, V-2, solid-fuel, liquid-fuel; guided missile, ballistic missile, cruise missile, intercontinental ballistic missile (ICBM), submarine-launched ballistic missile (SLBM), MIRV, heat-seeking missile, anti-tank missile, smart bomb*.

rocky *a.* stony, flinty, hard, inflexible, solid, petrified, ragged, jagged, rugged; see also STONE. —*Ant.* SOFT, flexible, sandy.

rod *n.* **1** [A rodlike body] staff, bar, pole, wand, stave, baton, spike, pin, cylinder, bacillus, cylindrical object, scepter, twig, switch, whip, stock, stalk, trunk; see also STICK. **2** [A fishing rod] pole, rod and reel, tackle; see EQUIPMENT.

rodent *n.* *Common varieties of rodents include the following:* rat, mouse, squirrel, chipmunk, beaver, porcupine, muskrat, prairie dog, gopher, marmot, groundhog, woodchuck, ground squirrel, chinchilla, mole, guinea pig.

rodeo *n.* riding unbroken horses, rounding up cattle, roundup, features of a roundup. *Rodeo events include the following:* broncobusting, bulldogging, calf-roping, cutting out steers, Brahma bull riding.

rogue *n.* outlaw, problem, miscreant; see CRIMINAL.

roguish *a.* **1** [Dishonest] unscrupulous, sly, corrupt; see DISHONEST. **2** [Mischievous] playful, impish, arch; see NAUGHTY.

role *n.* function, task, part, character, title role, impersonation, leading man, leading woman, hero, heroine, ingénue, performance, presentation, acting, characterization, capacity, position, office, purpose.

roll *n.* **1** [The act of rolling] turn, turning over, revolution, rotation, wheeling, trundling, whirl, gyration. **2** [A relatively flat object rolled up on itself] scroll, volute, spiral, coil, whorl, convolution, fold, shell, cone, cornucopia, tube, cylinder. **3** [A long, heavy sound] thunder, roar, drumbeat; see NOISE 1. **4** [A small portion of bread] *Types of rolls include the following:* parkerhouse, hard, soft, dinner, crescent, sesame, poppy-seed, cloverleaf, rye, whole-wheat, sourdough, breakfast, sweet, cinnamon, popover, croissant, Danish, brioche, biscuit, hot cross bun, bagel, bun, English muffin; egg roll; see also BREAD, PASTRY. **5** [A list] register, table, schedule; see CATALOG, INDEX 2, LIST, RECORD 1.

roll *v.* **1** [To move by rotation, or in rotating numbers] rotate, come around, swing around, wheel, come in turn, circle, alternate, follow, succeed, be in sequence, follow in due course; see also MOVE 1, TURN 1. **2** [To revolve] turn, pivot, spin; see sense 1. **3** [To make into a roll] bend, curve, arch; see TWIST. **4** [To flatten or spread with a roller] press, level, flatten, spread, pulverize, grind.—*Ant.* CUT, roughen, toss up. **5** [To flow] run, billow, surge; see FLOW. **6** [To produce a relatively deep, continuous sound] reverberate, resound, echo; see ROAR, SOUND. **7** [To function] work, go, start production; see OPERATE 2.

rolled *a.* **1** [Made into a roll] twisted, folded, curved, bent, bowed, coiled, spiraled, arched, wound, convoluted.—*Ant.* SPREAD, unrolled, opened out. **2** [Flattened] pressed, leveled, evened; see FLAT 1, SMOOTH 1.

roller *n.* cylinder, rolling pin, hair roller; see ROLL 2.

rollicking *a.* high-spirited, jolly, exuberant; see HAPPY.

Roman *a.* Latin, classic, classical, late classic, Augustan, ancient, Italic.

romance *n.* **1** [A love affair] affair, courtship, amour; see LOVE 1. **2** [A tale of love and adventure] historical romance, novel, fiction; see STORY.

romantic *a.* adventurous, novel, daring, charming, enchanting, lyric, poetic, fanciful, chivalrous, courtly, knightly.

romp *v.* gambol, celebrate, frolic; see PLAY 1, 2.

roof *n.* cover, shelter, tent, house, habitation, home.

roofing *n.* shingles, tiles, asphalt, thatch, roof.

room *n.* **1** [Space] vastness, reach, sweep; see EXTENT. **2** [An enclosure] chamber, apartment, cabin, cubicle, niche, vault. *Rooms include* *the following:* living room, dining room, sitting room, drawing room, bedroom, music room, playroom, bathroom, guest room, family room, waiting room, boardroom, conference room, foyer, vestibule, study, library, den, kitchen, hall, master bedroom, parlor, wardrobe, closet, pantry, basement, cellar, attic, garret, anteroom, dormitory, alcove, ward, office, breakfast nook, nursery, studio, schoolroom, loft. **3** [The possibility of admission] opening, place, opportunity; see VACANCY 2. **4** [A rented sleeping room] quarters, lodgings, digs*; see APARTMENT.

roomer *n.* lodger, occupant, dweller; see TENANT.

roommate *n.* roomie*, flatmate, bunkmate; see FRIEND.

roomy *a.* spacious, capacious, ample; see BIG 1, LARGE 1.

rooster *n.* cock, chanticleer*, chicken; see FOWL.

root *n.* **1** [An underground portion of a plant] *Types of roots include the following:* conical, napiform, fusiform, fibrous, moniliform, nodulose, tuberous, adventitious, prop, aerial, tap. **2** [The cause or basis] source, reason, motive; see ORIGIN 2, 3. —**take root** begin growing, start, commence; see GROW 1.

rooted *a.* grounded, based, fixed; see FIRM 1.

rope *n.* cord, cordage, braiding, string, thread, strand, tape, cord, lace, cable, hawser, lariat, lasso, line, towline. —**at the end of one's rope** desperate, despairing, in despair; see EXTREME, HOPELESS. —**know the ropes*** be experienced, comprehend, understand; see KNOW 1. —**on the ropes*** near collapse, close to ruin, in danger; see ENDANGERED.

rose *a.* rose-colored, rosy, flushed; see PINK, RED.

rose *n.* *Kinds of roses include the following:* wild, tea, hybrid tea, perpetual, multiflora, floribunda, musk, cabbage; eglantine, sweetbrier, rambler; see also FLOWER.

roster *n.* names, subscribers, program; see CATALOG, LIST, INDEX 2.

rostrum *n.* dais, pulpit, stage; see PLATFORM 1.

rosy *a.* **1** [Rose-colored] colored, deep pink, pale cardinal; see PINK, RED. **2** [Promising] optimistic, favorable, cheerful; see HOPEFUL 1, 2.

rot *n.* **1** [The process of rotting] decomposition, corruption, disintegration; see DECAY. **2** [*Nonsense] trash, silliness, foolishness; see NONSENSE 1.

rot *v.* decay, disintegrate, decompose; see SPOIL.

rotate *v.* twist, wheel, revolve; see MOVE 1, TURN 1.

rotation *n.* turn, circumrotation, circle; see REVOLUTION.

rotten *a.* **1** [Having rotted] bad, rotting, putrefying, decaying, putrefied, spoiled, decomposed, decayed, offensive, disgusting, rancid, fecal, rank, foul, corrupt, polluted, infected, loathsome, overripe, bad-smelling, putrid, crumbled, disintegrated, stale, noisome, smelling, fetid, noxious.—*Ant.* FRESH, unspoiled, good. **2** [Not sound] unsound, defective, impaired; see WEAK 2. **3** [Corrupt] contaminated, polluted, filthy, tainted, defiled, impure, sullied, unclean, soiled, debauched, blemished, morbid, infected, dirtied, depraved, tarnished; see also DIRTY.—*Ant.* PURE, clean, healthy.

rough *a.* **1** [Not smooth] unequal, broken, coarse, choppy, ruffled, uneven, ridged, rugged, irregular, not sanded, not finished, unfinished, not completed, needing the finishing touches, bumpy, rocky, stony, jagged, grinding, knobby, sharpening, cutting, sharp, crinkled, crumpled, rumpled, scraggly, straggly, hairy, shaggy, hirsute, bushy, tufted, bearded, woolly, nappy, unshaven, unshorn, gnarled, knotty, bristly.—*Ant.* LEVEL, flat, even. **2** [Not gentle] harsh, strict, stern; see SEVERE 2. **3** [Crude] boorish, uncivil, uncultivated; see RUDE 1. **4** [Not quiet] buffeting, stormy, tumultuous; see TURBULENT. **5** [Unfinished] incomplete, imperfect, uncompleted; see UNFINISHED. **6** [Approximate] inexact, unprecise, uncertain; see APPROXIMATE.

roughly *a.* **1** [Approximately] about, in round numbers, by guess; see APPROXIMATELY. **2** [In a brutal manner] coarsely, cruelly, inhumanly; see BRUTALLY.

roughness *n.* **1** [The quality of being rough on the surface] unevenness, coarseness, brokenness, bumpiness, irregularity, raggedness, jaggedness, wrinkledness, shagginess, bushiness, beardedness, hairiness, woolliness, bristling.—*Ant.* REGULARITY, smoothness, evenness. **2** [Things causing or exhibiting roughness] break, crack, ragged edge, scratch, abrasion, nick. **3** [The quality of being rough in conduct] harshness, severity, hardness; see RUDENESS.

round *a.* **1** [Shaped like a globe or disk] spherical, spheroid, globular, orbicular, globe-shaped, ball-shaped, domical, circular, cylindrical, ringed, annular, oval, disk-shaped. **2** [Curved] arched, bowed, rounded, looped, recurved, incurved, coiled, curled. **3** [Approximate] rough, in tens, in hundreds; see APPROXIMATE.

round *prep.* about, near, in the neighborhood of, close to; see also ALMOST, APPROXIMATELY, AROUND.

round *n.* **1** [A round object] ring, orb, globe; see CIRCLE 1, RIM. **2** [A period of action] bout, course, whirl, cycle, circuit, routine, performance; see also SEQUENCE 1, SERIES. **3** [A unit of ammunition] cartridge, charge, load; see AMMUNITION, BULLET, SHOT 1.

round *v.* **1** [To turn] whirl, wheel, spin; see TURN 1. **2** [To make round] curve, convolute, bow, arch, bend, loop, whorl, shape, form, recurve, coil, fill out, curl, mold.—*Ant.* STRAIGHTEN, flatten, level. —**round off** approximate; round off by tens, hundreds, etc.; express as a round number; see also ESTIMATE. —**round out** expand, fill out, enlarge; see GROW 1.

roundabout *a.* circuitous, deviating, out-of-the-way; see INDIRECT.

roundness *n.* fullness, completeness, circularity, oneness, inclusiveness, wholeness.

roundup *n.* gathering, corralling, herding, wrangling, assembling.

rouse *v.* **1** [To waken] arouse, raise, awake; see AWAKEN, WAKE 1. **2** [To stimulate] urge, stir, provoke; see ANIMATE, EXCITE.

route *n.* **1** [A course being followed] way, course, path, track, beat, tack, divergence, detour, digression, meandering, rambling, wandering, circuit, round, rounds, range; see also ROAD 1. **2** [A projected course] map, plans, plot; see PLAN 2, PROGRAM 2.

routine *a.* usual, customary, methodical; see CONVENTIONAL 1, HABITUAL.

routine *n.* round, cycle, habit; see METHOD, SYSTEM.

rove *v.* walk, meander, wander; see ROAM.

row *n.* series, order, file; see LINE 1. —**in a row** in succession, successively, in a line; see CONSECUTIVE.

rowdy *a.* rebellious, boisterous, mischievous; see LAWLESS 2, UNRULY.

royal *a.* **1** [Pertaining to a king or his family] high, elevated, highborn, monarchic, reigning, regnant, regal, ruling, dominant, absolute, imperial, sovereign, supreme, noble, of noble birth, of gentle birth; see also sense 2, NOBLE 3. **2** [Having qualities befitting royalty] great, grand, stately, lofty, illustrious, renowned, eminent, superior, worthy, honorable, dignified, chivalrous, courteous, kingly, great-hearted, princely, princelike, majestic, magnificent, splendid, noble, courtly, impressive, commanding, aristocratic, lordly, august, imposing, superb, glorious, resplendent, gorgeous, sublime; see also sense 1, NOBLE 1, 2, WORTHY.

royalty *n.* kingship, sovereignty, nobility, authority, eminence, distinction, blood, birth, high descent, rank, greatness, power, supremacy, primacy, the crown, suzerainty; see also KING 1, QUEEN.

rub *n.* **1** [A rubbing action] brushing, stroke, massage, smoothing, scraping, scouring, grinding, rasping, friction, attrition; see also TOUCH 2. **2** [A difficulty] impediment, hindrance, dilemma; see DIFFICULTY 1, 2, PREDICAMENT.

rub *v.* **1** [To subject to friction] scrape, smooth, abrade, scour, grate, grind, wear away, graze, rasp, knead, fret, massage, polish, shine, burnish, scrub, erase, rub out, rub down, file, chafe, clean. **2** [To apply by rubbing; *usually with "on"*] brush, cover, finish; see PAINT 2. —**rub out** eradicate, erase, delete; see CANCEL, ELIMINATE.

rubber *a.* elastic, rubbery, soft, stretchable, stretching, rebounding, flexible, ductile, lively, buoyant, resilient.

rubbish *n.* litter, debris, waste; see TRASH 1.

rude *a.* **1** [Boorish] rustic, ungainly, awkward, crude, coarse, gross, rough, harsh, blunt, rugged, common, barbarous, lumpish, ungraceful, hulking, loutish, antic, rowdy, disorderly, brutish, clownish, stupid, ill-proportioned, unpolished, uncultured, unrefined, untrained, indecorous, unknowing, untaught, uncouth, slovenly, ill-bred, inelegant, ignorant, inexpert, illiterate, clumsy, gawky, slouching, graceless, ungraceful, lumbering, green, unacquainted, unenlightened, uneducated, vulgar, indecent, ribald, homely, outlandish, disgraceful, inappropriate.—*Ant.* CULTURED, urbane, suave. **2** [Not polite] churlish, sullen, surly, sharp, harsh, gruff, snarling, ungracious, unkind, obstreperous, overbearing, sour, disdainful, unmannerly, ill-mannered, improper, shabby, ill-chosen, discourteous, ungentlemanly, fresh*, abusive, forward, loud, loudmouthed, bold, brazen, audacious, brash, arrogant, supercilious, blustering, impudent, crass, raw, saucy, crusty, pert, unabashed, sharptongued, loose, mocking, barefaced, insolent, impertinent, offensive, naughty, impolite, hostile, insulting, disrespectful, scornful, flippant, presumptuous, sarcastic, defiant, outrageous, swaggering, disparaging, contemptuous, rebellious, disdainful, unfeeling, insensitive, scoffing, disagreeable, domineering, overbearing, highhanded, hypercritical, self-assertive, brutal, severe, hard, cocky, bullying, cheeky*, nervy*, assuming, dictatorial, magisterial, misbehaved, officious, meddling, intrusive, meddlesome, bitter, uncivilized, slandering, ill-tempered, bad-tempered, sassy*, snotty*, snooty*, uppity*.—*Ant.* POLITE, courteous, mannerly. **3** [Harsh] rough, violent, stormy; see TURBULENT. **4** [Approximate] surmised, guessed, imprecise; see APPROXIMATE. **5** [Coarse] rough, unrefined, unpolished; see CRUDE. **6** [Primitive] ignorant, uncivilized, barbarous; see PRIMITIVE 3.

rudely *a.* crudely, impudently, coarsely, impolitely, indecently, barbarously, roughly, harshly, bluntly, indecorously, insolently, contemptuously, brutally, dictatorially, churlishly, sullenly, gruffly, discourteously, loudly, brazenly, blusteringly, crassly, unabashedly, ribaldly, mockingly, snootily*.—*Ant.* KINDLY, politely, suavely.

rudeness *n.* discourtesy, bad manners, vulgarity, incivility, impoliteness, impudence, disrespect, misbehavior, barbarity, ungentlemanliness, unmannerliness, ill-breeding, crudity, brutality, barbarism, tactlessness, boorishness, unbecoming conduct, conduct not becoming a gentleman, crudeness, grossness, coarseness, bluntness, effrontery, impertinence, insolence, audacity, boldness, shamelessness, presumption, officiousness, intrusiveness, brazenness, sauciness, defiance, contempt, back talk, ill temper, irritability, disdain, bitterness, sharpness, unkindness, ungraciousness, harshness, gall*, sass*, lip*, nerve*, brass*, cheek*.

rudimentary *a.* **1** [Basic] elementary, primary, original; see FUNDAMENTAL. **2** [Immature] embryonic, undeveloped, simple; see UNFINISHED 1.

rudiments *n.* fundamentals, first principles, source; see ELEMENTS.

ruffle *v.* **1** [To disarrange] rumple, tousle, ripple; see CONFUSE, TANGLE. **2** [To anger] irritate, fret, anger; see BOTHER 1, 2.

rug *n.* carpet, carpeting, floor covering, Oriental rug, runner, scatter rug, throw rug, floor mat, drugget.

rugged *a.* **1** [Rough; *said especially of terrain*] hilly, broken, mountainous; see ROUGH 1. **2** [Strong; *said especially of persons*] hale, sturdy, hardy; see HEALTHY, STRONG 1.

ruin *n.* **1** [The act of destruction] extinction, demolition, overthrow; see DESTRUCTION 1, WRECK 1. **2** [A building fallen into decay; *often plu-*

ral] remains, traces, residue, foundation, vestiges, remnants, relics, wreck, walls, detritus, rubble; see also DESTRUCTION 2. **3** [The state of destruction] dilapidation, waste, wreck; see DESTRUCTION 2.

ruin *v.* **1** [To destroy] injure, overthrow, demolish; see DESTROY, RAVAGE. **2** [To cause to become bankrupt] impoverish, bankrupt, beggar; see WRECK.

ruined *a.* **1** [Destroyed] demolished, overthrown, torn down, razed, extinct, abolished, exterminated, annihilated, subverted, wrecked, desolated, ravaged, smashed, crushed, crashed, extinguished, dissolved, extirpated, totaled*; see also DESTROYED.—*Ant.* PROTECTED, saved, preserved. **2** [Spoiled] pillaged, harried, robbed, plundered, injured, hurt, impaired, defaced, harmed, marred, past hope, mutilated, broken, gone to the dogs*, done for*.—*Ant.* REPAIRED, restored, mended. **3** [Bankrupt] pauperized, poverty-stricken, beggared, reduced, left in penury, penniless, fleeced, in want, gone under*, under water*, through the mill*.—*Ant.* RICH, prosperous, well-off.

ruins *n.* remains, debris, wreckage; see DESTRUCTION 2, WRECK 2.

rule *n.* **1** [Government] control, dominion, jurisdiction; see GOVERNMENT 1. **2** [A regulation] edict, command, commandment; see LAW 3. **3** [The custom] habit, course, practice; see CUSTOM. —**as a rule** ordinarily, generally, usually; see REGULARLY.

rule *v.* **1** [To govern] conduct, control, dictate; see GOVERN. **2** [To regulate] order, decree, direct; see MANAGE 1. —**rule out** eliminate, not consider, preclude; see DENY, FORBID.

ruled *a.* administered, controlled, managed; see GOVERNED.

ruler *n.* **1** [One who governs] governor, commander, chief, manager, adjudicator, monarch, regent, director; see also DICTATOR, KING 1, LEADER 2. **2** [A straightedge] *Types of rulers include the following:* foot rule, yardstick, carpenter's rule, parallel rule, stationer's rule, T-square, try square, steel square, compositor's rule, compositor's ruler.

ruling *n.* order, decision, precept; see LAW 3.

rumble *n.* reverberation, thunder, roll; see NOISE 1.

rumble *v.* resound, growl, reverberate; see SOUND.

rummage *v.* search, ransack, search high and low, scour, turn inside out.

rumor *n.* report, news, tidings, intelligence, dispatch, hearsay, gossip, scandal, tattle, notoriety, noise, cry, popular report, fame, repute, grapevine, buzz*, breeze*, hoax, fabrication, suggestion, supposition, story, tale, invention, fiction, falsehood; see also LIE.

rumored *a.* reported, told, said, reputed, spread abroad, gossiped, given out, noised about, broadcast, as they say, all over town, current, circulating, in circulation, rife, prevailing, prevalent, persisting, general, going around, making the rounds.

rump *n.* posterior, buttocks, sacrum, hind end, tail end, posterior, butt end, bottom, croup, crupper, rear, rear end, derrière, backside, seat, breech, hunkers, fundament, butt*, buns*, duff*, bum*, tush*, keister*, can*.

rumple *v.* crumple, crush, fold; see WRINKLE.

run *n.* **1** [The act of running] sprint, pace, jog, bound, flow, amble, gallop, canter, lope, spring, trot, dart, rush, dash, flight, escape, break, charge, swoop, race, scamper, tear, whisk, flow, fall, drop. **2** [A series] continuity, succession, sequence; see SERIES. **3** [The average] par, norm, run of the mill; see AVERAGE. **4** [A course] way, route, field; see TRACK 1. —**in the long run** in the final outcome, finally, eventually; see ULTIMATELY. —**on the run 1** [Hurrying] busy, in a hurry, running; see HURRYING. **2** [Fleeing] retreating, defeated, routed; see BEATEN 1.

run *v.* **1** [To move, usually rapidly] flow in, flow over, chase along, fall, pour, tumble, drop, leap, spin, whirl, whiz, sail. **2** [To go swiftly by physical effort] rush, hurry, spring, bound, scurry, skitter, scramble, scoot, travel, run off, run away, dash ahead, dash on, put on a burst of speed, go on the double*, light out*, make tracks*, dart, dart ahead, gallop, canter, lope, spring, trot, single-foot, amble, pace, flee, speed, spurt, swoop, bolt, race, shoot, tear, whisk, scamper, scuttle. **3** [To function] move, work, go; see OPERATE 2. **4** [To cause to function] control, drive, govern; see MANAGE 1. **5** [To extend] encompass, cover, spread; see REACH 1, SURROUND 1. **6** [To continue] last, persevere, go on; see CONTINUE 1. **7** [To compete] oppose, contest, contend with; see COMPETE, RACE 2. —**run down 1** [To chase] hunt, seize, apprehend; see PURSUE 1. **2** [To ridicule] make fun of, belittle, depreciate; see RIDICULE. —**run into 1** [To collide with] bump into, crash into, have a collision with; see HIT 1. **2** [To encounter] come across, see, contact; see MEET 6. —**run out 1** [To stop]

expire, finish, end; see STOP 2. **2** [To become exhausted] weaken, wear out, waste away; see TIRE 1. —**run out of** lose, dissipate, exhaust; see WASTE 2. —**run over** trample, drive over, run down; see HIT, KILL. —**run through** waste, squander, use up; see SPEND.

runaway *a.* out of control, delinquent, wild; see DISORDERLY 1.

rundown *n.* report, outline, account; see SUMMARY.

run-down *a.* **1** [Exhausted] weak, debilitated, weary; see WEAK 1, 2, TIRED. **2** [Dilapidated] broken-down, shabby, beat-up*; see OLD 2, CRUMBLY.

runner *n.* racer, entrant, contestant, sprinter, dasher, distance runner, long-distance runner, middle-distance runner, miler, marathoner, cross-country runner, jogger, trackman, hurdler, messenger, courier, express, dispatch bearer; see also ATHLETE.

running *a.* **1** [In the act of running] pacing, racing, speeding, galloping, cantering, trotting, jogging, scampering, fleeing, bounding, whisking, sprinting, flowing, tumbling, falling, pouring. **2** [In the process of running] producing, operating, working, functioning, proceeding, moving, revolving, guiding, conducting, administering, going, in operation, in action, executing, promoting, achieving, transacting, determining, bringing about. **3** [Ranging] reaching, spreading, encompassing; see EXTENDING.

runoff *n.* spring runoff, drainage, surplus water; see FLOW, RIVER, WATER 1.

run-of-the-mill *a.* popular, mediocre, ordinary; see COMMON 1.

runt* *n.* shrimp*, twerp*, nobody, small fry*, little person.

rupture *n.* hole, separation, crack; see BREAK 1, TEAR.

rupture *v.* crack, tear, burst; see BREAK.

rural *a.* rustic, farm, agricultural, ranch, pastoral, bucolic, backwoods, country, agrarian, suburban.—*Ant.* URBAN, industrial, commercial.

ruse *n.* artifice, ploy, scam*; see DEVICE 2, TRICK 1.

rush *n.* haste, dash, charge; see HURRY.

rush *v.* hasten, speed, hurry up; see HURRY.

rushed *a.* hurried, pressed, pressured; see DRIVEN.

rushing *a.* being quick, bestirring oneself, losing no time; see HURRYING.

Russian *a.* Slavic, Slav, Muscovite, Siberian, White Russian, Belorussian, Soviet.

rust *n.* decomposition, corruption, corrosion, oxidation, decay, rot, dilapidation, breakup, wear.

rust *v.* oxidize, become rusty, degenerate, decay, rot, corrode.

rustic *a.* agricultural, pastoral, agrarian; see RURAL.

rustle *v.* swish, stir, sough; see SOUND.

rusty *a.* 1 [Decayed] unused, neglected, worn; see OLD 2, WEAK 2. 2 [Unpracticed] out of practice, soft, out of shape; see WEAK 5.

rut *n.* 1 [A deeply cut track] hollow, trench, furrow; see GROOVE. 2 [Habitual behavior] custom, habit, course, routine, practice, performance, round, circuit, circle, usage,

procedure.—*Ant.* CHANGE, progress, variety.

ruthless *a.* cruel, fierce, savage, brutal, merciless, inhuman, hard, cold, fiendish, unmerciful, pitiless, grim, unpitying, tigerish, ferocious, stonyhearted, coldblooded, remorseless, vindictive, vengeful, revengeful, rancorous, implacable, unforgiving, malevolent, hardhearted, hard, cold, unsympathetic, vicious, sadistic, surly, tyrannical, relentless, barbarous, inhuman, atrocious, flagrant, terrible, abominable, outrageous, oppressive, bloodthirsty, venomous, galling.—*Ant.* KIND, helpful, civilized.

S

Sabbath *n.* day of rest, the Lord's Day, Saturday or Sunday; see WEEKEND.

sabotage *n.* demolition, overthrow, treason; see DESTRUCTION 1, REVOLUTION 2.

sabotage *v.* subvert, siege, undermine; see ATTACK 1, DESTROY.

sac *n.* welt, pouch, blister; see SORE.

sack *n.* sac, pouch, pocket; see BAG, CONTAINER. —**hit the sack*** go to bed, go to sleep, retire; see SLEEP.

sacrament *n.* holy observance, ceremonial, ceremony, rite, ritual, liturgy, act of divine worship, mystery, the mysteries. *In the Roman Catholic and Eastern Orthodox churches, the seven sacraments are as follows:* baptism, confirmation or the laying on of hands, penance, Communion or the Eucharist, extreme unction or Anointing of the Sick, holy orders, matrimony.

sacramental *a.* sacred, pure, solemn; see HOLY 1, RELIGIOUS 1.

sacred *a.* 1 [Holy] pure, pious, saintly; see HOLY 1. 2 [Dedicated] consecrated, ordained, sanctioned; see DIVINE.

sacrifice *n.* 1 [An offering to a deity] offering, tribute, atonement; see CEREMONY. 2 [A loss] discount, deduction, reduction; see LOSS 1.

sacrifice *v.* 1 [To offer to a deity] consecrate, dedicate, give up; see BLESS. 2 [To give up as a means to an end] forfeit, forgo, relinquish, yield, suffer the loss of, renounce, spare, give up, let go, resign oneself to, sacrifice oneself, surrender, part with, go astray from. 3 [To sell at a loss] cut, reduce, sell out; see DECREASE 2, LOSE 2.

sad *a.* 1 [Afflicted with sorrow] unhappy, sorry, sorrowful, downcast, dismal, gloomy, glum, pensive, heavy-hearted, dispirited, dejected, desolate, depressed, troubled, melancholy, morose, grieved, pessimistic, crushed, brokenhearted, heartbroken, heartsick, despondent, careworn, disheartened, rueful, anguished, lamenting, mourning, grieving, weeping, bitter, woebegone, doleful, spiritless, joyless, heavy, crestfallen, discouraged, moody, low-spirited, despairing, hopeless, worried, downhearted, cast down, in heavy spirits, morbid, oppressed, blighted, grief-stricken, foreboding, apprehensive, horrified, anxious, wretched, miserable, mournful, disconsolate, forlorn, jaundiced, out of sorts*, distressed, afflicted, bereaved, repining, harassed, dreary, down in the dumps*, in bad humor, out of humor, cut up*, in the depths*, blue, stricken with grief, wearing a long face, in tears, feeling like hell*, down in the mouth*.—*Ant.* HAPPY, joyous, cheerful. 2 [Suggestive of sorrow] pitiable, unhappy, dejecting, saddening, disheartening, discouraging, joyless, dreary, dark, dismal, gloomy, moving, touching, mournful, disquieting, disturbing, somber, doleful, oppressive, funereal, lugubrious, pathetic, tragic, pitiful, piteous, woeful, rueful, sorry, unfortunate, hapless, heartrending, dire, distressing, depressing, grievous.

sadden *v.* oppress, dishearten, discourage, cast down, deject, depress, break someone's heart.

sadistic *a.* cruel, brutal, vicious; see CRUEL.

sadly *a.* unhappily, morosely, dejectedly, wistfully, sorrowfully, gloomily, joylessly, dismally, dolefully, mournfully, cheerlessly, in sorrow.

sadness *n.* sorrow, dejection, melancholy, depression, grief, despondency, oppression, gloom, the blues*.

safe *a.* 1 [Not in danger] out of danger, secure, in safety, in security, free from harm, free from danger, unharmed, safe and sound, protected, guarded, housed, screened from danger, unthreatened, unmolested, entrenched, impregnable, invulnerable, under the protection of, saved, safeguarded, secured, defended, supported, sustained, preserved, maintained, upheld, vindicated, shielded, nourished, sheltered, fostered, cared for, cherished, watched, impervious to, patrolled, looked after, supervised, tended, attended, kept in order, surveyed, regulated, with one's head above water, undercover, out of harm's way, on the safe side, on ice*, at anchor, in harbor, snug as a bug in a rug*, under lock and key.—*Ant.* DANGEROUS, unsafe, risky. 2 [Not dangerous] sound, secure, safety-inspected; see HARMLESS. 3 [Reliable] trustworthy, dependable, competent; see RELIABLE. —**keep safe** care for, escort, protect; see GUARD, WATCH.

safe *n.* strongbox, coffer, chest, repository, vault, case, lockbox, safe-deposit box.

safekeeping *n.* supervision, care, guardianship; see CUSTODY, PROTECTION 2.

safely *a.* securely, with impunity, without harm, without risk, without danger, harmlessly, carefully, cautiously, reliably.

safety *n.* 1 [Freedom from danger] security, protection, impregnability, surety, sanctuary, refuge, shelter, invulnerability. 2 [A lock] lock mechanism, safety catch, safety lock; see FASTENER, LOCK 1.

sag *n.* depression, dip, swale; see HOLE 1.

sag *v.* stoop, hang down, become warped; see BEND, LEAN 1.

said *a.* pronounced, aforesaid, aforementioned; see PRECEDING, SPOKEN.

sail *n.* 1 [Means of sailing a vessel] sheets, canvas, cloth; see GOODS. *Sails include the following:* mainsail, foresail, topsail, jib, spanker, flying jib, trysail, staysail, balloon sail, spinnaker, royal, topgallant. 2 [A journey by sailing vessel] voyage, cruise, trip; see JOURNEY. —**set sail** begin a voyage, shove off, weigh anchor; see LEAVE 1, SAIL 1.

sail *v.* 1 [To travel by sailing] cruise, voyage, go alongside, bear down on, bear for, direct one's course for, set sail, put to sea, sail away from,

navigate, travel, make headway, lie in, make for, heave to, fetch up, bring to, bear off, close with, run in, put in. 2 [To fly] float, soar, ride the storm, skim, glide.

sailor *n.* seaman, mariner, seafarer, pirate, navigator, pilot, boatman, yachtsman, able-bodied seaman, Jack Tar*, tar*, sea dog*, limey*, salt*, swab*, swabbie*, bluejacket. *Kinds and ranks of sailors include the following—crew:* deck hand, stoker, cabin boy, yeoman, purser; ship's carpenter, cooper, tailor, steward, quartermaster, signalman, gunner, boatswain or bo's'n*; *officers:* captain or commander or skipper, navigating officer, deck officer; first, second, third mate.

saint *n.* a true Christian, child of God, son of God, paragon, salt of the earth, godly person, martyr, moral exemplar, canonized person, altruist, the pure in heart, a believer.

saintly *a.* angelic, pious, divine; see HOLY.

sake *n.* 1 [End] objective, consequence, final cause; see RESULT. 2 [Purpose] score, motive, principle; see PURPOSE 1. 3 [Welfare] benefit, interest, well-being; see ADVANTAGE, WELFARE 1.

salad *n.* salad greens, slaw, mixture, combination. *Common salads include the following:* green, tossed, vegetable, tomato, potato, macaroni, fruit, bean, taco, combination, chef's, tuna, shrimp, lobster, crab, chicken, ham, Waldorf, Caesar, Cobb, pineapple, banana, molded, frozen; cole slaw.

salary *n.* wages, compensation, remuneration; see PAY 2.

sale *n.* 1 [The act of selling; *used in the plural*] commerce, business, exchange, barter, merchandising, direct selling, mail-order selling, e-commerce, marketing, vending, trade. 2 [An individual instance of selling] deal, transaction, negotiation, turnover, trade, purchase, auction, disposal; see also BUYING, SELLING. 3 [An organized effort to promote selling] clearance, stock reduction, fire sale, unloading, dumping, closeout, liquidation, end-of-the-year clearance, remnant sale, going out of business sale, bankruptcy sale. —**for** (or **on** or **up for**) **sale** put on the market, to be sold, available, offered for purchase, not withheld. —**on sale** marked down, reduced, cut, at a bargain, at a cut rate, knocked down; see also REDUCED 2.

salesman *n.* 1 [A sales clerk] salesperson, seller, counterman; see CLERK. 2 [A commercial traveler] out-of-town representative, agent, canvasser, solicitor, seller, businessman, itinerant, fieldworker, traveler, traveling man, traveling salesman, sales representative, sales manager.

salesperson *n.* salesman, saleswoman, saleslady; see CLERK.

saliva *n.* water, spittle, salivation, excretion, phlegm, mucus, spit.

saloon *n.* bar, nightclub, cocktail lounge, pub*, brewpub*, gin mill*, beer joint*, hangout*, place; see also RESTAURANT.

salt *a.* alkaline, saline, briny; see SALTY.

salt *n.* 1 [A common seasoning and preservative] sodium chloride, common salt, table salt, savor, condiment, flavoring, spice, seasoning. *Common types of flavoring salts include the following:* garlic, sea, celery, onion, barbecue, salad, seasoning, hickory smoked; monosodium glutamate, MSG, poultry seasoning, salt substitute. 2 [Anything that provides savor] relish, pungency, smartness; see HUMOR 1, WIT. —**not worth one's salt** good-for-nothing, bad, worthless; see POOR 2. —**with a grain (or pinch) of salt** doubtingly, skeptically, dubiously; see SUSPICIOUSLY.

salt *v.* 1 [To flavor with salt] season, make tasty, make piquant; see FLAVOR. 2 [To scatter thickly] strew, spread, pepper; see DISTRIBUTE, SOW.

salty *a.* briny, brackish, pungent, alkaline, well-seasoned, flavored, well-flavored, highly flavored, sour, acrid.

salute *v.* snap to attention, dip the colors, touch one's cap, do honor to, recognize; see also PRAISE 1.

salvage *v.* retrieve, recover, regain; see SAVE 1.

salvation *n.* 1 [The act of preservation] deliverance, liberation, emancipation; see RESCUE. 2 [A means of preservation] buckler, safeguard, assurance; see PROTECTION 2.

salve *n.* ointment, unguent, lubricant, balm, medicine, emollient, unction, remedy, help, cure, cream.

same *a.* 1 [Like another in state] equivalent, identical, corresponding; see ALIKE, EQUAL. 2 [Like another in action] similarly, in the same manner, likewise; see ALIKE.

same *pron.* the very same, identical object, substitute, equivalent, similar thing.

sameness *n.* uniformity, unity, resemblance, analogy, similarity, alikeness, identity, standardization, equality, equivalence, no difference.

sample *n.* specimen, unit, individual; see EXAMPLE.

sample *v.* taste, test, inspect; see EXAMINE, EXPERIMENT.

sanction *n.* consent, acquiescence, assent; see PERMISSION.

sanction *v.* confirm, authorize, countenance; see APPROVE, ENDORSE 2.

sanctity *n.* holiness, sacredness, piety; see VIRTUE 1.

sanctuary *n.* 1 [A sacred place] shrine, church, temple; see CHURCH 1. 2 [A place to which one may retire] asylum, resort, haven; see SHELTER.

sand *n.* 1 [Rock particles] sandy soil, sandy loam, silt, dust, grit, powder, gravel, rock powder, rock flour, debris, dirt; see also EARTH 2. 2 [The beach] strand, seaside, seashore; see SHORE.

sandal *n.* slipper, thong, flip-flop; see SHOE.

sandwich *n.* lunch, light lunch, quick lunch. *Sandwiches include the following:* hamburger, burger*, cheeseburger, wiener, hot dog*, Denver, Western, club, tuna salad, ham, chicken, roast beef, ham and egg, cheese, deviled meat, steak, submarine, grilled cheese, BLT, egg salad, open face, peanut butter and jelly, jelly.

sandy *a.* 1 [Containing sand; *said especially of soil*] loose, open, permeable, porous, easy to work, easily worked, granular, powdery, gritty. 2 [Suggestive of sand; *said especially of the hair*] fair-haired, fair, blond, light, light-haired, reddish, sandy-red, sun-bleached, flaxen, faded.

sane *a.* 1 [Sound in mind] rational, normal, lucid, right-minded, sober, in one's right mind, with a healthy mind, mentally sound, balanced, centered, healthy-minded, reasonable, in possession of one's faculties.—*Ant.* INSANE, irrational, delirious. 2 [Sensible] reasonable, practical, wise; see SENSIBLE.

sanitary *a.* hygienic, wholesome, sterile; see HEALTHFUL.

sanity *n.* sound mind, rationality, healthy mind, saneness, a clear mind, clearmindedness, wholesome outlook, common sense, intelligence, reason, reasonableness, prudence, good judgment, acumen, understanding, comprehension.

sap *n.* 1 [The life fluid of a plant] fluid, secretion, essence; see LIQUID. 2 [*A dupe] dolt, gull, sucker*; see FOOL.

sapling *n.* scion, seedling, slip, sprig, young tree; see also TREE.

sappy *a.* 1 [Juicy] lush, succulent, watery; see JUICY. 2 [*Idiotic] foolish, silly, sentimental; see STUPID.

sarcasm *n.* satire, irony, banter, derision, contempt, scoffing, flouting, ridicule, burlesque, disparagement, criticism, cynicism, invective, censure, lampooning, aspersion, sneering, mockery.—*Ant.* FLATTERY, fawning, cajolery.

sarcastic *a.* scornful, mocking, ironical, satirical, taunting, severe, derisive, bitter, saucy, hostile, sneering, snickering, quizzical, arrogant, disrespectful, offensive, carping, cynical, disillusioned, snarling, unbelieving, corrosive, acid, cutting, scorching, captious, sharp, pert, brusque, caustic, biting, harsh, austere, grim.

sardonic *a.* sarcastic, cynical, scornful; see SARCASTIC.

Satan *n.* Mephistopheles, Lucifer, Beelzebub; see DEVIL.

satanic *a.* malicious, evil, devilish; see SINISTER.

satellite *n.* **1** [A moon] planetoid, minor planet, secondary planet, inferior planet, asteroid. **2** [A man-made object put into orbit around a celestial body] artificial moon, spacecraft, moonlet, sputnik, space station, communications satellite, weather satellite, GPS satellite, geostationary satellite.

satire *n.* mockery, ridicule, caricature; see IRONY.

satisfaction *n.* **1** [The act of satisfying] gratification, fulfillment, achievement; see ACHIEVEMENT. **2** [The state or feeling of being satisfied] comfort, pleasure, well-being, content, contentment, gladness, delight, bliss, joy, happiness, relief, complacency, peace of mind, ease, heart's ease, serenity, contentedness, cheerfulness. **3** [Something that contributes to satisfaction] reward, prosperity, good fortune; see BLESSING 2. **4** [Settlement of a debt] reimbursement, repayment, compensation.

satisfactorily *a.* **1** [In a satisfactory manner] convincingly, suitably, competently; see ADEQUATELY. **2** [In a manner productive of satisfactory results] amply, abundantly, thoroughly; see AGREEABLY.

satisfactory *a.* adequate, satisfying, pleasing; see ENOUGH.

satisfied *a.* content, happy, contented, filled, supplied, fulfilled, paid, compensated, appeased, convinced, gratified, sated, at ease, with enough, without care, satiated.

satisfy *v.* **1** [To make content] comfort, cheer, elate, befriend, please, rejoice, delight, exhilarate, amuse, entertain, flatter, make merry, make cheerful, gladden, content, gratify, indulge, humor, conciliate, propitiate, capture, enthrall, enliven, animate, captivate, fascinate, fill, be of advantage, gorge. **2** [To pay] repay, clear up, disburse; see PAY 1, SETTLE 7. **3** [To fulfill] do, fill, serve the purpose, be enough,

observe, perform, comply with, conform to, meet requirements, keep a promise, accomplish, complete, be adequate, be sufficient, provide, furnish, qualify, answer, serve, equip, meet, avail, suffice, fill the want, come up to, content one, appease one, fill the bill*, pass muster*, get by, do in a pinch*.—*Ant.* NEGLECT, leave open, fail to do.

satisfying *a.* pleasing, comforting, gratifying; see ENOUGH, PLEASANT 2.

saturate *v.* overfill, drench, steep; see IMMERSE, SOAK 1.

saturated *a.* drenched, full, soggy; see SOAKED, WET 1.

saturation *n.* fullness, soaking, overload; see EXCESS 1.

sauce *n.* topping, gravy, dressing; see FLAVORING, FOOD.

sausage *n.* link sausage, salami, liverwurst; see MEAT.

savage *a.* **1** [Primitive] crude, simple, original; see CRUDE. **2** [Cruel] barbarous, inhuman, brutal; see CRUEL. **3** [Wild] untamed, uncivilized, uncultured; see UNCONTROLLED.

savage *n.* primitive, ruffian, animal; see BEAST 2.

savagely *a.* cruelly, viciously, barbarically; see BRUTALLY.

save *v.* **1** [To remove from danger] deliver, extricate, rescue, free, set free, liberate, release, emancipate, ransom, redeem, come to the rescue of, defend.—*Ant.* LEAVE, desert, condemn. **2** [To assure an afterlife] rescue from sin, reclaim, regenerate; see sense 1. **3** [To hoard] collect, store, invest, have on deposit, amass, accumulate, gather, treasure up, store up, pile up, hide away, cache, stow away, sock away*.—*Ant.* WASTE, spend, invest. **4** [To preserve] conserve, keep, put up; see PRESERVE 2.

saved *a.* **1** [Kept from danger] rescued, released, delivered, protected, defended, guarded, safeguarded, preserved, reclaimed, regenerated, cured, healed, conserved, maintained, safe, secure, freed, free from harm, unthreatened, free from danger.—*Ant.* RUINED, destroyed, lost. **2** [Not spent] kept, unspent, unused, untouched, accumulated, deposited, on deposit, retained, laid away, hoarded, invested, amassed, stored, spared.—*Ant.* WASTED, squandered, spent.

savings *n.* means, property, resources, funds, reserve, investment, provision, provisions, accumulation, store, riches, harvest, hoard, savings account, cache, nest egg, money in the bank, provision for a rainy day.

savior *n.* **1** [One who saves another] deliverer, rescuer, preserver; see

PROTECTOR. **2** [Jesus Christ; *usually capital*] Redeemer, Messiah, Son of God; see CHRIST.

savor *v.* enjoy, relish, appreciate; see LIKE 1.

saw *n.* power, circular, concave, mill, ice, crosscut, band, rip, hand, pruning, whip, buck, keyhole, back, butcher's, hack, jig, etc. saw; see also TOOL 1.

say *v.* tell, speak, relate, state, announce, declare, state positively, open one's mouth, have one's say, break silence, put forth, let out, assert, maintain, express oneself, answer, respond, suppose, assume. —**to say the least** at a minimum, at the very least, to put it mildly, minimally.

saying *n.* aphorism, adage, maxim, byword, motto, proverb, precept, dictum.

scab *n.* eschar, slough, crust.

scaffold *n.* framework, stage, structure; see BUILDING, PLATFORM 1.

scald *v.* char, blanch, parboil; see BURN.

scale *n.* **1** [A series for measurement] rule, computation, system; see MEASURE 2. **2** [A flake or film] thin coating, covering, encrustation; see FLAKE, LAYER. **3** [A device for weighing; *often plural*] steelyard, analytical balance, balance, scale beam. *Varieties of scales include the following:* beam, automatic indicating, counter, cylinder, drum, barrel, platform, spring, computing, digital, household, miner's, assayer's, truck, jeweler's, butcher's, baker's. **4** [Musical tones] range, major scale, minor scale, harmonic scale, melodic scale; see also MUSIC. —**on a large scale** extensively, grandly, expansively; see GENEROUSLY. —**on a small scale** economically, in a limited way, with restrictions; see INADEQUATE, UNIMPORTANT.

scale *v.* **1** [To climb] ascend, surmount, mount; see CLIMB. **2** [To peel] exfoliate, strip off, flake; see PEEL, SKIN. **3** [To measure] compare, balance, compute; see COMPARE 1.

scalpel *n.* dissecting instrument, surgical tool, blade; see KNIFE.

scamper *v.* hasten, scurry, hightail*; see HURRY 1, RUN 2.

scan *v.* browse, thumb through, consider; see LOOK 2.

scandal *n.* shame, disgrace, infamy, discredit, slander, disrepute, detraction, defamation, opprobrium, reproach, aspersion, backbiting, gossip, eavesdropping, rumor, hearsay.—*Ant.* PRAISE, adulation, flattery.

scandalize *v.* detract, defame, backbite; see SLANDER.

scandalous *a.* infamous, disreputable, ignominious; see SHAMEFUL 2.

scanty *a.* scarce, few, pinched, meager, little, small, bare, ragged, insufficient, inadequate, slender, narrow, thin, scrimp, scrimpy, tiny, wee, sparse, diminutive, short, stingy.—*Ant.* MUCH, large, many.

scar *n.* cicatrix, cicatrice, mark, blemish, discoloration, disfigurement, defect, flaw, hurt, wound, injury.

scar *v.* cut, disfigure, slash; see HURT 1.

scarce *a.* limited, infrequent, not plentiful; see RARE 2, UNCOMMON. —**make oneself scarce*** go, depart, run off; see LEAVE 1.

scarcely *a.* barely, only just, scantily; see HARDLY.

scarcity *n.* deficiency, inadequacy, insufficiency; see LACK 2, POVERTY 1.

scare *n.* fright, terror, alarm; see FEAR.

scare *v.* panic, terrify, alarm; see FRIGHTEN. —**scare off** (or **away**) drive off, drive out, drive away, get rid of, dispose of, disperse, scatter; see also FRIGHTEN.

scared *a.* startled, frightened, fearful; see AFRAID.

scarf *n.* throw, sash, muffler, shawl, comforter, ascot, stole, wrap; see also CLOTHES.

scarlet *a.* cardinal, royal red, vermilion; see RED.

scat* *v.* be off, begone, get out of my way, get out from under my feet, out with you, be off with you, get out of my sight, scoot*, get out, beat it*, shoo*, scram*, get going.

scatter *v.* **1** [To become separated] run apart, run away, go one's own way, diverge, disperse, disband, migrate, spread widely, go in different directions, blow off, go in many directions, be strewn to the four winds.—*Ant.* ASSEMBLE, convene, congregate. **2** [To cause to separate] dispel, dissipate, diffuse, strew, divide, disband, shed, distribute, disseminate, separate, disunite, sunder, scatter to the wind, sever, put asunder.—*Ant.* UNITE, join, mix. **3** [To waste] expend, dissipate, fritter away; see SPEND, WASTE 2.

scattered *a.* spread, strewed, rambling, sowed, sown, sprinkled, spread abroad, separated, disseminated, dispersed, strung out, distributed, widespread, diffuse, all over the place, separate, shaken out.—*Ant.* GATHERED, condensed, concentrated.

scene *n.* spectacle, exhibition, display; see VIEW.

scenery *n.* landscape, prospect, spectacle; see VIEW.

scenic *a.* beautiful, spectacular, dramatic; see BEAUTIFUL.

scent *n.* odor, fragrance, redolence; see PERFUME, SMELL 1, 2.

schedule *n.* timetable, table of arrivals and departures, agenda, order of business, calendar, outline, program, plan, flowchart, game plan, catalogue, register; see also PLAN 2, PROGRAM 2. —**on schedule** on time, not delayed, prompt; see EARLY 2, PUNCTUAL.

schedule *v.* record, register, catalogue; see LIST 1.

scheduled *a.* listed, announced, arranged; see PLANNED, PROPOSED.

scheme *n.* project, course of action, purpose; see PLAN 2, SYSTEM.

scheme *v.* intrigue, contrive, plot; see PLAN 1.

scholar *n.* learned person, academic, authority, expert, professor, graduate student, fellow, scholar-in-residence, visiting scholar; see also STUDENT.

scholarly *a.* erudite, cultured, studious; see EDUCATED, LEARNED 1.

scholarship *n.* research, learning, pedantry; see KNOWLEDGE 1.

scholastic *a.* academic, literary, lettered; see LEARNED 1.

school *n.* **1** [An institution of learning] *Varieties of schools include the following:* nursery school, elementary school, high school, secondary school, parochial school, preparatory school, private school, prep school, public school, boarding school, military school, academy, seminary, normal school, conservatory, trade school, technical school, graduate school, professional school, divinity school, art school, law school, college of arts and science, junior high school, middle school, senior high school, community college, junior college; see also COLLEGE, UNIVERSITY. **2** [Persons or products associated by common intellectual or artistic theories] party, following, circle; see FOLLOWING. **3** [A building housing a school] schoolhouse, establishment, institution; see BUILDING. —**attend school** undergo schooling, learn, go to school, get one's education, receive instruction, matriculate, study, take courses, be a student, enroll; see also LEARN, STUDY.

schoolbook *n.* primer, textbook, assigned reading; see BOOK.

schooling *n.* teaching, nurture, discipline; see EDUCATION 1.

schoolmate *n.* roommate, comrade, classmate; see FRIEND.

schoolteacher *n.* educator, lecturer, instructor; see TEACHER.

school year *n.* academic year, terms, semesters; see YEAR.

science *n.* **1** [An organized body of knowledge] department of learning, branch of knowledge, system of knowledge, body of fact; see also CHEMISTRY, MATHEMATICS, MEDICINE 3, SOCIAL SCIENCE, ZOOLOGY for commonly recognized sciences. **2** [A highly developed skill] craftsmanship, art, deftness; see ABILITY.

scientific *a.* **1** [Objectively accurate] precise, exact, clear; see ACCURATE 2, OBJECTIVE 1. **2** [Concerning science] experimental, deductive, methodically sound; see LOGICAL.

scientist *n.* expert, specialist, investigator, laboratory technician, natural philosopher, student of natural history, explorer, research worker, research assistant, learned person, serious student, PhD, scientific thinker. *Scientists include the following:* anatomist, astronomer, botanist, biologist, chemist, biochemist, geneticist, geologist, mineralogist, metallurgist, geographer, mathematician, physicist, psychiatrist, psychologist, astrophysicist, ecologist, biophysicist, bacteriologist, marine biologist, oceanographer, pharmacist, chemical engineer, agronomist, entomologist, ornithologist, endocrinologist, radiologist, graphologist, geophysicist, neurologist, zoologist, paleontologist, anthropologist, ethnologist, archaeologist, sociologist, linguist; see also DOCTOR.

scissors *n.* shears, pair of scissors, blades, hair scissors, paper scissors, garden shears, cutting instrument.

scoff *v.* mock, deride, jeer, ridicule, put down, be dismissive, show contempt, scorn, tut-tut, dis*; see also RIDICULE.

scold *v.* admonish, chide, chew out*, bawl out*, get after, lay down the law*, jump on*, jump all over*, rebuke, censure, reprove, upbraid, reprimand, taunt, cavil, criticize, denounce, disparage, recriminate, rate, revile, rail, abuse, vilify, find fault with, nag, lecture, call on the carpet*, rake over the coals*, give one a talking to, chasten, preach, tell off*, keep after, light into*, put down; see also PUNISH.—*Ant.* PRAISE, commend, extol.

scoop *v.* ladle, shovel, bail; see DIP 2.

scoot *v.* dart, speed, rush; see HASTEN 2, HURRY 1.

scope *n.* reach, range, field; see EXTENT.

scorch *v.* roast, parch, shrivel; see BURN.

scorching *a.* fiery, searing, sweltering; see BURNING, HOT 1.

score *n.* **1** [A tally] reckoning, record, average, rate, account,

count, number, summation, aggregate, sum, addition, summary, amount, final tally, final account; see also NUMBER, WHOLE. **2** [Written music] transcription, arrangement, orchestration; see MUSIC 1, COMPOSITION. —**know the score*** grasp, be aware of, comprehend; see KNOW 1, UNDERSTAND 1.

score *v.* **1** [To make a single score] make a goal, make a point, rack up*, chalk up, total, calculate, reckon, tally, enumerate, count, add. **2** [To compose a musical accompaniment] arrange, adapt, orchestrate; see COMPOSE 2.

scorn *v.* hold in contempt, despise, disdain; see HATE.

scornful *a.* contemptuous, disdainful, haughty; see EGOTISTIC.

scoundrel *n.* rogue, scamp, villain; see RASCAL.

scour *v.* scrub, cleanse, rub; see CLEAN, WASH 1, 2.

scout *n.* **1** [One who gathers information] explorer, pioneer, outpost, runner, advance guard, precursor, patrol, reconnoiterer. **2** [A Boy Scout or Girl Scout] *Degrees of scouts include the following:* Cub, Tenderfoot, Second Class, First Class, Star, Life, Eagle, Explorer, Queen's (British), bronze palm, gold palm, silver palm; Brownie, Junior, Cadette, Senior.

scowl *v.* glower, disapprove, grimace; see FROWN.

scramble *v.* **1** [To mix] combine, blend, interfuse; see MIX 1. **2** [To climb hastily] clamber, push, struggle; see CLIMB.

scrap *n.* **1** [Junk metal] waste material, chips, cuttings; see TRASH 1. **2** [A bit] fragment, particle, portion; see BIT 1, PIECE 1. **3** [*A fight] quarrel, brawl, squabble; see FIGHT 1.

scrap *v.* **1** [To discard] reject, forsake, dismiss; see ABANDON 1, DISCARD. **2** [*To fight] wrangle, battle, squabble; see FIGHT, QUARREL.

scrapbook *n.* portfolio, memorabilia, notebook; see ALBUM, COLLECTION.

scrape *v.* abrade, scour, rasp; see RUB 1.

scraper *n.* grater, rasp, abrasive; see TOOL 1.

scratch *n.* hurt, cut, mark; see INJURY, SCAR. —**from scratch** from the beginning, without preparation, from nothing; see ALONE, ORIGINAL 1.

scratch *v.* scrape, scarify, prick; see DAMAGE, HURT 1.

scratching *a.* grating, abrasive, rasping; see ROUGH 1.

scrawl *v.* scribble, scratch, doodle; see WRITE 2.

scrawled *a.* scribbled, scratched, inscribed; see WRITTEN 2.

scrawny *a.* lanky, gaunt, lean; see THIN 2.

scream *n.* screech, outcry, shriek; see CRY 1, YELL.

scream *v.* shriek, screech, squeal; see CRY 2, YELL.

screaming *a.* shrieking, screeching, squealing; see YELLING.

screen *n.* **1** [A concealment] cloak, cover, covering, curtain, shield, envelope, veil, mask, shade. **2** [A protection] shelter, guard, security; see COVER 1, PROTECTION 2.

screen *v.* **1** [To hide] veil, conceal, mask; see HIDE 1. **2** [To choose] select, eliminate, sift; see CHOOSE.

screw *n.* spiral, worm, bolt, pin; see also FASTENER. *Screws include the following:* jack, lead, double, drive, lag, right-handed, left-handed, metric, regulating, set, winged, thumb, spiral, triple, wood, machine, Phillips (trademark).

screw* *v.* cheat, swindle, beat; see DEFEAT, HURT 2, TRICK. —**screw up*** bungle, foul up*, mishandle; see BOTCH.

screwy* *a.* odd, crazy, nutty*; see INSANE, WRONG 2.

scribble *n.* scrawl, scratch, doodle; see HANDWRITING.

scribble *v.* scrawl, scratch, doodle; see WRITE 2.

scrimp *v.* limit, pinch, skimp; see ECONOMIZE.

script *n.* **1** [Handwriting] writing, characters, chirography; see HANDWRITING. **2** [Playbook] lines, text, dialogue, book, scenario.

scripture *n.* **1** [Truth] reality, verity, final word; see TRUTH. **2** [The Bible; *capital*] the Word, Holy Writ, the Book; see BIBLE.

scrub *a.* second-rate, unimportant, mediocre; see POOR 2.

scrub *v.* rub, cleanse, scour; see CLEAN, WASH 1, 2.

scrubbed *a.* cleaned, polished, immaculate; see CLEAN 1.

scruple *n.* compunction, qualm, uneasiness; see DOUBT.

scruples *n.* overconscientiousness, point of honor, scrupulousness; see ATTENTION, CARE 1.

scrupulous *a.* exact, punctilious, strict; see CAREFUL.

scrutinize *v.* view, study, stare; see EXAMINE, WATCH.

scrutiny *n.* analysis, investigation, inspection; see EXAMINATION 1.

scuffle *n.* struggle, shuffle, strife; see FIGHT 1.

sculptor *n.* artist, modeler, carver, stone carver, woodcarver, worker in bronze, worker in metal. *Major sculptors include the following:* Phidias, Praxiteles, Lorenzo Ghiberti, Donatello, Luca della Robbia, Michelangelo, Benvenuto Cellini, Gian Lorenzo Bernini, Auguste Rodin, Constantin Brancusi, Henry Moore, Alberto Giacometti, Claes Oldenburg, Louise Nevelson.

sculpture *n.* carving, modeling, carving in stone, modeling in clay, kinetic sculpture, mobile, op art, casting in bronze, woodcutting, stone carving, plastic art; see also ART, STATUE.

scum *n.* froth, film, impurities; see RESIDUE, TRASH 1.

sea *n. Important seas include the following:* Barents, Ross, Weddell, Bering, Caribbean, Baltic, North, Irish, Mediterranean, Adriatic, Ionian, Aegean, Black, Caspian, Dead, Red, Tasman, Okhotsk, Japan, Yellow, South China, Arabian, East China, Java, Coral; Gulf of Mexico, Gulf of California, Persian Gulf, Hudson Bay, Baffin Bay, Bay of Bengal; see also OCEAN. **—at sea** confused, puzzled, upset; see BEWILDERED, UNCERTAIN. **—put (out) to sea** embark, go, start out; see LEAVE 1, SAIL 1.

sea bottom *n.* ocean floor, deep-sea floor, bottom of the sea, offshore lands, ocean bottom, ocean depths, continental shelf, undersea topography, marine farm, tidewater; see also OCEAN. *Terms for undersea topography include the following:* bank, sands, seamount, ridge, guyot, hill, tablemount, escarpment, plateau, reef, basin, canal, province, shoal, sill, channel, deep, depth, plain, trench, trough, fracture zone, rift.

seacoast *n.* seashore, seaboard, seaside; see SHORE.

seafood *n.* mollusk, lobster, oyster; see FISH, SHELLFISH.

seal *n.* **1** [Approval] authorization, permit, allowance; see PERMISSION. **2** [Fastener] adhesive tape, sticker, tie; see FASTENER, TAPE.

sealed *a.* secured, fixed, held together; see FIRM 1, TIGHT 2.

seal off *v.* quarantine, close, segregate; see FORBID, RESTRICT.

seam *n.* joint, line of joining, union, stitching, line of stitching, closure, suture.

seamstress *n.* sewer, needleworker, designer; see TAILOR.

sear *v.* scorch, brown, toast; see COOK.

search *n.* exploration, research, quest; see HUNTING. **—in search of** looking for, seeking, on the lookout for; see SEARCHING.

search *v.* explore, examine, rummage, look up and down, track down, look for, go through, poke into, scrutinize, ransack; see also HUNT 1, SEEK.

searching *a.* hunting, looking for, seeking for, pursuing, in search of, ready for, in the market for, in need of, needing, wanting, on the lookout for, looking out for.

searchlight *n.* arc light, beam, ray; see LIGHT 3.

seashell *n. Common seashells include the following:* conch, periwinkle, abalone, ammonite, ram's horn, clam, mussel, oyster, starfish, sea urchin, sand dollar, sea snail, nautilus, scallop, cowrie, limpet, cockle, whelk; see also SHELL 3.

seashore *n.* seaboard, seaside, seacoast; see SHORE.

seasick *a.* nauseated, miserable, queasy; see SICK.

seaside *n.* seaboard, seashore, seacost; see SHORE.

season *n.* period, term, division of the year; see FALL 3, SPRING 2, SUMMER, WINTER. **—in season** legal to hunt, ready to pick, mature; see LEGAL, READY 2, RIPE 1, 3.

seasonal *a.* once a season, periodically, biennial; see ANNUAL, YEARLY.

seasoned *a.* **1** [Spicy] tangy, sharp, aromatic; see SPICY. **2** [Experienced] established, settled, mature; see ABLE, EXPERIENCED.

seasoning *n.* sauce, relish, herb, spice, pungency; see also FLAVORING.

seat *n.* **1** [A structure on which one may sit] bench, chair, stool; see FURNITURE. **2** [Space in which one may sit] situation, chair, accommodation; see PLACE 2. **3** [The part of the body with which one sits] buttocks, rear, breech; see RUMP. **—have (or take) a seat** be seated, sit down, occupy a place; see SIT.

seated *a.* situated, located, settled, installed, established, rooted, set, fitted in place, placed, arranged, accommodated with seats.

seating *n.* places, reservations, chairs, seats, room, accommodation, arrangement, seating space.

seaward *a.* offshore, out to sea, over the sea; see MARITIME.

seaweed *n.* kelp, tangle, sea tangle, sea meadow, algae, marine meadow; see also PLANT. *Seaweed includes the following:* sea moss, Irish moss, Sargasso weed, rockweed, sea lettuce, kelp, giant kelp, gulfweed, sea cabbage.

seaworthy *a.* fit for sea, navigable, secure; see SAFE 1.

secede *v.* withdraw, retract, leave; see RETREAT.

secession n. departure, seceding, retraction; see WITHDRAWAL.

seclude v. screen out, conceal, cover; see HIDE 1.

secluded a. screened, isolated, sequestered; see WITHDRAWN.

seclusion n. solitude, aloofness, privacy; see RETIREMENT 2.

second a. secondary, subordinate, subsidiary, junior, ancillary, auxiliary, inferior, next, next in order, following, next to the first, next in rank, another, other.

second n. flash, trice, blink of an eye; see MOMENT 1.

secondary a. 1 [Derived] dependent, subsequent, subsidiary; see SUBORDINATE. 2 [Minor] inconsiderable, petty, small; see TRIVIAL, UNIMPORTANT.

secondhand a. used, not new, preowned, reclaimed, renewed, reused, old, worn, hand-me-down*, borrowed, derived, not original.

secondly a. in the second place, furthermore, also, besides, next, on the other hand, in the next place, for the next step, next in order, further, to continue; see also INCLUDING.

second-rate a. mediocre, inferior, common; see POOR 2.

secrecy n. concealment, confidence, hiding, seclusion, privacy, retirement, solitude, mystery, dark, darkness, isolation, reticence, stealth.

secret a. 1 [Not generally known] mysterious, ambiguous, hidden, unknown, arcane, cryptic, esoteric, occult, mystic, mystical, classified, dark, veiled, enigmatic, inscrutable, strange, deep, buried in mystery, obscure, clouded, shrouded, unenlightened, unintelligible, Orphic, cabalistic.—*Ant.* KNOWN, revealed, exposed. 2 [Hidden] latent, concealed, secluded; see HIDDEN. 3 [Operating secretly] clandestine, underhand, underhanded, stealthy, sly, surreptitious, close, furtive, disguised, undercover, backdoor, confidential, classified, backstairs, incognito, camouflaged, enigmatic, under false pretenses, unrevealed, undisclosed, dissembled, dissimulated, under wraps; see also SECRETIVE.—*Ant.* OPEN, aboveboard, overt.

secret n. mystery, deep mystery, something veiled, something hidden, confidence, private matter, code, telegram, personal matter, privileged information, top secret, enigma, puzzle, something forbidden, classified information, confidential information, inside information, an unknown, the unknown. — **in secret** slyly, surreptitiously, quietly; see SECRET 3.

secretary n. 1 [A secondary executive officer] director, manager, superintendent; see EXECUTIVE. 2

[An assistant] clerk, typist, stenographer, copyist, amanuensis, recorder, confidential clerk, correspondent.

secrete v. 1 [To hide] conceal, cover, seclude; see DISGUISE, HIDE 1. 2 [To perspire] discharge, swelter, emit; see SWEAT.

secretion n. discharge, issue, movement; see EXCRETION, FLOW.

secretive a. reticent, taciturn, undercover, with bated breath, in private, in the dark, in chambers, by a side door, under one's breath, in the background, between ourselves, in privacy, in a corner, under the cloak of, reserved.

secretly a. privately, covertly, obscurely, darkly, surreptitiously, furtively, stealthily, underhandedly, slyly, behind one's back, intimately, personally, confidentially, between you and me, in strict confidence, in secret, behind the scenes, on the sly, behind closed doors, under the table*, quietly, hush-hush*.—*Ant.* OPENLY, obviously, publicly.

sect n. denomination, following, order; see CHURCH 3, FACTION.

section n. 1 [A portion] subdivision, slice, segment; see PART 1, SHARE. 2 [An area] district, sector, locality; see REGION 1.

sector n. section, district, quarter; see AREA, DIVISION 2.

secure a. 1 [Firm] fastened, bound, adjusted; see FIRM 1, TIGHT 1. 2 [Safe] guarded, defended, protected; see SAFE 1. 3 [Self-confident] assured, stable, determined; see CONFIDENT.

secure v. 1 [To fasten] settle, lock, bind; see FASTEN, TIGHTEN 1. 2 [To obtain] achieve, acquire, grasp; see GET 1.

security n. 1 [Safety] protection, shelter, safety, refuge, retreat, defense, safeguard, preservation, sanctuary, ward, guard, immunity, freedom from harm, freedom from danger, redemption, salvation.—*Ant.* DANGER, risk, hazard. 2 [A guarantee] earnest, forfeit, token, pawn, pledge, surety, bond, collateral, assurance, bail, certainty, promise, warranty, pact, compact, contract, covenant, agreement, sponsor, bondsman, hostage; see also PROTECTION 2.—*Ant.* DOUBT, broken faith, unreliability.

sedative n. tranquilizer, medication, narcotic; see DRUG, MEDICINE 2.

sediment n. silt, dregs, grounds; see RESIDUE.

seduce v. decoy, allure, inveigle, entice, abduct, attract, tempt, bait, bribe, lure, fascinate, induce, stimulate, defile, deprave, lead astray, violate, prostitute, rape, deflower, ravish.—*Ant.* PRESERVE, protect, guide.

see *v.* **1** [To perceive with the eye] observe, look at, behold, examine, inspect, regard, view, look out on, gaze, stare, eye, lay eyes on, mark, perceive, pay attention to, heed, mind, detect, take notice, discern, scrutinize, scan, spy, survey, contemplate, remark, clap eyes on*, make out, cast the eyes on, direct the eyes, catch sight of, cast the eyes over, get a load of*. **2** [To understand] perceive, comprehend, discern; see RECOGNIZE 1, UNDERSTAND 1. **3** [To witness] look on, be present, pay attention, notice, observe, regard, heed; see also WITNESS. **4** [To accompany] escort, attend, bear company; see ACCOMPANY. **5** [To have an appointment (with)] speak to, have a conference with, get advice from; see CONSULT, DISCUSS. **—see about** attend to, look after, provide for; see PERFORM 1. **—see through 1** [To complete] finish up, bring to a successful conclusion, wind up; see COMPLETE, END 1. **2** [To understand] comprehend, penetrate, detect; see UNDERSTAND 1. **—see to** do, attend to, look after; see UNDERSTAND 1.

seed *n.* grain, bulbs, cuttings, ears, tubers, roots; seed corn, seed potatoes, etc. *Seeds and fruits commonly called seeds include the following:* grain, kernel, berry, ear, corn, nut. **—go** (or **run**) **to seed** decline, worsen, run out; see WASTE 3.

seed *v.* scatter, sow, broadcast; see PLANT.

seeding *n.* sowing, implanting, spreading; see FARMING.

seeing *a.* observing, looking, regarding, viewing, noticing, surveying, looking at, observant, wide awake, alert, awake, perceiving, inspecting, witnessing.

seek *v.* search for, dig for, fish for, look around for, look up, hunt up, sniff out, dig out, hunt out, root out, smell around, go after, run after, see after, prowl after, go in pursuit of, go in search of, go gunning for.

seem *v.* appear to be, have the appearance, give the impression, take on the aspect, impress one, appear to one, look, look like, resemble, make a show of, show, have the features of, lead one to suppose something to be, have all the evidence of being, have all the earmarks of, make a noise like.

seen *a.* observed, evident, viewed; see OBVIOUS 1.

seep *v.* leak, flow gently, trickle; see DRAIN 1, FLOW.

seepage *n.* drainage, infiltration, leakage; see FLOW.

seethe *v.* simmer, stew, burn; see BOIL, COOK.

segment *n.* section, portion, fragment; see DIVISION 2, PART 1.

segregate *v.* isolate, sever, split up; see DIVIDE, SEPARATE 2.

segregated *a.* divided along racial lines, isolated, excluded; see RACIAL, SEPARATED.

segregation *n.* dissociation, disconnection, separation; see DIVISION 1.

seize *v.* **1** [To grasp] take, take hold of, lay hold of, lay hands on, catch hold of, hang onto, catch, grip, clinch, clench, clasp, embrace, grab, clutch, grapple, snag, pluck, appropriate, snatch, swoop up, enclose, pinch, squeeze, hold fast, possess oneself of, envelop.—*Ant.* LEAVE, pass by, let alone. **2** [To take by force] capture, rape, occupy, win, take captive, pounce, conquer, take by storm, subdue, overwhelm, overrun, overpower, ambush, snatch, incorporate, exact, retake, carry off, apprehend, arrest, secure, commandeer, force, gain, take, recapture, appropriate, expropriate, take possession of, take over, hijack, skyjack, carjack, pounce on, usurp, overcome, impound, intercept, steal, abduct, snap up*, nab*, trap, throttle, lay hold of, lift, hook, collar*, fasten upon, wrench, claw, snare, bag, wring, get one's hands on, kidnap, rustle*, hold up, swipe*, scramble for, help oneself to. **3** [To comprehend] perceive, see, know; see UNDERSTAND 1.

seized *a.* confiscated, annexed, clutched; see BEATEN 1, CAPTURED.

seizure *n.* **1** [Capture] seizing, taking, apprehending; see CAPTURE. **2** [A spasm] spell, convulsion, breakdown; see FIT 1, ILLNESS 1.

seldom *a.* rarely, unusually, in a few cases, a few times, at times, seldom seen, usually, sporadically, irregularly, whimsically, sometimes, from time to time, on a few occasions, on rare occasions, infrequently, not often, not very often, occasionally, uncommonly, scarcely, hardly, hardly ever, scarcely ever, when the spirit moves, on and off, once in a while, once in a blue moon, once in a lifetime, every now and then, not in a month of Sundays*.—*Ant.* FREQUENTLY, often, frequent.

select *v.* decide, pick, elect; see CHOOSE.

selected *a.* picked, chosen, elected; see NAMED 2.

selection *n.* **1** [The act of selecting] choice, election, determination, choosing, preference, appropriation, adoption, reservation, separation. **2** [Anything selected] pick, preference, election; see CHOICE.

selective *a.* discriminating, judicious, particular; see CAREFUL.

self *a.* of one's self, by one's self, by one's own effort; see ALONE, INDIVIDUAL.

self *n.* oneself, one's being, inner nature; see CHARACTER 2.

self-assurance *n.* security, self-reliance, morale; see CONFIDENCE.

self-assured *a.* self-confident, assured, certain; see CONFIDENT.

self-centered *a.* self-indulgent, egotistical, self-conscious; see EGOTISTIC, SELFISH.

self-confidence *n.* assurance, courage, self-reliance; see CONFIDENCE.

self-confident *a.* fearless, secure, self-assured; see CONFIDENT.

self-conscious *a.* unsure, uncertain, shy; see DOUBTFUL, HUMBLE 1.

self-contained *a.* self-sustaining, complete, independent; see FREE 1, WHOLE 1.

self-control *n.* poise, self-restraint, reserve, self-government, restraint, discipline, self-discipline, discretion, balance, stability, sobriety, dignity, repression, constraint, self-regulation.—*Ant.* NERVOUSNESS, anger, talkativeness.

self-defense *n.* self-protection, self-preservation, putting up a fight; see FIGHT 1, PROTECTION 2.

self-esteem *n.* self-respect, self-confidence, confidence; see PRIDE 1, DIGNITY.

self-evident *a.* plain, apparent, visible; see OBVIOUS 2.

self-explanatory *a.* plain, clear, distinct; see OBVIOUS 2.

self-imposed *a.* accepted, self-determined, willingly adopted; see DELIBERATE, VOLUNTARILY.

selfish *a.* self-seeking, self-centered, self-indulgent, indulging oneself, wrapped up in oneself, narrow, narrow-minded, prejudiced, egotistical, egotistic, looking out for number one*; see also GREEDY.

selfishly *a.* egotistically, stingily, greedily, miserly, in one's own interest, meanly, wrongly, ungenerously, from selfish motives.

selfishness *n.* self-regard, self-indulgence, self-worship; see GREED.

self-made *a.* competent, self-reliant, capable; see ABLE, CONFIDENT.

self-reliant *a.* determined, resolute, independent; see ABLE, CONFIDENT.

self-respect *n.* self-esteem, worth, pride; see CONFIDENCE, DIGNITY.

self-restraint *n.* patience, endurance, self-control; see RESTRAINT 1.

self-sacrifice *n.* altruism, kind-

heartedness, benevolence; see GENEROSITY, KINDNESS 1, 2.

self-satisfaction *n.* complacency, smugness, conceit; see EGOTISM.

self-satisfied *a.* smug, vain, conceited; see EGOTISTIC.

self-sufficient *a.* competent, self-confident, efficient; see CONFIDENT.

sell *v.* market, vend, auction, dispose of, put up for sale, put on the market, barter, exchange, transfer, liquidate, trade, bargain, peddle, retail, merchandise, sell over the counter, contract, wholesale, dump, clear out, have a sale, give title to, put in escrow.—*Ant.* BUY, obtain, get. —**sell out*** trick, turn in, betray, double-cross*; see also DECEIVE.

seller *n.* dealer, tradesman, salesman, saleswoman, saleslady, salesgirl, salesclerk, sales rep*, salesperson, retailer, agent, vendor, merchant, auctioneer, shopkeeper, marketer, peddler, trader, storekeeper; see also BUSINESSMAN, MERCHANT.

selling *n.* sale, auction, bartering, trading, vending, auctioning, transfer, transferring, commercial transaction, transacting, merchandising, disposal.—*Ant.* BUYING, purchasing, acquiring.

sellout* *n.* betrayal, deception, deal; see TRICK 1.

semester *n.* six-month period, eighteen weeks, four and one-half months; see TERM 2.

semifinal *n.* next to the last match, elimination round, final four; see ROUND 2.

seminary *n.* secondary school, institute, theological school; see SCHOOL 1.

senate *n.* legislative body, assembly, council; see LEGISLATURE.

Senate *n.* legislative body, upper branch of Congress, the Upper House; see LEGISLATURE.

senator *n.* statesman, politician, member of the senate; see REPRESENTATIVE 2.

send *v.* **1** [To dispatch] transmit, forward, convey, advance, express, ship, mail, send forth, send out, export, send in, delegate, expedite, hasten, accelerate, post, address, rush, rush off, hurry off, get under way, give papers, provide with credentials, send out for, address to, commission, consign, drop, convey, transfer, pack off, give, bestow, grant, confer, entrust, assign, impart, give out. **2** [To broadcast, usually electronically] transmit, relay, wire, cable, broadcast, televise, carry, conduct, communicate. —**send (away) for** order, request,

write away for; see ASK, GET 1. —
send back reject, mail back, decide against; see RETURN 2.

senile *a.* aged, infirm, feeble; see OLD 1, SICK.

senility *n.* old age, dotage, feebleness, growing old, aging, infirmity, decline, senile dementia, senescence, Alzheimer's disease, second childhood; see also AGE 2, WEAKNESS 1.

senior *a.* elder, older, higher in rank; see SUPERIOR.

seniority *n.* preferred standing, ranking, station; see ADVANTAGE.

sensation *n.* **1** [The sense of feeling] sensibility, consciousness, perception; see EMOTION, THOUGHT 1. **2** [A feeling] response, sentiment, passion; see FEELING 1.

sensational *a.* **1** [Fascinating] marvelous, exciting, incredible; see IMPRESSIVE, INTERESTING. **2** [Melodramatic] exaggerated, excessive, emotional; see EXCITING.

sense *n.* **1** [One of the powers of physical perception] kinesthesia, function, sensation; see HEARING 3, SIGHT 1, TASTE 1, TOUCH 1. **2** [Mental ability] intellect, understanding, reason, mind, spirit, soul, brains, judgment, wit, imagination, common sense, cleverness, reasoning, intellectual ability, mental capacity, savvy*, knowledge; see also THOUGHT 1.—*Ant.* DULLNESS, idiocy, ignorance. **3** [Reasonable and agreeable conduct] reasonableness, fair-mindedness, discretion; see FAIRNESS. **4** [Tact and understanding] insight, discernment, prudence; see FEELING 4, JUDGMENT 1. **—in a sense** in a way, to a degree, somewhat; see SOME, SOMEHOW. **—make sense** be reasonable, be intelligible, be clear, be understandable, be logical, be coherent, articulate, add up, follow, infer, deduce, hang together*, hold water*, put two and two together, seem, appear, stand to reason.

senseless *a.* ridiculous, silly, foolish; see ILLOGICAL, STUPID.

senses *n.* consciousness, mental faculties, sanity; see AWARENESS, LIFE 1, 2.

sensible *a.* **1** [Showing good sense] reasonable, prudent, perceptive, acute, shrewd, sharp, careful, aware, wise, cautious, capable, practical, judicious, having a head on one's shoulders*, endowed with reason, discerning, thoughtful; see also SANE 1, RATIONAL 1. **2** [Perceptive] aware, informed, attentive; see CONSCIOUS.

sensitive *a.* **1** [Tender] delicate, sore, painful; see SORE 1. **2**

[Touchy] high-strung, tense, nervous; see IRRITABLE, UNSTABLE 2.

sensitivity *n.* **1** [Susceptibility] allergy, irritability, ticklishness; see FEELING 4. **2** [Emotional response or condition] delicacy, sensibility, sensitiveness, nervousness, acute awareness, consciousness, acuteness, subtlety, feeling, sympathetic response, sympathy, empathy.

sensory *a.* **1** [Neurological] sensible, relating to the senses, conscious; see SENSUAL 1. **2** [Conveyed by the senses] audible, perceptible, discernible; see OBVIOUS 1, 2, TANGIBLE.

sensual *a.* **1** [Sensory] tactile, sensuous, stimulating, sharpened, pleasing, dazzling, feeling, beautiful, heightened, enhanced, appealing, delightful, luxurious, emotional, fine, arousing, stirring, moving; see also EXCITING. **2** [Carnal] voluptuous, pleasure-loving, physical, lewd, hedonistic, lustful, lascivious, earthy, self-loving, self-indulgent, epicurean, intemperate, gluttonous, rakish, debauched, orgiastic, sensuous, piggish, hoggish, bestial.

sensuality *n.* sexuality, appetite, ardor; see DESIRE 2, EMOTION, LOVE 1.

sensuous *a.* passionate, physical, exciting; see SENSUAL 2.

sent *a.* shipped, mailed, commissioned, appointed, ordained, delegated, dispatched, directed, issued, transmitted, discharged, gone, on the road, in transit, uttered, sent forth, driven, impelled, forced to go, consigned, ordered, committed.—*Ant.* KEPT, restrained, held back.

sentence *n.* **1** [A pronounced judgment] edict, decree, order; see JUDGMENT 3, PUNISHMENT, VERDICT. **2** [An expressed thought] *Types of sentences include the following:* simple, complex, compound, compound-complex, kernel, cleft, conditional, complete, incomplete, declarative, interrogative, imperative, exclamatory; statement, question, command, exclamation.

sentence *v.* pronounce judgment, judge, send to prison; see CONDEMN, CONVICT, IMPRISON, PUNISH.

sentiment *n.* sensibility, predilection, tender feeling; see EMOTION, FEELING 4, THOUGHT 2.

sentimental *a.* emotional, romantic, silly, dreamy, idealistic, visionary, artificial, unrealistic, susceptible, overemotional, affected, mawkish, simpering, insincere, overacted, schoolgirlish, sappy*, corny*, gushy.

sentimentality *n.* sentimentalism, sentiment, melodramatics, bathos, mawkishness, melodrama, triteness, mush*, romance; see also EMOTION.

sentry *n.* sentinel, lookout, protector; see WATCHMAN.

separate v. **1** [To keep apart] isolate, insulate, single out, sequester, seclude, rope off, segregate, intervene, stand between, draw apart, split up, break up. **2** [To part company] take leave, go away, depart; see LEAVE 1.

separated a. divided, parted, apart, disconnected, partitioned, distinct, disunited, disjointed, sundered, disembodied, cut in two, cut apart, set apart, distant, removed, disassociated, distributed, scattered, put asunder, divorced, divergent, marked, severed, far between, in halves.—*Ant.* UNITED, together, whole.

separately a. singly, independently, distinctly; see CLEARLY 1, 2, INDIVIDUALLY.

separation n. **1** [The act of dividing] disconnection, severance, division, cut, detachment. **2** [The act of parting] coming apart, drawing apart, parting company, breaking up, departure, embarkation.

sequel n. consequence, continuation, progression; see SEQUENCE 1, SERIES.

sequence n. **1** [Succession] order, continuity, continuousness, continuance, successiveness, progression, graduation, consecutiveness, flow, perpetuity, unbrokenness, subsequence, course. **2** [Arrangement] placement, distribution, classification; see ORDER 3. **3** [A series] chain, string, array; see SERIES.

serenade n. melody, love song, nocturne; see MUSIC 1, SONG.

serene a. calm, clear, unruffled, peaceful, translucent, undisturbed, undimmed, tranquil, composed, cool, coolheaded, sedate, levelheaded, content, satisfied, patient, reconciled, easygoing, placid, limpid, comfortable, cheerful.—*Ant.* CONFUSED, disturbed, ruffled.

serenity n. quietness, calmness, tranquility; see PEACE 2, 3.

sergeant n. noncommissioned officer, top kick*, sarge*. *Types include the following:* master sergeant, staff sergeant, technical sergeant, first sergeant, top sergeant, platoon sergeant, drill sergeant, sergeant major, sergeant-at-arms, police sergeant; see also OFFICER 3, SOLDIER.

serial n. installment, series, continued story; see MOVIE.

series n. rank, file, line, row, set, train, range, list, string, chain, order, sequence, succession, group, procession, continuity, column, progression, category, classification, scale, array, gradation.

serious a. **1** [Involving danger] grave, severe, pressing; see DANGEROUS, IMPORTANT 1. **2** [Thoughtful]

earnest, sober, reflective; see SOLEMN.

seriously a. **1** [In a manner fraught with danger] dangerously, precariously, perilously, in a risky way, threateningly, menacingly, grievously, severely, harmfully.—*Ant.* SAFELY, harmlessly, in no danger. **2** [In a manner that recognizes importance] gravely, soberly, earnestly, sedately, solemnly, thoughtfully, sternly, with great earnestness, all joking aside; see also SINCERELY.—*Ant.* LIGHTLY, thoughtlessly, airily. —**take seriously** consider, calculate on, work on; see BELIEVE, TRUST 1.

seriousness n. **1** [The quality of being dangerous] gravity, weight, enormity; see IMPORTANCE. **2** [The characteristic of being sober] earnestness, sobriety, solemnity, gravity, staidness, thoughtfulness, calmness, coolness, sedateness, sobermindedness; see also SINCERITY.—*Ant.* FUN, gaiety, levity.

sermon n. lesson, doctrine, lecture; see SPEECH 2.

serpent n. reptile, viper, pit viper; see SNAKE.

servant n. attendant, retainer, helper, hireling, dependent, menial, lackey, domestic, drudge, slave; see also ASSISTANT. *Servants include the following:* butler, housekeeper, chef, cook, kitchenmaid, general maid, laundress, chambermaid, parlormaid, lady's maid, seamstress, nursemaid, nurse, valet, doorman, footman, squire, chauffeur, groom, gardener, yardman, kennelman.

serve v. **1** [To fulfill an obligation] hear duty's call, obey the call of one's country, carry out, discharge one's duty, assume one's responsibilities. **2** [To work for] be employed by, labor for, be in the employ of; see WORK 2. **3** [To help] give aid, assist, be of assistance; see HELP. **4** [To serve at table] wait on, attend, provide guests with food, help. —**serve someone right** deserve it, having it coming, get one's just deserts; see DESERVE.

served a. dressed, prepared, offered, apportioned, dealt, furnished, supplied, provided, dished up.

service n. **1** [Aid] cooperation, assistance, support; see HELP 1. **2** [Tableware] set, silver, setting; see DISH 1, POTTERY. **3** [A religious service] rite, worship, sermon; see CEREMONY 2. **4** [Military service] the armed forces, duty, active service, stint. —**at someone's service** zealous, anxious to help, obedient; see HELPFUL 1, READY 1, WILLING. —**of service** useful, handy, usable; see HELPFUL 1.

service *v.* maintain, work on, keep up; see REPAIR.

serviceable *a.* practical, advantageous, beneficial; see HELPFUL 1, USABLE.

serving *n.* plateful, course, portion; see MEAL 2.

session *n.* assembly, concourse, sitting; see GATHERING.

set *a.* **1** [Firm] stable, solid, settled; see FIRM 2. **2** [Determined] concluded, agreed upon, decided; see DETERMINED 1.

set *n.* **1** [Setting] attitude, position, bearing; see INCLINATION 1. **2** [A social group] clique, coterie, circle; see FACTION, ORGANIZATION 2. **3** [A collection of (like) items] kit, assemblage, assortment; see COLLECTION.

set *v.* **1** [To place] insert, settle, put, plant, store, situate, lay, deposit, arrange. **2** [To establish] anchor, fix, introduce; see ESTABLISH 2, INSTALL. **3** [To become firm] jell, solidify, congeal; see HARDEN, STIFFEN, THICKEN. —**set about** start, begin, start doing; see BEGIN 1. —**set off** **1** [To show by contrast] set in relief, contrast, intensify, make distinct. **2** [To explode] touch off, set the spark to, detonate; see EXPLODE. —**set up** **1** [To make arrangements] prearrange, inaugurate, work on; see ARRANGE 2. **2** [To finance] patronize, promote, support; see PAY 1.

setback *n.* hindrance, impediment, reversal; see DELAY, DIFFICULTY 1.

setting *n.* environment, surroundings, mounting, backdrop, frame, framework, background, context, perspective, horizon, shadow, shade, distance.—*Ant.* FRONT, foreground, focus.

settle *v.* **1** [To decide] reach a decision, form judgment on, come to a conclusion about; see DECIDE. **2** [To prove] establish, verify, make certain; see PROVE. **3** [To finish] end, make an end of, complete; see ACHIEVE. **4** [To sink] descend, fall, decline; see SINK 1. **5** [To establish residence] locate, lodge, become a citizen, reside, fix one's residence, abide, set up housekeeping, make one's home, establish a home, keep house; see also DWELL. **6** [To take up sedentary life; *often used with "down"*] follow regular habits, live an orderly life, become conventional, follow convention, buy a house, marry, marry and settle down, raise a family, get in a rut, hang up one's hat*. **7** [To satisfy a claim] pay, compensate, make an adjustment, reach a compromise, make payment, arrange a settlement, get squared away, pay damages, pay out, settle out of court,

settle up, work out, settle the score*, even the score*, dispose of, resolve, rectify, reconcile.

settled *a.* decided, resolved, ended; see DETERMINED 1.

settlement *n.* **1** [An agreement] covenant, arrangement, compact; see AGREEMENT 1, CONTRACT. **2** [A payment] compensation, remuneration, reimbursement; see ADJUSTMENT, PAY 1. **3** [A colony] principality, plantation, establishment; see COLONY.

settler *n.* planter, immigrant, homesteader; see PIONEER 2.

setup *n.* structure, composition, plan; see ORDER 3, ORGANIZATION 2.

sever *v.* part, split, cleave; see CUT 1, DIVIDE.

several *a.* **1** [Few] some, any, a few, quite a few, not many, sundry, two or three, a small number of, scarce, sparse, hardly any, scarcely any, half a dozen, only a few, scant, scanty, rare, infrequent, in a minority, a handful, more or less, not too many.—*Ant.* many, large numbers of, none. **2** [Various] plural, a number of, numerous; see MANY, VARIOUS.

several *n.* various ones, a small number, quite a few; see FEW.

severe *a.* **1** [Stern] exacting, uncompromising, unbending, inflexible, unchanging, unalterable, harsh, cruel, oppressive, close, grinding, obdurate, resolute, austere, rigid, grim, earnest, stiff, forbidding, resolved, relentless, determined, unfeeling, with an iron will, strict, inconsiderate, firm, unsparing, immovable, unyielding, adamant. **2** [Difficult or rigorous] overbearing, tyrannical, sharp, exacting, drastic, domineering, rigid, oppressive, despotic, intractable, unmerciful, bullying, uncompromising, relentless, unrelenting, hard, rigorous, austere, grinding, grim, implacable, cruel, pitiless, critical, unjust, barbarous, crusty, gruff, stubborn, autocratic, hidebound; see also DIFFICULT 1.—*Ant.* EASY, easygoing, indulgent.

severely *a.* critically, harshly, rigorously; see FIRMLY 2, SERIOUSLY 1.

severity *n.* hardness, hardheartedness, strictness; see CRUELTY.

sew *v.* stitch, seam, fasten, work with needle and thread, tailor, tack, embroider, bind, piece, baste.

sewage *n.* excrement, offal, waste matter; see RESIDUE.

sewer *n.* drain, drainpipe, drainage tube, conduit, gutter, disposal system, sewage system, septic tank, dry well, trench, leach field, leach bed, leach ditches, sewage disposal, sanitary sewer, sanitary facilities.

sewing *n.* stitching, seaming, tailoring, embroidering, darning, mending, piecing, patching, dressmaking.

sex *n.* **1** [Ideas associated with sexual relationships] sex attraction, sex appeal, magnetism, sensuality, affinity, love, courtship, marriage, generation, reproduction. **2** [A group, either male or female] men, women, males, females, the feminine world, the masculine world. **3** [Gender] sexuality, masculinity, femininity, womanliness, manhood, manliness. **4** [Sexual intercourse] making love, the sexual act, going to bed with someone; see COPULATION, FORNICATION.

sexual *a.* **1** [Reproductive] generative, reproductive, procreative; see ORIGINAL 1. **2** [Intimate] carnal, wanton, passionate; see SENSUAL 2.

sexuality *n.* lust, sensuality, passion; see DESIRE 2.

shabby *a.* ragged, threadbare, faded, ill-dressed, dilapidated, decayed, deteriorated, poor, pitiful, worn, meager, miserable, wretched, poverty-stricken, scrubby, seedy, gone to seed, down at the heel, grubby, in bad repair.—*Ant.* NEAT, new, well-kept.

shack *n.* hut, shed, hovel, cabin, shanty, cottage.

shade *n.* **1** [Lack of light] blackness, shadow, dimness; see DARKNESS 1. **2** [A degree of color] brilliance, saturation, hue; see COLOR, TINT. **3** [A slight difference] variation, trace, hint; see SUGGESTION 1. **4** [An obstruction to light] covering, blind, screen; see CURTAIN.

shade *v.* **1** [To intercept direct rays] screen, cover, shadow; see SHELTER. **2** [To make darker] darken, blacken, obscure, cloud, shadow, make dim, tone down, black out, make dusky, deepen the shade, overshadow, make gloomy, screen, shut out the light, keep out the light. **3** [To become darker] grow dark, grow black, become dark, grow dim, blacken, turn to twilight, deepen into night, become gloomy, be overcast, grow dusky, cloud up, cloud over, overcloud, grow shadowy.

shadow *n.* umbra, murkiness, gloom; see DARKNESS 1.

shadow *v.* **1** [To shade] dim, veil, screen; see SHADE 1, 2, SHELTER. **2** [To follow secretly] trail, watch, keep in sight; see PURSUE 1.

shady *a.* **1** [Shaded] dusky, shadowy, murky, gloomy, overcast, in the shade, sheltered, out of the sun, dim, cloudy, under a cloud, cool, indistinct, vague; see also DARK 1. **2** [*Questionable] suspicious, disreputable, dubious, dishonest, fishy*, underhanded.

shaft *n.* **1** [Rod] stem, bar, pole; see ROD 1. **2** [Light ray] wave, streak, beam of light; see RAY.

shake *n.* tremor, shiver, pulsation; see MOVEMENT 1, 2.

shake *v.* **1** [To vibrate] tremble, quiver, quake, shiver, shudder, palpitate, wave, waver, fluctuate, reel, flap, flutter, totter, wobble, stagger, waggle. **2** [To cause to vibrate] agitate, rock, sway, swing, joggle, jolt, bounce, jar, move, set in motion, convulse.

shaken *a.* unnerved, upset, overcome; see EXCITED.

shaky *a.* **1** [Not firm] quivery, trembling, jellylike, unsettled, not set, yielding, unsteady, tottering, insecure, unsound, unstable, infirm, jittery, nervous.—*Ant.* FIRM, settled, rigid. **2** [Not reliable] uncertain, not dependable, questionable; see UNRELIABLE, UNSTABLE 2.

shall *v.* intend, want to, must; see WILL 3.

shallow *a.* **1** [Lacking physical depth] slight, inconsiderable, superficial, with the bottom in plain sight, with no depth, with little depth, not deep, one-dimensional.—*Ant.* DEEP, bottomless, unfathomable. **2** [Lacking intellectual depth] simple, silly, trifling, frivolous, superficial, petty, foolish, idle, unintelligent, dull, piddling, wishy-washy*; see also STUPID.

sham *a.* not genuine, counterfeit, misleading; see FALSE 3.

sham *n.* pretense, deception, counterfeit; see FAKE.

shame *n.* **1** [A disgrace] embarrassment, stigma, blot; see DISGRACE. **2** [A sense of wrongdoing] bad conscience, mortification, confusion, humiliation, compunction, regret, chagrin, discomposure, irritation, remorse, embarrassment, abashment, self-reproach, self-disgust; see also GUILT. **3** [A condition of disgrace] humiliation, dishonor, degradation; see DISGRACE, SCANDAL.

shame *v.* humiliate, mortify, dishonor; see DISGRACE, HUMBLE.

shameful *a.* **1** [Offensive] immodest, corrupt, immoral, intemperate, debauched, drunken, villainous, knavish, degraded, reprobate, diabolical, indecent, indelicate, lewd, vulgar, impure, unclean, carnal, sinful, wicked. **2** [Disgraceful] dishonorable, scandalous, flagrant, obscene, ribald, infamous, opprobrious, outrageous, gross, infernal, disgusting, too bad, unworthy, evil, foul, hellish, disreputable, corrupt, dishonest, despicable; see also WRONG.—*Ant.* WORTHY, admirable, creditable.

shameless *a.* brazen, bold, forward; see RUDE 2, LEWD 2.

shape *n.* **1** [Form] contour, aspect,

configuration; see FORM 1, LOOKS. **2** [An actual form] pattern, stamp, frame; see MOLD 1. **3** [Condition] fitness, physical state, health; see STATE 2. —**out of shape** distorted, misshapen, battered; see BENT, BROKEN 1, FLAT 1, RUINED 1, 2, TWISTED 1. —**take shape** take on form, mature, fill out; see DEVELOP 1, IMPROVE 2.

shape v. **1** [To give shape] mold, cast, fashion; see FORM 1. **2** [*To take shape] become, develop, take form; see FORM 4, GROW 2. —**shape up*** **1** [To obey] mind, observe the rules, conform; see BEHAVE, OBEY, IMPROVE 2. **2** [To develop] enlarge, expand, advance; see DEVELOP 1.

shaped a. made, fashioned, created; see FORMED.

shapeless a. **1** [Formless] indistinct, indefinite, invisible, vague, without form, without shape, amorphous, lacking form, unformed, unmade, not formed, with no definite outline; see also UNCERTAIN. **2** [Deformed] misshapen, irregular, unshapely, unsymmetrical, mutilated, disfigured, malformed, ill-formed, warped, abnormal; see also DEFORMED.—Ant. REGULAR, symmetrical, shapely.

shapely a. symmetrical, comely, proportioned; see TRIM 2.

share n. division, apportionment, part, portion, helping, serving, piece, ration, slice, allotment, parcel, dose, fraction, fragment, allowance, dividend, percentage, commission, cut*.

share v. **1** [To divide] allot, distribute, apportion, part, deal, dispense, assign, administer.—Ant. UNITE, combine, withhold. **2** [To partake] participate, share in, experience, take part in, receive, have a portion of, have a share in, go in with, take a part of, take a share of.—Ant. AVOID, have no share in, take no part in. **3** [To give] grant, bestow, contribute; see GIVE 1.

sharp a. **1** [Having a keen edge] acute, edged, razor-edged, sharpened, ground fine, honed, razorsharp, sharp-edged, fine, cutting, knifelike, knife-edged.—Ant. DULL, unsharpened, blunt. **2** [Having a keen point] pointed, sharp-pointed, spiked, spiky, peaked, salient, needlepointed, keen, fine, spiny, thorny, prickly, barbed, needlelike, stinging, sharp as a needle, pronged, tapered, tapering, horned. **3** [Having a keen mind] clever, astute, bright; see INTELLIGENT. **4** [Distinct] audible, visible, explicit; see CLEAR 2, DEFINITE 2, OBVIOUS 1. **5** [Intense] cutting, biting, piercing; see INTENSE. **6** [*Stylish] dressy, chic, in style; see FASHIONABLE.

sharpen v. **1** [To make keen] grind, file, hone, put an edge on, grind to a fine edge, make sharp, make acute, whet, give an edge to, put a point on, give a fine point to.—Ant. FLATTEN, thicken, dull. **2** [To make more exact] focus, bring into focus, intensify, make clear, make clearer, clarify, outline distinctly, make more distinct.—Ant. CONFUSE, cloud, obscure.

sharply a. piercingly, pointedly, distinctly; see CLEARLY 1, 2.

shatter v. smash, split, burst; see BREAK 2.

shattered a. splintered, crushed, destroyed; see BROKEN 1.

shave v. shear, graze, barber, cut, use a razor, clip closely, strip, strip the hair from, tonsure, make bare, peel, skin, remove, slice thin.

she pron. this one, this girl, this woman, that girl, that woman, a female animal; see also WOMAN 1.

shears n. cutters, clippers, snips; see SCISSORS.

shed n. shelter, outbuilding, hut, lean-to, woodshed.

shed v. drop, let fall, give forth, shower down, cast, molt, slough, discard, exude, emit, scatter, sprinkle.

sheep n. lamb, ewe, ram; see ANIMAL, GOAT.

sheer a. **1** [Abrupt] perpendicular, very steep, precipitous; see STEEP. **2** [Thin] transparent, delicate, fine; see THIN 1.

sheet n. **1** [A bed cover] covering, bed sheet, bedding; see CLOTH, COVER 1. **2** [A thin, flat object] lamina, leaf, foil, veneer, layer, stratum, coat, film, ply, covering, expanse.

shelf n. **1** [A ledge] rock, reef, shoal; see LEDGE. **2** [A cupboard rack] counter, cupboard, mantelpiece, rack, bookshelf.

shell n. **1** [A shell-like cover or structure] husk, crust, nut, pod, case, casing, scale, shard, integument, eggshell, carapace, plastron. **2** [An explosive projectile] bullet, cartridge, ammo*; see WEAPON. **3** [A crustacean covering] Varieties include the following: tortoise, crustacean, bivalve, mollusk, clam, mussel, conch, snail; see also SEASHELL.

shell v. shuck, strip, peel off; see SKIN.

shellfish n. crustacean, mollusk, crustacean animal, invertebrate, marine animal, arthropod, gastropod, bivalve. Creatures often called shellfish include the following: crab, lobster, clam, shrimp, prawn, crawfish, crayfish, mussel, whelk, cockle, abalone, snail.

shelter n. refuge, harbor, haven, sanctuary, asylum, retreat, shield, screen, defense, security, safety, guardian, protector, house, roof, tent, shack, shed, hut, shade.

shelter *v.* screen, cover, hide, conceal, guard, take in, ward, harbor, defend, protect, shield, watch over, take care of, secure, preserve, safeguard, surround, enclose, lodge, house.—*Ant.* EXPOSE, turn out, evict.

sheltered *a.* **1** [Shaded] screened, protected, shady, veiled, covered, protective, curtained. **2** [Protected] guarded, supervised, shielded; see SAFE, WATCHED.

sheriff *n.* county officer, county administrator, peace officer; see POLICE OFFICER.

shield *n.* bumper, protection, guard; see COVER 1.

shift *n.* **1** [A change] transfer, transformation, substitution, displacement, fault, alteration, variation; see also CHANGE 1. **2** [A working period] turn, shift, stint; see TIME 1.

shift *v.* **1** [To change position] move, turn, stir; see CHANGE 2. **2** [To cause to shift] displace, remove, substitute; see EXCHANGE 1. **3** [To put in gear] change gears, downshift, put in drive; see DRIVE 2.

shin *n.* tibia, leg, limb; see BONE, LEG.

shindig* *n.* banquet, dance, dinner; see PARTY 1.

shine *v.* **1** [To give forth light] radiate, beam, scintillate, glitter, sparkle, twinkle, glimmer, glare, glow, flash, blaze, shimmer, illuminate, blink, shoot out beams, irradiate, dazzle, bedazzle, flash, flicker, luminesce, light. **2** [To reflect light] glisten, gleam, glow, look good, grow bright, give back, give light, deflect, mirror; see also REFLECT 3. **3** [To cause to shine, usually by polishing] scour, brush, polish, put a gloss on, put a finish on, finish, burnish, wax, buff, polish up, make brilliant, make glitter, glaze; see also CLEAN, PAINT 2.

shining *a.* radiant, gleaming, luminous; see BRIGHT 1.

shiny *a.* polished, sparkling, glistening; see BRIGHT 1.

ship *n. Types of ships include the following:* steamer, steamship, liner, freighter, landing barge, dredge, trawler, floating cannery, factory ship, supply ship, ferry, clipper, square-rigged vessel, sailing ship, transport, tanker, pilot boat, junk, galleon, sampan, battleship, cruiser, destroyer, aircraft carrier, submarine, whaling vessel, bark, schooner, windjammer, yacht, cutter, sloop, tug, cruise ship, paddle-wheeler; see also BOAT.

ship *v.* send, consign, ship out; see SEND 1.

shipment *n.* cargo, carload, purchase; see FREIGHT.

shipped *a.* transported, exported, delivered; see SENT.

shirk *v.* elude, cheat, malinger; see AVOID, EVADE.

shirt *n. Shirts include the following:* dress, undershirt, sport, work, cowboy, Western, long-sleeved, short-sleeved, cotton, silk, flannel, polo, button-down, T-shirt, tank top, blouse, jersey, pull-over, turtleneck; see also CLOTHES.

shiver *v.* be cold, vibrate, quiver; see SHAKE 1, WAVE 3.

shock *n.* **1** [The effect of physical impact] crash, clash, wreck; see COLLISION. **2** [The effect of a mental blow] excitement, hysteria, emotional upset; see CONFUSION. **3** [The after-effect of physical harm] concussion, stupor, collapse; see ILLNESS 1, INJURY.

shock *v.* **1** [To disturb one's self-control] startle, agitate, astound; see DISTURB. **2** [To disturb one's sense of propriety] insult, outrage, horrify, revolt, offend, appall, abash, astound, anger, floor, shake up, disquiet, dismay. **3** [To jar] rock, agitate, jolt; see SHAKE 2.

shocked *a.* startled, aghast, upset, astounded, offended, appalled, dismayed; see also TROUBLED.

shocking *a.* repulsive, hateful, revolting; see OFFENSIVE 2.

shoe *n.* footwear, boot, slipper, sandal, pump, moccasin, Oxford, saddle shoe, high-top, wingtip, brogue, hush puppy, flat, clog, galosh, tennis shoe, cleat, jogging shoe, running shoe, cross-training shoe, gym shoe, walking shoe, ski boot, track shoe, sneaker, loafer, heels, wedgie. —**in another's shoes** in the place of another, in other circumstances, reversal of roles; see SYMPATHETIC 1, UNDERSTOOD 1.

shoo *interj.* get away, begone, leave.

shoot *v.* **1** [To discharge] fire, shoot off, expel, pull the trigger, set off, torpedo, explode, ignite, blast, sharpshoot, open fire, rake, pump full of lead*. **2** [To move rapidly] dart, spurt, rush; see HURRY 1. **3** [To kill by shooting] dispatch, murder, execute; see KILL 1. —**shoot at 1** [To fire a weapon at] shoot, fire at, take a shot at; see ATTACK 1. **2** [*To strive for] aim, endeavor, strive; see TRY 1.

shop *n.* store, department store, retail store, thrift shop, drugstore, discount house, novelty shop. —**set up shop** go into business, start, open a business; see BEGIN 1, 2. —**shut up shop** close up, go out of business, cease functioning; see CLOSE 4, STOP 2. —**talk shop** talk business, exchange views, discuss one's specialty; see GOSSIP, TALK 1.

shop v. shop for, look for, try to buy; see BUY.

shopkeeper n. manager, merchant, storekeeper; see BUSINESSMAN.

shopper n. bargain hunter, professional shopper, purchaser; see BUYER.

shopping n. purchasing, hunting, looking; see BUYING.

shopping center n. shops, mall, shopping mall; see BUSINESS 4, PARKING LOT.

shore n. beach, strand, seaside, sand, coast, seacoast, seashore, bank, border, seaboard, margin, lakeside, lakeshore, riverbank, riverside.

short a. **1** [Not long in space] low, skimpy, slight, not tall, not long, undersized, little, abbreviated, dwarfish, stubby, stunted, stocky, diminutive, tiny, small, dwarf, dwarfed, close to the ground, dumpy, chunky, compact, squat, thickset, pint-size, stumpy, sawed-off*, runty. **2** [Not long in time] brief, curtailed, cut short, fleeting, not protracted, concise, unprolonged, unsustained, condensed, terse, succinct, pithy, summary, pointed, precise, bare, abridged, summarized, abbreviated, hasty, compressed, short-term, short-lived. **3** [Inadequate] deficient, insufficient, meager; see INADEQUATE. —**be** (or **run**) **short** (**of**) lack, want, run out of; see NEED. —**fall short** not reach, be inadequate, fall down; see FAIL 1, MISS 3. —**for short** as a nickname, familiarly, commonly; see NAMED 1, SO-CALLED. —**in short** that is, in summary, to make a long story short; see BRIEFLY, FINALLY 1.

shortage n. short fall, scant supply, curtailment; see LACK 1.

shortcoming n. fault, deficiency, lapse; see WEAKNESS 1.

shortcut n. bypass, alternative, time-saver; see MEANS 1, WHY.

shorten v. curtail, abridge, abbreviate; see DECREASE 2.

shorter a. smaller, lower, not so long, briefer, more limited, more concise, more abrupt, lessened, diminished, reduced, curtailed.—*Ant.* HIGHER, longer, taller.

short-lived a. brief, momentary, temporary; see SHORT 2.

shortly a. presently, quickly, right away; see SOON.

shortness n. brevity, briefness, conciseness; see LENGTH 1.

shortsighted a. unthinking, foolish, unwary; see RASH, STUPID.

shot n. **1** [A flying missile] bullet, dumdum, slug, ball, pellet, lead, projectile, buckshot, grapeshot. **2**

[An opportunity to shoot] occasion, chance, turn; see OPPORTUNITY 1. **3** [One who shoots] gunner, rifleman, marksman; see HUNTER. —**call the shots** direct, command, supervise; see CONTROL. —**have** (or **take**) **a shot at*** endeavor, attempt, do one's best at; see TRY 1. —**like a shot** rapidly, speedily, like a bat out of hell*; see FAST 1, QUICKLY. —**shot in the arm** help, boost, assistance; see ENCOURAGEMENT.

shoulder n. upper arm, shoulder cut, shoulder joint; see ARM 1, 2, JOINT 1. —**cry on someone's shoulder** weep, object, shed tears; see CRY 1, COMPLAIN. —**turn** (or **give**) **a cold shoulder to** ignore, neglect, pass over; see INSULT.

shout n. roar, bellow, scream; see CRY 1, YELL.

shout v. screech, roar, scream; see YELL.

shouting n. cries, yelling, jeering; see CRY 1.

shove v. jostle, push out of one's way, shoulder; see PUSH 1.

shovel n. Shovels include the following: coal, snow, fire, miner's, irrigating, split, twisted, pronged, scoop, spade, round-pointed; see also TOOL 1.

shovel v. take up, pick up, take up with a shovel, clean out, throw, lift out, move, pass, shift; see also DIG 1, LOAD 1.

show n. **1** [An exhibition] presentation, exhibit, showing, exposition, expo*, display, occurrence, sight, appearance, program, flower show, boat show, home show, dog show, carnival, representation, burlesque, production, concert, act, pageant, spectacle, light show, entertainment; see also COMEDY, DRAMA, MOVIE. **2** [Pretense] sham, make-believe, semblance; see PRETENSE 1, 2. —**for show** for sake of appearances, ostensibly, ostentatiously; see APPARENTLY. —**get** (or **put**) **the show on the road*** start, open, get started; see BEGIN 1. —**steal the show** triumph, get the best of it, win out; see DEFEAT, WIN 1.

show v. **1** [To display] exhibit, manifest, present; see DISPLAY. **2** [To explain] reveal, tell, explicate; see EXPLAIN. **3** [To demonstrate] attest, determine, confirm; see PROVE. **4** [To convince] teach, prove to, persuade; see CONVINCE. **5** [To indicate] register, note, point; see RECORD 1. —**show off** brag, swagger, make a spectacle of oneself; see BOAST. —**show up 1** [To arrive] appear, come, turn up; see ARRIVE. **2** [To expose] discredit, defeat, belittle; see EXPOSE 1.

showdown n. crisis, turning point, culmination; see CLIMAX.

shower n. **1** [Water falling in drops]

drizzle, mist, rainfall; see RAIN 1. **2** [Act of cleansing the body] bathing, washing, sponging; see BATH 1.

shown *a.* **1** [Put on display] displayed, demonstrated, advertised, exposed, set out, presented, delineated, exhibited, laid out, put up for sale, put up, put on the block.—*Ant.* WITHDRAWN, concealed, held back. **2** [Proved] demonstrated, determined, made clear; see OBVIOUS 2.

showoff *n.* boaster, exhibitionist, egotist; see BRAGGART.

showpiece *n.* masterpiece, prize, work of art; see MASTERPIECE.

show window *n.* display window, store window, picture window; see DISPLAY.

showy *a.* flashy, glaring, gaudy; see ORNATE.

shred *n.* fragment, piece, tatter; see BIT 1.

shred *v.* slice, strip, cut into small pieces; see TEAR.

shrewd *a.* astute, ingenious, sharp; see INTELLIGENT.

shrewdly *a.* knowingly, cleverly, trickily, sagaciously, astutely, skillfully, ably, slyly, foxily, guilefully, smartly, deceptively, cunningly, intelligently, judiciously, neatly, coolly, handily, facilely, adroitly, deftly, with skill, in a crafty manner, in a cunning manner, with consummate skill, knowing one's way around; see also CAREFULLY 1, DELIBERATELY.

shriek *n.* scream, screech, howl; see CRY 1, 3, YELL 1.

shriek *v.* scream, screech, squawk; see CRY 1, 2, YELL.

shrill *a.* high-pitched, piercing, penetrating, sharp, screeching, deafening, earsplitting, blatant, noisy, clanging, harsh, blaring, raucous, metallic, discordant, cacophonous, acute; see also LOUD 1.—*Ant.* SOFT, low, faint.

shrine *n.* sacred place, hallowed place, altar; see CHURCH 1.

shrink *v.* withdraw, recoil, flinch; see CONTRACT 1.

shrinkage *n.* lessening, reduction, depreciation; see LOSS 1, 3.

shrivel *v.* parch, dry up, shrink; see CONTRACT 1, DRY 1.

shrub *n.* bush, fern, hedge; see PLANT.

shrubbery *n.* shrubs, bushes, hedge; see BRUSH 3.

shrunken *a.* withdrawn, withered, contracted; see DRY 1, WRINKLED.

shudder *n.* tremor, shuddering, shaking, trembling.

shudder *v.* quiver, quake, shiver; see SHAKE 1, WAVE 1.

shun *v.* dodge, evade, keep away from; see AVOID.

shut *a.* stopped, locked, fastened; see TIGHT 2.

shut *v.* close up, lock, seal; see CLOSE 4. —**shut down** close down, shut up, abandon; see STOP 1. —**shut off** turn off, discontinue, put a stop to; see CLOSE 4, STOP 1. —**shut out** keep out, evict, fence out; see REFUSE. —**shut up 1** [To cease speaking] be quiet, stop talking, quiet, hush, quit chattering, silence. **2** [To close] padlock, close up, stop; see CLOSE 4.

shutter *n.* blind, cover, shade; see CURTAIN, SCREEN 1.

shy *a.* retiring, bashful, modest, diffident, submissive, timid, passive, reticent, fearful, tentative, subservient, docile, compliant, humble, coy, restrained, timorous, demure.

shyness *n.* bashfulness, reserve, timidity, modesty, timidness, coyness, demureness, sheepishness, diffidence, apprehension, backwardness, nervousness, insecurity, reticence, stage fright; see also RESTRAINT 1.

sick *a.* ill, ailing, unwell, disordered, diseased, feeble, frail, impaired, weak, suffering, feverish, sickly, declining, unhealthy, rabid, indisposed, distempered, infected, invalid, delicate, infirm, rickety, peaked, broken-down, physically run-down, confined, laid up, under medication, bedridden, in poor health, nauseated, nauseous, at death's door, hospitalized, quarantined, incurable, out of kilter*, feeling poorly, sick as a dog*, in a bad way, not so hot*, under the weather*.—*Ant.* HEALTHY, hearty, well. —**get sick** become sick or ill, contract a disease, take sick; see SICKEN 1. —**sick of** tired of, disgusted, fed up; see DISGUSTED.

sicken *v.* **1** [To contract a disease] become ill, become infected, take sick, fall ill, become diseased, fall victim to a disease, be stricken, run a temperature, run a fever, be taken with, come down with, catch a disease, acquire, waste away, languish, suffer a relapse, break out with, catch one's death*, pick up a bug*. **2** [To offend] repel, nauseate, revolt; see DISGUST.

sickening *a.* **1** [Contaminated] sickly, tainted, diseased; see SICK. **2** [Disgusting] revolting, nauseous, putrid; see OFFENSIVE 2.

sickly *a.* ailing, weakly, feeble; see SICK.

sickness *n.* ill health, ailment, infirmity; see ILLNESS 1.

side *a.* to the side, indirect, roundabout; see OBLIQUE.

side *n.* **1** [One of two opponents] party, contestant, combatant; see FACTION. **2** [A face] facet, front,

front side, rear, surface, outer surface, inner surface, top, bottom, elevation, view; see also PLANE 1. —**from side to side** back and forth, wobbly, unstable; see IRREGULAR 1. —**on the side** in addition to, as a bonus, additionally; see EXTRA. —**side by side** adjacent, nearby, faithfully; see LOYALLY, NEAR 1. —**take sides** join, fight for, declare oneself; see HELP, SUPPORT 2.

sideline *n.* avocation, interest, trade; see HOBBY.

sidestep *v.* evade, elude, shun; see AVOID.

sidewalk *n.* footpath, pavement, walkway; see PATH.

sideways *a.* indirectly, sloping, sidelong; see OBLIQUE.

siege *n.* offense, onslaught, assault; see ATTACK.

sieve *n.* strainer, sifter, colander, screen, bolter, mesh, hair sieve, drum sieve, flat sieve, gravel sieve, flour sieve.

sift *v.* 1 [To evaluate] investigate, scrutinize, probe; see EXAMINE. 2 [To put through a sieve] bolt, screen, winnow, grade, sort, colander, size, strain; see also CLEAN, FILTER 2, PURIFY.

sigh *n.* deep breath, sigh of relief, expression of sorrow; see CRY 1.

sigh *v.* groan, moan, lament; see CRY 1, GASP.

sight *n.* 1 [The power of seeing] perception, eyesight, eyes for, range of vision, apprehension, keen sight, clear sight; see also VISION 1. 2 [Something worth seeing; *often plural*] show, view, spectacle, display, scene, point of interest, local scene, landmark. 3 [*An unsightly person] eyesore, hag, ogre; see SLOB. —**a sight for sore eyes*** beauty, welcome sight, delight; see BLESSING 2, FRIEND, VIEW. —**at first sight** hastily, without much consideration, provisionally; see QUICKLY. —**by sight** somewhat acquainted, not intimately, superficially; see UNFAMILIAR 1. —**catch sight of** glimpse, notice, see momentarily; see SEE 1. —**lose sight of** miss, fail to follow, slip up on; see FORGET, NEGLECT 1. —**on sight** at once, without hesitation, precipitately; see IMMEDIATELY, QUICKLY. —**out of sight (of)** disappeared, vanished, indiscernible; see GONE 1, INVISIBLE.

sightseeing *n.* vacationing, excursion, tour; see TRAVEL.

sightseer *n.* observer, tourist, voyager; see TRAVELER.

sign *n.* 1 [A signal] indication, clue, omen, divination, premonition, handwriting on the wall, foreshadowing, manifestation, foreboding, foreknowledge, token, harbinger, herald, hint, symptom, assurance, prediction, portent, prophecy, mark, badge, symbol, caution, warning, beacon, flag, hand signal, gesture, wave of the arm, flash, whistle, warning bell, signal bell, signal light, high sign*. 2 [An emblem] insignia, badge, crest; see EMBLEM. 3 [A symbol] type, visible sign, token; see sense 1.

sign *v.* 1 [Authorize] endorse, confirm, acknowledge; see APPROVE. 2 [Indicate] express, signify, signal; see MEAN 1. 3 [Hire] engage, contract, employ; see HIRE.

signal *n.* beacon, flag, gesture; see SIGN 1.

signal *v.* give a sign to, flag, wave, gesture, motion, nod, beckon, warn, indicate.

signature *n.* sign, stamp, mark, name, written name, subscription, autograph, impression, indication, designation, trademark, one's John Hancock*.

signed *a.* autographed, endorsed, marked, written, undersigned, countersigned, sealed, witnessed, notarized, registered, enlisted, signed on the dotted line*.

signer *n.* cosigner, underwriter, endorser; see WITNESS.

significance *n.* weight, consequence, point; see IMPORTANCE.

significant *a.* meaningful, notable, vital; see IMPORTANT 1.

signify *v.* imply, import, purport; see MEAN 1.

silence *n.* 1 [Absence of sound] quietness, stillness, hush, utter stillness, absolute quiet, quietude, calm, noiselessness, quiet, deep stillness, soundlessness, loss of signal, radio silence, security silence, security blackout, censorship, hush of early dawn.—*Ant.* NOISE, din, uproar. 2 [Absence of speech] muteness, secrecy, reserve, reticence, inarticulateness, golden silence, respectful silence.

silence *v.* hush, quell, still; see QUIET 2.

silenced *a.* quieted, calmed, stilled, restrained, repressed, held down, held back, restricted, subdued, gagged, inhibited, coerced, suppressed, under duress, under compulsion, murdered*; see also INTERRUPTED.

silent *a.* 1 [Without noise] still, hushed, soundless; see CALM 2, QUIET. 2 [Without speech] reserved, mute, speechless; see DUMB 1.

silently *a.* without noise, without a sound, as still as a mouse, like a shadow, in utter stillness, noiselessly, calmly, quietly, soundlessly, mutely, dumbly, secretly, sneakily, in deathlike silence, like one struck dumb, speechlessly, wordlessly, as silently as falling snow.

silhouette *n.* contour, shape, profile; see FORM 1, OUTLINE 3.

sill *n.* threshold, beam, bottom of the frame; see LEDGE.

silly *a.* senseless, ridiculous, nonsensical, absurd, brainless, simple-minded, unreasonable, foolish, irrational, inconsistent, stupid, illogical, vacuous, inane, frivolous, ludicrous, preposterous; see also CHILDISH.

silver *a.* silvery, pale, white, lustrous, bright, shiny, silvery white, silver-like, shimmering, glittering, resplendent, white as silver.

silverware *n.* silver, service, cutlery, flatware, silver plate, holloware. *Common pieces of silverware include the following:* knife, dinner knife, butter knife, steak knife, fork, salad fork, cold meat fork, tablespoon, soup spoon, dessert spoon, grapefruit spoon, ice-cream spoon, iced-tea spoon, coffee spoon, teaspoon, soup ladle, gravy ladle, sugar spoon, spatula.

silvery *a.* shiny, glittering, brilliant; see BRIGHT 1.

similar *a.* much the same, comparable, related; see ALIKE.

similarity *n.* correspondence, likeness, resemblance, parallelism, semblance, agreement, affinity, kinship, analogy, closeness, approximation, conformity, concordance, concurrence, coincidence, congruity, parity, harmony, comparability, identity, community, relation, correlation, relationship, proportion, comparison, simile, interrelation, association, connection, similar form, like quality, point of likeness, similar appearance.—*Ant.* DIFFERENCE, variance, dissimilarity.

similarly *a.* likewise, thus, furthermore, in a like manner, correspondingly, by the same token, in addition, then, as well, too; see also SO.

simmer *v.* seethe, stew, warm; see BOIL, COOK.

simmering *a.* broiling, heated, boiling; see HOT 1.

simple *a.* 1 [Not complicated] single, unmixed, unblended, mere, unadulterated, not complex, simplistic, not confusing, obvious, direct, pure. 2 [Plain] homely, unadorned, unaffected; see MODEST 2. 3 [Easy] not difficult, effortless, done with ease; see EASY 2.

simple-minded *a.* unintelligent, childish, mindless; see DULL 3, NAIVE, STUPID.

simpleton *n.* clod, idiot, bungler; see FOOL.

simplicity *n.* 1 [The quality of being plain] plainness, stark reality, lack of ornament, lack of sophistication, bareness, monotony, homeliness,

severity. 2 [Artlessness] naiveté, plainness, primitiveness; see INNOCENCE 2.

simplified *a.* made easy, made plain, uncomplicated, clear, interpreted, broken down, cleared up, reduced, abridged; see also OBVIOUS 2.

simplify *v.* clear up, clarify, interpret; see EXPLAIN.

simplistic *a.* simplest, naive, over-simplified; see CHILDISH, SIMPLE 1.

simply *a.* 1 [With simplicity] clearly, plainly, intelligibly, directly, candidly, sincerely, modestly, easily, quietly, naturally, honestly, frankly, unaffectedly, artlessly, ingenuously, without self-consciousness, commonly, ordinarily, matter-of-factly, unpretentiously, openly, guilelessly. 2 [Merely] utterly, just, solely; see ONLY 2.

simulate *v.* imitate, feign, lie; see PRETEND 1.

simultaneous *a.* coincident, at the same time, concurrent, in concert, in the same breath, in chorus, at the same instant, in sync; see also EQUALLY.

simultaneously *a.* at the same time, as one, concurrently; see TOGETHER 2.

sin *n.* error, wrongdoing, trespass, wickedness, evildoing, iniquity, immorality, transgression, ungodliness, unrighteousness, veniality, disobedience to the divine will, transgression of the divine law, violation of God's law; see also CRIME. *Sins recognized as deadly include the following:* pride, covetousness, lust, anger, gluttony, envy, sloth.

sin *v.* err, do wrong, commit a crime, offend, break the moral law, break one of the Commandments, trespass, transgress, misbehave, go astray, fall, lapse, fall from grace, wander from the straight and narrow*, backslide.

since *a., prep., conj.* 1 [Because] for, as, inasmuch as, considering, in consideration of, after all, seeing that, in view of, for the reason that, by reason of, on account of, in view of; see also BECAUSE. 2 [Between the present and a previous time] ago, from the time of, subsequent to, after, following, more recently than, until now.

sincere *a.* truthful, faithful, trustworthy; see HONEST 1, RELIABLE.

sincerely *a.* truthfully, truly, really, genuinely, earnestly, aboveboard, seriously, naturally, candidly, frankly, profoundly, deeply, to the bottom of one's heart.

sincerity *n.* openness, frankness, truthfulness; see HONESTY, RELIABILITY.

sinful *a.* wicked, erring, immoral; see BAD 1, WRONG 1.

sinfully *a.* wickedly, immorally, unjustly; see WRONGLY.

sing *v.* chant, carol, warble, vocalize, hum, harmonize, trill, croon, twitter, chirp, raise a song, lift up the voice in song, burst into song.

singe *v.* brand, sear, scorch; see BURN.

singer *n.* vocalist, songster, chorister, choirmaster, soloist, minstrel, chanter, entertainer; see also MUSICIAN.

singing *n.* warbling, crooning, chanting; see MUSIC 1.

single *a.* 1 [Unique] sole, original, exceptional, singular, only, without equal, unequaled, peerless, unrivaled; see also RARE 2, UNIQUE, UNUSUAL 1.—*Ant.* MANY, numerous, widespread. 2 [Individual] particular, separate, indivisible; see INDIVIDUAL, PRIVATE. 3 [Unmarried] unwed, divorced, celibate, eligible, virginal, living alone, companionless, unattached, available, free, footloose, unfettered*.—*Ant.* MARRIED, UNITED, wed.

single-handed *a.* without assistance, courageously, self-reliantly; see ALONE, BRAVELY.

single-minded *a.* stubborn, self-reliant, bigoted; see SELFISH.

singly *a.* alone, by itself, by oneself, separately, only, solely, one by one, privately, individually, once.

singular *a.* sole, one only, single; see UNIQUE.

sinister *a.* evil, inauspicious, wicked, bad, corrupt, perverse, dishonest, foreboding, disastrous, malignant, hurtful, harmful, injurious, dire, poisonous, adverse, unlucky, woeful, ominous, unfortunate, unfavorable; see also BAD 1.

sink *n.* sewer, basin, cesspool, washbasin, tub, pan, bowl.

sink *v.* 1 [To go downward] descend, decline, fall, crash, subside, drop, droop, slump, go under, immerse, go to the bottom, be submerged, settle, go to Davy Jones's locker, touch bottom, go down with the ship.—*Ant.* RISE, float, come up. 2 [To cause to sink] submerge, scuttle, depress, immerse, engulf, overwhelm, swamp, lower, bring down, force down, cast down, let down; see also IMMERSE. 3 [To weaken] decline, fail, fade; see WEAKEN 1. 4 [To decrease] lessen, diminish, wane; see DECREASE 1. —**sink in*** impress, take hold, make an impression; see INFLUENCE.

sinner *n.* wrongdoer, terrorist, lawbreaker; see CRIMINAL.

sip *v.* taste, drink in, extract; see DRINK 1.

siren *n.* horn, whistle, signal; see ALARM.

sister *n.* 1 [A female sibling] blood relative, member of the family, stepsister, half sister, big sister, little sister, kid sister*, sis*; see also RELATIVE. 2 [A female member of a group] associate, co-worker, companion.

sit *v.* be seated, seat oneself, take a seat, sit down, sit up, squat, perch, take a load off one's feet*, have a place, have a chair, sit in, take a chair, take a seat, take a place.—*Ant.* RISE, stand up, get up. —**sit in** sit in on, take part in, be a part of; see COOPERATE, JOIN 2. —**sit out** ignore, abstain from, hold back; see NEGLECT 1, 2.

site *n.* locality, section, situation; see PLACE 3, POSITION 1.

sit-in *n.* demonstration, march, display; see PROTEST, STRIKE 1.

sitter *n.* baby sitter, attendant, daycare provider; see SERVANT.

situated *a.* established, fixed, located; see PLACED.

situation *n.* 1 [Circumstance] condition, state, state of one's affairs; see CIRCUMSTANCES 1, 2. 2 [A physical position] location, site, spot; see PLACE 3, POSITION 1.

size *n.* 1 [Measurement] extent, area, dimension; see MEASUREMENT 2. 2 [Magnitude] bulk, largeness, greatness, extent, vastness, scope, immensity, enormity, stature, hugeness, breadth, substance, volume, mass, extension, intensity, capacity, proportion; see also EXTENT, QUANTITY.

size up* *v.* judge, survey, scrutinize; see EXAMINE.

sizzle *n.* hiss, hissing, sputtering; see NOISE 1.

sizzle *v.* brown, grill, broil; see COOK, FRY.

skate *v.* slide, glide, skim, slip, skid, go quickly, race, ice-skate, rollerskate, skateboard, rollerblade, board*, blade*.

skeleton *n.* 1 [Bony structure] skeletal frame, bone, support; see BONE. 2 [Framework] design, outline, sketch; see FRAME 1.

skeptic *n.* doubter, unbeliever, cynic; see CYNIC.

skeptical *a.* cynical, dubious, unbelieving; see DOUBTFUL, SUSPICIOUS 1.

sketch *n.* portrayal, picture, draft, design, outline, drawing, representation, painting, skeleton, figure, illustration, copy, likeness, depiction; see also PICTURE 2, PLAN 1.

sketch *v.* paint, etch, depict; see DRAW 2.

sketchy *a.* coarse, crude, preliminary; see UNFINISHED 1.

skid *v.* slip, glide, move; see SLIDE.

skill *n.* dexterity, facility, craft; see ABILITY.

skilled *a.* skillful, a good hand at, proficient; see ABLE, EXPERIENCED.

skillful *a.* skilled, practiced, accomplished; see ABLE, EXPERIENCED.

skim *v.* **1** [To pass lightly and swiftly] soar, float, sail, dart; see also FLY 1. **2** [To remove the top; especially, to remove cream] brush, scoop, separate; see DIP 2, REMOVE 1. **3** [To read swiftly] look through, speed-read, scan; see EXAMINE, READ 1.

skimp *v.* pinch pennies, cut corners, scrimp; see SACRIFICE 2, SAVE 3.

skimpy *a.* short, scanty, insufficient; see INADEQUATE.

skin *n.* epidermis, derma, cuticle, bark, peel, husk, rind, hide, coat, pelt, fur, covering, surface, parchment. —**be no skin off one's back** (or **nose**)* not hurt one, do no harm, not affect one; see SURVIVE 1. —**by the skin of one's teeth** barely, scarcely, narrowly; see HARDLY. —**get under someone's skin** irritate, disturb, upset; see ENRAGE. —**save one's skin*** get away, evade, leave just in time; see ESCAPE, SURVIVE 1.

skin *v.* peel, pare, flay, scalp, strip, strip off, pull off, remove the surface from, skin alive, husk, shuck, lay bare, bare.

skin diver *n.* scuba diver, submarine diver, deep-sea diver, pearl diver, aquanaut, frogman; see also DIVER.

skinflint *n.* scrimper, tightwad*, hoarder; see MISER.

skinny *a.* lean, gaunt, slender; see THIN 2.

skip *v.* hop, spring, leap; see JUMP 1.

skirmish *n.* engagement, encounter, conflict; see BATTLE, FIGHT 1.

skirt *n.* kilt, petticoat, miniskirt; see CLOTHES, DRESS 2.

skull *n.* scalp, cranium, brain case; see HEAD 1.

sky *n.* firmament, atmosphere, the blue yonder; see AIR 1, HEAVEN. —**out of a clear blue sky** without warning, suddenly, abruptly; see QUICKLY, SOON.

skyscraper *n.* tall building, high-rise building, high-rise; see BUILDING.

slab *n.* slice, chunk, lump; see PART 1.

slack *a.* relaxed, lax, limp; see LOOSE 1.

slack off (or **up**) *v.* decline, lessen, become slower; see DECREASE 1, SLOW 1.

slam *v.* **1** [To throw with a slam] thump, fling, hurl; see THROW 1. **2** [To shut with a slam] bang, crash, push; see CLOSE 2, 4.

slander *n.* defamation, calumny, scandal; see LIE.

slander *v.* defame, libel, defile, detract, depreciate, disparage, revile, dishonor, blaspheme, curse, attack, sully, tarnish, vilify, blot, cast a slur on, scandalize, belittle, backbite, malign, speak evil of, give a bad name, sling mud.—*Ant.* PRAISE, applaud, eulogize.

slang *n.* cant, argot, colloquialism, pidgin English, vulgarism, lingo, shoptalk, vulgarity; see also JARGON 1, 2.

slant *v.* veer, lie obliquely, incline; see BEND, LEAN 1, TILT.

slanting *a.* inclining, sloping, tilting; see BENT.

slap *v.* strike, pat, spank; see HIT 1.

slapdash *a.* hasty, haphazard, impetuous; see CARELESS.

slap-happy* *a.* punch-drunk, dazed, dizzy; see BEATEN 1, SILLY.

slapstick *a.* absurd, droll, comical; see FUNNY 1.

slash *v.* slit, gash, sever; see CUT 1.

slaughter *n.* butchery, killing, massacre; see MURDER.

slaughter *v.* slay, murder, massacre; see BUTCHER 1, KILL.

Slav *n. Slavs include the following:* Russian, Belorussian, Yugoslav, Bosnian, Montenegrin, Macedonian, Bulgarian, Pole, Slovene, Slovak, Ukrainian, Bohemian, Czech, Serb, Croat, Lusatian.

slave *n.* bondsman, bondservant, chattel, serf, toiler, menial, drudge, thrall, drone, laborer, captive, bondmaid, bondwoman, victim of tyranny, one of a subject people.

slavery *n.* **1** [Bondage] subjugation, restraint, involuntary servitude; see CAPTIVITY. **2** [Drudgery] toil, menial labor, grind; see WORK 2.

Slavic *a.* Slav, Slavonic, Old Church Slavonic. *Words referring to Slavic peoples languages, etc. include the following:* Cyrillic, Glagolitic, Russian, Polish, Bulgarian, Czech or Bohemian, Serbian, Croatian or Croat, Bosnian, Montenegrin, Yugoslav, Ukrainian, Serbo-Croatian, Slovenian, Belorussian, Lusatian, Macedonian, Slovak.

slay *v.* murder, slaughter, assassinate; see KILL 1.

sleazy *a.* shoddy, flimsy, cheap; see SHABBY, POOR 2.

sled *n.* hand sled, bobsled, sleigh, coasting sled, child's sled, toboggan, coaster.

sleek *a.* silken, silky, satin; see SMOOTH 1.

sleep *n.* slumber, doze, nap, rest, sound sleep, deep sleep, siesta, catnap, dream, hibernation, the sandman*, snooze*, shut-eye*.

sleep v. slumber, doze, drowse, rest, nap, snooze*, hibernate, dream, snore, nod, yawn, relax, go to bed, fall asleep, take forty winks*, catnap, turn in, hit the hay*, saw logs*, sack out*. **—sleep (something) off** get over it, improve, sober up; see RECOVER 3.

sleeping a. dormant, inert, inactive; see ASLEEP.

sleepy a. dozy, somnolent, drowsy; see TIRED.

slender a. slim, slight, spare; see THIN 1, 2.

slice n. thin piece, chop, chunk; see PART 1.

slick a. sleek, slippery, glossy; see OILY 2, SMOOTH 1.

slide v. glide, skate, skim, slip, coast, skid, move along, move over, move past, pass along. **—let slide** ignore, pass over, allow to decline; see NEGLECT 1, 2.

slight a. **1** [Trifling] insignificant, petty, piddling; see TRIVIAL, UNIMPORTANT. **2** [Inconsiderable] small, sparse, scanty; see INADEQUATE. **3** [Delicate] frail, slender, flimsy; see DAINTY.

slightly a. a little, to some extent, hardly at all, scarcely any, not noticeably, unimportantly, inconsiderably, insignificantly, lightly, somewhat.

slim a. slender, narrow, lank; see THIN 2.

slime n. fungus, mire, ooze; see MUD.

slimy a. oozy, slippery, mucky; see MUDDY 1, 2.

sling v. hurl, send, catapult; see THROW 1.

slink v. prowl, cower, lurk; see SNEAK.

slip n. **1** [Error] lapse, misdeed, indiscretion; see ERROR. **2** [Misstep] slide, skid, stumble; see FALL 1. **3** [Undergarment] underclothing, chemise, half slip; see CLOTHES, UNDERWEAR. **—give someone the slip** get away, slip away, escape from; see LEAVE 1. **—slip up** make a mistake, err, bungle; see FAIL 1.

slipper n. house shoe, sandal, light shoe; see SHOE.

slippery a. glassy, smooth, glazed, polished, oily, waxy, soapy, greasy, slimy, icy, sleek, glistening, wet, unsafe, insecure, uncertain, tricky, shifty, slithery, slippery as an eel*.

slip-up* n. oversight, mishap, omission; see ERROR.

slit n. split, cleavage, crevice; see HOLE 1, TEAR.

slit v. tear, slice, split; see CUT 1.

sliver n. splinter, slice, fragment; see BIT 1, FLAKE.

slob* n. pig, hog, slattern, tramp, bum, yokel, ragamuffin.

slobber v. drip, salivate, dribble; see DROOL.

slogan n. catchword, rallying cry, trademark; see MOTTO, PROVERB.

slop v. slosh, wallow, splash, drip, spill, run over; see also DROP 1, EMPTY 1.

slope n. rising ground, incline, grade; see HILL.

sloppy a. clumsy, amateurish, mediocre; see AWKWARD, CARELESS.

slot n. aperture, opening, cut; see HOLE 1.

slow a. **1** [Slow in motion] sluggish, laggard, deliberate, gradual, loitering, leaden, creeping, inactive, slow-moving, crawling, slow-paced, leisurely, as slow as molasses in January*.—Ant. FAST, swift, rapid. **2** [Slow in starting] dilatory, procrastinating, delaying, postponing, idle, indolent, tardy, lazy, apathetic, phlegmatic, inactive, sluggish, heavy, quiet, drowsy, inert, sleepy, lethargic, stagnant, negligent, listless, dormant, potential, latent; see also LATE 1.—Ant. IMMEDIATE, alert, instant. **3** [Slow in producing an effect] belated, behindhand, backward, overdue, delayed, long-delayed, retarded, detained, hindered.—Ant. BUSY, diligent, industrious. **4** [Dull or stupid] stolid, not lively, uninteresting; see DULL 3.

slow v. **1** [To become slower] slacken, slow up, slow down, lag, loiter, relax, procrastinate, stall, let up, wind down, ease up. **2** [To cause to become slower] delay, postpone, moderate, reduce, retard, detain, decrease, diminish, hinder, hold back, keep waiting, brake, curtail, check, curb, cut down, rein in, cut back.

slowly a. moderately, gradually, nonchalantly, gently, leisurely, at one's leisure, taking one's own sweet time*.

slowness n. sluggishness, apathy, lethargy; see INDIFFERENCE.

sluggish a. inactive, torpid, indolent; see LAZY 1, SLOW 1, 2.

sluggishness n. apathy, drowsiness, lethargy; see FATIGUE, LAZINESS.

slum n. cheap housing, poor district, tenement neighborhood, skid row, the wrong side of the tracks*.

slump n. depreciation, slip, descent; see DROP 2.

slump v. decline, depreciate, decay; see SINK 1.

slush n. melting snow, mire, refuse; see MUD.

slut n. wench, whore, hooker*; see PROSTITUTE.

sly *a.* wily, tricky, foxy, shifty, crafty, shrewd, designing, deceitful, scheming, deceiving, intriguing, cunning, unscrupulous, deceptive, conniving, calculating, plotting, dishonest, treacherous, underhanded, sneaking, double-dealing, faithless, traitorous, sharp, smart, ingenious, cagey*, dishonorable, crooked, mean, dirty, double-crossing*, slick*, smooth*, slippery, shady*.

slyly *a.* secretly, cunningly, furtively; see CLEVERLY.

small *a.* 1 [Little in size] tiny, diminutive, miniature; see LITTLE 1. 2 [Little in quantity] scanty, short, meager; see INADEQUATE. 3 [Unimportant] trivial, inessential, insignificant; see SHALLOW 2, UNIMPORTANT.

smaller *a.* tinier, lesser, petite; see LESS, SHORTER.

smallness *n.* littleness, narrowness, diminutive size, shortness, brevity, slightness, scantiness, tininess.

small talk *n.* chitchat, light conversation, banter, table talk, badinage, babble.

smart *a.* 1 [Intelligent] clever, bright, quick; see INTELLIGENT. 2 [*Impudent] bold, brazen, forward; see RUDE 2.

smart *v.* sting, be painful, burn; see HURT 1.

smart aleck* *n.* showoff, boaster, life of the party; see BRAGGART.

smash *n.* crash, shattering, breaking; see BLOW.

smash *v.* crack, shatter, crush, burst, shiver, fracture, break, demolish, dash to pieces, destroy, batter, crash, wreck, break up, overturn, overthrow, lay in ruins, raze, topple, tumble.

smashed *a.* wrecked, crushed, mashed; see BROKEN 1.

smear *v.* 1 [To spread] cover, coat, apply; see PAINT 2, SPREAD 3. 2 [To slander] defame, vilify, libel; see INSULT, SLANDER.

smell *n.* 1 [A pleasant smell] fragrance, odor, scent, perfume, essence, aroma, bouquet. 2 [An unpleasant smell] malodor, stench, stink, reek, mustiness, foulness, uncleanness, fume. 3 [The sense of smell] smelling, olfactory perception, olfaction; see AWARENESS.

smell *v.* 1 [To give off odor] perfume, scent, exhale, reek, stink. 2 [To use the sense of smell] scent, sniff, inhale, snuff, nose out, get a whiff of; see also BREATHE.

smelly *a.* stinking, foul, fetid; see RANK 2.

smile *n.* grin, smirk, tender look, friendly expression, delighted look, joyous look; see also LAUGH.

smile *v.* beam, be gracious, look happy, look delighted, look pleased,

---

break into a smile, look amused, smirk, grin; see also LAUGH.

smiling *a.* bright, with a smile, sunny, beaming; see also HAPPY.

smirk *n.* leer, grin, smile; see SNEER.

smith *n.* metalworker, forger, blacksmith; see CRAFTSMAN, WORKMAN.

smog *n.* pollution, smaze, fog, fumes, dirty fog, haze, mist, air pollution; see also SMOKE.

smoke *n.* vapor, fume, gas, soot, reek, haze, smudge, smog.

smoke *v.* 1 [To give off smoke] burn, fume, smudge, smoke up, smolder, reek. 2 [To use smoke, especially from tobacco] puff, inhale, smoke a pipe, smoke cigarettes, smoke cigars. —**smoke out** uncover, reveal, find; see DISCOVER.

smoked *a.* cured, dried, kippered; see PRESERVED 2.

smoky *a.* smoking, smoldering, reeking; see BURNING.

smolder *v.* fume, give off smoke, steam; see BURN, SMOKE 1.

smooth *a.* 1 [Without bumps] flat, plane, flush, horizontal, unwrinkled, level, monotonous, unrelieved, unruffled, mirrorlike, quiet, still, tranquil, glossy, glassy, lustrous, smooth as glass.—*Ant.* ROUGH, steep, broken. 2 [Without jerks] uniform, regular, even, invariable, steady, stable, fluid, flowing, rhythmic, constant, continuous. 3 [Without hair] shaven, beardless, whiskerless, cleanshaven, smooth-faced, smooth-chinned; see also BALD.—*Ant.* HAIRY, bearded, unshaven.

smooth *v.* even, level, flatten, grade, iron, polish, varnish, gloss, clear the way, smooth the path.

smoothly *a.* flatly, sleekly, placidly; see EASILY, EVENLY 1.

smorgasbord *n.* buffet, appetizers, salad bar; see FOOD, LUNCH, MEAL 2.

smother *v.* stifle, suffocate, suppress; see CHOKE, EXTINGUISH.

smothered *a.* 1 [Extinguished] drenched, consumed, drowned, put out, not burning, quenched, snuffed. 2 [Strangled] choked, asphyxiated, breathless; see DEAD 1.

smudge *n.* smirch, spot, soiled spot; see BLEMISH.

smug *a.* self-satisfied, complacent, conceited, pleased with oneself, snobbish, egotistical, self-righteous, stuck up*, stuck on oneself*.

snack *n.* luncheon, slight meal, bite; see LUNCH, MEAL 2.

snack bar *n.* cafeteria, lunchroom, cafe; see RESTAURANT.

snag *n.* obstacle, hindrance, knot; see BARRIER, DIFFICULTY 1.

snake *n.* reptile, serpent, legless reptile. *Common snakes include the fol-*

lowing: viper, pit viper, water moccasin, copperhead, blacksnake, bullsnake, rattlesnake, python, cobra, coral snake, blue racer, garter snake, gopher snake, kingsnake, milk snake, water snake, boa constrictor, adder, puff adder, anaconda, asp, garden snake, cottonmouth, sidewinder, green snake, rat snake.

snap *n.* clasp, fastening, catch; see FASTENER.

snap *v.* catch, clasp, lock; see CLOSE 4, FASTEN. —**snap at** vent one's anger at, jump down someone's throat*, take it out on; see GET ANGRY. —**snap out of it** pull through, get over, revive; see RECOVER 3.

snapshot *n.* snap, photo, action shot; see PHOTOGRAPH, PICTURE 2, 3.

snare *n.* trap, lure, decoy; see TRICK 1.

snarl *n.* **1** [Confusion] tangle, entanglement, complication; see CONFUSION. **2** [A snarling sound] grumble, gruffness, angry words; see GROWL.

snarl *v.* growl, grumble, mutter, threaten, bark, yelp, snap, gnash the teeth, bully, quarrel.

snatch *v.* jerk, grasp, steal; see SEIZE 1, 2.

sneak *v.* skulk, slink, creep, slip away, move secretly, hide, prowl, lurk; see also EVADE.

sneaky *a.* tricky, deceitful, unreliable; see DISHONEST.

sneer *v.* mock, scoff, jeer, taunt, slight, scorn, decry, belittle, detract, lampoon, ridicule, deride, caricature, laugh at, look down, insult, disdain, satirize, condemn, give the raspberry*, give the Bronx cheer*.

sneeze *n.* explosive exhalation, cough, fit of sneezing; see COLD 2, FIT 1.

snicker *v.* giggle, titter, chuckle; see LAUGH.

sniff *v.* detect, scent, inhale; see SMELL 2.

snip *v.* clip, slice, nip; see CUT 1.

snob *n.* elitist, highbrow, stuffed shirt*; see BRAGGART.

snobbish *a.* ostentatious, pretentious, overbearing; see EGOTISTIC.

snooty* *a.* conceited, nasty, egotistical; see EGOTISTIC.

snore *v.* snort, wheeze, sleep; see BREATHE.

snotty* *a.* impudent, like a spoiled brat, nasty; see RUDE 2.

snout *n.* muzzle, proboscis, nozzle; see NOSE 1.

snow *n.* **1** [A snowstorm] blizzard, snowfall, snow flurries; see STORM. **2** [Frozen vapor] snow crystal, snowflake, slush, sleet, snowdrift, snow-

bank, powder snow, snowpack, snowfall, fall of snow.

snow *v.* storm, squall, howl, blow, cover, pelt, shower, sleet.

snub *v.* ignore, disregard, disdain; see NEGLECT 1.

snug *a.* **1** [Cozy] homelike, secure, sheltered; see COMFORTABLE 1, WARM 1. **2** [Close in fit] trim, well-built, close; see TIGHT 3.

so *a.* **1** [To a degree] very, this much, so large, vaguely, indefinitely, extremely, infinitely, remarkably, unusually, so much, extremely, in great measure; see also SUCH. **2** [Thus] and so on, and so forth, in such manner, in this way, in this degree, to this extent; see also THUS. **3** [Accordingly] then, therefore, consequently; see ACCORDINGLY.

soak *v.* **1** [To drench] wet, immerse, dip, immerge*, water, percolate, permeate, drown, saturate, pour into, pour on, wash over, flood; see also MOISTEN. **2** [To remain in liquid] steep, soften, be saturated, be waterlogged, be permeated. **3** [To absorb] dry up, sop up, mop up; see ABSORB.

soaked *a.* sodden, saturated, wet, wet through, drenched, soggy, dripping, seeping, immersed, steeped, dipped, flooded, drowned, waterlogged.

soap *n.* solvent, softener, cleanser, cleaner, soapsuds. *Varieties and forms of soap include the following:* bar, liquid, glycerine, saddle, powdered, perfumed, bath, laundry, dish; soap flakes; see also CLEANSER.

sob *n.* weeping, bewailing, convulsive sigh; see CRY 3.

sob *v.* lament, sigh convulsively, weep; see CRY 1.

sober *a.* solemn, serious, sedate, clearheaded, not drunk, calm, grave, temperate, abstemious, abstinent, teetotaling, abstaining, steady; see also MODERATE 4.

soberly *a.* moderately, temperately, abstemiously, solemnly, gravely, sedately, in a subdued manner, quietly, regularly, steadily, calmly, coolly, seriously, somberly, staidly, earnestly, dispassionately, fairly, justly.

so-called *a.* commonly named, nominal, professed, doubtfully called, allegedly, thus termed, wrongly named, popularly supposed, erroneously accepted as, supposed, also know as.

sociable *a.* affable, genial, companionable; see FRIENDLY.

social *a.* genial, amusing, entertaining, companionable, pleasurable, civil, polite, polished, mannerly, pleasure-seeking, hospitable, pleasant.

socialist *n.* Marxist, communist, populist; see RADICAL.

socialistic *a.* Marxist, communistic, social-democrat, noncapitalistic; see also DEMOCRATIC, RADICAL.

socially *a.* politely, civilly, courteously, hospitably, companionably, entertainingly, amusingly, cordially, genially, sociably.

social science *n.* study of people and social phenomena, study of human society, political science, anthropology, social studies; see also ECONOMICS, GEOGRAPHY, HISTORY, POLITICS, PSYCHOLOGY, SCIENCE 1, SOCIOLOGY.

social security *n.* social insurance, old-age insurance, disability insurance, unemployment insurance, social security payments, retirement.

social service *n.* social work, welfare, aid for the needy, charity, philanthropy.

society *n.* 1 [Friendly association] friendship, social intercourse, fellowship; see ORGANIZATION 2. 2 [Organized humanity] culture, the public, civilization, nation, community, human groupings, the people, the world at large, social life.

sociology *n.* study of society, cultural anthropology, social psychology, analysis of human institutions, study of human groups; see also SOCIAL SCIENCE.

sock *n.* stocking, hose, short stocking; see HOSIERY.

socket *n.* holder, opening, cavity; see JOINT 1.

soda *n.* soda water, carbonated water, mineral water; see DRINK 2.

sofa *n.* couch, divan, love seat; see FURNITURE.

soft *a.* 1 [Soft to the touch] smooth, satiny, velvety, silky, delicate, fine, thin, flimsy, limp, fluffy, feathery, downy, woolly, doughy, spongy, mushy.—*Ant.* HARSH, rough, flinty. 2 [Soft to the eye] dull, dim, quiet, shaded, pale, light, pastel, faint, blond, misty, hazy, dusky, delicate, pallid, ashen, tinted; see also SHADY.—*Ant.* BRIGHT, glaring, brilliant. 3 [Soft to the ear] low, melodious, faraway; see FAINT 3. —**be soft on** treat lightly, not condemn, fail to attack; see FAVOR, NEGLECT 1.

soften *v.* dissolve, lessen, diminish, disintegrate, become tender, become mellow, thaw, melt, moderate, bend, give, yield, relax, relent, mellow, modify, mollify, appease, mash, knead, temper, tone down, qualify, tenderize, enfeeble, weaken.—*Ant.* STRENGTHEN, increase, tone up.

softhearted *a.* tender, kindhearted, humane; see KIND.

softness *n.* mellowness, impressibility, plasticity; see FLEXIBILITY.

soggy *a.* mushy, spongy, saturated; see SOAKED, WET 1.

soil *n.* dirt, loam, clay; see EARTH 2.

soil *v.* stain, sully, spoil; see DIRTY.

soiled *a.* stained, tainted, ruined; see DIRTY 1.

sold *a.* 1 [Sold out] disposed of, gone, taken; see SOLD OUT. 2 [*Convinced] persuaded, impressed, taken with; see SATISFIED. —**sold out** out of, all sold, out of stock, not in stock, gone, depleted.

soldier *n.* warrior, fighter, private, enlisted man, enlisted woman, officer, fighting man, rank and file, foot soldier, draftee, volunteer, conscript, commando, mercenary, cadet, commissioned officer, noncommissioned officer, recruit, selectee, ranker*, veteran, militant, marine, infantryman, guerrilla, guardsman, scout, sharpshooter, artilleryman, gunner, engineer, airman, bomber pilot, fighter pilot, paratrooper, machine-gunner, G.I. Joe*, grunt*.

sole *a.* only, no more than one, remaining; see INDIVIDUAL, SINGLE 1.

solely *a.* singly, undividedly, singularly; see INDIVIDUALLY, ONLY 1.

solemn *a.* grave, serious, sober, earnest, intense, deliberate, heavy, austere, somber, dignified, staid, sedate, moody, pensive, brooding, grim, stern, thoughtful, reflective.

solemnly *a.* sedately, gravely, impressively; see SERIOUSLY 2.

solid *a.* 1 [Firm in position] stable, fixed, rooted; see FIRM 1. 2 [Firm or close in texture] compact, hard, dense; see FIRM 2, THICK 1. 3 [Reliable] dependable, trustworthy, steadfast; see RELIABLE. 4 [Continuous] uninterrupted, continued, unbroken; see CONSECUTIVE, REGULAR 3.

solid *n.* cube, cone, pyramid, cylinder, block, prism, sphere.

solidification *n.* hardening, freezing, calcification, ossification, stiffening, setting, crystallization, fossilization, compression, coagulation, concentration.

solidify *v.* set, fix, crystallize; see COMPRESS, HARDEN, THICKEN.

solitary *a.* sole, only, alone, single, secluded, companionless, lonely, separate, individual, isolated, singular.—*Ant.* ACCOMPANIED, social, attended.

solitude *n.* isolation, seclusion, retirement; see SILENCE 1.

soluble *a.* dissolvable, emulsifiable, dispersible, water-soluble, fat-soluble.

solution *n.* 1 [Explanation] interpretation, resolution, clarification;

see ANSWER. 2 [Fluid] suspension, fluid, fluid mixture; see LIQUID.

solve v. figure out, work out, reason out, think out, find out, puzzle out, decipher, unravel, explain, interpret, resolve, answer, decode, get to the bottom of, get right, hit upon a solution, work, do, settle, clear up, untangle, elucidate, fathom, unlock, determine, hit the nail on the head*, put two and two together, have it.

somber a. melancholy, dreary, gloomy; see DISMAL.

some a. few, a few, a little, a bit, part of, more than a few, more than a little, any.

some pron. any, a few, a number, an amount, a part, a portion.

somebody pron. someone, some person, a person, one, anybody, he, she, a certain person, this person, so-and-so, whoever.

someday a. sometime, one time, one time or another, at a future time, anytime, one day, one of these days, after a while, subsequently, finally, eventually.

somehow a. in some way, in one way or another, by some means, somehow or other, by hook or by crook, anyhow, after a fashion, with any means at one's disposal.

someone pron. some person, one, anyone; see SOMEBODY.

something pron. event, object, portion, anything, being; see also THING 1, 8.

sometime a. one day, in a time to come, in the future; see SOMEDAY.

sometimes a. at times, at intervals, now and then; see SELDOM.

somewhat a. a little, to a degree, to some extent; see MODERATELY, SLIGHTLY.

somewhere a. in some place, here and there, around, in one place or another, someplace, about, kicking around*, any old place*.

son n. male child, male offspring, descendant, stepson, heir, junior; see also CHILD, BOY.

song n. melody, lyric, strain, verse, poem, tune; see also MUSIC 1. —**for a song** cheaply, at a bargain, for almost nothing; see CHEAPLY. —**song and dance** drivel, boasting, pretense; see NONSENSE 1, 2.

soon a. before long, in a short time, presently, in due time, shortly, forthwith, quickly, in a minute, in a second, in short order, anon*; see also SOMEDAY.

sooner or later a. eventually, certainly, inevitably; see SOMEDAY, SURELY.

soot n. carbon, smoke, grit; see RESIDUE.

soothe v. quiet, tranquilize, alleviate, calm, relax, mollify, help, pacify, lighten, unburden, console, cheer; see also COMFORT 1, EASE 1, 2, RELIEVE.

sophisticated a. refined, adult, well-bred; see CULTURED, MATURE.

sophistication n. elegance, refinement, finesse; see COMPOSURE.

soppy a. soaked, drippy, damp; see WET 1, 2.

sorcerer n. sorceress, wizard, witch, alchemist; see also MAGICIAN.

sorcery n. enchantment, divination, alchemy; see MAGIC 1, WITCHCRAFT.

sore a. 1 [Tender] painful, hurtful, raw, aching, sensitive, irritated, irritable, bruised, inflamed, burned, unpleasant, ulcerated, abscessed, uncomfortable. 2 [*Angry] irked, resentful, irritated; see ANGRY.

sore n. cut, bruise, wound, boil, lesion, ulcer, hurt, abscess, gash, sting, soreness, discomfort, injury; see also PAIN 2.

sorely a. extremely, painfully, badly; see SO 1, VERY.

sorrow n. sadness, anguish, pain; see GRIEF.

sorrow v. bemoan, lament, be sad; see MOURN.

sorrowful a. grieved, afflicted, in sorrow, in mourning, depressed, dejected; see also SAD 1.

sorrowfully a. regretfully, weeping, in sadness; see SADLY.

sorry a. 1 [Penitent] contrite, repentant, softened, remorseful, regretful, conscience-stricken, sorrowful, touched, apologetic. 2 [Inadequate in quantity or quality] poor, paltry, trifling, cheap, mean, shabby, stunted, beggarly, scrubby, small, trivial, unimportant, insignificant, worthless, dismal, pitiful, despicable; see also INADEQUATE.—Ant. ENOUGH, plentiful, adequate.

sort n. species, description, class; see KIND 2, VARIETY 2. —**out of sorts** irritated, upset, in a bad mood; see ANGRY, TROUBLED.

sort v. file, arrange, class; see CLASSIFY, DISTRIBUTE, ORDER 3.

sort of a. somewhat, to a degree, kind of*; see SLIGHTLY, MODERATELY.

so-so a. ordinary, mediocre, average; see COMMON 1, DULL 4, FAIR 2.

sought a. wanted, needed, desired; see HUNTED.

soul n. 1 [Essential nature] spiritual being, heart, substance, individuality, disposition, cause, personality, force, essence, genius, principle, ego, psyche, life. 2 [The more lofty human qualities] courage, love, honor, duty, idealism, heroism, art, poetry, sense of beauty. 3 [A person] human being, person, being; see PERSON 1.

sound *a.* **1** [Healthy] hale, hearty, well; see HEALTHY. **2** [Firm] solid, stable, safe; see RELIABLE. **3** [Sensible] reasonable, rational, prudent; see SENSIBLE. **4** [Free from defect] flawless, unimpaired, undecayed; see WHOLE 2.

sound *n.* **1** [Something audible] vibration, din, racket; see NOISE 1. **2** [The quality of something audible] tonality, resonance, note, timbre, tone, pitch, intonation, accent, character, quality, softness, lightness, loudness, reverberation, ringing, vibration, modulation, discord, consonance, harmony. **3** [Water between an island and the mainland] strait, bay, bight; see CHANNEL.

sound *v.* vibrate, echo, resound, reverberate, shout, sing, whisper, murmur, clatter, clank, rattle, blow, blare, bark, ring out, explode, thunder, buzz, rumble, hum, jabber, jangle, whine, crash, bang, boom, burst, chatter, creak, clang, roar, babble, clap, patter, prattle, clink, toot, cackle, clack, thud, slam, smash, thump, snort, shriek, moan, quaver, trumpet, croak, caw, quack, squawk.

sounding *a.* ringing, thudding, bumping, roaring, calling, thundering, booming, crashing, clattering, clinking, clanging, tinkling, whispering, pinging, rattling, rumbling, ticking, crying, clicking, echoing, pattering, clucking, chirping, peeping, growling, grunting, bellowing, murmuring, whirring, making noise, making a sound, screeching, screaming, squealing.

sound out *v.* probe, feel out, feel, put out a feeler, send up a trial balloon, see how the land lies, get the lay of the land, see which way the wind blows; see also EXAMINE, EXPERIMENT.

soundproof *a.* soundproofed, insulated from noise, soundless; see QUIET.

soup *n. Soups include the following:* broth, bouillon, consommé, purée, bisque, chowder, gumbo, pottage, *potage* (French); chicken, beef, vegetable, tomato, potato, celery, lentil, mushroom, navy bean, barley, cheese, split pea, French onion, oxtail, mock turtle, wonton, eggdrop, matzo ball, etc. soup; minestrone, clam chowder, oyster stew, vichyssoise, bouillabaisse, borscht, gazpacho, mulligatawny, corn chowder, pepper pot, cock-a-leekie, Scotch broth; see also FOOD, STEW.

soupçon *n.* trace, drop, hint; see DASH 3.

sour *a.* acid, tart, vinegary, fermented, rancid, musty, turned,

acrid, salty, bitter, caustic, cutting, stinging, acrid, harsh, irritating, unsavory, tangy, briny, brackish, sharp, keen, biting, pungent, curdled, unripe. —**turn sour** putrefy, rot, decay; see SPOIL.

sour *v.* turn, ferment, spoil, make sour, curdle.

source *n.* beginning, cause, root; see ORIGIN 2, 3.

south *a.* **1** [Situated to the south] southern, southward, on the south side of, in the south, toward the equator, southernmost, toward the South Pole, southerly, tropical, equatorial, in the torrid zone. **2** [Moving toward the south] southward, to the south, southbound, headed south, southerly, in a southerly direction, toward the equator. **3** [Coming from the south] southerly, headed north, northbound, out of the south, from the south, toward the North Pole.

south *n.* southland, southern section, southern region, tropics, tropical region, equatorial region, Southern Hemisphere.

South *n.* South Atlantic States, the Confederacy, the Old South, antebellum South, Southern United States, the New South, the Deep South, Sunbelt, way down south, Dixie, southland.

southeast *a.* SE, southeastern, southeasterly, southeastward, south-southeast, southeast by south, southeast by east; see also DIRECTION.

southern *a.* in the south, of the south, from the south, toward the south, southerly; see also SOUTH 1.

southwest *a.* SW, southwestern, southwesterly, southwestward, south-southwest, southwest by south, southwest by west; see also DIRECTION.

souvenir *n.* memento, keepsake, relic; see MEMORIAL.

sow *v.* seed, scatter, plant, broadcast, drill in, drill, strew, put in small grain, do the seeding.

sowed *a.* scattered, cast, broadcast, spread, distributed, strewn, dispersed, planted.

spa *n.* baths, spring, health resort; see RESORT 2.

space *n.* **1** [The infinite regions] outer space, infinite distance, infinity, interstellar space, interplanetary space, the universe, cosmos, solar system, galaxy, the beyond; see also EXPANSE.—*Ant.* BOUNDARY, measure, definite area. **2** [Room] expanse, scope, range; see EXTENT. **3** [A place] area, location, reservation; see PLACE 2.

spacecraft *n.* rocket, spaceship,

space shuttle, capsule, orbiter, space station, weather satellite, spy satellite, lunar module, UFO, unidentified flying object, flying saucer; see also SATELLITE 2.

spaced a. divided, distributed, dispersed; see SEPARATED.

spacious a. capacious, roomy, vast; see BIG 1.

spade n. shovel, garden tool, digging tool; see TOOL 1.

Spanish a. Spanish-speaking, Iberian, Romance, Hispanic, Latino, Central American, South American, Spanish-American, Mexican, Latin American.

spank v. whip, chastise, thrash; see BEAT 1, PUNISH.

spare a. superfluous, auxiliary, additional; see EXTRA.

spare v. pardon, forgive, be merciful; see PITY, SAVE 1.

spark n. glitter, flash, sparkle; see FIRE 1.

sparkle v. glitter, glisten, twinkle; see SHINE 1.

sparse a. scattered, scanty, meager; see INADEQUATE, RARE 1.

spasm n. convulsion, seizure, contraction; see FIT 1.

spatter v. splash, spot, wet, sprinkle, soil, scatter, stain, dash, dot, speckle, shower, dribble, spray.

speak v. 1 [To utter] vocalize, say, express; see UTTER. 2 [To communicate] converse, discourse, chat; see TALK 1. 3 [To deliver a speech] lecture, declaim, deliver; see ADDRESS 2. —**so to speak** that is to say, in a manner of speaking, as the saying goes; see ACCORDINGLY. —**speak out** insist, assert, make oneself heard; see DECLARE. —**speak well for** commend, recommend, support; see PRAISE 1. —**to speak of** worth mentioning, significant, noteworthy.

speaker n. speechmaker, orator, lecturer, public speaker, preacher, spokesman, spokeswoman, spokesperson, spellbinder, talker.

speaking a. oral, verbal, vocal; see TALKING.

spear n. lance, javelin, bayonet; see WEAPON.

special a. specific, particular, appropriate, peculiar, proper, individual, unique, restricted, exclusive, defined, limited, reserved, specialized, determinate, distinct, select, choice, definite, marked, designated, earmarked; see also UNUSUAL 1, 2.

special* n. sale item, feature, prepared dish; see MEAL 2, SALE 1, 2.

specialist n. expert, devotee, master, ace, virtuoso, veteran, scholar, professional, authority, connoisseur,

maven*.—Ant. AMATEUR, beginner, novice.

specialize v. work in exclusively, go in for*, limit oneself to; see PRACTICE 2.

specialized a. specific, for a particular purpose, functional; see SPECIAL.

specialty n. pursuit, specialization, special interest; see HOBBY, JOB 1.

species n. group, type, sort; see DIVISION 2, KIND 2.

specific a. particular, distinct, precise; see DEFINITE 1, 2, SPECIAL.

specifically a. particularly, individually, characteristically; see ESPECIALLY.

specification n. designation, stipulation, written requirement; see PLAN 1, 2, REQUIREMENT 1.

specified a. particularized, precise, detailed; see NECESSARY.

specify v. name, designate, stipulate; see CHOOSE.

specimen n. individual, part, unit; see EXAMPLE.

speck n. spot, dot, mark; see BIT 1.

speckled a. specked, dotted, motley; see SPOTTED 1.

spectacle n. scene, representation, exhibition; see DISPLAY, VIEW. —**make a spectacle of oneself** show off, act ridiculously, play the fool; see MISBEHAVE.

spectacular a. striking, magnificent, dramatic; see IMPRESSIVE.

spectator n. beholder, viewer, onlooker; see OBSERVER.

speculate v. reflect, meditate, theorize; see THINK 1.

speech n. 1 [Language] tongue, mother tongue, native tongue; see LANGUAGE 1. 2 [The power of audible expression] talk, utterance, articulation, diction, pronunciation, expression, locution, vocalization, discourse, oral expression, parlance, enunciation, communication, prattle, conversation, chatter. 3 [An address] lecture, discourse, oration, pep talk*, harangue, sermon, dissertation, homily, exhortation, eulogy, recitation, talk, rhetoric, tirade, bombast, diatribe, commentary, appeal, invocation, valedictory, paper, stump speech, panegyric, keynote address, spiel*; see also COMMUNICATION.

speechless a. silent, inarticulate, mum; see DUMB 1, MUTE.

speed n. swiftness, briskness, activity, eagerness, haste, hurry, acceleration, dispatch, velocity, readiness, agility, liveliness, quickness, momentum, rate, pace, alacrity, promptness, expedition, rapidity, rush, urgency, headway, fleetness, good clip, lively clip, steam*.

speed v. move rapidly, hurry, rush, go fast, cover ground, roll, sail, hasten, gear up, ride hard, breeze*, go like the wind, go all out, gun the motor*, give it the gun*, step on the gas*, break the sound barrier; see also RACE 1. —**speed up 1** [To accelerate] go faster, increase speed, move into a higher speed; see RACE 1. **2** [To cause to accelerate] promote, further, get things going; see URGE 3.

speedy *a.* quick, nimble, expeditious; see FAST 1.

spell *n.* **1** [A charm] abracadabra, talisman, amulet; see CHARM 1. **2** [A period of time] term, interval, season; see TIME 1. —**cast a spell on (or over)** enchant, bewitch, beguile; see CHARM. —**under a spell** enchanted, mesmerized, bewitched; see CHARMED.

spell out *v.* make clear, go into detail, simplify; see EXPLAIN.

spend *v.* consume, deplete, waste, dispense, contribute, donate, give, liquidate, exhaust, squander, disburse, allocate, misspend, pay, discharge, lay out, pay up, settle, use up, throw away, foot the bill*, fork out*, fork over*, pony up*, ante up*, open the purse, shell out*, blow*.— *Ant.* SAVE, keep, conserve.

spent *a.* used, consumed, disbursed; see FINISHED 1.

sphere *n.* ball, globe, orb; see CIRCLE 1.

spice *n.* seasoning, herb, pepper, cinnamon, nutmeg, ginger, cloves, salt, paprika, oregano, anise, coriander, allspice, savor, relish; see also FLAVORING.

spicy *a.* **1** [Suggestive of spice] pungent, piquant, keen, hot, fresh, aromatic, fragrant, seasoned, tangy, savory, flavorful, tasty; see also SALTY, SOUR. **2** [Risqué] racy, suggestive, daring, indelicate; see also LEWD 2, SENSUAL 2.

spider *n. Common spiders include the following:* black widow, trapdoor, wolf, jumping, brown, brown recluse; daddy longlegs, tarantula.

spigot *n.* plug, valve, tap; see FAUCET.

spill *v.* lose, scatter, drop, spill over, pour out, run out; see also EMPTY 2.

spilled *a.* poured out, lost, run out; see EMPTY.

spin *n.* circuit, rotation, gyration; see REVOLUTION 1, TURN 1.

spin *v.* revolve, twirl, rotate; see TURN 1.

spine *n.* **1** [A spikelike protrusion] thorn, prickle, spike, barb, quill, ray, thistle, needle; see also POINT 2. **2** [A column of vertebrae] spinal column, ridge, backbone, vertebrae; see also BONE.

spineless *a.* timid, fearful, frightened; see COWARDLY, WEAK 3.

spinster *n.* unmarried woman, vir-

gin, single woman, old maid*, bachelor girl*; see also WOMAN 1.

spiny *a.* pointed, barbed, spiked; see SHARP 1.

spiral *a.* winding, circling, coiled, whorled, radial, curled, rolled, scrolled, helical, screw-shaped, wound.

spirit *n.* **1** [Life] breath, vitality, animation; see LIFE 1. **2** [Soul] psyche, essence, substance; see SOUL 2. **3** [A supernatural being] vision, apparition, specter; see GHOST, GOD. **4** [Courage] boldness, ardor, enthusiasm; see COURAGE. **5** [Feeling; *often plural*] humor, frame of mind, temper; see FEELING 4, MOOD 1.

spirited *a.* lively, vivacious, animated; see ACTIVE.

spiritless *a.* dull, apathetic, unconcerned; see INDIFFERENT.

spiritual *a.* refined, pure, holy; see RELIGIOUS 1.

spit *v.* splutter, eject, expectorate, drivel, slobber, drool.

spite *n.* malice, resentment, hatred; see HATE. —**in spite of** regardless of, in defiance of, despite; see REGARDLESS 2.

splash *n.* plash, plop, dash, spatter, sprinkle, spray; slosh, slop.

splash *v.* splatter, dabble, get wet; see MOISTEN.

splendid *a.* grand, great, fine; see BEAUTIFUL, EXCELLENT, GLORIOUS.

splendor *n.* luster, brilliance, brightness; see GLORY 2.

splice *v.* knit, graft, mesh; see JOIN 1, WEAVE 1.

splint *n.* prop, rib, reinforcement; see BRACE, SUPPORT 2.

splinter *n.* sliver, flake, chip; see BIT 1.

split *n.* **1** [A dividing] separation, breaking up, severing; see DIVISION 1. **2** [An opening] crack, fissure, rent; see HOLE 1.

split *v.* burst, rend, cleave; see BREAK 1, CUT 1, DIVIDE. —**split up** part, break up, separate; see DIVIDE, DIVORCE.

spoil *v.* **1** [To decay] rot, blight, fade, wither, molder, crumble, mold, mildew, corrode, decompose, putrefy, degenerate, weaken, become tainted. **2** [To ruin] damage, defile, plunder; see DESTROY.

spoiled *a.* damaged, marred, injured; see RUINED 2, WASTED.

spoiling *a.* rotting, breaking up, wasting away; see DECAYING.

spoils *n.* plunder, pillage, prize; see BOOTY.

spoke *n.* bar, brace, crosspiece; see ROD 1.

spoken *a.* uttered, expressed, told, announced, mentioned, communicated, oral, verbal, phonetic, voiced, unwritten.

spokesman *n.* deputy, mediator, substitute, spokesperson, spokeswoman; see also AGENT, SPEAKER.

sponsor *n.* advocate, backer, supporter, champion; see also PATRON.

spontaneous *a.* involuntary, instinctive, unplanned, impromptu, adlib*, casual, unintentional, impulsive, automatic, unforced, natural, unavoidable, unconscious, uncontrollable.—*Ant.* DELIBERATE, willful, intended.

spontaneously *a.* instinctively, impulsively, automatically; see UNCONSCIOUSLY.

spoof *n.* joke, put-on*, satire; see DECEPTION.

spoof *v.* fool, play a trick on, kid*; see TRICK.

spooky* *a.* weird, eerie, ominous; see MYSTERIOUS 2, UNCANNY.

spoon *n.* teaspoon, tablespoon, ladle; see SILVERWARE.

sport *n.* **1** [Entertainment] diversion, recreation, play, amusement, merrymaking, festivity, revelry, pastime, pleasure, enjoyment; see also ENTERTAINMENT, FUN, GAME 1. **2** [A joke] pleasantry, mockery, jest, mirth, joke, joking, antics, tomfoolery, nonsense, laughter, practical joke. **3** [Athletic or competitive amusement] *Sports include the following:* hunting, shooting, (the) Olympics, horse racing, automobile racing, running, fishing, basketball, golf, tennis, squash, handball, volleyball, soccer, gymnastics, football, baseball, track, cricket, lacrosse, ice hockey, skating, skiing, fencing, cycling, bowling, field hockey, swimming, diving, windsurfing, polo, billiards, mountain climbing, boxing, wrestling.

sporting *a.* considerate, sportsmanlike, gentlemanly; see GENEROUS, REASONABLE 1.

sportsman *n.* huntsman, big game hunter, woodsman; see FISHERMAN, HUNTER.

sportsmanship *n.* **1** [Skill] facility, dexterity, cunning; see ABILITY. **2** [Honor] justice, integrity, truthfulness; see HONESTY.

spot *n.* **1** [A dot] speck, flaw, pimple; see BIT 1, BLEMISH. **2** [A place] point, location, scene; see PLACE 3. **—hit the high spots*** treat hastily, go over lightly, touch up; see NEGLECT 1. **—hit the spot*** please, delight, be just right; see SATISFY 1. **—in a bad spot*** in danger, threatened, on the spot*; see DANGEROUS.

spot *v.* blemish, blotch, spatter; see DIRTY.

spotless *a.* stainless, immaculate, without spot or blemish; see CLEAN, PURE 2.

spotted *a.* **1** [Dotted] marked, dappled, mottled, dotted, speckled, motley, blotchy. **2** [Blemished] soiled, smudged, smeared; see DIRTY 1.

spouse *n.* marriage partner, groom, bride; see HUSBAND, MATE 3, WIFE.

sprain *n.* twist, overstrain, strain; see INJURY.

sprained *a.* wrenched, strained, pulled out of place; see HURT, TWISTED 1.

sprawl *v.* slouch, relax, lounge; see LIE 3.

spray *n.* splash, steam, fine mist; see FOG.

spray *v.* scatter, diffuse, sprinkle; see SPATTER.

spread *a.* expanded, dispersed, extended, opened, unfurled, sown, scattered, diffused, strewn, disseminated, broadcast; see also DISTRIBUTED.—*Ant.* RESTRICTED, narrowed, restrained.

spread *n.* **1** [Extent] scope, range, expanse; see EXTENT, MEASURE 1. **2** [A spread cloth] bedspread, coverlet, counterpane; see COVER 1. **3** [A spread food] preserves, peanut butter, pâté; see BUTTER, CHEESE. **4** [*A meal] feast, banquet, elaborate meal; see DINNER, LUNCH, MEAL 2.

spread *v.* **1** [To distribute] cast, diffuse, disseminate; see RADIATE 1, SCATTER 2, SOW. **2** [To extend] open, unfurl, roll out, unroll, unfold, reach, circulate, lengthen, widen, expand, untwist, unwind, uncoil, enlarge, increase, develop, branch off, radiate, diverge, expand; see also FLOW, REACH 1.—*Ant.* CLOSE, shorten, shrink. **3** [To apply over a surface] cover, coat, smear, daub, plate, gloss, enamel, paint, spray, plaster, pave, wax, spatter, gild, varnish. **4** [To separate] part, sever, disperse; see DIVIDE, SEPARATE 1.

spreading *a.* extending, extensive, spread out, growing, widening.

spree *n.* revel, frolic, binge*; see CELEBRATION.

sprightly *a.* lively, quick, alert; see AGILE.

spring *n.* **1** [A fountain] flowing water, artesian well, sweet water; see ORIGIN 2. **2** [The season between winter and summer] springtime, seedtime, flowering, budding, vernal equinox, blackberry winter*; see also SEASON.

sprinkle *v.* dampen, bedew, spray; see MOISTEN.

sprout *v.* germinate, take root, shoot up, bud, burgeon; see also GROW 1.

spry *a.* nimble, fleet, vigorous; see AGILE.

spunk* *n.* spirit, courage, nerve; see COURAGE.

spurn *v.* despise, reject, look down on; see EVADE.

spurt *n.* squirt, jet, stream; see WATER 2.

spurt *v.* spout, jet, burst; see FLOW.

sputter *v.* stumble, stutter, falter; see STAMMER.

spy *n.* secret agent, foreign agent, scout, detective, undercover man, CIA operative, observer, watcher, mole, counterspy, double agent, spook*.

spy *v.* scout, observe, watch, examine, bug*, tap, scrutinize, take note, search, discover, look for, hunt, peer, pry, spy upon, set a watch on, hound, trail, tail*, follow; see also MEDDLE 1, 2.

squabble *n.* spat, quarrel, feud; see DISPUTE.

squabble *v.* argue, disagree, fight; see QUARREL.

squad *n.* company, unit, crew; see TEAM 1.

squalid *a.* filthy, sordid, foul; see DIRTY 1.

squall *n.* blast, gust, gale; see STORM.

squalor *n.* ugliness, disorder, uncleanness; see FILTH.

squander *v.* use wastefully, spend lavishly, throw away; see WASTE 2.

square *a.* 1 [Having right angles] right-angled, four-sided, equal-sided, squared, equilateral, rectangular, rectilinear. 2 [*Old-fashioned] dated, stuffy, conventional; see CONSERVATIVE, OLD-FASHIONED.

square *n.* 1 [A rectangle] equal-sided rectangle, plane figure, four-sided figure; see RECTANGLE. 2 [A park] city center, town square, plaza, recreational area; see also PARK 1.

squat *v.* stoop, hunch, cower; see SIT.

squawk *v.* cackle, crow, yap; see CRY 2.

squeak *n.* peep, squeal, screech; see CRY 2, NOISE 1.

squeak *v.* creak, peep, squeal; see CRY 2, SOUND. **—squeak through*** manage, survive, get by*; see ENDURE 2, SUCCEED 1.

squeal *v.* shout, yell, screech; see CRY 1, 2.

squeamish *a.* finicky, fussy, delicate, hard to please, fastidious, particular, exacting, prim, prudish, queasy, qualmish, easily nauseated, persnickety*, prissy*.

squeeze *n.* influence, restraint, force; see PRESSURE 1, 2. **—put the squeeze on*** compel, urge, use force with; see FORCE, INFLUENCE.

squeeze *v.* clasp, pinch, clutch; see HUG, PRESS 1.

squint *v.* narrow the eyes, peek, peep; see LOOK 2.

squirm *v.* wriggle, twist, fidget; see WIGGLE.

squirt *v.* spurt, spit, eject; see EMIT.

stab *n.* thrust, wound, puncture; see CUT. **—make (or take) a stab at** endeavor, try to, do one's best to; see TRY 1.

stab *v.* pierce, wound, stick, cut, hurt, run through, thrust, prick, drive, puncture, hit, bayonet, knife; see also KILL 1.

stability *n.* 1 [Firmness of position] steadiness, durability, solidity, endurance, immobility, suspension, balance, permanence. 2 [Steadfastness of character] stableness, aplomb, security, endurance, maturity, resoluteness, determination, perseverance, adherence, backbone, assurance, resistance; see also CONFIDENCE.

stable *a.* 1 [Fixed] steady, stationary, solid; see FIRM 1. 2 [Steadfast] calm, firm, consistent; see CONSTANT.

stable *n.* barn, coop, corral; see PEN 1.

stack *n.* pile, heap, mound; see BUNCH.

stack *v.* heap, pile up, accumulate; see LOAD 1. **—stack up** compare, measure up, match; see EQUAL.

stadium *n.* gymnasium, stands, amphitheater; see ARENA.

staff *n.* 1 [A stick] wand, pole, stave; see STICK. 2 [A corps of employees] personnel, assistants, men, women, force, help, workers, crew, team, faculty, cadre, cast, factotums, organization, agents, operatives, deputies, servants.

stage *n.* 1 [The theater] theater, limelight, spotlight; see DRAMA. 2 [A platform] frame, scaffold, staging; see PLATFORM 1. 3 [A level, period, or degree] grade, plane, step; see DEGREE 1. **—by easy stages** easily, gently, taking one's time; see SLOWLY.

stagger *v.* totter, waver, sway, weave, bob, careen, vacillate.

staggering *a.* monstrous, huge, tremendous; see LARGE 1, UNBELIEVABLE.

stagnant *a.* inert, dead, inactive; see IDLE.

stagnate *v.* deteriorate, putrefy, rot; see DECAY.

staid *a.* sober, grave, steady; see DIGNIFIED.

stain *n.* blot, blemish, spot, splotch, stained spot, smudge, stigma, brand, blotch, ink spot, spatter, drip, speck.

stain v. spot, discolor, taint; see DIRTY.

stairs n. stairway, staircase, flight, steps, stair, fire escape, escalator, ascent.

stake n. rod, paling, pale; see STICK. **—at stake** in danger, at risk, involved, implicated, in jeopardy, in question, hazarded, concerned*, endangered. **—pull up stakes*** depart, move, decamp; see LEAVE 1.

stale a. spoiled, dried, smelly; see OLD 2.

stalk n. stem, support, upright, spire, shaft, spike, straw, stock, trunk.

stalk v. shadow, track, chase; see HUNT 1, PURSUE 1.

stall v. 1 [To break down] not start, conk out*, die; see BREAK DOWN 2. 2 [To delay] postpone, hamper, hinder; see DELAY.

stamina n. strength, vigor, vitality; see ENDURANCE.

stammer v. stutter, repeat oneself, hem and haw, falter, stop, stumble, hesitate, pause; see also SPEAK 1.

stamp n. emblem, brand, cast; see MARK 1.

stamp v. impress, imprint, brand; see MARK 1. **—stamp out** eliminate, kill off, dispatch; see DESTROY.

stamped a. marked, branded, okayed*; see APPROVED.

stampede n. rush, dash, flight; see RUN 1.

stampede v. bolt, rush, panic; see RUN 2.

stand n. notion, view, belief; see ATTITUDE, OPINION 1. **—make (or take) a stand** insist, assert, take a position; see DECLARE.

stand v. 1 [To be in an upright position] be erect, be on one's feet, stand up, come to one's feet, rise, jump up. 2 [To endure] last, hold, abide; see ENDURE 1. 3 [To be of a certain height] be, attain, come to; see REACH 1. **—stand a chance** have a chance, be a possibility, have something in one's favor, have something on one's side, be preferred. **—stand by** 1 [To defend or help] befriend, second, abet; see DEFEND 2, HELP. 2 [To wait] be prepared, be ready, be near; see WAIT 1. **—stand for** 1 [To mean] represent, suggest, imply; see MEAN 1. 2 [To allow] permit, suffer, endure; see ALLOW. **—stand out** be prominent, be conspicuous, emerge; see LOOM 2.

standard a. regular, regulation, typical; see APPROVED.

standard n. pattern, type, example; see MODEL 2.

standardization n. uniformity, sameness, likeness, evenness, levelness, monotony; see also REGULARITY.

standardize v. regulate, institute, normalize; see ORDER 3, SYSTEMATIZE.

standardized a. patterned, regularized, made alike; see REGULATED.

standby n. supporter, stand-in, proxy; see SUBSTITUTE.

stand-in n. proxy, second, understudy; see SUBSTITUTE.

standing n. position, status, reputation; see RANK 3.

standoff n. stalemate, deadlock, dead end; see DELAY.

standoffish a. cool, aloof, distant; see INDIFFERENT.

standpoint n. attitude, point of view, view; see OPINION 1.

standstill n. stop, halt, cessation; see DELAY.

star n. 1 [A luminous heavenly body] sun, astral body, pulsar, quasar, fixed star, variable star. *Familiar stars include the following—individual stars*: Betelgeuse, Sirius, Vega, Spica, Arcturus, Aldebaran, Antares, Alpha Centauri or Rigil Kent, Deneb, Rigel, Canopus, Procyon, Castor, Pollux, Capella, Algol, North Star or Polaris; *constellations*: Ursa Major or the Great Bear, Ursa Minor or the Little Bear, Big Dipper, Little Dipper, Orion or the Hunter, Coma Berenices or Berenice's Hair, Gemini or the Twins, Cassiopeia, Pleiades, Taurus or the Bull, Canis Major or the Greater Dog, Canis Minor or the Lesser Dog, Scorpius or the Scorpion, Sagittarius or the Archer, Corona Borealis or the Northern Crown, Pegasus, Leo or the Lion, Hercules, Boötes or the Herdsman, Cetus or the Whale, Aquila or the Eagle, Cygnus or the Swan, Corona Australis or the Southern Crown, Crux or the Southern Cross, Cancer or the Crab, Virgo or the Virgin, Libra or the Scales, Capricornus or the Sea Goat, Aquarius or the Water Bearer, Pisces or the Fishes, Aries or the Ram. 2 [A conventional figure] asterisk, Star of David, five-pointed star; see FORM 1. 3 [A superior performer] headliner, leading lady, leading man, movie actor, movie actress, actor, actress, matinee idol, chief attraction, superstar.

stare v. gaze, gawk, ogle; see LOOK 2, WATCH.

stark-naked a. nude, without a stitch of clothing, in the altogether*; see NAKED 1.

start n. inception, commencement, beginning; see ORIGIN 2.

start v. commence, begin, initiate, originate, inaugurate, launch, create, kick off*, turn on, switch on, fire up, power up, set off; see also BEGIN 1, 2.

started *a.* evoked, initiated, instituted; see BEGUN.

startle *v.* alarm, shock, astonish; see SURPRISE.

starvation *n.* deprivation, need, want; see HUNGER.

starve *v.* famish, crave, perish; see DIE.

starving *a.* famished, weakening, dying; see HUNGRY.

state *n.* 1 [A sovereign unit] republic, body politic, kingdom; see NATION 1. 2 [A condition] circumstance, situation, welfare, phase, case, station, nature, estate, footing, status, standing, occurrence, occasion, eventuality, element, requirement, category, standing, reputation, environment, chances, outlook, position. —**in a state*** disturbed, upset, badly off; see TROUBLED.

state *v.* pronounce, assert, affirm; see DECLARE.

stately *a.* 1 [*Said of persons*] dignified, haughty, noble; see PROUD 1. 2 [*Said of objects*] large, imposing, magnificent; see GRAND.

statement *n.* 1 [The act of stating] allegation, declaration, assertion, profession, acknowledgment, assurance, affirmation; see also ANNOUNCEMENT. 2 [A statement of account] bill, charge, reckoning, invoice, account, record, report, budget, audit, balance sheet, tab*, check.

statesman *n.* legislator, lawgiver, administrator, executive, minister, official, politician, diplomat, representative, elder statesman, veteran lawmaker.

station *n.* 1 [Place] situation, site, location; see POSITION 1. 2 [Depot] terminal, stop, stopping place; see DEPOT. 3 [Social position] order, standing, state; see RANK 3. 4 [An establishment to vend petroleum products] gas station, gasoline station, service station, filling station, petrol station, pumps, petroleum retailer; see also GARAGE. 5 [A broadcasting establishment] television station, radio station, television transmission, radio transmission, microwave transmitter, radio transmitter, television transmitter, broadcasting station, studios, channel; see also COMMUNICATIONS, RADIO, TELEVISION.

station *v.* place, commission, post; see ASSIGN.

stationary *a.* fixed, stable, permanent; see MOTIONLESS 1.

stationery *n.* writing materials, office supplies, school supplies; see PAPER 4.

statue *n.* statuette, cast, figure, bust, representation, likeness, image, sculpture, statuary, marble, bronze, ivory, icon.

statuesque *a.* stately, beautiful, grand; see GRACEFUL 2.

stature *n.* development, growth, tallness; see HEIGHT, SIZE 2.

status *n.* situation, standing, station; see RANK 3.

staunch *a.* steadfast, strong, constant; see FAITHFUL.

stay *n.* 1 [A support] prop, hold, truss; see SUPPORT 2. 2 [A visit] stop, sojourn, halt; see VISIT.

stay *v.* tarry, linger, sojourn; see VISIT. —**stay put*** remain, stand still, persist; see WAIT 1.

steadfast *a.* staunch, stable, constant; see FAITHFUL.

steadily *a.* firmly, unwaveringly, undeviatingly; see REGULARLY.

steady *a.* uniform, unvarying, patterned; see CONSTANT, REGULAR 3. —**go steady (with)*** keep company with, court, go together*; see COURT, LOVE 1, 2.

steak *n.* filet mignon, sirloin, T-bone; see FOOD, MEAT.

steal *v.* take, filch, pilfer, thieve, loot, rob, purloin, embezzle, defraud, keep, carry off, shoplift, appropriate, take possession of, lift, remove, impress, abduct, shanghai, kidnap, run off with, hold up, strip, poach, swindle, plagiarize, misappropriate, burglarize, blackmail, fleece, plunder, pillage, ransack, burgle*, stick up*, hijack, rip off*, pinch*, mooch*, gyp*; see also SEIZE 2.

stealing *n.* piracy, embezzlement, shoplifting; see CRIME, THEFT.

steam *n.* vaporized water, fumes, fog; see VAPOR.

steam *v.* heat, brew, pressure-cook; see COOK.

steamboat *n.* steamer, steamship, riverboat; see BOAT, SHIP.

steep *a.* precipitous, sudden, sharp, angular, craggy, rough, rugged, irregular, vertical, uphill, downhill, abrupt, sheer, perpendicular.

steer *v.* point, head for, direct; see DRIVE 2. —**steer clear of** stay away from, miss, evade; see AVOID.

stem *n.* peduncle, petiole, trunk; see STALK. —**from stem to stern** the full length, completely, entirely; see EVERYWHERE, THROUGHOUT.

stench *n.* odor, stink, foulness; see SMELL 2.

step *n.* 1 [A movement of the foot] pace, stride, gait, footfall, tread, stepping. 2 [One degree in a graded rise] rest, run, tread, round, rung, level. 3 [The print of a foot] footprint, footmark, print, imprint, impression, footstep, spoor, trail, trace, mark; see also TRACK 2. —**in step (with)** in agreement with, coinciding with, similar to; see

ALIKE, SIMILARLY. —**out of step** inappropriate, behind the times, inaccurate; see WRONG 2, WRONGLY. —**step by step** by degrees, cautiously, tentatively; see SLOWLY. —**take steps** do something, start, intervene; see ACT 1. —**watch one's step** be careful, take precautions, look out; see WATCH OUT.

step v. pace, stride, advance, recede, go forward, go backward, go up, go down, ascend, descend, pass, walk, march, move, hurry, hop; see also CLIMB, RISE 1. —**step up** augment, improve, intensify; see INCREASE.

steppingstone n. help, agent, factor; see MEANS 1.

stereotype n. convention, prejudgment, institution; see AVERAGE, PREJUDICE.

stereotype v. conventionalize, prejudge, pigeonhole, categorize.

stereotyped a. hackneyed, trite, ordinary; see CONVENTIONAL 1, 3, DULL 4.

sterile a. 1 [Incapable of producing young] infertile, impotent, childless, nulliparous, barren.—*Ant.* FERTILE, productive, potent. 2 [Incapable of producing vegetation] desolate, fallow, waste, desert, arid, dry, barren, unproductive, fruitless, bleak; see also EMPTY. 3 [Scrupulously clean] antiseptic, disinfected, decontaminated, germ-free, sterilized, uninfected, sanitary, pasteurized; see also PURE 2.

sterilize v. antisepticize, disinfect, pasteurize; see CLEAN, PURIFY.

stern a. rigid, austere, strict; see SEVERE 1.

stew n. ragout, goulash, Hungarian goulash, chowder, beef stew, Irish stew, mulligan stew, ratatouille, bouillabaisse, casserole; see also FOOD, SOUP.

stick n. shoot, twig, branch, stem, stalk, rod, wand, staff, stave, walking stick, cane, matchstick, club, baton, drumstick, pole, bludgeon, bat, ruler, stock, cue, mast. —**the sticks*** rural areas, the backcountry, outlying districts; see COUNTRY 1.

stick v. 1 [To remain fastened] adhere, cling, fasten, attach, unite, cohere, hold, stick together, hug, clasp, hold fast.—*Ant.* LOOSEN, let go, fall, come away. 2 [To penetrate with a point] prick, impale, pierce; see PENETRATE. —**stick by (someone)** be loyal to, stand by, believe in; see SUPPORT 2. —**stick out** jut, show, come through; see PROJECT 1. —**stick up for*** support, aid, fight for; see SUPPORT 2.

stickup* n. holdup, robbery, stealing; see CRIME, THEFT.

sticky a. ropy, viscous, tacky, sticking, gummy, waxy, pasty, gluey.

stiff a. 1 [Not easily bent] solid, rigid, petrified, firm, tense, unyielding, inflexible, hard, hardened, starched, taut, thick, stubborn, obstinate, unbending, thickened, wooden, steely, frozen, solidified.—*Ant.* SOFT, flexible, softened. 2 [Formal] ungainly, ungraceful, unnatural; see AWKWARD. 3 [Severe] strict, rigorous, exact; see SEVERE 1, 2. 4 [Potent] hard, potent, powerful; see STRONG 4.

stiffen v. gel, harden, starch, petrify, brace, prop, cement, strengthen, thicken, clot, coagulate, solidify, congeal, condense, set, curdle, freeze, cake, crystallize.

stifle v. smother, suffocate, extinguish; see CHOKE.

still a. 1 [Silent] calm, tranquil, noiseless; see QUIET. 2 [Yet] nevertheless, furthermore, however; see BESIDES, BUT 1, YET 1.

stimulant n. tonic, bracer, energizer; see DRUG.

stimulate v. excite, incite, rouse, spur on, foster, induce, jolt, provoke, key up, fire up; see also URGE 2.

stimulated a. keyed up, speeded up, aroused; see EXCITED.

stimulating a. intriguing, enlivening, arousing, high-spirited, bracing, rousing, energetic, refreshing, exhilarating, enjoyable, refreshing, provocative, sharp, evocative, exciting, inspiring, provoking, animating.—*Ant.* DULL, dreary, humdrum.

sting n. 1 [An injury] wound, swelling, sore; see INJURY. 2 [Pain] prick, bite, burn; see PAIN 2.

sting v. prick, prickle, tingle; see HURT 1.

stingy a. parsimonious, niggardly, miserly, penurious, close, close-fisted, greedy, covetous, tightfisted, tight*, grasping, penny-pinching, cheap*, selfish, mean, cheeseparing.—*Ant.* GENEROUS, bountiful, liberal.

stink n. stench, fetor, offensive odor; see SMELL 2.

stink v. smell bad, emit a stench, be offensive; see SMELL 1.

stir v. move, beat, agitate; see MIX 1. —**stir up trouble** cause difficulty, foment, agitate; see BOTHER 2, DISTURB.

stitch v. join, make a seam, baste; see SEW.

stock a. trite, hackneyed, stereotyped; see COMMON 1, DULL 4.

stock n. 1 [Goods] merchandise, produce, accumulation; see PRODUCE. 2 [Livestock] domestic animals, barnyard animals, farm animals; see CATTLE. 3 [A stalk] stem, plant, trunk; see STALK. —**in stock** not sold out, stocked, not difficult to get; see AVAILABLE. —**out of stock** sold out, gone, not available; see SOLD OUT. —

take stock (of) 1 [To inventory] enumerate, audit, take account of; see EXAMINE. 2 [To consider] examine, study, review; see CONSIDER, THINK 1. —**take stock in** believe in, put faith in, rely on; see TRUST 1.

stockings *n.* hose, pantyhose, nylons; see HOSIERY.

stock-still *a.* frozen, stagnant, inactive; see MOTIONLESS 1.

stock (up) *v.* replenish, supply, furnish; see BUY.

stolen *a.* taken, kept, robbed, filched, pilfered, purloined, appropriated, lifted*, abducted, kidnapped, snatched*, run off with, poached, copped*, plagiarized, misappropriated, embezzled, converted.

stomach *n.* paunch, belly, midsection, solar plexus, bowels, intestines, viscera, entrails, insides*, guts, gut*, tummy, pot*, middle, breadbasket*, corporation*.

stomachache *n.* indigestion, dyspepsia, gastric upset; see ILLNESS 1, 2.

stone *a.* rock, stony, rocky, hard, rough, craggy, petrified, marble, granite.

stone *n.* mass, crag, cobblestone, boulder, gravel, pebble, rock, sand, grain, granite, marble, flint, gem, jewel. —**cast the first stone** criticize, blame, reprimand; see ATTACK, SCOLD. —**leave no stone unturned** take great pains, be scrupulous, try hard; see PURSUE 1, WORK 1.

stoned* *a.* drugged, high*, intoxicated; see DRUNK.

stony *a.* inflexible, cruel, pitiless; see FIRM 2, ROUGH 1.

stool *n.* seat, footstool, footrest; see FURNITURE.

stoop *v.* bend forward, incline, crouch; see LEAN 1.

stop *n.* 1 [A pause] halt, stay, standstill; see END 2, PAUSE. 2 [A stopping place] station, platform, bus stop; see DEPOT. —**put a stop to** halt, interrupt, interdict; see STOP 1.

stop *v.* 1 [To halt] pause, stay, stand still, lay over, stay over, break the journey, shut down, rest, discontinue, curtail, pull up, reach a standstill, hold, stop dead in one's tracks*, stop short, freeze, call it a day*, cut short; see also END 1. 2 [To cease] terminate, finish, conclude, withdraw, leave off, let up, pull up, fetch up, wind up, relinquish, have done, desist, refrain, settle, discontinue, end, close, tie up, give up, call off, bring up, close down, break up, hold up, pull up, lapse, be at an end, cut out, die away, go out, defect, surrender, close, peter out*, call it a day*, knock off*, lay off*, throw in the towel*, melt away, drop it, run out, write off, run its course.—*Ant.* BEGIN, start, commence. 3 [To pre-

421 ◀ **straighten**

vent] hinder, obstruct, arrest; see PREVENT.

stopover *n.* layover, overnight, pause; see DELAY.

stopped *a.* at a halt, cancelled, cut short; see INTERRUPTED.

storage *n.* warehouse, repository, accommodation; see STOREHOUSE.

store *n.* shop, mart, shopping mall, mall, strip mall, retail establishment, sales outlet, market, department store, specialty shop, chain store, drygoods store, boutique, emporium, grocery store, convenience store, warehouse club, superstore, drugstore.

store *v.* put, deposit, cache, stock, store away, stow away, lay by, lay in, lay up, put by, put away, put aside, lock away, bank, warehouse, stockpile, hoard, collect, pack away, set aside, set apart, amass, file, stash*, salt away*, put in mothballs*; see also SAVE 3.—*Ant.* SPEND, draw out, withdraw.

stored *a.* stocked, reserved, hoarded; see SAVED 2.

storehouse *n.* depository, warehouse, granary, silo, store, storage space, corncrib, barn, depot, cache, cellar, grain elevator, safe-deposit vault, armory, arsenal, repository.

storekeeper *n.* small businessman, purveyor, grocer; see MERCHANT.

storm *n.* tempest, downpour, thunderstorm, cloudburst, disturbance, waterspout, blizzard, snowstorm, squall, hurricane, cyclone, tornado, twister*, gust, blast, gale, blow, monsoon, typhoon.

storm *v.* blow violently, howl, blow a gale, roar, set in, squall, pour, drizzle, rain, rain cats and dogs*.

stormy *a.* rainy, wet, damp, cold, bitter, raging, roaring, frigid, windy, blustery, pouring, turbulent, storming, wild, boisterous, rough, squally, dark, violent, threatening, menacing.

story *n.* imaginative writing, fable, narrative, tale, tall tale, myth, fairy tale, anecdote, legend, account, satire, burlesque, memoir, parable, fiction, novel, romance, allegory, epic, saga, fantasy; see also LITERATURE 1.

stout *a.* corpulent, fleshy, portly; see FAT.

stove *n.* range, heater, cookstove, oven, furnace; see also APPLIANCE.

straight *a.* 1 [Not curved or twisted] rectilinear, linear, vertical, perpendicular, plumb, upright, erect, in line, unbent, in a row, on a line, even, level.—*Ant.* BENT, curved, curving. 2 [Direct] uninterrupted, continuous, through; see DIRECT 1.

straighten *v.* order, compose, make

straight, untwist, unsnarl, unbend, uncoil, unravel, uncurl, unfold, put straight, level, arrange, arrange on a line, align.—*Ant.* BEND, twist, curl. —**straighten out** put in order, clarify, make less confused, clean up, arrange.

straightforward *a.* sincere, candid, outspoken; see FRANK, HONEST 1.

strain *n.* 1 [Effort] exertion, struggle, endeavor; see EFFORT. 2 [Mental tension] anxiety, tension, pressure; see STRESS 2.

strain *v.* 1 [To exert] endeavor, strive, labor; see TRY 1. 2 [To filter] refine, purify, screen; see SIFT 2.

strained *a.* forced, constrained, tense; see DIFFICULT 1.

strainer *n.* mesh, filter, colander; see SIEVE.

strait-laced *a.* strict, severe, stiff; see PRUDISH.

stranded *a.* deserted, left behind, marooned; see ABANDONED.

strange *a.* foreign, rare, unusual, uncommon, external, outside, without, detached, apart, faraway, remote, alien, unexplored, isolated, unrelated, irrelevant; see also UNFAMILIAR 2, UNKNOWN 1, 2, 3, UNNATURAL 1.—*Ant.* familiar, present, close.

strangely *a.* oddly, queerly, unfamiliarly, unnaturally, uncommonly, exceptionally, remarkably, rarely, fantastically, amazingly, surprisingly, singularly, peculiarly, unusually.—*Ant.* REGULARLY, commonly, usually.

strangeness *n.* newness, unfamiliarity, novelty, abnormality, eccentricity, remoteness.

stranger *n.* foreigner, outsider, unknown person, uninvited person, visitor, guest, immigrant, intruder, alien, interloper, new kid in town*, new kid on the block*, drifter, squatter, perfect stranger, complete stranger.

strangle *v.* asphyxiate, suffocate, garrote; see CHOKE.

strap *n.* thong, strop, leash; see BAND 1.

strategy *n.* approach, method, procedure; see TACTICS.

straw *n. Straws and strawlike fibers include the following:* oat, wheat, barley, rye, rice, buckwheat, bean; see also HAY. —**a straw in the wind** evidence, indication, signal; see SIGN 1. —**grasp at straws (or a straw)** try any expedient, panic, show desperation; see FEAR, TRY 1.

straw vote *n.* opinion poll, unofficial ballot, dry run*; see OPINION 1, VOTE 1, 2.

stray *v.* rove, roam, go astray; see WALK 1.

streak *n.* stripe, strip, ridge; see BAND 1.

stream *n.* current, rivulet, brook; see RIVER, WATER 2.

stream *v.* gush, run, flow; see FLOW.

street *n.* highway, way, lane, path, avenue, thoroughfare, boulevard, terrace, drive, place, road, route, artery, parkway, court, cross street, alley, circle, dead end, passage.

streetcar *n.* tram, trolley, bus; see VEHICLE.

streetwalker *n.* whore, hustler*, hooker*; see PROSTITUTE.

strength *n.* vigor, brawn, energy, nerve, vitality, muscle, stoutness, health, toughness, sturdiness, hardiness, tenacity, soundness.—*Ant.* WEAKNESS, feebleness, loss of energy.

strengthen *v.* intensify, add, invigorate, fortify, reinforce, confirm, encourage, increase, multiply, arm, empower, harden, steel, brace, buttress, stimulate, sustain, nerve, animate, reanimate, restore, refresh, recover, hearten, establish, toughen, temper, rejuvenate, tone up, build up, make firm, stiffen, brace up, rally, sharpen, enliven, substantiate, uphold, back, augment, enlarge, extend, mount, rise, ascend, wax, grow, back up, beef up*.—*Ant.* WEAKEN, cripple, tear down.

strenuous *a.* vigorous, arduous, zealous; see DIFFICULT 1.

strenuously *a.* hard, laboriously, energetically; see VIGOROUSLY.

stress *n.* 1 [Importance] significance, weight, import; see IMPORTANCE. 2 [Pressure] strain, tension, force, burden, trial, fear, tenseness, stretch, tautness, pull, draw, extension, protraction, intensity, tightness, spring; see also PRESSURE 1.

stress *v.* accent, underline, accentuate; see EMPHASIZE.

stretch *n.* compass, range, reach; see EXTENT.

stretch *v.* 1 [To spread out] grow, expand, extend, spread, unfold, radiate, increase, swell, spring up, shoot up, open.—*Ant.* CONTRACT, shrink, wane. 2 [To cause to become longer, spread out, etc.] tighten, strain, make tense, draw, draw out, elongate, extend, develop, distend, inflate, lengthen, magnify, amplify, widen, draw tight.—*Ant.* RELAX, let go, slacken.

stretcher *n.* litter, cot, gurney; see BED 1.

strew *v.* spread, toss, cover; see SCATTER 2.

stricken *a.* wounded, injured, harmed; see HURT.

strict *a.* stringent, stern, austere; see SEVERE 2.

strictly *a.* rigidly, rigorously, stringently; see SURELY.

stride *n.* step, pace, long step; see GAIT. **—take in one's stride** handle, do easily, deal with; see MANAGE 1.

strife *n.* quarrel, struggle, conflict; see FIGHT 1.

strike *n.* 1 [An organized refusal] walkout, deadlock, work stoppage, quitting, sit-down strike, wildcat strike, moratorium, embargo, tie-up, slowdown, confrontation, sit-in; see also REVOLUTION 2. 2 [A blow] hit, stroke, punch; see BLOW. **—(out) on strike** striking, protesting, on the picket line; see UNEMPLOYED.

strike *v.* 1 [To hit] box, punch, thump; see BEAT 1, HIT 1. 2 [To refuse to work] walk out, tie up, sit down, slow down, go out, be on strike, sit in, arbitrate, negotiate a contract, picket, boycott, stop, quit, resist, hold out; see also OPPOSE 1, 2. 3 [To light] kindle, ignite, scratch; see IGNITE. **—strike out** 1 [To begin something new] start out, initiate, find a new approach; see BEGIN 1. 2 [To cancel] obliterate, invalidate, expunge; see CANCEL. 3 [In baseball, to be out on strikes] fan, whiff*, go down swinging*, go down on strikes, take a called third strike.

striking *a.* attractive, stunning, dazzling; see BEAUTIFUL, HANDSOME.

string *n.* 1 [A sequence] chain, succession, procession; see SEQUENCE 1, SERIES. 2 [Twine] cord, twist, strand; see ROPE. **—string along*** accede, go along, agree; see FOLLOW 2.

stringy *a.* wiry, ropy, woody, pulpy, hairy, veined, coarse, threadlike.

strip *n.* tape, slip, shred; see BAND 1, LAYER.

strip *v.* 1 [Undress] divest, disrobe, become naked; see UNDRESS. 2 [Remove] pull off, tear off, lift off; see PEEL.

stripe *n.* line, division, strip, contrasting color, band, border, ribbon, zigzag; see also LAYER.

striped *a.* lined, marked, streaked, veined, ribbed; see also BARRED 1.

strive *v.* endeavor, aim, attempt; see TRY 1.

stroll *v.* ramble, saunter, roam; see WALK 1.

strong *a.* 1 [Physically strong; *said especially of persons*] robust, sturdy, firm, muscular, sinewy, vigorous, stout, hardy, big, heavy, husky, lusty, active, energetic, tough, virile, mighty, athletic, able-bodied, powerful, manly, brawny, burly, wiry, strapping, made of iron.—*Ant.* WEAK, emaciated, feeble. 2 [Physically strong; *said especially of things*] solid, firm, staunch, well-built, secure, tough, durable, unyielding, steady, stable, fixed, sound, powerful, mighty, rugged, substantial.—*Ant.* UNSTABLE, insecure, tottering. 3 [Wielding power] great, mighty, influential; see POWERFUL 1. 4 [Potent in effect] powerful, potent, high-powered, stiff, effective, hard, high-potency, stimulating, inebriating, intoxicating. 5 [Intense] sharp, acute, keen; see INTENSE. 6 [Financially sound] stable, solid, safe; see RELIABLE.

strongest *a.* mightiest, stoutest, firmest, hardiest, healthiest, most vigorous, most active, most intense, most capable, most masterful, sturdiest, most courageous, strongest-willed, most efficient.—*Ant.* WEAK, feeblest, most timid.

strongly *a.* stoutly, vigorously, actively, heavily, fully, completely, sturdily, robustly, firmly, solidly, securely, immovably, steadily, heartily, forcibly, resolutely, capably, powerfully.

structure *n.* arrangement, composition, framework; see BUILDING.

struggle *n.* conflict, contest, strife; see FIGHT 1.

struggle *v.* strive, grapple, contend; see FIGHT.

stub *n.* stump, short end, snag, root, remainder, remnant.

stubborn *a.* unreasonable, obstinate, firm, dogged, opinionated, contradictory, contrary, determined, resolved, bullheaded, mulish, fixed, hard, willful, dogmatic, prejudiced, tenacious, unyielding, headstrong.

stubbornly *a.* persistently, resolutely, willfully, doggedly, tenaciously; see also FIRMLY 2.

stubbornness *n.* obstinacy, doggedness, inflexibility, pertinacity, tenacity, perverseness, bullheadedness, pigheadedness; see also DETERMINATION.

stuck *a.* [Tight] fast, fastened, cemented; see TIGHT 2.

student *n.* learner, undergraduate, novice, high-school student, high schooler, coed*, college student, graduate student, pupil, docent, apprentice; see also SCHOLAR.

studious *a.* thoughtful, well-read, well-informed, scholarly, lettered, learned, bookish, erudite, earnest, industrious, diligent, attentive.

study *n.* research, investigation, scholarship; see EDUCATION 1.

study *v.* read, go into, refresh the memory, read up on, burn the midnight oil, bone up*, go over, cram, think, inquire, investigate, analyze, research, bury oneself in, plunge into.

stuff *v.* ram, pad, wad; see FILL 1, PACK 2.

stuffed *a.* crowded, crammed, packed; see FULL 1.

stuffed shirt* *n.* phony*, pompous person, blowhard*; see FAKE.

stuffing *n.* packing, wadding, padding, quilting, filler, packing material.

stuffy *a.* confined, stagnant, muggy; see CLOSE 5.

stumble *v.* trip, lurch, shamble; see FALL 1, TRIP 1.

stump *n.* butt, piece, projection; see END 4.

stumped* *a.* puzzled, baffled, at a loss; see UNCERTAIN.

stun *v.* 1 [To render unconscious] daze, put to sleep, knock out; see DEADEN. 2 [To astound] astonish, amaze, bewilder; see SURPRISE.

stunned *a.* dazed, astonished, nonplussed; see SHOCKED.

stunning *a.* striking, marvelous, remarkable; see BEAUTIFUL, HANDSOME.

stunt *n.* feat, trick, prank; see ACHIEVEMENT, JOKE.

stupid *a.* senseless, brainless, idiotic, simple, shallow, dense, imprudent, witless, irrational, inane, ridiculous, mindless, ludicrous, muddled, absurd, half-witted, funny, comical, silly, laughable, nonsensical, illogical, indiscreet, unintelligent, irresponsible, scatterbrained, crackbrained, addled, foolish, unwary, incautious, misguided, wild, injudicious, imbecile, addlebrained, addleheaded, addlepated, lunatic, insane, mad, crazy, moronic, touched, freakish, comic, narrow-minded, incoherent, childish, senile, far-fetched, preposterous, unreasonable, asinine, unwise, thoughtless, careless, fatuous, light, lightheaded, flighty, madcap, giddy, boneheaded*, cuckoo*, cracked*, dumb*, goofy*, half-baked, in a daze, wacky*, harebrained, screwy*, cockeyed*, loony*, batty*, dopey*, nutty*.—*Ant.* SANE, wise, judicious.

stupidity *n.* 1 [Dullness of mind] stupor, slowness, heaviness, obtuseness, sluggishness, feeblemindedness, weakness, silliness, nonsense, folly, absurdity, imbecility, brainlessness, imprudence, lunacy, idiocy, shallowness, weakmindedness, impracticality, senility, giddiness, thickheadedness, asininity, slowness, lack of judgment.—*Ant.* INTELLIGENCE, wisdom, judgment. 2 [Extreme folly] nonsense, absurdity, silliness; see CARELESSNESS, NONSENSE 2.

stupidly *a.* imprudently, stubbornly, obtusely; see FOOLISHLY.

sturdy *a.* firm, resolute, unyielding; see STRONG 1, 2.

stutter *v.* stumble, falter, sputter; see STAMMER.

style *n.* 1 [Distinctive manner] way, form, technique; see METHOD. 2 [Fashion] vogue, habit, custom; see FASHION 2. —**in style** current, chic, stylish; see FASHIONABLE, POPULAR 1.

stylish *a.* chic, smart, in fashion; see FASHIONABLE.

suave *a.* sophisticated, ingratiating, urbane; see CULTURED.

subconscious *a.* subliminal, innermost, unconscious; see MENTAL 2.

subconscious *n.* the unconscious, psyche, mind; see SOUL 2.

subject *a.* governed, ruled, controlled, directed, obedient, submissive, servile, slavish, subservient, subjected, at someone's feet, at the mercy of.

subject *n.* substance, matter, theme, material, topic, question, problem, point, case, matter for discussion, matter in hand, item on the agenda, topic under consideration, field of inquiry, head, chapter, argument, thought, discussion.

subject *v.* cause to experience something, lay open, expose, submit.

subjective *a.* nonobjective, introspective, arbitrary; see INTERNAL 1.

subjectively *a.* internally, intrinsically, individually, egocentrically, mentally, nonobjectively, emotionally, introspectively, inherently; see also PERSONALLY 2.

sublime *a.* exalted, lofty, stately; see GRAND.

submarine *n.* U-boat, submersible, sub; see SHIP.

submerge *v.* submerse, engulf, swamp; see IMMERSE, SINK 2.

submission *n.* 1 [A yielding] obedience, meekness, assent; see RESIGNATION 1. 2 [Something submitted] report, memorandum, account; see RECORD 1.

submissive *a.* passive, tractable, yielding; see DOCILE.

submit *v.* 1 [To offer] tender, proffer, present; see OFFER 1. 2 [To surrender] capitulate, yield, give in; see OBEY.

subordinate *a.* inferior, junior, smaller, low, insignificant, subnormal, paltry, not up to snuff*, below par, unequal to, not comparable to, lower, minor, depending on, lower in rank, subject, subservient, submissive, subsidiary, auxiliary, ancillary; see also UNDER 2.—*Ant.* superior, higher, excellent.

subordinate *n.* assistant, helper, aide; see ASSISTANT.

subsequent *a.* succeeding, consequent, coming after; see FOLLOWING.

subsequently *a.* afterward, consequently, in the end; see FINALLY 2.

subside *v.* recede, sink, dwindle; see FALL 1.

subsidiary *a.* secondary, auxiliary, supplementary; see SUBORDINATE.

subsidize *v.* support, finance, back; see PROMOTE 1.

subsidy *n.* allowance, support, grant; see PAYMENT 1.

subsist *v.* stay alive, remain alive, live on; see LIVE 4.

subsistence *n.* 1 [The supporting of life] living, sustenance, maintenance, support, keep, necessities of life. 2 [The means of supporting life] means, resources, circumstances, property, money, riches, wealth, capital, substance, affluence, independence, gratuity, fortune, dowry, legacy, earnings, wages, salary, tips, income, pension; see also FUNDS.—*Ant.* POVERTY, penury, pennilessness.

substance *n.* matter, material, being, object, item, person, animal, something, element; see also THING 1.

substantial *a.* 1 [Real] material, actual, visible; see TANGIBLE. 2 [Considerable] ample, abundant, plentiful; see LARGE 1, MUCH 2.

substantially *a.* extensively, considerably, largely; see MUCH 1, 2.

substitute *n.* deputy, double, dummy, relief, stand-in, standby, understudy, proxy, replacement, ringer*, sub*, pinch-hitter*, designated hitter*; see also DELEGATE.

substitute *v.* act for, do the work of, replace, supplant, displace, take another's place, double for, answer for, pass for, go for, go as, fill in for, pinch-hit for, take the rap for*, go to bat for*, front for, be in someone's shoes.

substitution *n.* change, swap, replacement; see EXCHANGE 3.

subterranean *a.* sunken, subsurface, subterraneous; see UNDERGROUND.

subtle *a.* indirect, implied, insinuated; see MENTAL 2.

subtlety *n.* fine distinction, nuance, innuendo; see SUGGESTION 1.

subtract *v.* deduct, take away, withhold; see DECREASE 2.

subtraction *n.* deducting, deduction, diminution; see DISCOUNT, REDUCTION 1.

suburb *n.* outlying district, residential district, bedroom community; see AREA.

suburban *a.* residential, rural, exurban; see DISTRICT, LOCAL 1, RURAL.

subversion *n.* overthrow, undermining, sabotage; see DEFEAT, REVOLUTION 2.

subversive *a.* ruinous, riotous, insurgent; see REBELLIOUS.

subway *n.* underground (British), tube (British), rapid transit; see RAILROAD, TRAIN.

succeed *v.* 1 [To attain success] achieve, accomplish, get, prosper, attain, reach, be successful, fulfill, earn, do well, secure, succeed in, score, obtain, thrive, profit, realize, acquire, flourish, be victorious, capture, reap, benefit, recover, retrieve, gain, receive, master, triumph, possess, overcome, win, win out, work out, carry out, surmount, prevail, conquer, vanquish, distance, outdistance, reduce, suppress, worst, work, outwit, outmaneuver, score a point, be accepted, be well-known, grow famous, carry off, pull off, come off, come through, make one's way, make one's fortune, satisfy one's ambition, make one's mark, hit the mark, live high, come through with flying colors, beat the game*, work well, overcome all obstacles, play one's cards well, crown, top, do oneself proud*, make it*, make good, do all right by oneself, be on top of the heap*, go places*, click*, set the world on fire*, cut the mustard*, make a killing*, put across*.—*Ant.* FAIL, give up, go amiss. 2 [To follow in time] follow after, come after, take the place of, ensue, supervene, supplant, supersede, succeed, replace, postdate, displace, come next, become heir to, result, be subsequent to, follow in order, bring up the rear.

succeeding *a.* ensuing, following after, next in order; see FOLLOWING.

success *n.* 1 [The fact of having succeeded to a high degree] fortune, good luck, achievement, accomplishment, gain, benefit, prosperity, victory, advance, attainment, progress, profit, end, completion, triumph, conclusion, the life of Riley*, bed of roses*, easy street*, favorable outcome.—*Ant.* DEFEAT, loss, disaster. 2 [A successful person or thing] celebrity, famous person, leader, authority, master, expert, somebody, star, superstar, VIP*, tops.—*Ant.* FAILURE, loser, nonentity.

successful *a.* prosperous, fortunate, lucky, victorious, triumphant, auspicious, happy, unbeaten, favorable, strong, propitious, advantageous, encouraging, contented, satisfied, thriving, flourishing, wealthy, ahead of the game*, sitting pretty*, on easy street*, at the top of the ladder, out in front, on the track*, over the hump*.—*Ant.* UNSUCCESSFUL, poor, failing.

successfully *a.* fortunately, triumphantly, luckily, victoriously, happily, favorably, strongly, thrivingly, flourishingly, famously, propitiously, auspiciously, prosperously, contentedly, beyond all expectation.

succession *n.* continuation, suite, set; see SEQUENCE 1, SERIES.

successive *a.* serial, succeeding, in line; see CONSECUTIVE.

successor *n.* heir, follower, replacement; see CANDIDATE.

such *a.* so, so very, of this kind, of that kind, of the sort, of the degree, so much, before-mentioned.

such *pron.* this, that, such a one, such a person, such a thing. —**as such** in and of itself, by its own nature, more than in name only; see ACCORDINGLY, ESSENTIALLY.

such as *conj., prep.* for example, for instance, to give an example; see INCLUDING, SIMILARLY, THUS.

suck *v.* absorb, take up, swallow up; see SWALLOW.

sucker *n.* 1 [*A victim] dupe, fool, cat's-paw; see VICTIM. 2 [Candy] lollipop, sweet, confectionary; see CANDY.

suction *n.* sucking, vacuum, drawing power; see ATTRACTION, POWER 2, PULL 1.

sudden *a.* precipitate, impromptu, swift; see IMMEDIATE, UNEXPECTED. —**all of a sudden** unexpectedly, suddenly, precipitously; see QUICKLY.

suddenly *a.* without any warning, abruptly, swiftly; see QUICKLY.

suds *n.* foam, bubbles, lather; see FROTH, SOAP.

sue *v.* prosecute, follow up, claim, demand, indict, litigate, contest, pray, entreat, plead, petition, appeal, accuse, file a plea, claim damages, go to court, file suit, prefer a claim, enter a lawsuit, take to court, file a claim, have the law on, haul into court*.

suffer *v.* 1 [To feel pain] undergo, experience, ache, smart, be in pain, be wounded, agonize, grieve, be racked, be convulsed, droop, flag, sicken, torture oneself, get it in the neck*, look green about the gills, complain of, be affected with, go hard with, match it, flinch at, not feel like anything, labor under.— *Ant.* RECOVER, be relieved, be restored. 2 [To endure] bear, sustain, put up with; see ENDURE 2. 3 [To permit] admit, let, submit; see ALLOW.

suffering *n.* distress, misery, affliction; see DIFFICULTY 1, 2, PAIN 2.

sufficient *a.* adequate, ample, satisfactory; see ENOUGH 1.

sufficiently *a.* to one's satisfaction, enough, amply; see ADEQUATELY.

suffocate *v.* stifle, smother, strangle; see CHOKE.

sugar *n. Common varieties and forms of sugar include the following:* sucrose, cane sugar, brown sugar, beet sugar, grape sugar, dextrose, fructose, fruit sugar, maltose, malt sugar, lactose, maple sugar; see also FOOD.

sugary *a.* saccharine, treacly, candied; see SWEET 1.

suggest *v.* 1 [To make a suggestion] submit, advise, recommend; see PROPOSE 1. 2 [To bring to mind] imply, infer, intimate; see HINT.

suggested *a.* submitted, advanced, proposed, propounded, advised, recommended, counseled, tendered, reminded, prompted, summoned up, called up, offered, laid before, put forward.

suggestion *n.* 1 [A suggested detail] hint, allusion, suspicion, intimation, implication, innuendo, insinuation, opinion, proposal, advice, recommendation, injunction, charge, instruction, submission, reminder, approach, advance, bid, idea, tentative statement, presentation, proposition, tip. 2 [A suggested plan] scheme, idea, outline; see PLAN 2. 3 [A very small quantity] trace, touch, taste; see BIT 1.

suicide *n.* self-murder, self-destruction, hara-kiri; see DEATH. —**commit suicide** kill oneself, take an overdose, slash one's wrists, take one's own life, end it all*, commit hara-kiri, poison oneself, jump off a bridge, blow one's brains out*.

suit *n.* 1 [A series] suite, set, group; see SERIES. 2 [A case at law] lawsuit, action, litigation; see TRIAL 2. 3 [Clothes to be worn together] costume, ensemble, outfit, livery, uniform; see also CLOTHES. *Kinds of suits include the following—women:* sport suit, tailored suit, pantsuit, jumpsuit, evening suit, bathing suit, sunsuit, play suit; *men:* sport suit, business suit, full dress, tails*, monkey suit*, dinner jacket, tuxedo, tux*, bathing suit. —**bring suit** prosecute, start legal proceedings, litigate; see SUE.

suit *v.* 1 [To be in accord with] befit, be agreeable, be appropriate to; see AGREE. 2 [To please] amuse, fill, gratify; see ENTERTAIN 1, SATISFY 1. 3 [To adapt] accommodate, revise, readjust; see ALTER 1.

suitable *a.* fitting, becoming, proper; see FIT 1.

suitably *a.* well, all to the good, fittingly; see FIT 1.

suitcase *n.* grip, satchel, luggage; see BAG.

suited *a.* adapted, satisfactory, fit; see FIT 1.

sullen *a.* unsociable, silent, morose, glum, sulky, sour, cross, ill-humored, petulant, moody, grouchy, fretful, ill-natured, peevish, gloomy, gruff, churlish; see also IRRITABLE.—*Ant.* FRIENDLY, sociable, jolly.

sullenly *a.* morosely, glumly, sourly; see ANGRILY, SILENTLY.

sum *n.* amount, value, total; see WHOLE.

summarily *a.* promptly, readily, speedily; see IMMEDIATELY.

summarize *v.* review, condense, shorten; see DECREASE 2.

summary *n.* outline, digest, synopsis, recap, analysis, abstract, abbreviation, résumé, précis, skeleton, brief, case, reduction, version, core, report, survey, sketch, syllabus, condensation, sum and substance, wrap-up*.

summer *n.* summertime, summer season, dog days, sunny season, harvest, haying time, vacation time; see also SEASON.

summit *n.* apex, zenith, crown; see TOP 1.

summon *v.* request, beckon, send for, invoke, bid, draft, petition, signal, motion, sign, order, command, direct, enjoin, conjure up, ring, charge, recall, call in, call for, call out, call forth, call up, call away, call down, call together, volunteer.

sun *n.* day-star, solar disk, eye of heaven*, light of the day, solar energy, source of light; see also STAR 1. —**under the sun** on earth, terrestrial, mundane; see EARTHLY.

sunburned *a.* tanned, burned, sunburnt, brown, suntanned, bronzed, ruddy.—*Ant.* PALE, white-skinned, pallid.

Sunday *n.* first day of the week, Sabbath, day of rest; see WEEKEND.

sunken *a.* lowered, depressed, down; see UNDER 1.

sunlight *n.* daylight, sunshine, light of day; see LIGHT 1.

sunny *a.* shining, brilliant, sunshiny; see BRIGHT 1.

sunrise *n.* dawn, daybreak, aurora; see MORNING 1.

sunset *n.* sundown, evening, end of the day, close of the day, nightfall, twilight, dusk; see also NIGHT 1.—*Ant.* MORNING, dawn, sunrise.

sunshine *n.* sunlight, the sun, sunbeams; see LIGHT 1.

superb *a.* magnificent, splendid, elegant; see EXCELLENT, GRAND.

superficial *a.* flimsy, cursory, hasty, shallow, shortsighted, ignorant, narrow-minded, prejudiced, partial, external, unenlightened.—*Ant.* LEARNED, deep, profound.

superficially *a.* lightly, on the surface, frivolously; see CARELESSLY.—*Ant.* CAREFULLY, thoughtfully, thoroughly.

superfluous *a.* unnecessary, excessive, extra; see EXTREME.

superintendent *n.* supervisor, inspector, director; see EXECUTIVE.

superior *a.* higher, better, preferred, above, finer, of higher rank, a cut above*, more exalted; see also EXCELLENT.

superiority *n.* supremacy, preponderance, advantage; see PERFECTION.

supernatural *a.* preternatural, superhuman, spectral, ghostly, occult, metaphysical, hidden, mysterious, secret, unknown, unrevealed, dark, mystic, mythical, mythological, fabulous, legendary, unintelligible, unfathomable, inscrutable, incomprehensible, undiscernible, transcendental, obscure, unknowable, impenetrable, invisible, concealed.—*Ant.* NATURAL, plain, common.

superstition *n.* irrational belief, fear, old wives' tale; see FEAR.

superstitious *a.* fearful, apprehensive, credulous; see AFRAID.

supervise *v.* oversee, conduct, control; see MANAGE 1.

supervised *a.* directed, administered, superintended; see MANAGED 2.

supervision *n.* guidance, surveillance, direction; see MANAGEMENT 1.

supervisor *n.* director, superintendent, administrator; see EXECUTIVE.

supper *n.* evening meal, high tea (British), midnight snack; see DINNER.

supplement *n.* sequel, continuation, complement; see ADDITION 1.

supplement *v.* add to, reinforce, strengthen; see INCREASE.

supplementary *a.* additional, completing, supplemental; see EXTRA.

supply *n.* stock, amount, reserve; see QUANTITY.

supply *v.* furnish, fulfill, outfit; see SATISFY 3.

support *n.* **1** [Aid] care, assistance, comfort; see HELP 1. **2** [A reinforcement] lining, coating, rib, stilt, stay, supporter, buttress, pole, post, prop, guide, backing, stiffener, rampart, stave, stake, rod, pillar, timber; see also BRACE. **3** [Financial aid] maintenance, livelihood, sustenance; see PAYMENT 1. —**in support of** for, condoning, approving; see FOR.

support *v.* **1** [To hold up from beneath] prop, hold up, buoy up, keep up, shore up, bear up, bolster, buttress, brace, sustain, stay, keep from falling, shoulder, carry, bear.—*Ant.* DROP, let fall, break down. **2** [To uphold] maintain, sustain, back up, abet, aid, assist, help, bolster, comfort, carry, bear out, hold, foster, shoulder, corroborate, cheer, establish, promote, advance, champion, advocate, approve, stick by, stand by, stand behind, substantiate, verify, get back of, confirm, further, encourage, hearten, strengthen, recommend, take care of, pull for, agree with, stand up for, keep up, stand back of, take the part of, rally round, give a lift to, stick up for*, go to bat for*, boost. **3** [To provide for] take care of, keep an eye on, care for, attend to, look after, back, bring up, sponsor, put up the money for, finance, pay for, subsidize, nurse, pay the expenses of, grubstake*, stake*, raise.—*Ant.* ABANDON, ignore, fail.

supported *a.* **1** [Backed personally] financed, promoted, sustained; see BACKED 2. **2** [Supported physically] held up, propped up, braced, bolstered, borne up, floating on, floated, buoyed up, based on, founded on, raised up, having a sufficient base, having an adequate foundation; see also FIRM 1.

supporter *n.* advocate, sponsor, helper; see PATRON.

suppose *v.* conjecture, surmise, deem; see GUESS.

supposed *a.* assumed, presumed, presupposed; see LIKELY 1.

supposedly *a.* seemingly, supposably, believably; see PROBABLY.

supposing *conj.*, *a.* if, in case that, in these circumstances, under these conditions, let us suppose, allowing that, presuming, assuming, taking for granted that.

suppress *v.* crush, overpower, subdue; see DEFEAT.

suppression *n.* abolition, suppressing, overthrow; see DEFEAT.

supremacy *n.* domination, mastery, supreme authority; see POWER 2.

supreme *a.* highest, greatest, paramount, chief; see also BEST.

sure *a.*, *interj.* **1** [Confident] positive, assured, convinced; see CERTAIN 1. **2** [*Certainly] of course, by all means, positively, absolutely, definitely; see also SURELY. —**for sure** certainly, for certain, without doubt; see SURELY. —**make sure** make certain, determine, establish; see GUARANTEE. —**to be sure** of course, certainly, obviously; see SURELY.

surefire* *a.* dependable, certain, infallible; see EXCELLENT, RELIABLE.

surely *a.* doubtlessly, certainly, undoubtedly, definitely, absolutely, evidently, explicitly, without doubt, beyond doubt, beyond question, plainly, infallibly, most assuredly, decidedly, inevitably, indisputably, positively, unquestionably, without any doubt, admittedly, clearly, with assurance, beyond the shadow of a doubt, nothing else but, precisely, conclusively, distinctly, by all means, at any rate, with certainty, unerringly, unmistakably, at all events, undeniably, with confidence, as a matter of course, rain or shine*.

surf *n.* breakers, rollers, combers; see WAVE 1.

surface *n.* exterior, covering, facade; see COVER 1, OUTSIDE 1.

surgeon *n.* specialist, operator, sawbones*; see DOCTOR.

surgery *n.* surgical procedure, arthroscopic surgery, the knife*; see MEDICINE 3, OPERATION 4.

surname *n.* cognomen, last name, patronymic; see NAME 1.

surpass *v.* excel, outdo, better; see EXCEED.

surplus *n.* residue, leftover, something extra; see EXCESS 1, REMAINDER.

surprise *n.* **1** [A feeling] astonishment, wonderment, shock; see WONDER 1. **2** [The cause of a feeling] something unexpected, blow, sudden attack, unexpected good fortune, sudden misfortune, unawaited event, unsuspected plot. —**take by surprise** startle, assault, sneak up on; see SURPRISE *v.*

surprise *v.* astonish, astound, bewilder, confound, shock, amaze, overwhelm, dumbfound, unsettle, stun, electrify, petrify, startle, stupefy, stagger, take aback, cause wonder, awe, dazzle, daze, perplex, leave aghast, flabbergast, floor*, bowl over*, jar, take one's breath away, strike dumb, beggar belief, creep up on, catch unawares.

surprised *a.* upset, taken by surprise, taken unawares, astounded, caught napping, astonished, bewildered, caught off guard, shocked, confounded, startled.

surprising *a.* shocking, extraordinary, remarkable; see UNUSUAL 1, 2, UNEXPECTED.

surrender *n.* capitulation, yielding, giving up, submission, giving way, unconditional surrender, abdication, resignation, delivery.

surrender *v.* **1** [To accept defeat] capitulate, yield, raise the white flag; see QUIT 2. **2** [To relinquish possession] give up, let go, resign; see ABANDON 1.

surround *v.* **1** [To be on all sides] girdle, circle, environ, enclose, close in, close around, circle about, envelop, hem in, wall in. **2** [To take a position on all sides] encompass, encircle, inundate, flow around, close in, close around, hem in, go around, beleaguer, blockade.—*Ant.* ABANDON, flee from, desert.

surrounded *a.* girdled, encompassed, encircled, hemmed in, fenced in, hedged in, circled about, enclosed, fenced about, enveloped.—*Ant.* FREE, unfenced, agape.

surrounding *a.* enclosing, encircling, encompassing; see AROUND.

surroundings *n.* setting, environs, vicinity; see ENVIRONMENT.

survey *n.* study, critique, outline; see EXAMINATION 1.

survey *v.* 1 [To look upon] look over, take a view of, view; see SEE 1. 2 [To examine or summarize] study, scan, inspect; see EXAMINE.

survival *n.* endurance, durability, continuance; see CONTINUATION.

survive *v.* 1 [To live on] outlive, outlast, outwear, live down, live out, weather the storm, make out, persist, persevere, last, remain, pull through, come through, keep afloat, get on; see also ENDURE 1. 2 [To endure] suffer through, withstand, sustain; see ENDURE 2.

survivor *n.* heir, widow, widower, descendant, orphan.

suspect *a.* dubious, questionable, suspected; see UNLIKELY, SUSPICIOUS 2.

suspect *v.* 1 [To doubt someone] distrust, disbelieve, mistrust; see DOUBT. 2 [To suppose] presume, surmise, speculate; see ASSUME.

suspected *a.* doubtful, imagined, fancied; see SUSPICIOUS 2.

suspend *v.* 1 [To exclude temporarily] reject, exclude, drop, remove; see also BAR 2, EJECT, REFUSE. 2 [To cease temporarily] postpone, defer, put off, discontinue, adjourn, interrupt, delay, procrastinate, shelve, waive, retard, protract, lay on the table, file, lay aside, break up, restrain, desist, break off, halt, put a stop to, check, put an end to.—*Ant.* CONTINUE, carry on, proceed.

suspended *a.* pensile, in midair, pendulous; see HANGING.

suspense *n.* apprehension, uncertainty, anxiety; see DOUBT.

suspicion *n.* misgiving, mistrust, surmise; see DOUBT. —**above suspicion** honorable, cleared, unassailable; see HONEST 1, INNOCENT 1. —**under suspicion** suspected, held for questioning, dubious; see SUSPICIOUS 2.

suspicious *a.* 1 [Entertaining suspicion] jealous, distrustful, suspecting, doubting, questioning, doubtful, dubious, in doubt, skeptical, unbelieving, wondering.—*Ant.* TRUSTING, trustful, without any doubt. 2 [Arousing suspicion] not quite trustworthy, questionable, queer*, suspect, irregular, unusual, peculiar, out of line, debatable, disputable.—*Ant.* REGULAR, usual, common.

suspiciously *a.* doubtingly, doubtfully, skeptically, dubiously, uncer-

tainly, unbelievingly, questioningly, in doubt, having doubt, causing suspicion, with caution, with reservations, with a grain of salt.

sustain *v.* 1 [To carry] bear, transport, pack; see CARRY 1, SUPPORT 1, 2. 2 [To nourish] maintain, provide for, nurse; see PROVIDE 1, SUPPORT 2.

swallow *v.* consume, engulf, gulp, take, wash down, pour, swill, bolt, swig, choke down, swallow up, toss off, chug*, chug-a-lug*; see also DRINK 1, EAT 1.

swamp *n.* bog, fen, quagmire, morass, marsh, slough, soft ground, wet ground, mire, peat bog, bottoms, river bottoms, lowland, bottomland, muskeg.

swampy *a.* boggy, wet, miry; see MUDDY 2.

swanky *a.* showy, elegant, fancy, ritzy*; see also EXCELLENT, EXPENSIVE, ORNATE.

swap* *v.* interchange, trade, barter; see EXCHANGE.

swarm *n.* throng, crowd, multitude, horde, pack, troop, school, hive, mass, flock.

swarm *v.* rush together, crowd, throng; see GATHER, RUN.

swarthy *a.* dark-skinned, tawny, dark-hued, dark-complexioned.

swat *v.* beat, knock, slap; see HIT 1.

sway *n.* swaying, swinging, swing, oscillation, vibration, undulation, wave.

sway *v.* bend, oscillate, swagger; see WAVE 3.

swear *v.* 1 [To curse] blaspheme, utter profanity, cuss*; see CURSE. 2 [To take an oath] avow, affirm, testify, state, vow, attest, warrant, vouch, assert, swear by, bear witness, cross one's heart.

sweat *n.* perspiration, beads of sweat, sweating, steam.

sweat *v.* perspire, secrete, swelter, wilt, exude, break out in a sweat.

sweater *n.* *Types of sweaters include the following:* coat, twin, evening, sport, long-sleeved, short-sleeved, sleeveless, crew-neck, turtleneck, V-neck, pullover, cardigan; see also CLOTHES.

sweaty *a.* perspiring, moist, wet with perspiration, glowing, bathed in sweat; see also HOT 1.

sweep *v.* brush up, clear, clear up; see CLEAN, MOP.

sweepings *n.* dirt, litter, refuse; see FILTH, TRASH 1.

sweet *a.* 1 [Sweet in taste] toothsome, sugary, luscious, candied, honeyed, saccharine, cloying, like nectar, delicious; see also RICH 4.—*Ant.* SOUR, bitter, sharp. 2 [Sweet in disposition] agreeable, pleasing, engaging, winning, delightful, reasonable, gentle, kind, generous, unselfish, even-tempered, good-humored, considerate, thoughtful, affable, companionable; see also FRIENDLY.—*Ant.* SELFISH, repulsive, inconsiderate. **3** [Sweet in smell] fragrant, sweet-smelling, fresh, delicate, delicious, spicy, rich, perfumed, clean.

sweeten *v.* add sugar, make sweet, mull; see FLAVOR.

sweetheart *n.* beloved, dear, loved one; see LOVER 1.

sweetly *a.* agreeably, pleasantly, comfortably, gently, gratefully, softly, smoothly, kindly, in a winning manner, charmingly.

sweets *n.* bonbons, candy, confections, desserts, sugar, sweetmeats, preserves, candied fruit; see also CANDY.

swell *a.* just what one wants, desirable, fine; see EXCELLENT.

swell *v.* dilate, expand, distend, increase, enlarge, grow, grow larger, puff up, be inflated, become larger, bulge, puff, inflate, bulge out, blister, round out, fill out.

swelling *n.* welt, wart, pimple, carbuncle, boil, pock, pustule, inflammation, growth, corn, lump, bunion, tumor, blister, abscess; see also INJURY.

swerve *v.* move, bend, turn aside; see TURN 6.

swift *a.* flying, sudden, speedy; see FAST 1.

swiftly *a.* speedily, rapidly, fast; see QUICKLY.

swim *n.* bath, dip, plunge, dive, jump, splash.

swim *v.* bathe, float, glide, slip through the water, stroke, paddle, go for a swim, take a dip, train for the swimming team, swim freestyle.

swimming *n.* diving, aquatics, bathing; see SPORT 3.

swindle *n.* imposition, deception, knavery; see TRICK 1.

swindle *v.* dupe, victimize, defraud; see DECEIVE.

swindler *n.* cheat, cheater, thief, impostor, charlatan, deceiver, trickster, falsifier, counterfeiter, card shark*, cardsharp*, forger, fraud, con man*, con artist*, four-flusher*, sharper, gypster*; see also CRIMINAL.

swing *n.* sway, motion, fluctuation, stroke, vibration, oscillation, lilt, beat, rhythm; see also WAVE 2. **—in full swing** lively, vigorous, animated; see ACTIVE, EXCITING.

swing *v.* sway, pivot, rotate, turn, turn about, revolve, fluctuate, waver, vibrate, turn on an axis; see also WAVE 3.

swinger* *n.* pleasure seeker, libertine, sophisticated person, life of the party*, cohabitant.

switch *n.* dial, knob, lever; see CONTROL 2.

switch *v.* change, shift, rearrange; see ALTER 1, TURN 2.

swivel *v.* rotate, spin, revolve; see TURN 1.

swollen *a.* distended, puffed, swelled; see ENLARGED.

swoop *n.* plunge, fall, drop; see DESCENT 2, DIVE 1.

swoop *v.* slide, plummet, plunge; see DESCEND, DIVE, FALL 1.

sword *n.* saber, rapier, weapon; see KNIFE.

syllabus *n.* summary, outline, course plan; see PLAN 1, PROGRAM 2.

sylvan *a.* wooded, shady, forestlike; see RURAL.

symbol *n.* representation, token, figure; see SIGN 1.

symbolic *a.* representative, typical, indicative, suggestive, symptomatic, characteristic.

symbolize *v.* typify, signify, express; see MEAN 1.

symmetry *n.* proportion, arrangement, order, equality, regularity, harmony, agreement, equivalence, equipoise, evenness, balance, equilibrium, similarity.

sympathetic *a.* compassionate, loving, considerate; see THOUGHTFUL 2.

sympathetically *a.* sensitively, perceptively, responsively, harmoniously, in accord, in harmony, in concert, understandingly, appreciatively, with feeling, warmly, heartily, cordially, kindheartedly, warmheartedly, softheartedly, humanely, in tune with others*.

sympathize *v.* pity, show mercy, comfort, understand, be understanding, love, be kind to, commiserate, express sympathy.

sympathy *n.* **1** [Fellow feeling] understanding, commiseration, compassion; see PITY. **2** [An expression of sympathy] condolence, consolation, solace, comfort, cheer, encouragement, reassurance; see also HELP 1, ENCOURAGEMENT.

symptom *n.* mark, sign, token; see CHARACTERISTIC.

synonymous *a.* same, like, similar, equivalent, identical, correspondent, corresponding, alike, interchangeable, convertible, compatible; see also EQUAL.—*Ant.* OPPOSITE, divergent, contrary.

synopsis *n.* outline, digest, brief; see SUMMARY.

syntax *n.* order of words, arrangement, grammatical rules; see GRAMMAR, LANGUAGE 2.

synthetic *a.* artificial, counterfeit, plastic; see FALSE 3.

syrup *n.* sugar solution, sweet liquid, glucose; see SUGAR. *Kinds of syrup include the following:* cane, corn, maple, simple, sugar; molasses, honey, treacle, sorghum.

system *n.* orderliness, regularity, conformity, logical order, definite

plan, arrangement, rule, systematic order, systematic procedure, logical process; see also ORDER 3.

systematic *a.* orderly, methodical, precise; see REGULAR 3.

systematize *v.* plan, arrange, organize; see ORDER 3.

T

tab *n.* loop, stop, clip; see LABEL, MARKER, TAG 2.

table *n.* **1** [A piece of furniture] desk, pulpit, stand, board, counter, slab, dresser, bureau, lectern, sideboard, washstand; see also FURNITURE. *Tables include the following:* writing, dining, kitchen, card, folding, drafting, vanity, gateleg, dressing, drop-leaf, operating, end, laboratory, refectory, coffee, picnic, butcher-block, Parsons, work, typing, round, conference; secretary, computer stand, altar, workbench, TV tray. **2** [A statement in tabulated form] synopsis, report, record; see SUMMARY. **—turn the tables** reverse, change, switch; see ALTER 1. **—under the table*** covertly, surreptitiously, not obviously; see SECRETLY.

tableau *n.* scene, picture, illustration; see VIEW.

tablecloth *n.* covering, spread, place mats; see COVER 1.

tablet *n.* **1** [A thin piece of material bearing a legend] slab, stone, monument; see MEMORIAL. **2** [Writing paper] folder, pad, sheets; see PAPER 4. **3** [A pharmaceutical preparation] pill, dose, capsule; see MEDICINE 2.

taboo *a.* forbidden, out of bounds, reserved; see ILLEGAL, RESTRICTED.

taboo *n.* restriction, reservation, prohibition; see RESTRAINT 2.

taboo *v.* inhibit, forbid, prevent; see HINDER, RESTRAIN.

tabulate *v.* systematize, arrange, index; see LIST 1, RECORD 1.

tack *n.* **1** [A short, broad-headed nail] thumbtack, pushpin, carpet tack, copper tack; see also NAIL, PIN 1. **2** [An oblique course] digression, tangent, deviation; see TURN 6.

tack *v.* **1** [To fasten lightly] pin, nail, stitch; see FASTEN. **2** [To steer an oblique course] go in zigzags, zigzag, change course; see TURN 6.

tackle *n.* **1** [Equipment] rigging, ropes and pulleys, apparatus; see EQUIPMENT. **2** [A contrivance having mechanical advantage] pulleys, block and tackle, movable pulley; see TOOL 1. **3** [In football, an attempt to down a ballcarrier] flying, running, shoulder, etc. tackle; sack, hit; see DEFENSE 1, JUMP. **4** [In football, one who plays between end and guard] linesman, right tackle, left tackle; see FOOTBALL PLAYER. **5** [In fishing, equipment] gear, sporting goods, fishing outfit; see EQUIPMENT. *Fishing tackle includes the following:* hook, line, fly, casting rod, casting reel, cut bait, live bait, minnow, grasshopper, fish eggs, worm, lure, spinner, fish net, landing net, pole, float, cork, sinker, creel, tackle box, deep-sea tackle, leader, stringer, fish sack, basket.

tackle *v.* **1** [To undertake] begin, turn to, make an attempt at; see TRY 1, UNDERTAKE. **2** [In football, to endeavor to down an opponent] seize, throw down, grab; see UPSET 1.

tact *n.* perception, discrimination, judgment, acuteness, penetration, intelligence, acumen, common sense, subtlety, discernment, prudence, aptness, good taste, refinement, delicacy, the ability to get along with others, finesse, horse sense*.—Ant.* RUDENESS, coarseness, misconduct.

tactful *a.* diplomatic, civil, considerate; see THOUGHTFUL 2.

tactics *n.* strategy, maneuvering, military art, generalship, plan of attack, plan of defense, procedure, stratagem, approach, disposition, map work, chalk work.

tactile *a.* palpable, physical, tactual; see REAL 2, TANGIBLE.

tactless *a.* unperceptive, inconsiderate, rude, discourteous, unsympathetic, unthoughtful, insensitive, boorish, misunderstanding, impolite, rash, hasty, awkward, clumsy, imprudent, rough, crude, unpolished, gruff, uncivil, vulgar.

tag *n.* **1** [A remnant or scrap] rag, piece, patch; see REMNANTS. **2** [A mark of identification] ticket, badge, card, tab, trademark, stamp, stub, voucher, slip, label, emblem, insignia, tally, motto, sticker, inscription, laundry mark, price tag, bar code, identification number, button, pin. 3 [A children's game] hide-and-seek, freeze tag, capture the flag; see GAME 1.

tag *v.* 1 [To fit with a tag] designate, denote, earmark; see MARK 2. 2 [*To follow closely] chase, dog, trail; see PURSUE 1.

tail *n.* rear end, rear appendage, extremity, hind part, butt*, coccyx; see also REAR. —**on someone's tail** behind, shadowing, trailing; see FOLLOWING. —**with one's tail between one's legs** in defeat, humbly, dejectedly; see FEARFULLY.

tailor *n.* garment maker, clothier, dressmaker, seamstress, designer, one who alters and repairs clothing.

tainted *a.* contaminated, polluted, impaired; see SPOILED.

take *n.* 1 [Something that is taken] part, cut, proceeds; see PROFIT 2, SHARE. 2 [Scene filmed or televised] film, shot, motion picture; see PHOTOGRAPH. 3 [*Something that is seized] holdings, catch, haul*; see BOOTY.

take *v.* 1 [To seize] appropriate, take hold of, catch, grip, grab, pluck, pocket, carry off; see also SEIZE 1, 2. 2 [To collect] gather up, accept, reap; see RECEIVE 1. 3 [To catch] capture, grab, get hold of; see CATCH 1. 4 [To choose] select, settle on, opt for, make a selection, pick, decide on, prefer; see also CHOOSE, DECIDE. 5 [To acquire] win, procure, gain, achieve, receive, attain, obtain, secure; see also EARN 2, GET 1. 6 [To require] necessitate, demand, call for; see NEED. 7 [To contract; *said of a disease*] get, come down with, be seized with; see CATCH 4. 8 [To record] note, register, take notes; see RECORD 1. 9 [To transport] move, drive, bear; see CARRY 1. 10 [To captivate] charm, delight, overwhelm; see ENTERTAIN 1, FASCINATE. 11 [To win] prevail in, triumph over, beat; see DEFEAT 2, 3. 12 [To buy] pay for, select, procure; see BUY. 13 [To rent] lease, hire, charter; see RENT 2. 14 [To steal] misappropriate, loot, rob; see STEAL. 15 [To undergo] tolerate, suffer, bear; see ENDURE 2, UNDERGO. 16 [To lead] guide, steer, pilot; see LEAD 1. 17 [To escort] conduct, attend, go with; see ACCOMPANY. 18 [To admit] let in, accommodate, give access to; see RECEIVE 4. 19 [To adopt] utilize, assume, appropriate; see ADOPT 2. 20 [To apply] put in practice, exert, exercise; see PRACTICE 1, USE 1. 21 [To experience] sense, observe, be

aware of; see FEEL 2. 22 [*To cheat] defraud, trick, swindle; see DECEIVE. 23 [To begin to grow] germinate, take root, develop; see BECOME. —**take after** [To resemble] look like, be like, seem like; see RESEMBLE. —**take away** 1 [To subtract] deduct, take from, minus*; see DECREASE 2. 2 [To carry off] transport, cart off, carry away; see REMOVE 1. —**take back** 1 [To regain] retrieve, get back, reclaim; see RECOVER 1. 2 [To restrict] draw in, retire, pull in; see REMOVE 1, WITHDRAW. 3 [To disavow] retract, recant, recall; see DENY, WITHDRAW. —**take down** 1 [To dismantle] disassemble, take apart, undo; see DISMANTLE. 2 [To write down] inscribe, jot down, note down; see RECORD 1, WRITE 2. —**take for** 1 [To mistake for] misapprehend, misidentify as, believe to be; see MISTAKE. 2 [To assume] presuppose, infer, accept; see ASSUME. —**take in** 1 [To include] embrace, comprise, incorporate; see INCLUDE 1. 2 [To understand] comprehend, apprehend, perceive; see UNDERSTAND 1. 3 [To cheat] swindle, lie, defraud; see DECEIVE. 4 [To give hospitality to] welcome, shelter, accept; see RECEIVE 1, 4. 5 [To shorten] reduce, lessen, cut down; see DECREASE 2. —**take off** 1 [To remove] strip off, take one's clothes off, disrobe; see UNDRESS. 2 [To deduct] lessen by, subtract, take away; see DECREASE 2. 3 [To leave the earth] blast off, ascend, soar; see FLY 1, 4, RISE 1. 4 [To leave] go away, depart, shove off*; see LEAVE 1. —**take on** 1 [To hire] employ, engage, give work to; see HIRE. 2 [To acquire an appearance] emerge as, develop, acquire; see BECOME, SEEM. 3 [To undertake] attempt, handle, endeavor; see TRY 1, UNDERTAKE. 4 [To meet in fight or sport] engage, battle, contest; see ATTACK 1, COMPETE. —**take over** 1 [To take control] take charge, take command, assume control; see LEAD 1. 2 [To seize control of] take the reins of, take the helm of, overthrow; see SEIZE 2. 3 [To convey] transport, bear, move; see CARRY 1, SEND 1. —**take to** enjoy, be fond of, admire; see FAVOR, LIKE 1, 2. —**take up** 1 [To begin] start, initiate, commence; see BEGIN 1. 2 [To raise] lift, elevate, hoist; see RAISE 1. 3 [To shorten] tighten, reduce, lessen; see DECREASE 2. 4 [To occupy] consume, engage, fill; see OCCUPY 2, USE 1. 5 [To adopt as a cause] appropriate, become involved with, assume; see ADOPT 2.

taken *a.* **1** [Captured] arrested, seized, appropriated; see CAPTURED. **2** [Employed or rented] occupied, reserved, held; see RENTED.

takeoff *v.* ascent, upward flight, fly-off, climb, hop, jump, vertical take-off; see also RISE 1.

tale *n.* **1** [A story] anecdote, fairy tale, folk tale; see STORY. **2** [A lie] tall tale, fiction, exaggeration; see LIE.

talent *n.* aptitude, faculty, gift; see ABILITY.

talented *a.* gifted, capable, skilled; see ABLE.

talk *n.* **1** [Human speech] utterance, locution, parlance; see COMMUNICATION, SPEECH 2. **2** [A conference] symposium, parley, consultation; see CONVERSATION, DISCUSSION. **3** [An address] lecture, oration, sermon; see SPEECH 3. **4** [Gossip] report, hearsay, chatter; see GOSSIP 1, RUMOR. **5** [Nonsense] noise, rubbish, jive; see JARGON 1, NONSENSE 1.

talk *v.* **1** [To converse] discuss, confer, chat, interview, speak, communicate, talk together, engage in a dialogue, have a meeting of the minds, chatter, gossip, yammer, remark, be on the phone with, be in contact with, talk over, reason with, visit with, parley, read, hold a discussion, confide in, argue, observe, notice, inform, rehearse, debate, have an exchange, exchange opinions, have a conference with, talk away, go on*, gab*, chew the fat*, compare notes with, talk someone's leg off*, shoot off one's mouth*, spit it out*, shoot the breeze*, pass the time of day, engage in conversation. **2** [To lecture] speak, give a talk, deliver a speech; see ADDRESS 2. **3** [To inform] reveal to, divulge to, notify; see TELL 2. **4** [To utter] pronounce, express, speak; see UTTER. —**talk about** treat, take under consideration, deal with; see CONSIDER, DISCUSS. —**talk back** sass, retort, defy; see ANSWER 1. —**talk down to** stoop, snub, be overbearing; see HUMILIATE, PATRONIZE 2. —**talk someone into** win over, sway, affect; see CONVINCE, INFLUENCE, PERSUADE.

talkative *a.* wordy, verbal, long-winded; see FLUENT.

talker *n.* speaker, conversationalist, orator, speechmaker, mouthpiece, spokesman, spokeswoman, lecturer, actor, performer, debater, storyteller, gossip, barker, announcer, preacher, lawyer, reader, after-dinner speaker, windbag*.

talking *a.* eloquent, chattering, mouthing, repeating, echoing, pronouncing, fluent, articulating, expressing, enunciating, ranting, spouting, haranguing, speaking,

vocalizing, verbalizing, orating, verbose, conversing, discussing, holding forth.

tall *a.* **1** [Lofty] big, great, towering; see HIGH 1. **2** [Exaggerated] farfetched, outlandish, unbelievable; see EXAGGERATED.

tally *n.* reckoning, account, poll; see SCORE 1.

tally *v.* record, write down, register, mark down, count, total, add up, sum up, correspond, match, jibe*; see also RECORD 1, COUNT, AGREE.

tame *a.* **1** [Domesticated] subdued, submissive, housebroken, harmless, trained, overcome, mastered, civilized, broken in, harnessed, yoked, acclimated, muzzled, bridled.—*Ant.* WILD, untamed, undomesticated. **2** [Gentle] tractable, obedient, kindly; see GENTLE 3. **3** [Uninteresting] insipid, monotonous, routine; see CONVENTIONAL 3, DULL 4, UNINTERESTING.

tamper with *v.* interfere with, change, meddle with; see ALTER 1, DESTROY.

tan *a.* brownish, suntanned, weathered; see BROWN.

tan *n.* light brown, beige, neutral color; see BROWN, GOLD, YELLOW.

tang *n.* zest, flavor, savor; see TASTE 2.

tangible *a.* perceptible, palpable, material, real, substantial, sensible, touchable, verifiable, physical, corporeal, solid, visible, stable, well-grounded, incarnated, embodied, manifest, factual, objective, tactile.—*Ant.* SPIRITUAL, ethereal, intangible.

tangle *n.* snarl, snag, muddle; see CONFUSION, KNOT 2.

tangle *v.* involve, complicate, confuse, obstruct, hamper, derange, mix up, disorganize, upset, unbalance, unhinge, perplex, tie up, trap, mess up.—*Ant.* ORDER, fix, unravel.

tangled *a.* tied up, confused, knit together, disordered, chaotic, out of place, mixed up, snarled, trapped, entangled, twisted, muddled, messed up, balled up*, screwy*, with wires crossed*.

tank *n.* **1** [A large container for liquids] tub, basin, vat; see CONTAINER. **2** [An armored vehicle on a roller belt with cogged wheels] armored tank, armored personnel carrier, armored car; see WEAPON.

tantrum *n.* rage, outburst, spell; see ANGER, FIT 2.

tap *n.* **1** [A light blow] pat, rap, dab; see BLOW. **2** [A spigot] faucet, petcock, drain; see FAUCET.

tap *v.* **1** [To strike lightly] pat, touch, rap; see HIT 1. **2** [To puncture in order to draw liquid] open, pierce, bore; see PENETRATE.

tape *n.* ribbon, line, rope. *Tapes include the following:* recording tape, cartridge, cassette, edging, tapeline, tape measure, steel tape, surveyor's chain, adhesive tape, gummed tape, duct tape, electrical tape, draftsman's tape, Scotch tape, masking tape, packing tape, transparent tape, audiotape, videotape, mending tape, bias tape, seam binding.

tape *v.* **1** [To fasten] tie up, bind, bond; see FASTEN. **2** [To record] register, make a recording, put on tape; see RECORD 3. **3** [To bandage] tie, bind up, dress; see BIND 1, FASTEN.

taper *v.* narrow, lessen, thin out; see DECREASE 1, 2. **—taper off** recede, peter out*, diminish; see DECREASE 2.

tape recorder *n.* recording equipment, stereo, stereophonic recorder, cassette recorder, cassette deck, cassette player, dictaphone, VCR, videotape machine, videocassette recorder.

tapestry *n.* hanging, fabric, weaving; see CLOTH, CURTAIN, DECORATION 2.

tar *n.* pitch, asphalt, coal tar; see GUM.

tardy *a.* overdue, too late, delayed; see LATE 1, SLOW 2, 3.

target *n.* **1** [A goal] objective, aim, purpose, end, destination, mark. **2** [Bull's-eye] point, spot, butt, mark, dummy. **3** [A prey] quarry, game, scapegoat; see VICTIM.

tarnish *v.* soil, turn dark, lose luster; see DIRTY.

tart *a.* bitter, pungent, sharp; see SOUR.

tartly *a.* aciduously, sharply, curtly; see ANGRILY.

tartness *n.* sourness, acidity, acridity; see BITTERNESS.

task *n.* chore, responsibility, business; see DUTY 1.

taste *n.* **1** [The sense that detects flavor] tongue, taste buds, palate, senses. **2** [The quality detected by taste] flavor, savor, savoriness, aftertaste, tang, suggestion, zip*, wallop*, kick*, smack, jolt, zing*, punch*. **3** [Judgment, especially aesthetic judgment] discrimination, susceptibility, appreciation, good taste, discernment, acumen, sensibilities, penetration, acuteness, feeling, refinement, appreciation; see also JUDGMENT 1. **4** [Preference] tendency, leaning, attachment; see INCLINATION 1. **—in bad taste** pretentious, rude, crass; see TASTELESS 3. **—in good taste** elegant, pleasing, refined; see ARTISTIC, DAINTY. **—to someone's taste**

pleasing, satisfying, appealing; see PLEASANT 2.

taste *v.* **1** [To test by the tongue] sip, try, touch, sample, lick, suck, roll over in the mouth, partake of. **2** [To recognize by flavor] sense, discern, distinguish; see KNOW 3. **3** [To experience] feel, perceive, know; see UNDERGO.

tasteful *a.* delicate, elegant, fine; see DAINTY.

tasteless *a.* **1** [Lacking flavor] unsavory, bland, unseasoned, vapid, flat, watery, flavorless, without spice; see also DULL 4, ORDINARY 2.—*Ant.* DELICIOUS, seasoned, spicy. **2** [Plain] homely, insipid, trite; see COMMON 1. **3** [Lacking good taste] pretentious, ornate, showy, trivial, artificial, florid, ostentatious, clumsy, makeshift, coarse, useless, rude, uncouth, ugly, unsightly, unlovely, hideous, foolish, stupid, crass.—*Ant.* REFINED, civilized, cultivated.

tasty *a.* savory, palatable, appetizing; see DELICIOUS.

tattle *v.* blab, tell on, report; see GOSSIP.

tattler *n.* busybody, tattletale, snoop; see GOSSIP 2, TRAITOR.

tattletale *n.* informer, tattler, busybody, snitch*, fink*, squealer*, stool pigeon*, stoolie*, rat*.

taught *a.* instructed, informed, directed; see EDUCATED, LEARNED 1.

taunt *n.* insult, mockery, jibe; see RIDICULE.

tavern *n.* taproom, alehouse, roadhouse; see BAR 2.

tax *n.* **1** [A pecuniary levy] fine, charge, rate, toll, levy, impost, duty, assessment, tariff, tribute, obligation, price, cost, contribution, expense; see also DUES. **2** [A burden] strain, task, demand; see BURDEN 2.

tax *v.* **1** [To cause to pay a tax] assess, exact from, demand, exact tribute, charge duty, demand toll, require a contribution, enact a tax. **2** [To burden] encumber, weigh down, overload; see BURDEN.

taxation *n.* levying, assessment, money-gathering; see DUES, TAX 1.

taxed *a.* **1** [Paying taxes] levied upon, demanded to pay, required to pay, assessed, subject to tax. **2** [Burdened] overtaxed, strained, harassed, fatigued; see also TIRED.

taxicab *n.* taxi, cab, hack*; see AUTOMOBILE.

tea *n.* **1** [An infusion made from tea leaves] beverage, brew, infusion, decoction; see also DRINK 2. *Tea and tealike drinks include the following:* black, green, Lapsang souchong, oolong, Darjeeling, orange pekoe, pekoe, gunpowder, Earl Grey, English breakfast, rose hip, spiced, jasmine, blended, sassafras, sage, mint, camomile, herb; iced tea or ice tea, cambric tea. **2** [A light afternoon or evening meal] snack, refreshment, tea party; see LUNCH, MEAL 2.

teach v. instruct, tutor, coach, educate, profess, explain, expound, lecture, direct, give a briefing, edify, enlighten, guide, show, give lessons in, ground, rear, prepare, fit, interpret, bring up, instill, inculcate, indoctrinate, brainwash*, develop, form, address to, initiate, inform, nurture, illustrate, imbue, implant, break in, give the facts, give an idea of, improve someone's mind, open one's eyes, knock into someone's head*, bring home to*, cram, stuff; see also INFLUENCE, MOTIVATE.—*Ant.* LEARN, gain, acquire.

teacher n. schoolmaster, schoolmistress, schoolman, educator, public school teacher, high-school teacher, tutor, mentor, pedagogue, master, guru, swami, mistress, kindergarten teacher, teacher-in-training, substitute teacher, professor, lecturer, instructor, faculty member, graduate assistant.

teaching n. pedagogy, instruction, training; see EDUCATION 1, 3.

team n. **1** [A group of people working together, as on the stage] partners, combo, troupe, company, duo, trio; see also ORGANIZATION 2. **2** [An organization, especially in sport] squad, crew, club; see ORGANIZATION 2.

team up with v. attach oneself to, collaborate with, join; see ACCOMPANY, COOPERATE, HELP.

teamwork n. partisanship, collaboration, union; see ALLIANCE 1, COOPERATION, PARTNERSHIP.

tear n. teardrop, droplet, eyewash; see DROP 1.

tear n. rent, rip, hole, slit, laceration, split, break, gash, rupture, fissure, crack, cut, breach, damage, imperfection.—*Ant.* REPAIR, patch, renovation.

tear v. rend, rip, shred, mangle, rive, rip up, split, lacerate; see also CUT 1.

tearful a. weeping, mournful, lamenting, teary, weepy, on the edge of tears.

tears n. sobbing, sob, crying, cry, weeping, lamenting, whimpering, grieving, mourning, waterworks*; see GRIEF.

tease v. taunt, tantalize, torment; see BOTHER 2, RIDICULE.

teaspoon n. kitchen utensil, measuring spoon, 1/3 of a tablespoon, stirrer; see also UTENSILS.

technical a. specialized, special, scientific, professional, scholarly, mechanical, restricted, methodological, technological, industrial.—*Ant.* ARTISTIC, nontechnical, simplified.

technician n. practitioner, professional, engineer; see CRAFTSMAN, SPECIALIST.

technique n. procedure, system, routine; see METHOD.

tedious a. slow, wearisome, tiresome; see DULL 4.

tedium n. boredom, tediousness, dullness; see MONOTONY.

teenage a. immature, youthful, adolescent; see YOUNG 1, 2.

teens n. boyhood, girlhood, adolescence, early adolescence, late adolescence, awkward age*; see also YOUTH 1.

teeter v. seesaw, totter, wobble; see SHAKE 1.

teeth n. dentition, fangs, tusks; see TOOTH.

teetotaler n. nondrinker, prohibitionist, prude, abstainer.

telegram n. wire, cable, cablegram, message, teletype copy, radiogram, call, report, summons, night message, night letter, day letter, news message, code message, signal, flash; see also COMMUNICATION.

telegraph n. Morse telegraph, wireless, transmitter; see COMMUNICATION, RADIO 2.

telegraph v. wire, send a wire, send a cable; see COMMUNICATE 2.

telepathy n. insight, premonition, extrasensory perception; see COMMUNICATION.

telephone n. phone, private phone, extension phone, radiophone, radiotelephone, car phone, cellular phone, cellphone, cordless phone, wireless phone, fax machine, mouthpiece, line, party line, long distance, extension, pay phone.

telephone v. call, call up, phone, ring, ring up, make a call to, dial, call on the phone, fax, put in a call to, phone up*, give a ring, give a buzz.

telephoned a. phoned, called, phoned in, rang, buzzed, faxed, reached by phone.

telescope n. field glasses, binoculars, opera glasses, glass, optical instrument, reflecting telescope, refracting telescope, radio telescope; see also GLASSES.

television n. TV, video, color television, home entertainment center, boob tube*, the tube*, the box*; see also STATION 5.

tell v. **1** [To inform] communicate, explain, instruct, direct, order, divulge, reveal, make known, utter, speak, report, recite, reel off, spit out, put before, let in on, open up to, give the facts, lay open, fill someone in, let on, let slip, level with, leave word, hand it to, lay before, break it to, break the news, add up, keep someone posted, let know, give out, leak, give notice, declare, acquaint with, advise, confess, impart, notify, represent, assert, mention, tell all, break down, give away, cough up*, come across with*, shoot*, come clean*, make a clean breast of; see also DISCUSS, SAY.—*Ant.* HIDE, keep secret, be silent. 2 [To deduce] know, understand, make out, perceive, ascertain, find out, recognize, be sure, differentiate, discriminate, determine, know for certain. —**tell off** rebuke, reprimand, chide; see SCOLD.

teller *n.* cashier, clerk, bank clerk; see WORKMAN.

telling *a.* crucial, conspicuous, significant; see EFFECTIVE, IMPORTANT 1.

temper *n.* 1 [State of mind] disposition, frame of mind, humor; see MOOD 1. 2 [An angry state of mind] furor, ire, passion; see ANGER, RAGE 1. 3 [The quality of being easily angered] impatience, excitability, touchiness, sourness, sensitivity, fretfulness, peevishness, irritability, ill humor, petulance, irascibility, crossness, churlishness, pugnacity, sullenness, grouchiness, huffiness.—*Ant.* PATIENCE, calmness, equanimity. 4 [The quality of induced hardness or toughness in materials] tensile strength, sturdiness, hardness; see FIRMNESS, STRENGTH. —**lose one's temper** become angry, get mad, fly off the handle*; see RAGE 1.

temper *v.* 1 [To soften or qualify] mitigate, pacify, moderate; see EASE 1, 2, SOFTEN. 2 [To toughen or harden] steel, stiffen, solidify, heat-treat; see STRENGTHEN.

temperament *n.* character, disposition, constitution, nature, inner nature, quality, temper, spirit, mood, attitude, type, structure, makeup, humor, outlook, peculiarity, individuality, idiosyncrasy, distinctiveness, psychological habits, mentality, intellect, susceptibility, ego, inclination, tendency, turn of mind, frame of mind.

temperamental *a.* moody, sensitive, touchy; see IRRITABLE.

temperance *n.* moderation, abstinence, self-control; see RESTRAINT 1.

temperate *a.* 1 [Moderate] regulated, reasonable, fair; see MODERATE 4. 2 [Neither hot nor cold] medium, warm, balmy; see FAIR 3, MILD 2. 3 [Not given to drinking] abstemious, abstinent, restrained; see MODERATE 5.

temperature *n.* heat, warmth, cold, coolness, degrees above or below zero, sensation, comfort level, body heat, weather condition, climatic characteristic, thermal reading.

tempestuous *a.* raging, tumultuous, furious; see STORMY, TURBULENT.

temple *n.* house of prayer, synagogue, pagoda; see CHURCH 1.

tempo *n.* pace, rate, meter; see SPEED.

temporal *a.* 1 [Transitory] fleeting, transient, ephemeral; see TEMPORARY. 2 [Worldly] secular, earthly, mundane; see WORLDLY.

temporarily *a.* momentarily, briefly, tentatively, for a while, for the moment, for a time, provisionally, transitorily, for the time being, pro tempore, pro tem.—*Ant.* FOREVER, perpetually, perennially.

temporary *a.* transitory, transient, fleeting, short, brief, ephemeral, fugitive, volatile, shifting, momentary, passing, summary, stopgap, makeshift, substitute, for the time being, overnight, ad hoc, impermanent, irregular, changeable, unenduring, unfixed, unstable, perishable, provisional, short-lived, mortal, pro tem, on the fly*, on the wing, here today and gone tomorrow*.—*Ant.* PERMANENT, fixed, eternal.

tempt *v.* lure, fascinate, seduce, appeal to, induce, intrigue, incite, provoke, allure, charm, captivate, entice, draw out, bait, stimulate, move, motivate, rouse, instigate, wheedle, coax, inveigle, vamp, make a play for*, make someone's mouth water.

temptation *n.* lure, attraction, fascination; see APPEAL 2.

tempted *a.* desiring, inclined, enticed; see CHARMED.

tempting *a.* appetizing, attractive, fascinating; see CHARMING.

ten *a.* tenth, tenfold, decuple, denary, decimal.

tenant *n.* renter, lessee, householder, rent payer, dweller, inhabitant, occupant, resident, roomer, lodger, holder, possessor, leaseholder, tenant farmer; see also RESIDENT.—*Ant.* OWNER, proprietor, landlord.

tend *v.* 1 [To watch over] care for, direct, superintend, do, perform, accomplish, guard, administer, minister to, oversee, wait upon, attend, serve, nurse, mind; see also MANAGE 1. 2 [To have a tendency (toward)] lead, point, direct, make for, result in, serve to, be in the habit of, favor, be predisposed to, be prejudiced in favor of, be apt to, gravitate toward, incline to, verge on.

tendency *n.* 1 [Direction] aim, bent, trend; see DRIFT 1. 2 [Inclination] leaning, bias, bent; see INCLINATION 1.

tender *a.* **1** [Soft] delicate, fragile, supple; see SOFT 2. **2** [Kind] loving, solicitous, compassionate; see KIND. **3** [Touching] moving, pathetic, affecting; see PITIFUL. **4** [Sensitive] touchy, ticklish, oversensitive; see RAW 5, SORE 1.

tenderhearted *a.* softhearted, tender, sensitive; see HUMANE, KIND, MERCIFUL.

tenderly *a.* **1** [Softly] gently, carefully, delicately; see LIGHTLY. **2** [Lovingly] fondly, affectionately, appreciatively; see LOVINGLY.

tenderness *n.* fondness, consideration, care; see FRIENDSHIP, KINDNESS 1.

tennis *n.* lawn tennis, court tennis, tennis tournament; see SPORT 3.

tennis shoes *n.* sneakers, gym shoes, canvas shoes, tennies*, crosstraining shoes, high-tops, athletic shoes, trainers, running shoes; see also SHOE.

tense *a.* **1** [Nervous] agitated, anxious, high-strung, on edge, fluttery, jumpy, jittery; see also EXCITED.—*Ant.* CALM, unconcerned, indifferent. **2** [Stretched tight] rigid, stiff, firm; see TIGHT 1.

tension *n.* **1** [Stress] tautness, force, tightness; see BALANCE 2, STRESS 2. **2** [Mental stress] pressure, strain, anxiety; see STRESS 2.

tent *n.* shelter, canvas, canopy, tarpaulin, covering; see also COVER 1. *Tentlike coverings include the following:* umbrella tent, awning, marquee, wigwam, tepee, booth, pavilion, pup tent, fly tent, lean-to tent, circus tent, big top*.

tentative *a.* provisional, probationary, makeshift; see EXPERIMENTAL.

tentatively *a.* experimentally, conditionally, provisionally; see TEMPORARILY.

tepee *n.* Indian tent, wigwam, wickiup; see TENT.

term *n.* **1** [A name] expression, terminology, phrase, word, locution, indication, denomination, article, appellation, designation, title, head, caption, nomenclature, moniker*; see also NAME 1. **2** [A period of time] span, interval, course, cycle, season, duration, phase, quarter, course of time, semester, school period, session, period of confinement; see also TIME 2. **—come to terms** compromise, arrive at an agreement, arbitrate; see AGREE. **— in terms of** in reference to, about, concerning; see REGARDING.

terminal *a.* final, concluding, ending; see LAST 1.

terminal *n.* **1** [An end] limit, extremity, terminus; see END 4. **2** [Part of a computer] PC, workstation, personal computer; see COMPUTER.

terminate *v.* complete, end, perfect; see ACHIEVE.

terminology *n.* nomenclature, vocabulary, argot; see JARGON 2, LANGUAGE 1.

terms *n.* **1** [Conditions] details, items, points, particulars; see CIRCUMSTANCES 2. **2** [An agreement] understanding, treaty, conclusion; see AGREEMENT 1.

terrace *n.* patio, garden, lawn; see GARDEN, YARD 1.

terra firma *n.* solid ground, land, soil; see EARTH 2.

terrain *n.* ground, region, territory; see AREA.

terrible *a.* **1** [Inspiring terror] terrifying, appalling, fearful, awesome, horrifying, ghastly, awe-inspiring, petrifying, revolting, gruesome, shocking, unnerving; see also FRIGHTFUL.—*Ant.* HAPPY, joyful, pleasant. **2** [*Unpleasant] disastrous, inconvenient, disturbing, awful, horrible*, atrocious*, lousy*; see also OFFENSIVE 2.—*Ant.* WELCOME, good, attractive.

terribly* *a.* horribly, frightfully, drastically; see BADLY 1, VERY.

terrific *a.* shocking, immense, tremendous; see GREAT 1, LARGE 1.

terrify *v.* shock, horrify, terrorize; see FRIGHTEN.

territorial *a.* regional, sectional, provincial; see NATIONAL 1.

territory *n.* **1** [A specified area] region, township, empire; see AREA. **2** [An area organized politically under the central government] commonwealth, colony, protectorate; see NATION 1. **3** [An indefinite area] section, area, boundary; see REGION 1.

terror *n.* fright, horror, panic; see FEAR.

terrorist *n.* subversive, revolutionary, incendiary; see REBEL.

terrorize *v.* coerce, intimidate, browbeat; see THREATEN.

test *n.* **1** [A check for adequacy] inspection, analysis, countdown, probing, inquiry, inquest, elimination, proving grounds, search, dry run*; see also EXAMINATION 1, EXPERIMENT. *Tests include the following:* technical, structural, mechanical, chemical, psychological, mental, intelligence, IQ, intelligence quotient, aptitude, vocational, qualifying, comprehensive, written, truefalse, multiple-choice, objective, diagnostic, semester, term, psychiatric. **2** [A formal examination] quiz, questionnaire, essay; see EXAMINATION 2.

test *v.* inquire, question, try out; see EXAMINE, EXPERIMENT.

tested *a.* examined, tried, proven; see ESTABLISHED 2, RELIABLE.

tester *n.* validator, examiner, lab assistant; see INSPECTOR.

testify *v.* **1** [To demonstrate] indicate, show, make evident; see PROVE. **2** [To bear witness] affirm, give evidence, swear, swear to, attest, witness, bear witness, give one's word, certify, warrant, depose, vouch, give the facts, stand up for, say a good word for. **3** [To declare] assert, attest, claim; see DECLARE.

testimony *n.* **1** [The act of stating] attestation, statement, assertion; see DECLARATION. **2** [Evidence] grounds, facts, data; see PROOF. **3** [Statement] deposition, affidavit, affirmation; see DECLARATION.

text *n.* **1** [A textbook] required reading, manual, handbook; see BOOK. **2** [A subject, expecially a verse from the Bible] quotation, stanza, passage; see SUBJECT. **3** [Writing, considered for its authenticity] lines, textual evidence, document; see MANUSCRIPT, WRITING 2.

texture *n.* **1** [Quality] character, disposition, fineness, roughness, coarseness, feeling, feel, sense, flexibility, stiffness, smoothness, taste; see also FIBER. **2** [Structure] composition, organization, arrangement; see CONSTRUCTION 2, FORM 2.

thank *v.* be obliged, show gratitude, give thanks, acknowledge, show appreciation, be obligated to, be indebted to, bless, praise, smile on, show courtesy, express one's obligation to; see also APPRECIATE 1.—*Ant.* NEGLECT, ignore, show indifference.

thanked *a.* blessed, applauded, appreciated; see PRAISED.

thankful *a.* obliged, grateful, gratified, contented, satisfied, indebted, pleased, kindly disposed, appreciative, giving thanks, overwhelmed.

thankless *a.* **1** [Not returning thanks] unappreciative, ungrateful, self-centered; see CRUEL, RUDE 2. **2** [Not eliciting thanks] poorly paid, unappreciated, unrewarded; see USELESS 1.

thanks *n.* appreciation, thankfulness, acknowledgment, recognition, gratitude, gratefulness.—*Ant.* BLAME, censure, criticism.

thanks *interj.* thank you, I thank you, much obliged, I appreciate it*.

Thanksgiving *n.* harvest festival, last Thursday in November, day of gratitude; see CELEBRATION, FEAST, HOLIDAY.

that *a.* the, this, one, a certain, the indicated, the past, the future, the previously mentioned, a certain, a particular, not this.

that *conj.* in that, so, so that, in order

that, to the end that, for the reason that; see also BECAUSE.

that *pron.* the one, that one, this one, the one in question, that fact, that person, the thing indicated, the aforementioned one, who, which. —at that* even so, all things considered, anyway; see ANYHOW. —not all that* not so very, not so, rather less; see NOT.

thaw *v.* liquefy, flow, run, liquate, fuse, become liquid; see also DISSOLVE, MELT 1.—*Ant.* FREEZE, congeal, refrigerate.

the *a.*, *definite article* **1** [The definite article] some, a few, a particular, a special, a specific, a certain, an individual, this, that, each, every, these, those, the whole, the entire. **2** [Special or unique; *often italics*] preeminent, outstanding, particular, supreme, unparalleled, unequaled, unsurpassed, unusual, uncommon, rare, singular, unprecedented, exceptional, one, sole, single, significant, distinguished, specific, choice, individual, peculiar, exceptional, occasional, unfamiliar, strange, spectacular, phenomenal, unheard-of, unknown, unattainable, invincible, almighty, all-powerful; see also SPECIAL, UNIQUE.—*Ant.* COMMON, USUAL, ordinary.

theater *n.* **1** [A building intended for theatrical productions] playhouse, concert hall, coliseum; see AUDITORIUM. **2** [The legitimate stage] stage, drama, Broadway; see COMEDY, MOVIES 2.

theatrical *a.* ceremonious, meretricious, superficial; see AFFECTED 2.

theft *n.* robbery, racket, thievery, larceny, stealing, swindling, swindle, cheating, defrauding, fraud, piracy, burglary, pillage, pilfering, plunder, vandalism, holdup, pocket-picking, safecracking, extortion, embezzlement, looting, appropriation, shoplifting, fleecing, mugging, stickup*; see also CRIME.

their *poss. pronominal adj.* belonging to them, belonging to others, their own, of them.

them *pron.* these persons, these things, those persons, those things, the others, the above, some people, him and her; see also EVERYBODY.

theme *n.* **1** [A subject] topic, proposition, argument, thesis, text, subject matter, matter at hand, problem, question, point at issue, affair, business, point, case, thought, idea, line; see also SUBJECT. **2** [A recurrent melody] melody, motif, strain; see SONG. **3** [A short composition] essay, report, paper; see WRITING 2, STATEMENT 1.

then *a.* at that time, formerly, before, years ago, at that point, suddenly, all at once, soon after, before long, next, later, thereupon; see also

WHEN 2, 3. —**but then** but at the same time, on the other hand, however; see BUT 1, 2. —**what then?** what would happen in that case?, and then?, what would the result be?; see WHAT 1.

theology *n.* dogma, creed, theism; see BELIEF, FAITH 2.

theoretical *a.* ideal, analytical, academic; see ASSUMED.

theory *n.* **1** [Principles] method, approach, philosophy; see LAW 4. **2** [Something to be proved] hypothesis, conjecture, speculation; see OPINION 1.

therapeutic *a.* curative, healing, corrective, remedial.

therapy *n.* remedy, healing, cure; see MEDICINE 3.

there *a.* in that place, not here, beyond, over there, yonder, in the distance, at a distance, over yonder, in that spot, at that point; see also WHERE 2. —**not all there*** crazy, eccentric, demented; see INSANE.

thereafter *a.* from then on, from that day on, after that; see FOLLOWING, HEREAFTER.

thereby *a.* by way of, that, by that means, by which; see also THROUGH 4, WHEREBY.

therefore *a.*, *conj.* accordingly, consequently, hence, wherefore, for, since, inasmuch as, for this reason, on account of, to that end, in that event, in consequence, as a result.

thermometer *n.* mercury, thermostat, thermoregulator; see MEASURE 2.

these *a.* those, the, the indicated, the present, the previously mentioned, the above, certain, not those.

these *pron.* those, the ones here, they, them, not those.

they *pron.* people, men, women, men and women, these people, everyone, those people, all, others, he and she, both; see also EVERYBODY.

thick *a.* **1** [Dense] compact, impervious, condensed, compressed, multitudinous, numerous, rank, crowded, close, solid, packed, populous, profuse, populated, swarming, heaped, abundant, impenetrable, concentrated, crammed, packed together, closely packed, like a can of sardines*, jampacked*.—*Ant.* SCATTERED, spacious, wide-open. **2** [Deep] in depth, edgewise, third-dimensional; see DEEP 2. **3** [Of heavy consistency] compact, heavy, viscous, viscid, dense, syrupy, ropy, coagulated, curdled, turbid, gelatinous, glutinous, gummy, clotted, opaque; see also STRINGY.—*Ant.* LIGHT, porous, filmy. **4** [Not clear] cloudy, turbid, indistinct; see DULL 2, MUDDY 1, OBSCURE 1. **5** [*Stupid] obtuse, ignorant, doltish; see DULL 3. **6** [*Intimate] cordial, familiar,

fraternal; see FRIENDLY. —**through thick and thin** faithfully, devotedly, in good and bad times; see LOYALLY.

thicken *v.* coagulate, curdle, petrify, ossify, solidify, freeze, clot, set, congeal, jell, grow thick; see also HARDEN, STIFFEN.

thickness *n.* density, compactness, solidity, closeness, heaviness, stiffness, condensation, concentration, clot.—*Ant.* FRAILTY, thinness, slimness.

thief *n.* burglar, highwayman, robber; see CRIMINAL.

thieve *v.* loot, rob, filch; see STEAL.

thievery *n.* burglary, robbery, pilfering; see CRIME, THEFT.

thigh *n.* thighbone, femur, ham; see LEG.

thin *a.* **1** [Of little thickness] flimsy, slim, slight, diaphanous, sheer, rare, sleazy, permeable, paper-thin, wafer-thin.—*Ant.* THICK, heavy, coarse. **2** [Slender] slim, lean, skinny, scraggy, lank, spare, gaunt, bony, wan, rangy, skeletal, scrawny, lanky, delicate, wasted, haggard, emaciated, rawboned, shriveled, wizened, rickety, spindly, pinched, starved.—*Ant.* FAT, obese, heavy. **3** [Sparse] scarce, insufficient, deficient; see INADEQUATE. **4** [Having little content] sketchy, slight, insubstantial; see SHALLOW 1, 2. **5** [Having little volume] faint, shrill, weak; see LIGHT 7.

thin *v.* thin out, weed out, dilute; see DECREASE 2, WEAKEN 2.

thing *n.* **1** [An object] article, object, item, lifeless object, commodity, device, gadget, material object, being, entity, body, person, something, anything, everything, element, substance, piece, shape, form, figure, configuration, creature, stuff, goods, matter, thingamajig*, doohickey*, thingamabob*. **2** [A circumstance] matter, condition, situation; see CIRCUMSTANCE 1. **3** [An act] deed, feat, movement; see ACTION 2. **4** [A characteristic] quality, trait, attribute; see CHARACTERISTIC. **5** [An idea] notion, opinion, impression; see THOUGHT 2. **6** [A pitiable person] wretch, poor person, sufferer, urchin; see also PATIENT, REFUGEE. **7** [Belongings; *usually pl.*] possessions, clothes, luggage; see PROPERTY 1, BAGGAGE. **8** [Something so vague as to be nameless] affair, matter, concern, business, occurrence, anything, everything, something, stuff, point, information, subject, idea, question, indication, intimation, contrivance, word, name, shape, form, entity. **9** [Something to be done] task, obligation, duty; see JOB 2. —**do one's own thing*** live according to one's own principles, do what one likes, live fully; see LIVE 1.

things *n.* possessions, luggage, belongings; see BAGGAGE, PROPERTY 1.

think *v.* 1 [To examine something with the mind] cogitate, muse, ponder, consider, contemplate, deliberate, stop to consider, study, reflect, examine, think twice, estimate, evaluate, appraise, resolve, ruminate, scan, confer, consult, meditate, meditate upon, take under consideration, have on one's mind, brood over, speculate, weigh, have in mind, keep in mind, bear in mind, mull over, turn over, sweat over*, stew, bone up*, beat one's brains, rack one's brains, use the old bean*, figure out, put on one's thinking cap, use one's head, hammer away at, hammer out, bury oneself in.—*Ant.* NEGLECT, take for granted, accept. 2 [To believe] be convinced, deem, hold; see BELIEVE. 3 [To suppose] imagine, guess, presume; see ASSUME. 4 [To form in the mind] conceive, invent, create; see IMAGINE. 5 [To remember] recollect, recall, reminisce; see REMEMBER 1, 2.

thinking *a.* pensive, introspective, reflective; see THOUGHTFUL 1. —**put on one's thinking cap** begin thinking, study, examine; see THINK 1.

thinking *n.* reasoning, reason, contemplation; see THOUGHT 1.

thinness *n.* slenderness, slimness, shallowness; see LIGHTNESS 2.

thin-skinned *a.* sensitive, touchy, moody; see IRRITABLE.

third *a.* part, after the second, next but one; see THREE.

thirst *n.* dryness, need for liquid, longing, craving.

thirsty *a.* dry, parched, arid, eager, hankering for, burning for, craving, longing for, partial to, hungry for, itching for, inclined to, bone-dry*, crazy for*, wild for; see also HUNGRY.—*Ant.* SATISFIED, full, replete.

this *a.* the, that, the indicated, the present, one, the previously mentioned, a certain, not that, a particular.

this *pron.* the one, this one, that one, the one in question, the aforementioned one, this person, the thing indicated, this fact, who, which.

thorn *n.* spine, briar, neetle; see POINT 2.

thorny *a.* bothersome, perplexing, formidable; see DIFFICULT 1, 2.

thorough *a.* 1 [Painstaking] exact, meticulous, precise; see ACCURATE 2, CAREFUL. 2 [Complete] thoroughgoing, out-and-out, total; see ABSOLUTE 1.

thoroughly *a.* fully, wholly, in detail; see COMPLETELY.

those *a.* the, the previously mentioned, the past, the future, certain, not these, these, the above-mentioned, the indicated.

those *pron.* these, the others, they, them, not these.

though *conj.* despite the fact that, even if, if; see ALTHOUGH, BUT 1.

thought *n.* 1 [Mental activity] speculation, reflection, deliberation, meditation, rumination, perceiving, apprehending, seeing, consideration, reasoning, intuition, logical process, perception, insight, understanding, viewpoint, concept, brain work, thinking, knowing, realizing, discerning, rationalizing, concluding, drawing conclusions, inferring, deducing, deriving, deduction, inducing, logic, judging, rationalization, judgment, argumentation, cogitation, contemplation, cognition, intellection, brainstorm. 2 [The result of mental activity] idea, plan, view, fancy, notion, impression, image, understanding, appreciation, conception, observation, belief, feeling, opinion, guess, inference, theory, hypothesis, supposition, assumption, intuition, conjecture, deduction, postulate, premise, knowledge, evaluation, appraisal, assessment, estimate, verdict, finding, decision, determination, reflection, consideration, abstraction, conviction, tenet, presumption, surmise, doctrine, principle, drift, calculation, caprice, reverie, sentiment, care, worry, anxiety, uneasiness, dream. 3 [Care or attention] heed, thoughtfulness, solicitude; see ATTENTION.

thoughtful *a.* 1 [Notable for thought] thinking, meditative, engrossed, absorbed, rapt in, pensive, considered, seasoned, matured, studied, philosophic, contemplative, studious, cogitative, examined, pondered, speculative, deliberative, reflective, introspective, clearheaded, levelheaded, keen, wise, farsighted, rational, calculating, discerning, penetrating, politic, shrewd, careful, sensible, retrospective, intellectual, brainy*, deep.—*Ant.* THOUGHTLESS, unthinking, irrational. 2 [Considerate] heedful, polite, courteous, solicitous, friendly, kind, kindly, unselfish, concerned, anxious, neighborly, regardful, social, cooperative, responsive, aware, sensitive, benign, indulgent, obliging, careful, attentive, gallant, chivalrous, charitable.—*Ant.* SELFISH, boorish, inconsiderate.

thoughtfulness *n.* understanding, helpfulness, indulgence; see KINDNESS 1.

thoughtless *a.* **1** [Destitute of thought] irrational, unreasoning, unreasonable, inane, incomprehensible, witless, undiscerning, foolish, doltish, babbling, bewildered, confused, puerile, senseless, driveling, inept, dull, heavy-handed, obtuse, flighty; see also STUPID. **2** [Inconsiderate] heedless, negligent, inattentive, neglectful, careless, self-centered, egocentric, selfish, asocial, antisocial, unmindful, unheeding, indifferent, unconcerned, listless, apathetic, boorish, discourteous, unrefined; see also RUDE 2.—*Ant.* CAREFUL, thoughtful, unselfish.

thoughtlessness *n.* inattention, oversight, heedlessness; see CARELESSNESS, NEGLECT 1.

thousand *a.* ten hundred, millenary, thousandfold; see MANY.

thrash *v.* trounce, whip, chasten; see BEAT 1, PUNISH.

thread *n.* yarn, string, strand; see FIBER.

thread *v.* attach, weave together, string together; see JOIN 1.

threat *n.* menace, fulmination, intimidation; see WARNING.

threaten *v.* intimidate, caution, admonish, scare, torment, push around, forewarn, bully, abuse, bluster, endanger, be dangerous, be gathering, be in the offing, imperil, be brewing, approach, come on, advance; see also FRIGHTEN, WARN.—*Ant.* HELP, mollify, placate.

threatened *a.* warned, endangered, imperiled, jeopardized, in bad straits, insecure, unsafe, unprotected, vulnerable, exposed, in a crucial state, in danger, besieged, surrounded, under attack, set upon, in a bad way.—*Ant.* SAFE, invulnerable, protected.

threatening *a.* alarming, dangerous, aggressive; see OMINOUS, SINISTER, UNSAFE.

three *a.* triple, treble, threefold, third, triform, triune, tertiary, thrice, triply.

threshold *n.* sill, gate, door; see ENTRANCE 1.

thrift *n.* saving, parsimony, frugality; see ECONOMY.

thrifty *a.* parsimonious, careful, frugal; see ECONOMICAL 1.

thrill *n.* pleasant sensation, stimulation, tingle; see EXCITEMENT, FUN.

thrill *v.* animate, inspire, rouse; see EXCITE.

thrilled *a.* inspired, moved, electrified; see EXCITED, HAPPY.

thrilling *a.* overwhelming, exciting, breathtaking; see STIMULATING.

thrive *v.* flourish, increase, succeed; see GROW 1.

throat *n.* neck, windpipe, larynx, trachea, esophagus, jugular region,

gullet, gorge. —**cut each other's throats*** ruin each other, fight, feud; see DESTROY. —**cut one's own throat*** ruin oneself, cause one's own destruction, act contrary to one's best interests; see COMMIT SUICIDE, DAMAGE. —**ram down someone's throat*** impose, pressure, coerce; see FORCE. —**stick in someone's throat*** be difficult to say, not come easily, be disturbing; see DISTURB.

throaty *a.* husky, hoarse, deep; see HOARSE.

throb *n.* pulse, pulsation, palpitation; see BEAT 1.

throb *v.* vibrate, pulsate, palpitate; see BEAT 2.

throne *n.* authority, sway, dominion, royal power, sovereignty, the crown, Royal Majesty or Highness; see also CHAIR 2, ROYALTY.

throng *n.* multitude, mass, concourse; see CROWD, GATHERING.

throttle *v.* strangle, stifle, silence; see CHOKE.

through *a.*, *prep.* **1** [Finished] completed, over, ended; see DONE 1, FINISHED 1. **2** [From one side to the other] straight through, through and through, clear through; see IN 2, INTO, WITHIN. **3** [During] throughout, for the period of, from beginning to end; see DURING. **4** [By means of] by, by way of, by reason of, in virtue of, in consequence of, for, by the agency of, at the hand of. **5** [Referring to continuous passage] nonstop, unbroken, one-way; see CONSECUTIVE, CONSTANT, REGULAR 3. —**through and through** permeating, pervasive, enduring; see THROUGHOUT, COMPLETELY.

throughout *a.*, *prep.* all through, during, from beginning to end, from one end to the other, everywhere, all over, in everything, in every place, up and down, on all accounts, in all respects, inside and out, at full length, every bit, to the end, from the word go, to the brim*; see also COMPLETELY.

throw *v.* **1** [To hurl] fling, butt, bunt, pitch, fire, let go, sling, toss, heave, lob, dash, launch, chuck, bowl, cast, hurl at, let fly, deliver, cast off.—*Ant.* CATCH, receive, grab. **2** [To use a switch to connect or disconnect power] flip a switch, turn a knob, push a button; see TURN OFF, TURN ON 1. **3** [To force to the ground] pin, nail*, flatten; see DEFEAT 3. **4** [*To lose by allowing an opponent to succeed] lose deliberately, lose as planned, give over; see LOSE 3. —**throw away** reject, refuse, turn down; see DISCARD. —**throw in** add, expend, give; see INCREASE. —**throw out** discharge, throw away, reject; see DISCARD. —**throw together** make quickly, do in a hurry, do a rush job; see BUILD, MANUFACTURE. —**throw up 1** [To vomit] regurgitate, retch, barf*; see VOMIT. **2** [To quit] give up, cease, terminate; see STOP 2. **3** [To construct, usually hastily] build overnight, patch up, knock together; see BUILD.

thrown *a.* **1** [Hurled] pitched, tossed, heaved; see SENT. **2** [Beaten] knocked over, sent sprawling, heaved; see BEATEN 1.

thrust *n.* **1** [A jab] punch, stab, poke; see BLOW. **2** [An attack] onset, onslaught, advance; see ATTACK. **3** [A strong push] drive, impetus, pressure; see PUSH.

thrust *v.* poke, push, shove; see HIT 1.

thud *n.* thump, dull sound, plop; see NOISE 1.

thumb *n.* opposable digit, first digit, preaxial digit; see FINGER. —**all thumbs** fumbling, clumsy, inept; see AWKWARD. —**under someone's thumb** under someone's control, controlled, governed; see MANAGED.

thump *n.* thud, knock, rap; see NOISE 1, BLOW.

thump *v.* pound, knock, rap, wallop, slap, strike, whack, hit; see also BEAT 1, HIT 1.

thunder *n.* crash, peal, outburst, explosion, boom, booming, roar, rumble, clap, crack, discharge, thunderbolt, uproar, blast; see also NOISE 1.

thunder *v.* peal, boom, rumble, resound, roll, crash, clamor, clash; see also SOUND, STORM.

thunderous *a.* booming, roaring, crashing; see LOUD 1, 2.

thunderstorm *n.* electrical storm, squall, downpour; see THUNDER, STORM.

thunderstruck *a.* astonished, confounded, astounded, dumbfounded; see also BEWILDERED.

thus *a.* in this manner, so, consequently, hence, in such a way, just like that, in kind, along these lines; see also THEREFORE.

thwart *v.* stop, impede, frustrate; see CONFUSE, PREVENT.

tick *n.* **1** [A light beat] beat, tap, click, ticktock; see also BEAT 1, 2. **2** [An insect] parasite, louse, mite; see INSECT, PEST 1.

ticket *n.* **1** [A valid token] check, tag, slip, pass, note, card, badge, label, voucher, rain check, stub, receipt, record, license, permit, passage, credential, visa, passport, document. **2** [Candidates representing a political party] party list, choice, ballot; see CANDIDATE, FACTION, PARTY 3.

tickle *v.* rub, caress, stroke; see TOUCH 1.

ticklish *a.* sensitive, unsteady, touchy; see IRRITABLE, UNSTABLE 2.

tidbit *n.* morsel, mouthful, bite; see BIT 1.

tide *n.* current, flow, flux, stream, course, sluice, undercurrent, undertow, drag, whirlpool, eddy, vortex, torrent, wave, tidal wave, tsunami. *Tides of the sea include the following:* low, neap, ebb, spring, full, high, flood.

tidiness *n.* neatness, orderliness, uniformity; see CLEANLINESS.

tidy *a.* orderly, trim, spruce; see NEAT 1.

tie *n.* **1** [A fastening] band, bond, strap, brace, yoke, bandage, zipper; see also FASTENER. **2** [A necktie] cravat, neckerchief, bow tie, Windsor tie, ascot, four-in-hand, scarf, neckcloth, choker. **3** [Affection] bond, relation, kinship; see AFFECTION, LOVE 1. **4** [An equal score, or a contest having that score] deadlock, draw, even game, dead heat, drawn battle, neck-and-neck contest, even-steven*, stalemate, standoff, wash*.

tie *v.* **1** [To fasten] bind, make fast, attach; see FASTEN, JOIN 1. **2** [To tie a knot in] knot, make a bow, make a tie, make a knot, do up, fix a tie, make a hitch; see also sense 1. **3** [To equal] match, keep up with, parallel; see EQUAL. —**tie up 1** [To fasten] wrap, package, secure; see CLOSE 4, ENCLOSE. **2** [To obstruct] hinder, stop, delay; see HINDER.

tied *a.* **1** [Firm] fixed, bound, made firm; see FIRM 1. **2** [Even] evenly matched, running neck and neck, in a dead heat; see ALIKE, EQUAL.

tight *a.* **1** [Firm] taut, secure, fast, bound up, close, clasped, fixed, steady, stretched thin, established, compact, strong, stable, enduring, steadfast, unyielding, unbending, set, stuck hard, hidebound, invulnerable, snug, sturdy; see also FIRM 1.—*Ant.* LOOSE, tottery, shaky. **2** [Closed] sealed, airtight, impenetrable, impermeable, impervious, watertight, waterproof, hermetically sealed, padlocked, bolted, locked, fastened, shut tight, clamped, fixed, tied, snapped, swung to, tied up, nailed, spiked, slammed, obstructed, blocked, blind, shut, stopped up, plugged.—*Ant.* OPEN, penetrable, unprotected. **3** [Closefitting] pinching, shrunken, snug, uncomfortable, cramping, skintight, short, crushing, choking, smothering, cutting.—*Ant.* LOOSE, ample, wide. **4** [*Intoxicated*] inebriated, drunken, tipsy; see DRUNK. **5** [*Stingy*] parsimonious, miserly, cheap*; see STINGY. **6** [Difficult to obtain; *said especially of money*] scarce, frozen, tied up; see

RARE 2. —**sit tight** do nothing, refrain from action, stay put; see WAIT 1.

tighten v. 1 [To make tight] compress, condense, squeeze, bind, contract, strangle, constrict, crush, cramp, pinch, grip more tightly, clench, screw down, add pressure; see also STRETCH 2.—*Ant.* LOOSEN, relax, unloose. 2 [To become tight] contract, harden, congeal, stiffen, toughen, become more disciplined.—*Ant.* SOFTEN, melt, liquefy.

tightfisted a. thrifty, niggardly, frugal; see STINGY.

tile n. baked clay, flooring, roofing; see CLAY, FLOORING.

till v. cultivate, work, raise crops from; see FARM.

tilt n. slant, slope, incline; see INCLINATION 2.

tilt v. slant, tip, turn, set at an angle, lean, slope, slouch, shift, dip, sway, make oblique, deviate, turn edgewise; see also BEND.—*Ant.* STRAIGHTEN, level, bring into line.

timber n. 1 [Standing trees] wood, lumber, timberland; see FOREST. 2 [A beam] stake, pole, club; see BEAM 1, LUMBER.

time n. 1 [Duration] continuance, lastingness, extent, past, present, future, infinity, space-time, chronology; see also TODAY. *Units of measuring time include the following:* second, minute, hour, day, term, millisecond, nanosecond, week, month, year, decade, generation, lifetime, century, millennium, eon, epoch, era, period. 2 [A point in time] incident, event, occurrence, occasion, moment, instant, term, season, tide, course, sequence, point, generation. 3 [A period of time] season, era, interval; see AGE 3. 4 [Experience] background, living, participation; see EXPERIENCE. 5 [Leisure] opportunity, free moment, chance; see FREEDOM 2. 6 [Circumstances; *usually plural; used with "the"*] condition, the present, nowadays; see CIRCUMSTANCE 1, CIRCUMSTANCES 2. 7 [A measure of speed] tempo, rate, meter; see BEAT 2. —**ahead of time** ahead of schedule, fast, earlier than expected; see EARLY 2. —**at one time** simultaneously, concurrently, at once; see TOGETHER 2. —**at the same time** simultaneously, concurrently, at once; see TOGETHER 2. —**at times** occasionally, sometimes, once in a while; see SELDOM. —**behind the times** out of date, archaic, obsolete; see OLD-FASHIONED. —**behind time** tardy, delayed, coming later; see LATE 1. —**do time** * serve a prison term, go to jail, be imprisoned; see SERVE TIME. —**for the time being** for the present, for now, under consideration; see TEMPORARILY. —

from time to time occasionally, sometimes, once in a while; see FREQUENTLY. —**in due time** eventually, at an appropriate time, in the natural course of events; see FINALLY 2, ULTIMATELY. —**in no time** instantly, rapidly, without delay; see QUICKLY, SOON. —**in time** eventually, after the proper time, inevitably; see FINALLY 2. —**lose time** go too slow, tarry, cause a delay; see DELAY. —**make time** gain time, act hastily, hasten; see HURRY 1. —**many a time** often, regularly, consistently; see FREQUENTLY. —**on time** 1 at the appointed time, punctually, correct; see PUNCTUAL. 2 by credit, in installments, on account; see UNPAID 1. —**pass the time of day** exchange greetings, chat, converse; see GREET. —**serve time** serve a jail sentence, be incarcerated, be in jail, pay one's debt to society, go to jail, do time*, be sent up*. —**take one's time** dawdle, slow down, dillydally; see DELAY, LOITER. —**waste time** malinger, dawdle, drift; see LOAF.

time v. register distance, clock, measure time; see MEASURE 1.

time-honored a. revered, eminent, noble; see VENERABLE.

timely a. opportune, seasonable, in good time, fitting the times, suitable, appropriate, convenient, propitious, well-timed, modern, up-to-date, newsworthy, fit.—*Ant.* UNTIMELY, ill-timed, inappropriate.

timepiece n. timekeeper, chronometer, stopwatch; see CLOCK, WATCH 1.

timid a. 1 [Irresolute] indecisive, vacillating, wavering; see IRRESPONSIBLE. 2 [Cowardly] fainthearted, spiritless, weak; see AFRAID, COWARDLY. 3 [Reticent] shy, withdrawn, modest; see HUMBLE 1.

tinge n. tint, shade, hint; see TRACE 1, TINT.

tingle v. shiver, prickle, sting, itch, creep, grow excited, thrill, get goose pimples all over*.

tinker v. try to mend, play with, take apart; see REPAIR.

tint n. tinge, hue, shade, color value, cast, flush, dye, tinct, taint, coloring, glow, pastel color, luminous color, pale hue, tone, tincture, dash, touch, luminosity, color tone, coloration, pigmentation, ground color, complexion; see also COLOR.

tinted a. tinged, painted, touched up; see COLORED.

tiny a. small, miniature, diminutive; see LITTLE 1.

tip n. 1 [The point] apex, peak, top; see POINT 2. 2 [A gratuity] reward, gift, compensation, fee, small change, money, lagniappe, handout; see also PAY 2. 3 [*A bit of informa-

tion] hint, clue, warning; see KNOWLEDGE 1, NEWS 1.

tip *v.* slant, incline, shift; see BEND, LEAN 1, TILT.

tiptop* *a.* superior, prime, choice; see BEST, EXCELLENT.

tire *n. Terms for types of tires include the following:* tubeless, belted, radial, snow, mud, puncture-proof, steel-belted, all-weather, all-terrain, recapped, synthetic, low-pressure, natural rubber, solid rubber, pneumatic, oversize, airplane, motorcycle, bicycle, recap.

tire *v.* **1** [To become exhausted] grow weary, break down, droop, flag, pall, faint, drop, huff and puff*, jade, sink, yawn, collapse, give out, wilt, go stale, poop out*, burn out.—*Ant.* REST, awake, relax. **2** [To make a person exhausted] tax, overtax, harass, fatigue, exhaust, overwork, strain, drain, overstrain, overburden, prostrate, depress, dispirit, pain, vex, worry, distress, deject, dishearten, wear out, run a person ragged, do in*.

tired *a.* fatigued, weary, run-down, exhausted, overworked, overtaxed, wearied, worn, spent, burned out, jaded, wasted, worn-out, drooping, distressed, drowsy, droopy, sleepy, haggard, faint, prostrated, broken-down, drained, consumed, empty, collapsing, all in*, finished, stale, fagged, dog-tired*, dead on one's feet*, pooped*, done in*, done for*, worn to a frazzle*, played out*, tuckered out*, fed up*.—*Ant.* ACTIVE, lively, energetic.

tireless *a.* unwearied, energetic, untiring; see ACTIVE.

tiresome *a.* irksome, wearying, monotonous; see DULL 4.

tissue *n.* **1** [A network] web, mesh, filigree; see NETWORK 2. **2** [Thin fabric] gauze, gossamer, lace; see VEIL, WEB. **3** [Protective layer, especially in living organisms] film, membrane, intercellular substance; see MUSCLE.

title *n.* **1** [A designation] indication, inscription, sign; see NAME 1. **2** [Ownership or evidence of ownship] right, claim, license; see OWNERSHIP. **3** [Mark of rank or dignity] commission, decoration, medal, ribbon, coat of arms, crest, order, authority, privilege, degree; see also EMBLEM. *Titles include the following:* Sir, Madam, Ma'am*, Doctor, Mr., Ms., Mrs., Miss, Reverend, Pastor, Father, Brother, Sister, Monsignor, Bishop, Archbishop, His Holiness, Pope, Cardinal, Patriarch, Rabbi, Imam, Swami, King, Queen, Prince, Princess, Duke, Duchess, Grand Duke, Marquis, Marquess, Marquise, Count, Earl, Countess, Viscount, Viscountess, Baron, Baroness, Dame, Lord, Lady, Sultan, Emperor, Empress, Monsieur, Madame, Mademoiselle, Don, Doña, Herr, Frau, Fräulein, Señor, Señora, Señorita, Signor, Signora, Signorina, General, Colonel, Major, Captain, Lieutenant, Admiral, Commander, Ensign, President, Vice President, Senator, Representative, Congressman, Congresswoman, Congressperson, Speaker, Secretary, Justice, Judge, Governor, Mayor, Professor, Esquire.

to *prep.* **1** [In the direction of] toward, via, into, facing, through, directed toward, traveling to, along the line of. **2** [Indicating position] over, upon, in front of; see ON 1. **3** [Until] till, up to, stopping at; see UNTIL. **4** [So that] in order to, intending to, that one may, for the purpose of. **5** [Indicating degree] up to, down to, as far as, in that degree, to this extent. **6** [Indicating result] becoming, until, back, ending with.

to and fro *a.* seesaw, zigzag, back and forth, backwards and forwards, in and out, up and down, from side to side, off and on, round and round, forward and back.

toast *n.* **1** [A sentiment or person drunk to] pledge, salute, acknowledgment; see HONOR 1. *Invitations for toasts include the following:* here's to you, good luck, lest we forget, your health, *prosit* (German), *skoal* (Scandinavian), *salud* (Spanish), *à votre santé* (French), down the hatch*, here's how*, here's mud in your eye*, here's looking at you*, cheers. **2** [Browned bread] *Varieties of toast include the following:* zwieback, Melba, French, milk, cinnamon; see also BREAD.

toast *v.* **1** [To honor by drinking liquor] drink to, compliment, propose a toast; see DRINK 2, PRAISE 1. **2** [To brown bread] put in a toaster, heat, crisp; see COOK.

tobacco *n. Forms of tobacco include the following:* cigarette, cigar, chewing tobacco, pipe tobacco, snuff, shag, flake, plug, crimp cut, navy cut, cavendish, aromatic, maduro, claro, natural. *Types of tobacco include the following:* Turkish, Oriental, Virginia, Burley, Perique, Latakia, Olor, Cubano, Connecticut Shade.

today *n.* this day, the present, our time, this moment; see also NOW 1.

to-do* *n.* commotion, stir, fuss; see DISORDER, FIGHT 1.

toe *n.* digit, front of the foot, tip of a shoe; see FOOT 2. **—on one's toes*** alert, aware, attentive; see CAREFUL. **—step (or tread) on someone's toes** annoy, offend, disturb; see ANGER.

together *a.* **1** [Jointly] collectively,

unitedly, commonly; see sense 2. **2** [Simultaneously] at the same time, concurrently, coincidentally, concomitantly, contemporaneously, at once, in connection with, at a blow, in unison, at one jump, in sync.

togs* *n.* clothing, outfit, attire; see CLOTHES.

toil *n.* labor, occupation, drudgery; see WORK 2.

toil *v.* sweat, labor, slave; see WORK.

toilet *n.* lavatory, washroom, rest room, men's room, women's room, powder room, gentlemen's room, ladies' room, comfort station, bathroom, bath, latrine, privy, outhouse, little boy's room*, little girl's room*, head*, potty*, can*, pot*, john*.

token *n.* mark, favor, sample; see GIFT 1. —**by the same token** following from this, similarly, thus; see THEREFORE. —**in token of** as evidence of, by way of, as a gesture; see BY 2.

told *a.* recounted, recorded, set down, reported, known, made known, chronicled, revealed, exposed, said, published, revealed, printed, announced, released, described, stated, set forth, included in the official statement, made public property, become common knowledge, related, depicted, enunciated, pronounced, given out, handed down, telegraphed, broadcast, telecast, confessed, admitted, well-known, discovered; see also SPOKEN.—*Ant.* SECRET, concealed, unknown. —**all told** in all, in toto, on the whole; see ALTOGETHER.

tolerable *a.* endurable, sufferable, sustainable; see BEARABLE.

tolerance *n.* **1** [Open-mindedness] concession, liberality, permission, forbearance, indulgence, mercy, compassion, sympathy, empathy, license, sufferance, grace, understanding, sensitivity, charity, altruism, benevolence, humanity, endurance, patience, goodwill; see also KINDNESS 1. **2** [Saturation point] threshold, tolerance level, end; see LIMIT 2.

tolerant *a.* understanding, receptive, sympathetic; see LIBERAL, PATIENT 1.

tolerate *v.* **1** [To allow] permit, consent to, put up with; see ALLOW. **2** [To endure] bear, undergo, abide; see ENDURE 2.

toll *n.* **1** [Charges] duty, fee, customs, exaction, tollage; see also PRICE, TAX. **2** [Loss] casualties, deaths, losses; see DAMAGE 2.

tomb *n.* vault, crypt, mausoleum; see GRAVE.

tombstone *n.* monument, gravestone, headstone, footstone, stone, marker, cross, funerary statue.

tomorrow *n.* the morrow, next day

in the course of time, the future, *mañana* (Spanish); see also DAY 1.

ton *n.* two thousand pounds, short ton, metric ton, long ton, shipping ton, displacement ton, measurement ton, freight ton; see also WEIGHT 1, 2.

tone *n.* **1** [A musical sound] pitch, timbre, resonance; see SOUND 2. **2** [Quality] nature, trend, temper; see CHARACTER 1. **3** [Manner] expression, condition, aspect; see MOOD 1. **4** [A degree of color] hue, tint, coloration; see COLOR.

tone down *v.* subdue, moderate, temper; see SOFTEN.

tongs *n.* pinchers, pliers, tweezers; see UTENSILS.

tongue *n.* **1** [The movable muscle in the mouth] organ of taste, organ of speech, lingua; see MUSCLE, ORGAN 2. *Parts of the tongue used in speech are:* tip, apex, front, center, back. **2** [Speech] talk, utterance, discourse; see LANGUAGE 1. —**hold one's tongue** refrain from speaking, hold back, keep silent; see RESTRAIN. —**on the tip of someone's tongue** forgotten, not quite remembered, not readily recalled; see FAMILIAR, FORGOTTEN.

tongue-tied *a.* **1** [Mute] silent, speechless, voiceless; see DUMB 1, MUTE 1. **2** [Inarticulate] reticent, nervous, inarticulate; see RESERVED 3.

tonight *n.* this evening, this night, later; see NIGHT 1.

too *a.* **1** [Also] as well, likewise, in addition, additionally, moreover, futhermore, further, besides; see also ALSO. **2** [In excess] extremely, excessively, over and above; see BESIDES.

tool *n.* **1** [An implement] utensil, machine, instrument, mechanism, weapon, apparatus, appliance, engine, means, contrivance, gadget; see also DEVICE 1. *Common tools include the following:* can opener, hammer, knife, jack, crank, pulley, wheel, bar, crowbar, lever, sledge, winch, grinder, stapler, clamp, vise, plumb, vise-grip, hex key, Allen wrench, utility knife, box cutter, chisel, plane, screw, brace, bit, file, saw, screwdriver, ax, corkscrew, hatchet, wrench, pliers, drill, sander, router, jimmy. **2** [One who permits himself to be used] accomplice, hireling, dupe; see SERVANT.

tooth *n.* **1** [A dental process] fang, tusk, saber-tooth, ivory, artificial tooth, false tooth, bony appendage. *Human teeth include the following:* incisor, canine, cuspid, eyetooth, bicuspid, premolar, molar, grinder, wisdom tooth; deciduous teeth, baby teeth, milk teeth, permanent teeth.

2 [A toothlike or tooth-shaped object] point, stub, projection; see ROOT 1. —**get (or sink) one's teeth into** become occupied with, involve oneself in, be busy at; see ACT 1. —**tooth and nail** energetically, fervently, forcefully; see EAGERLY, FIERCELY.

top *a.* **1** [Highest] topmost, uppermost, highest, on the upper end; see also HIGHEST. **2** [Best] prime, head, first, among the first; see also BEST 1.

top *n.* **1** [The uppermost portion] peak, summit, crown, head, crest, tip, apex, acme, cap, crowning point, headpiece, capital, pinnacle, zenith, spire; see also HEIGHT.—*Ant.* BOTTOM, lower end, nadir. **2** [A cover] lid, roof, ceiling; see COVER 1. **3** [A spinning toy] spinner, musical top, whistling top; see TOY 1. **4** [The leader] head, captain, chief; see LEADER 2. —**blow one's top*** lose one's temper, become angry, be enraged; see RAGE 1. —**off the top of one's head** speaking offhand, chatting casually, spontaneous; see SPONTANEOUS. —**on top** prosperous, thriving, superior; see SUCCESSFUL.

top *v.* **1** [To remove the top] prune, lop off, trim; see CUT 1. **2** [To exceed] better, beat, excel; see EXCEED. **3** [To apply topping] cover, screen, coat; see PAINT 2. —**top off** finish, end, bring to a conclusion; see COMPLETE.

top-heavy *a.* overweight, unstable, unbalanced; see SHAKY 1.

topic *n.* question, theme, material; see SUBJECT.

topless *a.* almost nude, bare to the waist, exposed; see NAKED 1.

top-level *a.* leading, superior, supreme; see EXCELLENT, IMPORTANT 1.

top-secret *a.* restricted, kept quiet, hush-hush*; see SECRET 1.

topsy-turvy *a.* confused, upside down, disordered; see DISORDERLY 1.

torch *n.* beacon, light, flare; see LIGHT 3.

torment *n.* agony, suffering, misery; see PAIN 1, 2, TORTURE.

torment *v.* mistreat, torture, irritate; see HURT 1.

tormentor *n.* oppressor, persecutor, antagonist; see ENEMY.

torn *a.* ripped, slit, split, severed, lacerated, mutilated, broken, rent, fractured, cracked, slashed, gashed, ruptured, snapped, sliced, burst, cleaved, wrenched, divided, riven, pulled out, impaired, damaged, spoiled; see also RUINED 1.—*Ant.* WHOLE, repaired, fixed.

torrent *n.* overflow, deluge, downpour; see FLOOD, FLOW, STORM.

torrid *a.* blazing, fiery, sweltering; see HOT 1.

torture *n.* pain, anguish, agony, torment, crucifixion, martyrdom, pang, ache, twinge, physical suffering, mental suffering, tribulation; see also CRUELTY.—*Ant.* COMFORT, enjoyment, delight.

torture *v.* annoy, irritate, disturb; see ABUSE, BOTHER 2.

Tory *n.* traditionalist, reactionary, extreme conservative; see CONSERVATIVE.

toss *v.* **1** [To throw easily] hurl, fling, cast; see THROW 1. **2** [To move up and down] bob, buffet, stir, move restlessly, tumble, pitch, roll, heave, sway, flounder, rock, wobble, undulate, swing, rise and fall; see also WAVE 3.

tossup *n.* deadlock, stalemate, draw; see TIE 4.

tot *n.* child, infant, youngster; see BABY.

total *a.* **1** [Whole] entire, inclusive, every; see WHOLE 1. **2** [Complete] utter, gross, thorough; see ABSOLUTE 1.

total *n.* sum, entirety, result; see WHOLE.

total *v.* **1** [To add] figure, calculate, count up, ring up, tag up, sum up, add up; see also ADD 1. **2** [To amount to] consist of, come to, add up to; see AMOUNT TO, EQUAL.

totality *n.* everything, oneness, collectivity; see WHOLE.

totally *a.* entirely, wholly, exclusively; see COMPLETELY.

totem *n.* figure, symbol, crest; see EMBLEM.

totter *v.* shake, rock, careen, quake, tremble, stumble, lurch, stagger, falter, trip, weave, zigzag, reel, rock, roll, walk drunkenly, wobble, waver, hesitate, seesaw, teeter, dodder, crumple, sway, be loose, be weak; see also WAVE 3.

touch *n.* **1** [The tactile sense] feeling, touching, feel, perception, tactility. **2** [Contact] rub, stroke, pat, fondling, rubbing, petting, stroking, licking, handling, graze, scratch, brush, taste, nudge, kiss, peck, embrace, hug, cuddling, caress. **3** [A sensation] sense, impression, pressure; see FEELING 2. **4** [Skill] knack, technique, talent; see ABILITY, METHOD. **5** [A trace] suggestion, scent, inkling; see BIT 1. —**get in touch (with)** call, telephone, write to, contact, wire, telegraph, correspond with, communicate with, reach, keep in contact with, make overtures.

touch *v.* **1** [To be in contact] stroke, graze, rub, nudge, thumb, finger, paw, pat, pet, caress, lick, taste, brush, kiss, glance, sweep, fondle, smooth, massage, sip, partake; see also FEEL 1. **2** [To come into contact with] meet, encounter, reach; see MEET 1. **3** [To relate to] refer to, regard, affect; see CONCERN 1. —**touch on** treat, refer to, mention; see DISCUSS. —**touch up** renew, modify, rework; see REMODEL, REPAIR.

touch-and-go *a.* **1** [Hasty] rapid, casual, superficial; see SHALLOW 2. **2** [Risky] ticklish, hazardous, tricky; see DANGEROUS, UNCERTAIN.

touched *a.* **1** [Having been in slight contact] fingered, nudged, used, brushed, bumped, handled, rubbed, stroked, rearranged, kissed, grazed, licked, tasted, fondled. **2** [Affected] moved, impressed, stirred; see AFFECTED 1.

touching *a.*, *prep.* **1** [Referring to] regarding, in regard to, in reference to; see ABOUT 2. **2** [Affecting] moving, pathetic, tender; see PITIFUL. **3** [Adjacent] tangent, in contact, against; see NEAR 1, NEXT 2.

touchy *a.* **1** [Irritable] ill-humored, testy, sensitive; see IRRITABLE. **2** [Dangerous] harmful, hazardous, risky; see UNSAFE.

tough *a.* **1** [Strong] robust, wiry, mighty; see STRONG 1, 2. **2** [Cohesive] solid, firm, sturdy, hard, hardened, adhesive, leathery, coherent, inseparable, molded, tight, cemented, unbreakable, in one piece, dense, closely packed.—*Ant.* WEAK, fragile, brittle. **3** [Difficult to chew] half-cooked, uncooked, sinewy, indigestible, inedible, fibrous, old, hard as nails, tough as shoeleather*.—*Ant.* SOFT, tender, overcooked. **4** [Difficult] hard, troublesome, laborious; see DIFFICULT 1, SEVERE 1. **5** [Hardy] robust, sound, capable; see HEALTHY. **6** [Rough and cruel] savage, fierce, ferocious; see CRUEL. **7** [*Unfavorable] bad, unfortunate, untimely; see UNFAVORABLE. **8** [*Excellent] fine, terrific*, first-class; see EXCELLENT. —**tough it out*** persevere, persist, endure; see ENDURE 1.

tour *n.* trip, voyage, travel; see JOURNEY.

tour *v.* voyage, vacation, take a trip; see TRAVEL.

tourist *n.* sightseer, vacationist, visitor; see TRAVELER.

tournament *n.* meet, tourney, match; see SPORT 3.

tout* *v.* praise highly, laud, puff; see PROMOTE 1.

tow *v.* haul, pull, drag; see DRAW 1.

toward *a.*, *prep.* to, in the direction of, pointing to, via, on the way to, proceeding, moving, approaching, in relation to, close to, headed for, on the road to; see also NEAR 1.

towel *n.* wiper, drier, absorbent paper, sheet, toweling, napkin,

cloth, rag. *Towels include the following:* linen, cotton, terry, terry cloth, guest, face, Turkish, hand, bath, beach, dish, tea, paper. —**throw in the towel*** admit defeat, give in, surrender; see QUIT 2.

tower *n.* spire, mast, steeple, bell tower, lookout tower, keep, belfry, campanile, turret, radio tower, skyscraper, obelisk, pillar, column, minaret.

tower *v.* look over, extend above, surmount; see OVERLOOK.

town *a.* civic, community, civil; see MUNICIPAL, URBAN.

town *n.* **1** [In the United States, a small collection of dwellings] township, village, hamlet, county seat, municipality, borough, small town, burg*, hick town*. **2** [The people in a city, especially the prominent people] townspeople, inhabitants, society; see POPULATION.

toxic *a.* noxious, virulent, lethal; see DEADLY, POISONOUS.

toy *a.* childish, miniature, small; see LITTLE 1.

toy *n.* **1** [Something designed for amusement] game, plaything, pastime; see DOLL, GAME 1. *Toys include the following:* dolls, games, board games, balls, toy weapons, blocks, jacks, tops, puzzles, models, jump ropes, scooters, wagons, kites, sporting goods, electronic devices, electronic games, bicycles, tricycles, roller skates, rollerblades, marbles, skateboards, hobby horses. **2** [Anything trivial] trifle, bauble, gadget; see KNICKKNACK.

trace *n.* **1** [A very small quantity] indication, fragment, dash, dab, sprinkling, tinge, pinch, taste, crumb, trifle, shred, drop, speck, shade, hint, shadow, nuance, iota, scintilla, particle, jot, suggestion, touch, tittle, suspicion, minimum, smidgen*, snippet, tad, smell, spot; see also BIT 1. **2** [A track] evidence, trail, footprint; see TRACK 2.

trace *v.* **1** [To track] smell out, track down, run down; see TRACK 1. **2** [To draw] sketch, outline, copy; see DRAW 2.

tracing *n.* imitation, reproduction, duplicate; see COPY.

track *n.* **1** [A prepared way] path, course, road; see RAILROAD. **2** [Evidence left in passage] footprint, step, trace, vestige, impression, tire track, mark, footmark, footstep, trail, fingerprint, blood stain, imprint, remnant, record, indication, print, sign, remains, token, symbol, clue, scent, wake. —**keep track of** keep an account of, stay informed about, maintain contact with; see TRACK 1, WATCH. —**lose track of** lose sight of, lose contact with, abandon; see FORGET. —**make tracks*** run away, abandon, depart quickly; see LEAVE 1. —**off the track** deviant, variant, deflected; see MISTAKEN 1. —**the wrong side of the tracks** ghetto, poor side of town, lower class neighborhood; see SLUM.

track *v.* 1 [To follow by evidence] hunt, pursue, smell out, add up, put together, trail, follow, watch, trace, follow the scent, follow a clue, follow footprints, draw an inference, piece together, dog, be hot on the trail of, tail*, shadow. 2 [To dirty with tracks] leave footprints, leave mud, muddy, stain, soil, besmear, spatter, leave a trail of dirt; see also DIRTY.

trade *n.* 1 [Business] commerce, sales, enterprise; see BUSINESS 1. 2 [A craft] occupation, profession, position; see JOB 1. *Common trades include the following:* auto mechanic, boilermaker, baker, barber, butcher, bookbinder, bricklayer, carpenter, construction worker, cook, cabinetmaker, cameraman, dressmaker, electrician, embalmer, engraver, jeweler, locksmith, metallurgist, miner, machinist, optician, painter, plumber, printer, seamstress, shoemaker, tailor, textile worker, technician, toolmaker, welder. 3 [An individual business transaction] deal, barter, contract; see SALE 2.

trade *v.* 1 [To do business] patronize, shop, purchase; see BUY, SELL. 2 [To give one thing for another] barter, swap, give in exchange; see EXCHANGE. —**trade in** turn in, make part of a deal, get rid of; see SELL.

trademark *n.* brand, tag, commercial stamp; see LABEL.

trader *n.* salesman, dealer, merchant; see BUSINESSMAN.

tradesman *n.* storekeeper, retailer, merchant; see BUSINESSMAN.

trade union *n.* union, organized labor, guild; see LABOR 4.

tradition *n.* 1 [The process of preserving orally] folklore, legend, fable; see STORY. 2 [Cultural heritage] ritual, mores, law; see CULTURE 2, CUSTOM.

traditional *a.* folkloric, legendary, mythical, epical, ancestral, unwritten, balladic, told, handed down, anecdotal, proverbial, inherited, folkloristic, old, acknowledged, customary, generally accepted, habitual, widespread, usual, widely used, popular, acceptable, established, fixed, sanctioned, universal, taken for granted, rooted, classical, prescribed, doctrinal, conventional; see also COMMON 1, REGULAR 3.

traffic *n.* 1 [The flow of transport] travel, passage, transportation, flux,

movement, transfer, transit, passenger service, freight shipment, influx. 2 [Dealings] commerce, transactions, exchange; see BUSINESS.

tragedy *n.* 1 [Unhappy fate] lot, bad fortune, misfortune, doom, problem, error, mistake.—*Ant.* HAPPINESS, fortune, success. 2 [A series of tragic events] adversity, affliction, hardship; see DIFFICULTY 1, 2.—*Ant.* SUCCESS, prosperity, good fortune. 3 [An artistic creation climaxed by catastrophe] play, tragic drama, melodrama; see DRAMA, MOVIE, NOVEL.

tragic *a.* catastrophic, fatal, disastrous; see UNFORTUNATE.

trail *n.* trace, tracks, path; see WAY 2.

trail *v.* 1 [To follow] track, trace, follow a scent; see HUNT 1, PURSUE 1. 2 [To lag behind] fall back, loiter, tarry; see WAIT 1.

trailer *n.* house trailer, recreational vehicle, mobile home; see HOME 1.

train *n.* 1 [A sequence] string, chain, succession; see SERIES. 2 [A locomotive and attached cars] transport train, passenger train, freight train, local train, limited, supply train, express train, excursion train, commuter train, troop train, boat train, mail train, bullet train, subway, rapid transit, underground, elevated, el*, electric, diesel, choo-choo*; see also RAILROAD.

train *v.* 1 [To drill] practice, exercise, discipline; see REACH 2. 2 [To educate] instruct, tutor, enlighten; see TEACH. 3 [To toughen oneself] prepare, grow strong, get into practice, reduce, make ready, fit out, equip, qualify, bring up to standard, whip into shape*, work out, get a workout.—*Ant.* WEAKEN, break training, be unfit. 4 [To direct the growth of] rear, lead, discipline, mold, bend, implant, guide, shape, care for, encourage, infuse, imbue, order, bring up, nurture, nurse, prune, weed; see also RAISE 1.—*Ant.* NEGLECT, ignore, disdain. 5 [To aim] bring to bear, level, draw a bead; see AIM.

trained *a.* prepared, qualified, cultured, initiated, skilled, informed, schooled, primed, graduated, disciplined, enlightened; see also EDUCATED.—*Ant.* INEXPERIENCED, raw, untrained.

trainer *n.* teacher, tutor, instructor, coach, manager, mentor, officer, master, boss, handler, pilot, guide, leader.

training *n.* drill, practice, exercise, preparation, instruction, foundation, schooling, discipline, basic principles, groundwork, basic training, coaching, indoctrination, preliminaries, tuneup, buildup*; see also EDUCATION.

trait *n.* habit, manner, peculiarity; see CHARACTERISTIC.

traitor *n.* betrayer, deserter, renegade, Judas, Benedict Arnold, informant, informer, spy, counterspy, agent, double agent, hypocrite, quisling, impostor, plotter, conspirator, turncoat, sneak, doublecrosser*, fink*, rat*, rat fink*, stool pigeon*, two-timer*; see also REBEL.—*Ant.* SUPPORTER, follower, partisan.

traitorous *a.* seditious, disloyal, treacherous; see FALSE 1.

tramp *n.* 1 [Vagrant] hobo, wanderer, bum*; see BEGGAR. 2 [A long walk, often in rough country] hike, excursion, stroll; see WALK 3. 3 [*Prostitute] whore, harlot, slut; see PROSTITUTE.

trample *v.* stamp on, crush, tread on, grind underfoot, injure, squash, bruise, tramp over, overwhelm, defeat.

trance *n.* coma, daze, stupor; see CONFUSION.

tranquil *a.* composed, agreeable, gentle; see SERENE.

tranquilize *v.* calm, pacify, quell; see CALM DOWN, QUIET 1, SOOTHE.

tranquilizer *n.* sleeping pill, depressant, alleviator, palliative, soother, mollifier, calmative, sedative, placebo, pacifier, downer*; see also DRUG, MEDICINE 2.

tranquillity *n.* calmness, peacefulness, serenity; see PEACE 2, 3.

transact *v.* accomplish, carry on, conclude; see BUY, SELL.

transaction *n.* sale, proceeding, deal; see BUSINESS 4.

transcend *v.* rise above, transform, excel; see EXCEED.

transcontinental *a.* trans-American, trans-Siberian, trans-Canadian, trans-European, intracontinental, cross-country.

transcribe *v.* reprint, reproduce, decipher; see COPY.

transcript *n.* record, reprint, reproduction; see COPY.

transfer *n.* 1 [Ticket] token, fare, check; see TICKET 1. 2 [A document providing for a change] new orders, instructions, new assignment; see COMMAND, DIRECTIONS.

transfer *v.* 1 [To carry] transport, convey, shift; see CARRY 1. 2 [To assign] sell, hand over, deliver; see ASSIGN, GIVE 1.

transferred *a.* moved, removed, shifted, transported, relocated, transmitted, turned over, sent, relayed, shipped, mailed, faxed, transplanted, reassigned, transposed, restationed, conveyed, delivered, transmuted; see also SENT.—*Ant.* FIXED, retained, kept.

transform *v.* convert, metamorphose, reconstruct; see ALTER 1.

transformation *n.* 1 [A change] alteration, transmutation, conversion; see CHANGE 1. 2 [A grammatical construction] transform, transformed construction, equivalent grammatical sequence; see ADJECTIVE, PHRASE, SENTENCE 2.

transfusion *n.* dialysis, blood transfusion, transfer; see EXCHANGE 1.

transgress *v.* overstep, rebel, infringe; see DISOBEY.

transgression *n.* misbehavior, trespass, infraction; see CRIME, SIN, VIOLATION.

transgressor *n.* offender, sinner, rebel; see CRIMINAL.

transient *a.* provisional, ephemeral, transitory; see TEMPORARY.

transient *n.* tourist, traveler, visitor, migrant, migrant worker.

transistor *n.* portable radio, pocket radio, receiver; see RADIO 2.

transition *n.* shift, passage, flux, alteration, modification, switch, variation, passing, development, transformation, turn, realignment; see also CHANGE 2.—*Ant.* STABILITY, constancy, durability.

translate *v.* decode, transliterate, interpret, decipher, paraphrase, render, transpose, turn, gloss, put in equivalent terms.

translated *a.* interpreted, adapted, rendered, transliterated, glossed, paraphrased, transposed, reworded, reworked, transferred, rewritten.

translation *n.* transliteration, version, adaptation, rendition, rendering, interpretation, paraphrase, rewording, gloss, reading.

transmission *n.* 1 [The act of transporting] transference, conveyance, carrying; see DELIVERY 1, TRANSPORTATION. 2 [The carrying of sound on radio waves] broadcast, telecast, radiocast; see BROADCASTING. 3 [A mechanism for adapting power] gears, gear box, automatic transmission; see DEVICE 1.

transmit *v.* 1 [To send] dispatch, forward, convey; see SEND 1, 2. 2 [To carry] pass on, transfer, communicate; see SEND 2.

transmitter *n.* antenna, radio tower, wire; see COMMUNICATION, ELECTRONICS.

transparent *a.* 1 [Allowing light to pass through] translucent, lucid, crystalline, gauzy, thin, permeable, pellucid, sheer, see-through, diaphanous, glassy; see also CLEAR 2.—*Ant.* DARK, black, smoky. 2 [Obvious] easily seen, plain, clear; see OBVIOUS 1.

transplant *n.* transplanting, transplantation, graft; see OPERATION 4.

transplant *v.* reset, graft, remove; see ALTER 1.

transport *v.* convey, move, bring; see CARRY 1.

transportation *n.* conveying, conveyance, carrying, hauling, shipping, carting, moving, transferring, truckage, freightage, airlift, transference, transit, passage, a ride, a lift.

transported *a.* conveyed, forwarded, transferred; see MOVED 1.

trap *n.* 1 [A device to catch game or persons] net, box trap, steel trap, spring trap, snare, mousetrap, pit, blind, pitfall, cul-de-sac, deadfall. 2 [A trick] prank, practical joke, snare; see TRICK 1.

trap *v.* ensnare, seduce, fool; see AMBUSH, DECEIVE.

trapped *a.* ambushed, cornered, with one's back to the wall; see CAPTURED.

trash *n.* 1 [Rubbish] garbage, waste, refuse, dregs, filth, litter, debris, dross, sweepings, rubble, odds and ends, stuff, rags, scraps, scrap, excess, scourings, fragments, pieces, shavings, loppings, slash, rakings, slag, parings, rinsings, residue, offal, junk, sediment, leavings, droppings.—*Ant.* MONEY, goods, riches. 2 [Nonsense] drivel, rubbish, senselessness; see NONSENSE 1.

travel *n.* riding, roving, wandering, visiting, rambling, sailing, boating, busing, touring, biking, hiking, cruising, driving, wayfaring, going abroad, seeing the world, sightseeing, voyaging, journeying, trekking, flying, globe-trotting, space travel, rocketing.

travel *v.* tour, cruise, voyage, roam, explore, jet to, rocket to, orbit, go into orbit, take a jet, go by jet, migrate, trek, vacation, motor, visit, traverse, jaunt, wander, junket, journey, adventure, quest, trip, rove, inspect, make an expedition, cross the continent, cross the ocean, encircle the globe, make the grand tour, sail, see the country, go camping, go abroad, take a trip, cover, go walking, go riding, go bicycling, make a train trip, drive, fly, set out, set forth, sightsee; see also WALK 1.

traveled *a.* 1 [*Said of persons*] worldly, cosmopolitan, experienced; see CULTURED. 2 [*Said of roads*] well-used, busy, operating, in use, frequented, widely known, sure, safe, well-trodden, accepted.—*Ant.* ABANDONED, little-used, unexplored.

traveler *n.* voyager, adventurer, tourist, explorer, nomad, wanderer, truant, peddler, roamer, rambler, wayfarer, migrant, excursionist, junketeer, sightseer, straggler, vagabond, vagrant, hobo, tramp,

gypsy, gadabout, itinerant, pilgrim, rover, passenger, commuter, globetrotter.

traveling *a.* passing, en route, on board, shipped, freighted, transported, moving, carried, conveyed, consigned, wandering, touring, roving, on tour, vagrant, migrant, nomadic, wayfaring, itinerant, cruising, excursioning, commuting, driving, flying, sailing, riding, on vacation, migrating, voyaging; see also MOVING 2.

travesty *n.* burlesque, spoof, caricature; see PARODY.

tray *n.* platter, plate, salver; see DISH 1.

treacherous *a.* deceptive, undependable, dangerous, risky, misleading, tricky, false, deceitful, ensnaring, faulty, precarious, unstable, insecure, shaky, slippery, ticklish, difficult, ominous, alarming, menacing.—*Ant.* RELIABLE, dependable, steady.

treachery *n.* faithlessness, disloyalty, betrayal; see DISHONESTY, TREASON.

tread *v.* walk, step, step on; see TRAMPLE.

treason *n.* sedition, seditiousness, disloyalty, perfidy, treachery, seditionary act, seditious act, aid and comfort to the enemy; see also DISHONESTY, DECEPTION, REVOLUTION 2.

treasure *n.* richness, riches, nest egg; see WEALTH.

treasure *v.* prize, value, appreciate, guard, cherish, adore, fancy, like; see also LOVE 1.

treasurer *n.* bursar, cashier, banker; see CLERK.

treasury *n.* exchequer, safe, depository; see BANK 2.

treat *n.* entertainment, surprise, amusement, feast, source of gratification, gift, special dish.

treat *v.* 1 [To deal with a person or thing] negotiate, manage, have to do with, have business with, behave toward, handle, make terms with, act toward, react toward, use, employ, have recourse to.—*Ant.* NEGLECT, ignore, have nothing to do with. 2 [To assist toward a cure] attend, administer, prescribe, dose, operate, nurse, dress, minister to, apply therapy, care for, doctor*; see also HEAL. 3 [To pay for another's entertainment] entertain, indulge, satisfy, amuse, divert, play host to, escort, take, pick up the check*.

treatise *n.* tract, paper, monograph, thesis, study, report, essay.

treatment *n.* 1 [Usage] handling, processing, dealing, approach, execution, procedure, method, manner, proceeding, way, strategy, custom, habit, employment, practice, mode, line, angle. **2** [Assistance toward a cure] diet, operation, medical care, surgery, therapy, remedy, prescription, regimen, hospitalization, doctoring*; see also MEDICINE 2.

treaty *n.* agreement, pact, settlement, covenant, compact, convention, alliance, charter, sanction, bond, understanding, arrangement, bargain, negotiation, truce, cease-fire, deal.

tree *n.* *Trees include the following:* ash, elm, oak, maple, evergreen, birch, tulip, fir, cypress, juniper, spruce, larch, tamarack, pine, cedar, beech, chestnut, buckeye, eucalyptus, hickory, walnut, sycamore, palm, willow, locust, sequoia, redwood, poplar, acacia, cottonwood, dogwood, box elder, apple, cherry, peach, plum, pear, olive, banyan, mahogany, bamboo, ebony, ironwood, bottletree; see also WOOD 1.
—**up a tree*** cornered, in difficulty, trapped; see IN TROUBLE.

trees *n.* wood, woods, windbreak; see FOREST.

trek *v.* hike, migrate, journey; see TRAVEL.

tremble *v.* quiver, shiver, vibrate; see SHAKE 1.

tremendous *a.* huge, great, colossal; see LARGE 1.

tremor *n.* trembling, shaking, shivering; see EARTHQUAKE.

trench *n.* rut, hollow, gully, ravine, depression, gutter, furrow, drainage canal, creek, moat, dike, drain, channel, gorge, gulch, arroyo. *Military trenches include the following:* dugout, earthwork, entrenchment, fortification, breastwork, pillbox, excavation, bunker, machine-gun nest, foxhole, slit trench, moat, tank-trap.

trend *n.* bias, bent, leaning; see INCLINATION 1.

trendy* *a.* stylish, popular, contemporary; see FASHIONABLE.

trespass *v.* encroach, invade, infringe; see MEDDLE 1.

trespasser *n.* encroacher, invader, infringer; see INTRUDER.

trial *a.* tentative, test, preliminary; see EXPERIMENTAL.

trial *n.* **1** [An effort to learn the truth] analysis, test, examination; see EXPERIMENT. **2** [A case at law] suit, lawsuit, fair hearing, hearing, action, case, contest, indictment, legal proceedings, claim, cross-examination, litigation, counterclaim, arraignment, prosecution, citation, court action, judicial contest, seizure, bill of divorce, habeas corpus, court-martial, impeachment. **3** [An ordeal] suffering, misfortune, heavy blow; see DIFFICULTY 1, 2. —**on trial** **1** [In court] in litiga-

tion, up for investigation, at the bar, before the bar, before a judge, before a jury, being tried, contested, appealed, indicted; see also ACCUSED. **2** [Experimental] on a trial basis, for a trial period, on approval; see UNCERTAIN.

triangle *n.* *Triangles include the following:* equilateral, isosceles, right-angled, obtuse-angled, scalene, acute-angled.

triangular *a.* three-cornered, three-sided, triagonal; see ANGULAR.

tribal *a.* tribalistic, group, kindred; see RACIAL.

tribe *n.* primitive group, ethnic group, clan; see RACE 2.

tributary *n.* stream, branch, sidestream; see RIVER.

tribute *n.* applause, recognition, eulogy; see PRAISE 2.

trick *n.* **1** [A deceit] wile, fraud, deception, ruse, cheat, cover, feint, hoax, artifice, decoy, trap, stratagem, intrigue, fabrication, double-dealing, forgery, fake, illusion, invention, subterfuge, distortion, delusion, ambush, snare, blind, evasion, plot, equivocation, concealment, treachery, swindle, feigning, impersonation, pretense, duplicity, falsehood, falsification, perjury, disguise, conspiracy, circumvention, quibble, trickery, beguiling, chicanery, humbug, maneuver, sham, counterfeit, scam*, gyp*, touch*, phoney*, come-on*, fast one*, dodge*, plant*, clip*, sucker deal*, con game*, bluff, shakedown*, sellout*, con*, funny business*, dirty work*, crooked deal, front*, gimmick*; see also LIE.—*Ant.* HONESTY, truth, veracity. **2** [A prank] jest, sport, practical joke; see JOKE. **3** [A practical method or expedient] skill, facility, know-how*; see ABILITY, METHOD.

trick *v.* dupe, outwit, fool; see DECEIVE.

trickle *v.* drip, leak, run; see FLOW.

tricky *a.* **1** [Shrewd] clever, sharp, keen-witted; see INTELLIGENT. **2** [Delicate or difficult] complicated, intricate, critical, touchy, involved, dangerous, demanding, exacting, perplexing, knotty, thorny, complex, unstable, ticklish, catchy, likely to go wrong, hanging by a thread*; see also DIFFICULT 1, 2.—*Ant.* EASY, clearcut, simple.

tricycle *n.* velocipede, trike*, three-wheeler; see VEHICLE.

tried *a.* dependable, proved, used; see USED 1.

trifle *n.* **1** [A small quantity] particle, piece, speck; see BIT 1. **2** [A small degree] jot, eyelash, fraction; see BIT 2. **3** [Something of little importance] triviality, small matter, nothing; see INSIGNIFICANCE.

trifling *a.* petty, small, insignificant; see TRIVIAL, UNIMPORTANT.

trill *n.* warble, quaver, vibrato, tremolo.

trill *v.* quaver, warble, whistle, chirp, twitter; see also SOUND.

trim *a.* 1 [Neat] orderly, tidy, spruce; see CLEAN 1, NEAT 1. 2 [Well-proportioned] shapely, well-designed, streamlined, clean, slim, shipshape, delicate, fit, comely, well-formed, symmetrical, well-made, clean-cut, well-balanced, graceful, well-molded, harmonious, beautiful, classical, compact, smart, built*, buff*; see also HANDSOME.—*Ant.* DISORDERED, shapeless, overweight.

trim *v.* 1 [To cut off excess] prune, shave, lop; see CUT 1. 2 [To adorn] ornament, embellish, deck; see DECORATE. 3 [To prepare for sailing] ballast, rig, outfit; see SAIL 1.

trimming *n.* 1 [Ornamentation] accessory, frill, tassel; see DECORATION 2. 2 [The act of cutting off excess] shearing, lopping off, shaving off; see REDUCTION 1.

trinity *n.* trio, trilogy, triplet, triplicate, threesome, triad, troika, the Godhead; Father, Son, and Holy Spirit; the Triune God, Trinity; see also GOD 1.

trinket *n.* gadget, novelty, bauble; see JEWEL, JEWELRY.

trio *n.* 1 [A combination of three] threesome, triangle, triplet; see TRINITY. 2 [Three musicians performing together] string trio, vocal trio, piano trio; see BAND 3.

trip *n.* 1 [A journey] voyage, excursion, tour; see JOURNEY. 2 [A psychedelic experience] hallucinations, LSD trip, being turned on*; see DRUG.

trip *v.* 1 [To stumble] tumble, slip, lurch, slide, founder, fall, pitch, fall over, slip upon, plunge, sprawl, topple, go head over heels.—*Ant.* ARISE, ascend, get up. 2 [To cause to stumble] block, hinder, bind, tackle, overthrow, push, send headlong, kick, shove, mislead.—*Ant.* HELP, pick up, give a helping hand.

triple *a.* in triplicate, by three, threefold; see THREE.

trite *a.* hackneyed, typical, stereotyped; see COMMON 1, DULL 4.

triumph *n.* conquest, achievement, success; see VICTORY.

triumphant *a.* victorious, successful, lucky, winning, conquering, in the lead, triumphal, jubilant, dominant, laurel-crowned, champion, championship, prize-winning, unbeaten, topseeded, out front, triumphing, elated, in the ascendancy, with flying colors.—*Ant.* BEATEN, defeated, overwhelmed.

trivial *a.* petty, trifling, small, superficial, piddling, wee, little, frivolous, insignificant, irrelevant, unimportant, nugatory, skin-deep, meaningless, mean, diminutive, slight, of no account, of no consequence, scanty, meager, inappreciable, microscopic, dribbling, nonessential, flimsy, inconsiderable, vanishing, momentary, immaterial, indifferent, beside the point, minute, inessential, paltry, inferior, minor, small-minded, beggarly, useless, inconsequential, worthless, mangy, trashy, pitiful, of little moment, dinky*, small-town*, cutting no ice*, cut and dried; see also SHALLOW 2.—*Ant.* IMPORTANT, great, serious.

troop *n.* flock, collection, company, troupe, band, assemblage; see also GATHERING.

troops *n.* soldiers, armed forces, fighting men; see ARMY 1.

trophy *n.* citation, medal, cup; see PRIZE.

tropic *a.* 1 [Related to the tropics] tropical, equatorial, jungle; see HOT 1. 2 [Hot] thermal, torrid, burning; see HOT 1.

tropics *n.* torrid zone, equator, Equatorial Africa; South America, Latin America, Caribbean, Amazon, the Congo, the Pacific Islands, jungles; see also JUNGLE.

trot *v.* lope, jog, amble; see RUN 2.

trouble *n.* 1 [A person or thing causing trouble] annoyance, difficult situation, bother, bind, hindrance, difficulty, task, puzzle, predicament, plight, problem, fear, worry, concern, inconvenience, nuisance, disturbance, calamity, catastrophe, disaster, crisis, delay, quarrel, dispute, bad news, affliction, intrusion, irritation, trial, pain, ordeal, discomfort, injury, adversity, hang-up*, case, gossip, problem child, meddler, pest, tease, tiresome person, inconsiderate person, intruder, troublemaker, fly in the ointment, headache*, brat, holy terror*, peck of trouble*, hassle*.—*Ant.* HELP, aid, comfort. 2 [Illness] ailment, malady, affliction; see ILLNESS 1, 2. 3 [Civil disorder] riot, turmoil, strife; see DISTURBANCE 2. 4 [A quarrel] argument, feud, bickering; see DISPUTE, FIGHT 1. —**in trouble** in a quandary, in difficulty, in a predicament, in bad*, in hot water*, in for it*, in the doghouse*, in a jam*, out on a limb*; see also TROUBLED.

trouble *v.* 1 [To disturb] disconcert, annoy, irritate; see BOTHER 2, DISTURB. 2 [To take care] be concerned with, make an effort, take pains; see BOTHER 1.

troubled *a.* disturbed, agitated, grieved, apprehensive, pained, anxious, perplexed, afflicted, confused, puzzled, overwrought, aggravated*, uptight*, bothered, harassed, vexed, plagued, teased, annoyed, concerned, uneasy, discomposed, harried, careworn, mortified, badgered, baited, inconvenienced, put out, upset, flustered, tortured, goaded, irritated, displeased, unhappy, tried, roused, disconcerted, pursued, chafed, ragged, galled, rubbed the wrong way, tired, molested, crossed, thwarted, distressed, wounded, sickened, restless, irked, pestered, heckled, persecuted, frightened, alarmed, terrified, scared, anguished, harrowed, tormented, provoked, stung, ruffled, fretting, perturbed, afraid, shaky, shaken, fearful, unsettled, suspicious, in turmoil, full of misgivings, dreading, bugged*, in a quandary, in a stew, on pins and needles*, all hot and bothered*, worried stiff*, in a tizzy*, burned up*, miffed*, peeved*, riled*, floored*, up a tree*, hung-up*, up the creek without a paddle*.—*Ant*. CALM, at ease, settled.

troublemaker *n*. rogue, knave, recreant; see CRIMINAL.

troublesome *a*. bothersome, difficult, annoying, irritating, oppressive, repressive, distressing, upsetting, painful, dangerous, damaging, disturbing, alarming, vexing.

trough *n*. dip, channel, hollow; see HOLE 2.

trousers *n*. slacks, breeches, pants; see CLOTHES.

trout *n*. Trout include the following: speckled, brook, rainbow, cutthroat, lake, steelhead, brown, golden, tiger, bull, Apache; see also FISH.

trowel *n*. blade, scoop, implement; see TOOL 1.

truant *a*. missing, straying, playing hooky*; see ABSENT.

truce *n*. armistice, cease-fire, lull; see PEACE 1.

truck *n*. carriage, van, lorry, motor vehicle; see also VEHICLE. *Types of trucks include the following:* moving van, police van, laundry truck, pickup truck, delivery truck, freight truck, logging truck, trailer, piggyback trailer, tractor trailer, truck train, cement mixer, refrigerator truck, refrigerated truck, four-wheel drive truck, garbage truck, dump truck, rig, semi*, halftrack, armored personnel carrier, APC.

trudge *v*. plod, step, tread; see WALK 1.

true *a*. **1** [Accurate] precise, verified, proved, certain, certified, definite, checked, exact, correct; see also VALID 1. **2** [Loyal] sure, reliable, trustworthy, faithful, dependable, sincere; see also FAITHFUL, RELI-

ABLE. **3** [Genuine] authentic, virtual, substantial, tangible, actual, pure; see also REAL 2, VALID 2. —**come true** become a fact, be actualized, come about; see DEVELOP 1, HAPPEN 2.

truism *n*. commonplace, self-evident truth, adage; see CLICHÉ, MOTTO, PROVERB.

truly *a*. honestly, exactly, definitely, factually, correctly, accurately, unequivocally, reliably, sincerely, scrupulously, fairly, justly, validly, scientifically, rightfully, righteously, faithfully, worthily, without bias, without prejudice, fairly and squarely*.—*Ant*. WRONGLY, dishonestly, deceptively.

trumped up *a*. falsified, concocted, magnified; see EXAGGERATED, FALSE 2.

trumpet *n*. horn, bugle, cornet; see MUSICAL INSTRUMENT.

trump up *v*. think up, devise, concoct, falsify, present fraudulent evidence, misrepresent; see also LIE 1, DECEIVE.

trunk *n*. **1** [A container for goods] chest, case, foot locker; see CONTAINER. **2** [The torso] body, abdomen, thorax; see BACK 1, STOMACH. **3** [The stem of a tree] column, stock, log; see STALK. **4** [A proboscis] prow, snoot, snout; see NOSE 1.

trust *n*. **1** [Reliance] confidence, dependence, credence; see FAITH 1. **2** [Responsibility] guardianship, liability, account; see DUTY 1. **3** [A large company] monopoly, corporation, institution; see BUSINESS 4. —**in trust** in another's care, held for, reserved; see SAVED 2.

trust *v*. **1** [To believe in] swear by, place confidence in, confide in, esteem, depend upon, expect help from, presume upon, lean on, fall back on, have no doubt, rest assured, be sure about, have no reservations, rely on, put faith in, look to, count on, assume that, presume that, be persuaded by, be convinced, put great stock in, set great store by, bank on*, take at one's word; see also BELIEVE.—*Ant*. DOUBT, mistrust, disbelieve. **2** [To hope] presume, take, imagine; see ASSUME, HOPE. **3** [To place in the protection of another] lend, put in safekeeping, entrust; see sense 1. **4** [To give credit to] advance, lend, loan, let out, grant, confer, let, patronize, aid, give financial aid to.—*Ant*. BORROW, raise money, pawn.

trusted *a*. trustworthy, dependable, reliable, trusty, tried, proved, intimate, close, faithful, loyal, true, staunch, constant, devoted, incorruptible, safe, honorable, honored, inviolable, on the level*, regular*, right, sure-fire*.—*Ant.* DISHONEST, questionable, unreliable.

trustee *n.* guardian, custodian, controller, lawyer, stockholder, guarantor, regent, board member, appointee, administrator, member of the directorate.

trusting *a.* trustful, credulous, confiding, gullible, unsuspecting, easygoing, open, candid, indulgent, obliging, well-meaning, goodnatured, tenderhearted, green; see also NAIVE.—*Ant.* SUSPICIOUS, skeptical, critical.

trustworthiness *n.* integrity, uprightness, loyalty; see HONESTY.

trustworthy *a.* accurate, honest, true; see RELIABLE.

trusty *n.* trusted person, trustworthy convict, prison attendant, privileged prisoner; see also PRISONER.

truth *n.* 1 [Conformity to reality] truthfulness, correctness, sincerity, verity, candor, openness, honesty, fidelity, frankness, revelation, authenticity, exactness, infallibility, precision, perfection, certainty, genuineness, accuracy, fact, the gospel truth*, straight dope*, inside track*, the nitty-gritty*, the facts, the case.—*Ant.* LIE, deception, falsehood. 2 [Integrity] trustworthiness, honor, veracity; see HONESTY. —**in truth** in fact, indeed, really; see TRULY.

truthful *a.* correct, frank, just; see HONEST 1.

truthfully *a.* honestly, honorably, veraciously; see SINCERELY, TRULY.

truthfulness *n.* integrity, frankness, accuracy; see HONESTY.

try *v.* 1 [To endeavor] attempt, undertake, exert oneself, contend, strive, make an effort, risk, have a try at, contest, wrangle, labor, work, aspire, propose, try to reach, do what one can, tackle, venture, struggle for, compete for, speculate, make every effort, put oneself out, vie for, aspire to, attack, make a bid for, beat one's brains*, bear down, shoot at*, shoot for*, drive for, chip away at*, do one's best, make a pass at, go after, go out of the way, do all ·in one's power, buckle down, lift a finger, break an arm*, lay out, do oneself justice, have a go at*, make a go of it*, go all out, leave no stone unturned, move heaven and earth, knock oneself out*, break one's neck*, bust a gut*, take a crack at*, give it a whirl*, fight the good fight*. 2 [To test] assay, investigate, put to the proof; see ANALYZE, EXAMINE. 3 [To conduct a trial] hear a case, examine, decide; see JUDGE. —**try on** fit, have a fitting, try on for size; see WEAR 1. —**try out**

for go out for, audition for, compete; see REHEARSE 3.

trying *a.* troublesome, bothersome, irritating; see DIFFICULT 1, 2.

tryout *n.* test, demonstration, rehearsal; see EXAMINATION 1.

tryst *n.* rendezvous, assignation, union; see APPOINTMENT 2, MEETING 1.

tub *n.* keg, bucket, tank; see CONTAINER.

tubby *a.* plump, beefy, stout; see FAT, SHORT 1.

tube *n.* 1 [A pipe] conduit, hose, test tube, tubing, tunnel, subway; see also PIPE 1. 2 [A metal container] package, holder, squeeze tube; see CONTAINER. 3 [An electronic device] cathode ray tube, picture tube, fluorescent tube; see DEVICE 1, MACHINE.

tuck *n.* crease, folding, pleat; see FOLD.

tuft *n.* clump, cluster, group; see BUNCH.

tug *v.* pull, haul, tow; see DRAW 1.

tuition *n.* fee, cost, expenditure; see PRICE.

tumble *v.* drop, plunge, descend; see FALL 1, TRIP 1.

tumbler *n.* 1 [An acrobat] equilibrist, gymnast, trampolinist; see ACROBAT, ATHLETE. 2 [A glass] goblet, cup, mug; see GLASS.

tumor *n.* neoplasm, growth, cyst; see SWELLING.

tumult *n.* agitation, uproar, turbulence; see CONFUSION, DISTURBANCE 2, FIGHT 1.

tune *n.* melody, ballad, strain; see SONG. —**change one's tune** change one's mind, alter one's actions, be transformed; see ALTER 1. —**sing a different tune** change one's mind, alter one's actions, be transformed; see ALTER 1.

tune *v.* adjust the pitch, attune, put in tune, tune up, tighten the strings, use the tuning fork, set the tune; see also HARMONIZE.

tunnel *n.* hole, burrow, underground passage, cave, passageway, subway, tube, crawl space, crawlway, shaft, mine, pit.

turbulence *n.* disorder, commotion, fracas; see CONFUSION, DISTURBANCE 2, FIGHT 1.

turbulent *a.* riotous, violent, stormy, disturbed, noisy, restless, raging, howling, buffeting, thunderous, tumultuous, excited, passionate, uncontrolled, vehement, roaring, tempestuous, rampant, rowdy, lawless, disorderly, untamed, disordered, chaotic, agitated, fierce, wild, rude, rough, blustering, angry, storming, uproarious, clamorous, mutinous, rebellious, destructive, hard, stern, intense, bitter, fiery, boisterous, perturbed, foaming, shaking, vociferous, demonstrative.—*Ant.* PEACEFUL, tranquil, at ease.

turf *n.* earth, peat, lawn; see GRASS 1.

turkey *n.* turkey cock, turkey hen, tom, tom turkey, bird, fowl, Thanksgiving bird, Christmas bird, gobbler, turkey gobbler, wild turkey, domestic turkey.

turmoil *n.* agitation, turbulence, riot; see CONFUSION, DISTURBANCE 2.

turn *n.* 1 [A revolution] rotation, cycle, circle, round, circulation, pirouette, barrel roll, gyre, gyration, spin, about-face, roll, forward roll, backward roll, somersault, flip, back flip, cartwheel, aerial, turning, circumrotation, spiral; see also REVOLUTION 1. 2 [A bend] curve, winding, twist, wind, hook, shift, angle, corner, fork, branch. 3 [A turning point] climax, crisis, juncture, emergency, critical period, crossing, change, new development, shift, twist. 4 [A shock] fright, jolt, blow; see SURPRISE 1. 5 [An action] deed, accomplishment, service; see HELP 1. 6 [A change in course] curve, detour, deviation, correction, course correction, corner, loop, stem turn, jump turn, telemark, kick turn, spiral, dodge, cut back, zigzag. —**at every turn** in every instance, constantly, consistently; see REGULARLY. —**by turns** taking turns, in succession, alternately; see CONSECUTIVE. —**call the turn** anticipate, predict, foretell; see EXPECT 1. —**take turns** do by turns, do in succession, share; see ALTERNATE 1. —**to a turn** correctly, properly, to the right degree; see PERFECTLY.

turn *v.* 1 [To pivot] revolve, rotate, roll, spin, wheel, whirl, circulate, go around, swivel, round, twist, twirl, gyrate, loop; see also SWING. 2 [To reverse] go back, recoil, change, upset, retrace, face about, turn around, flip, capsize, shift, alter, vary, convert, transform, invert, subvert, return, alternate. 3 [To divert] deflect, veer, turn aside, turn away, sidetrack, swerve, put off, call off, turn off, deviate, dodge, twist, avoid, shift, switch, avert, shy away, redirect, draw aside. 4 [To become] grow into, change into, pass into; see BECOME. 5 [To sour] curdle, acidify, become rancid; see SOUR. 6 [To change direction] swerve, swing, bend, veer, tack, round to, incline, deviate, detour, loop, curve, dodge, cut back, zigzag. 7 [To incline] prefer, be predisposed to, favor; see LEAN 1, TEND 2. 8 [To sprain] strain, bruise, dislocate; see HURT 1. 9 [To nauseate] sicken, make one sick, revolt; see DISGUST. 10 [To bend] curve, twist, fold; see BEND. 11 [To transform] transmute, remake, transpose; see ALTER 1. 12

[To make use of] apply, adapt, utilize; see USE 1. 13 [To point] direct, set, train; see AIM. 14 [To repel] repulse, push back, throw back; see REPEL 1. —**turn about** turn around, pivot, reverse; see TURN 1. —**turn against** revolt, disobey, defy; see OPPOSE 1, 2, REBEL. —**turn aside** avert, deflect, divert; see TURN 3. —**turn back** retrogress, retrograde, revert; see RETURN 1, 2. —**turn down** 1 [To decrease in volume, etc.] hush, lower, curb; see DECREASE 2. 2 [To refuse] reject, decline, rebuff; see REFUSE. —**turn in** 1 [To deliver] hand over, transfer, give up; see GIVE 1. 2 [*To go to bed] lie down, retire, hit the hay*; see REST 1. —**turn into** 1 [To change] transform, alter, transmute; see ALTER 1. 2 [To become changed] be converted, transform, modify; see CHANGE 2. —**turn off** stop, shut off, douse, turn out, log off, halt, close, shut, extinguish, shut down, kill the light*, turn off the juice*, cut the motor*, hit the switch*. —**turn on** 1 [To start the operation of] set going, switch on, set in motion, log on, put in gear; see also BEGIN 1. 2 [To attack] strike, assail, assault; see ATTACK. 3 [*To take drugs] smoke marijuana, get high*, take a trip*, smoke pot*, get stoned*, freak out*, blow pot*, trip out*, get wasted*. 4 [*To arouse] titillate, stimulate, stir up; see EXCITE. 5 [To depend on or upon] hinge on, be dependent on, be based on; see DEPEND ON 2. —**turn out** 1 [To stop the operation of] extinguish, shut off, stop; see TURN OFF. 2 [To dismiss] discharge, evict, send away; see DISMISS, OUST. 3 [To produce] make, put out, build; see MANUFACTURE, PRODUCE 2. 4 [To finish] end, complete, perfect; see ACHIEVE. —**turn over** 1 [To invert] overturn, reverse, subvert; see UPSET 1. 2 [To transfer] hand over, give over, deliver; see ASSIGN, GIVE 1. —**turn to** 1 [To rely upon] confide, appeal to, depend upon; see TRUST 1. 2 [To start] start to work, become interested in, take up; see BEGIN 1. —**turn up** 1 [To find] bring to light, detect, come across; see DISCOVER, FIND. 2 [To arrive] enter, come, roll in; see ARRIVE. 3 [To increase the volume, etc.] amplify, augment, boost; see INCREASE, STRENGTHEN.

turncoat *n.* traitor, renegade, betrayer, defector; see also DESERTER, TRAITOR.

turned *a.* 1 [Revolved] rotated, rounded, circled, circulated, spun, rolled, whirled, gyrated, set going. 2 [Deflected] switched, twisted, dodged, avoided, shied away from, shifted, shunted, changed.

turning *a.* spinning, twisting, shifting, whirling, rotating, revolving, bending, curving, shunting; see also GROWING, CHANGING.—*Ant.* PERMANENT, static, fixed.

turning *n.* whirling, revolving, rotating; see REVOLUTION 1.

turning point *n.* peak, juncture, culmination; see CLIMAX, CRISIS.

turnout *n.* 1 [Production] output, result, volume; see PRODUCTION 1. 2 [A gathering] assembly, attendance, group; see GATHERING.

tusk *n.* canine tooth, fang, incisor; see TOOTH 1.

tussle *n.* scuffle, struggle, scrap; see FIGHT 1.

tutelage *n.* 1 [Instruction] teaching, tutoring, tutorship, schooling; see also EDUCATION 1. 2 [Care] guardianship, charge, protection; see CUSTODY.

tutor *n.* instructor, tutorial assistant, private tutor; see TEACHER.

tutoring *n.* coaching, training, instruction; see EDUCATION 1.

TV *n.* video, cable, idiot box*; see TELEVISION.

tweak *v.* twitch, squeeze, jerk; see PINCH.

tweezers *n.* forceps, nippers, tongs; see TOOL 1.

twelve *a.* dozen, twelvefold, twelfth; see NUMBER.

twenty *a.* twentieth, vicenary, twentyfold, vicennial.

twice *a.* double, doubly, once and again, over again, once over.

twig *n.* offshoot, limb, sprig; see BRANCH 2.

twilight *n.* dusk, nightfall, gloaming, late afternoon, early evening, sunset, dawn, break of day; see also NIGHT 1.

twin *a.* identical, fellow, twofold, second, accompanying, joint, coupled, matched, copied, duplicating; see also SECOND, TWO.—*Ant.* SINGLE, lone, solitary.

twin *n.* identical twin, fraternal twin, look-alike, double, counterpart, duplicate, copy, doppelgänger.

twine *n.* braid, cord, string; see ROPE.

twinge *v.* twitch, shiver, smart; see TINGLE.

twinkle *v.* shimmer, flicker, sparkle; see SHINE 1.

twinkling *a.* sparkling, glimmering, flashing; see BRIGHT 1.

twirl *v.* spin, rotate, twist; see TURN 1.

twist *v.* wring, wrap, twine, twirl, spin, turn around, wrap around; see also TURN 1.

twisted *a.* 1 [Crooked] contorted, wrenched, bent, knotted, braided, twined, wound, wreathed, writhing, convolute.—*Ant.* STRAIGHT, even, regular. 2 [Confused] erroneous, perplexing, wrongheaded, awry, puzzling, unintelligible, disorganized, tangled, perverted; see also WRONG 2.—*Ant.* CLEAR, simple, logical.

twitch *v.* 1 [To pluck] pull, tug, snatch; see PULL 2. 2 [To jerk] shiver, shudder, have a fit, kick, work, palpitate, beat, twinge, pain.

twitter *n.* sing, chirp, whistle, peep, cheep, coo.

two *a.* twin, dual, binary, both, double, forked, bifid.

two *n.* two of a kind, twins, couple; see PAIR. **—in two** halved, divided, split; see SEPARATED. **—put two and two together** reason, figure out, see the light; see DECIDE.

two-faced *a.* deceitful, hypocritical, Janus-faced; see FALSE 1.

tycoon *n.* magnate, mogul, director; see BUSINESSMAN, EXECUTIVE.

type *n.* 1 [Kind] sort, nature, character; see KIND 2, VARIETY 2. 2 [Representative] representation, sample, example; see MODEL 1, 2. 3 [Letter] symbol, emblem, figure, character, sign; see also LETTER 1. *Styles of types include the following:* Times Roman, Courier, Gothic, Helvetica, Caslon, Goudy, Bembo, Bodoni, Old Style, Century Gothic, Granjon, Garamond, Plantin, Optima, Futura, Perpetua, Frutiger, Gill Sans, Century Schoolbook, Baskerville. *Font types include the following:* standard, lightface, boldface, extrabold, serif, sans serif, roman, italic, oblique, upright, small caps, black letter, monospace, slab serif, cursive, open, extended, condensed, shaded, wide, expanded.

type *v.* 1 [To write using a keyboard] typewrite, copy, transcribe, teletype, input, touchtype, keyboard, input, hunt and peck*. 2 [To classify] categorize, normalize, standardize; see CLASSIFY.

typed *a.* 1 [In typewritten format] typewritten, copied, typed-up, keyboarded, formatted, transcribed; see also PRINTED. 2 [Classified] labeled, characterized, stereotyped, symbolized, classed, sampled, marked, regulated, exemplified, patterned, standardized, stylized, typecast, formalized.

typewritten *a.* written on a typewriter, transcribed, copied; see PRINTED.

typical *a.* characteristic, habitual, usual, representative, symbolic, normal, illustrative, conventional, archetypical, prototypical, stereotypical, ideal, expected, suggestive, standardized, standard, patterned, common, ordinary, average, everyday, regular.—*Ant.* SUPERIOR, exceptional, extraordinary.

typify *v.* exemplify, symbolize, embody; see MEAN 1.

typist *n.* secretary, typewriter operator, office girl, inputter, clerk, clerical worker.

tyrannical *a.* dictatorial, domineering, totalitarian; see ABSOLUTE 2.

tyranny *n.* oppression, cruelty, severity, reign of terror, despotism, absolutism.

tyrant *n.* despot, absolute ruler, dictator; see DICTATOR.

U

ubiquitous *a.* omnipresent, universal, allover; see EVERYWHERE.

ugliness *n.* unsightliness, homeliness, hideousness, repulsiveness, loathsomeness, unseemliness, offensiveness, deformity, bad looks, ill looks, ill-favored countenance, plainness, disfigurement, grim aspect, foulness, horridness, monstrousness, inelegance, frightfulness, fearfulness.—*Ant.* BEAUTY, fairness, attractiveness.

ugly *a.* **1** [Ill-favored] unsightly, loathsome, hideous, homely, repulsive, unseemly, uncomely, bad-looking, deformed, plain, disfigured, monstrous, foul, horrid, frightful, revolting, repellent, unlovely, appalling, haggish, misshapen, misbegotten, grisly, looking a mess*, looking like the devil*, not fit to be seen*.—*Ant.* BEAUTIFUL, handsome, graceful. **2** [Dangerous] pugnacious, quarrelsome, bellicose, rough, cantankerous, violent, vicious, evil, sinister, treacherous, wicked, formidable.—*Ant.* REASONABLE, mild, complaisant.

ukase *n.* decree, proclamation, edict; see JUDGMENT.

ulcer *n.* boil, abscess, infection; see SORE.

ulterior *a.* unstated, undisclosed, not explicit, having a hidden agenda, implied, veiled.

ultimate *a.* final, terminal, latest; see LAST 1.

ultimately *a.* eventually, at last, in the end, sooner or later, as a conclusion, to cap the climax, sequentially, after all, at long last, climactically, at the close, in conclusion, conclusively, in due time, after a while, in after days, presently, by and by; see also FINALLY.—*Ant.* EARLY, in the beginning, at present.

ultimatum *n.* demands, requirements, deadline.

umbrella *n.* parasol, sunshade, beach umbrella; see HAT.

umpire *n.* referee, moderator, mediator; see JUDGE 1.

unable *a.* incapable, powerless, weak, incompetent, unskilled, impotent, not able, inept, incapacitated, inefficacious, helpless, unfitted, inefficient, unqualified, inadequate, ineffectual, inoperative.—*Ant.* ABLE, capable, effective.

unaccompanied *a.* sole, solitary, deserted; see ALONE.

unaccustomed *a.* **1** [Unfamiliar] strange, unknown, unusual; see UNFAMILIAR 1. **2** [Unpracticed] incompetent, unskilled, untrained; see NAIVE.

unacquainted *a.* ignorant, out of touch, unknown; see UNFAMILIAR 1.

unadulterated *a.* uncorrupted, unalloyed, undiluted; see PURE 1.

unaffected *a.* **1** [Genuine] spontaneous, candid, simple; see NATURAL 3. **2** [Uninfluenced] steady, unmoved, unchanged; see CALM 1.

unanimous *a.* united, single, collective, combined, unified, concerted, harmonious, concordant, concurrent, public, popular, undivided, of one accord, agreed, common, communal, shared, universal, accepted, unquestioned, undisputed, uncontested, consonant, consistent, with one voice, homogeneous, accordant, assenting.—*Ant.* DIFFERENT, dissenting, irreconcilable.

unanimously *a.* with one voice, harmoniously, all together, by acclamation, universally, unitedly, singly, collectively, without a dissenting voice, by common consent, by vote, in unison, cooperatively, concurrently, popularly, commonly, undisputedly, consonantly, consistently, in agreement.

unanswered *a.* without reply, unrefuted, not responded to, unnoticed, unchallenged, unquestioned, in doubt, filed, ignored, unsettled, undecided, disputed, moot, debatable, vexed, open, pending, under consideration, undetermined, up in the air, tabled.—*Ant.* DETERMINED, answered, responded to.

unapproachable *a.* withdrawn, hesitant, aloof; see DISTANT.

unarmed *a.* weaponless, defenseless, peaceable; see WEAK 5.

unasked *a.* uninvited, not asked, unwelcome; see UNPOPULAR.

unattached *a.* unbound, independent, ungoverned; see FREE 1, 2, 3.

unauthorized *a.* unofficial, unapproved, unlawful; see ILLEGAL.

unavoidable *a.* inescapable, sure, impending; see CERTAIN 2.

unaware *a.* uninformed, oblivious, ignorant, not cognizant, unmindful, unconscious, unknowing, heedless, negligent, careless, insensible, forgetful, unconcerned, blind, deaf, inattentive, without notice, deaf to, caught napping, in a daze, out of it*, not seeing the forest for the trees*.—*Ant.* CONSCIOUS, aware, cognizant.

unbalanced *a.* **1** [Deranged] crazy, unsound, psychotic; see INSANE, TROUBLED. **2** [Unsteady] wobbly, shaky, treacherous; see UNSTABLE 1.

unbearable *a.* intolerable, unacceptable, too much*; see TERRIBLE 2.

unbeaten *a.* victorious, triumphant, winning; see SUCCESSFUL.

unbecoming *a.* unsuitable, unfitted, awkward; see IMPROPER.

unbelievable *a.* beyond belief, incredible, inconceivable, staggering, unimaginable, not to be credited, dubious, doubtful, improbable, questionable, implausible, open to doubt, a bit thick*; see also UNLIKELY.—*Ant.* LIKELY, believable, probable.

unbeliever *n.* atheist, agnostic, heathen; see SKEPTIC.

unbend *v.* become more casual, be informal, relax; see REST 1.

unblemished *a.* spotless, flawless, unmarked; see PERFECT 2.

unborn *a.* embryonic, incipient, expected, future, prospective, potential, latent, anticipated, awaited.

unbound *a.* loose, untied, unfastened; see FREE 1, 2, 3.—*Ant.* BOUND, stapled, tied.

unbreakable *a.* indestructible, durable, everlasting, cast-iron, lasting, unshakeable, solid, firm, unchangeable, invulnerable, incorruptible, resistant, rugged, tight, unyielding.—*Ant.* DAINTY, fragile, brittle.

unbridled *a.* unrestrained, uncontrolled, unchecked; see UNRULY.

unbroken *a.* **1** [Whole] entire, intact, unimpaired; see WHOLE 2. **2** [Continuous] uninterrupted, continuous, even; see REGULAR 3, SMOOTH 1, 2.

unburden *v.* **1** [To unload] dump, dispose of, relinquish; see LIGHTEN, RELIEVE. **2** [To reveal] disclose, confess, divulge; see ADMIT 2.

unbutton *v.* undo, open up, unfasten; see OPEN 2.

uncalled-for *a.* unjustified, redundant, not needed; see UNNECESSARY.

uncanny *a.* weird, unnatural, supernatural, preternatural, superhuman, ghostly, inexplicable, strange, odd, mystifying, incredible, mysterious, magical, devilish; see also MAGIC.

uncertain *a.* undecided, undetermined, unsettled, doubtful, changeable, unpredictable, improbable, unlikely, unfixed, unsure, indeterminate, haphazard, random, chance, casual, provisional, contingent, alterable, subject to change, possible, vague, conjectural, questionable, problematic, suppositional, hypothetical, theoretical, open to question, equivocal, perplexing, debatable, dubious, indefinite, unascertained, ambiguous, unresolved, debated, conjecturable, unknown, unannounced, imprecise, in abeyance, up in the air, in doubt.

uncertainty *n.* **1** [The mental state of being uncertain] perplexity, doubt, puzzlement, quandary, mystification, indecision, ambivalence.—*Ant.* BELIEF, certainty, decision. **2** [The state of being undetermined or unknown] contingency, questionableness, obscurity, vagueness, ambiguity, difficulty, incoherence, intricacy, involvement, darkness, inconclusiveness, indeterminateness, improbability, low probability, unlikelihood, conjecturability; see also DOUBT.—*Ant.* DETERMINATION, sureness, necessity. **3** [That which is not determined or not known] chance, mutability, change, unpredictability, possibility, emergence, contingency, blind spot, puzzle, enigma, question, guesswork, conjecture, dilemma, blank, vacancy, maze, theory, risk, leap in the dark.—*Ant.* TRUTH, fact, matter of record.

unchanged *a.* unaltered, the same, unmoved, constant, steady, fixed, continuing, stable, permanent, durable, unvarying, eternal, invariable, consistent, persistent, firm, unvaried, resolute, perpetual, continuous, maintained, uninterrupted, fast.—*Ant.* CHANGED, altered, modified.

uncivilized *a.* barbarous, uncontrolled, barbarian; see PRIMITIVE 3.

unclassified *a.* not classified, disordered, out of order; see CONFUSED 2, UNKNOWN 1.

uncle *n.* father's brother, mother's brother, elder; see RELATIVE.

unclean *a.* soiled, sullied, stained, spotted, filthy, bedraggled, smeared, befouled, nasty, grimy, polluted, rank, unhealthful, defiled, muddy, stinking, fetid, rotten, vile, decayed, contaminated, tainted, rancid, putrid, putrescent, moldy, germy, musty, mildewed, besmirched, smirched, filmed over, bleary, dusty, sooty, smudgy, scurvy, scurfy, clogged, slimy, mucky, tarnished, murky, smudged, daubed, blurred, spattered; see also DIRTY 1, IMPURE 1.—Ant. CLEAN, pure, white.

uncomfortable a. 1 [Troubled in body or mind] distressed, ill at ease, uneasy, nervous, disturbed, pained, miserable, wretched, restless, annoyed, angry, in pain, smarting, suffering, upset, vexed, on pins and needles, weary, tired, fatigued, exhausted, strained, worn, aching, sore, galled, stiff, chafed, cramped, agonized, hurt, anguished.—Ant. QUIET, rested, happy. 2 [Causing discomfort] ill-fitting, tight, constrictive, binding, chafing, abrasive, piercing, awkward, annoying, irritating, distressful, galling, wearisome, difficult, hard, thorny, troublesome, harsh, grievous, dolorous, bitter, excruciating, afflictive, distressing, torturing, painful, agonizing, disagreeable.—Ant. EASY, pleasant, grateful.

uncomfortably a. distressfully, uneasily, dolefully, agonizingly, painfully, miserably, wretchedly, restlessly, sadly, fretfully, annoyingly, disturbingly, awkwardly, irritatingly, troublesomely, harshly, grievously, bitterly, poignantly, sharply, keenly, excruciatingly, disagreeably, unhappily, dismally, in anguish.

uncommitted a. 1 [Neutral] unpledged, unaffiliated, free; see NEUTRAL 1. 2 [Reserved] evasive, reticent, shy; see WITHDRAWN.

uncommon a. unusual, out of the ordinary, different, extraordinary, unheard of, unique, rare, exceptional, out-of-the-way, strange, exotic, arcane, remarkable, startling, surprising, fantastic, unaccustomed, unfamiliar, freakish, irregular, uncustomary, unconventional, unorthodox, abnormal, aberrant, peculiar, odd, bizarre, eccentric, original, prodigious, fabulous, monstrous, wonderful, unaccountable, noteworthy, curious, queer, unparalleled, outlandish, extreme.—Ant. COMMON, usual, ordinary.

uncommunicative a. reticent, silent, evasive; see QUIET, RESERVED.

uncompromising a. strong, inflexible, determined; see FIRM 1.

unconcern n. apathy, aloofness, coldness; see INDIFFERENCE.

unconcerned a. careless, apathetic, inattentive; see NONCHALANT, INDIFFERENT.

unconditional a. positive, definite, absolute, unconstrained, without reserve, outright, final, certain,

complete, entire, whole, total, unrestricted, unqualified, unlimited, actual, thorough, thoroughgoing, genuine, indubitable, assured, determinate, unequivocal, full, categorical, decisive, unmistakable, clear, unquestionable.

unconnected a. 1 [Separate] divided, detached, disconnected; see SEPARATED. 2 [Irrelevant] discrete, unrelated, inapplicable; see IRRELEVANT.

unconscious a. insensible, swooning, in a state of suspended animation, torpid, lethargic, inanimate, senseless, drowsy, motionless, benumbed, stupefied, numb, inert, paralyzed, palsied, entranced, in a stupor, in a coma, in a trance, raving, out of one's head, out like a light*, knocked out, zonked*, unaware, blind, oblivious.—Ant. CONSCIOUS, vivacious, awake.

unconscious n. [Usually used with "the"] psyche, instinct, motive force; see MEMORY 1, MIND 1.

unconsciously a. abstractedly, mechanically, carelessly, automatically, habitually, by rote, unintentionally, inattentively, heedlessly, without reflection, negligently, disregardfully, thoughtlessly, neglectfully, hurriedly, unthinkingly, without calculation, unguardedly.—Ant. DELIBERATELY, intentionally, willfully.

unconstitutional a. unjust, undemocratic, lawless; see ILLEGAL.

uncontrollable a. ungovernable, stubborn, insurgent; see UNRULY.

uncontrolled a. open, clear, free, unchecked, unhindered, boundless, ungoverned, unregulated, unsuppressed, limitless, unbridled, unfettered, unobstructed, independent, unburdened, unlimited, unbounded, unhampered, uncurbed, unconstrained, unconfined.

unconventional a. novel, individual, different; see UNIQUE, UNUSUAL 2.

uncouth a. awkward, clumsy, crude; see RUDE 1, 2.

uncover v. unseal, uncork, unscrew, pry open, lift the lid, dig up, reveal, tap, lay open, lay bare, bring to light, flush out, ferret out, unclose, fish out, fish up, take the wraps off of; see also OPEN 2.—Ant. CLOSE, cover, seal up.

undamaged a. uninjured, safe, unharmed; see WHOLE 2.

undecided a. undetermined, in the balance, unsettled; see DOUBTFUL, UNCERTAIN.

undefeated a. unbeaten, victorious, winning; see SUCCESSFUL.

undefined a. 1 [Infinite] limitless, boundless, forever; see INFINITE. 2

[Vague] dim, unclear, indistinct; see IRREGULAR 4, OBSCURE 1.

undemonstrative *a.* restrained, distant, stoic; see RESERVED, WITHDRAWN.

undeniable *a.* proven, sound, sure; see ACCURATE 1.

undependable *a.* unsound, careless, inconstant; see IRRESPONSIBLE, UNRELIABLE.

under *a.*, *prep.* **1** [Referring to physical position] on the bottom of, below, covered by, 'neath*, concealed by, held down by, supporting, pinned beneath, on the underside of, pressed down by, beneath.—*Ant.* ABOVE, over, on top of. **2** [Subject to authority] governed by, in the power of, obedient to; see SUBORDINATE. **3** [Included within] belonging to, subsequent to, following; see BELOW 3.

underachiever *n.* slow learner, retarded child, underprivileged person, backward child, misfit, problem child, foreigner, nonnative speaker, foreign-born pupil; see also FOOL.

underage *a.* juvenile, youthful, minor; see YOUNG 1.

underbrush *n.* thicket, brush, brushwood, jungle, second growth, tangle, hedge, cover, scrub, bush; see also FOREST.

underclothes *n.* lingerie, intimate apparel, undies*; see CLOTHES, UNDERWEAR.

undercover *a.* **1** [Secret] hidden, surreptitious, clandestine; see SECRET 3. **2** [Secretly] privately, surreptitiously, stealthily; see SECRETLY.

underdeveloped *a.* backward, retarded, third-world; see WEAK 1, 2, 3, 5.

underdog *n.* loser, underling, low man on the totem pole*; see FAILURE 2, VICTIM.

underestimate *v.* miscalculate, come short of, undervalue, depreciate, underrate, disparage, slight, minimize, think too little of, hold too lightly, not give someone enough credit, make light of, deprecate.

underfoot *a.* **1** [Beneath] down, at bottom, below; see UNDER 1. **2** [In the way] annoying, tiresome, impeding; see DISTURBING.

undergo *v.* sustain, submit to, support, experience, feel, know, be subject to, bear, meet with, endure, go through, encounter, bear up under, put up with, share, withstand.—*Ant.* AVOID, ESCAPE, RESIST.

undergone *a.* sustained, submitted to, supported, experienced, felt, suffered, borne, met with, known, endured, gone through, encountered, put up with, shared, seen, withstood.

underground *a.* **1** [Subterranean] buried, covered, earthed over, under the sod, in the recesses of the earth, hidden from the light of day, gone to earth; see also UNDER 1. **2** [Secret] hidden, undercover, clandestine; see SECRET 3. **3** [Unconventional] experimental, radical, avant-garde; see UNUSUAL 2.

undergrowth *n.* underwood, tangle, scrub; see BRUSH 3.

underhanded *a.* deceptive, sneaky, secretive; see SLY.

underlie *v.* carry, bear, hold up; see HOLD 7.

underline *v.* **1** [Emphasize] stress, mark, indicate; see EMPHASIZE. **2** [To make a line under] underscore, mark, interline, bracket, check off, italicize.

underling *n.* subordinate, hireling, servant, menial, minion, flunky*; see also ASSISTANT.

undermine *v.* impair, threaten, ruin; see WEAKEN 2.

underneath *a.*, *prep.* beneath, below, lower than; see UNDER 1.

undernourished *a.* underfed, mistreated, afflicted with malnutrition; see HUNGRY.

underpass *n.* bridge, culvert, cave; see TUNNEL.

underprivileged *a.* indigent, destitute, educationally handicapped; see POOR 1.

underrate *v.* undervalue, discount, disparage; see UNDERESTIMATE.

undershirt *n.* shirt, T-shirt, turtleneck; see CLOTHES, UNDERWEAR.

underside *n.* underneath, base, root; see BOTTOM, FOUNDATION 2.

understand *v.* **1** [To comprehend] apprehend, fathom, take in, grasp, figure out, seize, identify with, know, perceive, appreciate, follow, master, conceive, be aware of, sense, recognize, grow aware, explain, interpret, see through, learn, find out, see into, catch, note, be conscious of, have cognizance of, realize, discern, read, distinguish, infer, deduce, induce, make out, become alive to, have been around*, experience, have knowledge of, be instructed in, get to the bottom of, get at the root of, penetrate, possess, be informed of, come to one's senses, see the light, make out, register*, savvy*, get the gist of, catch on, get the point of, dig*, read between the lines, be with it*, get the idea, get it*. **2** [To suppose] guess, conjecture, surmise; see ASSUME. **3** [To accept] concede, take for granted, count on; see AGREE.

understandable *a.* comprehensible, conceivable, appreciable, expected, to be expected, natural, normal, regular, making sense, intelligible, in harmony with, readable, reasonable, logical, right, customary, recognizable, justifiable, imaginable, acceptable, apprehensible, credible.

understanding *n.* **1** [The power to understand] sharpness, intelligence, comprehension; see JUDGMENT 1. **2** [The act of comprehending] recognition, knowing, perception; see JUDGMENT 2, THOUGHT 1. **3** [That which comes from understanding] conclusion, knowledge, perception; see BELIEF, OPINION 1. **4** [Informal agreement] meeting of minds, common view, harmony; see AGREEMENT 1. **5** [The intellect] head, brain, mentality; see MIND 1.

understate *v.* undervalue, minimize, lessen; see DECREASE 2, UNDERESTIMATE.

understood *a.* **1** [Comprehended] penetrated, realized, appreciated, known, discovered, grasped, reasoned out, rationalized, explained, experienced, discerned, distinguished, made out, learned, fathomed, searched, explored, analyzed, mastered, conned, taken to heart.—*Ant.* UNKNOWN, overlooked, uncomprehended. **2** [Agreed upon] concerted, ratified, assumed, stipulated, pledged, tacitly agreed upon, engaged for, settled, concluded, fixed upon, endorsed, subscribed to, accepted.

undertake *v.* endeavor, engage, set out, promise, try out, try, begin, offer, set in motion, volunteer, initiate, commit oneself to, embark upon, venture, take upon oneself, answer for, hazard, stake, move, devote oneself to, take up for, take on, set about, go in for, put one's hand to, have one's hands in, have in hand, launch into, address oneself to, enter upon, busy oneself with, tackle, pitch into*, fall into, buckle down, take on, take the plunge, fall to, have a try at, go for in a big way.

undertaken *a.* set in motion, begun, launched, embarked upon, initiated, pushed forward, ventured, started, endeavored, assumed, taken up, promised, offered, volunteered, hazarded, chanced, risked, pledged, tackled, essayed, tried, aimed at, attempted, striven for, engaged for.

undertaker *n.* mortician, funeral director, embalmer, mortuary director.

undertaking *n.* engagement, enterprise, attempt; see ACTION 1, 2.

undertone *n.* buzz, murmur, hum; see WHISPER 1.

undertow *n.* whirlpool, undercurrent, riptide; see FLOW, TIDE.

underwater *a.* submarine, sunken, marine; see UNDER 1.

underwear *n.* undergarments, underclothing, unmentionables*, lingerie, intimate apparel, under-

linen, underclothes, skivvies*; see also CLOTHES. *Types of underwear include the following—men:* shirt, shorts, briefs, drawers, red flannels, union suit, jockey shorts, T-shirt, boxer shorts, long underwear; *women:* underskirt, slip, petticoat, girdle, brassiere, garter belt, braslip, bra, halfslip, corset, corselet, bodice, camisole, *cache-sexe* (French), vest, briefs, foundation garment, panty girdle, panties, pantyhose, shorts, knickers (British), falsies*; *infants:* shirt, drawers, pants, diaper, slip, rubber pants.

underweight *a.* skinny, undersized, puny; see THIN 2.

underworld *n.* **1** [Hell] Hades, Inferno, netherworld; see HELL. **2** [Crime] gangdom, rackets, organized crime; see CRIME.

undesirable *a.* objectionable, shunned, disliked, to be avoided, unwanted, outcast, rejected, defective, disadvantageous, inexpedient, inconvenient, troublesome, annoying, unwished for, repellent, loathed, unsought, dreaded, insufferable, unacceptable, scorned, displeasing, distasteful, loathsome, abominable, obnoxious, unpopular, bothersome, unlikable, unwelcome, unapprovable, useless, inadmissible, unsatisfactory, disagreeable, awkward, embarrassing, unfit.—*Ant.* WELCOME, proper, suitable.

undeveloped *a.* potential, incipient, nascent; see HIDDEN.

undisputed *a.* unchallenged, unquestioned, assured; see CERTAIN 2.

undistinguished *a.* ordinary, commonplace, plain; see COMMON 1, CONVENTIONAL 3, DULL 4.

undisturbed *a.* settled, unruffled, untroubled; see CALM 1, 2.

undivided *a.* **1** [Unified] united, full, collective; see WHOLE. **2** [Undistracted] exclusive, complete, entire; see WHOLE 1.

undo *v.* **1** [To bring to ruin] mar, destroy, ruin, wreck, break, bring to naught, subvert, injure, overthrow, unsettle, turn topsy-turvy, upset, defeat. **2** [To open] untie, unfasten, unbuckle, untangle, unwind, unhook, disengage, loosen.

undoing *n.* ruination, downfall, reversal, destruction, misfortune, calamity, overthrow, trouble, grief, catastrophe, defeat, shipwreck, smash, wrack, subversion, collapse, casualty, accident, mishap, misadventure, misstep, mischance, bad luck, adversity, reverse, blow, trial, affliction, stroke of fate, slip, blunder, fault, omission, difficulty, failure, error, miscalculation, trip, stumble, fumble, blunder, repulse, discouragement, deathblow, last straw.—*Ant.* ADVANTAGE, good omen, godsend.

undone *a.* **1** [Unfinished] left, incomplete, unperformed; see UNFINISHED 1. **2** [Distraught] upset, disturbed, agitated; see TROUBLED. **3** [Ruined] betrayed, destroyed, killed; see DEAD 1, RUINED 1, 2.

undoubtedly *a.* assuredly, without doubt, of course; see UNQUESTION-ABLY.

undress *v.* strip, take off one's clothes, disrobe, dismantle, divest, become naked, peel*, pile out of one's clothes*.—*Ant.* DRESS, put on one's clothes, attire oneself.

undue *a.* improper, illegal, indecorous, unfair, unseemly, unjust, underhanded, sinister, forbidden, excessive, unnecessary, extreme, extravagant, disproportionate, immoderate.—*Ant.* NECESSARY, proper, requisite.

unduly *a.* improperly, excessively, extremely; see UNNECESSARILY.

undying *a.* everlasting, perpetual, deathless; see ETERNAL.

unearned *a.* won, accrued, unmerited; see FREE 4.

unearth *v.* **1** [To disclose] reveal, find, uncover; see LEARN. **2** [To dig up] excavate, exhume, mine; see DIG 1.

unearthly *a.* frightening, ghostly, supernatural; see UNNATURAL 1.

uneasiness *n.* disquiet, restlessness, agitation; see FEAR.

uneasy *a.* unquiet, anxious, fearful, irascible, troubled, harassed, vexed, perturbed, alarmed, upset, afraid, apprehensive, nervous, frightened, shaky, perplexed, agitated, unsettled, suspicious, peevish, irritable, fretful, worried, anguished, in turmoil, disquieted, shaken, full of misgivings, fidgety, jittery, on edge, all nerves, jumpy, snappish, uncomfortable, molested, tormented, in distress.—*Ant.* QUIET, placid, soothed.

uneducated *a.* unschooled, illiterate, untaught; see IGNORANT 2.

unemotional *a.* reticent, apathetic, insensitive; see INDIFFERENT, QUIET.

unemployed *a.* out of work, in the unemployment line, on welfare, receiving charity, jobless, idle, inactive, laid off, loafing, unoccupied, without gainful employment, on the dole, cooling one's heels*, on the shelf.—*Ant.* BUSY, employed, at work.

unending *a.* everlasting, infinite, neverending; see ETERNAL.

unequal *a.* **1** [Not alike] odd, ill-

matched, dissimilar; see UNLIKE. **2** [One-sided] uneven, unbalanced, inequitable; see IRREGULAR 1.

unequaled *a.* unmatched, unrivaled, supreme; see UNIQUE.

unethical *a.* sneaky, immoral, unfair; see DISHONEST, WRONG 1.

uneven *a.* **1** [Rough] bumpy, rugged, jagged; see ROUGH 1. **2** [Irregular] notched, jagged, serrate; see IRREGULAR 4. **3** [Variable] intermittent, spasmodic, fitful; see IRREGULAR 1. **4** [Odd] remaining, leftover, additional; see ODD 4.

unevenly *a.* roughly, intermittently, irregularly, spottily, bumpily, with friction, haphazardly, jumpily, all up and down, fitfully, off an on.

uneventful *a.* routine, monotonous, unexciting, quiet; see also DULL 4, 6.

unexampled *a.* unprecedented, singular, unequaled; see UNIQUE, UNUSUAL 1.

unexpected *a.* unforeseen, surprising, unlooked for, sudden, startling, unpredicted, coming unaware, astonishing, staggering, stunning, electrifying, amazing, not in the cards, not on the books, unanticipated, not bargained for, left out of calculation, wonderful, unprepared for, instantaneous, eye-opening, like a bolt from the blue.—*Ant.* EXPECTED, predicted, foreseen.

unexpectedly *a.* surprisingly, instantaneously, suddenly, startlingly, without warning, like a bolt from the blue; see also QUICKLY.—*Ant.* REGULARLY, according to prediction, as anticipated.

unfair *a.* **1** [Unjust] wrongful, wrong, low, base, injurious, unethical, bad, wicked, culpable, blamable, blameworthy, foul, illegal, inequitable, improper, unsporting, shameful, cruel, shameless, dishonorable, unreasonable, grievous, vicious, vile, undue, unlawful, petty, mean, inexcusable, unjustifiable, immoral, criminal, forbidden, irregular.—*Ant.* FAIR, proper, sporting. **2** [Not in accord with approved trade practices] unethical, criminal, discriminatory; see sense 1.

unfaithful *a.* **1** [Not faithful] false, untrue, deceitful; see UNRELIABLE. **2** [Having broken the marriage vow] adulterous, incontinent, unchaste; see BAD 1.

unfamiliar *a.* **1** [Unacquainted] not introduced, not associated, unknown, not on speaking terms, not versed in, not in the habit of, out of contact with.—*Ant.* FRIENDLY, intimate, acquainted. **2** [Strange] alien, outlandish, exotic, remote, novel, original, different, unusual, extraordinary, unaccustomed, unexplored, uncommon.—*Ant.* COMMON, ordinary, usual.

unfashionable *a.* outmoded, anti-

quated, obsolete; see OLD-FASH-
IONED.

unfasten *v.* unsnap, untie, unlock;
see LOOSEN 1.

unfavorable *a.* untimely, inopportune, unseasonable, adverse,
calamitous, unpropitious, inexpedient, bad, ill-chosen, ill-fated, ill-
suited, ill-timed, unsuitable,
improper, wrong, untoward, inauspicious, unlucky, unfortunate,
regrettable, premature, tardy, late,
unfit, inadvisable, objectionable,
inconvenient, disadvantageous,
damaging, destructive, unseemly,
ill-advised, obstructive, troublesome, embarrassing, awkward,
unpromising.

unfavorably *a.* adversely, negatively, opposingly, oppositely,
antagonistically, conflictingly,
obstructively, malignantly, on the
contrary, counteractively, contrarily, in opposition, in the negative, by turning thumbs down, by
giving the red light; see also
AGAINST 3.

unfinished *a.* 1 [Not completed]
uncompleted, undone, half done,
incomplete, under construction,
unperformed, imperfect, uncon-
cluded, deficient, unexecuted, unaccomplished, in preparation, in the
making, not done, in the rough,
sketchy, tentative, partial, shapeless, formless, unperfected, unfulfilled, undeveloped, unassembled,
defective, found wanting, cut short,
immature, faulty, crude, rough.—
Ant. DONE, completed, perfected. 2
[Without a finish] unpainted, unvar-
nished, bare, raw, rough, crude,
unprotected, uncovered, plain,
undecorated, unadorned.

unfit *a.* 1 [Incompetent] unqualified,
feeble, unpracticed, inexperienced,
weak, impotent, inept, clumsy,
debilitated, incapacitated, badly
qualified, incompetent, unable,
unprepared, ineffective, unapt.—
Ant. ABLE, fit, effective. 2 [Unsuit-
able] ill-adapted, improper, wrong,
ill-advised, unlikely, unpromising,
inexpedient, inappropriate, inapplicable, useless, valueless, mistaken,
incorrect, inadequate, flimsy.—*Ant.*
FIT, suitable, correct.

unfold *v.* shake out, straighten,
release, display, unwind, spread
out, uncurl, unwrap, reel out,
unbend, open, flatten, loosen,
unroll.—*Ant.* FOLD, roll, lap.

unforeseen *a.* surprising, abrupt,
sudden; see UNEXPECTED.

unforgettable *a.* notable, exceptional, extraordinary; see IMPRES-
SIVE.

unforgivable *a.* inexcusable, unpardonable, unjustifiable, indefensible,
inexpiable; see also WRONG 1.

unfortunate *a.* unlucky, luckless,

unhappy, afflicted, troubled,
stricken, unsuccessful, without success, burdened, pained, not prosperous, in adverse circumstances, broken, shattered, ill-fated, on the road
to ruin, in a desperate plight,
ruined, out of luck, in a bad way,
jinxed*, snakebit*, behind the eight
ball*, gone to the dogs*, down on
one's luck; see also SAD 1.—*Ant.*
HAPPY, lucky, prosperous.

unfortunately *a.* unluckily, unhappily, miserably, sadly, grievously,
disastrously, dismally, calami-
tously, badly, sickeningly, discouragingly, catastrophically, horribly,
if worst comes to worst.—*Ant.* HAP-
PILY, favorably, prosperously.

unfounded *a.* baseless, unproven,
groundless; see UNTRUE.

unfriendly *a.* 1 [Hostile] opposed,
alienated, ill-disposed, against,
opposite, contrary, warlike, bellicose, competitive, conflicting,
antagonistic, estranged, at variance,
irreconcilable, not on speaking
terms, turned against, with a chip
on one's shoulder*.—*Ant.* FRIENDLY,
intimate, approving. 2 [Lacking
friendly qualities] grouchy, bearish,
surly, misanthropic, gruff, ill-disposed, envious, uncharitable, faultfinding, combative, quarrelsome,
grudging, malignant, spiteful, malicious, vengeful, resentful, hateful,
peevish, aloof, unsociable, querulous, suspicious, sour.—*Ant.* GENER-
OUS, frank, open.

ungainly *a.* clumsy, gawky, inexpert;
see AWKWARD, RUDE 1.

ungodly* *a.* dreadful, atrocious,
immoral; see BAD 1.

ungovernable *a.* unmanageable,
wild, uncontrollable; see UNRULY.

ungracious *a.* unpleasant, discourteous, impolite; see RUDE 1, 2.

ungrateful *a.* thankless, selfish,
lacking in appreciation, grasping,
demanding, forgetful, unmindful,
heedless, careless, insensible, dissatisfied, grumbling, looking a gift
horse in the mouth, faultfinding,
oblivious.—*Ant.* THANKFUL, grateful, obliged.

unguarded *a.* thoughtless, frank,
careless; see CARELESS.

unhandy *a.* awkward, ill-arranged,
unwieldy, ill-contrived, clumsy; see
also TROUBLESOME.

unhappily *a.* regrettably, lamen-
tably, unluckily; see UNFORTU-
NATELY.

unhappiness *n.* sorrow, woe, sadness; see DEPRESSION 2, GRIEF.

unhappy *a.* 1 [Sad] miserable, sorrowful, wretched; see TROUBLED. 2
[Unfortunate] afflicted, troubled, in
a desperate plight; see UNFORTU-
NATE.

unharmed *a.* unhurt, uninjured, intact; see SAFE 1, WHOLE 2.

unhealthy *a.* sickly, sick, in a decline, in ill health, infirm, delicate, feeble, shaky, undernourished, rickety, spindling, ailing, weak, rundown, debilitated.—*Ant.* HEALTHY, robust, hale.

unheard *a.* noiseless, soundless, hushed; see QUIET.

unheard-of *a.* unprecedented, unique, new; see UNKNOWN 1.

unhinge *v.* **1** [To detach] dislodge, disjoint, disunite; see REMOVE 1. **2** [To upset] unbalance, disorder, derange; see UPSET 1.

unhurried *a.* leisurely, deliberate, nonchalant; see SLOW 1.

unhurt *a.* uninjured, all right, whole; see SAFE 1.

unidentified *a.* unnamed, nameless, not known; see UNKNOWN 1, 2.

unified *a.* made one, united, joined, combined, concerted, synthesized, amalgamated, conjoined, incorporated, blended, identified, coalesced, federated, centralized, intertwined, consolidated, associated, cemented, coupled, allied, wedded, married, merged, confederated.—*Ant.* SEPARATED, distinct, disjoined.

uniform *a.* **1** [Even] symmetrical, smooth, straight; see REGULAR 3. **2** [Alike] equal, well-matched, similar; see ALIKE.

uniform *n.* costume, suit, dress; see CLOTHES.

uniformity *n.* **1** [Regularity] sameness, steadiness, evenness; see REGULARITY. **2** [Harmony] unity, accord, concord; see AGREEMENT 1.

uniformly *a.* without exception, with great regularity, consistently; see EVENLY 2, REGULARLY.

unify *v.* consolidate, ally, conjoin; see UNITE.

unimaginable *a.* inconceivable, incomprehensible, incredible, unbelievable, unheard-of, indescribable, unthinkable, improbable; see also IMPOSSIBLE.

unimaginative *a.* barren, tedious, usual; see COMMON 1, DULL 4.

unimpeachable *a.* blameless, irreproachable, faultless; see INNOCENT 1, 2, UPRIGHT 2.

unimportant *a.* trifling, inconsiderable, slight, worthless, inconsequential, insignificant, unnecessary, immaterial, indifferent, beside the point, frivolous, useless, of no account, worthless, trivial, paltry, superfluous, fleeting, ephemeral.—*Ant.* IMPORTANT, weighty, great.

uninformed *a.* unenlightened, naive, unacquainted; see IGNORANT 1, 2.

unintentional *a.* unthinking, involuntary, erratic; see AIMLESS.

uninterested *a.* apathetic, impassive, detached; see INDIFFERENT.

uninteresting *a.* tedious, boring, tiresome, dreary, wearisome, prosaic, fatiguing, monotonous, dull, stale, trite, commonplace, irksome, stupid, humdrum, prosy, flat, mundane, insipid, unentertaining, soporific, banal.—*Ant.* INTERESTING, exciting, lively.

uninterrupted *a.* unending, continuous, unbroken; see CONSECUTIVE, CONSTANT.

uninvited *a.* unasked, unwanted, not invited; see UNPOPULAR.

union *n.* **1** [The act of joining] unification, junction, meeting, uniting, joining, coupling, embracing, coming together, merging, fusion, mingling, concurrence, symbiosis, amalgamation, confluence, congregation, reconciliation, conciliation, correlation, combination, connection, linking, attachment, coalition, conjunction, consolidation, incorporation, centralization, affiliation, confederation, copulation, coition.—*Ant.* DIVORCE, separation, severance. **2** [A closely knit group] association, federation, society; see ORGANIZATION 2. **3** [A marriage] wedlock, conjugal ties, matrimony, cohabitation, nuptial connection, match, matrimonial affiliation. **4** [A labor union] labor federation, brotherhood, local; see LABOR 4.

Union *n.* [The North in the American Civil War] the Free States, Antislavery States, the Northern States.

unique *a.* single, peerless, matchless, unprecedented, unparalleled, sui generis, novel, individual, sole, unexampled, lone, different, unequaled.—*Ant.* COMMON, frequent, many.

unison *n.* concert, unity, harmony; see UNITY 1.

unit *n.* **1** [A whole] entirety, complement, total, totality, assemblage, assembly, system. **2** [A detail] section, segment, part, fraction, piece, joint, block, square, layer, link, length, digit, member, factor.

unite *v.* join, meet, ally, combine, solidify, harden, strengthen, condense, confederate, couple, affiliate, merge, band together, blend, mix, become one, concentrate, consolidate, entwine, intertwine, grapple, amalgamate, league, band, embody, embrace, copulate, associate, assemble, gather together, conjoin, keep together, tie in, pull together, hang together, join forces, coalesce, fuse, wed, marry, merge, mingle, stick together, stay together.—*Ant.* DIVIDE, separate, part.

united *a.* unified, leagued, combined, affiliated, federal, confederated, integrated, amalgamated, as one, singular, cooperative, consolidated, concerted, congruent, associated, assembled, linked, banded, in partnership; see also ORGANIZED.—*Ant.* SEPARATED, distinct, individual.

United Nations *n.* UN, peace-keeping force, international society, community of nations. *Principal bodies of the United Nations are:* General Assembly, Security Council, Economic and Social Council, Trusteeship Council, International Court of Justice, Secretariat.

unity *n.* 1 [The quality of oneness] homogeneity, homogeneousness, sameness, indivisibility, identity, inseparability, singleness, similarity, uniqueness, integration, universality, all-togetherness, ensemble, uniformity, wholeness; see also WHOLE.—*Ant.* DIFFERENCE, diversity, divorce. 2 [Union] federation, confederation, compact, combination, correspondence, alliance, agreement, concord, identity of purpose, unification, aggregation; see also ORGANIZATION 2. 3 [Harmony] concord, agreement, accord; see HARMONY 1.

universal *a.* 1 [Concerning the universe] cosmic, stellar, celestial, sidereal, astronomical, cosmogonic. 2 [Worldwide] mundane, earthly, terrestrial, sublunary, terrene, human, worldly.—*Ant.* LOCAL, restricted, district. 3 [General] entire, all-embracing, prevalent, customary, usual, whole, sweeping, extensive, comprehensive, total, unlimited, limitless, endless, vast, widespread, catholic, common, regular, undisputed, accepted, unrestricted.—*Ant.* SPECIAL, limited, peculiar.

universally *a.* entirely, prevailingly, comprehensively; see COMPLETELY.

universe *n.* cosmos, creation, the visible world, astral system, universal frame, all created things, everything, nature, the natural world.

university *a.* professional, college, collegiate, advanced, graduate, undergraduate, freshman, sophomore, junior, senior, learned, academic, educational.

university *n.* educational institution, institution of higher learning, multiversity, normal school, state university; see also COLLEGE, SCHOOL 1.

unjust *a.* wrong, inequitable, wrongful; see UNFAIR.

unjustifiable *a.* unallowable, unforgivable, unjust; see WRONG 1.

unjustly *a.* unfairly, dishonestly, unrighteously; see WRONGLY.

unkind *a.* malignant, spiteful, mean, malicious, cruel, curt, indifferent, uncharitable, ungracious, inconsid-

erate, boorish; see also RUDE 1, 2.—*Ant.* KIND, benevolent, helpful.

unknown *a.* 1 [Not known; *said of information*] uncomprehended, unapprehended, undiscovered, untold, unexplained, uninvestigated, unexplored, unheard-of, unperceived, concealed, hidden, unrevealed.—*Ant.* KNOWN, established, understood. 2 [Not known; *said of people*] alien, unfamiliar, not introduced, unheard-of, obscure, foreign, strange, friendless, private, retired, aloof, anonymous, reclusive, secretive, forgotten. 3 [Not known; *said of terrain*] unexplored, far-off, remote, far, distant, foreign, undiscovered, exotic, transoceanic, transmarine, at the far corners of the earth, faraway, unfrequented, untraveled, desolate, desert, unvisited, legendary, strange.

unlawful *a.* forbidden, illicit, outlawed; see ILLEGAL.

unlawfully *a.* illegally, unjustly, unjustifiably; see WRONGLY.

unlearned *a.* unlettered, rude, boorish, uneducated, ignorant, illiterate, clownish, untutored, untaught, unread, doltish, crass, half-taught, ill-bred, half-educated, uninitiated, unversed, uninstructed, unguided, unenlightened, dull, misguided, empty, unaccomplished, backward, lowbrow*.—*Ant.* LEARNED, educated, adept.

unleash *v.* release, unfetter, set free; see FREE.

unless *prep., conj.* saving, without the provision that, if not, except, except that, excepting that.

unlike *a.* dissimilar, different, incongruous, contradictory, hostile, opposed, inconsistent, heterogeneous, diverse, contrasted, conflicting, contrary, disparate, dissonant, discordant, clashing, separate, opposite, divergent, various, variant.—*Ant.* LIKE, similar, correspondent.

unlikely *a.* improbable, unheard-of, incredible, implausible, against the odds, unbelievable, absurd, unconvincing, not likely, scarcely possible, apparently false, contrary to expectation, inconceivable, doubtful, dubious, questionable, extraordinary, marvelous, out of the ordinary, strange.—*Ant.* LIKELY, probable, credible.

unlimited *a.* infinite, limitless, boundless, unending, extensive, universal, unrestricted, unconditional, unfathomable, inexhaustible, unconfined, immense, illimitable, measureless, incalculable, interminable, without number, unfathomed, unsounded, untold, countless, numberless, incomprehensible, immeasurable, endless.

unload v. disburden, discharge, dump, slough, lighten, cast, unpack, relieve, remove cargo, disgorge, empty, deplane, unburden, break bulk.—*Ant.* FILL, load, pack.

unlock v. unbar, unfasten, open the lock; see OPEN 2.

unloved a. disliked, detested, despised; see HATED.

unlucky a. 1 [Unfortunate] luckless, hapless, ill-starred; see UNFORTUNATE. 2 [Unpropitious] ill-chosen, ill-fated, untimely; see UNFAVORABLE.

unmanageable a. uncontrollable, irrepressible, ungovernable; see UNRULY.

unmarried a. celibate, unwed, single, virgin, maiden, eligible, chaste, unwedded, spouseless, footloose and fancy-free.—*Ant.* MARRIED, wed, wedded.

unmistakable a. conspicuous, distinct, evident; see CLEAR 2, OBVIOUS 1.

unmitigated a. out-and-out, complete, unabridged; see ABSOLUTE 1.

unmoved a. 1 [Not moved physically] firm, stable, motionless, static, solid, durable, immovable, firm as a rock, staunch, fast, moveless, statuelike, rooted, steady, immobile, unshaken, changeless, unwavering. 2 [Not moved emotionally] impasssive, stoic, quiet, cold, cool, calm, collected, deliberate, resolute, dispassionate, calculating, unaffected, unemotional, indifferent, judicious, unflinching, nerveless, cool as a cucumber.

unnatural a. 1 [Contrary to nature] monstrous, phenomenal, malformed, unaccountable, abnormal, perverted, abominable, preposterous, marvelous, uncanny, wonderful, strange, incredible, sublime, freakish, unconforming, inhuman, outrageous, unorthodox, miraculous, contrary to known laws.—*Ant.* COMMON, ordinary, usual. 2 [Artificial] synthetic, imitation, manufactured, ersatz, concocted, made-up, fabricated, false, pseudo, mock, spurious, phony*.—*Ant.* NATURAL, occurring, naturally.

unnecessarily a. needlessly, by chance, carelessly, fortuitously, casually, haphazardly, wantonly, accidentally, unessentially, redundantly, inexpediently, uselessly, exorbitantly, superfluously, undesirably, objectionably, disadvantageously, optionally, avoidably, without cause, without reason, gratuitously; see also FOOLISHLY.—*Ant.* NECESSARILY, unavoidably, indispensably.

unnecessary a. needless, fortuitous, casual, chance, haphazard, wanton, accidental, unessential, nonessential, beside the point, irrelevant, futile, extraneous, additional, redundant, useless, exorbitant, superfluous, worthless, undesirable, optional, avoidable, objectionable, disadvantageous, random, noncompulsory, dispensable, adventitious, without compulsion, uncalled-for, gratuitous.—*Ant.* NECESSARY, essential, required.

unnoticed a. unobserved, unseen, unheeded, overlooked, inconspicuous, secret, hidden, passed by, unobtrusive, disregarded, unconsidered, unattended, neglected, unmarked, unremembered, unscrutinized, unremarked, unrecognized, slurred over, uninspected, winked at, glossed over, lost sight of, ignored, in the background, undistinguished, unexamined, unwatched, unlooked at.—*Ant.* SEEN, watched, noticed.

unoccupied a. 1 [Vacant] uninhabited, empty, deserted, unfurnished, void, voided, untenanted.—*Ant.* FULL, inhabited, tenanted. 2 [Idle] loitering, inactive, unemployed; see IDLE.

unofficial a. unsanctioned, off-the-record, without legal force; see INFORMAL.

unopposed a. unchallenged, unrestricted, unhampered; see FREE 1, 2, 3.

unorganized a. chaotic, random, disorganized; see CONFUSED 2.

unorthodox a. unconventional, irregular, eccentric; see UNUSUAL 2.

unpack v. unload, uncrate, unwrap; see REMOVE 1.

unpaid a. 1 [Owed; *said of debts*] due, payable, not discharged, past due, overdue, delinquent, unsettled, unliquidated, undefrayed, outstanding.—*Ant.* PAID, defrayed, discharged. 2 [Working without salary] voluntary, unsalaried, amateur, freewill, donated, contributed.

unpleasant a. 1 [Not pleasing in society] disagreeable, obnoxious, boring; see RUDE 2. 2 [Not pleasing to the senses] repulsive, obnoxious, abhorrent; see OFFENSIVE 2.

unpleasantness n. disturbance, nuisance, bother; see DIFFICULTY 1, 2, TROUBLE 1.

unpopular a. disliked, despised, out of favor, abhorred, loathed, shunned, avoided, ostracized, scorned, detested, unloved, unvalued, uncared-for, obnoxious.—*Ant.* POPULAR, liked, agreeable.

unprecedented a. unparalleled, novel, original; see UNIQUE.

unpredictable a. random, inconstant, variable; see IRREGULAR 1.

unprepared a. unready, unwarned,

unwary, unexpectant, surprised, taken aback, unguarded, unnotified, unadvised, unaware, unsuspecting, taken off guard, napping, in the dark, going off half-cocked.

unproductive *a.* unprolific, impotent, barren; see STERILE 1, 2.

unprofitable *a.* losing, loss-making, in the red, not worth the effort, profitless, costly, unlucrative, unremunerative.—*Ant.* PROFITABLE, gainful, productive.

unpromising *a.* discouraging, unfavorable, adverse; see UNLIKELY.

unprotected *a.* defenseless, unarmed, unguarded; see UNSAFE.

unpublished *a.* unprinted, in manuscript, circulated privately; see UNKNOWN 1.

unqualified *a.* **1** [Absolute] downright, utter, outright; see CERTAIN 2. **2** [Incompetent] inexperienced, unprepared, incapable; see UNFIT.

unquestionable *a.* **1** [Certain] sure, obvious, clear; see CERTAIN 2. **2** [Faultless] superior, unexceptionable, flawless; see EXCELLENT.

unquestionably *a.* certainly, without a doubt, surely, indubitably, indisputably, definitely, reliably, absolutely, positively, incontrovertibly, indeed, assuredly, of course, undoubtedly, undeniably, beyond doubt, beyond a shadow of a doubt, beyond dispute.

unravel *v.* unwind, disengage, undo; see FREE.

unreal *a.* visionary, delusive, deceptive, illusory, imagined, hallucinatory, ideal, dreamlike, insubstantial, nonexistent, fanciful, misleading, fictitious, theoretical, hypothetical, fabulous, notional, whimsical, fantastic; see also UNBELIEVABLE.—*Ant.* REAL, substantial, genuine.

unrealistic *a.* unworkable, not practical, nonsensical; see UNRELIABLE.

unreasonable *a.* **1** [Illogical] irrational, biased, fatuous; see ILLOGICAL. **2** [Immoderate] exorbitant, extravagant, inordinate; see EXTREME. **3** [Senseless] foolish, silly, thoughtless; see STUPID.

unreasonably *a.* illogically, irrationally, stupidly; see FOOLISHLY.

unregulated *a.* uncontrollable, unchecked, chaotic; see UNCONTROLLED.

unrelated *a.* independent, unattached, irrelevant; see SEPARATE.

unrelenting *a.* cruel, merciless, pitiless; see RUTHLESS.

unreliable *a.* undependable, unstable, wavering, deceitful, tricky, shifty, furtive, underhanded, untrue, fickle, giddy, untrustworthy, vacillating, fallible, weak, unpredictable; see also DISHONEST.

unrest *n.* **1** [Lack of mental calm] malaise, distress, discomfort, perturbation, agitation, worry, sorrow, anxiety, grief, trouble, annoyance, tension, ennui, disquiet, soul-searching, irritation, harassment, upset, vexation, chagrin, mortification, perplexity, unease, disease, moodiness, disturbance, bother, dither, tizzy*. **2** [Social or political restlessness] disquiet, agitation, turmoil, strife, disturbance, uproar, debate, contention, bickering, change, altercation, crisis, confusion, disputation, contest, controversy, quarrel, sparring, uncertainty, insurrection, suspicion, dissatisfaction.

unrestricted *a.* allowable, not forbidden, free; see OPEN 3.

unripe *a.* green, tart, immature; see RAW 1.

unrivaled *a.* matchless, unequaled, without peer; see UNIQUE, UNUSUAL 1.

unroll *v.* display, uncover, present; see EXPOSE 1.

unruffled *a.* collected, smooth, serene; see CALM 1, 2.

unruly *a.* uncontrollable, willful, headstrong, forward, violent, impulsive, uncurbed, impetuous, ill-advised, rash, reckless, dashing, heedless, perverse, intractable, recalcitrant, self-assertive, refractory, rebellious, wayward, inexorable, restive, impervious, hidebound, unyielding, incorrigible, intemperate, drunken, lawless, vicious, brawling, unlicensed, rowdy, bawdy, quarrelsome, immovable, unwieldy, resolute, inflexible, forceful, dogged, mulish, fanatic, irrational, unreasonable, irrepressible, high-spirited, impudent, abandoned, profligate, stubborn, obstinate, turbulent, disorderly, self-willed, opinionated, bullheaded, ungovernable, stiff-necked, ornery*, mean, skittish, dangerous.

unsafe *a.* hazardous, perilous, risky, threatening, treacherous, fearsome, unreliable, insecure, venturesome, unstable, alarming, precarious, ticklish, giddy, dizzy, slippery, uncertain, unpromising, shaky, explosive.—*Ant.* SAFE, harmless, proof.

unsaid *a.* unspoken, not expressed, unstated; see QUIET.

unsatisfactory *a.* disappointing, below expectation, displeasing, undesirable, regrettable, disconcerting, disquieting, vexing, distressing, upsetting, disturbing, offensive, unacceptable, disagreeable, unwelcome, shocking, deficient; see also POOR 2.—*Ant.* EXCELLENT, satisfactory, gratifying.

unsavory a. disagreeable, unpleasant, revolting; see OFFENSIVE 2.

unscientific a. irrational, impulsive, inconclusive; see ILLOGICAL.

unscrew v. screw out, unfasten, untwist; see LOOSEN 1.

unscrupulous a. unprincipled, dishonest, wicked; see DISHONEST.

unseal v. free, remove, crack; see OPEN 2.

unseemly a. 1 [In bad taste; said of conduct] improper, unbecoming, inept; see RUDE 1. 2 [In bad taste; said of things] vulgar, tawdry, cheap; see POOR 2.

unseen a. imagined, imaginary, hidden, obscure, unobserved, veiled, occult, sensed, unperceived, unnoticed, unsuspected, curtained, unobtrusive, viewless, invisible, sightless, dark, shrouded, impalpable, imperceptible, inconspicuous, undiscovered, impenetrable, dense.

unselfish a. disinterested, selfless, charitable; see KIND.

unsettle v. disrupt, displace, disarrange; see BOTHER 2, DISTURB.

unsettled a. 1 [Undetermined] undecided, unfixed, unresolved; see UNCERTAIN. 2 [Unstable] confused, agitated, troubled, changing, explosive, shifting, precarious, ticklish, unpredictable, uneasy, unbalanced, perilous, complex, complicated, fluid, kinetic, active, busy, critical.—Ant. SIMPLE, stable, solid.

unshaken a. unmoved, unaffected, undaunted; see FIRM 1.

unsightly a. hideous, deformed, homely; see REPULSIVE 1, UGLY 1.

unskilled a. untrained, uneducated, amateur; see IGNORANT 2.

unsophisticated a. ingenuous, innocent, simple; see INEXPERIENCED, NAIVE.

unsound a. 1 [False] ill-founded, erroneous, incongruous; see ILLOGICAL. 2 [Insecure] weak, unreliable, unbacked; see UNSTABLE 2.

unspeakable a. horrid, unutterable, abominable, horrible, fearful, inexpressible, unimaginable, dreadful, dire, shocking, appalling, frightful, frightening, alarming, beastly, inhuman, calamitous.

unspeakably a. greatly, unbelievably, terribly; see MUCH 1, 2.

unspoiled a. unblemished, spotless, faultless; see PERFECT 2, PURE 2.

unspoken a. tacit, implicit, inferred; see UNDERSTOOD 1.

unstable a. 1 [Having a high center of gravity] unsteady, wavering, unbalanced, giddy, wobbly, wiggly, weaving, shifty, precarious, top-heavy, teetering, shifting, uncertain, rattletrap, beetling, jutting,

lightly balanced.—Ant. FIRM, steady, solid. 2 [Easily disturbed] variable, changeable, giddy, capricious, fluctuating, shifty, volatile, rootless, dizzy, unpredictable, uncertain, sensitive, oversensitive, thin-skinned, timid, delicate.

unsteady a. 1 [Wobbly] wiggly, wavering, shaky, treacherous, unbalanced, top-heavy, leaning, ramshackle, giddy, weaving, heaving, precarious, teetering, uncertain; see also IRREGULAR 1. 2 [Inconstant] changeable, fluctuating, vacillating, variable, uncertain, unfixed, capricious, volatile, unreliable, tricky, shifty, shaky, jerky, fluttering.

unstuck a. unfastened, unglued, rattling; see LOOSE 1.

unsuccessful a. defeated, disappointed, frustrated, aborted, disastrous, unprosperous, unfortunate, unlucky, futile, failing, fruitless, worthless, sterile, bootless, unavailing, ineffectual, ineffective, immature, useless, foiled, shipwrecked, overwhelmed, overpowered, broken, ruined, destroyed, thwarted, crossed, disconcerted, dashed, circumvented, premature, inoperative, of no effect, balked, left holding the sack*, skunked*, stymied, jinxed*, out of luck, stuck*.—Ant. SUCCESSFUL, fortunate, lucky.

unsuitable a. inapt, inadequate, improper, malapropos, disagreeable, discordant, incongruous, inharmonious, incompatible, clashing, out of place, jarring, dissonant, discrepant, irrelevant, uncalled-for, dissident, inappropriate, ill-suited, unseemly, conflicting, opposite, contrary, unbecoming, unfitting, unfit, disparate, disturbing, mismatched, disproportionate, divergent, mismated, inapplicable, unassimilable, inconsistent, intrusive, amiss, interfering, disagreeing, inept, unbefitting, inadmissible, absurd, unseasonable, ill-timed, unfortunate, unsympathetic, not in keeping, out of joint, at odds, at variance, repugnant, out of kilter*, cockeyed*.—Ant. FIT, suitable, proper.

unsung a. slighted, disregarded, unacknowledged; see NEGLECTED.

unsure a. unreliable, hesitant, doubtful; see UNCERTAIN.

unsurpassed a. unequaled, unexcelled, matchless; see UNIQUE.

unsuspecting a. 1 [Gullible] confiding, undoubting, credulous; see TRUSTING. 2 [Naive] innocent, inexperienced, simple; see NAIVE.

unsympathetic a. unmoved, apathetic, cold; see INDIFFERENT.

untangle v. clear up, put in order, disentangle; see ORDER 3.

untaught a. artless, instinctive, innate; see NATURAL 1.

unthinkable *a.* inconceivable, unimaginable, improbable; see UNLIKELY.

unthinking *a.* heedless, rude, inconsiderate; see CARELESS.

untidy *a.* slovenly, unkempt, disorderly; see DIRTY 1.

untie *v.* unlace, unknot, loosen, unfasten; see also LOOSEN 1.

untied *a.* unfastened, slack, unbound; see FREE 2, 3, LOOSE 1.

until *prep.* till, to, between the present and, in anticipation of, prior to, during the time preceding, down to, continuously, before the coming of, in expectation of, as far as; see also UNTO.

untimely *a.* unseasonable, awkward, ill-timed, inauspicious, badly timed, too early, abortive, too late, unpromising, ill-chosen, improper, unseemly, inappropriate, wrong, unfit, disagreeable, mistimed, intrusive, badly calculated, inopportune, out-of-date, malapropos, premature, unlucky, unfavorable, unfortunate, inexpedient, anachronistic.—*Ant.* EARLY, timely, seasonable.

untiring *a.* inexhaustible, powerful, persevering; see STRONG 1.

unto *prep.* to, toward, till, until, contiguous to, against, up to, next to, beside, in the direction of, to the degree of, to the extreme of.

untold *a.* uncounted, countless, unnumbered, many, innumerable, beyond measure, inexpressible, incalculable, undreamed of, staggering, unimaginable, multitudinous, manifold, multiple.

untouchable *a.* taboo, forbidden, denied; see ILLEGAL.

untouched *a.* **1** [Not harmed] intact, whole, secure, unbroken, in good order, unharmed, in good condition, in a good state of preservation, safe and sound, out of danger, shipshape. **2** [Not contaminated] virgin, clear, pure; see CLEAN 1.

untrained *a.* green, raw, novice; see INEXPERIENCED.

untried *a.* untested, uninitiated, new; see INEXPERIENCED.

untroubled *a.* composed, serene, placid; see CALM 1, 2.

untrue *a.* false, misleading, specious, lying, hollow, deceptive, delusive, untrustworthy, deceitful, sham, spurious, incorrect, prevaricating, wrong.

untruth *n.* falsehood, misrepresentation, evasion; see LIE.

untruthful *a.* insincere, crooked, deceitful; see DISHONEST.

untutored *a.* unlearned, uneducated, illiterate; see IGNORANT 2.

unused *a.* **1** [Not used] fresh, available, usable; see NEW 1. **2** [Surplus]

additional, remaining, superfluous; see EXTRA.

unusual *a.* **1** [Remarkable] rare, extraordinary, strange, outstanding, great, uncommon, special, distinguished, prominent, important, noteworthy, awe-inspiring, awesome, unique, fine, unheard-of, unexpected, seldom met with, surprising, superior, astonishing, amazing, prodigious, incredible, inconceivable, atypical, conspicuous, exceptional, eminent, significant, memorable, renowned, refreshing, singular, fabulous, unprecedented, unparalleled, unexampled, unaccountable, stupendous, unaccustomed, wonderful, notable, superior, marvelous, striking, overpowering, electrifying, dazing, fantastic, startling, astounding, indescribable, appalling, stupefying, ineffable, out of sight*.—*Ant.* COMMON, familiar, customary. **2** [Different] unique, extreme, uncommon, particular, exaggerated, distinctive, choice, little-known, out of the ordinary, marked, forward, unconventional, radical, exceptional, peculiar, strange, foreign, unnatural, puzzling, perplexing, confounding, disturbing, novel, advanced, startling, shocking, staggering, uncustomary, breaking with tradition, infrequent, mysterious, mystifying, surprising, extraordinary, unparalleled, deep, profound, aberrant, singular, unorthodox, unconformable, not to be expected, eccentric, unbalanced, unprecedented, inconsistent, individual, original, refreshing, newfangled, new, modern, recent, late, fresh, curious, unfamiliar, irregular, odd, unaccountable, alien, queer, quaint, freakish, bizarre, far-fetched, neurotic, exotic, outlandish, old-fashioned, out-of-the-way, abnormal, irrational, monstrous, anomalous, fearful.—*Ant.* COMMON, ordinary, normal.

unusually *a.* **1** [Not usually] oddly, curiously, peculiarly; see ESPECIALLY 1. **2** [To a marked degree] extraordinarily, remarkably, surprisingly; see VERY.

unveil *v.* uncover, reveal, make known; see EXPOSE 1.

unwanted *a.* undesired, rejected, outcast; see HATED, UNPOPULAR.

unwarranted *a.* unjust, wrong, groundless; see UNFAIR 1.

unwell *a.* ailing, ill, diseased; see SICK.

unwholesome *a.* unhealthful, toxic, dangerous; see POISONOUS.

unwieldy *a.* awkward, clumsy, cumbersome; see HEAVY 1.

unwilling *a.* backward, resistant, reluctant, recalcitrant, unenthusiastic, doubtful, wayward, unready, indisposed, disinclined, averse, opposed, against, contrary, indifferent, indocile, intractable, demurring, shrinking, flinching, hesitating, shy, slack, evasive, loath, shy of, malcontent, slow, remiss, grudging, uncooperative, contrary, against the grain.—*Ant.* READY, willing, eager.

unwillingly *a.* grudgingly, resentfully, involuntarily; see ANGRILY.

unwind *v.* 1 [To undo] separate, loose, undo; see UNWRAP. 2 [To uncoil] untwist, unravel, untwine; see FREE, LOOSEN 2. 3 [To relax] recline, get rid of one's tensions, calm down; see RELAX.

unwise *a.* ill-considered, ill-advised, rash; see STUPID.

unwitting *a.* chance, inadvertent, accidental; see AIMLESS.

unworthy *a.* undeserving, reprehensible, contemptible; see OFFENSIVE 2.

unwrap *v.* untie, undo, unpack, take out of wrappings, unroll, disclose, free, uncover, strip, lay bare, divest, dismantle, peel, husk, shuck, flay, expose, lay open, unclothe, denude.—*Ant.* COVER, wrap, pack.

unwritten *a.* 1 [Oral] unrecorded, vocal, word-of-mouth; see SPOKEN. 2 [Traditional] unsaid, customary, unspoken, generally accepted; see also TRADITIONAL, UNDERSTOOD 2.

unzip *v.* unfasten, undo, free; see OPEN 3.

up *a., prep.* 1 [Situated above] at the top of, at the crest of, at the summit of, at the apex of, nearer the top of, nearer the head of, nearer the source of.—*Ant.* DOWN, nearer the bottom of, farther from the head of. 2 [Moving from the earth] upward, uphill, skyward, heavenward, away from the center of gravity, perpendicularly, into the air, higher, away from the earth. 3 [Expired] lapsed, elapsed, run out, terminated, invalid, ended, come to a term, outdated, exhausted, finished, done. 4 [Happening] under consideration, being scrutinized, moot, live, current, pertinent, timely, relevant, pressing, urgent. 5 [Next] after, in order, prospective; see FOLLOWING. —**up to** 1 [Until] before, preceding, previous to; see UNTIL. 2 [*Doing] occupied with, engaged in, carrying out, dealing with. 3 [*Dependent upon] assigned to, expected of, delegated to, enjoined upon.

up* *v.* elevate, raise up, boost; see INCREASE.

up-and-coming *a.* industrious, prospering, alert; see ACTIVE.

upbringing *n.* rearing, bringing up,

instruction; see CHILDHOOD, TRAINING.

upchuck* *v.* vomit, puke*, toss one's cookies*, barf*, lose one's lunch*.

upcoming *a.* expected, future, imminent; see FORTHCOMING.

update *v.* modernize, bring up to date, refresh; see RENEW 1.

upheaval *n.* outburst, explosion, eruption; see OUTBREAK 1.

upheld *a.* supported, maintained, advanced; see BACKED 2.

uphill *a.* up, toward the summit, toward the crest, skyward, ascending, climbing.—*Ant.* DOWN, downhill, descending.

uphold *v.* 1 [To hold up] brace, buttress, prop; see SUPPORT 1. 2 [To maintain] confirm, sustain, back up; see SUPPORT 2.

upholstery *n.* padding, stuffing, cushioning, pillows, filling.

upkeep *n.* 1 [Maintenance] conservation, subsistence, repair; see CARE 1. 2 [Cost of maintenance] expenses, outlay, expenditure; see PRICE.

upon *a., prep.* 1 [On] on top of, in, attached to, visible on, against, affixed to, above, next to, located at, superimposed on. 2 [At the time of] consequent to, beginning with, at the occurrence of; see SIMULTANEOUS.

upper *a.* top, topmost, uppermost, above, higher, more elevated, loftier, overhead.—*Ant.* UNDER, lower, bottom.

upper-class *a.* well-born, cultivated, genteel; see NOBLE 3.

upper hand *n.* sway, dominion, superiority; see ADVANTAGE.

upright *a.* 1 [Vertical] erect, perpendicular, on end; see STRAIGHT 1. 2 [Honorable] straightforward, honest, fair; see HONEST 1.

uprising *n.* rebellion, upheaval, riot; see REVOLUTION 2.

uproar *n.* babble, confusion, turmoil, ado, hassle, commotion, clamor, disturbance, tumult, din, racket, clatter, hubbub, fracas, clangor, jangle, bustle, bickering, discord, row.

uproarious *a.* noisy, confused, disorderly; see LOUD 2.

uproot *v.* deracinate, pull up, weed out; see REMOVE 1.

upset *a.* disconcerted, amazed, shocked; see CONFUSED 2.

upset *n.* overthrow, destruction, subversion; see DEFEAT.

upset *v.* 1 [To turn over] overturn, upturn, subvert, turn bottom-side up, turn inside out, upend, reverse, keel over, overset, topple, tip over, turn topsy-turvy, overbalance, invert, capsize, tilt, pitch over, overthrow.—*Ant.* STAND, erect, elevate. 2 [To disturb] agitate, fluster, per-

turb; see BOTHER 2. **3** [To beat] conquer, outplay, overpower; see
DEFEAT 2, 3.

upside-down *a.* topsy-turvy, tangled, bottomside up, inverted,
rearend foremost, backward, the
wrong way, wrongside uppermost,
cart-before-the-horse, head over
heels.—*Ant.* STEADY, upright, right
side up.

upstairs *a.* in the upper story, above,
up the steps; see UPPER.

upstairs *n.* the upper story, the penthouse, the rooms above the ground
floor; see FLOOR 2.

upstanding *a.* honorable, upright,
straightforward; see HONEST 1.

upswing *n.* growth, boom, acceleration; see INCREASE.

uptight* *a.* **1** [Troubled] worried,
concerned, apprehensive; see TROU-
BLED. **2** [Cautious] conventional,
old-fashioned, strict; see CONSERVA-
TIVE.

up-to-date *a.* in vogue, in fashion,
fashionable, conventional, stylish,
modern, modernistic, streamlined,
popular, faddish, brand-new, current, up-to-the-minute, au courant,
according to the prevailing taste,
modish, the latest, all the rage,
hip*, trendy*, in*, with-it*.

upturn *n.* upswing, upsurge, recuperation; see IMPROVEMENT 1,
RECOVERY 1, 2.

upturned *a.* tilted, tipped, upside-
down, inclined, sloped, slanted,
oblique, expectant, upward-looking,
turned up, extended.

upward *a.* up, higher, skyward, in
the air, uphill, away from the earth,
up the slope, on an incline, up north.

urban *a.* **1** [Concerning city govern-
ment] city, municipal, metropolitan;
see PUBLIC 2. **2** [Concerning city liv-
ing] big-city, civic, municipal, metropolitan, within the city limits,
inner-city, central-city, downtown,
zoned, planned, business-district,
civil, nonrural, ghetto, shopping,
residential, apartment-dwelling.

urbane *a.* suave, smooth, refined; see
POLITE, CULTURED.

urge *v.* **1** [To present favorably]
favor, further, support; see
APPROVE. **2** [To induce] charge, beg,
plead, adjure, influence, beseech,
implore, ask, command, entreat,
desire, request, press, inveigle, talk
into, incite, spur, move, allure,
tempt, attract, influence, prompt,
instigate, exhort, advise, solicit,
inspire, stimulate, conjure, coax,
wheedle, maneuver, draw, put up
to*, prevail upon.—*Ant.* RESTRAIN,
deter, discourage. **3** [To drive] compel, drive, propel, impel, force,
coerce, constrain, press, push,
make, oblige, goad, prod, spur.—
Ant. DENY, block, withhold.

urged *a.* **1** [Supported] favored, furthered, proposed; see BACKED 2. **2**
[Pressed] begged, charged,
implored, asked, commanded,
entreated, desired, requested, invei-
gled, talked into, incited, moved,
motivated, allured, lured, tempted,
seduced, attracted, influenced,
prompted, instigated, inspired,
advised, solicited, inspired, whipped
up, stimulated, coaxed, wheedled,
maneuvered, put up to*, prevailed
upon, compelled, obliged, propelled,
driven, induced, impelled, coerced,
forced, constrained.

urgency *n.* import, need, seriousness; see IMPORTANCE, NECESSITY 3.

urgent *a.* **1** [Of immediate impor-
tance] pressing, critical, necessary,
compelling, imperative, important,
indispensable, momentous, wanted,
required, called for, demanded,
salient, chief, paramount, essential,
primary, vital, principal, absorbing,
all-absorbing, not to be delayed, crucial, instant, leading, capital, overruling, foremost, exigent, crying. **2**
[Insistent] compelling, persuasive,
imperious, solemn, grave, weighty,
impressive, earnest, importunate,
clamorous, hasty, breathless, precipitate, frantic, impetuous, imperative, convincing, beseeching, seductive, commanding, imploring, eager,
zealous, anxious, enthusiastic, moving, excited, impulsive, vigorous,
overpowering, masterful.

urgently *a.* **1** [Critically] pressingly,
instantly, imperatively, necessarily,
indispensably, crucially, requisitely,
essentially, primarily, capitally. **2**
[Insistently] compellingly, persuasively, solemnly, gravely, weightily,
impressively, earnestly, importu-
nately, clamorously, hastily, breath-
lessly, precipitately, frantically,
impetuously, convincingly, beseech-
ingly, seductively, commandingly,
imploringly, eagerly, anxiously,
zealously, movingly, emotionally,
excitedly, impulsively, compul-
sively, vigorously, irresistibly, overpoweringly, enthusiastically, mas-
terfully.

urinate *v.* go to the restroom, go to
the bathroom, go to the lavatory,
have to go*, excrete, micturate, use
the urinal, use the bedpan, make
water, tinkle*, wizz*, pee*, take a
leak*, piss*.

urn *n.* vessel, jar, amphora, pot, container, funerary urn.

usable *a.* available, at hand, useful,
employable, unused, good, serviceable, applicable, ready, subservient,
helpful, valuable, beneficial, profitable, advantageous, fit, desirable,
efficacious, instrumental, fitting,
conformable, suitable, proper, prac-

tical, convenient.—*Ant.* USELESS, worthless, no good.

usage *n.* 1 [Custom] practice, rule, habit; see USE 1. 2 [Accepted language] good usage, grammatical usage, approved diction; see GRAMMAR, LANGUAGE.

use *n.* 1 [The act of using] practice, employment, application, usage, appliance, effecting, manner, adoption, utilization, manipulation, bringing to bear, management, handling, performance, conduct, recourse, resort, exercise, treatment, method, technique, control, resolution, realization, association.—*Ant.* NEGLECT, disuse, dismissal. 2 [The state of being useful] utility, usefulness, usability, employment, application, value, advantage, excellence, helpfulness, convenience, suitability, expedience, aid, serviceability, merit, profit, practicability, practicality, fitness, subservience, effectiveness, applicability.

use *v.* 1 [To make use of] avail oneself of, employ, put to use, exercise, exert, put forth, utilize, apply, bring to bear, practice, play on, do with, draw on, adopt, take advantage of, make do, accept, work, put in practice, relate, make with, put to work, make shift with.—*Ant.* DISCARD, reject, refuse. 2 [To make a practice of; *now used principally in the past tense*] be accustomed to, practice, adapt, conform, habituate, regulate, suit, familiarize, attune. 3 [To behave toward] deal with, handle, bear oneself toward; see MANAGE 1. **—use up** consume, exhaust, squander; see SPEND, WASTE 1, 2.

used *a.* 1 [Employed] put to use, utilized, applied, adopted, adapted, accepted, put in service, practiced, turned to account.—*Ant.* DISCARDED, rejected, unused. 2 [Accustomed] practiced, customary, suited; see HABITUAL. 3 [Secondhand] cast-off, depreciated, reconditioned; see OLD 2.

useful *a.* valuable, beneficial, serviceable; see HELPFUL 1.

usefulness *n.* application, value, advantage, excellence, convenience, suitability, usability, range, versatility, helpfulness, utility, serviceability, merit, profitableness, fitness, practicality, practicability, propriety, adaptability; see also USE 2.

useless *a.* 1 [Unserviceable] worthless, unusable, ineffectual, expendable, incompetent, of no use, ineffective, inoperate, dysfunctional, counterproductive, inefficient, unprofitable, broken, shot*.—*Ant.* EFFICIENT, usable, operative. 2

[Futile] vain, pointless, fruitless; see HOPELESS.

usher *n.* conductor, guide, usherette, escort, doorman, cicerone, herald, page, footman.

using *a.* employing, utilizing, applying, adopting, running, working, accepting, practicing, manipulating, controlling, putting in service, trying out, testing, proving, wearing out.

usual *a.* 1 [Ordinary] general, frequent, normal; see COMMON 1. 2 [Habitual] prevailing, accustomed, customary; see CONVENTIONAL 1.

usually *a.* ordinarily, customarily, habitually; see REGULARLY.

usurp *v.* assume, appropriate, expropriate, commandeer, lay hold of; see also SEIZE 2.

utensils *n.* [Implements; *especially for the kitchen*] equipment, tools, appliances, conveniences, wares; see also TOOL 1. *Kitchen utensils include the following:* sieve, egg beater, knife, fork, spoon, measuring cup, grater, spatula, skewer, pancake turner, can opener, egg slicer, meat grinder, butcher knife, peeler, paring knife, pastry cutter, squeezer, knife sharpener, coffee grinder, blender, food processor, mixer, vegetable brush, pan scourer, frying pan, saucepan, cake pan, pie pan, roaster, bottle brush, dishpan, draining pan, sink strainer, dishmop, mixing bowl, pan lid, rolling pin, pastry board, coffee pot, bread pan, cookie sheet.

utilities *n.* *Public utilities' services include the following:* phone service, cable, electricity, electric power, light and power, nuclear energy, steam generation, cogeneration, natural gas transmission, energy supply, water filtration, wastewater treatment, sewerage, recycling, refuse collection, rubbish removal.

utility *n.* [Usefulness] service, advantage, convenience; see USE 2.

utilize *v.* employ, appropriate, turn to account; see USE 1.

utmost *a.* ultimate, chief, entire, whole, full, unreserved, complete, unstinted, total, absolute, unlimited, unsparing, thorough, exhaustive, highest, maximum, most, top, undiminished, undivided, thoroughgoing, unmitigated, sheer, unqualified, unconditional, all-out.

utopia *n.* wonderland, dreamland, paradise, Eden, land of milk and honey*; see also HEAVEN 2.—*Ant.* HELL, dystopia, brave new world.

utopian *a.* visionary, idealistic, quixotic; see IMPRACTICAL.

utter *a.* complete, total, thorough; see ABSOLUTE 1.

utter *v.* pronounce, talk, express, articulate, voice, whisper, mutter, shout, exclaim, enunciate, air, speak, tell, disclose, declare, say, assert, affirm, ejaculate, vocalize, proclaim, give tongue to, recite, blurt out, let fall, announce, come out with.

utterance *n.* declaration, saying, assertion, announcement, pro-

nouncement, ejaculation, vociferation, talk, speech, statement, query, expression, sentence, proclamation, recitation, spiel*, rant, response, reply, oration.

utterly *a.* entirely, thoroughly, wholly; see COMPLETELY.

V

vacancy *n.* 1 [A vacated position] opening, vacated post, post without an incumbent, unfilled position, unheld office, job. 2 [A vacated residence] empty apartment, tenantless house, uninhabited house, vacant house, unoccupied house, deserted house, room for rent, house for sale.

vacant *a.* 1 [Without contents] devoid, void, unfilled; see EMPTY. 2 [Without an occupant] unoccupied, untenanted, tenantless, uninhabited, idle, free, deserted, abandoned, without a resident, not lived in.—*Ant.* INHABITED, occupied, tenanted.

vacate *v.* go away, relinquish, depart; see LEAVE 1.

vacation *n.* respite, rest, recreation time, intermission, recess, holiday, leave of absence, sabbatical, time off*.

vaccinate *v.* inoculate, immunize, prevent, treat, mitigate, protect, inject, shoot.

vaccinated *a.* immunized, inoculated, given injections; see PROTECTED.

vaccination *n.* 1 [The act of administering a vaccine] injection, inoculation, shots; see TREATMENT 2. 2 [A result of vaccination] protection, immunization, inoculation; see IMMUNITY 2.

vacuous *a.* inane, senseless, empty-headed; see STUPID.

vacuum *n.* space, void, hollowness, emptiness.

vacuum cleaner *n.* vacuum, carpet sweeper, vacuum sweeper; see APPLIANCE.

vagrant *a.* 1 [Having no home] roaming, itinerant, nomadic; see TRAVELING. 2 [Having no occupation] begging, mendicant, profligate, idling, prodigal, loafing, beachcombing, panhandling*, bumming*, mooching*. 3 [Having no fixed course] wayward, capricious, erratic; see AIMLESS.

vagrant *n.* beggar, idler, loafer, tramp, bum*, street person, bag lady*, wino*, slacker*.

vague *a.* 1 [Not clearly expressed] indefinite, unintelligible, superfi-

cial; see OBSCURE 1. 2 [Not clearly understood] uncertain, undetermined, unsure, doubtful, dubious, questionable, misunderstood, enigmatic, puzzling, nebulous, inexplicable, unsettled, bewildering, perplexing, problematic.—*Ant.* CERTAIN, sure, positive. 3 [Not clearly visible] dim, nebulous, dark; see HAZY.

vaguely *a.* uncertainly, unclearly, hazily, foggily, confusedly, mistily, shiftily, unreliably, dubiously, eccentrically, unsurely, illegally, evasively, unpredictably, obscurely, indefinitely, without clear outlines, incapable of being determined.

vagueness *n.* ambiguity, obscurity, difficulty; see CONFUSION, UNCERTAINTY 1, 2.

vain *a.* 1 [Possessing unwarranted self-esteem] proud, haughty, arrogant; see EGOTISTIC. 2 [Useless] worthless, hopeless, profitless; see FUTILE, USELESS 1. **—in vain** futilely, purposelessly, unprofitably; see USELESS.

valentine *n.* sentimental letter, St. Valentine's Day greeting, love verse; see LETTER 2.

valet *n.* manservant, body servant, attendant, gentleman's gentleman; see also SERVANT.

valiant *a.* courageous, unafraid, dauntless; see BRAVE.

valiantly *a.* courageously, boldly, fearlessly; see BRAVELY.

valid *a.* 1 [Capable of proof] sound, cogent, logical, conclusive, solid, well-grounded, well-founded, tested, accurate, convincing, telling, correct, determinative, compelling, persuasive, potent, stringent, strong, ultimate, unanswerable, irrefutable.—*Ant.* WRONG, erring, misleading. 2 [Genuine] true, original, factual, real, actual, pure, uncorrupted, authentic, confirmed, authoritative, trustworthy, credible, attested, efficient, legitimate, adequate, substantial, proven, unadulterated.—*Ant.* FALSE, fictitious, counterfeit.

validate *v.* confirm, sanction, legalize; see APPROVE.

validity *n.* soundness, advantage, value; see USEFULNESS.

valley *n.* vale, glen, canyon, depression, trough, notch, channel, lowland, river valley, stream valley, hollow, plain, dell, valley floor, coulee, dale, river bottom; see also GAP, RAVINE.—*Ant.* MOUNTAIN, ridge, hilltop.

valor *n.* bravery, heroism, boldness; see COURAGE.

valuable *a.* salable, marketable, in demand, high-priced, commanding a good price, costly, expensive, dear, priceless, precious, of value, in great demand, hardly obtainable, scarce, without price, good as good*.—*Ant.* CHEAP, unsalable, unmarketable.

valuation *n.* cost, appraisal, judgment; see ESTIMATE.

value *n.* 1 [Monetary value] price, expense, cost, profit, value in exhange, equivalent, rate, amount, market price, charge, face value, assessment, appraisal. 2 [The quality of being desirable] use, benefit, advantage; see sense 3. 3 [Quality] worth, merit, significance, consequence, goodness, condition, state, excellence, distinction, desirability, grade, finish, perfection, eminence, superiority, advantage, power, regard, importance, mark, caliber, repute. 4 [Precise signification] significance, force, sense; see MEANING.

value *v.* 1 [To believe to be valuable] esteem, prize, appreciate; see ADMIRE. 2 [To set a price upon] estimate, reckon, assess, appraise, fix the price of, place a value on, assay, rate, figure, compute, evaluate, judge, repute, consider, enumerate, account, charge, levy, ascertain, price.

valued *a.* evaluated, appraised, charged; see MARKED 2.

valve *n.* flap, lid, plug; see PIPE 1. *Valves include the following:* automatic, alarm, check, cutoff, side, overhead, dry-pipe, gate, lift, piston, rocking, safety, slide, throttle, sleeve, intake, exhaust, butterfly.

vandal *n.* despoiler, looter, hooligan*; see PIRATE.

vandalism *n.* piracy, demolition, wreckage; see DESTRUCTION 1.

vanguard *n.* advance guard, forerunners, precursors, front line, avant-garde.

vanish *v.* fade out, go away, dissolve; see DISAPPEAR.

vanishing *a.* disappearing, going, fading; see HAZY.

vanity *n.* ostentation, display, conceit, show, self-love, narcissism, self-glorification, self-applause, pretension, vainglory, conceitedness, affection, complacency, smugness.

vanquish *v.* conquer, overcome, subdue; see DEFEAT 2, 3.

vapid *a.* flat, boring, uninteresting; see DULL 3, 4.

vapor *n.* mist, steam, condensation, smog, exhalation, breath, fog, gas, haze, smoke.

vaporize *v.* diffuse, vanish, dissipate; see EVAPORATE.

vaporous *a.* fleeting, wispy, without substance; see IMAGINARY.

variable *a.* inconstant, shifting, unsteady; see IRREGULAR 1, 4.

variance *n.* change, fluctuation, deviation; see VARIATION 2.

variation *n.* 1 [Change] modification, alteration, mutation; see CHANGE 1. 2 [Disparity] inequality, difference, dissimilarity, distinction, disproportion, exception, contrast, irregularity, aberration, abnormality, disparity.—*Ant.* SIMILARITY, conformity, likeness.

varied *a.* discrete, different, diverse; see MIXED 1, VARIOUS.

variety *n.* 1 [Quality or state of being diverse] diversity, change, diversification, difference, variance, medley, mixture, miscellany, disparateness, divergency, variation, incongruity, fluctuation, shift, change, modification, departure, many-sidedness. 2 [Sort] kind, class, division, species, genus, race, tribe, family, assortment, type, stripe, nature, ilk, character, description, rank, grade, category, classification, quality.—*Ant.* EQUALITY, equalness, similarity.

various *a.* different, disparate, dissimilar, diverse, diversified, variegated, varicolored, many-sided, several, manifold, numerous, unlike, many, sundry, variable, changeable, inconstant, uncertain, of any kind, all manner of, of every description, distinct; see also MULTIPLE 1.—*Ant.* ALIKE, undiversified, identical.

variously *a.* varyingly, inconsistently, unpredictably; see DIFFERENTLY, UNEVENLY.

varnish *v.* finish, paint, shellac, lacquer, wax, size, enamel, japan, surface, coat, luster, polish, gloss, adorn, refinish, glaze, gloss over.—*Ant.* EXPOSE, remove the finish, strip.

vary *v.* diverge, differ, deviate, digress, swerve, depart, fluctuate, alternate, diverge from, be distinguished from, range, be inconstant, mutate, be uncertain.—*Ant.* REMAIN, be steady, hold.

varying *a.* diverse, differing, diverging; see CHANGING.

vase *n.* vessel, urn, jar, pottery, porcelain, receptacle, flower holder, ornament.

vast *a.* 1 [Large] huge, enormous,

immense; see LARGE 1. 2 [Extensive] broad, far-flung, wide, spacious, expansive, spread-out, ample, far-reaching, widespread, comprehensive, detailed, all-inclusive, astronomical, prolonged, stretched out, expanded.—*Ant.* NARROW, limited, confined.

vastness *n.* hugeness, extent, enormity; see EXPANSE, SIZE 2.

vat *n.* vessel, tub, barrel; see CONTAINER.

vault *n.* 1 [A place for the dead] tomb, crypt, grave; see MONUMENT 1. 2 [A place for preserving valuables] safe-deposit box, safety-deposit box, burglar-proof safe; see SAFE.

vault *v.* jump over, hurdle, clear; see JUMP 1.

veal *n.* calf, beef, baby beef; see MEAT. *Cuts of veal include the following:* chops, leg, loin, rack, shank, neck, breast, chuck. *Veal dishes include the following:* breaded veal cutlet, veal stew, calf's liver, Wiener schnitzel, veal parmigiana, veal scaloppine.

veer *v.* swerve, bend, deviate; see TURN 1, 2, 3.

vegetable *a.* plantlike, herblike, floral, blooming, blossoming, growing, flourishing.

vegetable *n.* plant, herbaceous plant, herb, legume, edible root. *Common vegetables include the following:* cabbage, potato, turnip, bean, carrot, pea, celery, lettuce, parsnip, spinach, squash, zucchini, tomato, pumpkin, asparagus, onion, corn, lentil, leek, chicory, kale, garlic, radish, cucumber, artichoke, eggplant, beet, scallion, pepper, okra, kohlrabi, parsley, chard, rhubarb, cauliflower, Brussels sprout, broccoli, endive, Chinese cabbage, watercress, rutabaga.

vegetate *v.* 1 [To germinate] bud, sprout, blossom; see BLOOM, GROW 1. 2 [To stagnate] hibernate, stagnate, languish; see WEAKEN 1.

vegetation *n.* plants, plant growth, trees, shrubs, saplings, flowers, wildflowers, grasses, herbage, herbs, pasturage, weeds, vegetables, crops.

vehicle *n.* *Vehicles include the following:* carriage, buggy, wagon, sleigh, cart, motor car, jeep, bus, automobile, truck, van, motorcycle, taxicab, railroad car, cab, taxi, SUV, limousine, limo*.

veil *n.* 1 [A thin fabric] scarf, kerchief, mask; see WEB. 2 [A curtain] screen, cover, shade; see CURTAIN.

vein *n.* 1 [A fissure] cleft, aperture, opening, channel, cavity, crack, cranny, rift, chink, break, breach, slit, crevice, flaw, rupture, bed, seam. 2 [A persistent quality]

strain, humor, mood, temper, tang, spice, dash; see also CHARACTERISTIC, TEMPERAMENT. 3 [A blood duct leading to the heart] *Important veins include the following:* jugular, pulmonary, subclavian, portal, iliac, hepatic, renal, axillary, femoral, saphenous; vena cava.

velocity *n.* quickness, rapidity, swiftness; see SPEED.

velvet *a.* silken, shining, plushy; see SOFT 2.

velvet *n.* cotton velvet, rayon, corduroy; see GOODS.

venal *a.* mercenary, on the take*, dishonest; see CORRUPT, GREEDY.

veneer *n.* surface, exterior, covering; see COVER 1.

venerable *a.* revered, old, aged, ancient, hoary, reverenced, honored, honorable, noble, august, grand, esteemed, respected, dignified, imposing, grave, serious, sage, wise, philosophical, experienced.—*Ant.* INEXPERIENCED, callow, raw.

venerate *v.* revere, reverence, adore; see LOVE 1, WORSHIP.

veneration *n.* respect, adoration, awe; see REVERENCE, WORSHIP 1.

vengeance *n.* retribution, return, retaliation; see REVENGE 1.

vengeful *a.* spiteful, revengeful, rancorous; see CRUEL.

venom *n.* poison, virus, toxin, bane, microbe, contagion, infection.

vent *n.* ventilator, vent hole, venting hole, smoke hole, flue, aperture, chimney.

vent *v.* let out, drive out, discharge; see FREE.

ventilate *v.* freshen, let in fresh air, circulate fresh air, vent, air cool, air out, free, oxygenate; see also AIR.

ventilated *a.* aired out, having adequate ventilation, not closed up; see AIRED 1, COOL 1, OPEN 1.

ventilation *n.* airing, purifying, oxygenating, freshening, opening windows, changing air, circulating air, air conditioning.

venture *n.* adventure, risk, hazard, peril, stake, chance, speculation, dare, experiment, trial, attempt, test, essay, gamble, undertaking, enterprise, investment, leap in the dark, plunge*, flyer*, crack*, fling*.

venture *v.* attempt, hazard, try out; see TRY 1.

ventured *a.* risked, chanced, dared; see DONE 1.

verb *n.* *Verbs include the following:* finite, active, passive, transitive, intransitive, modal, auxiliary, linking, copulative, reflexive, strong, weak, regular, irregular, helping, phrasal.

verbal *a.* told, linguistic, lingual; see ORAL, SPOKEN.

verbally *a.* orally, by word of mouth, person-to-person; see SPOKEN.

verbatim *a.* exactly, word for word, to the letter; see LITERALLY.

verdict *n.* judgment, finding, ruling, decision, answer, opinion, sentence, determination, decree, conclusion, deduction, adjudication, arbitrament.

verge *n.* edge, brink, border; see BOUNDARY.

verge *v.* border, edge, touch; see APPROACH 2.

verification *n.* verifying, attestation, affirmation; see CONFIRMATION.

verify *v.* establish, substantiate, authenticate, prove, check, document, test, validate, settle, corroborate, confirm.

vermin *n.* flea, louse, mite; see INSECT.

versatile *a.* many-sided, adaptable, dexterous, varied, ready, clever, handy, talented, gifted, adroit, resourceful, ingenious, accomplished; see also ABLE.

versatility *a.* flexibility, utility, adjustability; see ADAPTABILITY.

verse *n.* 1 [Composition in poetic form] poetry, metrical composition, versification, stanza, rhyme, lyric, sonnet, ode, heroic verse, dramatic poetry, blank verse, free verse. 2 [A unit of verse] line, verse, stanza, stave, strophe, antistrophe, hemistich, distich, quatrain.

version *n.* 1 [One of various accounts] report, account, tale; see STORY. 2 [A translation] paraphrase, redaction, transcription; see TRANSLATION.

vertebrae *n.* spine, spinal column, backbone, chine.

vertical *a.* perpendicular, upright, on end; see STRAIGHT 1.

very *a.* extremely, exceedingly, greatly, acutely, indispensably, just so, surprisingly, astonishingly, incredibly, wonderfully, particularly, certainly, positively, emphatically, really, truly, pretty, decidedly, pressingly, notably, uncommonly, extraordinarily, prodigiously, highly, substantially, dearly, amply, vastly, extensively, noticeably, conspicuously, largely, considerably, hugely, excessively, imperatively, markedly, enormously, sizably, materially, tremendously, superlatively, immensely, remarkably, unusually, immoderately, quite, indeed, somewhat, rather, simply, intensely, urgently, exceptionally, severely, seriously, in a great measure, to a great degree, beyond compare, on a large scale, ever so, beyond measure, by far, in the extreme, in a marked degree, to a great extent, without restraint, more or less, in part, infinitely, very much, real*, right*, awfully*, good and*, powerful*, powerfully*, hell of a*, precious*, so*, no end*.

vessel *n.* 1 [A container] pitcher, urn, kettle; see CONTAINER. 2 [A ship] boat, craft, bark*; see SHIP. 3 [A duct; *especially for blood*] blood vessel, artery, capillary; see VEIN 2.

vest *n.* waistcoat, jacket, garment; see CLOTHES.

vestige *n.* trace, remains, scrap; see REMAINDER.

veteran *n.* 1 [An experienced person] master, one long in service, old hand, one of the old guard, old bird*, old dog*, old timer*.—*Ant.* AMATEUR, rookie*, youngster. 2 [An experienced soldier] ex-soldier, seasoned campaigner, ex-service man, reenlisted man, old soldier, war horse*, ex-G.I.*, vet.

veterinarian *n.* animal specialist, vet, animal doctor; see DOCTOR.

veto *n.* rejection, prohibition, negative; see DENIAL, REFUSAL.

veto *v.* interdict, prohibit, decline; see DENY, REFUSE.

vetoed *a.* declined, rejected, disapproved; see NO, REFUSED.

vex *v.* provoke, irritate, annoy; see BOTHER 2.

via *prep.* by way of, by the route passing through, on the way to, through the medium of; see also BY 2, THROUGH 4.

vibrant *a.* energetic, vigorous, lively; see ACTIVE.

vibrate *v.* 1 [To quiver] fluctuate, flutter, waver; see WAVE 3. 2 [To sound] echo, resound, reverberate; see SOUND.

vibration *n.* quake, wavering, vacillation, fluctuation, oscillation, quiver, shake; see also WAVE 3.

vice *n.* corruption, iniquity, wickedness; see EVIL 1.

vice versa *a.* conversely, in reverse, the other way round, turn about, about-face, in opposite manner, far from it, on the contrary, in reverse.

vicinity *n.* proximity, nearness, neighborhood; see ENVIRONMENT, REGION 1.

vicious *a.* wicked, corrupt, bad, debased, base, impious, profligate, demoralized, faulty, vile, foul, impure, lewd, indecent, licentious, libidinous; see also BAD 1.—*Ant.* PURE, noble, virtuous.

vicious circle *n.* chain of events, cause and effect, interreliant problems; see DIFFICULTY 1, 2.

viciously *a.* cruelly, spitefully, harmfully; see BRUTALLY, WRONGLY.

victim *n.* prey, sacrifice, immolation,

sufferer, wretch, quarry, game, hunted, offering, scapegoat, martyr.

victimize *v.* cheat, swindle, dupe, trick, fool; see also DECEIVE.

victor *n.* conqueror, champion, prizewinner; see WINNER.

victorious *a.* winning, triumphant, mastering; see SUCCESSFUL.

victory *n.* conquest, mastery, subjugation, overcoming, overthrow, master stroke, lucky stroke, winning, success, triumph, gaining, defeating, subduing, destruction, killing*, knockout, pushover*.

vie *v.* contend, strive, rival; see COMPETE.

view *n.* glimpse, look, sight, panorama, aspect, show, appearance, prospect, distance, opening, stretch, outlook, way, extended view, long view, avenue, contour, outline, scene, spectacle. —**in view** visible, in sight, not out of sight, perceptible, perceivable; see also OBVIOUS 1. —**in view of** in consideration of, because, taking into consideration; see CONSIDERING. —**on view** displayed, on display, exposed; see SHOWN 1. —**with a view to** in order to, so that, anticipating; see TO 4.

view *v.* observe, survey, inspect; see SEE 1.

viewer *n.* watcher, onlooker, spectator; see OBSERVER.

viewpoint *n.* point of view, perspective, standpoint, angle, slant, position, stand, aspect, light, respect, attitude, point of observation, outlook.

vigilant *a.* alert, watchful, on guard; see CAREFUL, OBSERVANT.

vigor *n.* 1 [Activity] exercise, action, energy; see VITALITY. 2 [Health] well-being, endurance, vitality; see HEALTH.

vigorous *a.* 1 [Done with vigor] energetic, lively, brisk; see ACTIVE. 2 [Forceful] powerful, strong, potent; see EFFECTIVE.

vigorously *a.* energetically, alertly, eagerly, quickly, nimbly, agilely, strenuously, resolutely, firmly, forcibly, forcefully, urgently, unfalteringly, purposefully, actively, boldly, adventurously, zealously, lustily, robustly, stoutly, hardily, wholeheartedly, earnestly, warmly, fervidly, fervently, ardently, intensely, passionately, sincerely, devoutly, appreciatively, with heart and soul, healthily, fearlessly, mightily, decidedly, by brute force, like blazes*; see also POWERFULLY.— *Ant.* CALMLY, aimlessly, slowly.

vile *a.* sordid, corrupt, debased; see SHAMEFUL 1, 2.

village *n.* hamlet, settlement, small town; see TOWN 1.

villain *n.* scoundrel, knave, brute; see CRIMINAL.

vindicate *v.* 1 [To clear] acquit, free, absolve; see EXCUSE. 2 [To justify] prove, bear out, warrant; see PROVE.

vindication *n.* defense, acquittal, clearance; see PROOF 1.

vindictive *a.* revengeful, resentful, spiteful; see CRUEL.

vine *n.* creeper, climbing plant, creeping plant, trailing plant, stem climber, leaf climber, tendril climber; see also PLANT. *Vines include the following:* grapevine, honeysuckle, trumpet vine, English ivy, Virginia creeper, poison ivy, blackberry, raspberry, briar, rambler, teaberry, dewberry, morning-glory, bougainvillea, jasmine, pea vine, watermelon, cantaloupe, cucumber, wild cucumber, squash, gourd, pumpkin, passionflower.

violate *v.* 1 [To transgress] outrage, disrupt, infringe, break, tamper with; see also MEDDLE 1. 2 [To rape] dishonor, molest, defile, ravish.

violation *n.* infringement, transgression, negligence, misbehavior, non-observance, violating, shattering, transgressing, forcible trespass, trespassing, contravention, breach, breaking, rupture, flouting; see also CRIME.

violence *n.* 1 [Violent disturbance] rampage, tumult, disorder, clash, onslaught, struggle; see also CONFUSION, DISTURBANCE 2, UPROAR. 2 [Violent conduct] fury, force, vehemence, frenzy, brutality, savagery; see also INTENSITY.

violent *a.* strong, powerful, forceful, forcible, rough, mighty, great, potent, coercive, furious, mad, savage, fierce, passionate, vehement, frenzied, demonic, frantic, fuming, enraged, disturbed, agitated, impassioned, impetuous, urgent, maddened, aroused, inflamed, distraught, hysterical, vehement, extreme, unusual, brutal, destructive, murderous, homicidal, rampageous.— *Ant.* CALM, GENTLE, QUIET.

violently *a.* destructively, forcibly, forcefully, combatively, powerfully, strongly, coercively, flagrantly, outrageously, overwhelmingly, compellingly, disturbingly, turbulently, stormily, ruinously, stubbornly, with violence, in a violent manner, abruptly, noisily, with a vengeance, like fury, rebelliously, riotously, furiously, angrily, vehemently, fiercely, brutally, frantically, hilariously, hysterically, passionately, urgently, madly, frenziedly, ardently, enthusiastically, impulsively.— *Ant.* MILDLY, gently, undisturbedly.

violet *a.* lavender, mauve, purplish; see PURPLE.

violin n. fiddle, viola, Stradivarius; see MUSICAL INSTRUMENT.

VIP* n. very important person, notable, important figure; see LEADER 2.

virgin a. 1 [Chaste] pure, modest, virginal; see CHASTE. 2 [Original or natural] undisturbed, untamed, new; see NATURAL 3, ORIGINAL 1, 3.

Virgin n. Madonna, Blessed Virgin Mary, Queen of Saints, Our Lady, Mother of God, Mary, the Queen of Heaven, Queen of Angels, Star of the Sea, The Virgin Mother, Immaculate Conception, Immaculate Mary; see also SAINT.

virginity n. maidenhood, girlhood, chastity; see VIRTUE 1.

virile a. masculine, potent, macho; see MALE, MANLY.

virility n. potency, masculinity, manliness; see MANHOOD 2.

virtually a. for all practical purposes, practically, implicitly; see ESSENTIALLY.

virtue n. 1 [Moral excellence] morality, goodness, righteousness, uprightness, ethical conduct, good thing, respectability, rectitude, honor, honesty, merit, fineness, character, excellence, value, chastity, quality, worth, kindness, innocence, generosity, trustworthiness, faithfulness, consideration, justice, prudence, temperance, fortitude, faith, hope, charity, love.—*Ant.* EVIL, immorality, depravity. 2 [An individual excellence] quality, characteristic, attribute, way, trait, feature, accomplishment, achievement, property, distinction, capacity, power.—*Ant.* LACK, inability, incapacity. 3 [Probity in sexual conduct] virginity, purity, decency; see CHASTITY. **—by virtue of** on the grounds of, because of, looking toward; see BECAUSE.

virtuoso n. maestro, artiste, expert; see MASTER 3, MUSICIAN.

virtuous a. good, upright, moral; see HONEST 1, WORTHY.

virus n. 1 [An infection] sickness, communicability, illness; see ILLNESS 2. 2 [An organism] microorganism, bacillus, bacteriophage; see GERM.

visceral a. instinctive, intuitive, emotional, gut*.

vise n. clamp, holder, clasp; see FASTENER.

visibility n. perceptibility, discernibility, distinctness; see CLARITY.

visible a. apparent, evident, noticeable; see OBVIOUS 1.

vision n. 1 [The faculty of sight] sight, perception, perceiving, range of view, optics, eyesight. 2 [Understanding] foresight, discernment, breadth of view, insight, penetration, intuition, divination, astuteness, keenness, foreknowledge, prescience, farsightedness, acumen, wisdom. 3 [Something seen through powers of the mind] imagination, poetic insight, fancy, fantasy, image, concept, conception, inspiration, idea; see also THOUGHT 1, 2. 4 [Something seen by other than normal sight] revelation, trance, ecstasy, fantasy, hallucination, phantom, apparition, ghost, wraith, specter, apocalypse, nightmare, spirit, warlock; see also ILLUSION.

visionary a. 1 [Impractical] ideal, romantic, utopian; see IMPRACTICAL. 2 [Imaginary] not real, delusory, dreamy; see IMAGINARY.

visit n. social call, call, appointment, interview, formal call, talk, evening, stay, holiday, visitation, vacation.

visit v. stay with, dwell with, stop by, call on, call upon, come around, be the guest of, make a visit, sojourn awhile, revisit, look in on, visit with, stop off, stop in, stop over, have an appointment with, pay a visit to, tour, take in, drop in on, hit, look around*, look up*, look in, drop over, pop in, have a date.

visitor n. caller, visitant, official inspector; see GUEST.

visual a. seen, optical, of the vision; see OBVIOUS 1.

visualize v. see in the mind's eye, picture mentally, conceive; see IMAGINE.

vital a. 1 [Necessary] essential, indispensable, requisite; see NECESSARY. 2 [Alive] live, animate, animated; see ALIVE. 3 [Vigorous] lively, energetic, lusty; see ACTIVE.

vitality n. life, liveliness, animation, vim, vigor, intensity, continuity, endurance, energy, spirit, ardor, audacity, spunk*, fervor, verve, venturesomeness, pep*, get-up-and-go*.

vitals n. organs, entrails, intestines; see INSIDES.

vitamin n. *Types of vitamins include the following:* vitamin A, vitamin B_1 or thiamine, vitamin B_2 or riboflavin, vitamin B_6 or pyridoxine, vitamin B_{12}, nicotinic acid or niacin, pantothenic acid, choline, folic acid, inositol, para-aminobenzoic acid, vitamin C or ascorbic acid, vitamin D, vitamin D_2 or ergocalciferol, vitamin D_3 or cholecalciferol, vitamin E or tocopherol, vitamin H or biotin, vitamin K or menadione; see also MEDICINE 2.

vivid a. 1 [Brilliant] shining, glowing, gleaming; see BRIGHT 1. 2 [Distinct] strong, striking, lucid; see CLEAR 2, DEFINITE 2.

vividly a. glowingly, strikingly, flamingly; see BRIGHTLY.

vocabulary n. wordbook, dictionary, lexicon, thesaurus, stock of words, glossary; scientific, literary, active, passive, etc. vocabulary; see also DICTION.

vocal a. 1 [Verbal] expressed, uttered, voiced; see ORAL, SPOKEN. 2 [Produced by the voice; *said especially of music*] sung, scored for voice, vocalized; see MUSICAL 1.

vocalist n. chorister, caroler, songster; see MUSICIAN, SINGER.

vocation n. calling, mission, pursuit; see PROFESSION 1.

voice n. 1 [A vocal sound] speech, sound, call, cry, utterance, tongue, whistle, moan, groan, song, yell, hail, howl, yowl, bark, whine, whimper, mutter, murmur, shout, bleat, bray, neigh, whinny, roar, trumpet, cluck, honk, meow, hiss, quack; see also NOISE 1.—*Ant.* SILENCE, dumbness, stillness. 2 [Approval or opinion] decision, conclusion, assent, negation, approval, recommendation, wish, view; see also CHOICE, OPINION 1. —**with one voice** all together, by unanimous vote, without dissent; see UNANIMOUSLY.

voice v. assert, cry, sound; see TALK 1, TELL 1.

voiced a. vocal, sonant, sounded; see ORAL, SPOKEN.

void a. barren, sterile, fruitless, meaningless, useless, invalid, vain, voided, unconfirmed, unratified, null and void, worthless, unsanctioned, set aside, avoided, forceless, voted out, ineffectual, ineffective, voidable.—*Ant.* VALID, in force, used.

volatile a. 1 [Having the qualities of a gas] gaseous, vaporous, buoyant; see LIGHT 5. 2 [Having a sprightly temperament] lively, vivacious, playful; see ACTIVE.

volitional a. willing, voluntary, free; see OPTIONAL.

volley n. round, discharge, barrage; see FIRE 2.

voltage n. electric potential, potential difference, charge; see ENERGY 2.

voluble a. talkative, glib, loquacious; see FLUENT.

volume n. 1 [Quantity] bulk, mass, amount; see EXTENT, SIZE 2. 2 [Contents] cubical size, space, dimensions; see CAPACITY. 3 [A book] printed document, tome, pamphlet; see BOOK. 4 [Degree of sound] loudness, amplification, strength; see SOUND 2.

voluntarily a. by preference, willingly, deliberately, optionally, spontaneously, freely, intentionally, by choice, of one's own choice, on one's own, in one's own sweet way, of one's own free will, to one's heart's

content, at one's discretion, on one's own initiative.

voluntary a. willing, intentional, spontaneous; see OPTIONAL.

volunteer n. enlistee, unpaid worker, charity worker; see CANDIDATE, RECRUIT.

volunteer v. come forward, enlist, sign up, submit oneself, take the initiative, offer oneself, do on one's own accord, do of one's own free will, take upon oneself, speak up, stand up and be counted, go in*, chip in*, do on one's own hook*, take the bull by the horns, stand on one's own feet, take the bit between one's teeth, take the plunge; see also JOIN 2.

volunteered a. offered, proffered, given freely; see JOINED.

voluptuous a. epicurean, sensuous, erotic; see SENSUAL.

vomit v. throw up, eject, bring up, spit up, dry heave, be seasick, be sick, hurl forth, retch, ruminate, regurgitate, give forth, discharge, belch forth, spew up, puke*, barf*, toss one's cookies*.

voracious a. insatiable, hoggish, ravening; see GREEDY.

vote n. 1 [A ballot] tally, ticket, slip of paper, butterfly ballot, punch card, absentee ballot, yes or no, secret ballot. 2 [A decision] referendum, choice, majority; see ELECTION. 3 [The right to vote] suffrage, the franchise, manhood suffrage, universal suffrage, woman suffrage, enfranchisement; see also RIGHT.

vote v. ballot, cast a vote, cast a ballot, give a vote, enact, establish, choose, determine, bring about, effect, grant, confer, declare, suggest, propose; see also DECIDE. —**vote down** decide against, refuse, blackball; see DENY. —**vote for** give one's vote to, cast a ballot for, second; see SUPPORT 2. —**vote in** elect, put in, put in office; see CHOOSE. —**vote out** reject, remove from office, vote down; see DEFEAT, DISMISS.

voted a. decided, willed, chosen; see NAMED 2.

voter n. elector, balloter, registered voter, member of a constituency, member of the electorate, vote caster, native, naturalized citizen, taxpayer, voter by proxy, absentee voter; see also CITIZEN.

vouch v. assert, attest, affirm; see ENDORSE 2.

vow n. pledge, solemn assertion, oath; see PROMISE 1.

vowel n. nonconsonant, open-voiced sound, vowel sound, diphthong, digraph; see also LETTER 1. *Linguistic terms referring to vowel sounds include the following:* high, mid, low, front, central, back, tense, slack, rounded, unrounded, stressed, unstressed, nasalized, clipped, diphthongized. *In the English alphabet, vowels are represented as follows: a, e, i, o, u, and sometimes y.*

voyage *n.* tour, trip, excursion; see JOURNEY.

vulgar *a.* sordid, ignoble, mean, base, obscene, indecent, gross, filthy, villainous, dishonorable, unworthy, fractious, inferior, disgusting, base-minded, mean-spirited, malicious, ill-tempered, sneaking, deceitful, slippery, loathsome, odious, foul-mouthed, brutish, debased, contemptible, profane, abhorrent, nasty, tasteless, low, uncouth.—*Ant.* NOBLE, high-minded, lofty.

vulgarity *n.* impudence, discourtesy, crudity; see RUDENESS.

vulnerable *a.* woundable, exposed, assailable; see UNSAFE, WEAK 2, 5.

W

wad *n.* **1** [A little heap] bundle, pile, clump; see BUNCH. **2** [*A considerable amount of money] fortune, bankroll, mint*; see WEALTH.

wad *v.* stuff, pad, cushion; see PACK 2.

wade *v.* walk in the surf, paddle, get one's feet wet; see SWIM.

wag *v.* waggle, swing, sway; see WAVE 3.

wage *v.* conduct, make, carry on; see DO 1.

wager *n.* risk, hazard, challenge; see BET.

wages *n.* salary, earnings, payment; see PAY 2.

wagon *n.* pushcart, buggy, truck, coach, carriage, caravan, car, covered wagon, prairie schooner, Conestoga wagon, cab.

wail *v.* moan, weep, lament; see MOURN.

waist *n.* waistline, middle, midriff; see STOMACH.

wait *n.* halt, holdup, time wasted; see DELAY, PAUSE.

wait *v.* **1** [To await] expect, anticipate, tarry, pause, wait for, look for, watch for, abide, dally, remain, idle, bide one's time, mark time, stay up for, lie in wait for, ambush, lie low, hole up*, hang around*, stick around*, cool one's heels*.—*Ant.* LEAVE, hurry, act. **2** [To serve food at a table] serve, deliver, tend, act as waiter, act as waitress, arrange, set, ready, place on the table, help, portion, bus tables, wait tables. —**wait for** await, expect, stay up for; see WAIT 1. —**wait on** accommodate, serve, attend; see WAIT 2. —**wait up (for)** expect, stay up for, stay awake; see WAIT 1, WORRY 2.

waiter *n.* headwaiter, steward, attendant, footman, busboy, servant, innkeeper, host, lackey, counterman, soda jerk*.

waiting *a.* standing, languishing, in line, next in turn, expecting, hoping for, marking time, in wait, cooling one's heels*.—*Ant.* MOVING, hurrying, acting.

waiting room *n.* restroom, salon, lounge, terminal, reception room, hall, antechamber, foyer, preparation room, depot, station.

waitress *n.* female attendant, servant, maidservant, hostess, counter girl, restaurant employee, carhop.

waive *v.* forgo, neglect, reject; see ABANDON 1.

wake *v.* **1** [To waken another] call, rouse, bring to life, arouse, awaken, wake up, prod, shake, nudge, break into one's slumber. **2** [To become awake] get up, awake, be roused, get out of bed, open one's eyes, rise, arise, stir, stretch oneself. —**wake up** rise and shine, arise, get up, awake, get going*, get cracking*.

walk *n.* **1** [Manner of walking] gait, tread, stride; see STEP 1. **2** [Course over which one walks] pavement, sidewalk, pathway, footpath, track, trail, driveway, boardwalk, pier, promenade, avenue, road, drive, lane, alley, dock, platform, gangway; see also STREET. **3** [A short walking expedition] stroll, ramble, turn, hike, promenade, airing, saunter, tramp, trek, march, circuit, jaunt, tour.

walk *v.* **1** [To move on foot] step, pace, march, tread, amble, stroll, hike, saunter, wander, ramble, go out for an airing, take a walk, promenade, trudge, tramp, trek, tour, take a turn, roam, rove, meander, traipse about, patrol, knock about*, knock around*, hoof it*, toddle along, shuffle, wend one's way, cruise. **2** [To cause to move on foot] lead, drive, exercise, train, order a march, escort, accompany, take for a walk. —**walk (all) over** subdue, trample on, beat up*; see ABUSE. —**walk away** vanish, depart, split*; see ABANDON 1, 2, LEAVE 1. —**walk off** depart, go one's own way, stalk off; see LEAVE 1. —**walk out on** desert, leave, walk off from; see ABANDON 2.

walkie-talkie *n.* portable transmitter and receiver, field radio, cellular phone; see RADIO 2.

walking *a.* strolling, rambling, trudging, hiking, touring, ambling, sauntering, tramping, marching, promenading, passing, roaming, wandering, wayfaring, trekking*.

walkout *n.* protest, boycott, demonstration; see STRIKE 1.

wall *n.* 1 [A physical barrier] dam, embankment, dike, ditch, bank, levee, stockade, fence, parapet, retainer, rampart, bulwark, palisade, fort, cliff, barricade, floodgate, sluice. 2 [An obstacle; *figurative*] barrier, obstruction, bar, cordon, entanglement, hurdle, resistance, defense, snag, hindrance, impediment, difficulty, limitation, restriction, retardation, knot, hitch, drawback, stumbling block, check, stop, curb, red tape, fly in the ointment, bottleneck, red herring, detour.

wallet *n.* billfold, purse, moneybag; see BAG, FOLDER.

wallop *v.* thump, thrash, strike; see HIT 1.

wallow *v.* grovel, welter, flounder, lie in, roll about in, bathe in, toss, immerse, be immersed in, besmirch oneself.

wan *a.* colorless, sickly, anemic; see PALE 1.

wander *v.* 1 [To stroll] hike, ramble, saunter; see WALK 1. 2 [To speak or think incoherently] stray, maunder, digress; see RAMBLE 2.

wanderer *n.* adventurer, voyager, gypsy; see TRAVELER.

wandering *a.* 1 [Wandering in space] roving, roaming, nomadic, meandering, restless, traveling, drifting, straying, going off, strolling, ranging, prowling, ambulatory, straggling, on the road, peripatetic, itinerant, roundabout, circuitous.— *Ant.* IDLE, home-loving, sedentary. 2 [Wandering in thought] discursive, digressive, disconnected; see INCOHERENT.

wane *v.* decline, subside, fade away; see DECREASE 1, FADE 1.

want *n.* 1 [Need] privation, dearth, shortage; see LACK 2. 2 [Desire] wish, craving, demand; see DESIRE 1.

want *v.* 1 [To desire] require, aspire, fancy, hanker after, have an urge for, incline toward, covet, crave, long for, lust for, have a fondness for, have a passion for, have ambition, thirst for, hunger for, be greedy for, ache for*, have a yen for*, have an itch for*. 2 [To lack] be deficient in, be deprived of, require; see NEED.

wanted *a.* needed, necessary, desired, in need of, sought after, in

demand, requested, asked for.— *Ant.* SATISFIED, fulfilled, filled.

wanting *a.* 1 [Deficient] destitute, poor, in default of, deprived of, bereft of, devoid of, empty of, bankrupt in, cut off, lacking, short, inadequate, defective, remiss, incomplete, missing, substandard, insufficient, absent, needed, unfulfilled, on the short end. 2 [Desiring] desirous of, covetous, longing for; see ENVIOUS, GREEDY.

wanton *a.* 1 [Unrestrained] reckless, extravagant, capricious, unreserved, unfettered, free, wayward, fluctuating, changeable, whimsical, fitful, variable, fanciful, inconstant, fickle, frivolous, volatile. 2 [Lewd] wayward, lustful, licentious; see LEWD 2.

war *n.* fighting, hostilities, combat. *Types of wars include the following:* air, guerrilla, shooting, ground, sea, jungle, desert, mountain, amphibious, trench, naval, aerial, land, push-button, hot, cold, total, limited, civil, revolutionary, religious, preventive, world, offensive, defensive, biological, bacteriological, germ, chemical, atomic, nuclear, psychological, war to end all wars, war of nerves, war of attrition, war of liberation, campaign, crusade, *Blitzkrieg* (German).

war *v.* fight, battle, go to war, wage war on, make war against, engage in combat, take the field against, contend, contest, meet in conflict, march against, attack, bombard, shell, kill, shoot, murder.

ward *n.* 1 [A territorial division] district, division, territory; see REGION 1. 2 [A juvenile charge] orphan, foster child, adopted child; see CHILD. 3 [Hospital room] convalescent chamber, infirmary, emergency ward; see HOSPITAL.

warden *n.* official, officer, overseer, superintendent, guardian, tutor, keeper, head keeper, jailer, bodyguard, guard, governor, prison head.

wardrobe *n.* 1 [A closet] chest, bureau, dresser; see CLOSET. 2 [Clothing] apparel, garments, attire; see CLOTHES.

warehouse *n.* wholesale establishment, storehouse, stockroom, storage place, distribution center, repository, depot, shed, stockpile, depository, bin, elevator, storage loft, barn.

wares *n.* goods, lines, stock, products, commodities, manufactured articles, merchandise, stuff.

warfare *n.* military operations, hostilities, combat; see WAR.

warlike *a.* belligerent, hostile, offensive; see AGGRESSIVE.

warm *a.* **1** [Moderately heated] heated, sunny, melting, hot, mild, tepid, lukewarm, summery, temperate, clement, pleasant, glowing, perspiring, sweaty, sweating, flushed, warmish, snug as a bug in a rug*.—*Ant.* COOL, chilly, chilling. **2** [Sympathetic] gracious, cordial, compassionate; see FRIENDLY.

warm *v.* heat up, warm up, put on the fire; see COOK, HEAT 2.

warmth *n.* **1** [Fervor] fever, passion, feeling; see EMOTION. **2** [Affection] friendliness, kindness, sympathy; see FRIENDSHIP. **3** [Heat] light, glow, warmness; see HEAT 1, TEMPERATURE.

warn *v.* forewarn, give notice, put on guard, give fair warning, signal, advise, prepare, alert, inform, remind, enjoin, hint, prepare for the worst, offer a word of caution, admonish, counsel, exhort, dissuade, reprove, threaten, forbid, predict, remonstrate, deprecate, prescribe, urge, recommend, prompt, suggest, advocate, cry wolf, tip off*, give the high sign, put a bug in one's ear*.

warned *a.* informed, admonished, made aware, cautioned, advised, given warning, prepared for the worst, told, forewarned, tipped off*, put on the lookout.

warning *n.* caution, admonition, notice, advice, forewarning, alert, intimation, premonition, notification, sign, omen, alarm, indication, token, hint, lesson, information, example, distress signal, prediction, signal, injunction, exhortation, high sign, word to the wise, tip-off, SOS*, handwriting on the wall.

warp *v.* curve, twist, pervert; see BEND.

warrant *n.* authorization, certificate, credential, official document, license, summons, subpoena, security, pass, testimonial, passport, credentials, permit, permission, verification, authentication.

warrant *v.* **1** [To guarantee] assure, insure, vouch for; see GUARANTEE. **2** [To justify] bear out, call for, give grounds for; see EXPLAIN.

warranty *n.* written guaranty, guarantee, pledge; see GUARANTY.

warrior *n.* battler, fighter, combatant; see SOLDIER.

warship *n.* fighting ship, armored vessel, gunboat, man-of-war, frigate, ship-of-the-line; see also BOAT, SHIP. *Warships include the following:* battleship, cruiser, destroyer, destroyer escort, submarine, guided-missile frigate, guided-missile destroyer, missile cruiser, attack submarine, dreadnought, capital ship, landing ship, submarine chaser, aircraft carrier, escort carrier, torpedo boat, PT-boat, raider, flagship.

wart *n.* protuberance, spot, mole, projection, blemish, growth, bulge, lesion, tumor.

wary *a.* circumspect, cautious, alert; see CAREFUL, SLY.

wash *n.* **1** [Laundry] wet wash, washing, linen, family wash, soiled clothing, dirty clothes, clean clothes, washed clothing, flat pieces, finished laundry. **2** [The movement of water] swishing, lapping, roll, swirl, rush, surging, eddy, wave, undulation, surge, heave, flow, murmur, gush, spurt. **3** [A stream bed that is usually dry] arroyo, gulch, canyon; see GAP 3. **4** [A prepared liquid] rinse, swab, fluid; see LIQUID.

wash *v.* **1** [To bathe] clean, cleanse, shine, immerse, douse, soak, take a bath, take a shower, soap, rub the dirt off, scour, scrub, rinse, wipe, sponge, dip, freshen up, wash up, clean up. **2** [To launder] clean, starch, scrub, put in a washing machine, boil, soap, send to the laundry, scour, rinse out, soak, drench.—*Ant.* DIRTY, stain, spoil. **3** [To brush with a liquid] swab, whitewash, color; see PAINT 2. **4** [*To be convincing] be plausible, stand up, endure examination; see ENDURE 1, SUCCEED 1.

washable *a.* pre-washed, wash-and-wear, unfading, launderable, permanent-press, colorfast, preshrunk.

washed *a.* **1** [Laundered] cleaned, scrubbed, bleached, boiled, put through the wash, soaped.—*Ant.* DIRTY, soiled, foul. **2** [Watered] bathed, dipped, drenched, sponged, doused, soaked, cleansed, submerged, showered.—*Ant.* DRY, scorching, desert.

washed-up* *a.* finished, defeated, done for*, over the hill*, dead in the water*; see also RUINED 1, 2.

washer *n.* dishwasher, washing machine, laundry machine; see APPLIANCE, MACHINE.

washing *n.* laundry, soiled clothes, dirty clothes; see WASH 1.

waste *a.* futile, discarded, worthless, valueless, useless, empty, barren, dreary, uninhabited, desolate, profitless, superfluous, unnecessary, functionless, purposeless, pointless, unserviceable.

waste *n.* **1** [The state of being wasted] disuse, misuse, dissipation, consumption, uselessness, devastation, ruin, decay, loss, exhaustion, extravagance, squandering, wear and tear, wrack and ruin; see also WEAR.—*Ant.* USE, PROFIT, VALUE. **2** [Refuse] rubbish, garbage, scrap; see TRASH 1. **3** [Unused land] desert, wilds, wilderness, wasteland, fen, tundra, marsh, marshland, bog, moor, quagmire, dustbowl, badlands, swamp, wash.

waste v. 1 [To use without result] dissipate, spend, consume, lose, be of no avail, come to nothing, go to waste, misuse, throw away, use up, misapply, misemploy, labor in vain, cast pearls before swine.—*Ant.* PROFIT, use well, get results. 2 [To squander] burn up, lavish, scatter, splurge, spend, be prodigal, indulge, abuse, empty, drain, fatigue, spill, impoverish, misspend, exhaust, fritter away, ruin, be spendthrift, divert, go through, gamble away, throw money away*, run through, hang the expense*, blow*, burn the candle at both ends.—*Ant.* SAVE, be thrifty, manage wisely. 3 [To be consumed gradually] decay, thin out, become thin, wither, dwindle, lose weight, be diseased, run dry, wilt, droop, decrease, disappear, drain, empty, wear out, wear down.—*Ant.* GROW, develop, enrich.

wasted a. squandered, spent, destroyed, lost, consumed, eaten up, worn down, worn out, thrown away, shriveled, gaunt, emaciated, decayed, depleted, scattered, drained, gone for nothing, missapplied, useless, to no avail, down the drain, unappreciated, of no use, worthless.

wasteful a. extravagant, profligate, dissipated, prodigal, liberal, immoderate, overgenerous, cavalier, incontinent, thriftless, lavish, squandering, profuse, unthrifty, improvident, careless, reckless, wild, destructive, with money to burn*, easy come easy go.

wastefully a. extravagantly, carelessly, improvidently, wildly, immoderately, thriftlessly, recklessly, prodigally, destructively, foolishly, lavishly, inconsiderately, openhandedly, imprudently, ruthlessly, profusely, overgenerously, with no thought for tomorrow, without a second thought, without good sense, without consideration, without restraint.

watch n. 1 [A portable timepiece] wristwatch, pocket watch, stopwatch, digital watch, analog watch, sportsman's watch, fashion watch, ladies' watch, men's watch, children's watch, chronometer; see also CLOCK. 2 [Strict attention] lookout, observation, observance, awareness, attention, vigilance, guard, heed, watchfulness.—*Ant.* NEGLECT, sleepiness, apathy. 3 [A period of duty or vigilance] nightwatch, guard duty, patrol; see GUARD. 4 [Persons or a person standing guard] guard, sentry, sentinel; see GUARDIAN 1.

watch v. 1 [To be attentive] observe, see, scrutinize, follow, attend, mark, regard, listen, wait, attend, take

notice, contemplate, mind, view, pay attention, concentrate, look closely, focus on. 2 [To guard] keep an eye on, patrol, police; see GUARD. — **watch out** take care, heed, be cautious, be careful, proceed carefully, mind, go on tiptoe, take precautions, be on one's guard, make sure of, be doubly sure, keep an eye peeled, handle with kid gloves*, look alive*. —**watch over** protect, look after, attend to; see GUARD.

watched a. guarded, spied on, followed, held under suspicion, scrutinized, observed, marked, kept under surveillance, noticed, noted, bugged*.

watchful a. on guard, vigilant, prepared; see CAREFUL.

watchfulness n. vigilance, alertness, caution; see ATTENTION.

watching a. vigilant, wary, alert; see CAREFUL.

watchman n. day watchman, sentinel, scout, spy, ranger, observer, spotter, signalman, flagman, shore patrol, night watchman, security guard, curator, guard, guardian, patrolman, detective, policeman, sentry, keeper, caretaker, lookout.

water n. 1 [Water as a liquid] rain, rainwater, liquid, drinking water, city water, mineral water, salt water, spa water, distilled water, bottled water, limewater, H_2O. 2 [Water as a body] spring, lake, ocean, sea, gulf, bay, sound, strait, marsh, loch, puddle, pond, basin, pool, river, lagoon, reservoir, brook, stream, creek, waterfall, bayou.

water v. sprinkle, spray, irrigate; see MOISTEN.

watered a. 1 [Given water] sprinkled, showered, hosed, sprayed, washed, sluiced, bathed, drenched, wetted, irrigated, flooded, baptized, doused, soused, sodden, slaked, quenched; see also WET 1. 2 [Diluted] thinned, weakened, adulterated, lessened, contaminated, mixed, debased, impure, corrupt, blended, weakened, spread out, inflated, cheapened.

waterfall n. cataract, cascade, chute, falls.

water power n. hydraulics, waterworks, water pressure, hydroelectric power; see also ENERGY 2.

waterproof a. impermeable, tight, airtight, vacuum-packed, oiled, rubber-coated, watertight, insulated, impervious, hermetically sealed.

watery a. moist, damp, humid, soggy, sodden, wet, thin, colorless, washed, waterlike.—*Ant.* DRY, parched, baked.

wave n. 1 [A wall of water] comber, swell, roller, heave, tidal wave, billow, tide, surge, crest, bore, breaker, whitecap, tsunami. **2** [A movement suggestive of a wave] surge, gush, swell, uprising, onslaught, influx, tide, flow, stream, swarm, drift, rush, crush, fluctuation. **3** [Undulating movement] rocking, bending, winding; see sense 2.

wave *v.* **1** [To flutter] stream, pulse, flow, shake, fly, dance, flap, swish, swing, tremble, whirl.—*Ant.* FALL, droop, hang listless. **2** [To give an alternating movement] motion, beckon, call, raise the arm, signal, greet, return a greeting, hail. **3** [To move back and forth] falter, waver, oscillate, vacillate, fluctuate, pulsate, vibrate, shake, wag, waggle, sway, lurch, bend, swing, dangle, seesaw, wobble, reel, quaver, quiver, swing from side to side, palpitate, move to and fro; see also ROCK.

waver *v.* fluctuate, vacillate, hesitate, dillydally, seesaw, deliberate, reel, teeter, totter, hem and haw, pause, stagger.

wavy *a.* **1** [Sinuous] undulating, bumpy, crinkly; see ROUGH 1, TWISTED 1. **2** [Unsteady] wavering, fluctuating, vibrating; see UNSTABLE 1.

wax *n.* *Waxes include the following:* paraffin, resin, spermaceti, beeswax, honeycomb, sealing wax, earwax, cerumen, carnauba wax, automobile wax, floor wax, ski wax, furniture polish.

waxy *a.* slick, glistening, polished, slippery, smooth, glazed, sticky, tacky, glassy; see also SMOOTH 1.

way *n.* **1** [Road] trail, walk, byway; see HIGHWAY. **2** [Course] alternative, direction, progression, trend, tendency, distance, space, extent, bearing, orbit, approach, passage, gateway, entrance, access, door, gate, channel. **3** [Means] method, mode, plan, technique, design, system, procedure, process, measure, contrivance, stroke, step, move, action, idea, outline, plot, policy, instrument. **4** [Manner] form, fashion, gait, tone, guise, habit, custom, usage, behavior, style. —**by the way** casually, by the by, as a matter of fact; see INCIDENTALLY. —**by way of** routed through, detoured through, utilizing; see THROUGH 4. —**get out of the** (or **one's**) **way** go, remove oneself, retire; see LEAVE 1, REMOVE 1. —**give way** **1** [To collapse] sag, fall, crumble; see GIVE 2. **2** [To concede] yield, accede, grant; see ADMIT 2. —**in the way** bothersome, nagging, obstructing; see DISTURBING. —**make one's way** progress, succeed, do well; see SUCCEED 1. — **make way** draw back, give way, withdraw; see LEAVE 1. —**on the way out** declining, no longer fashionable, going out; see OLD-FASHIONED, UNPOPULAR. —**out of the way** **1** [Taken care of] disposed of, attended to, settled; see MANAGED 2. **2** [Secluded] unfrequented, isolated, rural; see REMOTE 1. —**parting of the ways** breakup, agreement to separate, difference of opinion; see FIGHT 1, SEPARATION 1. —**under way** advancing, starting, making headway; see MOVING 1. —**way out** means of escape, salvation, loophole; see ESCAPE.

wayfarer *n.* pilgrim, rambler, voyager; see TRAVELER.

ways and means *n.* methods, approaches, devices; see MEANS 1.

wayward *a.* unruly, disobedient, perverse, headstrong, capricious, delinquent, refractory, willful, unruly, unmanageable, insubordinate, incorrigible, recalcitrant, self-indulgent, changeable, stubborn.—*Ant.* OBEDIENT, stable, resolute.

we *pron.* you and I, he and I, she and I, they and I, us.

weak *a.* **1** [Lacking physical strength; *said of persons*] delicate, puny, flabby, flaccid, effeminate, frail, sickly, debilitated, senile; see also SICK.—*Ant.* STRONG, healthy, robust. **2** [Lacking physical strength; *said of things*] flimsy, makeshift, brittle, unsubstantial, jerry-built, rickety, tumbledown, sleazy, shaky, unsteady, ramshackle, rotten, wobbly, tottery.—*Ant.* STRONG, shatterproof, sturdy. **3** [Lacking mental firmness or character] weak-minded, fainthearted, irresolute, nervous, spineless, unstrung, palsied, wishy-washy, hesitant, vacillating, frightened, timid, fearful.—*Ant.* BRAVE, courageous, adventurous. **4** [Lacking in volume] thin, low, soft, indistinct, feeble, faint, dim, muffled, whispered, bated, inaudible, light, stifled, dull, pale.—*Ant.* LOUD, strong, forceful. **5** [Lacking in military power] small, paltry, ineffectual, ineffective, inadequate, impotent, ill-equipped, insufficiently armed, limited, unorganized, undisciplined, untrained, vulnerable, exposed, assailable, unprepared. **6** [Lacking in capacity or experience] unsure, untrained, young; see UNSTABLE 2.

weaken *v.* **1** [To become weaker] lessen, lose, decrease, relapse, soften, relax, droop, fail, crumble, halt, wane, abate, limp, languish, fade, decline, totter, tremble, flag, faint, wilt, lose spirit, become disheartened, fail in courage, slow down, break up, crack up*, wash out*.—*Ant.* STRENGTHEN, revive, straighten. **2** [To make weaker] reduce, minimize, enervate, debilitate, exhaust, cripple, unman, emasculate, castrate, devitalize, undermine, impair, sap, enfeeble, unnerve, incapacitate, impoverish, thin, dilute, take the wind out of someone's sails, wear down; see also DECREASE 2.—*Ant.* REVIVE, quicken, animate.

weakling *n.* puny person, feeble creature, coward, crybaby, milksop, jellyfish*, softy*, sissy*, pushover*, cream puff*, namby-pamby.

weakness *n.* **1** [The state of being weak] feebleness, senility, delicacy, invalidity, frailty, faintness, prostration, decrepitude, debility, impotence, enervation, dizziness, infirmity.—*Ant.* STRENGTH, good health, vitality. **2** [An instance or manner of being weak] fault, failing, bad habit, deficiency, defect, disturbance, lapse, vice, sore point, gap, flaw, instability, sin, indecision, inconstancy, vulnerability.—*Ant.* VIRTUE, good, strength. **3** [Inclination] liking, tendency, bent; see HUNGER, INCLINATION 1.

wealth *n.* capital, capital stock, economic resources, stock, stocks and bonds, securities, vested interests, land, property, commodities, cash, money in the bank, money, natural resources, assets, means, riches, substance, affluence, belongings, investments, portfolio, fortune, hoard, treasure, resources, revenue, cache, competence, luxury, opulence, prosperity, abundance, money to burn*, dough*.—*Ant.* POVERTY, pauperism, unemployment.

wealthy *a.* opulent, moneyed, affluent; see RICH 1.

weapon *n.* armament, protection, weaponry, deadly weapon, military hardware, lethal weapon, defense. *Weapons include the following:* club, spear, arrow, knife, catapult, bullet, dart, missile, cruise missile, heat-seeking missile, laser-guided missile, guided missile, ICBM (intercontinental ballistic missile), ABM (antiballistic missile), MIRV (multiple independently-targetable reentry vehicle), CBW (chemical and biological warfare), bomb, car bomb, truck bomb, letter bomb, smart bomb, stick, ax, firearm, cannon, gun, musket, rifle, blackjack, whip, sword, pistol, handgun, automatic weapon, semiautomatic weapon, weapon of mass destruction, mortar, rocket, bazooka, flamethrower, land mine, mine, napalm, revolver, bayonet, machine gun, warhead, tank.

wear *n.* depreciation, damage, loss, erosion, wear and tear, loss by friction, diminution, waste, corrosion, impairment, wearing away, disappearance, result of friction.—*Ant.* GROWTH, accretion, building up.

wear *v.* **1** [To use as clothing or personal ornament] bear, carry, effect, put on, don, be clothed, slip on, have

on, dress in, attire, cover, wrap, harness, get into*; see also DRESS 2.—*Ant.* UNDRESS, take off, disrobe. **2** [To wear down] use up, use, consume, wear thin, wear out, waste, diminish, cut down, scrape off, exhaust, fatigue, weather down, impair. **3** [To be consumed by wear] fade, go to seed, decay, crumble, dwindle, shrink, decline, deteriorate, decrease, waste, become threadbare. **—wear down** wear out, get thinner, get worn out; see DECREASE 1, WASTE 3. **—wear off** go away, get better, diminish; see STOP 2. **—wear out** become worn, be worthless, get thinner; see WASTE 1, 3.

wear and tear *n.* depletion, wearing, effect of use; see DAMAGE 1, 2, DESTRUCTION 2.

weariness *n.* tiredness, exhaustion, dullness; see FATIGUE.

weary *a.* exhausted, fatigued, overworked; see TIRED.

weary *v.* **1** [To make weary] annoy, vex, distress, irk, tax, strain, overwork, exhaust, fatigue, tire, harass, bore, disgust, dishearten, dispirit, wear out, leave someone cold, depress, cloy, jade, glut, burden, sicken, nauseate. **2** [To become weary] flag, be worn out, sink, droop, lose interest, fall off, tire, grow tired, drowse, doze, sicken.—*Ant.* ENJOY, excite, be amused.

weather *n.* climate, clime*, atmospheric conditions, air conditions, drought, clear weather, sunny weather, foul weather, tempest, calm, windiness, the elements, cloudiness, heat, cold, warmth, chilliness.

weather *v.* **1** [To expose to the weather] dry, bleach, discolor, blanch, whiten, pulverize, tan, burn, expose, harden, petrify. **2** [To pass through adversity successfully] overcome, stand up against, bear the brunt of; see ENDURE 1, SUCCEED 1.

weather-beaten *a.* decayed, battered, weathered; see OLD 2, 3, WORN 2.

weatherman *n.* weather reporter, weather prophet, weather forecaster, meteorologist, climatologist.

weather report *n.* weather prediction, weathercast, meteorological forecast; see FORECAST.

weave *n.* pattern, design, texture; see WEB.

weave *v.* **1** [To construct by interlacing] knit, sew, interlace, spin, twine, intertwine, crisscross, interlink, wreathe, mesh, net, knot, twill, fold, interfold, ply, reticulate, loop, splice, braid, plait, twist. **2** [To move in and out] dodge, sidle through, make one's way, twist and turn, snake, zigzag, beat one's way, insinuate oneself through, wedge through.

web *n.* cobweb, lacework, netting, plait, mesh, mat, matting, wicker, weft, warp, woof, network, interconnection, reticulation, intermixture, entanglement, tracery, filigree, interweaving, trellis.

wed *v.* espouse, join in wedlock, take in marriage; see MARRY 1, 2.

wedded *a.* married, espoused, in holy matrimony; see MARRIED.

wedding *n.* wedlock, nuptials, matrimony; see MARRIAGE.

wedge *n.* spearhead, shim, chock; see MACHINE, TOOL 1.

weed *n.* **1** [Wild plant] noxious weed, unwanted plant, prolific plant; see PLANT. *Common weeds include the following:* ragweed, clover, chickweed, crab grass, knotgrass, sheep sorrel, speedwell, yarrow, nettle, wild morning glory, pigweed, buckthorn, dandelion, lamb's-quarters, dog fennel, plantain, couch grass, jimson weed, ironweed, wild sunflower, wild hemp, horsemint, foxtail, milkweed, wild barley, wild buckwheat, mullein, Russian thistle, tumbleweed, burdock, wild carrot, wild parsley, vervain, wild mustard. **2** [*Cigarette or cigar] coffin nail*, fag*, smoke; see TOBACCO. **3** [*Marijuana] pot*, Mary Jane*, grass*; see MARIJUANA.

week *n.* wk., seven days, six days, forty-hour week, working week, work week.

weekday *n.* working day, Monday through Friday, workday; see DAY 1.

weekend *n.* end of the week, Saturday to Monday, short vacation, long weekend, holiday weekend.

weekly *a.* once every seven days, once a week, occurring every week.

weep *v.* wail, moan, lament; see CRY 1.

weigh *v.* **1** [To measure weight] scale, put on the scales, hold the scales, put in the balance, counterbalance, heft*; see also MEASURE 1. **2** [To have weight] be heavy, carry weight, be important, tell, count, show, register, press, pull, be a load, burden, tip the scales at. **3** [To consider] ponder, contemplate, balance; see CONSIDER. —**weigh down** pull down, burden, oppress; see DEPRESS 2.

weight *n.* **1** [Heaviness] pressure, load, gross weight, net weight, dead weight, molecular weight, specific gravity, burden, mass, density, ponderability, ponderousness, tonnage, ballast, substance, G-force, atomic weight; see also MEASUREMENT 2, PRESSURE 1.—*Ant.* LIGHTNESS, buoy-

ancy, airiness. **2** [An object used for its weight] counterbalance, counterweight, counterpoise, ballast, paperweight, stone, rock, lead weight, sinker, anchor, plumb, sandbag. *Common weights include the following:* grain, dram, ounce, pound, ton, short ton, long ton, troy weight, pennyweight, troy ounce, troy pound, carat, kilogram, centigram, gram, milligram, metric ton, metric carat. **3** [Importance] influence, authority, sway; see IMPORTANCE.

weird *a.* uncanny, ominous, eerie; see MYSTERIOUS 2.

welcome *a.* gladly received, gladly admitted, desired, appreciated, honored, esteemed, cherished, desirable, agreeable, pleasant, good, pleasing, delightful.—*Ant.* UNDESIRABLE, disagreeable, unpleasant. —**you're welcome** my pleasure, forget it, think nothing of it, don't mention it, it's nothing, no problem*.

welcome *interj.* greetings, come right in, make yourself at home, how do you do?, glad to see you, won't you come in?.

welcome *n.* greetings, salute, salutation, a hero's welcome, handshake, warm reception, free entrance, entree, hospitality, friendliness, the glad hand*.—*Ant.* rebuke, snub, cool reception. —**wear out one's welcome** bore others, stay too long, make others weary with one; see WEARY 1.

welcome *v.* embrace, hug, take in; see GREET.

welcomed *a.* received, accepted, initiated; see WELCOME.

weld *v.* fuse, unite, seam; see JOIN 1.

welfare *n.* **1** [Personal condition] health, happiness, well-being, prosperity, good, good fortune, progress, state of being. **2** [Social service] poverty program, social insurance, health service; see INSURANCE.

well *a.* **1** [In good health] fine, sound, fit, trim, healthy, robust, strong, hearty, high-spirited, vigorous, hardy, hale, blooming, fresh, flourishing, rosy-cheeked, whole, in fine fettle, in shape*, hunky-dory*, great*, fit as a fiddle, chipper*.—*Ant.* SICK, ill, infirm. **2** [Satisfactorily] up to the mark, suitably, adequately, commendably, excellently, thoroughly, admirably, splendidly, favorably, rightly, properly, expertly, strongly, irreproachably, capably, soundly, competently, ably, fine, great*.—*Ant.* BADLY, poorly, unsatisfactorily. **3** [Sufficiently] abundantly, adequately, completely, fully, quite, entirely, considerably, wholly, plentifully, luxuriantly, extremely.—*Ant.* HARDLY, insufficiently, barely. —**as well** in addition, additionally, along with; see ALSO. —**as well as** similarly, alike, as much as; see EQUALLY.

well *n.* **1** [A source of water] spring, fountain, font, spout, geyser, well-spring, mouth, artesian well, reservoir. **2** [A shaft sunk into the earth] pit, hole, depression, chasm, abyss, oil well, gas well, water well, gusher. **3** [Any source] beginning, derivation, fountainhead; see ORIGIN 3.

well-balanced *a.* steady, sensible, well-adjusted; see RELIABLE.

well-behaved *a.* mannerly, courteous, civil; see POLITE.

well-being *n.* prosperity, happiness, fortune; see HEALTH, WELFARE 1.

well-informed *a.* informed, well-read, advised; see LEARNED 1, EDUCATED.

well-known *a.* famous, reputable, recognized, renowned, eminent, illustrious, familiar, widely known, noted, acclaimed, popular, public, celebrated, in the public eye, notorious, infamous.—*Ant.* UNKNOWN, obscure, undiscovered.

well-off *a.* prosperous, well-to-do, wealthy; see RICH 1.

well-read *a.* bookish, scholarly, erudite; see EDUCATED, INTELLIGENT.

well-rounded *a.* well-informed, with broad interests, having a good background; see BALANCED.

well-to-do *a.* wealthy, well-off, prosperous; see RICH 1.

welt *n.* wound, bruise, weal; see INJURY.

west *a.* **1** [Situated to the west] westward, in the west, on the west side of, toward the sunset, west side, western, westerly, westernmost. **2** [Going toward the west] westbound, westward, to the west, headed west, in a westerly direction, out of the east. **3** [Coming from the west] eastbound, eastward, in the east, headed east, in an easterly direction, out of the west.

West *n.* **1** [Western Hemisphere] New World, the Americas, North and South America, America. **2** [European and American Culture] the Occident, Western civilization, Christian society, Europe, European Community, European Union. **3** [Western United States; *especially the cowboy and mining culture*] the range, the prairies, Rocky Mountain country, Far West, Northwest, Southwest, where men are men*, wild-and-woolly country*, the wide open spaces*, buffalo range*, Cow Country*.

western *a.* **1** [Concerning the direction to the west] westerly, westward, on the west side of; see WEST 1. **2** [Concerning the western part of the United States] West, Pacific, Pacific Seaboard, West Coast, Northwestern, Southwestern, cowboy, middle-western, far-western, in the sagebrush country, on the Western plains, in the wide open spaces, in the Wild West, in the Rockies, in God's country, in the wild-and-woolly West*, out where the men are men*. **3** [Concerning Europe and America] American, European, Continental, British, Canadian, Caribbean, Latin American, French, German, Italian, Spanish.

wet *a.* **1** [Covered or soaked with liquid] moist, damp, soaking, soaked, drenched, soggy, muggy, dewy, watery, dank, slimy, dripping, saturated, sodden.—*Ant.* DRY, dried, clean. **2** [Rainy] drizzly, slushy, snowy, slippery, muddy, humid, foggy, damp, clammy, showery, stormy, drizzling, cloudy, misty.—*Ant.* CLEAR, sunny, cloudless.

wet *v.* sprinkle, dampen, splash; see MOISTEN.

whack *n.* stroke, thump, wham; see BLOW. —**out of whack*** out of order, not working, spoiled; see RUINED 1, 2.

wham *n.* hit, knock, whack; see BLOW.

wharf *n.* boat landing, quay, pier; see DOCK.

what *pron.* **1** [An indication of a question] which?, what sort?, what kind?, what thing?, what means?. **2** [Something indefinite] that which, whatever, something, anything, everything, whichever, anything at all. —**and what not** et cetera, and other things too numerous to mention, some more; see ANYTHING, EVERYTHING. —**what about** but what, remember, and then; see BUT 1, 2, 3. —**what for** but why, to what end, for what purpose; see WHY.

whatever *pron.* anything, everything, no matter what, whatsoever.

wheat *n.* staff of life, breadstuff, wheat flour; see GRAIN 1.

wheel *n.* **1** [A thin circular body that turns on an axis] disk, ratchet, ring, hoop, roller, caster, drum, ferris wheel, wheel trolley, flywheel, cogwheel, steering wheel, sprocket wheel, chain wheel, water wheel. **2** [*An important person*] personage, VIP, big shot*; see CELEBRITY, EXECUTIVE. —**at** (or **behind**) **the wheel** driving, in control, running things; see RUNNING 1, 2.

wheels* *n.* car, vehicle, auto; see AUTOMOBILE.

wheeze *v.* breathe heavily, puff, pant; see GASP.

when *a., conj.* **1** [At what time?] how soon?, how long ago?, in what period?, just when?, at which instant?. **2** [Whenever] if, at any time, at the moment that, just as soon as, in the event that, on the condition that; see also IF. **3** [During] at the same time that, immediately upon, just as, just after, at, while, meanwhile; see also DURING.

whenever *conj.* at any time, at any moment, on any occasion, at the first opportunity, if, when, should.

where *a., conj.* **1** [A question as to position] in what place?, at which place?, at what moment?, whither?, in what direction?, toward what? **2** [An indication of position] wherever, anywhere, in whatever place, at which point, in which, to which, to what end.

whereabouts *n.* location, spot, site; see PLACE 3.

whereas *conj.* since, inasmuch as, insomuch as, forasmuch as, considering that, when in fact, while, while on the contrary.

whereby *conj.* by which, through which, in accordance with which, with the help of which, how.

wherefore *a.* why?, for what?, for which reason?, therefore, so, accordingly, thereupon.

whereupon *conj.* at which point, thereupon, at the conclusion of which, whereon, upon which, consequently.

wherever *a., conj.* where, in whatever place, anywhere, in any place that, wheresoever, regardless of where, in any direction.

wherewithal *n.* resources, money, funds; see FUNDS.

whether *conj.* if, either, even if, if it follows that. **—whether or not 1** [Surely] in any case, certainly, positively; see SURELY. **2** [If] whether, yes or no, whichever; see IF.

which *pron., a.* what, whichever, that, whatever, and that, and which, one, who.

whichever *pron., a.* which, whatever, whichsoever, no matter which, whoever.

whiff *n.* scent, puff, fume; see SMELL 1, 2.

while *conj.* **1** [As long as] during, at the same time that, during the time that, whilst, throughout the time that, in the time that. **2** [Although] even though, whereas, though; see ALTHOUGH. **—for a while** for a short time, for a few minutes, briefly; see AWHILE.

whim *n.* notion, vagary, caprice; see INCLINATION 1.

whimper *v.* fuss, weep, snivel; see COMPLAIN, WHINE.

whimsical *a.* playful, capricious, comical; see FUNNY 1.

whine *v.* sing, hum, whistle, whim-

per, drone, cry, moan, murmur, grumble, complain, gripe*, beef*.

whip *n.* switch, strap, rod, cane, lash, scourge, knotted cord, knout, cat-o-nine-tails, thong, blacksnake, dog whip, ox whip, bullwhip, horsewhip, buggy whip, riding whip, quirt.

whip *v.* thrash, strike, scourge; see BEAT 2, PUNISH.

whipping *n.* beating, thrashing, strapping; see PUNISHMENT.

whir *v.* whiz, swish, vibrate; see HUM.

whirl *n.* **1** [Rapid rotating motion] swirl, turn, flurry, spin, gyration, reel, surge, whir; see also REVOLUTION 1. **2** [Confusion] hurry, flutter, fluster, ferment, agitation, tempest, storm, rush, tumult, turbulence, commotion, hurly-burly, bustle.

whirl *v.* turn around, rotate, spin; see TURN 1.

whirlpool *n.* eddy, vortex, swirl, maelstrom, undertow, undercurrent, rapids.

whiskers *n.* beard, mustache, sideburns, goatee, burnsides, mutton chops, facial hair, bristles, (hogs, etc.), vibrissa (cats, etc.).

whiskey *n.* bourbon whiskey, rye whiskey, corn whiskey, Scotch whiskey, Irish whiskey, Canadian whiskey, hard liquor, spirits, aqua vitae, booze*, firewater*, hooch*, homebrew, moonshine*, mountain dew*; see also DRINK 2.

whisper *n.* **1** [A low, sibilant sound] rustle, noise, murmur, hum, buzz, drone, undertone, hissing. **2** [A guarded utterance] disclosure, divulgence, rumor; see SECRET.

whisper *v.* speak softly, speak in a whisper, speak under one's breath, speak in an undertone, tell, talk low, speak confidentially, mutter, murmur, speak into someone's ear.—*Ant.* YELL, speak aloud, shout.

whispering *a.* rustling, sighing, buzzing, humming, murmuring, droning, hissing.

whistle *n.* **1** [A shrill sound] cry, shriek, howl, blast, piping, siren call, fire alarm, birdcall, signal, toot, blare; see also NOISE 1. **2** [An instrument that produces a shrill sound] fife, pipes, pennywhistle; see ALARM.

whistle *v.* **1** [To produce a shrill blast] fife, pipe, flute, trill, hiss, whiz, wheeze, shriek, howl, blare, toot, tootle; see also SOUND. **2** [To call with a whistle] signal, summon, warn; see SUMMON.

white *a.* **1** [The color of fresh snow] ivory, silvery, snow-white, snowy, frosted, milky, milky-white, chalky, pearly, blanched, ashen, pale, wan, albescent.—*Ant.* DARK, black, dirty. **2** [Colorless] clear, transparent, clean, blank, spotless, pure, unalloyed, neutral, achromatic, achromic. **3** [Concerning the white race] fair-skinned, light-complexioned, Caucasian; see EUROPEAN, WESTERN 2. **4** [Pale] ashen, wan, pallid; see PALE 1.

white-collar *a.* professional, office, administrative, skilled.

whiten *v.* **1** [To become white] grow hoary, blanch, turn white, turn gray, grow pale, be covered with snow, be silvered, change color, fade. **2** [To make white] bleach, blanch, silver, paint white, whitewash, apply powder, chalk.—*Ant.* DIRTY, smudge, blacken.

whitewash *v.* gloss over, cover up, play down, minimize, dissemble over, downplay, sweep under the carpet, turn a blind eye to; see also EXCUSE.

whittle *v.* pare, carve, shape, fashion, shave, model, chip off, lessen, diminish, shave, decrease, pare down.

who *pron.* what, that, which, he, she, they, I, you, whoever, whichever.

whoever *pron.* he who, she who, the one who, whatever person, no matter who.

whole *a.* **1** [Entire] all, every, inclusive, full, undivided, integral, complete, total, aggregate, indivisible, inseparable, indissoluble, gross, undiminished, utter.—*Ant.* UNFINISHED, partial, incomplete. **2** [Not broken, damaged, or split up] thorough, mature, developed, unimpaired, unmarred, full, unbroken, undamaged, entire, in one piece, sound, solid, untouched, without a scratch, intact, uninjured, undecayed, completed, preserved, perfect, complete, safe, in A-1 condition*, shipshape, in good order, together, unified, exhaustive, conclusive, unqualified, fulfilled, accomplished, consummate.—*Ant.* BROKEN, mutilated, defective. **3** [Not ill or injured] hale, hearty, sound; see HEALTHY, WELL 1.

whole *n.* unity, totality, everything, oneness, entity, entirety, collectivity, sum, assemblage, aggregate, aggregation, body, lump, gross, length and breadth, generality, mass, amount, bulk, quantity, universality, complex, assembly, gross amount.—*Ant.* PART, portion, fraction. —**as a whole** collectively, altogether, in toto, en masse; see also COMPLETELY.

wholehearted *a.* sincere, earnest, candid; see HEARTY.

wholesale *a.* **1** [Dealing in large lots] large-scale, in the mass, quantitative, in bulk, bulk, to the retailer, by the carload, loose, in quantity, in job lots; see also COMMERCIAL. **2** [Indiscriminate] sweep-

ing, widespread, comprehensive; see WHOLE 1.

wholesome *a.* nutritive, nourishing, beneficial; see HEALTHFUL.

wholly *a.* totally, entirely, fully; see COMPLETELY.

whom *pron.* that, her, him; see WHO, WHAT 2.

whopper* *n.* great lie, falsehood, fabrication; see LIE, STORY.

whore *n.* hooker*, tramp*, slut*; see PROSTITUTE.

whorl *n.* twirl, twist, spiral; see COIL.

whose *poss. pronominal adj.* to whom, belonging to what person, of the aforementioned one, from these.

why *a., conj.* for what reason?, how so?, how?, how is it that?, on whose account?, what is the cause that?, to what end?, for what purpose?, on what foundation?, how do you explain that?, how come?*.

wicked *a.* sinful, immoral, corrupt, evil, base, foul, gross, dissolute, wayward, irreligious, blasphemous, profane, evil-minded, vile, bad, naughty, degenerate, depraved, incorrigible, unruly, heartless, shameless, degraded, debauched, hard, toughened, disreputable, infamous, indecent, mean, remorseless, scandalous, atrocious, contemptible, nasty, vicious, fiendish, hellish, villainous, rascally, devilish, malevolent, conspiratorial, flagrant, criminal, heinous, murderous, tricky, sinister, ignoble, monstrous, rotten*, lowdown*, good-for-nothing, dirty, felonious, dangerous, cut-throat, ratty*, slippery, crooked.—*Ant.* HONEST, just, kind.

wickedness *n.* evil, depravity, immorality; see EVIL 1.

wide *a.* **1** [Broad] extended, spacious, deep; see BROAD 1. **2** [Loose] broad, roomy, full; see LOOSE 1. **3** [Extensive] large-scale, all-inclusive, universal; see GENERAL 1.

wide-awake *a.* alert, watchful, vigilant; see CAREFUL.

widely *a.* extensively, generally, publicly, nationally, internationally, universally, in many places, broadly, comprehensively.

widen *v.* **1** [To make wider] add to, broaden, stretch, extend, increase, enlarge, distend, spread out, give more space, augment. **2** [To become wider] unfold, grow, open, stretch, grow larger, increase, swell, multiply.

widespread *a.* extensive, general, sweeping, broad, comprehensive, far-reaching, pandemic, widely accepted, boundless, popular, public, unrestricted, unlimited, on a large scale, over-all.—*Ant.* OBSCURE, secret, limited.

widow *n.* widow woman, dowager, divorcée, husbandless wife, dead man's wife; see also WIFE.

widower *n.* surviving husband, grass widower, widowman*; see HUSBAND.

width *n.* breadth, wideness, girth, diameter, distance across, amplitude, cross dimension, cross measurement, expanse.—*Ant.* LENGTH, height, altitude.

wield *v.* handle, manipulate, exercise; see HOLD 1.

wiener *n.* frankfurter, sausage, hot dog*; see MEAT.

wife *n.* married woman, spouse, lady, dame, madam, matron, helpmate, consort, mate, housewife, better half*, the missis*, the little woman*, wifey*, the old lady*.—*Ant.* WIDOW, spinster, old maid.

wig *n.* hairpiece, fall, human-hair wig, synthetic wig, toupee, rug*, periwig, peruke; see also HAIR 1.

wiggle *v.* wag, waggle, wriggle, squirm, shimmy, shake, flounce, dance sensually.

wild *a.* **1** [Not controlled] unrestrained, unmanageable, boisterous; see UNRULY. **2** [Uncivilized] barbarous, savage, undomesticated; see PRIMITIVE. **3** [Not cultivated] luxuriant, lush, exuberant, dense, excessive, desolate, waste, desert, weedy, untrimmed, uninhabited, native, natural, untouched, virgin, overgrown, uncultivated, untilled, overrun, uncared for, neglected, impenetrable, free, rampant. **4** [Inaccurate] erratic, off, unsound; see WRONG 2. **5** [Stormy] disturbed, raging, storming; see TURBULENT. **6** [Very excited] hot, eager, avid; see EXCITED. **7** [Dissolute] loose, licentious, profligate; see LEWD 2. **8** [Imprudent] reckless, foolish, incautious; see CARELESS.

wildcat *n.* mountain lion or cougar, bobcat, Canada lynx, caracal.

wilderness *n.* wilds, wasteland, back country, the woods, the North woods, primeval forest, uninhabited region; see also DESERT, FOREST.

wildly *a.* hastily, rashly, fiercely, violently, ferociously, uncontrollably, carelessly, quixotically, savagely, unwittingly, recklessly, confusedly, pell-mell.—*Ant.* CAREFULLY, prudently, judiciously.

will *n.* **1** [Desire] inclination, wish, disposition, pleasure, yearning, craving, longing, hankering. **2** [Conscious power] resolution, volition, intention, preference, will power, mind, determination, self-determination, decisiveness, moral strength, discretion, conviction, willfulness.—*Ant.* DOUBT, vacillation, indecision. **3** [Testament for

the disposition of property] bequest, disposition, instructions, last wishes, bestowal, dispensation, last will and testament. —**free will** willingness, volition, intention, purpose, choice, free choice, power of choice, freedom, pleasure, discretion, inclination, desire, wish, intent, option, determination, mind, consent, assent.—*Ant.* RESTRAINT, predestination, unwillingness.

will *v.* **1** [To exert one's will] decree, order, command, demand, authorize, request, make oneself felt, decide upon, insist, direct, enjoin. **2** [To wish] want, incline to, prefer; see WISH. **3** [An indication of futurity] shall, would, should, expect to, anticipate, look forward to, hope to, await, foresee, propose.

willful *a.* intentional, premeditated, contemplated; see DELIBERATE.

willing *a.* energetic, prompt, reliable, active, obedient, enthusiastic, zealous, responsible, agreeable, prepared, voluntary, ready, compliant, amenable, tractable, feeling, like, in accord with.—*Ant.* OPPOSED, averse, unwilling.

willingly *a.* gladly, readily, obediently, agreeably, voluntarily, with relish, at one's pleasure, on one's own account, of one's own accord, without reservation, without a second thought, with good cheer, freely, with pleasure, cheerfully, with all one's heart, at the drop of a hat*, like a shot*.

willingness *n.* zeal, enthusiasm, readiness, earnestness, eagerness, alacrity, cordiality, hospitality, courteousness, compliance, good will, geniality.

will-o'-the-wisp *n.* fancy, ephemera, dream, pipe dream, *ignis fatuus* (Latin), shadow, illusion, vision, delusion.

wilt *v.* droop, wither, weaken, shrivel, flag, dry up, fade, become flaccid, lose freshness, faint.—*Ant.* GROW, STAND, stiffen.

win *n.* triumph, conquest, victory; see SUCCESS 1.

win *v.* **1** [To gain a victory] be victorious, prevail, get the best of, come out first, conquer, overcome, come out on top, overwhelm, triumph; see also SUCCEED 1. **2** [To obtain] get, acquire, gain; see GET 1. **3** [To reach] attain, accomplish, effect; see APPROACH 2, 3.

wind *n.* draft, air current, breeze, gust, gale, blast, flurry, whisk, whiff, puff, whirlwind, flutter, wafting, zephyr, trade wind, sirocco, northeaster, nor'easter, southwester, sou'wester, tempest, blow, cyclone, typhoon, twister, hurricane, sandstorm, prevailing westerlies, stiff breeze, chinook, Santa Ana. —**get** (or **have**) **wind of*** hear about, have news of, trace; see HEAR 1. — **take the wind out of someone's sails** best, get the better of, overcome; see DEFEAT 2, 3.

wind *v.* **1** [To wrap about] coil, reel in, entwine, wreathe, shroud, fold, cover, bind, tape, bandage. **2** [To twist] convolute, screw, wind up; see BEND. **3** [To meander] zigzag, weave, snake, twist, loop, turn, twine, ramble, swerve, deviate. — **wind up** conclude, be through with, come to the end of; see END 1.

windbag* *n.* blowhard*, loudmouth, big talker*; see TALKER.

winded *a.* tired, exhausted, out of breath, breathless, gasping, panting, heaving, fagged.

winding *a.* turning, gyrating, gyring, spiraling, twisting, snaky, serpentine, convoluted.—*Ant.* STRAIGHT, direct, vertical.

window *n.* skylight, porthole, bay window, bow window, picture window, casement, double-hung window, dormer, stained-glass, show window, rose window, transom, jalousie window, peephole.

windpipe *n.* airpipe, bronchus, trachea; see THROAT.

windshield *n.* windscreen, protection against the wind, wraparound; see SCREEN 1.

windy *a.* breezy, blustery, raw, stormy, wind-swept, airy, gusty, blowing, fresh, drafty, wind-shaken, tempestuous, boisterous.—*Ant.* CALM, quiet, still.

wine *n. Wines include the following:* still, sparkling, fortified, dry, sweet, red, white, rosé, blush, vintage, nonvintage, varietal, *appellation contrôlée;* blackberry, cherry, currant, gooseberry, dandelion; sacramental, dessert, dinner, medicinal, aperitif, cooking; California, New York State, French, Italian, German, Spanish; sherry, Tokay, port, claret, muscatel; Burgundy, Bordeaux, champagne, sauterne, Rhine wine, Chablis, Chianti, Beaujolais, Barolo; retsina, sake, rice wine; cabernet sauvignon, pinot noir, merlot, chardonnay, sauvignon blanc, Gewürztraminer, zinfandel, pinot grigio, Riesling, Concord, catawba; sangria; see also DRINK 2.

wing *n.* **1** [An organ or instrument of flight] appendage, aileron, airfoil; see FEATHER. **2** [An architectural unit or extension] annex, addition, projection, hall, section, division, part. **3** [An organized group of aircraft] flying unit, formation, air squadron; see UNIT. —**take under one's wing** favor, help, protect; see ADOPT 2.

wink *v.* squint, blink, flirt, make eyes at, bat the eyes.

winner *n.* victor, conqueror, prizewinner, champion, winning com-

petitor, hero, successful contestant, leading entrant, Olympic champion, titleholder, champ*, frontrunner.

winning *a.* **1** [Engaging] attractive, appealing, agreeable; see CHARMING. **2** [Victorious] champion, conquering, leading; see SUCCESSFUL.

winsome *a.* engaging, entrancing, fetching; see CHARMING.

winter *n.* cold season, frosty weather, wintertime, Christmastime, Jack Frost.

wintry *a.* chilly, frosty, icy, snowy, frigid, cold, bleak, raw, biting, cutting.—*Ant.* WARM, summery, balmy.

wipe *v.* rub, clean, dry, dust, mop, clear, wash, swab, soak up, obliterate. —**wipe out** slay, annihilate, eradicate; see DESTROY, KILL 1, REMOVE 1.

wire *n.* **1** [A metal strand] line, electric wire, cable, aerial, circuit, wiring, live wire, coil, conductor, filament, musical string, wire tape, wire cord. **2** [A metal net] barbed wire, wire fence, wire cage; see FENCE. **3** [A telegraphic message] cablegram, message, cable; see TELEGRAM. —**down to the wire** to the very end, at the last, eventually; see FINALLY 2. —**get (in) under the wire** just make it, be just in time, squeak through*; see ARRIVE.

wire *v.* **1** [To install wire] set up a circuit, install electricity, lay wires, connect electric cables, prepare for electrical service, pipe*; see also ELECTRIFY. **2** [To send a message by wire] flash, telegraph, notify; see TELL 1.

wiring *n.* wirework, electric line, cable work, cables, electrical installations, facilities for electric power, circuit system, electrical wire distribution, tubing, circuit pattern, circuiting, threading, process, route, line, path, pattern, trail.

wiry *a.* agile, sinewy, tough; see STRONG 1.

wisdom *n.* prudence, astuteness, sense, reason, clear thinking, good judgment, sagacity, understanding, sanity, shrewdness, experience, practical knowledge, carefulness, vigilance, tact, balance, poise, stability, caution, solidity, hardheadedness, brains, common sense, horse sense*, savvy*.—*Ant.* STUPIDITY, irrationality, rashness.

wise *a.* **1** [Judicious] clever, sagacious, witty; see THOUGHTFUL 1. **2** [Shrewd] calculating, cunning, crafty; see SLY. **3** [Prudent] tactful, sensible, wary; see CAREFUL. **4** [Erudite] taught, scholarly, smart; see EDUCATED, LEARNED 1. **5** [Informed] wise to*, on to*, aware of; see FAMILIAR WITH.

wisely *a.* tactfully, prudently, circumspectly, sagaciously, shrewdly, judiciously, discreetly, carefully, admirably, discerningly, sagely, knowingly, reasonably, sensibly, intelligently.—*Ant.* FOOLISHLY, stupidly, unthinkingly.

wish *n.* longing, yearning, hankering, desire, thirst, disposition, request, hope, intention, preference, choice, want, prayer, invocation, liking, pleasure, injunction, command, order.

wish *v.* **1** [To desire] covet, crave, envy; see WANT 1. **2** [To express a desire] hope, request, entreat, prefer, want, pray for, invoke, command, order, solicit, beg, look forward to, require; see also NEED.

wishful *a.* desirous, longing, eager; see ZEALOUS.

wishy-washy* *a.* indecisive, spineless, feeble; see WEAK 3.

wisp *n.* tuft, cluster, shred, a few strands, lock, bit, shock, cowlick, stray lock.

wit *n.* wittiness, smartness, whimsicality, pleasantry, drollery, banter, burlesque, satire, jocularity, witticism, sally, whimsy, repartee, joke, aphorism, jest, quip, epigram, pun, wisecrack*, gag. —**at one's wits' end** downhearted, desperate, helpless; see TROUBLED. —**have (or keep) one's wits about one** be ready, take precautions, be on one's guard; see WATCH OUT. —**live by one's wits** use sharp practices, live dangerously, be street-smart*; see TRICK.

witch *n.* sorcerer, warlock, magician, enchantress, charmer, hag, crone.

witchcraft *n.* sorcery, magic, black magic, necromancy, witchery, divination, devil worship, enchantment, spell, bewitchment, voodooism, shamanism, demonology.

witch hunt *n.* persecution, show trial, kangaroo court, miscarriage of justice.

with *prep.* by, in association, in the midst of, among, amidst, along with, in company with, arm in arm, hand in glove, in conjunction with, among other things, beside, alongside of, including.

withdraw *v.* **1** [To retire] depart, draw back, take leave; see RETREAT. **2** [To remove from use or circulation] revoke, rescind, abolish, repeal, annul, abrogate, veto, suppress, repress, retire, stamp out, declare illegal, ban, bar, nullify, repudiate, reverse, retract, throw overboard, invalidate, quash, dissolve.

withdrawal *n.* removal, retreat, retraction, resignation, alienation, abandonment, recession, revulsion, abdication, relinquishment, departure.—*Ant.* PROGRESS, advance, appearance.

withdrawn *a.* retired, secluded, isolated, removed, departed, cloistered, reclusive, drawn back, gone into retirement, taken out, absent, retreated.—*Ant.* ACTIVE, involved, progressing.

wither *v.* shrivel, shrink, droop, wilt, decay, die, grow brown, dry up, dry out, fade, lose freshness, deteriorate, fall away.—*Ant.* REVIVE, reawaken, bloom.

withered *a.* shriveled, wilted, decayed, deteriorated, shrunken, dead, browned, faded, parched, dried up, drooping, wrinkled.—*Ant.* FRESH, blooming, alive.

withheld *a.* concealed, held back, hidden, checked, restrained, interdicted, delayed, denied, kept on leash, on ice*.—*Ant.* FREE, opened, made visible.

withhold *v.* hold back, reserve, keep; see DENY.

within *a., prep.* inside, indoors, in, not further than, not beyond, not over, in reach of, in a period of, not outside; see also INSIDE 2.

with-it* *a.* up-to-date, well-informed, contemporary, hip*, stylish, in the know*, on the ball*, in the swing of things*; see also MODERN 1.

without *a., prep.* **1** [Outside] out, outdoors, outwardly, externally, on the outside, standing outside, left out. **2** [Lacking] not with, not having, in the absence of, free from, deprived of.

withstand *v.* face, oppose, confront, resist, endure, stand up to, hold out.

witness *n.* observer, onlooker, eyewitness, bystander, spectator, testifier, beholder, signatory. —**bear witness** affirm, attest, give evidence; see TESTIFY 2.

witness *v.* see, observe, be a witness, be on the scene, behold, be present, testify, vouch for, stand for, look on, say under oath, depose, be on hand.

witnessed *a.* sworn to, vouched for, alleged, borne out, validated, valid, established, verified, authenticated, substantiated, supported, upheld, endorsed, brought forward.

witty *a.* quick-witted, clever, amusing; see INTELLIGENT.

wizard *n.* magician, soothsayer, witch, witch doctor, sorcerer, fortuneteller, astrologer, alchemist, medicine man, conjurer, shaman, enchanter, hypnotist, diviner, seer, clairvoyant, augurer, medium, palmist.

wobble *v.* shake, quaver, flounder, vacillate, tremble, quiver, move unsteadily, dodder, teeter, totter, be unsteady, waver, quake, stagger, shuffle, waggle.

wobbly *a.* wavering, unbalanced, precarious; see UNSTABLE 1.

wolf *n.* wild dog, coyote, timber wolf; see DOG.

woman *n.* **1** [An adult female] lady, dame, matron, gentlewoman, maid, debutante, nymph, virgin, girl, chick*, doll*, babe*, gal*, broad*. **2** [A wife or mistress] love, lover, wife; see WIFE. **3** [Womankind] femininity, the fair sex, womanhood, the female of the species*.

womanhood *n.* adulthood, maturity, majority, womanliness, sexual prime, nubility, marriageable age, maidenhood, matronhood, spinsterhood.

womanizer *n.* promiscuous man, playboy, skirtchaser*, tomcat*, Casanova, Lothario, Romeo, Don Juan, philanderer, seducer, adulterer.

womanly *a.* ladylike, feminine, female, gentle, modest, compassionate, wifely, sisterly, maternal, motherly, protective, womanish, fair.—*Ant.* MANLY, virile, masculine.

womb *n.* uterus, female cavity, belly; see STOMACH.

won *a.* gained, achieved, conquered, taken, got, triumphed, overwhelmed.—*Ant.* BEATEN, lost, failed.

wonder *n.* **1** [Amazement] surprise, awe, stupefaction, admiration, wonderment, astonishment, puzzlement, wondering, stupor, bewilderment, perplexity, fascination, consternation, perturbation, confusion, shock, start, jar, jolt, incredulity. **2** [A marvel] miracle, curiosity, oddity, rarity, freak, phenomenon, sensation, prodigy, act of God, portent, wonderwork, spectacle, prodigious event, something unnatural, the unbelievable.

wonder *v.* **1** [To marvel] be surprised, be startled, be fascinated, be amazed, be dumbfounded, be confounded, be dazed, be awestruck, be astonished, be agape, be dazzled, stand aghast, be struck by, be unable to take one's eyes off, admire, gape, be taken aback, stare, be flabbergasted. **2** [To question] be curious, query, hold in doubt; see ASK.

wonderful *a.* fine, enjoyable, pleasing; see PLEASANT 2.

wonderfully *a.* beautifully, admirably, excellently; see WELL 2.

wonderland *n.* paradise, Eden, utopia, Garden of Eden, Land of Milk and Honey, nirvana, best of all worlds, fantasyland.

wood *n.* **1** [A forest; *often plural*] grove, woodland, timber; see FOREST. **2** [The portion of trees within the bark] timber, lumber, sapwood, heartwood, pith, knot, growth ring.

Varieties of wood include the following: oak, chestnut, mahogany, sugar maple, red maple, cherry, cedar, walnut, hickory, butternut, hemlock, spruce, hornbeam, ebony, linden, beech, birch, poplar, tamarack, white pine, yellow pine, gumwood, elm, cypress, redwood, fir, Douglas fir, ash, red oak, live oak, white oak, willow, cottonwood, zebrawood, bamboo.

wooded *a.* timbered, forested, tree-covered, wild, tree-laden, treed, reforested, woody, jungly, having cover, timber-bearing, lumbering, uncut, not lumbered, not cut over, with standing timber, primeval, below the timberline, jungle-covered.

wooden *a.* wood, frame, frame-built, long-built, boarded, clapboarded, plank, built of slabs, pine, oak, elm, ash, mahogany.

woodwork *n.* molding, fittings, paneling, stairway, wood finishing, doors, window frames, sashes, jambs, wood trim.

woodworking *n.* woodcraft, wood-carving, wood turning, cabinet-making, carpentry, joinery.

wool *n.* fleece, lambswool, Angora wool, Shetland wool, tweed, flannel, gabardine, worsted, woolen suiting, serge, broadcloth, frieze, mohair, felt, blanketing, carpeting; see also GOODS 1.

word *n.* **1** [A unit of expression] term, name, expression, designation, concept, vocable, utterance, sound, a voicing, form of speech, speech, locution, free morpheme, lexeme. *Classes of words include the following:* common noun, proper noun, personal pronoun, possessive pronoun, demonstrative pronoun, relative pronoun, interrogative pronoun, indefinite pronoun, definite article, indefinite article, transitive verb, intransitive verb, reflexive verb, auxiliary verb, descriptive adjective, quantitative adjective, participial adjective, adverb, coordinating conjunction, subordinating conjunction, preposition, interjection, modifier, subject, predicate, source word, synonym, antonym, homograph, homophone, etymon, cognate word, colloquialism, jargon, slang word, dialect word, provincialism, translation, native word, foreign word, idiom, acronym, compound word, exclamation, greeting, spoken word, written word. **2** [Promise] pledge, commitment, word of honor; see PROMISE 1. **3** [Tidings] report, message, information; see NEWS 1. —**a good word** favorable comment, recommendation, support; see PRAISE 2. —**by word of mouth** orally, verbally, spoken; see ORAL. —**have words with** argue with, differ with, bicker; see ARGUE, FIGHT. —**in so many words** succinctly, cursorily, economically; see BRIEFLY. —**take at one's word** trust in, have confidence in, put one's trust in; see BELIEVE. —**the word** information, the facts, the lowdown*; see KNOWLEDGE 1.

wordiness *n.* redundance, redundancy, diffuseness, circumlocution, repetition, verbiage, verbosity, bombast, tautology, indirectness, flow of words, rhetoric, copiousness, tediousness.—*Ant.* SILENCE, conciseness, succinctness.

wording *n.* locution, phrasing, turn of phrase, contents, style, expression, way of putting it.

wordy *a.* tedious, bombastic, long-winded; see DULL 4.

work *n.* **1** [Something to be done] commitment, task, obligation; see JOB 2. **2** [The doing of work] performance, endeavor, employment, production, occupation, practice, activity, manufacture, industry, operation, transaction, toil, labor, exertion, drudgery, functioning, stress, struggle, slavery, trial, push, attempt, effort, pains, elbow grease*, muscle*. **3** [The result of labor; *often plural*] feat, accomplishment, output; see ACHIEVEMENT. **4** [Occupation] profession, craft, business; see JOB 1. —**at work** working, on the job, engaged; see BUSY 1. —**in the works*** prepared for, budgeted, approved; see READY 2. —**make short (or quick) work of** finish off, deal with, dispose of; see DO 1. —**out of work** not hired, dismissed, looking for a job; see UNEMPLOYED.

work *v.* **1** [To labor] toil, slave, sweat, do a day's work, do the chores, exert oneself, apply oneself, do one's best, overexert, overwork, overstrain, get to work, work overtime, work day and night, work one's way up, tax one's energies, pull, plod, tug, struggle, strive, carry on, do the job, punch a time clock*, put in time, pour it on*, work one's fingers to the bone*, buckle down, bear down, work like a horse*, work like a dog, work like a slave, keep at it, stay with it, put one's shoulder to the wheel, burn the candle at both ends, burn the midnight oil. **2** [To be employed] earn a living, have a job, hold a post, occupy a position, report for work, be on the staff, be among the employed, be on the job. **3** [To function] go, run, serve; see OPERATE 2. **4** [To handle successfully] control, accomplish, manage; see ACHIEVE, OPERATE 3. **5** [To fashion] give form to, sculpture, mold; see FORM 1. —**work at** attempt, endeavor, do one's

best; see TRY 1. —**work in** introduce, find a place for, squeeze in; see INCLUDE 1. —**work on (or upon)** try to encourage, use one's influence with, talk to; see INFLUENCE. —**work out 1** [To solve] come to terms, compromise, reach an agreement; see AGREE. **2** [To satisfy a requirement] finish, do what is necessary, get something done; see ACHIEVE.

workable *a.* useful, practicable, functional; see WORKING 1.

worker *n.* laborer, toiler, mechanic; see WORKMAN.

working *a.* **1** [Functioning] operational, running, in operation, functioning, moving, in process, in working order, humming along*, firing on all cylinders, in gear, in collar. **2** [Employed] laboring, on the job, punching a clock; see BUSY 1.

workman *n.* operator, mechanic, machinist, craftsman, tradesman, artist, artisan, technician, journeyman, master worker, handworker, skilled workman. *Workers include the following:* carpenter, cabinetmaker, upholsterer, paperhanger, plasterer, bricklayer, plumber, electrician, metalworker, locksmith, boilermaker, pipefitter, coppersmith, printer, pressman, prepress technician, compositor, typesetter, linotype operator, glassworker, glazier, tiler, concrete worker, automobile mechanic, punch press operator, shipping clerk, file clerk, packager, assembler, conductor, brakeman, locomotive engineer, switchman, surveyor, fireman, barber, custodian, truck driver, bus driver, carpet installer, carpet cleaner, gardener, tree surgeon, seamstress, tailor, baker, butcher, farm worker, cowboy, dairyman, waiter, waitress, laundry worker, welder, drill operator, hydraulic press operator, diesinker, mason, lathe operator, gear-cutting machine operator, threading machine operator, operator, textile worker, tool-and-die maker, postal clerk, policeman, painter, galvanizer, draftsman, appliance repairman, TV repairman, cameraman, meat cutter, packer, assembly-line worker, maintenance worker, machine operator, patternmaker, foundry worker, road worker, heavy-equipment operator, construction worker, lineman, cook, dishwasher, caterer, janitor, groundskeeper, landscaper, security guard, HVAC technician.

workmanship *n.* craftsmanship, skill, quality of work, performance, handicraft, working ability, handiwork, achievement, manufacture, execution.

workout *n.* exercise, conditioning, gymnastics; see DISCIPLINE 2.

works *n.* 1 [Working parts] cogs, belts, cams, wheels, gears, pistons, springs, coils, chains, rods, pulleys, wires; see also INSIDES. 2 [*Everything; *with *"the"*] totality, entirety, the whole; see ALL, EVERYTHING.

workshop *n.* 1 [Place where work is done] plant, works, laboratory, foundry, studio, yards, mill. 2 [Seminar] discussion group, study group, class.

world *n.* 1 [The earth] globe, wide world, planet; see EARTH 1. 2 [The universe] cosmos, nature, creation; see UNIVERSE. 3 [A specific group] realm, division, system; see CLASS 1. 4 [All one's surroundings] environment, atmosphere, childhood, adolescence, adulthood, experience, life, inner life, memory, idealization. — **bring into the world** give birth to, bear, have a baby; see PRODUCE 1. — **on top of the world** feeling fine, exuberant, successful; see HAPPY. — **out of this world** extraordinary, strange, remarkable; see UNUSUAL 1, 2.

worldly *a.* mundane, earthly, ungodly, practical, matter-of-fact, secular, strategic, grubbing, money-making, unprincipled, power-loving, self-centered, opportunistic, sophisticated, cosmopolitan, terrestrial, profane, human, natural, temporal.

worldwide *a.* global, universal, extensive; see GENERAL 1.

worm *n.* caterpillar, grub, larva, maggot, leech, parasite, helminth. *Common worms include the following:* angleworm, earthworm, threadworm, tapeworm, silkworm, flatworm or platyhelminth, gordian worm, ribbon worm or nemertean, marine worm, hookworm, pinworm, planarian, tubifex worm, horsehair worm, blindworm, slowworm, roundworm or nematode worm, annelid worm, cutworm, army worm, wireworm, measuring worm.

worn *a.* 1 [Used as clothing] carried, put on, donned, displayed, exhibited, used, sported*. 2 [Showing signs of wear] frayed, threadbare, old, secondhand, ragged, shabby, used, consumed, deteriorated, patched, torn, the worse for wear.— *Ant.* FRESH, new, whole.

worn-out *a.* used up, gone, destroyed; see RUINED 1, 2, USELESS 1.

worried *a.* troubled, bothered, perturbed, vexed, distressed, miserable, annoyed, concerned, nervous, upset, suffering, torn, in conflict, pained, burdened, ill at ease, racking one's brains, uptight*, all hot and bothered*, anxious, hung up*; see also EXCITED.

worrisome *a.* troubling, distressing, ominous, foreboding, disturbing,

worrying, fear-inducing, anxious, apprehensive.

worry *n.* 1 [The state of anxiety] concern, anxiety, misery; see DISTRESS. 2 [A cause of worry] problem, upset, disturbance; see FEAR, TROUBLE 1.

worry *v.* 1 [To cause worry] annoy, trouble, bother; see DISTURB. 2 [To indulge in worry] fret, chafe, fear, take to heart, break one's heart, despair, stew, be anxious, worry oneself, have qualms, wince, agonize, writhe, suffer, turn gray with worry, become sick with worry, sweat out*; see also BOTHER 1.

worship *n.* 1 [Adoration] prayer, devotion, homage, adulation, benediction, invocation, supplication, beatification, veneration, offering, burnt offering, reverence, honor. 2 [A religious service] Mass, services, devotions; see CHURCH 2.

worship *v.* sanctify, pray to, invoke, venerate, glorify, praise, exalt, offer one's prayers to, pay homage to, give thanks, offer thanks to, sing praises to, reverence, celebrate, adore, revere, laud, extol, magnify, chant, sing, bow down; see also PRAY 2.

worshiper *n.* churchgoer, communicant, member of the congregation, believer, supplicant, devotee, devotionalist, adorer, pietist, pious person, devout person, celebrant, priest, priestess.—*Ant.* SKEPTIC, atheist, agnostic.

worst *a.* most terrible, most harmful, most lethal, poorest, lowest, least, last, most ghastly, most horrible, most pitiful, least meaningful, meanest, least understanding, least effective.

worst *n.* lowest point, nadir, bottom; see BOTTOM. —**at worst** under the worst possible circumstances, unluckily, grievously; see BADLY 1, UNFORTUNATELY. —**(in) the worst way** unluckily, disastrously, horribly; see UNFORTUNATELY.

worth *a.* deserving, meriting, equal in value to, priced at, exchangeable for, valued at, worth in the open market, pegged at, cashable for, good for, appraised at, having a face value of, reasonably estimated at, bid at, held at. —**for all one is worth** greatly, mightily, hard; see POWERFULLY.

worth *n.* goodness, value, quality, character, importance, significance, meaning, estimation, benefit, excellence, merit; see also VALUE 1, 3.

worthless *a.* profitless, counterproductive, barren, unprofitable, unproductive, unimportant, insignificant, counterfeit, bogus, cheap, sterile, waste, wasted, no good, trashy, inconsequential, petty, piddling, paltry, trivial, trifling, unessential, beneath notice, empty, good-for-nothing, no-account*, not worth the trouble*, not worth speaking of*, not able to say much for*.

worthlessness *n.* uselessness, inefficiency, impracticality; see WASTE 1.

worthwhile *a.* good, serviceable, useful, important, profitable, valuable, remunerative, estimable, worthy, helpful, beneficial, meritorious, excellent, rewarding, praiseworthy.

worthy *a.* good, true, honest, honorable, reliable, trustworthy, dependable, noble, charitable, dutiful, philanthropic, virtuous, moral, pure, upright, righteous, decent, incorruptible, meritorious, creditable, qualified, fit, deserving, rightminded, worthy of, model, exemplary, sterling, sinless, stainless, blameless.—*Ant.* WORTHLESS, bad, evil.

would-be *a.* assuming, supposed, *manqué* (French); see HOPEFUL 1.

wound *a.* twisted, wrapped, coiled; see WOVEN.

wound *n.* bruise, hurt, scar; see INJURY.

wound *v.* **1** [To hurt the body] gash, scrape, injure; see HURT 1. **2** [To hurt the feelings] trouble, upset, pain; see BOTHER 2, DISTURB.

wounded *a.* injured, hurt, disabled, stabbed, cut, shot, scratched, bitten, gashed, hit, beaten, attacked, winged, nicked.

woven *a.* spun, interlinked, netted, netlike, wreathed, sewn, intertwined, united, interlaced, interwoven.

wrap *v.* roll up, swathe, muffle, bind, fold about, encircle, coil, enclose, swaddle, bandage, envelop, enwrap, protect, encase, sheathe, cover up, shelter, clothe, cover with paper, shrink-wrap, enclose in a box.—*Ant.* UNWRAP, unsheathe, open up. — **wrap up*** finish off, bring to an end, polish off*; see COMPLETE.

wrapped *a.* covered, sheathed, swaddled, swathed, enclosed, protected, enveloped, encased, concealed, shrouded, hidden, clothed, done up.—*Ant.* OPEN, unwrapped, uncovered. —**wrapped up in** devoted to, engrossed by, implicated in; see LOVING.

wrath *n.* fury, vengeance, madness; see ANGER.

wreck *n.* **1** [Anything wrecked] junk, ruins, skeleton, hulk, bones, scattered parts, crash, smashup, pileup*, relic, litter, pieces, shreds, waste, wreckage, debris. **2** [A person in poor physical or mental con-

dition] incurable, consumptive, nervous wreck, basket case*, a shadow of one's former self, overworked person, mess*, goner*, washout*, shadow, skin-and-bones*, walking wounded*.

wreck *v.* spoil, ruin, destroy, devastate, demolish, raze, knock down, disfigure, mangle, smash, tear down, break, split, efface, batter, torpedo, tear to pieces, put out of order, impair, injure, bash in, mess up, play hell with*, put out of commission.—*Ant.* REPAIR, restore, rebuild.

wreckage *n.* remains, ruins, hulk, remnants, flotsam and jetsam; see also WRECK 1.

wrecked *a.* demolished, destroyed, broken up, knocked to pieces, ruined, smashed to bits, shipwrecked, stranded, beached, grounded, scuttled, capsized, put out of order, blown to bits, junked, dismantled, shattered, on the rocks, gone to pot, shot to hell*.

wrench *n.* **1** [A violent twist] jerk, strain, sprain, tug, pull, dislodgement, extrication, dislocation. **2** [A spanner] *Wrenches include the following:* monkey, single-head, double-head, pipe, Stillson, crescent, sparkplug, hubcap, flat, S-socket, bearing, connecting-rod; see also TOOL 1.

wrench *v.* twist, strain, distort; see BEND.

wrestle *v.* grapple, struggle with, contend with, perform in a wrestling bout, wrassle*, tangle*, tussle; see also FIGHT.

wrestling *n.* contention, grappling, bout; see FIGHT 1.

wretched *a.* **1** [Afflicted] distressed, woeful, sorrowful; see SAD 1. **2** [Poor in quality] weak, faulty, cheap; see POOR 2.

wring *v.* squeeze out, compress, press; see TWIST.

wrinkle *n.* crease, furrow, crinkle, ridge, fold, corrugation, line, crow's foot, pucker, pleat.

wrinkle *v.* rumple, crease, furrow, pucker, twist, crumple, compress, crinkle.—*Ant.* STRAIGHTEN, smooth out, iron.

wrinkled *a.* creased, rumpled, furrowed, puckered, warped, twisted, crumpled, crinkled, dried up, withered, unironed, unpressed, shrivelled.—*Ant.* SMOOTH, ironed, pressed.

write *v.* **1** [To compose in words] set forth, formulate, draft, turn out, crank out*, pen, put in writing, communicate, rewrite, produce fiction; work as an author, journalist, etc. **2** [To set down in writing] inscribe, sign, scrawl, address, print, letter, autograph, transcribe, jot down, scribble, record, dash off, put in black and white, typewrite, typeset, produce hard copy, put down on paper. —**write off** charge off, take a loss on, recognize as a bad debt; see LOSE 2.

writer *n.* author, journalist, reporter, newspaperman, magazine writer, contributor, poet, novelist, essayist, biographer, dramatist, playwright, literary critic, foreign correspondent, feature writer, sports writer, fashion writer, shorthand writer, stenographer, anecdotist, amanuensis, ghostwriter, songwriter, copyist, scribe, editor, contributing editor, war correspondent, special writer, freelance writer, technical writer, speechwriter, member of the Fourth Estate, scribbler, pen pusher*, hack, newshound*. *Major writers include the following—British:* Daniel Defoe, Jonathan Swift, Henry Fielding, Samuel Johnson, Lawrence Sterne, Sir Walter Scott, Jane Austen, William Makepeace Thackeray, Charles Dickens, Anthony Trollope, Charlotte Brontë, George Eliot, Matthew Arnold, Thomas Hardy, Joseph Conrad, Rudyard Kipling, James Joyce, Virginia Woolf, D.H. Lawrence, George Orwell, Evelyn Waugh, Samuel Beckett; *American:* James Fenimore Cooper, Ralph Waldo Emerson, Nathaniel Hawthorne, Edgar Allan Poe, Henry David Thoreau, Herman Melville, Samuel Langhorne Clemens (Mark Twain), Henry Adams, Henry James, Edith Wharton, Stephen Crane, Theodore Dreiser, Willa Cather, F. Scott Fitzgerald, William Faulkner, Ernest Hemingway, John Steinbeck, Eudora Welty, Saul Bellow, Flannery O'Connor; *French:* Michel Eyquem de Montaigne, (François-Marie Arouet de) Voltaire, Jean Jacques Rousseau, Stendhal, Honoré de Balzac, Victor Hugo, Alexandre Dumas, Gustave Flaubert, Émile Zola, Guy de Maupassant, Marcel Proust, Albert Camus; *Italian:* Niccolò Machiavelli, Giovanni Boccaccio, Alessandro Manzoni; *German:* Thomas Mann, Franz Kafka, Günter Grass; *Russian:* Nikolai Gogol, Ivan Turgenev, Fyodor Dostoevsky, Leo Tolstoy, Anton Chekhov, Boris Pasternak; *Spanish:* Miguel de Cervantes, Jorge Luis Borges; *Yiddish:* I.B. Singer.

write-up* *n.* report, account, publicity; see WRITING 2.

writhe *v.* contort, move painfully, squirm, distort, suffer, twist and turn, undergo agony, turn with pain, throw a fit*.—*Ant.* REST, be at ease, move easily.

writing *n.* 1 [The practice of writing] transcribing, inscribing, reporting, corresponding, letter-writing,

copying, handwriting, typewriting, penmanship, lettering, printing, graphology, signing, autographing, stenography. 2 [Anything written] literature, written matter, document, composition, article, poem, prose, paper, theme, editorial, discourse, essay, thesis, dissertation, book, manuscript, novel, play, literary production, scenario, drama, work, signature, letter, pamphlet, tract, treatise, disquisition, comment, commentary, review, recitation, certificate, record, bill, bit*, item, piece. 3 [The occupation of a writer] journalism, reporting, literature, authorship, freelance writing, professional writing, auctorial pursuits, the pen, the Fourth Estate, creative writing, feature writing, technical writing, speechwriting, newspaper work, the writers' craft, hack writing, ghostwriting.

written *a.* 1 [Composed] set forth, authored, penned, drawn up, reported, signed, turned out, fictionalized, arranged, rearranged, adapted, ghostwritten, recorded, dictated. 2 [Inscribed] copied, scriptural, transcribed, printed, lettered, autographed, signed, put in writing, in black and white, in one's hand.

wrong *a.* 1 [Immoral] evil, sinful, wicked, naughty, salacious, base, indecent, risqué, blasphemous, ungodly, amoral, dissolute, dissipated, wanton, profane, sacrilegious, depraved, corrupt, profligate, shady*, lowdown*, smutty.— *Ant.* GOOD, righteous, virtuous. 2 [Inaccurate] inexact, erroneous, mistaken, in error, incorrect, fallacious, untrue, erring, astray, amiss, ungrounded, spurious, unsubstantial, unsound, erratic, misguided, self-deluded, in the wrong, under an error, beside the mark, laboring under a false impression, out of line, at fault, to no purpose, not right, awry, faulty, mishandled, miscalculated, misfigured, misconstructed, misconstrued, altered, not precise, perverse, wide of the mark, not according to the facts, badly estimated, a mile off*, all off, crazy*. 3 [Inappropriate] unfitted, disproportionate, ill-fitting; see IMPROPER. —**go wrong** fall apart, take a wrong turn, go astray; see FAIL 1.

wrong *n.* vice, sin, misdemeanor, crime, immorality, indecency, transgression, unfairness, imposition, oppression, foul play, prejudice, bias, partiality, unlawful practice, villainy, delinquency, error, miscarriage, mistake, blunder, offense, wrongdoing, violation, tort, hurt, persecution, malevolence, cruelty, libel, abuse, harm, damage, spite, slander, lie, slight, misusage, outrage, inhumanity, malfeasance, misfeasance, dereliction, insult, discourtesy.—*Ant.* KINDNESS, good deed, consideration.

wrong *v.* hurt, oppress, defame; see ABUSE.

wrongly *a.* unfairly, prejudicially, wrongfully, partially, badly, unjustifiably, illegally, disgracefully, sin-

fully, unreasonably, unlawfully, criminally, inexcusably, unsuitably, improperly, awkwardly, incongruously, incorrectly, unbecomingly, indecorously, questionably, imprudently, rashly, unnaturally, illogically; see also INADEQUATELY.—*Ant.* APPROPRIATELY, tastefully, prudently.

wrung *a.* twisted, squeezed out, pressed; see TWISTED 1.

X

x *n.* unknown quantity, variable, y; see QUANTITY.

Xmas* *n.* the Nativity, Christmas, Christmastime, yule, yuletide; see also CHRISTMAS, HOLIDAY.

X-rays *n.* Roentgen rays, radioactivity, radium emanation, actinic rays,

actinism, encephalogram, ultraviolet rays, refractometry, radiant energy, cathode rays; see also ENERGY 2, RAY.

xylophone *n.* carillon, vibraphone, vibes, vibraharp, mallet instrument, glockenspiel, marimba; see also MUSICAL INSTRUMENT.

Y

yacht *n.* pleasure boat, sloop, racing boat; see BOAT, SHIP.

yank *n.* twitch, jerk, wrench; see JERK 1.

yank* *v.* haul, tug, drag, jiggle, jerk*, flip, wrench, twitch; see also DRAW 1, PULL 2.

Yankee *a.* 1 [Having New England qualities] homespun, individualistic, conservative; see MODERATE 3, 4, 5, PRACTICAL. 2 [Concerning the United States] North American, Western, Americanized; see AMERICAN.

Yankee *n.* 1 [A New Englander] Northerner, Easterner, early settler, Abolitionist, Unionist. 2 [A person from the United States] American, American citizen, North American, westerner, Yank*.

yard *n.* 1 [An enclosure, usually next to a building] court, courtyard, barnyard, backyard, corral, fold, patch, patio, terrace, play area, lawn, grass, garden, clearing, quadrangle, lot; see also PLAYGROUND. 2 [An enclosure for work] brickyard, coalyard, junkyard, navy yard, dockyard, railyard, stockyard, lumberyard. 3 [Tracks for making up trains] railroad yard, switchyard, railway yard, marshalling yard, terminal. 4 [A unit of measurement] three feet, pace, step, arm-span, thirty-six inches; see also MEASURE 1.

yardstick *n.* criterion, basis for judgment, standard, index, measuring

stick, basis for comparison; see also MEASURE 2.

yarn *n.* 1 [Spun fiber] spun wool, twist, flaxen thread, cotton fiber, rug yarn, crochet thread, knitting yarn, alpaca yarn; see also FIBER. 2 [A tale] anecdote, sea story, adventure story, tall tale, fictional account; see also STORY. 3 [A lie] fabrication, tall tale*, alibi, fish story*, cock-and-bull story*; see also LIE.

yaw *v.* curve, swerve, bank; see TURN 6.

yawn *v.* 1 [To open wide] gape, split open, spread out; see DIVIDE, GROW 1. 2 [To give evidence of drowsiness] gape, be sleepy, make a yawning sound, show weariness; see also SLEEP, TIRE 1.

yea *a.* okay, aye, well; see YES.

year *n.* twelve months, annual cycle, continuum of days; see AGE 3, TIME 1, 2. *Kinds of years include the following:* civil, legal, calendar, lunar, solar, astronomical, natural, sidereal, tropical, equinoctial, leap, school, fiscal. —**year after year** year by year, annually; year in, year out; see YEARLY.

yearbook *n.* annual, almanac, yearly report; see CATALOG, RECORD 1.

yearling *n.* suckling, nursling, weanling; see ANIMAL, BABY.

yearly *a.* annually, once a year, every winter, every spring, every summer, every autumn, year by year; see also REGULARLY.

yearn *v.* want, crave, long for, fret,

chafe, grieve, mourn, droop, pine, covet, be eager for, be desirous of, be ardent, be fervent, be passionate, wish for, thirst for, hunger for, aspire to, set one's heart upon, hanker for, have a yen for*; see also TRY 1.—*Ant.* AVOID, be content, be indifferent.

yearning *n.* want, longing, craving; see DESIRE 1, WISH.

yell *n.* **1** [A shout] bellow, cry, yelp, roar, whoop, howl, screech, shriek, squeal, holler*, hoot, yawp, hubbub, hullabaloo, hue and cry, protest; see also NOISE 1. **2** [Organized cheering] hip-hip-hurray, rooting, cheer; see ENCOURAGEMENT.

yell *v.* bellow, cry out, scream, shout, yelp, yap, bawl, roar, halloo, vociferate, whoop, howl, screech, shriek, squeal, squall, yammer, hoot, cheer, call, yip, give encouragement, call down, raise one's voice, holler, whoop it up; see also SOUND.

yelling *a.* boisterous, clamorous, noisy, bawling, uproarious, turbulent, drunken, aroused, riotous, cantankerous, blatant, vociferous; see also HARSH, LOUD 2.—*Ant.* QUIET, subdued, silent.

yelling *n.* cry, scream, shout, outcry, vociferation, screeching, bawling, yowling, bellowing, howling, yelping; see also NOISE 1, YELL.

yellow *a.* **1** [Having a yellowish color] yellowish, golden, jaundiced. **2** [*Cowardly] low, cringing, lily-livered, white-livered, craven, treacherous; see also COWARDLY, VULGAR.

yellow *n.* *Tints and shades of yellow include the following:* cream color, ivory color, old ivory, ivory-yellow, tan, lemon color, orange-yellow, saffron, jasmine, tawny, sand, gold, sallow, buff, brilliant yellow, chrome yellow, Dutch pink-yellow, Dutch yellow, golden yellow, Imperial yellow, platinum yellow, yellow carmine, yellow madder, yellow ocher; see also COLOR, GOLD.

yelp *v.* howl, screech, hoot; see CRY 2, SOUND.

yen* *n.* longing, craving, hunger; see DESIRE 1.

yes *a.* surely, of course, certainly, good, fine, aye, true, granted, very well, all right, OK*, okay*, oke*, okey-dokey*, Roger, we copy, over to you, most assuredly, by all means, agreed, oh yes, amen, naturally, without fail, just so, good enough, even so, in the affirmative, you bet*.

yes man* *n.* toady, company man*, brown-noser*, bootlicker*, go-along man*, get-along man*.

yesterday *a.* recently, previously, earlier; see BEFORE.

yesterday *n.* the other day, the day before, recently, last day, not long ago; see also PAST 1.

yet *a.* **1** [Nevertheless] notwithstanding, however, in spite of, despite, still, but, though, although, at any rate, on the other hand. **2** [Thus far] until now, till, hitherto, prior to, still; see also UNTIL. **3** [In addition] besides, additionally, further; see BESIDES. —**as yet** still, not yet, till now; see YET 2.

yield *v.* **1** [To surrender] give up, capitulate, succumb, resign, abdicate, relinquish, quit, cede, bow, lay down arms, cease from, let go, submit, give oneself over, relent, admit defeat, suffer defeat, forgo, humble oneself, waive, throw in the towel*, call it quits*, back down*, holler uncle*, eat crow*; see also ABANDON 1.—*Ant.* RESIST, withstand, repulse. **2** [To produce] bear, bring forth, blossom; see BLOOM, PRODUCE 1, 2. **3** [To grant] accede, concur, acquiesce; see ADMIT 2, AGREE.

yielding *a.* **1** [Producing] green, fruitful, productive; see FERTILE, RICH 3. **2** [Flexible] pliant, plastic, malleable; see FLEXIBLE. **3** [Docile] submissive, pliable, tractable; see HUMBLE 1, OBEDIENT 1.

yogi *n.* mystic, fakir, anchorite, ascetic, practitioner of yoga, guru, devotee.

yoke *v.* couple, link, connect, hitch, harness; see also FASTEN, JOIN 1.

yokel *n.* rustic, bumpkin, hayseed*; see BOOR.

yonder *a.* farther, away, faraway; see DISTANT, REMOTE 1.

you *pron.* yourself, you yourself, thee, thou, all of you, you too, you alone, you all*.

young *a.* **1** [In the early portion of life] boyish, girlish, adolescent, juvenile, budding, in one's teens, childlike, youthful, pubescent, boylike, girllike, new-fledged, blooming, burgeoning, childish, half-grown, growing, blossoming, at the breast, babe in arms, knee high to a grasshopper*.—*Ant.* OLD, aged, senile. **2** [Inexperienced] callow, green, immature, tender, raw, puerile, untutored, unlearned, junior, subordinate, inferior, unfledged, ignorant, undisciplined, tenderfoot, wet behind the ears*; see also INEXPERIENCED, NAIVE.—*Ant.* EXPERIENCED, veteran, expert. **3** [New] fresh, modern, recent, newborn; see also FASHIONABLE.

youngster *n.* child, boy, girl, pupil, kid*, tyke*, young'un*, bambino; see also YOUTH 3.

youth *n.* **1** [The state or quality of being young] boyhood, adolescence, girlhood, childhood, early manhood, early adulthood, puberty, tender age, minority, youthfulness, teen age, virginity, bloom, teens, age of ignorance, age of indiscretion, awkward age, salad days.—*Ant.* MATURITY, old age, senility. **2** [Young people] children, the younger generation, the rising generation, the next generation, the young, college youth, working youth. **3** [A young person] boy, junior, teenager, lad, youngster, stripling, minor, young man, miss, girl, maiden, fledgling, juvenile, urchin, adolescent, student, kid*, teen, preteen, gosling, pup*, calf*; see also CHILD.

youthful *a.* **1** [Possessing youth]

young, childlike, adolescent; see ACTIVE, YOUNG 1, 2. **2** [Suited to youth] keen, enthusiastic, zestful, vigorous, active, buoyant, lighthearted, prankish, fresh, lithe, full-blooded, full of life, spirited, limber, athletic, lightfooted, coltish, bubbling over, full of the devil; see also MODERN 1.—*Ant.* SLOW, cautious, serious.

yowl *n.* howl, yelp, wail; see CRY 1, YELL 1.

yule *n.* Christmas, Xmas*, Nativity, Christmas season, Christmastide, Christmastime, yuletide, Advent.

Z

zeal *n.* **1** [Enthusiasm] ardor, fervor, eagerness. **2** [Industry] earnestness, hustle, hustling, bustle, bustling, intensity, industry, willingness, inclination, application, determination, promptitude, dispatch, diligence, perseverance, intentness, assiduity, readiness, aptitude, enterprise, initiative, push*, stick-to-itiveness*; see also ATTENTION, CARE 1, COOPERATION.—*Ant.* IDLENESS, slackness, indolence.

zealot *n.* partisan, fan, bigot, fanatic, lobbyist, devotee, enthusiast, dogmatist, opinionist, missionary, fighter, cultist, follower, disciple, true believer, propagandist, bitter-ender*, crank*, addict, bug*, faddist, fiend*.

zealous *a.* fervent, earnest, intense, fanatical, industrious, diligent, intent, dogmatic, devoted, ardent; see also ENTHUSIASTIC.

zealously *a.* with zeal, assiduously, fiercely; see INDUSTRIOUSLY, VIGOROUSLY.

zenith *n.* top, pinnacle, summit, acme, apogee, culmination, highest point, apex, tip, crest, cap, crown, peak.

zero *n.* **1** [A cipher] naught, nothing, nadir, love, below freezing, the lowest point, goose egg*, nix*, zip*, zilch*, *nada* (Spanish), *bupkes* (Yiddish). **2** [Nothing] nullity, oblivion, void; see BLANK 1.

zest *n.* **1** [Relish] gusto, enjoyment, pleasure; see HAPPINESS. **2** [Savor] taste, tang, piquancy, spice, bite, nip, pungency, punch, snap, ginger, kick, guts*, body; see also FLAVOR.

zigzag *a.* oblique, inclined, sloping, awry, crooked, sinuous, twisted, askew, transverse, diagonal, curved, bent, crinkled, serrated, jagged,

straggling, meandering, devious, erratic, rambling, oscillating, fluctuating, waggling, undulatory, vibratory, indirect, spiral, tortuous; see also ANGULAR, IRREGULAR 4.—*Ant.* STRAIGHT, parallel, undeviating.

zip* *n.* energy, vigor, vim; see STRENGTH.

zip* *v.* run, dash, rush; see RUN 2, HURRY.

zodiac *n.* celestial meridian, signs of the zodiac, sky signs, groups of stars, constellations; see also PLANET, STAR 1. *The twelve signs of the zodiac are as follows:* Aquarius or the Water Bearer, Pisces or the Fish, Aries or the Ram, Taurus or the Bull, Gemini or the Twins, Cancer or the Crab, Leo or the Lion, Virgo or the Virgin, Libra or the Scales, Scorpio or the Scorpion, Sagittarius or the Archer, Capricorn or the Goat.

zone *n.* **1** [A band] circuit, meridian, latitude; see BAND 1, STRIPE. **2** [An area] region, district, territory; traffic, building, danger, quiet, school, hospital, parking, etc. zone; Frigid, Temperate, Torrid Zone; see also PLACE 3, POSITION 1.

zoo *n.* menagerie, zoological garden, terrarium, aquarium, aviary.

zoological *a.* animal, zoologic, marsupial, mammalian, mammalogical, ornithological, herpetological, ichthyological, echinological, conchological, entomological, arachnological, crustaceological; see also ALIVE, BIOLOGICAL.

zoology *n.* life science, biological science, natural history; see LIFE 1, SCIENCE.

zoom *v.* speed, rush, hum; see CLIMB, HURRY 1, RISE 1.